The Bride's Essential

Book of Lists

Amy Nebens

Illustrations by Greg Stadler

Sterling Signature
NEW YORK

Sterling Signature
NEW YORK

An Imprint of Sterling Publishing
387 Park Avenue South
New York, NY 10016

This edition published in 2013 by Sterling Publishing Co., Inc.

ISBN 978-1-4549-0844-9

Distributed in Canada by Sterling Publishing
C/o Canadian Manda Group, 165 Dufferin Street
Toronto, Ontario, Canada M6K 3H6
Distributed in the United Kingdom by GMC Distribution Services
Castle Place, 166 High Street, Lewes, East Sussex, England BN7 1XU
Distributed in Australia by Capricorn Link (Australia) Pty. Ltd.
P.O. Box 704, Windsor, NSW 2756, Australia

For information about custom editions, special sales, and premium and corporate purchases,
please contact Sterling Special Sales at 800-805-5489 or specialsales@sterlingpublishing.com.

Manufactured in China

2 4 6 8 10 9 7 5 3 1

www.sterlingpublishing.com

Contents

Introduction

H e proposed and you accepted—or maybe it was the other way around. Either way, the result is wonderfully the same. You are engaged—and about to embark upon an amazing journey together. Along the way, you will encounter endless well wishes, delightful stacks of presents, and perhaps even a celebration or two in your honor. Enjoy this time; there is nothing else like it. That said, there is also much work to be done. After all, you have a wedding to plan—an endeavor that is both exciting and challenging. But all the time and energy devoted to organizing this momentous occasion will seem worth it on the big day when you stand before family and friends to be pronounced husband and wife.

The purpose of this book is to facilitate your planning efforts by providing you with the information you need and the right questions to ask—in a streamlined, efficient format. To make navigating easier, topics are organized into ten sections, clearly marked with tabs. Within each section, you'll find detailed lists of things to do, helpful tips and advice, and prepared interviews for meeting with service providers. In an attempt to be comprehensive, we've included a wide range of topics and questions; of course, not all brides will have the same concerns and desires, so make use of only those elements that apply to your situation. Before turning to any one section, take the time to look through the introduction. Here, you'll find such helpful tools as a planning timeline, a budget worksheet, valuable money-saving tips, and guidelines to follow when hiring wedding professionals. The appendix at the back of the book offers additional planning aids, which are listed in the table of contents.

We've made sure to include information geared to the modern bride and groom. Almost all of today's couples, for instance, are online, and the wedding planning process has easily evolved to accommodate that. This book will explain the benefits of online planning in terms of finding information online, tools to use, interactive capabilities, and more. Some couples want to take a more personal approach to their nuptials, rather than choosing a strictly traditional route—in this book we offer suggestions on where to look for inspiration and ways to incorporate unique ideas into the wedding. Many couples, whether for budget, creative, or stylistic reasons, are choosing to bring a Do-It-Yourself (DIY) element into their big day. We explain exactly what this means, how and why to include DIY components, as well as places to find project ideas and directions. Plus, for those brides and grooms thinking about planning a destination wedding, we've added lots of facts about where to have it, what to know, and how to plan across long distances.

The folders located on the inside front and back covers are a convenient place to store magazine clippings and any leaflets you may receive from service providers; for added convenience, you can stash business cards in the translucent plastic sleeves at the front of the book. As a record of your meetings, this book will not only help you stay organized, it will prove useful to have on hand during subsequent meetings for reference purposes and to allow you to make quick comparisons on the spot. And when the planning is over and the party has begun, just tuck your book away until a time, years from now, when you want to remember the details of how your wedding day came to be.

Planning Timeline

Here, you'll find a general overview of the steps involved in the planning process. Once you get an idea of what's ahead, refer to the "things to do" checklists within each section for detailed accounts. While the planner below can be used as a guide for budgeting your time, the earlier you make arrangements, the better. The schedule below begins nine months before the wedding, but that's not to say that you'll have to settle for less if you've got less time—just get started now.

NINE MONTHS BEFORE OR EARLIER

☐ Plan get-together for families to meet, celebrate, and discuss wedding plans

☐ Go for engagement photograph sitting

☐ Announce engagement in newspapers

☐ Create blog or website to post wedding news, information, pictures, etc.; or sign up at a wedding site to get ideas from other brides and to have access to wedding tools and information

☐ Discuss budget—with each other and family (include both families in talks if both families will be sharing the costs)

☐ Create inspiration notebook/folder, or use a website such as Pinterest, and start gathering ideas.

☐ Select a date—and alternative ones to ensure flexibilty when it comes to availability of a location or wedding professional you want to hire

☐ Hire wedding consultant (see page 50 to determine whether you need one)

☐ Choose and ask attendants

☐ Put together guest list

☐ Book site for ceremony

☐ Book site for reception

☐ If considering a destination wedding, start researching places and inquiring about availability

☐ Book officiant

☐ Book caterer

☐ Book musicians for ceremony

☐ Book band/disc jockey for reception

☐ Order dress and veil/headpiece

SIX TO NINE MONTHS BEFORE

☐ Book photographer

☐ Book videographer

☐ Book florist

☐ Start shopping online for everything from vendors to dresses

☐ Select and order attendants' dresses and accessories

☐ Reserve rental equipment

- ☐ Meet with caterer to plan menu and schedule tasting
- ☐ Order invitations and other wedding stationery
- ☐ Book calligrapher
- ☐ Send save-the-date cards
- ☐ If having an at-home wedding, begin any necessary home improvements and/or landscaping work
- ☐ Make arrangements with hotel to hold block of rooms for out-of-town guests
- ☐ Book room for your wedding night
- ☐ Investigate honeymoon destinations and travel arrangements
- ☐ If traveling abroad, update passports, visas, and any other required travel documents and inquire about necessary immunizations
- ☐ Register for wedding gifts

FOUR TO SIX MONTHS BEFORE
- ☐ Start any DIY planning
- ☐ Make final honeymoon reservations
- ☐ Purchase/order/make favors
- ☐ Schedule time for ceremony rehearsal
- ☐ Plan rehearsal dinner (whether this involves making the arrangements yourself or discussing the event with the groom's family)
- ☐ Purchase tuxedo/suit, or reserve rental (groom and groomsmen)
- ☐ Meet with florist to plan bouquets, arrangements, etc.
- ☐ Order wedding cake
- ☐ Purchase/make gifts for bridal party
- ☐ Purchase bridal shoes and other accessories
- ☐ Have invitations addressed

TWO TO FOUR MONTHS BEFORE
- ☐ Send hotel, transportation, and area attractions information to out-of-town guests (if wedding is in a popular tourist destination during peak season, you may want to do this earlier)
- ☐ Investigate local requirements for obtaining marriage license
- ☐ Book/arrange for transportation for bride, groom, attendants, and immediate family on wedding day
- ☐ Meet with officiant to discuss service
- ☐ Begin writing vows
- ☐ Select readings/songs for ceremony; ask those you want to read/perform if they will do the honor
- ☐ Make selections for ceremony music
- ☐ Select songs for the major highlights of reception (first dance, cake-cutting, bouquet toss, etc.)
- ☐ Purchase appropriate undergarments and hosiery for wedding gown, and bring to first fitting
- ☐ Purchase wedding rings
- ☐ Select gift for groom, if you two are exchanging presents
- ☐ Select thank-you gifts for parents
- ☐ Purchase going-away outfit
- ☐ Mail invitations (this should be done six to eight weeks before wedding)
- ☐ Investigate local newspapers' time requirements and content guidelines for wedding announcements
- ☐ Have wedding portrait taken
- ☐ Do trial runs with makeup artist and hairstylist, and schedule beauty appointments for the wedding day

FOUR TO SIX WEEKS BEFORE

- [ ] Make arrangements for blood tests, if state requires (the time frame for this varies according to local regulations; check with the local town clerk's office)
- [ ] Obtain marriage license (the time varies according to local regulations; check with the local town clerk's office)
- [ ] Create/order ceremony programs
- [ ] Plan bridesmaids' luncheon
- [ ] Put together welcome baskets for out-of-town guests
- [ ] Send wedding announcements to newspapers
- [ ] Give list of songs you want (and don't want) played to band/disc jockey
- [ ] Have final dress fitting
- [ ] Pick up ordered tuxedo/suit, if purchasing (groom and groomsmen)
- [ ] Start arranging seating plan
- [ ] Pick up wedding rings

TWO WEEKS BEFORE

- [ ] Give caterer final head count
- [ ] Finalize seating plan; write place cards, or give calligrapher the information and materials to do so
- [ ] Send shot lists to photographer and videographer
- [ ] Compose toasts for rehearsal dinner and wedding reception
- [ ] Make a detailed schedule of the wedding reception events (times for cocktails, first dance, dinner, cake-cutting, etc.) to give to all applicable service providers
- [ ] Break in shoes and scuff bottoms to add traction

ONE WEEK BEFORE

- [ ] Pick up dress, if not being delivered
- [ ] Pick up tuxedo, if renting (groom and groomsmen)
- [ ] Confirm reservations for wedding night and honeymoon
- [ ] Get crisp bills from bank for gratuities; put tips in labeled envelopes and seal
- [ ] Organize final payments for service providers who need to be paid on wedding day
- [ ] Pack for honeymoon
- [ ] Purchase traveler's checks
- [ ] Make a list of everything you need to bring to wedding, and gather all the necessary items together
- [ ] Host bridesmaids' luncheon
- [ ] Confirm final details with all service providers
- [ ] Arrange for mail to be held at post office during honeymoon
- [ ] Call stores where you're registered to hold deliveries

ONE DAY BEFORE

- [ ] Drop off welcome baskets for out-of-town guests at hotel (or ask attendant to do so)
- [ ] Get manicure and pedicure
- [ ] Have rehearsal; hand out gifts to wedding party if you haven't already
- [ ] Assign tasks and duties to wedding party for next day
- [ ] Give attendants anything they need to execute said duties
- [ ] Attend rehearsal dinner
- [ ] Give groom his gift, if you two are exchanging presents

Budget Planner

Knowing just how much you are able to spend will facilitate the planning process and help you to make decisions. Be sure to account for taxes and gratuities, which often are not included in quoted fees. For a typical wedding, you can expect to devote roughly the following percentages of your budget toward specified aspects: 50% for reception; 10% for music; 10% for flowers; 10% for photography/videography; 10% for bride's and groom's attire; 10% for the remaining expenses (invitations, transportation, etc.). Use the worksheet below to help outline your costs.

Wedding Element	Estimate	Actual	Deposit	Balance	Paid
RECEPTION (50%)					
Site fee					
Food/caterer					
Bar/corkage fee					
Champagne/wine					
Cake/cake-cutting fee					
Rentals					
Furniture					
Linens					
China					
Silver					
Glassware					
Wedding consultant					
Parking fees/valet parking					
Coat check attendant					
Gratuities					
Subtotal					
MUSIC (10%)					
Ceremony musicians					
Music for cocktail hour					
Band/disc jockey for reception					
Gratuities					
Subtotal					
FLOWERS/DECORATIONS (10%)					
Ceremony site flowers/decorations					
Bride's bouquet					
Attendants' bouquets					
Toss bouquet					

Wedding Element	Estimate	Actual	Deposit	Balance	Paid
Corsages/boutonnieres					
Flower girls' baskets					
Floral hair accessories					
DIY project materials					
Reception centerpieces					
Arrangements for buffet tables					
Arrangements for cake table					
Arrangements for rest rooms					
Other reception decorations					
Subtotal					
PHOTOGRAPHY/VIDEOGRAPHY (10%)					
Photography package/fee					
Wedding album (if not included in above)					
Additional albums					
Additional prints					
Online proofs					
Online posting					
Videography package/fee					
Additional videos					
Subtotal					
ATTIRE/BEAUTY (10%)					
Bridal gown					
Alterations					
Veil/headpiece					
Shoes					
Undergarments					
Hosiery					
Jewelry					
Other accessories					
Rehearsal dinner outfit					
Going-away outfit					
Hair					
Makeup					
Manicure/pedicure					
Groom's tuxedo/suit					
Groom's shoes/socks					

Wedding Element	Estimate	Actual	Deposit	Balance	Paid
Groom's accessories (bow tie/tie, cumberbund/vest, cuff links, etc.)					
Subtotal					
OTHER EXPENSES (10%)					
CEREMONY					
Site fee					
Officiant's fee/donation					
Ceremonial objects/accessories (unity candle, wine goblet, etc.)					
Ring bearer's pillow					
Marriage license					
Wedding rings					
Subtotal					
STATIONERY					
Wedding invitations					
Save-the-date cards					
At-home cards					
Announcements					
Thank-you notes					
Ceremony programs					
Menus					
Seating cards					
Calligrapher's fee					
Postage (for invitations, response cards, thank-you notes)					
Subtotal					
TRANSPORTATION					
Rented vehicle(s) for bride, groom, immediate family, and wedding party					
Gratuities for drivers					
Shuttle for guests					
Subtotal					
GIFTS					
Favors					
Welcome baskets for out-of-town guests					
Gifts for wedding party					

Wedding Element	Estimate	Actual	Deposit	Balance	Paid
Gifts for parents					
Bride and groom's gifts to each other					
Subtotal					
PARTIES					
Bridesmaids' luncheon					
Rehearsal dinner					
Subtotal					
MISCELLANEOUS					
TOTAL					

Money-Saving Hints and Tips

✧ The going rate for location fees in January, February, and March is typically lower than at other times of the year. Some locations charge a higher fee for Saturday nights.

✧ Typically buffet-style meals are less pricey than seated ones, and cocktail receptions cost less than buffets; breakfasts, brunches, and afternoons are usually less costly still.

✧ Ask caterers about bringing in your own liquor. You may be able to save money if you buy it wholesale; just be sure to find out if the caterer charges a corkage fee.

✧ Skip the "champagne toast," and let guests raise glasses of whatever they're drinking; doing so can shave off as much as $5 per person.

✧ If you need to rent chairs for both the ceremony and reception, try to get ones that work for both. Make sure that doing this won't pose any setup problems.

✧ Make engagement announcements or rehearsal dinner invites yourself with store-bought stationery run through a home computer; doing so will leave more money to spend on professionally printed wedding invitations.

✧ Classic black ink is typically less expensive than colored ink.

✧ Classic white or ivory paper is typically less expensive than colored paper.

✧ Keep calligraphy costs down by enlisting the help of an artistic friend.

✧ Consider hiring a disc jockey instead of a band, as a DJ is typically less expensive.

✧ Avoid having a wedding around such holidays as Valentine's Day and Mother's Day, when flower prices are higher.

✧ Use seasonal flowers for bouquets and arrangements; they are less expensive than out-of-season blooms.

✧ Consider alternatives to traditional floral centerpieces, such as arrangements of greenery, bowls of fruit, or compotes artistically stacked with pretty wrapped favors.

✧ Wear your mother's wedding gown—for the sentiment as well as the savings.

✧ If purchasing favors, ask for a bulk discount or wholesale rate.

Hiring Guidelines

✧ When starting your search for locations and service providers, check with friends and family members for suggestions and referrals. Site coordinators and catering managers are also good resources for recommendations.

✧ You can also search online for vendors. Many vendors have their own websites and blogs where you can view their work. Even if you love what you see and read, it is still important to check references from these vendors and to meet with them in person. Other ways to search might be through national associations that list related vendors in your area.

✧ Instead of dealing with many different vendors, often one company will take care of many of the details. Not only does dealing with one place make logistics a bit easier, often, the more you get from them, the better the deal they will give you.

✧ Before scheduling an interview with a service provider, inquire as to whether he/she is available for your wedding date and time.

✧ Just because a professional is highly recommended by a friend or relative doesn't mean you don't have to interview him/her. You need to make sure that the service provider's way of thinking is in line with yours.

✧ Be creative in your thinking. For instance, if you are not a fan of typical wedding videos, maybe search for a documentary filmmaker who could do wonders with your day.

✧ It's a good idea to meet with more than one service provider before making a hiring decision so you get a sense of your options. Keep the meetings limited, though; too many will just make your head swim.

✧ Ask for three references. If a professional doesn't agree to provide names and contact information, it's a sure sign to move on.

✧ Once you find the service providers you want, go ahead and book them—soon. Chances are, if you like them, they're good, and their schedules fill up quickly.

✧ Make sure that your contracts state: dates, times (arrival and departure), location of wedding, fees (including taxes and overtime charges; noting gratuities is optional), deposit amount, balance due date and amount, insurance coverage, cancellation and refund policies, names of the people who will provide the service, agreed-upon attire of professionals, number and length of breaks, meal accommodations, and detailed descriptions of absolutely everything that is being provided.

✧ If you're unsure of contract terms, have a lawyer review the documents.

✧ Don't work with any professional who expects payment in full before services are rendered. A partial deposit, however, is acceptable and, in most cases, expected.

Chapter One

Ceremony

Ceremony

THINGS TO DO

- [ ] Make appointments to meet with site coordinators and/or officiants
- [ ] Visit potential ceremony sites
- [ ] Reserve location for date of wedding
- [ ] Send signed contract and deposit for ceremony site
- [ ] Choose and ask attendants
- [ ] Book officiant
- [ ] Reserve any necessary rental equipment (see page 56)
- [ ] Schedule rehearsal
- [ ] Schedule any necessary meetings/counseling sessions with officiant
- [ ] Make arrangements for ceremony music (see page 81)
- [ ] Make arrangements for floral decorations (see page 97)
- [ ] Make arrangements for any other decorations for ceremony site
- [ ] Consult local town clerk's office regarding marriage license requirements:
  - [ ] how far in advance you need to and are able to obtain license
  - [ ] what jurisdiction license needs to be from (ie: where you'll be married or where you live)
  - [ ] witness requirements
  - [ ] whether a blood test is required, what must be tested for, what forms are required, and where you can get the appropriate blood test
- [ ] Get blood tests, if required
- [ ] Obtain marriage license
- [ ] Obtain any necessary official religious documents
- [ ] Plan/write vows
- [ ] Plan/adapt/review any other parts of ceremony
- [ ] Select readings and/or songs for special participants
- [ ] Send selected readings and/or songs to appropriate participants
- [ ] Decide upon order of attendants for processional
- [ ] Make any desired seating arrangements
- [ ] Arrange for place to get dressed before ceremony
- [ ] Determine where to have receiving line (could be done at reception site instead)
- [ ] Obtain any objects necessary for ceremony customs, such as drinking wine from a shared goblet, lighting the unity candle, or breaking the glass
- [ ] Obtain pillow for ring bearer; purchase basket and flower petals for flower girl(s)
- [ ] Purchase birdseed/bubbles for guests to shower you with as you leave ceremony site (this custom could instead be performed as you leave the reception site)

☐ Make arrangements for distribution of ceremony programs and signing of guest book
☐ Assign attendant to arrange dress and/or veil at altar
☐ Assign attendant to hold bouquet and/or glove during ceremony
☐ If no ring bearer, or ring bearer is only to carry bride's ring, assign attendant to hold groom's ring during ceremony
☐ Put together emergency supply kit for wedding day (see page 157 for contents)
☐ Confirm final details/times with officiant and site coordinator
☐ Get contact numbers for officiant and site coordinator for wedding day
☐ Other _____
☐ _____
☐ _____
☐ _____
☐ _____
☐ _____
☐ _____
☐

Site

QUESTIONS TO ASK: CEREMONY SITE

Ceremony Site I

Site name: _____
Contact person: _____
Address: _____
_____

Phone: _____
E-mail: _____
Website: _____
✧ What dates and times are available? _____
_____

✧ How many people does the space hold—seated and standing? _____
✧ If the space is bigger than we need, can pews or rows be roped off? _____

Words to the Wise

✧ Think outside the traditional venues when looking for inspiration for where to exchange your vows. Think about places that have held special memories for you—like where you went on your first date, where you like to vacation, even a favorite scene from a movie, whether it was shot on a beach, vineyard, or town square.

✧ If you're planning to hold your ceremony and reception in two different places, the distance that you and your guests will need to travel between the two should factor into your selection of sites.

✧ Consider undertaking DIY projects to personalize your wedding, such as making the ring pillow or the programs yourself or personalizing the aisles with attractive buckets and hand-picked flowers. Search online or look through books and magazines for DIY wedding ideas.

✧ If you're considering having your ceremony in a public outdoor space (such as a beach or park), find out if you need to acquire a permit or any special permissions.

✧ Asking a dear friend to do a reading or requesting that a musically gifted relative sing a song at your wedding is a good way to personalize your ceremony while honoring someone close to you.

Ceremony Site II   *Ceremony Site III*

_____   _____
_____   _____
_____   _____
_____   _____
_____   _____
_____   _____
_____   _____
_____   _____
_____   _____
_____   _____
_____   _____
_____   _____

Ceremony Site I

◇ *If a house of worship:* Will any congregant or other worshiper be permitted to attend the ceremony?

◇ *If an outdoor location:* Is there a backup plan for inclement weather?

◇ What are the acoustics like?

◇ Will the officiant use/need a microphone?

◇ Will we or any readers be heard easily without a microphone? Is one available if necessary?

◇ How long is the aisle?

◇ Is there a room in which my attendants and I can dress?

◇ Is there an organ or piano?

◇ Can we hire an outside musician to play it?

◇ Can other musicians be brought in to play other instruments?

◇ Are there any restrictions regarding instruments or music?

◇ Is there space for musicians to set up?

◇ Are there ample electrical outlets to suit their needs?

◇ Is photography or videography permitted in the room?

◇ Is there a good spot to take formal pictures?

◇ Can we bring in our own flowers?

◇ *If a house of worship:* Do couples typically donate ceremony flowers to the house of worship, or can we use them for the reception?

◇ Are there restrictions/rules for decorating? For example, can we use candles? Are there areas we cannot decorate? Can we hang decorations on walls and doors?

Ceremony Site II | *Ceremony Site III*

Ceremony Site I

✧ How far in advance of ceremony
can set up begin?

✧ Is there someone on staff to help
coordinate a rehearsal?

✧ Is there someone on staff to help
coordinate such details as cuing
members of the processional and
setting up a table for programs?

✧ Is there a suitable spot for a
receiving line?

✧ Will any other ceremonies be
taking place at the same time?
On the same day?

✧ Is throwing birdseed or blowing
bubbles allowed after the ceremony?
Is there a place to do this?

✧ Is there parking? If so, what is
the capacity?

✧ Does the facility have liability
insurance?

✧ What is the fee for use of the site?

✧ How much of a deposit is required?

✧ When is the balance due?

✧ What is the cancellation policy?

✧ Other questions/notes:

KEEP IN MIND

For the receiving line, the bride and her attendants should either set aside their
bouquets or hold their flowers in the left hand in order to shake with the right.

Ceremony Site II   *Ceremony Site III*

Officiant

QUESTIONS TO ASK: RELIGIOUS CEREMONY

Officiant I

Name:

Address:

Phone:

E-mail:

✧ What dates and times are you available?

✧ Can you give us an overview of the service?

✧ What are your thoughts about the service?

✧ How long is the typical ceremony?

✧ Can we help personalize the ceremony? If so, will you provide guidelines?

✧ Can we write our own vows? If so, will you provide guidance?

✧ Can we include family members/ friends in the service by assigning readings/prayers or songs?

✧ *If interfaith marriage:* Can another officiant (of the other faith) take part in the service?

✧ Will you perform the ceremony outside a house of worship?

✧ If the wedding is out of town, will you travel?

✧ Will you give a sermon or speech? If so, can we see a copy of what you'll say before the wedding?

✧ Do you permit photography or videography during the ceremony?

Officiant II

Officiant III

Officiant I

◇ Do you have any restrictions regarding music?

◇ Are there restrictions regarding wedding attire?

◇ Will you attend the rehearsal?

◇ What is expected of us in terms of premarital classes?

◇ How many pre-wedding meetings will we have with you?

◇ When and where will the marriage license be signed?

◇ How many witnesses are needed to sign the marriage license?

◇ Are there any requirements regarding who can be a witness?

◇ Is there a fee, or is a donation acceptable?

◇ Other questions/notes:

_____
_____
_____
_____
_____
_____
_____
_____
_____
_____
_____
_____
_____
_____
_____
_____
_____
_____
_____
_____
_____
_____

KEEP IN MIND

Be sure to include your officiant and his or her spouse on the wedding guest list.

Officiant II | *Officiant III*

QUESTIONS TO ASK: CIVIL CEREMONY

Officiant I

Name:

Address:

Phone:

E-mail:

✧ What dates and times are you available?

✧ Can you give us an overview of the ceremony?

✧ How long is the typical ceremony?

✧ How much guidance can we expect in shaping the ceremony?

✧ Can we write our own vows? Do you provide any guidelines?

✧ Can you provide us with standard vows if we don't write our own?

✧ Can any religious elements (readings, music, etc.) be included?

✧ Will you give a sermon or speech? Can we see a copy ahead of time?

✧ In terms of location, what is the extent of your jurisdiction?

✧ Will you travel within the area of your jurisdiction?

✧ What is expected of us in terms of premarital meetings?

✧ Will you attend the rehearsal?

✧ When, where, and by whom will the marriage license be signed?

✧ What is your fee?

✧ Other questions/notes:

Officiant II	*Officiant III*

Notes

Chapter Two

Reception

Reception

THINGS TO DO

- [ ] Make appointments with site managers and, if necessary, caterers
- [ ] Hire wedding consultant (optional; see page 50)
- [ ] Visit potential reception sites
- [ ] Reserve location for date of wedding
- [ ] Send signed contract and deposit for location
- [ ] Interview potential caterers (if off-site)
- [ ] Book caterer
- [ ] Send signed contract and deposit to caterer
- [ ] Schedule menu tasting
- [ ] Take care of necessary home improvements/landscaping, if having at-home wedding
- [ ] Make arrangements for reception music (see page 84)
- [ ] Make arrangements for floral decorations (see page 97)
- [ ] Make arrangements for other reception decorations
- [ ] Make menu selections (see page 39 for menu checklist)
- [ ] Visit rentals showroom to choose chairs, tables, linens, china, etc.
- [ ] Reserve rental equipment (see page 56 for rentals worksheet)
- [ ] Schedule delivery and pickup of rental equipment
- [ ] Schedule cake tasting
- [ ] Order wedding cake (and groom's cake, if desired)
- [ ] Select cake topper
- [ ] Make arrangements for parking, if necessary
- [ ] Arrange for place to change into going-away outfits
- [ ] Give caterer and/or site coordinator final head count
- [ ] Make seating chart
- [ ] Compose toasts (from you to your groom; from the two of you thanking your hosts and guests)
- [ ] Confirm details, date, times, and location with rental company
- [ ] Get phone number of rental company contact for wedding day
- [ ] Confirm details with caterer
- [ ] Get phone number of caterer for wedding day
- [ ] Go over times for all reception "events" (cocktails, first dance, dinner, cake-cutting, etc.) with caterer/site coordinator, and give this schedule to applicable service providers (photographer, videographer, band/disc jockey)
- [ ] Get phone number of site coordinator for wedding day
- [ ] Give site coordinator arrival times for all service providers

- ☐ Ask caterer/site coordinator to have cake topper packed up for you, if yours to keep
- ☐ Ask caterer/site coordinator to have top tier of wedding cake packed up for you (to save for first anniversary)
- ☐ Assign someone to take top tier of wedding cake home and freeze for you—and to take cake topper home if applicable
- ☐ Arrange to have groom's cake cut up and boxed for favors, if desired (legend has it that a single woman who sleeps with some of this cake under her pillow will dream of her husband-to-be)
- ☐ Other _____
- ☐ _____
- ☐ _____
- ☐ _____
- ☐ _____
- ☐ _____
- ☐ _____

KEEP IN MIND

Help make your guests comfortable during the reception by placing baskets filled with useful items—such as adhesive bandages, hair spray, and mouthwash—in the rest rooms.

Site

Things to think about when deciding upon a reception location:

- ✧ Is the space easily transformed with decorations? Does it need decorations, or does it fulfill your vision as is?
- ✧ Does the style of the space match the desired mood for your wedding?
- ✧ Does the decor coordinate with your desired color scheme?
- ✧ What are the views like?
- ✧ Are you comfortable with the site coordinator? (If you will be dealing with this person a lot, this is an important point.)
- ✧ If you have invited older guests, is the space easily accessible for them?

Things to think about if considering an at-home wedding:

✧ Do you have enough space to accommodate the number of people on your guest list?

✧ Will you be holding the event indoors, outdoors, or both?

✧ If outdoors, what will your backup plan be for inclement weather? Tent? Move everyone indoors?

✧ Will you be comfortable having a potentially large group of people in your home? (Remember there's always the possibility of breakage and spills.)

✧ Will you need to make any home improvements or do any landscaping before the event?

✧ How much rearranging of furniture will you need to do to accommodate the event?

✧ What items will you need to rent, and how much of an expense will this add?

✧ Will you be having the event catered, or will a family member be doing the cooking?

✧ Is there enough cooking space in your kitchen, or will you need to make other arrangements?

✧ Do you have enough parking space, and how will parking be organized?

✧ Do you have enough bathrooms, or will you need to rent portable toilets?

Things to think about if considering an outdoor wedding:

✧ What will your backup plan be in case of rain?

✧ Are you willing to risk having guests be uncomfortable due to extreme temperatures or excessive wind, or will you rent a tent equipped to temper the effects of such problems?

✧ Is the ground even enough for chairs and tables to be stable?

✧ What will the landscape (flowers and trees) look like at the time of the wedding? (Ask to see photographs.)

✧ Will allergies to outdoor elements affect your or the groom's enjoyment of the day?

✧ How will you combat insects that might be milling around after dark?

✧ If a public space, is a permit required?

QUESTIONS TO ASK: RECEPTION SITE

For places with on-site caterers, the site coordinator may be the person with whom you will speak regarding the menu; if this is the case for your situation, refer to the list of catering questions that begins on page 38 during your interview.

Reception Site I

Site name: Atlantic Beach Club

Contact person: Lori

Address: 55 Purgatory Road
Middletown RI 02842

Phone: 401 847 2750

E-mail:

Website:

✧ What dates and times are available?

✧ What is the fee for the site rental? Ø

✧ How many hours does that include? 5hr 6pm - 11pm

✧ How much of that time is party time and how much is setup and cleanup?

✧ How do overtime charges work? $ 25 per server (1 xtr hr)

✧ How many people can the space comfortably accommodate for a seated dinner? 300 people

✧ How many people can the space hold for a cocktail reception (standing room with some tables sprinkled about)?

✧ Are there any circumstances that affect the capacity of the space (for instance, the addition of a dance floor or head table)?

✧ Do you provide tables, chairs, linens, china, and glassware? Yes

✧ Is there a choice of styles for any of the above?

✧ *If tables are provided:* How many guests per table?

Reception Site II	*Reception Site III*

Reception Site I

◇ Can tables and chairs easily be placed in the reception area?

◇ How does the flow work if more than one room/area is used?

◇ *If using site for ceremony and reception:* Where will each take place?

◇ *If ceremony and reception are in the same room:* How will the space be transformed? How long will the changeover take?

◇ Where will cocktails be served?

◇ *If outdoors:* Is the ground even enough to set out chairs and tables for a cocktail hour and/or the reception?

◇ *If outdoors:* Is this a public space where anybody can wander in and out?

◇ *If outdoors:* Is there a backup plan for inclement weather?

◇ Are other spaces (gardens, terraces) accessible to guests?

◇ Are there additional charges for the use of other spaces?

◇ Are any spaces off-limits to guests?

◇ Will other parties be going on at the same time?

◇ Is there a party immediately preceding or following our event?

◇ If so, what preparations are taken to ensure that each party finishes on time, but no one is rushed out?

◇ *If a summer wedding:* Is the space air-conditioned?

◇ Is there an on-site coordinator?

◇ Will he/she or someone else be there on the wedding day to accept deliveries and ensure that all other details run smoothly?

Reception Site II   *Reception Site III*

Reception Site I

✧ Is there an on-site caterer? _____

✧ If not, are there kitchen facilities to
bring in an off-site caterer? _____

✧ Is there a particular caterer we are
required to use? _____

✧ Is there a particular florist or
photographer we must use? _____

✧ Are there rules regarding alcohol? _____

✧ Are there rules dictating style,
noise level, or the hours during
which music can be played? _____

✧ Is there enough space for a band or
disc jockey to set up? Where would
the band or disc jockey be? _____

✧ Is there a dance floor or enough space
to lay a rented floor? Where would
the dance floor be? _____

✧ What is the dance floor's capacity? _____

✧ Are there ample electrical outlets for
musical equipment? _____

✧ Are there any rules regarding
photography or videography? _____

✧ Are there any good spots for
formal pictures? _____

✧ Is there a good place to hold the
receiving line? _____

✧ Can we visit the site during another
event to see the space set up? _____

✧ Does your facility have any
decorations we can use? _____

✧ What is the parking capacity? _____

✧ Is the parking area located close to
the site's entrance? _____

✧ Is valet parking offered?
If so, what is the cost? _____

✧ If valet parking is not offered,
can we hire outside valet parkers? _____

Reception Site II	*Reception Site III*

Reception Site I

✧ Once inside, how are guests directed
to the event?

✧ Where are the bathrooms located?

✧ How many stalls are there?

✧ Is there an attendant?
At any additional cost to us?

✧ May we see the bathrooms?

✧ *If outdoors:* Is there room for
portable toilets?

✧ Is there a coat room?

✧ Is there a coat room attendant?
At any additional cost to us?

✧ Is there a place to set up a gift table?
If so, do you provide the table?

✧ Is throwing birdseed or blowing
bubbles allowed after the reception,
and is there a place to do this?

✧ Is there a place to change into
going-away outfits?

✧ Is there security on-site and in the
parking lot?

✧ Do you have liability insurance?
What are we responsible for?

✧ How much of a deposit is required?

✧ When is the balance due?

✧ What is your cancellation policy?

✧ Can you provide a list of references
who have recently had weddings here?

✧ Other questions/notes:

Reception Site II	*Reception Site III*

Food

Facts at Your Fingertips: The Lingo

✧ **American service (also "plated service"):** Food is set on the plates in the kitchen, then brought out to seated guests. This is typically the most cost-efficient service style.

✧ **French service:** Traditionally, this style consisted of a six-member serving team who prepared meals tableside. Because this is an expensive endeavor, many caterers today simply incorporate some French-style touches; in such a case, food can be cooked in the kitchen and the final details, such as tossing salads or carving beef, attended to by the wait staff tableside. Food is served with two long serving forks.

✧ **Russian service:** Members of the wait staff serve each course from platters, placing the food on plates already set at guests' seats.

✧ **Family style:** Platters of food prepared in the kitchen are set at the table, and guests serve themselves. This style cuts back on the need for extensive wait staff, but makes it difficult to gauge the precise amount of food needed.

✧ **Station:** Tables are set up with different elements of the meal, with plates and utensils at one end of the station for guests to take for themselves. Certain stations are manned with a chef, as in a carving or sushi station, while at other stations, guests help themselves.

✧ **Signature cocktails:** Some couples have favorite drink they want served at their wedding, perhaps one they discovered on vacation or out one night, or one that was created just for them based on their favorite flavors, or maybe one that matches their color scheme or theme.

QUESTIONS TO ASK: CATERING

Caterer I

Name:

Address:

Phone:

E-mail:

Website:

✧ How long have you been in business?

✧ What are some of the styles of weddings you have worked on in the past?

✧ **By consumption:** This refers to how a couple is charged for alcohol. Typically, there are two options—the bill can reflect a per-person flat rate or it can be calculated by consumption, meaning the bartenders will track how many drinks or how many bottles have been "sold." If you don't have many big drinkers in the crowd, this is often a more economical way to go.

✧ **Corkage fee:** This is the fee caterers charge for opening a bottle of alcohol. When the bar tab is included in the catering fee, there is usually no corkage fee. If the bar is a separate tab or you'll be bringing in your own liquor, ask if there will be a corkage fee (and have the price stated in your contract).

MENU CHECKLIST *(Use this list according to your specific needs.)*

Cocktail Hour
☐ Bar
☐ Hors d'oeuvres

Main Reception
☐ Appetizer
☐ Salad
☐ Soup
☐ Entrée

☐ Cake
☐ Other desserts
☐ Bar/beverages
☐ Champagne toast

Keep in Mind

The wait staff/guest ratio is an important one. For a seated meal, it is best to have one server for every eight- to ten-person table. For a buffet, there should ideally be one waiter for every twenty-five people.

Caterer II	*Caterer III*

Caterer I

✧ Do you offer all types of service: seated, buffet, station, and cocktail?   _____

✧ What is the service style for seated: French, Russian, or plated?   _____

✧ *If on-site catering:* Who will be the chef on duty on our wedding day?   _____

✧ Are there set menu packages, or can one be custom-made?   _____

✧ What are menu suggestions that fit our budget, style, and season—for both the cocktail hour and dinner?   _____

✧ Will guests be offered entrée options?   _____

✧ Do you offer special meals (kosher, low-fat, vegetarian)? Are there any on hand for last-minute requests?   _____

✧ How do you accommodate any last-minute changes?   _____

✧ Will you/the chef prepare special family recipes?   _____

✧ What are the fees, and what do they include?   _____

✧ Are gratuities additional?   _____

✧ Do you offer tastings to help select the menu?   _____

✧ Is there an additional charge for tastings?   _____

✧ Would the tastings be prepared by the same person doing the food for our wedding?   _____

✧ Is a traditional wedding cake extra? And a groom's cake?   _____

✧ If we contract the wedding cake from a private baker, do you charge a cake-cutting fee?   _____

Caterer II

Caterer III

Caterer I

◇ Is champagne for a toast included?
If not, what is the charge? _____

◇ What do overtime charges include? _____

◇ When would they go into effect? _____

◇ Is there a minimum number of plates
that must be ordered? _____

◇ Can you explain the bar fees? _____

◇ Are bar fees based on consumption
or the number of opened bottles? _____

◇ What label of alcohol is used? _____

◇ Are sodas/tonics provided at no charge? _____

◇ Are refunds given for unopened bottles? _____

◇ Can we bring in our own liquor? _____

◇ Will you provide a shopping list if
we choose to bring in liquor? _____

◇ Is there a corkage fee? _____

◇ Do you offer meals for musicians/
photographers/videographers at
a lower price? _____

◇ Do you offer children's meals at a
lower price? _____

◇ Who will be overseeing the wait staff
and kitchen staff on our wedding day? _____

◇ How long has your staff worked
with you? _____

◇ How will the staff be dressed? _____

◇ What is the server/guest ratio? _____

◇ *If off-site caterer:* Have you worked at
our site? If so, does it meet your needs?
If you haven't worked at the site, will
you visit it to check out the facilities? _____

◇ Do you provide tables, chairs, linens,
china, glassware, serving pieces, etc.?
If so, is a security deposit required in
case of breakage or stains? _____

Caterer II	*Caterer III*

Caterer I

◇ If you don't provide these items, do you work with a rental company that offers discounts to your clients?

◇ Will you provide a list of rental items needed?

◇ Will you be responsible for receiving rental deliveries and organizing rental returns?

◇ *If caterer is responsible for tables:* How are the tables arranged?

◇ *If tables are provided by caterer:* How many guests can sit comfortably at each table?

◇ How are the setup and cleanup handled?

◇ How many meetings can we plan to have with you?

◇ When do you need the final head count?

◇ Do you have liability insurance?

◇ How are you licensed?

◇ Can we see your health permit?

◇ How much of a deposit is required?

◇ What is your cancellation policy?

◇ Do you have references?

◇ Other questions/notes:

Caterer II	Caterer III

The Cake

Facts at Your Fingertips: Cake Talk

✧ **Buttercream:** This versatile cake filling and frosting can be colored and flavored for a variety of effects. It can also be used for cake trimmings, such as beaded edgings and faux flowers. Made from a mixture of softened butter, milk or cream, confectioners' sugar, and egg yolks, buttercream does not hold up well in the heat and, hence, is not ideal for an outdoor summer wedding.

✧ **Fondant:** This malleable sugar, water, and cream of tartar mixture can be wrapped around a cake for a porcelain finish or molded into decorations, such as flowers, fruits, bows, and other fancy designs.

✧ **Royal icing:** Made from sugar and egg whites, this icing can be tinted any color and hardens when dry to make sturdy decorations for cakes.

✧ **Marzipan:** This almond paste, sugar, and egg white mixture can be tinted with food coloring and molded to make trimmings, such as flowers, fruits, bows, and other designs.

QUESTIONS TO ASK: CAKE

Bakery I

Company name: _____

Contact person: _____

Address: _____

_____

_____

Phone: _____

E-mail: _____

Website: _____

✧ Do you have a portfolio from which we can select a style? _____

✧ Will you create a custom design based on our vision? _____

✧ What are some flavor combinations you can suggest for fillings and icings? _____

✧ What are some cake trimmings you like to use? _____

Bakery II   *Bakery III*

Bakery I

◇ Have you worked with real flowers? _____

◇ Are you familiar with the safety issues _____
    regarding edible flowers and the need _____
    to use flowers free from pesticides? _____

◇ Have you worked with sugared fruits _____
    and flowers? _____

◇ Do you offer a cake tasting? _____

◇ Is the cake prepared and then frozen, or _____
    is it prepared fresh for the wedding day? _____

_____

◇ What is the fee? Is it based on a _____
    per-person charge? _____

_____

_____

◇ Are delivery and setup included? _____
    If not, what is the additional cost? _____

◇ Will you decorate a cake with faux _____
    layers for display and prepare a less _____
    expensive sheet cake for cutting and _____
    serving? _____

◇ Will you do a groom's cake? If so, what _____
    are our choices and what is the fee? _____

_____

_____

◇ How far in advance do we need _____
    to place our order? _____

◇ Do you have references? _____

_____

_____

_____

_____

_____

◇ Other questions/notes: _____

_____

_____

_____

_____

Bakery II	Bakery III

Wedding Consultant

What a wedding consultant can do:

◇ Plan the entire event, from finding the site to handling the details on the wedding day.

◇ Make arrangements for select aspects of the wedding, such as the flowers, music, and photography.

◇ Run the show on the wedding day only.

Why you might want to hire a wedding consultant:

◇ To save time. A consultant can take on a large or small amount of responsibility and also weed out some of the early search steps.

◇ To plan a long-distance event.

◇ To reap the rewards of consultant/vendor relationships and possible discounts.

◇ To gain the benefit of not starting from scratch. A consultant will know exactly what needs to be done and when and how to do it.

◇ To leave the worrying to a professional.

◇ To have a referee for family disputes.

◇ To obtain an unbiased professional opinion.

◇ To have someone on hand to deal with the details.

◇ To obtain the advice of someone knowledgeable about wedding etiquette.

QUESTIONS TO ASK: WEDDING CONSULTANT

Wedding Consultant I

Name: _____

Address: _____

_____

_____

Phone: _____

E-mail: _____

Website: _____

◇ Do you have a portfolio with photos of weddings you've planned? _____

◇ Do you have a business license? _____

◇ How long have you been in business? _____

Why you might not want to hire a wedding consultant:

✧ Hiring a consultant can be pricey, and the cost might mean you can't afford something else you want.

✧ Hiring a stranger to help you plan one of the most personal days of your life might make you a bit more uncomfortable than you expected.

✧ It can be difficult to find just the right person to interpret your vision, and you may end up having to compromise on certain aspects.

✧ The person you choose may not be in sync with your groom or other family members, creating yet another "relationship" you need to be concerned about.

✧ Depending on your consultant's personality, you could feel as if you're losing control over your wedding.

✧ Even if you like planning, you can hire someone to take care of certain details—such as the time-consuming ones—or to just be there on the special day to ensure everything runs smoothly.

THINGS TO DO

☐ Interview potential candidates
☐ Book wedding consultant
☐ Schedule progress meetings
☐ Send signed contract and deposit to wedding consultant
☐ Confirm final details with wedding consultant
☐ Get contact number of wedding consultant for wedding day

Wedding Consultant II	*Wedding Consultant III*

Wedding Consultant I

◆ Are you certified? By what association? _____

◆ What is your fee? Do you charge
hourly, a flat fee, or a percentage of
the total wedding budget? _____

◆ Can we hire you to plan the
entire event? _____

◆ Can we hire you to help with just
some of the planning? _____

◆ Can we hire you to help on the
wedding day only? _____

◆ What details do you handle? _____

◆ What details won't you handle? _____

◆ How many meetings should we plan
to have? _____

◆ Can we conduct business by phone
and/or e-mail? _____

◆ *If site has been selected:*
Have you planned any weddings at
our site before? _____

◆ *If site has been selected:*
Do you know the catering manager/
events planner at our site? _____

◆ Do you have vendors you've worked
with in the past? _____

◆ Are there a few that you like for each
service or just one vendor for each? _____

◆ Do these service providers offer
your clients discounts? _____

Wedding Consultant II	*Wedding Consultant III*

Wedding Consultant I

✧ What would the process be for
   selecting and hiring vendors for our
   wedding?

_____
_____
_____
_____
_____

✧ Do you like to take complete control,
   or do you welcome our ideas
   and participation?

✧ Will you be on hand the day of
   the wedding?

✧ How many other events will you be
   organizing on that day?

✧ How many people on your staff will
   be at the wedding?

✧ How long has your staff worked
   with you?

✧ How will you (and your staff) be
   dressed?

✧ *If hiring consultant to be at wedding:*
   What happens if you are ill on our
   wedding day?

✧ Do you require meals?

✧ Will you travel if necessary?

✧ Will there be additional expenses for
   parking and travel?

✧ Do you have liability insurance?

✧ Do you have references?

_____
_____
_____
_____
_____
_____
_____
_____
_____
_____
_____
_____
_____
_____
_____
_____
_____
_____
_____
_____

✧ Other questions/notes:

_____
_____
_____
_____

Wedding Consultant II	*Wedding Consultant III*

Rentals

(for an at-home wedding or a site where items are not provided)

RENTALS WORKSHEET

(Use this list according to your specific needs.)

Rental Item	Description	Cost/ item	Qty.	Total Cost
CEREMONY				
Chairs				
Canopy for altar				
Aisle runner (may be provided by florist)				
Other				
COCKTAIL HOUR				
Chairs				
Tables				
Linens				
China				
Flatware				
Glassware				
Serving pieces				
Decorative accessories				
Other				

Vendor I

| | | | | Vendor II | | | | | | | | | Vendor III | | | | |

Vendor II   **Vendor III**

Description	Cost/item	Qty.	Total Cost	Description	Cost/item	Qty.	Total Cost

Vendor I

Rental Item	Description	Cost/ item	Qty.	Total Cost
RECEPTION				
Tent				
Chairs				
Tables				
Lounge furniture				
Linens				
China				
Flatware				
Glassware				
Serving pieces				
Decorative accessories				
Dance floor				
Heaters				
Lights				
Portable toilets				
Other				
TOTAL				

Vendor II				Vendor III			
Description	Cost/item	Qty.	Total Cost	Description	Cost/item	Qty.	Total Cost
TOTAL				TOTAL			

QUESTIONS TO ASK: RENTAL COMPANY

Rental Company I

Company name: _____

Contact person: _____

Address: _____
_____
_____
_____

Phone: _____

E-mail: _____

Website: _____

✧ Can your inventory accommodate the _____
size of our guest list? _____

✧ Do you deliver? _____

✧ Will you ship to an out-of-town site? _____

✧ How far in advance can items be _____
delivered? _____

✧ How soon after the event can items _____
be picked up? _____

✧ Will we incur extra charges because _____
of off delivery dates? For example, _____
if items from a Saturday night wedding _____
are not picked up until Monday because _____
there is no service on Sunday, will we _____
be charged for that extra day? _____

✧ Do you offer selections in various _____
price ranges? _____
_____

✧ Do you offer a variety of tent styles? _____
_____
_____

✧ Do you offer a variety of table shapes _____
and sizes? _____
_____
_____

✧ Do you offer a variety of chair styles? _____
_____

✧ Do you offer table linens in different _____
fabrics and colors? _____

Rental Company II   *Rental Company III*

Rental Company I

◇ Do you offer china, flatware, glassware, and serving pieces in different patterns/colors?

◇ Do you offer any other items we need?

◇ Is there anyone on staff to help us achieve the look we want?

◇ Is there a minimum number of items that must be ordered?

◇ What are the fees for the items we want? *(Refer to the worksheet on page 56 to record fees.)*

◇ Is setup included?

◇ Is there breakage coverage?

◇ How does the payment schedule work?

◇ What is your cancellation policy?

◇ Is there an emergency contact for the wedding day in case items are not delivered or arrive damaged?

◇ Do you have liability insurance?

◇ Do you have references?

◇ Other questions/notes:

Rental Company II

Rental Company III

Notes

Chapter Three

Stationery

Stationery

THINGS TO DO

☐ Speak to stationers about ideas and costs
☐ Search online for invitations and designs
☐ If DIY-ing, start thinking of designs and gathering necessary materials
☐ Order desired stationery items *(refer to the worksheet on page 68, and use it as needed)*
☐ Send deposit to stationer
☐ Give wording for invitation (and for any other items you're ordering) to stationer
☐ Review proofs for invitation and for any other applicable items
☐ Obtain addresses for everyone on guest list
☐ Call calligraphers to see work/discuss fees
☐ Book calligrapher, or recruit a talented friend for your calligraphy needs
☐ Send guest list (with addresses) and envelopes to person addressing invitations
☐ Send seating cards and/or table number cards to calligrapher, if applicable
☐ Purchase special stamps for response envelopes
☐ Assemble invitations and stuff envelopes
☐ Bring envelopes to post office to be hand-stamped
☐ Purchase guest book
☐ Purchase pen for guest book
☐ Assign friend or family member to oversee guest book at wedding
☐ Follow up with invitees who haven't responded (about two weeks before wedding)
☐ Address wedding announcements
☐ Arrange for someone to send wedding announcements on the day of or the day after the wedding
☐ Other _____
☐ _____
☐ _____
☐ _____
☐ _____
☐ _____
☐ _____
☐ _____
☐ _____

Facts at Your Fingertips: Invitation Inserts

The following are inserts that can accompany the main wedding invitation:

✧ **Ceremony/reception card:** This is the most common invitation for guests who are asked to attend both the ceremony and the reception. If you're having an intimate ceremony with a smaller guest list than that of the reception, send separate ceremony and reception cards.

✧ **Response card:** Guests will use this card to let you know if they'll be attending your wedding. If you need guests to give you their entrée selections ahead of time, include their choices on the card.

✧ **Response envelope:** Guests will use this small, stamped envelope to return the response card. The envelope should be preaddressed to the wedding host.

✧ **Pew card:** This card is sent to family and friends who have special assigned seats at the ceremony. The card should read "Please present this card" and include the name of the location, the date, and the pew or row number.

✧ **Within-the-ribbon card:** This card serves the same purpose as a pew card, except that instead of designating a specific pew number, it will say "Within the ribbon," referring to a roped-off section of pews in the front.

✧ **Map/directions card:** Often the venue will provide this, but if you want to have the map and information printed to match the style of your invitation, a stationer can usually accommodate you.

✧ **Accommodations card:** This card can be included in the invitations of out-of-town guests to provide them with information regarding any hotels where you've held blocks of rooms. Include the hotel's telephone number. (You could, instead, send a separate letter ahead of the invitations providing this information, as well as details regarding local area attractions; this will give guests plenty of time to make their travel arrangements.)

✧ **Rain card:** If you're planning an outdoor wedding and have an alternate location booked for inclement weather, include that location's name and address on this card.

✧ **Parking card:** If you have arranged for special parking nearby or on-site with valet service, include this information on a card with the words "Please present this card to the parking attendant" as well as "Gratuities included," if applicable.

✧ **Tissue paper:** This thin sheet of tissue, once used to prevent the invitation ink from smudging, is still considered an elegant touch.

✧ **Inner envelope:** This envelope, which is slightly smaller than the mailing envelope, holds the invitation and all other components. The inner envelope should remain unsealed and be addressed with the guests' names. For a formal wedding, put the title and last name of each guest on this envelope. For a more casual tone, use only their first names.

Facts at Your Fingertips: Printing Primer

✧ **Engraving:** This technique, which uses a metal plate with die-cut letters, creates raised letters on the front of a piece of paper (and small indentations on the back). This method takes longer than others and is the most expensive.

✧ **Thermography:** Less expensive than engraving but offering a similar look, this technique creates letters with a heating process that combines ink and powder. The letters are raised on the front side of the paper, but the back of the paper is smooth.

✧ **Offset:** This technique uses an inked rubber cylinder to print on the paper. The look is less formal than engraving or thermography, and the process is less expensive.

✧ **Embossing:** This technique, which creates raised lettering, is usually "blind," meaning the letters or symbols are the same color as the paper but stand out in relief. The method is most often used for monograms, borders, or artwork on stationery pieces.

Words to the Wise

✧ Send save-the-date cards to out-of-town guests as early as six to nine months before the wedding.

✧ Mail invitations six to eight weeks before the wedding (the earlier the better during holiday seasons).

✧ Don't include registry information on the invitations; rely upon word of mouth.

✧ Before ordering table number cards to identify reception tables, find out if your reception site or caterer will provide these.

✧ Order extra envelopes (inner and outer) to allow for any addressing mistakes.

✧ With the exception of people's titles, when addressing invitations do not use abbreviations.

✧ Some couples choose to send formal wedding announcements to friends and relatives who were not invited to the wedding. These announcements should be mailed either on the day of the ceremony or the day after.

Stationery Worksheet

Stationery Item	Description	Cost/ item	Qty.	Total Cost
	Vendor I			
Wedding invitations				
Outer envelopes				
Inner envelopes				
Ceremony cards				
Reception cards				
Response cards				
Response envelopes				
Pew cards				
Within-the-ribbon cards				
Map/directions cards				
Accommodations cards				
Rain cards				
Parking cards				
Tissue paper				
Engagement announcements				
Save-the-date cards				

Vendor II

Vendor III

Description	Cost/item	Qty.	Total Cost	Description	Cost/item	Qty.	Total Cost

Vendor I

Stationery Item	Description	Cost/ item	Qty.	Total Cost
Rehearsal dinner invitations				
Ceremony programs				
Menu cards				
Seating cards				
Table number cards				
Thank-you notes				
At-home cards				
Wedding announcements				
Other				
TOTAL				

KEEP IN MIND

Thank-you notes for engagement gifts and wedding presents given before the wedding should be sent within two weeks of receipt. Traditional etiquette dictates that you take no longer than one month to send your notes of gratitude for wedding presents received on or after the wedding day, but modern practices have extended this period to two months. (For those presents received on the wedding day, the clock starts ticking upon your return from the honeymoon.)

Vendor II				Vendor III			
Description	Cost/item	Qty.	Total Cost	Description	Cost/item	Qty.	Total Cost
TOTAL				TOTAL			

QUESTIONS TO ASK: STATIONERY

Stationer I

Company name:

Contact person:

Address:

Phone:

E-mail:

Website:

✧ What are our options regarding the different pieces that can make up the wedding invitation (inner envelopes, response cards, etc.), and how do they affect the cost?

✧ Can you print up additional pieces to include with the invitation, such as a map/directions card and an accommodations card?

✧ What are our printing options, and how do they affect the cost?

✧ What are our paper options (material, weight, color), and how do they affect the cost?

✧ What are our options in type style?

✧ Can we see samples of different printing techniques, paper styles, and type styles?

✧ Aside from the basic options, do you help with other creative details or only offer what printing companies offer? If so, what are add-on options? What have you done in the past? Do you have samples?

Stationer II	Stationer III

Stationer I

◇ Are there certain styles or sizes that are more budget-friendly in terms of printing and postage?

◇ When do we need to place an order?

◇ When would the invitations be ready?

◇ Do you address envelopes? If so, do you print or do calligraphy by hand?

◇ Is there an extra fee for addressing envelopes?

◇ If you don't do calligraphy, do you work with someone who does? Does he/she give discounts to your customers?

◇ Do we assemble the invitations and stuff envelopes ourselves?

◇ Do we stamp and send out invitations?

◇ What is the difference in cost, if any, between ordering extra invitations up front or after the initial order has been placed?

◇ Can we order extra envelopes (inner and outer) in case of addressing mistakes?

◇ Can the envelopes be delivered before the invitations are ready so the calligrapher can get started?

◇ Will we be able to see a proof before any pieces are printed?

◇ Will you be able to help us compose the proper wording for our invitation?

◇ Can you advise us as to what information we should (and shouldn't) include on the invitation?

◇ Can you help us find a special emblem to use on our stationery?

◇ What are the rules regarding a monogram?

◇ How should we arrange our names on thank-you notes?

Stationer II | *Stationer III*

Stationer I

◇ Have you ever printed a program for
   our faith's service?
◇ What are the costs for the invitations
   we are interested in? *(Refer to the*
   worksheet on page 68 to record costs.)
◇ What is the payment policy?
◇ What is the cancellation policy?

◇ Other questions/notes *(if there are*
   any other stationery items, such as
   those listed in this section's worksheet,
   that you wish to order, be sure to
   discuss them with the stationer):

QUESTIONS TO ASK: CALLIGRAPHY

Calligrapher I

Name:
Address:

Phone:
E-mail:
Website:
◇ Can we see samples of your work?
◇ Do you do calligraphy by hand or
   computer?
◇ Do you provide a menu of calligraphy
   styles to choose from?
◇ What style would work best with
   our invitation?
◇ What are your fees?
   What do they include?

Stationer II   *Stationer III*

Calligrapher II   *Calligrapher III*

Calligrapher I

✧ Do you do outer and inner envelopes?

✧ Will you do pieces that can then be printed from your artwork, such as the invitations themselves, maps, menus, etc.?

✧ Will you do table numbers and seating cards or a seating chart?

✧ When do you need the list of guests and addresses?

✧ Can you accommodate last-minute invitations?

✧ How long after you receive the materials can we expect to have completed pieces?

✧ Do you have references?

✧ Other questions/notes:

KEEP IN MIND

Instead of having individual seating cards, some couples choose to have a single seating chart that tells everyone where they'll be dining. Such a chart can make an attractive accent when artistically designed. Should you wish to incorporate this option into your festivities, ask the calligraphers you interview whether they can create one.

Calligrapher II	Calligrapher III

Notes

Chapter Four

Music & Flowers

Ceremony Music

THINGS TO DO

☐ Interview ceremony musicians
☐ Arrange to listen to performances
☐ Book ceremony musician(s)
☐ Send signed contract and deposit to musicians
☐ Select music for:
  ☐ prelude
  ☐ attendants' processional
  ☐ bride's processional
  ☐ ceremony
  ☐ recessional
  ☐ postlude
☐ Give any necessary sheet music to musicians
☐ Make any necessary arrangements for equipment required by musicians
☐ Confirm date/times/location with musicians
☐ Get contact numbers of musicians for wedding day
☐ Other _____
☐ _____
☐ _____
☐ _____
☐ _____
☐ _____
☐ _____

QUESTIONS TO ASK: CEREMONY MUSIC

Ceremony Musician I

Name: _____

Address: _____
_____
_____

Phone: _____

E-mail: _____

Website: _____

◇ What instrument(s) do you (and your
   co-performers) play? _____

◇ What is in your repertoire? _____
_____
_____

◇ Will you learn new pieces? _____

◇ Can you suggest pieces that will fit
   our wedding style? _____
_____
_____

◇ Do you know the religious songs we
   want played? _____

◇ Have you performed at our site? _____
   If so, do you require any amplification?
   Provided by whom? _____

◇ If you're not familiar with the site, will
   you visit to assess the acoustics? _____

◇ If you're ill on our wedding day, do
   you have a backup? _____

◇ Can we meet/hear him or her? _____

◇ What will your attire be? _____

◇ Do you have liability insurance? _____

◇ What is your fee? _____

◇ How much of a deposit do you require? _____

◇ When is the balance due? _____

◇ What is your cancellation policy? _____

Ceremony Musician II	Ceremony Musician III

Ceremony Musician I

✧ Do you have references?

_____

_____

_____

_____

_____

_____

✧ Other questions/notes:

_____

_____

_____

_____

Reception Music

THINGS TO DO

☐ Interview bands or disc jockeys
☐ Listen to bands/disc jockeys perform
☐ Book band/disc jockey
☐ Send contract and deposit to band/disc jockey
☐ Arrange to have music for:
    ☐ cocktail hour
    ☐ interlude between cocktail hour and main reception
    ☐ introduction of married couple
    ☐ first dance
    ☐ father–daughter dance
    ☐ mother–son dance
    ☐ dinner
    ☐ general dancing
    ☐ traditional/religious dances
    ☐ cake-cutting
    ☐ bouquet toss
    ☐ bride and groom's exit
☐ Arrange for band/disc jockey to see site and check facilities

Ceremony Musician II	Ceremony Musician III

☐ Give band the sheet music for songs you want them to learn
☐ Make any necessary arrangements for equipment required by band/disc jockey
☐ Give band/disc jockey list of requested songs and songs you don't want played
☐ Confirm date, times, and location with band/disc jockey
☐ Give schedule of events to band/disc jockey (include any announcements to be made, such as telling guests to pick up favors)
☐ Give any necessary music to disc jockey
☐ Get contact numbers of musicians/disc jockey for wedding day
☐ Other _____
☐ _____

Words to the Wise

✧ It is a good idea to see any bands/disc jockeys that you are considering perform live at an event similar to yours; that way, you can get a feel for their style, the quality of their work, and the overall impression that they make.

✧ When selecting music, consider including a range of songs (from standards to current party hits) so there is something for everyone.

✧ Discuss where in the reception space the band or disc jockey will be stationed and where the speakers will be; you don't want the performers and their equipment to be too close to the reception tables, especially those where older guests are seated.

QUESTIONS TO ASK: BAND

Band I

Name: _____

Address: _____

_____

_____

_____

_____

Phone: _____

E-mail: _____

Website: _____

✧ What is your musical style? _____

_____

✧ Can you play all different styles? _____

✧ Will you provide a song list to _____
choose from? _____

✧ Will you take requests from us of _____
songs to play and not to play? _____

✧ Will you take requests from guests? _____

✧ Will you learn new songs? How many? _____

✧ Do you know the traditional/ethnic _____
songs we want played? _____

✧ Will you be the master of ceremonies _____
(announcing the first dance, toasts, _____
cake-cutting, etc.)? _____

✧ What is your fee? _____

_____

✧ How many hours does that include? _____
Of playing time? Of setting up and _____
breaking down equipment? _____

✧ How many pieces/what instruments _____
does that include? _____

✧ How many breaks (and of what length) _____
do you require? _____

✧ Will all the members take a break _____
at the same time, or will you rotate _____
so there is always live music? _____

✧ Will there be recorded music during _____
the break(s)? _____

Band II

Band III

Band I

✧ Will you play overtime? _____

✧ What is your overtime charge? _____

✧ Do you charge for travel time and parking? _____

✧ Do you have a link to a demo we can watch online? _____

✧ Can we see you perform live at an event? _____

✧ *If booking through an agency:* Will the musicians we hear on the recording/at a performance be the ones at our wedding? _____

✧ Have you played at our site before? If not, will you check out the site ahead of time? _____

✧ Does our site have the facilities (space, electrical capabilities) you need? _____

✧ If anything extra is required, is it our cost to incur or yours? _____

✧ Do you use any special lighting? _____

✧ Will any band members play at the ceremony, too? _____

✧ Is there an additional fee or a discount? _____

✧ Will any band members play during the cocktail hour? _____

✧ Is there an additional fee or a discount? _____

✧ Do you motivate the crowd, or do you limit your talking to emceeing duties? _____

✧ Do you have any group dances or contests in your repertoire? Will you refrain from doing these if we wish? _____

✧ What will your attire be? _____

Band II	Band III

Band I

◇ Do you require meals? _____
◇ When would you arrive to set up? _____
◇ Do you have another event the _____
   same day? _____
◇ Do you have liability insurance? _____
◇ How much of a deposit is required? _____
◇ When is the balance due? _____
◇ What is your cancellation policy? _____
_____
◇ Do you have references? _____
_____
_____
_____
_____
_____
_____
◇ Other questions/notes: _____
_____
_____
_____
_____
_____

KEEP IN MIND

In preparation for your first dance, when all eyes will be focused on you, you may want to take dancing lessons with your groom. Such lessons can not only help you to dazzle guests with your grace and style, but also give you an opportunity to spend some extra time with your future husband.

Band II

Band III

QUESTIONS TO ASK: DISC JOCKEY

Disc Jockey I

Name:

Address:

Phone:

E-mail:

Website:

✧ Do you have the types of music we're looking for in your collection?

✧ Are you willing to play songs that are not in your collection? Will you obtain them yourself, or must we provide them?

✧ Do you have the traditional/ethnic songs we want?

✧ Will you provide a song list to choose from?

✧ Will you take requests from us of songs to play and not to play?

✧ Will you take requests from guests?

✧ Will you be the master of ceremonies (announcing the first dance, toasts, cake-cutting, etc.)?

✧ What is your fee?

✧ How many hours does that include? Of playing time? Of setting up and breaking down equipment?

✧ How many breaks (and of what length) do you require?

✧ Will music play during the break(s)?

✧ Will you play overtime?

✧ What is your overtime charge?

✧ Do you charge for travel time and parking?

✧ Will you play during the cocktail hour?

✧ Is there an additional fee or a discount?

Disc Jockey II	Disc Jockey III

Disc Jockey I

◇ Can we see you in action at an event? _____

◇ *If booking through an agency:*
Will the deejay we see on the
recording/at an event be the one at
our wedding? _____

◇ Have you played at our site before?
If not, will you check out the site
ahead of time? _____

◇ Does the site have the facilities (space/
electrical capabilities) you need? _____

◇ If anything extra is required, is it our
cost to incur or yours? _____

◇ Do you use any special lighting? _____

◇ Do you motivate the crowd, or do you
limit any talking to emceeing duties? _____

◇ Do you have any group dances or
contests in your repertoire? Will you
refrain from doing these if we wish? _____

◇ What will your attire be? _____

◇ Do you require a meal? _____

◇ When would you arrive to set up? _____

◇ Do you have another event the
same day? _____

◇ Do you have liability insurance? _____

◇ How much of a deposit is required? _____

◇ When is the balance due? _____

◇ What is your cancellation policy? _____

◇ Do you have references? _____

◇ Other questions/notes: _____

Disc Jockey II | *Disc Jockey III*

Notes

Flowers

THINGS TO DO

☐ Save photos/magazine clippings of flowers and arrangements for inspiration
☐ Make appointments to interview florists
☐ Hire florist
☐ Make appointment to see sample bouquets and arrangements
☐ Give table size to florist (so that centerpieces can be sized accordingly)
☐ Provide florist with swatches of dresses/table linens (to achieve complementary bouquets/arrangements)
☐ Make selections for all floral items *(see worksheet on page 98)*
☐ Send deposit to florist
☐ Send signed contract to florist
☐ Give measurement for length of aisle to florist if he/she is providing runner
☐ Confirm final details with florist
☐ Confirm date, times, and locations with florist
☐ Get contact number of florist for wedding day
☐ Other _____
☐ _____
☐ _____

Words to the Wise

✧ Bring pictures of floral arrangements and bouquets that you like to your interviews with florists; it is much easier to convey your ideas with visual aids.

✧ Make sure that centerpieces do not obstruct guests' views of one another.

✧ Avoid flowers with powerful scents, as they may interfere with your guests' enjoyment of the food.

✧ Discuss the staying power of the flowers you're interested in with your florist; you don't want your beautiful blooms to wilt halfway through the event. (Along these lines, you might want to include a statement in your contract that arrangements will consist of flowers in full bloom as well as buds that will bloom throughout the day.)

✧ Ask your attendants if they are allergic to any flowers; you don't want your bridesmaids to be sneezing when standing up for you.

✧ If you're planning on doing the bouquet toss but want to save your bridal bouquet, order a toss bouquet—a smaller bouquet intended specifically for this custom.

✧ Find out if the florist will dry your bouquet for a keepsake, or assign someone the task of attending to it while you're on your honeymoon.

Flower Worksheet

		Vendor I		
Element	Description	Cost/ item	Qty.	Total Cost
PERSONAL FLOWERS				
Bride's bouquet				
Maid of honor's bouquet				
Bridesmaids' bouquets				
Groom's boutonniere				
Groomsmen's boutonnieres				
Special people corsages				
Special people boutonnieres				
Floral hair accessories				
Flower girls' baskets				
Toss bouquet				
Other				
CEREMONY SITE FLOWERS/ACCESSORIES				
Entryway				
Altar				
Aisles				
Huppah or wedding canopy				

Vendor II					Vendor III		
Description	Cost/item	Qty.	Total Cost		Description	Cost/item	Qty.	Total Cost

Element	Description	Cost/item	Qty.	Total Cost
Vendor I				
Rose petals to sprinkle down aisle				
Program table				
Guest book table				
Cloth aisle runner (often supplied by florist)				
Candles				
Other				
RECEPTION FLOWERS				
Dinner tables (centerpieces and/or individual blooms at place settings)				
Dinner buffet tables/serving stations				
Cocktail hour guest tables				
Cocktail hour buffet tables				
Entryway				
Seating card table				
Favor table				
Cake table				
Gift table				
Rest rooms				
Favors for guests				
TOTAL				

Vendor II				**Vendor III**			
Description	Cost/item	Qty.	Total Cost	Description	Cost/item	Qty.	Total Cost
TOTAL				**TOTAL**			

QUESTIONS TO ASK: FLOWERS

Florist I

Name:

Address:

Phone:

E-mail:

Website:

◇ Can we see photos of weddings you've done?

◇ Do you have one particular style, or will you work with us to create arrangements that match our vision?

◇ Will you look at pictures we've found to help explain what we want?

◇ Can we see sample arrangements?

◇ Do you specialize in weddings?

◇ What other types of events have you done?

◇ Have you done any events at our site?

◇ Where do you get the flowers for the arrangements?

◇ Are arrangements made the day of or before? How are they stored?

◇ Will you be on hand on the wedding day arranging and setting up, or will someone else be doing this?

◇ If someone else, can we see this person's work and meet him/her?

◇ Do you provide an aisle runner for the ceremony?

◇ Do you provide candles and create displays with them?

◇ Can you build a wedding canopy or huppah?

Florist II	Florist III

Florist 1

✧ Can you work with our cake decorator
   if we want flowers on the cake? Are
   you familiar with the safety issues
   regarding edible flowers and the need
   to use flowers free from pesticides?
✧ Do you do floral favors?

✧ What will the costs be for the different
   elements we are interested in?
   (Refer to the worksheet on page 98
   to record costs.)
✧ Can you suggest some money-saving
   strategies?

✧ Will the flowers we're interested
   in be in season at the time of our
   wedding? If not, can you suggest
   some similar-looking alternatives
   to save money?
✧ How do you feel about transforming
   pew arrangements from the ceremony
   into centerpieces for the reception to
   help ease our budget?
✧ Are there delivery and setup fees?
✧ Are the centerpiece vases ours to keep,
   or do they need to go back to you?
✧ How many planning meetings should
   we expect to have?
✧ How many other events are you
   scheduled to work on our wedding day?
✧ What time would the flowers be
   delivered, and when would you
   (and your team) arrive to set up?

Florist II

Florist III

Florist I

◇ Do you have liability insurance?
◇ How much of a deposit do you require?
◇ When is the balance due?
◇ What is your cancellation policy?

◇ Do you have references?

◇ Other questions/notes:

KEEP IN MIND

If the vases do not need to go back to the florist, you may want to offer your centerpieces to guests as favors or donate the arrangements to a local hospital or nursing home.

Florist II	Florist III

Notes

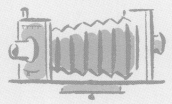

Photography & Videography

Photography

THINGS TO DO

☐ Look through wedding albums of family members and friends to get a sense of the
photography style you want

☐ Make appointments to interview photographers

☐ Book photographer

☐ Send signed contract and deposit to photographer

☐ Make appointment for engagement picture sitting

☐ Scout potential photo spots—at home, at a local park, at wedding location

☐ Give photographer list of desired shots and important people to be photographed
(see page 195 for sample list)

☐ Assign attendant to point out important people to photographer

☐ Give a copy of shot list to said attendant

☐ Select albums (including page and border style)

☐ Confirm details with photographer

☐ Get contact number from photographer for wedding day

☐ Purchase disposable cameras for tables

☐ Assign someone to put disposable cameras on tables, if applicable

☐ Other _____

Words to the Wise

✧ When meeting with a photographer, ask to see an album of one entire wedding; if you
review a portfolio that contains shots from different weddings, you are seeing only the
best couple of shots from each event and you're not necessarily getting a realistic view of
the photographer's ability.

✧ If you're booking a photographer through an agency, make sure that the photographer
who will be shooting your wedding is the one whose work you've reviewed. And be sure
to meet the photographer in person.

✧ Before the wedding day, scout out your location (and have your photographer do the
same) to determine the best settings for photographs; you don't want to waste precious
time on the day of your big event fretting about where to pose.

✧ To play it safe, make sure your photographer brings backup equipment; that way, you
won't be left without any pictures of this momentous occasion if something malfunctions.

✧ Consider taking some, if not all, formal portraits before the ceremony to avoid spend-
ing valuable reception time posing for the camera. If you don't want your groom to see
you before the ceremony, arrange to do only those shots that don't include the two of you.

QUESTIONS TO ASK: PHOTOGRAPHY

Photographer I

Name:

Address:

Phone:

E-mail:

Website:

◇ What is your style?

◇ Do you prefer formal portraits, photojournalistic shots, candids, or a combination?

◇ Do you shoot weddings primarily?

◇ What other types of photography have you done?

◇ Can we see a portfolio of your work?

◇ Can we see an album of one entire wedding?

◇ Can we see indoor and outdoor shots?

◇ What is your fee?

◇ For how many hours?

◇ How many shots will be taken?

◇ How many proofs will we see?

◇ How many albums are included in the cost?

◇ What is the cost for additional albums?

◇ How many shots in each album?

◇ Are all the album shots the same size?

◇ Can we add pages to an album, and if so, what is the cost?

◇ How many portraits are included in the fee?

◇ What are our size options for portraits (8×10, 5×7, 5×5, wallet, etc.)?

◇ What is the cost for additional prints?

Photographer II | Photographer III

Photographer I

✧ Do we own the images you post online?
Do we get them on disk or in an
account on a photo website?

✧ Do we get to keep the original digital
files as part of the package?

✧ What kind of camera do you use?

✧ What quality and type of paper
do you use?

✧ Are album pages acid-free/archival
quality?

✧ Do we have choices for album, page,
and border styles?

✧ Can we see our album options?

✧ Is there an extra fee to have our
names and wedding date printed
on the cover of the album?

✧ Do you retouch images?

✧ Do you use lighting equipment? If so, is
it wireless? If not, how do you ensure
that guests don't trip over cords?

✧ Do you bring backup equipment?

✧ Have you worked at our site before?

✧ Do you know good places for shots?

✧ If you're unfamiliar with our site,
are you willing to visit it and scout
for shot locations?

✧ Will you shoot the rehearsal and
rehearsal dinner? What would
the fee be?

✧ Will you come early on the day of the
wedding to take shots of us getting
ready? Is this included in the fee for
the wedding, or is this extra?

✧ How long should formal pictures take?

✧ Will you work off a prepared shot list?

Photographer II	*Photographer III*

Photographer I

✧ If you take table shots, must we order all of them?

✧ Are black-and-white photographs an option?

✧ How many photographers and assistants will be there?

✧ If others will be shooting photos, can we see their work?

✧ If you're ill, who will photograph our wedding?

✧ How long after the wedding will we see proofs?

✧ How long after we make our proof selections will we receive the prints and/or albums?

✧ What will your attire be?

✧ Do you require meals?

✧ Are there any additional charges (e.g., parking, travel)?

✧ How much of a deposit is required?

✧ When is the balance due?

✧ What is your cancellation policy?

✧ Do you have liability insurance?

✧ Do you have references?

✧ Other questions/notes:

Photographer II   *Photographer III*

Videography

THINGS TO DO

- ☐ Watch wedding videos of family and friends to determine desired style
- ☐ Make appointments to interview videographers
- ☐ Book videographer
- ☐ Send signed contract and deposit to videographer
- ☐ Give videographer list of desired shots and important people *(use sample list on page 195 as a guide)*
- ☐ Assign attendant to point out important people to videographer
- ☐ Give shot list to said attendant
- ☐ Confirm details with videographer
- ☐ Get contact number from videographer for wedding day
- ☐ Other _____
- ☐ _____
- ☐ _____
- ☐ _____
- ☐ _____

QUESTIONS TO ASK: VIDEOGRAPHY

Videographer I

Name: _____

Address: _____

_____

_____

Phone: _____

E-mail: _____

Website: _____

✧ What is your filming style? _____

✧ Can we see samples of your work? _____

✧ Can we see a sample of a wedding similar to ours? _____

✧ Have you shot indoors and outdoors, by candlelight and twilight? _____

Facts at Your Fingertips: Videography Terms

✧ **Highlights reel:** Typically included in basic packages, this five- to ten-minute video is a wrap-up of the high points of your wedding in chronological order. It can be set to music (the song for your first dance, perhaps) and may include special visual effects.

✧ **Documentary style (short-form):** This video style, often done in black-and-white, involves shooting hours of straight coverage and then editing it down for a tape of an agreed-upon length (often one hour) while still keeping the story and feeling intact.

✧ **Straight-cut format:** Just as it sounds, this style entails shooting your wedding from start to finish with little, if any, editing. The video may be long, but you won't have missed a thing.

✧ **In-camera style:** The videographer shoots just certain moments of the wedding.

Videographer II	Videographer III

Videographer I

◇ Do you shoot weddings primarily?
◇ What other types of videography have you done?
◇ What is your fee?

◇ How many hours of service and raw footage does that include?
◇ How many discs of what length does that include?
◇ What is the cost of additional disks?

◇ Is the final copy uncut or edited?
◇ If edited, who does the editing?
◇ Can we see some of his/her work?
◇ Do we help edit, or do you decide what to cut?
◇ If we're getting an edited video, what happens to the raw footage?
◇ Is a shorter highlights video included in the fee?
◇ What kind of special effects can we include? Is there an additional cost?

◇ How do you transition between scenes?

◇ Can you lay music over some scenes? Is there an additional cost?
◇ Can you do titles? Is there an additional cost?
◇ Can we provide baby photos and honeymoon photos to be incorporated into the video? Is there an extra cost?
◇ Will you work off a shot list?
◇ Have you shot at our wedding site?
◇ Do you know good places at our site to shoot?

Videographer II	*Videographer III*

Videographer I

◇ Will you come early to shoot us getting
   ready and having formal pictures taken?
   If so, is there an additional cost?

◇ Is black-and-white footage an option?

◇ What type of equipment do you use?

◇ Is it portable?

◇ Do you bring backup equipment?

◇ Can you be inconspicuous during the
   ceremony and reception?

◇ How many videographers and
   assistants will be there?

◇ If others will be shooting footage,
   can we see their work?

◇ If you're ill on the wedding day, who
   will take your place?

◇ When will we be able to see any
   footage? When will we see final video?

◇ What will your attire be?

◇ Do you require meals?

◇ Do you have liability insurance?

◇ Are there any other charges
   (e.g., parking, travel)?

◇ How much of a deposit is required?

◇ When is the balance due?

◇ What is your cancellation policy?

◇ Do you have references?

◇ Other questions/notes:

Videographer II   *Videographer III*

Notes

Chapter Six

Fashion

Bridal Attire

THINGS TO DO

- [ ] Collect photos of dress styles you admire from magazines and/or peruse online for styles you like
- [ ] Think about your theme or location as these can sometimes inspire a look
- [ ] Make appointments at bridal salons
- [ ] Ask parent, maid of honor, or other bridal attendant to accompany you to bridal salons
- [ ] Select:
    - [ ] gown
    - [ ] veil/headpiece
    - [ ] shoes (before first fitting)
    - [ ] undergarments appropriate for gown (before first fitting)
    - [ ] hosiery (have extra pairs on hand on wedding day)
    - [ ] garter
    - [ ] jewelry
    - [ ] hair accessories
    - [ ] purse
    - [ ] wrap
    - [ ] gloves
    - [ ] going-away outfit
    - [ ] rehearsal dinner outfit
- [ ] Make appointments for gown fittings and inquire as to what you will need to bring with you
- [ ] Obtain swatches of gown for florist and, if applicable, for professional who will be dyeing shoes
- [ ] Discuss bustle style of train with seamstress
- [ ] Bring parent or maid of honor to fitting to learn how to bustle train
- [ ] Find out from bridal salon how to hang and care for dress
- [ ] Find out from bridal salon what to do if dress is wrinkled before wedding
- [ ] Find out from bridal salon what to do if you get a spot on the dress

If borrowing a gown:

- [ ] Take gown out of storage
- [ ] Determine what alterations, if any, are needed
- [ ] Examine gown for stains and rips
- [ ] Take gown to reputable seamstress for alterations (if an older gown, take to a professional equipped to handle vintage garments)
- [ ] Take gown to reputable professional for cleaning and/or steaming

If renting a gown:

- ☐ Search online and locally for salons who rent gowns
- ☐ Get references
- ☐ Schedule appointments
- ☐ Find out alteration policy
- ☐ Ask about timing in terms of when you can get dress and when it needs to be returned
- ☐ Inquire about a policy for return conditions
- ☐ Ask if anyone else can rent the dress before your wedding after you've put a deposit down

☐ Plan time and place to bustle gown after ceremony
☐ Arrange for place to store going-away outfits at reception site
☐ Arrange for place to change into going-away outfits
☐ Take shoes to be dyed to match gown
☐ Pick up dyed shoes
☐ Pick up gown
☐ Break in shoes and scuff shoe bottoms (so that they're comfortable and you don't slip in them)
☐ Find professional dry cleaner who specializes in bridal gown care to clean and pack up dress and accessories after wedding
☐ Assign someone to take wedding gown home for you after wedding (if you won't be able to do so yourself)
☐ Assign someone to take gown to dry cleaner after wedding
☐ Other _____
☐ _____
☐ _____
☐ _____
☐ _____
☐ _____
☐ _____
☐ _____

Words to the Wise

✧ Most bridal salons require appointments, so call before visiting one.

✧ If making an appointment on the weekend, request an early time slot or be prepared for long waits.

✧ Try on a variety of dress styles; something that looks great on the hanger may not be flattering when you put it on, and something that you never thought you'd consider might look fabulous.

✧ Make sure that you feel comfortable in the gown that you select; you don't want to be tugging at the dress or worrying that you don't look your best on your wedding day.

✧ Before purchasing a gown, inquire as to whether or not the salon carries any insurance and what exactly that insurance covers; if the store doesn't have insurance, you are running the risk of losing your money if the place goes out of business or if your dress is ruined by a fire or flood while in the store's possession.

✧ Once you've selected a gown, ask the sales associate for recommendations regarding undergarments.

Facts at Your Fingertips: Silhouettes

✧ **Ball gown:** Exuding a timeless romantic quality, this dress boasts a full skirt that springs from a fitted waist.

✧ **A-line/princess:** Admired for its clean lines and soft-yet-angular form, this sub-dued variation of the ball gown features a slightly tapered waist that gives way to a gentle A-shaped skirt.

✧ **Empire:** This high-waisted dress, beloved for its period look, features a straight column or A-line skirt flowing from just below the bustline.

✧ **Slip dress:** Designed with simple spaghetti straps, a low-cut neckline (typically a scoop or V-neck), and unembellished fabric, this style is chosen by brides who want to make a quietly elegant statement.

✧ **Sheath:** This straight, modern-looking style comes in a little at the waist before hitting the floor in one clean, sleek column.

QUESTIONS TO ASK: WHEN MAKING BRIDAL SALON APPOINTMENTS

Salon I

Salon name: _____

Address: _____

_____

_____

Phone: _____

E-mail: _____

Website: _____

◇ Do I need an appointment to see and
try on dresses? _____

◇ What is the price range of the dresses? _____

◇ How long does it take to order a gown? _____

◇ Will I be assigned a sales associate,
or will I try on gowns on my own? _____

◇ Will I be able to look at your collection
of gowns and select what I'd like to
try on, or will a sales associate be
deciding what to show and not
show me? _____

◇ Can I bring pictures of gowns I've
seen so you can tell me if you carry
them or so you can get an idea of
what I like? _____

◇ Is there a limit to how many dresses
I can try on? _____

◇ Do you hold designer trunk shows? _____

◇ Do I need to bring special undergarments and shoes to try on
dresses, or do you provide these? _____

KEEP IN MIND

If you are planning to have shoes dyed to match your gown, make sure the shoes
you select are dyeable.

Salon II

Salon III

QUESTIONS TO ASK: WEDDING GOWN

Salon I

Salon name: _____
Sales associate: _____
Address: _____
_____
_____

Phone: _____
E-mail: _____
Website: _____
◇ What style of dress do you recommend
for my body type? _____
◇ Are some styles better for certain
seasons? _____
◇ Are some fabrics better for certain
seasons? _____
◇ Can any of the designs I try on be
customized? _____
◇ Are some dress designs available in
more than one fabric (i.e., are there
less expensive yet similar fabric
alternatives for some dresses)? _____
◇ Do dresses come in more than one
color (e.g., choice of white or ivory)? _____
◇ How much is the gown I'm
interested in? _____
_____
_____
_____
◇ What does the gown price include? _____
◇ Are alterations extra? _____
◇ How many fittings will there be? _____
◇ Do you steam the dress after final
alterations? _____
◇ Do you sell accessories such as veils,
shoes, and hosiery? *(Costs can be
recorded in the space provided at
the end of this list of questions.)* _____

Salon II	Salon III

Salon I

⟡ If you don't sell accessories, do you have discount relationships with stores that do?

⟡ Can you recommend someone to dye shoes to match the gown?

⟡ How far in advance of the wedding will the dress be ready?

⟡ Do you deliver?

⟡ Can I hire someone to bustle me after the ceremony? What is the fee?

⟡ Do you handle care for the gown after the wedding, or can you recommend a reputable wedding gown cleaner/preserver?

⟡ Do you offer discounts for bridesmaid dresses if I purchase my gown here?

⟡ How long has this salon been in business?

⟡ Do you carry any type of insurance? What does it cover?

⟡ How much of a deposit is required?

⟡ When is the balance due?

⟡ Do you accept credit cards?

⟡ What is the cancellation policy?

⟡ Accessory costs:

⟡ Other questions/notes:

Salon II   Salon III

Notes

Bridal Attendants' Attire

THINGS TO DO

☐ Peruse magazines and online to check out different styles—be sure to look at bridesmaids's dresses as well as other dresses, such as cocktail, evening, and daytime. Consider your location, themes, and color scheme when looking

☐ Make appointments to see bridesmaid dresses

☐ Select dresses

☐ Give attendants' measurements to salon, or have attendants do so

☐ Give any necessary contact information for attendants to salon, or have attendants do so

☐ Arrange to have dresses for out-of-town attendants sent to them, or have attendants do so

☐ Obtain swatches of the bridesmaid dresses to show florist (for bouquets/arrangements) and professional who will be dyeing shoes

☐ If attendants are selecting their own dresses in a color of your choosing, send swatches of the color to attendants

☐ If attendants are not having alterations done at the same place, give them instructions as to where the hemline should fall

☐ Select shoes for attendants, or give them guidelines for doing so

☐ Select any accessories for attendants (purse, gloves, jewelry)

☐ Select attire for child attendants, or give their parents guidelines for doing so

☐ Follow up with attendants to make sure that they have their attire and accessories ready for the wedding day

☐ Other _____

Words to the Wise

✧ When ordering bridesmaid dresses, make sure that there is plenty of time to have alterations done after the garments' scheduled arrival date.

✧ Be considerate of your bridesmaids' feelings by selecting a style that is flattering on all of them; toward the same end, and for a little variety, you could have your attendants wear different styles in the same color.

✧ For your bridesmaids' gifts, consider purchasing something that the attendants can wear to the wedding—such as earrings or a necklace.

✧ Traditionally, bridesmaids pay for their own attire. Some brides choose to make a contribution to this expense.

✧ Don't feel that you must order bridesmaid dresses from a salon. It is perfectly acceptable to select off-the-rack dresses.

QUESTIONS TO ASK: BRIDAL ATTENDANTS' ATTIRE

Salon I

Salon name:
Sales associate:
Address:

Phone:
E-mail:
Website:
✧ What styles do you recommend for a
   group with different sizes/body types?
✧ How do you handle dress orders and
   fittings for out-of-town bridesmaids?
   Do you have pictures or sketches of
   dresses to send them?
✧ Can you ship?
✧ How far in advance do we need to
   order the dresses?
✧ How long after we place the order
   will the dresses arrive?
✧ *If there's a discount because you*
   bought wedding dress at same store:
   If my bridesmaids order different dress
   styles, will there still be a discount?
✧ What is the price of the dress?

✧ Do you do alterations? If not, do you
   work with someone who offers
   your customers a discount?
✧ If you do alterations, are they included
   in the cost of the dress? If alterations
   are not included, what is the cost?
✧ How much is shipping?
✧ Do you carry any insurance? What
   does it cover?
✧ How much of a deposit is required?

Salon II | Salon III

Salon I

✧ When is the balance due? _____
✧ What is your cancellation policy? _____
_____
✧ Other questions/notes: _____
_____
_____
_____
_____

Groom's and Groomsmen's Attire

(You may want to photocopy the following section for your husband-to-be.)

THINGS TO DO

☐ Decide upon the style of tuxedo/suit (often determined by the time and formality of the wedding)
☐ Call formalwear stores to see if you need an appointment and if you need to bring anything
☐ Try on ensembles
☐ Purchase tuxedo/suit or book rental
☐ Select:
    ☐ shirt
    ☐ shoes
    ☐ tie
    ☐ cumberbund/vest
    ☐ pocket square
    ☐ cuff links
    ☐ tie clip
    ☐ studs
    ☐ socks
☐ Organize groomsmen's attire (refer to checklist above for ensemble components)
☐ Obtain measurements for out-of-town groomsmen
☐ Select going-away ensemble
☐ Pick up tuxedo/suit
☐ Assign someone to return tuxedo if a rental
☐ Other _____
☐ _____

Salon II   *Salon III*

Words to the Wise

✧ The groom might want to consider purchasing a tuxedo rather than renting one; by figuring out how much use he would get out of a tuxedo and looking into the costs of renting and buying, he will be able to make an informed decision that could save money in the long run.

✧ If the groom doesn't wish to wear a tuxedo, and you're not planning a formal evening wedding, discuss opting for a dark suit. For a more casual affair, an ensemble consisting of neutral trousers and a dark blazer is a possibility.

✧ If renting, the groom and groomsmen should pick up their tuxedos a few days before the wedding so that there's time to fix any problems that might arise (the wrong tux was ordered, it doesn't fit properly, etc.).

✧ Men should wear either a boutonniere or a pocket square—not both.

QUESTIONS TO ASK: GROOM'S ATTIRE
(The following questions can be used in the search for the groomsmen's attire, too.)

Store I

Store name:

Sales associate:

Address:

_____

_____

_____

_____

Phone:

E-mail:

Website:

If renting:

◇ How far in advance do I need to
  reserve the rental?

◇ What are the different styles that
  you offer?

◇ How old is the formalwear you
  rent out?

◇ Will I be able to see/examine the
  actual suit that I will be getting?

◇ What is included as part of the
  package?

◇ What is the cost?

◇ How do fittings/alterations work?
  Are they included in the cost or extra?

◇ When can I pick up the ensemble?

◇ Is the ensemble cleaned and pressed
  before pickup?

◇ When is the ensemble due back?

◇ Will I incur extra charges if the tuxedo
  gets stained, or do you assume there
  will be some amount of wear and tear?

Store II	Store III

Store I

◇ Do you offer discounts for ushers if
  I rent my attire from your store?

◇ How much of a deposit is required?

◇ When is the balance due?

◇ What is the cancellation policy?

If buying:

◇ How far in advance of the wedding
  do I need to place my order?

◇ What is included in the price?

◇ Are alterations extra?

◇ How many fittings will there be?

◇ Is there anything I need to bring to
  the fittings?

◇ Do you sell shoes and accessories?

◇ If not, do you have discount
  relationships with stores that sell
  shoes and accessories?

◇ Do you offer rentals for ushers?

◇ Do you carry insurance? What does
  it cover?

◇ What is the cost of the tuxedo/suit
  I'm interested in?

◇ When would the tuxedo/suit be ready?

◇ How much of a deposit is required?

◇ When is the balance due?

◇ What is the cancellation policy?

◇ Other questions/notes:

Store II

Store III

Notes

Chapter Seven

Details

Beauty

THINGS TO DO

- [ ] Make appointment to try out hairstylist
- [ ] Make appointment to try out makeup artist
- [ ] Bring to trial run with hairstylist:
    - [ ] headpiece
    - [ ] photo or sketch of dress to show neckline
    - [ ] photos of hairstyles you like
- [ ] Make appointment with hairstylist for wedding day
- [ ] Make appointment with makeup artist for wedding day
- [ ] Make appointment to have manicure (and pedicure, if desired)
- [ ] Make appointments for bridesmaids to have hair, makeup, and/or nails done, if desired
- [ ] Confirm all beauty appointments
- [ ] Obtain lipstick for touch-ups during the wedding
- [ ] Other _____
- [ ] _____

Words to the Wise

✧ Even if you don't usually wear much in the way of cosmetics, it's wise to have your makeup professionally done on your wedding day. For one thing, you'll look and feel beautiful, and for another, a qualified professional will know what to do so that you look your best in the photographs.

✧ Be sure to purchase or get a sample of the same shade of lipstick that your makeup artist uses on you; you'll need it for touch-ups throughout the event.

✧ Wear a button-down shirt when having your hair and makeup done; you don't want to mess up your hair or smudge your makeup by pulling a shirt over your head when it's time to change.

✧ Carry blotting tissues in your purse to keep the inevitable shine (from all the excitement and dancing) off your face. (This shine has a way of showing up in photographs.)

✧ Don't get a fancy new haircut before your wedding; instead, get your hair trimmed about three to four weeks before the big day so that your locks have time to grow in perfectly.

✧ Don't get a facial or any other skin treatments in the two weeks before your wedding. You don't want to risk breaking out or having any other adverse reactions.

✧ Do treat yourself to a manicure and pedicure. The manicure will look just dandy every time someone asks to see your rings, and the pedicure (aside from providing some much needed pampering) will have you ready for the honeymoon.

QUESTIONS TO ASK: HAIR/MAKEUP

Use this interview for discussions with a hairstylist or a professional who will be doing both your hair and makeup. If you'll be having a different person do your makeup, refer to the interview that begins on page 146 when meeting with a makeup artist.

Salon I

Name:

Salon:

Address:

Phone:

E-mail:

Website:

✧ Can we schedule a trial run?

✧ What is your fee and payment policy?

✧ Will you travel? Are there additional fees for parking and travel?

✧ Will you stay on hand to help me with my hair, veil, and headpiece (and makeup touch-ups) after the ceremony? At what additional cost, if any?

✧ Do you bring your own equipment and hair products (and makeup)?

✧ What kind of space and lighting do you need?

✧ Will you bring an assistant?

✧ Can I meet this assistant? Has this person done styling (and makeup) on his/her own?

✧ Will you style my attendants' hair (and do their makeup), or will your assistant? How long will it take, and what is the fee?

✧ How long will it take to have my hair (and makeup) done?

✧ *If stylist won't be at wedding:* Can you provide me with a hair product (and makeup) for quick fixes (touch-ups)?

Salon II	Salon III

QUESTIONS TO ASK: MAKEUP

Salon I

Name:

Salon:

Address:

Phone:

E-mail:

Website:

✧ Can we schedule a trial run?

✧ What is your fee and payment policy?

✧ Will you travel? Are there additional
  fees for parking and travel?

✧ Will you stay on hand for touch-ups
  after the ceremony and during the
  reception? At what additional cost?

✧ Do you bring your own makeup and
  brushes?

✧ What kind of space and lighting do
  you need?

✧ Will you bring an assistant?

✧ Can I meet this assistant? Has this
  person done makeup on his/her own?

✧ Will you do my attendants' makeup,
  or will your assistant? How long will
  it take, and what is the fee?

✧ How long will it take to have my
  makeup done?

✧ *If makeup artist won't be at wedding:*
  Can you provide me with makeup for
  touch-ups during the wedding?

✧ Other questions/notes:

Salon II

Salon III

Rehearsal Dinner

(While this is traditionally the responsibility of the groom's parents, many brides are involved in planning this event. Use the following according to your needs.)

THINGS TO DO

If groom's parents are planning the event:
- ☐ Discuss rehearsal dinner with groom's parents
- ☐ Give groom's parents the menu for the wedding reception so that the meals are not too similar
- ☐ Compile guest list for rehearsal dinner
- ☐ Give addresses or phone numbers of guests on your list to groom's parents
- ☐ Compose toast (with groom) to thank hosts and guests
- ☐ Other _____
- ☐ _____
- ☐ _____

If bride is involved in planning the event:
- ☐ Reserve location
- ☐ Send signed contract and deposit for location
- ☐ Decide upon menu
- ☐ Make arrangements for any decorations or music
- ☐ Compile guest list (with addresses or phone numbers) for rehearsal dinner
- ☐ Order, purchase, or print out invitations, or call invitees
- ☐ Address invitations
- ☐ Send invitations
- ☐ Compose toast (with groom) to thank hosts and/or guests
- ☐ Give final head count to site manager
- ☐ Confirm all details with site manager
- ☐ Other _____
- ☐ _____
- ☐ _____
- ☐ _____
- ☐ _____
- ☐ _____
- ☐ _____
- ☐ _____
- ☐ _____

Facts at Your Fingertips: Rehearsal Dinner Basics

✧ **Hosts:** According to traditional practices, the parents of the groom throw this party, but today the celebration can be hosted by both the bride's and groom's parents or by the happy couple themselves.

✧ **Invitees:** Members of the wedding party, immediate family members, and the officiant—as well as the spouses or significant others of all these people—are on the guest list for this event. Often, the hosts choose to invite out-of-town wedding guests as well.

✧ **Style:** Usually a more casual affair than the wedding, the rehearsal dinner can be anything you want, from a sit-down dinner at a restaurant to a laid-back cookout in the backyard.

✧ **Invitations:** These tend to be less formal than those for the wedding. Often, hosts choose the do-it-yourself method rather than having invitations professionally printed. Phone calls are also perfectly appropriate.

✧ **Toasts:** Generally, the hosts of the party toast the bride and groom, as does the best man, but any number of people can stand up to say a few words. It is also gracious for the bride and groom to toast their hosts and thank their guests. Like the overall style of the event, the toasts at the rehearsal dinner tend to be more casual than those given at the wedding, often including amusing stories.

✧ **Gifts:** Many couples take this opportunity to present their gifts to their attendants.

KEEP IN MIND

If the groom's parents are throwing the rehearsal dinner, the immediate family members should be spread out among the tables to better host the guests.

QUESTIONS TO ASK: REHEARSAL DINNER

Site I

Site name:

Contact person:

Address:

Phone:

E-mail:

Website:

◇ How many people can the space accommodate?

◇ Is there a minimum head count required?

◇ Do you offer a buffet or a seated meal?

◇ What are our choices for the menu?

◇ Will you work with us to keep the menu different from that of the wedding?

◇ Can you cater to special dietary needs?

◇ What is the overall fee, and what exactly does that include?

◇ Are gratuities additional?

◇ How many hours are we allotted?

◇ How do overtime charges work?

◇ How do the bar fees work?

◇ What label of alcohol is used?

◇ Can we bring in our own liquor? If so, is there a corkage fee?

Site II

Site III

Site I

◇ How private is the space we'll be
using?

◇ Are there any outdoor spaces we
can use?

◇ Is there a space for cocktails before
the meal?

◇ Will there be a maître d' assigned to
our party only?

◇ Will there be wait staff assigned to
our party only?

◇ How many guests are seated at
each table?

◇ What will the server/guest ratio be?

◇ Do you provide any sort of table
decoration, such as candles?

◇ Can we bring in decorations?

◇ Can we visit the space set up for
an event?

◇ Is there a coat check? At what
additional cost, if any?

◇ Is there valet parking? At what
additional cost, if any?

◇ Does the facility have liability
insurance?

◇ When do you need the final head
count?

◇ How much of a deposit is required?

◇ When is the balance due?

◇ What is your cancellation policy?

◇ Other questions/notes:

Site II   *Site III*

Rings

THINGS TO DO

☐ Have engagement ring insured, if groom has not done so already
☐ Select wedding bands
☐ Pick up wedding bands from jeweler
☐ Bring wedding bands to be engraved
☐ Pick up wedding bands from engraver
☐ Have engagement ring cleaned (so it's nice and shiny on your wedding day)
☐ Give wedding bands to best man
☐ Other _____

QUESTIONS TO ASK: RINGS

Store 1

Store name: _____
Sales associate: _____
Address: _____
_____
_____

Phone: _____
E-mail: _____
Website: _____
◇ How long does it take to order rings? _____
◇ Can a ring be resized later, or does
  the decoration on it prevent this? _____
◇ What are the prices of the bands? _____
_____
_____
◇ Do you engrave? If so, what is the cost? _____
◇ If not, can you recommend a jeweler
  who engraves? _____
_____
◇ How much of a deposit is required? _____
◇ When is the balance due? _____
◇ What is the cancellation policy? _____
◇ Other questions/notes: _____
_____

> ### KEEP IN MIND
>
> If you're having your wedding bands engraved, you should know that hand engraving makes the deepest cut and, hence, results in a longer-lasting inscription than machine engraving.

Store II	*Store III*

Gifts

THINGS TO DO

☐ Register for gifts (this should be done before any pre-wedding parties; it can also be helpful to register before the holidays)

☐ Purchase/order/make favors

☐ Wrap favors

☐ Purchase/order/make gifts for bridal party (groom should do same for groomsmen)

☐ Wrap gifts for bridal party (groom should do same for groomsmen's gifts)

☐ Purchase gift for groom, if you two are exchanging presents

☐ Purchase thank-you gifts for parents

☐ Wrap groom's and parents' gifts

☐ Plan time to give attendants their gifts (often done at a bridesmaids' luncheon or the rehearsal dinner)

☐ Plan time to give groom his gift, if applicable (often done in private the evening before the wedding)

☐ Plan time to give parents their presents

☐ Bring favors to location the day before the wedding, or assign an attendant the responsibility of getting them there

☐ Arrange for table to hold favors

☐ Assign someone to set up favors

☐ Other _____

☐ _____

☐ _____

KEEP IN MIND

When deciding where to register, find out if items can be purchased over the phone or online, in case your friends and relatives are unable to go to the store in person. Other questions to ask are: whether gifts can be shipped directly to you; how quickly the registry is updated (you want to avoid getting more than one of the same gift); and what the store's replacement (for gifts that arrive damaged), return, and exchange policies are. Last but not least, find out if the store gives you a discount on registry items that you and your husband purchase after the wedding.

Bride's Emergency Kit

There are a number of items that you should have on hand at the ceremony and reception in case of attire and beauty "emergencies." Organize them into a small bag, and ask one of your attendants or a family member to hold on to it for you or find a place to stash it.

INCLUDE:

- [ ] sewing kit
- [ ] fabric tape (for a quick fix to a hem)
- [ ] safety pins
- [ ] corsage pins
- [ ] extra earring backs
- [ ] extra hosiery (in case of runs)
- [ ] clear nail polish (for small runs)
- [ ] chalk (to cover up any last minute wedding dress splotches)
- [ ] spot remover
- [ ] static cling spray
- [ ] tweezers
- [ ] makeup for touch-ups
- [ ] mirror
- [ ] facial tissues
- [ ] blotting tissues
- [ ] bobby pins
- [ ] comb/hairbrush
- [ ] dental floss/toothpicks
- [ ] breath mints
- [ ] tampons/sanitary napkins
- [ ] headache relief medication
- [ ] stomach relief medication
- [ ] bandages
- [ ] bottle of water
- [ ] straws (to stay hydrated without smudging lipstick)

Gratuities

THINGS TO DO

☐ Add up gratuities and get crisp bills from bank
☐ Place tips in labeled envelopes and seal
☐ Assign attendant/family member to hand out tips on wedding day, if host isn't distributing the tips
☐ Give tips to assigned person to hand out

Facts at Your Fingertips: Tipping Guide

Use these numbers as a general guide. Not only do local practices vary (you can ask your catering manager or wedding consultant about area standards), but you need to give what works for your budget, what you are comfortable with, and what you feel is deserved. Also, be sure to review your contracts, as the gratuity may already be specified or included in the total fee.

✧ **Wedding consultant:** 15 to 20 percent if booked through an agency; it is not necessary to tip independent consultants, though a personal gift is a thoughtful and appropriate gesture.

✧ **Caterer/banquet manager:** 15 to 20 percent (usually specified in contract and included in total fee).

✧ **Reception site coordinator:** 15 to 20 percent (usually specified in contract and included in total fee).

✧ **Maître d':** 15 to 20 percent (usually specified in contract and included in total fee).

✧ **Wait staff:** 15 to 20 percent total, to be divided among the servers (often noted in contract); give to maître d' to dispense.

✧ **Bartenders:** 5 to 10 percent of bar total.

✧ **Musicians:** $25+ per musician (may be noted in contract).

✧ **Disc jockey:** $25+ if booked through an agency (may be noted in contract); it is not necessary to tip an independent disc jockey.

✧ **Chauffeur(s):** 15 to 20 percent each (may be noted in contract).

✧ **Hairstylist/makeup artist:** 15 to 20 percent if booked through a salon; it is not necessary to tip independent hairstylists or makeup artists.

✧ **Parking attendants:** $1 per car (may be noted in contract); pay ahead of time and request that attendants not accept tips from guests.

✧ **Rest room/coat room attendants:** $1 per guest (may be noted in contract); pay ahead of time and request that attendants not accept tips from guests.

✧ **Delivery people:** $5 to $10 each, depending on time and effort spent.

Notes

Notes

Chapter Eight

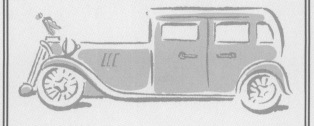

Hotels &
Transportation

Hotel Accommodations/Activities

THINGS TO DO

☐ Book your hotel room for wedding night

☐ Hold block of hotel rooms for out-of-town guests

☐ Ask for special code for guests to use when booking rooms in the block

☐ Send hotel and transportation information to out-of-town guests; include directions from local airports and cities from which many guests will be arriving by car, as well as information (description, location, phone number) regarding local attractions

☐ Put together welcome baskets for guests' rooms

☐ Confirm hotel reservation for your wedding night

☐ Bring guest baskets to hotel, or assign someone to do so

☐ Other _____

☐ _____

☐ _____

☐ _____

KEEP IN MIND

Though certainly not a requirement, welcome baskets are a great way to make your out-of-town guests feel at home when they arrive at the hotel. You could include snacks, a map of the area, a schedule of the weekend's events, and any other items that you think might be useful to your guests—perhaps sunscreen for a wedding at the beach.

QUESTIONS TO ASK: WEDDING NIGHT RESERVATIONS

Hotel I

Hotel name:

Contact person:

Address:

Phone:

E-mail:

Website:

◇ Is there a honeymoon suite? If so, is it available on the date of our wedding?

◇ What is the rate for this suite?

◇ Is breakfast included in the rate?

◇ Are there any special amenities, such as a whirlpool bath, in the honeymoon suite?

◇ Can we see the honeymoon suite?

◇ What are the rates for other rooms available on our wedding night?

◇ Is breakfast included in those rates?

◇ What amenities and what size bed do those rooms have?

◇ Can we see one of the rooms?

◇ Is there room service?

◇ *If a summer wedding:* Are the rooms air-conditioned?

◇ What is the check-out time? Can we request a late check-out?

◇ How much of a deposit, if any, is required?

◇ What is the cancellation policy?

◇ Other questions/notes:

Hotel II

Hotel III

QUESTIONS TO ASK: GUEST RESERVATIONS

Hotel I

Hotel name: _____

Contact person: _____

Address: _____

_____

_____

Phone: _____

E-mail: _____

Website: _____

✧ Do you offer a special rate for a block of rooms for wedding guests? _____

✧ What is the regular rate, and what is the discounted rate? _____

✧ How many rooms can we hold in a block? _____

✧ How many rooms at the special rate are available on the dates we need them? _____

✧ Do we incur any charges if not all of the rooms in the block are actually booked by guests? _____

✧ Is there a minimum number of rooms that must be booked by guests to qualify for the special rate? _____

✧ Is there a minimum stay? _____

✧ Is there a date by which guests must reserve rooms in order to receive the special rate? _____

✧ What amenities are available to guests? _____

✧ *If a summer wedding:* Are the rooms air-conditioned? _____

✧ Do you offer shuttle service between the hotel and local airports? If so, is it complimentary? _____

✧ Is breakfast included in the room rate? _____

✧ What are the views from the rooms in the discounted block? _____

Hotel II	Hotel III

Hotel I

◇ Can you show us one of the rooms
   that would be in the discounted block?
   _____

◇ Will guests have the choice of
   smoking or nonsmoking rooms
   in the block?
   _____

◇ Will guests have the choice of singles
   or doubles in the block?
   _____

◇ What are the check-in and check-out
   times?
   _____

◇ Can we get into rooms prior to our
   guests' arrival to leave welcome
   baskets, or can we leave them at
   the front desk for guests to receive
   at check-in?
   _____

◇ Are we required to put down a deposit
   to hold the block? If so, how much?
   Is this deposit refundable?
   _____

◇ If we need to cancel the block,
   what's your policy?
   _____

◇ Are guests required to put down
   a deposit? If so, how much?
   _____

◇ What is the cancellation policy for
   guests?
   _____

◇ Other questions/notes:
   _____

KEEP IN MIND

A casual brunch on the morning after the wedding provides the opportunity to spend some extra time with out-of-town guests who have come a long way to see you. Such a get-together can be hosted by you and your groom or anyone else who offers.

Hotel II	Hotel III

Notes

Transportation

THINGS TO DO

☐ Book/arrange for transportation for bride, groom, wedding party, and immediate family to ceremony and reception

☐ Book/arrange for bride and groom's getaway vehicle after reception

☐ Book/arrange for transportation for immediate family and wedding party after reception

☐ Send signed contract and deposit to transportation service

☐ Arrange for someone to drive bride and/or groom's car(s) home after reception, if necessary

☐ Arrange for shuttle service to take out-of-town guests from hotel to ceremony and reception sites and back to hotel, if desired

☐ Book transportation to airport for honeymoon

☐ Give driver(s) all necessary directions, addresses, and contact numbers

☐ Confirm all transportation arrangements

☐ Fill bride and/or groom's personal car(s) with plenty of gas, if being used on wedding day

☐ Other _____

☐ _____

☐ _____

☐ _____

☐ _____

Words to the Wise

✧ Like all the details of your wedding, the car that you ride in should be perfect in every way. Before hiring the services of any transportation company, inspect the vehicles. Try to see and book the actual cars that you and your group will be using.

✧ A stretch limousine offers plenty of room, but it's not the only option for riding in style; vintage automobiles and horse-drawn carriages are sure to add a touch of romance.

✧ If you're hiring a special vehicle for the day, be sure to let the photographer know; shots of you and your groom stepping out of your "chariot" are not to be missed.

✧ If there are any restrictions regarding decorating your getaway vehicle, be sure to let your wedding party know ahead of time.

✧ Some hosts provide a shuttle service to take guests to and from the hotel and the ceremony and reception sites in order to reduce the possibility of drinking and driving.

QUESTIONS TO ASK: TRANSPORTATION

Transportation Service I

Company name: _____

Contact person: _____

Address: _____

_____

_____

Phone: _____

E-mail: _____

Website: _____

✧ What types of cars/limousines/vehicles
are available? _____

_____

_____

_____

✧ How many passengers can the
vehicle(s) comfortably accommodate? _____

_____

_____

✧ Is there a minimum number of hours
required? _____

✧ What is the fee? Is the gratuity
included? _____

_____

_____

✧ What amenities does that rate include? _____

_____

_____

✧ How many hours does that rate
include? _____

_____

✧ *If an hourly rate:* When does the clock
start—when the driver leaves the base
or when passengers are picked up? _____

_____

Transportation Service II	*Transportation Service III*

Transportation Service I

◇ How do overtime charges work?   _____
_____

◇ What are the charges for any extra
amenities (champagne, TV, etc.)
we might want?

◇ How old are the vehicles?
◇ Can we see the vehicles?
◇ How long has each driver who would
be providing services for our wedding
been with your company?

◇ What is the driving record of each
of these drivers?

◇ Is each of these drivers familiar with
the area?
◇ How will each driver be dressed?
◇ Do you have liability insurance?
◇ How much of a deposit is required?
◇ When is the balance due?
◇ What is your cancellation policy?

◇ Do you have references?

◇ Other questions/notes:

Transportation Service II	*Transportation Service III*

Notes

Chapter Nine

Honeymoon & Beyond

Honeymoon

THINGS TO DO

☐ Get recommendations from friends and family for honeymoon destinations
☐ Find travel agent/tour operator specializing in chosen destination, if not making the arrangements yourself
☐ Make arrangements to take time off from work for honeymoon
☐ Book transportation to destination
☐ Book hotel accommodations
☐ If renting a car, find out if your automobile insurance covers you on a rental car in the honeymoon location or if you should purchase insurance from the rental company
☐ Book car rental/transportation from airport to hotel, if necessary
☐ Make sure travel documents (passports, visas, etc.) are current, if traveling out of the country
☐ Obtain travel insurance, if desired
☐ Purchase guidebooks about destination
☐ Purchase foreign language books or lesson programs, if applicable
☐ Make appointments to get any necessary immunizations for foreign travel
☐ Book activities
☐ Make any necessary dining reservations
☐ Purchase any items you need for the trip
☐ Pick up or print out tickets/itinerary from travel agent, if they're not being mailed to you
☐ Obtain traveler's checks
☐ Change currency, if necessary
☐ Pack (include any special gear required for planned activities)
☐ Make sure you have extra camera batteries and film
☐ Assign someone to keep track of tickets/travel documents so they don't get lost in the wedding mayhem
☐ Confirm all reservations
☐ Have mail held at post office and newspaper delivery put on hold
☐ Call stores where you're registered to hold deliveries
☐ Other _____
☐ _____
☐ _____
☐ _____
☐ _____
☐ _____
☐ _____
☐ _____

Words to the Wise

✧ Even if you're changing your name, book your airline tickets in your maiden name to match your driver's license, passport, or other form of identification necessary for airport checkpoints.

✧ Some airlines and hotels will upgrade honeymoon couples if space permits; inquire when you check in at the airport as well as at your hotel.

✧ Before making hotel reservations, check out photographs to see if you like the look of the place—including the rooms. You should be able to find images on the company's websites, or you can contact them directly to request a brochure. Some hotel websites even offer "virtual tours" of the rooms and grounds.

✧ When booking your trip, inquire about travel insurance. Such a policy can protect you from losing money if you need to cancel due to health reasons, family emergencies, or natural disasters; it can also cover theft during the trip. Types and costs vary, but before purchasing a policy, find out if you're already covered by your homeowner's/renter's insurance or your credit card company.

QUESTIONS TO ASK: TRAVEL AGENT

Be sure to go over the information under "Travel Considerations" on page 180 with the travel agent as well.

Travel Agency I

Name of travel agency: _____
Name of agent: _____
Address: _____
_____
_____
Phone: _____
E-mail: _____
Website: _____
✧ Do you specialize in any specific type of vacation? _____
✧ What do your services include? _____
_____
_____
✧ How long has the agency been in business? _____

Travel Agency II | *Travel Agency III*

Travel Agency I

✧ Can you make any recommendations
as to where and when we should
travel?

_____
_____
_____
_____

✧ Have you ever visited the destination
we're discussing?

✧ Have you sent many couples to a
particular resort?

_____
_____
_____
_____

✧ Do you have any photos/brochures of
potential hotels (including pictures
of rooms)?

✧ What is the cost of the trip we're
interested in, and what is included?
*(Be sure to get costs for all elements,
such as transportation to destination,
hotel accommodations, car rentals, etc.)*

_____
_____
_____
_____
_____

✧ What type of travel insurance is
offered? What is the additional cost,
if any?

✧ How does payment work?

✧ What is the cancellation policy?

✧ Do you have references?

_____
_____
_____
_____
_____

✧ Other questions/notes:

_____
_____
_____
_____

Travel Agency II

Travel Agency III

TRAVEL CONSIDERATIONS

Option I

Destination

- ✧ What is the weather like in the destination we're considering at the time we'd be there?
- ✧ Do we need to be concerned about drinking the water, eating any foods, or any safety issues?
- ✧ Do we need a passport, a visa, or any other travel documents?

- ✧ Do we need any immunizations?

- ✧ What side of the road do people drive on?

Hotel Accommodations

- ✧ Can we request the following:
  - Room with a view?
  - Room with a patio/terrace?
  - Bed size?
  - Smoking/nonsmoking?
  - Private bath?
- ✧ What is the room rate?

- ✧ Are any meals included in the room rate?

- ✧ What are the amenities in the room (television, phone, alarm clock, radio, air-conditioning, fireplace, minibar/ refrigerator, whirlpool tub, etc.)?
- ✧ What other amenities does the hotel offer (dining facilities, gym, pool, spa, private beach, etc.)?

Option II

Option III

Option I

✧ Is there room service?

✧ Can we rent sporting equipment
(tennis rackets, skis, snorkeling gear,
etc.) from the hotel?

✧ Does the hotel offer transportation
to and from the airport? If so, is it
complimentary?

✧ How much of a deposit, if any, is
required for a room reservation?

✧ What is the cancellation policy?

✧ Other questions/notes:

Airplane Reservations

✧ What is the airline fare for the dates
and times we want?

✧ What are the terms for changing
the dates of reservations after
we've booked them?

✧ What is the cancellation policy for
the reservations we're considering?

✧ If we're not already members of the
frequent flier program, can we join
now and receive miles for this trip?

✧ Can we get our seating assignments
now?

✧ Can we request special meals for
the flight?

✧ Other questions/notes:

Option II   _Option III_

Option I

Train Reservations

◇ Can we reserve seats?

◇ Are cabins available for longer trips?

◇ Are sleeper seats available for longer trips?

◇ What is the fare for the dates and times we want?

◇ What are the terms for changing the dates of reservations after we've booked them?

◇ What is the cancellation policy?

◇ Is there a dining car?

◇ Can we check luggage?

◇ Is there a limit to the amount of checked or carry-on luggage?

◇ Other questions/notes:

Cruise Reservations

◇ What are the differences between cabin categories—with respect to accommodations and cost?

◇ What is the rate for the cruise we're interested in?

◇ Is the cost of flying to and from port included in the rate?

◇ Are port charges and taxes included?

◇ Is transportation provided between the airport and the ship? If so, is there an additional fee?

◇ Are meals and drinks included in the rate?

Option II

Option III

Option I

◇ What are the seating arrangements for meals?

◇ Can we request an early or late seating for dinner?

◇ Are a jacket and tie required for meals?

◇ Is there room service?

◇ What amenities are offered on board?

◇ What is the average age of the passengers?

◇ Do we need a passport for certain destinations?

◇ What is the payment policy?

◇ What is the cancellation policy?

◇ Other questions/notes:

Rental Cars

◇ What are our options (make, size, convertible, automatic/standard, air-conditioning, music player, etc.)?

◇ What is the rate?

◇ How does payment work?

◇ What is the cancellation policy?

◇ Other questions/notes:

Option II

Option III

After "I Do"

THINGS TO DO

- [ ] Pick up held mail at post office, upon return from honeymoon
- [ ] Call stores where you've registered to resume gift delivery, upon return from honeymoon
- [ ] Fill out necessary documents to change name legally, if applicable
- [ ] Contact the appropriate agencies/businesses to inform them of name change, if applicable:
    - [ ] Department of Motor Vehicles
    - [ ] passport office
    - [ ] Social Security Administration
    - [ ] insurance agencies
    - [ ] credit card companies
    - [ ] banks/financial institutions
    - [ ] payroll offices
    - [ ] registrar of voters
- [ ] Contact any agencies/businesses that require knowledge of or should know about your change in marital status
- [ ] Send thank-you notes
- [ ] Send change-of-address cards
- [ ] Follow up with photographer regarding proofs
- [ ] Follow up with videographer
- [ ] Other _____
- [ ] _____
- [ ] _____
- [ ] _____

Notes

Notes

Appendix

Gift Registry Guide

Formal China	Quantity
Place settings:	
Chargers	_____
Dinner plates	_____
Salad/dessert plates	_____
Bread plates	_____
Cups and saucers	_____
Rimmed soup bowls	_____
Serving pieces:	
Large platter	_____
Medium platter	_____
Covered vegetable dish	_____
Open vegetable dish	_____
Gravy boat	_____
Creamer	_____
Sugar bowl	_____
Butter dish	_____
Salt and pepper shakers	_____

Everyday Dishes	Quantity
Place settings:	
Dinner plates	_____
Salad/dessert plates	_____
Soup/cereal bowls	_____
Cups and saucers	_____
Mugs	_____
Serving pieces:	
Large platter	_____
Medium platter	_____

Everyday Dishes *(continued)*	Quantity
Covered vegetable dish	_____
Open vegetable dish	_____
Salad bowl	_____
Salad tongs	_____
Creamer	_____
Sugar bowl	_____
Butter dish	_____
Salt and pepper shakers	_____

Crystal/Barware	
Red wine glasses	_____
White wine glasses	_____
Water goblets	_____
Highballs	_____
Double old-fashioneds	_____
Champagne flutes	_____
Decanter	_____
Ice bucket (and tongs)	_____
Martini glasses	_____
Pilsners	_____

Everyday Glassware	
Iced tea glasses	_____
Juice glasses	_____
Pitcher	_____

	Sterling Quantity	Stainless Quantity
Flatware		
Place settings:		
Dinner forks	_____	_____
Salad forks	_____	_____
Dinner knives	_____	_____
Butter knives	_____	_____
Tablespoons	_____	_____
Teaspoons	_____	_____
Soup spoons	_____	_____
Dessert spoons	_____	_____
Iced tea spoons	_____	_____
Serving pieces:		
Serving spoon	_____	_____
Pierced spoon	_____	_____
Serving fork	_____	_____
Cake server	_____	_____
Lasagna server	_____	_____
Ladle	_____	_____

	Quantity
Entertaining	
Cheese board	_____
Cheese knives	_____
Platter for hors d'oeuvres	_____
Chip and dip	_____
Cake plate	_____
Coasters	_____
Trivets	_____

	Quantity
Knives	
Steak knives	_____
Bread knife	_____
Chef's knife	_____
Carving knife	_____
Carving fork	_____
Boning knife	_____
Cleaver	_____
Paring knife	_____
Kitchen shears	_____
Sharpening rod	_____
Knife block	_____
Cookware	
1-quart saucepan	_____
2-quart saucepan	_____
3-quart saucepan	_____
Stockpot	_____
2-quart Dutch oven	_____
4-quart Dutch oven	_____
8-quart Dutch oven	_____
8-inch skillet	_____
10-inch skillet	_____
12-inch skillet	_____
3-quart sauté pan	_____
5-quart sauté pan	_____
7-quart sauté pan	_____
Grill pan	_____
Roasting pan	_____
Roasting rack	_____
Griddle	_____
Wok	_____
Double boiler	_____
Steamer basket	_____
Kettle/teapot	_____

	Quantity			Quantity
Bakeware			**Appliances**	
Baking sheet	_____		Microwave oven	_____
Loaf pan	_____		Toaster oven	_____
Round cake pan	_____		Food processor	_____
Pie pan	_____		Blender	_____
Muffin tin	_____		Hand mixer	_____
Glass baking dish	_____		Standing mixer	_____
Cooling rack	_____		Coffeemaker	_____
			Coffee grinder	_____
Kitchen Items			Cappuccino/espresso	
Cutting board	_____		maker	_____
Colander	_____		Juicer	_____
Sifter	_____		Waffle iron	_____
Mixing bowls	_____		Ice cream maker	_____
Measuring spoons	_____		Electric can opener	_____
Measuring cups	_____			
Whisk	_____		**Table Linens**	
Spatulas	_____		Tablecloth	_____
Mixing spoons	_____		Silencing cloth	_____
Baster	_____		Table runner	_____
Rolling pin	_____		Place mats	_____
Cheese grater	_____		Dinner napkins	_____
Garlic press	_____		Cocktail napkins	_____
Garlic roaster	_____		Napkin rings	_____
Ice cream scoop	_____			
Pasta server	_____			
Pizza slicer	_____			
Egg slicer	_____			
Apple corer	_____			
Spoon rest	_____			
Spice rack	_____			
Sushi set	_____			
Chopsticks	_____			
Kitchen timer	_____			
Cookbooks	_____			

	Quantity		Quantity
Bed Linens		**Giftware**	
Fitted sheets	_____	Vases	_____
Flat sheets	_____	Picture frames	_____
Pillowcases	_____	Candy dishes	_____
Pillows	_____	Candlesticks	_____
Mattress pad	_____	Decorative bowls	_____
Comforter	_____		
Duvet	_____	**Luggage**	
Duvet cover	_____	Suitcases	_____
Pillow shams	_____	Garment bag	_____
Bed skirt	_____	Duffel bag	_____
Decorative pillows	_____	Carry-on bag	_____
Throw	_____	Luggage cart	_____

Bath Linens/Accessories

	Quantity
Bath sheets	_____
Bath towels	_____
Hand towels	_____
Washcloths	_____
Bath mat	_____
Shower curtain	_____
Soap dish	_____
Toothbrush holder	_____
Tissue holder	_____
Wastebasket	_____

Sample Photography/ Videography Shot List

Use the following as a guide and add any detailed variations specific to your situation.

✧ Bride getting ready
✧ Groom getting ready

Formal portraits (can be taken before or after ceremony):
✧ Bride (with and without bouquet)
✧ Groom
✧ Bride and groom
✧ Bride and groom with bride's immediate family
✧ Bride and groom with groom's immediate family
✧ Bride and groom with immediate families
✧ Bride with maid of honor and bridesmaids (with each individually and all together)
✧ Groom with best man and ushers (with each individually and all together)
✧ Bride and groom with entire wedding party

Ceremony:
✧ Venue set up before guests arrive
✧ Guests arriving/being seated
✧ Musicians
✧ Groom at the altar or walking down aisle with parents
✧ Mother of the bride or bride's parents walking down aisle
✧ Processional (bridesmaids, flower girl/ ring bearer, bride)

✧ Attendants at altar/seated in pews
✧ Readers/participants in ceremony
✧ Reciting of vows
✧ Exchanging of rings
✧ Additional ceremony highlights/rituals
✧ Kiss
✧ Recessional

Reception:
✧ Receiving line
✧ Introduction of bride and groom
✧ First dance
✧ Father–daughter dance
✧ Mother–son dance
✧ Traditional/religious dance
✧ Bride dancing with father-in-law
✧ Groom dancing with mother-in-law
✧ Parents of bride dancing
✧ Parents of groom dancing
✧ Toasts
✧ Pre-meal prayers
✧ General dancing
✧ Table shots
✧ Centerpiece
✧ Cake
✧ Cake-cutting
✧ Bouquet toss
✧ Bride and groom with college friends (for alumni magazines)
✧ Bride and groom leaving reception
✧ Candids throughout event

Contact Information

Wedding Consultant
Name: _____
Company: _____
Address: _____
_____
_____
Phone: _____
E-mail: _____
Website: _____
Wedding day contact #: _____

Ceremony Site
Site name: _____
Contact person: _____
Address: _____
_____
_____
Phone: _____
E-mail: _____
Website: _____
Wedding day contact #: _____

Officiant
Name: _____
Address: _____
_____
_____
Phone: _____
E-mail: _____
Website: _____
Wedding day contact #: _____

Reception Site

Site name:

Contact person:

Address:

Phone:

E-mail:

Website:

Wedding day contact #:

Caterer/Banquet Manager

Name:

Company:

Address:

Phone:

E-mail:

Website:

Wedding day contact #:

Baker/Cake Decorator

Name:

Company:

Address:

Phone:

E-mail:

Website:

Wedding day contact #:

Ceremony Musicians
Name: _____
Address: _____
_____
_____
Phone: _____
E-mail: _____
Website: _____
Agency: _____
Agency representative: _____
Agent's phone: _____
Agent's e-mail: _____
Wedding day contact # for musicians: _____
Wedding day contact # for agent: _____

Band/Disc Jockey
Name: _____
Address: _____
_____
_____
Phone: _____
E-mail: _____
Website: _____
Agency: _____
Agency representative: _____
Agent's phone: _____
Agent's e-mail: _____
Wedding day contact # for band/disc jockey: _____
Wedding day contact # for agent: _____

Florist
Name: _____
Company: _____
Address: _____
_____
Phone: _____
E-mail: _____
Website: _____
Wedding day contact #: _____

Photographer
Name: _____
Address: _____
_____
_____
_____

Phone: _____
E-mail: _____
Website: _____
Agency: _____
Agency representative: _____
Agent's phone: _____
Agent's e-mail: _____
Wedding day contact # for photographer: _____
Wedding day contact # for agent: _____

Videographer
Name: _____
Address: _____
_____
_____
_____

Phone: _____
E-mail: _____
Website: _____
Agency: _____
Agency representative: _____
Agent's phone: _____
Agent's e-mail: _____
Wedding day contact # for videographer: _____
Wedding day contact # for agent: _____

Rental Company
Company name: _____
Contact person: _____
Address: _____
_____
_____

Phone: _____
E-mail: _____
Website: _____
Wedding day contact #: _____

Bridal Salon
Salon name:
Sales associate:
Address:

Phone:
E-mail:
Website:
Wedding day contact # for seamstress:

(if coming to bustle)

Formalwear Shop
Shop name:
Contact person:
Address:

Phone:
E-mail:
Website:
Wedding day contact #:

Hairstylist
Name:
Salon:
Address:

Phone:
E-mail:
Website:
Wedding day contact #:
Makeup Artist
Name:

Salon: _____

Address: _____

_____

_____

Phone: _____

E-mail: _____

Website: _____

Wedding day contact #: _____

Transportation Service

Company: _____

Contact person: _____

Address: _____

_____

_____

Phone: _____

E-mail: _____

Website: _____

Wedding day contact #: _____

Hotel #1

Hotel name: _____

Contact person: _____

Address: _____

_____

_____

Phone: _____

E-mail: _____

Website: _____

Reservation code: _____

Hotel #2
Hotel name: _____
Contact person: _____
Address: _____
_____
_____
_____
Phone: _____
E-mail: _____
Website: _____
Reservation code: _____

Bridesmaid #1
Name: _____
Address: _____
_____
_____
_____
Phone/Fax: _____
E-mail: _____
Wedding day contact #: _____

Bridesmaid #2
Name: _____
Address: _____
_____
_____
_____
Phone: _____
E-mail: _____
Wedding day contact #: _____

Bridesmaid #3
Name: _____
Address: _____
_____
_____
_____
Phone: _____
E-mail: _____
Wedding day contact #: _____

Bridesmaid #4
Name: _____
Address: _____
                                             _____
                                             _____
Phone: _____
E-mail: _____
Wedding day contact #:   _____

Bridesmaid #5
Name: _____
Address: _____
                                             _____
                                             _____
Phone: _____
E-mail: _____
Wedding day contact #:   _____

Groomsman #1
Name: _____
Address: _____
                                             _____
                                             _____
Phone: _____
E-mail: _____
Wedding day contact #:   _____

Groomsman #2
Name: _____
Address: _____
                                             _____
                                             _____
Phone: _____
E-mail: _____
Wedding day contact #:   _____

Groomsman #3
Name: _____
Address: _____
                _____

Phone: _____
E-mail: _____
Wedding day contact #:   _____

Groomsman #4
Name: _____
Address: _____
                _____

Phone: _____
E-mail: _____
Wedding day contact #:   _____

Groomsman #5
Name: _____
Address: _____
                _____

Phone: _____
E-mail: _____
Wedding day contact #:   _____

Reader/Singer #1
Name: _____
Address: _____
                _____

Phone: _____
E-mail: _____
Wedding day contact #:   _____

Reader/Singer #2
Name: _____
Address: _____
                _____

Phone: _____
E-mail: _____
Wedding day contact #:   _____

Bride's Parents
Name: _____
Address: _____
_____
_____
Phone: _____
E-mail: _____
Wedding day contact #: _____

Name: _____
Address: _____
_____
_____
Phone: _____
E-mail: _____
Wedding day contact #: _____

Groom's Parents
Name: _____
Address: _____
_____
_____
Phone: _____
E-mail: _____
Wedding day contact #: _____

Name: _____
Address: _____
_____
_____
Phone: _____
E-mail: _____
Wedding day contact #: _____

Bridesmaids' Measurements

Bridesmaid #1:
 Bust: _____
 Hips: _____
 Waist: _____
 Height: _____

Bridesmaid #4:
 Bust: _____
 Hips: _____
 Waist: _____
 Height: _____

Bridesmaid #2:
 Bust: _____
 Hips: _____
 Waist: _____
 Height: _____

Bridesmaid #5:
 Bust: _____
 Hips: _____
 Waist: _____
 Height: _____

Bridesmaid #3:
 Bust: _____
 Hips: _____
 Waist: _____
 Height: _____

Things to Bring: Rehearsal/ Rehearsal Dinner

It is a good idea to make your own detailed list of "things to bring," complete with all the items specific to your individual situation. Feel free to use the list below as a guide.

☐ Ordered list of paired-off attendants for processional and recessional
☐ List of family members being escorted down aisle
☐ Extra copies of readings/songs for special ceremony participants
☐ Shoes to practice walking down aisle
☐ Ribbon bouquet from shower, if applicable
☐ Gifts for bridesmaids and groomsmen, to give at dinner
☐ Gift for groom (if desired), to be given after dinner
☐ Copy of toast, if giving one

Things to Bring: Wedding Day

It is a good idea to make your own detailed list of "things to bring," complete with all the items specific to your individual situation. Feel free to use the list below as a guide.

- [ ] Wedding gown
- [ ] Veil
- [ ] Headpiece
- [ ] Undergarments
- [ ] Hosiery
- [ ] Shoes
- [ ] Jewelry
- [ ] Purse
- [ ] Bridal emergency kit (see page 157)
- [ ] Steamer, if recommended by bridal salon to take wrinkles out of dress
- [ ] Anything recommended by bridal salon to remove spots from dress
- [ ] Makeup that you want the stylist to use
- [ ] Brush/comb
- [ ] Toothbrush and toothpaste
- [ ] This book (complete with wedding-day contact numbers of service providers)
- [ ] Wine goblet, candleholder, other ceremonial objects
- [ ] Guest book
- [ ] Pen for guest book
- [ ] Copy of vows, if you wish to review before wedding
- [ ] Extra copies of shot list and schedule for photographer and/or videographer
- [ ] Extra copy of schedule of events and announcements for band/disc jockey
- [ ] Extra copy of playlist for band/disc jockey
- [ ] Any music still needed by disc jockey
- [ ] Copy of toast, if giving one
- [ ] Copy of gratuity list
- [ ] Gratuities (in sealed, labeled envelopes)
- [ ] Payments for service providers
- [ ] Camera (with extra memory card and batteries/charger)
- [ ] Rings, if not already with best man
- [ ] Going-away outfit
- [ ] Packed suitcase for wedding night
- [ ] Honeymoon tickets, information, and packed suitcase, if necessary

208

Index

Cooking Basics

Tooling Up: Kitchen Appliances and Equipment

A kitchen outfitted with equipment and tools tailored to your cooking style makes working in the kitchen practical, efficient, and a pleasure.

Cooking Knives

Choose your knives carefully and give them regular care.

Selecting the Right Knives

Choose knives that feel balanced and comfortable in your hand. Those made of high-carbon stainless steel with blades that run through the handles and are riveted in place are a good choice. High-carbon stainless steel resists corrosion similarly to regular stainless steel, but it isn't as hard, so it sharpens more easily.

Caring for Your Knives

Always cut on a cutting board. Wash knives in hot, soapy water immediately after using them; rinse and wipe dry or allow to air-dry. Do not let them soak in water, and do not wash them in the dishwasher. Store knives in a knife block or protective case.

In general, you should sharpen knives using a professional-style grind wheel or a whetstone, or take them to a professional service. Once they're sharp, occasionally realign the edge and remove nicks with a sharpening steel—a ridged rod made of diamond-coated steel or ceramic. Here's how:

Rest the sharpening steel vertically with its tip pressed against a stable cutting surface, such as a cutting board. Place a knife blade against the steel  near the handle at a 20-degree angle to the steel. In one smooth, slow motion, gently draw the blade down the full length of the steel, pulling it toward you as the blade moves down the steel.

When you finish the stroke, the tip of the blade—still at an angle—should be near the tip of the steel. Repeat with the other side of the blade.

Useful Knives for the Home Cook

These knives should meet most of your needs.
Bread knife: The serrated blade easily cuts through breads, bagels, tomatoes, cakes, or other foods with tough exteriors and soft interiors.
Chef's or cook's knife: Chop, dice, and mince foods with the wedge-shape blade.
Paring knife: The short blade comfortably peels and cuts fruits and vegetables.
Utility knife: The thin blade makes it easy to smoothly slice sandwiches and other soft foods, such as fruit and cheese.

Nonessential Knives

These knives are useful for specific tasks.
Boning knife: The narrow blade works well for cutting meat off bones.
Carving knife/slicer: This long, thin blade makes it easy to slice cooked meats.
Fillet knife: The long, thin, flexible blade is useful for efficiently filleting fish.

| Bread knife | Carving knife | Chef's knife | Utility knife | Paring knife |

Pots and Pans

Pots and pans are made of a variety of materials. Aluminum and copper pans are the best heat conductors, though all-copper pans are expensive and tarnish easily, and plain aluminum pans can react with certain foods. Good options for the home cook include heavy stainless-steel pans with copper bottoms, pans clad with aluminum sandwiched between stainless steel, and aluminum pans treated with a process known as hard anodization. Anodization creates a non-corrosive cookware that conducts heat well. Heavy pans such as those described above, as well as enameled cast iron, often are called for because they heat foods evenly.

Range-Top Cookware Checklist

Commonly used cookware includes pans of different sizes, shapes, and functions.

Double boiler: Two pans work together, with one fitting into the other. Water in the bottom pan simmers gently to cook the contents in the top pan. You can substitute a metal or heat-resistant glass bowl and a saucepan. The bowl should fit in the pan but not touch the simmering water.

Dutch oven or kettle: The large, heavy pot has a tight-fitting lid and two handles. It is used for soups, stews, and braising meats. A kettle often is used in canning.

Seasoning a Skillet

Regular cast-iron cookware needs to be seasoned to help it avoid rust and corrosion. Instructions for seasoning should come with the skillet. If no instructions are available, wash and dry the pan thoroughly. Brush shortening or cooking oil over the entire inside surface. Heat in a 350°F oven for 1 hour. Cool and wipe out the skillet. Season the skillet before the first use and periodically thereafter.

Saucepans: These versatile pans come in many sizes, including 1½, 2, and 3 quarts. It's helpful to have several different sizes.

Skillets: This long-handled, low-sided pan sometimes is referred to as a frying pan. Its sides often slope to allow for better evaporation of liquids. Large (10-inch) and very large (12-inch) skillets are most useful. A 10-inch nonstick skillet also comes in handy. Other sizes include small (6-inch) and medium (8-inch). If you want to use a skillet in the oven, wrap the handle in a couple of layers of heavy-duty foil or purchase a skillet with an oven-going or removable handle.

Vegetable steamer (collapsible or insert): The perforated basket holds food over boiling water in a pan to steam it rather than boil it.

Saucepan

Saucepan

Dutch oven

Flared-edge skillet

Straight-sided skillet with lid

Specialty Pans

While not essential, these specialty pans offer features that make it easier to prepare specific foods.

Griddle: This flat, often rimless pan makes flipping pancakes a cinch. A nonstick griddle also helps you cook with a minimum amount of fat.

Grill pan: The grooves of this heavy, stove-top, griddle-type pan allow fat to drain away from food and add appetizing grill marks to the cooked items.

Omelet pan: Sloped sides and a nonstick surface make it easy to fold and slide omelets from the pan onto the plate.

Wok: Available with a rounded or flat bottom, this pan offers deep, sloping sides that help keep food pieces in the pan when stir-frying.

About Nonstick Pans

Look for fairly heavy, moderately priced nonstick pans. With proper care and with the use of heat-proof spatulas and wooden spoons, the pans will last three to five years before needing to be replaced.

Baking Pans and Dishes

In this cookbook, a baking pan refers to a metal container, and a baking dish refers to an oven-safe glass or ceramic container. (If substituting glass or ceramic cookware for recipes that call for baking pans, reduce baking temperature by about 25°F.)

Baking Pans (Metal)

● Use for nicely browned baked goods. See page 163 for information on choosing the right pans for cakes.

● Use for broiling. Do not use glass dishes or casseroles when broiling because the high temperatures may cause the glass to shatter.

Baking Dishes (Glass or Ceramic)

● Use for dishes made with eggs or with acidic ingredients such as tomatoes and lemon. Baking pans made of aluminum, iron, and tin can react with these foods, causing the foods to discolor.

Ovenware Checklist

With these ovenware pieces in your kitchen, you'll be able to make almost any baked good you desire.

Baking dishes (glass), rectangular: One 2-quart (12×7½×2-inch), one 3-quart (13×9×2-inch).

Baking dish (glass), square: One 2-quart (8×8×2-inch).

Baking pans (metal): One 9×9×2-inch, one 13×9×2-inch, and one 15×10×1-inch (jelly-roll).

Cake pans (metal): Two round 8×1½- or 9×1½-inch; those with 2-inch-deep sides also will suffice.

Specialty Bakeware

Some desserts require specific bakeware.

Fluted tube pan: Fluted sides bring a decorative look to cakes. This pan comes in various sizes, with a 10-inch, 12-cup being the most common.

Springform pan: The pan bottom is separate from the pan sides. A clamp holds the two parts together and opens to allow the sides to be pulled away from the baked dessert. Use this round pan for making cheesecakes and other desserts that are tricky to remove from their pans. The 8- and 9-inch sizes are most common; 10- and 11-inch pans also are available.

Tart pan with removable bottom: A removable bottom makes it easy to neatly transfer a tart to a serving plate. Pans come in 9- to 11-inch sizes. (Shallow quiche or flan pans are one piece, without removable bottoms.)

Tube pan: This deep pan, also known as an angel food cake pan, has a hollow center tube that promotes even baking. Most tube pans have removable bottoms. A 10-inch pan is a common size.

Roasting pan with rack

Square baking dish

Covered casserole

Custard cups

Cookie sheet

15×10×1-inch baking pan

Cookie sheets (metal): At least two with either no sides or low sides; in a pinch, substitute a 15×10×1-inch (jelly-roll) baking pan, though its rims may inhibit even browning.

Covered casseroles: Several round, deep, glass, various sizes (1-, 2-, and 3-quart). If a recipe calls for a covered casserole and you do not have a lid, use foil to cover.

Welcome (Baking) Mats

Silicone baking mats are a high-tech twist on traditional parchment.

If you do a lot of cookie, jelly-roll, or biscuit baking, you might consider investing in a few sizes of nonstick silicone baking mats. They ensure even heating and easy release from the pan and are easily cleaned with a damp sponge.

Custard cups: Six round, glass, 6-ounce. Use them for cooking custards and other individual desserts and when measuring and preparing small amounts of ingredients, such as garlic, in advance so that the ingredients are ready when you need them in a recipe.

Loaf pans (metal) or dishes (glass): Several 7½×3½×2-inch, 8×4×2-inch, or 9×5×3-inch.

Muffin pan: One pan with twelve 2½-inch cups or one or two pans with twelve 1¾-inch cups.

Pie plate (glass) or pan (metal): One round 9-inch.

Pizza pan (metal): One round 12- to 14-inch; in a pinch, substitute a baking sheet, but build up the pizza crust edges to hold toppings.

Roasting pan with rack: One large enough to accommodate a roast yet fit in your oven. A rack helps promote even cooking and prevents the roast from stewing in the pan juices.

Soufflé dish: One round, glass, 1½-quart; in a pinch, substitute a straight-sided casserole with the same volume.

Specialty bakeware: See page 9.

Kitchen Gadgets

You can certainly get soup from pot to bowl without a ladle, but it's amazing how much easier (and neater) the task is with one in hand. That's the case with most kitchen gadgets. In general, having the right tools can make cooking more efficient and enjoyable.

Cooking Utensils and Gadgets Checklist

Here are some of the most helpful tools for cooking, including substitutions where possible.

Bottle/can opener.

Colander: Use this perforated bowl-shape utensil to rinse food or to drain liquids from solid food. When solids are fine, use a fine-mesh sieve.

Corkscrew: With many models available, choose the type you're comfortable using. See pages 120–121.

Cutting boards: Stock up on two. Reserve one solely for raw meat, poultry, fish, and shellfish, and the other for ready-to-eat foods.

Egg separator: Use to separate egg yolks from whites. See page 224. Separating eggs by passing the yolk from shell to shell can spread any harmful bacteria that may be present.

Food mill: If you don't have one, force food through a strainer set over a bowl or pan.

Fork, long-handled: Use when carving or moving large pieces of food, such as roasts.

Funnel: Helps avoid spills when pouring an ingredient from one container to another.

Other Useful Gadgets

These tools are not essential for everyday cooking, but the more you cook, the more you'll enjoy having them on hand.

- Cheese slicer
- Citrus juicer/reamer
- Citrus zester
- Mandoline
- Meat mallet
- Mortar and pestle
- Parchment paper
- Pastry bag with tips
- Pizza cutter
- Pizza stone
- Potato masher
- Salad spinner

Graters

Grater: This metal tool generally has a surface punched with small, sharp-edged holes or slits that are used to break foods into smaller pieces. Those with large holes are sometimes called shredders, while those with the largest holes are sometimes called slicers. Box graters have different-size holes or slits on each side. The size of the holes or slits determines the task for which the grater is best suited. The smaller the holes or slits, the finer the resulting food pieces.

Kitchen shears: Use for snipping everything from fresh herbs to kitchen string.

Knives: See page 7.

Ladle: In a pinch, substitute a heatproof cup.

Measuring cups and spoons: See page 23.

Mixing bowls: For most cooks, a set of four mixing bowls in the following sizes will suffice: small (1-quart), medium (1½-quart), large (2½-quart), and extra-large (4-quart).

Pastry blender: For cutting fat (such as shortening) into flour to make baked goods. If you don't have one, use two knives in a crisscross motion.

Pastry brush: Use for brushing glazes over baked goods and for greasing pans.

Pastry blender

Pepper grinder: Use when you desire the more flavorful freshly ground pepper.

Rolling pin: A clean, heavy bottle with smooth sides can be used instead.

Colander

Sieves

Rotary beater: If you have an electric mixer or handheld blender, you may not need one.

Rubber scraper: Use these utensils, also known as rubber spatulas, for scraping batter from a bowl and for folding ingredients together.

Sharpening steel: See page 7.

Sieves: Use these circular wire-mesh utensils, also called strainers, to separate small particles from large ones. Stock up on one large and one small.

Sifter: If you don't have one, pour flour or powdered sugar into a sieve set over a bowl, then stir it to force the grains through the wire mesh.

Skewers: These thin, pointed sticks are made of metal or wood and are used to hold pieces of meat, fruit, and vegetables. To use wooden skewers for grilling or broiling, be sure to first soak them in water for at least 30 minutes to prevent them from burning.

Slotted spoon, long-handled: Useful for removing solids from liquid mixtures.

Spatulas: These flat utensils can be made of metal, rubber, plastic, and wood. A metal turner-type spatula is used for flipping foods; a narrow, flexible metal spatula works well for spreading. Rubber or plastic spatulas also are called rubber

Essential Tools: While most of your tools can be stored in a drawer, it's handy to have the ones you use all the time—spoons, spatulas, rubber scrapers, and whisks—in a crock on the counter right next to the stove.

scrapers (see Rubber scraper, left). When using a spatula for cooking on the range top, make sure the one you use is heatproof; metal or silicone is a good choice.

Spoon, long-handled: These work well for stirring large volumes.

Thermometers: See below.

Timer: A digital timer can help you time cooking steps to the second.

Tongs (metal or with nylon grippers): Use to lift and turn foods.

Vegetable brush: Useful for scrubbing fruits and vegetables when skins will not be removed.

Vegetable peeler: Essential for peeling vegetables; in a pinch, peel skins with a paring knife.

Wire cooling rack: Allows air to circulate around baked goods to cool them quickly and keep them from getting soggy.

Wire whisks: These come in handy for beating eggs and other ingredients. They also can help you smooth out lumpy sauces; see page 517. In a pinch, substitute a rotary beater.

Wooden spoons (assorted sizes): These sturdy tools are useful for stirring thick dough and batter. Because wooden handles stay cool longer than metal handles, they are a good choice for stirring mixtures while they heat.

Kitchen Thermometers

Kitchen thermometers help ensure that foods are cooked to safe internal temperatures and are stored at proper temperatures.

Appliance Thermometers

Oven thermometer: This lets you check the accuracy of your oven's temperature.

Refrigerator/freezer thermometer: This verifies whether the appliance is chilling correctly. For food safety, refrigerators should maintain a temperature of no higher than 40°F, and freezers should maintain a temperature of 0°F or less.

Food Thermometers

For information on the proper way to use meat thermometers, see page 367; for information on internal temperatures for cooked meats and poultry, see the charts at the end of the Grilling, Meat, and Poultry chapters.

Candy/deep-frying thermometer: These thermometers can safely measure extra-high

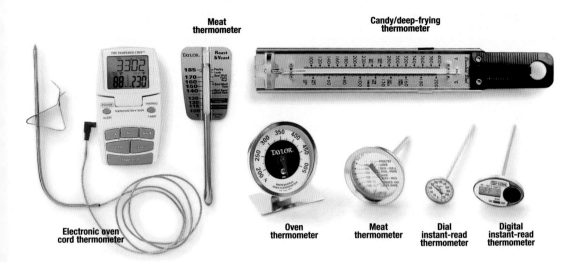

Meat thermometer

Candy/deep-frying thermometer

Electronic oven cord thermometer

Oven thermometer

Meat thermometer

Dial instant-read thermometer

Digital instant-read thermometer

temperatures. They are marked with candy-making stages and for deep-fat frying. Use one when making candy, some frostings and syrups, and when frying foods in a large quantity of cooking oil. (For more information on cooking candy mixtures, see pages 189 and 198.)

Disposable temperature indicator (not pictured): This single-use thermometer, designed for specific temperature ranges, has a sensor that changes color when the appropriate temperature is reached. Follow manufacturer's directions and use it only for the foods for which it is designed.

Electronic oven cord thermometer: Best for roasts or large cuts of meats, this thermometer features a probe designed to stay in the meat as it cooks. A stay-cool cord attaches to a magnet-backed unit that affixes to the oven door. An alarm sounds when the food reaches the desired temperature. Though designed for oven use, it also can be used to check foods cooking on the stove top.

Fork thermometer (not pictured): Handy for grilling, this thermometer can be used for most foods. To ensure an accurate reading, be sure that the tine of the fork containing the sensor is fully inserted. Do not leave it in food while the food is cooking.

Instant-read thermometer: It gives an internal reading in seconds. The sensor in a digital instant-read thermometer is in the tip. Use this type to verify internal temperatures of thin or thick foods. The sensor of a dial instant-read thermometer is in the stem, not the tip, so the

stem must be inserted at least 2 inches into the food you are testing for an accurate reading. (For thinner cuts, you may need to insert the thermometer sideways into the food.) Also see page 367. Do not leave either type of thermometer in food while the food is cooking.

Meat thermometer: Typically used to check the internal temperature of large cuts of meats, such as roasts and whole poultry, it generally is not appropriate for thin foods. An oven-safe meat thermometer may be left in a conventional oven but not in a microwave oven.

Pop-up thermometer (not pictured): Sometimes turkey or other meat comes with an embedded thermometer that pops up when the food is done. Even when such a device is present, the food should be tested with a reliable food thermometer to ensure that it reaches the proper temperatures for safety and doneness.

Temperature and Safety

Cooking foods to their proper temperatures is about maximizing flavor, texture, and safety.

Always use a thermometer to determine if something is done. Never just guess by looking at it or by the amount of time it has spent in the oven or on the grill. See "Safe Food Temperatures" on page 51 for the safe temperatures of various cooked foods.

Countertop Appliances

Review this roundup of today's most common and most useful kitchen appliances.

Blender: With short blades that rotate quickly, this small appliance trims preparation time by instantly blending, chopping, and pureeing foods. For best results:

● Blend large quantities of food in several small batches for better control.

● Stop the blender often and check the size of the food pieces. Blenders work quickly and can easily overblend or overchop food.

● Keep in mind that a blender cannot whip foods (such as whipped cream and potatoes).

● Cut foods into ½- to 1-inch pieces before adding them to the blender, unless otherwise directed.

● When blending heated mixtures, let them cool slightly before blending and fill blender container half full. Cover with lid and open vent. Cover open vent with a clean towel while operating blender. Begin blending warm mixtures on low speed, then increase speed as necessary.

Blender, handheld: Also called an immersion blender, this appliance can blend, liquefy, or puree foods directly in pots or bowls. Because a blender container isn't needed, cleanup is easier.

Bread machine: It handles all bread-baking steps, resulting in freshly baked bread. See page 160.

Electric mixer: This appliance is essential for mixing, whipping, and beating foods. There are two types of mixers. A handheld mixer works for most recipes. If you cook a lot, you may want to invest in a heavy-duty stand mixer, which handles large amounts of thick batter and allows you freedom while it's operating. Many stand mixers knead bread dough with special attachments.

Food processor: This appliance performs many of the same jobs as a blender or electric mixer. While it can't whip foods, it can slice and shred. When processing heated mixtures, cool mixture slightly and fill bowl only half full. Cover lid with a clean towel while operating.

Indoor grill: See page 360.

Slow cooker/crockery cooker: See "Slow Cooker Recipes Essentials," pages 529–530.

Toaster oven: It is ideal for toasting several slices of bread at once and baking small amounts of food because it takes little time to preheat.

Cooking Appliances

The home cook can choose from a variety of ranges, including innovative options that go beyond the standard gas and electric choices.

Combination oven: A microwave-convection oven combination joins the speed of microwaving with the even cooking of convection baking.

Convection oven: Fans circulate hot air through a gas or electric oven, enabling food to cook faster and more evenly. Even cooking means superior results, especially when baking. Also, because the air circulates, more of the oven space can be used.

Converting for Convection

Most recipes can be converted for use in a convection oven. Follow the instructions from your oven manufacturer, keeping the following suggestions in mind.

● Follow the manufacturer's recommendations for preheating a convection oven. Position oven racks before you turn the oven on because they will heat up quickly.

● So hot air circulates as designed, place foods in center of oven; leave space between pans and between pans and oven walls. Open the oven door as little as possible during baking.

● When converting recipes for convection baking, use the temperature and time from the original recipe but check for doneness after three-quarters of the baking time has elapsed. Or reduce the original temperature by 25°F.

● Use the doneness test given in the original recipe. Even when food appears golden brown, it may not be done.

● Because convection ovens offer superior browning and crisping results, most recipes designed for convection ovens do not call for baking dishes to be covered. If you do use your convection oven to bake a standard recipe that calls for the dish to be covered, the temperature and time will likely be about the same. For covered long-baking recipes designed for a standard oven, reduce the temperature for convection baking by 25°F to 50°F.

Halogen/microwave combination oven: This oven combines light waves and microwaves to cook food four times faster than a conventional oven would—with the same oven-quality browning and crisping.

Microwave oven: This appliance uses electro-magnetic waves to cook and warm food in much less time than conventional ovens and stove tops. While you should follow the manufactur-er's directions for operating your microwave, here's some general know-how:

● The microwave timings in this cookbook are designed for a microwave with a cooking power of 850 to 1,000 watts. If you own a lower- or higher-wattage oven, adjust cooking times.

● Use only microwave-safe utensils, materials, and containers in a microwave oven. Look for the words "microwave-safe" on product labels. Never use metal utensils or dishes or those that contain metal (such as dishes or plates with gold or silver trim) in the microwave.

● Use the lid of the microwave-safe container or plastic wrap to cover containers when cooking foods such as casseroles, fish, poultry, and meat. Covering the food helps retain steam, prevent dry-ing, and cook the food faster. Use waxed paper as a cover when heating foods that might spatter.

● When using plastic wrap to cover, vent it by turning back one corner to allow steam to escape.

● Microwave energy tends to penetrate the edges of food first, so stir food often to ensure even cooking. This way, the hotter portion on the outside will be mixed into the cooler center. If the food cannot be stirred (such as chicken pieces or fish fillets), rearrange it: Move the less-cooked food from the center to the edges of the baking dish. For foods in individual dishes, rearrange the dishes, moving those in the center of the oven to the edges. Some microwaves have a turntable to help food cook more evenly.

● If the food can't be stirred or rearranged, and your microwave doesn't have a turntable, turn the dish or food, rotating it halfway unless the recipe specifies otherwise. Turn over large pieces of food, checking for even cooking.

● Always test food after the minimum cooking time in a recipe, using the doneness test given. Some microwaved foods may look as if they need more cooking when they actually are done.

Microwave Timing Hints

Almonds (toasting): Place ½ to 1 cup slivered or sliced almonds in a 2-cup microwave-safe measure. Microwave, uncovered, on 100 percent power (high) for 1 minute; stir. Microwave 1½ to 3 minutes more, stirring every 30 seconds. At the first sign of toast-ing, spread nuts on paper towels. Let stand for at least 15 minutes before using.

Chocolate (melting): Place 1 cup (6 ounc-es) semisweet or milk chocolate pieces or 1 ounce unsweetened or semisweet choco-late, chopped, in a small microwave-safe bowl. Microwave, uncovered, on 70 percent power (medium high) for 1 minute; stir. Microwave on 70 percent power (medium high) for 1½ to 3 minutes more, stirring after every 15 seconds, until chocolate is melted and smooth.

Cream cheese (softening): In a microwave-safe bowl microwave cream cheese, uncov-ered, on 100 percent power (high). Allow 10 to 20 seconds for 3 ounces and 30 to 60 seconds for 8 ounces or until cream cheese begins to soften. Let stand for 5 minutes.

Meat, ground: Crumble 1 pound ground meat in a 1½-quart microwave-safe cas-serole. Microwave, covered, on 100 percent power (high) for 4 to 6 minutes or until thoroughly cooked, stirring twice; drain.

Pancake syrup (heating): In a microwave-safe measure microwave syrup, uncovered, on 100 percent power (high) for 20 to 30 seconds for ½ cup and 30 to 60 seconds for 1 cup or until syrup is warm.

Potatoes (baking): Prick medium-size bak-ing potatoes with a fork. Microwave, uncov-ered, on 100 percent power (high) until almost tender, rearranging once. Allow 4 to 6 minutes for one potato, 6 to 9 minutes for two potatoes, and 10 to 15 minutes for four potatoes. Let stand for 5 minutes.

Tortillas (softening): Place tortillas between paper towels. Microwave on 100 percent power (high), allowing 20 to 30 seconds for four 6- to 9-inch tortillas and 30 to 40 seconds for six tortillas.

Glossary: Cooking Terms and Techniques

Find definitions of terms and techniques used in the recipes in this cookbook and others here. For topics not included, look in relevant chapters or the index.

Al dente: See "Pasta Essentials," page 411.

Bake: To cook food, covered or uncovered, using the direct, dry heat of an oven. The term is usually used to describe the cooking of cakes, other desserts, casseroles, and breads.

Baste: To moisten foods during cooking or grilling with fats or seasoned liquids to add flavor and prevent drying. In general, recipes in this cookbook do not call for basting meat and poultry with pan juices or drippings. Basting tools, such as brushes and bulb basters, could be sources of bacteria if contaminated when dipped into uncooked or undercooked meat and poultry juices, then allowed to sit at room temperature and used later for basting.

Batter: An uncooked, wet mixture that can be spooned or poured, as with cakes, pancakes, and muffins. Batters usually contain flour, eggs, and milk as their base. Some thin batters are used to coat foods before frying.

Beat: To make a mixture smooth by briskly whipping or stirring it with a spoon, fork, wire whisk, rotary beater, or electric mixer. See "Beating Eggs," page 35.

Bias-slice: To slice a food, such as a carrot, at a 45-degree angle.

Bias-

Blackened: A popular Cajun cooking method in which seasoned fish or other foods are cooked over high heat in a super-heated heavy skillet until charred, resulting in a crisp, spicy crust. At home, this is best done outdoors because of the large amount of smoke produced.

Blanch: To partially cook fruits, vegetables, or nuts in boiling water or steam to intensify and set color and flavor. This is an important step in preparing fruits and vegetables for freezing. Blanching also helps loosen skins from tomatoes, peaches, and almonds.

Blend: To combine two or more ingredients by hand or with an electric mixer or blender until smooth and uniform in texture, flavor, and color.

Boil: To cook food in liquid at a temperature that causes bubbles to form in the liquid and rise in a steady pattern, breaking at the surface. A rolling boil occurs when liquid is boiling so vigorously that the bubbles can't be stirred down. See also Simmer, page 20.

Braise: To cook food slowly in a small amount of liquid in a tightly covered pan on the range top or in the oven. Braising is recommended for less-tender cuts of meat.

Breading: A coating of crumbs, sometimes seasoned, on meat, fish, poultry, and vegetables. Breading often is made with soft or dry bread crumbs. See Crumbs, right.

Broil

Brine (verb): To pickle or cure vegetables, meats, fish, and seafood in heavily salted water.

Broil: To cook food a measured distance below direct, dry heat. When broiling, position the broiler pan and its rack so that the surface of the food (not the rack) is the specified distance from the heat source. Use a ruler to measure this distance.

Brown: To cook a food in a skillet, broiler, or oven to add flavor and aroma and develop a rich, desirable color on the outside.

Butterfly: To split food, such as shrimp or pork chops, through the middle without completely separating the halves. Opened flat, the split halves resemble a butterfly.

Candied: A food, usually a fruit, nut, or citrus peel, that has been cooked or dipped in sugar syrup.

Carve: To cut or slice cooked meat, poultry, fish, or game into serving-size pieces. To carve poultry, see page 479.

Cheesecloth: A thin 100-percent-cotton cloth with a fine or coarse weave. In cooking, cheesecloth is used to bundle up herbs, strain liquids, and wrap rolled meats. Look for it among cooking supplies in supermarkets and specialty cookware shops.

Chiffonade: In cooking, this French word, meaning "made of rags," refers to thin strips of fresh herbs or lettuce.

Chiffonade

Chill: To cool food to below room temperature in the refrigerator or over ice. When recipes in this book call for chilling foods, it should be done in the refrigerator.

Chop: See "Slicing, Dicing, and More," page 19.

Clarified butter: It is butter that has had the milk solids removed. Sometimes called drawn butter, clarified butter is best known as a dipping sauce for seafood. Because clarified butter can be heated to high temperatures without burning, it's also used for quickly browning meats. See recipe, page 314. Store clarified butter in the refrigerator up to 1 month.

Coat: To evenly cover food with crumbs, flour, or a batter before cooking; often done to meat, fish, and poultry.

Cooking oil: A room-temperature liquid made from vegetables, nuts, or seeds. Common types for general cooking include corn, soybean, canola, sunflower, safflower, peanut, and olive. For baking, cooking oils cannot be used interchangeably with solid fats because they do not hold air when beaten. See also Flavored oils, page 36.

Cream (verb): To beat a fat, such as butter or shortening, either alone or with sugar to a light, fluffy consistency. May be done by hand with a wooden spoon or with an electric mixer. This process incorporates air into the fat so baked products have a lighter texture and a better volume.

Crimp: To pinch or press pastry or dough together using your fingers, a fork, or another utensil. Usually done for a piecrust edge.

Crisp-tender: The state of vegetables that have been cooked until just tender but still somewhat crunchy. At this stage, a fork can be inserted into the vegetables with a little pressure.

Crumbs: Fine particles of food that have been broken off

Making Crumbs

While some prepared crumbs, such as those made from graham crackers, chocolate wafers, and dry bread, are available at the supermarket, others are not. All are easy to make at home.

● Dry bread, cookie, and cracker crumbs can be made by processing them to a fine consistency in a blender or food processor. Or place the ingredient in a heavy plastic bag and crush it to a fine consistency with a rolling pin. Leave one end of the bag open a bit so air can escape during rolling.

● To make 1 cup of cracker or cookie crumbs, you'll need 28 saltine crackers, 14 graham cracker squares, 22 vanilla wafers, 19 chocolate wafers, 15 gingersnaps, or 24 rich, round crackers.

● Use a blender or food processor to make fluffy soft bread crumbs. One slice yields ¾ cup crumbs. Or to make fine dry bread crumbs, arrange ½-inch bread cubes in a single layer on a baking pan. Bake in a 300°F oven for 10 to 15 minutes or until dry, stirring twice. Let cool. Place in a food processor or blender; process into fine crumbs. One slice yields ¼ cup fine dry crumbs.

a larger piece. Crumbs are used as a coating, thickener, or binder or in a dessert crust. Recipes usually specify either soft or fine dry bread crumbs, which generally are not interchangeable. See "Making Crumbs," above.

Crush: To smash food into smaller pieces, generally using your hands, a mortar and pestle, or a rolling pin. Crushing dried herbs releases their flavor and aroma.

Crush

Cube: See "Slicing, Dicing, and More," page 19.

Curdle: To cause semisolid pieces of coagulated protein to develop in a dairy product. This can occur when food such as milk or sour cream is heated to too high a temperature or is combined with an acidic food, such as lemon juice.

Cut in: To work a solid fat, such as shortening, butter, or margarine, into dry ingredients. This usually is done with a pastry blender, two knives in a crisscross fashion, your fingertips, or a food processor. See photo 1, page 454.

Dash: Refers to a small amount of seasoning that is added to food. It is generally between ¹⁄₁₆ and ⅛ teaspoon.

Deep-fat fry: See Fry, page 18.

Deglaze: Adding a liquid, such as water, wine, or broth, to a skillet that has been used to cook meat. The liquid is poured into the pan after the meat has been removed to help loosen browned bits and make a flavorful sauce.

Dice: See "Slicing, Dicing, and More," page 19.

Dip: To immerse food for a short time in a liquid or dry mixture to coat, cool, or moisten it.

Dissolve: To stir together a solid and a liquid to form a mixture in which none of the solid remains. In some cases, heat may be needed in order for the solid to dissolve into the liquid.

Drawn: A term referring to a whole fish, with or without scales, that has had its internal organs removed. The term "drawn butter" refers to clarified butter. See Clarified butter, page 16.

Dredge: To coat food, either before or after cooking, with a dry ingredient, such as flour, cornmeal, or sugar.

Drip pan: A metal or disposable foil pan placed under food during grilling to catch drippings. A drip pan also can be made from heavy-duty foil.

Drizzle: To randomly pour a liquid, such as powdered sugar icing, in a thin stream over food.

Dust: To sprinkle food with a dry ingredient, such as flour, cornmeal, or powdered sugar, before or after cooking.

Dredge

Emulsify: To combine two liquids or semiliquids, such as oil and vinegar, that don't naturally dissolve into each other. One way to do this is to gradually add one ingredient to the other while stirring rapidly with a fork or wire whisk to incorporate air.

Fillet: A piece of meat or fish that has no bones. As a verb, fillet refers to the process of cutting meat or fish into boneless pieces.

Flake: To gently break food into small, flat pieces.

Flour (verb): To coat or dust a food or utensil with flour. Food may be floured before cooking to add texture and improve browning. Baking utensils sometimes are floured to prevent sticking.

Flute: To make a decorative impression in food, usually a piecrust edge. See page 435.

Fold: A method of gently mixing ingredients without decreasing their volume. To fold, use a rubber spatula to cut down vertically through the mixture from the back of the bowl. Move the spatula across the bottom of the bowl, and bring it back up the other side, carrying some of the mixture from the bottom over the surface. Repeat, rotating the bowl a quarter turn each time you complete the folding process.

Flute: Also see piecrusts, page 435.

French: To cut meat away from the end of a rib or chop to expose the bone, as with a lamb rib roast.

Frost: To apply a cooked or uncooked topping, which is soft enough to spread but stiff enough to hold its shape, to cakes, cupcakes, or cookies.

Fry: To cook food in a hot cooking oil or fat, usually until a crisp brown crust forms. To panfry is to cook food, which may have a light breading or coating, in a skillet in a small amount of hot fat or oil. To deep-fat fry (or french fry) is to cook a food until it is crisp in enough hot fat or oil to cover the food. To shallow fry is to cook a food, usually breaded or coated with batter, in about 1 inch of hot fat or oil. To oven fry is to cook a food in a hot oven, using a small amount of fat, which results in a healthier product than the other forms of frying.

Garnish: To add visual appeal to a finished dish.

Giblets: The edible internal organs of poultry, including the liver, heart, and gizzard. (The neck is not part of the giblets, though it sometimes is packaged with them.) Giblets sometimes are used to make gravy.

Glacé (gla-SAY): The French term for "glazed" or "frozen." In the United States, it describes a candied food. See Candied, page 16.

Glaze: A thin, glossy coating.

Gluten: An elastic protein present in flour, especially wheat flour, that provides most of the structure of baked products. Also see Knead, above right.

Grate: To rub food, such as hard cheeses, vegetables, or whole nutmeg or ginger, across a grating surface to make very fine pieces. A food processor also may be used.

Grate

Grease: To coat a utensil, such as a baking pan or skillet, with a thin layer of fat or oil. A pastry brush works well to grease pans. Also refers to fat released from meat and poultry during cooking.

Grease

Grilling, direct: A method of quickly cooking food by placing it on a grill rack directly over the heat source. A charcoal grill is often left uncovered for direct grilling, while a gas grill is generally covered.

Grilling, indirect: Method of slowly cooking food in a covered grill over a spot where there is no heat source. Usually the food is placed on the rack over a drip pan, with coals arranged around the pan.

Grind: To mechanically cut a food into smaller pieces, usually with a food grinder or a food processor.

Hors d'oeuvre (or-DERV): French term for small, hot or cold portions of savory food served as an appetizer.

Ice: To drizzle or spread baked goods with a thin frosting.

Jelly roll: Dessert made by spreading a filling on a sponge cake and rolling it up into a log shape. When other foods are shaped "jelly-roll-style," it refers to rolling them into a log shape with fillings inside. A jelly-roll pan is 15×10×1 inches and is used to make the thin cake for a jelly roll.

Juice: The natural liquid extracted from fruits, vegetables, meats, and poultry. Also refers to the process of extracting juice from foods.

Julienne: See "Slicing, Dicing, and More," page 19.

Knead: To work dough with the heels of your hands in a pressing and folding motion until it becomes smooth and elastic. This is an essential step in developing the gluten in many yeast breads. See photo 1, page 141.

Marble: To gently swirl one food into another. Marbling usually is done with light and dark cake or cookie batters.

Marble

Marinade: A seasoned liquid in which meat, poultry, fish, shellfish, or vegetables are soaked to flavor and sometimes tenderize them. Most marinades contain an acid, such as wine or vinegar.

Marinate: To soak food in a marinade. When marinating food, do not use a metal container that can react with acidic ingredients and give food an off flavor. Always marinate foods in the refrigerator, never on the kitchen counter. To reduce cleanup, contain the food you are marinating in a plastic bag set in a bowl or dish. Discard leftover marinade that has come in contact with raw meat. Or if it's to be used on cooked meat, bring leftover marinade to a rolling boil before using to destroy any bacteria that may be present.

Mash: To press or beat food to remove lumps and make a smooth mixture. This can be done with a fork, potato masher, food mill, food ricer, or electric mixer.

Measure: To determine the quantity or size of food or a utensil. See "Measuring Ingredients," page 23.

Melt: To heat solid food, such as chocolate, butter, or margarine, over low heat until it becomes liquid.

Mince: See "Slicing, Dicing, and More," page 19.

Mix: To stir or beat two or more foods together until they are thoroughly combined. May be done with an electric mixer, a rotary beater, or by hand with a wooden spoon.

Moisten: To add enough liquid to a dry ingredient or mixture to make it damp but not runny.

Mortar and pestle: A set that includes a bowl-shape vessel (the mortar) to hold ingredients to be crushed by a club-shape utensil (the pestle).

Mull: To slowly heat a beverage, such as apple cider, with spices and sugar.

Oven fry: See Fry, above left.

Pan-broil: To cook food, especially meat, in a skillet without added fat, removing any fat as it accumulates.

Mortar and pestle

Parboil: To boil food, such as a vegetable, only until it is partially cooked.

Parchment paper: A grease- and heat-resistant paper used to line baking pans, to wrap foods in packets for baking, or to make disposable pastry bags.

Pare: To cut off the skin or outer covering of a fruit or vegetable, using a small knife or a vegetable peeler.

Partially set: A mixture of gelatin and a liquid that has the consistency of unbeaten egg whites.

Peel: The skin or outer covering of a vegetable or fruit (also called the rind). Peel also refers to the process of removing this covering.

Pinch: The amount of a dry ingredient that can be pinched between your finger and thumb.

Pipe: To force semisoft food, such as frosting or whipped cream, through a pastry bag.

Pit: To remove the seed from fruit.

Plump: To allow food, such as raisins, to soak in a liquid, which generally increases its volume.

Pipe

Poach: To cook food by partially or completely submerging it in a simmering liquid.

Pound: To strike food with a heavy utensil to crush it or, in the case of meat or poultry, to break up connective tissue in order to tenderize or flatten it.

Poach

Precook: To partially or completely cook food before using it in a recipe.

Preheat: To heat an oven or utensil to a specific temperature before using it.

Process: To preserve food at home by canning or to prepare food in a food processor.

Proof: To allow a yeast dough to rise before baking. Proof also indicates the amount of alcohol present in a distilled liquor.

Puree: To process or mash food until it is as smooth as possible. This can be done using a blender, food processor, sieve, or food mill; also refers to the resulting mixture.

Reconstitute: To bring concentrated or condensed food, such as frozen fruit juice, to its original strength by adding water.

Reduce: To decrease the volume of a liquid by boiling it rapidly to cause evaporation. As the liquid evaporates, it thickens and intensifies in flavor. The resulting richly flavored liquid, called a reduction, can be used as a sauce or as the base of a sauce. When reducing liquids, use the pan size specified in the recipe because the surface area of the pan affects how quickly the liquid will evaporate.

Rind: The skin or outer coating—usually rather thick—of food, such as melons or citrus fruits.

Roast, roasting: A large piece of meat or poultry that's usually cooked by roasting, which refers to a dry-heat cooking method where food is cooked, uncovered, in an oven. Tender pieces of meat work best for roasting.

Roll, roll out: To form food into a shape. Dough, for instance, can be rolled into ropes or balls. The phrase "roll out" refers to mechanically flattening food, usually a dough or pastry, with a rolling pin.

Roux (roo): A French term that refers to a mixture of flour and a fat cooked to a golden or rich brown color and used for a thickening in sauces, soups, and gumbos.

Saute: From the French word *sauter,* meaning "to jump." Sauteed food is cooked and stirred in a small amount of fat over fairly high heat in an open, shallow pan. Food cut into uniform size sautes best.

Scald: To heat a liquid, often milk, to a temperature just below the boiling point, which is when tiny bubbles just begin to appear around the edge.

Score

Score: To cut narrow slits, often in a diamond pattern, through the outer surface of a food to deco-

rate it, tenderize it, help it absorb flavor, or allow fat to drain as it cooks.

Scrape: To use a sharp or blunt instrument to rub the outer coating from a food, such as carrots.

Sear: To brown a food, usually meat, quickly on all sides using high heat. This helps seal in the juices and may be done in the oven, under a broiler, or on top of the range.

Section: To separate and remove the membrane of segments of citrus fruits. To section oranges, use a paring knife to remove the peel and white rind. Working over a bowl to catch the juice, cut between one orange section and the membrane, slicing to the center of the fruit. Turn the knife and slide it up the other side of the section along the membrane, cutting outward. Repeat with remaining sections.

Section

Slicing, Dicing, and More

Not sure of the difference between chopping, mincing, slicing, or dicing? Here's a guide.

Chop: To cut food with a knife, cleaver, or food processor into fine, medium, or coarse irregular pieces.

Cube: To cut food into uniform pieces, usually ½ inch on all sides.

Dice: To cut food into uniform pieces, usually ⅛ to ¼ inch on all sides.

Julienne: To cut food into thin, matchlike sticks about 2 inches long. For easier cutting, first cut food into slices about 2×¼ inch; stack the slices and cut them lengthwise into strips ⅛ to ¼ inch wide.

Mince: To chop food into tiny, irregular pieces.

Slice: To cut food into flat, thin pieces.

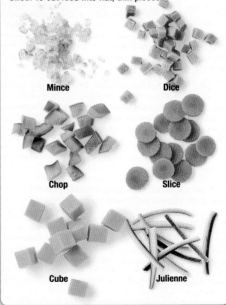

Mince

Dice

Chop

Slice

Cube

Julienne

Shred, finely shred: To push food across a shredding surface to make long, narrow strips. Finely shred means to make long, thin strips. A food processor also may be used. Lettuce and cabbage may be shredded by thinly slicing them. See also Grate, page 18.

Shred

Shuck: To remove the shells from seafood, such as oysters and clams, or the husks from corn.

Sieve: To separate liquids from solids by pressing the food through a sieve.

Sieve

Sift: To put one or more dry ingredients, especially flour or powdered sugar, through a sifter or sieve to remove lumps.

Simmer: To cook food in a liquid that is kept just below the boiling point; a liquid is simmering when a few bubbles form slowly and burst just before reaching the surface. See also Boil, page 16.

Skewer: A long, narrow metal or wooden stick that can be inserted through pieces of meat or vegetables for grilling. If using bamboo or wooden skewers, soak them in cold water for 30 minutes before you thread them to prevent burning.

Skim: To remove a substance, such as fat or foam, from the surface of a liquid, such as homemade broth or stock. To skim fat from poultry or meat drippings, see photo, page 483. To skim fat from broth, see page 552.

Slice: See "Slicing, Dicing, and More," page 19.

Snip: To cut food, often fresh herbs or dried fruit, with kitchen shears or scissors into small, uniform pieces using short, quick strokes.

Steam: To cook a food in the vapor given off by boiling water.

Steep: To allow a food, such as tea, to stand in water that is just below the boiling point in order to extract flavor or color.

Snip

Stew: To cook food in liquid for a long time until tender, usually in a covered pot. The term also refers to a mixture prepared this way.

Stir: To mix ingredients with a spoon or other utensil to combine them, to prevent them from sticking during cooking, or to cool them after cooking.

Stir-fry: A method of quickly cooking small pieces of food

Toasting Tip

Toasting rolls and buns adds a little crunch to sandwiches. A toaster oven makes toasting easy. You also can use your broiler. Simply place sliced rolls or buns, cut sides up, on the unheated rack of a broiler pan and broil 4 to 5 inches from heat for 1 to 2 minutes or until golden brown.

Thickening Math

Follow these guidelines when using flour and cornstarch to thicken sauces.

For each cup of medium-thick sauce, use 2 tablespoons flour mixed with ¼ cup cold water or 1 tablespoon cornstarch mixed with 1 tablespoon cold water. Thoroughly mix the starch (flour or cornstarch) with the water to prevent lumps. Stir the mixture into the sauce to be thickened; cook and stir over medium heat until thickened and bubbly. To be sure the starch is completely cooked, cook and stir a flour-thickened sauce 1 minute more and a cornstarch-thickened sauce 2 minutes more.

in a little hot oil in a wok or skillet over medium-high heat while stirring constantly. See page 573.

Thickeners: Food used to give a thicker consistency to sauces, gravies, puddings, and soups. Common thickeners include all-purpose flour, cornstarch, and quick-cooking tapioca. Cornstarch produces a more translucent mixture than flour and has twice the thickening power. Before adding a thickener to a hot mixture, stir cold water into a small amount of it. You also can combine flour or cornstarch with cold water in a screw-top jar and shake until thoroughly blended. It is critical that the starch-water mixture be free of lumps to prevent lumps in your sauce or gravy. Tapioca is a good choice for foods that are going to be frozen. See Tapioca, page 43.

Toast: The process of browning, crisping, or drying a food by exposing it to heat. Toasting coconut, nuts, and seeds helps develop their flavor (see page 265). It's also the process of exposing bread to heat so it becomes browner, crisper, and drier. See "Toasting Tip," below left.

Toss: To mix ingredients lightly by using two utensils to gently lift and drop them.

Weeping: When liquid separates out of a solid food, such as jellies, custards, and meringues.

Whip: To beat food lightly and rapidly using a wire whisk, rotary beater, or electric mixer in order to incorporate air and increase its volume.

Zest: The colored outer portion of citrus fruit peel. It is rich in fruit oils and often used as a seasoning. To remove the zest, draw the fruit across the fruit zester or grater; avoid the white membrane, called the pith, beneath the peel because it is bitter.

Zest

Stocking Up: Planning, Shopping, and Ingredients

When 5 p.m. arrives on a weekday, you'll have dinner under control if you've done a little planning and are familiar with what's available at your food market.

An Overview of Ingredients

Today's food markets are full of options. Ingredients come fresh, frozen, canned, dried, and otherwise preserved—and there's a vast array of ethnic foods to enliven your cooking. Much of your cooking success depends on the quality of your ingredients. There are several ways to get the best ingredients available and still stay within your budget—both in terms of time and money. When it comes to produce, learn what is in season. It will not only taste better but also will be more economical. Compare the taste and price of June strawberries or August tomatoes with those you can find in mid-January, and you'll appreciate the difference.

Stock Up on Shortcuts

Meals at home don't have to be entirely homemade to be nourishing and meaningful for your family. There's a middle ground between fast food and made-from-scratch meals, and convenience products are often a realistic way to get there. Here are a few ideas.

● Call on ready-made entrées, such as roasted chicken from the deli and heat-and-serve meat loaf and pot roast from the meat department. Round out the meal with a recipe you've wanted to try. Or simply enjoy easygoing side dishes, such as frozen vegetables or baked potatoes.

● Visit the supermarket deli or bakery for instant appetizers and simple side dishes or breads to add to your meal.

● Stock up on items that take little effort from kitchen to table, such as frozen meatballs, pizza shells, pasta sauce, pasta, cheese, and eggs.

● Purchase shortcut ingredients, such as shredded cheeses, rice pilaf mixes, packaged salad greens, precut fruits and vegetables, and bottled roasted red sweet peppers.

Timesaving Strategies

If a penny saved is a penny earned, a few minutes spent planning menus and strategizing your shopping saves hours when it's time to step into the kitchen and start cooking.

Shop Smart

● Keep an ongoing list of your grocery needs. Post it somewhere in the kitchen so you can write down items as you notice they're needed.

● Get organized before you head to the store, making a list of items you'll need for a week's worth of meals. Review "Nutrition Basics Made Simple," pages 45–49, as you plan.

● Shop during downtimes when the market isn't crowded. This lets you take your time to discover new foods and read the facts on nutrition labels.

● To cut down on impulse purchases, shop with a list and avoid going when you're hungry. Do, however, keep an eye out for specials on items you routinely use—there's a difference between impulse buying and finding good bargains.

● Check newspaper ads and inserts to take advantage of weekly specials and coupons.

Cook Smart

● Use the recipes' prep and cook times to help allocate your time. Recipes that are designated as Fast can be prepared and served in 30 minutes or less. The timings assume that some steps can be performed simultaneously.

● Read the recipe completely before you begin. This will eliminate last-minute trips to the store. Preheat your oven as you begin any recipe that needs to be baked or broiled so the oven will be ready when you are.

● Overlap steps to accomplish two things at once. Chop vegetables, measure ingredients, open cans, or prepare sauces while waiting for water to boil, meat to brown, or appliances to preheat.

● Clean as you go. Before you start preparation, fill the sink or dish pan with hot, soapy water.

● Let timesaving appliances and techniques work for you. Use a food processor to chop vegetables or grate cheese. The microwave is an easy, no-mess method for melting butter or chocolate. Use a toaster oven to toast buns and rolls quickly; use kitchen shears to snip fresh herbs or dried fruit, a garlic press to crush garlic, and a mini ice cream scoop for drop cookies.

Children and Mealtimes

Consider these ideas for helping children develop positive attitudes about food and for getting them involved in mealtimes.

● Take the kids grocery shopping and ask them to help you choose what to buy. For example, ask them to pick three fruits and three vegetables that they'd like to eat during the week.

● Ask each child to help plan the family meal on a designated night. Let him or her even handle the details; for example, stop at a party supply store and let the planner select special paper napkins.

● Remind kids that tastes can change. Encourage them to try at least one bite of everything—call it a "no, thank you" bite.

● Remember that it takes children a while to try new things, so continue introducing them to a variety of foods. It will help if you always have some nutritious foods on hand so when their hunger (and curiosity) strikes, you'll be ready.

Staying Organized in the Kitchen

For smooth and efficient meal preparation, one of the smartest things you can do is to keep your pantry—which comprises your freezer, refrigerator, and cupboards—well stocked. Have an organizational system for storing your ingredients. Keep dry goods, such as flour and sugar, in one place and canned goods, such as broth and canned tomatoes, in another.

When you come home from grocery shopping, go through your refrigerator and discard any less-than-fresh produce and any meat, dairy products, eggs, or condiments that have expired dates on the packaging. Wipe the refrigerator shelves and inside the door with a warm, soapy sponge or clean kitchen cloth.

Menu-Planning Basics

Whether you're planning a formal dinner for eight at 8 p.m. or simply looking forward to some family time around the table, here's how to create a balanced and harmonious menu.

● Combine interesting and complementary flavors, colors, and textures. Consider how flavors will work together. For example, one highly seasoned food usually is enough and can be rounded out by milder accompaniments (think chili served with corn bread). Evaluate how different foods' colors and shapes will look together on a plate (fish, mashed potatoes, and parsnips look dull in comparison to fish, a crisp green salad, and a wild rice pilaf). And don't forget about temperature and texture—serving foods that contrast (soft and crisp or cold and hot) will make a meal more lively and varied.

● Use MyPyramid and the good nutrition information on pages 45–49 to help you plan how to eat healthfully.

● One starchy dish (potatoes, rice, pasta, beans, or corn) is plenty with most meals. Bread can be served in addition to the one starchy dish.

● Balance the courses: Alternate rich, highly flavored foods with simple, fresh items. For example, if you serve a rich, cheesy lasagna, dessert should be light and refreshing—perhaps a lemon sorbet with sugar cookies. Avoid repeating flavors, even when two recipes aren't served at the same time; consider how each dish will add to the meal.

Measuring Ingredients

Getting great results from a recipe begins with correctly measuring ingredients. Using the right utensils and method is all it takes.

The Right Utensils

Graduated measuring cups: These stackable cups, also called dry measuring cups, come in increments of ¼, ⅓, ½, ⅔, ¾, and 1 cup. They are used to measure dry ingredients and soft solids, such as shortening, and should not be used for liquids.

Liquid measuring cups: These clear-glass or plastic cups hold 1, 2, or 4 cups of liquid and have incremental markings printed on the outside; a handle and spout make for easy pouring.

Measuring spoons: Nested spoons commonly come in sets that measure ¼, ½, and 1 teaspoon, plus 1 tablespoon. These can be used for dry and liquid ingredients.

The Right Measuring Method

Dry ingredients: Spoon ingredient into the appropriate measuring cup or measuring spoon; level off the excess with the straight edge of a knife or spatula.
Liquid ingredients: Pour liquid into a liquid measuring cup set on a level surface.
To confirm the measurement, bend down so your eye is level with the markings on the cup. (If you are using an angled measuring cup, view the markings from above.)
When measuring 1 tablespoon or less, fill the appropriate measuring spoon to the top without letting the liquid spill over.

Ingredients Needing Extra Know-How

Brown sugar: Press firmly into a dry measure. The sugar should hold the shape of the measure when it is turned out.
Butter, margarine, or solid shortening: These ingredients are often packaged in stick form with measurement markings on the wrapper. Use a sharp knife to cut off the amount needed. If the wrapper isn't marked, press the ingredient into a dry measuring cup or spoon with a rubber

Liquid measuring cups

Measuring spoons

Dry measuring cups

scraper, then level it off with a straight edge.
Dried herbs: Lightly fill a measuring spoon to the top. If a recipe specifies crushing dried herb, empty the spoon's contents into one hand, then crush the herb with the fingers of the other hand. To crush rosemary or leaf sage, use a mortar and pestle (see page 18).

Weights and Measures

Tablespoon Math

3 teaspoons = 1 tablespoon
4 tablespoons = ¼ cup
5⅓ tablespoons = ⅓ cup
8 tablespoons = ½ cup
10⅔ tablespoons = ⅔ cup
12 tablespoons = ¾ cup
16 tablespoons = 1 cup

Measure	Equivalent Measure	Equivalent Ounces
1 tablespoon		½ fluid ounce
1 cup	½ pint	8 fluid ounces
2 cups	1 pint	16 fluid ounces
2 pints (4 cups)	1 quart	32 fluid ounces
4 quarts (16 cups)	1 gallon	128 fluid ounces

Note: For metric equivalents, see page 656.

Flour: Stir flour in the bag or canister to lighten its volume. Sifting is not necessary, except for cake flour. Lightly spoon flour into a dry measuring cup or a measuring spoon. Level off the top with the straight edge of a knife or spatula.

A World of Flavors

Many foods require absolutely no embellishment. They are delicious in and of themselves; a perfectly ripe peach or watermelon is a good example. But within the vast world of food there are special ingredients that contribute great taste to dishes that might otherwise be bland. These include seasonings such as herbs and spices, spicy chiles, pungent olives (which also can be eaten on their own), and earthy mushrooms. This section introduces some of the more popular types of these ingredients, as well as tips for using them.

Herbs

These are some of the most commonly used culinary herbs. While the photograph on page 25 shows fresh herbs, most herbs are available in fresh and dried forms. Each herb brings its own distinct flavor to recipes, but substitutions are offered when available.

Basil adds a minty, clovelike aroma to sauces, salads, and, of course, pesto. Cinnamon, lemon, and anise basil have the basil flavor, plus the flavor for which they are named. Substitute: oregano or thyme.

Bay leaves, also called laurel leaves, most commonly are found in the form of dried whole leaves. They bring an aromatic, woodsy note to a dish. Common in slow-simmering dishes such as soups and stews, they should be added to a dish whole (never crumbled); always discard them before serving the dish. Turkish and California bay leaves, the most common varieties, can be used interchangeably.

Chervil has a flavor similar to parsley with a hint of tarragon. Use it in salads, soups, and vegetables, keeping in mind it loses flavor when boiled. Substitute: parsley and tarragon mix.

Chives have a mild onion flavor. Snip the leaves as you need them; they grow back after cutting just like grass does. Chives taste great sprinkled over egg dishes, in salad dressings, and on potatoes. Substitute: thinly sliced green onion tops (though use less because they're more strongly flavored than chives).

Cilantro also is known as fresh coriander, leaf coriander, or Chinese parsley. It brings a pungent flavor to many dishes, from Asian specialties and Indian sauces to Mexican salsas. Season with cilantro to taste, keeping in mind that too much can bring a harsh, soapy flavor. Substitute: parsley.

Dill is a familiar herb for peas. Its delicate taste also is excellent with fish, seafood, and vegetables. It is, of course, the main flavor of pickles. Substitute: fennel leaves or tarragon.

Marjoram is similar to oregano but with a sweeter, milder flavor. It can be used to season almost any meat and vegetable dish. Substitute: oregano (though use less).

Mint is sweet and refreshing, with a cool aftertaste. Peppermint has a sharp, pungent flavor, while spearmint is more delicate. Mint makes a great edible garnish for desserts; try mint in salads, marinades, and dressings too. Substitute: basil, marjoram, or rosemary.

Oregano offers a robust, pungent flavor; it is popular as a pizza and pasta flavoring. Also try it in bean soups, sauces, and pasta salads. Substitute: marjoram, basil, or thyme.

Parsley brings a mild, fresh taste to almost any dish. Italian parsley (also called flat-leaf parsley) has a milder flavor than the curly-leaf variety. Either will work in recipes that call for parsley.

Rosemary has a bold flavor that is best described as piney and perfumey. It is especially enjoyed in lamb, pork, and fish dishes and is delicious in Italian-style herb breads. Substitute: thyme, tarragon, or savory.

Sage has a subtly bitter, musty, mintlike taste. It often is used to season poultry, sausage, pork, and stuffing; it also complements most vegetables. Substitute: savory, marjoram, or rosemary.

Savory has thyme and mint tones that provide a nice complement to soups, meats, fish, mushrooms, and bean dishes. Winter savory, which has a stronger flavor than summer savory, is great for long-simmering stews. Substitute: thyme or sage.

Tarragon, a beloved herb in French cuisine, has an aromatic, licoricelike flavor. It's excellent with poultry, most fish, and grilled meats and in vinaigrettes. Substitute: chervil or a dash of crushed fennel seeds or a dash of crushed anise seeds.

Thyme, a little bit minty and a little bit lemony, seasons chicken, beef, vegetables, and sauces. An old adage exclaims, "When in doubt, use thyme!" Substitute: basil, marjoram, oregano, or savory.

Caring for Fresh Herbs: Fresh snipped herbs add flavor that can't be matched by dried. If you don't have an herb garden within reach, buy fresh herbs at a farmer's market or supermarket.

You can keep herbs fresh for up to 1 week by cutting ½ inch from the stems and standing them, stems submerged and tops covered with a loose-fitting plastic bag, in a jar of water in your refrigerator. Pinch off wilting or dried-out leaves as they appear. The exception is fresh basil, which may blacken in the refrigerator; instead, store it in the same way, but do not refrigerate.

If a recipe calls for snipped fresh herbs, start with clean, dry herbs; wet ones may clump together. (To dry wet herbs either blot them with a paper towel or use a salad spinner to spin off excess water.) Use kitchen shears to simply cut the herbs into small, uniform pieces using short, quick strokes. If the stalks are tough—as is the case with rosemary—don't use them. Snip herbs just before adding them to a recipe to get their maximum flavor.

Generally, add fresh herbs at the end of cooking time because they lose flavor and color as they simmer. Exceptions include fresh rosemary

continued on page 27

Chives

Cilantro

Basil

Oregano

Marjoram

Dill

Curly-leaf parsley

Peppermint

Italian (flat-leaf) parsley

Sage

Savory

Thyme

Tarragon

Rosemary

Spices

These common spices make a good pantry foundation. Some substitution suggestions offer similar flavors; others are acceptable flavor alternatives. When substituting, start with half of the amount the recipe calls for, unless directed otherwise, and add to suit your taste.

Spice	Flavor	Common Uses	Substitution
Allspice (ground)	Blend of cinnamon, nutmeg, cloves	Baked goods, jerk seasoning, stews	Ground cinnamon, nutmeg, or cloves
Anise seeds	Licoricelike flavor	Cabbage dishes, meats, fruit desserts	Fennel seeds or a few drops of anise extract
Cardamom (ground)	Spicy-sweet with peppery and gingerlike tones	Curried dishes, bean dishes, baked goods	Ground ginger
Cayenne pepper	Hot, pungent, smoky	Stews, barbecue rubs and sauces, and bean, meat, egg, and cheese dishes	Use 2 to 3 drops bottled hot pepper sauce for ⅛ to ¼ teaspoon cayenne pepper
Chili powder	Hot, spicy, peppery taste and aroma	Soups, stews, marinades, meat dishes	Dash bottled hot pepper sauce plus equal measures of ground oregano and cumin
Cinnamon (ground)	Strong, spicy-sweet flavor	Meats, breads, pumpkin and fruit desserts, hot coffee, tea, chocolate	Ground nutmeg or allspice (use only ¼ of the specified amount)
Cloves (ground)	Strong, pungent, almost hot flavor	Baked beans, barbecue dishes, chili, mulled wine, fruit desserts, cakes	Ground allspice, cinnamon, or nutmeg
Cumin (ground)	Pungent, spicy, slightly bitter flavor	Indian and Mexican cooking, meats, poultry	Chili powder
Curry powder	A fragrant, mild-to-hot blend of up to 20 ground spices	Meats, sauces, stews, root vegetables; often used in Asian and Indian cooking	Combine equal parts of ground spices common in curry (such as cumin, coriander, red and black peppers, ginger, turmeric)
Fennel seeds	Mild licoricelike flavor and aroma	Meat, sausage, poultry dishes, baked goods, fruit desserts, coleslaw	Anise or caraway seeds
Ginger (ground)	Sweet-hot flavor, nippy aroma	Stir-fries, marinades, meats, baked goods	Ground allspice, cinnamon, mace, or nutmeg
Mustard (dry, seeds)	Dry mustard attains hot flavor when mixed with water; seeds have hot, spicy flavor	Dry mustard—salad dressings and egg, cheese, and meat dishes; seeds—pickling, relishes, and boiled vegetables and meats	In cooked mixtures, 1 tablespoon yellow mustard for each 1 teaspoon dry; no substitutions for mustard seeds
Nutmeg (ground)	Slightly sweet and spicy flavor and aroma	Baked goods, white sauces, custard, eggnog	Ground cinnamon, ginger, or mace
Paprika (Hungarian, Spanish)	Hungarian paprika is generally more pungent than Spanish and can be labeled sweet (mild) or hot; Spanish paprika is slightly sweet and bitter	Vegetables, beef, fish, chicken, salads, egg dishes	Cayenne pepper, but use sparingly because it's much hotter
Pepper, black or white	Black pepper is more pungent than white	Savory foods, spiced desserts	White may be substituted for black, but it's milder in flavor

continued from page 25

and winter savory, which can withstand a long cooking time.

Substituting Dried Herbs for Fresh: In a pinch, dried herbs can be substituted for fresh. To do so, use one-third the amount called for in the recipe. (For example, substitute 1 teaspoon dried herb for 1 tablespoon fresh herb.) To substitute ground herbs for dried leaf herbs, use about half of the amount called for in the recipe.

Before adding a dried herb to a recipe, crush it between your finger and thumb to help release flavors. To crush rosemary or leaf sage, use a mortar and pestle. Add dried herbs at the beginning of cooking time to allow their flavors to develop.

Spices and Spice Blends

Spices are the seeds, bark, roots, fruit, or flowers of plants. They add flavor and color to all types of dishes. For a description of the spices common in a well-stocked pantry, see the chart, page 26. What follows here are descriptions of herb and spice blends, which let you add an intriguing combination of flavors with just one measure. Keeping a selection of these blends on hand allows you to turn a simple broiled chicken breast or steak on the grill into something savory and delicious. Buy them in small amounts, as they lose flavor over time.

Barbecue seasoning is a zesty blend of spices that brings a smoke-flavored heat to foods. These spices may include salt, sugar, garlic, cayenne pepper, hickory smoke flavor, onion, and others. Sprinkle it onto meats before grilling, roasting, or broiling.

Bouquet garni (boo-KAY gar-NEE) is a French term for a bundle of herbs that is tied together or in a piece of cheesecloth, allowing you to remove it easily from a cooked dish. A bouquet garni is handy for blends that use bay leaves, which should be removed from a dish before serving. Traditional bouquet garni includes thyme, parsley, and bay leaf, but you can create one from just about any herbs. Bundle the herbs in several thicknesses of 100-percent-cotton cheesecloth, then tie the cheesecloth closed with kitchen string to form a bag.

Bouquet garni

Storing Dried Herbs and Spices

Store dried herbs and spices in airtight containers in a dry place away from sunlight and heat. Replace them when their aroma fades. Generally, whole spices and herbs keep 1 to 2 years (whole cloves, nutmeg, and cinnamon sticks will maintain their quality slightly beyond 2 years). Ground herbs and spices maintain their quality up to 6 months. Refrigerate red spices, such as paprika, to preserve their flavor and color.

Cajun seasoning differs from brand to brand, but most blends are peppery hot and include onion, garlic, salt, and the classic Cajun trio of white, black, and red peppers. Sprinkle it into crumb coatings or directly onto fish, poultry, or meat before cooking.

Dry rub is a blend of several different herbs and spices that is rubbed over or patted onto the surface of meat before it's cooked. Purchase dry rubs in a variety of flavor combinations from the supermarket. You also can make your own dry rub with complementary flavorings from your spice rack.

Fines herbes (feenz ERB) is a French phrase that describes a mix containing chervil, parsley, chives, and tarragon. Use it in place of individual herbs in gravies, sauces, creamy soups, and poultry stuffings.

Five-spice powder varies by brand but usually includes cinnamon, star anise or anise seeds, fennel, Szechwan or black pepper, and cloves. To make your own, in a blender container combine 3 tablespoons ground cinnamon, 6 star anise or 2 teaspoons anise seeds, 1½ teaspoons fennel seeds, 1½ teaspoons whole Szechwan peppers or whole black peppercorns, and ¾ teaspoon ground cloves. Cover and blend until powdery. Store in a covered container. Makes about ⅓ cup.

Herbes de Provence is a melange of dried herbs that is common in the South of France. It usually includes basil, fennel,

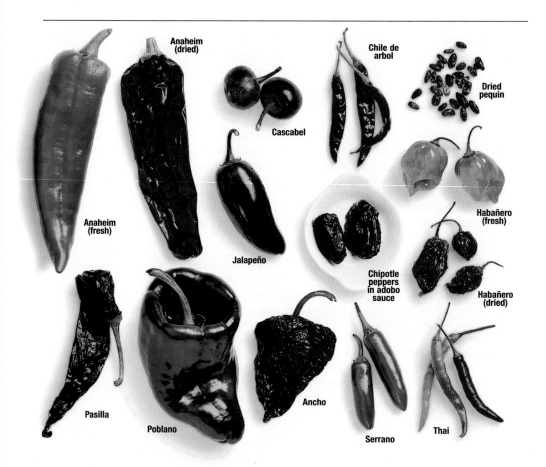

Anaheim (dried)

Chile de arbol

Dried pequin

Cascabel

Anaheim (fresh)

Habañero (fresh)

Jalapeño

Chipotle peppers in adobo sauce

Habañero (dried)

Pasilla

Poblano

Ancho

Serrano

Thai

lavender, marjoram, rosemary, sage, savory, and thyme. Add it to poultry stuffings, creamy pasta dishes, soups, and salad dressings.

Italian seasoning is great to have on hand for quick tomato sauces. Common herbs in this mix include basil, oregano, thyme, and rosemary; sometimes garlic and red pepper are included.

Jamaican jerk seasoning is a lively mixture that can include salt, sugar, allspice, thyme, cloves, ginger, cinnamon, onion, and chile peppers. It adds spice to fish, meat marinades, and salad dressings.

Lemon-pepper seasoning is a mixture made up of primarily salt with black pepper and dried grated lemon peel. It adds a delicate lemon flavor to poultry and vegetables.

Mexican seasoning is a spicy blend that often includes cumin, chile peppers, salt, onion, sweet peppers, garlic, and oregano.

Chiles

These spicy pods of the capsicum family of plants also are called chile peppers. They're available in many sizes and colors, with varying degrees of hotness. (Generally, the smaller the chile, the hotter it is.) See tip, page 74, regarding safe handling of chiles. When shopping for fresh chiles, look for bright colors and avoid any that are shriveled, bruised, or broken. Store them, covered, in the refrigerator for up to 5 days. Dried chiles will keep for up to 1 year in airtight containers in a cool, dark place. Many varieties are readily available.

Anaheim chiles, sold in fresh and dried forms, are versatile and offer medium heat.

Ancho chiles are the dried version of poblano chiles (see page 29). They are mild to medium hot, with complex flavors.

Cascabel chiles have medium heat. These red chiles most often are sold dried.

Chiles de arbol are long, slender, bright to deep red chiles that are extremely hot. They come in both dried and fresh forms.

Chipotle chiles are dried, smoked jalapeño chiles (see below), which sometimes are found canned in adobo, a spicy sauce. Not surprisingly, they add a deep, smoky flavor to foods. They generally are not as hot as fresh jalapeños.

Dried pequin chiles are the smallest chiles of all—only about ⅓ inch long. They're loaded with blistering heat and should be used sparingly and with caution.

Habañero chiles, native to the Caribbean, pack a searing heat. They are available fresh and dried, with the fresh being more popular.

Jalapeño chiles are hot to extremely hot, with a short, oval shape and a green to reddish green color.

Pasilla chiles are long, slender dried chiles with wrinkled skins and are medium to extremely hot, with a rich flavor. In some regions, they're also available fresh as chilaca chiles.

Poblano chiles are mild to medium-hot chiles with deep, complex flavors.

Serrano chiles are commonly used in Southwestern cooking. These hot, slender chiles are deep green, which sometimes ripens to bright red.

Thai chiles, sometimes called bird chiles, are colorful, little, and pack plenty of intense heat. They are the choice for spicing up Thai-inspired dishes.

Olives

The fruit of the olive tree is available in more than 75 varieties. Olives are sold pitted and unpitted. Although pitted olives are more convenient to use than unpitted olives, pitting causes more of the olive to be exposed to the brine, which softens the flesh. Remove the pit from an unpitted olive by gently crushing the long side of the olive with the heel of your hand; the pit will pop out. Many flavored olives are also available in markets.

Alphonso olives, from Chile, are huge, deep purple in color, and have a slightly bitter, sour taste. Their flesh is soft and meaty.

Arbequina olives are green and brine-cured, with a slightly bitter taste.

Catalan olives are brine-cured Spanish olives that are marinated with curry, celery, and pepper. They have a crisp, dense flesh and an assertive curry flavor.

Cerignola olives are huge, green or jet-black, and brine-cured, with a lemon-apple flavor. This variety is difficult to pit.

Gaeta olives are small and reddish brown, with a slightly earthy flavor.

Kalamata olives are greenish black purple and brine-cured, with a pungent, lingering flavor.

Niçoise olives are small, brownish purple, and brine-cured, with a fruity, juicy flavor.

Nyon olives are black, dry-roasted, and tender, with a slightly bitter flavor.

Catalan   Alphonso   Kalamata   Gaeta

Niçoise   Arbequina   Nyon   Cerignola

Oyster

Shiitake

White

Beech

Cremini

Chanterelle

Morel

Wood ear

Porcini

Portobello
(small)

Enoki

Portobello
(large)

Mushrooms

A plant in the fungus family, mushrooms come in many colors and shapes, with flavors ranging from mild and nutty to meaty, woodsy, and wild. They come both fresh and dried. Look for these varieties.

Beech mushrooms are small with all-white or light brown caps. They offer a crunchy texture and a mild, sweet, nutty flavor that works well in stir-fries and in sauces for poultry and fish. When using in recipes, add toward the end of cooking time to retain their texture.

Chanterelle (shant-uh-REL) mushrooms are best in simple recipes because of their delicate, buttery flavor. They have a trumpet shape and are bright yellow to orange in color.

Cremini mushrooms are tan to rich brown in color and can be used in most any recipe that calls for white mushrooms because they're similar in taste but earthier in flavor.

Enoki (eh-NOH-kee) mushrooms are delicate and white, with long, thin stems and tiny caps. They often come vacuum packed. Show off their delicate flavor and slight crunch in salads and as soup toppers.

Morel (more-EL) mushrooms are great for refined sauces and other gourmet recipes. These tan, black, or yellow spongy-looking mushrooms have an intense rich, nutty flavor and aroma—and generally a high price tag. Morels also are available in dried form.

Oyster mushrooms come in a variety of colors, from cream to gray, and sizes; all have a velvety texture and a mild taste that melds well with poultry, veal, and seafood dishes.

Porcini mushrooms, also known as cèpes, are pale brown wild mushrooms usually sold in dried form. (See "More on Mushrooms," right, for how to reconstitute dried mushrooms.) They are prized for their strong woodsy flavor. Try them in soups and pasta sauces.

Portobello mushrooms often are used to bring heartiness and meatiness to vegetarian entrées. These velvety brown mushrooms boast a deep mushroom flavor and are delicious grilled; find them in large, medium, and small sizes.

Shiitake (shee-TAH-kee) mushrooms are prized for the meaty flavor and texture they add to pasta dishes, soups, and other entrées. They are a favorite in Chinese cooking. Use only the caps, though; remove the woody stems before adding them to recipes.

White mushrooms are a good, all-purpose mushroom with a mild, woodsy flavor. They can be served raw, sauteed, or grilled. They have an umbrella shape and are creamy white to light brown in color; the small ones are sometimes referred to as button mushrooms.

Wood ear mushrooms are a favorite in Asian-style stir-fries. Favored for their yielding, yet crunchy texture, they are usually found dried.

More on Mushrooms

Mushrooms—both fresh and dried—can be used in a variety of ways to add both taste and texture to dishes. Certain varieties are associated with specific seasons or styles of cooking. Spring is the time for fresh morels, for instance (though the dried variety can be used any time of year), while porcini are delicious in hearty fall foods. Many are good all-year-round mushrooms (white mushrooms and cremini, for example). Here are a few tips on cooking with mushrooms. (For information on selecting and storing fresh mushrooms, see pages 601–602.)

● Don't wash fresh mushrooms. Because they are porous, washing makes them waterlogged and mushy. The best way to clean mushrooms is a quick wipe with a mushroom brush. If you don't have one, brush them off thoroughly with a damp paper towel.

● The stems of most fresh mushrooms are edible (shiitakes are the most notable exception), but before chopping or slicing fresh mushrooms for use in a dish, it's a good idea to trim off the ends of the stems for neatness and eye appeal.

● To reconstitute dried mushrooms, before using them soak them in enough hot water or broth to cover for 20 to 30 minutes, then rinse them under cold running water.

● The liquid from reconstituting dried mushrooms often is flavorful and can be used in soups and sauces. Just be sure to strain it through 100-percent-cotton cheesecloth or a clean paper towel first to remove any grit the mushrooms left behind.

Glossary: Ingredients

Find definitions of ingredients—both common staples and specialty ingredients—here. For topics not included, look in relevant chapters or in the index.

Acini di pepe: A tiny ball-shape pasta that is used primarily in soups. If you can't find it, orzo is a good substitute. See "Pasta," pages 412–413.

Acorn squash: A hard-shelled, acorn-shape winter squash with sweet, nutty-tasting golden yellow flesh. See pages 598–599, 603, and 610.

Active dry yeast: See Yeast, page 44.

Adobo sauce: A dark red Mexican sauce made from ground chiles, herbs, and vinegar. Chipotle peppers are packed in it.

All-purpose flour: See Flour, page 36.

Almond paste: A creamy mixture made of ground, blanched almonds and sugar. It's used as a filling in pastries, cakes, and confections. For best baking results, use an almond paste without syrup or liquid glucose.

Alphonso olive: See "Olives," page 29.

Anaheim chile: See "Chiles," pages 28–29.

Ancho chile: See "Chiles," pages 28–29.

Anchovy paste: A mixture of ground anchovies, vinegar, and seasonings. Anchovy paste is available in tubes in the canned fish or gourmet section of the supermarket.

Arbequina olive: See "Olives," page 29.

Arborio rice: A plump, short grain rice that is used for making risotto. Its high starch content contributes to the traditional creaminess of the dish. Carnaroli rice is another good choice for risotto.

Artificial sweeteners: A category of sugar substitutes that have no nutritional value. Because they have unique attributes, they should not be substituted for other sweeteners unless a recipe specifically calls for them.

Arugula: This salad green, also called rocket, is prized for its peppery flavor. See "Guide to Greens," pages 513–514.

Asiago (aged): An Italian cow's-milk cheese with a nutty, sharp, and pleasantly salty flavor. Grate it over pasta or serve with figs, grapes, pears, and apples. See "Cheeses," pages 224–226.

Baking ammonia: A compound also known as hartshorn powder. It once was used as a leavening agent. It's most often used in Scandinavian baking and is available at pharmacies and through mail order. Cream of tartar is an acceptable substitute, although cookies made with it are less crisp than those made with baking ammonia. If you use baking ammonia for baking, use caution when opening the oven door because irritating ammonialike fumes may be produced.

Baking powder: A combination of dry acid, baking soda, and starch that has the ability to release carbon dioxide in two stages.

Baking soda: A chemical leavening agent that creates carbon dioxide. It is used in conjunction with acidic ingredients, such as buttermilk, sour cream, brown sugar, or fruit juices, to create the bubbles that make the product rise.

Balsamic vinegar: Syrupy and slightly sweet, this dark brown vinegar is made from the juice of the white Trebbiano grape. It gets its body, color, and sweetness from being aged in wooden barrels.

Barley, pearl: A hearty, chewy grain that is used in breads, cereals, and soups. Pearl barley has had the bran removed, and the grain has been steamed and polished. Pearl barley comes in both quick-cooking and regular varieties. See pages 86 and 105.

Basil: See "Herbs," pages 24–25.

Basmati rice: An aromatic, long grain brown or white rice from India and California. Basmati rice is nutty and fluffy. Use as you would regular long grain rice. See pages 86 and 105.

Bay leaves: See "Herbs," pages 24–25.

Bean sauce, bean paste: Popular in Asian cooking, both products are made from fermented soybeans and have a salty bean flavor. Japanese bean paste is called miso.

Bean threads: Thin, almost transparent noodles made from mung bean flour. They also are called bean noodles or cellophane noodles.

Beech mushroom: See "Mushrooms," pages 30–31.

Beef and beef cuts: See "Beef Cuts," pages 364–365.

Bittersweet chocolate: See Chocolate, page 34.

Black beans: Dried legumes, also called turtle beans, popular in Mexican, Caribbean, and Latin cooking. They have black skin, creamy white interiors, and a mild flavor. See pages 86 and 106.

Black-eyed peas: Legumes with cream-color skin and a black "eye" on their curves. They can be purchased fresh or dried and are popular in Southern cooking. See pages 86 and 106.

Boiling onions: See Onions, page 40.

Bok choy: A vegetable with pale green or white stems and dark green leaves. It also is called Chinese white cabbage. Its crisp texture and mild, delicate flavor make it a favorite in stir-fries. See "Guide to Greens," pages 513–514.

Bouillon: A bouillon cube is a compressed cube of dehydrated beef, chicken, fish, or vegetable stock. Bouillon

> **Bean threads**

Baking Powder and Soda

Because recipes often call for such small amounts of baking powder and baking soda, you may think these ingredients are not essential for success. They are! These ingredients are leavening agents—without them, baked products will not rise. And because the chemical properties of the two ingredients are different, one cannot be substituted for another. It's best to keep both on hand.

When using baking soda, keep in mind that the soda and acid begin to react as soon as a liquid is added, so any product that uses only soda as the leaven should be baked immediately.

granules are small particles of the same substance, but they dissolve faster. Both can be reconstituted in hot liquid to substitute for stock or broth in soups or sauces.

Bouquet garni (boo-KAY gar-NEE): See "Herbs," pages 24–25.

Bow tie pasta (farfalle): A pasta that is shaped like a bow tie or butterfly. See "Pasta," pages 412–413.

Bread flour: See Flour, page 36.

Bread-machine yeast: See Yeast, page 44.

Brie: A rich, mild, and creamy French cow's-milk cheese best at room temperature. The interior should bulge when fully ripened. The bloomy white rind is edible. Brie is popular warmed and/or in pastry crusts with crackers or bread and fresh fruit. See "Cheeses," pages 224–226.

Broad beans: See Fava beans, page 36.

Broth: A strained clear liquid in which meat, poultry, or fish has been simmered with vegetables and herbs. It is similar to stock and can be used interchangeably with it. Reconstituted bouillon also can be used when broth is specified.

Brown rice: See Rice, page 41.

Brown sugar: See Sugar, page 43.

Bucatini: A pasta similar to spaghetti, but thicker and wider, with a hollow tube down the center. See "Pasta," pages 412–413.

Buckwheat groats: Eaten as a grain, buckwheat groats are actually the hulled, crushed kernels of a plant related to rhubarb. When groats are roasted, they are called kasha and have a toasty, nutty flavor. See pages 86 and 105.

Bulgur: The steamed, dried, and crushed kernels of whole wheat. It has a hearty, chewy texture and comes in coarse, medium, and fine grinds. It is essential in tabbouleh and popular in Middle Eastern pilafs. See pages 86 and 105.

Butter: For rich flavor, butter is usually the fat of choice. For baking, butter is recommended rather than margarine for consistent results (see Margarine, page 38). Salted and unsalted butter can be used interchangeably in recipes; however, if you use unsalted butter,

| 4 TBSP | 5 TBSP | 6 TBSP | 7 TBSP | 8 TBSP |
| 1/4 CUP | 1/3 CUP | 8 TBSP = 1 STICK = 1/2 CUP | | |

NET WT. 4 OZ. (113g)
THIS UNIT NOT LABELED FOR INDIVIDUAL SALE

you may want to increase the amount of salt in a recipe. The paper wrapping on a stick of butter is marked with tablespoon and partial-cup measurements for easy dividing.

Butter beans: See Lima beans, page 38.

Buttercup squash: A small, round winter squash with sweet orange flesh. See pages 598–599, 603, and 610.

Butterhead lettuce: A lettuce identified by small, round heads made up of soft, tender leaves that are green around the outside of the head, moving to pale green to yellow at the core of the head. Bibb and Boston lettuces are the two most common butterhead varieties. See "Guide to Greens," pages 513–514.

Buttermilk: See Milk and milk products, page 38.

Butternut squash: A beige, vase-shape winter squash that is bulbous on one end. It has orange flesh and a taste similar to sweet potatoes. See pages 598–599, 603, and 610.

Cabbage: A crisp-leaved cruciferous vegetable. Most varieties grow in a round or head shape. Cabbage comes in white, green, and red leaves that are flat or curly. See "Guide to Greens," pages 513–514.

Cake flour: See Flour, page 36.

Camembert: A rich, mild, and creamy French cow's-milk cheese best eaten at room temperature. The interior should bulge when fully ripened. The bloomy white rind is edible. Camembert is popular warmed and/or in pastry crusts with crackers or bread and fresh fruit. See "Cheeses," pages 224–226.

Campanelle: A pasta that has fluted, petal-like edges and hollow centers. In Italian, the name means "bellflowers." See "Pasta," pages 412–413.

Capellini: Long, thin, and delicate strands of pasta. It also is called angel hair. See "Pasta," pages 412–413.

Capers: The buds of a spiny shrub that grows from Spain to China. Found next to the olives in the supermarket, capers have an assertive flavor that can best be described as the marriage of citrus and olive, plus an added tang that comes from the salt and vinegar of their packaging brine. While smaller buds bring more flavor than larger buds, they can be used interchangeably in recipes.

Cascabel chile: See "Chiles," pages 28–29.

Catalan olive: See "Olives," page 29.

Cavatappi: A short, tubular, spiral-shape pasta that looks like a corkscrew. Elbow macaroni is a good substitute. See "Pasta," pages 412–413.

Cavatelli: A short, football-shape pasta with a rippled top. The scooplike underside is great for capturing tomato sauces. See "Pasta," pages 412–413.

Cerignola olive: See "Olives," page 29.

Chanterelle (shant-uh-REL) mushroom: See "Mushrooms," pages 30–31.

Cheddar, white cheddar: A tangy cow's-milk cheese that originated in England but now also is made in Canada, Ireland, and the United States. Age determines whether it has a mild or sharp flavor. The color ranges from cream to pumpkin orange. It's the ultimate cheese for traditional macaroni and cheese. See "Cheeses," pages 224–226.

Chervil: See "Herbs," pages 24–25.

Chèvre: This soft, tangy, yet mild-flavored French and North American cheese is made with pure goat's milk. It's wonderful served with mixed greens. See "Cheeses," pages 224–226.

Chickpeas: See Garbanzo beans, page 36.

Chile: See "Chiles," pages 28–29.

Chile de arbol: See "Chiles," pages 28–29.

Chili oil: A fiery seasoning flavored with chile peppers.

Chili paste: A condiment, available in mild or hot versions, that's made from chile peppers, vinegar, and seasonings.

Chipotle chile: See "Chiles," pages 28–29.

Chives: See "Herbs," pages 24–25.

Capers

Melting Chocolate

To melt chocolate on the range top, place it in a heavy saucepan or double boiler. Place the saucepan over low heat or the double boiler over hot, but not boiling, water. Stir the chocolate often to keep it from burning.

Make sure the utensils you use are dry and avoid splashing water into the pan. Even a little water will cause the chocolate to seize up and get grainy and lumpy.

To melt chocolate in a microwave, see page 15.

Chocolate: Six types of chocolate generally are available: *Milk chocolate* is at least 10 percent pure chocolate with added cocoa butter, sugar, and milk solids. *Semisweet and bittersweet chocolate* can be used interchangeably. They contain at least 35 percent pure chocolate with added cocoa butter and sugar. *Sweet chocolate* is dark chocolate with at least 15 percent pure chocolate, extra cocoa butter, and extra sugar. *Unsweetened chocolate* is used for baking and cooking rather than snacking. It contains pure chocolate and cocoa butter with no sugar added. *Unsweetened cocoa powder* is pure chocolate with most of the cocoa butter removed. Dutch-process or European-style cocoa powder has been treated to neutralize acids, making it mellower in flavor. *White chocolate,* which has a mild flavor, contains cocoa butter, sugar, and milk solids. Products such as white baking pieces, white candy coating, and white confectionery bars sometimes are confused with white chocolate. While they often are used interchangeably, they are not truly white chocolate because they do not contain cocoa butter.

Chorizo (chuh-REE-zoh): A spicy pork sausage used in Mexican and Spanish cuisine. Spanish chorizo is made with smoked pork; Mexican chorizo is made with fresh pork.

Chutney: A mixture of chopped fruit (mango is a classic), vegetables, and spices enlivened by hot peppers, fresh ginger, or vinegar. This condiment often is used in Indian cuisine.

Cilantro: See "Herbs," pages 24–25.

Cipollini onions: Small Italian onions with a flat, round shape and a mild, sweet taste. They are the bulb of the grape hyacinth plant. See pages 600, 602, and 609.

Coarse sugar: See Sugar, page 43.

Coconut milk: A product made from water and coconut pulp that's often used in Southeast Asian and Indian cooking. Coconut milk is not the clear liquid in the center of the coconut, nor should it be confused with cream of coconut, a sweetened coconut concoction often used to make mixed drinks such as piña coladas.

Collard greens: A type of nonhead-forming cabbage. Collard greens have dark blue-green, smooth leaves and a mild flavor. In the southern United States, collard greens cooked with bacon or salt pork are particularly popular. See "Guide to Greens," pages 513–514.

Cooking oil: Oil that is liquid at room temperature made from vegetables, nuts, or seeds. Common types for cooking include corn, soybean, canola, sunflower, safflower, peanut, and olive. For baking, cooking oils cannot be used interchangeably with solid fats because they do not hold air when beaten. See also Flavored oils, page 36.

Cornmeal: A meal made from dried corn—yellow, white, or blue. It is sold in fine, medium, and coarse grinds.

Couscous: (KOOS-koos): A granular pasta made from semolina. Look for it in the rice and pasta section of supermarkets. See "Pasta," pages 412–413.

Cracked wheat: Crushed whole kernels of unprocessed wheat (these whole kernels of wheat also are called wheat berries). It comes in fine, medium, and coarse textures. See pages 86 and 105.

Cranberry beans: A dried bean variety that is tan with streaks of red or burgundy. It has a cream-color interior, nutty flavor, and also is called a shell bean or borlotti bean. See pages 86 and 106.

Crème fraîche: A dairy product made from whipping cream and a bacterial culture, which causes the whipping cream to thicken and develop a sharp, tangy flavor. If you can't find crème fraîche in your supermarket, you can make a substitute by combining ½ cup whipping cream (do not use ultrapasteurized cream) and ½ cup dairy sour cream. Cover the mixture and let it stand at room temperature for 2 to 5 hours or until it thickens. Cover and refrigerate for up to 1 week.

Cremini mushroom: See "Mushrooms," pages 30–31.

Crookneck squash: Also called yellow squash, this common summer squash has a curved neck; thin, edible skin; and mild-tasting flesh.

Curry paste: A blend of herbs, spices, and fiery chiles that often is used in Indian and Thai cooking. Look for curry paste in Asian markets. Curry pastes are available in many varieties and are sometimes classified by color (green, red, or yellow), by heat (mild or hot), or by a particular style of curry (such as Panang or Masaman).

Crookneck squash

Delicata squash: A long, oval-shape winter squash with tan-and-green-striped skin. Its creamy flesh tastes a bit like sweet potatoes. Unlike most winter squash it has thin, edible skin. See pages 598–599, 603, and 610.

Demi-glace (DEHM-ee-glahs): A thick, intense meat-flavored gel that often is used as a foundation for soups and sauces. Demi-glace is available in gourmet shops or through mail order catalogs.

Dill: See "Herbs," pages 24–25.

Ditalini: Italian for "tiny thimbles," this pasta is best used in soups. See "Pasta," pages 412–413.

Dried pequin chile: See "Chiles," pages 28–29.

Egg roll skins: Pastry wrappers used to encase a savory filling and make egg rolls. Look for them in the produce aisle of the supermarket or at Asian markets. Egg roll skins are similar to, but larger than, wonton skins.

Eggs: For information on using eggs safely, see page 224. Keep in mind that you should avoid eating foods that contain raw eggs. Eggs should be cooked until both the yolk and white are firm; scrambled eggs should not be runny. Cook casseroles and other dishes that contain eggs until they register 160°F on an instant-read thermometer.

If you have a recipe that calls for raw or undercooked eggs (such as Caesar salads and homemade ice cream), use shell eggs that are clearly labeled as having been pasteurized to destroy salmonella. If you have a recipe that calls for raw or undercooked egg whites, use pasteurized dried egg whites or pasteurized refrigerated liquid egg whites. For cake recipes, allow eggs to stand at room temperature for 30 minutes before using. If the cake recipe calls for separated eggs, separate them immediately after removing them from the refrigerator and use them within 30 minutes. For all other recipes, use eggs straight from the refrigerator. See "Egg Equivalents," right, regarding comparable egg sizes.

Egg whites, dried: Pasteurized dried egg whites can be used where egg whites are needed; follow package directions for reconstituting them. Unlike raw egg whites, which must be thoroughly cooked before serving to kill harmful bacteria, pasteurized dried egg whites can be used in recipes that do not call for egg whites to be thoroughly cooked. Keep in mind that meringue powder may not be substituted, as it has added sugar and starch. Find dried egg whites in powdered form in the baking aisle of many supermarkets and through mail order sources.

Endive, Belgian: A bitter green that grows in tightly compact, small (6 inches long), elongated heads of white leaves with barely green tips. Its bitter flavor is a favorite in salads, though the heads can be briefly cooked. See "Guide to Greens," pages 513–514.

Endive, curly: A lacy, leafy, slightly bitter salad green whose leaves have a slightly prickly texture. See "Guide to Greens," pages 513–514.

Enoki (eh-NOH-kee) mushroom: See "Mushrooms," pages 30–31.

Escarole: A variety of endive (see above) that has pale green leaves on crisp white stalks and a mild, almost nutty flavor. Escarole can be used fresh in salads, cooked in soups, and sauteed as a side dish, similarly to spinach. See "Guide to Greens," pages 513–514.

Evaporated milk: See Milk and milk products, page 38.

Extracts and oils: Products based on the aromatic essential oils of plant materials that are distilled by various means. In extracts, the highly concentrated oils usually are suspended in alcohol to make them easier to combine with other foods in cooking and baking. Almond, anise, lemon, mint, orange, peppermint, and vanilla are some commonly available extracts. Some undiluted oils also are available, usually at pharmacies. These include oil of anise, oil of cinnamon, oil of cloves, oil of peppermint, and oil of wintergreen. Do not try to substitute oils for ground spices in recipes. Oils are so concentrated that they're measured in drops, not teaspoons. Oil of cinnamon, for example, is 50 times stronger than ground cinnamon. You can, however, substitute 1 or 2 drops of an oil for ½ teaspoon extract in frosting or candy recipes.

Beating Eggs

Recipes generally specify the consistency of beaten whole eggs, egg whites, and egg yolks.

Slightly beaten eggs: Use a fork to beat the whole egg until the yolk and white are combined and no streaks remain.

Beating egg whites until soft peaks form: Place the egg whites in a clean glass or metal mixing bowl (do not use plastic). Beat the whites with an electric mixer on medium speed or with a rotary beater until they form peaks with tips that curl over when the beaters are lifted out. Any speck of fat, oil, or yolk in the bowl will prevent whites from developing the necessary whipped consistency.

Beating egg whites until stiff peaks form: Continue beating egg whites, now on high speed, until they form peaks with tips that stand straight when the beaters are lifted out.

Beating egg yolks: Beat the egg yolks with an electric mixer on high speed for about 5 minutes or until they are thick and lemon color.

Egg Equivalents

Recipes in this cookbook were developed and tested using large eggs. If you purchase eggs in other sizes, adjust the number you use to ensure success when preparing baked goods, soufflés, egg-thickened sauces, or recipes in which egg binds the ingredients. For most other recipes, egg size isn't critical.

Large Eggs	Other Size Equivalents
1 large egg	1 jumbo, 1 extra large, 1 medium, or 1 small egg
2 large eggs	2 jumbo, 2 extra large, 2 medium, or 3 small eggs
3 large eggs	2 jumbo, 3 extra large, 3 medium, or 4 small eggs
4 large eggs	3 jumbo, 4 extra large, 5 medium, or 5 small eggs
5 large eggs	4 jumbo, 4 extra large, 6 medium, or 7 small eggs
6 large eggs	5 jumbo, 5 extra large, 7 medium, or 8 small eggs

Farina: A meal made from finely ground and sifted wheat. Farina occasionally is used in cooking but most often is combined with boiling water to make a mild, creamy hot breakfast cereal.

Fat-free half-and-half: See Milk and milk products, page 38.

Fat-free milk: Also called skim milk. See Milk and milk products, page 38.

Fats and oils: See specific ingredients, such as butter, margarine, shortening, lard, and cooking oil.

Fava beans (broad beans): Large flat brown, oval beans that are sold fresh, dried, and canned. Fava beans are popular in Mediterranean and Middle Eastern cooking. See pages 86 and 106.

Feta: This cheese, originally from Greece where it traditionally was made from sheep's or goat's milk, also is made from cow's milk now. The texture is firm to crumbly and the flavor is sharp, tangy, and salty. Feta is delicious crumbled over salads and pasta dishes. See "Cheeses," pages 224–226.

Feta

Fettuccine: A long, broad, flat, ribbonlike pasta. See "Pasta," pages 412–413.

Fines herbes (feenz ERB): See "Spices and Spice Blends," pages 27–28.

Fingerling potato: See Potatoes, page 40.

Fish sauce: A pungent brown sauce made by fermenting fish, usually anchovies, in brine. It's often used in Southeast Asian cooking.

Five-spice powder: See "Spices and Spice Blends," pages 27–28.

Flavored oils: Commercially prepared oils flavored with herbs, spices, or other ingredients, including avocado, walnut, sesame, hazelnut, and almond. In addition to using them in recipes when called for, try brushing them over grilled vegetables or bread, or experiment with them in your favorite vinaigrette recipe.

Flavoring: Imitation extract made of chemical compounds. Unlike an extract or oil, a flavoring often does not contain any of the original food it resembles. Some common imitation flavorings available are banana, black walnut, brandy, cherry, chocolate, coconut, maple, pineapple, raspberry, rum, strawberry, and vanilla.

Flour: A finely milled grain or food product. While wheat is the most popular flour, it can be made from many different cereals, roots, and seeds. Store flour in an airtight container in a cool, dry place. All-purpose flour may be stored for up to 8 months. Bread flour, cake flour, gluten flour, whole wheat flour, and other whole grain flours may be stored up to 5 months. For longer storage, refrigerate or freeze the flour in a moisture- and vaporproof container. Bring chilled flour to room temperature before using in baking. Here are the types of flour most commonly used in cooking:

All-purpose flour is made from a blend of soft and hard wheat flours and, as its name implies, can be used for many purposes, including baking, thickening, and coating. All-purpose flour usually is sold presifted and is available bleached or unbleached. Bleached flour has been made chemically whiter in appearance. Some cooks prefer the bleached flour to make their cakes and bread as white as possible, while other cooks prefer their flour to be processed as little as necessary. Both bleached and unbleached flour are suitable for home baking and can be used interchangeably.

Bread flour contains more gluten than all-purpose flour, making it ideal for baking breads, which rely on gluten for structure and height (see Gluten, page 18). If you use a bread machine, use bread flour instead of all-purpose flour for best results. Or use all-purpose flour and add 1 or 2 tablespoons of gluten flour (available in supermarkets or health food stores).

Cake flour is made from a soft wheat and produces a tender, delicate crumb because the gluten is less elastic. It's too delicate for general baking, but to use it for cakes, sift it before measuring and use 1 cup plus 2 tablespoons of cake flour for every 1 cup all-purpose flour specified.

Gluten flour is made by removing most of the starch from high-protein, hard-wheat flour. Because whole grain flours are low in gluten (see Gluten, page 18), some whole grain bread recipes often call for a little gluten flour to help the finished loaf attain the proper texture. If you can't find gluten flour, sometimes called wheat gluten, at a supermarket, look for it at a health food store.

Pastry flour is a soft wheat blend with less starch than cake flour. It is used for making pastry.

Self-rising flour is all-purpose flour with salt and a leavener, such as baking powder, added. It generally is not used for making products containing yeast.

Specialty flours include whole wheat, graham, rye, oat, buckwheat, and soy. They are combined with all-purpose flour in baking recipes because none has sufficient gluten to provide the right amount of elasticity on its own.

Food coloring: Liquid, paste, or powdered edible dyes used to tint foods.

Frisée: A slightly bitter, delicate green with curly leaves that are white at the stem end, then yellow, then green at the tips. It generally is used as a salad green but occasionally is lightly cooked with bacon. See "Guide to Greens," pages 513–514.

Fruit: See "Selecting Fresh Fruit," pages 603–605.

Fusilli: Long, twisted, spaghettilike strands of pasta. See "Pasta," pages 412–413.

Gaeta olive: See "Olives," page 29.

Garbanzo beans: Round, beige legumes that are slightly larger than green peas. Garbanzo beans, also called chickpeas, have a firm, toothsome texture and nutty flavor. They are popular in Mediterranean and Middle Eastern cooking and are the main ingredient in the spread hummus. See pages 86 and 106.

Garlic, elephant garlic: A strongly scented, pungent bulb that is related to an onion. Multiple garlic cloves make up a garlic bulb. Elephant garlic is larger, milder, and more closely related to the leek than regular garlic. Store firm, fresh, plump garlic bulbs in a cool, dry, dark place; leave bulbs whole because individual cloves dry out quickly. Convenient substitutes are available; for each clove called for in a recipe use either ⅛ teaspoon garlic powder or ½ teaspoon bottled minced garlic. For a Roasted Garlic Spread, peel away the dry outer layers of

Garbanzo beans

skin from 1 head of garlic, leaving skins and cloves intact. Cut off the pointed top portion (about ¼ inch), leaving the bulb intact but exposing the individual cloves. Place the garlic head, cut side up, in a custard cup. Drizzle with a little olive oil. Cover with foil and bake in a 425°F oven for 25 to 35 minutes or until the cloves feel soft when pressed. Set aside just until cool enough to handle. Squeeze out the garlic paste from individual cloves.

Garlic

Gelatin: A powdered thickening agent made from natural animal protein. Gelatin is available in unflavored and flavored forms. When using gelatin, make sure the powder dissolves completely (see tip, below).

Gemelli: A short pasta that looks like two spaghetti strands twisted together. Gemelli means "twins" in Italian. See "Pasta," pages 412–413.

Ginger: The root of a semitropical plant that adds a spicy-sweet flavor to recipes. Ginger, also called gingerroot, should be peeled before using. To peel, cut off one end of the root and use a vegetable peeler to remove the brown outer layer in strips. To grate ginger, use the fine holes of a grater. To mince ginger, slice peeled ginger with the grain (lengthwise) into thin sticks. Stack the sticks in a bundle and cut them finely. Unpeeled ginger stays fresh 2 to 3 weeks in the refrigerator when wrapped loosely in a paper towel. For longer storage, place unpeeled ginger in a freezer bag and store in freezer. Ginger will keep indefinitely when frozen, and you can grate or slice the ginger while it's frozen. In a pinch, ground ginger can be used for grated fresh ginger. For 1 teaspoon grated fresh ginger, use ¼ teaspoon ground ginger.

Ginger, crystallized: A confection made from pieces of ginger (gingerroot) cooked in a sugar syrup, then coated with sugar. Also known as candied ginger, it often is used in baked goods. Store in a cool, dry, dark place.

Gluten flour: See Flour, page 36.

Gnocchi (NYOH-kee): Italian dumplings made of flour or potatoes are used like pasta.

Gorgonzola: A tangy, creamy, blue-veined cow's-milk cheese from Italy. It's delicious with fruit and stands up to hearty red wine. See "Cheeses," pages 224–226.

Gouda, aged Gouda: A cow's-milk cheese originally from Holland. It has a creamy texture and nutty, caramellike flavor. As Gouda ages, the mild, buttery flavor becomes more earthy and cheddarlike. The high fat content makes it a good melting cheese; Gouda is great for fondue and aged Gouda is a good cheese for topping French onion soup. See "Cheeses," pages 224–226.

Granulated sugar: See Sugar, page 43.

Great Northern beans: Large white bean with a mild flavor that is close in size and shape to a baby lima bean. They are good for use in baked bean dishes and are interchangeable with other white beans, such as navy beans, in most recipes. See pages 86 and 106.

Green onions: See Onions, page 40.

Habañero chile: See "Chiles," pages 28–29.

Half-and-half: See Milk and milk products, page 38.

Havarti: A traditional Danish cheese that has a buttery yet tangy flavor. It melts nicely for sandwiches and sauces. See "Cheeses," pages 224–226.

Herbes de Provence: See "Spices and Spice Blends," pages 27–28.

Herbs: See "Herbs," pages 24–25.

Hoisin sauce: A sauce popular in Asian cooking that adds a multitude of sweet and spicy flavors to a dish.

Hominy grits: Also known as "grits," this meal of white or yellow corn has been treated with lye, dried, then ground fine, medium, or coarse. Simmered with water or milk, it's good as a side dish or served with syrup as breakfast.

Honey: A sweet, sticky sweetener that's produced by bees from floral nectar. Its flavor depends on the flowers from which the honey is derived; most honey is made from clover, but other sources include lavender, thyme, orange blossom, apple, cherry, buckwheat, and tupelo. Generally, the lighter the color, the milder the flavor. Store honey at room temperature in a dark place. If it becomes solid, liquefy it by warming the honey jar slightly in the microwave oven or in a pan of hot tap water. Honey should not be given to children who are younger than 1 year old because it can contain trace amounts of botulism spores, which could trigger a potentially fatal reaction in children with undeveloped immune systems.

Iceberg lettuce: The most common type of head lettuce in American supermarkets, iceberg is identified by its large head and crisp pale green leaves. Iceberg is mild in flavor. See "Guide to Greens," pages 513–514.

Italian seasoning: See "Spices and Spice Blends," pages 27–28.

Jalapeño chile: See "Chiles," pages 28–29.

Jamaican jerk seasoning: See "Spices and Spice Blends," pages 27–28.

Jumbo shell macaroni: Large, shell-shape pasta that is perfect for stuffing with a variety of fillings and baking. See "Pasta," pages 412–413.

Kabocha (kah-BOH-chah) squash: Also known as Japanese pumpkin, kabocha is a winter squash with a jade-green rind and a pale orange interior that is smooth and sweet. It can be cooked similarly to acorn squash. See pages 598–599, 603, and 610.

Kalamata olive: See "Olives," page 29.

To dissolve one envelope of unflavored gelatin:

● Place gelatin in a small saucepan and stir in at least ¼ cup water, broth, or fruit juice. Let it stand 5 minutes to soften, then stir it over low heat until the gelatin is dissolved.

● Do not mix gelatin with figs, fresh pineapple (canned pineapple is not a problem), fresh ginger, guava, kiwifruit, and papaya, as these foods contain an enzyme that prevents gelatin from setting up.

● Some recipes call for gelatin at various stages of gelling. "Partially set" means the mixture looks like unbeaten egg whites. At this point, solid ingredients may be added. "Almost firm" describes gelatin that is sticky to the touch. It can be layered at this stage. "Firm" gelatin holds a cut edge and is ready to be served.

Kale: A member of the cabbage family. Its dark green, frilly leaves grow in a loosely knit bouquet formation, making it a favorite of ornamental gardeners and cooks. Its mild, cabbagelike flavor is good in salads or cooked similarly to spinach. See "Guide to Greens," pages 513–514.

Salt

Kosher salt: A coarse salt with no additives that many cooks prefer for its light, flaky texture and clean taste. It also has a lower

Kosher salt

sodium content than regular salt. Find it in the supermarket with the other salts.

Lamb and lamb cuts: See "Lamb Cuts," page 400.

Lard: A product made from pork fat that can be used for baking. It's noted for producing light, flaky piecrusts, though shortening is more commonly used today.

Lasagna noodle: A long, wide (2- to 3-inch) noodle used in layered baked pasta dishes such as lasagna. See "Pasta," pages 412–413.

Leaf lettuce: A type of lettuce that grows in a loose, leafy formation rather than in a tight head. Generally, leaf lettuces are more full-flavored than head lettuces. Their color ranges from medium green to dark green and some have a red tinge at their leaf tips. See "Guide to Greens," pages 513–514.

Leavenings: Ingredients that are essential in helping batter and dough expand or rise during baking. Without leavening, the baked products will be heavy and tough. See specific ingredients, such as yeast, baking powder, and baking soda, for more information.

Leek: With a large leafy green top and a white slightly bulbous bottom, leeks resemble giant scallions. They are related to both garlic and onions and have a taste that combines the two but is milder than either one of them. Leeks require careful cleaning before use because their many layers accumulate grit. Trim the green top and the root end and slit them top to bottom. Run them under cold running water to wash out the grit.

Lemongrass: A highly aromatic, lemon-flavor herb often used in Asian cooking. To use, trim the fibrous ends and slice what remains into 3- to 4-inch sections. Cut each section in half lengthwise, exposing the layers. Rinse pieces under cold water to remove any grit and slice thinly. In a pinch, substitute ½ teaspoon finely shredded lemon peel for 1 tablespoon lemongrass.

Lemongrass

Lemon-pepper seasoning: See "Spices and Spice Blends," pages 27–28.

Lentils: Tiny, lens-shape dried legumes that—unlike most legumes—don't require soaking before cooking. Lentils have a creamy interior when cooked and a nutty flavor. See pages 86 and 106. Lentils come in several varieties:

Brown lentils are the most common type found in supermarkets. They still have their seed coats on, which helps keep them intact during cooking.

French lentils are gray-green in color and have a creamy yellow interior. They are slightly smaller than brown lentils and have a slightly more delicate, peppery flavor. French lentils, also called de Puy or green lentils, are sold with their seed coats on, which helps them hold their shape better than other lentil types.

Red lentils are smaller than either brown or French lentils, and they do not have a seed coat, so tend to break down when cooked. They are popular in Indian and North African cooking.

Yellow lentils are similar to red in that they are small and do not have seed coats so they tend to break down when cooked.

Light cream: See Milk and milk products, below.

Lima beans: Pale green and plump legumes with a firm, meaty texture and a mild flavor. See pages 86 and 106. Lima beans come in several varieties:

Baby lima beans are the smallest of the lima bean varieties and have the mildest flavor. Baby lima beans are a true variety, not simply immature large lima beans.

Christmas or calico lima beans are spotted and have purple or burgundy streaks.

Large lima beans are bigger and plumper than any other limas. Also called butter beans, they have a more distinct flavor than baby lima beans.

Linguine: A long, thin, flat pasta noodle. See "Pasta," pages 412–413.

Mafalda: Long, flat, wide pasta ribbons that have ruffled edges. See "Pasta," pages 412–413.

Manchego, aged: A sheep's-milk cheese from Spain. It has a mellow, nutty flavor and is satisfying with a fruity wine or eaten on its own. See "Cheeses," pages 224–226.

Manicotti: A large, tubular pasta used for stuffing. See "Pasta," pages 412–413.

Margarine: A substitute for butter generally made from vegetable oil. It was developed in the late 1800s. When baking with stick margarine, be sure to use one that contains at least 80 percent fat and 100 calories per tablespoon. (Check nutritional information.) See page 243.

Marjoram: See "Herbs," pages 24–25.

Marsala: A fortified wine that can be either dry or sweet. Sweet Marsala is used both for drinking and cooking. Dry Marsala makes a nice before-dinner drink.

Mascarpone: A soft, rich, and butterlike cheese from Italy. It is made from cow's milk. Mascarpone stars in tiramisu and is also great served with fresh fruit. See "Cheeses," pages 224–226.

Maytag Blue: An Iowa-made blue cheese that has a soft, crumbly texture and a salty, slightly peppery flavor. It is lovely served crumbled over salads. See "Cheeses," pages 224–226.

Meringue powder: A combination of pasteurized dried egg whites, sugar, and edible gums. Just add additional sugar and water and beat for a fluffy meringue. The added gums make for a stable meringue. Look for it in baking catalogs and specialty stores.

Milk and milk products:

Buttermilk is a low-fat or fat-free milk to which a bacterial culture has been added. It has a mildly acidic taste. Sour milk, made from milk and lemon juice or vinegar, can be substituted in baking recipes. See page 169.

Evaporated milk is canned whole milk with about half of

its water removed. It lends a creamy richness to many recipes, including pumpkin pie. Measure it straight from the can for recipes calling for evaporated milk; to use it in place of fresh milk, dilute it as directed on the can (usually with an equal amount of water) to make the quantity called for in the recipe. Evaporated milk, also available in low-fat and fat-free versions, is unsweetened so is not interchangeable with sweet- **Mustard greens** ened condensed milk.

Fat-free half-and-half is made mostly from fat-free milk, with carrageenan for body. It can bring a creamy flavor to recipes without added fat. Experiment using it in cornstarch- or flour-thickened soup, sauce, and gravy recipes that call for regular half-and-half.

Light cream and half-and-half are interchangeable in most recipes. Light cream contains 18 to 30 percent milk fat. Half-and-half is a mixture of milk and cream. Neither one contains enough fat to be whipped.

Nonfat dry milk powder can be reconstituted for use in cooking.

Sour cream and yogurt are available in low-fat and fat-free varieties. Sour cream traditionally is made from light cream with a bacterial culture added. Yogurt is made from milk with a bacterial culture added.

Sweetened condensed milk is whole milk that has had water removed and sugar added. It also is available in low-fat and fat-free versions. It is not interchangeable with evaporated milk or fresh milk.

Whipping cream contains at least 30 percent milk fat and can be beaten into whipped cream.

Whole, low-fat or light, reduced-fat, and fat-free milk may be used interchangeably in cooking because these milk types differ only in the amount of fat they contain and in the richness of flavor they lend to foods. Recipes in this cookbook were tested using reduced-fat (2 percent) milk.

Milk chocolate: See Chocolate, page 34.

Millet: A tiny round yellow cereal grain that adds crunch to many commercially made whole grain breads. Millet also can be boiled and turned into pilaf. See pages 86 and 105.

Mint: See "Herbs," pages 24–25.

Morel (more-EL) mushroom: See "Mushrooms," pages 30–31.

Mozzarella, fresh: A soft, mild-flavor cheese usually made from cow's milk. It is packaged in whey or water. Fresh mozzarella showcases beautifully on an antipasto tray. See "Cheeses," pages 224–226.

Muenster, American: A rich and mild cow's-milk cheese. It is not the same as French Muenster. Try it in grilled cheese sandwiches or with sliced apples. See "Cheeses," pages 224–226.

Mushrooms, fresh and dried: This plant in the fungus family has flavors ranging from mild and nutty to meaty, woodsy, and wild; it comes in many colors and shapes. Popular choices for drying include oyster, wood ear, and shiitake. Dried mushrooms swell into tender, flavorful morsels. To reconstitute, simply cover them in warm water and soak them about 30 minutes. Rinse well and squeeze out the moisture. Remove and discard tough stems. Cook them in recipes as you would fresh mushrooms. See "Mushrooms," pages 30–31.

Mustard greens: The leaves of the mustard plant are a favorite green in the southern United States, where they are cooked with bacon or salt pork. The leaves are dark green and have ruffled edges and a distinctly peppery, mustardlike taste. See "Guide to Greens," pages 513–514.

Napa cabbage: The thin, crisp white and pale green leaves of this large, cylindrical Chinese cabbage add crunch to stir-fries. Napa cabbage also is good baked or braised. See "Guide to Greens," pages 513–514.

Navy beans: Small white, mild-flavor legumes that are sold dried or canned. Navy beans are used widely in baked bean dishes and are interchangeable with Great Northern beans in most recipes. See pages 86 and 106.

Nested pasta: Long, thin strands of pasta (generally angel hair or vermicelli) that have been coiled up into a round or oval shape to form a "nest." See "Pasta," pages 412–413.

Niçoise olive: See "Olives," page 29.

Nonfat dry milk powder: See Milk and milk products, page 38.

Nonstick cooking spray: This convenient product reduces the mess associated with greasing pans; it also can help cut down on fat in cooking. Use the spray only on unheated baking pans or skillets because it can burn or smoke if sprayed onto a hot surface. For safety, hold pans over a sink or garbage can when spraying to avoid making the floor or counter slippery.

Nuts: Dried seeds or fruits with edible kernels surrounded by a hard shell or rind. Nuts are available in many forms, such as chopped, slivered, and halved. Use the form called for in the recipe. In most recipes, the nuts are selected for their particular flavor and appearance; however, in general, walnuts may be substituted for pecans and almonds for hazelnuts, and vice versa. When grinding nuts, take extra care not to overdo it, or you may end up with a nut butter. If you're using a blender or processor to grind them, add 1 tablespoon of the sugar or flour from the recipe for each cup of nuts to help absorb some of the oil. Use a quick start-and-stop motion for better control over the fineness. For best results, grind the nuts in small batches and be sure to let the nuts cool after toasting and before grinding.

Nyon olive: See "Olives," page 29.

Oats: A highly nutritious cereal grain that starts out unprocessed as oat groats. See pages 86 and 105. Depending on how they are processed, oat groats become:

Quick-cooking rolled oats have been broken down into smaller pieces before they are steamed and flattened. Quick-cooking oats cook faster than regular oats, but lose some of the hearty, nutty texture in the process. In

most recipes, regular oats and quick-cooking rolled oats are interchangeable unless specified. *Regular or rolled oats* (also called old-fashioned oats) are simply steamed, then flattened with rollers.

Quick-cooking oats

Olives: See "Olives," page 29.

Onions: Members of the allium family, along with garlic and leeks, onions are used to flavor all kinds of foods. Some of them are mild enough to stand on their own. Vadalia, Maui, and Walla Walla onions are known for their sweetness and juicy, crisp texture. Onions come in many other varieties, including:

Boiling onions are small, usually about 1 inch in diameter, and can be used in soups and stews or cooked and served as a side dish.

Green onions are simply immature onions. Also called scallions or spring onions, they have long green stems with small white bulbs at the end. Both stems and bulbs are edible. Green onions are good cooked in dishes and raw in salads or sprinkled on top of scrambled eggs.

Pearl onions are tiny—usually about the size of a marble—and can be cooked and served as a side dish. Creamed onions are made with pearl onions.

Red onions are large and globe shape, with red skin and a fairly mild, sweet taste. Also called Italian onions, they often are eaten raw.

White onions generally are globe shape. They range in flavor from relatively mild to strong.

Yellow onions represent several varieties, ranging in shapes from globe to flat and ranging in taste from faintly sweet to strong.

Oregano: See "Herbs," pages 24–25.

Orzo (rosamarina): A small, rice-shape pasta that generally is used in soups and as a quick-to-fix side dish. See "Pasta," pages 412–413.

Oyster mushroom: See "Mushrooms," pages 30–31.

Pancetta: See "Pancetta and Prosciutto," right.

Parmigiano-Reggiano: A rich, sharp flavor distinguishes the Italian cow's-milk cheese. It is the quintessential cheese in risotto and for grating as a finishing touch to pasta. Parmesan is the domestic variety of this cheese. See "Cheeses," pages 224–226.

Parsley: See "Herbs," pages 24–25.

Pasilla chile: See "Chiles," pages 28–29.

Pastry flour: See Flour, page 36.

Pattypan squash: A small, flying-saucer-shape summer squash with a scalloped edge. Pattypan range in color from pale green to darker green to yellow. They generally are picked small (1 to 4 inches across). The smallest ones often are called baby pattypan and are especially tender. See pages 598–599, 603, and 610.

Pearl onions: See Onions, above.

Pectin: A natural substance found in some fruits that makes fruit-and-sugar mixtures used in jelly and jam making set up. Commercial pectin also is available. See page 212.

Penne: A short, tubular pasta that is diagonally cut on both ends. Penne, Italian "pen" or "quill," is smooth; penne rigate has ridges. See "Pasta," pages 412–413.

Pequin chile (dried): See "Chiles," pages 28–29.

Pesto: Traditionally an uncooked sauce made from crushed garlic, basil, and nuts blended with Parmesan cheese and olive oil. Today's pestos may call on other herbs or greens and may be homemade or purchased. Tomato pesto is also available. Pesto adds a heady freshness to many recipes.

Phyllo (FEE-loh) dough: Tissue-thin sheets of dough are layered and baked into a delicate, flaky pastry. Phyllo,

Pancetta and Prosciutto

These two time-honored Italian meats are becoming favorites for adding flavor to today's cooking. Look for both in well-stocked supermarkets, Italian grocery stores, or specialty food shops.

Prosciutto (proh-SHOO-toh): To Italians, prosciutto means "ham"; cooks in America use the term to refer to a type of ham that has been seasoned, salt-cured, and air-dried (rather than smoked). The process takes at least nine months and results in somewhat sweetly spiced, rose-color meats with a sheen. Parma ham from Italy (prosciutto di Parma) is considered to be the best. Sliced prosciutto dries out quickly and should be used within a day or frozen for longer storage.

Pancetta (pan-CHEH-tuh): Italian-style bacon that's made from the belly (or pancia) of a hog. Unlike bacon, pancetta is not smoked but instead seasoned with pepper and other spices and cured with salt. Pancetta is generally available packaged in a sausagelike roll. In a pinch, substitute regular bacon.

sometimes spelled filo, is Greek for "leaf." It is prominent in Greek, Turkish, and Near Eastern dishes. Although phyllo can be made at home, a frozen commercial product is available and much handier to use. Allow frozen phyllo dough to thaw while it is still wrapped; once unwrapped, sheets of phyllo dough quickly dry out and become unusable. To preserve sheets of phyllo, keep them stacked and covered with plastic wrap while you prepare your recipe. Rewrap any remaining sheets and return them to the freezer.

Pine nut: A high-fat nut that comes from certain varieties of pine trees. Their flavor ranges from mild and sweet to pungent. Store them in the refrigerator or freezer because they go rancid quickly. In a pinch, substitute chopped almonds or, in cream sauces, walnuts.

Pine nuts

Pinto beans: Pale pink legumes with reddish brown streaks (pinto means "painted" in Spanish). Pinto beans are flavorful and creamy. They are popular in Latin cooking and are the main ingredient in Mexican-style refried beans. See pages 86 and 106.

Poblano chile: See "Chiles," pages 28–29.

Porcini mushrooms: See "Mushrooms," pages 30–31.

Pork and pork cuts: See "Pork Cuts," pages 386–387.

Port du Salut: A cow's-milk cheese from France. It has a buttery, savory flavor. It's lovely on a platter with fresh fruit. See "Cheeses," pages 224–226.

Portobello mushroom: See "Mushrooms," pages 30–31.

Potatoes: These starchy tubers have varying degrees of moisture, density, and sugar. These characteristics make certain varieties best for specific preparations. Most potatoes can be divided into four types: russet, long white, round white, and round red—though specialty varieties are increasingly available. See pages 600, 602, and 610. Common potato varieties include:

Fingerling potatoes are small, elongated potatoes with a moist, creamy interior. They can be brown, red, white, yellow, or purple and can be boiled, steamed, or roasted.

Long white potatoes are similar to russets (see below) but with a thinner skin. They are best baked, boiled, or fried.

New potatoes are simply young potatoes of any variety—white, red, yellow, or purple. They are prized for their thin skin and tender, sweet flesh. They are just the right size to cook whole—boiled, steamed, or roasted.

Purple or blue potatoes are native to South America and are increasingly available in American supermarkets. Their flesh ranges from dark blue to lavender to pale blue or white. They have a nutty flavor. Because exposing them to water drains them of color, they are best baked or roasted.

Round red potatoes are often referred to as "new potatoes," but that is a misnomer. Red potatoes are their own variety, with red skin and white flesh. They hold their shape well when cooked, making them good for boiling, steaming, roasting, and in salads.

Round white potatoes are denser and waxier than other varieties, meaning they hold their shape when cooked. They're a good choice for potato salads.

Russet potatoes are probably the most popular potato in the United States. They have a lower moisture content and starchier, mealier flesh than other varieties and cook up light and fluffy in baked or mashed potatoes. They're also great roasted or turned into french fries.

Sweet potatoes are the edible roots of a tropical flowering plant. Often confused with the yam (see Yams, page 44), sweet potatoes have pale yellow flesh and are not as sweet as yams.

Yukon gold potatoes have a yellow flesh and buttery texture that makes them excellent for mashed potatoes. Finnish yellow potatoes are another popular yellow variety.

Powdered sugar: See Sugar, page 43.

Prosciutto: See "Pancetta and Prosciutto," page 40.

Provolone: This cow's-milk cheese originated in Italy. The flavor of a young provolone is mild—when aged it is somewhat sharp. Young provolone lends itself well to melting on a pizza. See "Cheeses," pages 224–226.

Puff pastry: A butter-rich, multilayered pastry. When baked, the butter produces steam between the layers, causing the dough to puff up into many flaky layers. Because warm, softened puff pastry dough becomes sticky and unmanageable, roll out one sheet of dough at a time, keeping what you're not using wrapped tightly in plastic wrap in the refrigerator.

Pumpkin: A large squash with mild-tasting orange flesh and an abundance of large seeds, called pepitas. The smaller the pumpkin, the sweeter it is. If you're making

Puff pastry

your own pumpkin puree for pumpkin pie, choose a pumpkin labeled "pie pumpkin" or "sugar pumpkin." See page 599.

Queso fresco: A slightly salty Mexican cheese with a dry texture and mild flavor. Also called queso blanco, it is best crumbled over finished dishes. See "Cheeses," pages 224–226.

Quick-rising active dry yeast: See Yeast, page 44.

Quinoa (KEEN-wah): This tiny, beadlike cream-color grain is considered a complete protein because it contains all eight essential amino acids. It has the highest protein content of any grain. Quinoa is lighter than rice but can be used in similar fashion. See pages 86 and 105.

Queso fresco

Radicchio: A bitter Italian green that is actually deep burgundy red or purple in color. Radicchio grows in small, compact heads that can be separated into leaves for use in salads or braised or roasted whole. See "Guide to Greens," pages 513–514.

Ravioli: Pillows of fresh pasta that are stuffed with a variety of fillings, including cheese, vegetables, and finely ground seafood and meat. See "Pasta," pages 412–413.

Raw sugar: See Sugar, page 43.

Red beans: Small, oval deep red legumes popular in Mexican and Southwestern cooking. Red beans are also the bean component in red beans and rice, a Louisiana specialty. See pages 86 and 106.

Red kidney beans: Large, crescent-shape red legumes with a cream-color interior and full flavor. They are popular for use in chili and can be used interchangeably with red beans (see above). See pages 86 and 106.

Red onions: See Onions, pages 40, 600, 602, and 609.

Rice: A grain grown all over the world in marshy areas. Rice comes in many types, the most common of which is white. White rice comes in long, medium, and short grains. The shorter the grain, the more starch it contains. Because it is the starch that causes rice to stick together when cooked, long grain rice cooks up lighter and fluffier than short grain rice. See pages 86 and 105. Other varieties of rice include:

Arborio rice is a short grain white rice preferred in risotto for the traditional creaminess it gives to the dish.

Aromatic rices include basmati, Texmati, wild pecan, and jasmine rice. Their aromas are irresistible and hint at their flavors, which range from toasted nuts to popped corn. Look for them in larger supermarkets or those that stock Indian or Middle Eastern foods.

Brown rice is an unpolished rice grain with the bran layer intact. Pleasantly chewy and nutty in flavor, brown rice requires a longer cooking time than white rice—but also has more nutrients.

Converted rice is white rice that has been parboiled before it's packaged. This process helps retain nutrients and keeps the grains from sticking together when cooked.

Instant or quick-cooking rice is partially or fully cooked before it is packaged, allowing it to cook quickly at home.

Wild rice is not really a grain at all, but rather the seed of a marsh grass. It takes three times as long to cook as white rice, but the nutlike flavor and chewy texture are worth it. Wild rice must be thoroughly washed before it is cooked.

Rice noodles, rice sticks: Thin noodles, popular in Asian cooking, made from finely ground rice and water. When fried, they puff into light, crisp strands. They also can be soaked to use in stir-fries and soups. Thicker varieties are called rice sticks. Find both products in Asian markets; substitute vermicelli or capellini for the thin rice noodles, linguine or fettuccine for the thicker rice sticks.

Rice papers: Round, flat, edible papers made from the pith of a rice-paper plant. They are used for wrapping spring rolls.

Rice vinegar: A mild-flavor vinegar made from fermented rice. Rice vinegar is interchangeable with rice wine vinegar, which is made from fermented rice wine. Seasoned rice vinegar, with added sugar and salt, can be used in recipes calling for rice vinegar, though you may wish to adjust the seasonings. If you can't find rice vinegar, substitute white vinegar or white wine vinegar.

Rigatoni: A large, tubular pasta with ridges. It is best paired with chunky sauces and used in baked pasta dishes. See "Pasta," pages 412–413.

Romaine: Lettuce with long, crisp, slightly bitter leaves that are dark green on the edges, moving to light green at their centers. Romaine is the classic lettuce for Caesar salad (page 496). See "Guide to Greens," pages 513–514.

Roquefort: A pungent, slightly salty French blue cheese made from sheep's milk. It has a creamy texture. It clearly is the star of Roquefort salad dressing and is great with fruit for dessert. See "Cheeses," pages 224–226.

Rosemary: See "Herbs," pages 24–25.

Rotini: A short (1 or 2 inches long) tightly spiraled pasta. See "Pasta," pages 412–413.

Russet potato: See Potatoes, page 40.

Sage: See "Herbs," pages 24–25.

Salad oil: See page 501.

Salsa: A sauce usually made from finely chopped tomatoes, onions, chiles, and cilantro. It often is used in Mexican and Southwestern cuisine.

Savory: See "Herbs," pages 24–25.

Savoy cabbage: A cabbage whose crinkly leaves grow in loose, full heads. It is considered one of the best varieties of cabbage for cooking because it is so tender and mild-tasting. See "Guide to Greens," pages 513–514.

Scallion: See Onions, page 40.

Sea salt: A salt variety derived from the evaporation of sea water. Some cooks prefer it over table salt for its clean, salty flavor.

Self-rising flour: See Flour, page 36.

Semisweet chocolate: See Chocolate, page 34.

Serrano chiles: See "Chiles," pages 28–29.

Sesame oil: A pale yellow oil made from untoasted sesame seeds. Toasted sesame oil is made from sesame seeds. It has a rich brown color and concentrated flavor.

Shallots: This member of the onion family has a flavor that is a cross between onion and garlic. Shallots grow in heads similar to garlic but in much larger cloves, with rosy, pale brown papery skin and a light purple interior.

Sherry: A fortified wine that ranges from dry to sweet and from light to dark. Besides enjoying it as a before- or after-dinner drink, sherry can be used in cooking.

Shiitake (shee-TAH-kee) mushroom: See "Mushrooms," pages 30–31.

Shortening: A vegetable oil that has been processed into solid form. Shortening commonly is used for baking or frying. Plain and butter-flavor types can be used interchangeably. Store in a cool, dry place. Once opened, use within 6 months. Discard if it has an odor or appears discolored.

Shrimp paste: A pungent seasoning made from dried, salted shrimp that has been pounded into a paste. Shrimp paste gives Southeast Asian dishes an authentic, rich flavor. The salty shrimp taste mellows during cooking. In a pinch, substitute anchovy paste, though it's not as boldly flavored.

Soba noodles: Made from wheat and buckwheat flours, soba noodles are a favorite Japanese fast food. In a pinch, substitute a narrow, whole wheat ribbon pasta, such as linguine.

Somen noodles: Made from wheat flour, these dried Japanese noodles are fine and most often white. In a pinch, substitute angel hair pasta.

Sorrel: A sour, lemony-tasting herb that is used as a flavoring in soups and, in the spring when it's young and tender, in salads. See "Guide to Greens," pages 513–514.

Sour cream: See Milk and milk products, page 38.

Soybeans, green soybeans: Highly nutritious, high-protein legumes that have a mild taste and firm texture when cooked. Green soybeans, sometimes called edamame, their Japanese name, have been picked before they are completely mature. They have a sweet, nutty flavor and can be cooked and served similarly to lima beans. See pages 86, 101, and 106.

Soba noodles

Soymilk: Made of the liquid pressed from ground soybeans, soymilk can be a good substitute for cow's milk for people who do not consume dairy products. Plain, unfortified soymilk offers high-quality proteins and B vitamins. Substituting soymilk for regular milk in cooking is possible in some cases, though the flavor may be affected. Experiment to see what is acceptable to you.

Spaghetti: Long, thin strands of pasta. The name literally means "little strings" in Italian. See "Pasta," pages 412–413.

Spelt: A nutty-tasting cereal grain similar to wheat but higher in protein and more digestible, making it an alternative grain for some of those who are allergic to wheat. Spelt flour can be found in health food stores. See pages 86 and 105.

Spices: See "Spices and Spice Blends," pages 27–28.

Spinach: A leafy, dark green vegetable that is high in iron and vitamins A and C. Spinach is good fresh in salads, steamed, and sauteed. Baby spinach is especially tender and good in a time pinch because the stems don't need trimming. See "Guide to Greens," pages 513–514.

Split peas: A variety of sweet-tasting field peas that is cultivated just for drying. They are split along their natural seams—hence, their name. They don't require soaking before cooking and come in two varieties—green and yellow. See pages 86 and 106.

Stilton: An English blue-veined cheese that has a creamy yet slightly crumbly texture. It is especially good alone or served with port or dry red wine. See "Cheeses," pages 224–226.

Stock: The strained clear liquid in which meat, poultry, or fish has been simmered with vegetables or herbs. It is similar to broth but is richer and more concentrated. Stock and broth can be used interchangeably; reconstituted bouillon can also be substituted for stock.

Straight-neck summer squash: A thin-skinned yellow squash similar to crookneck squash (see page 34) but with a straight, rather than curved, neck.

Sugar: A sweetener that's primarily made from sugar beets or sugarcane. Sugar comes in a variety of forms:

Brown sugar is a mix of granulated sugar and molasses. Dark brown sugar has more molasses and, hence, more molasses flavor than light brown sugar (also known as golden brown sugar). Unless otherwise specified, recipes in this cookbook were tested using light brown sugar. Unless one is specified, dark and light brown sugars can be used interchangeably. Tip: To help keep brown sugar soft, store it in a heavy plastic bag or a rustproof, airtight container and seal well. If it becomes hard, you can soften it by emptying the hardened sugar into a rustproof container and adding a piece of soft bread; the sugar will absorb the moisture and soften in a day or two. After the sugar has softened, remove the bread and keep the container tightly closed.

Coarse sugar often is used for decorating baked goods. Coarse sugar, sometimes called pearl sugar, has much larger grains than regular granulated sugar; look for it where cake-decorating supplies are sold.

Granulated sugar is white granular, crystalline sugar. It is what to use when a recipe calls for sugar without specifying a particular type. White sugar most commonly is available in a fine granulation, though superfine (also called ultrafine or castor sugar), a finer grind, also is available. Because superfine sugar dissolves readily, it's ideal for frostings, meringues, and drinks.

Powdered sugar is granulated sugar that has been milled to a fine powder, then mixed with cornstarch to prevent lumping. Sift powdered sugar, also known as confectioner's sugar, before using.

Raw sugar is not sold to U.S. consumers. Products labeled and sold as raw sugar, such as Demerara sugar and turbinado sugar, are not true raw sugars as they have been refined in some way. For example, turbinado sugar, a course sugar with a subtle molasses flavor, is cleaned through a steaming process. It is available in many health food stores.

Vanilla sugar is infused with flavor from a dried vanilla bean. It tastes great stirred into coffee drinks and sprinkled over baked goods. To make vanilla sugar, fill a 1-quart jar with 4 cups sugar. Cut a vanilla bean in half lengthwise; insert both halves into the sugar. Secure lid and store in a cool, dry place for several weeks before using. It will keep indefinitely.

Sweet chocolate: See Chocolate, page 34.

Sweetened condensed milk: See Milk and milk products, page 38.

Sweeteners: See Artificial sweeteners, page 32; Honey, page 37; and Sugar, above.

Sweet potato: See Potatoes, page 40.

Swiss: A mild, slightly nutty flavor and small holes characterize this American cow's-milk cheese. It is a great choice for sandwiches or fondue. See "Cheeses," pages 224–226.

Swiss chard: This member of the beet family is grown for its leafy, nutrient-packed leaves. The two most common varieties are one with medium green leaves and crisp light green stalks, and one with darker green leaves and red stalks. It can be prepared similarly to spinach. Baby Swiss chard is sometimes found in the salad greens mix called mesclun. See "Guide to Greens," pages 513–514.

Tahini: A flavoring agent made from ground sesame seeds and often used in Middle Eastern cooking. Look for tahini in specialty food shops or Asian markets.

Tahini

Tamari: A dark, thin sauce made from soybeans. Tamari is a slightly thicker, mellower cousin of soy sauce and is used to flavor Asian dishes. In a pinch, substitute soy sauce.

Tamarind paste: A thick, tart brown Asian flavoring that comes from the fruit of a tamarind tree.

Tapioca: A tiny, pearl-like starch that is most commonly used in tapioca pudding. Tapioca is also good as a thickener, particularly for foods that are going to be frozen because—unlike flour- and cornstarch-thickened mixtures—frozen tapioca mixtures retain their thickness when reheated. Tapioca comes in regular and quick-cooking varieties. See Thickeners, page 20.

Tarragon: See "Herbs," pages 24–25.

Thai chiles: See "Chiles," pages 28–29.

Thyme: See "Herbs," pages 24–25.

Toasted sesame oil: See Sesame oil, page 42.

Tofu: See page 99.

Tomatoes, dried: Sometimes referred to as sun-dried tomatoes, these shriveled-looking tomato pieces boast an intense flavor and chewy texture. They're available packed in olive oil or dry. Follow recipe directions for rehydrating dry tomatoes. If no directions are given, cover with boiling water, let stand about 10 minutes or until pliable, then drain well and pat dry. Snip pieces with scissors, if necessary. Generally, dry and oil-packed tomatoes can be used interchangeably, though the dry tomatoes will need to be rehydrated, and the oil-packed will need to be drained, rinsed, and patted dry.

Tortellini: Small, twisted, circular pockets of pasta that are stuffed with fillings. Tortellini can be found in fresh, frozen, and dried forms. See "Pasta," pages 412–413.

Tortilla: A small, thin, flat bread, popular in Mexican cooking, that is made from corn or wheat flour and usually is wrapped around a filling. To warm and soften flour tortillas, wrap a stack of eight to 10 in foil and heat them in a 350°F oven for 10 minutes.

Dried tomatoes

Turban squash: Vividly colored—usually bright orange with green and white stripes—winter squash that has a bulb-shape cap swelling from the blossom end. It has dark yellow flesh that tastes vaguely of hazelnuts. See pages 598–599, 603, and 610.

Unsweetened chocolate: See Chocolate, page 34.

Unsweetened cocoa powder: See Chocolate, page 34.

Vanilla: A liquid extract made from the seed of an orchid. Imitation vanilla, an artificial flavoring, makes an inexpensive substitute for vanilla. They can be used interchangeably in recipes.

Vanilla bean: See "Vanilla Beans," right.

Vanilla sugar: See Sugar, page 43.

Veal and veal cuts: See "Veal Cuts," page 366.

Vegetables: For selecting and storing vegetables, see pages 601–603.

Vermicelli: Extremely thin strands of pasta. See "Pasta," pages 412–413.

Vermouth: White wine that has been fortified and flavored with herbs and spices. Dry vermouth is white and is used as a before-dinner drink or in nonsweet drinks, such as a martini. Sweet vermouth is reddish brown and can be drunk straight or used in sweet mixed drinks. Vermouth often is used as a cooking ingredient.

Vinegar: A sour liquid that is a by-product of fermentation. Through fermentation the alcohol from grapes, grains, apples, and other sources is changed to acetic acid to create vinegar.

Wagon wheel macaroni (ruote): A round pasta with spokes like a wheel. See "Pasta," pages 412–413.

Wasabi: A Japanese horseradish condiment with a distinctive pale lime-green color and a head-clearing heat (if used in significant amounts). Wasabi is available as a paste in a tube or as a fine powder in a small tin or bottle. It's often used to flavor fish or serve with sushi.

Watercress: A member of the mustard family, the small, dark green leaves have a peppery bite similar to arugula. Watercress is used to flavor soups, sandwiches, and salads. See "Guide to Greens," pages 513–514.

Wheat berries: Whole, unprocessed, chewy kernels of wheat. After being cooked, they can be baked into breads or made into delicious and nutritious pilafs and salads. See pages 86 and 105.

Wheat bran: This flaky outer covering of the wheat berry (see above) doesn't have a lot of nutritional value but is loaded with flavor and fiber. Bake it into breads and muffins. See page 86.

Wheat germ: Nutty-tasting wheat germ is the ground-up embryo of the wheat berry (see above). It comes in both raw and toasted forms. The raw form is used in baked goods; the toasted form is used in baked goods and also can also be sprinkled on cereal and yogurt to add vitamins, minerals, and protein. See page 86.

Whipping cream: See Milk and milk products, page 38.

White chocolate: See Chocolate, page 34.

White mushroom: See "Mushrooms," pages 30–31.

White onions: See Onions, page 40.

Wild rice: See Rice, page 41.

Wontons, wonton wrappers: Stuffed savory Asian pastries. The wrappers, paper-thin skins used to make wontons, can be found in the produce aisle or in Asian markets. Wonton wrappers are similar to, but smaller than, egg roll skins.

Wood ear mushrooms: See "Mushrooms," pages 30–31.

Yam: This tropical-vine tuber often is confused with the sweet potato. Though they do share some characteristics, they come from different plant species. The orange flesh of the yam is deeper in color than that of the sweet potato

Vanilla Beans

Using dried vanilla beans helps pack recipes with vanilla flavor. Here's a little know-how:

Vanilla beans are the long, thin pod of an orchid plant. The pod itself, which has been dried and cured, should not be eaten. Instead the tiny seeds inside the pod are used. They bring an intense vanilla flavor and dark brown, confettilike flecks to dishes. Follow recipe directions for extracting the seeds from the pod. Often the pod will be heated in a liquid mixture to make it easier to split open, but even a dry vanilla bean can be cut lengthwise with a paring knife. After it is open, scrape out the tiny seeds. Discard the pod or use it to make vanilla sugar (see Vanilla sugar, left).

You can generally substitute 2 teaspoons vanilla for 1 vanilla bean. Vanilla paste, which contains flecks of the vanilla bean seeds, is also available. Find it in specialty markets or through mail order catalogs and follow package directions for using it.

and has a higher moisture and sugar content. Yams and sweet potatoes are interchangeable in most recipes. See pages 600, 603, and 610.

Yeast: A tiny, single-cell organism that feeds on the sugar in dough, creating carbon dioxide gas that makes dough rise.

Active dry yeast is the most popular form. In baking, these tiny, dehydrated granules are mixed with flour or dissolved in warm water.

Bread-machine yeast is highly active yeast that was developed especially for use in these small appliances.

Quick-rising active dry yeast is more active than active dry yeast, substantially cutting down on the time it takes for dough to rise. This yeast, sometimes called fast-rising or instant yeast, usually is mixed with the dry ingredients before the warm liquids are added. The recipes in this cookbook were tested using active dry yeast.

Yellow onions: See Onions, page 40.

Yogurt: See Milk and milk products, page 38.

Yukon gold potato: See Potatoes, page 40.

Ziti: Thin, smooth tubes of pasta that range in length from about 2 inches to 12 inches—in which case it's called long ziti. See "Pasta," pages 412–413.

Zucchini: A long, slightly cylindrical summer squash whose skin ranges from pale green to dark green to yellow. The smaller the zucchini, the thinner its skin. It has tender, mild-tasting flesh and is good sauteed, roasted, or grilled. It is popular as a baby vegetable.

Nutrition Basics Made Simple

Living a healthy life has been made easy by MyPyramid from the U.S. Department of Agriculture (USDA). It stresses a personalized approach to good health, encouraging consumers to combine healthy food choices with daily physical activity.

Healthy Eating

Discover a healthier you! Practicing good nutrition and getting regular exercise is a sure-fire way to improve your health. With the variety of food products available, eating healthfully can be simple, delicious, and satisfying!

Understanding MyPyramid

MyPyramid is an updated version of the Food Guide Pyramid that stresses the importance of both physical activity and healthy eating. Don't be confused by the new design. It still has all the same food groups (grains, vegetables, fruits, fats, milk, and meat and beans), each represented by a different-color strip. The wider the strip, the more servings should be eaten from that group daily.

The strips start wide at the pyramid's base and narrow as they reach the tip. This indicates that some foods in each group should be eaten more than others in the group because they are more nutrient dense. For instance, in the grain group (orange strip), whole grains, such as brown rice and quinoa, are found at the base, while refined grains, such as white bread and sugary cereals, are found at the tip.

Because we are all individuals with needs based on our age, gender, and level of daily physical activity, MyPyramid does not show how many servings should be eaten from each group. Instead, you can visit the MyPyramid website at www.mypyramid.gov and let My Pyramid Plan figure your nutrient needs. If you do not have Internet access, check with your physician or dietitian.

Grain Up for Good Health: In MyPyramid, the orange strip, the widest of the six, represents grains. Because grains are rich in carbohydrates, they are a major energy source for our bodies. Grains can be broken into two groups: whole and refined. Barley, brown rice, quinoa,

and oatmeal are examples of whole grains. Because whole grains include the entire grain, they provide more fiber, protein, vitamins, and minerals than their refined counterparts. It is recommended to consume at least three servings of whole grains per day. Refined grains, such as white rice, white bread, and many breakfast cereals, are stripped of their fiber and nutrients. Although some refined products are enriched, a process that adds vitamins and minerals, whole grains are still superior.

Vitamin-Packed Vegetables: Vegetables, the pyramid's green strip, are nutrient powerhouses. They are low in calories but packed with vitamins, minerals, and fiber. In adults, vegetable nutrients play an important role in the prevention of cancer, heart disease, and obesity. They promote growth and development in children. Choosing a variety of dark green leafy vegetables, orange vegetables, legumes, and starchy vegetables will intensify the nutritional benefits. To meet the dietary guidelines, people following a 2,000-calorie diet should eat 2½ cups of vegetables daily.

Favor the Fruit Flavor: In all their brilliant colors, fruits, the pyramid's red strip, are full of flavor, sweet juices, and a wealth of nutrients. Most fruits contain powerful antioxidants that fight and prevent disease. Reap more of these

Whole Grain Goodness

The new USDA MyPyramid recommends consuming 3 servings of whole grains per day. Whole grains contain the entire grain kernel, which includes the bran, the germ, and the endosperm. Examples of whole grains include:

- Amaranth
- Brown rice
- Buckwheat
- Bulgur
- Millet
- Oatmeal
- Popcorn
- Quinoa
- Sorghum
- Triticale
- Whole cornmeal
- Whole grain barley
- Whole grain cornmeal
- Whole rye
- Whole wheat flour
- Whole wheat tortilla
- Wild rice

Breads & Crackers

  1 slice 100% whole grain bread
  1 small slice whole wheat French bread
  4 snack-size slices rye bread
  ½ whole wheat English muffin
  1 whole wheat mini bagel
  1 6-inch whole wheat (flour) tortilla or corn tortilla
  5 whole wheat crackers
  2 rye crispbreads
  7 square or round crackers
  1 small piece corn bread

Cereal

  1 cup ready-to-eat whole grain dry cereal
  ½ cup cooked oatmeal
  1 packet instant oatmeal

Pasta & Rice

  ½ cup cooked whole wheat spaghetti
  ½ cup cooked brown rice, wild rice, or enriched white rice

Other Grains

  3 cups popped popcorn
  ½ cup cooked cracked wheat bulgur
  1 4½-inch whole wheat pancake
  1 whole wheat, bran, or corn muffin

Note: An amount considered a serving size on a product's Nutrition Facts label may be larger than specified in these guidelines.

Source: U.S. Departments of Health and Human Services and Agriculture, MyPyramid.gov.

health benefits by opting for whole fruits instead of fruit juice. Whole fruits have fewer calories, more fiber, and none of the added sugars you'll find in juices. The dietary guidelines recommend 2 cups of fruit per day based on a 2,000-calorie diet.

Facts on Fats: Believe it or not, fats, the pyramid's yellow strip, are absolutely essential to a healthy diet. They are needed to help the body absorb fat-soluble vitamins and antioxidants. Fats add flavor and tenderness to foods and help you to feel full faster.

All fats, however, were not created equal. In your diet you'll find three types: saturated, trans fats, and unsaturated fats. Saturated fats, found commonly in meat and cheese, increase the risk of heart disease by raising cholesterol. Trans fats should also be avoided because, like saturated fats, they contribute to heart disease. They are commonly found in stick margarine and processed or packaged foods.

The unsaturated fats found in oils, nuts, and seeds are the healthy fats that, when consumed in appropriate amounts, have beneficial effects. Dietary guidelines suggest consuming less than 10 percent of calories from saturated fat per day, less than 300 milligrams of cholesterol per day, and keeping your intake of trans-fatty acids as low as possible.

Milk Your Diet: MyPyramid puts more emphasis on the milk group, the blue strip, than in the past because the new guidelines suggest that you should strive to consume 3 cups daily of fat-free or low-fat milk or other dairy products. Milk and dairy products have long been known to help build strong bones and prevent bone loss, but their high calcium levels also help regulate blood pressure levels. Dairy foods can be high in saturated fat and cholesterol, so choose reduced fat or fat-free options when available.

Meat Your Needs: Meat, beans, eggs, and other meat substitutes, the pyramid's purple strip, provide essential proteins that help build, maintain, and replace the body's tissues. They are rich in many B vitamins, zinc, iron, vitamin E, and magnesium, but eggs and some meats are high in saturated fat and cholesterol. When selecting and preparing foods from this group, make choices that are lean, low-fat, or fat-free. With a wide selection of meat cuts and cooking methods available, it's simple to incorporate lean meats into your meals. If you choose a vegetarian lifestyle, dry beans, legumes, and nuts are excellent meat alternatives.

Deficiencies in a Nation of Abundance

Surprisingly, many Americans do not consume enough nutrients to meet the needs of their bodies even though they consume more than enough calories. Without these nutrients, the body does not function at its full potential. To avoid being caught in this trap, eat foods that are low in calories and high in nutrients. For examples of nutrient-rich food choices see "Power Foods," page 49. Some Americans try to make up for a lack of nutrients in their diets with vitamin and mineral supplements. This certainly can be helpful, but supplements cannot do the same jobs a healthy diet does because there are components in food that cannot be duplicated by supplements.

Besides simply getting enough of the right nutrients, it is also important to maintain a healthy weight by balancing calories consumed with calories expended, or burned, throughout the day. If you need to lose weight, start slowly so you don't get discouraged. By taking small steps to make permanent lifestyle changes, weight loss will be more easily attainable.

Physical activity is an essential part of weight management. By gradually decreasing the amount of calories consumed and increasing physical activity, you'll be on your way to a healthy weight.

Special Reports

With the current emphasis on nutrition, it seems new information on the subject is reported daily. It's no wonder that many consumers are confused about which nutrients to eat and which to avoid. To clear things up, here's a closer look at a few of these nutrients.

Sugar: While sugar is a carbohydrate and provides energy to the body, it contains zero essential nutrients. Sugar is a naturally occurring ingredient that provides browning, volume, tenderness, flavor, and moisture to baked goods; however, it can contribute excessive calories without lasting satisfaction. Recently, sugar substitutes have become a popular alternative, especially because several of them can be used in cooking and baking. Sugar substitutes do not provide browning, tenderness, volume, and moisture as true sugar does, but they

can be used to add sweetness to products while keeping calories and carbohydrates in check.

Fiber: Fiber is a beneficial carbohydrate that comes in two forms: soluble and insoluble. Soluble fiber is found in many fruits, vegetables, and grains. It can help lower low-density-lipoprotein (LDL) blood cholesterol levels. Insoluble fiber, found in the skins of fruits and vegetables and in whole grains, nuts, and seeds, provides roughage that promotes digestion. Strive to consume 25 to 35 grams of fiber per day.

Sodium: With an increased dependence on packaged and convenience foods for quick-to-the-table meals comes increased sodium intake. Too much sodium raises blood pressure, which results in higher risk of heart disease and stroke. Shopping around the perimeter of the supermarket is a great way to avoid excessive sodium. In the outer aisles you generally find fresh ingredients; convenience foods lurk in the center. Take it easy with the salt shaker; just 1 teaspoon of

Sodium Chart

Food Item	Amount	Sodium	% of Daily Value
Apple, raw with skin	1 med.	0 mg	0%
Broccoli, raw	1 cup	24 mg	1%
Salmon, Atlantic	3 oz.	52 mg	2.3%
Skinless chicken breast half	3 oz.	64 mg	2.8%
Whole wheat bread	1 slice	148 mg	6.4%
Egg, fried	1 large	162 mg	7%
Potato chips	1 oz.	168 mg	7.3%
Ketchup	1 Tbsp.	178 mg	7.7%
Cheerios	1 cup	273 mg	11.8%
Hamburger, fast food (no condiments)	1 sandwich	387 mg	16.8%
Purchased chicken pot pie	7 oz. pie	948 mg	41.2%
Egg and ham biscuit, fast food	1 biscuit	1,382 mg	60%

Source: Bowes and Church's Food Values of Portions Commonly Used. 18th edition. Jean A.T. Pennington and Judith S. Douglass. Lippincott Williams & Wilkins Copyright 2005. ISBN: 0-7817-4429-6

salt provides about 2,300 milligrams of sodium, the recommended daily maximum.

Nutrition Labels

With so many great ingredients stocked in such abundance at our supermarkets, creating healthy, delicious meals is easy. Nearly all products provide a nutrition label to help you make healthy decisions. The following information will help you to better understand these labels.

Serving Sizes: Given in familiar units, such as cups, tablespoons, or pieces.

Daily Values: Expressed in percentages. They tell how much of the recommended amount of a nutrient is in a serving of the food. Use these values to figure out how much one serving of the food will contribute to the overall daily recommended intake of particular nutrients. Daily Values are based on a 2,000-calorie diet. Depending on your age, gender, and activity level, you may require more or less than 2,000 calories. Therefore, for some nutrients

you may require more or less than 100 percent of the Daily Values.

Trans Fats: Listed in grams. As of January 2006, it is mandatory to include a value for trans-fatty acids on the food label. Remember, you want to avoid these whenever possible.

Food Allergy Information: A product must list whether it contains ingredients to be avoided by people with the following food allergies: milk, eggs, fish, crustacean shellfish, tree nuts, peanuts, wheat, or soybeans. This information, which is found near the list of ingredients, also is new on food labels as of January 2006.

Analyzing the Recipes

Each recipe in this cookbook includes the nutrition facts of a single serving, which is calculated in the Better Homes and Gardens® Test Kitchen using nutrition analysis software. The nutrition facts include the number of calories and the amount of fat, saturated fat, cholesterol, sodium, carbohydrates, fiber, and protein for each serving. Recipes also include the amount of vitamin A, vitamin C, calcium, and iron, noted as percentages in Daily Values. When looking at the nutrition facts, keep in mind the following factors:

● Analyses do not include optional ingredients.

● The first serving size listed is analyzed when a range is given. For example, if a recipe makes 4 to 6 servings, the nutrition facts are based on 4 servings.

● When ingredient choices (such as butter or margarine) appear in a recipe, the first one listed is used for analysis.

● When milk is a recipe ingredient, the analysis is calculated using 2% (reduced-fat) milk.

● When a marinade is specified in a recipe, the nutritional analysis is adjusted based on how much of the marinade is actually used.

● Where appropriate, the size of a single serving of the recipe is listed behind the total number of servings. It is listed in familiar units, such as cups, tablespoons, or pieces.

● Diabetic exchanges, listed with the nutrition facts for each recipe, are based on the exchange list developed by the American Dietetic Association and the American Diabetes Association.

● If the amount of food consumed is different from the stated serving size, the nutrition facts no longer will be accurate.

• FAT FREE • CHOLESTEROL FREE

Nutrition Facts

| Serving Size | 1 Cup (28g/1.0 oz.) |
| Servings Per Container | About 12 |

	Cereal	Cereal with 1/2 Cup Vitamins A&D Fat Free Milk
Amount Per Serving		
Calories	100	140
Calories from Fat	0	0

		% Daily Value**	
Total Fat 0g*		0%	0%
Saturated Fat 0g		0%	0%
Trans Fat 0g			
Cholesterol 0mg		0%	0%
Sodium 200mg		8%	11%
Potassium 25mg		1%	7%
Total Carbohydrate 24g		8%	10%
Dietary Fiber 1g		4%	4%
Sugars 2g			
Other Carbohydrate 21g			
Protein 2g			

Vitamin A	10%	15%
Vitamin C	10%	10%
Calcium	0%	15%
Iron	45%	45%
Vitamin D	10%	25%
Thiamin	25%	30%
Riboflavin	25%	35%
Niacin	25%	25%
Vitamin B₆	25%	25%
Folic Acid	25%	25%
Vitamin B₁₂	25%	35%

* Amount in cereal. One half cup of fat free milk contributes an additional 40 calories, 65mg sodium, 6g total carbohydrate (6g sugars), and 4g protein.
**Percent Daily Values are based on a 2,000 calorie diet. Your daily values may be higher or lower depending on your calorie needs:

	Calories	2,000	2,500
Total Fat	Less than	65g	80g

Serving Size →

Trans Fats →

Daily Values →

Special Icons

Low-Fat Recipes: A main-dish recipe flagged with a 🔲LOW FAT symbol contains 12 or fewer grams of fat per serving; a bread or vegetable serving contains 3 grams of fat or fewer; all other side-dish servings contain 5 grams of fat or fewer. A low-fat serving of a sauce, a beverage, or a cookie contains 2 or fewer grams of fat.

Whole Grains: Recipes in which one portion contains the recommended serving of whole grain are flagged with a 🔲WHOLE GRAIN symbol.

Vegetarian: Recipes flagged with a 🔲VEGETARIAN symbol do not contain meat, poultry, or fish. Since there are many classifications of vegetarian eating, be sure to look at the individual ingredient lists to find the recipes that meet your individual goals and needs.

Power Foods

Beyond choosing a variety of foods as part of a healthy diet, remember that some foods offer more nutritional bang for the buck. Foods high in antioxidants have a great nutritional advantage. Antioxidants protect against free radicals that roam through the body, damaging cells. Three well-known antioxidants are vitamins A, C, and E. Each has been shown to decrease the risk of some cancers, heart disease, and arthritis, to name just a few health problems. Choose items from this list of power foods to begin incorporating more antioxidants and other beneficial nutrients into your diet.

Deeply colored fruits and vegetables: These tend to have the highest levels of vitamins, minerals, and antioxidants. When looking for a simple snack or putting together your next meal, choose the following foods often: sweet peppers, kale, spinach, berries, asparagus, grapes, dried plums, carrots, broccoli, and apples.

Fish: Fatty fish, such as tuna, salmon, and mackerel, contain omega-3 fatty acids, a healthful unsaturated fat that can reduce the risk of heart and vascular disease. They are also rich in vitamin E and full of flavor.

Cabbage and other cruciferous vegetables: Vegetables in this category, such as arugula, broccoli, cabbage, cauliflower, kale, and radishes, have been shown to contain cancer-fighting agents. So eat up when there is a bowl of Brussels sprouts on the table.

Whole grains: Whole grains are not a single food but an entire category of nutrient-dense foods that contain all of the nutrient-rich parts of the grain kernel. Whole grains can help regulate blood glucose, prevent heart disease, and provide an increased feeling of fullness.

Nuts: Although nuts are high in fat, it is most often unsaturated fat. Including nuts in your diet provides key vitamins, fiber, and a feeling of satisfaction, which makes them a great snack. Choose nuts that are not salted or sugar-coated; if you want to enhance their flavor, try toasting them. Keep in mind that a healthy portion of nuts is 1 ounce, which is equivalent to about ¼ cup.

Tea: Tea recently has emerged as a rich source of antioxidants. Green teas hit the top of the list for antioxidant levels, and some research suggests they may boost metabolism. Be sure to avoid adding sugar to your tea.

Chocolate: Believe it or not, indulging in a small amount of the right kind of chocolate provides antioxidants. Which kind is the most antioxidant rich? Look for those that contain at least 60 percent cacao. If this is not clearly labeled, choose chocolates labeled bittersweet or dark. Remember that less is more: The benefit of chocolate is outweighed if you consume too much of the high-calorie food.

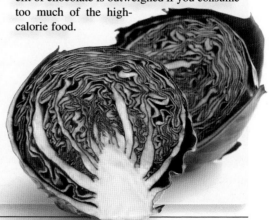

Food Safety

Keep basic food safety, including simple steps you can take to prevent food-borne illness, in mind when preparing food and maintaining your kitchen.

The Golden Rule of Food Safety

You'll often hear food safety experts repeat the adage "Keep hot food hot and cold food cold." The reason for this is because bacteria thrive at temperatures between 40°F and 140°F (sometimes called the "danger zone" when it comes to food safety). Therefore, cold foods need to be held at 40°F or below, and hot foods need to be served immediately or held at 140°F or above. While you can't see, taste, or smell the bacteria that cause food-borne illness, you can take control of keeping food safe in your kitchen by following these basic steps.

Keep It Clean!

Keep your hands and all surfaces and utensils that come into contact with food clean.

Keep hands clean: Nearly half of all cases of food-borne illness could be eliminated by proper hand washing. Remember to wash your hands:

● Before handling food or utensils or eating.

● After handling food, especially raw meat, poultry, fish, shellfish, or eggs.

● Between tasks—for example, after cutting up raw chicken and before dicing the vegetables.

● After using the bathroom, changing diapers, playing with pets, or touching any unclean item.

Proper hand washing means thoroughly scrubbing your hands—front and back, all the way up to the wrists, over and under the fingernails, and in between fingers—in hot, soapy water for at least 20 seconds. Rinse your hands and use paper towels or a clean cloth to dry them. If you have an open wound or cut, prevent contamination by wearing rubber gloves while handling food.

Keep dishcloths, towels, and sponges clean. One way to eliminate the bacteria that thrive in sponges and dishcloths is to soak them in a diluted bleach solution (¾ cup bleach per 1 gallon water) three times a week. Sponges should be allowed to air-dry. Wash dishcloths often using the hot cycle of your washing machine. Use paper towels to clean up spills, especially juices from raw meat, poultry, fish, and shellfish.

Keep surfaces and utensils clean. Immediately after preparing raw meat, poultry, fish, shellfish, eggs, and unwashed produce, clean any utensils and surfaces used with hot, soapy water.

Care for your cutting boards. After each use, cutting boards should be thoroughly washed with hot, soapy water, then rinsed and allowed to air-dry or patted dry with paper towels. Or, if they're dishwasher-safe, place them in the dishwasher. As an added safety measure, flood a cutting board's surface with a sanitizing solution (1 teaspoon of liquid chlorine bleach per 1 quart of water); allow the board to stand several minutes. Rinse and air-dry or pat dry with paper towels.

Replace cutting boards whenever they have become worn or develop hard-to-clean grooves.

Wash food thermometer probes after each use with hot, soapy water and rinse before reinserting the probe into food.

Wipe up refrigerator spills immediately. Clean refrigerator surfaces with hot, soapy water and rinse. Once a week, throw out perishable foods that should no longer be eaten.

Keep pets off counters and away from food.

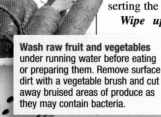

Wash raw fruit and vegetables under running water before eating or preparing them. Remove surface dirt with a vegetable brush and cut away bruised areas of produce as they may contain bacteria.

Separate, Don't Cross-Contaminate

Cross contamination occurs when cooked or ready-to-eat foods pick up bacteria from other foods, hands, cutting boards, knives, or other utensils. To avoid cross contamination, it is especially important to keep raw meat, poultry, eggs, fish, and shellfish and their juices away from other foods. Follow these guidelines.

    When shopping, keep raw meat, poultry, fish, and shellfish separate from other foods in your grocery cart.

    Once home, store raw meat, poultry, fish, and shellfish in sealed containers or plastic bags so that the juices don't drip onto other foods. Large turkeys and roasts should be placed on a tray or pan that is large enough to catch any juices that may leak out. To store eggs, see page 224.

    Purchase two cutting boards, if possible, that are distinctly different from one another. Designate one for raw meat, poultry, fish, and shellfish and the other for ready-to-eat foods, such as breads and vegetables.

    Follow guidelines under "Keep It Clean!" (page 50) to keep hands and any utensils and surfaces that come into contact with foods clean.

    Place cooked foods on a clean plate, never on an unwashed one that was used to hold raw meat, poultry, fish, or shellfish.

    Don't wash raw poultry, beef, pork, lamb, or veal before cooking. Doing so poses a risk of cross contamination with other foods and utensils in the kitchen. Any bacteria that might be present are destroyed with proper cooking.

    Marinate foods safely (see Marinate, page 18).

Cook to Proper Temperatures

Properly cooking food to a safe temperature destroys the harmful bacteria that cause foodborne illnesses. Safe temperatures vary from food to food. Follow doneness tests given with the recipes. See "Safe Food Temperatures," right, for general guidelines. Leftovers should be reheated to 165°F, and reheated sauces, soups, and gravies should be brought to a rolling boil. See charts at the end of the fish and shellfish chapter for guidelines on doneness tests for those foods. For information on cooking eggs, see page 224 and Eggs, page 34.

    It's essential to use a clean food thermometer to ensure that meat, poultry, casseroles, and other foods are properly cooked all the way through. See pages 12–13 to learn about the types of food thermometers available.

Chill It!

Cold temperatures keep most harmful bacteria from multiplying. Follow these steps to keep foods cold.

    When shopping, buy perishable foods last. Go straight home and refrigerate them promptly. Follow packaging labels for safe handling.

    Refrigerate leftover foods immediately after you have finished eating. Leftovers should not stay out of the refrigerator longer than 2 hours (1 hour if the temperature is above 80°F). To refrigerate or freeze cooked foods, see "Cool It Quickly," page 53. For guidelines on storing foods properly, see pages 53–56.

    Use appliance thermometers (see page 12) to ensure that your refrigerator and freezer are maintaining proper temperatures for food safety. Refrigerate at or below 40°F; freeze at or below 0°F. Because cold air needs to circulate the unit

Safe Food Temperatures

Always use a food thermometer to ensure that food has reached a high enough temperature to destroy harmful bacteria. Here are the internal temperatures recommended by the USDA.

Food	Final Doneness Temperature
Beef, lamb, and veal steaks, chops, and roasts	
medium rare	145°F
medium	160°F
Hamburger, meat loaf, ground pork, veal, and lamb	160°F
Pork chops, ribs, and roasts	160°F
Egg dishes	160°F
Ground turkey and chicken	165°F
Stuffing and casseroles	165°F
Leftovers	165°F
Chicken and turkey breasts	170°F
Chicken and turkey whole bird, legs, thighs, and wings	180°F
Duck and goose	180°F

to keep foods safe, avoid packing the refrigerator and freezer too full.

Thaw Safely

Thaw frozen foods in the refrigerator—never at room temperature. A few exceptions include breads and sweets that specifically call for thawing at room temperature. Make sure that thawing foods do not drip onto other foods. Some foods may be successfully thawed in the microwave; follow your microwave manufacturer's directions and cook the food immediately after thawing. You also can thaw food by placing the item in a leakproof plastic bag and immersing it in cold tap water in the sink. Every half hour, change the water to keep it cold and turn the food over if it's not fully submerged; cook food immediately after thawing.

Safe Picnics

The basic steps to keeping food safe in the home—clean, separate, cook, and chill—also apply to safe outdoor eating.
Keep it clean: Clean your hands and surfaces often—take along moist towelettes or soap and water to do the job.
Separate: To avoid cross contamination, tote plenty of plates and utensils along. Designate some for handling raw foods only and the others for handling cooked foods. Keep uncooked meats, poultry, fish, and shellfish separate from other foods—transport them in tightly sealed bags or containers and pack them at the bottom of the cooler so that their juices do not drip onto other foods.
Cook properly: Use a food thermometer to make sure your foods are cooked to a safe internal temperature (follow recipe directions or see grilling charts, pages 353–360). Do not partially cook or grill food to finish cooking later.
Chill it: When toting foods, remember:
● Keep perishable foods at a temperature of 40°F or below by packing them in a well-insulated cooler with plenty of ice. A full cooler will maintain its cold temperature longer than a partially filled one. Thaw meat, poultry, fish, and shellfish in the refrigerator before taking them to a picnic. Wait until just before leaving home to pack perishable foods in the cooler.
● Take two insulated coolers: one for drinks, the other for perishable foods. That way warm

Food Safety Information

Information on food safety is constantly emerging. For the latest information and precautions, call the USDA Meat and Poultry Hotline, 800/535-4555; the U.S. FDA Center for Food Safety and Applied Nutrition Outreach Center, 888/723-3366; or consult your health care provider. You can also get information by checking the government's food safety website at www.foodsafety.gov.

air won't reach the perishables each time someone grabs a chilled beverage.
● On your way to the picnic, place coolers in your air-conditioned car rather than the trunk. At the picnic, keep coolers tightly closed in a shady area.
● Keep foods in the coolers until you need them; remove raw food only when you're ready to put it on the grill. (If grilling in batches, keep foods not being grilled in the cooler.)
● Discard any perishable food left outside for more than 2 hours (1 hour if the temperature is above 80°F).

Toting and Serving Hot Foods

Bacteria thrive at temperatures between 40°F and 140°F, so keeping hot foods hot is just as important as keeping cold foods cold.
● When serving hot foods on a buffet, keep them at 140°F or higher. Use chafing dishes, slow cookers, and warming trays.
● When toting hot food to a party, keep the food at or above 140°F. Use heavy-duty foil, several layers of newspaper, or a heavy towel to wrap the container well. Then place the wrapped container in an insulated container.

When in Doubt, Throw It Out

If you aren't sure that food has been prepared, served, or stored safely, discard it. If a food has been improperly handled, even proper cooking cannot make it safe. Never taste food to see if it's safe to eat because contaminated food can look, smell, and taste perfectly normal, and even a small amount can make you ill.

Food Storage and Make-Ahead Cooking

Make-ahead cooking—from stashing leftovers in the freezer for another meal to baking ahead for the holidays—is a great way to get the most out of time spent in the kitchen.

Storage Guidelines

When you store perishable foods, follow the guidelines for keeping foods safe (see "Food Safety," pages 50–52). These additional guidelines will help you get the best flavor and texture from stored foods.

Cold Enough for You?

Use appliance thermometers (see page 12) to make sure your freezer and refrigerator maintain proper temperatures for safe food storage. Refrigerators should maintain a temperature of 40°F or below, and freezers should maintain a temperature of 0°F or below.

Cool It Quickly

Hot foods bound for the refrigerator or freezer must be cooled quickly. First, it decreases the chance for bacteria to grow. Second, it freezes food faster, preventing the formation of ice crystals that may ruin the flavor and texture of foods. Here's how to cool food quickly.

● Divide cooked foods into small portions in shallow containers. Divide soups and stews into

Foods Not to Freeze

These foods lose flavor, texture, or overall quality when frozen.

● Battered and fried foods
● Cooked egg whites and yolks, as well as icings made with egg whites
● Cottage and ricotta cheeses
● Custard and cream pies or desserts with cream fillings
● Mayonnaise
● Soups and stews made with potatoes, which can darken and become mushy
● Soups and stews thickened with cornstarch or flour
● Sour cream
● Stuffed chops or chicken breasts
● Whole eggs in the shell, raw or cooked

portions that are 2 to 3 inches deep and stir while cooling. Divide roasts and whole poultry into portions that are 2 to 3 inches thick. Place portions of hot food in the refrigerator. Remove stuffing from poultry and refrigerate in separate containers.

● If the final destination is the freezer, transfer cold food from the refrigerator to the freezer. Arrange containers in a single layer in the freezer until frozen; this allows the cold air to circulate around the packages, freezing the food faster. Stack them after they are completely frozen.

Note: Never let perishable foods stand at room temperature before they're refrigerated or frozen.

Wraps and Containers

Follow these guidelines for buying storage containers and wraps for refrigerator or freezer.

Containers: Most airtight food storage containers with tight-fitting lids—even disposables—provide adequate protection in the refrigerator. When shopping for freezer-safe containers, however, look for a phrase or an icon on the label or container bottom indicating that they are designed for freezer use.

Baking dishes: When freezing, use freezer-to-oven or freezer-to-microwave dishes and cover them with plastic freezer wrap or heavy-duty foil.*

Glass jars with tight-fitting lids: All major brands of canning jars are acceptable for use in the refrigerator and freezer. If freezing liquid and semiliquid foods, leave headspace in the jar so the food can expand as it freezes (see page 217).

Self-sealing storage bags and plastic wraps: Products are available for both refrigerator and freezer storage.

Regular or heavy-duty foil: When freezing food, use only heavy-duty foil.

*Note: Do not use foil to wrap foods that contain acidic ingredients, such as tomatoes. Acid reacts with the foil, giving the food an off flavor. To refrigerate or freeze a casserole that contains tomatoes or another acidic ingredient, first cover the food with plastic wrap, then with foil; remove the plastic wrap before reheating.

Be Label Conscious

Always take a moment to properly label food before you freeze it. Using a wax crayon or waterproof marking pen, note on the package the name of the item or recipe; the quantity, date, and number of servings; the date it was frozen; and any special information about its use. Follow recommended storage times included in recipes (if given), or see the Storage Charts, which begin below, for additional guidelines.

Thawing and Reheating

See page 52 for important information on safely thawing foods.

Always reheat food to a safe internal temperature before serving. To do so, invest in a food thermometer (see pages 12–13) and follow these guidelines.
● Bring sauces, soups, and gravies to a rolling boil in a covered saucepan, stirring occasionally.
● Heat other leftovers to 165°F.

Storage Chart for Purchased Items

By keeping the pantry, refrigerator, and freezer well stocked with commonly used ingredients, you can cut down on those last-minute trips to the store. Purchase products by "sell by" or expiration dates and follow these guidelines for storing them.

Product:	To store:	Refrigerate (40°F) up to:	Freeze (0°F) up to:
Dairy Products			
Butter	Refrigerate in original packaging; to freeze, overwrap with moisture- and vaporproof wrap.	1 month	6 months
Buttermilk	Refrigerate in original packaging. To freeze, transfer to freezer containers; allow for headspace (see page 217).	7 days	3 months
Cheese, cottage and ricotta	Refrigerate in original packaging.	Use by date on container. If no date given, use within 5 days of purchase.	Do not freeze.
Cheese, hard	See pages 223–224.	See pages 223–224.	See page 224.
Sour cream	Refrigerate in original packaging.	7 days	Do not freeze.
Yogurt	Refrigerate in original packaging; transfer to freezer container to freeze.	7 days	1 month
Eggs			
Hard-cooked, in shells	Refrigerate.	7 days	Do not freeze.
Whites	Refrigerate in tightly covered containers; transfer to freezer container to freeze.	4 days	1 year
Whole, beaten	Beat whites and yolks together and place in freezer container.	Not applicable	1 year
Whole, in shells	Store whole eggs in carton placed in coldest part of refrigerator. Do not wash; do not store in the refrigerator door.	5 weeks after packing date (see page 224)	Do not freeze eggs in shells.
Yolks	Refrigerate unbroken raw yolks covered with water in a tightly covered container.	2 days	Do not freeze.
Meats, Poultry, Fish			
Bacon	Refrigerate in original wrapping; overwrap in freezer wrap to freeze.	7 days	1 month
Sausage, raw	Same as bacon	1 to 2 days	2 months

Storage Chart for Purchased Items (continued)

Product:	To store:	Refrigerate (40°F) up to:	Freeze (0°F) up to:
Meats, Poultry, Fish *(continued)*			
Sausage, smoked links and patties	Refrigerate in original wrapping; overwrap in freezer wrap to freeze.	7 days	1 month
Ham, fully cooked, whole	Wrap in appropriate refrigerator wrap or in moisture- and vaporproof wrap to freeze.	7 days	1 month
Ham, canned (labeled "keep refrigerated")	Chill, unopened, in original can. After opening, wrap in appropriate wrap.	6 months (unopened) 3 to 5 days (opened)	1 month after opening; do not freeze in can.
Hot dogs	Refrigerate in original wrapping. After opening, wrap in appropriate wrap.	2 weeks (unopened) 1 week (opened)	1 month
Lunch meats	Refrigerate in original wrapping. After opening, wrap in appropriate wrap.	2 weeks (unopened) 3 to 5 days (opened)	1 month
Beef, uncooked roasts and steaks	Refrigerate in original wrapping; overwrap in freezer wrap to freeze.	3 to 5 days	1 year
Lamb, uncooked roasts and chops	Refrigerate in original wrapping; overwrap in freezer wrap to freeze.	3 to 5 days	9 months
Pork, uncooked roasts and chops	Refrigerate in original wrapping; overwrap in freezer wrap to freeze.	3 to 5 days	6 months
Ground beef, lamb, pork, veal	Refrigerate in original wrapping; overwrap in freezer wrap to freeze.	1 to 2 days	4 months
Poultry (chicken or turkey), **uncooked, whole**	Refrigerate in original wrapping; overwrap in freezer wrap to freeze.	1 to 2 days	1 year
Poultry (chicken or turkey), **uncooked, pieces**	Refrigerate in original wrapping; overwrap in freezer wrap to freeze.	1 to 2 days	9 months
Ground chicken or turkey	Refrigerate in original wrapping; overwrap in freezer wrap to freeze.	1 to 2 days	4 months
Fish	Store in moisture- and vaporproof wrap in coldest part of refrigerator.	1 to 2 days	3 months
Pantry Staples			
Instant chicken or beef bouillon	Store in a cool, dry place or refrigerate. Check package for expiration date.		
Dried herbs and spices	See page 27.		
Olive oil	Store in a cool, dark place for up to 6 months or refrigerate up to 1 year; see page 501.		
Cooking oil	Store at room temperature for up to 6 months.		
Pasta and rice	Store in airtight containers in a cool, dry place. Store brown rice up to 6 months; dried pasta and long grain white rice indefinitely.		
Produce *(See charts, pages 601–605.)*			
Garlic	Store in a cool, dark, dry place; do not refrigerate or freeze. Store whole bulbs up to 8 weeks; individual cloves 3 to 10 days. Discard shriveled, discolored, or dried-out cloves.		

Storage Chart for Home-Cooked Foods

These general guidelines are for refrigerating and freezing home-baked and home-cooked products. Specific instructions in individual recipes may vary. Follow the recipe's guidelines for best results. For appropriate wrappings and containers for freezing and refrigerating, refer to page 53.

Product:	To store:	Refrigerate (40°F) up to:	Freeze (0°F) up to:
Baked Goods/Desserts			
Bread dough	Follow recipe through mixing and kneading stages. Form dough into a ball. Wrap in moisture- and vaporproof wrap or place in self-sealing freezer bag.	24 hours. Bring to room temperature before shaping.	3 months. Thaw dough for up to 2 hours at room temperature or overnight in the refrigerator. Shape and bake according to recipe.
Breads, quick (baked)	Place in self-sealing plastic bag; seal and store at room temperature up to 3 days. To freeze, see page 125.	Not recommended.	See page 125.
Breads, yeast (baked)	See page 125.	Not recommended.	See page 125.
Cakes	See page 165.	See page 165.	See page 165.
Cheesecakes	To freeze, carefully transfer cooled cheesecake to a freezer-safe plate. Place whole cheesecake in a freezer bag. Or place individual pieces in an airtight container.	3 days	1 month (individual pieces up to 2 weeks). Thaw whole cheesecake in refrigerator overnight or pieces at room temperature 30 minutes.
Cookies, dough and baked	See pages 243 and 257.	See page 243.	See page 243.
Pies, baked and unbaked	See pages 436 and 443.	See pages 436 and 443.	See page 436.
Leftovers			
Chicken nuggets, patties (cooked)	Transfer to appropriate containers. (See "Food Storage and Make-Ahead Cooking," pages 53–54.)	1 to 2 days	3 months
Meat leftovers (cooked meat and meat dishes)	Divide into smaller portions, if appropriate. Transfer to appropriate containers. (See "Food Storage and Make-Ahead Cooking," pages 53–54.)	3 to 4 days	3 months
Poultry dishes (cooked)	Divide into smaller portions, if appropriate. Transfer to appropriate containers. (See "Food Storage and Make-Ahead Cooking," pages 53–54.)	3 to 4 days	4 months
Poultry pieces, plain (cooked)	Transfer to appropriate containers. (See "Food Storage and Make-Ahead Cooking," pages 53–54.)	3 to 4 days	4 months
Soups and stews	Divide into smaller portions. Transfer to appropriate containers. See page 547.	3 days	6 months

Great Meals with Family and Friends

Whether it's a special event or holiday, or simply a casual Friday-night get-together, inviting guests to your home for a meal is a wonderful way to make people feel warm and welcome.

Entertaining 101

The point of entertaining is to enjoy family and friends. The more you keep stress out of the picture, the more relaxed and easygoing your event will be. Keep these tips in mind.

Stay in your comfort zone: Prepare items within your skill level and budget. Consider coming up with a list of "house specialties"—those tried-and-true favorites you can always count on to please guests. If you wish to experiment, complement your house specialties with dishes you've wanted to try.

Keep it simple: Serve the number of people you

Easy Entertaining

Sure, it's a pleasure to acquire beautiful linens and eye-catching tableware, but you don't need a matching set of anything (or even a table) to gather family and friends over food. Just keep this advice in mind.

● No tablecloth? It's absolutely optional, so go without or use a clean sheet, colorful quilt, or light bedspread. Napkins are a must, and paper ones will do.

● Got a drawer full of mismatched flatware and a cupboard packed with mismatched china? A jumble of colors and patterns can add a cheerful and charming note—and may even lead to some interesting conversations. Use a vase of flowers or heirloom serving pieces as a focal point.

● If you're short on table space, use your kitchen counter for a buffet line and use your coffee table and end tables for beverages.

● No table? No problem. Make sure the food you serve can be balanced in one hand and eaten with a spoon or fork. (Chili, soups, or sandwiches, followed by cookies or brownies, are ideal.)

● If someone volunteers to pitch in with the prep or bring a course, say yes! Just be sure to return the favor when that person is the host.

easily can accommodate. Balance make-ahead recipes with those that require a few last-minute finishing details, and round out your menu with convenience items, if you wish.

Invest a little time: Work out a schedule so you know in what order to prepare the food. Make sure your oven, refrigerator, and freezer will hold everything as needed and that oven temperatures for oven-going foods don't conflict.

Invite guests in advance: Give them plenty of time to make arrangements. Allow 10 days for informal events, two weeks or more for formal events. For formal events, send written invitations; for informal events, call or invite guests personally. Be clear about the details—whether it's a barbecue, cocktail buffet, sit-down dinner, etc., and what time the party begins—so your guests will know what to wear and what to expect.

Serve dinner promptly: Follow the customs of your region. Allow about one hour for before-dinner appetizers and beverages, but not much more—you don't want your guests famished, or stuffed, by the time they sit down to dinner.

Don't panic: It happens to the best of cooks—the soup scorches, the soufflé falls. Make light of

Glass

Dinner fork

Knife

Teaspoon

Dinner plate

Napkin

Casual meals: This simple setting is perfect for everyday lunches and dinners. Having soup? Simply place the bowl on the plate. This setting can also be used for casual entertaining for close friends or family.

Bread & salad plate

Water goblet

Wineglass

Salad fork

Dinner fork

Dinner plate

Knife   **Teaspoon**

Napkin

Informal dinners or luncheons: This setting adds a wineglass and bread and/or salad plate. Use it for a special brunch, ladies' luncheon, or a celebratory dinner at home.

Water goblet

Bread & salad plate

Dessert spoon

Butter knife

Dessert fork

Red wineglass

White wineglass

Dinner plate

Napkin

Salad fork

Soup spoon

Dinner fork

Knife

Teaspoon

Formal meals: This setting is for holiday meals and for formal entertaining. When serving dessert, be sure to have cleared all unnecessary plates, utensils, and glasses. See photo, page 59.

it and move on. If you don't let it ruin your evening, neither will your guests. Remember, entertaining isn't about perfection. Most people are happy to simply be part of the fun.

Setting the Table

Getting the simple details just right is easy, and it will add pleasure to your guests' overall enjoyment of a meal. Consider this a primer.

Table-Setting Basics

The correct placement of flatware, plates, and glasses is more than just about tradition. Guests appreciate finding pieces in a particular spot. See photos, page 58, for guidelines.

Tablecloths, place mats, and table runners are optional; napkins, however, are not. Generally dinner napkins are 24 inches square; luncheon and breakfast napkins are a few inches smaller. For casual and family meals, paper napkins are fine. Fold the napkins in an attractive shape and place them on the plates or on the table to the left of or under the forks.

> ## *Setting the Scene*
>
> *When entertaining, a few thoughtful touches can make guests feel truly welcomed into your home.*
>
> ● Call on candles or soft lighting to create warmth; avoid scented candles that may clash with the food you serve.
> ● Whether tied to the season, linked to the occasion, or an expression of your own creativity, centerpieces add a festive note. Just be sure they're not so tall that guests can't see around them.
> ● Music can add to the mood. Keep it at a volume that allows guests to converse comfortably.
> ● Monitor guests' comfort throughout the evening. You may have had your heart set on serving guests on the deck, for example, but if the evening turns chilly, move the party indoors.
> ● If you serve alcoholic beverages, always have a nonalcoholic drink or two on hand. Never press a guest who declines an alcoholic beverage.

Casual family meals: Knives and teaspoons go to the right of the dinner plates; forks and napkins are placed on the left. Glasses are above the knives. A soup spoon and a salad fork may be added (placed on respective sides in order of use); a cup and saucer may be placed to the right.

Informal dinners or luncheons: Arrange knives and spoons to the right of the dinner plate; place dinner forks and salad forks to the left of the plate in order of use. Above each plate place a dessert spoon and dessert fork, pointing left and right, respectively. Arrange glasses, bread/salad plates, and bread knives as directed for formal meals, below.

Formal meals: Place knives (blade edges in) next to plates. Then place spoons to the right of the knives in order of use from outside in. Place forks to the left of the plates in order of use from the outside in. Arrange glasses above the knives in this order: (left to right) water goblets, then wineglasses, placed large to small. Place bread/salad plates above forks. A butter knife may be placed across each bread plate. The cups, saucers, and coffee spoons are placed to the right of the setting, though for formal dinners these items usually are brought to the table when served.

Formal meal dessert

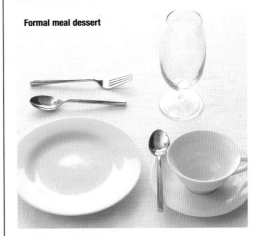

Buffet-Style Service

Serving food buffet style is an easy way to feed groups of eight or more people. Arrange the buffet table in a logical serving sequence with plates first, followed by the main dish, side dishes, salad, and bread. Arrange condiments next to the dish they accompany. Avoid objects that make it awkward to maneuver around the food, such as slender candlesticks or large centerpieces.

If guests will sit at tables, arrange napkins and flatware in settings at the tables. Place water glasses and empty wineglasses on each table before the party and have an open bottle of wine or a pitcher of water at each table. If guests are not going to be seated at tables, arrange the napkins and flatware at the end of the buffet line and set up a separate table with drinks, glasses, and coffee service. Some hosts place desserts on a separate table.

If there is no table seating for the meal, make sure guests can serve themselves, cut the foods with a fork, and eat easily while sitting with a plate in their laps.

Basic Table Manners

Whether you're enjoying an informal family meal or entertaining a group, good manners help put everyone at ease. Here are a few basic customs to practice.

Flatware: As the meal begins, take silverware from the outside of the place setting for the first course and work your way in toward the plate. Never put used flatware back on the table. Generally, when it is not in use you may lay the knife across the back of the plate, slightly to one side, handle on the side. During the meal, lay the fork across the plate at an angle to you, with the handle on the rim.

Passing dishes (family setting): Pass to the right, from person to person. Don't pass over someone, unless it is a child who is unable to hold a large bowl or platter.

Passing dishes (formal setting): Pass to the right and set the dishes in front of the person next to you; don't hand them directly to him or her.

Finger food: When it's not obvious whether a food should be eaten with utensils or with your fingers, watch the host, other guests, or other diners in a restaurant. If still in doubt, use utensils.

Napkins: At informal meals, put your napkin on your lap when you sit down. At formal meals, wait until after the host puts the dinner napkin in his or her lap. Leave the napkin in your lap when not in use until you leave the table. If you leave the table temporarily, place the napkin on your chair or to the left of your plate (folded to conceal soiled parts). At the end of the meal,

leave the napkin loosely folded to the left of your plate; if your plate has been removed, leave the napkin in the center of your place setting.

Talking: Chew and swallow before you talk. Keep your mouth closed while you are chewing.

Smoking: As a general rule, it is not acceptable to smoke at the table.

End of the meal: Lay the knife and fork across your plate with the handles at the four o'clock position to signal you have finished eating. Remain at the table, making conversation, until everyone has finished.

Serving and clearing: Serve from a diner's left and clear from the right. The exception is beverages—wine and water are poured from the right side. Do not clear plates from guests at the table until everyone has finished eating.

Table manners and children: The best way to teach table manners to children is to eat meals with them every day. Make dinner a pleasant family time and practice good table manners yourself; your children will learn by example.

R.S.V.P. Etiquette

An invitation to dine in someone's home, whether offered in person or in writing, usually requires a prompt response. The host needs to know how many to expect at the gathering.

● If you see "R.S.V.P." (a French acronym meaning "please respond") on an invitation, you must respond whether or not you plan to attend. If a telephone number is included, call the host promptly with your response. If a return card is offered, return it by the date requested.

● When no R.S.V.P. is present, you need not respond; however, it is OK to do so, and chances are your host will appreciate it. If the invitation says "regrets only," you should only contact the host if you do not plan to attend.

● If you cannot accept the invitation or want to keep the evening open, decline politely. Once you have accepted an invitation, you are obliged to attend unless a crisis arises.

Appetizers & Snacks

Crab Tartlets, 65

Italian Cheese Log, 67

Cranberry-Barbecue Meatballs, 77

Appetizers & Snacks Essentials

As the host, you can be the life of the party, if you like, or just the life behind the party. Preplanning will keep your get-together lively and running smoothly.

What to Serve

To help you determine what foods to serve, here are some things to keep in mind:

● Select favorite recipes you are comfortable with preparing or try new recipes before the day of the party.

● Include make-ahead appetizers that require only minimal last-minute prep or heating.

● Make sure you will have enough refrigerator space for cold appetizers.

● If appetizers are to be warm, make sure you have enough oven space to warm them and warming plates to maintain their temperature.

● Choose foods that provide contrasting colors, flavors, temperatures, and textures. Balance rich foods with light items and include at least one or two low-calorie and vegetarian choices.

● Plan appetizers from each of the following categories for variety: meat or poultry, fish or seafood, cheese, and vegetables or fruit. If your party lasts over several hours, consider serving hearty appetizers, such as meatballs, kabobs, or some made with pastry or bread.

Beverage Planner

To determine how much to buy for drinks, refer to these guidelines:

Bruschetta, page 75

● When serving bar drinks, allow 1½ ounces of liquor for each drink. You'll get 16 drinks from a 750-milliliter bottle. Allow a quart of mixer—ginger ale or carbonated or tonic water—for every three people.

● Plan on serving a 750-milliliter bottle of wine for every two guests (one bottle for every three to four guests if the wine is served during a meal). Or buy the large 1.5-liter bottle of wine, which will serve four guests (six to eight guests if served during a meal).

● Allow about 12 ounces of beer per guest for every half hour to an hour. For a large crowd, you might want to buy a keg.

● Always have some nonalcoholic beverages on hand. Also consider nonalcoholic wines and beers for nondrinkers.

How Much Is Enough?

Guests will be hungry at events held close to dinnertime, less so at late-evening gatherings. Use the following as a guide:

● For small gatherings of eight to ten guests, three or four types of appetizers are suitable; for parties of up to 45 guests, plan on six varieties; and for more than 45 guests, offer eight choices.

● Plan on about 12 bite-size servings per person for cocktail parties. Hot appetizers and shrimp go fast, so provide plenty.

● Estimate that guests will eat about half of what they would at an all-appetizer party if a full meal is to be served later.

● Keep extra nibbles in your freezer and have the makings for things that can be assembled at the last minute in your pantry or refrigerator. Good options include crackers, cheeses, nuts, candies, smoked meats, olives, and vegetables for dipping.

Creamy Dip for Fruit EASY

Prep: 15 minutes **Chill:** 1 hour **Makes:** 2 cups

- **1 8-ounce package cream cheese, softened**
- **1 8-ounce carton dairy sour cream**
- **¼ cup packed brown sugar**
- **1 teaspoon vanilla**
- **2 to 3 tablespoons milk**
  Assorted fruit, such as dark sweet cherries, strawberries, and/or sliced apple, pear, and banana

1. In a small mixing bowl beat the cream cheese with an electric mixer on low speed until smooth. Gradually add the sour cream, beating until combined. Add the brown sugar and vanilla; beat just until combined. Stir in enough milk to reach dipping consistency. Cover and chill at least 1 hour before serving. Serve with assorted fruit.

Spice Dip for Fruit: Prepare as above, except add ½ teaspoon cinnamon or pumpkin pie spice.

Per 2 tablespoons plain or spice variation: 95 cal., 8 g total fat (5 g sat. fat), 22 mg chol., 52 mg sodium, 5 g carbo., 0 g fiber, 2 g pro. **Daily Values:** 6% vit. A, 4% calcium, 2% iron **Exchanges:** 2 Fat

Lower-Calorie Dip for Fruit: You can substitute reduced-fat cream cheese and light sour cream for the regular cream cheese and sour cream.

Creamy Marshmallow Dip for Fruit: Prepare as above, except omit brown sugar and stir in one 7-ounce jar marshmallow crème.

Per 2 tablespoons lower-calorie or marshmallow variation: 70 cal., 5 g total fat (3 g sat. fat), 13 mg chol., 35 mg sodium, 6 g carbo., 0 g fiber, 1 g pro. **Daily Values:** 4% vit. A, 2% calcium, 1% iron **Exchanges:** ½ Other Carbo., 1 Fat

Dill Dip EASY

Substitute tarragon, basil, or thyme for dill if you want to change the dip's flavor.

Prep: 10 minutes **Chill:** 1 to 24 hours
Makes: about 2 cups

- **1 8-ounce package cream cheese, softened**
- **1 8-ounce carton dairy sour cream**
- **2 tablespoons finely chopped green onion (1)**
- **2 tablespoons snipped fresh dill or 2 teaspoons dried dill**
- **½ teaspoon seasoned salt or salt**
  Milk (optional)
  Assorted vegetable dippers or crackers

1. In a medium mixing bowl beat cream cheese, sour cream, green onion, dill, and seasoned salt with an electric mixer on low speed until fluffy. Cover and chill for 1 to 24 hours. If dip thickens after chilling, stir in 1 to 2 tablespoons milk. Serve with vegetable dippers.

Per 2 tablespoons: 80 cal., 8 g total fat (4 g sat. fat), 22 mg chol., 98 mg sodium, 2 g carbo., 0 g fiber, 2 g pro. **Daily Values:** 6% vit. A, 2% calcium, 2% iron **Exchanges:** 2 Fat

Creamy Blue Cheese Dip: Prepare as above, except omit dill and seasoned salt. Stir ½ cup crumbled blue cheese (2 ounces) and ⅓ cup finely chopped toasted walnuts into the beaten cream cheese mixture.

Per 2 tablespoons: 110 cal., 10 g total fat (6 g sat. fat), 24 mg chol., 100 mg sodium, 2 g carbo., 0 g fiber, 2 g pro. **Daily Values:** 6% vit. A, 4% calcium, 2% iron **Exchanges:** 2 Fat

White Bean Dip

Prep: 20 minutes **Chill:** 4 to 24 hours
Makes: about 2 cups

- **¼ cup soft bread crumbs**
- **2 tablespoons dry white wine or water**
- **1 15- to 19-ounce can white kidney beans or Great Northern beans, rinsed and drained**
- **¼ cup slivered almonds, toasted (see tip, page 265)**
- **2 tablespoons lemon juice**
- **2 tablespoons olive oil**
- **¼ teaspoon salt**
- **⅛ teaspoon cayenne pepper**
- **3 cloves garlic, minced**
- **2 teaspoons snipped fresh oregano or basil or ½ teaspoon dried oregano or basil, crushed**
  Fresh basil (optional)
  Pita chips and/or assorted vegetable dippers

Creamy Dip for Fruit

1. In a small bowl combine bread crumbs and wine; set aside to soak for 10 minutes.

2. In a food processor or blender combine beans, almonds, lemon juice, olive oil, salt, cayenne pepper, and garlic. Cover and process until almost smooth. Add bread crumb mixture; process until smooth. Stir in the oregano. Cover and chill for 4 to 24 hours.

3. To serve, transfer bean mixture to a serving bowl. If desired, garnish with fresh basil. Serve with pita chips.

Per 2 tablespoons: 114 cal., 4 g total fat (0 g sat. fat), 0 mg chol., 16 g carbo., 2 g fiber, 4 g pro.
Daily Values: 2% vit. C, 4% calcium, 6% iron
Exchanges: 1 Starch, 1 Fat

Crab Dip

Serve this flavorful dip with crackers or spoon it into purchased phyllo shells. See photo of Crab Tartlets, page 61.

Prep: 20 minutes **Chill:** 2 to 24 hours
Makes: about 1⅓ cups

> 1 cup cooked crabmeat or one 6-ounce can crabmeat, drained, flaked, and cartilage removed
> ½ cup mayonnaise or salad dressing
> ½ cup dairy sour cream
> 2 tablespoons finely chopped red onion
> 1 tablespoon snipped fresh dill or 1 teaspoon dried dill
> 1 teaspoon finely shredded lemon peel or lime peel
> 1 teaspoon lemon juice or lime juice
> Several dashes bottled hot pepper sauce
> Dash cayenne pepper (optional)
> Salt and black pepper
> Assorted crackers and/or vegetable dippers

1. In a medium bowl stir together the crabmeat, mayonnaise, sour cream, onion, dill, lemon peel, lemon juice, hot pepper sauce, and, if desired, cayenne pepper. Season dip to taste with salt and black pepper.

2. Transfer dip to a serving bowl. Cover and chill for 2 to 24 hours. Serve with crackers.

Per 2 tablespoons: 116 cal., 11 g total fat (2 g sat. fat), 26 mg chol., 127 mg sodium, 1 g carbo., 0 g fiber, 3 g pro.
Daily Values: 64% vit. A, 1% vit. C, 3% calcium, 1% iron
Exchanges: ½ Very Lean Meat, 2 Fat

Crab Tartlets: Prepare as at left, except after Step 1, spoon dip into 30 miniature phyllo dough shells (two 2.1-ounce packages). Or to serve warm, place the phyllo dough shells on a large baking sheet. Spoon dip into shells. Bake in a 350°F oven for 5 to 8 minutes or until heated through. If desired, garnish with additional finely shredded lemon peel and fresh dill sprigs.

Per tartlet: 62 cal., 5 g total fat (1 g sat. fat), 8 mg chol., 52 mg sodium, 3 g carbo., 0 g fiber, 2 g pro.
Daily Values: 1% vit. C, 1% calcium, 1% iron
Exchanges: 1 Fat

Cheesy Sausage and Spinach Dip

Prep: 25 minutes **Bake:** 30 minutes
Oven: 350°F **Makes:** 5 cups

> 8 ounces bulk sweet or hot Italian sausage
> ½ cup chopped onion (1 medium)
> ½ cup chopped red sweet pepper (1 medium)
> 2 cloves garlic, minced
> 2 8-ounce packages reduced-fat cream cheese (Neufchâtel), softened
> 1½ cups finely shredded Parmesan cheese
> ¼ cup milk
> ¼ cup mayonnaise
> ¼ cup light dairy sour cream
> 2 cups chopped fresh spinach leaves
> ⅓ cup mild banana pepper rings, drained and chopped
> French bread slices, toasted, or bagel chips

1. In a large skillet cook sausage, onion, sweet pepper, and garlic until sausage is brown, stirring often. Drain off fat. Set sausage mixture aside to cool.

2. In a large bowl stir together cream cheese, Parmesan cheese, milk, mayonnaise, and sour cream. Add sausage mixture, spinach, and banana peppers; gently stir to combine. Spread mixture into a 9-inch fluted quiche dish or deep-dish pie plate.

3. Bake in a 350°F oven about 30 minutes or until bubbly. Serve with toasted bread slices.

Make-ahead directions: Prepare as above through Step 2. Cover and chill for up to 24 hours. Uncover and bake about 40 minutes or until heated through.

Per ¼ cup: 146 cal., 7 g total fat (6 g sat. fat), 32 mg chol., 2 g carbo., 0 g fiber, 7 g pro.
Daily Values: 14% vit. A, 15% vit. C, 11% calcium, 2% iron
Exchanges: 1 Medium-Fat Meat, 1½ Fat

Chunky Guacamole

For a kicked-up version of this guacamole, stir in one seeded, finely chopped jalapeño chile pepper; dairy sour cream; and/or snipped fresh cilantro.

Prep: 20 minutes **Chill:** 1 hour **Makes:** 2 cups

- **2 medium roma tomatoes, seeded and finely chopped**
- **¼ of a small red onion, finely chopped**
- **2 tablespoons lime juice**
- **1 tablespoon olive oil**
- **¼ teaspoon salt**
- **⅛ teaspoon black pepper**
- **1 or 2 cloves garlic, minced**
- **2 ripe avocados, halved, seeded, peeled, and coarsely mashed**
- **Tortilla chips**

1. In a bowl combine tomato, red onion, lime juice, olive oil, salt, pepper, and garlic. Gently stir in avocados. Cover the surface with plastic wrap. Chill for up to 1 hour. Serve with tortilla chips.

Per 2 tablespoons: 48 cal., 5 g total fat (1 g sat. fat),
0 mg chol., 39 mg sodium, 3 g carbo., 1 g fiber, 1 g pro.
Daily Values: 4% vit. A, 7% vit. C, 2% iron
Exchanges: 1 Fat

 ## Mexican Seven-Layer Dip

Prep: 15 minutes **Chill:** 4 to 24 hours
Makes: 16 servings

- **1 9-ounce can bean dip**
- **¼ cup picante sauce or taco sauce**
- **1 8-ounce container refrigerated guacamole**
- **1 8-ounce carton dairy sour cream**
- **1 cup shredded cheddar or taco cheese**
- **¼ cup sliced green onion (2)**
- **2 tablespoons sliced, pitted ripe olives**
- **⅔ cup chopped, seeded tomato (1 medium)**
- **8 cups tortilla chips or crackers**

1. Combine bean dip and picante sauce. Spread mixture into a ¼-inch-thick, 9×5-inch rectangle on a serving platter. Carefully spread guacamole and sour cream over bean dip mixture. Top with cheese, green onion, and olives. Cover and chill for 4 to 24 hours.

2. Before serving, sprinkle with chopped tomato. Serve with tortilla chips.

Per ¼ cup dip + ½ cup chips: 176 cal., 12 g total fat
(4 g sat. fat), 14 mg chol., 281 mg sodium, 14 g carbo., 2 g fiber,
5 g pro.
Daily Values: 7% vit. A, 4% vit. C, 9% calcium, 4% iron
Exchanges: ½ Starch, ½ Other Carbo., 2½ Fat

Black-Eyed Peas Salsa

Black-Eyed Peas Salsa

Prep: 15 minutes **Chill:** overnight **Makes:** 2 cups

- **1 15-ounce can black-eyed peas, rinsed and drained**
- **¼ cup thinly sliced green onion (2)**
- **¼ cup finely chopped red sweet pepper**
- **2 tablespoons cooking oil**
- **2 tablespoons cider vinegar**
- **1 to 2 fresh jalapeño chile peppers, seeded and chopped (see tip, page 74)**
- **¼ teaspoon cracked black pepper**
- **2 cloves garlic, minced**
- **Tortilla chips or assorted crackers**

1. In a bowl combine black-eyed peas, green onion, sweet pepper, oil, vinegar, jalapeño pepper, black pepper, dash *salt,* and garlic. Cover and chill overnight. Serve with tortilla chips.

Per 2 tablespoons: 44 cal., 2 g total fat (0 g sat. fat),
2 mg chol., 86 mg sodium, 5 g carbo., 1 g fiber, 2 g pro.
Daily Values: 2% vit. A, 9% vit. C, 1% calcium, 1% iron
Exchanges: ½ Starch

Salsa

Prep: 30 minutes **Chill:** 2 to 48 hours
Makes: 2 cups

- **1 cup seeded and finely chopped tomato (3 small)**
- **⅓ cup finely chopped red onion (1 small)**
- **2 to 4 fresh serrano, habañero, or jalapeño chile peppers, seeded and finely chopped (see tip, page 74)**
- **2 tablespoons lime juice**

2 tablespoons snipped fresh cilantro

¼ teaspoon salt

4 cloves garlic, minced

1. In a bowl stir together the tomato, onion, chile pepper, lime juice, cilantro, salt, and garlic. Cover and chill for 2 to 48 hours.

Tomatillo Salsa: Prepare as above, except omit one tomato. Add 4 to 6 tomatillos, husked, rinsed, and finely chopped (about 1 cup), or one 11- to 13-ounce can tomatillos, rinsed, drained, and finely chopped.

Per 2 tablespoons salsa or tomatillo variation: 6 cal., 0 g total fat (0 g sat. fat), 0 mg chol., 38 mg sodium, 1 g carbo., 0 g fiber, 0 g pro.
Daily Values: 2% vit. A, 7% vit. C, 1% iron
Exchanges: Free

Peppered Herb Cheese Ball

See photo of Italian Cheese Log, page 61.

Prep: 25 minutes **Chill:** 4 to 24 hours
Makes: 1½ cups

3 tablespoons snipped fresh chives

2 tablespoons snipped fresh parsley

1 8-ounce package cream cheese, softened

4 ounces goat cheese

3 tablespoons snipped fresh basil

¼ to ½ teaspoon cracked black pepper

1 clove garlic, minced

Assorted crackers

1. In a shallow dish combine 1 tablespoon of the chives and all of the parsley; set aside. In a medium mixing bowl beat cream cheese and goat cheese with an electric mixer on medium speed until smooth. Beat in remaining 2 tablespoons chives, the basil, pepper, and garlic.

2. Form mixture into a ball. Roll cheese ball in chives mixture. Wrap and chill for 4 to 24 hours. Serve with crackers.

Per 2 tablespoons: 92 cal., 9 g total fat (6 g sat. fat), 25 mg chol., 91 mg sodium, 1 g carbo., 0 g fiber, 3 g pro.
Daily Values: 8% vit. A, 2% vit. C, 3% calcium
Exchanges: 2 Fat

Italian Cheese Log: Prepare as above, except substitute fontina cheese for the goat cheese and beat 2 ounces finely chopped hard salami and 2 tablespoons finely chopped roasted red sweet pepper into the cheese mixture; form into a log. Serve with water crackers or baguette slices.

Per 2 tablespoons: 121 cal., 5 g total fat (6 g sat. fat), 36 mg chol., 220 mg sodium, 1 g carbo., 0 g fiber, 5 g pro.
Daily Values: 9% vit. A, 10% vit. C, 7% calcium, 2% iron
Exchanges: ½ High-Fat Meat, 1½ Fat

Smoky Cheese Ball

Prep: 15 minutes **Chill:** 4 to 24 hours
Stand: 45 minutes **Makes:** 3½ cups

2 8-ounce packages cream cheese

2 cups finely shredded smoked cheddar, Swiss, or Gouda cheese

½ cup butter or margarine

2 tablespoons milk

2 teaspoons steak sauce

1 cup finely chopped nuts, toasted (see tip, page 265)

Assorted crackers

1. In a mixing bowl let cream cheese, shredded cheese, and butter stand at room temperature for 30 minutes. Add milk and steak sauce; beat until fluffy. Cover and chill for 4 to 24 hours.

2. Shape mixture into a ball; roll in nuts. Let stand for 15 minutes. Serve with crackers.

Per 2 tablespoons: 146 cal., 14 g total fat (8 g sat. fat), 34 mg chol., 2 g carbo., 0 g fiber, 4 g pro.
Daily Values: 10% vit. A, 8% calcium, 2% iron
Exchanges: 3 Fat

Smoked Salmon-Pesto Spread

Prep: 20 minutes **Chill:** 6 to 24 hours
Stand: 15 minutes **Makes:** about 2½ cups

1 4-ounce piece plain smoked salmon, skin and bones removed and flaked

½ of an 8-ounce package cream cheese, softened

¼ cup purchased basil pesto

1 8-ounce package cream cheese, softened

¼ cup butter or margarine, softened

2 tablespoons snipped fresh chives

¼ teaspoon coarsely ground black pepper

Assorted crackers or sliced baguette

1. Line a 3-cup mold with plastic wrap. In a bowl stir together salmon and the half package cream cheese. Spread evenly in bottom of mold. Spread pesto over salmon mixture. In a bowl stir together the 8 ounces cream cheese, the butter, chives, and pepper. Drop by spoonfuls over pesto; spread evenly. Cover and chill for 6 to 24 hours.

2. To serve, uncover and invert mold onto a serving platter; remove plastic wrap. Let stand at room temperature for 15 minutes. Serve with assorted crackers.

Per 2 tablespoons: 109 cal., 11 g total fat (5 g sat. fat), 97 mg chol., 135 mg sodium, 1 g carbo., 0 g fiber, 3 g pro.
Daily Values: 6% vit. A, 2% calcium, 1% iron
Exchanges: 2½ Fat

Chicken Liver Pâté

The flavors of bacon and a splash of white wine make this pâté a best-loved classic.

Prep: 10 minutes **Cook:** 10 minutes
Chill: 3 to 24 hours **Makes:** 1 cup

- 2 slices bacon
- 8 ounces chicken livers
- ½ cup chopped onion (1 medium)
- 4 cloves garlic, minced
- 2 tablespoons dry white wine or milk
- ¼ teaspoon salt
- ¼ teaspoon black pepper
- ¼ teaspoon ground nutmeg or ⅛ teaspoon ground allspice
  Snipped fresh parsley or chives (optional)
  Assorted crackers

1. In a large skillet cook bacon until crisp. Remove from skillet, reserving 2 tablespoons drippings. Drain and crumble bacon; set aside.

2. Add chicken livers, onion, and garlic to reserved drippings in skillet. Cook and stir over medium heat about 5 minutes or until livers are no longer pink; cool slightly.

3. In a food processor or blender combine crumbled bacon, chicken liver mixture, wine, salt, pepper, and nutmeg. Cover and process or blend until combined (mixture will be soft). Line a 1-cup mold or bowl with plastic wrap; spoon in liver mixture. (Or spoon liver mixture directly into a crock or ramekin or several small ramekins.) Cover and chill for 3 to 24 hours.

4. To serve, uncover and invert mold or bowl onto a platter; remove plastic wrap. (Or place ramekin or crock on a serving plate.) If desired, sprinkle with parsley. Serve with crackers.

Per 2 tablespoons: 82 cal., 5 g total fat (2 g sat. fat), 103 mg chol., 140 mg sodium, 2 g carbo., 0 g fiber, 6 g pro. **Daily Values:** 50% vit. A, 8% vit. C, 1% calcium, 15% iron **Exchanges:** 1 Medium-Fat Meat

Swiss Fondue

Kirsch, a cherry-flavored brandy, complements the Emmentaler and Gruyère cheeses perfectly. A dry sherry is a fine option too.

Start to Finish: 50 minutes
Oven: 350°F **Makes:** 3½ cups

- 3 cups shredded Gruyère or Swiss cheese (12 ounces)
- 2 cups shredded Emmentaler, Gruyère, or Swiss cheese (8 ounces)
- 3 tablespoons all-purpose flour
- 12 1-inch-thick slices herb bread or French bread, cut into 1-inch cubes, and/or 3 cups broccoli or cauliflower florets
- 1½ cups dry white wine
- ¼ cup milk
- 2 tablespoons Kirsch or dry sherry
- ⅛ teaspoon ground nutmeg
- ⅛ teaspoon white pepper
  Paprika (optional)

1. Let shredded cheeses stand at room temperature for 30 minutes. Toss cheeses with the flour; set aside.

2. Meanwhile, place bread cubes on a baking sheet and bake in a 350°F oven for 5 to 7 minutes or until crisp and toasted; set aside. To precook broccoli or cauliflower, bring a small amount of water to boiling in a saucepan; add florets. Simmer, covered, about 3 minutes or until crisp-tender. Drain and rinse with cold water; set aside.

3. In a large saucepan heat wine over medium heat until small bubbles rise to the surface. Just before wine boils, reduce heat to low and stir in the cheese mixture, a little at a time, stirring constantly and making sure cheese melts before adding more. Stir until mixture bubbles gently. Stir in milk, Kirsch, nutmeg, and white pepper.

4. Transfer cheese mixture to a fondue pot. Keep mixture bubbling gently over a fondue burner. (If cheese mixture becomes too thick, stir in a little more milk.) If desired, sprinkle cheese mixture with paprika. Serve with toasted bread cubes and/or vegetable florets.

Per ¼ cup sauce + 1 slice cubed bread: 287 cal., 15 g total fat (9 g sat. fat), 48 mg chol., 299 mg sodium, 16 g carbo., 1 g fiber, 16 g pro. **Daily Values:** 10% vit. A, 49% calcium, 5% iron **Exchanges:** 1 Starch, 2 High-Fat Meat

Supreme Pizza Fondue

Supreme Pizza Fondue

Use a meatless spaghetti sauce, such as marinara, in this recipe.

Prep: 20 minutes **Cook:** 10 minutes
Makes: 5½ cups

- **4 ounces bulk Italian sausage**
- **1 small onion, finely chopped**
- **1 clove garlic, minced**
- **1 26-ounce jar spaghetti sauce**
- **1 cup chopped fresh mushrooms**
- **⅔ cup chopped pepperoni or Canadian-style bacon**
- **1 teaspoon dried basil or oregano, crushed**
- **½ cup chopped pitted ripe olives (optional)**
- **¼ cup finely chopped green sweet pepper (optional)**
  Cooked tortellini, Italian flatbread (focaccia) or Italian bread cubes, or mozzarella and/ or provolone cheese cubes

1. In a large skillet cook the sausage, onion, and garlic until meat is brown. Drain off fat.

2. Add spaghetti sauce, mushrooms, pepperoni, and basil. Heat to boiling; reduce heat. Simmer, covered, for 10 minutes. If desired, stir in ripe olives and sweet pepper. If using sweet pepper, cover and cook 5 minutes more or until sweet pepper is tender. Serve with tortellini.

Slow cooker directions: Prepare as above through Step 1, except in a 3½- or 4-quart slow cooker combine spaghetti sauce, mushrooms,

pepperoni, and basil. Stir in the sausage mixture. Cover and cook on low-heat setting for 3 hours. If desired, stir in ripe olives and sweet pepper. Cover; cook on low-heat setting for 15 minutes more. Serve with tortellini.

Per ¼ cup: 59 cal., 4 g total fat (2 g sat. fat), 10 mg chol., 296 mg sodium, 3 g carbo., 1 g fiber, 3 g pro.
Daily Values: 1% vit. A, 8% vit. C, 1% calcium, 11% iron
Exchanges: ½ High-Fat Meat, ½ Vegetable

Chili con Queso FAST

Pasteurized prepared cheese product melts to a wonderfully smooth consistency in this classic tortilla dip.

Start to Finish: 30 minutes **Makes:** 2½ cups

- **½ cup finely chopped onion (1 medium)**
- **1 tablespoon butter or margarine**
- **1⅓ cups chopped, seeded tomato (2 medium)**
- **1 4-ounce can diced green chile peppers**
- **8 ounces pasteurized prepared cheese product, cut into cubes**
- **2 ounces Monterey Jack cheese with jalapeño peppers, shredded (½ cup)**
- **1 teaspoon cornstarch**
  Tortilla chips or corn chips

1. In a medium saucepan cook onion in butter until tender. Stir in tomato and undrained chile peppers. Heat to boiling; reduce heat. Simmer, uncovered, for 10 minutes.

2. Toss cheeses with cornstarch. Gradually add cheese mixture to saucepan, stirring until cheese melts. Heat through. Serve with chips.

White Chili con Queso: Prepare as above, except substitute one 8-ounce package cream cheese, cubed and softened, for the cheese product.

Slow cooker directions: Prepare as above, except omit butter and skip Step 1. Toss cheeses with cornstarch in a 2½- to 3½-quart slow cooker. Add the onion, tomato, and chile peppers. Cover and cook on low-heat setting for 3 to 3½ hours or on high-heat setting for 1½ hours. Whisk well before serving. Keep warm on low-heat setting.

Per ¼ cup chili or white chili variation: 124 cal., 8 g total fat (6 g sat. fat), 28 mg chol., 386 mg sodium, 4 g carbo., 0 g fiber, 6 g pro.
Daily Values: 16% vit. A, 12% vit. C, 18% calcium, 2% iron
Exchanges: 1 High-Fat Meat

Brie en Croûte

Jalapeño pepper jelly adds a little sweetness and some zing to this rich, buttery appetizer.

Prep: 30 minutes **Bake:** 20 minutes **Oven:** 400°F
Stand: 10 minutes **Makes:** 12 servings

- ½ of a 17.3-ounce package frozen puff pastry sheets, thawed (1 sheet)
- 2 tablespoons jalapeño pepper jelly, apple jelly, or apricot jelly
- 2 4½-ounce rounds Brie or Camembert cheese
- 2 tablespoons chopped nuts, toasted (see tip, page 265)
- 1 egg, slightly beaten
- 1 tablespoon water
  Apple and/or pear slices

1. Grease a baking sheet; set aside. Unfold pastry on a lightly floured surface; roll into a 16×10-inch rectangle. Cut into two 8-inch circles (see photo 1, right); reserve trimmings.

2. Spread jelly on top of each cheese round. Sprinkle with nuts; lightly press nuts into jelly.

3. Combine egg and water; set aside. Place pastry circles over rounds; invert rounds and pastry. Brush pastry edges with a little egg mixture. Bring pastry edges up and over rounds, pleating and pinching edges to cover and seal (see photo 2, right). Trim excess pastry. Place rounds, smooth sides up, on prepared baking sheet. Brush egg mixture over tops and sides. Cut small slits for steam to escape. Using hors d'oeuvre cutters, cut shapes from reserved pastry. Brush shapes with egg mixture; place on rounds.

4. Bake in a 400°F oven for 20 to 25 minutes or until pastry is golden brown. Let stand for 10 to 20 minutes before serving. Serve with fruit.

Brie en Croûte with Caramelized Onion: Prepare as above, except omit jelly. Cut 1 small onion into thin wedges. In a small saucepan cook onion in 2 teaspoons hot butter or margarine, covered, over medium-low heat 15 to 20 minutes or until tender and golden, stirring occasionally. Meanwhile, cut up any large pieces in 2 tablespoons mango chutney; spread chutney over top of each cheese round. Top with onions and nuts. Continue as directed in Step 3.

Brie en Croûte with Mushrooms: Prepare as above, except omit the jelly and nuts. In a large skillet cook 1 medium chopped shallot in 1 table-spoon hot butter over medium heat for 2 minutes. Meanwhile, chop 8 ounces fresh mushrooms; add to shallots and cook until tender. Stir in 1 tablespoon dry or cream sherry; 1 teaspoon dried thyme, crushed; ¼ teaspoon salt; and ⅛ teaspoon black pepper. Cook and stir until liquid has evaporated. Continue as directed in Step 3.

Per ¹⁄₁₂ of jelly, onion, or mushroom variations: 182 cal., 13 g total fat (4 g sat. fat), 39 mg chol., 215 mg sodium, 10 g carbo., 0 g fiber, 6 g pro.
Daily Values: 145% vit. A, 4% calcium, 1% iron
Exchanges: ½ Other Carbo., 1 High-Fat Meat, 1 Fat

1. Using an 8-inch round cake pan as a pattern, carefully cut two circles from the dough rectangle. Reserve the trimmings to use for garnishing.

2. Gently bring the pastry edges up and over the cheese round, pleating and pinching to seal. Trim excess pastry so it is not too thick.

Praline-Topped Brie

Prep: 10 minutes **Bake:** 15 minutes
Oven: 350°F **Makes:** 10 servings

- 1 13-ounce round Brie or Camembert cheese
- ½ cup orange marmalade
- 2 tablespoons packed brown sugar
- ⅓ cup coarsely chopped pecans, toasted (see tip, page 265)
  Baguette slices, toasted, and/or assorted plain crackers

1. Place the round of cheese in a shallow ovenproof serving dish or pie plate. In a small bowl stir together orange marmalade and brown sugar. Spread on top of cheese. Sprinkle with toasted pecans.

2. Bake in a 350°F oven about 15 minutes or until cheese is slightly softened and topping is bubbly. Serve with toasted baguette slices.

Per ¹⁄₁₀ of round: 198 cal., 13 g total fat (7 g sat. fat), 37 mg chol., 242 mg sodium, 14 g carbo., 0 g fiber, 8 g pro.
Daily Values: 5% vit. A, 1% vit. C, 8% calcium, 2% iron
Exchanges: 1 Other Carbo., 1 High-Fat Meat, 1 Fat

Fresh Spring Rolls

others covered). Fold bottom of rice paper over filling; arrange two shrimp halves across filling; fold in paper sides. Tightly roll up the rice paper and filling. Place, seam side down, on a large plate. Repeat with remaining rice paper, filling, and shrimp. Cover and chill for up to 6 hours.

5. For sauce, in a saucepan combine ½ cup *water* and the sugar. Bring to boiling over medium heat, stirring occasionally until sugar is dissolved. Remove from heat. Stir in vinegar, fish sauce, and the 1 tablespoon shredded carrot. Serve spring rolls with sauce.

Per spring roll + about 2 teaspoons sauce: 65 cal., 0 g total fat (0 g sat. fat), 11 mg chol., 57 mg sodium, 13 g carbo., 1 g fiber, 2 g pro. **Daily Values:** 16% vit. A, 7% vit. C, 2% calcium, 5% iron **Exchanges:** ½ Starch, ½ Other Carbo.

Fresh Spring Rolls

Start to Finish: 50 minutes
Chill: up to 6 hours **Makes:** 24 rolls

  2 ounces dried rice vermicelli noodles
 24 medium shrimp, peeled and deveined
  2 cups shredded napa cabbage
  1 cup shredded carrot
  ½ cup fresh cilantro leaves
  ½ cup fresh mint leaves or Italian parsley
 24 round rice paper wrappers (8½-inch diameter)
  2 tablespoons sugar
  2 tablespoons rice vinegar
  1 tablespoon fish sauce (nuoc nam or nam pla)
  1 tablespoon finely shredded carrot

1. In a saucepan cook the vermicelli in boiling lightly salted water for 3 minutes; drain. Rinse under cold water; drain well. Use kitchen shears to snip the noodles into small pieces; set aside.

2. In a large saucepan cook the shrimp in boiling lightly salted water for 1 to 2 minutes or until opaque; drain. Rinse with cold water; drain again. Halve the shrimp lengthwise; set aside.

3. In a large bowl combine cooked vermicelli, cabbage, the 1 cup shredded carrot, cilantro, and mint leaves; set aside.

4. Pour 1 cup warm water into a shallow dish. Dip rice papers, one at a time, into water; gently shake off excess water. Place wet rice papers between clean, damp, 100-percent-cotton kitchen towels; let stand for 10 minutes. Brush any dry edges with a little additional water. Place a well-rounded tablespoon of cabbage mixture across lower third of a softened rice paper (keep

Egg Rolls

Prep: 25 minutes **Cook:** 2 minutes per batch
Oven: 300°F **Makes:** 8 rolls

  8 egg roll skins
  1 recipe Pork Filling
     Cooking oil for deep-fat frying
 1⅓ cups bottled sweet-and-sour sauce

1. For each egg roll, place an egg roll skin on a surface with a corner pointing toward you. Spoon about ¼ cup Pork Filling across and just below center of egg roll skin. Fold bottom corner over filling, tucking it under on the other side. Fold side corners over filling, forming an envelope shape. Roll egg roll toward remaining corner. Moisten top corner with water; press firmly to seal.

2. In a deep-fat fryer heat 2 inches cooking oil to 365°F. Fry egg rolls, a few at a time, for 2 to 3 minutes or until golden. Drain on paper towels. Keep warm in a 300°F oven while frying remaining egg rolls. Serve egg rolls with sauce.

Pork Filling: In a skillet cook 8 ounces ground pork, 1 teaspoon grated fresh ginger, and 1 clove garlic, minced, for 2 to 3 minutes or until meat is brown; drain fat. Add ½ cup finely chopped bok choy, ½ cup chopped water chestnuts, ½ cup shredded carrot, and ¼ cup finely chopped onion. Cook and stir for 2 minutes. Combine 2 tablespoons soy sauce, 2 teaspoons cornstarch, ½ teaspoon sugar, and ¼ teaspoon salt; add to skillet. Cook and stir for 1 minute; cool.

Per egg roll + 2 tablespoons sauce: 240 cal., 3 g total fat (1 g sat. fat), 16 mg chol., 794 mg sodium, 44 g carbo., 1 g fiber, 9 g pro. **Daily Values:** 46% vit. A, 17% vit. C, 8% calcium, 10% iron **Exchanges:** 2 Starch, 1 Other Carbo., ½ Lean Meat

California Sushi Rolls `NO FAT`

Start to Finish: 30 minutes **Makes:** 12 sushi pieces

- 2 **sheets nori (seaweed) (each about 8 inches square)**
- 1 **recipe Sushi Rice**
  Desired fillings (such as small carrot, zucchini, or cucumber sticks; avocado slices; flake-style imitation crabmeat; lox-style smoked salmon; and/or small peeled, deveined, and cooked shrimp)
- 1 **recipe Honey-Ginger Sauce**

1. After spreading the rice onto the nori sheet, arrange desired fillings to one side of the center.

2. Using the mat, roll up the nori, starting with the side with the fillings and lifting the mat away from you.

1. Lay each nori sheet on a sushi mat lined with plastic wrap; with damp fingers, spread 1 cup of Sushi Rice over each sheet, leaving a 1-inch border along one edge uncovered. Arrange desired fillings to one side of center (see photo 1, right).

2. Roll up the nori, starting with the filled side and rolling toward the 1-inch, unfilled edge. (To shape a tight, even roll, place your hands under the closest mat edge. Carefully lift and roll the rice-topped nori away from you; see photo 2, right.) Press the unfilled edge over top, brushing with water to seal, if necessary.

3. Cut each roll into six pieces; arrange on a platter. If desired, cover and chill for up to 4 hours. Serve with Honey-Ginger Sauce.

Sushi Rice: In a fine-mesh sieve wash ½ cup short grain rice under cold running water, rubbing grains together with your fingers. In a saucepan combine rinsed rice, 1 cup cold water, 2 tablespoons rice vinegar, and ¼ teaspoon salt. Bring to boiling; reduce heat. Simmer, covered, for 15 minutes (rice should be sticky). Remove from heat; stir in ¼ cup finely shredded carrot, 1 tablespoon sugar, and, if desired, 1 tablespoon sake or dry sherry. Cover; cool to room temperature. (Rice can be prepared ahead; cover and chill for up to 3 days.) Makes about 2 cups.

Honey-Ginger Sauce: In a small saucepan combine ⅓ cup honey, ¼ cup water, 2 tablespoons plum sauce, 2 tablespoons soy sauce, and one 2-inch piece fresh ginger, peeled and thinly sliced. Bring to boiling, stirring frequently; reduce heat. Simmer, uncovered, for 15 to 20 minutes or until slightly thickened. Strain into a small bowl; cool. Cover and chill. Makes a scant ¾ cup.

Per piece + 1 tablespoon sauce: 71 cal., 0 g total fat (0 g sat. fat), 0 mg chol., 206 mg sodium, 17 g carbo., 0 g fiber, 1 g pro.
Daily Values: 7% vit. A, 4% vit. C, 1% calcium, 3% iron
Exchanges: ½ Starch, ½ Other Carbo.

⭐*FAVORITE* Spinach Phyllo Triangles

Prep: 50 minutes **Bake:** 15 minutes
Oven: 375°F **Makes:** 36 triangles

- 1 **10-ounce package frozen chopped spinach**
- ½ **cup finely chopped onion (1 medium)**
- 1 **clove garlic, minced**
- 1½ **cups finely crumbled feta cheese (6 ounces)**
- ½ **teaspoon dried oregano, crushed**
- 24 **sheets frozen phyllo dough (9×14-inch rectangles), thawed**
- ½ **cup butter, melted**

1. For filling, cook the spinach, onion, and garlic according to spinach package directions. Drain well in a colander. Press mixture with the back of a spoon to remove excess moisture. Combine spinach mixture with feta cheese and oregano.

2. Place one sheet of phyllo dough on a cutting board or other flat surface. Lightly brush with some of the melted butter. Place another sheet of phyllo on top; brush with butter. (Keep remaining phyllo covered with plastic wrap until needed.)

3. Cut the two layered sheets lengthwise into three equal strips, each 14 inches long. Spoon a well-rounded teaspoon of filling about 1 inch from an end of each dough strip. To fold into a triangle, bring a corner over filling so the short edge lines up with the side edge (see photo, page 73). Continue folding the triangular shape along the strip until the other end is reached. Repeat with remaining phyllo, butter, and filling.

4. Place triangles on a baking sheet; brush with butter. Bake in a 375°F oven about 15 minutes or until golden. Serve warm.

Make-ahead directions: Prepare through Step 3, page 72. Place the unbaked triangles in a covered freezer container; freeze for up to 2 months. Brush with additional melted butter and bake as directed. Do not thaw the triangles before baking.

Per 2 triangles: 124 cal., 8 g total fat (4 g sat. fat), 23 mg chol., 239 mg sodium, 9 g carbo., 1 g fiber, 3 g pro.
Daily Values: 50% vit. A, 2% vit. C, 6% calcium, 4% iron
Exchanges: ½ Other Carbo., ½ High-Fat Meat, 1 Fat

Starting at the filling end of each strip, fold a corner over the filling to form a triangle. Continue the triangular fold for the length of the strip.

Quesadillas

Try some quesadillas with exotic new flavors, such as the two variations that follow this recipe.

Prep: 15 minutes   **Cook:** 4 minutes per batch
Oven: 300°F   **Makes:** 9 servings

    Nonstick spray coating
6   7- or 8-inch flour tortillas
**1½   cups shredded Colby Jack cheese
    (6 ounces)**
**3   tablespoons canned diced green chile
    peppers, drained**
3   tablespoons chopped green onion (1½)
**3   slices bacon, crisp-cooked, drained, and
    crumbled**
    Salsa (optional)

1. Coat one side of each tortilla with cooking spray. Place tortillas, sprayed sides down, on a cutting board or waxed paper. Sprinkle ¼ cup of the cheese over half of each tortilla. Top cheese with chile peppers, green onion, and bacon. Fold tortillas in half, pressing gently.

2. Heat a 10-inch nonstick skillet over medium heat for 1 minute. Cook quesadillas, two at a time, over medium heat for 4 to 6 minutes or until light brown, turning once. Remove quesadillas from skillet; place on a baking sheet. Keep warm in a 300°F oven. Repeat with remaining quesadillas. To serve, cut each quesadilla into three wedges. If desired, serve with salsa.

Manchego and Mushroom Quesadillas: Prepare as above, except substitute 6 ounces manchego cheese, shredded, for the Colby Jack cheese.

Omit the chile peppers and bacon. In a medium skillet heat 1 tablespoon butter over medium heat. Add 6 ounces sliced button mushrooms (about 2¼ cups). Cook about 10 minutes or until mushrooms are tender and liquid is evaporated, stirring occasionally. Stir in ½ cup chopped cooked ham or Canadian-style bacon, ¼ cup finely chopped red sweet pepper, the 3 tablespoons green onion, 2 tablespoons snipped fresh cilantro, and ¼ teaspoon crushed red pepper. To assemble, sprinkle ¼ cup of the manchego cheese over half of each tortilla. Top with mushroom mixture. Fold tortillas in half, pressing gently. Cook quesadillas as directed in Step 2, at left.

Per 2 wedges Colby Jack or manchego variation: 150 cal., 9 g total fat (5 g sat. fat), 19 mg chol., 267 mg sodium, 10 g carbo., 0 g fiber, 6 g pro.
Daily Values: 4% vit. A, 4% vit. C, 16% calcium, 4% iron
Exchanges: ½ Starch, 1 High-Fat Meat

Olive and Walnut Quesadillas: Prepare as at left, except substitute 4 ounces shredded mozzarella cheese and 2 ounces shredded Parmesan cheese for the Colby Jack cheese. Omit chile peppers, green onion, and bacon. Sprinkle ¼ cup of the cheese over half of each tortilla. In a small bowl combine ¼ cup chopped pitted ripe olives, 3 tablespoons toasted walnuts, and 2 tablespoons snipped fresh oregano or ½ teaspoon dried oregano, crushed. Sprinkle over cheese. Continue as directed in Step 2, at left.

Per 2 wedges: 122 cal., 6 g total fat (2 g sat. fat), 8 mg chol., 257 mg sodium, 11 g carbo., 1 g fiber, 6 g pro.
Daily Values: 2% vit. A, 1% vit. C, 16% calcium, 5% iron
Exchanges: ½ Starch, 1 Medium-Fat Meat

Manchego and Mushroom Quesadillas

Nachos

Nachos

For an eye-catching plate of nachos, use colorful tortilla chips.

Prep: 15 minutes **Bake:** 20 minutes
Oven: 350°F **Makes:** 8 servings

- 5 cups bite-size tortilla chips (6 ounces)
- 1 pound ground beef
- 1 15-ounce can black beans or pinto beans, rinsed and drained
- 1 cup bottled chunky salsa
- 1½ cups shredded cheddar, Colby Jack, or Mexican cheese blend (6 ounces)
  Optional toppings (such as thinly sliced green onion, snipped fresh cilantro, seeded and chopped fresh jalapeño chile pepper [see tip, right], dairy sour cream, and bottled chunky salsa)

1. Spread half of the tortilla chips on an 11- or 12-inch ovenproof platter or pizza pan; set aside.

2. In a large skillet cook beef over medium heat until brown. Drain off fat. Add beans and the 1 cup salsa to beef. Spoon half of the mixture over chips. Sprinkle with half the cheese.

3. Bake in a 350°F oven about 10 minutes or until cheese melts. Remove from oven. Top with remaining chips, beef mixture, and cheese. Bake about 10 minutes more or until cheese melts. If desired, top with green onion, cilantro, jalapeño pepper, sour cream, and/or additional salsa.

Per cup: 374 cal., 21 g total fat (9 g sat. fat), 61 mg chol., 713 mg sodium, 26 g carbo., 5 g fiber, 23 g pro.
Daily Values: 7% vit. A, 24% calcium, 13% iron
Exchanges: 1½ Starch, 1½ Medium-Fat Meat, 1 High-Fat Meat, 1 Fat

Two-Bean Nachos: Prepare as at left, except omit beef. Add a second 15-ounce can black beans or pinto beans, rinsed and drained, choosing the alternate to what was added first. Stir the 1 cup salsa into beans; spoon half the mixture over chips. Sprinkle with half the cheese. Continue as directed in Step 3.

Per cup: 283 cal., 14 g total fat (6 g sat. fat), 26 mg chol., 759 mg sodium, 30 g carbo., 6 g fiber, 14 g pro.
Daily Values: 7% vit. A, 25% calcium, 9% iron
Exchanges: 2 Starch, 1 High-Fat Meat, ½ Fat

Tapenade

Start to Finish: 30 minutes **Makes:** 1 cup

- ½ cup pimiento-stuffed green olives
- ½ cup kalamata olives, pitted
- 1 tablespoon olive oil
- 1 tablespoon Dijon-style mustard
- 2 teaspoons balsamic vinegar
- 2 cloves garlic, minced
- ½ cup finely chopped, seeded tomato
- 2 tablespoons thinly sliced green onion (1)
- 1 8-ounce loaf baguette-style French bread, cut into ½-inch slices and toasted

1. In a blender or food processor combine green olives, kalamata olives, olive oil, mustard, vinegar, and garlic. Cover and blend until nearly smooth, scraping down sides of container as necessary. Stir in tomato and green onion. Serve with toasted bread slices.

Per bread slice + about 2 teaspoons topping: 41 cal., 2 g total fat (0 g sat. fat), 0 mg chol., 167 mg sodium, 6 g carbo., 1 g fiber, 1 g pro.
Daily Values: 1% vit. A, 2% vit. C, 1% calcium, 2% iron
Exchanges: ½ Starch

Handling Hot Chile Peppers

Because hot chile peppers, such as jalapeños, contain volatile oils that can burn your skin and eyes, avoid direct contact with chiles as much as possible. When working with chile peppers, wear plastic or rubber gloves. If your bare hands do touch the chile peppers, wash your hands well with soap and water.

Bruschetta `LOW FAT`

See photo, page 63.

Start to Finish: 35 minutes **Makes:** 36 servings

- 1 **tablespoon olive oil**
- 1 **tablespoon snipped fresh chives**
- 1 **tablespoon snipped fresh basil**
- 1 **tablespoon lemon juice**
- 1 **clove garlic, minced**
- 2 **cups seeded and chopped roma and/or yellow tomato (3 to 4 medium)**
- ½ **cup finely chopped red onion (1 small)**
- **Salt and freshly ground black pepper**
- 1 **8-ounce loaf baguette-style French bread, cut into ½-inch slices and toasted**
- **Fresh basil (optional)**

1. In a medium bowl stir together olive oil, chives, basil, lemon juice, and garlic. Add tomato and onion; toss to coat. Season to taste with salt and pepper. Set aside.

2. To serve, with a slotted spoon, spoon tomato mixture onto each toast slice. If desired, garnish with fresh basil. Serve within 30 minutes.

Seafood Bruschetta: Prepare as above, except decrease tomato to 1 cup. Add 6 ounces lump crabmeat or 6 ounces peeled, deveined, cooked shrimp, coarsely chopped, and 1 tablespoon snipped fresh dill to the tomato mixture.

Per bruschetta + about 1 tablespoon tomato or seafood mixture: 23 cal., 1 g total fat (0 g sat. fat), 0 mg chol., 43 mg sodium, 4 g carbo., 0 g fiber, 1 g pro.
Daily Values: 91% vit. A, 2% vit. C, 1% calcium, 1% iron
Exchanges: ½ Other Carbo.

Herbed Leek Tarts

Impress your guests with these free-form tarts. Sweet peppers, leeks, and Gruyère make them irresistible.

Prep: 20 minutes **Bake:** 25 minutes
Oven: 375°F **Makes:** 24 servings

- 4½ **cups thinly sliced leek (6 medium)**
- 4 **cloves garlic, minced**
- 2 **tablespoons olive oil**
- ½ **cup chopped red sweet pepper (1 small)**
- 2 **tablespoons Dijon-style mustard**
- 1 **teaspoon dried herbes de Provence or dried basil, crushed**
- 6 **ounces Gruyère or Swiss cheese, shredded (1½ cups)**
- 1 **15-ounce package rolled refrigerated unbaked piecrust (2 crusts)**
- 2 **tablespoons chopped almonds or walnuts**

1. For filling, in a large skillet cook leek and garlic in hot oil about 5 minutes or until tender. Remove from heat; stir in sweet pepper, mustard, and herbes de Provence. Cool slightly; stir in shredded cheese. Set filling aside.

2. Preheat oven to 375°F. Unfold piecrust according to package directions. On a lightly floured surface, roll one piecrust into a 12-inch circle. Transfer to a baking sheet. Spread half of the filling in the center of the piecrust, leaving a 1½-inch unfilled border. Fold edge up and over filling, pleating as necessary. Sprinkle 1 tablespoon of the almonds over filling. Repeat with remaining piecrust, filling, and nuts.

3. Bake about 25 minutes or until crusts are golden. Cool for 10 minutes on baking sheets. Cut each tart into 12 wedges. Serve warm or at room temperature.

Make-ahead directions: Prepare as above through Step 2. Cover and chill assembled tarts for up to 4 hours. Uncover; bake as directed.

Per wedge: 135 cal., 8 g total fat (3 g sat. fat), 11 mg chol., 122 mg sodium, 12 g carbo., 0 g fiber, 3 g pro.
Daily Values: 9% vit. A, 11% vit. C, 9% calcium, 3% iron
Exchanges: 1 Other Carbo., 1½ Fat

Herbed Leek Tarts

Buffalo Wings

Prep: 20 minutes **Marinate:** 30 minutes
Broil: 20 minutes **Makes:** 12 servings

- 12 **chicken wings (about 2 pounds)**
- 2 **tablespoons butter or margarine, melted**
- 3 **tablespoons bottled hot pepper sauce**
- 2 **teaspoons paprika**
- ¼ **teaspoon salt**
- ¼ **teaspoon cayenne pepper**
- 1 **recipe Blue Cheese Dip or Lower-Fat Blue Cheese Dip**
  Celery sticks (optional)

1. Cut off and discard tips of chicken wings (see photo 1, right). Cut wings at joints to form 24 pieces (see photo 2, right). Place chicken wing pieces in a resealable plastic bag set in a shallow dish.

2. For marinade, stir together melted butter, hot pepper sauce, paprika, salt, and cayenne pepper. Pour over chicken wings; seal bag. Marinate at room temperature for 30 minutes. Drain and discard marinade.

3. Place chicken wings on the unheated rack of a broiler pan. Broil 4 to 5 inches from the heat about 10 minutes or until light brown. Turn wings. Broil for 10 to 15 minutes more or until chicken is tender and no longer pink. Serve with Blue Cheese Dip and, if desired, celery sticks.

Blue Cheese Dip: In a blender or food processor combine ½ cup dairy sour cream, ½ cup mayonnaise or salad dressing, ½ cup crumbled blue cheese, 1 tablespoon white wine vinegar or white vinegar, and 1 clove garlic, minced. Cover and blend or process until smooth. Cover and chill for up to 1 week. If desired, top with additional crumbled blue cheese before serving. Makes 1¼ cups.

Per 2 pieces + about 2 tablespoons dip: 221 cal., 19 g total fat (6 g sat. fat), 47 mg chol., 258 mg sodium, 1 g carbo., 0 g fiber, 11 g pro.
Daily Values: 11% vit. A, 1% vit. C, 5% calcium, 4% iron
Exchanges: 1½ Lean Meat, 3 Fat

Lower-Fat Blue Cheese Dip: Prepare as above, except substitute fat-free dairy sour cream and fat-free mayonnaise dressing or salad dressing for the regular sour cream and mayonnaise.

Per 2 pieces + about 2 tablespoons dip: 149 cal., 10 g total fat (4 g sat. fat), 38 mg chol., 283 mg sodium, 3 g carbo., 0 g fiber, 11 g pro.
Daily Values: 11% vit. A, 1% vit. C, 5% calcium, 3% iron
Exchanges: 1½ Lean Meat, 1½ Fat

1. Use a sharp knife to carefully cut off the tip of each chicken wing. Discard the wing tips.

2. Spread the remaining wing portions open. With a sharp knife, carefully cut each wing at its joint into two sections.

Antipasto

Prep: 25 minutes **Cook:** 10 minutes **Chill:** 1 to 2 days
Stand: 30 minutes **Makes:** 12 to 16 servings

- 1 **pound uncooked chicken or turkey hot Italian sausage links**
- 1 **tablespoon cooking oil**
- ⅓ **cup olive oil**
- 2 **teaspoons finely shredded lemon peel**
- ⅓ **cup lemon juice**
- 2 **tablespoons snipped fresh basil**
- 2 **teaspoons dried Italian seasoning, crushed**
- 2 **cloves garlic, minced**
- 1 **12-ounce jar roasted red sweet peppers, drained and cut into bite-size strips**
- 12 **ounces mozzarella cheese, cut into ½-inch cubes**
- 1 **cup pitted kalamata olives**

1. In a large skillet cook sausage in hot oil over medium heat about 10 minutes or until sausage is cooked through, turning frequently to brown evenly. Remove from heat; cool. Cut sausage links into ¼-inch-thick slices; set aside.

2. Meanwhile, for dressing, in a small bowl whisk together olive oil, lemon peel, lemon juice, basil, Italian seasoning, and garlic; set aside.

3. In a 2-quart jar layer sausage, sweet pepper, cheese, and olives. Pour dressing into jar. Cover tightly; chill for 1 to 2 days. Turn jar upside down occasionally to distribute dressing.

4. Before serving, let stand at room temperature for 30 minutes. Arrange antipasto on a platter.

Per ½ cup: 200 cal., 18 g total fat (5 g sat. fat), 30 mg chol., 459 mg sodium, 4 g carbo., 1 g fiber, 12 g pro.
Daily Values: 4% vit. A, 91% vit. C, 19% calcium, 4% iron
Exchanges: 1 Vegetable, 1½ Lean Meat, 2 Fat

Sausage Bites `FAST`

Prep: 10 minutes **Cook:** 20 minutes
Makes: 16 to 20 servings

> 1 **cup bottled barbecue sauce**
> ½ **cup apricot preserves**
> 1 **teaspoon dry mustard**
> 16 **ounces cooked bratwurst, cut into
>   ¾-inch-thick slices**
> 16 **ounces cooked kielbasa, cut into
>   ¾-inch-thick slices**
> 8 **ounces small cooked smoked sausage links**

1. In a large saucepan combine barbecue sauce, apricot preserves, and dry mustard. Cook and stir until bubbly. Stir in bratwurst, kielbasa, and smoked sausage links. Cook, covered, over medium-low heat about 20 minutes more or until heated through, stirring occasionally.

Per serving: 272 cal., 21 g total fat (8 g sat. fat), 42 mg chol., 742 mg sodium, 11 g carbo., 0 g fiber, 9 g pro.
Daily Values: 4% vit. C, 1% calcium, 4% iron
Exchanges: 1 Other Carbo., 1½ High-Fat Meat, 1½ Fat

Cranberry-Barbecue Meatballs `EASY`

See photo, page 61.

Prep: 15 minutes **Cook:** 10 minutes
Makes: 64 meatballs

> 2 **16-ounce packages frozen cooked
>   homestyle meatballs, thawed
>   (32 meatballs each)**
> 1 **16-ounce can jellied cranberry sauce**
> 1 **cup barbecue sauce**

1. In a large saucepan combine thawed meatballs, cranberry sauce, and barbecue sauce. Heat to boiling; reduce heat. Simmer, uncovered, for 10 to 15 minutes or until heated through, stirring mixture occasionally.

Cranberry-Chipotle Meatballs: Prepare as above, except add 1 to 2 tablespoons finely chopped chipotle chile peppers in adobo sauce to the sauce mixture.

Mexi Meatballs: Prepare as above, except substitute one 16-ounce jar salsa and one 10-ounce can enchilada sauce for the cranberry sauce and barbecue sauce.

Per meatball cranberry-barbecue, cranberry-chipotle, or Mexi variations: 57 cal., 4 g total fat (2 g sat. fat), 5 mg chol., 145 mg sodium, 4 g carbo., 0 g fiber, 2 g pro.
Daily Values: 1% calcium, 1% iron
Exchanges: ½ High-Fat Meat

Easy Appetizers

Asparagus with Prosciutto: Wrap strips of thinly sliced prosciutto around steamed asparagus.

Cheese-Stuffed Pecans: In a medium mixing bowl bring 1 cup (4 ounces) finely shredded Gouda cheese to room temperature. Add 3 tablespoons dairy sour cream. Beat with an electric mixer until creamy. Mound a scant teaspoon of cheese mixture onto the flat side of 20 large pecan halves. Top with an additional 20 pecan halves, flat sides down. Cover and chill for 30 minutes.

Cheesy Basil-Shrimp Pizzas: Arrange three 6- to 8-inch Italian bread shells (Boboli) on a baking sheet. Brush 1 tablespoon garlic-flavor olive oil over bread. Top with 3 sliced roma tomatoes. Peel, devein, and remove the tails from 8 ounces cooked medium shrimp. Halve shrimp horizontally. Top pizza with the cooked shrimp and 1 cup shredded Italian-blend cheese. Bake in a 425°F oven for 5 to 6 minutes or until cheese melts. Sprinkle with 2 tablespoons finely shredded fresh basil.

Nutty Sweet Brie: Place one 8-ounce round Brie cheese in a shallow baking dish or pie plate. Bake in a 350°F oven for 10 minutes. Meanwhile, in a small saucepan combine ¼ cup butter or margarine, ¼ cup packed brown sugar, ¼ cup chopped desired nuts, and 1 tablespoon honey. Bring mixture to boiling over medium heat, stirring constantly. Pour sauce over warm Brie. Serve with assorted crackers.

Mussels with Creole Sauce

Mussels with Creole Sauce

When you buy live mussels, place them in an open container, cover them with a moist cloth, and chill them for up to five days. Remove the beards just before cooking. Once debearded, mussels will die.

Prep: 30 minutes **Soak:** 45 minutes
Cook: 15 minutes **Makes:** 4 servings

> 1 **pound mussels in shells**
> 1 **cup salt**
> ½ **cup finely chopped green sweet pepper (1 small)**
> ½ **cup finely chopped onion (1 medium)**
> 3 **cloves garlic, minced**
> 1 **tablespoon butter or margarine**
> 1 to 2 **teaspoons Cajun seasoning**
> 1 **cup dry white wine**
> 1 **medium tomato, chopped**
> 2 **teaspoons snipped fresh oregano**
> 2 **teaspoons snipped fresh thyme**
> 8 to 12 **slices baguette-style French bread**
>   **Lemon wedges (optional)**

1. Scrub live mussels under cold running water. Using your fingers, pull out the beards that are visible between the shells. In an 8-quart Dutch oven combine 4 quarts (16 cups) *cold water* and ⅓ cup of the salt. Add the mussels; soak for 15 minutes. Drain and rinse, discarding water. Repeat twice.

2. In a large Dutch oven cook and stir sweet pepper, onion, and garlic in hot butter over medium-high heat for 4 to 5 minutes or until onion is tender. Add Cajun seasoning; cook and stir for 2 minutes more.

3. Carefully add wine; bring to boiling. Add mussels. Cook, covered, for 5 to 7 minutes or until shells open and mussels are cooked through. Discard any that do not open.

4. Use a slotted spoon to transfer mussels to a large shallow serving bowl; set aside. Stir tomato, oregano, and thyme into cooking liquid in Dutch oven; heat through. Pour mixture over mussels. Serve with bread and, if desired, lemon wedges.

Per 4 ounces cooked mussels with sauce: 290 cal., 7 g total fat (2 g sat. fat), 48 mg chol., 507 mg sodium, 26 g carbo., 2 g fiber, 20 g pro.
Daily Values: 13% vit. A, 49% vit. C, 7% calcium, 34% iron
Exchanges: ½ Vegetable, 1 Starch, ½ Other Carbo., 2½ Very Lean Meat, 1½ Fat

Smoked Salmon and Avocado Stacks

Capers are flower buds pickled in brine or white balsamic vinegar.

Prep: 20 minutes **Chill:** 2 hours **Makes:** 12 servings

> 1 **large ripe avocado, halved, seeded, and peeled**
> 1 **tablespoon capers, drained**
> 2 **teaspoons lemon juice or lime juice**
> 1 **clove garlic, minced**
> 24 **cracked pepper or sesame water crackers**
> 4 to 6 **ounces thinly sliced lox-style smoked salmon**
> 1 **cup watercress**
> ½ **cup thin slices of quartered red onion (1 medium)**

1. For avocado spread, in a small bowl mash avocado. Stir in capers, lemon juice, and garlic. Cover with plastic wrap. Chill for up to 2 hours.

2. To assemble, spread avocado mixture on crackers. Top with smoked salmon, watercress, and red onion slices.

Per 2 stacks: 66 cal., 3 g total fat (0 g sat. fat), 2 mg chol., 253 mg sodium, 7 g carbo., 1 g fiber, 3 g pro.
Daily Values: 3% vit. A, 5% vit. C, 1% calcium, 1% iron
Exchanges: ½ Starch, ½ Fat

Lemon-Ginger-Marinated Shrimp Bowl LOW FAT

To make the cucumber ribbons for a garnish (used in the Orange-Mint variation), use a vegetable peeler to thinly slice a cucumber lengthwise.

Prep: 25 minutes **Cook:** 1 to 3 minutes
Chill: overnight **Makes:** about 20 servings

- 5 **pounds fresh large shrimp in shells, peeled and deveined**
- ½ **cup olive oil**
- ½ **cup white or red wine vinegar**
- 1½ **teaspoons finely shredded lemon peel**
- ¼ **cup lemon juice**
- 2 **tablespoons tomato paste**
- 1 **tablespoon honey**
- 3 **cloves garlic, minced**
- 2 **teaspoons grated fresh ginger**
- ½ **teaspoon salt**
- ¼ **teaspoon cayenne pepper**

1. In a large kettle bring 5 quarts *water* and 1 teaspoon *salt* to boiling. Add the shrimp. Bring to boiling; reduce heat. Simmer, uncovered, for 1 to 3 minutes or until shrimp turn opaque, stirring occasionally. Drain shrimp. Rinse under cold running water; drain again.

2. Arrange shrimp in circular layers in a glass bowl that is 7 to 8 inches in diameter and about 4 inches deep. Place shrimp tails toward the center; only round shrimp backs should be visible from the outside of the bowl. Repeat layers until bowl is filled, pressing down every couple of layers with the bottom of a plate. When the bowl is full, press with the plate again.

3. For marinade, in a screw-top jar combine oil, vinegar, lemon peel, lemon juice, tomato paste, honey, garlic, ginger, salt, and cayenne pepper. Cover and shake well. Pour marinade over shrimp. Cover and chill overnight, occasionally placing a large, flat plate tightly over the bowl and inverting the bowl to distribute marinade.

4. To serve, place the large plate off-center over the bowl and invert the bowl slightly to drain marinade. Repeat inverting until all marinade has drained. Discard marinade. Select a serving platter that has ½-inch sides because shrimp will water out slightly. Place the platter over the bowl and carefully invert the bowl to unmold.

Orange-Mint-Marinated Shrimp Bowl: Prepare as at left, except substitute orange peel for the lemon peel, orange juice for the lemon juice, and Dijon-style mustard for tomato paste. Omit cayenne pepper and add 1 tablespoon snipped fresh mint to the marinade. If desired, arrange cucumber ribbons and fresh mint sprigs on top of shrimp and garnish with orange wedges.

Spicy Marinated Shrimp Bowl: Prepare as at left, except omit honey and ginger. Add 1 teaspoon ground black pepper and ½ teaspoon ground white pepper to marinade mixture. If desired, serve with lime wedges.

Quick Marinated Shrimp Bowl: Prepare desired variation as above, except use 4 pounds frozen cooked shrimp (with tails), thawed, in place of the 5 pounds fresh large shrimp in shells.

Small version: Halve the amount of shrimp and marinade ingredients for desired variation; arrange shrimp in a glass bowl that is 5 to 6 inches in diameter and about 3 inches deep. Makes about 10 servings.

Per 3 to 4 ounces cooked shrimp for all variations: 97 cal., 2 g total fat (0 g sat. fat), 129 mg chol., 133 mg sodium, 1 g carbo., 0 g fiber, 17 g pro.
Daily Values: 3% vit. A, 3% vit. C, 4% calcium, 10% iron
Exchanges: 2½ Very Lean Meat

Orange-Mint-Marinated Shrimp Bowl

Zesty Shrimp Cocktail `FAST`

For a special gathering, serve this shrimp appetizer in martini glasses lined with colorful greens.

Prep: 25 minutes **Chill:** 2 hours to overnight
Makes: 8 to 10 servings

- 1½ **pounds fresh or frozen large shrimp in shells, peeled and deveined**
- ¼ **cup ketchup**
- 2 **tablespoons orange juice**
- 1 **tablespoon salad oil**
- 2 **teaspoons prepared horseradish**
- ⅛ **teaspoon salt**
- ⅛ **teaspoon cayenne pepper**

1. Thaw shrimp, if frozen. Cook shrimp in boiling lightly salted water for 1 to 3 minutes or until shrimp turn opaque, stirring occasionally. Rinse under cold running water; drain. Chill for 2 hours to overnight.

2. For sauce, in a screw-top jar combine ketchup, juice, salad oil, horseradish, salt, and cayenne pepper. Cover and shake well. Refrigerate until serving time. Serve shrimp with sauce.

Per 2 shrimp and 1 tablespoon sauce: 92 cal., 3 g total fat (0 g sat. fat), 97 mg chol., 226 mg sodium, 3 g carbo., 0 g fiber, 13 g pro.
Daily Values: 4% vit. A, 8% vit. C, 4% calcium, 9% iron
Exchanges: 2 Very Lean Meat, ½ Fat

FAVORITE Stuffed Mushrooms

Prep: 25 minutes **Bake:** 13 minutes
Oven: 425°F **Makes:** 24 mushrooms

- 24 **large fresh mushrooms (1½ to 2 inches in diameter)**
  Nonstick cooking spray
- ¼ **cup sliced green onion (2)**
- 1 **clove garlic, minced**
- ¼ **cup butter or margarine**
- ½ **cup fine dry bread crumbs**
- ½ **cup shredded cheddar or smoked Gouda cheese or crumbled blue cheese (2 ounces)**
- 2 **strips crisp-cooked bacon, crumbled**

1. Clean mushrooms, remove stems, and set stems aside. Place mushroom caps, stem sides down, in a 15×10×1-inch baking pan. Lightly coat mushroom caps with cooking spray. Bake in a 425°F oven for 5 minutes. Drain mushroom caps, stem sides down, on a double thickness of paper towels.

2. Chop enough of the reserved stems to make 1 cup. In a saucepan cook chopped stems, green onion, and garlic in hot butter until tender. Stir in bread crumbs, cheese, and bacon. Turn mushrooms stem sides up; fill with bacon mixture. Return mushroom caps to baking pan. Bake for 8 to 10 minutes more or until heated through.

Prosciutto-Stuffed Mushrooms: Prepare as at left, except omit butter, cheese, and bacon. Cook mushroom stems, green onion, and garlic in ¼ cup olive oil. Stir in bread crumbs, ⅓ cup chopped prosciutto, ¼ cup shredded Parmesan or Asiago cheese, and 1 teaspoon dried Italian seasoning, crushed. Continue as directed.

Pesto-Stuffed Mushrooms: Prepare as at left, except discard mushroom stems. Omit green onion, garlic, butter, bread crumbs, cheese, and bacon. In a small bowl combine ½ cup purchased pesto, ¼ cup shredded Parmesan cheese, and ¼ cup toasted pine nuts. Continue as directed.

Per mushroom for all variations: 45 cal., 4 g total fat (2 g sat. fat), 8 mg chol., 101 mg sodium, 2 g carbo., 0 g fiber, 2 g pro.
Daily Values: 2% vit. A, 2% calcium, 1% iron
Exchanges: 1 Fat

Potato Skins

Instead of baking the potatoes for 40 minutes, cook them in the microwave at 100-percent power (high) for 15 to 20 minutes, rearranging them once.

Prep: 20 minutes **Bake:** 50 minutes
Oven: 425°F **Makes:** 12 servings

- 6 **large baking potatoes (such as russet or long white)**
- 2 **teaspoons cooking oil**
- 1 **to 1½ teaspoons chili powder**
  Several drops bottled hot pepper sauce
- ⅔ **cup chopped Canadian-style bacon or 8 strips crisp-cooked bacon, crumbled**
- ⅔ **cup finely chopped tomato (1 medium)**
- 2 **tablespoons finely chopped green onion (1)**
- 1 **cup shredded cheddar cheese (4 ounces)**
- ½ **cup dairy sour cream (optional)**

1. Scrub potatoes; prick them with a fork. Bake in a 425°F oven for 40 to 45 minutes or until tender; cool.

2. Cut each potato lengthwise into four wedges. Scoop out the inside of each potato wedge (see photo, page 81). Cover and chill the leftover white portion for another use.

3. In a small bowl combine the oil, chili powder, and hot pepper sauce. Using a pastry brush, brush the insides of the potato wedges with the oil mixture. Place the potato wedges in a single layer on a large baking sheet. Sprinkle wedges with bacon, tomato, and green onion; top with cheese.

4. Bake about 10 minutes more or until cheese melts and potatoes are heated through. If desired, serve with sour cream.

Make-ahead directions: Prepare as at left through Step 3. Cover and chill potato wedges for up to 24 hours. Uncover and continue as directed.

Per 2 wedges: 72 cal., 5 g total fat (2 g sat. fat), 14 mg chol., 174 mg sodium, 3 g carbo., 1 g fiber, 5 g pro.
Daily Values: 5% vit. A, 7% vit. C, 8% calcium, 5% iron
Exchanges: ½ Starch, ½ Fat

Beginning at one end, use a teaspoon to carefully scrape away the inside of each potato wedge. Leave a shell about ¼ inch thick.

Onion Rings

A sweet onion, such as Vidalia, works well.

Prep: 15 minutes **Cook:** 2 to 3 minutes per batch
Makes: 6 servings

- ¾ cup all-purpose flour
- ⅔ cup milk
- 1 egg
- 1 tablespoon cooking oil
- ¼ teaspoon salt
   Cooking oil or shortening for deep-fat frying
- 4 medium mild yellow or white onions, sliced ¼ inch thick and separated into rings

1. For batter, in a medium mixing bowl combine flour, milk, egg, the 1 tablespoon oil, and the salt. Using a rotary beater, beat batter just until smooth.

2. In a deep-fat fryer or large deep skillet heat 1 inch of oil to 365°F. Using a fork, dip onion rings into batter; drain off excess batter. Fry onion rings, a few at a time, in a single layer in the hot oil for 2 to 3 minutes or until golden, stirring once or twice with a fork to separate rings. Remove rings from oil; drain on paper towels. Sprinkle to taste with additional salt.

Spicy Onion Rings: Prepare as at left, except omit sprinkling with additional salt. In a small bowl combine ¼ teaspoon salt and ¼ teaspoon cayenne pepper. Sprinkle over fried onion rings and serve immediately.

Per cup plain or spicy variation: 301 cal., 22 g total fat (4 g sat. fat), 37 mg chol., 222 mg sodium, 23 g carbo., 2 g fiber, 4 g pro.
Daily Values: 2% vit. A, 9% vit. C, 6% calcium, 6% iron
Exchanges: ½ Vegetable, ½ Starch, 1 Other Carbo., 4 Fat

Sweet and Savory Onion Rings: Prepare as at left, except in a small microwave-safe bowl combine 3 tablespoons honey and 1 teaspoon finely snipped fresh rosemary. Cook at 100-percent power (high) about 30 seconds or until heated through. Drizzle over salted onion rings. Serve immediately.

Per cup: 333 cal., 4 g total fat (4 g sat. fat), 37 mg chol., 222 mg sodium, 31 g carbo., 2 g fiber, 4 g pro.
Daily Values: 2% vit. A, 9% vit. C, 6% calcium, 6% iron
Exchanges: ½ Vegetable, ½ Starch, 1½ Other Carbo., 4 Fat

Sweet Herbed Nuts

These brown sugar-sweetened nuts get an unexpected flavor from the hint of thyme.

Prep: 15 minutes **Bake:** 8 minutes
Oven: 350°F **Makes:** 8 servings

- 8 ounces whole almonds, pecan halves, and/or cashews (about 2 cups)
- 1 tablespoon butter
- 1 tablespoon packed brown sugar
- 1 tablespoon snipped fresh thyme or 1 teaspoon dried thyme, crushed
- ¼ teaspoon salt
- ⅛ teaspoon cayenne pepper (optional)

1. Spread nuts in a single layer in a shallow baking pan. Bake in a 350°F oven for 8 to 10 minutes, stirring occasionally.

2. In a medium saucepan melt butter over medium heat. Add brown sugar; cook and stir until sugar melts. Remove from heat. Stir in thyme, salt, and, if desired, cayenne pepper. Add nuts to butter mixture; toss to coat. Spread coated nuts on a piece of foil; cool.

3. Store in an airtight container in the refrigerator for up to 1 week or in the freezer for up to 3 months.

Per ¼ cup: 184 cal., 16 g total fat (2 g sat. fat), 4 mg chol., 84 mg sodium, 7 g carbo., 3 g fiber, 6 g pro.
Daily Values: 1% vit. A, 1% vit. C, 7% calcium, 7% iron
Exchanges: ½ Other Carbo., 1 High-Fat Meat, 1½ Fat

Wasabi Party Mix

Crunchy Party Mix

Look for wasabi-flavored dried peas (used in the Wasabi Party Mix variation) in the produce section or ethnic food aisle of your supermarket.

Prep: 20 minutes **Bake:** 45 minutes
Oven: 300°F **Makes:** 16 to 18 cups

- 5 **cups pretzel sticks**
- 4 **cups round toasted oat cereal**
- 4 **cups bite-size wheat or bran square cereal**
- 4 **cups bite-size rice or corn square cereal or bite-size shredded wheat biscuits**
- 3 **cups mixed nuts**
- 1 **cup butter or margarine**
- ¼ **cup Worcestershire sauce**
- 1 **teaspoon garlic powder**
  Several drops bottled hot pepper sauce

1. In a roasting pan combine pretzels, oat cereal, wheat cereal, rice cereal, and nuts. Set aside.

2. In a small saucepan heat and stir butter, Worcestershire sauce, garlic powder, and hot pepper sauce until butter melts. Drizzle butter mixture over cereal mixture; stir gently to coat.

3. Bake in a 300°F oven for 45 minutes, stirring every 15 minutes. Spread on a large piece of foil to cool. Store in an airtight container at room temperature for up to 2 weeks or in the freezer for up to 3 months.

Cajun-Style Party Mix: Prepare as above, except substitute 3 cups pecan halves for the mixed nuts and add ½ teaspoon cayenne pepper to the butter mixture.

Five-Spice Party Mix: Prepare as at left, except substitute 2 cups honey-roasted cashews and 1 cup unsalted unblanched almonds for the 3 cups mixed nuts and omit Worcestershire sauce, garlic powder, and hot pepper sauce. Add 3 tablespoons five-spice powder to the melted butter.

Per ½ cup crunchy, Cajun-style, or five-spice variations:
210 cal., 14 g total fat (4 g sat. fat), 16 mg chol., 383 mg sodium, 18 g carbo., 2 g fiber, 4 g pro.
Daily Values: 7% vit. A, 4% vit. C, 5% calcium, 23% iron
Exchanges: 1 Starch, 3 Fat

Wasabi Party Mix: Prepare as at left, except substitute 3 cups wasabi-flavored dehydrated peas for the 3 cups mixed nuts; omit hot pepper sauce.

Per ½ cup: 152 cal., 7 g total fat (3 g sat. fat), 16 mg chol., 314 mg sodium, 19 g carbo., 1 g fiber, 2 g pro.
Daily Values: 7% vit. A, 4% vit. C, 4% calcium, 24% iron
Exchanges: 1 Starch, 1½ Fat

Herbed Soy Snacks `FAST`

Prep: 5 minutes **Bake:** 5 minutes
Oven: 350°F **Makes:** 16 servings

- 8 **ounces dry-roasted soybeans (2 cups)**
- 1½ **teaspoons dried thyme, crushed**
- ¼ **teaspoon garlic salt**
- ⅛ **to ¼ teaspoon cayenne pepper**

1. Spread soybeans in an even layer in a 15×10×1-inch baking pan. In a bowl combine thyme, garlic salt, and cayenne pepper. Sprinkle soybeans with thyme mixture.

2. Bake in a 350°F oven about 5 minutes or just until heated through, shaking pan once. Cool mixture completely. Store in an airtight container at room temperature for up to 1 week.

Indian-Spiced Soy Snacks: Prepare as above, except substitute ½ teaspoon garam masala and ¼ teaspoon salt for the thyme and garlic salt.

Sesame-Ginger Soy Snacks: Prepare as above, except substitute 2 teaspoons toasted sesame oil, ¾ teaspoon ground ginger, and ½ teaspoon onion salt for the thyme, garlic salt, and cayenne pepper.

Sweet Chili Soy Snacks: Prepare as above, except substitute ½ teaspoon garlic salt, 2 teaspoons brown sugar, and 1½ teaspoons chili powder for the thyme, garlic salt, and cayenne pepper.

Per 2 tablespoons for all variations: 75 cal., 3 g total fat (1 g sat. fat), 0 mg chol., 27 mg sodium, 4 g carbo., 2 g fiber, 7 g pro.
Daily Values: 3% calcium, 5% iron
Exchanges: ½ Lean Meat, ½ Fat

Beans, Rice & Grains

Two-Bean Tamale Pie, 92

Risotto with Beans and Vegetables, 90

Peppers Stuffed with Cranberry Bulgur, 102

Beans, Rice & Grains Essentials

Beans, rice, and grains can enhance anyone's diet deliciously and nutritionally with textures and flavors that keep you coming back for more.

Shopper's Guide to Rice

Rice is classified by its size: long, medium, or short grain. Here's a sampling of what's available (see photos, page 86):

Arborio rice: This short grain white rice contributes to the creaminess of risotto.

Aromatic rice: Basmati, jasmine, Texmati, and wild pecan are long grain rices that have a floral flavor and aroma.

Brown rice: This pleasantly chewy and nutty rice retains the bran around the kernel and requires a longer cooking time than white rice. It is available as short or long grain.

Converted rice: Also called parboiled rice, it is steamed and pressure-cooked before it's packaged, which helps it to retain nutrients and keeps the grains from sticking together when cooked.

Instant and quick-cooking rices: These rices are partially or fully cooked before they are packaged, resulting in short cooking times.

White rice: White rice lacks the bran and germ and is available as long, medium, or short grain. The shorter the grain, the more starch it contains and the more it will stick together when cooked.

Wild rice: This marsh grass is not a grain at all. It has a nutlike flavor and chewy texture.

The Magic Bean

Dried beans are rich in complex carbohydrates and fiber and contain a higher proportion of protein than any other plant food. Although the protein is incomplete, grains, nuts, or a small

portion of lean meat can be combined with beans to supply the missing amino acids. Beans also provide many important vitamins and minerals for nutrition and versatility that are hard to beat.

When a recipe calls for a cup measure of beans, use this quick guide: One pound of dry beans equals 2¼ to 2½ cups dry, uncooked beans or 6 to 7 cups cooked beans, depending on the variety. A 15-ounce can of beans contains about 1¾ cups drained beans.

The Whole Story

Try these delicious whole grains for breakfast, dinner—even dessert.

Barley: Barley is one of the oldest grains known. It has a bold flavor and chewy texture.

Bulgur: These whole wheat kernels have been boiled, dried, and cracked. The flavor is earthy and the texture is tender and chewy.

Millet: This cereal grass has a mild and slightly sweet flavor.

Quinoa: *KEEN-wah* has a delicate flavor, light texture, and more protein than any other grain.

Spelt: This distant cousin of wheat has a mild flavor and higher protein content than wheat.

Wheat berries: These whole, unprocessed kernels of wheat have a nutty and slightly sweet flavor and chewy texture.

Lentil and Veggie Tostadas, page 96

Eating Meatless

Pasta, dairy products, eggs, dry beans, lentils, tofu, rice, vegetables, and grains are important ingredients in a meatless diet. To get the most fiber, phytochemicals, and flavor, try to choose a variety of whole grains whenever you can. If your meatless recipes include dairy products, choose the low-fat and fat-free options. For more information on eating a nutritionally balanced diet, see pages 45–49.

Beans, Rice & Grains

A diet rich in beans, rice, and grains has been enjoyed by many civilizations for centuries. These foods are naturally low in fat, high in fiber, and full of flavor.

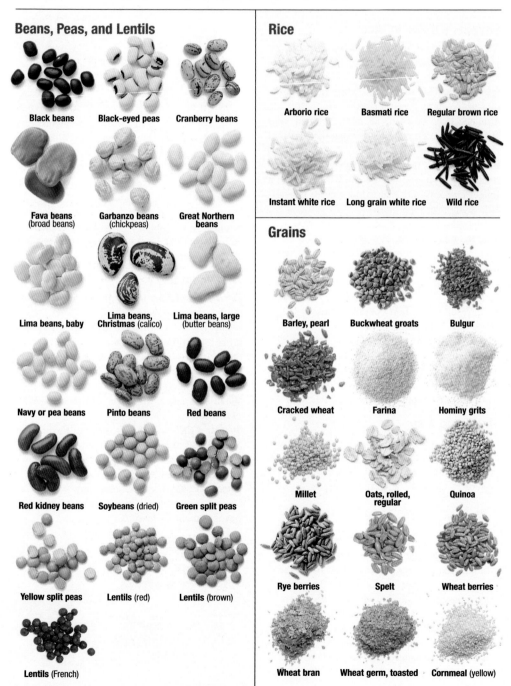

Beans, Peas, and Lentils

Black beans

Black-eyed peas

Cranberry beans

Fava beans
(broad beans)

Garbanzo beans
(chickpeas)

Great Northern
beans

Lima beans, baby

Lima beans,
Christmas (calico)

Lima beans, large
(butter beans)

Navy or pea beans

Pinto beans

Red beans

Red kidney beans

Soybeans (dried)

Green split peas

Yellow split peas

Lentils (red)

Lentils (brown)

Lentils (French)

Rice

Arborio rice

Basmati rice

Regular brown rice

Instant white rice

Long grain white rice

Wild rice

Grains

Barley, pearl

Buckwheat groats

Bulgur

Cracked wheat

Farina

Hominy grits

Millet

Oats, rolled,
regular

Quinoa

Rye berries

Spelt

Wheat berries

Wheat bran

Wheat germ, toasted

Cornmeal (yellow)

Wild Rice and Barley Pilaf

Wild Rice and Barley Pilaf LOW FAT

Autumn flavors come together in this fruited rice dish. Serve it alongside roasted pork or poultry.

Prep: 20 minutes **Cook:** 45 minutes
Stand: 5 minutes **Makes:** 8 side-dish servings

- ¾ cup uncooked wild rice
- ½ cup regular barley
- 1 tablespoon butter
- 2 14-ounce cans reduced-sodium chicken broth
- ½ cup dried cranberries, snipped dried apricots, dried tart cherries, and/or currants
- ⅓ cup sliced almonds, toasted (see tip, page 265)

1. Rinse wild rice with cold water; drain. In a large saucepan cook and stir rice and barley in hot butter over medium heat for 3 minutes. Carefully add broth. Bring to boiling, reduce heat. Simmer, covered, for 45 to 50 minutes or until rice and barley are tender and most of the liquid is absorbed. Remove from heat.

2. Stir dried fruit into the rice mixture; cover and let stand 5 minutes. Stir in the almonds before serving.

Per ⅔ cup: 172 cal., 5 g total fat (1 g sat. fat), 4 mg chol., 250 mg sodium, 28 g carbo., 4 g fiber, 5 g pro.
Daily Values: 1% vit. A, 2% calcium, 5% iron
Exchanges: ½ Fruit, 1½ Starch, ½ Fat

Rice Pilaf

With its variety of colors and textures, this rice pilaf dresses up a simple main dish.

Prep: 20 minutes **Cook:** 15 minutes
Makes: 4 to 6 side-dish servings

- ¾ cup uncooked long grain rice or basmati rice
- 2 cloves garlic, minced
- 2 tablespoons butter or margarine
- 1 14-ounce can reduced-sodium chicken broth*
- ¼ cup dried currants or raisins (optional)
- ¼ cup chopped carrot or red or green sweet pepper
- ¼ cup dry white wine, apple juice, or water
- ¼ teaspoon dried basil, oregano, or Italian seasoning, crushed
- ½ cup green onion, sliced (4)
- ¼ cup pine nuts, slivered almonds, or chopped pecans, toasted (see tip, page 265)
- 2 slices bacon, crisp-cooked, drained, and crumbled, or ¼ cup chopped cooked ham

1. In a medium saucepan cook and stir the rice and garlic in hot butter for 3 to 5 minutes or until rice is light brown.

2. Carefully stir in the chicken broth, currants (if desired), carrot, wine, and basil. Bring mixture to boiling; reduce heat. Simmer, covered, for 15 to 20 minutes or until the rice is tender and the liquid is absorbed. Stir in the green onion, pine nuts, and bacon.

*Note: You may substitute 1¾ cups water and 1½ teaspoons instant chicken bouillon granules for the chicken broth.

Per ¾ cup: 275 cal., 13 g total fat (4 g sat. fat), 20 mg chol., 362 mg sodium, 32 g carbo., 1 g fiber, 7 g pro.
Daily Values: 25% vit. A, 6% vit. C, 3% calcium, 15% iron
Exchanges: 2 Starch, 2½ Fat

Autumn Harvest

Bring together family and friends with this autumn-inspired dinner.

- *Pork Medallions with Cranberry and Fig Chutney (page 389)*
- *Rice Pilaf (above)*
- *Mesclun with pears and blue cheese*
- *Mashed sweet potatoes*
- *Apple tart*

Rice and Vegetable Pilaf

The rich flavor of this pilaf comes from brown rice and wild rice, vegetables, and crunchy nuts.

Prep: 20 minutes **Cook:** 45 minutes **Stand:** 5 minutes
Makes: 6 side-dish servings

  1 **cup sliced fresh mushrooms**
  ⅓ **cup onion, chopped (1 small)**
  1 **clove garlic, minced**
  1 **tablespoon butter or margarine**
  ½ **cup uncooked regular brown rice**
  ⅓ **cup uncooked wild rice, rinsed and drained**
  1 **14-ounce can chicken broth**
  ½ **cup shredded zucchini or frozen peas**
  ½ **cup shredded carrot (1 medium)**
  ⅛ **to ¼ teaspoon black pepper**
  ⅓ **cup chopped walnuts or pecans, toasted (see tip, page 265)**

1. In a medium saucepan cook mushrooms, onion, and garlic in hot butter about 10 minutes or until tender. Stir in brown and wild rice. Cook for 3 minutes, stirring frequently.

2. Carefully add chicken broth. Bring to boiling; reduce heat. Simmer, covered, for 45 to 50 minutes or until rices are tender and most of the liquid is absorbed. Remove from heat.

3. Stir in zucchini, carrot, and black pepper. Let stand, covered, for 5 minutes. Stir in walnuts.

Per ⅔ cup: 275 cal., 13 g total fat (4 g sat. fat), 20 mg chol., 362 mg sodium, 32 g carbo., 1 g fiber, 7 g pro.
Daily Values: 25% vit. A, 6% vit. C, 3% calcium, 15% iron
Exchanges: 2 Starch, 2½ Fat

Spanish Rice `LOW FAT`

Make this side dish for a Mexican-inspired meal.

Prep: 15 minutes **Cook:** 20 minutes
Makes: 6 to 8 side-dish servings

  ½ **cup chopped onion (1 medium)**
  ½ **cup chopped green sweet pepper**
  1 **clove garlic, minced**
  1 **tablespoon cooking oil**
  1 **teaspoon chili powder**
  2 **14-ounce cans diced tomatoes, undrained**
  1 **cup water**
  ¾ **cup uncooked long grain rice**
  1 **4-ounce can diced green chile peppers, undrained**
  ¼ **teaspoon salt**
  ⅛ **teaspoon black pepper**

Several dashes bottled hot pepper sauce (optional)
  ½ **cup shredded cheddar cheese (optional)**

1. In a large skillet cook onion, sweet pepper, and garlic in hot oil until tender. Add chili powder; cook 1 minute more. Stir in undrained tomatoes, water, rice, undrained chile peppers, salt, black pepper, and, if desired, several dashes hot pepper sauce. Bring to boiling; reduce heat. Simmer, covered, about 20 minutes or until rice is tender and most of the liquid is absorbed. If desired, sprinkle with shredded cheese.

Per ¾ cup: 144 cal., 3 g total fat (0 g sat. fat), 0 mg chol., 353 mg sodium, 27 g carbo., 2 g fiber, 4 g pro.
Daily Values: 20% vit. A, 59% vit. C, 8% calcium, 11% iron
Exchanges: 1½ Starch, ½ Fat

Italian Rice and Sweet Onion Casserole

Prep: 45 minutes **Bake:** 30 minutes **Oven:** 325°F
Makes: 6 to 8 side-dish servings

 1½ **cups uncooked arborio rice or short grain rice**
  1 **cup whole fresh mushrooms, such as porcini and/or button**
  ¼ **cup butter or margarine**
 12 **purple or white boiling onions, peeled and halved**
  1 **medium sweet onion, such as Vidalia or Walla Walla, cut into 8 wedges**
  2 **cloves garlic, minced**
 1¾ **cups Vegetable Stock (see recipe, page 549) or one 14-ounce can vegetable broth**
  ¾ **cup freshly shredded Romano or Parmesan cheese (3 ounces)**

1. In a saucepan combine 3 cups *water* and ½ teaspoon *salt*. Bring to boiling. Remove from heat; stir in rice. Cover and let stand for 30 minutes; drain. Rinse with cold water; drain again.

2. Meanwhile, in a large skillet cook one-third of the mushrooms in hot butter over medium-high heat. Cook and stir for 4 to 5 minutes or until tender. Remove mushrooms from skillet; set aside. Add the remaining mushrooms, boiling onions, sweet onion, and garlic to hot skillet. Cook and stir until vegetables are tender. Reduce heat to medium and add cooked rice. Cook and stir for 4 to 5 minutes or until rice is golden. Carefully stir in Vegetable Stock. Bring to boiling. Transfer rice mixture to a 2-quart casserole.

3. Bake, covered, in a 325°F oven for 25 to 30 minutes or until rice is tender and liquid is absorbed. Fluff with a fork. Stir in ⅔ cup of the Romano cheese. Sprinkle with the reserved cooked mushrooms and the remaining cheese. Bake, uncovered, about 5 minutes more or until cheese melts and is lightly brown.

Per ¾ cup: 313 cal., 12 g total fat (5 g sat. fat), 28 mg chol., 523 mg sodium, 43 g carbo., 2 g fiber, 8 g pro.
Daily Values: 7% vit. A, 3% vit. C, 11% calcium, 12% iron
Exchanges: 3 Starch, 2 Fat

Fried Rice

Start to Finish: 30 minutes **Makes:** 6 side-dish servings

>   2 eggs, beaten
>   1 teaspoon soy sauce
>   1 teaspoon sesame oil or vegetable oil
>   1 clove garlic, minced
>   1 tablespoon cooking oil
>   ½ cup thinly bias-sliced celery (1 stalk)
>   1 cup sliced fresh mushrooms
>   1 8.8-ounce pouch cooked white rice (2 cups)
>   1 medium carrot, shredded
>   ½ cup frozen peas, thawed
>   2 tablespoons soy sauce
>   ¼ cup sliced green onion (2)

1. In a small bowl combine eggs and the 1 teaspoon soy sauce.

2. Pour the sesame oil into a wok or large skillet. Preheat over medium heat. Add the egg mixture and garlic; stir gently to scramble. When set, remove egg mixture from wok and cut up any large pieces. Remove wok from heat.

3. Pour the cooking oil into the wok or skillet. (Add more oil if necessary during cooking.) Return to medium-high heat. Stir-fry celery in hot oil for 1 minute. Add mushrooms; stir-fry for 1 to 2 minutes more or until vegetables are crisp-tender.

4. Add cooked rice, carrot, and peas. Sprinkle with the 2 tablespoons soy sauce. Cook and stir for 4 to 6 minutes or until heated through. Add cooked egg mixture and green onion; cook and stir for about 1 minute more or until heated through.

Per ⅔ cup: 141 cal., 6 g total fat (1 g sat. fat), 71 mg chol., 418 mg sodium, 18 g carbo., 2 g fiber, 5 g pro.
Daily Values: 31% vit. A, 8% vit. C, 3% calcium, 5% iron
Exchanges: ½ Vegetable, 1 Starch, 1 Fat

Shrimp Fried Rice: Prepare as at left, except add 12 ounces peeled and deveined fully cooked shrimp when adding the rice. Makes 4 main-dish servings.

Per 1¼ cups: 286 cal., 10 g total fat (2 g sat. fat), 272 mg chol., 818 mg sodium, 26 g carbo., 3 g fiber, 26 g pro.
Daily Values: 51% vit. A, 15% vit. C, 7% calcium, 22% iron
Exchanges: ½ Vegetable, 1½ Starch, 3 Very Lean Meat, 1½ Fat

Easy Risotto EASY

Prep: 5 minutes **Cook:** 25 minutes **Stand:** 5 minutes
Makes: 3 or 4 side-dish servings

>   ⅓ cup chopped onion (1 small)
>   1 tablespoon butter or margarine
>   ⅔ cup uncooked arborio rice or long grain rice
>   2 cups water
>   1 teaspoon instant chicken bouillon granules
>   Dash black pepper
>   1 cup frozen peas (optional)
>   ¼ cup grated Parmesan or Romano cheese

1. In a medium saucepan cook onion in hot butter until tender; add rice. Cook and stir for 2 minutes more. Stir in water, bouillon granules, and pepper. Bring to boiling; reduce heat. Simmer, covered, for 20 minutes (do not lift lid).

2. Remove saucepan from heat. If desired, stir in peas. Let stand, covered, for 5 minutes. Rice should be tender but slightly firm, and the mixture should be creamy. (If necessary, stir in a little hot water to reach desired consistency.) Stir in Parmesan cheese.

Per ⅔ cup: 179 cal., 6 g total fat (3 g sat. fat), 10 mg chol., 571 mg sodium, 25 g carbo., 0 g fiber, 6 g pro.
Daily Values: 5% vit. A, 21% vit. C, 12% calcium, 11% iron
Exchanges: 1½ Starch, 1 Fat

Fried Rice

Risotto

Prep: 10 minutes **Cook:** about 15 minutes
Makes: 4 side-dish servings

- **1 medium onion, chopped (½ cup)**
- **1 clove garlic, minced**
- **2 tablespoons olive oil**
- **2 tablespoons butter**
- **1 cup uncooked arborio rice**
- **2 14-ounce cans reduced-sodium chicken broth**
- **½ cup finely shredded Parmesan or Asiago cheese (2 ounces)**
- **⅛ teaspoon black pepper**

1. In a large saucepan cook onion and garlic in hot oil and 1 tablespoon of the butter until onion is tender; add rice. Cook and stir over medium heat 2 to 3 minutes or until rice begins to brown.

2. Meanwhile, in another saucepan bring broth to boiling; reduce heat and simmer. Slowly add 1 cup broth to the rice mixture, stirring constantly. Continue to cook and stir over medium heat until liquid is absorbed. Add another ½ cup broth to the rice mixture, stirring constantly. Continue to cook and stir until the liquid is absorbed. Add remaining broth, ½ cup at a time, stirring constantly until the broth has been absorbed. (This should take about 15 minutes.)

3. Stir in the remaining butter, the Parmesan cheese, and pepper.

Lemon-Asparagus Risotto: Prepare as above, except add 1 cup chopped fresh asparagus and 1 teaspoon finely shredded lemon peel after half of the chicken broth has been stirred into the rice mixture.

Per ¾ cup plain or lemon-asparagus variation: 290 cal., 16 g total fat (6 g sat. fat), 23 mg chol., 685 mg sodium, 30 g carbo., 0 g fiber, 8 g pro.
Daily Values: 5% vit. A, 2% vit. C, 13% calcium, 12% iron
Exchanges: 2 Starch, ½ Lean Meat, 2½ Fat

Risotto with Beans and Vegetables LOW FAT

With the addition of vegetables and beans, this creamy risotto is hearty enough to be a main dish. See photo, page 83.

Prep: 20 minutes **Cook:** 30 minutes
Makes: 4 main-dish or 6 side-dish servings

- **3 cups vegetable broth or chicken broth**
- **2 cups sliced fresh mushrooms**
- **½ cup chopped onion (1 medium)**
- **2 cloves garlic, minced**
- **2 tablespoons olive oil**
- **1 cup uncooked arborio rice**
- **1 cup finely chopped zucchini (1 medium)**
- **1 cup finely chopped carrot (2 medium)**
- **1 15-ounce can white kidney (cannellini) beans or pinto beans, rinsed and drained**
- **½ cup grated Parmesan cheese**
- **2 tablespoons snipped fresh Italian parsley**

1. In a medium saucepan bring broth to boiling; reduce heat and simmer until needed. Meanwhile, in a large saucepan cook mushrooms, onion, and garlic in hot oil over medium heat about 5 minutes or until onion is tender. Add uncooked rice. Cook and stir about 5 minutes more or until rice is golden brown.

2. Slowly add 1 cup of the broth to the rice mixture, stirring constantly. Continue to cook and stir until liquid is absorbed. Add another ½ cup of the broth, the zucchini, and carrot to rice mixture, stirring constantly. Continue to cook and stir until liquid is absorbed. Add another 1 cup broth, ½ cup at a time, stirring constantly until the broth has been absorbed. (This process should take about 20 minutes.)

3. Stir the remaining ½ cup broth into rice mixture. Cook and stir until rice is slightly creamy and just tender. Stir in beans and Parmesan cheese; heat through. Sprinkle with parsley.

Per cup: 340 cal., 11 g total fat (3 g sat. fat), 9 mg chol., 1,074 mg sodium, 53 g carbo., 7 g fiber, 15 g pro.
Daily Values: 74% vit. A, 17% vit. C, 16% calcium, 22% iron
Exchanges: 1 Vegetable, 3 Starch, ½ Lean Meat, 1 Fat

Spicy Black Beans and Rice
LOW FAT VEGETARIAN WHOLE GRAIN

For a variation, spoon the bean mixture over squares of corn bread instead of the brown rice.

Prep: 5 minutes **Cook:** 20 minutes
Makes: 4 main-dish servings

- **½ cup chopped onion (1 medium)**
- **4 cloves garlic, minced**
- **2 tablespoons olive oil or cooking oil**
- **1 15-ounce can black beans, rinsed and drained (see photo, page 92)**
- **1 14.5-ounce can Mexican-style stewed tomatoes, undrained**
- **½ cup bottled salsa**
- **¼ teaspoon salt**

⅛ to ¼ teaspoon cayenne pepper

2 cups hot cooked brown rice or long grain rice

½ cup shredded cheddar cheese, Monterey Jack cheese, or Mexican cheese blend (2 ounces) (optional)

¼ cup chopped onion (optional)

1. In a medium saucepan cook the ½ cup onion and garlic in hot oil until tender but not brown. Carefully stir in beans, undrained tomatoes, salsa, salt, and cayenne pepper. Bring to boiling; reduce heat. Simmer, uncovered, for 15 minutes.

2. To serve, mound rice on serving plates; make a well in each mound. Spoon the black bean mixture into wells. If desired, sprinkle with shredded cheese and the ¼ cup chopped onion.

Per ¾ cup: 284 cal., 8 g total fat (1 g sat. fat), 0 mg chol., 835 mg sodium, 48 g carbo., 7 g fiber, 11 g pro.
Daily Values: 3% vit. A, 34% vit. C, 7% calcium, 12% iron
Exchanges: 1 Vegetable, 2½ Starch, ½ Very Lean Meat, 1 Fat

Portobello Wrap with White Bean-Chili Spread VEGETARIAN

Hungry for something fresh? This flavorful Italian-style wrap is ideal as a light dinner or as an accompaniment to a simple mug of soup. Chèvre adds a tart contrast to the mild cannellini beans.

Prep: 30 minutes **Broil:** 6 minutes
Makes: 4 main-dish servings

4 portobello mushroom caps, stems and gills removed*

¼ cup bottled Italian salad dressing

1 19-ounce can white kidney beans (cannellini), drained and rinsed

2 cloves garlic, quartered

3 tablespoons olive oil

1 teaspoon chili powder

¼ teaspoon salt

2 cups fresh baby spinach

1 tablespoon bottled Italian salad dressing

4 8-inch garlic-herb, spinach, or plain flour tortillas

4 ounces goat cheese (chèvre), crumbled, or 1 cup shredded Monterey Jack cheese (4 ounces)

1. Brush portobello mushrooms on both sides with the ¼ cup dressing. Let stand for 15 minutes. Meanwhile, in a food processor combine beans, garlic, olive oil, chili powder, and salt. Cover and process until nearly smooth; set aside.

2. Toss spinach with the 1 tablespoon salad dressing; set aside.

3. Preheat broiler. Place mushrooms on the unheated rack of the broiler pan. Broil 4 inches from heat for 6 to 8 minutes, turning mushrooms over halfway through broiling. Slice mushrooms into strips.

4. Spread about one-third of the bean puree evenly over each flour tortilla. Top the bean puree layer with warm mushroom slices, spinach mixture, and cheese. Roll up each tortilla around fillings. Place wraps, seam side down, on plates.

For a charcoal grill: Grill mushrooms on the ungreased rack of an uncovered grill directly over medium coals for 6 to 8 minutes or until mushrooms are tender and brown, turning once. (For a gas grill, preheat grill. Reduce heat to medium. Place mushrooms on grill rack over heat. Cover and grill as above.)

*Note: To remove gills (the black portion underneath the caps) from mushrooms, gently scrape with a spoon.

Per wrap: 537 cal., 28 g total fat (8 g sat. fat), 13 mg chol., 1,158 mg sodium, 58 g carbo., 10 g fiber, 23 g pro.
Daily Values: 32% vit. A, 8% vit. C, 22% calcium, 22% iron
Exchanges: ½ Vegetable, 3½ Starch, 1½ Medium-Fat Meat, 3½ Fat

Portobello Wrap with White Bean-Chili Spread

Two-Bean Tamale Pie

Golden corn bread is a delicious topper for this saucy casserole. See photo, page 83.

Prep: 25 minutes **Bake:** 25 minutes **Oven:** 400°F
Makes: 6 main-dish servings

- 1 **cup chopped green sweet pepper (1 medium)**
- ½ **cup chopped onion (1 medium)**
- 2 **cloves garlic, minced**
- 1 **tablespoon cooking oil**
- 1 **15-ounce can kidney beans or black beans, rinsed, drained, and slightly mashed**
- 1 **15-ounce can pinto beans, rinsed, drained, and slightly mashed**
- 1 **6-ounce can (⅔ cup) vegetable juice**
- 1 **4-ounce can diced green chile peppers, undrained**
- 1 **teaspoon chili powder**
- ½ **teaspoon ground cumin**
- 1 **8.5-ounce package corn muffin mix**
- ½ **cup shredded cheddar cheese (2 ounces)**
- ¼ **cup snipped fresh cilantro or Italian parsley**

1. Grease a 2-quart square baking dish or 10-inch quiche dish; set aside.

2. In a medium skillet cook sweet pepper, onion, and garlic in hot oil until tender. Stir in kidney beans, pinto beans, vegetable juice, chile peppers, chili powder, and cumin; heat through. Spoon bean mixture into the prepared dish.

3. Prepare corn muffin mix according to package directions; add cheese and cilantro, stirring just until combined. Evenly spoon corn bread mixture over bean mixture. Bake, uncovered, in a 400°F oven 25 minutes or until golden. If desired, serve with *salsa* and *dairy sour cream*.

Per 1½ cups: 387 cal., 13 g total fat (2 g sat. fat), 37 mg chol., 858 mg sodium, 58 g carbo., 9 g fiber, 17 g pro.
Daily Values: 19% vit. A, 59% vit. C, 21% calcium, 16% iron
Exchanges: 1 Vegetable, 3½ Starch, 1 Lean Meat

Fiesta of Flavors

Take your family south of the border with this Mexican-inspired menu.

- *Chunky Guacamole (page 66)*
- *Tortilla-Black Bean Casserole (right)*
- *Spanish Rice (page 88)*
- *Fruit sorbet or ice cream*
- *Quick Frozen Margaritas (page 119)*

Tortilla-Black Bean Casserole LOW FAT VEGETARIAN

Prep: 25 minutes **Bake:** 30 minutes **Stand:** 10 minutes
Oven: 350°F **Makes:** 8 main-dish servings

- 2 **cups chopped onion (2 large)**
- 1½ **cups chopped green sweet pepper (2 medium)**
- 1 **14.5-ounce can diced tomatoes, undrained**
- ¾ **cup bottled picante sauce or green salsa**
- 2 **teaspoons ground cumin**
- 2 **cloves garlic, minced**
- 2 **15-ounce cans black beans and/or red kidney beans, rinsed and drained**
- 12 **6-inch corn tortillas**
- 2 **cups reduced-fat Monterey Jack cheese, shredded (8 ounces)**
- 2 **medium tomatoes, chopped (optional)**
- 2 **cups shredded lettuce (optional)**
   Sliced green onions (optional)
   Sliced pitted ripe olives (optional)
- ½ **cup light dairy sour cream or plain low-fat yogurt (optional)**

1. In a large skillet combine onion, sweet pepper, tomatoes, picante sauce, cumin, and garlic. Bring to boiling; reduce heat. Simmer, uncovered, for 10 minutes. Stir in beans.

2. Spread one-third of the bean mixture over the bottom of a 3-quart rectangular baking dish. Top with six of the tortillas, overlapping as necessary, and 1 cup of the cheese. Add another one-third of the bean mixture; top with remaining six tortillas and remaining bean mixture.

3. Bake, covered, in a 350°F oven for 30 to 35 minutes or until heated through. Sprinkle with remaining cheese. Let stand 10 minutes.

4. If desired, top with chopped tomato, lettuce, green onion, olives, and sour cream.

Per 4×3¼-inch piece: 295 cal., 8 g total fat (4 g sat. fat), 20 mg chol., 689 mg sodium, 46 g carbo., 8 g fiber, 18 g pro.
Daily Values: 18% vit. A, 55% vit. C, 31% calcium, 21% iron
Exchanges: 3 Starch, 1 Lean Meat

Canned beans may save you time, but they add salt to your dishes. You can eliminate the salty liquid by rinsing the beans in a colander under cold running water; drain well.

Bean and Cheese Burritos FAST VEGETARIAN

To slim down this family favorite use fat-free refried beans and reduced-fat cheese.

Prep: 15 minutes **Bake:** 10 minutes **Oven:** 350°F
Makes: 3 or 4 main-dish servings

- 6 to 8 7- or 8-inch flour tortillas
- 1 cup chopped onion (1 large)
- 1 tablespoon cooking oil
- 1 16-ounce can refried beans or 1 recipe Refried Beans (below)
- 1 cup shredded cheddar cheese (4 ounces)
- 1 cup shredded lettuce
- ⅓ cup bottled salsa
  Dairy sour cream (optional)
  Guacamole (optional)

1. Stack tortillas and wrap tightly in foil. Heat in a 350°F oven for 10 minutes to soften.

2. Meanwhile, for filling, in a skillet cook onion in hot oil until tender; add refried beans. Cook and stir until heated through. Spoon about ¼ cup of the filling onto each tortilla just below center and to within 1 inch of the edge. Divide cheese among tortillas. Fold bottom edge of each tortilla up and over filling (see photo 1, page 381). Fold opposite sides in over filling (see photo 2, page 381). Roll up from the bottom. Place on a baking sheet. Bake in a 350°F oven about 10 minutes or until heated through. To serve, top with lettuce and salsa and, if desired, sour cream and guacamole.

Per 2 burritos: 542 cal., 24 g total fat (11 g sat. fat), 52 mg chol., 991 mg sodium, 20 g carbo., 10 g fiber, 23 g pro.
Daily Values: 31% vit. A, 31% vit. C, 41% calcium, 28% iron
Exchanges: ½ Vegetable, 3½ Starch, ½ Very Lean Meat, 1 High-Fat Meat, 3 Fat

Refried Beans

Prep: 20 minutes **Stand:** 1 hour
Cook: 2½ hours + 10 minutes
Makes: 4 side-dish servings

- 8 ounces dry pinto beans (about 1¼ cups)
- 2 tablespoons bacon drippings or olive oil
- 2 cloves garlic, minced

1. Rinse beans. In a large saucepan combine beans and 4 cups *water.* Bring to boiling; reduce heat. Simmer for 2 minutes. Remove from heat. Cover; let stand for 1 hour. (Or place beans in water in pan. Cover; let soak in a cool place overnight.) Drain and rinse beans.

2. In the same saucepan or Dutch oven combine beans, 4 cups fresh *water,* and ½ teaspoon *salt.* Bring to boiling; reduce heat. Simmer, covered, for 2½ to 3 hours or until beans are very tender. Drain beans, reserving liquid.

3. In a heavy large skillet heat bacon drippings. Stir in garlic. Add beans; mash thoroughly with a potato masher. Stir in enough of the cooking liquid (about ¼ cup) to make a pastelike mixture. Cook, uncovered, over low heat for 8 to 10 minutes or until thick, stirring often. Season to taste with *salt* and *black pepper.*

Per ½ cup: 239 cal., 7 g total fat (3 g sat. fat), 6 mg chol., 300 mg sodium, 33 g carbo., 9 g fiber, 12 g pro.
Daily Values: 5% vit. C, 5% calcium, 12% iron
Exchanges: 2 Starch, 1 Very Lean Meat, 1 Fat

Calico Beans LOW FAT

Prep: 10 minutes **Bake:** 1 hour **Oven:** 375°F
Makes: 12 to 16 side-dish servings

- 1 cup chopped onion (1 large)
- 6 slices bacon, cut up
- 1 clove garlic, minced
- 1 16-ounce can lima beans, drained
- 1 16-ounce can pork and beans in tomato sauce
- 1 15-ounce can red kidney beans, drained
- 1 15-ounce can butter beans, drained
- 1 15-ounce can garbanzo beans, drained
- ¾ cup ketchup
- ½ cup molasses
- ¼ cup packed brown sugar
- 1 tablespoon yellow mustard
- 1 tablespoon Worcestershire sauce

1. In a skillet cook onion, bacon, and garlic until bacon is crisp and onion is tender; drain. In a bowl combine onion mixture, lima beans, pork and beans, red kidney beans, butter beans, garbanzo beans, ketchup, molasses, brown sugar, mustard, and Worcestershire sauce. Transfer bean mixture to a 3-quart casserole. Bake, covered, in a 375°F oven for 1 hour.

Slow cooker directions: Prepare as above, except transfer bean mixture to a 3½- or 4-quart slow cooker. Cover and cook on low-heat setting for 10 to 12 hours or on high-heat setting for 4 to 5 hours.

Per ⅔ cup: 245 cal., 3 g total fat (1 g sat. fat), 5 mg chol., 882 mg sodium, 47 g carbo., 9 g fiber, 10 g pro.
Daily Values: 5% vit. A, 13% vit. C, 10% calcium, 22% iron
Exchanges: 2 Starch, 1 Other Carbohydrate, ½ Very Lean Meat

Old-Fashioned Baked Beans

Prep: 1 hour **Stand:** 1 hour **Cook:** 1 hour
Bake: 2½ hours **Oven:** 300°F
Makes: 10 to 12 side-dish servings

- 1 **pound dry navy beans or dry Great Northern beans (about 2⅓ cups)**
- ¼ **pound bacon or salt pork, cut up**
- 1 **cup chopped onion (1 large)**
- ½ **cup molasses or maple syrup**
- ¼ **cup packed brown sugar**
- 1 **teaspoon dry mustard**

1. Rinse beans. In a large Dutch oven combine beans and 8 cups *water.* Bring to boiling; reduce heat. Simmer for 2 minutes. Remove from heat. Cover and let stand for 1 hour. (Or place beans in water in Dutch oven. Cover and let soak in a cool place overnight.) Drain and rinse beans.

2. Return beans to Dutch oven. Stir in 8 cups fresh *water.* Bring to boiling; reduce heat. Simmer, covered, for 1 to 1½ hours or until beans are tender, stirring occasionally. Drain beans, reserving liquid.

3. In a 2½-quart casserole combine the beans, bacon, and onion. Stir in 1 cup of the reserved bean liquid, molasses, brown sugar, dry mustard, ½ teaspoon *salt,* and ¼ teaspoon *black pepper.*

4. Bake, covered, in a 300°F oven 2½ hours or to desired consistency, stirring occasionally. If necessary, add additional reserved bean liquid.

Slow cooker directions: Prepare as above, except transfer the bean mixture to a 3½- or 4-quart slow cooker. Cover and cook on low-heat setting for 8 to 10 hours or on high-heat setting for 4 to 5 hours. Stir before serving.

Per ¾ cup: 285 cal., 7 g total fat (3 g sat. fat), 8 mg chol., 220 mg sodium, 45 g carbo., 11 g fiber, 11 g pro.
Daily Values: 4% vit. C, 12% calcium, 22% iron
Exchanges: 2 Starch, 1 Other Carbo., ½ Very Lean Meat, 1 Fat

Shortcut Baked Beans

LOW FAT   FAST

Prep: 10 minutes **Cook:** 15 minutes
Makes: 4 or 5 side-dish servings

- 1 **16-ounce can pork and beans in tomato sauce**
- 1 **15-ounce can red kidney beans, drained**
- ¼ **cup ketchup**
- 2 **tablespoons packed brown sugar**
- 1 **tablespoon cooked bacon pieces**

- 2 **teaspoons dried minced onion**
- 2 **teaspoons yellow mustard**

1. In a medium saucepan combine pork and beans, kidney beans, ketchup, brown sugar, bacon pieces, minced onion, and mustard. Cook over low heat about 15 minutes or to desired consistency, stirring often.

Oven directions: Combine all ingredients in a 1½-quart casserole. Bake, uncovered, in a 350°F oven about 45 minutes or to desired consistency.

Slow cooker directions: Double all ingredients and combine in a 3½- or 4-quart slow cooker. Cover and cook on low-heat setting for 5 to 6 hours or on high-heat setting for 2½ to 3 hours. Makes 8 to 10 side-dish servings.

Per ¾ cup: 235 cal., 2 g total fat (1 g sat. fat), 9 mg chol., 894 mg sodium, 49 g carbo., 12 g fiber, 14 g pro.
Daily Values: 6% vit. A, 10% vit. C, 10% calcium, 29% iron
Exchanges: 3 Starch

Red Beans and Orzo

Inspired by Southern-style red beans and rice, this skillet dish uses orzo pasta instead of rice.

Start to Finish: 30 minutes **Makes:** 4 main-dish servings

- 1 **14-ounce can chicken broth**
- 1 **cup water**
- 1½ **cups dried orzo (rosamarina) pasta**
- ½ **cup finely chopped onion (1 medium)**
- 1 **teaspoon dried Italian seasoning, crushed**
- 1 **15-ounce can red beans or pinto beans, rinsed and drained**
- 1 **large tomato, peeled, seeded, and chopped (1 cup)**
- 4 **slices bacon, crisp-cooked and crumbled, or ½ cup chopped ham**
- ¼ **cup snipped fresh Italian parsley**
- ⅓ **cup finely shredded Parmesan cheese**

1. Bring chicken broth and water to boiling in a large saucepan. Stir in orzo, onion, and Italian seasoning. Reduce heat. Boil gently, uncovered, for 12 to 15 minutes or until orzo is just tender and liquid is absorbed, stirring frequently.

2. Stir in beans, tomato, bacon, and parsley; heat through. Top with Parmesan cheese.

Per 1½ cups: 580 cal., 18 g total fat (9 g sat. fat), 38 mg chol., 1,474 mg sodium, 71 g carbo., 8 g fiber, 36 g pro.
Daily Values: 15% vit. A, 25% vit. C, 61% calcium, 27% iron
Exchanges: ½ Vegetable, 4½ Starch, 3 Lean Meat, 1 Fat

Autumn Succotash

Autumn Succotash (LOW FAT) (FAST)

Start to Finish: 25 minutes
Makes: 6 to 8 side-dish servings

- 1 10-ounce package frozen lima beans
- 1 10-ounce package frozen whole kernel corn
- 2 small tomatoes, seeded and chopped
- ¼ cup sliced green onion (2)
- 1 tablespoon snipped fresh parsley
- ¼ cup red wine vinegar
- 2 tablespoons bottled Italian salad dressing
- ¼ teaspoon dry mustard

1. Cook lima beans and corn according to package directions; drain. In a bowl combine lima beans, corn, tomato, green onion, and parsley.

2. In a small mixing bowl whisk together red wine vinegar, dressing, and mustard. Pour over lima bean mixture; toss to coat. Serve at room temperature or chilled.

Per ⅔ cup: 129 cal., 3 g total fat (0 g sat. fat), 0 mg chol.,
74 mg sodium, 24 g carbo., 3 g fiber, 5 g pro.
Daily Values: 28% vit. C
Exchanges: 1½ Starch

Beans with Pesto Bulgur
(VEGETARIAN)

This colorful dish can be served warm or chilled.

Prep: 20 minutes **Stand:** 1 hour **Cook:** 1¼ hours
Makes: 4 main-dish servings

- ¾ cup dry cranberry beans, dry Christmas (calico) lima beans, or dry pinto beans
- 1⅓ cups vegetable broth or chicken broth
- ⅔ cup bulgur

- ¾ cup chopped red sweet pepper (1 medium)
- ¼ cup thinly sliced green onion (2)
- ⅓ cup purchased basil pesto

1. Rinse dry beans. In a large saucepan combine beans and 5 cups *water*. Bring to boiling; reduce heat. Simmer for 2 minutes. Remove from heat. Cover and let stand for 1 hour. (Or place beans in water in a large saucepan. Cover and let soak in a cool place for 6 to 8 hours or overnight.) Drain and rinse beans.

2. Return beans to pan. Add 5 cups fresh *water*. Bring to boiling; reduce heat. Simmer, covered, for 1¼ to 1½ hours for cranberry and pinto beans or 45 to 60 minutes for Christmas lima beans or until tender; drain.

3. Meanwhile, in a medium saucepan bring broth to boiling; add bulgur. Return to boiling; reduce heat. Simmer, covered, about 15 minutes or until most of the liquid is absorbed. Remove from heat. Stir in the cooked beans, sweet pepper, green onion, and pesto. Season with freshly ground *black pepper*.

Shortcut option: Prepare as above, except omit Steps 1 and 2. Substitute one 15-ounce can pinto beans, drained, for the beans in Step 3.

Per cup: 359 cal., 14 g total fat (2 g sat. fat), 3 mg chol.,
483 mg sodium, 46 g carbo., 14 g fiber, 14 g pro.
Daily Values: 20% vit. A, 82% vit. C, 5% calcium, 12% iron
Exchanges: 3 Starch, 1 Very Lean Meat, 2 Fat

Bean Basics

Many civilizations have enjoyed beans for ages, and nutrition is only the beginning of their power. They also add great taste and texture to dishes. Keep the following information about beans in mind.

● Dried beans store well, but the older they are the longer it will take to cook them. Buy beans from a store that has a quick turnaround and do not combine new packages of beans with older packages.

● Think cooking dried beans is too time-consuming? Beans may be cooked in advance and refrigerated for up to 3 days.

● Canned beans are also a quick option for families on the go. The downside is that they can contribute sodium to your diet. A simple solution is to rinse the beans, as pictured on page 92.

White Beans and Wilted Spinach `FAST`

Start to Finish: 15 minutes **Makes:** 4 side-dish servings

- 1 **medium onion, halved and thinly sliced**
- 6 **cloves garlic, minced (1 tablespoon)**
- 1 **tablespoon extra virgin olive oil**
- 1 **15- to 19-ounce can white kidney (cannellini) or navy beans, rinsed and drained**
- 1 **14.5-ounce can diced tomatoes**
- 1 **tablespoon chopped fresh thyme**
- 4 **cups torn fresh spinach**
- 2 **slices turkey bacon, cooked, drained, and crumbled**
- 4 **teaspoons bottled balsamic or red wine vinaigrette**

1. In a skillet cook onion and garlic in hot olive oil about 3 minutes or until tender. Stir in beans.

2. Drain tomatoes, reserving ⅓ cup liquid (discard remaining liquid). Add thyme. Stir in tomatoes and reserved tomato liquid. Cook and stir over medium heat about 2 minutes or until heated through. Stir in 3 cups of the spinach; cover and cook about 30 seconds or until just wilted. Stir in remaining spinach and bacon. Spoon mixture into four individual bowls. Drizzle each serving with 1 teaspoon vinaigrette. Season to taste with *salt* and *black pepper*.

Per ⅔ cup: 170 cal., 7 total fat (1 g sat. fat), 8 mg chol., 580 mg sodium, 25 g carbo., 6 g fiber, 8 g pro.
Daily Values: 57% vit. A, 41% vit. C, 11% calcium, 15% iron
Exchanges: 2 Vegetable, 1 Starch, ½ Very Lean Meat, ½ Fat

Lentil Basics

Lentils are low in fat, high in protein and fiber, and they cook quickly for down-to-the-wire meals. There are three main varieties: brown, yellow, and red.

● Brown lentils, sold with their seed coats on, are widely available and relatively large in size. They tend to lose their shape after long cooking times.

● Yellow lentils, sold skinned and split, also are relatively large. They have a mild, nutty flavor.

● Red lentils are small and cook faster than the other lentils. Use them in soups, purees, and when shape retention is not a factor.

● To substitute one type of lentil for another, you may have to adjust cooking times. Check package labels for directions.

Lentil and Veggie Tostadas
`LOW FAT` `FAST` `EGETARIAN`

See photo, page 85.

Start to Finish: 20 minutes **Makes:** 4 main-dish servings

- 1¾ **cups water**
- ¾ **cup red lentils, rinsed and drained**
- ¼ **cup chopped onion**
- ½ **teaspoon salt**
- ½ **teaspoon ground cumin**
- 1 **clove garlic, minced**
- 1 to 2 **tablespoons snipped cilantro**
- 4 **tostada shells**
- 2 **cups assorted chopped vegetables (such as broccoli, tomato, zucchini, and/or yellow summer squash)**
- ¾ **cup shredded Monterey Jack cheese (3 ounces)**

1. In a medium saucepan stir together the water, lentils, onion, salt, cumin, and garlic. Bring to boiling; reduce heat. Simmer, covered, for 12 to 15 minutes or until lentils are tender and most of the liquid is absorbed. Use a fork to mash the cooked lentils; stir in cilantro.

2. Spread lentil mixture on tostada shells; top with vegetables and cheese. Place on a large baking sheet. Broil 6 inches from the heat about 2 minutes or until cheese melts.

Per tostada: 280 cal., 10 g total fat (4 g sat. fat), 19 mg chol., 427 mg sodium, 33 g carbo., 7 g fiber, 15 g pro.
Daily Values: 11% vit. A, 31% vit. C, 21% calcium, 13% iron
Exchanges: ½ Vegetable, 2 Starch, 1 High-Fat Meat

French Lentils with Rice and Vegetables

French (green) lentils are gaining in popularity because they hold their shape after cooking, making them a great choice for salads.

Prep: 15 minutes **Cook:** 30 minutes **Cool:** 1 hour
Makes: 6 side-dish servings

- 3 **cups water**
- ½ **teaspoon salt**
- ½ **cup dry French lentils, rinsed and drained**
- 1 **recipe Dijon Dressing (page 97)**
- ½ **cup uncooked basmati rice or long grain rice**
- ½ **cup chopped carrot (1 medium)**
- ½ **cup chopped yellow summer squash**
- ½ **cup chopped seedless cucumber**
- ⅔ **cup coarsely chopped yellow, red, or green sweet pepper**

2 **roma tomatoes, seeded and finely chopped**
2 **tablespoons chopped shallots**
½ **cup crumbled feta cheese (2 ounces)
(optional)**

1. In a medium saucepan heat the water and salt to boiling. Stir in lentils. Return to boiling; reduce heat. Simmer, covered, for 15 minutes. Add rice; simmer, covered, for about 15 minutes more or until rice and lentils are tender. Let stand, covered, for 5 minutes. If necessary, drain well. Spoon into a large bowl; set aside to cool about 1 hour.

2. Prepare the Dijon Dressing and set aside.

3. Stir carrot, summer squash, cucumber, sweet pepper, tomato, and shallot into rice mixture. Add dressing; toss salad gently to coat. Serve at room temperature or chilled. If desired, before serving, sprinkle with feta cheese.

Dijon Dressing: In a blender combine ¼ cup olive oil, 2 tablespoons lemon juice, 2 tablespoons Dijon-style mustard, 1 clove garlic, ¼ teaspoon salt, and ¼ teaspoon black pepper. Cover and blend until mixture is smooth.

Per ¾ cup: 216 cal., 9 g total fat (1 g sat. fat), 0 mg chol.,
423 mg sodium, 28 g carbo., 6 g fiber, 7 g pro.
Daily Values: 32% vit. A, 111% vit. C, 4% calcium, 12% iron
Exchanges: ½ Vegetable, 1½ Starch, 2 Fat

Baked Cheese Grits

Prep: 10 minutes **Bake:** 25 minutes **Oven:** 325°F
Stand: 5 minutes **Makes:** 4 or 5 side-dish servings

2 **cups water or chicken broth**
½ **cup quick-cooking grits**
1 **egg, beaten**
1 **cup shredded Monterey Jack or cheddar
cheese (4 ounces)**
1 **tablespoon butter or margarine**

1. In a saucepan bring water to boiling. Slowly add grits, stirring constantly. Gradually stir about ½ cup of the grits mixture into the egg. Return egg mixture to saucepan and stir to combine. Remove saucepan from heat. Stir cheese and butter into grits mixture until melted.

2. Spoon grits into a 1-quart casserole. Bake in a 325°F oven for 25 to 30 minutes or until a knife inserted near the center comes out clean. Let stand for 5 minutes before serving.

Per ⅔ cup: 223 cal., 13 g total fat (8 g sat. fat), 88 mg chol.,
458 mg sodium, 16 g carbo., 0 g fiber, 10 g pro.
Daily Values: 11% vit. A, 18% calcium, 6% iron
Exchanges: 1 Starch, 1 High-Fat Meat, ½ Fat

Polenta NO FAT

Prep: 30 minutes **Cool:** 30 minutes **Chill:** 30 minutes
Bake: 20 minutes **Oven:** 350°F
Makes: 6 side-dish servings

1 **cup cornmeal**
½ **teaspoon salt**
 **Spaghetti sauce, pizza sauce, or taco sauce
(optional)**
 Grated Parmesan cheese (optional)

1. In a medium saucepan bring 2¾ cups *water* to boiling. Meanwhile, in a medium bowl combine cornmeal, 1 cup cold *water,* and salt.

2. Slowly add cornmeal mixture to boiling water, stirring constantly. Cook and stir until mixture returns to boiling. Reduce heat to low. Cook for 10 to 15 minutes or until mixture is very thick, stirring frequently (see photo, below).

3. Pour hot mixture into a 9-inch pie plate, spreading it in an even layer; cool. Cover and chill about 30 minutes or until firm. Bake, uncovered, in a 350°F oven about 20 minutes or until hot. Cut into wedges. If desired, serve with spaghetti sauce and sprinkle with Parmesan cheese.

Per 2 wedges: 84 cal., 0 g total fat (0 g sat. fat), 0 mg chol.,
199 mg sodium, 18 g carbo., 2 g fiber, 2 g pro.
Daily Values: 2% vit. A, 5% iron
Exchanges: 1 Starch

Fried Polenta: Prepare as above, except pour the hot mixture into a 7½×3½×2-inch or 8×4×2-inch loaf pan; cool. Cover and chill for several hours or overnight. Remove from pan and cut into twelve ½-inch-thick slices. In a large skillet fry half of the polenta slices in 2 tablespoons butter over medium heat for 8 to 10 minutes on each side or until brown and crisp. Repeat with remaining slices, adding 1 tablespoon more butter. If desired, serve with additional butter and honey or maple-flavored syrup. Makes 6 servings.

Per 2 slices: 124 cal., 6 g total fat (1 g sat. fat), 0 mg chol.,
171 mg sodium, 15 g carbo., 1 g fiber, 2 g pro.
Daily Values: 2% vit. A, 1% calcium, 5% iron
Exchanges: 1 Starch, 1 Fat

Cook the cornmeal mixture over low heat, stirring occasionally, until it is extremely thick.

Cheese and Basil Polenta VEGETARIAN

Prep: 40 minutes **Cool:** 1 hour **Chill:** 3 hours
Bake: 40 minutes **Stand:** 10 minutes **Oven:** 350°F
Makes: 6 main-dish servings

- **6 ounces fontina or mozzarella cheese, shredded (1½ cups)**
- **⅓ cup grated Parmesan or Romano cheese**
- **2 tablespoons snipped fresh basil or 2 teaspoons dried basil, crushed**
- **1 cup yellow cornmeal**
- **½ teaspoon salt**
- **1 recipe Tomato-Basil Sauce**

1. In a medium bowl stir together fontina cheese, Parmesan cheese, and basil; set aside. Grease a 2-quart square baking dish; set aside.

2. For polenta, in a saucepan bring 2¾ cups *water* to boiling. Meanwhile, in a bowl stir together cornmeal, 1 cup cold *water,* and salt. Slowly add cornmeal mixture to boiling water, stirring constantly. Cook and stir until mixture returns to boiling. Reduce heat to low. Cook for 10 to 15 minutes or until mixture is thick, stirring occasionally (see photo, page 97).

3. Pour one-third of the hot mixture into the prepared baking dish. Sprinkle with half of the cheese mixture. Repeat layers, ending with the hot mixture. Cool for 1 hour. Cover with foil and chill 3 hours or overnight until firm.

4. Bake polenta, uncovered, in a 350°F oven about 40 minutes or until light brown and heated through. Let stand for 10 minutes before serving. Serve with Tomato-Basil Sauce. If desired, garnish with additional fresh *basil.*

Tomato-Basil Sauce: In a medium saucepan cook ¾ cup chopped onion and 2 cloves garlic, minced, in 2 tablespoons hot butter or margarine until onion is tender. Carefully stir in two undrained 14.5-ounce cans whole Italian-style tomatoes, cut up; half of a 6-ounce can (⅓ cup) tomato paste; ½ teaspoon sugar; ¼ teaspoon salt; and ⅛ teaspoon ground black pepper. Bring to boiling; reduce heat. Simmer, uncovered, about 20 minutes or to desired consistency. Stir in ¼ cup snipped fresh basil or 1 tablespoon dried basil, crushed. Cook 5 minutes more. Makes about 3⅓ cups sauce.

Per 4×2½-inch piece: 310 cal., 15 g total fat (9 g sat. fat), 47 mg chol., 969 mg sodium, 29 g carbo., 4 g fiber, 14 g pro.
Daily Values: 41% vit. A, 34% vit. C, 27% calcium, 14% iron
Exchanges: 1 Vegetable, 1½ Starch, 1 Medium-Fat Meat, 1½ Fat

Sesame Tofu Stir-Fry

Sesame Tofu Stir-Fry FAST VEGETARIAN

Start to Finish: 30 minutes **Makes:** 4 main-dish servings

- **1 12- to 16-ounce package refrigerated water-packed firm or extra-firm tofu (fresh bean curd), drained and cut into ½-inch cubes (see tip, page 99)**
- **¼ cup finely chopped peanuts**
- **1 tablespoon sesame seeds**
- **1 teaspoon grated fresh ginger or ½ teaspoon ground ginger**
- **⅛ teaspoon crushed red pepper**
- **1 tablespoon cooking oil**
- **1 16-ounce bag frozen stir-fry vegetables, thawed**
- **⅔ cup bottled stir-fry sauce**
- **2 cups hot cooked rice**
- **2 green onions, thinly sliced (¼ cup)**
- **1 medium orange, cut into 8 wedges**

1. Place tofu on paper towels. In a bowl combine 1 tablespoon of the peanuts, the sesame seeds, ginger, and red pepper. Add tofu; toss.

2. In a skillet heat oil over medium-high heat. Add tofu mixture; stir-fry 4 minutes or until sesame seeds are toasted and tofu is golden.

3. Remove tofu mixture from skillet. Add vegetables to skillet; stir-fry 2 to 3 minutes or until heated through. Add stir-fry sauce; cook until mixture is bubbly. Stir in tofu; heat through. Serve over rice. Sprinkle with remaining peanuts and green onion. Serve with orange wedges.

Per 1 cup tofu mixture + ½ cup rice: 386 cal., 14 g total fat (2 g sat. fat), 1 mg chol.,1,054 mg sodium, 45 g carbo., 6 g fiber, 19 g pro.
Daily Values: 23% vit. A, 58% vit. C, 13% calcium, 17% iron
Exchanges: 1 Vegetable, 1½ Starch, 1 Other Carbo., 2 Medium-Fat Meat, ½ Fat

Crispy Tofu and Vegetables

LOW FAT VEGETARIAN

Prep: 15 minutes **Marinate:** 15 minutes
Cook: 9 minutes **Makes:** 4 main-dish servings

  2 **cups fresh sugar snap peas (8 ounces)**
  1 **12- to 16-ounce package refrigerated water-packed light, reduced-fat, or regular extra-firm tofu (fresh bean curd), drained (see tip, right)**
  3 **tablespoons reduced-sodium teriyaki sauce or soy sauce**
  ¼ **cup yellow cornmeal**
  ⅛ **teaspoon cayenne pepper**
  2 **teaspoons toasted sesame oil**
  2 **medium red and/or yellow sweet peppers, cut into thin strips**
  8 **green onions, cut into 2-inch pieces**
  2 **teaspoons cooking oil**
  1 **tablespoon white or black sesame seeds, toasted (optional) (see tip, page 265)**

1. Remove strings and tips from pea pods; cut pea pods in half and set aside.

2. Cut tofu crosswise into eight ½-inch slices. Arrange in a single layer in a 2-quart rectangular baking dish. Pour 2 tablespoons of the teriyaki sauce over tofu; turn slices to coat. Marinate at room temperature for 15 minutes.

3. In a shallow dish combine cornmeal and cayenne pepper. Drain tofu slices, discarding marinade. Dip tofu slices in cornmeal mixture; press gently to coat both sides; set aside.

4. Pour 1 teaspoon of the sesame oil into a nonstick skillet. Preheat over medium-high heat. Stir-fry sweet pepper strips for 2 minutes. Add pea pods and green onion; stir-fry for 2 to 3 minutes more or until crisp-tender. Remove skillet from heat; stir the remaining 1 tablespoon teriyaki sauce into vegetables. Transfer vegetables to a serving platter; cover and keep warm. Wipe skillet clean.

5. In the same skillet heat remaining sesame oil and the cooking oil over medium heat. Cook tofu slices for 2½ to 3 minutes on each side or until crisp and golden brown, using a spatula to turn carefully. Serve tofu over vegetables. If desired, sprinkle with sesame seeds.

Per cup: 151 cal., 6 g total fat (1 g sat. fat), 0 mg chol., 473 mg sodium, 15 g carbo., 3 g fiber, 9 g pro.
Daily Values: 69% vit. A, 196% vit. C, 6% calcium, 14% iron
Exchanges: 1 Vegetable, ½ Starch, 1 Lean Meat, ½ Fat

Discovering Tofu

Tofu, also known as bean curd, is a good source of protein, phytochemicals, and isoflavonoids. Additionally, it has no cholesterol. Making tofu is similar to making simple cheeses (pressed curd tofu) or yogurt (silken tofu).

Before cooking tofu, drain, slice or cube it, and blot with paper towels to remove excess water. This allows more room for marinades to be absorbed, and will help prevent spattering.

Each tofu has its best use. Here is a quick reference to check before you buy.

Extra-firm: Ideal for when you want tofu that won't fall apart or if you want to break it into crumbles.

Firm: All-purpose tofu, strong enough to withstand frying and sauteing; retains some delicacy that extra-firm tofu lacks.

Flavored: Marinated, ready to use, and available in a variety of flavors.

Silken: Sold in shelf-stable packages; add to salads, puree for salad dressings and smoothies, or scramble with eggs.

Soft: Delicate, custardlike texture, which makes it a perfect choice for salads, smoothies, baked goods, sauces, and dips.

Mushroom-Tofu Pockets

VEGETARIAN

Prep: 25 minutes **Bake:** 25 minutes
Oven: 400°F **Makes:** 4 pockets

- 3 cups sliced white button mushrooms, (8 ounces)
- ¼ cup finely chopped red onion or thinly sliced green onion (2)
- ¼ teaspoon salt
- ¼ teaspoon black pepper
- 2 tablespoons olive oil
- ½ of a 12- to 16-ounce package refrigerated water-packed firm tofu (fresh bean curd), drained and diced*
- 2 tablespoons Worcestershire sauce or steak sauce
- 1 egg
- 1 teaspoon water
- ½ of a 17.3-ounce package frozen puff pastry sheets, thawed (1 sheet)
- 4 teaspoons Dijon-style mustard

1. In a large skillet cook mushrooms, onion, salt, and pepper in hot oil for 6 to 8 minutes or until tender. Set aside. Place tofu on paper towels to remove excess water.

2. Preheat oven to 400°F. Line a baking sheet with parchment paper; set aside. Place Worcestershire sauce in a bowl. Add tofu; stir gently to coat. Set aside. In a small bowl beat together egg and water; set aside.

3. On a lightly floured surface, roll pastry into a 12-inch square; cut into four squares. Spread each square with 1 teaspoon mustard. Divide the tofu mixture among the squares of pastry. Top tofu with mushroom mixture. Fold pastry over to form a rectangle, stretching pastry gently, if necessary; press edges with your fingers, then with tines of fork, to seal (pastry will be full). Place pockets on prepared baking sheet.

4. Prick tops of pockets several times with the fork; brush tops of pockets with egg mixture. Bake about 25 minutes or until golden. Cool slightly before serving.

*Note: Store tofu in the refrigerator, except if it's in a shelf-stable package. Once opened, refrigerate tofu covered with water for up to 1 week, changing water daily, or freeze for up to 5 months.

Per pocket: 438 cal., 31 g total fat (2 g sat. fat), 53 mg chol., 613 mg sodium, 28 g carbo., 1 g fiber, 13 g pro.
Daily Values: 1% vit. A, 1% vit. C, 6% calcium, 12% iron
Exchanges: ½ Vegetable, 1½ Starch, 1 Medium-Fat Meat, 5 Fat

Meatless Tacos

Meatless Tacos LOW FAT VEGETARIAN

These tacos are so good, you won't miss the meat!

Prep: 10 minutes **Cook:** 35 minutes **Makes:** 8 tacos

- ½ cup water
- ¼ cup lentils, rinsed and drained
- ¼ cup chopped onion (1 small)
- 8 taco shells
- 1 8-ounce can tomato sauce
- ½ of a 1.125- or 1.25-ounce envelope (5 teaspoons) taco seasoning mix
- 8 ounces refrigerated water-packed firm or extra-firm tofu (fresh bean curd), drained and finely chopped
- 1½ cups shredded lettuce
- 1 medium tomato, chopped
- ½ cup shredded cheddar cheese (2 ounces)

1. In a saucepan combine water, lentils, and onion. Bring to boiling; reduce heat. Simmer, covered, for 25 to 30 minutes or until lentils are tender and liquid is absorbed. Meanwhile, heat taco shells according to package directions.

2. Stir tomato sauce and taco seasoning mix into lentils. Bring to boiling; reduce heat. Simmer, uncovered, for 5 minutes. Stir in tofu; heat through. Spoon into taco shells. Top with lettuce, tomato, and cheese. If desired, serve with *bottled salsa.*

Per taco: 148 cal., 7 g total fat (2 g sat. fat), 7 mg chol., 460 mg sodium, 16 g carbo., 3 g fiber, 7 g pro.
Daily Values: 4% vit. A, 6% vit. C, 9% calcium, 8% iron
Exchanges: 1 Starch, ½ Lean Meat, 1 Fat

Bulgur Tacos: Prepare as on page 100, except increase water to ¾ cup and substitute bulgur for lentils. Simmer water, bulgur, and onion, covered, for about 15 minutes or until bulgur is tender and liquid is absorbed.

Per taco: 143 calories, 7 g total fat (2 g sat. fat), 7 mg chol., 460 mg sodium, 16 g carbo., 2 g fiber, 6 g pro.
Daily Values: 4% vit. A, 6% vit. C, 9% calcium, 6% iron
Exchanges: 1 Starch, ½ Lean Meat, 1 Fat

Vegetable Tacos: Prepare as on page 100, except stir 1 cup frozen whole kernel corn and ¾ cup shredded carrot into the tomato sauce mixture and increase the number of taco shells to 12.

Per taco: 133 cal., 6 g total fat (2 g sat. fat), 5 mg chol., 326 mg sodium, 17 g carbo., 3 g fiber, 6 g pro.
Daily Values: 46% vit. A, 6% vit. C, 7% calcium, 6% iron.
Exchanges: 1 Starch, ½ Lean Meat, ½ Fat

Garlic Edamame and Walnuts EASY

Start to Finish: 15 minutes **Makes:** 4 side-dish servings

- 1 12-ounce package frozen shelled sweet soybeans (edamame)
- 1 clove garlic, minced
- 1 tablespoon olive oil
- ¼ cup fine dry bread crumbs or panko (Japanese-style bread crumbs)
- ¼ cup finely chopped walnuts
- ⅛ teaspoon salt
- ⅛ teaspoon black pepper

1. Cook edamame according to package directions; drain.

2. In a large skillet cook garlic in hot oil until tender. Stir in bread crumbs, walnuts, salt, and pepper. Cook and stir over medium heat about 4 minutes or until crumbs and walnuts are light brown and crisp. Stir in edamame; heat through.

Per ¾ cup: 230 cal., 14 g total fat (2 g sat. fat), 0 mg chol., 266 mg sodium, 15 g carbo., 4 g fiber, 13 g pro.
Daily Values: 42% vit. A, 26% vit. C, 19% calcium, 20% iron
Exchanges: 1 Starch, 1½ Very Lean Meat, 2 Fat

Edamame

A great staple of the world.

The high protein content of edamame, also called sweet soybeans, is 35 percent, far beyond that of any other plant. The pods can be cooked as a vegetable or processed into many products, including tofu, miso, tempe, soymilk, and soybean oil.

Summer Spelt Medley

FAVORITE Summer Spelt Medley
WHOLE GRAIN

Nutty-flavored spelt is an ancestor of today's hybrid wheat, with a protein content 10 to 25 percent higher than wheat. It is available as berries (used here), flakes, and flour.

Prep: 20 minutes **Cook:** 1 hour **Chill:** 1 hour
Makes: 6 to 8 side-dish servings

- 1½ cups uncooked spelt
- ¾ cup chopped red sweet pepper (1 medium)
- ¾ cup chopped, seeded cucumber
- ½ cup shredded carrot (1 medium)
- ½ cup sliced radishes
- ¼ cup sliced green onions (2)
- ⅔ cup low-fat mayonnaise
- 2 tablespoons lemon juice
- ¼ teaspoon salt
- ⅛ teaspoon cayenne pepper

1. In a medium saucepan combine spelt and enough *water* to cover by 2 inches. Bring to boiling; reduce heat. Simmer, uncovered, about 1 hour or until tender. Drain well and place spelt in a large bowl.

2. Add sweet pepper, cucumber, carrot, radishes, and green onion to spelt; stir to combine. In a small mixing bowl whisk together mayonnaise, lemon juice, salt, and cayenne pepper. Add to spelt mixture and toss to coat. Cover and chill at least 1 hour or up to 6 hours.

Per cup: 278 cal., 10 g total fat (2 g sat. fat), 9 mg chol., 272 mg sodium, 41 g carbo., 5 g fiber, 7 g pro.
Daily Values: 56% vit. A, 68% vit. C, 2% calcium, 12% iron
Exchanges: ½ Vegetable, 2½ Starch, 1½ Fat

Wheat Berry Tabbouleh

Bulgur Tabbouleh: Prepare as at left, except omit wheat berries. Place ¾ cup bulgur in a colander; rinse with cold water. In a large bowl combine bulgur, cucumber, parsley, green onion, and mint. Prepare dressing as at left, except add 2 tablespoons water to the oil, lemon juice, and salt. Pour dressing over bulgur mixture; toss to coat. Cover and chill for 4 to 24 hours. Stir tomato into bulgur mixture just before serving.

Per cup: 228 cal., 14 g total fat (2 g sat. fat), 0 mg chol., 156 mg sodium, 24 g carbo., 6 g fiber, 4 g pro.
Daily Values: 8% vit. C, 3% calcium, 9% iron
Exchanges: 1½ Starch, ½ Vegetable, 2 Fat

Tabbouleh Wrap or Pita: For a wrap, place several lettuce leaves in the center of an 8-inch flour tortilla. Using a slotted spoon, top lettuce with ½ cup tabbouleh. Fold bottom of tortilla halfway over the tabbouleh, then fold over sides, forming a pocket. Or for a pita, line pita bread halves with lettuce leaves and fill each one with ½ cup tabbouleh. Makes 5 wraps or pita halves.

Per wrap or pita half: 173 cal., 7 g total fat (1 g sat. fat), 0 mg chol., 286 mg sodium, 24 g carbo., 2 g fiber, 4 g pro.
Daily Values: 24% vit. A, 20% vit. C, 5% calcium, 10% iron
Exchanges: 1½ Starch, ½ Vegetable, 1 Fat

Wheat Berry Tabbouleh

FAST   WHOLE GRAIN

Start to Finish: 25 minutes **Makes:** 5 side-dish servings

- 2⅔ **cups cooked wheat berries***
- ¾ **cup chopped tomato**
- ¾ **cup chopped cucumber**
- ½ **cup snipped fresh parsley**
- ¼ **cup thinly sliced green onion (2)**
- 1 **tablespoon snipped fresh mint**
- 3 **tablespoons cooking oil**
- 3 **tablespoons lemon juice**
- ¼ **teaspoon salt**
- 4 **lettuce leaves**

1. In a large bowl combine cooked wheat berries, tomato, cucumber, parsley, green onion, and mint.

2. For dressing, in a screw-top jar combine oil, lemon juice, and salt. Cover and shake well. Pour dressing over wheat berry mixture; toss to coat. Serve immediately or cover and chill for up to 4 hours. Serve in a lettuce-lined bowl and, if desired, garnish with *lemon slices*.

***Note:** To cook wheat berries, bring one 14-ounce can vegetable or chicken broth and ¼ cup water to boiling. Add 1 cup wheat berries. Return to boiling; reduce heat. Simmer, covered, for 45 to 60 minutes or until tender; drain. Cover and chill for up to 3 days.

Per cup: 148 cal., 9 g total fat (1 g sat fat), 0 mg chol., 295 mg sodium, 17 g carbo., 2 g fiber, 3 g pro.
Daily Values: 17% vit. A, 31% vit. C, 3% calcium, 8% iron
Exchanges: ½ Vegetable, 1 Starch, 1½ Fat

Peppers Stuffed with Cranberry Bulgur   LOW FAT   FAST

Bulgur is a staple of the Middle East. This steamed, dried, and crushed wheat kernel has a tender, chewy texture. See photo, page 83.

Start to Finish: 30 minutes **Makes:** 4 main-dish servings

- 1 **14-ounce can vegetable or chicken broth**
- ½ **cup shredded carrot (1 medium)**
- ¼ **cup chopped onion (1 small)**
- ¾ **cup bulgur**
- ⅓ **cup dried cranberries, cherries, or raisins**
- 2 **large or 4 small red, green, or yellow sweet peppers**
- ¾ **cup shredded Muenster, brick, or mozzarella cheese**
- ½ **cup water**
- 2 **tablespoons sliced almonds or chopped pecans, toasted (see tip, page 265)**

1. In a large skillet stir together the broth, carrot, and onion. Bring to boiling; reduce heat. Simmer, covered, for 5 minutes. Stir in bulgur and cranberries. Remove from heat. Cover and let stand for 5 minutes. Drain off excess liquid.

2. Meanwhile, halve the sweet peppers lengthwise, removing the seeds and membranes.

3. Stir shredded cheese into bulgur mixture; spoon into sweet pepper halves, dividing evenly. Place sweet pepper halves in skillet. Add the ½ cup water. Bring to boiling; reduce heat. Simmer, covered, for 5 to 10 minutes or until sweet peppers are crisp-tender and bulgur mixture is heated through. Sprinkle with nuts.

Per stuffed pepper: 260 cal., 9 g total fat (4 g sat. fat),
20 mg chol., 552 mg sodium, 37 g carbo., 8 g fiber, 10 g pro.
Daily Values: 70% vit. A, 181% vit. C, 19% calcium, 8% iron
Exchanges: 1 Vegetable, ½ Fruit, 1½ Starch, ½ High-Fat Meat, 1 Fat

Greek Quinoa and Avocados

Greek Quinoa and Avocados FAST VEGETARIAN

Prep: 15 minutes **Cook:** 15 minutes
Makes: 4 main-dish servings

- ½ cup uncooked quinoa, rinsed and drained
- 1 cup water
- 2 roma tomatoes, seeded and finely chopped
- ½ cup shredded fresh spinach
- ⅓ cup finely chopped red onion (1 small)
- 2 tablespoons lemon juice
- 2 tablespoons olive oil
- ½ teaspoon salt
  Spinach leaves
- 2 ripe avocados, halved, seeded, peeled, and sliced*
- ⅓ cup crumbled feta cheese (about 1½ ounces)

1. In a saucepan combine quinoa and water. Bring to boiling; reduce heat. Simmer, covered, about 15 minutes or until liquid is absorbed.

2. Place quinoa in a medium bowl. Add tomato, shredded spinach, and onion; stir to combine.

In a small bowl whisk together lemon juice, oil, and salt. Add to quinoa mixture; toss to coat.

3. Place spinach leaves on four salad plates. Arrange avocado slices on spinach leaves. Spoon quinoa mixture over avocado slices. Sprinkle with some of the feta cheese.

*Note: Brush avocado slices with additional lemon juice to prevent browning.

Per ½ cup quinoa + ½ avocado: 332 cal., 24 g total fat
(5 g sat. fat), 11 mg chol., 457 mg sodium, 27 g carbo., 8 g fiber,
7 g pro.
Daily Values: 46% vit. A, 37% vit. C, 11% calcium, 18% iron
Exchanges: ½ Vegetable, 1½ Starch, 4½ Fat

FAVORITE Fruit and Nut Baked Oatmeal

Oatmeal stars in this sweet bake infused with dried apricots, tart cherries, golden raisins, and, of course, brown sugar. It's perfect for a cold winter morning.

Prep: 15 minutes **Bake:** 20 minutes
Oven: 350°F **Makes:** 4 main-dish servings

- 1¾ cups milk
- 2 tablespoons butter or margarine
- 1 cup regular rolled oats
- ⅓ cup snipped dried apricots
- ⅓ cup dried tart cherries
- ⅓ cup golden raisins
- 4 tablespoons packed brown sugar
- ½ teaspoon vanilla
- ¼ teaspoon salt
- ½ cup coarsely chopped walnuts or pecans

1. In a medium saucepan bring 1¾ cups milk and butter to boiling. Slowly stir in oats. Stir in apricots, cherries, raisins, 2 tablespoons of the brown sugar, vanilla, and salt. Cook and stir for 1 minute. Pour into a lightly greased 1½-quart casserole.

2. Bake, uncovered, in a 350°F oven for 15 minutes. Sprinkle with the remaining 2 tablespoons brown sugar and nuts. Bake about 5 minutes more or until bubbly. Cool slightly. If desired, serve with additional milk.

Per cup: 455 cal., 20 g total fat (5 g sat. fat), 25 mg chol.,
250 mg sodium, 63 g carbo., 6 g fiber, 10 g pro.
Daily Values: 22% vit. A, 2% vit. C, 18% calcium, 14% iron
Exchanges: ½ Milk, 1½ Fruit, 1½ Starch, 1 Other Carbo., 3 Fat

Cranberry-Almond Cereal Mix `FAST` `LOW FAT`

Prep: 10 minutes **Cook:** 12 minutes
Makes: 14 side-dish servings

- 1 **cup regular rolled oats**
- 1 **cup quick-cooking barley**
- 1 **cup bulgur or cracked wheat**
- 1 **cup dried cranberries, snipped dried apricots, or raisins**
- ½ **cup sliced almonds, toasted (see tip, page 265)**
- ⅓ **cup sugar**
- 1 **tablespoon ground cinnamon**
- ¼ **teaspoon salt**
  Milk (optional)

1. Combine oats, barley, bulgur, cranberries, almonds, sugar, cinnamon, and salt. Cover tightly; store at room temperature for up to 6 months.

2. For two servings, in a small saucepan bring 1⅓ cups *water* to boiling. Add ⅔ cup of the cereal mix to boiling water; reduce heat. Simmer, covered, for 12 to 15 minutes or until cereal reaches desired consistency. If desired, serve with milk.

Microwave directions: For one breakfast serving, in a large microwave-safe cereal bowl combine ¾ cup *water* and ⅓ cup cereal mix. Microwave, uncovered, on 50 percent power (medium) for 8 to 11 minutes or until cereal reaches desired consistency, stirring once. Stir before serving. If desired, serve with milk.

Per ⅓ cup: 171 cal., 3 g total fat (0 g sat. fat), 0 mg chol., 46 mg sodium, 33 g carbo., 5 g fiber, 4 g pro.
Daily Values: 3% calcium, 6% iron
Exchanges: 2 Starch

Fruit Muesli `FAST`

Start to Finish: 10 minutes
Makes: 12 main-dish servings

- 4 **cups multigrain cereal with rolled rye, oats, barley, and wheat**
- 1 **cup regular rolled oats**
- ¾ **cup coarsely chopped almonds or pecans, toasted (see tip, page 265)**
- 1 **cup toasted wheat germ**
- 1 **7-ounce package mixed dried fruit bits**
- ½ **cup unsalted shelled sunflower seeds**
- ½ **cup dried banana chips, coarsely crushed**
  Milk or nonfat plain yogurt (optional)

1. In a large bowl stir together multigrain cereal, rolled oats, almonds, wheat germ, dried fruit bits, sunflower seeds, and banana chips.

Cover tightly and refrigerate for up to 4 weeks. If desired, serve with milk or yogurt.

Per ⅔ cup: 318 cal., 12 g total fat (3 g sat. fat), 0 mg chol., 13 mg sodium, 45 g carbo., 4 g fiber, 11 g pro.
Daily Values: 2% vit. C, 4% calcium, 16% iron
Exchanges: 1 Fruit, 2 Starch, ½ High-Fat Meat, 1 Fat

Granola

Granola

Prep: 10 minutes **Bake:** 30 minutes
Oven: 300°F **Makes:** 12 main-dish servings

- 2 **cups regular rolled oats**
- 1 **cup coarsely chopped sliced almonds, chopped walnuts, or chopped pecans**
- ½ **cup coconut (optional)**
- ½ **cup shelled sunflower seeds**
- ¼ **cup toasted wheat germ**
- ¼ **cup flax seeds**
- ½ **cup honey or maple-flavored syrup**
- 2 **tablespoons cooking oil**
- 1 **cup dried fruit (cherries, snipped pitted dates, raisins, or cranberries) (optional)**

1. Grease a 15×10×1-inch baking pan; set aside. In a bowl combine oats, almonds, coconut (if desired), sunflower seeds, wheat germ, and flax seeds. In a bowl combine honey and oil; stir into oat mixture. Spread evenly in the prepared pan. Bake in a 300°F oven for 30 to 35 minutes or until light brown, stirring after 20 minutes. If desired, stir in dried fruit.

2. Spread on a large piece of foil to cool. Store in an airtight container for up to 1 week. (Or store in freezer bags and freeze for up to 2 months.)

Per ½ cup: 244 cal., 13 g total fat (1 g sat. fat), 0 mg chol., 1 mg sodium, 28 g carbo., 4 g fiber, 7 g pro.
Daily Values: 5% calcium, 11% iron
Exchanges: 1½ Starch, ½ Other Carbo., 2 Fat

Cooking Grains

Use this chart as a guide when cooking grains. Measure the amount of water into a medium saucepan and bring to a full boil unless the chart indicates otherwise. If desired, add ¼ teaspoon salt to the water. Slowly add the grain and return to boiling; reduce heat. Simmer, covered, for the time specified or until most of the water is absorbed and the grain is tender.

Grain	Amount of Grain	Amount of Water	Cooking Direction	Yield
Barley, quick-cooking pearl	1¼ cups	2 cups	Simmer, covered, for 10 to 12 minutes. Drain, if necessary.	3 cups
Barley, regular pearl	¾ cup	3 cups	Simmer, covered, about 45 minutes. Drain, if necessary.	3 cups
Buckwheat groats or kasha	⅔ cup	1½ cups	Add to cold water. Bring to boiling. Simmer, covered, for 6 to 8 minutes.	2¼ cups
Bulgur	1 cup	2 cups	Add to cold water. Bring to boiling. Simmer, covered, about 15 minutes.	3 cups
Cornmeal	1 cup	2¾ cups	Combine cornmeal and 1 cup cold water. Add to the 2¾ cups boiling water. Simmer, covered, about 10 minutes, stirring occasionally.	3½ cups
Farina, quick-cooking	¾ cup	3½ cups	Simmer, uncovered, for 2 to 3 minutes, stirring constantly.	3½ cups
Hominy grits, quick-cooking	¾ cup	3 cups	Simmer, covered, about 5 minutes, stirring occasionally.	3 cups
Millet	¾ cup	2 cups	Simmer, covered, for 15 to 20 minutes. Let stand, covered, for 5 minutes.	3 cups
Oats, rolled, quick-cooking	1½ cups	3 cups	Simmer, uncovered, for 1 minute. Let stand, covered, for 3 minutes.	3 cups
Oats, rolled, regular	1⅔ cups	3 cups	Simmer, uncovered, for 5 to 7 minutes. Let stand, covered, for 3 minutes.	3 cups
Quinoa	¾ cup	1½ cups	Rinse well. Simmer, covered, about 15 minutes. Drain, if necessary.	1¾ cups
Rice, long grain white	1 cup	2 cups	Simmer, covered, about 15 minutes. Let stand, covered, for 5 minutes.	3 cups
Rice, regular brown	1 cup	2 cups	Simmer, covered, about 45 minutes. Let stand, covered, for 5 minutes.	3 cups
Rice, wild	1 cup	2 cups	Rinse well. Simmer, covered, about 40 minutes or until most of the water is absorbed. Drain, if necessary.	3 cups
Rye berries	¾ cup	2½ cups	Simmer, covered, about 1 hour. Drain. (Or soak berries in 2½ cups water in the refrigerator for 6 to 24 hours. Do not drain. Bring to boiling; reduce heat. Simmer, covered, for 30 minutes.)	2 cups
Spelt	1 cup	3 cups	Simmer, covered, for 50 to 60 minutes.	2½ cups
Wheat berries	¾ cup	2½ cups	Simmer, covered, for 45 to 60 minutes. Drain. (Or soak and cook as for rye berries.)	2 cups
Wheat, cracked	⅔ cup	1½ cups	Add to cold water. Bring to boiling. Simmer, covered, for 12 to 15 minutes. Let stand, covered, for 5 minutes.	1¾ cups

Cooking Dry Beans, Lentils, and Split Peas

Rinse beans, lentils, or split peas. (See special cooking instructions below for black-eyed peas, fava beans, lentils, and split peas.) In a large Dutch oven combine 1 pound beans and 8 cups cold water. Bring to boiling; reduce heat. Simmer for 2 minutes. Remove from heat. Cover and let stand for 1 hour. (Or omit simmering; soak beans in cold water overnight in a covered Dutch oven.) Drain and rinse. In the same Dutch oven combine beans and 8 cups fresh water. Bring to boiling; reduce heat. Simmer, covered, for time listed below or until beans are tender, stirring occasionally. Cooking time depends on the dryness of the beans.

Variety	Amount	Appearance	Cooking Time	Yield
Black beans	1 pound	Small, black, oval	1 to 1½ hours	6 cups
Black-eyed peas	1 pound	Small, cream color, oval (one side has a black oval with a cream-color dot in the center)	Do not presoak. Simmer, covered, for 45 minutes to 1 hour.	7 cups
Cranberry beans	1 pound	Small, tan color with specks and streaks of burgundy, oval	1¼ to 1½ hours	7 cups
Fava or broad beans	1 pound	Large, brown, flat oval	Follow these soaking directions instead of those above: Bring beans to boiling; simmer, covered, 15 to 30 minutes to soften skins. Let stand 1 hour. Drain and peel. To cook, combine peeled beans and 8 cups fresh water. Bring to boiling; reduce heat. Simmer, covered, 45 to 50 minutes or until tender.	6 cups
Garbanzo beans (chickpeas)	1 pound	Medium, yellow or golden, round and irregular	1½ to 2 hours	6¼ cups
Great Northern beans	1 pound	Small to medium, white, kidney shape	1 to 1½ hours	7 cups
Kidney beans, red	1 pound	Medium to large, brownish red, kidney shape	1 to 1½ hours	6⅔ cups
Lentils (brown or French)	1 pound	Tiny, brownish green, disk shape	Do not presoak. Use 5 cups water. Simmer, covered, about 30 minutes.	7 cups
Lima beans, baby	1 pound	Small, off-white, wide oval	45 minutes to 1 hour	6½ cups
Lima beans, Christmas (calico)	1 pound	Medium, burgundy and cream color, wide oval	45 minutes to 1 hour	6½ cups
Lima beans, large (butter beans)	1 pound	Medium, off-white, wide oval	1 to 1¼ hours	6½ cups
Navy or pea beans	1 pound	Small, off-white, oval	1 to 1½ hours	6¼ cups
Pinto beans	1 pound	Small, tan color with brown specks, oval	1¼ to 1½ hours	6½ cups
Red beans	1 pound	Small, dark red, oval	1 to 1½ hours	6½ cups
Soybeans	1 pound	Small, cream color, oval	3 to 3½ hours	7 cups
Split peas	1 pound	Tiny, green or yellow, disk shape	Do not presoak. Use 5 cups water. Simmer, covered, about 45 minutes.	5½ cups

Beverages

Hot Spiced Cider, 113   Icy Cranberry Margaritas, 118   Vanilla-Orange Smoothies, 116

Beverages Essentials

Does the day's first cup of tea or coffee give you a feeling of aah? Use these basic brewing methods to improve that first cup. And learn how to concoct your coffeehouse favorites.

Types of Tea

Black teas are fermented, making them the strongest, richest, and most mellow type of tea.

Green teas are not fermented and are milder than black or oolong teas.

Oolong teas are partially fermented and have a richer, mellower flavor than green tea but are not as strong and rich as black tea.

Oolong Tea

Green Tea

Black Tea

White teas are the least processed of all and produce a pale yellow beverage that is light and fragrant.

Tea Products

Loose tea and individual or pitcher-size *tea bags,* either in regular or decaffeinated forms, are commonly available. Brewing loose tea requires adding boiling water to the tea, then straining it before serving, or using an infuser, such as a tea ball or spoon-shape container (see above), which eliminates the need for straining.

Instant tea powder is available flavored, sweetened with sugar, or artificially sweetened.

Flavored teas, such as black currant tea, are teas mixed with fruit, spices, or herbs.

Herbal "teas," called tisanes, contain no tea. They are herbal beverages made from flowers, herbs, spices, fruit, berries, or other plants. Chamomile and lemon verbena are common herbal teas.

Refrigerator-Brewed Iced Tea: In glass container place six to eight tea bags in 1½ quarts cold water. Cover. Let tea "brew" in refrigerator about 24 hours. Remove tea bags. Serve tea in tall glasses over ice.

Tea Beverages

Hot Tea: To prepare five (6-ounce) servings, warm a teapot by filling it with boiling water. If using loose tea, measure 3 to 6 teaspoons loose tea into a tea ball or infuser. Empty teapot; add tea ball or three to six tea bags to pot. Immediately add 4 cups boiling water to teapot. Cover and let steep for 3 to 5 minutes. Remove tea ball or tea bags and discard used tea leaves. Serve at once.

Iced Tea: To make five servings, prepare Hot Tea (above), except use 4 to 8 teaspoons loose tea or four to eight tea bags. Steep as above and cool at room temperature for 2 hours. Serve over ice cubes and store leftovers in the refrigerator. (It is fine to use herbal, green, and black teas for brewing iced tea in the refrigerator [see inset, below] because refrigeration inhibits the growth of bacteria.)

Coffee Products

Whole coffee beans are blended and roasted to varying degrees. Longer-roasted beans yield a brewed coffee with a darker color and a stronger, slightly bitter flavor.

Ground coffee is available in drip, regular, and fine grinds for different brewing methods; the finer the grind, the shorter the brewing.

Flavored coffee is coffee mixed with various flavorings, such as hazelnut. It is available in whole bean, ground, and instant forms.

Instant coffee is powdered or freeze-dried crystals made from brewed coffee. It needs water added to make the beverage. Instant espresso coffee powder also is available.

Decaffeinated coffee has had much of coffee's naturally occurring caffeine extracted. Some blends of caffeinated and decaffeinated coffee also can be purchased.

Flavored Coffee   Medium Roast   Dark Roast

Making Coffee

Drip Coffee: For each 6-ounce cup desired, use 1 to 2 tablespoons ground coffee and ¾ cup water. Measure ground coffee into a filter-lined coffeemaker basket. For an electric drip coffeemaker, pour cold water into water compartment. Place pot on heating element; let water drip through basket. For a nonelectric drip coffeemaker, pour boiling water over coffee in basket. Let water drip into pot. When dripping stops, remove basket and discard grounds.

Percolator Coffee: For each 6-ounce cup desired, use 1 to 2 tablespoons ground coffee and ¾ cup water. Pour cold water into pot. Stand stem and basket firmly in pot. Measure ground coffee into basket, replace basket lid, and cover pot. Turn pot on, let water come to boiling, and perk gently for 5 to 8 minutes. Let coffee stand 1 to 2 minutes. Remove basket; discard grounds.

French Press Coffee (plunger brewing): For each 6-ounce cup desired, use 1 to 2 tablespoons coarse ground coffee and ¾ cup water. Measure ground coffee into carafe. Pour freshly boiled water over coffee. Let stand a few minutes. Press the plunger filter through the water, trapping grounds beneath. After pouring coffee, discard grounds.

Coffee Beverages

Espresso: To make this strong, dark coffee, brew it under pressure in an espresso coffee machine according to the manufacturer's directions. If you don't have an espresso machine, prepare four (2-ounce) servings using a drip coffeemaker, 1 cup cold water, and ⅓ cup French roast or espresso roast coffee, ground as directed for your coffeemaker; brew according to manufacturer's directions. Pour into small cups; serve with sugar cubes or coarse sugar.

Cappuccino: To make cappuccino, top espresso with foamy, steamed milk. For four (4-ounce) servings, prepare espresso (above). In a small saucepan warm 1 cup low-fat milk over medium heat until hot but not boiling. Process milk in a food processor or blender until frothy. (If your espresso machine has a steaming nozzle, heat and froth milk according to manufacturer's directions.) Divide espresso among 5- to 8-ounce cups and top

Espresso   Cappuccino   Café Latte

with frothy milk. Sprinkle with ground cinnamon or grated chocolate. If desired, serve with sugar.

Café Latte: To make latte, top espresso with extra-foamy steamed milk. For four (6-ounce) servings, prepare cappuccino (above), except increase low-fat milk to 2 cups. If desired, serve with sugar.

Iced Coffee: To make six (8-ounce) servings, measure ½ cup ground coffee into a filter-lined drip coffeemaker basket. Prepare coffee according to coffeemaker instructions using 6 measuring cups cold water. Cover; chill at least 2 hours. Serve over ice. If desired, stir in half-and-half, sugar, and flavoring.

Chill Out

For individual beverages: Freeze fruit juice or iced tea in ice-cube trays and use cubes to chill a fruity drink or tea without diluting it.

For the punch bowl: Keep punch chilled by floating a ring of frozen fruit juice in it. To make a decorative ring, arrange desired fruit in a ring mold, add about 1 inch of desired fruit juice to hold fruit in place, and freeze. Fill mold with additional juice; place in freezer until ready to use. Unmold by holding bottom of mold under warm water for a few seconds.

Hot Orange and Mocha Drink [FAST]

To make orange peel curls for a garnish, use a vegetable peeler to remove orange peel in a long, thin strip. Cut strips into even thinner strips. Wrap the peel around a wooden skewer and let stand several minutes. Remove the skewer before using.

Start to Finish: 20 minutes **Makes:** 6 servings

    1 orange
    5 cups hot strong coffee
  ½ cup unsweetened cocoa powder
  ½ cup packed brown sugar
  ¼ teaspoon ground cinnamon
  ½ cup whipping cream, half-and-half, or
       light cream
    1 recipe Whipped Honey-Orange Topping
       Orange peel curls (optional)

1. Using a vegetable peeler, remove the peel from the orange in strips, being careful not to remove the white pith. In a large saucepan combine the peel and hot coffee. Let stand over medium-low heat for 5 minutes. Remove the peel with a slotted spoon and discard.

2. Meanwhile, in a small bowl whisk together cocoa powder, brown sugar, and cinnamon. Whisk cocoa mixture into hot coffee until well combined. Stir in cream. If desired, use an immersion blender to froth the coffee mixture. Ladle coffee mixture into six coffee mugs. Top each serving with a spoonful of Whipped Honey-Orange Topping. If desired, garnish with orange peel curls.

Whipped Honey-Orange Topping: In a chilled mixing bowl combine ½ cup whipping cream, 1 tablespoon honey, and, if desired, 1 tablespoon orange liqueur or orange juice. Beat with chilled beaters of an electric mixer on low speed or with a whisk until soft peaks form.

Icy Orange and Mocha Drink: Prepare as above, except cover and chill coffee mixture up to 3 days. Serve chilled in tall glasses over ice.

Per 7 ounces: 256 cal., 17 g total fat (9 g sat. fat), 55 mg chol., 24 mg sodium, 25 g carbo., 0 g fiber, 3 g pro.
Daily Values: 12% vit. A, 12% calcium, 8% iron
Exchanges: 1½ Other Carbo., 3½ Fat

Iced Green Tea [NO FAT]

Prep: 25 minutes **Cool:** several hours **Makes:** 12 servings

  12 cups water
  ¼ cup sugar
    3 inches fresh ginger, peeled and thinly sliced
  12 to 16 bags green tea
       Ice cubes

1. In a large saucepan combine water, sugar, and ginger. Bring to boiling; reduce heat. Simmer, covered, 5 minutes. Remove from heat. Add tea bags; cover and let stand for 3 minutes. Remove and discard tea bags. Strain ginger from tea; discard ginger. Transfer tea to a 2-gallon pitcher or punch bowl. Cover; cool several hours. If desired, chill. Serve in glasses over ice.

Per 8 ounces: 18 cal., 0 g total fat (0 g sat. fat), 0 mg chol., 7 mg sodium, 5 g carbo., 0 g fiber, 0 g pro.
Exchanges: Free

Chai [FAST]

Start to Finish: 15 minutes **Makes:** 2 servings

  ½ cup water
    1 bag black tea, such as orange pekoe,
       English breakfast, Lapsang Souchong,
       or Darjeeling
    1 3-inch piece stick cinnamon
    2 cups milk
    2 tablespoons raw sugar or honey
    1 teaspoon vanilla
  ⅛ teaspoon ground ginger
  ⅛ teaspoon ground cardamom

1. In a small saucepan combine the water, tea bag, and cinnamon. Bring to boiling. Remove from heat. Cover and let stand for 5 minutes. Discard tea bag and cinnamon stick. Stir milk, sugar, vanilla, ginger, and cardamom into tea. Cook and stir over medium heat just until mixture is heated through (do not boil). Serve in warm mugs.

Per 10 ounces: 175 cal., 5 g total fat (3 g sat. fat), 18 mg chol., 124 mg sodium, 24 g carbo., 0 g fiber, 8 g pro.
Daily Values: 10% vit. A, 4% vit. C, 30% calcium, 1% iron
Exchanges: 1 Milk, 1 Other Carbo., ½ Fat

Chocolate Chai: Prepare as above, except stir in 1 tablespoon unsweetened Dutch-process cocoa powder with the milk and spices. Heat through. Serve topped with whipped cream. If desired, sprinkle with ground nutmeg.

Per 10 ounces: 212 cal. 8 g total fat (5 g sat. fat), 29 mg chol., 127 mg sodium, 26 g carbo., 0 g fiber, 9 g pro.
Daily Values: 12% vit. A, 4% vit. C, 33% calcium, 3% iron
Exchanges: 1 Milk, 1 Other Carbo., 1½ Fat

Cranberry Tea

Prep: 15 minutes **Chill:** 2 hours **Makes:** 5 servings

- 3 **cups water**
- 4 **bags green tea**
- 1 **bag mint tea**
- 2 **cups cranberry juice, chilled**
  Ice cubes
  Fresh mint leaves or fresh cranberries (optional)

1. In a medium saucepan bring the water to boiling. Remove from heat. Add tea bags. Cover and let stand for 10 minutes. Remove and discard tea bags. Cover and chill for 2 hours.

2. Transfer tea to a pitcher; stir in the cranberry juice. Serve over ice. If desired, garnish with mint leaves or cranberries. Chill remaining tea up to 2 days.

Per 8 ounces: 58 cal., 0 g total fat (0 g sat. fat), 0 mg chol.,
6 mg sodium, 15 g carbo., 0 g fiber, 0 g pro.
Daily Values: 60% vit. C, 1% calcium, 1% iron
Exchanges: 1 Fruit

Hot Chocolate Mix

Start to Finish: 15 minutes
Makes: about 16 cups mix (enough for 32 servings)

- 1 **25.6-ounce package nonfat dry milk powder**
- 1 **16-ounce jar powdered nondairy creamer**
- 1 **8-ounce container unsweetened cocoa powder, sifted**
- 2 **cups powdered sugar**
  Tiny marshmallows (optional)

1. In an extra-large bowl combine dry milk powder, nondairy creamer, cocoa powder, and powdered sugar. Store in a tightly covered container for up to 3 months.

2. For one serving, place ½ cup of the mix in a mug or cup and add ½ cup boiling water. If desired, top with marshmallows.

Malted Hot Chocolate Mix: Prepare as above, except add one 13-ounce jar malted milk powder to the dry mix. Makes about 18 cups mix (enough for 36 servings).

Per 6 ounces plain or malted variation: 207 cal., 5 g total fat
(4 g sat. fat), 4 mg chol., 127 mg sodium, 28 g carbo., 0 g fiber,
10 g pro.
Daily Values: 11% vit. A, 2% vit. C, 36% calcium, 6% iron
Exchanges: 1 Milk, 1 Other Carbo., 1 Fat

Hot Chocolate

Start to Finish: 15 minutes **Makes:** 6 servings

- 2 **ounces unsweetened or semisweet chocolate, coarsely chopped, or ⅓ cup semisweet chocolate pieces**
- ⅓ **cup sugar**
- 4 **cups milk**
- 1 **tablespoon instant coffee crystals (optional)**
  Whipped cream or tiny marshmallows (optional)

1. In a medium saucepan combine chocolate, sugar, and ½ cup of the milk. Cook and stir over medium heat until mixture just comes to boiling. Stir in remaining milk and, if desired, coffee crystals; heat through but do not boil. Remove saucepan from heat.

2. If desired, beat mixture with a rotary beater or immersion blender until frothy. Serve in mugs. If desired, top with whipped cream or marshmallows.

Spiced Hot Chocolate: Prepare as above, except without coffee crystals; stir ½ teaspoon ground cinnamon and ¼ teaspoon ground nutmeg into chocolate mixture with remaining milk.

Per 6 ounces plain or spiced variation: 171 cal., 8 g total fat
(5 g sat. fat), 12 mg chol., 83 mg sodium, 21 g carbo., 1 g fiber,
6 g pro.
Daily Values: 7% vit. A, 3% vit. C, 20% calcium, 4% iron
Exchanges: ½ Milk, 1 Other Carbo., 1½ Fat

Low-Fat Hot Cocoa: Prepare as above, except substitute ¼ cup unsweetened cocoa powder for the chocolate and use fat-free milk.

Per 6 ounces: 113 cal., 1 g total fat (0 g sat. fat), 3 mg chol.,
84 mg sodium, 20 g carbo., 0 fiber, 6 g pro.
Daily Values: 7% vit. A, 3% vit. C, 24% calcium, 3% iron
Exchanges: 1 Other Carbo., ½ Milk

Hot Chocolate from mix

White Hot Chocolate

Coffee rounds out the flavor; you won't know it's there.

Start to Finish: 20 minutes **Makes:** 4 servings

- 3 ounces white baking chocolate with cocoa butter, chopped
- 2 cups milk, half-and-half, or light cream
- ⅓ cup hot strong coffee
- ½ teaspoon vanilla
  Vanilla ice cream (optional)
  Grated nutmeg or chocolate-flavored sprinkles (optional)

1. In a saucepan combine chocolate and ⅓ cup of the milk. Cook and stir over low heat until chocolate is melted. Add remaining milk. Stir until heated through. Add coffee and vanilla. Serve in mugs. If desired, top with ice cream and nutmeg.

Brandied White Hot Chocolate: Prepare as above, except add 2 or 3 tablespoons brandy to the saucepan when adding coffee and vanilla.

Per 5½ ounces plain or brandied variation: 183 cal., 9 g total fat (6 g sat. fat), 17 mg chol., 80 mg sodium, 18 g carbo., 0 g fiber, 6 g pro.
Daily Values: 5% vit. A, 16% calcium, 1% iron
Exchanges: ½ Milk, 1 Other Carbo., 1½ Fat

Hot Spiced Cider

See photo, page 107.

Prep: 10 minutes **Cook:** 10 minutes **Makes:** 8 servings

- 8 cups apple cider or apple juice
- ¼ cup packed brown sugar
- 6 inches stick cinnamon
- 1 teaspoon whole allspice
- 1 teaspoon whole cloves
- 1 teaspoon shredded orange peel
- 8 thin orange wedges (optional)
- 8 whole cloves (optional)

1. In a large saucepan combine cider and brown sugar. For spice bag, place cinnamon, allspice, 1 teaspoon cloves, and orange peel in center of a double-thick, 6-inch square of 100-percent-cotton cheesecloth. Tie closed with clean kitchen string. Add bag to saucepan with cider. Bring to boiling; reduce heat. Simmer, covered, for 10 minutes. Meanwhile, if desired, stud orange wedges with cloves. Discard spice bag. Serve cider in mugs. If using, garnish with orange wedges.

Per 8 ounces: 142 cal., 0 g total fat (0 g sat. fat), 0 mg chol., 10 mg sodium, 36 g carbo., 0 g fiber, 0 g pro.
Daily Values: 4% vit. C, 2% calcium, 6% iron
Exchanges: 2 Fruit, ½ Other Carbo.

Easy Party Punch

Start to Finish: 10 minutes **Makes:** 25 servings

- 1 12-ounce can frozen citrus blend juice concentrate, thawed
- 1 12-ounce can frozen berry blend juice concentrate, thawed
- 2 2-liter bottles ginger ale, chilled
  Ice cubes or ice ring
  Halved orange slices (optional)
  Fresh strawberries, sliced (optional)

1. In an extra-large punch bowl combine thawed concentrates. Add ginger ale and ice. If desired, garnish with orange slices and/or strawberries.

Per 6 ounces: 101 cal., 0 g total fat (0 g sat. fat), 0 mg chol., 13 mg sodium, 26 g carbo., 0 g fiber, 0 g pro.
Daily Values: 49% vit. C, 1% calcium, 5% iron
Exchanges: ½ Fruit, 1 Other Carbo.

 # Quantity Fruit Punch

For a small group, halve the ingredients.

Prep: 15 minutes **Chill:** 4 hours **Makes:** 60 servings

- 8 cups water
- 1 12-ounce can frozen orange juice concentrate
- 1 12-ounce can frozen lemonade concentrate
- 2 cups sugar
- ¼ cup lime juice
  Ice cubes
- 2 46-ounce cans unsweetened pineapple juice, chilled
- 2 2-liter bottles ginger ale, chilled
- 2 1-liter bottles carbonated water, chilled
  Fresh strawberries, halved lengthwise (optional)
  Halved orange slices (optional)

1. In a large pitcher or bowl combine water and the frozen concentrates; stir to dissolve concentrates. Stir in sugar and lime juice until sugar is dissolved. Cover and chill for 4 hours.

2. To serve, pour half of the juice mixture over ice in a large punch bowl. Slowly pour in one can of pineapple juice, one bottle of ginger ale, and one bottle of carbonated water; stir gently to combine. If desired, garnish with strawberries and/or orange slices. Repeat when needed.

Per 6 ounces: 95 cal., 0 g total fat (0 g sat. fat), 0 mg chol., 14 mg sodium, 24 g carbo., 0 g fiber, 0 g pro.
Daily Values: 25% vit. C, 1% calcium, 2% iron
Exchanges: ½ Fruit, 1 Other Carbo.

Slushy Punch

Lemon-lime beverage makes a sweeter punch. For a spiked punch, you can add ½ cup rum or vodka with the fruit juices.

Prep: 15 minutes **Freeze:** overnight
Stand: 20 minutes **Makes:** 14 servings

- 1½ cups unsweetened pineapple juice
- 1 ripe medium banana, peeled and cut up
- ½ cup sugar
- ½ of a 6-ounce can (⅓ cup) frozen orange juice concentrate, thawed
- 1 tablespoon lemon juice
- 1⅓ cups water
- 1 1-liter bottle carbonated water or three 12-ounce cans lemon-lime carbonated beverage, chilled

1. In a blender combine pineapple juice, banana, sugar, thawed orange juice concentrate, and lemon juice. Cover and blend until smooth. Stir in the 1⅓ cups water. Transfer to a 1½- or 2-quart glass baking dish. Cover; freeze overnight.

2. To serve, let mixture stand at room temperature about 20 minutes. To form a slush, scrape a large spoon across frozen mixture; spoon into a punch bowl. Slowly pour carbonated water down side of bowl; stir gently to mix.

Per 4 ounces plain or spiked variation: 56 cal., 0 g total fat (0 g sat. fat), 0 mg chol., 4 mg sodium, 14 g carbo., 0 g fiber, 0 g pro.
Daily Values: 27% vit. C, 1% calcium, 1% iron
Exchanges: ½ Fruit, ½ Other Carbo.

Lemonade

Start to Finish: 20 minutes **Makes:** 4 servings

- 3 cups cold water
- 1 cup lemon juice
- ¾ cup sugar
- Ice cubes and lemon slices

1. In a 1½-quart pitcher stir together the water, lemon juice, and sugar until sugar is dissolved. If desired, chill in the refrigerator. Serve in glasses over ice. Garnish with lemon slices.

Per 8 ounces: 155 cal., 0 g total fat (0 g sat. fat), 0 mg chol., 4 mg sodium, 41 g carbo., 0 g fiber, 0 g pro.
Daily Values: 47% vit. C, 1% calcium
Exchanges: 2½ Other Carbo.

Peachy Lemonade: Prepare as above. Place half of one 15- to 16-ounce can peach slices (juice pack), chilled and undrained, in a blender or food processor with 1 cup Lemonade. Cover and blend or process until smooth. Pour into a large pitcher. Repeat with remaining undrained peaches and 1 cup Lemonade. Stir in remaining Lemonade. Serve in glasses over ice. If desired, garnish with peach slices. Makes 6 servings.

Per 8 ounces: 114 cal., 0 g total fat (0 g sat. fat), 0 mg chol., 13 mg sodium, 29 g carbo., 1 g fiber, 1 g pro.
Daily Values: 5% vit A, 22% vit. C
Exchanges: 2 Other Carbo.

Lemonade

Raspberry Shrub

Prep: 20 minutes **Cool:** 2 hours **Makes:** 14 servings

- 2 lemons
- 3 12-ounce packages frozen red raspberries (about 9 cups)
- 1½ cups honey
- 1 cup sugar
- ⅓ cup water
- 4 3-inch cinnamon sticks
- ¼ cup snipped fresh rosemary or ½ cup snipped fresh sage (optional)
- ½ teaspoon whole cloves
- ½ cup light rum (optional)
- 3 cups ice cubes
- 1 750-milliliter bottle sparkling wine or 1-liter bottle carbonated water, chilled

1. Using a vegetable peeler, remove peel from lemons in strips; juice the lemons (you should have about ⅓ cup juice). Set peel and juice aside. In a 4-quart Dutch oven combine raspberries, honey, sugar, and the water. Cook and stir over medium heat until sugar dissolves.

2. Add strips of lemon peel, lemon juice, cinnamon, rosemary (if desired), and cloves to Dutch oven. Bring mixture just to boiling, stirring occasionally. Remove from heat. Cover and cool to room temperature. Remove and discard cinnamon sticks. Press mixture, in batches, through a fine-mesh sieve; discard solids (you should have about 4 cups syrup).

3. To serve, in a punch bowl combine syrup, rum (if desired), and ice cubes. Slowly add sparkling wine, stirring gently. Serve in small glasses or punch cups.

Make-ahead directions: Prepare as above through Step 2. Cover and chill syrup for up to 3 days. Serve as above.

Per 4½ ounces: 232 cal., 0 g total fat (0 g sat. fat), 0 mg chol., 2 mg sodium, 52 g carbo., 1 g fiber, 1 g pro.
Daily Values: 7% vit. C, 2% iron
Exchanges: ½ Fruit, 3 Other Carbo.

Strawberry Shrub: Prepare as above, except substitute two 16-ounce packages frozen unsweetened whole strawberries for raspberries and reduce honey to 1 cup. Serve as above.

Per 4½ ounces: 188 cal., 0 g total fat (0 g sat. fat), 0 mg chol., 2 mg sodium, 41 g carbo., 1 g fiber, 0 g pro.
Daily Values: 1% vit. A, 49% vit. C, 1% calcium, 3% iron
Exchanges: ½ Fruit, 2½ Other Carbo.

Sangría

Orange and lime juices are included in this version of the Spanish red wine beverage.

Prep: 10 minutes **Chill:** 3 hours **Makes:** 10 servings

    1 cup orange juice
    ¼ cup lime juice
    1 750-milliliter bottle dry red wine
    ¼ to ⅓ cup sugar
       Ice cubes
       Orange slices (optional)
       Lime slices (optional)

1. In a 2-quart pitcher stir together orange and lime juices. Add wine and sugar, stirring until sugar is dissolved. Cover and chill for 3 to 24 hours. Serve over ice. If desired, garnish each serving with orange and lime slices.

Per 4 ounces: 85 cal., 0 g total fat (0 g sat. fat), 0 mg chol., 4 mg sodium, 9 g carbo., 0 g fiber, 0 g pro.
Daily Values: 1% vit. A, 24% vit. C, 1% calcium, 2% iron
Exchanges: ½ Other Carbo., 1 Fat

White Strawberry Sangría NO FAT EASY

While sangría typically is made with red wine, this version features white wine for a sangría blanco.

Prep: 10 minutes **Chill:** 1 hour **Makes:** 5 servings

    1 750-milliliter bottle dry white wine, such as
       Pinot Grigio or Sauvignon Blanc
    ½ cup strawberry schnapps
    ¼ cup sugar
    2 cups sliced fresh strawberries
       Ice cubes
       Whole strawberries (optional)

1. In a 2-quart pitcher stir together wine, strawberry schnapps, and sugar until sugar is dissolved. Add sliced strawberries. Cover and chill for 1 to 4 hours. Serve in glasses over ice. If desired, garnish with whole strawberries.

Per 8 ounces: 221 cal., 0 g total fat (0 g sat. fat), 0 mg chol., 8 mg sodium, 22 g carbo., 1 g fiber, 1 g pro.
Daily Values: 54% vit. C, 2% calcium, 4% iron
Exchanges: 1½ Other Carbo., 3 Fat

Milk Shakes FAST

Check out three ways to enjoy an ice cream favorite—plain, with malted milk powder, and with chocolate ice cream and coffee.

Start to Finish: 5 minutes **Makes:** 2 servings

    1 pint vanilla, chocolate, or strawberry
       ice cream
    ½ to ¾ cup milk

1. Place ice cream and milk in a blender. Cover and blend until smooth. Serve immediately in tall glasses.

Per 8 ounces: 296 cal., 16 g total fat (10 g sat. fat), 63 mg chol., 136 mg sodium, 34 g carbo., 0 g fiber, 7 g pro.
Daily Values: 13% vit. A, 2% vit. C, 24% calcium, 1% iron
Exchanges: 1 Milk, 1½ Other Carbo., 2½ Fat

Malts: Prepare as above, except add 2 tablespoons malted milk powder with the milk.

Per 8 ounces: 383 cal., 17 g total fat (11 g sat. fat), 67 mg chol., 240 mg sodium, 50 g carbo., 0 g fiber, 9 g pro.
Daily Values: 15% vit. A, 3% vit. C, 31% calcium, 2% iron
Exchanges: 1 Milk, 2½ Other Carbo., 3 Fat

Mocha Milk Shakes: Prepare Milk Shakes as above, except use chocolate ice cream. Add 2 teaspoons instant coffee crystals with milk.

Per 8 ounces: 320 cal., 16 g total fat (10 g sat. fat), 49 mg chol., 131 mg sodium, 41 g carbo., 2 g fiber, 9 g pro.
Daily Values: 13% vit. A, 3% vit. C, 22% calcium, 7% iron
Exchanges: 1 Milk, 2 Other Carbo., 2½ Fat

Eggnog `EASY`

If you like, omit the rum and bourbon and increase the milk to 2¼ cups to make this alcohol-free.

Prep: 15 minutes **Chill:** 4 hours **Makes:** 7 servings

- **4 egg yolks, beaten**
- **2 cups milk**
- **⅓ cup sugar**
- **1 cup whipping cream**
- **2 tablespoons light rum**
- **2 tablespoons bourbon**
- **1 teaspoon vanilla**
- **Ground nutmeg**

1. In a large heavy saucepan mix the egg yolks, milk, and sugar. Cook and stir over medium heat until mixture just coats a metal spoon. Remove from heat. Place the pan in a sink or bowl of ice water and stir for 2 minutes. Stir in whipping cream, rum, bourbon, and vanilla. Cover and chill for 4 to 24 hours. Serve in glasses. Sprinkle each serving with nutmeg.

Per 4 ounces: 242 cal., 17 g total fat (10 g sat. fat), 174 mg chol., 52 mg sodium, 14 g carbo., 0 g fiber, 5 g pro.
Daily Values: 17% vit. A, 1% vit. C, 12% calcium, 2% iron
Exchanges: ½ Milk, ½ Other Carbo., 3½ Fat

Lower-Fat Eggnog: Prepare as above, except substitute 3 cups fat-free half-and-half cream for the milk and whipping cream.

Per 4 ounces: 158 cal., 3 g total fat (1 g sat. fat), 122 mg chol., 107 mg sodium, 20 g carbo., 0 g fiber, 4 g pro.
Daily Values: 4% vit. A, 7% calcium, 2% iron
Exchanges: ½ Milk, 1 Other Carbo., 1 Fat

Mocha Smoothies

Vanilla-Orange Smoothies `LOW FAT` `FAST`

See photo, page 107.

Start to Finish: 10 minutes **Makes:** 2 servings

- **1 cup vanilla low-fat yogurt**
- **½ cup orange juice, chilled**
- **¼ teaspoon vanilla**
- **1 cup small ice cubes or crushed ice**

1. Combine ingredients in blender. Cover; blend until nearly smooth. Serve at once in glasses.

Per 8 ounces: 134 cal., 2 g total fat (1 g sat. fat), 6 mg chol., 82 mg sodium, 23 g carbo., 0 g fiber, 6 g pro.
Daily Values: 4% vit. A, 53% vit. C, 22% calcium, 1% iron
Exchanges: ½ Milk, ½ Fruit, 1 Other Carbo.

Energy Apricot-Berry Smoothies `LOW FAT` `FAST`

Prep: 10 minutes **Makes:** 4 servings

- **1 15-ounce can unpeeled apricot halves in light syrup**
- **1 cup vanilla-flavored soymilk or soymilk**
- **½ cup fresh or frozen red raspberries**
- **1 tablespoon soy protein powder**
- **1 tablespoon honey**

1. Combine all ingredients in a blender. Cover and blend until smooth. Serve immediately.

Per 6½ ounces: 124 cal., 1 g total fat (0 g sat. fat), 0 mg chol., 70 mg sodium, 26 g carbo., 3 g fiber, 5 g pro.
Daily Values: 31% vit. A, 10% vit. C, 9% calcium, 6% iron
Exchanges: ½ Fruit, 1½ Other Carbo., ½ Very Lean Meat

Mocha Smoothies `LOW FAT` `FAST`

Prep: 10 minutes **Makes:** 2 servings

- **1 cup fat-free milk**
- **1 medium banana, peeled, cut into ½-inch slices, and frozen**
- **1 to 2 tablespoons sugar or honey**
- **1 tablespoon unsweetened cocoa powder**
- **2 teaspoons instant coffee crystals**
- **½ teaspoon vanilla**
- **1 cup small ice cubes or crushed ice**

1. In a blender combine all ingredients, except ice. Cover; blend until smooth. Add ice. Cover; blend until nearly smooth. Serve at once in glasses. If desired, top with small *chocolate curls.*

Per 11 ounces: 136 cal., 1 g total fat (0 g sat. fat), 2 mg chol., 55 mg sodium, 28 g carbo., 2 g fiber, 6 g pro.
Daily Values: 6% vit. A, 9% vit. C, 15% calcium, 7% iron
Exchanges: ½ Milk, 1 Fruit, ½ Other Carbo.

Banana-Berry Smoothies

The color of these sippers will vary according to the berries used. Raspberries yield a rosy pink hue, while blueberries, blackberries, or mixed berries make them blue.

Prep: 10 minutes **Makes:** 3 servings

- 2 **cups plain fat-free yogurt**
- 2 **medium bananas, peeled, cut into ½-inch slices, and frozen**
- 1 **cup sliced fresh strawberries, chilled, or frozen unsweetened whole strawberries**
- 1 **cup mixed fresh berries, such as raspberries, blueberries, and/or blackberries, chilled, or frozen unsweetened mixed berries**
- 1 **tablespoon honey (optional)**
  Fresh berries (optional)

1. In a blender combine yogurt, bananas, strawberries, mixed berries, and, if desired, honey. Cover and blend until smooth. Serve immediately in chilled glasses. If desired, top with a few additional fresh berries.

Per 13 ounces: 199 cal., 1 g total fat (0 g sat. fat), 3 mg chol., 126 mg sodium, 39 g carbo., 3 g fiber, 11 g pro.
Daily Values: 3% vit. A, 61% vit. C, 34% calcium, 6% iron
Exchanges: 1 Milk, 1½ Fruit

Super Soy Smoothies

Because most vanilla-flavored soymilks contain sweeteners, if you use regular soymilk you may want to add sugar to taste.

Start to Finish: 10 minutes **Makes:** 4 servings

- ½ **of a 16-ounce package frozen unsweetened peach slices (about 2 cups)**
- 1 **medium banana, peeled and cut up**
- ¾ **cup vanilla-flavored soymilk or soymilk**
- ¼ **cup frozen pineapple-orange juice concentrate, thawed**
- 1 **cup ice cubes (optional)**

1. In a blender combine all ingredients, except ice. Cover and blend until smooth. If thinner smoothies are desired, with blender running, gradually add ice cubes through opening in lid. Blend until smooth after each addition. Serve immediately in chilled glasses.

Per 6 ounces: 101 cal., 1 g total fat (0 g sat. fat), 0 mg chol., 29 mg sodium, 23 g carbo., 2 g fiber, 2 g pro.
Daily Values: 8% vit. A, 61% vit. C, 6% calcium, 2% iron
Exchanges: ½ Milk, 1 Fruit

Pineapple Mimosas

While mimosas are typically an orange juice and sparkling wine beverage, this version has other fruity flavors. Another time, try substituting a different frozen fruit juice concentrate.

Prep: 10 minutes **Chill:** 2 hours **Makes:** 6 servings

- 1 **12-ounce can frozen pineapple-orange-banana juice concentrate, thawed**
- 1 **cup cold water**
- 1 **750-milliliter bottle pink sparkling wine, sparkling wine, or sparkling apple juice, chilled**
  Ice cubes
  Fresh pineapple wedges (optional)

1. In a large pitcher combine juice concentrate and water. Cover and chill for 2 to 24 hours.

2. Before serving, carefully add pink sparkling wine. Add ice to the pitcher or each glass before serving. If desired, garnish each glass with a fresh pineapple wedge.

Per 8 ounces: 147 cal., 0 g total fat (0 g sat. fat), 0 mg chol., 4 mg sodium, 18 g carbo., 0 g fiber, 1 g pro.
Daily Values: 1% vit. A, 34% vit. C, 1% calcium, 3% iron
Exchanges: ½ Fruit, 1 Other Carbo.

Apple Martinis

Start to Finish: 10 minutes **Makes:** 12 servings

- 1 **orange, cut into wedges**
  Sugar
- 3 **cups vodka or gin**
- ¾ **cup frozen apple juice concentrate, thawed**
- ⅓ **cup dry vermouth**
  Ice cubes
  Fresh orange peel twists (optional)

1. Rub orange wedges around the rims of 12 martini glasses. Dip rims into a dish of sugar to coat; set aside. In a pitcher combine vodka, apple juice concentrate, and vermouth. Place ice cubes in a martini shaker. For each drink, add ⅓ cup of the syrup mixture; shake. Strain into one of the prepared martini glasses. If desired, garnish with orange peel twists.

Orange Martinis: Prepare as above, except substitute 6 tablespoons frozen orange juice concentrate, thawed, for apple juice concentrate.

Per 3 ounces apple or orange variation: 164 cal., 0 g total fat (0 g sat. fat), 0 mg chol., 5 mg sodium, 7 g carbo., 0 g fiber, 0 g pro.
Daily Values: 1% vit. C, 1% iron
Exchanges: ½ Other Carbo.

Strawberry Daiquiris

Start to Finish: 10 minutes **Makes:** 7 servings

- 1 10-ounce package frozen sliced strawberries in syrup or frozen red raspberries in syrup
- ½ of a 6-ounce can (⅓ cup) frozen limeade concentrate
- ⅔ cup rum
- ⅓ cup powdered sugar (optional)
- 2½ to 3 cups ice cubes

1. In a blender combine strawberries in syrup, limeade concentrate, rum, and, if desired, powdered sugar. Cover; blend until smooth. With blender running, add ice cubes, one at a time, through opening in lid until mixture becomes slushy. Serve in glasses.

Lime Daiquiris: Prepare as above, except omit strawberries and powdered sugar. In a blender combine one 6-ounce can (⅔ cup) frozen limeade concentrate or half of a 12-ounce can (¾ cup) frozen lemonade concentrate and the rum. Garnish with lime wedges. Makes 6 servings.

Per 4 ounces strawberry or lime variation: 112 cal., 0 g total fat
(0 g sat. fat), 0 mg chol., 3 mg sodium, 16 g carbo.,
1 g fiber, 0 g pro.
Daily Values: 30% vit. C, 1% calcium, 1% iron
Exchanges: 1 Other Carbo.

Mai Tai Me

Lime Daiquiris

Mai Tai Me

Shake fruit juices, rum, and orange liqueur together for a tropical beverage. If you like, garnish with fresh fruit.

Start to Finish: 5 minutes **Makes:** 1 serving

- Ice cubes
- ⅓ cup pineapple juice
- 1 jigger (3 tablespoons) dark rum
- 1 jigger (3 tablespoons) orange liqueur
- 2 tablespoons grenadine syrup
- Dash lime juice
- Dash sugar
- Fresh fruit pieces, such as pineapple, lime wedges, and orange wedges (optional)

1. For each cocktail, fill a cocktail shaker with ice. Add pineapple juice, rum, orange liqueur, grenadine syrup, lime juice, and sugar. Cover and shake; serve in a tall glass. If desired, garnish with fresh fruit threaded on a long skewer.

Per 6 ounces: 370 cal., 0 g total fat (0 g sat. fat), 0 mg chol.,
20 mg sodium, 55 g carbo., 0 g fiber, 0 g pro.
Daily Values: 17% vit. C, 2% calcium, 1% iron
Exchanges: 4 Other Carbo.

 Icy Cranberry Margaritas

See photo, page 107.

Start to Finish: 10 minutes **Makes:** 6 servings

- Orange wedge
- Sugar
- ½ cup frozen cranberry-raspberry juice concentrate, thawed
- ½ cup tequila
- ¼ cup orange liqueur
- 3 tablespoons melon liqueur
- 5 cups ice cubes

1. Rub an orange wedge around rims of six margarita glasses. Dip rims into a dish of sugar to coat; set aside.

2. In a blender combine cranberry-raspberry juice concentrate, tequila, orange liqueur, and melon liqueur. Cover and blend until combined. With blender running, add ice cubes, one at a time, through opening in lid, blending until mixture becomes slushy. Pour into prepared glasses.

Per 4 ounces: 147 cal., 0 g total fat (0 g sat. fat), 0 mg chol.,
2 mg sodium, 18 g carbo., 0 g fiber, 0 g pro.
Daily Values: 19% vit. C
Exchanges: 1 Other Carbo.

Quick Frozen Margaritas

Turn this drink into a slushy combination by adding ice cubes to the blender one by one. There's no waiting to enjoy this frosty refresher.

Start to Finish: 10 minutes **Makes:** 8 servings

- 1 or 2 limes
- Coarse salt
- 1 12-ounce can frozen limeade concentrate
- ⅔ cup tequila
- ½ cup orange liqueur
- 4 cups ice cubes

1. Cut a thick lime slice; cut slice in half. Rub half slices around rims of eight glasses. Dip rims into a dish of coarse salt to coat; set aside.

2. In a blender combine limeade concentrate, tequila, and orange liqueur. Cover and blend until combined. With blender running, add ice cubes, one at a time, through opening in lid, blending until mixture becomes slushy.

3. Pour mixture into prepared glasses. Slice remaining lime into eight thin slices. Garnish with lime slices.

Make-ahead directions: Prepare Step 2 as above. Pour into a 1½-quart freezer container. Cover and freeze overnight. To serve, prepare glasses as above in Step 1. Use a large spoon to scrape the frozen surface and pile into salt-rimmed glasses.

Per 6 ounces: 167 cal., 0 g total fat (0 g sat. fat), 0 mg chol., 1,167 mg sodium, 26 g carbo., 0 g fiber, 0 g pro.
Daily Values: 10% vit. C, 1% calcium
Exchanges: 2 Other Carbo.

Strawberry Margaritas: Prepare as above, except substitute coarse sugar for the salt on the glasses and eliminate the lime garnish. Blend half of the mixture at a time, adding 1 cup frozen unsweetened whole strawberries along with 2 cups of the ice cubes to each half. If desired, garnish each glass with a whole strawberry.

Per 7 ounces: 184 cal., 0 g total fat (0 g sat. fat), 0 mg chol., 5 mg sodium, 30 g carbo., 1 g fiber, 0 g pro.
Daily Values: 34% vit. C, 1% calcium, 2% iron
Exchanges: 2 Other Carbo.

Orange Mint Juleps

Prep: 20 minutes **Stand:** 1 hour
Chill: up to 24 hours **Makes:** 8 servings

- 1 cup snipped fresh mint leaves
- 2 cups water
- ⅔ cup sugar
- 1 teaspoon shredded orange peel
- 2 cups orange juice
- ⅔ cup lemon juice
- ⅓ cup bourbon or vodka (optional)
- Cracked ice

1. Place mint leaves in a medium bowl; set aside. In a saucepan combine the water and sugar. Bring to boiling, stirring until sugar is dissolved. Remove from heat; pour over mint leaves. Stir in orange peel, orange juice, and lemon juice.

2. Cover and let stand at room temperature for 1 hour. Strain mixture through a mesh strainer. If desired, add bourbon. Cover and chill up to 24 hours. Serve in glasses over cracked ice.

Per 4 ounces: 98 cal., 0 g total fat (0 g sat. fat), 0 mg chol., 2 mg sodium, 25 g carbo., 0 g fiber, 1 g pro.
Daily Values: 79% vit. C, 2% calcium, 11% iron
Exchanges: 1½ Other Carbo.

Frozen Grasshoppers (FAST)

Serve this classic drink in place of dessert.

Start to Finish: 5 minutes **Makes:** 8 servings

- ½ cup green crème de menthe
- ½ cup white crème de cacao
- 1 pint vanilla ice cream
- 3 cups ice cubes
- Whipped cream (optional)
- Chopped layered chocolate-mint candies (optional)
- Fresh mint (optional)

1. In a blender combine crème de menthe, crème de cacao, ice cream, and about half the ice. Cover and blend until smooth. Add remaining ice; cover and blend until smooth.

2. Serve in small cocktail glasses. If desired, top each serving with whipped cream, chopped candies, and a sprig of fresh mint.

Per 4 ounces: 205 cal., 6 g total fat (4 g sat. fat), 23 mg chol., 23 mg sodium, 21 g carbo., 6 g fiber, 1 g pro.
Daily Values: 7% vit. A, 4% calcium
Exchanges: 1½ Other Carbo., 2½ Fat

The Basics of Wine

Wine fascinates many of us, and enthusiasts delight in learning about the producers, locations, climates, and cultures that merge to make great bottles. Yet for all its wondrous complexity, wine is quite simple to enjoy.

Choosing Wine

The best wine is the wine you like best. For help in finding what you like, refer to the list on page 122, which highlights the characteristics of eight popular wines. Remember that this list is just a start—there are many more to explore, from spicy-scented Gewürztraminers to dark, toasty-dry Malbecs. Remember, too, that many great wines are made not from just one grape but a blend of grapes. The most famous and time-honored blend is Bordeaux, the renowned French wine made from Cabernet Sauvignon and/or Merlot blended with other grapes. Today's winemakers continually are creating new blends that appeal to many palates. The breakdown of grapes is sometimes on a bottle's label, making it easy to choose a wine to try—start with blends that include grapes you know you like.

Considering Vintage

Vintage refers to the year the grapes were harvested; that year often is printed prominently on the label and the cork. A bad year, with too much or too little rain or heat, for instance, produces inferior grapes, while a great year produces terrific fruit, hence, terrific wines. Thanks to advances in agriculture and wine production, winemakers now offer wines that remain remarkably consistent year after year, especially those produced in Australia, New Zealand, North and South America, and South Africa. However, in Europe, which has a more finicky climate, vintage still can matter. When buying an expensive bottle of European wine, it pays to ask a trusted wine merchant for some advice about vintage.

Aging Wine

There's no need to wait to open up most bottles of wine; in fact, the vast majority of wines made today are meant to be drunk upon release. Only a small, select group of high-quality wines actually improves with extended aging. If you are buying a premium-price wine, ask the merchant if and how long you should cellar it before drinking it.

Storing Wine

Warm temperatures (70°F or so), fluctuations in temperature, and exposure to light can cause wine to degrade. Store the wine bottles in a vibration-free, cool, dark place—a cellar is ideal. If you don't have a cellar, keep wine in the most temperature-stable location in your home. Store bottles on their sides to keep the corks from drying out.

What about leftovers? It's true that after continued contact with air, a wine's aromas and flavors diminish rapidly; however, most wines stay drinkable for a day or two after opening. Simply recork the bottle with the original cork and store it in the refrigerator (whether it's a red or a white). Set the red outside the refrigerator long enough before serving it to allow it to come to the proper temperature.

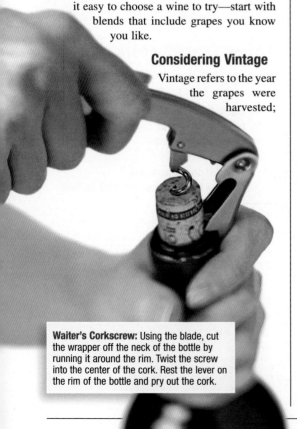

Waiter's Corkscrew: Using the blade, cut the wrapper off the neck of the bottle by running it around the rim. Twist the screw into the center of the cork. Rest the lever on the rim of the bottle and pry out the cork.

Choose a corkscrew you feel comfortable using.

Removing the Cork

Removing the cork from a wine bottle should be a pleasurable experience. First, set the bottle on a firm, flat surface. Use a knife or foil cutter to cut around the foil, then remove the foil. Finally, use the spiral of a corkscrew to remove the cork. All of the corkscrews shown above are inexpensive.

Serving Temperature

If a white wine is served too cold, the true character, flavor, and aroma will be diminished. If a red wine is served too warm, it will change the balance of the flavor components and hamper the taste of the wine. The old rule about serving red wine at room temperature no longer applies because most rooms today are kept warmer than in the past. It's best if red wine is chilled ever so briefly (10 minutes in an ice bucket or 30 minutes in the refrigerator) to bring it to the correct temperature. Here are a few temperature guidelines.

Type of Wine	Serving Temperature
Champagnes and sparkling wines	45°F
Sauvignon Blancs and Rieslings	45°F to 55°F
Chardonnays	55°F to 60°F
Lighter reds (Beaujolais, Pinot Noir)	55°F to 60°F
Sauternes	58°F to 62°F
Cabernet Sauvignons and Merlots	60°F to 65°F
Ports	62°F to 65°F

Wineglasses

While you can buy glasses in all kinds of shapes and sizes appropriate for specific wines, the three shown below will serve you well in most cases. Most important, look for wineglasses that become narrower at the top—this helps concentrate the bouquet.

Large glasses are appropriate for red wines because they allow the wine to have more contact with the air, which helps the flavor and bouquet develop.

Small glasses are good for white wine because they help keep the wine chilled. A larger surface area would cause the wine to warm too quickly.

Narrow, fluted glasses are useful for Champagne or sparkling wine because they keep the bubbles intact and preserve the fizz.

When you're ready to add to your wineglass collection, the next step would be to purchase a Pinot Noir glass. This is large, with a more bulbous shape than the traditional wineglass. The pot-bellied bulb allows more flavor and aroma to develop for this characteristically delicate and refined wine. Whichever glass you use, fill the glass no more than half full (one-third full for larger red wine glasses). Sparkling wines are an exception. You can fill the glasses a little fuller.

These three basic glass shapes will serve most of your needs.

Purchasing Wine for Entertaining

To figure out how much wine to stock when hosting guests, remember that each 750 ml (25 ounce) bottle of wine yields approximately six 4-ounce servings.

As a general rule, figure on three to four glasses of wine per person for a dinner party lasting four hours. For shorter appetizer parties, count on half that amount—about two glasses per person.

Do the math; this adds up to a little over one bottle for every two guests for dinner and about one bottle for every three guests for appetizers. However, it's always good to buy a few more bottles than you think you'll need. When stored as directed on page 120, most unopened bottles of wine will keep just fine until your next gathering.

For any kind of party, plan to serve as much bottled water as wine, if not a bit more. Refill water glasses at least as often as wineglasses. And always offer an array of nonalcoholic beverages for people who don't drink alcohol.

Pairing Wine with Food

While there are no steadfast rules when it comes to pairing wine and food, some foods do taste better with certain wines. Generally, the fuller a food's flavor, the fuller-flavor and fuller-bodied the wine ought to be. While the chart below offers some tried-and-true pairings, a great way to find combinations you like is to experiment. Try wines you like with foods you enjoy and take note of how they go together; soon, you'll start coming up with your own winning matches.

Guide to Eight Popular Wines

This chart shows eight wine varietals (wines made from one dominant grape) that pop up often on store shelves and restaurant wine lists, along with general characteristics of each. Note, however, that flavors and styles of the same varietals can vary depending on the region they come from and the winery that produced them.

Varietals	Characteristics	Food Pairing
Whites		
Chardonnay	Often rich and buttery, with pear and apple notes; many have a pronounced oak flavor.	Roast chicken, bold-flavored cheeses, seafood, and pork; great as a cocktail party sipper.
Pinot Grigio	Light-bodied, with mild peach or citrus flavors.	Light fish and chicken dishes, mild cheeses, appetizers, and vegetables; a terrific picnic wine.
Riesling	Brightly fruity; ranges from sweet to dry and often brings floral, peach, and citrusy tones.	Chicken, light fish dishes, pork and ham, barbecue, and spicy foods; a good white for the holidays.
Sauvignon Blanc	Light and zippy, often with zingy citrus and herblike aroma.	Goat and feta cheeses, chicken and fish dishes, especially those flavored with fresh tomatoes or herbs; delightful in hot summer months.
Reds		
Cabernet Sauvignon	Bold and full-bodied with cassis, black cherry, and sometimes cedarlike flavors.	Lamb, grilled and broiled steaks, burgers, and boldly flavored cheeses; great with meaty stews.
Merlot	A soft and fruity wine; often less mouth-drying (tannic) than Cabernet Sauvignon.	Beef, tomato-sauced pasta, lamb, pork, roast turkey, and burgers; a popular all-purpose house wine.
Pinot Noir	A silky, elegant wine with bright, red-fruit flavors and sometimes earthy and smoky notes.	Try with fish (especially salmon), meat, poultry, and any dishes featuring mushrooms; a good red wine for the holidays.
Shiraz/Syrah	Full-bodied, with vivid plum and black-fruit flavors and often with smoky and spicy notes.	Roasts, braises, and hearty, full-flavored dishes; a shoo-in with barbecue.

Breads

Dill Batter Bread, 149

Buttermilk Pancakes, 137

Banana Bread, 130

Breads Essentials

Mastering the art of bread baking is rewarding, whether you're making your first muffin or baking your umpteenth bread loaf. These tips should help for successful baking.

Major Ingredients

Flour: Sifting flour isn't necessary because today most flours are presifted. However, stir through the bag or canister just before measuring. Lightly spoon flour into a dry measuring cup and level it off. When preparing bread in a bread machine, use bread flour; for other breads, all-purpose flour, bleached or unbleached, works just fine.

Leavening: These ingredients—baking powder, baking soda, and yeast—add lightness to baked goods by "raising" them. If your baking powder tends to clump, sift it before adding it. Active dry yeast is the form called for in these recipes; bread machine recipes also list bread machine yeast as an alternate ingredient.

Quick Bread

Check quick bread loaves 10 to 15 minutes before the minimum baking time is reached to see if they're browning too quickly. If they are, cover them with foil. Note that the crack down the center of the loaf is typical of many loaves (see photo, below). After baking, let loaves completely cool on a wire rack. Then, before slicing, wrap in foil or plastic wrap and store at room temperature overnight. This allows the flavors to mellow and results in easier slicing.

Yeast Bread

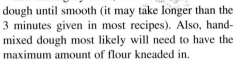

If you don't have an electric mixer, use a wooden spoon to beat the dough. When mixing by hand, beat dough until smooth (it may take longer than the 3 minutes given in most recipes). Also, hand-mixed dough most likely will need to have the maximum amount of flour kneaded in.

Let yeast breads rise in a draft-free location that has a temperature between 80°F and 85°F. To use your unheated oven for rising, place the bowl of dough on the center rack and a bowl of warm water on the lower rack. On the second rise, don't let the shaped dough rise above the top of the pan because it needs room to rise more as it bakes.

Check for doneness of a yeast bread by tapping the top of the loaf with your fingers. If it sounds hollow, the bread is done. If it is not yet done but is getting too brown, cover the loaf with foil to allow the inside to finish cooking. Yeast breads containing some sugar and butter probably will need this preventive measure.

Store yeast breads at room temperature; they become stale more quickly when chilled. If bread has cheese or meat in it, eat what you can the day it's baked and freeze the rest.

Freezing Breads

To freeze unfrosted muffins, scones, or biscuits, let them cool completely, tightly wrap in heavy foil or place in a freezer container, and freeze for up to 3 months. To reheat frozen muffins, leave them wrapped in heavy foil; heat in a 300°F oven 15 to 18 minutes. Reheat foil-wrapped scones or biscuits in a 300°F oven 20 to 25 minutes.

To freeze quick bread loaves, place completely cooled loaves in freezer containers or bags and freeze up to 3 months. Thaw wrapped loaves at room temperature.

To freeze and reheat yeast rolls, see tip on page 155. If desired, frost after heating.

Muffins `FAST`

Prep: 10 minutes **Bake:** 18 minutes
Oven: 400°F **Makes:** 12 muffins

- 1¾ **cups all-purpose flour**
- ⅓ **cup sugar**
- 2 **teaspoons baking powder**
- ¼ **teaspoon salt**
- 1 **egg, beaten**
- ¾ **cup milk**
- ¼ **cup cooking oil**
- 1 **recipe Streusel Topping (optional for plain and sweet variations)**

1. Preheat oven to 400°F. Grease twelve 2½-inch muffin cups or line with paper bake cups; set aside. In a medium bowl combine flour, sugar, baking powder, and salt. Make a well in center of flour mixture; set aside.

2. In another bowl combine egg, milk, and oil. Add egg mixture all at once to the flour mixture. Stir just until moistened (batter should be lumpy; see photo 1, right).

3. Spoon batter into prepared muffin cups, filling each two-thirds full (see photo 2, right). If desired, sprinkle Streusel Topping over muffin batter in cups. Bake for 18 to 20 minutes or until golden and a wooden toothpick inserted in centers comes out clean. Cool in muffin cups on a wire rack for 5 minutes. Remove from muffin cups; serve warm.

Blueberry Muffins: Prepare as above, except fold ¾ cup fresh or frozen blueberries and, if desired, 1 teaspoon finely shredded lemon peel into batter.

Cranberry Muffins: Prepare as above, except combine 1 cup coarsely chopped cranberries and 2 tablespoons additional sugar; fold into batter.

Oatmeal Muffins: Prepare as above, except reduce flour to 1⅓ cups and add ¾ cup rolled oats to flour mixture.

Poppy Seed Muffins: Prepare as above, except increase sugar to ½ cup and add 1 tablespoon poppy seeds to flour mixture.

Per muffin plain, blueberry, cranberry, oatmeal, or poppy seed variations: 136 cal., 5 g total fat (1 g sat. fat), 19 mg chol., 128 mg sodium, 19 g carbo., 0 g fiber, 3 g pro.
Daily Values: 1% vit. A, 6% calcium, 5% iron
Exchanges: 1 Starch, ½ Other Carbo., ½ Fat

Cheese Muffins: Prepare as at left, except stir ½ cup shredded cheddar cheese or Monterey Jack cheese into flour mixture.

Per muffin: 155 cal., 7 g total fat (2 g sat. fat), 24 mg chol., 158 mg sodium, 19 g carbo., 0 g fiber, 4 g pro.
Daily Values: 2% vit. A, 10% calcium, 5% iron
Exchanges: 1 Starch, ½ Other Carbo., 1 Fat

Banana Muffins: Prepare as at left, greasing muffin cups (do not use paper bake cups). Reduce milk to ½ cup. Stir ¾ cup mashed banana and ½ cup chopped nuts into flour mixture along with the egg mixture.

Per muffin: 184 cal., 9 g total fat (1 g sat. fat), 18 mg chol., 126 mg sodium, 24 g carbo., 1 g fiber, 4 g pro.
Daily Values: 1% vit. A, 3% vit. C, 6% calcium, 6% iron
Exchanges: 1 Starch, ½ Other Carbo., 1½ Fat

Streusel Topping: In a small bowl stir together 3 tablespoons all-purpose flour, 3 tablespoons packed brown sugar, and ¼ teaspoon ground cinnamon. Cut in 2 tablespoons butter until the mixture resembles coarse crumbs. Stir in 2 tablespoons chopped pecans or walnuts.

1. Stir the muffin batter with a wooden spoon just until the ingredients are moistened. Don't overmix or the muffins will be peaked and have tunnels and a tough texture.

2. Spoon the muffin batter into cups using a spoon and rubber spatula. Or to divide the batter easily, use an ice cream scoop (about ¼ cup volume) to drop the batter into the muffin cups.

Pick a Muffin Pan

Muffin cups come in various shapes and sizes. To make muffins in a size other than specified, prepare the batter as directed but adjust baking time and temperature as indicated in this chart. (These baking times are approximate and may vary with the recipe.)

Pan Size	Time/Temperature
Mini (1¾-inch)	10 to 12 min./400°F
Standard (2½-inch)	about 20 min./400°F
Jumbo (3½-inch)	about 30 min./350°F
Muffin tops (3½-inch)	8 to 10 min./400°F

Oat Bran Muffins `EASY`

Skip lining the muffin cups with paper bake cups for this recipe. These muffins will stick to the paper liners. Spray the cups instead.

Prep: 15 minutes **Bake:** 16 minutes
Oven: 400°F **Makes:** 12 muffins

    Nonstick cooking spray
1½ cups oat bran
  1 cup all-purpose flour
  2 teaspoons baking powder
  ¼ teaspoon baking soda
  ½ teaspoon salt
  1 egg, beaten
  ¾ cup applesauce
  ½ cup fat-free milk
  ¼ cup honey
  2 tablespoons cooking oil
  ½ cup raisins or snipped dried cranberries
    or cherries

1. Preheat oven to 400°F. Lightly coat bottoms of twelve 2½-inch muffin cups with cooking spray; set aside. In a medium bowl combine oat bran, flour, baking powder, baking soda, and salt. Make a well in the center of the flour mixture; set aside.

2. In a small bowl combine egg, applesauce, milk, honey, and oil. Add applesauce mixture all at once to flour mixture. Stir just until moistened (batter should be lumpy; see photo 1, page 126). Fold in raisins.

3. Spoon batter into prepared muffin cups, filling each half to two-thirds full (see photo 2, page 126). Bake for 16 to 18 minutes or until golden and a wooden toothpick inserted in centers comes out clean. Cool in muffin cups on a wire rack for 5 minutes. Remove from muffin cups; serve warm.

Per muffin: 145 cal., 4 g total fat (1 g sat. fat), 18 mg chol., 176 mg sodium, 29 g carbo., 2 g fiber, 4 g pro.
Daily Values: 1% vit. A, 1% vit. C, 4% calcium, 8% iron
Exchanges: ½ Fruit, 1 Starch, ½ Other Carbo.

Dried Fruit Muffins

Prep: 20 minutes **Bake:** 20 minutes
Oven: 400°F **Makes:** 12 muffins

  2 cups all-purpose flour
  1 teaspoon baking powder
  ½ teaspoon salt
  ½ teaspoon ground cinnamon or nutmeg
  ¼ teaspoon baking soda
  ½ cup butter or margarine, softened
  1 cup sugar
  2 eggs
  1 8-ounce carton dairy sour cream
  ½ teaspoon vanilla
  ¾ cup snipped dried cherries, apricots, raisins,
    and/or cranberries, or dried blueberries
  ½ cup chopped walnuts, pecans, almonds,
    or hazelnuts (filberts), toasted (see tip,
    page 265)
    Sugar (optional)

1. Preheat oven to 400°F. Line twelve 2½-inch muffin cups with paper bake cups; set aside. In a medium bowl combine flour, baking powder, salt, cinnamon, and baking soda; set aside.

2. In a large mixing bowl beat butter with an electric mixer on medium speed for 30 seconds. Add the 1 cup sugar; beat until well combined. Beat in eggs, sour cream, and vanilla. Stir in flour mixture until just moistened (batter should be lumpy; see photo 1, page 126). Stir in dried fruit and nuts.

3. Spoon batter into prepared muffin cups, filling each almost full (see photo 2, page 126). If desired, sprinkle with additional sugar. Bake about 20 minutes or until golden and a wooden toothpick inserted in centers comes out clean. Cool in muffin cups on a wire rack for 5 minutes. Remove from muffin cups; serve warm.

Per muffin: 316 cal., 16 g total fat (7 g sat. fat), 65 mg chol., 225 mg sodium, 39 g carbo., 1 g fiber, 5 g pro.
Daily Values: 13% vit. A, 5% calcium, 8% iron
Exchanges: ½ Fruit, ½ Starch, 1½ Other Carbo., 3½ Fat

Dried Fruit Muffins

Bran Cereal Muffins `EASY`

To serve hot muffins anytime, make this easy batter ahead and refrigerate it for up to 3 days.

Prep: 15 minutes **Bake:** 20 minutes
Oven: 400°F **Makes:** 24 muffins

- 1 cup boiling water
- 3 cups whole bran cereal (not flakes)
- 2½ cups all-purpose flour
- ½ cup granulated sugar
- ½ cup packed brown sugar
- 2 teaspoons baking powder
- 1 teaspoon ground cinnamon (optional)
- ½ teaspoon baking soda
- ½ teaspoon salt
- 2 eggs, beaten
- 2 cups buttermilk
- ½ cup cooking oil

1. Preheat oven to 400°F. Grease twenty-four 2½-inch muffin cups or line with paper bake cups; set aside. In a medium bowl pour boiling water over cereal. Stir to moisten cereal; set aside.

2. In another medium bowl combine flour, granulated sugar, brown sugar, baking powder, cinnamon (if desired), baking soda, and salt. In a large bowl combine eggs, buttermilk, and oil. Stir cereal and flour mixtures into buttermilk mixture just until moistened (see photo 1, page 126).

3. Spoon batter into prepared muffin cups, filling each three-fourths full (see photo 2, page 126). Bake about 20 minutes (20 to 22 minutes for refrigerated batter) or until a wooden toothpick inserted in centers comes out clean. Cool in muffin cups on a wire rack for 5 minutes. Remove from muffin cups; serve warm.

Per muffin: 150 cal., 5 g total fat (1 g sat. fat), 18 mg chol., 181 mg sodium, 27 g carbo., 5 g fiber, 3 g pro.
Daily Values: 4% vit. A, 4% vit. C, 2% calcium, 13% iron
Exchanges: 1 Starch, ½ Other Carbo., 1 Fat

Scones

Prep: 20 minutes **Bake:** 12 minutes
Oven: 400°F **Makes:** 12 scones

- 2½ cups all-purpose flour
- 2 tablespoons sugar
- 1 tablespoon baking powder
- ¼ teaspoon salt
- ⅓ cup butter
- 2 eggs, beaten
- ¾ cup whipping cream
- ½ cup dried currants or snipped raisins
  Whipping cream or milk
  Sugar

1. Preheat oven to 400°F. In a large bowl combine flour, the 2 tablespoons sugar, the baking powder, and salt. Using a pastry blender, cut in butter until mixture resembles coarse crumbs. Make a well in center of the flour mixture; set mixture aside.

2. In a medium bowl combine eggs, the ¾ cup whipping cream, and currants. Add egg mixture all at once to flour mixture. Using a fork, stir just until moistened.

3. Turn dough out onto a lightly floured surface. Knead dough by folding and gently pressing it for 10 to 12 strokes or until dough is nearly smooth. Divide dough in half. Pat or lightly roll each dough half into a 6-inch circle. Cut each circle into six wedges.

4. Place dough wedges 2 inches apart on an ungreased baking sheet. Brush wedges with whipping cream and sprinkle with additional sugar. Bake for 12 to 14 minutes or until golden. Remove scones from baking sheet; serve warm.

Orange Scones: Prepare as above, except omit the currants or raisins and stir in 1½ teaspoons finely shredded orange peel with the egg mixture. For icing, combine 1 cup powdered sugar, 1 tablespoon orange juice, and ¼ teaspoon vanilla; stir in additional orange juice, 1 teaspoon at a time, to reach drizzling consistency. Drizzle over baked scones.

Cherry Scones: Prepare as above, except omit the currants or raisins. In a small bowl pour enough boiling water over ½ cup snipped dried tart red cherries to cover. Let the cherries stand for 5 minutes; drain well. Stir drained cherries and ¼ teaspoon almond extract in with the egg mixture. If desired, drizzle baked scones with icing from Orange Scones variation (above).

Per scone plain, orange, or cherry variations: 229 cal., 12 g total fat (7 g sat. fat), 71 mg chol., 165 mg sodium, 26 g carbo., 1 g fiber, 4 g pro.
Daily Values: 9% vit. A, 1% vit. C, 5% calcium, 8% iron
Exchanges: 1 Starch, ½ Other Carbo., 2½ Fat

Biscuits Supreme `FAST`

Prep: 15 minutes **Bake:** 10 minutes
Oven: 450°F **Makes:** 12 biscuits

3 **cups all-purpose flour**
1 **tablespoon baking powder***
1 **tablespoon sugar**
1 **teaspoon salt**
¾ **teaspoon cream of tartar***
¾ **cup butter or ½ cup butter and**
    ¼ cup shortening
1 **cup milk**

1. Preheat oven to 450°F. In a large bowl combine the flour, baking powder, sugar, salt, and cream of tartar. Using a pastry blender, cut in butter until mixture resembles coarse crumbs. Make a well in the center of the flour mixture. Add milk all at once. Using a fork, stir just until mixture is moistened.

2. Turn dough out onto a lightly floured surface. Knead dough by folding and gently pressing it for four to six strokes or just until dough holds together. Pat or lightly roll dough until ¾ inch thick (see photo 1, above right). Cut dough with a floured 2½-inch biscuit cutter (see photo 2, above right); reroll scraps as necessary and dip cutter into flour between cuts.

3. Place dough circles 1 inch apart on an ungreased baking sheet. Bake for 10 to 14 minutes or until golden. Remove biscuits from baking sheet and serve warm.

*Note: If baking powder or cream of tartar appear lumpy, sift through a fine-mesh sieve before using.

Drop Biscuits Supreme: Prepare as above through Step 1, except increase the milk to 1¼ cups. Using a large spoon, drop dough into 12 mounds onto a greased baking sheet (see photo 3, above right). Bake as directed above. Makes 12 biscuits.

Buttermilk Biscuits: Prepare as above, except for rolled dough biscuits substitute 1¼ cups buttermilk or sour milk (see tip, page 169) for the 1 cup milk. For drop biscuits substitute 1½ cups buttermilk or sour milk for the 1¼ cups milk.

Per biscuit plain, drop, or buttermilk variations: 227 cal.,
13 g total fat (6 g sat. fat), 34 mg chol., 350 mg sodium,
24 g carbo., 1 g fiber, 4 g pro.
Daily Values: 8% vit. A, 5% calcium, 8% iron
Exchanges: 1½ Starch, 2½ Fat

1. Place biscuit dough on a lightly floured surface. Use your hands to pat the dough or a rolling pin to gently roll the dough to the thickness specified in the recipe.

2. To cut rolled dough, use a floured biscuit cutter or a metal cookie cutter. After each use, dip the cutter into flour.

3. To make drop biscuits, scoop the dough with a spoon; use a spatula or knife to push the dough off the spoon onto a greased baking sheet.

Spreads for Breads

Enliven homemade and purchased biscuits and breads with a flavorful spread. Stirring a seasoned butter together takes only about 5 minutes, though it needs to chill at least 1 hour for flavors to blend.

Citrus Butter: Combine ½ cup softened butter, 1 tablespoon powdered sugar, and 1 teaspoon finely shredded orange or lemon peel. Makes ½ cup.

Nut Butter: Combine ½ cup finely chopped almonds or walnuts, ¼ cup softened butter, and ¼ cup apricot or peach preserves. Makes 1 cup.

Onion-Parmesan Butter: Combine ½ cup softened butter, 2 tablespoons grated Parmesan cheese, and 2 teaspoons sliced green onion. Makes ½ cup.

Herb Butter: Combine ½ cup softened butter and ½ teaspoon each dried thyme and marjoram, crushed, or 1 teaspoon dried basil, crushed. Makes ½ cup. (See page 580 for butters flavored with fresh herbs.)

Cranberry-Orange Biscuits

Cranberry-Orange Biscuits

Give these festive biscuits holiday flair by cutting them with a star-shaped cookie cutter.

Prep: 25 minutes **Bake:** 10 minutes
Oven: 450°F **Makes:** 11 biscuits

 2 cups all-purpose flour
 1 tablespoon granulated sugar
 2 teaspoons baking powder
 1 teaspoon finely shredded orange peel
 ¼ teaspoon salt
 ¼ teaspoon baking soda
 ½ cup shortening
 ½ cup dried fruit, such as snipped
     cranberries, raisins, cherries, or mixed
     dried fruit bits; or currants or blueberries
 1 6-ounce carton orange or vanilla low-fat
     yogurt
 1 tablespoon milk
 1 recipe Orange Glaze (optional)

1. Preheat oven to 450°F. In a bowl stir together flour, granulated sugar, baking powder, orange peel, salt, and baking soda. Using a pastry blender, cut in shortening until mixture resembles coarse crumbs. Add dried fruit; toss until well mixed. Make a well in center of the flour mixture. Add yogurt and milk all at once. Using a fork, stir just until moistened.

2. Turn dough out onto a lightly floured surface. Knead dough by folding and gently pressing it for 10 to 12 strokes or until dough is nearly smooth. Pat or lightly roll dough until

½ inch thick (see photo 1, page 129). Cut dough with a floured 2½-inch biscuit cutter (see photo 2, page 129), rerolling scraps as necessary and dipping cutter into flour between cuts.

3. Place dough circles 1 inch apart on an ungreased baking sheet. Bake about 10 minutes or until golden. Remove biscuits from baking sheet; cool 5 minutes. If desired, drizzle with Orange Glaze. Serve warm.

Per biscuit: 196 cal., 10 g total fat (2 g sat. fat), 1 mg chol., 136 mg sodium, 24 g carbo., 1 g fiber, 3 g pro.
Daily Values: 1% vit. C, 4% calcium, 6% iron
Exchanges: 1 Starch, ½ Other Carbo., 2 Fat

Orange Glaze: In a small bowl combine ¾ cup powdered sugar, 1 teaspoon finely shredded orange peel, and enough orange juice (3 to 4 teaspoons) to reach glazing consistency.

Banana Bread

Make this favorite quick bread extra special by sprinkling streusel topping over the batter before baking. See photo, page 123.

Prep: 25 minutes **Bake:** 55 minutes
Oven: 350°F **Makes:** 1 loaf (16 slices)

 2 cups all-purpose flour
 1½ teaspoons baking powder
 ½ teaspoon baking soda
 ¼ teaspoon salt
 ¼ teaspoon ground cinnamon
 ⅛ teaspoon ground nutmeg
 2 eggs, beaten
 1½ cups mashed ripe banana (5 medium)
 1 cup sugar
 ½ cup cooking oil or melted butter or
     margarine
 ¼ cup chopped walnuts
 1 recipe Streusel-Nut Topping (optional)

1. Preheat oven to 350°F. Grease bottom and ½ inch up the sides of one 9×5×3-inch or two 7½×3½×2-inch loaf pans; set aside. In a large bowl combine flour, baking powder, baking soda, salt, cinnamon, and nutmeg. Make a well in center of flour mixture; set aside.

2. In a medium bowl combine eggs, banana, sugar, and oil. Add egg mixture all at once to flour mixture. Stir just until moistened (batter should be lumpy; see photo 1, page 126). Fold in walnuts. Spoon batter into prepared pan(s). If desired, sprinkle Streusel-Nut Topping over batter in pan(s).

3. Bake for 55 to 60 minutes for 9×5×3-inch pan or 40 to 45 minutes for 7½×3½×2-inch pans or until a wooden toothpick inserted near center comes out clean (if necessary, cover loosely with foil the last 15 minutes of baking to prevent overbrowning). Cool in pan on a wire rack for 10 minutes. Remove from pan. Cool completely on rack. Wrap; store overnight before slicing.

Per slice: 215 cal., 9 g total fat (1 g sat. fat), 27 mg chol., 122 mg sodium, 32 g carbo., 1 g fiber, 3 g pro.
Daily Values: 1% vit. A, 6% vit. C, 3% calcium, 5% iron
Exchanges: 1 Starch, 1 Other Carbo., 1½ Fat

Streusel-Nut Topping: In a small bowl combine ¼ cup packed brown sugar and 3 tablespoons all-purpose flour. Using a pastry blender, cut in 2 tablespoons butter until mixture resembles coarse crumbs. Stir in ⅓ cup chopped walnuts.

Nut Bread

Be sure to toast whichever kind of nuts you choose for this basic bread before folding them into the batter. Toasting brings out their flavor.

Prep: 25 minutes **Bake:** 50 minutes
Oven: 350°F **Makes:** 1 loaf (14 slices)

    2 cups all-purpose flour
    1 cup sugar
    1 tablespoon baking powder
    ½ teaspoon salt
    1 egg, beaten
    1 cup milk
    ¼ cup cooking oil
    ¾ cup chopped almonds, pecans, or walnuts,
       toasted (see tip, page 265)

1. Preheat oven to 350°F. Grease the bottom and ½ inch up the sides of an 8×4×2-inch loaf pan; set aside. In a large bowl stir together flour, sugar, baking powder, and salt. Make a well in center of flour mixture; set aside.

2. In a medium bowl combine the egg, milk, and oil. Add egg mixture all at once to flour mixture. Stir just until moistened (batter should be lumpy; see photo 1, page 126). Fold in nuts. Spoon batter into prepared pan.

3. Bake for 50 to 55 minutes or until a wooden toothpick inserted near center comes out clean. Cool in pan on a wire rack for 10 minutes. Remove from pan. Cool completely on wire rack. Wrap and store overnight before slicing.

Cranberry Nut Bread: Grease the bottom and ½ inch up the sides of a 9×5×3-inch loaf pan; set aside. Prepare as at left, except add 2 teaspoons finely shredded orange peel to flour mixture. Substitute orange juice for the milk and fold 1 cup coarsely chopped cranberries into batter along with nuts.

Per slice nut or cranberry nut variation: 207 cal., 8 g total fat (1 g sat. fat), 16 mg chol., 183 mg sodium, 30 g carbo., 1 g fiber, 4 g pro.
Daily Values: 1% vit. A, 1% vit. C, 10% calcium, 7% iron
Exchanges: 1 Starch, 1 Other Carbo., 1½ Fat

Blueberry Nut Bread: Prepare as at left, except add 1½ teaspoons finely shredded lemon peel to flour mixture. In a small bowl combine ½ cup dried blueberries with ¼ cup boiling water. Cover and let stand 10 minutes; drain, if necessary. Fold blueberries into batter along with the nuts. Bake in a prepared 8×4×2-inch loaf pan.

Per slice: 231 cal., 8 g total fat (1 g sat. fat), 16 mg chol., 183 mg sodium, 35 g carbo., 1 g fiber, 5 g pro.
Daily Values: 1% vit A, 1% vit. C, 10% calcium, 7% iron
Exchanges: 1 Starch, 1½ Other Carbo., 1½ Fat

Pick a Quick Bread Pan

If you would like to bake a quick bread in a different pan size than specified in a recipe, you'll need to adjust the baking time and remember to fill the pan only two-thirds full. If you have any leftover batter, bake it into muffins. (These baking times are approximate and may vary with the recipe.)

Pan Size	Baking Time
9×5×3-inch loaf pan	55 to 75 min.
8×4×2-inch loaf pan	50 to 60 min.
7½×3½×2-inch loaf pans	40 to 45 min.
4½×2½×1½-inch loaf pans	30 to 35 min.
2½-inch muffin cups	15 to 20 min.

Zucchini Bread

When the markets are brimming with zucchini, look for the small ones—they're young and their skins are extra tender.

Prep: 20 minutes **Bake:** 50 minutes
Oven: 350°F **Makes:** 1 loaf (16 slices)

- 1½ **cups all-purpose flour**
- 1 **teaspoon ground cinnamon**
- ½ **teaspoon baking soda**
- ½ **teaspoon salt**
- ¼ **teaspoon baking powder**
- ¼ **teaspoon ground nutmeg**
- 1 **egg, beaten**
- 1 **cup sugar**
- 1 **cup finely shredded, unpeeled zucchini**
- ¼ **cup cooking oil**
- ½ **cup chopped walnuts or pecans, toasted (see tip, page 265)**

1. Preheat oven to 350°F. Grease the bottom and ½ inch up the sides of an 8×4×2-inch loaf pan; set aside. In a medium bowl combine the flour, cinnamon, baking soda, salt, baking powder, and nutmeg. Make a well in center of flour mixture; set aside.

2. In another medium bowl combine egg, sugar, shredded zucchini, and oil. Add zucchini mixture all at once to flour mixture. Stir just until moistened (batter should be lumpy; see photo 1, page 126). Fold in nuts. Spoon batter into prepared pan.

3. Bake for 50 to 55 minutes or until a wooden toothpick inserted near center comes out clean. Cool in pan on a wire rack for 10 minutes. Remove from pan. Cool completely on a wire rack. Wrap and store overnight before slicing.

Apple Bread: Prepare as above, except substitute 1½ cups finely shredded, peeled apple for the shredded zucchini.

Per slice zucchini or apple variation: 147 cal., 6 g total fat (1 g sat. fat), 13 mg chol., 123 mg sodium, 21 g carbo., 1 g fiber, 2 g pro.
Daily Values: 1% vit. A, 1% vit. C, 1% calcium, 4% iron
Exchanges: ½ Starch, 1 Other Carbo., 1 Fat

Pumpkin Bread

Looking for a bread to serve with the holiday meal? Here's a festive suggestion.

Prep: 20 minutes **Bake:** 55 minutes
Oven: 350°F **Makes:** 2 loaves (32 slices)

- 3 **cups sugar**
- 1 **cup cooking oil**
- 4 **eggs**
- 3⅓ **cups all-purpose flour**
- 2 **teaspoons baking soda**
- 1½ **teaspoons salt**
- 1 **teaspoon ground cinnamon**
- 1 **teaspoon ground nutmeg**
- ⅔ **cup water**
- 1 **15-ounce can pumpkin**

1. Preheat oven to 350°F. Grease the bottom and ½ inch up the sides of two 9×5×3-inch, three 8×4×2-inch, or four 7½×3½×2-inch loaf pans; set aside. In an extra-large mixing bowl beat sugar and oil with an electric mixer on medium speed. Add eggs and beat well; set sugar mixture aside.

2. In a large bowl combine flour, baking soda, salt, cinnamon, and nutmeg. Alternately add flour mixture and the water to sugar mixture, beating on low speed after each addition just until combined. Beat in pumpkin. Spoon batter into prepared pans.

3. Bake for 55 to 65 minutes or until a wooden toothpick inserted near centers comes out clean. Cool in pans on wire racks for 10 minutes. Remove from pans. Cool completely on wire racks. Wrap and store overnight before slicing.

Per slice: 191 cal., 8 g total fat (1 g sat. fat), 27 mg chol., 197 mg sodium, 29 g carbo., 1 g fiber, 2 g pro.
Daily Values: 59% vit. A, 1% vit. C, 1% calcium, 6% iron
Exchanges: ½ Starch, 1½ Other Carbo., 1½ Fat

Raisin-Nut Pumpkin Bread: Prepare as above, except fold ¾ cup raisins and ¾ cup chopped walnuts into batter after pumpkin has been added.

Per slice: 220 cal., 10 g total fat (1 g sat. fat), 27 mg chol., 197 mg sodium, 32 g carbo., 1 g fiber, 8 g pro.
Daily Values: 59% vit. A, 2% vit. C, 2% calcium, 6% iron
Exchanges: ½ Starch, 1½ Other Carbo., 2 Fat

Lemon Bread

Pass slices of this citrus-sparked bread as an accompaniment to your favorite summer salad.

Prep: 20 minutes **Bake:** 50 minutes
Oven: 350°F **Makes:** 1 loaf (16 slices)

- 1¾ **cups all-purpose flour**
- ¾ **cup sugar**
- 2 **teaspoons baking powder**
- ¼ **teaspoon salt**
- 1 **egg, beaten**
- 1 **cup milk**
- ¼ **cup cooking oil, or ¼ cup butter or margarine, melted**
- 2 **teaspoons finely shredded lemon peel**
- 1 **tablespoon lemon juice**
- ½ **cup chopped almonds or walnuts**
- 2 **tablespoons lemon juice (optional)**
- 1 **tablespoon sugar (optional)**

1. Preheat oven to 350°F. Grease the bottom and ½ inch up the sides of an 8×4×2-inch loaf pan; set aside. In a medium bowl combine flour, the ¾ cup sugar, baking powder, and salt. Make a well in center of flour mixture; set mixture aside.

2. In another medium bowl combine the egg, milk, oil, lemon peel, and the 1 tablespoon lemon juice. Add egg mixture all at once to flour mixture. Stir just until moistened (batter should be lumpy; see photo 1, page 126). Fold in nuts. Spoon batter into prepared pan.

3. Bake for 50 to 55 minutes or until a wooden toothpick inserted near center comes out clean. If desired, in a small bowl stir together the 2 tablespoons lemon juice and the 1 tablespoon sugar. While bread is still in the pan, brush lemon-sugar mixture over the top of the loaf. Cool in pan on a wire rack for 10 minutes. Remove from pan. Cool completely on wire rack. Wrap and store overnight before serving.

Per slice: 147 cal., 6 g total fat (1 g sat. fat), 14 mg chol., 98 mg sodium, 20 g carbo., 1 g fiber, 3 g pro.
Daily Values: 1% vit. A, 2% vit. C, 6% calcium, 4% iron
Exchanges: ½ Starch, 1 Other Carbo., 1 Fat

Lemon-Poppy Seed Bread: Prepare as above, except substitute 1 tablespoon poppy seeds for the almonds or walnuts.

Per slice: 126 cal., 4 g total fat (1 g sat. fat), 14 mg chol., 98 mg sodium, 20 g carbo., 0 g fiber, 2 g pro.
Daily Values: 1% vit. A, 2% vit. C, 6% calcium, 4% iron
Exchanges: ½ Starch, 1 Other Carbo., ½ Fat

Lemon Bread

Cheddar Spoon Bread

Prep: 25 minutes **Bake:** 45 minutes
Oven: 325°F **Makes:** 8 portions

- 1½ **cups milk**
- ½ **cup cornmeal**
- 2 **cups shredded cheddar cheese or Monterey Jack cheese (8 ounces)**
- 1 **tablespoon butter or margarine**
- 1½ **teaspoons baking powder**
- 1 **teaspoon sugar**
- 4 **eggs**

1. Preheat oven to 325°F. In a large saucepan stir together the milk and cornmeal. Cook, stirring constantly, over medium-high heat until mixture is thickened and bubbly; remove from heat. Add cheese, butter, baking powder, sugar, and ¼ teaspoon *salt*; stir until cheese melts. Separate eggs. Add yolks, one at a time, to cornmeal mixture, stirring after each addition just until combined (mixture will be thick).

2. In a large mixing bowl beat egg whites with an electric mixer on high speed until stiff peaks form (tips stand straight). Stir about one-third of the beaten egg whites into the cornmeal mixture. Gently fold remaining beaten egg whites into cornmeal mixture until combined. Spoon into an ungreased 2-quart casserole or soufflé dish.

3. Bake for 45 to 50 minutes or until a knife inserted near the center comes out clean. Serve immediately.

Per portion: 221 cal., 14 g total fat (8 g sat. fat), 143 mg chol., 393 mg sodium, 10 g carbo., 1 g fiber, 12 g pro.
Daily Values: 13% vit. A, 1% vit. C, 32% calcium, 5% iron
Exchanges: ½ Starch, 1½ High-Fat Meat

Corn Bread `FAST`

If you prefer a sweeter corn bread, use the 3 tablespoons sugar.

Prep: 10 minutes **Bake:** 15 minutes
Oven: 400°F **Makes:** 8 to 10 wedges

   1 cup all-purpose flour
   ¾ cup cornmeal
   2 to 3 tablespoons sugar
   2½ teaspoons baking powder
   ¾ teaspoon salt
   1 tablespoon butter
   2 eggs, beaten
   1 cup milk
   ¼ cup cooking oil or melted butter

1. Preheat oven to 400°F. In a medium bowl stir together flour, cornmeal, sugar, baking powder, and salt; set aside.

2. Add the 1 tablespoon butter to a 10-inch cast-iron skillet or a 9×1½-inch round baking pan. Place in oven about 3 minutes or until butter melts. Remove skillet from oven; swirl butter in skillet to coat bottom and sides of pan.

3. Meanwhile, in a small bowl combine eggs, milk, and oil. Add egg mixture all at once to flour mixture. Stir just until moistened. Pour batter into hot skillet or pan. Bake for 15 to 20 minutes or until a wooden toothpick inserted near center comes out clean. Cut into wedges. Serve warm.

Per wedge: 219 cal., 10 g total fat (3 g sat. fat), 60 mg chol., 390 mg sodium, 26 g carbo., 1 g fiber, 5 g pro.
Daily Values: 5% vit. A, 12% calcium, 8% iron
Exchanges: 1½ Starch, 2 Fat

Double Corn Bread: Prepare as above, except fold ½ cup frozen whole kernel corn, thawed, into the batter.

Per wedge: 227 cal., 11 g total fat (3 g sat. fat), 60 mg chol., 391 mg sodium, 28 g carbo., 2 g fiber, 5 g pro.
Daily Values: 6 vit. A, 1% vit. C, 12% calcium, 8% iron
Exchanges: 2 Starch, 1½ Fat

Green Chile Corn Bread: Prepare as above, except fold 1 cup shredded cheddar cheese or Monterey Jack cheese (4 ounces) and one 4-ounce can diced green chile peppers, drained, into the batter.

Per wedge: 279 cal., 15 g total fat (6 g sat. fat), 74 mg chol., 517 mg sodium, 26 g carbo., 1 g fiber, 9 g pro.
Daily Values: 8 vit. A, 8% vit. C, 24% calcium, 9% iron
Exchanges: 1½ Starch, ½ High-Fat Meat, 2½ Fat

Corn Muffins: Prepare as at left, except omit the 1 tablespoon butter. Spoon batter into 12 greased 2½-inch muffin cups, filling cups two-thirds full. Bake in a 400°F oven about 15 minutes or until light brown and a wooden toothpick inserted near centers comes out clean. Makes 12 muffins.

Per muffin: 137 cal., 6 g total fat (1 g sat. fat), 37 mg chol., 250 mg sodium, 17 g carbo., 1 g fiber, 3 g pro.
Daily Values: 3% vit. A, 8% calcium, 5% iron
Exchanges: 1 Starch, 1 Fat

Corn Sticks: Prepare as at left, except omit the 1 tablespoon butter. Generously grease corn stick pans; heat in the preheated oven for 3 minutes. Carefully fill preheated pans two-thirds full. Bake in a 400°F oven about 12 minutes or until toothpick inserted in centers comes out clean. Makes 18 to 26 corn sticks.

Per corn stick: 91 cal., 4 g total fat (1 g sat. fat), 25 mg chol., 167 mg sodium, 11 g carbo., 1 g fiber, 2 g pro.
Daily Values: 2% vit. A, 5% calcium, 3% iron
Exchanges: 1 Starch

FAVORITE Fruit Coffee Cake

Choose your favorite seasonal fruit.

Prep: 30 minutes **Bake:** 40 minutes
Oven: 350°F **Makes:** 9 pieces

   1½ to 2 cups sliced, peeled apricots or peaches; chopped, peeled apples; blueberries; or red raspberries
   ¼ cup water
   ¼ cup sugar
   2 tablespoons cornstarch
   1½ cups all-purpose flour
   ¾ cup sugar
   ½ teaspoon baking powder
   ¼ teaspoon baking soda
   ¼ cup butter or margarine
   1 egg, beaten
   ½ cup buttermilk or sour milk (see tip, page 169)
   ½ teaspoon vanilla
   ¼ cup all-purpose flour
   ¼ cup sugar
   2 tablespoons butter or margarine

1. For filling, in a medium saucepan combine fruit and water. Bring to boiling; reduce heat. Simmer (do not simmer raspberries), covered, about 5 minutes or until fruit is tender. Combine ¼ cup sugar and cornstarch; stir into fruit. Cook and stir over medium heat until mixture is thickened and bubbly. Cook and stir 2 minutes more; set filling aside.

2. Preheat oven to 350°F. In a medium bowl combine the 1½ cups flour, the ¾ cup sugar, baking powder, and baking soda. Cut in ¼ cup butter until mixture resembles coarse crumbs. Make a well in the center of the flour mixture; set aside.

3. In another bowl combine egg, buttermilk, and vanilla. Add egg mixture all at once to flour mixture. Using a wooden spoon, stir just until moistened (batter should be lumpy). Spread half of the batter in an ungreased 8×8×2-inch baking pan. Spread filling over batter. Drop remaining batter in small mounds onto filling.

4. In a small bowl stir together the ¼ cup flour and ¼ cup sugar. Cut in the 2 tablespoons butter until mixture resembles coarse crumbs. Sprinkle over coffee cake. Bake for 40 to 45 minutes or until golden. Cool slightly; serve warm.

Per piece: 297 cal., 9 g total fat (5 g sat. fat), 46 mg chol., 162 mg sodium, 50 g carbo., 1 g fiber, 4 g pro.
Daily Values: 20% vit. A, 5% vit. C, 4% calcium, 8% iron
Exchanges: 1 Starch, 2½ Other Carbo., 1½ Fat

Rhubarb-Strawberry Coffee Cake: Prepare as on page 134, except substitute ¾ cup fresh or frozen cut-up rhubarb and ¾ cup frozen unsweetened whole strawberries for the listed fruit.

Per piece: 263 cal., 9 g total fat (2 g sat. fat), 46 mg chol., 162 mg sodium, 49 g carbo., 1 g fiber, 4 g pro.
Daily Values: 7% vit. A, 13% vit. C, 5% calcium, 7% iron
Exchanges: 1 Starch, 2½ Other Carbo., 1½ Fat

Blueberry Buckle

Enjoy this coffee cake while it's still warm.

Prep: 20 minutes **Bake:** 50 minutes
Oven: 350°F **Makes:** 9 pieces

- 2 **cups all-purpose flour**
- 2½ **teaspoons baking powder**
- ¼ **teaspoon salt**
- ½ **cup shortening**
- ¾ **cup sugar**
- 1 **egg**
- ½ **cup milk**
- 2 **cups fresh or frozen blueberries**
- ½ **cup all-purpose flour**
- ½ **cup sugar**
- ½ **teaspoon ground cinnamon**
- ¼ **cup butter**

1. Preheat oven to 350°F. Grease the bottom and ½ inch up the sides of a 9×9×2-inch or 8×8×2-inch baking pan; set aside. In a medium bowl combine the 2 cups flour, baking powder, and salt; set aside.

2. In a medium mixing bowl beat shortening with an electric mixer on medium speed for 30 seconds. Add the ¾ cup sugar. Beat on medium to high speed until light and fluffy. Add egg; beat well. Alternately add flour mixture and milk to beaten egg mixture, beating until smooth after each addition.

3. Spoon batter into prepared pan. Sprinkle with blueberries. In another bowl combine the ½ cup flour, the ½ cup sugar, and cinnamon. Using a pastry blender, cut in butter until mixture resembles coarse crumbs; sprinkle over blueberries. Bake for 50 to 60 minutes or until golden. Cool slightly; serve warm.

Raspberry Buckle: Prepare as above, except substitute fresh or frozen red raspberries for the blueberries.

Per piece blueberry or raspberry variation: 408 cal., 17 g total fat (6 g sat. fat), 38 mg chol., 247 mg sodium, 58 g carbo., 2 g fiber, 5 g pro.
Daily Values: 6% vit. A, 8% vit. C, 11% calcium, 11% iron
Exchanges: 1 Starch, 3 Other Carbo., 3 Fat

Raspberry Buckle

Buttermilk Coffee Cake

Prep: 30 minutes **Bake:** 35 minutes
Oven: 350°F **Makes:** 18 pieces

- 2½ cups all-purpose flour
- 1½ cups packed brown sugar
- ½ teaspoon salt
- ⅔ cup butter
- 2 teaspoons baking powder
- ½ teaspoon baking soda
- ½ teaspoon ground cinnamon
- ½ teaspoon ground nutmeg
- 2 eggs, beaten
- 1⅓ cups buttermilk or sour milk (see tip, page 169)
- ½ cup chopped pecans, walnuts, or almonds

1. Preheat oven to 350°F. Grease the bottom and ½ inch up the sides of a 13×9×2-inch baking pan; set aside. In a large bowl combine flour, brown sugar, and salt. Cut in butter until mixture resembles coarse crumbs; set aside ½ cup. Stir baking powder, baking soda, cinnamon, and nutmeg into remaining crumb mixture.

2. In a medium bowl combine eggs and buttermilk. Add egg mixture all at once to flour mixture, stirring just until moistened. Spoon batter into prepared pan. Stir together reserved crumb mixture and nuts; sprinkle over batter.

3. Bake for 35 to 40 minutes or until a wooden toothpick inserted near the center comes out clean. Cool slightly; serve warm.

Buttermilk Coffee Cake

Buttermilk Coffee Cake Ring: Prepare as at left, except grease and flour a 10-inch fluted tube pan and toast the nuts (see tip, page 265). Spoon half of the batter into prepared pan. Combine reserved ½ cup crumb mixture and the toasted nuts; sprinkle over batter. Top with remaining batter. Bake for 40 to 50 minutes or until a wooden skewer inserted near the center comes out clean. Cool in pan on a wire rack for 10 minutes. Remove from pan. Cool slightly; serve warm.

Per piece: 228 cal., 10 g total fat (4 g sat. fat), 43 mg chol., 212 mg sodium, 31 g carbo., 1 g fiber, 3 g pro.
Daily Values: 5% vit. A, 6% calcium, 7% iron
Exchanges: ½ Starch, 1½ Other Carbo., 2 Fat

Chocolate Chip Coffee Cake

Prep: 20 minutes **Bake:** 40 minutes
Oven: 350°F **Makes:** 16 pieces

- 1 cup chopped walnuts or pecans
- ¾ cup semisweet chocolate pieces
- ½ cup granulated sugar
- ½ cup packed brown sugar
- 1 teaspoon ground cinnamon
- 2 cups all-purpose flour
- 1 teaspoon baking powder
- ½ teaspoon baking soda
- ⅛ teaspoon salt
- 1 cup granulated sugar
- ½ cup butter, softened
- 2 eggs
- 1 8-ounce carton dairy sour cream
- 1 teaspoon vanilla

1. Preheat oven to 350°F. Grease a 13×9×2-inch baking pan; set aside. For filling, in a medium bowl combine nuts, chocolate pieces, the ½ cup granulated sugar, brown sugar, and cinnamon; set aside.

2. In a small bowl combine flour, baking powder, baking soda, and salt; set aside. In a large mixing bowl combine the 1 cup granulated sugar and butter; beat with an electric mixer on medium speed until well combined. Add eggs; beat until combined. Beat in sour cream and vanilla. Add flour mixture to the beaten mixture, beating until smooth. (Batter will be thick.) Set aside 1 cup batter.

3. Evenly spread remaining batter in the prepared pan. Sprinkle filling over batter. Spoon reserved batter over filling in small mounds.

4. Bake about 40 minutes or until a wooden toothpick inserted in the center comes out clean. Cool slightly; serve warm.

Per piece: 327 cal., 17 g total fat (7 g sat. fat), 49 mg chol., 135 mg sodium, 43 g carbo., 2 g fiber, 4 g pro.
Daily Values: 6% vit. A, 4% calcium, 8% iron
Exchanges: ½ Starch, 2½ Other Carbo., 3 Fat

Buttermilk Pancakes `FAST`

See photo, page 123.

Start to Finish: 25 minutes
Makes: 12 standard-size pancakes or 40 dollar-size pancakes

1¾	**cups all-purpose flour**
2	**tablespoons granulated sugar**
2	**teaspoons baking powder**
½	**teaspoon baking soda**
¼	**teaspoon salt**
1	**egg, slightly beaten**
1½	**cups buttermilk or sour milk (see tip, page 169)**
3	**tablespoons cooking oil**
	Desired fruit options (optional)*
	Desired syrup (optional)

1. In a large bowl stir together flour, sugar, baking powder, baking soda, and salt. In another bowl use a fork to combine egg, buttermilk, and oil. Add egg mixture all at once to flour mixture. Stir just until moistened (batter should be slightly lumpy). If desired, stir in desired fruit.

2. For each standard-size pancake, pour about ¼ cup batter onto a hot, lightly greased griddle or heavy skillet, spreading batter if necessary. For dollar-size pancakes, use about 1 tablespoon batter. Cook over medium heat for 1 to 2 minutes on each side or until pancakes are golden brown, turning to second side when pancakes have bubbly surfaces and edges are slightly dry. Serve warm. If desired, top with syrup.

Pancakes: Prepare as above, except substitute milk for buttermilk, increase baking powder to 1 tablespoon, and omit the baking soda.

Whole Wheat Pancakes: Prepare as above, except substitute whole wheat flour for the all-purpose flour and packed brown sugar for the granulated sugar.

Buckwheat Pancakes: Prepare as above, except use ¾ cup all-purpose flour and add 1 cup buckwheat flour.

Cornmeal Pancakes: Prepare as at left, except use 1¼ cups all-purpose flour and add ½ cup cornmeal.

Bran Pancakes: Prepare as at left, except use 1½ cups all-purpose flour and add ¼ cup oat bran, wheat bran, or toasted wheat germ.

Per standard-size buttermilk pancake, plain, whole wheat, buckwheat, cornmeal, or bran variations: 117 cal., 4 g total fat (1 g sat. fat), 19 mg chol., 179 mg sodium, 16 g carbo., 0 g fiber, 3 g pro.
Daily Values: 1% vit. A, 1% vit. C, 5% calcium, 5% iron
Exchanges: ½ Starch, ½ Other Carbo., 1 Fat

*Fruit Options: If desired, stir one of the following fruits into the pancake batter: ½ cup chopped fresh apple, apricot, peach, nectarine, or pear; ½ cup fresh or frozen blueberries; or ¼ cup chopped dried apple, pear, apricot, raisins, currants, dates, cranberries, blueberries, cherries, or mixed fruit.

French Toast `FAST`

Prep: 10 minutes **Cook:** 4 minutes per slice
Makes: 4 servings

4	**eggs, beaten**
1	**cup milk**
2	**tablespoons sugar**
2	**teaspoons vanilla**
2	**teaspoons orange liqueur (optional)**
½	**teaspoon ground cinnamon (optional)**
¼	**teaspoon ground nutmeg (optional)**
8	**½-inch slices challah bread or brioche or 8 slices dry white bread**
2	**tablespoons butter**
	Maple-flavored syrup (optional)

1. In a shallow mixing bowl beat together eggs, milk, sugar, vanilla, and, if desired, orange liqueur and/or cinnamon and nutmeg. Dip challah bread or brioche into egg mixture, letting it soak about 10 seconds on each side (if using white bread, dip into egg mixture, coating both sides).

2. In a skillet or on a griddle melt 1 tablespoon of the butter over medium heat; add half of the bread slices and cook for 2 to 3 minutes on each side or until golden brown. Repeat with remaining butter and bread slices. Serve warm. If desired, serve with syrup.

Per 2 slices: 291 cal., 13 g total fat (6 g sat. fat), 233 mg chol., 384 mg sodium, 29 g carbo., 1 g fiber, 12 g pro.
Daily Values: 13% vit. A, 1% vit. C, 13% calcium, 10% iron
Exchanges: ½ Milk, 1½ Starch, 2 Fat

Overnight Stuffed French Toast

and 4 teaspoons cornstarch. Cook and stir over medium heat until thickened and bubbly. Cook and stir for 2 minutes more.

Per slice + ⅓ cup sauce: 340 cal., 18 g total fat (8 g sat. fat), 176 mg chol., 303 mg sodium, 35 g carbo., 2 g fiber, 11 g pro.
Daily Values: 16% vit. A, 45% vit. C, 13% calcium, 10% iron
Exchanges: ½ Fruit, 1½ Starch, ½ Other Carbo., 1 Medium-Fat Meat, 2 Fat

Popovers EASY

Prep: 10 minutes **Bake:** 35 minutes
Oven: 400°F **Makes:** 6 popovers

- **1 tablespoon shortening or nonstick cooking spray**
- **2 eggs, slightly beaten**
- **1 cup milk**
- **1 tablespoon cooking oil**
- **1 cup all-purpose flour**
- **½ teaspoon salt**

1. Preheat oven to 400°F. Using ½ teaspoon shortening for each cup, grease the bottoms and sides of six 6-ounce custard cups or cups of a popover pan. (Or lightly coat cups with cooking spray.) Place the custard cups in a 15×10×1-inch baking pan; set aside.

2. In a medium bowl use a wire whisk or rotary beater to beat eggs, milk, and oil until combined. Add flour and salt; beat until smooth.

3. Fill the prepared cups half full with batter. Bake about 35 minutes or until firm.

4. Immediately after removing from oven, prick each popover to let steam escape. Turn off the oven. For crisper popovers, return popovers to oven for 5 to 10 minutes or until desired crispness is reached. Remove popovers from cups; serve immediately.

Whole Wheat and Onion Popovers: Prepare as above, except omit oil and cook ¼ cup chopped onion in 1 tablespoon butter or margarine until tender. Stir into egg mixture. Use only ⅔ cup all-purpose flour and add ⅓ cup whole wheat flour in Step 2.

Herb Popovers: Prepare as above, except stir 1 tablespoon finely snipped fresh dill or basil or ¾ teaspoon dried dill or basil, crushed, into batter before pouring it into cups or pans.

Per popover plain, whole wheat and onion, or herb variations:
153 cal., 7 g total fat (2 g sat. fat), 74 mg chol., 237 mg sodium, 17 g carbo., 1 g fiber, 5 g pro.
Daily Values: 3% vit. A, 6% calcium, 7% iron
Exchanges: 1 Starch, ½ Medium-Fat Meat, 1 Fat

Overnight Stuffed French Toast

Prep: 40 minutes **Chill:** up to 24 hours
Bake: 30 minutes **Oven:** 350°F **Makes:** 6 servings

- **2 3-ounce packages cream cheese, softened**
- **2 tablespoons orange marmalade or apricot preserves**
- **1 teaspoon finely chopped crystallized ginger**
- **⅛ teaspoon ground nutmeg**
- **¼ cup chopped almonds, toasted (see tip, page 265)**
- **6 1½-inch slices French bread**
- **4 eggs**
- **1 cup milk**
- **1 teaspoon vanilla**
- **1 recipe Orange Sauce**

1. Generously grease a 3-quart rectangular baking dish; set aside. In a mixing bowl beat together cream cheese, marmalade, ginger, and nutmeg. Stir in almonds. Cut a pocket in top crust of each bread slice. Divide cheese mixture evenly among pockets. Place stuffed bread slices in prepared baking dish. In a mixing bowl beat together eggs, milk, and vanilla; slowly pour egg mixture over bread slices, covering them. Cover; chill overnight.

2. Preheat oven to 350°F. Bake, uncovered, for 30 to 35 minutes or until golden. Serve with Orange Sauce.

Orange Sauce: In a small saucepan stir together ½ teaspoon finely shredded orange peel, 1¼ cups orange juice, 2 tablespoons honey,

Nun's Puffs

Prep: 25 minutes **Bake:** 30 minutes
Oven: 375°F **Makes:** 12 puffs

- ½ **cup butter**
- 1 **cup milk**
- ¾ **cup all-purpose flour**
- 4 **eggs**
- 1 **tablespoon sugar**
  Honey (optional)

1. Preheat oven to 375°F. Generously grease twelve 2½-inch muffin cups, including the edge and around the top of each cup; set aside. In a medium saucepan melt butter; add milk. Bring to boiling. Add flour all at once, stirring vigorously. Cook and stir until mixture forms a ball that does not separate. Remove from heat; cool for 5 minutes.

2. Add the eggs, one at a time, beating for 1 minute with a wooden spoon after each addition or until smooth. Divide dough evenly among prepared muffin cups, filling cups about two-thirds full; sprinkle with sugar.

3. Bake about 30 minutes or until golden brown and puffy. Remove from pan. Serve immediately. If desired, serve with honey.

Per puff: 137 cal., 10 g total fat (6 g sat. fat), 94 mg chol., 114 mg sodium, 8 g carbo., 0 g fiber, 4 g pro.
Daily Values: 9% vit. A, 4% calcium, 3% iron
Exchanges: ½ Starch, 2 Fat

Nun's Puffs

Waffles EASY

Serve this favorite topped with syrup for breakfast or brunch. Or turn it into dessert with sweetened strawberries and a pile of whipped cream.

Prep: 10 minutes **Bake:** per waffle baker directions
Makes: 12 to 16 (4-inch) waffles

- 1¾ **cups all-purpose flour**
- 2 **tablespoons sugar**
- 1 **tablespoon baking powder**
- ¼ **teaspoon salt**
- 2 **eggs**
- 1¾ **cups milk**
- ½ **cup cooking oil or butter, melted**
- 1 **teaspoon vanilla**

1. In a medium bowl stir together flour, sugar, baking powder, and salt. Make a well in center of flour mixture; set aside.

2. In another medium bowl beat eggs slightly; stir in milk, oil, and vanilla. Add egg mixture all at once to flour mixture. Stir just until moistened (batter should be slightly lumpy).

3. Pour 1 to 1¼ cups batter onto grids of a preheated, lightly greased waffle baker (use a regular or Belgian waffle baker). Close lid quickly; do not open until done. Bake according to manufacturer's directions. When done, use a fork to lift waffle off grid. Repeat with remaining batter. Serve warm.

Buttermilk Waffles: Prepare as above, except reduce the baking powder to 1 teaspoon and add ½ teaspoon baking soda. Substitute 2 cups buttermilk or sour milk (see tip, page 169) for the milk.

Per waffle plain or buttermilk variation: 180 cal., 11 g total fat (2 g sat. fat), 38 mg chol., 177 mg sodium, 17 g carbo., 0 g fiber, 4 g pro.
Daily Values: 3% vit. A, 1% vit. C, 11% calcium, 5% iron
Exchanges: 1 Starch, 2 Fat

Weekend Breakfast

Plan a leisurely breakfast for the family. Offer a variety of syrup flavors for the waffles.

- *Citrus sections and melon cubes*
- *Waffles (above)*
- *Canadian-style bacon*
- *Coffee, tea, or milk*

Overnight Waffles `EASY`

Here's one solution for an early morning breakfast. Set out an assortment of syrups and a variety of fruits to accompany the waffles.

Prep: 10 minutes **Chill:** up to 24 hours
Bake: per waffle baker directions
Makes: about 16 (4-inch) waffles

- 2¼ cups all-purpose flour
- 2 tablespoons sugar
- 1 package active dry yeast
- 1 teaspoon vanilla (optional)
- ½ teaspoon salt
- 1¾ cups milk
- 2 eggs
- ⅓ cup cooking oil or butter, melted

1. In a large mixing bowl stir together flour, sugar, yeast, vanilla (if desired), and salt; add milk, eggs, and oil. Beat with an electric mixer until thoroughly combined. Cover batter loosely and chill overnight or up to 24 hours.

2. Stir batter. Pour about ¾ cup batter onto grids of a preheated, lightly greased waffle baker. Close lid quickly; do not open until done. Bake according to manufacturer's directions. When done, use a fork to lift waffle off grid. Repeat with remaining batter. Serve warm. Discard any remaining batter.

Overnight Cornmeal Waffles: Prepare as above, except reduce the flour to 1½ cups and add ¾ cup cornmeal.

Per waffle plain or cornmeal variation: 133 cal., 6 g total fat (1 g sat. fat), 29 mg chol., 94 mg sodium, 16 g carbo., 1 g fiber, 4 g pro.
Daily Values: 2% vit. A, 1% vit. C, 4% calcium, 6% iron
Exchanges: 1 Starch, 1 Fat

Crepes `LOW FAT`

Turn these versatile, thin beauties into a savory main dish by filling them with a creamed mixture or into a delightful dessert by heating them in a buttery mixture.

Prep: 5 minutes **Cook:** 30 minutes **Makes:** 18 crepes

- 2 eggs, beaten
- 1½ cups milk
- 1 cup all-purpose flour
- 1 tablespoon cooking oil
- ¼ teaspoon salt

1. In a medium mixing bowl combine eggs, milk, flour, oil, and salt; beat until combined.

2. Heat a lightly greased 6-inch skillet; remove from heat. Spoon in 2 tablespoons batter; lift and tilt skillet to spread batter. Return to heat; brown on one side only. (Or cook on a crepe maker according to manufacturer's directions.) Invert the crepe onto a paper towel. Repeat with remaining batter, greasing skillet occasionally.

Make-ahead directions: Prepare as above. Layer cooled crepes with sheets of waxed paper in an airtight container; freeze up to 4 months. Thaw at room temperature for 1 hour before using.

Per crepe: 50 cal., 2 g total fat (1 g sat. fat), 25 mg chol., 50 mg sodium, 6 g carbo., 0 g fiber, 2 g pro.
Daily Values: 2% vit. A, 3% calcium, 2% iron
Exchanges: ½ Starch

French Bread Fix-Ups

Preheat the broiler. Cut a 1-pound loaf of French bread in half horizontally. Place bread halves, cut sides up, on a large baking sheet. Spread cut sides of bread with desired topping (see below). Broil about 6 inches from heat for 1½ to 2 minutes or until light brown. Cut crosswise into slices and serve warm. Makes 16 slices.

Garlic Bread: Stir together ¼ cup softened butter or margarine and ¼ teaspoon garlic salt. Spread over cut sides of bread halves.

Cheese Bread: Stir together ¼ cup softened butter or margarine and ¼ teaspoon garlic salt. Spread over cut sides of bread halves. Sprinkle buttered sides with 1 cup finely shredded Parmesan cheese, Romano cheese, or cheddar cheese.

Pesto Bread: Spread cut sides of each bread half with 3 tablespoons purchased basil pesto or dried tomato pesto.

White Bread `LOW FAT`

Prep: 30 minutes **Rise:** 1¼ hours **Rest:** 10 minutes
Bake: 35 minutes **Oven:** 375°F
Makes: 2 loaves (24 slices)

  5¾ to 6¼ cups all-purpose flour
  1 package active dry yeast
  2¼ cups milk or buttermilk
  2 tablespoons sugar
  1 tablespoon butter, margarine, or shortening
  1½ teaspoons salt

1. In a large mixing bowl combine 2½ cups of the flour and the yeast; set aside. In a medium saucepan heat and stir milk, sugar, butter, and salt just until warm (120°F to 130°F) and butter almost melts. Add milk mixture to flour mixture. Beat with an electric mixer on low to medium speed for 30 seconds, scraping sides of bowl constantly. Beat on high speed for 3 minutes. Using a wooden spoon, stir in as much of the remaining flour as you can.

2. Turn dough out onto a lightly floured surface. Knead in enough of the remaining flour to make a moderately stiff dough that is smooth and elastic (6 to 8 minutes total; see photo 1, right). Shape dough into a ball. Place in a lightly greased bowl, turning once to grease surface of dough. Cover; let rise in a warm place until double in size (45 to 60 minutes; see photos 2 and 3, right).

3. Punch dough down (see photo 4, right). Turn dough out onto a lightly floured surface; divide in half. Cover; let rest 10 minutes. Meanwhile, lightly grease two 8×4×2-inch loaf pans.

4. Shape each dough half into a loaf by patting or rolling. To shape by patting, gently pat and pinch dough into a loaf shape (see photo 5, right), tucking edges underneath. To shape by rolling, on a lightly floured surface, roll dough into a 12×8-inch rectangle. Tightly roll up, starting from a short side (see photo 6, right), sealing the seam with your fingertips.

5. Place the shaped dough halves in the prepared pans, seam sides down. Cover and let rise in a warm place until nearly double in size (about 30 minutes).

6. Preheat oven to 375°F. Bake for 35 to 40 minutes or until bread sounds hollow when lightly tapped. (If necessary, cover loosely with foil the last 5 to 10 minutes of baking to prevent overbrowning.) Immediately remove bread from pans. Cool completely on wire racks.

Per slice: 111 cal., 1 g total fat (0 g sat. fat), 2 mg chol., 151 mg sodium, 22 g carbo., 1 g fiber, 3 g pro.
Daily Values: 1% calcium, 7% iron
Exchanges: 1½ Starch

1. To knead dough, fold it over and push down with the heel of your hand. Turn the dough, fold, and push down again. Repeat this process until the dough is smooth and elastic.

2. To let dough rise, cover it with a clean towel and place it in a warm, draft-free location, such as the upper rack of a cool oven with a bowl of warm water sitting on a lower oven rack.

3. To see if dough has doubled in size and is ready to be shaped, press two fingers ½ inch into the center. Remove your fingers. If indentations remain, the dough is ready to be punched down.

4. To punch dough down, push your fist into the center. Use your fingers to pull dough edges into the center.

5. To pat dough into a loaf shape, use your hands to gently pat and pinch, tucking edges underneath. Place the shaped dough, seam side down, in a prepared loaf pan.

6. To roll dough into a loaf shape, use a rolling pin to form a 12×8-inch rectangle. Tightly roll up the rectangle, starting from a short side. Pinch seam to seal. Place shaped dough, seam side down, in prepared loaf pan.

Mixed-Grain Bread `LOW FAT` `WHOLE GRAIN`

Prep: 30 minutes **Rise:** 1½ hours **Rest:** 10 minutes
Bake: 30 minutes **Oven:** 375°F
Makes: 2 loaves (24 slices)

- 3½ to 4 cups all-purpose flour
- 2 packages active dry yeast
- 1½ cups milk
- ¾ cup water
- ½ cup cracked wheat
- ¼ cup cornmeal
- ¼ cup packed brown sugar
- 3 tablespoons cooking oil
- 1½ teaspoons salt
- 1½ cups whole wheat flour
- ½ cup rolled oats
  Water
  Rolled oats

1. In a large mixing bowl combine 2 cups of the all-purpose flour and the yeast; set aside. In a medium saucepan combine milk, the ¾ cup water, cracked wheat, cornmeal, brown sugar, oil, and salt. Heat and stir over medium-low heat just until warm (120°F to 130°F). Add milk mixture to flour mixture. Beat with an electric mixer on low to medium speed for 30 seconds, scraping sides of bowl. Beat on high speed for 3 minutes. Using a wooden spoon, stir in whole wheat flour, the ½ cup rolled oats, and as much of the remaining all-purpose flour as you can.

2. Turn dough out onto a lightly floured surface. Knead in enough of the remaining all-purpose flour to make a moderately stiff dough that is almost smooth and elastic (6 to 8 minutes total; see photo 1, page 141). Shape dough into a ball. Place in a lightly greased bowl, turning once to grease surface of dough. Cover; let rise in a warm place until double in size (about 1 hour; see photos 2 and 3, page 141).

3. Punch dough down (see photo 4, page 141). Turn out onto a lightly floured surface. Divide in half. Cover; let rest 10 minutes. Meanwhile, lightly grease two 8×4×2-inch loaf pans.

4. Shape each dough half into a loaf by patting or rolling (see photos 5 and 6, page 141). Place shaped dough halves in prepared pans. Cover; let rise in warm place until nearly double in size (about 30 minutes).

5. Preheat oven to 375°F. Brush loaf tops with additional water; sprinkle with additional rolled oats. Bake for 30 to 35 minutes or until bread sounds hollow when lightly tapped. (If necessary, cover loosely with foil the last 10 minutes of baking to prevent overbrowning.) Immediately remove bread from pans. Cool on wire racks. Serve within 2 days or freeze for longer storage.

Per slice: 143 cal., 3 g total fat (0 g sat. fat), 1 mg chol., 155 mg sodium, 26 g carbo., 2 g fiber, 4 g pro.
Daily Values: 1% vit. A, 3% calcium, 8% iron
Exchanges: 1½ Starch, ½ Fat

Quick Swedish Rye Bread `LOW FAT`

Little kneading is required to make this savory loaf.

Prep: 20 minutes **Rise:** according to package directions
Bake: 30 minutes **Oven:** 350°F
Makes: 2 loaves (32 slices)

- 1 16-ounce package hot roll mix
- ¾ cup rye flour
- 1 tablespoon packed brown sugar
- 1 to 2 teaspoons caraway seeds
- 2 tablespoons molasses
- 2 eggs

1. Grease a baking sheet; set aside. Prepare hot roll mix according to package directions, stirring rye flour, brown sugar, and caraway seeds into flour-yeast mixture; stir in molasses with the water, and use 2 eggs. Let the dough rest according to package directions. Divide dough in half. On a floured surface, roll each dough half into a 12×8-inch rectangle. Starting from a short side, tightly roll up each dough rectangle. Seal seams with your fingertips. Place shaped dough on prepared baking sheet, seam sides down. Let rise according to package directions.

2. Preheat oven to 350°F. Bake about 30 minutes or until bread sounds hollow when lightly tapped. Cool on wire racks.

Per slice: 79 cal., 1 g total fat (0 g sat. fat), 19 mg chol., 98 mg sodium, 14 g carbo., 0 g fiber, 3 g pro.
Daily Values: 1% calcium, 3% iron
Exchanges: 1 Starch

Reuben Roll: Prepare as above through Step 1, except sprinkle 1 cup finely shredded Swiss cheese and ⅔ cup finely chopped corned beef over the two dough rectangles. Continue as above. Let bread cool 15 minutes after baking; slice and serve warm.

Per slice: 101 cal., 3 g total fat (1 g sat. fat), 26 mg chol., 144 mg sodium, 14 g carbo., 0 g fiber, 4 g pro.
Daily Values: 1% vit. A, 3% calcium, 4% iron
Exchanges: 1 Starch, ½ Fat

Caraway-Rye Bread **LOW FAT**

*When you're looking for a hearty accompaniment
for a soup or stew, bake a batch of this bread.*

Prep: 40 minutes **Rise:** 1½ hours **Rest:** 10 minutes
Bake: 30 minutes **Oven:** 375°F
Makes: 2 loaves (24 slices)

- 4 to 4½ cups bread flour
- 1 package active dry yeast
- 2 cups warm water (120°F to 130°F)
- ¼ cup packed brown sugar
- 2 tablespoons cooking oil
- 1½ teaspoons salt
- 1½ cups rye flour
- 1 tablespoon caraway seeds
- Cornmeal
- 2 teaspoons milk

Caraway-Rye Bread

1. In a large mixing bowl stir together 2¾ cups
of the bread flour and the yeast. Add the warm
water, brown sugar, oil, and salt. Beat with
an electric mixer on low to medium speed for
30 seconds, scraping sides of bowl constantly.
Beat on high speed for 3 minutes. Using a
wooden spoon, stir in rye flour, caraway seeds,
and as much of the remaining bread flour as
you can.

2. Turn dough out onto a lightly floured surface. Knead in enough remaining bread flour to
make a moderately stiff dough that is smooth
and elastic (6 to 8 minutes total; see photo
1, page 141). Shape dough into a ball. Place in
a lightly greased bowl, turning once to grease
surface of dough. Cover; let rise in a warm place
until double in size (about 1 hour; see photos
2 and 3, page 141).

3. Punch dough down (see photo 4, page 141).
Turn dough out onto a lightly floured surface.
Divide dough in half. Cover; let rest 10 minutes. Meanwhile, lightly grease a baking sheet;
sprinkle greased baking sheet with cornmeal.

4. Shape each dough half by gently pulling it
into a ball, tucking edges under. Place dough
rounds on prepared baking sheet. Flatten each
dough round slightly to about 6 inches in diameter. (Or shape each dough half into a loaf by
patting or rolling [see photos 5 and 6, page 141].
Place in two greased 8×4×2-inch loaf pans.)
If desired, lightly score loaf tops with a sharp
knife. Cover and let rise in a warm place until
nearly double in size (30 to 45 minutes).

5. Preheat oven to 375°F. Brush loaf tops with
milk. Bake for 30 to 35 minutes or until tops
and sides are deep golden brown and bread
sounds hollow when lightly tapped. Immediately
remove from baking sheet (or pans). Cool on
wire racks.

Peasant Rye Bread: Prepare as at left, except
reduce rye flour to 1 cup. Stir in ¼ cup whole
bran cereal and ¼ cup yellow cornmeal with
rye flour.

Per slice caraway-rye or peasant rye variation: 126 cal.,
2 g total fat (0 g sat. fat), 0 mg chol., 148 mg sodium, 24 g carbo.,
2 g fiber, 4 g pro.
Daily Values: 1% calcium, 7% iron
Exchanges: 1½ Starch

Don't Kill the Yeast

For bread baking, take care when dissolving
the active dry yeast. Check the temperature
of the heated mixture with an instant-read
thermometer. If the mixture is too hot, the
yeast will die and the bread won't rise. If the
mixture is too cold, the yeast won't activate
and the bread won't rise. Follow the temperature guidelines listed in each recipe.

Whole Wheat Bread

Whole Wheat Bread

LOW FAT **WHOLE GRAIN**

Prep: 30 minutes **Rise:** 1½ hours **Rest:** 10 minutes
Bake: 35 minutes **Oven:** 375°F
Makes: 2 loaves (24 slices)

  3 to 3½ cups all-purpose flour
  1 package active dry yeast
1¾ cups water
  ⅓ cup packed brown sugar
  3 tablespoons butter, margarine, or shortening
1¼ teaspoons salt
  2 cups whole wheat flour

1. In a large mixing bowl combine 2 cups of the all-purpose flour and the yeast; set aside. In a medium saucepan heat and stir water, brown sugar, butter, and salt just until warm (120°F to 130°F) and butter almost melts. Add water mixture to flour mixture. Beat with an electric mixer on low to medium speed for 30 seconds, scraping sides of bowl constantly. Beat on high speed for 3 minutes. Using a wooden spoon, stir in whole wheat flour and as much of the remaining all-purpose flour as you can.

2. Turn dough out onto a lightly floured surface. Knead in enough remaining all-purpose flour to make a moderately stiff dough that is smooth and elastic (6 to 8 minutes total; see photo 1, page 141). Shape dough into a ball. Place in a lightly greased bowl; turn once to grease surface. Cover; let rise in a warm place until double in size (1 to 1½ hours; see photos 2 and 3, page 141).

3. Punch dough down (see photo 4, page 141). Turn out onto a lightly floured surface. Divide in half. Cover; let rest 10 minutes. Meanwhile, lightly grease two 8×4×2-inch loaf pans.

4. Shape each dough half into a loaf by patting or rolling. To shape by patting, gently pat and pinch, tucking edges underneath (see photo 5, page 141). To shape by rolling, on a lightly floured surface, roll into a 12×8-inch rectangle. Tightly roll up each dough rectangle, starting from a short side (see photo 6, page 141). Seal seams with your fingertips.

5. Place shaped dough halves in prepared pans. Cover and let rise in a warm place until nearly double in size (30 to 45 minutes).

6. Preheat oven to 375°F. Bake for 35 to 40 minutes or until bread sounds hollow when lightly tapped. (If necessary, cover loosely with foil the last 10 minutes of baking to prevent overbrowning.) Immediately remove bread from pans. Cool on wire racks.

Hearty Whole Wheat Bread: Prepare as at left, except reduce whole wheat flour to 1½ cups and add ½ cup toasted wheat germ.

Per slice whole wheat or hearty variation: 102 cal.,
1 g total fat (1 g sat. fat), 3 mg chol., 122 mg sodium, 19 g carbo.,
2 g fiber, 4 g pro.
Daily Values: 1% vit. A, 2% calcium, 6% iron
Exchanges: 1½ Starch

Oatmeal Bread: Prepare as at left, except substitute rolled oats for the whole wheat flour. Increase the all-purpose flour to 4 to 4½ cups total.

Per slice: 133 cal., 2 g total fat (1 g sat. fat), 4 mg chol.,
139 mg sodium, 25 g carbo., 1 g fiber, 3 g pro.
Daily Values: 1% vit. A, 1% calcium, 8% iron
Exchanges: 1½ Starch

Sourdough Starter

Prep: 10 minutes **Stand:** 5 days
Makes: about 2½ cups

  1 package active dry yeast
2½ cups warm water (105°F to 115°F)
  2 cups all-purpose flour
  1 tablespoon sugar or honey

1. Dissolve yeast in ½ cup of the warm water. Stir in the remaining warm water, flour, and sugar. Using a wooden spoon, beat until smooth. Cover with 100-percent-cotton cheesecloth. Let stand at room temperature (75°F to 85°F) for 5 to 10 days or until mixture has a fermented aroma and vigorous bubbling stops, stirring two or three times a day. (Fermentation time depends on room temperature; a warmer room will hasten the fermentation process.)

2. To store, transfer Sourdough Starter to a 1-quart plastic container. Cover and chill.

3. To use, stir starter. Measure amount of cold starter called for in recipe; bring to room temperature. Replenish starter after each use: For each 1 cup removed, stir ¾ cup all-purpose flour, ¾ cup water, and 1 teaspoon sugar or honey into remaining starter. Cover with cheesecloth; let stand at room temperature 1 day or until bubbly. Cover with lid; chill for later use. If starter is not used within 10 days, stir in 1 teaspoon sugar or honey. Continue to add 1 teaspoon sugar or honey every 10 days unless starter is replenished.

Sourdough Bread LOW FAT

Prep: 45 minutes **Rise:** 1¼ hours **Rest:** 10 minutes
Bake: 30 minutes **Oven:** 375°F
Makes: 2 loaves (24 slices)

    1 cup Sourdough Starter (page 144)
 5½ to 6 cups all-purpose flour
    1 package active dry yeast
 1½ cups water
    3 tablespoons sugar
    3 tablespoons butter or margarine
 1½ teaspoons salt
    ½ teaspoon baking soda

1. Measure Sourdough Starter; let stand at room temperature 30 minutes. In a large mixing bowl combine 2½ cups of the flour and the yeast; set aside. Heat and stir water, sugar, butter, and salt just until warm (120°F to 130°F) and butter almost melts. Add water mixture to yeast mixture; add Sourdough Starter. Beat with an electric mixer on low to medium speed for 30 seconds, scraping bowl. Beat on high speed for 3 minutes. Combine 2½ cups of the remaining flour and baking soda; add to yeast mixture. Using a wooden spoon, stir until combined. Stir in as much of the remaining flour as you can.

2. Turn dough out onto a lightly floured surface. Knead in enough remaining flour to make a moderately stiff dough (6 to 8 minutes total; see photo 1, page 141). Shape dough into a ball. Place in a lightly greased bowl, turning once to grease surface. Cover; let rise in a warm place until double (45 to 60 minutes; see photos 2 and 3, page 141). Punch dough down (see photo 4, page 141). Turn out onto a lightly floured surface; divide in half. Cover; let rest 10 minutes. Meanwhile, lightly grease two baking sheets.

3. Shape each dough half by gently pulling it into a ball, tucking edges underneath. Place dough rounds on prepared baking sheets. Flatten each round slightly to about 6 inches in diameter. Using a sharp knife, make crisscross slashes across loaf tops. Cover; let rise in a warm place until nearly double in size (about 30 minutes).

4. Preheat oven to 375°F. Bake for 30 to 35 minutes or until bread sounds hollow when lightly tapped. (If necessary, cover loosely with foil the last 10 minutes of baking to prevent overbrowning.) Immediately remove bread from baking sheets. Cool on wire racks.

Per slice: 131 cal., 2 g total fat (1 g sat. fat), 4 mg chol., 189 mg sodium, 25 g carbo., 1 g fiber, 3 g pro.
Daily Values: 1% vit. A, 1% calcium, 8% iron
Exchanges: 1½ Starch

Kneading Know-How

Kneading causes gluten to develop in yeast dough, and it is gluten that gives dough its structure. Gluten is necessary for bread to bake properly.

To knead, on a lightly floured surface fold dough over and push down on it with the heel of your hand, curving your fingers over dough (see photo 1, page 141). Give dough a quarter turn and repeat the procedure. Knead until you have a dough that has the stiffness specified in the recipe. In general, follow recipe timings. Here are descriptions of terms:

Soft dough: Extremely sticky; used for breads that don't require kneading.

Moderately soft dough: Slightly sticky but smooth; used for rich, sweet breads. Knead dough for 3 to 5 minutes.

Moderately stiff dough: Not sticky, slightly firm to the touch; used for most nonsweet breads. Knead dough for 6 to 8 minutes.

Stiff dough: Firm to the touch; holds its shape after 8 to 10 minutes of kneading.

Artisan-Style Bread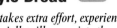

While this bread takes extra effort, experienced bread bakers especially will appreciate the results of this French-style bread.

Prep: 45 minutes **Stand:** 8 hours **Rest:** 50 minutes
Rise: 2½ hours **Bake:** 20 minutes **Oven:** 450°F
Makes: 2 loaves (28 slices)

- 1 **cup warm water (105°F to 115°F)**
- ¼ **teaspoon active dry yeast**
- 1 **cup bread flour**
- 1 **tablespoon rye flour**
- ¾ **cup warm water (105°F to 115°F)**
- 1 **cup warm water (105°F to 115°F)**
- 3 to 3¼ **cups bread flour**
- 2 **teaspoons salt**
- ½ **teaspoon active dry yeast**
  Spray bottle filled with water

1. Combine the 1 cup warm water and the ¼ teaspoon yeast; set aside for 5 minutes. Meanwhile, in a medium bowl combine the 1 cup bread flour and the rye flour.

2. Stir yeast mixture (make sure yeast has dissolved); add 1 tablespoon of the yeast mixture to the flour mixture. Discard remaining yeast mixture. Add the ¾ cup warm water to the flour mixture, stirring until combined. Cover with plastic wrap and let stand at room temperature for 8 to 24 hours (surface of mixture should be bubbly).

3. Add the 1 cup warm water to the flour mixture and stir until combined. In a large bowl stir together 3 cups of the bread flour, the salt, and the ½ teaspoon yeast; pour the water-flour mixture into the dry flour mixture. Using a wooden spoon, stir until combined.

4. Turn dough out onto a well-floured surface. Knead dough only a couple of strokes (dough will be very sticky). Cover; let rest 20 minutes.

5. Knead dough for 3 to 5 minutes more (dough will be wetter and softer than you may be used to). If dough is too sticky to work with, knead in up to ¼ cup more flour. Dough should be smooth, but still sticky, after kneading. (Or place dough in the large mixing bowl of a freestanding electric mixer. Use the dough hook attachment to knead the dough on medium speed for only 1½ minutes and no longer.) If kneaded by hand, place dough in an ungreased large bowl. Cover bowl with plastic wrap (do not let plastic wrap touch the surface of the sticky dough); let rise until nearly double in size (2 to 2½ hours).

6. Turn dough out onto a heavily floured surface; divide dough in half (gently handle dough, trying not to disturb air holes). Using floured hands, gently form each dough half into a small rectangle. Cover each dough rectangle with a large bowl or plastic wrap; let rest for 30 minutes.

7. Using floured hands, gently pull each piece of dough into a 12-inch baguette or a 6-inch round loaf, gently handling dough so as not to disturb big bubbles inside. Roll the baguette-shaped dough onto parchment paper. Place the baguette dough in baguette pans, parchment-paper sides down (see photo, below). Gently place the round loaves into two greased 8×1½-inch round baking pans. Cover; let rise until double in size (30 to 45 minutes). Preheat oven to 450°F.

8. Place pans in oven. Working quickly, heavily mist the inside of the oven, including the bread, with water. Bake about 20 minutes or until bread is a deep golden brown and sounds hollow when lightly tapped (or until the internal temperature reaches 200°F). Immediately remove from pans. Cool on wire racks.

Garlic-Basil Bread: Prepare as at left, except in Step 3 stir 2 large cloves garlic, minced, and 2 tablespoons snipped fresh basil or 2 teaspoons dried basil, crushed, in with the 3 cups flour.

Dried Tomato-Rosemary Bread: Prepare as at left, except in Step 3 stir ½ cup dried tomatoes (not oil packed), snipped, and 1 tablespoon snipped fresh rosemary or 1 teaspoon dried rosemary, crushed, in with the 3 cups flour.

Per slice plain, garlic-basil, or dried tomato-rosemary variations: 72 cal., 0 g total fat (0 g sat. fat), 0 mg chol., 167 mg sodium, 14 g carbo., 1 g fiber, 2 g pro.
Daily Values: 5% iron
Exchanges: 1 Starch

Artisan-Style Bread dough is soft and sticky, so you'll need to place the shaped dough on parchment paper before transferring it into baguette pan. Handle the dough as little as possible so you don't disturb the air bubbles in it.

French Bread `NO FAT`

The dough for this French bread is easier to handle than Artisan-Style Bread dough (page 146) and will produce a finer texture.

Prep: 40 minutes **Rise:** 1 hour 35 minutes
Rest: 10 minutes **Bake:** 35 minutes **Oven:** 375°F
Makes: 2 loaves (28 slices)

- 5½ to 6 cups all-purpose flour
- 2 packages active dry yeast
- 1½ teaspoons salt
- 2 cups warm water (120°F to 130°F)
- Cornmeal
- 1 egg white, slightly beaten
- 1 tablespoon water

1. In a large mixing bowl stir together 2 cups of the flour, the yeast, and salt. Add the 2 cups warm water to the flour mixture. Beat with an electric mixer on low to medium speed for 30 seconds, scraping bowl constantly. Beat on high speed for 3 minutes. Using a wooden spoon, stir in as much of the remaining flour as you can.

2. Turn dough out onto a lightly floured surface. Knead in enough remaining flour to make a stiff dough that is smooth and elastic (8 to 10 minutes total; see photo 1, page 141). Shape dough into a ball. Place in a lightly greased bowl, turning once to grease dough surface. Cover; let rise in a warm place until double in size (about 1 hour; see photos 2 and 3, page 141).

3. Punch dough down (see photo 4, page 141). Turn dough out onto a lightly floured surface. Divide dough in half. Cover; let rest for 10 minutes. Meanwhile, lightly grease a baking sheet; sprinkle greased baking sheet with cornmeal.

4. Roll each dough half into a 15×10-inch rectangle. Tightly roll up, starting from a long side; seal well. If desired, pinch and slightly pull ends to taper them. Place shaped dough, seam sides down, on prepared baking sheet. In a small bowl stir together egg white and the 1 tablespoon water. Brush some of the egg white mixture over loaf tops. Let rise until nearly double in size (35 to 45 minutes).

5. Preheat oven to 375°F. Using a sharp knife, make three or four diagonal cuts about ¼ inch deep across each loaf top. Bake for 20 minutes.

Brush again with some of the egg white mixture. Continue baking for 15 to 20 minutes more or until bread sounds hollow when lightly tapped. Immediately remove loaves from baking sheet. Cool on wire racks.

Baguettes: Prepare as at left, except divide dough into four portions. Shape each portion into a ball. Cover; let rest 10 minutes. Meanwhile, lightly grease two baking sheets or four baguette pans; sprinkle with cornmeal. Roll each dough portion into a 14×5-inch to 16×5-inch rectangle. Roll up, starting from a long side; seal well. If desired, pinch and slightly pull ends to taper them. Place shaped dough, seam sides down, on prepared baking sheets or baguette pans. Continue as directed, except reduce the second baking time to 8 to 10 minutes. Makes 4 baguettes (56 slices).

Per slice French bread or 2 slices baguettes: 85 cal., 0 g total fat (0 g sat. fat), 0 mg chol., 128 mg sodium, 18 g carbo., 1 g fiber, 3 g pro.
Daily Values: 6% iron
Exchanges: 1 Starch

Baguettes

Potato Bread with Sour Cream and Herbs LOW FAT

Prep: 35 minutes **Rise:** 1¼ hours **Rest:** 10 minutes
Bake: 25 minutes **Oven:** 375°F
Makes: 2 loaves (24 slices)

    7 to 7½ cups all-purpose flour
    2 packages active dry yeast
1½   cups milk
    2 tablespoons sugar
    2 tablespoons butter
    2 teaspoons salt
    1 10.75-ounce can condensed cream of
       potato soup
  ½ cup dairy sour cream
  ¼ cup snipped fresh chives
    1 tablespoon snipped fresh tarragon or fresh
       dill or 1 teaspoon dried tarragon, crushed,
       or dried dill

1. In a large mixing bowl combine 2½ cups of the flour and the yeast; set aside. In a saucepan heat and stir milk, sugar, butter, and salt just until warm (120°F to 130°F) and butter almost melts. Add milk mixture to flour mixture along with soup, sour cream, chives, and tarragon. Beat with an electric mixer on low speed for 30 seconds, scraping bowl constantly. Beat on high speed for 3 minutes, scraping bowl occasionally. Using a wooden spoon, stir in as much of the remaining flour as you can.

2. Turn dough out onto a lightly floured surface. Knead in enough remaining flour to make a moderately stiff dough that is smooth and elastic (6 to 8 minutes total; see photo 1, page 141). Shape dough into a ball. Place dough in a lightly greased bowl, turning once to grease surface of dough. Cover; let rise in a warm place until double in size (45 to 60 minutes; see photos 2 and 3, page 141).

3. Punch dough down (see photo 4, page 141). Cover; let rest 10 minutes. Meanwhile, lightly grease two 9×5×3-inch loaf pans.* Divide dough in half; shape into two loaves. Place in prepared pans. Cover and let rise in a warm place until nearly double in size (30 to 40 minutes).

4. Preheat oven to 375°F. Bake about 25 minutes or until bread sounds hollow when lightly tapped. (If necessary, cover loosely with foil the last 10 minutes of baking to prevent overbrowning.) Immediately remove bread from pans. Cool on wire racks.

*Shaping options: For round loaves, shape each dough half into a ball. Place in greased 2-quart casseroles. Cover and let rise; bake as at left. For rolls, shape dough into 24 to 32 balls. Place balls 1 to 2 inches apart on two greased baking sheets. Cover and let rise. Bake about 18 minutes or until golden.

Per slice: 162 cal., 3 g total fat (1 g sat. fat), 7 mg chol., 301 mg sodium, 29 g carbo., 1 g fiber, 5 g pro.
Daily Values: 2% vit. A, 1% vit. C, 3% calcium, 10% iron
Exchanges: 1½ Starch, ½ Other Carbo., ½ Fat

Focaccia LOW FAT

If you have a bread stone, transfer the dough onto the preheated stone before baking.

Prep: 30 minutes **Stand:** overnight **Rise:** 1 hour
Rest: 30 minutes **Bake:** 15 minutes **Oven:** 475°F
Makes: 12 wedges

    4 to 4¼ cups all-purpose flour
  ½ cup warm water (105°F to 115°F)
    1 teaspoon active dry yeast
    1 cup warm water (105°F to 115°F)
    2 teaspoons salt
    1 tablespoon olive oil
       Coarse salt

1. In a mixing bowl combine ½ cup of the flour, the ½ cup warm water, and the yeast. Beat with a wooden spoon until smooth. Cover loosely with plastic wrap. Let yeast mixture stand overnight at room temperature to ferment.

2. Into the yeast mixture, gradually stir in the 1 cup warm water, the 2 teaspoons salt, and just enough of the remaining flour to make a dough that pulls away from the sides of the bowl. Turn dough out onto a lightly floured surface. Knead in enough of the remaining flour to make a stiff dough that is smooth and elastic (8 to 10 minutes total; see photo 1, page 141). Place dough in a lightly greased bowl, turning once to grease surface of dough. Cover; let rise in a warm place until double in size (about 1 hour).

3. Turn dough out onto a well-floured baking sheet. Place an extra-large bowl upside down over the dough to cover it; let rest 30 minutes. Meanwhile, preheat oven and a bread stone (if available) to 475°F. Shape dough on the baking sheet into a circle about 11 inches in diameter by gently pulling and pressing with your fingertips, taking care to keep dough air bubbles intact. Dust your fingers with flour and make ½-inch-deep indentations every 2 inches in dough. Brush dough with oil; sprinkle lightly with coarse salt. Carefully slide focaccia from baking sheet to preheated bread stone.*

4. Bake for 15 to 20 minutes or until golden, checking after 8 minutes and popping any large air bubbles with a sharp knife. Transfer focaccia to a wire rack with a large spatula; let cool about 15 minutes. Serve warm.

***Note:** If you don't have a bread stone, transfer the shaped dough to a greased, unheated second baking sheet.

Herbed Focaccia: Prepare as on page 148, except add 2 teaspoons snipped fresh rosemary or ½ teaspoon dried rosemary, crushed, with the warm water, salt, and flour in Step 2.

Per wedge plain or herbed variation: 151 cal., 1 g total fat (0 g sat. fat), 0 mg chol., 583 mg sodium, 29 g carbo., 1 g fiber, 4 g pro.
Daily Values: 1% calcium, 10% iron
Exchanges: 2 Starch

Dill Batter Bread EASY

For a luncheon, serve this no-knead bread with a hearty chicken salad. See photo, page 123.

Prep: 15 minutes **Rise:** 50 minutes **Bake:** 25 minutes
Oven: 375°F **Makes:** 1 loaf (8 slices)

  1¾ **cups all-purpose flour**
    1 **package active dry yeast**
  ½ **cup water**
  ½ **cup cream-style cottage cheese**
    1 **tablespoon sugar**
    1 **tablespoon dill seeds or caraway seeds**
    1 **tablespoon butter or margarine**
    1 **teaspoon dried minced onion**
    1 **teaspoon salt**
    1 **egg, beaten**
  ½ **cup toasted wheat germ**

1. Grease a 9×1½-inch round baking pan or a 1-quart soufflé dish; set aside. In a large mixing bowl stir together 1 cup of the flour and the yeast; set aside.

2. In a medium saucepan heat and stir water, cottage cheese, sugar, dill seeds, butter, dried onion, and salt just until warm (120°F to 130°F) and butter almost melts. Add cottage cheese

mixture to flour mixture along with the egg. Beat with an electric mixer on low to medium speed for 30 seconds, scraping sides of bowl constantly. Beat on high speed for 3 minutes. Using a wooden spoon, stir in the wheat germ and the remaining flour (batter will be stiff).

3. Spoon batter into the prepared pan or soufflé dish, spreading to edges. Cover and let rise in a warm place until double in size (50 to 60 minutes). Preheat oven to 375°F. Bake for 25 to 30 minutes or until golden. Immediately remove from pan or soufflé dish. Serve warm.

Per slice: 185 cal., 4 g total fat (2 g sat. fat), 33 mg chol., 369 mg sodium, 30 g carbo., 2 g fiber, 8 g pro.
Daily Values: 3% vit. A, 1% vit. C, 3% calcium, 13% iron
Exchanges: 2 Starch, ½ Fat

English Muffin Bread LOW FAT

Prep: 20 minutes **Rise:** 45 minutes **Bake:** 25 minutes
Oven: 400°F **Makes:** 2 loaves (32 slices)

      Cornmeal
    6 **cups all-purpose flour**
    2 **packages active dry yeast**
  ¼ **teaspoon baking soda**
    2 **cups milk**
  ½ **cup water**
    1 **tablespoon sugar**
    1 **teaspoon salt**

1. Grease two 8×4×2-inch loaf pans. Lightly sprinkle greased pans with cornmeal to coat bottoms and sides; set pans aside.

2. In a large mixing bowl combine 3 cups of the flour, the yeast, and baking soda; set aside. In a medium saucepan heat and stir milk, water, sugar, and salt just until warm (120°F to 130°F). Using a wooden spoon, stir milk mixture into flour mixture. Stir in remaining flour. Divide dough in half. Place dough in prepared pans. Sprinkle tops with cornmeal. Cover and let rise in a warm place until double in size (about 45 minutes).

3. Preheat oven to 400°F. Bake about 25 minutes or until golden brown. Immediately remove bread from pans. Cool on wire racks.

Per slice: 90 cal., 1 g total fat (0 g sat. fat), 1 mg chol., 91 mg sodium, 18 g carbo., 1 g fiber, 3 g pro.
Daily Values: 1% vit. A, 2% calcium, 6% iron
Exchanges: 1 Starch

Home-Baked Pizza Made Easy

Instead of going out for pizza, make this family favorite right in your kitchen. The dough is simple to prepare using few ingredients. Personalize it with desired toppings.

Pizza Dough

Use this dough and your choice of toppings to make two thin-crust or pan pizzas; each pizza makes four servings of two wedges each for a total of eight servings. Or use half the dough to make four mini pizzas and freeze the other dough half to use another time.

Prep: 20 minutes **Rest:** 10 minutes **Oven:** 400°F/425°F
Makes: 2 Thin-Crust or Pan Pizzas, 8 Mini Pizzas, or 2 Calzones

- 2½ to 3 cups all-purpose flour
- 1 package active dry yeast
- ½ teaspoon salt
- 1 cup warm water (120°F to 130°F)
- 2 tablespoons cooking oil or olive oil

1. In a large mixing bowl combine 1¼ cups of the flour, the yeast, and salt; add warm water and oil. Beat with an electric mixer on low speed for 30 seconds, scraping bowl. Beat on high speed for 3 minutes. Using a wooden spoon, stir in as much of the remaining flour as you can.

2. Turn dough out onto a lightly floured surface. Knead in enough remaining flour to make a moderately stiff dough that is smooth and

Mini Pizzas

elastic (6 to 8 minutes total; see photo 1, page 141). Divide dough in half. Cover; let rest for 10 minutes. Use to make Thin-Crust Pizzas, Pan Pizzas, Mini Pizzas, or Calzones.

Thin-Crust Pizzas: Preheat oven to 425°F. Grease two 12-inch pizza pans or large baking sheets.* If desired, sprinkle with cornmeal. On a lightly floured surface, roll each dough half into a 13-inch circle. Transfer dough circles to prepared pans. Build up edges slightly; prick dough with a fork. Do not let rise. Bake about 10 minutes or until light brown. Spread pizza sauce onto hot crusts and top with desired meat, vegetables, and cheese. Bake about 10 minutes more or until bubbly. Cut each pizza into eight wedges. Makes 8 servings (2 wedges).

Pan Pizzas: Grease two 12-inch pizza pans or large baking sheets.* If desired, sprinkle with cornmeal. On a lightly floured surface, roll each dough half into an 11-inch circle. Transfer dough circles to prepared pans. Build up edges slightly. Cover and let rise in a warm place until nearly double (30 to 45 minutes). Meanwhile, preheat oven to 400°F. Prick dough with a fork. Bake for 10 to 15 minutes or until light brown. Spread pizza sauce onto hot crusts and top with desired meat, vegetables, and cheese. Bake about 10 minutes longer or until bubbly. Cut each pizza into eight wedges. Makes 8 servings (2 wedges).

Mini Pizzas: Wrap and freeze a pizza dough half for a later use. (To use frozen dough, thaw overnight in the refrigerator.) Preheat oven to 425°F. Grease four 7-inch pizza pans or two large baking sheets. If desired, sprinkle with cornmeal. Divide dough half into four portions. On a lightly floured surface, roll each dough portion into a 6-inch circle. Transfer dough circles to prepared pans. If desired, build up edges slightly. Prick dough with a fork. Do not let rise. Bake about 8 minutes or until light brown. Spread pizza sauce onto hot crusts. Top with meat, vegetables, and cheese. Bake about 5 minutes more or until bubbly. Makes 4 servings.

Whole Wheat Pizza Dough: Prepare dough as on page 150, except use only 1¼ cups all-purpose flour; mix it with the yeast and salt. Using a wooden spoon, stir in as much of 1¼ to 1¾ cups whole wheat flour as you can. Knead in remaining whole wheat flour to make a moderately stiff dough that is smooth and elastic (6 to 8 minutes). Continue as directed on page 150.

*Note: To bake pizzas on a round baking stone, place unheated pizza stone in an unheated oven. Preheat oven as directed. Roll pizza dough as directed on parchment paper; prick dough all over with a fork. Gently slide the dough and parchment paper onto hot baking stone. Bake dough on the paper; top pizza as desired. To use the stone for a second pizza, bake on it immediately after removing the first pizza.

Calzones

Prep: 40 minutes **Bake:** 30 minutes
Oven: 375°F **Makes:** 6 servings

  1 **recipe Pizza Dough (page 150)**
    Cornmeal (optional)
  1 **15-ounce can pizza sauce**
  1 **pound bulk Italian sausage or ground beef, cooked and drained; 4 ounces sliced pepperoni; or 1 cup cubed cooked ham or Canadian-style bacon**
 ½ **cup sliced green onions or sliced, pitted ripe olives**
  1 **cup sliced fresh mushrooms or chopped green sweet pepper**
  2 **cups shredded mozzarella cheese (8 ounces)**
    Milk
    Grated Parmesan cheese (optional)

1. Preheat oven to 375°F. Prepare Pizza Dough. Grease two 12-inch pizza pans or baking sheets. If desired, sprinkle with cornmeal. On a lightly floured surface, roll each dough half into a 13-inch circle. Transfer circles to prepared pans. Set aside half of the sauce. Spoon remaining sauce and the meat onto half of each circle to within 1 inch of edges. Sprinkle sauce with vegetables and mozzarella cheese. Fold dough circles in half, enclosing filling. Seal edges by pressing with tines of a fork. Prick tops; brush tops with milk. If desired, sprinkle with Parmesan cheese. Bake for 30 to 35 minutes or until crust is brown, switching pan positions

in oven halfway through baking time. Cut each into three wedges. Serve with reserved sauce.

Per wedge: 596 cal., 32 g total fat (13 g sat. fat), 81 mg chol., 1,145 mg sodium, 44 g carbo., 2 g fiber, 27 g pro.
Daily Values: 7% vit. A, 10% vit. C, 22% calcium, 22% iron
Exchanges: 2½ Starch, 1 Other Carbo., 2½ High-Fat Meat, 2½ Fat

Easy Individual Calzones: Prepare as at left, except omit dough. Use two 13.8-ounce packages refrigerated pizza dough. On lightly floured surface, unroll each package into a 13×9-inch rectangle. Cut each rectangle in half horizontally and vertically to form a total of eight small rectangles. Place rectangles on prepared pans. Continue as directed, placing fillings over half of a rectangle from a short side to within 1 inch of edges; fold in half with short edges joined together. Seal edges. Makes 8 individual calzones.

Per calzone: 532 cal., 24 g total fat (10 g sat. fat), 61 mg chol,, 1,251 mg sodium, 51 g carbo., 2 g fiber, 24 g pro.
Daily Values: 5% vit., A, 8% vit. C, 16% calcium, 17% iron
Exchanges: 3 Starch, ½ Other Carbo., 2 High-Fat Meat, 1½ Fat

Traditional Pizza

To make four Mini Pizzas (4 servings), use only half of the toppings.

Prep: 50 minutes **Makes:** 8 servings

  1 **recipe Pizza Dough (page 150)**
  1 **8- to 15-ounce container pizza sauce or Alfredo sauce (1 to 1½ cups)**
    Desired toppings, such as 6 ounces sliced pepperoni; 1 pound bulk Italian sausage or ground beef, cooked and drained; or 2 cups diced cooked ham; plus 1 cup sliced green onions; sliced, pitted ripe olives; sliced fresh mushrooms; chopped green sweet pepper; thinly sliced roma tomatoes; and/or quartered artichoke hearts; and 2 to 3 tablespoons snipped fresh basil
  2 **to 3 cups shredded mozzarella cheese (8 to 12 ounces)**

1. Prepare Pizza Dough to make Thin-Crust or Pan Pizzas on page 150. Spread pizza sauce or Alfredo sauce onto hot crusts. Top with desired toppings and cheese. Bake according to directions for Thin-Crust or Pan Pizzas or until bubbly.

Per 2 wedges (¼ pizza): 365 cal., 19 g total fat (8 g sat. fat), 47 mg chol., 858 mg sodium, 33 g carbo., 2 g fiber, 15 g pro.
Daily Values: 7% vit. A, 9% vit. C, 17% calcium, 15% iron
Exchanges: 2 Starch, 1 Medium-Fat Meat, 3 Fat

Dinner Rolls

Brushing fresh-from-the-oven rolls with melted butter gives them a soft, shiny crust.

Prep: 45 minutes **Rise:** 1½ hours **Rest:** 10 minutes
Bake: 12 minutes **Oven:** 375°F **Makes:** 24 rolls

> 4½ to 5 cups all-purpose flour
> 1 package active dry yeast
> 1 cup milk
> ⅓ cup sugar
> ⅓ cup butter, margarine, or shortening
> 1 teaspoon salt
> 2 eggs

1. In a large mixing bowl stir together 2 cups of the flour and the yeast. In a small saucepan heat and stir milk, sugar, butter, and salt just until warm (120°F to 130°F) and butter almost melts; add to flour mixture along with eggs. Beat with an electric mixer on low to medium speed for 30 seconds, scraping sides of bowl constantly. Beat on high speed for 3 minutes. Using a wooden spoon, stir in as much of the remaining flour as you can.

2. Turn dough out onto a lightly floured surface. Knead in enough remaining flour to make a moderately stiff dough that is smooth and elastic (6 to 8 minutes total; see photo 1, page 141). Shape dough into a ball. Place in a greased bowl; turn once to grease surface of dough. Cover; let rise in a warm place until double (about 1 hour; see photos 2 and 3, page 141).

3. Punch dough down (see photo 4, page 141). Turn dough out onto a lightly floured surface. Divide dough in half. Cover and let rest for 10 minutes. Meanwhile, depending on what shape of roll you want to make (see photos, right and on page 153), lightly grease a 13×9×2-inch baking pan or baking sheets.

4. Shape dough into 24 balls or desired rolls and place in prepared baking pan or on baking sheets. Cover; let rise in a warm place until nearly double in size (about 30 minutes).

5. Preheat oven to 375°F. Bake for 12 to 15 minutes for individual rolls or about 20 minutes for pan rolls or until golden. Immediately remove rolls from pans. Cool on wire racks.

Whole Wheat Dinner Rolls: Prepare as at left, except substitute 1¼ cups whole wheat flour for 1¼ cups of the all-purpose flour that is stirred in at the end of Step 1.

Onion Dinner Rolls: Prepare as at left, except add ⅓ cup chopped green onion or snipped fresh chives to milk mixture in Step 1.

Rye-Caraway Dinner Rolls: Prepare as at left, except add 2 teaspoons caraway seeds to milk mixture and substitute 1¼ cups rye flour for 1¼ cups of the all-purpose flour that is stirred in at the end of Step 1.

Buttermilk Dinner Rolls: Prepare as at left, except substitute 1¼ cups buttermilk for the milk and use only 1 egg.

Make-ahead directions: Prepare as at left through Step 3. Shape into 24 balls or desired rolls and place in prepared baking pan or sheets. Cover shaped rolls loosely with plastic wrap, leaving enough room for rolls to rise. Chill for 2 to 24 hours. Uncover; let rolls stand at room temperature for 30 minutes. Bake as directed.

Per roll plain, whole wheat, onion, rye-caraway, or buttermilk variations: 132 cal., 4 g total fat (2 g sat. fat), 26 mg chol., 127 mg sodium, 21 g carbo., 1 g fiber, 3 g pro. Daily Values: 2% vit. A, 2% calcium, 7% iron Exchanges: 1 Starch, ½ Other Carbo., ½ Fat

Rosettes: Divide each dough half into 16 pieces. On a lightly floured surface, roll each piece into a 12-inch-long rope. Tie each rope in a loose knot,

leaving two long ends. Tuck top end under knot and bottom end into the top center. Place 2 to 3 inches apart on prepared baking sheets. Makes 32 rolls.

Butterhorn Rolls: On a lightly floured surface, roll each dough half into a 12-inch circle; brush with melted butter or margarine. Cut each dough circle into 12 wedges. To shape rolls, begin

at wide end of each wedge and loosely roll toward the point. Place, point sides down, 2 to 3 inches apart on prepared baking sheets. Makes 24 rolls.

Parker House Rolls: On a lightly floured surface, roll each dough half until ¼ inch thick. Cut dough with a floured 2½-inch round cutter. Brush with melted butter or margarine. Using the dull edge of a table knife, make an off-center crease in  each round. Fold each round along the crease. Press the folded edge firmly. Place, large half up, 2 to 3 inches apart on prepared baking sheets. Makes 24 rolls.

Hamburger or Frankfurter Buns: Prepare Dinner Rolls as on page 152, except divide dough into 12 pieces. Cover; let rest 10 minutes. For hamburger buns, shape each piece into a ball, tucking edges under. Place on a greased baking sheet. Using your fingers, slightly flatten balls to 4 inches in diameter. For frankfurter buns, shape each portion into a roll about 5½ inches long, tapering ends. Place on a greased baking sheet. Continue as directed. Makes 12 buns.

Per bun: 263 cal., 7 g total fat (3 g sat. fat), 51 mg chol., 254 mg sodium, 42 carbo., 1 g fiber, 7 g pro.
Daily Values: 5% vit. A, 4% calcium, 14% iron
Exchanges: 2½ Starch, ½ Other Carbo., 1 Fat

Potato Rolls LOW FAT

Start by cooking and mashing the potato or try the instant mashed potato version.

Prep: 45 minutes **Rise:** 1 hour 35 minutes
Rest: 10 minutes **Bake:** pan rolls 20 minutes;
individual rolls 10 minutes **Oven:** 400°F **Makes:** 24 rolls

- 4 to 4½ cups all-purpose flour
- 1 package active dry yeast
- 1 cup milk
- ¼ cup water
- ¼ cup sugar
- ¼ cup shortening
- 1½ teaspoons salt
- 1 egg, beaten
- ½ cup mashed potato*

1. In a large mixing bowl combine 2 cups of the flour and yeast. In a saucepan heat and stir milk, water, sugar, shortening, and salt just until warm (120°F to 130°F) and shortening almost melts; add to flour mixture along with egg and mashed potato. Beat with electric mixer on low to medium speed for 30 seconds, scraping bowl. Beat on high speed for 3 minutes. Using a wooden spoon, stir in as much remaining flour as you can.

2. Turn dough out onto a lightly floured surface. Knead in enough of the remaining flour to make a moderately stiff dough that is smooth and elastic (6 to 8 minutes total; see photo 1, page 141). Shape dough into a ball. Place in a lightly greased bowl, turning once to grease surface. Cover; let rise in a warm place until double (about 1 hour; see photos 2 and 3, page 141).

3. Punch dough down (see photo 4, page 141). Turn dough out onto a lightly floured surface. Divide dough in half. Cover; let rest for 10 minutes. Lightly grease a 13×9×2-inch baking pan or a large baking sheet. Divide each dough half into 12 pieces. Gently pull each piece into a ball, tucking edges under to make smooth tops. Place in prepared baking pan or 2 inches apart on baking sheet. Cover; let rise in a warm place until nearly double in size (35 to 45 minutes).

4. Preheat oven to 400°F. Bake about 20 minutes for rolls in 13×9×2-inch pan. (If necessary, for consistency, cover with foil the last 5 minutes to prevent overbrowning.) Bake rolls on baking sheet for 10 to 12 minutes or until golden brown. Immediately remove rolls from pan or baking sheet. Cool on wire racks.

*Note: Peel and quarter 1 medium potato. Cook, covered, in a small amount of boiling salted water for 20 to 25 minutes or until tender; drain. Mash with a potato masher or beat with an electric mixer on low speed. Measure ½ cup.

Instant Mashed Potato Rolls: Prepare as above, except substitute packaged instant mashed potatoes (enough for one ½-cup serving) for the cooked mashed potatoes and add an additional ¼ to ⅓ cup all-purpose flour.

Make-ahead directions: Prepare as above through Step 3, except do not let rise after shaping. Cover shaped rolls loosely with plastic wrap, leaving enough room for dough to rise. Chill for 2 to 24 hours. Let stand, loosely covered, at room temperature for 30 minutes. Uncover and bake as directed.

Per roll plain or instant mashed potato variation: 109 cal., 3 g total fat (1 g sat. fat), 10 mg chol., 154 mg sodium, 18 g carbo., 1 g fiber, 3 g pro.
Daily Values: 1% vit. A, 2% vit. C, 2% calcium, 6% iron
Exchanges: 1 Starch, ½ Fat

Cinnamon Rolls

Cinnamon Rolls

For a special treat, use the caramel mixture with the cinnamon and chocolate variation.

Prep: 45 minutes **Rise:** 1½ hours **Rest:** 10 minutes
Bake: 20 minutes **Oven:** 375°F **Makes:** 24 rolls

  4 **to 4½ cups all-purpose flour**
  1 **package active dry yeast**
  1 **cup milk**
 ⅓ **cup granulated sugar**
 ⅓ **cup butter or margarine**
 ½ **teaspoon salt**
  2 **eggs**
 ¾ **cup packed brown sugar**
 ¼ **cup all-purpose flour**
  1 **tablespoon ground cinnamon**
 ⅓ **cup butter or margarine**
 ½ **cup golden raisins (optional)**
 ½ **cup chopped pecans, toasted (see tip, page 265) (optional)**
  1 **recipe Cream Cheese Icing or Vanilla Icing**

1. In a large mixing bowl combine 2 cups of the flour and the yeast; set aside. In a small saucepan heat and stir milk, granulated sugar, ⅓ cup butter, and the salt just until warm (120°F to 130°F) and butter almost melts; add to flour mixture along with eggs. Beat with an electric mixer on low to medium speed for 30 seconds, scraping bowl. Beat on high speed for 3 minutes. Using a wooden spoon, stir in as much of the remaining 2 to 2½ cups flour as you can.

2. Turn dough out onto a floured surface. Knead in enough remaining flour to make a moderately soft dough that is smooth and elastic (3 to 5 minutes total). Shape dough into a ball. Place dough in a lightly greased bowl, turning once to grease surface of the dough. Cover; let rise in a warm place until double in size (1 to 1½ hours; see photos 2 and 3, page 141).

3. Punch dough down (see photo 4, page 141). Turn onto a lightly floured surface. Divide in half. Cover and let rest 10 minutes. Lightly grease two 8×8×2- or 9×9×2-inch baking pans or two 9×1½-inch round baking pans; set aside. For filling, stir together brown sugar, the ¼ cup flour, and cinnamon; using a pastry blender, cut in ⅓ cup butter until mixture resembles coarse crumbs. If desired, stir in raisins and pecans.

4. Roll each dough half into a 12×8-inch rectangle. Sprinkle filling over dough, leaving 1 inch unfilled along one of the long sides. Roll up each rectangle, starting from the filled long side. Pinch dough to seal seams. Slice each rolled rectangle into 12 equal pieces. Arrange in prepared pans. Cover and let rise in a warm place until nearly double in size (about 30 minutes).

5. Preheat oven to 375°F. Bake for 20 to 25 minutes or until golden. Cool about 5 minutes; remove from pans. Spread with Cream Cheese Icing or drizzle with Vanilla Icing. If desired, serve warm.

Easy Cinnamon Rolls: Omit preparing the dough. Thaw two 16-ounce loaves frozen sweet roll dough. Roll each loaf into a 12×8-inch rectangle. Sprinkle filling over dough and continue with Step 4, letting loaves rise about 40 minutes. Bake as directed.

Cream Cheese Icing: In a small mixing bowl beat one 3-ounce package softened cream cheese with 2 tablespoons softened butter and 1 teaspoon vanilla. Gradually beat in 2½ cups powdered sugar until smooth. Beat in milk, 1 teaspoon at a time, to reach spreading consistency.

Vanilla Icing: In a small bowl stir together 1¼ cups powdered sugar, 1 teaspoon light-colored corn syrup, and ½ teaspoon vanilla. Add enough half-and-half or light cream (1 to 2 tablespoons) to reach drizzling consistency.

Make-ahead directions: Prepare as on page 154 through Step 4, except do not let rise after shaping. Cover shaped rolls loosely with oiled waxed paper, then with plastic wrap, leaving room for rolls to rise. Chill for 2 to 24 hours. Uncover and let stand at room temperature for 30 minutes. Bake as directed on page 154.

Per roll plain or easy variation with cream cheese icing:
233 cal., 8 g total fat (4 g sat. fat), 39 mg chol., 118 mg sodium,
36 g carbo., 1 g fiber, 3 g pro.
Daily Values: 6% vit. A, 3% calcium, 8% iron
Exchanges: 1 Starch, 1½ Other Carbo., 1½ Fat

Cinnamon and Chocolate Rolls: Prepare as on page 154, except do not add raisins to the filling. Stir ¾ cup miniature semisweet chocolate pieces into the filling after cutting in the butter.

Per roll: 256 cal., 10 g total fat (5 g sat. fat), 39 mg chol.,
118 mg sodium, 40 g carbo., 1 g fiber, 4 g pro.
Daily Values: 6% vit. A, 3% calcium, 8% iron
Exchanges: 1 Starch, 1½ Other Carbo., 2 Fat

Caramel-Pecan Rolls: Prepare as on page 154 through Step 3. In a small saucepan combine ⅔ cup packed brown sugar, ¼ cup butter or margarine, and 2 tablespoons light-colored corn syrup. Stir over medium heat until combined. Divide butter mixture evenly between the prepared baking pans. Sprinkle ⅔ cup toasted chopped pecans over butter mixture, dividing evenly between the two pans; set aside. Continue with Step 4, placing rolls on top of pecan-sprinkled butter mixture in pans. After baking, immediately invert rolls onto a plate. Omit the Cream Cheese Icing or Vanilla Icing.

Per roll: 237 cal., 10 g total fat (4 g sat. fat), 38 mg chol.,
119 mg sodium, 33 g carbo., 1 g fiber, 3 g pro.
Daily Values: 5% vit. A, 4% calcium, 8% iron
Exchanges: 1 Starch, 1 Other Carbo., 2 Fat

Reheating Yeast Rolls

For make-ahead convenience, you can freeze unfrosted yeast rolls in a freezer container or bag for up to 3 months.

Thaw the wrapped rolls at room temperature for 2 hours. To warm the thawed rolls, remove them from the freezer container or bag and wrap in foil. Heat rolls in a preheated 300°F oven about 20 minutes. If desired, frost the rolls after heating.

Creamy Caramel-Pecan Rolls

Prep: 25 minutes **Rise:** 1 hour **Bake:** 20 minutes
Oven: 375°F **Makes:** 24 rolls

- 1¼ **cups powdered sugar**
- ⅓ **cup whipping cream**
- 1 **cup coarsely chopped pecans**
- ½ **cup packed brown sugar**
- 1 **tablespoon ground cinnamon**
- 2 **16-ounce loaves frozen white bread dough or sweet roll dough, thawed**
- 3 **tablespoons butter or margarine, melted**
- ¾ **cup raisins (optional)**

1. Generously grease two 9×1½-inch round baking pans. Line bottoms with a circle of parchment paper or nonstick foil; set pans aside. For topping, in a small bowl stir together powdered sugar and whipping cream; divide evenly between prepared baking pans, gently spreading. Sprinkle pecans evenly over sugar mixture.

2. In another small bowl stir together brown sugar and cinnamon; set aside. On a lightly floured surface, roll each loaf of thawed dough into a 12×8-inch rectangle. Brush with melted butter; sprinkle with brown sugar-cinnamon mixture. If desired, sprinkle with raisins. Roll up each rectangle, starting from a long side. Seal seams. Slice each rolled rectangle into 12 pieces; place, cut sides down, on topping in pans.

3. Cover; let rise in a warm place until nearly double in size (about 1 hour). Preheat oven to 375°F. Break any surface bubbles with a greased toothpick. Bake for 20 to 25 minutes or until rolls sound hollow when gently tapped. (If necessary, cover rolls with foil the last 10 minutes of baking to prevent overbrowning.) Cool in pans on a wire rack for 5 minutes. Loosen edges and carefully invert rolls onto a serving platter. Spoon on any nut mixture that may remain in pan. Serve warm.

Make-ahead directions: Prepare as above through Step 2. Cover with oiled waxed paper, then with plastic wrap. Chill for 2 to 24 hours. Before baking, let chilled rolls stand, covered, for 1 hour at room temperature. Uncover and bake 25 to 30 minutes or until rolls sound hollow when gently tapped. Continue as directed.

Per roll: 183 cal., 6 g total fat (2 g sat. fat), 8 mg chol.,
13 mg sodium, 27 g carbo., 1 g fiber, 3 g pro.
Daily Values: 2% vit. A, 5% calcium, 2% iron
Exchanges: 1 Starch, 1 Other Carbo., 1 Fat

Easy Cinnamon Monkey Bread

Although monkey bread is easy to make, remember to thaw the rolls in the refrigerator overnight.

Prep: 20 minutes **Chill:** overnight **Bake:** 40 minutes
Oven: 350°F **Makes:** 24 small rolls

> 1 **34.5-ounce package frozen cinnamon sweet roll dough or orange sweet roll dough (12 rolls)**
> ½ **cup chopped pecans**
> ⅓ **cup butter or margarine, melted**
> ¾ **cup sugar**
> ¼ **cup caramel-flavored ice cream topping**

1. The night before, place frozen rolls about 2 inches apart on a large greased baking sheet. Discard frosting packets or reserve for another use. Cover rolls with plastic wrap. Refrigerate overnight to let dough thaw and begin to rise.

2. Preheat oven to 350°F. Generously grease a 10-inch fluted tube pan. Sprinkle ¼ cup of the pecans in the bottom of the pan.

3. Cut each roll in half. Dip each roll half into melted butter, then roll in sugar. Layer coated roll halves in the prepared pan. Drizzle with any remaining butter; sprinkle with any remaining sugar. Sprinkle the remaining ¼ cup pecans on top. Drizzle ice cream topping over all.

4. Place pan on a baking sheet. Bake for 40 to 45 minutes or until golden brown. Let stand for 1 minute. Invert onto a large serving platter. Spoon any topping and nuts that remain in pan onto rolls. Cool slightly. Serve warm.

Per small roll: 173 cal., 7 g total fat (1 g sat. fat), 7 mg chol., 148 mg sodium, 26 g carbo., 1 g fiber, 2 g pro.
Daily Values: 3% vit. A, 1% calcium, 5% iron
Exchanges: 1 Starch, ½ Other Carbo., 1½ Fat

Coffee with the Neighbors

Invite the neighbors for a midmorning chat and serve fresh-from-the-oven rolls.

● *Orange juice with sparkling water*
● *Hot Cross Buns and/or Cinnamon Rolls (pages 157 and 154)*
● *Cappuccino or Café Latte (page 110)*

FAVORITE Orange Bowknots

Orange peel and juice in both the dough and icing give these attractive rolls plenty of flavor.

Prep: 45 minutes **Rise:** 1½ hours **Rest:** 10 minutes
Bake: 12 minutes **Oven:** 375°F **Makes:** 24 rolls

> 6 **to 6½ cups all-purpose flour**
> 1 **package active dry yeast**
> 1¼ **cups milk**
> ½ **cup butter, margarine, or shortening**
> ⅓ **cup sugar**
> ½ **teaspoon salt**
> 2 **eggs**
> 2 **tablespoons finely shredded orange peel**
> ¼ **cup orange juice**
> 1 **recipe Orange Icing**

1. In a large mixing bowl combine 2 cups of the flour and the yeast; set aside. In a medium saucepan heat and stir the milk, butter, sugar, and salt just until warm (120°F to 130°F) and butter almost melts; add to flour mixture along with eggs. Beat with an electric mixer on low to medium speed for 30 seconds, scraping bowl. Beat on high speed for 3 minutes. Using a wooden spoon, stir in orange peel, orange juice, and as much of the remaining flour as you can.

2. Turn dough out onto a lightly floured surface. Knead in enough remaining flour to make a moderately soft dough that is smooth and elastic (3 to 5 minutes total). Shape dough into a ball. Place in a lightly greased bowl, turning once to grease surface of dough. Cover; let rise in a warm place until double in size (about 1 hour; see photos 2 and 3, page 141).

3. Punch dough down (see photo 4, page 141). Turn out onto a lightly floured surface. Divide in half. Cover and let rest 10 minutes. Lightly grease two large baking sheets; set aside.

4. Roll each dough half into a 12×7-inch rectangle. Cut each rectangle into twelve 7-inch-long strips. Tie each strip loosely in a knot. Place knots 2 inches apart on prepared baking sheets. Cover; let rise in a warm place until nearly double in size (about 30 minutes).

5. Preheat oven to 375°F. Bake for 12 to 14 minutes or until golden. Immediately remove from baking sheets. Cool on wire racks. Drizzle with Orange Icing.

Orange Icing: In a medium bowl combine 1½ cups powdered sugar, 1½ teaspoons finely shredded orange peel, and enough orange juice (2 to 3 tablespoons) to make icing a drizzling consistency.

Per roll: 191 cal., 5 g total fat (2 g sat. fat), 29 mg chol.,
90 mg sodium, 32 g carbo., 1 g fiber, 4 g pro.
Daily Values: 4% vit. A, 5% vit. C, 2% calcium, 8% iron
Exchanges: 1 Starch, 1 Other Carbo., 1 Fat

Hot Cross Buns

These slightly sweet rolls often are served during the Easter season.

Prep: 40 minutes **Rise:** 3 hours **Rest:** 10 minutes
Bake: 15 minutes **Oven:** 375°F **Makes:** 20 buns

- 4 to 4½ cups all-purpose flour
- 1 package active dry yeast
- ¾ teaspoon ground cinnamon
- ¼ teaspoon ground nutmeg
  Dash ground cloves
- ¾ cup milk
- ½ cup butter or margarine
- ⅓ cup granulated sugar
- ½ teaspoon salt
- 3 eggs
- ⅔ cup dried currants or raisins
- ¼ cup diced candied orange peel (optional)
- 1 egg white, beaten
- 1 tablespoon water
- 1 recipe Powdered Sugar Icing (page 184)

1. In a large mixing bowl combine 2 cups of the flour, the yeast, cinnamon, nutmeg, and cloves. In a saucepan heat and stir milk, butter, granulated sugar, and salt just until warm (120°F to 130°F) and butter almost melts. Add milk mixture to flour mixture along with eggs. Beat with an electric mixer on low to medium speed for 30 seconds, scraping bowl constantly. Beat on high speed for 3 minutes. Using a wooden spoon, stir in currants, orange peel (if desired), and as much of the remaining flour as you can.

2. Turn dough out onto a lightly floured surface. Knead in enough remaining flour to make a moderately soft dough (3 to 5 minutes total). Shape into a ball. Place in a lightly greased bowl, turning once to grease surface of dough. Cover; let rise in a warm place until double in size (about 2 hours; see photos 2 and 3, page 141).

3. Punch dough down. Turn dough out onto a lightly floured surface. Cover; let rest 10 minutes. Meanwhile, lightly grease two baking sheets; set aside. Divide dough into 20 pieces. Gently pull each piece into a ball, tucking edges under to make smooth tops. Place balls 1½ inches apart on prepared baking sheets. Cover; let rise until nearly double in size (about 1 hour).

4. Preheat oven to 375°F. Using a sharp knife, make crisscross slashes across the top of each dough ball. In a small bowl combine beaten egg white and water; brush over rolls. Bake about 15 minutes or until golden brown. Immediately remove buns from baking sheets. Cool slightly on wire racks. Drizzle Powdered Sugar Icing into crisscrosses on each bun. Serve warm.

Per bun: 202 cal., 6 g total fat (3 g sat. fat), 46 mg chol.,
127 mg sodium, 32 g carbo., 1 g fiber, 4 g pro.
Daily Values: 5% vit. A, 3% calcium, 8% iron
Exchanges: 1 Starch, 1 Other Carbo., 1 Fat

Hot Cross Buns

Challah [LOW FAT]

Prep: 30 minutes **Rise:** 1½ hours **Rest:** 10 minutes
Bake: 25 minutes **Oven:** 375°F **Makes:** 28 slices

- **4¾ to 5¼ cups all-purpose flour**
- **1 package active dry yeast**
- **1¼ cups water**
- **3 tablespoons sugar**
- **3 tablespoons pareve (made without dairy or meat ingredients) margarine**
- **½ teaspoon salt**
- **2 eggs**
- **1 egg yolk, beaten**
- **2 teaspoons water**
- **2 teaspoons poppy seeds**

1. In a large mixing bowl stir together 2 cups of the flour and the yeast; set aside. In a medium saucepan heat and stir the 1¼ cups water, the sugar, margarine, and salt just until warm (120°F to 130°F) and margarine almost melts. Add margarine mixture to flour mixture along with the two eggs. Beat with an electric mixer on low to medium speed for 30 seconds, scraping sides of bowl constantly. Beat on high speed for 3 minutes. Using a wooden spoon, stir in as much of the remaining flour as you can.

2. Turn dough out onto a lightly floured surface. Knead in enough of the remaining flour to make a moderately stiff dough that is smooth and elastic (6 to 8 minutes total; see photo 1, page 141). Shape dough into a ball. Place in a lightly greased bowl, turning once to grease surface of dough. Cover; let rise in a warm place until double in size (about 1 hour; see photos 2 and 3, page 141).

3. Punch dough down (see photo 4, page 141). Turn out onto a lightly floured surface. Divide into thirds. Cover; let rest for 10 minutes.

4. Roll each third into an 18-inch rope. Place ropes on a large baking sheet 1 inch apart; braid. Cover and let rise in a warm place until nearly double in size (about 30 minutes). Combine the egg yolk with the 2 teaspoons water; brush over braid and sprinkle with poppy seeds.

5. Preheat oven to 375°F. Bake for 25 to 30 minutes or until bread sounds hollow when lightly tapped. (If necessary, cover loosely with foil the last 10 minutes of baking to prevent overbrowning.) Immediately remove bread from baking sheet. Cool on a wire rack.

Egg Bread Loaves: Prepare as at left, except substitute 1⅓ cups milk for the water and use 3 tablespoons butter or margarine. Prepare as directed through Step 2. Punch dough down; divide in half. Cover; let rest 10 minutes. Lightly grease two 8×4×2-inch loaf pans. Shape dough into loaves by patting or rolling. Place shaped dough in prepared pans. Cover; let rise until nearly double (about 30 minutes). Omit egg yolk mixture and poppy seeds. Bake as directed.

Cinnamon-Swirl Bread: Prepare Egg Bread Loaves as above, except on a lightly floured surface, roll each dough half into a 12×7-inch rectangle. Brush lightly with water. Combine ½ cup sugar and 2 teaspoons ground cinnamon; sprinkle half of the sugar-cinnamon mixture over each rectangle. Roll up each rectangle, starting from a short side. Pinch seam and ends to seal. Place, seam sides down, in prepared loaf pans. Let rise and bake as directed. If desired, drizzle warm loaves with 1 recipe Powdered Sugar Icing (see page 184).

Per slice challah, egg bread, or cinnamon-swirl variations:
96 cal., 2 g total fat (0 g sat. fat), 22 mg chol., 62 mg sodium, 16 g carbo., 1 g fiber, 3 g pro.
Daily Values: 2% vit. A, 1% calcium, 6% iron
Exchanges: 1 Starch, ½ Fat

Stollen

In a conventional oven bake only one baking sheet at a time. Place the other one in the refrigerator so dough doesn't overrise.

Prep: 25 minutes **Rise:** 2 hours **Rest:** 10 minutes
Bake: 18 minutes **Oven:** 375°F
Makes: 3 loaves (36 slices)

- **4 to 4½ cups all-purpose flour**
- **1 package active dry yeast**
- **1¼ cups milk**
- **½ cup butter**
- **¼ cup granulated sugar**
- **½ teaspoon salt**
- **1 egg**
- **1 cup raisins or dried currants**
- **¼ cup diced mixed candied fruits and peels**
- **¼ cup slivered almonds**
- **1 tablespoon finely shredded orange peel**
- **1 tablespoon finely shredded lemon peel**
- **1 cup powdered sugar**
- **1 teaspoon butter, softened**

1. In a large mixing bowl combine 2 cups of the flour and the yeast. In a medium saucepan heat and stir milk, the ½ cup butter, granulated sugar, and salt until warm (120°F to 130°F) and butter almost melts. Add to flour mixture along with egg. Beat with an electric mixer on low speed for 30 seconds, scraping bowl constantly. Beat on high speed 3 minutes. Using a wooden spoon, stir in as much of the remaining flour as you can. Stir in raisins, candied fruits and peels, almonds, orange peel, and lemon peel.

2. Turn dough out onto a lightly floured surface. Knead in enough remaining flour to make a moderately soft dough (3 to 5 minutes total). Shape into a ball. Place in a lightly greased bowl; turn once. Cover; let rise in a warm place until double (1¼ to 1¾ hours; see photos 2 and 3, page 141).

3. Punch dough down (see photo 4, page 141). Turn dough out onto a lightly floured surface. Divide dough into thirds. Cover; let rest 10 minutes. Meanwhile, grease two large baking sheets; set aside. Roll each dough portion into a 10×6-inch oval. Without stretching, fold over a long side of each oval to within 1 inch of the opposite long side; press edges to lightly seal. Place on prepared baking sheets (two loaves on one baking sheet and one loaf on the other baking sheet). Cover; let rise until nearly double (45 to 60 minutes).

4. Preheat oven to 375°F. Bake one pan at a time for 18 to 20 minutes or until golden and bread sounds hollow when lightly tapped. Remove from sheets. Cool 30 minutes on wire racks. Combine powdered sugar, 2 tablespoons *hot water*, and 1 teaspoon butter; brush over warm bread.

Per slice: 116 cal., 4 g total fat (2 g sat. fat), 14 mg chol., 59 mg sodium, 19 g carbo., 1 g fiber, 2 g pro.
Daily Values: 2% vit. A, 1% vit. C, 2% calcium, 4% iron
Exchanges: ½ Starch, ½ Other Carbo., 1 Fat

Home-Style White Bread

LOW FAT   EASY

Prep: 10 minutes **Bake:** per bread machine directions

For 1½-pound loaf (16 slices)
- 1 **cup milk**
- ¼ **cup water**
- 4 **teaspoons butter, margarine, or olive oil**
- 3 **cups bread flour**
- 4 **teaspoons sugar**
- ¾ **teaspoon salt**
- 1 **teaspoon active dry yeast or bread machine yeast**

For 2-pound loaf (22 slices)
- 1¼ **cups milk**
- ¼ **cup water**
- 2 **tablespoons butter, margarine, or olive oil**
- 4 **cups bread flour**
- 2 **tablespoons sugar**
- 1 **teaspoon salt**
- 1¼ **teaspoons active dry yeast or bread machine yeast**

1. Select desired loaf size. Add the ingredients to a bread machine according to the manufacturer's directions. Select the basic white bread cycle. Remove hot bread from machine as soon as it is done. Cool on a wire rack.

Per slice: 114 cal., 2 g total fat (1 g sat. fat), 4 mg chol., 128 mg sodium, 20 g carbo., 1 g fiber, 4 g pro.
Daily Values: 1% vit. A, 2% calcium, 7% iron
Exchanges: 1½ Starch

Easy Whole Wheat Bread

LOW FAT   EASY   WHOLE GRAIN

Prep: 10 minutes **Bake:** per bread machine directions

For 1½-pound loaf (16 slices)
- 1 **cup milk**
- 3 **tablespoons water**
- 4 **teaspoons honey or sugar**
- 1 **tablespoon butter or margarine**
- 1½ **cups whole wheat flour**
- 1½ **cups bread flour**
- ¾ **teaspoon salt**
- 1 **teaspoon active dry yeast or bread machine yeast**

For 2-pound loaf (22 slices)
- 1⅓ **cups milk**
- ¼ **cup water**
- 2 **tablespoons honey or sugar**
- 4 **teaspoons butter or margarine**
- 2 **cups whole wheat flour**
- 2 **cups bread flour**
- 1 **teaspoon salt**
- 1¼ **teaspoons active dry yeast or bread machine yeast**

1. Select desired loaf size. Add ingredients to a bread machine according to manufacturer's directions. Select whole grain cycle, if available, or the basic white bread cycle. Remove hot bread from machine as soon as it is done. Cool on a rack.

Per slice: 105 cal., 1 g total fat (1 g sat. fat), 3 mg chol., 125 mg sodium, 20 g carbo., 2 g fiber, 4 g pro.
Daily Values: 1% vit. A, 2% calcium, 6% iron
Exchanges: 1½ Starch

Cheesy Potato Bread `LOW FAT`

For a satisfying sandwich, team slices of this flavorful bread with plenty of thinly sliced ham.

Prep: 25 minutes **Bake:** per bread machine directions

For 1½-pound loaf (16 slices)

- ¾ cup water
- ½ cup chopped, peeled potato
- ⅓ cup milk
- ⅓ cup shredded cheddar cheese
- 2 teaspoons butter or margarine
- 3 cups bread flour
- 1 tablespoon sugar
- ¾ teaspoon onion salt
- ¼ teaspoon caraway seeds, crushed (optional)
- 1 teaspoon active dry yeast or bread machine yeast

For 2-pound loaf (22 slices)

- 1 cup water
- ⅔ cup chopped, peeled potato
- ½ cup milk
- ½ cup shredded cheddar cheese
- 1 tablespoon butter or margarine
- 4 cups bread flour
- 4 teaspoons sugar
- 1 teaspoon onion salt
- ½ teaspoon caraway seeds, crushed (optional)
- 1¼ teaspoons active dry yeast or bread machine yeast

1. Select desired loaf size. In a small saucepan combine the water and potato. Bring to boiling; reduce heat. Simmer, covered, about 10 minutes or until potato is very tender; do not drain. Mash potato in the water. Measure potato mixture. If necessary, add water to equal ¾ cup mixture for the 1½-pound loaf or 1 cup mixture for the 2-pound loaf; discard any excess potato mixture. Let the measured potato mixture cool slightly.

2. Add the potato mixture and remaining ingredients to a bread machine according to the manufacturer's directions. Select the basic white bread cycle. Remove hot bread from machine as soon as it is done. Cool on a wire rack.

Per slice: 117 cal., 2 g total fat (1 g sat. fat), 4 mg chol., 98 mg sodium, 21 g carbo., 1 g fiber, 4 g pro.
Daily Values: 1% vit. A, 1% vit. C, 3% calcium, 7% iron
Exchanges: 1½ Starch

Bread Machine Adjustments

To convert conventional yeast bread recipes for use in a bread machine, follow these tips:

● Reduce flour amount to 3 cups (for a 1½-pound loaf) or 4 cups (for a 2-pound loaf). Reduce all ingredients by the same proportion, including yeast (one package equals about 2¼ teaspoons). For example, to make a 1½-pound loaf, a conventional recipe that uses 4½ cups flour and 1 package yeast would be decreased by one-third to 3 cups flour and 1½ teaspoons yeast.

● If a bread uses two or more types of flour, add flour amounts together and use that total as the basis for reducing the recipe. The total flour used should be only 3 or 4 cups, depending on machine size.

● Use bread flour instead of all-purpose flour. Rye breads usually need 1 tablespoon gluten flour even when bread flour is used.

● Make sure liquid ingredients are at room temperature before starting the machine.

● Add ingredients in the order specified by the bread machine manufacturer.

● Do not use light-colored dried fruits, such as apricots and light raisins, because their preservatives inhibit yeast performance.

● For breads containing whole wheat or rye flour, use the whole grain cycle, if available. For sweet or rich breads, use the light-color setting, if your machine has one.

● When making dough only, you might have to knead in a little more flour before shaping it. Knead in just enough flour to make dough easy to handle. If necessary, let dough rest 5 minutes before shaping. Bread machine-made dough often is elastic; letting it rest makes it easier to shape.

● The first time you try a new recipe in your machine, watch and listen. Check dough after 3 to 5 minutes of kneading. If it looks dry and the machine works excessively hard during the mixing cycle or if two or more balls of dough form, add 1 to 2 tablespoons extra liquid. If dough looks too soft, add more flour, 1 tablespoon at a time, until a ball forms. Keep a record of how much you add for future reference.

Cakes & Frostings

Carrot Cake, 172

Chocolate Cake, 166

Apple Cake, 172

Cakes Essentials

Plain or fancy, round or square—you'll find a cake for any reason or season on the following pages. To help ensure perfect cakes, read through these fundamentals before you start.

Use the Right Pans

When it comes to baking pans, your best bet is sturdy, single-wall aluminum pans. Keep in mind that shiny bakeware (aluminum, tin, and  stainless steel) reflects heat and results in cakes with thin, golden crusts. Dark or dull-finish bakeware (tin, glass, and many nonstick pans) absorbs more heat, increasing the amount of browning. If you use a pan with a dark or dull finish, follow the manufacturer's directions. Most suggest reducing the oven temperature by 25°F and checking doneness 3 to 5 minutes before the minimum recommended baking time. Silicone pans (see photo, above) are increasing in popularity. These pans may be used in the oven, microwave, and freezer. Follow the manufacturer's directions for baking and cooling when using silicone pans.

Preparing the Pan

Unless specified otherwise, grease and lightly flour baking pans for butter-type layer cakes and other cakes that will be removed from their pans. Use a paper  towel or pastry brush to evenly spread the shortening in the pan. Add a little flour, tilt the pan, and tap it so the flour covers all the greased surfaces; tap out the excess flour. You can use cocoa powder instead of flour for chocolate cakes.

Some recipes may direct you to line the bottoms of the pans with waxed paper or parchment paper. Cut pieces of waxed or parchment paper to the size of the pans; line the bottoms of the lightly greased pans with the paper, then grease and flour as described in the preceding paragraph.

Time and Temperature

Always be sure to bake cakes at the correct temperature. If the oven temperature is too hot, the cake may develop tunnels and cracks. If the oven temperature is too low, the cake may have a texture that is too coarse. Allow your oven to preheat while you prepare the cake batter.

Check the cake for doneness after the minimum baking time. To test a butter-type cake, insert a wooden toothpick near the center. If it comes out clean, the cake is done. If it comes out wet, bake the cake a few minutes more, then test in another spot near the center.

To test whether a foam cake (such as angel food, sponge, or chiffon cake) is done, touch the top lightly. If it springs back, the cake is finished baking.

Cooling Cakes

Before removing a layer cake from its baking pan, allow it to cool for 10 minutes on a wire rack. To remove the layer, loosen cake edges from pan using a metal spatula or knife. Place an inverted cake rack on the cake layer, turn the cake and rack over, and lift off the pan. (If the pans were lined with waxed paper, gently peel off the paper.) Place a second inverted rack on the cake layer and turn it over again so the baked cake is upright; cool completely. A butter-type cake that will be served in its pan should cool on a wire rack.

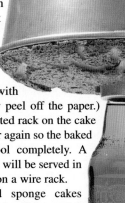

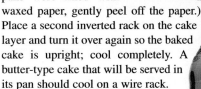

Angel food and sponge cakes baked in tube pans should be cooled upside down to set their structures. Use a long metal spatula to loosen the cooled cake from the pan. Press the spatula against the pan in a continuous motion to avoid tearing the cake.

Yellow Cake

Prep: 50 minutes **Bake:** 20 minutes **Oven:** 375°F
Cool: 1 hour **Makes:** 12 to 16 servings

 ¾ **cup butter**
 3 **eggs**
2½ **cups all-purpose flour**
2½ **teaspoons baking powder**
 ½ **teaspoon salt**
1¾ **cups sugar**
1½ **teaspoons vanilla**
1¼ **cups milk**

1. Allow butter and eggs to stand at room temperature for 30 minutes. Grease and flour two 9×1½-inch or 8×1½-inch round cake pans (see photo, page 163) or grease one 13×9×2-inch baking pan; set aside. In a bowl stir together flour, baking powder, and salt; set aside.

2. Preheat oven to 375°F. In a mixing bowl beat butter with an electric mixer on medium to high speed for 30 seconds. Gradually add sugar, beating until well combined (see photo, below). Beat 2 minutes more. Add eggs one at a time, beating well after each addition. Beat in vanilla. Alternately add flour mixture and milk, beating on low speed after each addition just until combined. Spread batter into prepared pan(s).

3. Bake for 20 to 25 minutes for the 9-inch pans, 30 to 35 minutes for 8-inch pans, 25 to 30 minutes for 13×9×2-inch pan, or until a wooden toothpick inserted near center(s) comes out clean. Cool cake layers in pans on wire racks for 10 minutes. Remove layers from pans; cool thoroughly on racks. Or place 13×9×2-inch cake in pan on wire rack; cool thoroughly. Frost with desired frosting (see pages 184 to 186).

Citrus Yellow Cake: Prepare as above, except stir 2 teaspoons finely shredded orange peel or lemon peel into batter.

Per serving yellow or citrus variation: 336 cal., 14 g total fat (8 g sat. fat), 88 mg chol., 333 mg sodium, 48 g carbo., 1 g fiber, 5 g pro.
Daily Values: 12% vit. A, 9% calcium, 7% iron
Exchanges: 1 Starch, 2 Other Carbo., 3 Fat

Beat the butter or shortening for 30 seconds. Gradually add the sugar and beat until well combined, scraping the sides of the bowl with a rubber scraper occasionally. The mixture will have a light and fluffy texture.

White Cake

For a whiter cake, use shortening instead of butter and clear vanilla instead of regular vanilla.

Prep: 55 minutes **Bake:** 20 minutes **Oven:** 350°F
Cool: 1 hour **Makes:** 12 to 16 servings

 4 **egg whites**
 2 **cups all-purpose flour**
 1 **teaspoon baking powder**
 ½ **teaspoon baking soda**
 ½ **teaspoon salt**
 ½ **cup butter or shortening, softened**
1¾ **cups sugar**
 1 **teaspoon vanilla**
1⅓ **cups buttermilk or sour milk (see tip,
      page 169)**

1. Allow egg whites to stand at room temperature for 30 minutes. Meanwhile, grease and lightly flour two 9×1½-inch or 8×1½-inch round cake pans (see photo, page 163) or grease one 13×9×2-inch baking pan; set pan(s) aside. In a medium bowl stir together flour, baking powder, baking soda, and salt; set aside.

2. Preheat oven to 350°F. In large mixing bowl beat butter with an electric mixer on medium to high speed for 30 seconds. Add sugar and vanilla; beat until well combined (see photo, below left). Add egg whites one at a time, beating well after each addition. Alternately add flour mixture and buttermilk to butter mixture, beating on low speed after each addition just until combined. Spread batter into prepared pan(s).

3. Bake for 20 to 25 minutes for 9-inch pans, 25 to 30 minutes for 8-inch pans, 30 to 35 minutes for 13×9-inch pan, or until a wooden toothpick inserted near center(s) comes out clean. Cool cake layers in pans on wire racks for 10 minutes. Remove cake layers from pans. Cool thoroughly on wire racks. Or place the 13×9×2-inch cake in pan on a wire rack; cool thoroughly. Frost with desired frosting (see pages 184 to 186).

Coconut White Cake: Prepare as above, except stir ¾ cup toasted flaked coconut (see tip, page 265) into batter.

Per serving white or coconut variation: 268 cal., 9 g total fat (4 g sat. fat), 23 mg chol., 274 mg sodium, 44 g carbo., 1 g fiber, 4 g pro.
Daily Values: 5% vit. A, 4% calcium, 5% iron
Exchanges: 1 Starch, 2 Other Carbo., 1½ Fat

Triple-Layer Lemon Cake

Don't let the fact that you have only two cake pans stop you from making this stunning three-layer beauty. Just bake in shifts, refrigerating the batter for the third layer while the first two layers bake.

Prep: 1¼ hours **Bake:** 28 minutes **Oven:** 350°F
Cool: 1 hour **Makes:** 12 servings

- **1 cup butter**
- **4 eggs**
- **2⅓ cups all-purpose flour**
- **1½ teaspoons baking powder**
- **½ teaspoon baking soda**
- **¼ teaspoon salt**
- **2 cups sugar**
- **2 teaspoons finely shredded lemon peel**
- **2 tablespoons lemon juice**
- **1 cup buttermilk or sour milk (see tip, page 169)**
- **½ recipe Lemon Curd (page 292) or 1 cup purchased lemon curd**
- **1 recipe Lemon-Cream Cheese Frosting**

1. Allow butter and eggs to stand at room temperature for 30 minutes. Meanwhile, grease and lightly flour three 8×1½-inch or 9×1½-inch round cake pans (see photo, page 163); set pans aside. In a medium bowl stir together flour, baking powder, baking soda, and salt; set aside.

2. Preheat oven to 350°F. In a large mixing bowl beat butter with an electric mixer on medium to high speed for 30 seconds. Add sugar, lemon peel, and lemon juice; beat until well combined (see photo, page 164). Add eggs one at a time, beating well after each addition. Alternately add flour mixture and buttermilk to butter mixture, beating on low speed after each addition just until combined. Spread into prepared pans.

3. Bake for 28 to 32 minutes for the 8-inch pans, 25 to 28 minutes for the 9-inch pans, or until a wooden toothpick inserted near centers comes out clean. Cool cake layers in pans on wire racks for 10 minutes. Remove cake layers from pans. Cool thoroughly on wire racks.

4. To assemble, turn two layers bottom sides up; spread with Lemon Curd. Stack these layers on a cake plate. Place remaining cake layer on top, rounded (top) side up. Frost top and sides with Lemon-Cream Cheese Frosting.

5. Cover and store cake in the refrigerator for up to 3 days. Let stand at room temperature for 30 minutes before serving.

Lemon-Cream Cheese Frosting: Finely shred 1 teaspoon lemon peel; set aside. In a medium mixing bowl combine two 3-ounce packages softened cream cheese, ½ cup softened butter, and 1 teaspoon lemon juice. Beat with electric mixer on low to medium speed until light and fluffy. Gradually add 4½ to 4¾ cups powdered sugar, beating until frosting reaches spreading consistency. Stir in the lemon peel.

Per serving: 818 cal., 42 g total fat (21 g sat. fat), 275 mg chol., 453 mg sodium, 107 g carbo., 1 g fiber, 8 g pro.
Daily Values: 28% vit. A, 11% vit. C, 8% calcium, 10% iron
Exchanges: 1 Starch, 6 Other Carbo., 8 Fat

Serving and Storing Cakes

Most cakes can be made several hours in advance, making them great choices for entertaining and special occasions. Here are some tips for keeping them at their best until serving time:

● After frosting a cake with a butter-type frosting, let it stand about an hour before slicing. This allows the frosting to set up.

● Cakes filled or frosted with whipped cream should be assembled no more than 2 hours before serving to keep them from becoming soggy.

● Most cakes can be covered and stored at room temperature for 2 to 3 days. If you don't have a cake cover, invert a large bowl over the cake.

● If the filling or frosting contains whipped cream, cream cheese, or eggs, store the cake, covered, in the refrigerator.

● Freeze layers unfrosted. Place the cooled layers on baking sheets and freeze until firm. Transfer frozen layers to large freezer bags or wrap and seal in freezer wrap. Freeze for up to 4 months.

● Angel food, sponge, and chiffon cakes also are best frozen unfrosted. Place cooled cakes in large freezer bags and freeze for up to 3 months. The delicate sponge texture may deteriorate if stored longer. Thaw cakes at room temperature for several hours before frosting and serving.

Chocolate Cake

See photo, page 161.

Prep: 50 minutes **Bake:** 35 minutes **Oven:** 350°F
Cool: 1 hour **Makes:** 12 to 16 servings

- ¾ cup butter
- 3 eggs
- 2 cups all-purpose flour
- ¾ cup unsweetened cocoa powder
- 1 teaspoon baking soda
- ¾ teaspoon baking powder
- ½ teaspoon salt
- 2 cups sugar
- 2 teaspoons vanilla
- 1½ cups milk

1. Allow butter and eggs to stand at room temperature for 30 minutes. Grease bottoms of two 8×8×2-inch square or 9×1½-inch round cake pans. Line bottoms of pans with waxed paper; grease and lightly flour pans. Or grease one 13×9×2-inch baking pan. Set pan(s) aside. In a medium bowl stir together flour, cocoa powder, baking soda, baking powder, and salt; set aside.

2. Preheat oven to 350°F. In a large mixing bowl beat butter with an electric mixer on medium to high speed for 30 seconds. Gradually add sugar, ¼ cup at a time, beating on medium speed until well combined. Scrape sides of bowl; beat 2 minutes. Add eggs one at a time, beating after each addition. Beat in vanilla. Alternately add flour mixture and milk to butter mixture, beating on low speed after each addition just until combined. Beat on medium to high speed for 20 seconds more. Spread into prepared pan(s).

3. Bake for 35 to 40 minutes for 8-inch pans and 13×9×2-inch pan, 30 to 35 minutes for 9-inch pans, or until a wooden toothpick inserted near center(s) comes out clean. Cool cake layers in pans on wire racks for 10 minutes. Remove layers from pans. Peel off waxed paper. Cool thoroughly on racks. Or place 13×9×2-inch cake in pan on wire rack; cool thoroughly. Frost with desired frosting (see pages 184 to 186).

Devil's Food Cake: Prepare as above, except omit baking powder and increase baking soda to 1¼ teaspoons.

Per serving chocolate or devil's food variation: 360 cal.,
15 g total fat (7 g sat. fat), 88 mg chol., 335 mg sodium,
51 g carbo., 1 g fiber, 6 g pro.
Daily Values: 10% vit. A, 11% calcium, 10% iron
Exchanges: 1 Starch, 2½ Other Carbo., 3 Fat

German Chocolate Cake

When baked in a 13×9×2-inch pan, this coconut-pecan-topped cake makes a great take-along sweet.

Prep: 1 hour **Bake:** 35 minutes **Oven:** 350°F
Cool: 1 hour **Makes:** 12 to 16 servings

- 1 4-ounce package sweet baking chocolate, chopped
- 1½ cups milk
- ¾ cup butter
- 3 eggs
- 2 cups all-purpose flour
- 1 teaspoon baking soda
- ¾ teaspoon baking powder
- ½ teaspoon salt
- 1¾ cups sugar
- 2 teaspoons vanilla
- 1 recipe Coconut-Pecan Frosting

1. In a small saucepan combine chocolate and milk. Cook and stir over low heat until melted; set aside to cool.

2. Allow butter and eggs to stand at room temperature for 30 minutes. Meanwhile, grease the bottoms of two 8×8×2-inch square or 9×1½-inch round cake pans. Line the bottoms of the pans with waxed paper; grease and lightly flour pans. Or grease one 13×9×2-inch baking pan. Set pan(s) aside. In a medium bowl stir together flour, baking soda, baking powder, and salt; set aside.

3. Preheat oven to 350°F. In a large mixing bowl beat butter with an electric mixer on medium to high speed for 30 seconds. Gradually add sugar, about ¼ cup at a time, beating on medium speed after each addition until well combined (about 3 minutes). Scrape sides of bowl; continue beating on medium speed for 2 minutes more. Add eggs one at a time, beating after each addition (about 1 minute total). Beat in vanilla. Alternately add flour mixture and chocolate mixture to butter mixture, beating on low speed after each addition just until combined. Beat on medium to high speed for 20 seconds more. Spread batter evenly into the prepared pan(s).

4. Bake for 35 to 40 minutes for 8-inch pans, 30 to 35 minutes for 9-inch pans, 40 to 45 minutes for 13×9×2-inch pan, or until a wooden toothpick inserted near the center(s) comes out clean. Cool cake layers in pans on wire racks for 10 minutes. Remove cake layers from pans. Peel off waxed paper. Cool thoroughly on racks. Or place 13×9×2-inch cake in pan on a wire rack; cool thoroughly.

5. Spread Coconut-Pecan Frosting over the top of each layer; stack the layers on a cake plate. Or spread Coconut-Pecan Frosting over the top of the 13×9-inch cake.

Coconut-Pecan Frosting: In a medium saucepan slightly beat 1 egg. Stir in one 5-ounce can (⅔ cup) evaporated milk, ⅔ cup sugar, and ¼ cup butter. Cook and stir over medium heat for 6 to 8 minutes or until thickened and bubbly. Remove from heat; stir in 1⅓ cups flaked coconut and ½ cup chopped pecans. Cover and cool thoroughly before using frosting to frost cake.

Per serving: 561 cal., 30 g total fat (16 g sat. fat), 120 mg chol., 425 mg sodium, 68 g carbo., 3 g fiber, 8 g pro.
Daily Values: 13% vit. A, 1% vit. C, 10% calcium, 9% iron
Exchanges: 1 Starch, 3½ Other Carbo., 6 Fat

Red Waldorf Cake

The popular story about this rosy-hued chocolate cake, also known as Red Velvet Cake, goes back to New York City's Waldorf-Astoria Hotel.

Prep: 1 hour **Bake:** 30 minutes **Oven:** 350°F
Cool: 1 hour **Makes:** 12 servings

> 2 eggs
> ½ cup unsweetened cocoa powder
> 2 ounces red food coloring (¼ cup)
> 2¼ cups sifted cake flour or 2 cups sifted all-purpose flour
> ½ teaspoon salt
> ½ cup shortening
> 1½ cups sugar
> 1 teaspoon vanilla
> 1 cup buttermilk or sour milk (see tip, page 169)
> 1 teaspoon baking soda
> 1 teaspoon vinegar
> 1 recipe Creamy Frosting

1. Allow eggs to stand at room temperature for 30 minutes. Meanwhile, grease and lightly flour two 9×1½-inch round cake pans (see photo, page 163) or one 13×9×2-inch baking pan. Set pan(s) aside. In a small bowl stir together cocoa powder and food coloring; set aside. In another small bowl stir together flour and salt; set aside.

2. Preheat oven to 350°F. In a large mixing bowl beat shortening with an electric mixer on medium to high speed for 30 seconds. Add sugar and vanilla; beat until well combined (see photo, page 164). Add eggs one at a time, beating on medium speed after each addition until combined. Beat in cocoa mixture. Alternately add flour mixture and buttermilk, beating on low to medium speed after each addition just until combined. Stir together baking soda and vinegar. Add to batter, mixing until combined. Spread batter into prepared pan(s).

3. Bake for 30 to 35 minutes for round pans, 30 minutes for 13×9×2-inch pan, or until a wooden toothpick inserted near center(s) comes out clean. Cool layers in pans for 10 minutes. Remove cake layers from pans; cool thoroughly on wire racks. Or place the 13×9×2-inch cake in pan on a wire rack; cool thoroughly. Frost with Creamy Frosting. Cover and store cake in the refrigerator for up to 3 days.

Creamy Frosting: In a medium saucepan whisk 1 cup milk into 3 tablespoons all-purpose flour. Cook and stir over medium heat until thickened and bubbly. Reduce heat; cook and stir for 2 minutes more. Cover surface with plastic wrap. Cool to room temperature (do not stir). In a medium mixing bowl beat 1 cup softened butter, 1 cup sugar, and 1 teaspoon vanilla with electric mixer on medium speed until light and fluffy. Add cooled milk mixture to butter mixture, ¼ cup at a time, beating on low speed after each addition until smooth.

Per serving: 500 cal., 26 g total fat (13 g sat. fat), 81 mg chol., 410 mg sodium, 61 g carbo., 0 g fiber, 5 g pro.
Daily Values: 14% vit. A, 1% vit. C, 11% calcium, 13% iron
Exchanges: 1 Starch, 3 Other Carbo., 5 Fat

Red Waldorf Cake

One-Bowl Chocolate Cake

For an elegant twist, top the cake with Ganache (page 186) instead of the Chocolate Glaze.

Prep: 20 minutes **Bake:** 30 minutes **Oven:** 350°F
Cool: 1 hour **Makes:** 8 servings

> 1 cup all-purpose flour
> 1 cup sugar
> ½ cup unsweetened cocoa powder
> ½ teaspoon baking soda
> ¼ teaspoon baking powder
> ¼ teaspoon salt
> ¾ cup milk
> ⅓ cup cooking oil
> 1 teaspoon vanilla
> 1 egg
> 1 recipe Chocolate Glaze

1. Preheat oven to 350°F. Grease and flour a 9×1½-inch round cake pan or 8×8×2-inch baking pan (see photo, page 163); set pan aside.

2. In a large mixing bowl stir together flour, sugar, cocoa powder, soda, baking powder, and salt. Add milk, oil, and vanilla. Beat with electric mixer on low speed just until combined. Beat on medium speed for 2 minutes. Add egg; beat 2 minutes more. Spread into prepared pan.

3. Bake for 30 to 35 minutes or until a wooden toothpick inserted near center comes out clean. Cool cake in pan on a wire rack for 10 minutes. Remove cake from pan. Cool thoroughly on wire rack. Spoon the Chocolate Glaze over the cooled cake.

Chocolate Glaze: Melt 4 ounces coarsely chopped semisweet chocolate and 3 tablespoons butter over low heat, stirring frequently. Remove from heat. Beat in 1½ cups powdered sugar and 3 tablespoons hot water. Stir in additional hot water, if needed, to reach drizzling consistency.

One-Bowl Mocha Cake: Prepare as above, except add 2 tablespoons instant espresso coffee powder to the milk; stir to dissolve. Prepare Chocolate Glaze as above, except stir 1 tablespoon instant espresso coffee powder into the hot water before beating into the chocolate mixture.

Per serving chocolate or mocha variation: 454 cal., 20 g total fat (7 g sat. fat), 41 mg chol., 230 mg sodium, 66 g carbo., 1 g fiber, 5 g pro.
Daily Values: 5% vit. A, 10% calcium, 12% iron
Exchanges: ½ Starch, 4 Other Carbo., 4 Fat

Spice Cake

The Browned Butter Frosting (page 184) is a yummy choice for this often-requested cake.

Prep: 50 minutes **Bake:** 30 minutes **Oven:** 350°F
Cool: 1 hour **Makes:** 12 servings

> ¼ cup butter
> 2 eggs
> 2 cups all-purpose flour
> 1½ teaspoons baking powder
> 1 teaspoon ground cinnamon
> ½ teaspoon baking soda
> ¼ teaspoon ground nutmeg
> ¼ teaspoon ground cloves
> ¼ teaspoon ground ginger
> ¼ cup shortening
> 1½ cups sugar
> ½ teaspoon vanilla
> 1¼ cups buttermilk or sour milk (see tip, page 169)

1. Allow butter and eggs to stand at room temperature for 30 minutes. Meanwhile, grease and lightly flour two 8×1½-inch round cake pans (see photo, page 163) or grease one 13×9×2-inch baking pan; set pan(s) aside. In a medium bowl stir together flour, baking powder, cinnamon, baking soda, nutmeg, cloves, and ginger; set aside.

2. Preheat oven to 350°F. In a large mixing bowl beat butter and shortening with an electric mixer on medium to high speed for 30 seconds. Add sugar and vanilla; beat until well combined (see photo, page 164). Add eggs one at a time, beating well after each addition. Alternately add flour mixture and buttermilk to butter mixture, beating on low speed after each addition just until combined. Spread into prepared pan(s).

3. Bake for 30 to 35 minutes for the round pans, 35 to 40 minutes for the 13×9×2-inch pan, or until a wooden toothpick inserted near center(s) comes out clean. Cool cake layers on wire racks for 10 minutes. Remove the cake layers from pans. Cool thoroughly on wire racks. Or place 13×9×2-inch cake in pan on a wire rack; cool thoroughly. Frost with desired frosting (see pages 184 to 186).

Applesauce Spice Cake: Prepare as on page 168, except reduce buttermilk to ¼ cup and combine it with 1 cup applesauce.

Per serving spice or applesauce variation: 265 cal., 9 g total fat (4 g sat. fat), 47 mg chol., 182 mg sodium, 41 g carbo., 1 g fiber, 4 g pro.
Daily Values: 4% vit. A, 1% vit. C, 7% calcium, 7% iron
Exchanges: 1 Starch, 2 Other Carbo., 1½ Fat

Fruit and Nut Spice Cake: Prepare as on page 168, except fold 1 cup chopped walnuts, ¾ cup snipped dried apricots, and ½ cup flaked coconut into the batter.

Per serving: 372 cal., 17 g total fat (6 g sat. fat), 46 mg chol., 182 mg sodium, 50 g carbo., 2 g fiber, 6 g pro.
Daily Values: 10% vit. A, 1% vit. C, 7% calcium, 10% iron
Exchanges: 1 Starch, 2½ Other Carbo., 2½ Fat

Oatmeal Cake

Oatmeal Cake

Prep: 1 hour **Bake:** 40 minutes **Oven:** 350°F
Cool: 20 minutes + 1 hour **Broil:** 2 minutes
Makes: 12 servings

- ½ **cup butter**
- 2 **eggs**
- 1¼ **cups boiling water**
- 1 **cup rolled oats**
- 2 **cups all-purpose flour**
- 2 **teaspoons baking powder**
- ¾ **teaspoon ground cinnamon**
- ½ **teaspoon baking soda**
- ½ **teaspoon salt**
- ¼ **teaspoon ground nutmeg**
- ¾ **cup granulated sugar**
- ½ **cup packed brown sugar**
- 1 **teaspoon vanilla**
- 1 **recipe Broiled Nut Topping**

1. Allow butter and eggs to stand at room temperature for 30 minutes. In a small bowl pour the boiling water over the oats. Stir until combined; let stand for 20 minutes. Meanwhile, grease and lightly flour a 9-inch springform pan; set pan aside. In a medium bowl stir together flour, baking powder, cinnamon, baking soda, salt, and nutmeg; set aside.

2. Preheat oven to 350°F. In a large mixing bowl beat the butter with an electric mixer on medium to high speed for 30 seconds. Add granulated sugar, brown sugar, and vanilla; beat until well combined (see photo, page 164). Add eggs one at a time, beating well after each addition. Alternately add the flour mixture and oatmeal mixture to the butter mixture, beating on low speed after each addition just until combined. Spread batter into prepared pan.

3. Bake for 40 to 45 minutes or until a wooden toothpick inserted near center comes out clean. Cool cake in pan on a wire rack for 20 minutes. Loosen sides of cake from pan; remove sides of pan. Cool on wire rack at least 1 hour more.

4. Transfer cake to a baking sheet. Spread Broiled Nut Topping over cake. Broil about 4 inches from heat for 2 to 3 minutes or until topping is bubbly and golden. Cool on a wire rack before serving.

Broiled Nut Topping: In medium saucepan combine ¼ cup butter and 2 tablespoons half-and-half, light cream, or milk. Cook and stir until butter melts. Add ½ cup packed brown sugar; stir until sugar dissolves. Remove from heat. Stir in ¾ cup chopped pecans or walnuts and ⅓ cup flaked coconut.

Per serving: 410 cal., 20 g total fat (10 g sat. fat), 70 mg chol., 273 mg sodium, 54 g carbo., 2 g fiber, 5 g pro.
Daily Values: 11% vit. A, 8% calcium, 11% iron
Exchanges: 1 Starch, 2½ Other Carbo., 4 Fat

Making Sour Milk

When a recipe calls for buttermilk and you have none, substitute sour milk.

Use the same amount of sour milk as buttermilk. For each 1 cup of sour milk, place 1 tablespoon lemon juice or vinegar in a glass measuring cup. Add enough milk to make 1 cup total liquid; stir. Let the mixture stand for 5 minutes before using.

Italian Cream Cake

Italian Cream Cake

A sprinkle of toasted pecans between the layers adds just the right amount of crunch.

Prep: 1 hour **Bake:** 25 minutes
Oven: 350°F **Cool:** 1 hour **Makes:** 16 servings

> 5 **eggs**
> ½ **cup butter**
> 2 **cups all-purpose flour**
> 1 **teaspoon baking soda**
> ½ **cup shortening**
> 2 **cups sugar**
> 1 **teaspoon vanilla**
> 1 **cup buttermilk or sour milk (see tip, page 169)**
> 1 **cup flaked coconut**
> ½ **cup finely chopped pecans, toasted (see tip, page 265)**
> 1 **recipe Cream Cheese Frosting (page 185)**
> ¾ **cup chopped pecans, toasted (see tip, page 265)**

1. Separate eggs. Allow egg yolks, egg whites, and butter to stand at room temperature for 30 minutes. Meanwhile, grease and flour three 8×1½-inch or 9×1½-inch round cake pans (see photo, page 163); set pans aside. In a medium bowl combine flour and baking soda; set aside.

2. Preheat oven to 350°F. In an extra-large mixing bowl beat butter and shortening with an electric mixer on medium to high speed for 30 seconds. Add sugar; beat until well combined (see photo, page 164). Add the egg yolks and vanilla; beat on medium speed until combined. Alternately add flour mixture and buttermilk to

butter mixture, beating on low speed after each addition just until combined. Fold in coconut and the ½ cup finely chopped pecans.

3. Thoroughly wash the beaters. In a medium mixing bowl beat egg whites until stiff peaks form (tips stand straight; see photo 2, page 182). Fold about one-third of the egg whites into cake batter to lighten. Fold in remaining whites. Spread batter evenly into the prepared pans.

4. Bake about 25 minutes for 9-inch pans, about 35 minutes for 8-inch pans, or until a wooden toothpick inserted near centers comes out clean. Cool cake layers in pans on wire racks for 10 minutes. Remove cake layers from pans. Cool thoroughly on wire racks.

5. Place one cake layer, bottom side up, on serving plate. Spread with about ½ cup Cream Cheese Frosting; sprinkle with ¼ cup pecans. Top with second cake layer, rounded (top) side up. Spread with ½ cup frosting and sprinkle with ¼ cup nuts. Place the remaining cake layer on top, rounded (top) side up; spread top and sides of cake with remaining frosting. Press remaining nuts into frosting around side of cake. Store cake in the refrigerator for up to 2 days.

Per serving: 618 cal., 34 g total fat (14 g sat. fat), 112 mg chol., 251 mg sodium, 77 g carbo., 2 g fiber, 5 g pro.
Daily Values: 13% vit. A, 5% calcium, 7% iron
Exchanges: ½ Starch, 4½ Other Carbo., 7 Fat

Burnt Sugar Candy Bar Cake

Cooking the sugar until it's caramelized, or "burnt," gives the cake a rich flavor and its name.

Prep: 70 minutes **Bake:** 25 minutes **Oven:** 350°F
Cool: 1 hour **Makes:** 16 servings

> ¾ **cup sugar**
> ¾ **cup hot water**
> 2 **eggs**
> ⅔ **cup butter**
> 3 **cups all-purpose flour**
> 1½ **teaspoons baking powder**
> ½ **teaspoon salt**
> ¼ **teaspoon baking soda**
> 1½ **cups sugar**
> 2 **teaspoons vanilla**
> 1 **recipe Browned Butter-Cream Cheese Frosting**
> 1 **cup finely chopped assorted candy bars**
> **Coarsely chopped assorted candy bars (optional)**

1. In a large skillet cook the ¾ cup sugar over medium-high heat until the sugar just begins to melt. Do not stir. Reduce heat; cook until sugar is golden brown, 1 to 3 minutes more, stirring mixture constantly. Carefully stir in hot water (syrup will form lumps). Bring mixture to boiling; reduce heat. Continue stirring until mixture is free of lumps. Remove from heat. Pour syrup into a large glass measuring cup. Add additional *water* to equal 1¾ cups liquid. Set sugar syrup aside to cool to room temperature.

2. Separate eggs. Allow egg yolks, egg whites, and butter to stand at room temperature for 30 minutes. Meanwhile, grease and lightly flour three 8×1½-inch round cake pans (see photo, page 163); set pans aside. Stir together flour, baking powder, salt, and baking soda; set aside.

3. Preheat oven to 350°F. In a large mixing bowl beat butter with an electric mixer on medium to high speed for 30 seconds. Add the 1½ cups sugar, the egg yolks, and the vanilla; beat until well combined. Alternately add the flour mixture and sugar syrup to butter mixture, beating on low speed after each addition just until combined.

4. Thoroughly wash beaters. In a clean medium mixing bowl beat egg whites on medium speed until stiff peaks form (tips stand straight; see photo 2, page 182). Fold egg whites into batter. Spread batter evenly into the prepared pans.

5. Bake for 25 to 30 minutes or until a wooden toothpick inserted near centers comes out clean. Cool cake layers in pans on wire racks for 10 minutes. Remove cake layers from pans. Cool thoroughly on wire racks.

6. To assemble, turn two layers bottom sides up; spread each with ½ cup of the Browned Butter-Cream Cheese Frosting. Sprinkle each frosted layer with half of the finely chopped candy. Stack these layers on cake plate, frosted sides up. Place the remaining cake layer on top, rounded (top) side up. Spread remaining frosting on top and sides of cake. If desired, garnish with the coarsely chopped candy bar pieces.

Browned Butter-Cream Cheese Frosting: In a small saucepan heat and stir ½ cup butter over low heat until melted. Continue heating until butter turns a light golden brown. Remove saucepan from heat. In a large bowl combine two 3-ounce packages softened cream cheese and 3 tablespoons softened butter. Beat with an electric mixer on medium speed until smooth. Beat in 2 cups powdered sugar. Beat in the browned butter and ¼ teaspoon vanilla. Gradually beat in 4½ cups additional powdered sugar and 2 to 3 teaspoons milk, beating until the frosting reaches spreading consistency.

Per serving: 594 cal., 24 g total fat (12 g sat. fat), 82 mg chol., 294 mg sodium, 92 g carbo., 1 g fiber, 5 g pro.
Daily Values: 14% vit. A, 4% calcium, 7% iron
Exchanges: 1 Starch, 5 Other Carbo., 5 Fat

Banana Cake

Prep: 50 minutes **Bake:** 25 minutes **Oven:** 350°F
Cool: 1 hour **Makes:** 12 to 16 servings

- 2 **eggs**
- 2¼ **cups all-purpose flour**
- 1½ **cups sugar**
- 1½ **teaspoons baking powder**
- 1 **teaspoon baking soda**
- ½ **teaspoon salt**
- 1 **cup mashed ripe banana (about 3)**
- ¾ **cup buttermilk or sour milk (see tip, page 169)**
- ½ **cup shortening**
- 1 **teaspoon vanilla**

1. Allow eggs to stand at room temperature for 30 minutes. Meanwhile, grease and lightly flour two 8×1½-inch or 9×1½-inch round cake pans (see photo, page 163) or grease one 13×9×2-inch baking pan; set pan(s) aside.

2. Preheat oven to 350°F. In a large mixing bowl stir together flour, sugar, baking powder, baking soda, and salt. Add banana, buttermilk, shortening, and vanilla. Beat with an electric mixer on low speed until combined. Add eggs; beat on medium speed for 2 minutes. Spread batter evenly into the prepared pan(s).

3. Bake for 25 to 30 minutes for round pans, about 30 minutes for 13×9×2-inch pan, or until a wooden toothpick inserted near center(s) comes out clean. Cool on wire racks for 10 minutes. Remove cake layers from pans; cool thoroughly on racks. Or place 13×9×2-inch cake in pan on wire rack; cool thoroughly. Frost with desired frosting (see pages 184 to 186).

Per serving: 294 cal., 10 g total fat (3 g sat. fat), 36 mg chol., 279 mg sodium, 48 g carbo., 1 g fiber, 4 g pro.
Daily Values: 2% vit. A, 5% vit. C, 6% calcium, 7% iron
Exchanges: 1 Starch, 2 Other Carbo., 2 Fat

Carrot Cake

Gumdrop carrots, as shown on page 161, make a fun garnish for this thoroughly American cake.

Prep: 1 hour **Bake:** 30 minutes
Oven: 350°F **Cool:** 1 hour **Makes:** 12 servings

- 4 **eggs, beaten**
- 2 **cups all-purpose flour**
- 2 **cups sugar**
- 2 **teaspoons baking powder**
- 1 **teaspoon ground cinnamon (optional)**
- ½ **teaspoon salt**
- ½ **teaspoon baking soda**
- 3 **cups finely shredded carrot* (lightly packed)**
- ¾ **cup cooking oil**
- 1 **recipe Cream Cheese Frosting (page 185)**
- ½ **cup finely chopped pecans, toasted (optional) (see tip, page 265)**

1. Allow eggs to stand at room temperature for 30 minutes. Meanwhile, grease two 9×1½-inch round cake pans. Line pans with waxed paper; grease the paper. Set pans aside.

2. Preheat oven to 350°F. In a large bowl stir together flour, sugar, baking powder, cinnamon (if desired), salt, and baking soda; set aside.

3. In another bowl combine eggs, carrot, and oil. Add egg mixture to flour mixture. Stir until combined. Pour batter into the prepared pans.

4. Bake for 30 to 35 minutes or until a wooden toothpick inserted near the centers comes out clean. Cool cake layers in pans on wire racks for 10 minutes. Remove cake layers from pans; cool thoroughly on wire racks.

5. Fill and frost with Cream Cheese Frosting. If desired, sprinkle chopped pecans over frosting. Cover and store cake in the refrigerator for up to 3 days.

*Note: The carrots should be finely shredded or they may sink to the bottom of the cake layer during baking.

Ginger-Carrot Cake: Prepare as above, except omit the cinnamon; add 2 teaspoons grated fresh ginger or ¾ teaspoon ground ginger with the eggs, carrot, and oil.

Per serving carrot or ginger-carrot variation: 679 cal., 30 g total fat (12 g sat. fat), 113 mg chol., 373 mg sodium, 98 g carbo., 1 g fiber, 6 g pro.
Daily Values: 86% vit. A, 3% vit. C, 5% calcium, 9% iron
Exchanges: 1 Starch, 5½ Other Carbo., 6 Fat

Apple Cake

A slice of this moist, spiced cake and a mug of warm cider or hot cocoa make the quintessential autumn snack. See photo, page 161.

Prep: 55 minutes **Bake:** 1 hour
Oven: 350°F **Cool:** 2 hours **Makes:** 12 servings

- 2 **eggs, beaten**
- 3 **cups all-purpose flour**
- 2 **teaspoons finely shredded lemon peel**
- 1 **teaspoon baking powder**
- 1 **teaspoon baking soda**
- 1 **teaspoon ground cinnamon**
- ¼ **teaspoon ground allspice**
- ¼ **teaspoon salt**
- 1 **cup granulated sugar**
- 1 **cup packed brown sugar**
- 1 **cup cooking oil**
- ½ **cup applesauce**
- 1 **tablespoon vanilla**
- 3 **cups chopped, peeled apple (4 to 5 medium)**
- 1 **cup chopped pecans, toasted (see tip, page 265)**
- **Powdered sugar**

1. Allow eggs to stand at room temperature for 30 minutes. Meanwhile, grease and lightly flour a 10-inch tube pan; set pan aside. In a medium bowl stir together flour, lemon peel, baking powder, baking soda, cinnamon, allspice, and salt; set aside.

2. Preheat oven to 350°F. In a large mixing bowl combine eggs, granulated sugar, brown sugar, oil, applesauce, and vanilla. Beat with an electric mixer on medium speed for 2 minutes. Add flour mixture to egg mixture and beat on low speed just until combined (batter will be thick). Fold in apple and pecans. Spoon batter into the prepared pan; spread evenly.

3. Bake about 1 hour or until a wooden toothpick inserted near center comes out clean. Cool cake in pan on a wire rack for 10 minutes. Remove from pan. Cool thoroughly on wire rack. Cover and store in refrigerator. Just before serving, sift powdered sugar over cake.

Per serving: 508 cal., 26 g total fat (4 g sat. fat), 35 mg chol., 206 mg sodium, 66 g carbo., 3 g fiber, 5 g pro.
Daily Values: 2% vit. A, 3% vit. C, 7% calcium, 14% iron
Exchanges: 1 Starch, 3½ Other Carbo., 5 Fat

Granny Cake

Granny Cake

Also known as the hummingbird cake, this old-fashioned treat is one of those recipes that's been traded over backyard fences for years.

Prep: 55 minutes **Bake:** 70 minutes
Oven: 325°F **Cool:** 2 hours **Makes:** 12 servings

- ¾ cup butter
- 3 eggs
- 3 cups all-purpose flour
- 2 cups granulated sugar
- 1 teaspoon baking soda
- 1 teaspoon ground nutmeg
- ½ teaspoon salt
- ½ teaspoon ground cloves
- 2 cups mashed ripe banana (about 6)
- 1 8-ounce can crushed pineapple, undrained
- 2 teaspoons vanilla
- 1 cup finely chopped pecans
  Powdered sugar (optional)

1. Allow butter and eggs to stand at room temperature for 30 minutes. Meanwhile, grease and flour a 10-inch fluted or plain tube pan; set pan aside. Stir together flour, granulated sugar, baking soda, nutmeg, salt, and cloves; set aside.

2. Preheat oven to 325°F. In a large mixing bowl beat butter with an electric mixer on medium speed for 30 seconds. Add eggs, banana, undrained pineapple, and vanilla. Beat until combined. Add flour mixture to banana mixture. Beat on low speed until combined. Beat on medium speed for 1 minute. Fold in pecans. Spoon batter into prepared pan; spread evenly.

3. Bake for 70 to 75 minutes or until a wooden toothpick inserted near the center comes out clean. Cool cake in pan on a wire rack for 10 minutes. Remove cake from pan. Cool thoroughly on wire rack. If desired, sift powdered sugar over cake just before serving.

Per serving: 477 cal., 20 g total fat (9 g sat. fat), 86 mg chol., 343 mg sodium, 70 g carbo., 3 g fiber, 6 g pro.
Daily Values: 12% vit. A, 9% vit. C, 3% calcium, 12% iron
Exchanges: 1 Starch, 3½ Other Carbo., 4 Fat

Gingerbread

Gingerbread tastes best when served warm. Further enhance the spicy wedges with Vanilla Sauce (page 525) or Lemon Sauce (page 524).

Prep: 20 minutes **Bake:** 35 minutes **Oven:** 350°F
Cool: 30 minutes **Makes:** 9 servings

- 1½ cups all-purpose flour
- ¾ teaspoon ground cinnamon
- ¾ teaspoon ground ginger
- ½ teaspoon baking powder
- ½ teaspoon baking soda
- ½ cup shortening
- ¼ cup packed brown sugar
- 1 egg
- ½ cup mild-flavored molasses
- ½ cup water

1. Preheat oven to 350°F. Grease a 9×1½-inch round cake pan; set pan aside. In a medium bowl stir together flour, cinnamon, ginger, baking powder, and baking soda; set aside.

2. In a large mixing bowl beat the shortening with an electric mixer on medium speed for 30 seconds. Add brown sugar; beat until well combined (see photo, page 164). Add egg and molasses; beat for 1 minute more. Alternately add flour mixture and water to shortening mixture, beating on low speed after each addition until combined. Spread batter into the prepared pan.

3. Bake for 35 to 40 minutes or until a wooden toothpick inserted near the center comes out clean. Cool in pan on a wire rack for 30 minutes. Serve warm.

Per serving: 253 cal., 11 g total fat (3 g sat. fat), 24 mg chol., 109 mg sodium, 34 g carbo., 1 g fiber, 3 g pro.
Daily Values: 1% vit. A, 1% vit. C, 7% calcium, 13% iron
Exchanges: 2 Other Carbo., 2 Fat

Busy-Day Cake

Prep: 25 minutes **Bake:** 30 minutes **Oven:** 350°F
Cool: 30 minutes **Makes:** 8 servings

- 1⅓ **cups all-purpose flour**
- ⅔ **cup sugar**
- 2 **teaspoons baking powder**
- ⅔ **cup milk**
- ¼ **cup butter, softened**
- 1 **egg**
- 1 **teaspoon vanilla**
- 3 **cups assorted fresh berries**
- 1 **recipe Whipped Cream (page 271) (optional)**

1. Preheat oven to 350°F. Grease an 8×1½-inch round cake pan; set the pan aside.

2. In a medium mixing bowl combine flour, sugar, and baking powder. Add milk, butter, egg, and vanilla. Beat with an electric mixer on low speed until combined. Beat on medium speed for 1 minute. Spread into the prepared pan.

3. Bake about 30 minutes or until a wooden toothpick inserted in center comes out clean. Cool in pan on a wire rack about 30 minutes. Serve warm with berries and, if desired, Whipped Cream.

Per serving: 224 cal., 7 g total fat (3 g sat. fat), 44 mg chol.,
123 mg sodium, 36 g carbo., 2 g fiber, 4 g pro.
Daily Values: 5% vit. A, 53% vit. C, 6% calcium, 7% iron
Exchanges: ½ Fruit, 1 Starch, 1 Other Carbo., 1½ Fat

Busy-Day Cake with Broiled Coconut Topping:
Prepare as above, except omit berries and Whipped Cream. While cake is baking, mix ¼ cup packed brown sugar and 2 tablespoons softened butter. Stir in 1 tablespoon milk. Stir in ½ cup coconut and, if desired, ¼ cup chopped nuts. Spread over warm cake. Broil 4 inches from heat 2 to 3 minutes or until golden. Cool on wire rack 30 minutes. Serve warm.

Per serving: 295 cal., 13 g total fat (8 g sat. fat), 52 mg chol.,
170 mg sodium, 42 g carb., 1 g fiber, 4 g pro.
Daily Values: 7% vit. A, 6% calcium, 6% iron
Exchanges: 1 Starch, 2 Other Carbo., 2½ Fat

Pineapple Upside-Down Cake

Prep: 20 minutes **Bake:** 30 minutes **Oven:** 350°F
Cool: 35 minutes **Makes:** 8 servings

- 2 **tablespoons butter**
- ⅓ **cup packed brown sugar**
- 1 **tablespoon water**
- 1 **8-ounce can pineapple slices, drained and halved**
- 4 **maraschino cherries, halved**
- 1⅓ **cups all-purpose flour**
- ⅔ **cup granulated sugar**
- 2 **teaspoons baking powder**
- ⅔ **cup milk**
- ¼ **cup butter, softened**
- 1 **egg**
- 1 **teaspoon vanilla**

1. Preheat the oven to 350°F. Place the 2 tablespoons butter in a 9×1½-inch round cake pan. Place pan in oven until butter melts. Stir in brown sugar and water. Arrange pineapple and cherries in pan. Set aside. In a medium mixing bowl stir together flour, granulated sugar, and baking powder. Add milk, ¼ cup butter, the egg, and vanilla. Beat with an electric mixer on low speed until combined. Beat on medium speed 1 minute. Spoon batter into prepared pan.

2. Bake 30 to 35 minutes or until wooden toothpick inserted in center comes out clean. Cool on a wire rack 5 minutes. Loosen sides of cake; invert onto plate. Cool 30 minutes; serve warm.

Per serving: 292 cal., 10 g total fat (6 g sat. fat), 53 mg chol.,
216 mg sodium, 47 g carbo., 1 g fiber, 4 g pro.
Daily Values: 9% vit. A, 5% vit. C, 11% calcium, 8% iron
Exchanges: 1 Starch, 2 Other Carbo., 2 Fat

Busy-Day Cake

Fruitcake

Prep: 30 minutes **Bake:** 1¼ hours **Oven:** 300°F
Cool: 2 hours **Store:** 2 weeks **Makes:** 16 servings

- 1½ **cups all-purpose flour**
- 1 **teaspoon ground cinnamon**
- ½ **teaspoon baking powder**
- ¼ **teaspoon baking soda**
- ¼ **teaspoon ground nutmeg**
- ¼ **teaspoon ground allspice**
- ¼ **teaspoon ground cloves**
- ¾ **cup diced mixed candied fruits and peels**
- ½ **cup raisins or snipped pitted dates**
- ½ **cup candied red or green cherries, quartered**
- ½ **cup chopped pecans or walnuts**
- 2 **eggs**
- ½ **cup packed brown sugar**
- ½ **cup orange juice or apple juice**
- ⅓ **cup butter, melted**
- 2 **tablespoons mild-flavored molasses**
  Brandy or fruit juice

1. Preheat oven to 300°F. Grease and lightly flour one 8×4×2-inch loaf pan or two 5¾×3×2-inch loaf pans. Set pan(s) aside. In a large bowl stir together flour, cinnamon, baking powder, baking soda, nutmeg, allspice, and cloves. Add fruits and peels, raisins, cherries, and nuts; mix well.

2. In another bowl beat eggs; stir in brown sugar, juice, butter, and molasses until combined. Stir egg mixture into fruit mixture. Spread batter into the prepared pan(s). (The smaller pans will be quite full.)

3. Bake for 1¼ to 1½ hours for the 8×4×2-inch pan, 55 to 65 minutes for the 5¾×3×2-inch pans, or until a wooden toothpick inserted near center(s) comes out clean. If necessary, cover pan(s) loosely with foil the last 10 to 15 minutes of baking to prevent overbrowning. Place cake in pan(s) on a wire rack; cool thoroughly.

4. Remove cake from pan(s). Wrap cake in brandy- or fruit-juice-moistened 100-percent-cotton cheesecloth. Wrap in foil. Store in the refrigerator for 2 to 8 weeks to mellow flavors. Remoisten cheesecloth with brandy or fruit juice weekly or as needed.

Per serving: 228 cal., 7 g total fat (3 g sat. fat),
37 mg chol., 95 mg sodium, 37 g carbo., 1 g fiber, 3 g pro.
Daily Values: 4% vit. A, 7% vit. C, 4% calcium, 7% iron
Exchanges: ½ Starch, ½ Fruit, 1½ Other Carbo., 1½ Fat

Cupcake Mania

Fun to make and fun to eat, cupcakes are a perfect sweet for any occasion. Most butter-type cakes can be baked as cupcakes. Grease and flour a muffin pan or line cups with paper bake cups. Fill cups half full with batter. Bake at the same temperature called for in the cake recipe but reduce the baking time by one-third to one-half. A two-layer cake usually makes 24 to 30 cupcakes. Cool and frost as desired or try one of the ideas below.

Caramel-Pecan Cupcakes: Drizzle caramel ice cream topping over yellow cupcakes. Sprinkle with coarsely chopped pecans.

Chocolate-Chocolate Cupcakes: Spoon Ganache (page 186) over chocolate cupcakes. Just before serving, garnish with fresh raspberries and mint leaves.

Candy Bar Cupcakes: Frost cupcakes with canned chocolate frosting or Chocolate Butter Frosting (page 185). Top with cut-up chocolate candy bars.

Cupcake Sundaes: Top each cupcake with a small scoop of ice cream. Spoon chocolate ice cream topping over ice cream. Garnish with maraschino cherries.

Teacup Cakes: Break candy canes in half. Set halves with crooks aside. Coarsely chop the straight portions of the candy canes. Frost cupcakes with canned creamy white or vanilla frosting. Press the crook halves of the candy canes into the tops of the cupcakes and position the candy canes to look like teacup handles. Sprinkle tops with the chopped candy canes.

Walnut Mocha Torte

Walnut Mocha Torte

The batter is mixed in a blender or food processor. The results are moist, nutty, and spectacular.

Prep: 40 minutes **Bake:** 20 minutes **Oven:** 350°F
Cool: 1 hour **Chill:** 2 hours **Makes:** 8 servings

  2 **cups walnuts or pecans, toasted (see tip, page 265)**
  2 **tablespoons all-purpose flour**
2½ **teaspoons baking powder**
  4 **eggs**
  ¾ **cup sugar**
  1 **recipe Mocha Frosting**
     Chocolate curls (optional)

1. Preheat oven to 350°F. Grease the bottoms of two 8×1½-inch round cake pans. Line pans with waxed paper; grease and lightly flour pans. Set pans aside. In a medium bowl combine nuts, flour, and baking powder; set aside.

2. In a blender or food processor combine eggs and sugar. Cover and blend or process until smooth, stopping and scraping sides as necessary. Add nut mixture. Cover and blend or process until smooth. Spread batter evenly in the prepared pans.

3. Bake for 20 to 25 minutes or until cakes spring back when lightly touched (centers may dip slightly). Cool cake layers on wire racks for 10 minutes. Remove cake layers from pans. Cool thoroughly on wire racks. Spread Mocha Frosting on each layer; stack layers. Loosely cover and chill cake for 2 to 24 hours. If desired, top with chocolate curls.

Mocha Frosting: In a chilled mixing bowl dissolve 1 teaspoon instant coffee crystals in 1 cup whipping cream. Add ⅓ cup sugar, ¼ cup unsweetened cocoa powder, and ½ teaspoon vanilla to cream mixture. Beat with an electric mixer on medium speed just until stiff peaks form (tips stand straight).

Per serving: 455 cal., 34 g total fat (10 g sat. fat), 147 mg chol., 122 mg sodium, 34 g carbo., 2 g fiber, 9 g pro.
Daily Values: 11% vit. A, 1% vit. C, 12% calcium, 10% iron
Exchanges: 2 Other Carbo., 1 Medium-Fat Meat, 5½ Fat

Sour Cream Pound Cake

Prep: 55 minutes **Bake:** 1 hour **Oven:** 325°F
Cool: 2 hours **Makes:** 10 servings

  ½ **cup butter**
  3 **eggs**
  ½ **cup dairy sour cream**
1½ **cups all-purpose flour**
  ¼ **teaspoon baking powder**
  ⅛ **teaspoon baking soda**
  1 **cup sugar**
  ½ **teaspoon vanilla**

1. Allow butter, eggs, and sour cream to stand at room temperature 30 minutes. Grease and lightly flour a 9×5×3-inch loaf pan; set pan aside. In a medium bowl stir together flour, baking powder, and baking soda; set aside.

2. Preheat the oven to 325°F. In a large mixing bowl beat butter with an electric mixer on medium to high speed for 30 seconds. Gradually add sugar, beating about 10 minutes or until light and fluffy (see photo, page 164). Beat in vanilla. Add eggs one at a time, beating 1 minute after each addition and scraping bowl frequently. Alternately add flour mixture and sour cream to butter mixture, beating on low to medium speed after each addition just until combined. Spread batter evenly into the prepared pan.

3. Bake for 60 to 75 minutes or until a wooden toothpick inserted near center comes out clean. Cool cake in pan on a wire rack 10 minutes. Remove from pan; cool thoroughly on rack.

Lemon-Poppy Seed Pound Cake: Prepare as above, except substitute ½ cup lemon yogurt for sour cream. Gently stir 1 teaspoon finely shredded lemon peel, 2 tablespoons lemon juice, and 2 tablespoons poppy seeds into batter.

Blueberry Pound Cake: Prepare as on page 176, except pour boiling water over ½ cup dried blueberries and let stand for 10 minutes. Drain well. Fold berries into the batter.

Per serving sour cream, lemon-poppy seed, or blueberry variations: 266 cal., 13 g total fat (7 g sat. fat), 93 mg chol., 117 mg sodium, 33 g carbo., 0 g fiber, 4 g pro.
Daily Values: 9% vit. A, 3% calcium, 6% iron
Exchanges: ½ Starch, 1½ Other Carbo., 2½ Fat

Vanilla-Fudge Marble Cake

Prep: 55 minutes **Bake:** 50 minutes **Oven:** 350°F
Cool: 2 hours **Makes:** 12 servings

- ¾ cup butter, softened
- 2 eggs
- 2¾ cups all-purpose flour
- 1½ teaspoons baking powder
- ½ teaspoon baking soda
- ½ teaspoon salt
- 1½ cups sugar
- 2 teaspoons vanilla
- 1¼ cups buttermilk or sour milk (see tip, page 169)
- ⅔ cup chocolate-flavored syrup
- 1 recipe Semisweet Chocolate Icing

1. Allow butter and eggs to stand at room temperature for 30 minutes. Meanwhile, grease and lightly flour a 10-inch fluted tube pan. In a medium bowl stir together flour, baking powder, baking soda, and salt. Set aside.

2. Preheat oven to 350°F. In a large mixing bowl beat butter with an electric mixer on low to medium speed about 30 seconds. Add sugar and vanilla; beat until fluffy (see photo, page 164). Add eggs one at a time, beating on low to medium speed 1 minute after each addition and scraping bowl frequently. Alternately add flour mixture and buttermilk to butter mixture, beating on low speed after each addition just until combined. Reserve 2 cups batter. Pour remaining batter into prepared pan.

3. In a bowl stir together the reserved 2 cups batter and chocolate-flavored syrup. Pour chocolate batter over vanilla batter in pan. Do not mix.

4. Bake about 50 minutes or until a wooden toothpick inserted near center comes out clean. Cool 15 minutes on a wire rack. Remove cake from pan; cool thoroughly on wire rack. Drizzle cake with Semisweet Chocolate Icing.

Semisweet Chocolate Icing: In a small saucepan heat ½ cup semisweet chocolate pieces, 2 tablespoons butter, 1 tablespoon light-colored corn syrup, and ¼ teaspoon vanilla over low heat, stirring until chocolate melts and mixture is smooth. Use immediately.

Per serving: 416 cal., 18 g total fat (10 g sat. fat), 75 mg chol., 400 mg sodium, 59 g carbo., 2 g fiber, 5 g pro.
Daily Values: 12% vit. A, 7% calcium, 9% iron
Exchanges: 1 Starch, 3 Other Carbo., 3½ Fat

Chiffon Cake

Prep: 55 minutes **Bake:** 65 minutes
Oven: 325°F **Cool:** 2 hours **Makes:** 12 servings

- 7 eggs
- 2¼ cups sifted cake flour or 2 cups sifted all-purpose flour
- 1½ cups sugar
- 1 tablespoon baking powder
- ¼ teaspoon salt
- ¾ cup cold water
- ½ cup cooking oil
- 2 teaspoons finely shredded orange peel
- 1 teaspoon finely shredded lemon peel
- 1 teaspoon vanilla
- ½ teaspoon cream of tartar

1. Separate eggs. Allow egg yolks and egg whites to stand at room temperature for 30 minutes. Meanwhile, in a large mixing bowl stir together flour, sugar, baking powder, and salt. Make a well in the center of flour mixture.

2. Preheat oven to 325°F. Add egg yolks, cold water, oil, orange peel, lemon peel, and vanilla to flour mixture. Beat with an electric mixer on low speed until combined. Beat on high speed about 5 minutes or until satin smooth; set aside.

3. Thoroughly wash beaters. In an extra-large mixing bowl beat egg whites and cream of tartar on medium speed until stiff peaks form (tips stand straight; see photo 2, page 182). Pour batter in thin stream over beaten egg whites; fold in gently. Pour into ungreased 10-inch tube pan.

4. Bake for 65 to 70 minutes or until top springs back when lightly touched. Immediately invert cake; cool thoroughly in pan. Loosen sides of cake from pan; remove cake.

Per serving: 292 cal., 12 g total fat (2 g sat. fat), 124 mg chol., 186 mg sodium, 41 g carbo., 0 g fiber, 5 g pro.
Daily Values: 4% vit. A, 2% vit. C, 9% calcium, 11% iron
Exchanges: ½ Starch, 2 Other Carbo., ½ Medium-Fat Meat, 2 Fat

Out of the Box

These shortcut cakes begin with packaged cake mix and get a few home-baked touches, a few sweet morsels in the batter, or a luscious filling or frosting for oven-fresh goodness.

Fruit Ribbon Cake **EASY**

Prep: 20 minutes **Bake:** per package directions
Oven: 350°F **Cool:** 1 hour **Makes:** 16 servings

  1 **package 2-layer-size white cake mix**
1⅓ **cups seedless red raspberry preserves**
 ⅔ **cup purchased lemon curd**
  1 **8-ounce container frozen whipped dessert topping, thawed**

1. Preheat oven to 350°F. Grease and lightly flour two 8×1½-inch or 9×1½-inch round cake pans (see photo, page 163). Set pans aside.

2. Prepare the cake mix according to the package directions. Divide batter evenly between the prepared pans. Bake according to the package directions.

3. Cool layers in pans on wire racks 10 minutes. Remove cake layers from pans; cool thoroughly on wire racks. Using a long-blade serrated knife, carefully cut each layer in half horizontally.

4. To assemble, place a half layer on a serving plate; spread with half of the raspberry preserves. Top with a second half layer; spread with lemon curd. Top with a third half layer; spread with remaining preserves. Top with the final half layer. If desired, cover and chill cake for up to 24 hours before icing. Spread top and sides of cake with whipped topping. Serve at once or chill for up to 4 hours before serving.

Per serving: 299 cal., 8 g total fat (3 g sat. fat), 10 mg chol., 244 mg sodium, 57 g carbo., 2 g fiber, 2 g pro.
Daily Values: 4% vit. C, 5% calcium, 8% iron
Exchanges: 3½ Other Carbo., 2 Fat

Cookies-and-Cream Cake **EASY**

Prep: 20 minutes **Bake:** per package directions
Oven: 350°F **Cool:** 1 hour **Makes:** 16 servings

  1 **package 2-layer-size white cake mix**
  1 **cup coarsely crushed chocolate sandwich cookies with white filling**
  1 **recipe Creamy White Frosting (page 185)**
  2 **ounces semisweet chocolate**
  1 **teaspoon shortening**

1. Preheat oven to 350°F. Grease and lightly flour two 9×1½-inch round cake pans (see photo, page 163). Set aside. Prepare cake mix according to package directions, folding crushed cookies into batter. Divide batter evenly between the prepared pans.

2. Bake according to package directions. Cool cake layers in pans on wire racks for 10 minutes. Remove layers from pans. Cool on wire racks.

3. Fill and frost cake with Creamy White Frosting.

4. In small heavy saucepan combine semisweet chocolate and shortening. Cook and stir over low heat until melted. Drizzle melted chocolate over top of cake.

Per serving: 448 cal., 20 g total fat (5 g sat. fat), 0 mg chol., 279 mg sodium, 68 g carbo., 1 g fiber, 3 g pro.
Daily Values: 5% calcium, 10% iron
Exchanges: 4½ Other Carbo., 4 Fat

Blueberry-Citrus Cake

Blueberries and citrus peel transform a simple lemon cake mix into a delectable treat. The tangy cream cheese-citrus frosting complements the moist cake.

Prep: 20 minutes **Bake:** 35 minutes **Oven:** 350°F
Cool: 1 hour **Makes:** 12 servings

  1 **package 2-layer-size lemon cake mix**
  1 **tablespoon finely shredded orange peel (set aside)**
 ½ **cup orange juice**
 ½ **cup water**
 ⅓ **cup cooking oil**
  3 **eggs**
1½ **cups fresh or frozen blueberries**
  1 **tablespoon finely shredded lemon peel**
  1 **recipe Citrus Frosting (page 179)**

1. Preheat oven to 350°F. Grease and lightly flour two 8×1½-inch or 9×1½-inch round cake pans (see photo, page 163). Set pans aside.

2. In a large mixing bowl combine cake mix, orange juice, water, and oil. Add eggs. Beat with electric mixer on low speed just until combined. Beat on medium speed for 2 minutes, scraping the sides of the bowl occasionally. Gently fold in blueberries, lemon peel, and orange peel. Pour batter into the prepared pans.

3. Bake for 35 to 40 minutes or until a wooden toothpick inserted near centers comes out clean. Cool cake layers in pans on wire racks for 10 minutes. Remove cake layers from pans; cool thoroughly on wire racks.

4. Fill and frost cake with Citrus Frosting. Store frosted cake in refrigerator.

Citrus Frosting: Finely shred 2 tablespoons orange peel and 1 tablespoon lemon peel; set aside. In a medium mixing bowl beat one 3-ounce package softened cream cheese and ¼ cup softened butter with an electric mixer on low to medium speed until fluffy. Add 3 cups powdered sugar and 2 tablespoons orange juice. Beat until combined. In a chilled small bowl beat 1 cup whipping cream with chilled beaters on medium speed until soft peaks form (tips curl); add whipped cream to cream cheese mixture. Add orange peel and lemon peel. Beat on low speed until combined.

Per serving: 502 cal., 24 g total fat (11 g sat. fat), 98 mg chol., 354 mg sodium, 70 g carbo., 1 g fiber, 4 g pro.
Daily Values: 12% vit. A, 19% vit. C, 11% calcium, 6% iron
Exchanges: 4½ Other Carbo., 5 Fat

Gooey Chocolate-Caramel Cake
EASY

It may seem like a lot of sweetened condensed milk and caramel sauce, but go ahead and pour it on— the gooey toppings make each forkful yummy!

Prep: 15 minutes **Bake:** per package directions
Cool: 1 hour **Makes:** 30 servings

> 1 package 2-layer-size German chocolate cake mix
> 1 14-ounce can sweetened condensed milk
> 1 12- to 12.5-ounce jar caramel ice cream topping
> 1 8-ounce carton frozen whipped dessert topping, thawed
> 3 1.4-ounce bars chocolate-covered English toffee, chopped

1. Prepare and bake the cake mix according to package directions for a 13×9×2-inch baking pan. Cool the cake thoroughly in the pan on a wire rack.

2. Using the handle of a wooden spoon, poke holes about 1 inch apart over surface of cake. Pour

the sweetened condensed milk over the cake. Pour caramel topping over cake. Spread dessert topping evenly over top. Before serving, sprinkle with the chopped toffee bars. Store leftover cake, covered, in the refrigerator for up to 24 hours.

Per serving: 222 cal., 7 g total fat (4 g sat. fat), 6 mg chol., 177 mg sodium, 33 g carbo., 1 g fiber, 2 g pro.
Daily Values: 1% vit. A, 1% vit. C, 5% calcium, 2% iron
Exchanges: 2 Other Carbo., 1½ Fat

Apple Upside-Down Spice Cake

Molasses lends its sweet, pungent flavor to this spice cake, while Brazil nuts give a buttery crunch to the brown sugar topping.

Prep: 25 minutes **Bake:** 40 minutes **Oven:** 350°F
Cool: 10 minutes **Makes:** 15 servings

> 2 large cooking apples, peeled, cored, and thinly sliced (about 2¾ cups)
> ½ cup chopped Brazil nuts
> 3 tablespoons butter
> 3 tablespoons packed brown sugar
> 1 package 2-layer-size spice cake mix
> 3 tablespoons molasses
> ½ cup whipping cream (optional)

1. Preheat oven to 350°F. Grease 13×9×2-inch baking pan. Set the pan aside.

2. In a large skillet cook and stir apple and nuts in hot butter over medium heat about 5 minutes or until apple is tender. Remove from heat; stir in brown sugar. Spread mixture in the bottom of the prepared pan.

3. Prepare cake mix according to package directions, reducing the water called for to 1 cup. Stir molasses into batter. Pour batter evenly over apple mixture.

4. Bake for 40 to 45 minutes or until a wooden toothpick inserted near center comes out clean. Cool in pan on wire rack for 10 minutes. Loosen sides of cake from pan with knife; invert cake onto serving plate.

5. If desired, in a chilled small mixing bowl beat whipping cream with an electric mixer on medium speed until soft peaks form. Serve cake warm with whipped cream.

Per serving: 283 cal., 14 g total fat (4 g sat. fat), 49 mg chol., 278 mg sodium, 38 g carbo., 1 g fiber, 2 g pro.
Daily Values: 4% vit. A, 1% vit. C, 8% calcium, 7% iron
Exchanges: 2½ Other Carbo., 3 Fat

Pumpkin Cake Roll

Pumpkin Cake Roll

Indulge in the classic holiday flavors of pumpkin and walnuts in this sumptuous roll-up cake.

Prep: 70 minutes **Bake:** 15 minutes **Oven:** 375°F
Cool: 1 hour **Chill:** 2 hours **Makes:** 8 servings

- 3 eggs
- ¾ cup all-purpose flour
- 2 teaspoons ground cinnamon
- 1 teaspoon baking powder
- 1 teaspoon ground ginger
- ½ teaspoon salt
- ½ teaspoon ground nutmeg
- 1 cup granulated sugar
- ⅔ cup canned pumpkin
- 1 teaspoon lemon juice
- 1 cup finely chopped walnuts
  Sifted powdered sugar
- 1 recipe Cream Cheese Filling

1. Allow eggs to stand at room temperature for 30 minutes. Meanwhile, grease a 15×10×1-inch baking pan. Line bottom of pan with waxed paper or parchment paper; grease paper. Set aside. In bowl combine flour, cinnamon, baking powder, ginger, salt, and nutmeg; set aside.

2. Preheat oven to 375°F. In a large mixing bowl beat eggs with an electric mixer on high speed about 5 minutes or until thick and lemon colored (see photo, page 181). Gradually beat in the granulated sugar. Stir in pumpkin and lemon juice. Fold flour mixture into pumpkin mixture.

Spread batter evenly in prepared pan. Sprinkle with walnuts.

3. Bake about 15 minutes or until the top springs back when lightly touched. Immediately loosen edges of cake from pan and turn cake out onto a towel sprinkled with sifted powdered sugar. Remove waxed paper. Roll towel and cake into a spiral, starting from a short side of the cake (see photo, below). Cool on a wire rack. Meanwhile, prepare Cream Cheese Filling.

4. Unroll cake; remove towel. Spread cake with the Cream Cheese Filling to within 1 inch of edges. Roll up cake; trim ends. Cover; chill for 2 to 48 hours.

Cream Cheese Filling: In a small bowl beat two 3-ounce packages softened cream cheese, ¼ cup softened butter, and ½ teaspoon vanilla with an electric mixer on medium speed until smooth. Gradually add 1 cup powdered sugar, beating after each addition until smooth.

Per serving: 455 cal., 25 g total fat (9 g sat. fat), 119 mg chol., 310 mg sodium, 52 g carbo., 2 g fiber, 8 g pro.
Daily Values: 74% vit. A, 3% vit. C, 7% calcium, 12% iron
Exchanges: ½ Starch, 3 Other Carbo., ½ Medium-Fat Meat, 4½ Fat

Starting from a short side, roll up the warm cake and the powdered sugar-coated towel. Let the cake cool.

Orange Sponge Cake LOW FAT

Prep: 70 minutes **Bake:** 55 minutes **Oven:** 325°F
Cool: 2 hours **Makes:** 12 servings

- 6 eggs
- 1 tablespoon finely shredded orange peel
- ½ cup orange juice or pineapple juice
- 1 teaspoon vanilla
- 1 cup sugar
- 1¼ cups all-purpose flour
- ½ teaspoon cream of tartar
- ½ cup sugar

1. Separate eggs. Allow egg yolks and whites to stand at room temperature for 30 minutes.

2. Preheat oven to 325°F. In a medium mixing bowl beat egg yolks with an electric mixer on high speed about 5 minutes or until thick and lemon colored (see photo, below). Add orange peel, orange juice, and vanilla; beat on low speed until combined. Gradually beat in the 1 cup sugar at low speed. Increase to medium speed; beat until mixture thickens slightly and doubles in volume (about 5 minutes total).

3. Sprinkle ¼ cup of the flour over egg yolk mixture; fold in until combined. Repeat with remaining flour, ¼ cup at a time. Set egg yolk mixture aside.

4. Thoroughly wash beaters. In a large mixing bowl beat egg whites and cream of tartar on medium speed until soft peaks form (tips curl; see photo 1, page 182). Gradually add the ½ cup sugar, beating on high speed until stiff peaks form (tips stand straight; see photo 2, page 182). Fold 1 cup of the beaten egg white mixture into the egg yolk mixture; fold egg yolk mixture into remaining egg white mixture. Pour batter into an ungreased 10-inch tube pan.

5. Bake 55 to 60 minutes or until cake springs back when lightly touched. Immediately invert cake; cool thoroughly in inverted pan. Loosen sides of cake from pan; remove from pan.

Lemon Sponge Cake: Prepare as on page 180, except substitute 2 teaspoons finely shredded lemon peel for the orange peel and ¼ cup lemon juice plus ¼ cup water for the orange juice or pineapple juice.

Chocolate Sponge Cake: Prepare as on page 180, except omit the orange peel. Reduce flour to 1 cup. Stir ⅓ cup unsweetened cocoa powder into the flour.

Almond Sponge Cake: Prepare as on page 180, except omit orange peel. Add ½ teaspoon almond extract with the orange juice or pineapple juice.

Per serving orange, lemon, chocolate, or almond variations: 184 cal., 3 g total fat (1 g sat. fat), 107 mg chol., 32 mg sodium, 36 g carbo., 0 g fiber, 5 g pro.
Daily Values: 4% vit. A, 10% vit. C, 2% calcium, 6% iron
Exchanges: ½ Starch, 2 Other Carbo., ½ Medium-Fat Meat

Beat egg yolks until they are thick and the color of lemons. Lift the beaters. If the yolks are sufficiently beaten, they will flow from the beaters in a thick stream.

Hot Milk Sponge Cake `LOW FAT`

For a low-calorie treat, dust this sponge cake lightly with powdered sugar or top with fresh fruit. For a sweeter treat, spread the cake with the topping from the Busy-Day Cake with Broiled Coconut Topping (page 174) and pop it under the broiler.

Prep: 45 minutes **Bake:** 20 minutes **Oven:** 350°F
Cool: 1 hour **Makes:** 9 servings

> **2 eggs**
> **1 cup all-purpose flour**
> **1 teaspoon baking powder**
> **1 cup sugar**
> **½ cup milk**
> **2 tablespoons butter**

1. Allow eggs to stand at room temperature for 30 minutes. Meanwhile, grease a 9×9×2-inch baking pan; set pan aside. In a small bowl stir together flour and baking powder; set aside.

2. Preheat oven to 350°F. In a medium mixing bowl beat eggs with electric mixer on high speed about 4 minutes or until thick and lemon colored (see photo, left). Gradually add sugar, beating on medium speed for 4 to 5 minutes or until light and fluffy. Add flour mixture; beat on low to medium speed just until combined.

3. In a small saucepan combine milk and butter. Heat and stir until butter melts; add to batter, beating until combined. Pour batter into the prepared pan.

4. Bake for 20 to 25 minutes or until a wooden toothpick inserted near the center comes out clean. Cool cake in pan on a wire rack.

Per serving: 180 cal., 4 g total fat (2 g sat. fat), 56 mg chol., 93 mg sodium, 33 g carbo., 0 g fiber, 3 g pro.
Daily Values: 4% vit. A, 5% calcium, 5% iron
Exchanges: ½ Starch, 1½ Other Carbo., 1 Fat

Cutting the Cake

How do you slice a beautiful cake without ending up with a plateful of crumbs?

Let a frosted cake stand at least 1 hour before cutting to give the frosting time to set up. Use a sharp knife for butter cakes and a long-blade serrated knife for angel food, sponge, and chiffon cakes. For cakes frosted with fluffy icings, between cuts dip the knife in hot water and shake it to remove excess water.

Angel Food Cake   [NO FAT]

Loosen the cooled cake from the pan by sliding a metal spatula between the cake and pan. So you don't cut into the cake, constantly press the spatula against the pan and draw it around in a continuous, not sawing, motion.

Prep: 50 minutes **Bake:** 40 minutes **Oven:** 350°F
Cool: 2 hours **Makes:** 12 servings

- 1½ **cups egg whites (10 to 12 large)**
- 1½ **cups sifted powdered sugar**
- 1 **cup sifted cake flour or sifted all-purpose flour**
- 1½ **teaspoons cream of tartar**
- 1 **teaspoon vanilla**
- 1 **cup granulated sugar**

1. In an extra-large mixing bowl allow the egg whites to stand at room temperature for 30 minutes. Meanwhile, sift powdered sugar and flour together three times; set aside.

2. Adjust baking rack to the lowest position in oven. Preheat oven to 350°F. Add cream of tartar and vanilla to egg whites. Beat with an electric mixer on medium speed until soft peaks form (tips curl; see photo 1, right). Gradually add granulated sugar, about 2 tablespoons at a time, beating until stiff peaks form (tips stand straight; see photo 2, right).

3. Sift about one-fourth of the flour mixture over beaten egg whites (see photo 3, right); fold in gently (see photo 4, right). (If bowl is too full, transfer to a larger bowl.) Repeat, folding in remaining flour mixture by fourths. Pour into an ungreased 10-inch tube pan. Gently cut through the batter to remove any large air pockets (see photo 5, right).

4. Bake on the lowest rack for 40 to 45 minutes or until top springs back when lightly touched. Immediately invert cake; cool thoroughly in the inverted pan. Loosen sides of cake from pan; remove cake from pan.

Chocolate Angel Food Cake: Prepare as above, except sift ¼ cup unsweetened cocoa powder with the flour mixture.

Honey Angel Food Cake: Prepare as at left, except in Step 2 after beating the egg white mixture to soft peaks, gradually pour ¼ cup honey in a thin stream over the egg white mixture and reduce granulated sugar to ½ cup.

Per serving plain, chocolate, or honey variations: 161 cal., 0 g total fat (0 g sat. fat), 0 mg chol., 51 mg sodium, 36 g carbo., 0 g fiber, 4 g pro.
Daily Values: 4% iron
Exchanges: ½ Starch, 2 Other Carbo.

1. Beat egg whites, cream of tartar, and vanilla until soft peaks form. The peaks will curl when the beaters are lifted from the mixture.

2. After adding granulated sugar, beat the egg white mixture until stiff peaks form. The peaks will stand straight up when the beaters are lifted from the mixture.

3. Sift flour mixture over stiffly beaten egg white mixture. If you don't have a sifter, press the dry mixture through a sieve.

4. To fold the flour mixture in, cut down through the egg white mixture with a rubber spatula; scrape across the bottom of the bowl and bring the spatula up and over, close to mixture's surface.

5. To eliminate any large air bubbles, gently cut through the batter in the pan with a narrow metal spatula or knife.

Orange Angel Food Sherbet Cake

Angel Food Ice Cream Cake

To save a step, replace the whipped cream with thawed frozen whipped dessert topping.

Prep: 45 minutes **Bake:** per package directions
Oven: 350°F **Cool:** per package directions
Freeze: 6½ hours **Makes:** 10 to 12 servings

- 1 **16-ounce package angel food cake mix**
- 1¼ **cups water**
- 4 **cups (2 pints) strawberry ice cream, softened**
- 2 **cups whipping cream**
- ¼ **cup sugar**
- 1 **teaspoon vanilla**
- 1 **cup small, whole strawberries**

1. Prepare cake mix according to package directions using the 1¼ cups water. Pour batter into an ungreased 10-inch tube pan. Gently cut through batter to remove any large air pockets (see photo 5, page 182).

2. Bake angel food cake according to the package directions. Immediately invert cake; cool thoroughly in inverted pan. Loosen sides of cake from pan; remove cake.

3. Carefully split cake horizontally into thirds. Place the bottom layer and middle layer on freezer-safe platters; spread each layer with 2 cups softened ice cream. Freeze layers for 30 to 60 minutes or until ice cream is firm. Place the middle layer, ice cream side up, on top of the bottom layer. Top with remaining layer. Cover with plastic wrap; freeze 6 to 24 hours.

4. To serve, in chilled mixing bowl beat whipping cream, sugar, and vanilla with chilled beaters of an electric mixer on medium speed until soft peaks form.

5. Remove cake from freezer. Spread top and sides of frozen cake with whipped cream. Garnish with strawberries. Serve immediately.

Per serving: 543 cal., 31 g total fat (19 g sat. fat), 142 mg chol., 374 mg sodium, 61 g carbo., 1 g fiber, 8 g pro.
Daily Values: 22% vit. A, 23% vit. C, 20% calcium, 1% iron
Exchanges: ½ Starch, 3½ Other Carbo., 6 Fat

Chocolate Angel Food Ice Cream Cake: Prepare as at left, except add ¼ cup unsweetened cocoa powder to cake mix. Substitute peppermint ice cream for strawberry ice cream. Spread ¼ cup fudge ice cream topping over each ice cream layer. Substitute 2 to 3 tablespoons coarsely crushed peppermint candies for strawberries.

Per serving: 524 cal., 26 g total fat (16 g sat. fat), 91 mg chol., 450 mg sodium, 66 g carbo., 8 g pro.
Daily Values: 14% vit. A, 16% calcium, 2% iron
Exchanges: ½ Starch, 4 Other Carbo., 5 Fat

Orange Angel Food Sherbet Cake: Prepare as at left, except reduce water to 1 cup and add ¼ cup thawed orange juice concentrate to the water. Add 2 teaspoons finely shredded orange peel to cake mix. Substitute orange, lime, lemon, or rainbow sherbet for the strawberry ice cream. Garnish with orange, lemon, or lime peel strips instead of strawberries.

Per serving: 435 cal., 19 g total fat (12 g sat. fat), 66 mg chol., 349 mg sodium, 62 g carbo., 5 g pro.
Daily Values: 15% vit. A, 25 vit. C, 12% calcium, 1% iron
Exchanges: ½ Starch, 3½ Other Carbo., 4 Fat

Angel Food Cake Success

● Separate eggs carefully. A trace of yolk can prevent the whites from obtaining their maximum volume.

● Make sure bowls, beaters, and spatulas are clean. The smallest amount of fat will reduce the volume of the beaten whites.

● To reach the desired volume as quickly as possible, begin adding the granulated sugar as soon as soft peaks form.

● Beat the egg white mixture just until stiff peaks form. Do not overbeat mixture as this will cause the cake to be dry.

Meringue Frosting

Start to Finish: 25 minutes **Makes:** about 5 cups

1½ **cups sugar**
⅓ **cup cold water**
2 **egg whites**
¼ **teaspoon cream of tartar**
1 **teaspoon vanilla**

1. In the 2-quart top of a double boiler combine sugar, water, egg whites, and cream of tartar. Beat with an electric mixer on low speed for 30 seconds.

2. Place the pan over boiling water (upper pan should not touch the water). Cook, beating constantly with the electric mixer on high speed, for 10 to 13 minutes or until an instant-read thermometer registers 160°F when inserted in the mixture, stopping beaters and quickly scraping bottom and sides of pan every 5 minutes to prevent sticking. Remove pan from the heat; add vanilla. Beat about 1 minute more or until frosting is fluffy and holds soft peaks. This frosts tops and sides of two 8- or 9-inch cake layers or one 10-inch tube cake. Store frosted cake in the refrigerator and serve the same day it is made.

Per ½₁₂ recipe: 97 cal., 0 g total fat (0 g sat. fat), 0 mg chol., 10 mg sodium, 24 g carbo., 0 g fiber, 1 g pro.
Exchanges: 1½ Other Carbo.

Powdered Sugar Icing

Start to Finish: 10 minutes **Makes:** ½ cup

1 **cup powdered sugar**
¼ **teaspoon vanilla**
1 **tablespoon milk or orange juice**
Milk

1. In a small bowl combine powdered sugar, vanilla, and 1 tablespoon milk. Stir in additional milk, 1 teaspoon at a time, until icing reaches drizzling consistency. This makes enough to drizzle over one 10-inch tube cake.

Chocolate Powdered Sugar Icing: Prepare as above, except add 2 tablespoons unsweetened cocoa powder to the powdered sugar and use milk, not orange juice.

Per ½₁₂ recipe for plain or chocolate variation: 34 cal., 0 g total fat (0 g sat. fat), 0 mg chol., 1 mg sodium, 8 g carbo., 0 g fiber, 0 g pro.
Exchanges: ½ Other Carbo.

Easy Crème Fraîche Frosting

Start to Finish: 10 minutes **Makes:** about 3 cups

1 **8-ounce carton dairy sour cream**
1 **cup whipping cream**
¾ **cup powdered sugar**
1 **teaspoon vanilla**

1. In a large mixing bowl combine sour cream, whipping cream, powdered sugar, and vanilla. Beat with an electric mixer on medium speed until mixture thickens and holds soft peaks. This frosts the tops and sides of two 8- or 9-inch cake layers. Store frosted cake in refrigerator.

Per ½₁₂ recipe: 120 cal., 11 g total fat (7 g sat. fat), 36 mg chol., 19 mg sodium, 4 g carbo., 1 g pro.
Daily Values: 8% vit. A, 4% calcium
Exchanges: 2½ fat

Browned Butter Frosting

Start to Finish: 20 minutes **Makes:** about 3 cups

¾ **cup butter**
6 **cups powdered sugar**
4 to 5 **tablespoons milk**
2 **teaspoons vanilla**

1. In a small saucepan heat butter over low heat until melted. Continue heating until butter turns a light golden brown. Remove from heat. In a large mixing bowl combine powdered sugar, 4 tablespoons of the milk, and the vanilla. Add browned butter. Beat with an electric mixer on low speed until combined. Beat on medium to high speed, adding additional milk, if necessary, to reach spreading consistency. This frosts the tops and sides of two 8- or 9-inch cake layers.

Per ½₁₂ recipe: 303 cal., 12 g total fat (7 g sat. fat), 31 mg chol., 84 mg sodium, 51 g carbo., 0 g fiber, 0 g pro.
Daily Values: 7% vit. A, 1% calcium
Exchanges: 3½ Other Carbo., 2½ Fat

Butter Frosting

Start to Finish: 20 minutes **Makes:** about 4½ cups

¾ **cup butter, softened**
2 **pounds powdered sugar (about 8 cups)**
⅓ **cup milk**
2 **teaspoons vanilla**

1. In an extra-large mixing bowl beat butter with an electric mixer on medium speed until smooth. Gradually add 2 cups of the powdered sugar, beating well. Beat in ⅓ cup milk and vanilla. Gradually beat in remaining sugar. Beat in additional milk to reach spreading consistency. If desired, tint with *food coloring*. This frosts tops and sides of two 8- or 9-inch layers. (Halve recipe to frost 13×9-inch cake.)

Chocolate Butter Frosting: Prepare as on page 184, except beat ½ cup unsweetened cocoa powder into butter before adding sugar.

Lemon or Orange Butter Frosting: Prepare as on page 184, except substitute fresh lemon juice or orange juice for the milk and add ½ teaspoon finely shredded lemon peel or 1 teaspoon finely shredded orange peel with the juice.

Per ¹⁄₁₂ butter, chocolate, lemon, or orange variations: 401 cal., 12 g total fat (7 g sat. fat), 31 mg chol., 85 mg sodium, 76 g carbo., 0 g fiber, 0 g pro.
Daily Values: 7% vit. A, 1% calcium
Exchanges: 5 Other Carbo., 2½ Fat

Frosting Finesse

Follow these steps to adorn your cake with swirls of luscious, creamy frosting.

1. To keep crumbs from mixing with the frosting, brush away any loose crumbs from the cake layers with a pastry brush or your hand.

2. Tuck strips of waxed paper under the edge of the cake before frosting it. This keeps the plate clean and the strips can be discarded later. Spread about a half cup frosting on top of the first layer.

3. Place the second cake layer, rounded (top) side up, on top of the frosted layer. Spread a thin coating of frosting on the sides of the cake to seal in any crumbs.

4. Add more frosting to the sides. Frost the sides again, swirling and building up top edge ¼ inch above the cake. Spread remaining frosting on top of cake, blending the frosting at the edges.

Cream Cheese Frosting

Start to Finish: 20 minutes **Makes:** about 3¾ cups

- 1 8-ounce package cream cheese, softened
- ½ cup butter, softened
- 2 teaspoons vanilla
- 5½ to 6 cups powdered sugar

1. In a large mixing bowl beat cream cheese, butter, and vanilla with an electric mixer on medium speed until light and fluffy. Gradually beat in powdered sugar to reach spreading consistency. This frosts tops and sides of two 8- or 9-inch layers. (Halve the recipe to frost a 13×9×2-inch cake.) Cover and store the frosted cake in refrigerator.

Cocoa-Cream Cheese Frosting: Prepare as above, except beat ½ cup unsweetened cocoa powder into the cream cheese mixture and reduce powdered sugar to 5 to 5½ cups.

Per ¹⁄₁₂ recipe plain or cocoa variation: 350 cal., 14 g total fat (9 g sat. fat), 41 mg chol., 111 mg sodium, 55 g carbo., 0 g fiber, 2 g pro.
Daily Values: 10% vit. A, 2% calcium, 1% iron
Exchanges: 3½ Other Carbo., 3 Fat

Creamy White Frosting

For a bright white frosting, use clear vanilla.

Start to Finish: 25 minutes **Makes:** about 3 cups

- 1 cup shortening
- 1½ teaspoons vanilla
- ½ teaspoon almond extract
- 1 pound powdered sugar (about 4 cups)
- 3 to 4 tablespoons milk

1. In a large mixing bowl beat shortening, vanilla, and almond extract with an electric mixer on medium speed for 30 seconds. Slowly add about half of the powdered sugar, beating well. Add 2 tablespoons of the milk. Gradually beat in the remaining powdered sugar and enough remaining milk to reach spreading consistency. This frosts the tops and sides of two 8- or 9-inch cake layers. (Halve the recipe to frost a 13×9×2-inch cake. Or freeze half of the frosting in a freezer container for up to 3 months; thaw at room temperature before using.)

Per ¹⁄₁₂ recipe: 301 cal., 17 g total fat (4 g sat. fat), 0 mg chol., 2 mg sodium, 38 g carbo., 0 g fiber, 0 g pro.
Exchanges: 2½ Other Carbo., 3½ Fat

No-Cook Fudge Frosting

Make tasty fudge frosting the easy way with this no-cook recipe.

Start to Finish: 15 minutes **Makes:** about 4½ cups

 2 **pounds powdered sugar (about 8 cups)**
 1 **cup unsweetened cocoa powder**
 1 **cup butter, softened**
 ⅔ **cup boiling water**
 2 **teaspoons vanilla**
   Boiling water

1. In a large mixing bowl combine powdered sugar and cocoa powder. Add butter, boiling water, and vanilla. Beat with an electric mixer on low speed until combined. Beat 1 minute on medium speed. If necessary, cool 20 minutes or until mixture reaches spreading consistency. Or if frosting is too thick, add boiling water, 1 tablespoon at a time, until frosting reaches spreading consistency. This frosts tops and sides of two 8- or 9-inch cake layers. (Halve the recipe to frost a 13×9×2-inch cake.)

Per ¹⁄₁₂ recipe: 462 cal., 16 g total fat (10 g sat. fat), 41 mg chol., 110 mg sodium, 79 g carbo., 0 g fiber, 2 g pro.
Daily Values: 9% vit. A, 8% calcium, 5% iron
Exchanges: 5½ Other Carbo., 3 Fat

Chocolate-Sour Cream Frosting

Start to Finish: 20 minutes **Makes:** about 4½ cups

 1 **12-ounce package (2 cups) semisweet chocolate pieces**
 ½ **cup butter**
 1 **8-ounce carton dairy sour cream**
 4½ **cups powdered sugar**

1. In a large saucepan melt chocolate and butter over low heat, stirring frequently. Cool for 5 minutes. Stir in sour cream. Gradually add powdered sugar, beating with a wooden spoon until smooth. This frosts tops and sides of two 8- or 9-inch cake layers. (Halve the recipe to frost a 13×9×2-inch cake.) Cover and store frosted cake in the refrigerator.

Chocolate-Mint-Sour Cream Frosting: Prepare as above, except stir in ½ teaspoon mint extract with the sour cream.

Per ¹⁄₁₂ recipe chocolate or chocolate-mint variation:
400 cal., 20 g total fat (12 g sat. fat), 30 mg chol., 93 mg sodium, 48 g carbo., 4 g fiber, 1 g pro.
Daily Values: 9% vit. A, 2% calcium
Exchanges: 3 Other Carbo., 4 Fat

Ganache

Start to Finish: 35 minutes **Makes:** about 2 cups

 1 **cup whipping cream**
 12 **ounces milk chocolate, semisweet chocolate, or bittersweet chocolate; chopped**

1. In a medium saucepan bring whipping cream just to boiling over medium-high heat. Remove from heat. Add chocolate (do not stir). Let stand 5 minutes. Stir until smooth. Cool 15 minutes. This frosts an 8- or 9-inch cake layer.

Per ¹⁄₁₂ recipe: 209 cal., 15 g total fat (9 g sat. fat), 27 mg chol., 28 mg sodium, 19 g carbo., 0 g fiber, 2 g pro.
Daily Values: 6% vit. A, 5% calcium
Exchanges: 1 Other Carbo., 3 Fat

Truffle Frosting: Prepare Ganache as above, except double ingredients and use milk chocolate pieces only (do not use semisweet or bittersweet). Instead of cooling for 15 minutes, transfer to a large mixing bowl. Cover and chill overnight. Beat with an electric mixer on medium speed about 30 seconds or until fluffy and of spreading consistency. This frosts tops and sides of two 8- or 9-inch cake layers.

Per ¹⁄₁₂ of recipe: 406 cal., 30 g total fat (17 g sat. fat), 55 mg chol., 53 mg sodium, 36 g carbo., 0 g fiber, 5 g pro.
Daily Values: 12% vit. A, 10% calcium
Exchanges: 2½ Other Carbo., 6 Fat

Penuche Frosting

Start to Finish: 15 minutes **Makes:** 2 cups

 ½ **cup butter**
 1 **cup packed brown sugar**
 ¼ **cup milk**
 1 **teaspoon vanilla**
 3½ **cups powdered sugar**

1. In a 2-quart saucepan melt butter; stir in brown sugar. Cook and stir over medium heat until bubbly. Remove from heat. Add milk and vanilla; beat vigorously with a wooden spoon until smooth. Add powdered sugar; beat by hand about 5 minutes or until frosting reaches spreading consistency. Use immediately. This frosts tops of two 8- or 9-inch layers or top of one 13×9×2-inch cake.

Per ¹⁄₁₂ recipe: 277 cal., 8 g total fat (5 g sat. fat), 21 mg chol., 64 mg sodium, 53 g carbo., 0 g fiber, 0 g pro.
Daily Values: 5% vit. A, 2% calcium, 2% iron
Exchanges: 3½ Other Carbo., 1½ Fat

Candies

Marbled Nut Clusters, 195

Maple Nutty Candy, 192

Nut Rocha, 199

Candies Essentials

Although it's important to thoroughly understand any recipe before you begin, it is especially important with candy. Follow these suggestions for successful candy making.

Candy Basics

● Use the proper equipment and gather it before you begin.

● Use a high-quality saucepan and use the size pan specified in the recipe to ensure success (see tip, below right.)

● Take the time to accurately measure all ingredients and do not make ingredient substitutions or alter quantities.

● Do not halve or double recipes. The only safe way to double your yield is to make two separate batches.

● Consider the humidity because it affects the preparation of all types of candies. Avoid making candy on days with high humidity and only make divinity on a relatively dry day. No amount of beating will make divinity set up if the day is humid.

Cooking Tips

● Butter the sides of the saucepan. This helps prevent the mixture from climbing the pan sides and boiling over.

● Dissolve the sugar thoroughly. This should be done when the sugar is combined with the other ingredients and the mixture is brought to boiling.

● Prevent sugar crystals from forming and clumping together in the saucepan by stirring the mixture constantly but gently. You want the sugar to dissolve without the mixture splashing on the sides of the saucepan.

● If some of the candy mixture does splash on the pan sides, cover the pan, leaving it on the heat for 30 to 45 seconds. Steam will condense inside the pan and dissolve crystals that may have formed. This will prevent the mixture from boiling over. (Mixtures using milk products or molasses should not be covered; they foam if steam cannot escape and may boil over.)

● Clip a candy thermometer to the side of the saucepan after the sugar is dissolved. For an accurate reading, be sure that the bulb of the thermometer is completely covered with boiling liquid, not just with foam, and that it does not touch the bottom of the pan. Always read the thermometer at eye level.

● Keep the mixture boiling at a moderate, steady rate over the entire surface. Our recipes specify a range-top temperature to use for cooking the candy mixture. If you use this information as a guide, you'll be able to maintain the best rate of cooking for optimum results.

Candy Equipment

Use helpful candy-making equipment for the best results.

Because cooking candy mixtures to the correct temperatures is critical, using a candy thermometer is a must. Choose a thermometer with a mercury bulb that's set low enough to measure the heat in the syrup but won't touch the bottom of the pan. The thermometer should have a clip that attaches it to the pan.

A high-quality, heavy aluminum saucepan is the best choice for making candy. Aluminum pans conduct heat evenly. Other types of metal pans, such as stainless steel, require careful watching because they may have hot spots and may not heat evenly.

Using the correct size pan is equally important. Various pan sizes were used during testing. Each recipe includes a recommendation for the best size.

Chocolate-Covered Cherries, page 196

Fudge

Prep: 15 minutes **Cook:** 30 minutes **Cool:** 50 minutes
Makes: about 1¼ pounds (32 pieces)

  2 **cups sugar**
  ¾ **cup half-and-half or light cream**
  2 **ounces unsweetened chocolate, cut up**
  1 **teaspoon light-colored corn syrup**
  ⅛ **teaspoon salt**
  2 **tablespoons butter**
  1 **teaspoon vanilla**
  ½ **cup chopped nuts (optional)**

1. Line a 9×5×3-inch loaf pan with foil, extending the foil over the edges of the pan. Butter the foil; set pan aside.

2. Butter the sides of a 2-quart heavy saucepan. In the saucepan combine sugar, half-and-half, chocolate, corn syrup, and salt. Cook and stir over medium heat until mixture boils. Clip a candy thermometer to the side of the pan. Reduce heat to medium-low; continue boiling at a moderate, steady rate (see bottom photo, page 197), stirring occasionally, until thermometer registers 236°F, soft-ball stage (20 to 25 minutes). (Adjust heat as necessary to maintain a steady boil.)

3. Remove saucepan from heat. Add butter and vanilla but do not stir. Cool, without stirring, to 110°F (50 to 60 minutes). Remove thermometer from saucepan. Beat mixture vigorously with a clean wooden spoon until candy just begins to thicken. If desired, add nuts. Continue beating until the fudge just starts to lose its gloss (6 to 8 minutes total).

4. Immediately spread fudge evenly in prepared pan. Score into squares while warm. Let fudge cool to room temperature. When fudge is firm, use foil to lift it out of pan. Cut into squares. Store, tightly covered, for up to 1 week.

Per piece: 71 cal., 2 g total fat (1 g sat. fat), 4 mg chol.,
20 mg sodium, 13 g carbo., 0 g fiber, 0 g pro.
Daily Values: 1% vit. A, 1% calcium, 1% iron
Exchanges: 1 Other Carbo., ½ Fat

 **Simple Fudge** EASY

Prep: 10 minutes **Cook:** 16 minutes **Chill:** 2 hours
Makes: about 2 pounds (64 pieces)

  1½ **cups sugar**
  1 **5-ounce can evaporated milk (⅔ cup)**
  ½ **cup butter**
  2 **cups tiny marshmallows**
  1 **cup semisweet chocolate pieces or chopped bittersweet chocolate**
  ½ **cup chopped walnuts**
  ½ **teaspoon vanilla**

1. Line an 8×8×2-inch baking pan with foil, extending the foil over the edges of the pan. Butter the foil; set pan aside.

2. Butter the sides of a 2-quart heavy saucepan. In saucepan combine sugar, evaporated milk, and butter. Cook and stir over medium-high heat until mixture boils (about 10 minutes). Reduce heat to medium; continue cooking, stirring constantly, for 6 minutes.

3. Remove saucepan from heat. Add marshmallows, chocolate pieces, walnuts, and vanilla; stir until marshmallows and chocolate melt and mixture is combined. Beat by hand for 1 minute.

4. Spread fudge evenly in prepared pan. Score into squares while warm. Cover; chill for 2 to 3 hours or until firm. When fudge is firm, use foil to lift it out of pan. Cut fudge. Store, tightly covered, in the refrigerator for up to 1 month.

Peanut Butter-Chocolate Fudge: Prepare as above, except substitute ½ cup peanut butter for the butter and, if desired, peanuts for the walnuts.

Per piece chocolate or peanut butter variation: 59 cal.,
3 g total fat (2 g sat. fat), 5 mg chol., 20 mg sodium, 8 g carbo.,
0 g fiber, 0 g pro.
Daily Values: 1% vit. A, 1% calcium, 1% iron
Exchanges: ½ Other Carbo., ½ Fat

 **Candy-Bar Fudge**

Prep: 10 minutes **Microwave:** 7¾ minutes
Chill: 2 hours **Makes:** about 2¾ pounds (64 pieces)

  ½ **cup butter**
  ⅓ **cup unsweetened cocoa powder**
  ¼ **cup packed brown sugar**
  ¼ **cup milk**
  3½ **cups powdered sugar**
  1 **teaspoon vanilla**
  30 **vanilla caramels, unwrapped**
  1 **tablespoon water**
  2 **cups unsalted peanuts**
  ½ **cup semisweet chocolate pieces**
  ½ **cup milk chocolate pieces**

1. Line a 9×9×2-inch baking pan with foil, extending the foil over edges of pan. Butter the foil; set pan aside.

2. In a large microwave-safe bowl microwave the butter, uncovered, on 100 percent power (high) for about 1 minute or until melted. Stir in cocoa powder, brown sugar, and milk. Microwave, uncovered, on high for 1 to 2 minutes or until mixture comes to a boil, stirring once. Stir again; microwave for 30 seconds more. Stir in powdered sugar and vanilla until smooth. Spread fudge mixture in prepared pan.

3. In a medium microwave-safe bowl combine caramels and water. Microwave, uncovered, on 50 percent power (medium) for 2½ to 3 minutes or until caramels are melted, stirring once. Stir in peanuts. Microwave, uncovered, on medium for 45 to 60 seconds more or until mixture is softened. Gently and quickly spread caramel mixture over fudge layer in pan.

4. In a medium microwave-safe bowl combine semisweet and milk chocolate pieces. Microwave, uncovered, on 50 percent power (medium) for 2 to 3 minutes or until melted, stirring once or twice. Spread over caramel layer. Score into squares while warm. Cover and chill for 2 to 3 hours or until bottom is firm. Use foil to lift candy out of pan. Cut fudge into pieces. Store, tightly covered, in the refrigerator for up to 3 weeks.

Stove-top directions: In a medium saucepan melt butter over medium heat. Stir in cocoa powder, brown sugar, and milk. Bring to boiling. Remove from heat; stir in powdered sugar and vanilla. Spread in prepared pan. In another saucepan melt caramels with water over low heat; stir in peanuts. Gently and quickly spread over fudge layer in pan. In a small saucepan melt semisweet and milk chocolate pieces over low heat, stirring constantly. Spread over caramel layer. Continue as directed.

Per piece: 100 cal., 5 g total fat (2 g sat. fat), 5 mg chol., 29 mg sodium, 12 g carbo., 0 g fiber, 2 g pro.
Daily Values: 1% vit. A, 2% calcium, 1% iron
Exchanges: 1 Other Carbo., 1 Fat

Easy White Fudge `EASY`

Prep: 20 minutes **Chill:** 2 hours
Makes: about 2 pounds (64 pieces)

- **3 cups white baking pieces**
- **1 14-ounce can sweetened condensed milk (1¼ cups)**
- **1 cup chopped pecans, almonds, or macadamia nuts**

- **2 teaspoons finely shredded orange peel (optional)**
- **1 teaspoon vanilla**
  Coarsely chopped pecans, almonds, or macadamia nuts (optional)

1. Line an 8×8×2-inch or 9×9×2-inch baking pan with foil, extending the foil over the edges of the pan. Butter foil; set aside.

2. In a 2-quart heavy saucepan cook and stir baking pieces and sweetened condensed milk over low heat just until pieces melt and mixture is smooth. Remove saucepan from heat. Stir in the 1 cup nuts, orange peel (if desired), and vanilla. Spread fudge evenly in prepared pan. If desired, sprinkle with additional nuts; press lightly into fudge. Score into 1-inch pieces. Cover and chill about 2 hours or until firm.

3. Use foil to lift fudge out of pan. Cut fudge into squares. Store, tightly covered, for up to 1 week.

Easy Chocolate Fudge: Prepare as above, except substitute 3 cups semisweet chocolate pieces for white pieces. If desired, omit orange peel.

Per piece: 92 cal., 5 g total fat (3 g sat. fat), 2 mg chol., 23 mg sodium, 11 g carbo., 0 g fiber, 1 g pro.
Daily Values: 2% calcium, 1% iron
Exchanges: 1 Other Carbo., 1 Fat

Easy White and Chocolate Fudges

Maple Nutty Candy

These yummy layered candies are filled with lots of flavors to love: peanut butter, maple, chocolate, and butterscotch. See photo, page 187.

Prep: 50 minutes **Chill:** 2 hours + 20 minutes
Makes: about 6 pounds (about 120 pieces)

- 12 ounces chocolate-flavored candy coating, cut up
- 1 12-ounce package butterscotch-flavored pieces (2 cups)
- 1¼ cups peanut butter
- 1 cup butter
- ½ cup evaporated milk
- 1 4-serving-size package regular vanilla pudding mix
- 1 tablespoon maple flavoring
- 1 teaspoon vanilla
- 1 2-pound package powdered sugar (9 cups)
- 3 cups salted peanuts (1 pound), chopped

1. Butter a 15×10×1-inch baking pan; set aside. In a medium heavy saucepan combine candy coating and butterscotch-flavored pieces. Cook and stir over low heat until melted.

2. Stir peanut butter into chocolate mixture until combined. Spread 1¾ cups of the peanut butter mixture into the prepared pan; chill until the mixture is set (about 20 minutes). Set remaining peanut butter mixture aside.

3. Meanwhile, in a large saucepan melt the butter. Stir in the evaporated milk and pudding mix. Cook and stir over medium heat until thickened and smooth. Remove from heat. Stir in maple flavoring and vanilla. Gradually stir in the powdered sugar (mixture will be thick).

4. Carefully spread pudding mixture over cooled peanut butter mixture in baking pan. If necessary, reheat the remaining peanut butter mixture to melt it. Stir peanuts into the remaining peanut butter mixture. Carefully spread peanut butter mixture over pudding mixture in baking pan. Chill for 2 hours. Cut candy into squares. In an airtight container layer candy pieces with waxed paper; cover. Chill for up to 2 weeks or freeze for up to 3 months. Thaw before serving.

Per piece: 118 cal., 7 g total fat (3 g sat. fat), 5 mg chol., 45 mg sodium, 13 g carbo., 0 g fiber, 2 g pro.
Daily Values: 1% vit. A, 1% calcium, 1% iron
Exchanges: 1 Other Carbo., 1½ Fat

Divinity

Start to Finish: 45 minutes
Makes: about 30 pieces

- 2½ cups sugar
- ½ cup water
- ½ cup light-colored corn syrup
- 2 egg whites
- 1 teaspoon vanilla or ¼ teaspoon peppermint or almond extract
- 1 or 2 drops food coloring (optional)
- ½ cup chopped nuts, such as walnuts, pecans, or almonds, toasted (see tip, page 265)

1. Line a tray or baking sheet with waxed paper; set aside. In a 2-quart heavy saucepan combine sugar, water, and corn syrup. Cook and stir over medium-high heat until the mixture boils. Clip a candy thermometer to the side of the pan. Reduce heat to medium; continue cooking, without stirring, until the thermometer registers 260°F, hard-ball stage (15 to 20 minutes). (Adjust heat as necessary to maintain a steady boil.)

2. Remove saucepan from heat; remove thermometer. In a large mixing bowl beat egg whites with an electric mixer on medium speed until stiff peaks form (tips stand straight). Gradually pour hot syrup mixture in a thin stream over egg whites,* beating on high speed about 3 minutes; scrape sides of bowl occasionally. Add vanilla and, if desired, food coloring. Continue beating on high just until candy starts to thicken and lose its gloss (5 to 7 minutes). When beaters are lifted, mixture should fall in a ribbon that mounds on itself (see photo 1, page 193). (To test, drop a spoonful of candy mixture onto waxed paper. If it stays mounded, the mixture has been beaten sufficiently. If mixture flattens, beat ½ to 1 minute more; check again. If mixture is too stiff to spoon, beat in a few drops *hot water* until candy is a softer consistency.)

3. Immediately stir in nuts. Using two teaspoons, quickly drop divinity onto prepared baking sheet (see photo 2, page 193). Store, tightly covered, for up to 1 week.

*Note: If using a stand mixer with a single beater that moves around the bowl, stop the mixer and pour a small amount of syrup over the whites. Immediately beat on high speed for 5 seconds. Stop the mixer and add more syrup. Beat on high speed for 5 seconds. Continue stopping and adding the remaining syrup in batches. If using a handheld mixer, beat the syrup into the whites in a steady stream. Avoid pouring the syrup onto the beaters, which will splatter it onto the sides of the bowl.

Per piece: 92 cal., 1 g total fat (0 g sat. fat), 0 mg chol., 10 mg sodium, 21 g carbo., 0 g fiber, 1 g pro.
Exchanges: 1½ Other Carbo.

1. When candy mixture just starts to lose its gloss, lift beaters. The mixture should fall in a ribbon and mound on itself, not disappear into what remains in the bowl.

2. With two teaspoons, quickly drop mounds of divinity onto waxed paper.

Penuche

Prep: 15 minutes **Cook:** 20 minutes **Cool:** 40 minutes
Makes: about 1¼ pounds (32 pieces)

    1 cup granulated sugar
    1 cup packed brown sugar
    ⅔ cup half-and-half or light cream
    2 tablespoons butter
    1 teaspoon vanilla
    ½ cup chopped pecans, walnuts, or cashews

1. Line an 8×4×2-inch loaf pan with foil, extending foil over the edges of the pan. Butter the foil; set pan aside.

2. Butter sides of a 2-quart heavy saucepan. In saucepan combine granulated sugar, brown sugar, and half-and-half. Cook and stir over medium heat until mixture boils. Clip a candy thermometer to side of pan. Reduce heat to medium-low. Continue boiling mixture at a moderate, steady rate (see bottom photo, page 197), stirring frequently, until thermometer registers 236°F, soft-ball stage (about 15 minutes). (Adjust heat as necessary to maintain a steady boil.)

3. Remove saucepan from heat. Add butter and vanilla but do not stir. Cool, without stirring, to 110°F (about 40 minutes).

4. Remove thermometer from saucepan. Beat mixture vigorously with a clean wooden spoon just until it begins to thicken. Add the chopped nuts. Continue beating until the penuche becomes thick and just starts to lose its gloss (about 10 minutes total).

5. Immediately spread penuche evenly in prepared pan. Score into squares while warm. When firm, use foil to lift it out of pan. Cut into squares. Store, tightly covered, for up to 1 week.

Per piece: 75 cal., 3 g total fat (1 g sat. fat), 4 mg chol., 13 mg sodium, 13 g carbo., 0 g fiber, 0 g pro.
Daily Values: 1% vit. A, 1% calcium, 1% iron
Exchanges: 1 Other Carbo., ½ Fat

Pralines

Prep: 15 minutes **Cook:** 21 minutes **Cool:** 30 minutes
Makes: about 36 pieces

    1½ cups granulated sugar
    1½ cups packed brown sugar
    1 cup half-and-half or light cream
    3 tablespoons butter
    2 cups pecan halves

1. Butter the sides of a 2-quart heavy saucepan. In saucepan combine granulated sugar, brown sugar, and half-and-half. Cook and stir over medium-high heat until mixture boils. Clip a candy thermometer to pan. Reduce heat to medium-low. Continue boiling mixture at a moderate, steady rate (see bottom photo, page 197), stirring occasionally, until thermometer registers 234°F, soft-ball stage (16 to 18 minutes). (Adjust heat as necessary to maintain a steady boil.)

2. Remove saucepan from heat. Add butter but do not stir. Cool, without stirring, to 150°F (about 30 minutes).

3. Remove thermometer from saucepan. Stir in pecans. Beat mixture vigorously with a clean wooden spoon just until it begins to thicken but is still glossy (about 3 minutes).

4. Working quickly, drop the pralines from a teaspoon onto waxed paper. Let stand until firm. Store, tightly covered, for up to 1 week.

Chocolate Pralines: Prepare as above, except add 2 ounces unsweetened chocolate, finely chopped, with the butter.

Per piece plain or chocolate variation: 125 cal., 6 g total fat (1 g sat. fat), 5 mg chol., 17 mg sodium, 18 g carbo., 1 g fiber, 1 g pro.
Daily Values: 1% vit. A, 2% calcium, 2% iron
Exchanges: 1 Other Carbo., 1½ Fat

Chocolate Truffles

Chocolate Truffles

Choose from nut-coated or chocolate-covered truffles—or make some of both.

Prep: 1 hour **Chill:** 20 minutes **Freeze:** 30 minutes
Stand: 30 minutes **Makes:** about 24 truffles

- 1 **12-ounce package semisweet chocolate pieces (2 cups) or one 11.5-ounce package milk chocolate pieces (1¾ cups)**
- ⅓ **cup whipping cream**
- ½ **teaspoon vanilla**
- ½ **cup ground, toasted almonds or hazelnuts (see tip, page 265)**

1. Line a baking sheet with waxed paper; set aside. In a medium heavy saucepan combine chocolate pieces and whipping cream. Cook and stir constantly over low heat until chocolate melts. Remove saucepan from heat; cool slightly. Stir in vanilla. Beat chocolate mixture with an electric mixer on low speed until smooth. Drop by teaspoons onto prepared baking sheet. Chill about 20 minutes or until firm.

2. Shape chilled chocolate mixture into balls; freeze for 30 minutes. Roll truffles in ground nuts. Place on waxed paper. Store, tightly covered, in the refrigerator for up to 2 weeks. Let truffles stand at room temperature about 30 minutes before serving.

Chocolate-Covered Truffles: Prepare as above, except omit nuts and dip chilled truffles in tempered chocolate.* Dip balls, one at a time, into chocolate. Let excess chocolate drip off balls. Place on waxed paper. Let stand until set. If desired, in a small saucepan combine ½ cup white baking pieces and 2 teaspoons shortening. Cook and stir over low heat until melted and smooth; decoratively drizzle over chocolate-covered truffles. Let stand until set.

*Note: To quick-temper chocolate, combine 12 ounces semisweet or milk chocolate pieces with 3 tablespoons shortening in a 4-cup glass measure. Pour warm water (100°F to 110°F) into a large glass bowl to a depth of 1 inch. Place the measure inside the bowl of water. Do not splash any water into the chocolate. The water should only cover the bottom half of the measure containing the chocolate. Stir mixture constantly until completely melted (15 to 20 minutes). If water cools, remove measure and replace water. Return measure to water; continue stirring. When melted, chocolate is ready for dipping. Repeat warming process if chocolate cools and hardens.

Per nut-coated or chocolate-covered truffle: 163 cal., 10 g total fat (7 g sat. fat), 5 mg chol., 9 mg sodium, 18 g carbo., 1 g fiber, 1 g pro.
Daily Values: 1% vit. A, 1% calcium, 3% iron
Exchanges: 1 Other Carbo., 2 Fat

FAVORITE Cream Cheese Mints

Prep: 50 minutes **Stand:** overnight
Makes: about 50 mints

- 1 **3-ounce package cream cheese, softened**
- ½ **teaspoon peppermint extract**
- 3 **cups powdered sugar**
  Few drops desired food coloring
  Granulated sugar

1. In a small bowl stir together softened cream cheese and peppermint extract. Gradually add powdered sugar, stirring until mixture is smooth. (Knead in the last of the powdered sugar with your hands.) Add food coloring; knead until food coloring is evenly distributed.

2. Form cream cheese mixture into ¾-inch balls. Roll each ball in granulated sugar; place on waxed paper. Flatten each ball with the bottom of a glass. (Or sprinkle small candy molds lightly with sugar. Press ¾ to 1 teaspoon cream cheese mixture into each mold. Remove from molds.) Cover mints with paper towels; let stand overnight. Store, tightly covered, in the refrigerator or freeze for up to 1 month.

Per mint: 33 cal., 1 g total fat (0 g sat. fat), 2 mg chol., 5 mg sodium, 7 g carbo., 0 g fiber, 0 g pro.
Daily Values: 1% vit. A
Exchanges: ½ Other Carbo.

Fruit-and-Nut Chocolate Bark

Fruit-and-Nut Chocolate Bark

Substitute the variety of nuts you like best.

Prep: 20 minutes **Chill:** 1 hour
Makes: 2¼ pounds (40 servings)

- 2 **cups almonds and/or hazelnuts (filberts), toasted and coarsely chopped (see tip, page 265)***
- ⅔ **cup golden raisins**
- ⅔ **cup snipped dried apricots**
- ⅔ **cup dried cranberries**
- ¼ **cup diced candied orange peel**
- 12 **ounces chocolate-flavored candy coating, cut up**
- 1 **7-ounce milk chocolate bar, cut up**

1. Line a large baking sheet with foil; grease foil and set aside. In a large bowl combine nuts, raisins, apricots, cranberries, and orange peel. Reserve ¾ cup of fruit mixture for topping. Set both portions aside.

2. In a 2-quart heavy saucepan heat and stir candy coating and chocolate bar over low heat until mixture is melted and smooth. Remove from heat. Stir in the large portion of fruit mixture; mix well. Pour mixture onto the prepared baking sheet. Spread to about a ⅜-inch thickness. Sprinkle topping over mixture in pan, pressing slightly with the back of a spoon.

3. Chill candy until firm, about 1 hour. Use foil to lift candy from baking sheet; carefully break candy into pieces. Store candy between layers of waxed paper in an airtight container in the refrigerator for up to 2 weeks. Do not freeze.

*Note: To toast filberts, spread in a single layer in a shallow baking pan. Bake in a 350°F oven for 5 to 10 minutes or until light golden brown, watching carefully and stirring once or twice. To remove the papery skins from hazelnuts, rub the nuts with a clean dish towel.

Per serving: 149 cal., 9 g total fat (4 g sat. fat), 1 mg chol., 3 mg sodium, 18 g carbo., 2 g fiber, 2 g pro.
Daily Values: 2% vit. A, 3% calcium
Exchanges: 1 Other Carbo., 2 Fat

Marbled Pecan Bark `EASY`

Three ingredients make two different candies. See photo of Marbled Nut Clusters, page 187.

Prep: 15 minutes **Chill:** 1 hour
Makes: 1½ pounds (30 servings)

- 4 **2-ounce squares vanilla-flavored candy coating, coarsely chopped**
- 1 **12-ounce package semisweet chocolate pieces**
- 1½ **cups chopped pecans, toasted (see tip, page 265)**

1. Line a baking sheet with waxed paper.

2. In a small heavy saucepan melt candy coating over low heat, stirring constantly. In another heavy saucepan melt chocolate pieces over low heat, stirring constantly; stir in pecans.

3. Spread chocolate mixture thinly over prepared baking sheet. Drizzle melted candy coating over chocolate mixture. Swirl candy coating through chocolate mixture with the tip of a spoon. Chill for 1 hour or until firm. Break into pieces. Store tightly covered in the refrigerator.

Marbled Nut Clusters: Prepare as above, except omit Step 1 and the vanilla-flavored candy coating; substitute coarsely chopped mixed nuts, peanuts, or cashews for the pecans. Melt chocolate pieces; stir in nuts. Spoon mixture by rounded teaspoons into 1¾-inch muffin cups lined with paper bake cups. In a small heavy saucepan melt one 1-ounce white baking chocolate over low heat. Drizzle a small amount of white chocolate over each cluster; swirl gently with a toothpick to create a marbled effect. Freeze until firm (about 10 minutes). Store in an airtight container in the refrigerator for 2 to 3 weeks.

Per serving: 122 cal., 9 g total fat (3 g sat. fat), 0 mg chol., 38 mg sodium, 12 g carbo., 2 g fiber, 3 g pro.
Daily Values: 1% calcium, 4% iron
Exchanges: 1 Other Carbo., 1½ Fat

Chocolate-Covered Cherries

Prep: 1¼ hours **Stand:** 2 hours + 10 minutes + 1 week
Chill: 1 hour **Makes:** 60 candies

- 3 **10-ounce jars maraschino cherries with stems (60 cherries)**
- 3 **tablespoons butter, softened**
- 3 **tablespoons light-colored corn syrup**
- 2 **cups powdered sugar**
- 1 **pound chocolate-flavored candy coating, cut up**

1. Let cherries stand on paper towels for 2 hours to drain thoroughly. Line a baking sheet with waxed paper; set aside.

2. In a medium bowl combine butter and corn syrup; stir in powdered sugar. Knead mixture until smooth (chill if too soft to handle). Wrap about ½ teaspoon powdered sugar mixture around each cherry. Place wrapped cherries, stem sides up, on the prepared baking sheet. Chill for 1 to 4 hours or until firm.

3. In a large heavy saucepan melt candy coating over low heat, stirring constantly until smooth. Line another baking sheet with waxed paper. Holding wrapped cherries by stems, dip, one at a time, into candy coating. If necessary, spoon coating over cherries to cover. (Be sure to completely seal cherries in coating to prevent juice from leaking.) Let excess coating drip off. Place coated cherries, stem sides up, on the prepared baking sheet. Let cherries stand until coating is set. To allow the powdered sugar mixture around cherries to liquefy, store, tightly covered, in a cool, dry place for 1 to 2 weeks before serving.

Per candy: 66 cal., 3 g total fat (2 g sat. fat), 2 mg chol., 9 mg sodium, 10 g carbo., 0 g fiber, 0 g pro.
Daily Values: 1% calcium
Exchanges: ½ Other Carbo., ½ Fat

Peanut Butter Balls

Prep: 35 minutes **Stand:** 10 minutes
Makes: about 25 candies

- ½ **cup peanut butter**
- 3 **tablespoons butter, softened**
- ¼ **cup crisp rice cereal (optional)**
- 1 **cup powdered sugar**
- 6 **ounces chocolate-flavored candy coating, cut up**

1. In a bowl stir together peanut butter and butter. Gradually add cereal, if desired, and powdered sugar, stirring until combined. If nec-

essary, knead with hands until smooth. Shape mixture into 1-inch balls; place on a baking sheet lined with waxed paper. Set aside.

2. In a small heavy saucepan melt candy coating over low heat, stirring constantly until smooth. Remove from heat; cool for 5 minutes. Using a fork, dip balls, one at a time, into coating, allowing excess to drip off. Return to waxed paper; let stand until coating is set (about 10 minutes). Store, tightly covered, in the refrigerator for up to 1 month or freeze for up to 3 months. If frozen, thaw at room temperature before serving.

Per candy: 98 cal., 7 g total fat (3 g sat. fat), 4 mg chol., 36 mg sodium, 9 g carbo., 0 g fiber, 1 g pro.
Daily Values: 1% vit. A, 1% iron
Exchanges: ½ Other Carbo.

White Cherry Candies

Prep: 20 minutes **Chill:** 35 minutes
Makes: about 36 candies

- 2 **teaspoons butter**
- 3 **tablespoons water**
- 1 **teaspoon vanilla**
- 2 **cups powdered sugar**
- ½ **cup nonfat dry milk powder**
- 1 **7-ounce package (2⅔ cups) flaked coconut**
- 9 **candied cherries, quartered**
- 6 **ounces vanilla-flavored candy coating**
- 1 **teaspoon shortening**
  Powdered sugar (optional)

1. In a medium saucepan melt butter over low heat. Remove from heat. Stir in water and vanilla.

2. In a medium bowl combine the 2 cups powdered sugar and nonfat dry milk powder. Stir sugar mixture into the butter mixture until combined. Add coconut, stirring until coated.

3. Drop by small teaspoons onto a baking sheet lined with waxed paper. Chill for 15 minutes. Top with a candied cherry quarter.

4. In a small saucepan melt candy coating and shortening over low heat, stirring constantly. Cool slightly. Drizzle over candies. Chill for 20 minutes more or until firm. Store in an airtight container in the refrigerator for up to 2 weeks. If desired, sift with additional powdered sugar before serving.

Per candy: 83 cal., 4 g total fat (3 g sat. fat), 1 mg chol., 22 mg sodium, 12 g carbo., 0 g fiber, 1 g pro.
Daily Values: 1% vit. A, 1% calcium
Exchanges: 1 Other Carbo., ½ Fat

Caramels

Caramels

If you've never had the pleasure of eating homemade caramels, you're in for a treat.

Prep: 15 minutes **Cook:** 55 minutes
Makes: about 2 pounds (64 pieces)

- **1 cup chopped walnuts (optional)**
- **1 cup butter**
- **1 16-ounce package brown sugar (2¼ cups packed)**
- **2 cups half-and-half or light cream**
- **1 cup light-colored corn syrup**
- **1 teaspoon vanilla**

1. Line an 8×8×2-inch or 9×9×2-inch baking pan with foil, extending foil over edges of pan. Butter the foil. If desired, sprinkle walnuts over bottom of pan. Set pan aside.

2. In a 3-quart heavy saucepan melt butter over low heat. Add brown sugar, half-and-half, and corn syrup; mix well. Cook and stir over medium-high heat until mixture boils. Clip a candy thermometer to the side of the pan. Reduce heat to medium. Continue boiling mixture at a moderate, steady rate (see photo, right), stirring frequently, until the thermometer registers 248°F, firm-ball stage (45 to 60 minutes). (Adjust heat as necessary to maintain a steady boil.)

3. Remove saucepan from heat; remove thermometer. Stir in vanilla. Quickly pour mixture into prepared pan. When firm, use foil to lift candy out of pan. Use a buttered knife to cut into 1-inch squares. Wrap each caramel in waxed paper or plastic wrap. Store for up to 2 weeks.

Shortcut Caramels: Prepare as at left, except substitute one 14-ounce can sweetened condensed milk (1¼ cups) for the half-and-half. This mixture will take less time to reach 248°F (about 15 to 20 minutes instead of 45 to 60 minutes).

Per piece: 80 cal., 4 g total fat (2 g sat. fat), 11 mg chol.,
43 mg sodium, 12 g carbo., 0 g fiber, 0 g pro.
Daily Values: 3% vit. A, 2% calcium, 1% iron
Exchanges: 1 Other Carbo., ½ Fat

Caramel Corn

This baked, buttery caramel corn beats purchased versions any day.

Prep: 10 minutes **Cook:** 10 minutes **Bake:** 20 minutes
Oven: 300°F **Makes:** 7 to 8 cups (7 servings)

- **7 to 8 cups popped popcorn**
- **¾ cup packed brown sugar**
- **6 tablespoons butter**
- **3 tablespoons light-colored corn syrup**
- **¼ teaspoon baking soda**
- **¼ teaspoon vanilla**

1. Remove all unpopped kernels from popped popcorn. Put popcorn into a 17×12×2-inch baking or roasting pan. Keep popcorn warm in a 300°F oven while making caramel mixture.

2. Butter a large piece of foil; set aside. For caramel, in a medium saucepan combine brown sugar, butter, and corn syrup. Cook and stir over medium heat until mixture boils. Continue boiling at a moderate, steady rate, without stirring, for 5 minutes more.

3. Remove saucepan from heat. Stir in baking soda and vanilla. Pour caramel over popcorn; stir gently to coat. Bake in a 300°F oven for 15 minutes. Stir mixture; bake 5 minutes more. Spread caramel corn on buttered foil; cool. Store, tightly covered, for 1 week.

Per cup: 236 cal., 11 g total fat (7 g sat. fat), 28 mg chol.,
171 mg sodium, 36 g carbo., 1 g fiber, 1 g pro.
Daily Values: 8% vit. A, 2% calcium, 4% iron
Exchanges: 2 Other Carbo., 2 Fat

Boil all candy mixtures at a moderate, steady rate (bubbles should form over the entire surface). Be sure the bulb of the candy thermometer is completely covered by the candy mixture.

Cooking and Testing Candy Mixtures

Cooking candy at the proper rate and accurately determining when it is done are two critical steps in successfully making candy.

Cooking and Testing Candy Mixtures

● Candy mixtures should boil at a moderate, steady rate with bubbles over the entire surface (see bottom photo, page 197). To guide you, our recipes suggest range-top temperatures for cooking the candy mixtures. However, to ensure that your candy will cook within the recommended time, you may need to adjust the temperature of your range to maintain the best rate of cooking. Cooking too fast or slow makes candy too hard or soft.

● When stirring hot candy mixtures, use a wooden spoon.

● The most accurate way to test the stages of hot candy mixtures is to use a candy thermometer. Be sure to check the accuracy of your thermometer every time you use it. To test it, place the thermometer in a saucepan of boiling water for a few minutes, then read the temperature. If the thermometer reads above or below 212°F, add or subtract the same number of degrees from the temperature specified in the recipe and cook to that temperature. And if a candy mixture needs to cool, be sure to add or subtract that same number of degrees from the cooling temperature.

● If a candy thermometer is not available, use the corresponding cold-water test described below. Start testing mixtures shortly before they reach minimum cooking times.

Cold-Water Test

All stages, except the thread stage, use cold water for testing. For the cold-water test, spoon a few drops of the hot candy mixture into a cup of cold (but not icy) water. Using your fingers, attempt to form the candy mixture into a ball, then remove the ball from the water. (In the last two stages, the mixture will not form a ball.) The firmness of the mixture according to the following stages will indicate the candy's temperature. If the mixture has not reached the desired stage, continue cooking and retesting, using fresh water and a clean spoon each time.

Thread stage (230°F to 233°F) When a teaspoon is dipped into the hot mixture in the pan, then lifted out, the candy falls off the spoon in a 2-inch-long, fine, thin thread.

Soft-ball stage (234°F to 240°F) When the ball of candy is removed from the cold water, it instantly flattens and runs over your fingers.

Firm-ball stage (244°F to 248°F) When the ball of candy is removed from the cold water, it is firm enough to hold its shape but quickly flattens.

Hard-ball stage (250°F to 266°F) When the ball of candy is removed from the cold water, it holds its shape but can be deformed with pressure.

Soft-crack stage (270°F to 290°F) When the hot mixture is dropped into the cold water, it separates into hard, pliable threads that cannot be shaped into a ball.

Hard-crack stage (295°F to 310°F) When the hot mixture is dropped into the cold water, it separates into hard, brittle threads that snap easily and cannot be shaped into a ball.

Popcorn and Candy Balls

Add a few drops of food coloring to the marshmallow mixture to give these treats a seasonal hue.

Start to Finish: 45 minutes **Oven:** 300°F
Makes: 16 popcorn balls

- **20 cups popped popcorn**
- **1½ cups light-colored corn syrup**
- **1½ cups sugar**
- **1 7-ounce jar marshmallow crème**
- **2 tablespoons butter**
- **1 teaspoon vanilla**
- **1½ cups candy-coated milk chocolate pieces or candy-coated peanut butter-flavored pieces**

1. Remove all unpopped kernels from popped popcorn. Place popcorn in a buttered 17×12×2-inch baking pan or roasting pan. Keep popcorn warm in a 300°F oven while preparing marshmallow mixture.

2. In a large saucepan bring corn syrup and sugar to boiling over medium-high heat, stirring constantly. Remove from heat. Stir in marshmallow crème, butter, and vanilla until combined.

3. Pour marshmallow mixture over hot popcorn; stir gently to coat. Cool until popcorn mixture can be handled easily. Stir in chocolate pieces. With damp hands, quickly shape mixture into 3-inch-diameter balls. Wrap each popcorn ball in plastic wrap. Store at room temperature for up to 1 week.

Popcorn Cake: Turn popcorn mixture into a buttered 10-inch tube pan. Press into pan with spatula or damp hands. Let stand about 30 minutes; remove and cut like cake into 16 slices.

Per ball or slice: 329 cal., 5 g total fat (3 g sat. fat), 6 mg chol., 67 mg sodium, 71 g carbo., 2 g fiber, 2 g pro.
Daily Values: 2% vit. A, 2% calcium, 2% iron
Exchanges: ½ Starch, 4 Other Carbo., 1 Fat

★ Nut Rocha

This chocolate-topped toffee is a classic. No doubt your family will ask for it often. See photo, page 187.

Prep: 40 minutes **Stand:** 6 to 8 hours
Makes: about 2 pounds (40 servings)

- **2 cups butter**
- **2 cups sugar**
- **⅓ cup water**
- **2 tablespoons light-colored corn syrup**
- **1 11½-ounce package milk chocolate pieces (1¾ cups)**
- **1 cup finely chopped, toasted nuts (see tip, page 265) (such as almonds, pecans, walnuts, and/or cashews)**

1. Line a 15×10×1-inch baking pan with foil, extending the foil over edges of pan. Set aside.

2. In a 3-quart saucepan melt butter. Stir in sugar, water, and corn syrup. Cook over medium-high heat to boiling, stirring until sugar is dissolved. Avoid splashing side of saucepan. Clip a candy thermometer to side of pan. Cook over medium heat, stirring frequently, until thermometer registers 290°F, soft-crack stage (about 15 minutes). Mixture should boil at a moderate, steady rate with bubbles over entire surface. Remove from heat; remove thermometer.

3. Carefully pour corn syrup mixture into prepared pan; spread evenly. Cool about 5 minutes or until top is set. Sprinkle with chocolate pieces; let stand for 2 minutes. Spread softened chocolate over toffee layer. Sprinkle with nuts; press into chocolate. Let stand at room temperature several hours or until set. Use foil to lift candy out of pan; break into pieces. In an airtight container layer rocha with waxed paper. Store at room temperature for up to 1 month.

Per serving: 181 cal., 13 g total fat (7 g sat. fat), 25 mg chol., 128 mg sodium, 16 g carbo., 0 g fiber, 1 g pro.
Daily Values: 2% calcium, 1% iron
Exchanges: 1 Other Carbo., 3 Fat

Popcorn and Candy Balls

Peanut Brittle

Prep: 10 minutes **Cook:** 50 minutes
Makes: about 2¼ pounds (72 servings)

- **2 cups sugar**
- **1 cup light-colored corn syrup**
- **½ cup water**
- **¼ cup butter**
- **2½ cups raw peanuts or raw cashews**
- **1½ teaspoons baking soda, sifted**

1. Butter two large baking sheets; set aside. Butter the sides of a 3-quart heavy saucepan. In pan combine sugar, corn syrup, water, and butter. Cook and stir over medium-high heat until mixture boils. Clip a candy thermometer to side of pan. Reduce heat to medium-low; continue boiling at a moderate, steady rate, stirring occasionally, until the thermometer registers 275°F, soft-crack stage (about 30 minutes). (Adjust heat as necessary to maintain a steady boil.)

2. Stir in nuts; continue cooking over medium-low heat, stirring frequently, until thermometer registers 295°F, hard-crack stage (15 to 20 minutes more).

3. Remove saucepan from heat; remove thermometer. Quickly sprinkle baking soda over corn syrup mixture, stirring constantly (see photo 1, below). Immediately pour onto prepared baking sheets. Use two forks to lift and pull brittle as it cools (see photo 2, below). Cool completely; break into pieces. Store, tightly covered, for up to 1 week.

Per serving: 68 cal., 3 g total fat (1 g sat. fat), 2 mg chol., 39 mg sodium, 10 g carbo., 0 g fiber, 1 g pro.
Daily Values: 1% vit. A, 1% calcium, 1% iron
Exchanges: ½ Other Carbo., ½ Fat

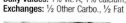

1. Stir constantly as you sprinkle baking soda over the corn syrup mixture. The mixture will foam as it reacts chemically to the soda. This makes the brittle porous.

2. As the brittle cools, stretch it into a thin sheet by gently lifting and pulling with two forks. Stretching it helps make it crisp.

Green Apple Lollipops

Green Apple Lollipops

Prep: 20 minutes **Cook:** 45 minutes
Cool: 35 minutes **Makes:** 18 to 20 lollipops

- **2 cups sugar**
- **¾ cup light-colored corn syrup**
- **1 tablespoon butter**
- **½ teaspoon apple flavoring oil or ¼ teaspoon blackberry flavoring oil**
- **2 drops green or 6 drops purple gel food coloring**
- **Lollipop sticks**

1. In a medium saucepan bring 1 cup *water* to boiling. Stir in sugar, syrup, and butter. Cook and stir over medium-high heat until mixture boils (about 7 minutes). Clip candy thermometer to side of pan. Reduce heat; continue boiling at a moderate, steady rate, stirring occasionally, until thermometer registers 300°F, hard-crack stage (45 to 50 minutes).

2. Remove from heat; stir in flavoring and gel food coloring. Let stand until thermometer registers 220°F (about 20 minutes). Butter two baking sheets. Place sticks 4 inches apart on sheets. Working quickly, spoon 1 tablespoon of candy mixture at the top 1 inch of each lollipop stick (do not spread; mixture will flow out). Cool completely. Wrap each lollipop in plastic wrap. Store at room temperature up to 2 weeks.

Per lollipop: 127 cal., 1 g total fat (0 g sat. fat), 2 mg chol., 24 mg sodium, 32 g carbo., 0 g fiber, 0 g pro.
Daily Values: 1% vit. A
Exchanges: 2 Other Carbo.

Canning & Freezing

Corn Relish, 219

Berry Freezer Jam, 214

Bread and Butter Pickles, 218

Canning & Freezing Essentials

Savor the days of summer by canning and freezing the brilliantly colored fruits and vegetables harvested from your garden or the local farmer's market.

Canning

||||||||||||||||||||||||||||||||||||||||||||||||||||||||||||||||||||||||||||||||||||||||||

Follow the step-by-step canning guidelines below for safe, delicious results that you'll be proud to serve or give as gifts to family and friends.

Equipment

Canner: Make your choice based on the kind of food you are canning. A boiling-water (or water-bath) canner is used for fruits, tomatoes, pickles, relishes, jams, and jellies. It is a large kettle that has a lid and a rack designed to hold canning jars. Any large cooking pot can be used if it has a rack, a tight-fitting lid, and enough depth for briskly boiling water to cover the jars by 1 inch.

Boiling-Water Canner   Pressure Canner

A pressure canner must be used for vegetables and other low-acid foods. It is a large heavy pot that has a rack and a tight-fitting lid with a vent (or petcock), a dial or weighted-pressure gauge, and a safety fuse. It may or may not have a gasket. Pressure canners allow foods to be heated to 240°F and to be held at that temperature as long as necessary. Always refer to manufacturer's instructions specific to your canner.

Jars: Use only standard canning jars. These are tempered to withstand the heat inside a canner, and their mouths are specially threaded to seal with canning lids. Inspect all jars before using them; discard any that are cracked or have chipped rims.

Lids: Use screw bands and flat metal lids that have a built-in sealing compound. Prepare them according to the manufacturer's directions. The flat lids are designed for one-time use only. Screw bands can be reused if they are not bent or rusty.

Other useful pieces of equipment include a kitchen scale, wide-mouth funnel, jar lifter, and food mill, colander, or sieve.

General Canning Steps

Follow these steps whether using a boiling-water canner or a pressure canner. Pack food into canning jars by the raw pack (cold pack) or hot pack method. In raw packing, uncooked food is packed into the canning jar and covered with boiling water, juice, or syrup (see chart introduction, pages 206–207, for syrup information). In hot packing, food is partially cooked, packed into jars, and covered with cooking liquid. The following guidelines apply to both methods.

Jar Lifter

1. Wash empty canning jars in hot, soapy water. Rinse thoroughly. Pour boiling water over jars and let them stand in the hot water until you're ready to fill them. Sterilize jars that will be processed for 10 minutes or less (see "Sterilizing Jars," page 219). Prepare lids and screw bands according to the manufacturer's directions.

2. Start heating water in the canner.

3. Prepare only as much food as needed to fill the maximum number of jars your canner will hold at one time. Keep the work area clean.

4. Place the hot jars on cloth towels to prevent them from slipping during packing.

5. Pack the food into jars using a wide-mouth funnel, allowing for adequate headspace.

6. Ladle or pour boiling liquid over the food, leaving adequate headspace (see page 217).

7. Release trapped air bubbles by gently working a sterilized rubber scraper or nonmetal utensil down the jars' sides. Add liquid, if needed, to maintain necessary headspace.

8. Wipe jar rims with a clean, damp cloth. (Food on the rims prevents a perfect seal.)

Wide-Mouth Funnel

9. Place prepared lids on jars; add screw bands; tighten according to manufacturer's directions.
10. Set each jar into the canner as it is filled and sealed. Jars should not touch each other.
11. Process filled jars, following the recipe's procedures and timings exactly.
12. Remove jars; place them on a rack or towels in a draft-free area to cool. Leave at least 1 inch of space between jars to allow air to circulate.
13. After the jars are completely cooled (12 to 24 hours), press the center of each lid to check the seal. If the dip in the lid holds, the jar is sealed. If the lid bounces up and down, the jar isn't sealed. Check unsealed jars for flaws. The contents can be refrigerated and used within 2 to 3 days, frozen, or reprocessed within 24 hours. To reprocess, use a clean jar and a new lid; process for the full length of time specified. Mark the label so you can use any recanned jars first. If jars have lost liquid but are still sealed, the contents are safe. However, any food not covered by liquid will discolor, so use these jars first.
14. Wipe the jars and lids. Remove, wash, and dry the screw bands; store for future use. Label jars with contents and date; include a batch number if you are doing more than one canner load per day (if one jar spoils, you can easily identify others from that same load). Store jars in a cool (50°F to 70°F), dry, dark place. Use within 1 year.

Boiling-Water Canning

Set the canner and rack on the stove top. Fill canner half full with water; cover and heat over high heat. Heat additional water in another kettle. Prepare syrup (see chart introduction, pages 206–207, for syrup information), if needed; keep it warm but not boiling. Prepare the food. When the water in the canner is hot, fill each jar and place it on the rack in the canner. Replace canner cover each time you add a jar. After the last jar has been added, pour additional boiling water into the canner until jars are submerged by 1 inch. Cover; heat to a full rolling boil. Now begin the processing timing. Keep the water boiling gently during processing, adding more boiling water if the level drops. If the water stops boiling when you add more, stop the timing, turn up the heat, and wait for a full boil before resuming counting. At the end of processing time, turn off heat and remove jars. Cool on a rack or dry towels. When jars are cool (12 to 24 hours), check seals.

Pressure Canning

Read manufacturer's instructions before using a pressure canner. Make sure all parts are clean and work properly. If your canner has a dial gauge, check it yearly for accuracy. (Contact a county extension service office for the nearest testing location.) Weighted-gauge canners remain accurate from year to year. Before canning, make sure the steam vent is clear. Set the canner and rack on the stove top. Add 2 to 3 inches of hot water (or the amount specified by the manufacturer). Turn heat to low.

Prepare enough food for one canner load. Fill each jar and place it in the canner. When the last jar is added, cover and lock the canner. Turn heat to high. When steam comes out the vent, reduce heat until steam flows freely at a moderate rate. Let the steam flow steadily for about 10 minutes to release all the air from inside the canner. Close the vent or place the weighted gauge over the vent according to manufacturer's instructions. Start timing when the recommended pressure is reached. Adjust heat to maintain a constant pressure.

When processing time is up, carefully remove the canner from the heat and set it away from drafts on a rack or a wooden board. If the canner is too heavy to move, simply turn off the heat. Let the pressure return to normal (allow 30 to 60 minutes). Do not lift the weight, open the vent, or run water over the canner.

Follow manufacturer's instructions for

Important Safety Reminder

● Always inspect a home-canned jar of food carefully before serving. If the jar has leaked, shows mold, or has a swollen lid or if the food has a foamy or murky appearance, discard the food and jar where it will not be eaten by people or pets.

● The odor from an opened jar should be pleasant. If food does not look or smell right, don't use it.

● Always boil all home-canned vegetables for 10 minutes before tasting or using them if you live less than 1,000 feet above sea level. If you live more than 1,000 feet above sea level, add an additional minute for each 1,000 feet of elevation.

opening the canner. Lift the cover away from you to avoid a blast of steam. If the food is still boiling vigorously in the jars, wait a few minutes before removing the jars. Cool jars 2 to 3 inches apart on a rack or dry towels in a draft-free area. Do not tighten lids. When the jars are completely cool (12 to 24 hours), check seals.

Freezing

For best results, use top-quality, garden-fresh produce and follow the guidelines below.

Equipment

To freeze vegetables and fruits you need a colander and a large kettle or a saucepan that has a wire basket. An accurate freezer thermometer will help you regulate your freezer temperature at 0°F or below.

A variety of freezer containers and materials are available. Choose moistureproof and vapor-proof materials that are able to withstand temperatures of 0°F or below and capable of being tightly sealed. For liquid or semiliquid foods, use rigid plastic freezer containers, freezer bags, or wide-top jars designed for freezing. Regular jars seldom are tempered to withstand freezer temperatures. For solid or dry-pack foods, use freezer bags, heavy-duty foil, plastic wrap for the freezer, or laminated freezer wrap.

General Freezing Steps

1. Select the best-quality fruits and vegetables that are at their peak of maturity. Hold produce in the refrigerator if it can't be frozen immediately. Rinse and drain small quantities through several changes of cold water. Lift fruits and vegetables out of the water; do not let them soak. Prepare cleaned produce as specified in the charts on pages 206–211.

2. Blanch vegetables (and fruits when directed) by scalding them in boiling water for a short time. This stops or slows enzymes that cause loss of flavor and color and toughen the food. Do not blanch in the microwave because it may not inactivate some enzymes. Timings vary with vegetable type and size.

Blanching is a heat-and-cool process. First, fill a large pot with water using 1 gallon of water per 1 pound of prepared food. Heat to boiling. Add prepared food to the boiling water (or place it in

a wire basket and lower it into the water); cover. Start timing immediately. Cook over high heat for the time specified in the charts. (Add 1 minute if you live 5,000 feet above sea level or higher.) Near the end of the time, fill your sink or a large container with ice water. As soon as the blanching time is complete, use a slotted spoon to transfer the food from the boiling water to a colander (or lift the wire basket out of the water). Immediately plunge the food into the ice water. Chill for the same amount of time it was boiled; drain well.

3. Package the cooled, drained food into freezer containers, leaving the specified headspace (see "Allow for Headspace," page 217).

Fruits often are frozen with added sugar or liquid for better texture and flavor. Refer to the directions in the chart introduction on pages 206–207.

Dry Pack

Unsweetened or dry pack: Do not add sugar or liquid to fruit; simply pack in a container. This is best for small whole fruits, such as berries.

Water pack: Cover the fruit with water or unsweetened fruit juice. Do not use glass jars. Maintain the recommended headspace.

Sugar pack: Place a small amount of fruit in the container and sprinkle lightly with sugar; repeat layering. Cover and let stand about 15 minutes or until juicy; seal.

Syrup pack: Cover fruit with a syrup of sugar and water (see chart introduction, pages 206–207, for syrup information).

4. Wipe container rims. Seal according to the manufacturer's directions, pressing out as much air as possible. If necessary, use freezer tape around the edges of the lids to ensure a tight seal.

5. Label each container with its contents, the amount, and the date.

6. Add packages to the freezer in batches to make sure that food freezes quickly and solidly. Leave some space between the packages so air can circulate around them. When frozen solid, the packages can be placed closer together.

7. Use frozen fruits and vegetables within 8 to 10 months. Vegetables are best cooked from a frozen state without thawing them first. Thaw fruits in their containers either in the refrigerator or in a bowl of cool water.

Canning and Freezing Fruits

Read "Canning & Freezing Essentials," pages 203–205. Wash fresh fruits with cool, clear tap water but do not soak them; drain. Follow preparation directions, below. If you choose to can or freeze fruits with syrup, select the syrup that best suits the fruit and your taste. Generally, heavier syrups are used with sour fruits, and lighter syrups are recommended for mild-flavor fruits. To prepare a syrup, place the following amounts of sugar and water in a large saucepan. Heat until

Food	Preparation	Boiling-Water Canning, Raw Pack
Apples	Allow 2 to 3 pounds per quart. Select varieties that are crisp, not mealy, in texture. Peel and core; halve, quarter, or slice. Dip into ascorbic-acid color-keeper solution; drain.	Not recommended.
Apricots	Allow 2 to 2½ pounds per quart. If desired, peel (see Peaches, Nectarines, below). Prepare as for Peaches, Nectarines. Quality is better when apricots are canned rather than frozen.	See Peaches, Nectarines, below.
Berries	Allow 1 to 3 pounds per quart. Can or freeze blackberries, blueberries, currants, elderberries, gooseberries, huckleberries, loganberries, and mulberries. Freeze (do not can) boysenberries, raspberries, and strawberries.	Fill jars with blackberries, loganberries, or mulberries. Shake down gently. Add boiling syrup, leaving a ½-inch headspace.* Process pints for 15 minutes and quarts for 20 minutes.
Cherries	Allow 2 to 3 pounds per quart. If desired, treat with ascorbic-acid color-keeper solution; drain. If unpitted, prick skin on opposite sides to prevent splitting.	Fill jars, shaking down gently. Add boiling syrup or water, leaving a ½-inch headspace.* Process pints and quarts for 25 minutes.
Melons	Allow about 4 pounds per quart for cantaloupe, honeydew, and watermelon. Peel and cut into ½-inch cubes or balls.	Not recommended.
Peaches, Nectarines	Allow 2 to 3 pounds per quart. To peel peaches (peeling nectarines is not necessary), immerse in boiling water for 30 to 60 seconds or until skins start to split; remove and plunge into cold water. Halve and pit. If desired, slice. Treat with ascorbic-acid color-keeper solution; drain.	Fill jars, placing fruit cut sides down. Add boiling syrup or water, leaving a ½-inch headspace.* Process pints for 25 minutes and quarts for 30 minutes. Do not raw pack apricots. (Note: Hot packing generally results in a better product.)
Pears	Allow 2 to 3 pounds per quart. Peel, halve, and core. Treat with ascorbic-acid color-keeper solution; drain.	Not recommended.
Plums	Allow 1 to 2 pounds per quart. Prick skin on 2 sides. Freestone varieties may be halved and pitted.	Pack firmly into jars. Add boiling syrup, leaving a ½-inch headspace.* Process pints for 20 minutes and quarts for 25 minutes.
Rhubarb	Allow 1½ pounds per quart. Discard leaves and woody ends. Cut into ½- to 1-inch pieces. Freeze for best quality.	Not recommended.

*See "Allow for Headspace," page 217.

the sugar dissolves. Skim off foam, if necessary. Use the syrup hot for canned fruits and chilled for frozen fruits. Allow ½ to ⅔ cup syrup for each 2 cups fruit. For very thin syrup, use 1 cup sugar and 4 cups water to yield 4 cups syrup. For thin syrup, use 1⅔ cups sugar and 4 cups water to yield 4¼ cups syrup. For medium syrup, use 2⅔ cups sugar and 4 cups water to yield 4⅔ cups syrup. For heavy syrup, use 4 cups sugar and 4 cups water to yield 5¾ cups syrup.

Boiling-Water Canning, Hot Pack	Freezing
Simmer in syrup for 5 minutes, stirring occasionally. Fill jars with fruit and syrup, leaving a ½-inch headspace.* Process pints and quarts for 20 minutes.	Use a syrup, sugar, or unsweetened pack (see Step 3, page 205), leaving the recommended headspace.*
See Peaches, Nectarines, below.	Peel as for peaches, below. Use a syrup, sugar, or water pack (see Step 3, page 205), leaving the recommended headspace.*
Simmer blueberries, currants, elderberries, gooseberries, and huckleberries in water for 30 seconds; drain. Fill jars with berries and hot syrup, leaving a ½-inch headspace.* Process pints and quarts for 15 minutes.	Slice strawberries, if desired. Use a syrup, sugar, or unsweetened pack (see Step 3, page 205), leaving the recommended headspace.*
Add cherries to hot syrup; bring to boiling. Fill jars with fruit and syrup, leaving a ½-inch headspace.* Process pints for 15 minutes and quarts for 20 minutes.	Use a syrup, sugar, or unsweetened pack (see Step 3, page 205), leaving the recommended headspace.*
Not recommended.	Use a syrup or unsweetened pack (see Step 3, page 205), leaving the recommended headspace.*
Add fruit to hot syrup; bring to boiling. Fill jars with fruit (placing cut sides down) and syrup, leaving a ½-inch headspace.* Process pints for 20 minutes and quarts for 25 minutes.	Use a syrup, sugar, or water pack (see Step 3, page 205), leaving the recommended headspace.*
Simmer fruit in syrup for 5 minutes. Fill jars with fruit and syrup, leaving a ½-inch headspace.* Process pints for 20 minutes and quarts for 25 minutes.	Use a syrup pack (see Step 3, page 205), leaving the recommended headspace.*
Simmer in water or syrup for 2 minutes. Remove from heat. Let stand, covered, for 20 to 30 minutes. Fill jars with fruit and cooking liquid or syrup, leaving a ½-inch headspace.* Process pints for 20 minutes and quarts for 25 minutes.	Halve and pit. Treat with ascorbic-acid color-keeper solution; drain well. Use a syrup pack (see Step 3, page 205), leaving the recommended headspace.*
In a saucepan sprinkle ½ cup sugar over each 4 cups fruit; mix well. Let stand until juice appears. Bring slowly to boiling, stirring gently. Fill jars with hot fruit and juice, leaving a ½-inch headspace.* Process pints and quarts for 15 minutes.	Blanch for 1 minute; cool quickly and drain. Use a syrup or unsweetened pack (see Step 3, page 205), leaving the recommended headspace.* Or use a sugar pack of ½ cup sugar to each 3 cups fruit.

Canning and Freezing Vegetables

Read "Canning & Freezing Essentials," pages 203–205. Wash fresh vegetables with cool, clear tap water; scrub firm vegetables with a clean produce brush to remove any dirt.

Vegetable	Preparation	Pressure Canning, Raw Pack*
Asparagus	Allow 2½ to 4½ pounds per quart. Wash; scrape off scales. Break off woody bases where spears snap easily; wash again. Sort by thickness. Leave whole or cut into 1-inch lengths.	Not recommended.
Beans: butter or lima	Allow 3 to 5 pounds unshelled beans per quart. Wash, shell, rinse, drain, and sort beans by size.	Fill jars with beans; do not shake down.** Add boiling water, leaving a 1-inch headspace for pints, 1¼-inch for large beans in quarts, and 1½-inch for small beans in quarts. Process pints for 40 minutes and quarts for 50 minutes.
Beans: green, Italian, snap, or wax	Allow 1½ to 2½ pounds per quart. Wash; remove ends and strings. Leave whole or cut into 1-inch pieces.	Pack beans tightly in jars;** add boiling water, leaving a 1-inch headspace. Process pints for 20 minutes and quarts for 25 minutes.
Beets	Allow 3 pounds (without tops) per quart. Trim off beet tops, leaving 1 inch of stem and roots, to reduce bleeding of color. Scrub well. Cover with boiling water. Boil about 15 minutes or until skins slip off easily; cool. Peel; remove stem and roots. Leave baby beets whole. Cut medium or large beets into ½-inch cubes or slices. Halve or quarter large slices.	Not recommended.
Carrots	Use 1- to 1¼-inch diameter carrots (larger carrots may be too fibrous). Allow 2 to 3 pounds per quart. Wash, trim, peel, and rinse again. Leave tiny ones whole; slice or dice the remainder.	Fill jar tightly to 1 inch from the top with raw carrots.** Add boiling water, leaving a 1-inch headspace. Remove air bubbles. Process pints for 25 minutes and quarts for 30 minutes.
Corn, cream-style	Allow 2 to 3 pounds per pint. Remove husks. Scrub with a vegetable brush to remove silks. Wash and drain.	Not recommended.
Corn, whole kernel	Allow 4 to 5 pounds per quart. Remove husks. Scrub with a vegetable brush to remove silks. Wash and drain.	Cover ears with boiling water; boil 3 minutes. Cut corn from cobs at three-quarters depth of kernels; do not scrape. Pack loosely in jars (do not shake or press down).** Add boiling water, leaving a 1-inch headspace. Process pints for 55 minutes and quarts for 85 minutes.
Peas, edible pods	Wash Chinese, snow, sugar, or sugar snap peas. Remove stems, blossom ends, and any strings.	Not recommended.
Peas: English or green	Allow 2 to 2½ pounds per pint. Wash, shell, rinse, and drain.	Pack loosely in jars (do not shake or press down).** Add boiling water, leaving a 1-inch headspace. Process pints and quarts for 40 minutes.

*For a dial-gauge canner, use 11 pounds of pressure; for a weighted-gauge canner, use 10 pounds of pressure. At altitudes above 1,000 feet, see tip, page 214.
**Add salt, if desired: ¼ to ½ teaspoon for pints and ½ to 1 teaspoon for quarts.

Pressure Canning, Hot Pack*	Freezing
Not recommended.	Blanch small spears for 2 minutes, medium for 3 minutes, and large for 4 minutes; cool quickly by plunging into ice water; drain. Fill containers; shake down, leaving no headspace.
Cover beans with boiling water; return to boiling. Boil for 3 minutes. Fill jars loosely with beans and cooking liquid,** leaving a 1-inch headspace. Process pints for 40 minutes and quarts for 50 minutes.	Blanch small beans for 2 minutes, medium beans for 3 minutes, and large beans for 4 minutes; cool quickly by plunging into ice water; drain. Fill containers loosely, leaving a 1/2-inch headspace.
Cover beans with boiling water; return water to boiling. Boil for 5 minutes. Loosely fill jars with beans and cooking liquid,** leaving a 1-inch headspace. Process pints for 20 minutes and quarts for 25 minutes.	Blanch for 3 minutes; cool quickly by plunging into ice water; drain. Fill containers; shake down, leaving a 1/2-inch headspace.
Pack hot jars to 1 inch from the top with beets.** Cover beets with boiling water, leaving a 1-inch headspace. Process pints for 30 minutes and quarts for 35 minutes.	Cook unpeeled beets in boiling water until tender. (Allow 25 to 30 minutes for small beets, 45 to 50 minutes for medium beets.) Cool quickly by plunging into ice water; drain. Peel; remove stem and roots. Cut into slices or cubes. Fill containers, leaving a 1/2-inch headspace.
Cover carrots with boiling water; return water to boiling. Reduce heat; simmer for 5 minutes. Fill jars with carrots and cooking liquid,** leaving a 1-inch headspace. Process pints for 25 minutes and quarts for 30 minutes.	Blanch tiny whole carrots for 5 minutes and cut-up carrots for 2 minutes; cool quickly by plunging into ice water; drain. Pack tightly into containers, leaving a 1/2-inch headspace.
Cover ears with boiling water; return to boiling and boil for 4 minutes. Use a sharp knife to cut off just the kernel tips, then scrape cob with a dull knife. Bring to boiling 1 cup water for each 2 cups corn. Add corn; simmer 3 minutes. Fill pint jars loosely (do not use quart jars),** leaving a 1-inch headspace. Process pints 85 minutes.	Cover ears with boiling water; return to boiling and boil 4 minutes. Cool quickly by plunging into ice water; drain. Use a sharp knife to cut off just the kernel tips, then scrape cob with a dull knife. Fill containers, leaving a 1/2-inch headspace.
Cover ears with boiling water; return to boiling and boil 3 minutes. Cut corn from cobs at three-quarters depth of kernels; do not scrape. Bring to boiling 1 cup water for each 4 cups corn. Add corn; simmer 5 minutes. Fill jars with corn and liquid,** leaving a 1-inch headspace. Process pints for 55 minutes and quarts for 85 minutes.	Cover ears with boiling water; return to boiling and boil 4 minutes. Cool by plunging into ice water; drain. Cut corn from cobs at two-thirds depth of kernels; do not scrape. Fill containers, leaving a 1/2-inch headspace.
Not recommended.	Blanch small pods 1 1/2 minutes or large pods 2 minutes. (If peas have started to develop, blanch 3 minutes. If peas are developed, shell and follow directions for green peas.) Cool quickly by plunging into ice water; drain. Fill containers, leaving a 1/2-inch headspace.
Cover with water; heat to boiling and boil for 2 minutes. Fill jars loosely with peas and cooking liquid,** leaving a 1-inch headspace. Process pints and quarts for 40 minutes.	Blanch 1 1/2 minutes; cool quickly by plunging into ice water; drain. Fill containers, shaking down and leaving a 1/2-inch headspace.

Canning and Freezing Vegetables (continued)

Vegetable	Preparation	Pressure Canning, Raw Pack*
Peppers, hot	Select firm jalapeño or other chile peppers; wash. Halve large peppers. Remove stems, seeds, and membranes (see tip, page 74). Place, cut sides down, on a foil-lined baking sheet. Bake in a 425°F oven for 20 to 25 minutes or until skins are bubbly and brown. Cover peppers or wrap in foil and let stand about 15 minutes or until cool. Pull the skin off gently and slowly using a paring knife.	Not recommended.
Peppers, sweet	Select firm green, bright red, or yellow peppers; wash. Remove stems, seeds, and membranes. Place, cut sides down, on a foil-lined baking sheet. Bake in a 425°F oven for 20 to 25 minutes or until skins are bubbly and brown. Cover peppers or wrap in foil and let stand about 15 minutes or until cool. Pull the skin off gently and slowly using a paring knife.	Not recommended.

*For a dial-gauge canner, use 11 pounds of pressure; for a weighted-gauge canner, use 10 pounds of pressure. At altitudes above 1,000 feet, see tip, page 214.
**Add salt, if desired: ¼ to ½ teaspoon for pints and ½ to 1 teaspoon for quarts.

Canning and Freezing Tomatoes

Allow 2½ to 3½ pounds unblemished tomatoes per quart. Wash tomatoes. To peel, dip tomatoes in boiling water for 30 seconds or until skins start to split. Dip in cold water; skin and core. Continue as directed below.

Tomatoes	Preparation	Boiling-Water Canning
Crushed	Wash and peel tomatoes. Cut into quarters; add enough to a large pan to cover bottom. Crush with a wooden spoon. Heat and stir until boiling. Slowly add remaining pieces, stirring constantly. Simmer for 5 minutes. Fill jars. Add bottled lemon juice: 1 tablespoon for pints, 2 tablespoons for quarts. Add salt, if desired: ¼ to ½ teaspoon for pints, ½ to 1 teaspoon for quarts. Leave a ½-inch headspace.	Process pints for 35 minutes and quarts for 45 minutes.
Whole or halved, no added liquid	Wash and peel tomatoes; halve, if desired. Fill jars, pressing to fill spaces with juice. Add bottled lemon juice: 1 tablespoon for pints, 2 tablespoons for quarts. Add salt, if desired: ¼ to ½ teaspoon for pints, ½ to 1 teaspoon for quarts. Leave a ½-inch headspace.	Process pints and quarts for 85 minutes.
Whole or halved, water-packed	Wash and peel tomatoes; halve, if desired. Fill jars. Add bottled lemon juice: 1 tablespoon for pints, 2 tablespoons for quarts. Add salt, if desired: ¼ to ½ teaspoon for pints, ½ to 1 teaspoon for quarts. Add boiling water, leaving a ½-inch headspace. Or heat tomatoes in saucepan with enough water to cover; simmer 5 minutes. Fill jars with tomatoes and cooking liquid. Add bottled lemon juice and salt (if desired) in the amounts listed above. Leave a ½-inch headspace.	Process pints for 40 minutes and quarts for 45 minutes.

*For a dial-gauge canner, use 11 pounds of pressure; for a weighted-gauge canner, use 10 pounds of pressure. At altitudes above 1,000 feet, see tip, page 214.

Pressure Canning, Hot Pack*	Freezing
Pack peppers in pint jars.** Add boiling water, leaving a 1-inch headspace. Process pints for 35 minutes.	Package in freezer containers, leaving no headspace.
Quarter large pepper pieces or cut into strips. Loosely pack pint jars to 1 inch from the top with pepper pieces.** Add boiling water, leaving a 1-inch headspace. Process pints for 35 minutes.	Quarter large pepper pieces or cut into strips. Fill containers, leaving a ½-inch headspace. Or spread peppers in a single layer on a baking sheet; freeze until firm. Fill container, shaking to pack closely and leaving no headspace.

Pressure Canning*	Freezing
Process pints and quarts for 15 minutes.	Set pan of tomatoes in ice water to cool. Fill containers, leaving a 1-inch headspace.
Process pints and quarts for 25 minutes.	Fill freezer containers, leaving a 1-inch headspace. (Use only for cooking, due to texture changes caused by freezing.)
Process pints and quarts for 10 minutes.	If heated, set pan of tomatoes in cold water to cool. Fill containers, leaving a 1-inch headspace.

Jellies and Jams Basics

Ingredients: For the best flavor and color, choose fruits at their peak of freshness. Pectin, which naturally is present in some fruits, is necessary for jelling. It can be added in powdered or liquid form. Add it as specified in the recipe; do not substitute one type for another. Sugar acts as a preservative, develops flavors, and aids in jelling. Use the amount specified in the recipe. Acid is needed for jelling and for flavor. If a fruit is low in acid, the recipe calls for adding lemon juice or citric acid.

Procedures: Prepare one batch at a time; do not double a recipe. A full rolling boil, critical to jellymaking, is one so rapid that you can't stir it down (see photo, top). To prevent a mixture from boiling over, fill

a pan no more than one-third full. A mixture will sheet off a spoon when it has reached its jelling point. To test, dip a metal spoon into the boiling mixture, then

hold it over the pan. If mixture is done, two drops will hang off edge of spoon, then run together in a sheetlike action (see photo, middle).

Or use a candy thermometer to find when the jelling point is reached (8°F above the boiling point of water—or 220°F at sea level). Boiling naturally results in foam. Skim it off with a large metal spoon (see photo, bottom) before ladling jelly into sterilized jars (see tip, page 219). Process in a boiling-water canner (see instructions, page 204). At altitudes below 1,000 feet above sea level, process for 5 minutes; add 1 minute for each additional 1,000 feet. After processing, let sit for 12 to 24 hours or until set. Use within 6 months.

Strawberry Jam

Strawberry Jam

Celebrate the summer season with this family favorite. Whether from your garden, the farmer's market, or the local grocery store, plump, juicy strawberries are a sweet reward after a long winter. Be sure to choose bright red berries that are free of blemishes.

Prep: 35 minutes **Process:** 5 minutes
Makes: 8 half-pints

- 2 **quarts (8 cups) fresh strawberries, hulled**
- 1 **1.75-ounce package regular powdered fruit pectin**
- ½ **teaspoon butter or margarine**
- 7 **cups sugar**

1. Place 1 cup of berries in an 8-quart heavy kettle. Crush berries. Continue adding berries and crushing until you have 5 cups crushed berries. Stir in pectin and butter. Heat on high, stirring constantly, until mixture comes to a full rolling boil (see photo, top left). Add sugar all at once. Return to boiling; boil 1 minute, stirring constantly. Remove from heat; skim off foam with a metal spoon (see photo, bottom left).

2. Ladle at once into hot, sterilized half-pint canning jars (see tip, page 219), leaving a ¼-inch headspace (see tip, page 217). Wipe jar rims; adjust lids. Process in a boiling-water canner for 5 minutes (start timing when water returns to boil). Remove jars; cool on racks.

Per tablespoon: 51 cal., 0 g total fat (0 g sat. fat), 0 mg chol., 1 mg sodium, 13 g carbo., 0 g fiber, 0 g pro.
Daily Values: 10% vit. C
Exchanges: 1 Other Carbo.

Grape Jam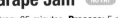

Prep: 65 minutes **Process:** 5 minutes
Makes: about 6 half-pints

- 3½ **pounds Concord grapes**
- 2 **cups water**
- 4½ **cups sugar**

1. Wash and stem grapes. Measure 8 cups. Remove skins from half of the grapes; set grape skins aside.

2. In an 8- to 10-quart heavy kettle combine skinned and unskinned grapes. Cover and cook 10 minutes or until soft. Press grapes through a sieve; discard seeds and cooked skins. Measure 3 cups of strained pulp; return to kettle. Stir in the uncooked grape skins and water. Cook, covered, for 10 minutes. Uncover; stir in sugar. Bring mixture to a full rolling boil, stirring often (see top photo, page 212). Boil, uncovered, about 12 minutes or until jam sheets off a metal spoon (see middle photo, page 212).

3. Remove kettle from heat; quickly skim off foam with a metal spoon (see bottom photo, page 212).

4. Ladle at once into hot, sterilized half-pint canning jars (see tip, page 219), leaving a ¼-inch headspace (see tip, page 217). Wipe jar rims; adjust lids. Process in a boiling-water canner for 5 minutes (start timing when water returns to boil). Remove jars; cool on racks.

Per tablespoon: 46 cal., 0 g total fat (0 g sat. fat), 0 mg chol., 0 mg sodium, 12 g carbo., 0 g fiber, 0 g pro.
Daily Values: 1% vit. C
Exchanges: 1 Other Carbo.

Blueberry-Ginger Freezer Jam

Prep: 25 minutes **Stand:** 10 minutes
Makes: about 5 half-pints

- 3 **cups fresh blueberries**
- 4 **cups sugar**
- 2 **tablespoons finely chopped crystallized ginger**
- 1 **tablespoon lemon juice**
- ½ **teaspoon ground ginger**
- ½ **of a 6-ounce package (1 foil pouch) liquid fruit pectin**

1. Place blueberries in a large heavy kettle. Coarsely mash with a potato masher. Stir in sugar. Bring to boiling over medium heat, stirring constantly to dissolve the sugar. Remove from heat. Stir in crystallized ginger, lemon juice, and ground ginger. Let stand 10 minutes, stirring occasionally.

2. Stir pectin into fruit mixture.

3. Ladle into half-pint freezer containers, leaving a ½-inch headspace (see tip, page 217). Seal and label. Let stand at room temperature 24 hours or until set. Store the jam for up to 3 weeks in the refrigerator or for up to 1 year in the freezer.

Per tablespoon: 47 cal., 0 g total fat (0 g sat. fat), 0 mg chol., 12 g carbo., 0 g fiber, 0 g pro.
Daily Values: 1% vit. C
Exchanges: 1 Other Carbo.

Peach Jam

Prep: 30 minutes **Process:** 5 minutes
Makes: about 7 half-pints

- 4 **cups finely chopped, peeled peaches (about 3 pounds fresh or 2 pounds frozen, thawed)**
- 7 **cups sugar**
- ¼ **cup lemon juice**
- ½ **of a 6-ounce package (1 foil pouch) liquid fruit pectin**

1. In a heavy 6- to 8-quart kettle combine peaches, sugar, and lemon juice. Heat over medium-high heat until mixture comes to a boil, stirring constantly to dissolve sugar. Add liquid pectin. Bring to a full rolling boil (see top photo, page 212); boil hard for 1 minute, stirring constantly. Remove from heat; quickly skim off foam with a metal spoon (see bottom photo, page 212).

2. Ladle at once into hot, sterilized half-pint canning jars (see tip, page 219), leaving a ¼-inch headspace (see tip, page 217). Wipe jar rims; adjust lids. Process in a boiling-water canner for 5 minutes (start timing when water returns to boil). Remove jars; cool on racks.*

*Note: Jam will become more set if held 1 week before serving.

Peach-Raspberry Jam: Prepare as above, except substitute 2 cups fresh raspberries for 2 cups of the finely chopped peaches. Stir before serving.

Per tablespoon peach or peach-raspberry variation: 56 cal., 0 g total fat (0 g sat. fat), 0 mg chol., 15 g carbo., 0 g fiber, 0 g pro.
Daily Values: 1% vit. A, 1% vit. C
Exchanges: 1 Other Carbo.

Altitude Adjustments

The timings in these recipes are for altitudes up to 1,000 feet above sea level; water boils at a lower temperature at higher altitudes. Follow these adjustments:

Blanching: Add 1 minute if you live 5,000 feet or more above sea level.

Boiling-water canning: Call your county extension service for detailed instructions.

Jellies and jams: Add 1 minute of processing time for each added 1,000 feet.

Pressure canning: Timings are the same, but different pressures must be used. For dial-gauge pressure canners, use 11 pounds of pressure if you live up to 2,000 feet above sea level; use 12 pounds pressure for 2,001 to 4,000 feet; use 13 pounds pressure for 4,001 to 6,000 feet; and use 14 pounds pressure for 6,001 to 8,000 feet. For weighted-gauge canners, use 10 pounds of pressure if you live up to 1,000 feet above sea level; use 15 pounds of pressure above 1,000 feet.

Sterilizing jars: Boil jars an additional 1 minute for each additional 1,000 feet.

Orange Marmalade

A marmalade is a preserve that contains pieces of deliciously tart fruit rind.

Prep: 55 minutes **Process:** 5 minutes
Makes: 6 half-pints

   4 **medium oranges**
   1 **medium lemon**
   ⅛ **teaspoon baking soda**
   5 **cups sugar**
   ½ **of a 6-ounce package (1 foil pouch) liquid fruit pectin**

1. Score orange and lemon peels into four lengthwise sections; remove the peels with your fingers. Set fruits aside. Scrape the bitter white portions off the peels and discard; cut peels into thin strips. Bring peels, 1½ cups *water,* and baking soda to boiling. Simmer, covered, for 20 minutes. Do not drain.

2. Section fruits, reserving juices; discard seeds. Add fruits and juices to peels; return to boiling. Simmer, covered, 10 minutes. Measure 3 cups.

3. In an 8- to 10-quart heavy kettle combine fruit mixture and sugar. Bring to a full rolling boil (see top photo, page 212), stirring constantly. Quickly stir in pectin. Return to a full rolling boil; boil for 1 minute, stirring constantly. Remove from heat; skim off foam with a metal spoon (see bottom photo, page 212).

4. Ladle into hot, sterilized half-pint canning jars (see tip, page 219), leaving a ¼-inch headspace (see tip, page 217). Wipe jar rims; adjust lids. Process in a boiling-water canner for 5 minutes (start timing when water returns to boil). Remove jars; cool on racks.

Per tablespoon: 46 cal., 0 g total fat (0 g sat. fat), 0 mg chol., 2 mg sodium, 12 g carbo., 0 g fiber, 0 g pro.
Daily Values: 5% vit. C
Exchanges: 1 Other Carbo.

Berry Freezer Jam

Spread this easy-to-make berry jam on hot toast, bagels, biscuits, or peanut butter and jelly sandwiches. See photo, page 201.

Prep: 30 minutes **Stand:** 24 hours
Makes: about 5 half-pints

   4 **cups fresh blackberries, raspberries, or hulled strawberries**
   4 **cups sugar**
   ½ **teaspoon finely shredded lemon peel**
   1 **1.75-ounce package regular powdered fruit pectin**
   ¾ **cup water**

1. In a bowl use a potato masher to crush the berries until you have 2 cups crushed berries. Mix berries, sugar, and lemon peel. Let stand for 10 minutes, stirring occasionally. In a small saucepan combine pectin and water. Bring to boiling over high heat; boil 1 minute, stirring constantly. Remove from heat and add to berry mixture; stir for 3 minutes or until sugar is dissolved and mixture is no longer grainy.

2. Ladle into half-pint freezer containers, leaving a ½-inch headspace (see tip, page 217). Seal and label. Let stand at room temperature 24 hours or until set. Store the jam for up to 3 weeks in the refrigerator or for up to 1 year in the freezer.

Per tablespoon: 49 cal., 0 g total fat (0 g sat. fat), 0 mg chol., 1 mg sodium, 13 g carbo., 0 g fiber, 0 g pro.
Daily Values: 3% vit. C
Exchanges: 1 Other Carbo.

Rhubarb-Raspberry Freezer Jam

Prep: 50 minutes **Stand:** 24 hours **Makes:** 5 half-pints

- **6 cups fresh or frozen unsweetened sliced rhubarb**
- **4 cups sugar**
- **2 cups fresh raspberries or one 12-ounce package frozen lightly sweetened red raspberries**
- **1 3-ounce package raspberry-flavored gelatin (not sugar-free)**

1. In a large heavy kettle combine rhubarb and sugar. Let stand 15 to 20 minutes or until sugar is moistened. Bring to boiling. Boil, uncovered, for 10 minutes, stirring often. Add berries; return to boiling. Boil hard 5 to 6 minutes or until thick, stirring often. Remove from heat. Add gelatin and stir until dissolved.

2. Ladle into half-pint freezer containers, leaving a ½-inch headspace (see tip, page 217). Seal and label. Let stand at room temperature 24 hours or until set. Store the jam for up to 3 weeks in the refrigerator or for up to 1 year in the freezer.

Per tablespoon: 51 cal., 0 g total fat (0 g sat. fat), 0 mg chol., 5 mg sodium, 13 g carbo., 0 g fiber, 0 g pro.
Daily Values: 3% vit. C, 1% calcium
Exchanges: 1 Other Carbo.

Fruit Juice Jelly

Fruit juice helps this jelly go together quickly. If you like, try substituting 100 percent fruit juice blends for the suggested juices.

Prep: 25 minutes **Process:** 5 minutes
Makes: 5 half-pints

- **4 cups cranberry juice (not low calorie) or unsweetened apple, grape, or orange juice**
- **¼ cup lemon juice**
- **1 1.75-ounce package regular powdered fruit pectin**
- **4½ cups sugar**

1. Pour desired fruit juice and lemon juice into a 6- to 8-quart heavy kettle. Sprinkle with pectin. Let stand for 1 to 2 minutes; stir to dissolve. Bring to a full rolling boil over medium-high heat (see top photo, page 212), stirring frequently. Stir in sugar. Return to a full rolling boil; stir often. Boil hard 1 minute, stirring constantly. Remove from heat; quickly skim off foam with a metal spoon (see bottom photo, page 212).

2. Ladle into hot, sterilized half-pint canning jars (see tip, page 219), leaving a ¼-inch headspace (see tip, page 217). Wipe jar rims and adjust lids. Process in a boiling-water canner for 5 minutes (start timing when water returns to boil). Remove jars; cool on racks until set.

Per tablespoon: 68 cal., 0 g total fat (0 g sat. fat), 0 mg chol., 2 mg sodium, 18 g carbo., 0 g fiber, 0 g pro.
Daily Values: 11% vit. C
Exchanges: 1 Other Carbo.

Pepper Jelly

Make this spicy-sweet jelly when you harvest the jalapeño peppers from your garden or receive a bounty from a friend. Pour the jelly over a block of cream cheese and serve with crackers for a simple and delicious appetizer or snack.

Prep: 50 minutes **Process:** 5 minutes
Makes: 5 half-pints

- **1½ cups cranberry juice (not low calorie)**
- **1 cup vinegar**
- **2 to 4 fresh jalapeño chile peppers, halved (see tip, page 74)**
- **5 cups sugar**
- **½ of a 6-ounce package (1 foil pouch) liquid fruit pectin**

1. In a medium stainless-steel, enamel, or non-stick saucepan combine cranberry juice, vinegar, and jalapeño peppers. Bring to boiling; reduce heat. Simmer, covered, for 10 minutes. Strain mixture through a sieve, pressing with the back of a spoon to remove all the liquid; measure 2 cups. Discard pulp.

2. In a 6-quart heavy kettle combine the 2 cups liquid and sugar. Bring to a full rolling boil over high heat (see top photo, page 212), stirring constantly. Quickly stir in pectin. Return to a full rolling boil; boil for 1 minute, stirring constantly. Remove from heat. Quickly skim off foam with a metal spoon (see bottom photo, page 212).

3. Ladle into hot, sterilized half-pint canning jars (see tip, page 219), leaving a ¼-inch headspace (see tip, page 217). Wipe jar rims; adjust lids. Process in a boiling-water canner for 5 minutes (start timing when water returns to boil). Remove jars; cool on racks until set (2 to 3 days).

Per tablespoon: 57 cal., 0 g total fat (0 g sat. fat), 0 mg chol., 0 mg sodium, 15 g carbo., 0 g fiber, 0 g pro.
Daily Values: 3% vit. C
Exchanges: 1 Other Carbo.

Pear-Cherry Chutney

Pear-Cherry Chutney NO FAT

Combine this sweet ruby chutney with a wheel of Brie cheese and crusty bread for a terrific gift.

Prep: 30 minutes **Cook:** 20 minutes
Cool: 1 hour **Makes:** 4 half-pints

　1　**cup dried tart red cherries, snipped**
　½　**cup sugar**
　2　**teaspoons finely shredded lemon peel**
　⅓　**cup lemon juice**
　½　**teaspoon ground cinnamon**
　½　**teaspoon ground allspice**
　5　**cups coarsely chopped, peeled ripe pears***

1. In a heavy kettle combine dried cherries, sugar, lemon peel, lemon juice, cinnamon, and allspice. Bring to boiling; reduce heat to medium. Simmer, uncovered, for 5 minutes, stirring occasionally. Stir in pears; return to boiling. Simmer, covered, for 10 minutes. Simmer, uncovered, 5 minutes more or until cooking liquid barely covers fruit. Remove from heat; let cool 1 hour.

2. Ladle into half-pint freezer containers, leaving a ½-inch headspace (see tip, page 217). Seal and label. Store the chutney up to 2 weeks in the refrigerator or for up to 6 months in the freezer. Serve on top of Brie or cream cheese or as a condiment with beef, pork, or lamb.

***Note:** Place peeled, cored, and cut-up pears in a food processor, one-third at a time. Pulse to coarsely chop.

Per 2 tablespoons: 41 cal., 0 g total fat (0 g sat. fat), 0 mg chol., 0 mg sodium, 11 g carbo., 1 g fiber, 0 g pro.
Daily Values: 2% vit. A, 4% vit. C, 1% calcium, 1% iron
Exchanges: ½ Other Carbo.

Blueberry Chutney NO FAT

Prep: 10 minutes **Cook:** 55 minutes
Cool: 1 hour **Makes:** about 3 half-pints

　1　**cup sugar**
　1　**cup raspberry-flavored vinegar**
　1　**large onion, finely chopped (1 cup)**
　2　**teaspoons finely shredded lemon peel**
　½　**teaspoon grated fresh ginger**
　¼　**teaspoon ground cinnamon**
　⅛　**teaspoon salt**
　⅛　**teaspoon cayenne pepper**
　6　**cups fresh or frozen blueberries**
　1　**cup fresh or frozen cranberries**

1. In a medium heavy saucepan combine sugar, vinegar, onion, lemon peel, ginger, cinnamon, salt, and cayenne pepper. Bring to boiling, stirring to dissolve sugar; reduce heat. Simmer, uncovered, for 15 minutes, stirring occasionally. Stir in 2 cups of the blueberries and the cranberries. Return to boiling; reduce heat. Simmer, uncovered, for 20 minutes, stirring occasionally. Add remaining 4 cups blueberries. Return to boiling; reduce heat. Simmer, uncovered, for 20 to 25 minutes more or until thickened and of desired consistency, stirring occasionally. Remove from heat; let cool 1 hour.

2. Ladle into half-pint freezer containers, leaving a ½-inch headspace (see tip, page 217). Seal and label. Store chutney up to 2 weeks in the refrigerator or for up to 6 months in the freezer. Serve as a condiment with turkey, chicken, beef, or pork.

Per 2 tablespoons: 57 cal., 0 g total fat (0 g sat. fat), 0 mg chol., 13 mg sodium, 15 g carbo., 1 g fiber, 0 g pro.
Daily Values: 1% vit. A, 8% vit. C, 1% iron
Exchanges: 1 Other Carbo.

Dining In

Share this delicious meal with friends during a quiet evening at home.

● *Broiled sirloin steak*
● *Blueberry Chutney (above)*
● *Creamy Potluck Potatoes (page 588)*
● *Roasted Asparagus with Gruyère (page 574)*
● *One-Bowl Chocolate Cake (page 168)*
● *Hot coffee or hot spiced tea*

Apple Butter NO FAT

Prep: 3 hours **Process:** 5 minutes
Makes: 8 half-pints

  4½ **pounds tart cooking apples, cored and
      quartered (about 14 medium)**
   3 **cups apple cider or apple juice**
   2 **cups sugar**
  1½ **teaspoons ground cinnamon**
   ½ **teaspoon ground cloves**
   ½ **teaspoon ground allspice**

1. In an 8- to 10-quart heavy kettle combine apples and cider. Bring to boiling; reduce heat. Simmer, covered, for 30 minutes, stirring occasionally. Press through a food mill or sieve until you have 8½ cups. Return pulp to kettle.

2. Stir in sugar, cinnamon, cloves, and allspice. Bring to boiling; reduce heat. Cook, uncovered, over low heat 1½ hours or until thick and mixture mounds on a spoon, stirring often.

Boiling-Water Canning: Ladle hot apple butter into hot, sterilized half-pint canning jars (see tip, page 219), leaving a ¼-inch headspace (see tip, right). Wipe jar rims; adjust lids. Process in a boiling-water canner for 5 minutes (start timing when water returns to boil). Remove jars; cool on racks.

Freezing: Place the kettle of apple butter in a sink filled with ice water; stir mixture to cool. Ladle into half-pint wide-top freezer containers, leaving a ½-inch headspace (see tip, right). Seal and label; freeze up to 10 months. Apple butter may darken slightly on freezing.

Per tablespoon: 25 cal., 0 g total fat (0 g sat. fat), 0 mg chol., 0 mg sodium, 7 g carbo., 0 g fiber, 0 g pro.
Daily Values: 1% vit. C
Exchanges: ½ Other Carbo.

Applesauce LOW FAT

Prep: 1½ hours **Process:** 15 minutes **Makes:** 6 pints

   8 **pounds tart cooking apples, cored and
      quartered (about 24 medium)**
   2 **cups water**
  10 **inches stick cinnamon (optional)**
  ¾ **to** 1¼ **cups sugar**

1. In an 8- to 10-quart heavy kettle combine apple, water, and, if desired, stick cinnamon. Bring to boiling; reduce heat. Simmer, covered, for 25 to 35 minutes or until apple is tender, stirring often.

2. Remove cinnamon, if using. Press apple through a food mill or sieve. Return pulp to kettle. Stir in sugar to taste. If necessary, add an additional ½ to 1 cup water to reach desired consistency. Bring to boiling.

Boiling-Water Canning: Ladle hot applesauce into sterilized pint canning jars (see tip, page 219), leaving a ½-inch headspace (see tip, below). Wipe jar rims; adjust lids. Process in a boiling-water canner for 15 minutes (start timing when water returns to boil). Remove jars; cool on racks.

Freezing: Place kettle of applesauce in a sink filled with ice water; stir mixture to cool. Ladle into pint wide-top freezer containers, leaving a ½-inch headspace (see tip, below). Seal and label; freeze for up to 8 months.

Per ½ cup: 112 cal., 1 g total fat (0 g sat. fat), 0 mg chol., 1 mg sodium, 29 g carbo., 4 g fiber, 0 g pro.
Daily Values: 1% vit. A, 10% vit. C, 1% calcium, 2% iron
Exchanges: 2 Fruit

Allow for Headspace

The amount of space between the top of the food and the rim of its container is called headspace. Leaving the correct amount is essential for optimum results.

Canning: Headspace allows a vacuum to form and the jar to seal. Use the headspace amount specified in recipes and in the charts on pages 206–211. After food and liquid are added, measure with a ruler (see photo, below) to make sure it's correct.

Freezing: Headspace provides room for food to expand without breaking the container or causing the lid to pop off. When  using unsweetened (dry) pack (no sugar or liquid added), leave a ½-inch headspace unless otherwise directed. When using water, sugar, or syrup pack in a wide-top container that has straight or slightly flared sides, leave a ½-inch headspace for pints and a 1-inch headspace for quarts. For narrow-top containers and freezer-safe jars, leave a ¾-inch headspace for pints and a 1½-inch headspace for quarts.

Dill Pickles

Prep: 30 minutes **Process:** 10 minutes
Makes: 6 pints

 3 pounds 4-inch pickling cucumbers
 (about 36)*
 3 cups white vinegar
 ¼ cup pickling salt
 ¼ cup sugar
 6 to 9 heads fresh dill or 6 tablespoons dill
 seeds

1. Thoroughly rinse cucumbers. Remove stems and cut off a slice from each blossom end. In a large stainless-steel, enamel, or nonstick sauce-pan combine 3 cups *water*, the vinegar, pickling salt, and sugar. Bring to boiling.

2. Pack cucumbers loosely into hot, sterilized pint canning jars (see tip, page 219), leaving a ½-inch headspace. Add two or three heads of dill or 1 tablespoon dill seeds to each jar. Pour hot vinegar mixture over cucumbers, leaving a ½-inch headspace (see tip, page 217). Discard any remaining hot vinegar mixture. Wipe jar rims; adjust lids.

3. Process in a boiling-water canner for 10 minutes (start timing when water returns to boil). Remove jars; cool on racks. Let stand 1 week.

Kosher-Style Dill Pickles: Prepare as above, except add 1 clove garlic, halved, to each jar.

*Note: If pickling cucumbers are not available, cut regular cucumbers into 4-inch spears.

Per regular or kosher-style variation: 7 cal., 0 g total fat (0 g sat. fat), 0 mg chol., 474 mg sodium, 2 g carbo., 0 g fiber, 0 g pro.
Daily Values: 2% vit. A, 1% vit. C, 1% iron
Exchanges: Free

Bread and Butter Pickles

See photo, page 201.

Prep: 40 minutes **Chill:** 3 hours
Process: 10 minutes **Makes:** 7 pints

 4 quarts (16 cups) sliced medium cucumbers
 8 medium white onions, sliced
 ⅓ cup pickling salt
 3 cloves garlic, halved
 Cracked ice
 4 cups sugar
 3 cups cider vinegar
 2 tablespoons mustard seeds
 1½ teaspoons ground turmeric
 1½ teaspoons celery seeds

1. In a 6- to 8-quart stainless-steel, enamel, or nonstick kettle combine cucumbers, onion, pickling salt, and garlic. Add 2 inches of cracked ice. Cover with lid and chill for 3 to 12 hours. Remove any remaining ice. Drain mixture well in a large colander. Remove garlic.

2. In the kettle combine sugar, vinegar, mustard seeds, turmeric, and celery seeds. Heat to boiling. Add cucumber mixture. Return to boiling.

3. Pack hot cucumber mixture and liquid into hot, sterilized pint canning jars (see tip, page 219), leaving a ½-inch headspace (see tip, page 217). Wipe jar rims; adjust lids. Process in a boiling-water canner for 10 minutes (start timing when water returns to boil). Remove jars; cool on racks.

Per ¼ cup: 33 cal., 0 g total fat (0 g sat. fat), 0 mg chol., 266 mg sodium, 9 g carbo., 0 g fiber, 0 g pro.
Daily Values: 1% vit. A, 1% vit. C, 1% iron
Exchanges: ½ Other Carbo.

Pickles and Relishes

Follow these guidelines when making homemade pickles and relishes.

Ingredients: Pickling cucumbers will make crunchier pickles than table or slicing varieties. Select unwaxed cucumbers and use them as soon as possible after harvest. Otherwise, refrigerate cucumbers or spread them in a cool, well-ventilated area. Wash them just before canning; remove the blossoms and slice off the blossom ends. Use granulated pickling or canning salt instead of table salt, which may cause the pickles to darken or make the brine cloudy. Cider vinegar is often used for pickles and relishes, but white vinegar can be used for a lighter-color product. Never dilute the vinegar more than is indicated in the recipe. Do not substitute ground spices for whole spices, which may cause the product to be dark and cloudy. Use soft or distilled water because hard water may prevent brined pickles from curing properly.

Procedures: Use only stoneware, glass, enamel, stainless-steel, or nonstick pans and food-grade plastic containers and utensils. Process pickles and relishes in a boiling-water canner (see instructions, page 204) to destroy yeasts, molds, and bacteria.

Corn Relish

Take advantage of summer's bounty of fresh corn on the cob when you make this colorful relish. Speckled with red and green sweet peppers, corn relish pairs well with pan-fried trout, grilled grouper, pork loin, or grilled ribeye steaks. See photo, page 201.

Prep: 1½ hours **Process:** 15 minutes **Makes:** 7 pints

16 to 18 fresh ears of corn
 2 cups water
 3 cups chopped celery (6 stalks)
 1½ cups chopped red sweet pepper (2 medium)
 1½ cups chopped green sweet pepper (2 medium)
 1 cup chopped onion (2 medium)
 3 cups vinegar
 2 cups sugar
 4 teaspoons dry mustard
 2 teaspoons pickling salt
 2 teaspoons celery seeds
 1 teaspoon ground turmeric
 3 tablespoons cornstarch
 2 tablespoons cold water

1. Cut corn from cobs (do not scrape cobs). Measure 8 cups corn. In an 8- to 10-quart stainless-steel, enamel, or nonstick heavy kettle combine corn and the 2 cups water. Bring to boiling; reduce heat. Simmer, covered, for 4 to 5 minutes or until corn is nearly tender; drain.

2. In the same kettle combine corn, celery, sweet peppers, and onion. Stir in vinegar, sugar, mustard, pickling salt, celery seeds, and turmeric. Bring to boiling. Boil gently, uncovered, for 5 minutes, stirring occasionally. Combine cornstarch and the 2 tablespoons cold water; add to corn mixture. Cook and stir until bubbly; cook and stir for 2 minutes more.

3. Ladle hot relish into hot, clean pint canning jars, leaving a ½-inch headspace (see tip, page 217). Wipe jar rims; adjust lids. Process in a boiling-water canner for 15 minutes (start timing when water returns to boil). Remove jars; cool on racks.

Per ¼ cup: 64 cal., 0 g total fat (0 g sat. fat), 0 mg chol., 103 mg sodium, 16 g carbo., 1 g fiber, 1 g pro.
Daily Values: 6% vit. A, 21% vit. C, 1% calcium, 2% iron
Exchanges: 1 Starch

Sweet Pickle Relish

Prep: 70 minutes **Stand:** 2 hours
Process: 10 minutes **Makes:** 10 half-pints

 6 cups chopped* cucumber (seeded, if desired) (about 6 medium)
 3 cups chopped* green and/or red sweet pepper (3 medium)
 3 cups chopped* onion (6 medium)
 ¼ cup pickling salt
 3 cups sugar
 2 cups cider vinegar
 1 tablespoon celery seeds
 1 tablespoon mustard seeds
 ½ teaspoon ground turmeric

1. Combine vegetables in an extra-large bowl. Sprinkle with pickling salt; add enough cold *water* to cover. Let stand at room temperature for 2 hours.

2. Pour vegetable mixture into colander set in sink. Rinse with fresh water and drain well.

3. In a 6- to 8-quart kettle combine sugar, vinegar, celery seeds, mustard seeds, and turmeric. Heat to boiling. Add drained vegetable mixture; return to boiling. Cook, uncovered, over medium-high heat for 10 minutes, stirring occasionally.

4. Ladle relish into hot, sterilized half-pint canning jars (see tip, below), leaving a ½-inch headspace (see tip, page 217). Wipe the jar rims; adjust lids. Process filled jars in a boiling-water canner for 10 minutes (start timing when water returns to boil). Remove jars; cool on racks.

*Note: If desired, use a food processor to chop vegetables in batches.

Per tablespoon: 20 cal., 0 g total fat (0 g sat. fat), 0 mg chol., 1 mg sodium, 5 g carbo., 0 g fiber, 0 g pro.
Daily Values: 4% vit. C
Exchanges: Free

Sterilizing Jars

Jars used for canning foods must be sterilized if they will be processed in a water-bath canner for 10 minutes or less.

Wash empty canning jars in hot, soapy water; rinse thoroughly. To sterilize the jars, place them in boiling water for 10 minutes. If you live more than 1,000 feet above sea level, add an additional 1 minute for each 1,000 feet of elevation.

Chunky Salsa

Chunky Salsa NO FAT

Vine-ripened tomatoes provide the high acidity needed for safe canning. Avoid using tomatoes from dead or frost-killed vines.

Prep: 2½ hours **Stand:** 30 minutes
Process: 15 minutes **Makes:** 5 pints

- 7 **pounds ripe tomatoes, peeled, if desired (about 20 medium)**
- 3 **cups seeded and chopped fresh Anaheim or poblano chile pepper (about 10) (see tip, page 74)**
- ⅓ **cup seeded and chopped fresh jalapeño chile pepper (3 large) (see tip, page 74)**
- 2 **cups chopped onion (2 large)**
- ½ **cup snipped fresh cilantro**
- 1 **cup vinegar**
- ½ **of a 6-ounce can (⅓ cup) tomato paste**
- 5 **cloves garlic, minced**
- 1 **teaspoon salt**
- 1 **teaspoon black pepper**

1. Seed, core, and coarsely chop tomatoes (you should have about 14 cups). Place tomato in a large colander. Let drain 30 minutes.

2. Place drained tomato in an 8-quart stainless-steel, enamel, or nonstick heavy kettle. Bring to boiling; reduce heat. Simmer, uncovered, about 1¼ hours or until thickened, stirring frequently. Add chile peppers, onion, cilantro, vinegar, tomato paste, garlic, salt, and black pepper. Return to boiling; reduce heat. Simmer, uncovered, for 10 minutes. Remove from heat.

3. Ladle hot salsa into hot, clean pint canning jars, leaving a ½-inch headspace (see tip, page 217). Wipe jar rims; adjust lids. Process in a boiling-water canner for 15 minutes (start timing when water returns to boil). Remove jars; cool on racks.

Per 2 tablespoons: 15 cal., 0 g total fat (0 g sat. fat), 0 mg chol., 41 mg sodium, 3 g carbo., 1 g fiber, 1 g pro.
Daily Values: 7% vit. A, 61% vit. C, 1% calcium, 3% iron
Exchanges: Free

Rhubarb-Strawberry Salsa NO FAT

This recipe makes use of two of summer's treasures—ripe, juicy strawberries and tart rhubarb. Fresh ginger accents this classic combination for a sweet yet tangy salsa that friends and family will love.

Prep: 15 minutes **Process:** 15 minutes
Makes: 4 half-pints

- 6 **cups chopped fresh rhubarb, cut into 1-inch pieces**
- 1½ **cups sugar**
- 1½ **cups dried cranberries**
- ¾ **cup cider vinegar**
- 1 **tablespoon grated fresh ginger**
- 2 **cups coarsely chopped fresh strawberries**

1. In a large saucepan combine rhubarb, sugar, cranberries, vinegar, and ginger. Bring to boiling; reduce heat. Simmer, uncovered, for 5 minutes. Remove from heat.

2. Ladle hot salsa into hot, clean half-pint canning jars, leaving a ½-inch headspace (see tip, page 217). Wipe jar rims; adjust lids. Process in a boiling-water canner for 15 minutes (start timing when water returns to a boil). Remove jars; cool on racks.

3. Stir ⅓ cup of the strawberries into each half-pint of processed salsa before serving. Serve as a condiment with turkey, chicken, or pork.

Per 2 tablespoons: 49 cal., 0 g total fat (0 g sat. fat), 0 mg chol., 1 mg sodium, 13 g carbo., 1 g fiber, 0 g pro.
Daily Values: 9% vit. C, 4% calcium, 1% iron
Exchanges: Free

Cheese & Eggs

Cheese Soufflé, 228

Eggs Benedict, 230

Farmer's Casserole, 237

Cheese and Eggs Essentials

Cheese and eggs are two versatile ingredients that are also the backbone for many recipes. Proper selection, storage, and handling of these two staples is a must for optimum results.

In addition to its role as an important cooking ingredient, cheese complements almost any meal or makes a meal itself. Serve a cheese course after the main course and before dessert. Or make cheese the basis of a simple get-together, serving it alongside dried apricots, figs, nuts, smoked salmon, crusty bread, and wine.

Using Cheese

Cheese is made from the milk of cows, goats, and sheep or a combination of any of these. The type of milk dictates a cheese's flavor and aging enhances it. The older the cheese, the stronger and sharper its flavor and the harder its texture.

Cheese should be served at room temperature. Colder temperatures mute the flavor and aroma and change texture. For instance, the texture of a creamy style of cheese, such as Camembert, will be somewhat tough and rubbery when the cheese is cold. At room temperature, the same cheese will develop its smooth, rich texture.

When you use high-quality cheese as an ingredient, it will add more flavor to your dish than a mass-produced variety would. And though better cheeses are often more expensive, you can use smaller quantities. For a cheese platter, where cheese alone is the star, seek out handcrafted cheese from small producers; you'll notice a dramatic flavor difference. Ask for samples at the cheese counter and ask questions about the different cheeses available. Choose three to five types that have different textures, flavor intensities, and milk sources. Plan on serving 4 to 6 ounces of cheese per guest. Fresh or dried fruit, bread, and wine are natural accompaniments.

Storing Cheese

Airtight packaging is the key to proper cheese storage. If the cheese has a rind, leave it on to keep the cheese fresh. Wrap unused cheese tightly in foil or plastic wrap, then seal it in a plastic bag or a container with a tight-fitting lid. Store the cheese in the refrigerator.

Most cheese comes stamped with a "sell by" date on the package. In general, the softer the cheese, the shorter the storage life. If there is no date on the container, soft cheeses, such as

Pairing Wine and Cheese

Matching wine with cheese is not difficult, and there are a couple of ways to go about it. The first is to match the wine's flavor intensity and mouth feel with that of the cheese. For instance, creamy-textured cheeses, such as Brie, often pair well with heavy, dessert-type wines because they both have a thick, rich feel on the tongue. Tangy fresh goat cheeses often taste best with crisp white wines, such as Sauvignon Blanc, because their sharp, acidic flavors and light textures complement each other perfectly. Aged cheeses with a bold flavor pair well with well-aged wines, such as Cabernet Sauvignon. Another way to pair cheese and wine is to select offerings from the same region. For example, if you are pouring Italian wine, serve Italian cheeses. If you've chosen California wines, search out California-made cheeses.

cottage and ricotta, should be stored no longer than 5 days after purchase. Firm and hard cheeses have less moisture and can be stored for longer periods if properly wrapped. For longer storage, cheese can be frozen, but expect a quality compromise. Freezing usually destroys the texture and affects the flavor and aroma. It's best to reserve cheeses that have been frozen for use as ingredients—in casseroles, for example.

As cheese ages, it may develop surface mold. Surface mold looks unappealing but generally is harmless. For firm cheese, cut away at least 1 inch around the moldy area and use the remaining cheese. Discard soft cheeses, such as cottage cheese and cream cheese, that have mold.

Using Eggs

Eggs are a favorite because of all of the ways you can cook them in addition to the many functions they perform in recipes.

- Select clean, fresh eggs from refrigerated display cases. Don't use dirty, cracked, or leaking eggs. They may have become contaminated with harmful bacteria.
- Refrigerate eggs with the large ends up in their cartons so they don't absorb refrigerator odors.

Fresh eggs can be refrigerated for up to 5 weeks after the packing date (a number stamped on the carton from 1 to 365 with 1 representing January 1 and 365 representing December 31).

- When cracking eggs avoid getting any eggshell in the raw eggs. Also, when separating eggs use an egg separator so that any bacteria present on the shell won't contaminate either the yolk or the white.

- To store raw egg whites, refrigerate them in a tightly covered container for 4 days. Or place them in a freezer container and freeze for up to 1 year. Although you can refrigerate unbroken raw yolks covered with water in a tightly covered container for up to 2 days, you should not freeze them. To freeze whole eggs, beat the whites and yolks together, place in a freezer container, and freeze for up to 1 year. Refrigerate hard-cooked eggs in their shells for up to 7 days.
- Wash your hands, utensils, and countertop after working with eggs.
- Serve hot egg dishes as soon as they're cooked. Chill leftovers promptly and reheat thoroughly before serving. Refrigerate cold egg dishes immediately.
- For more information about handling eggs safely, call the U.S. Department of Agriculture's Meat and Poultry Hotline at 888/674-6854.

Cheeses

While there is a cheese for every taste and occasion, almost all varieties can be eaten as an appetizer or served with other foods. Below are brief descriptions of cheeses you may be familiar with or may want to add to your "to try" list.

Name	Description
Fresh Cheeses Fresh cheeses are made from goat's, cow's, and sheep's milk and have not been aged. They have high moisture content and a creamy, soft texture.	
Chèvre	This soft, tangy yet mild-flavored French and North American cheese is made with pure goat's milk. It's wonderful served with mixed greens.
Feta	Originally from Greece, where it was traditionally made from sheep's or goat's milk, now this cheese is also made from cow's milk. The texture is firm to crumbly and the flavor is sharp, tangy, and salty. Feta is delicious crumbled over salads and pasta dishes.
Fresh mozzarella	Packaged in whey or water, fresh mozzarella is usually made from cow's milk. The texture is soft and the flavor is mild. Fresh mozzarella showcases beautifully on an antipasto tray.
Mascarpone	This soft, rich, and butterlike cheese from Italy is made from cow's milk. It's a starring ingredient in tiramisu but is also great served with fresh fruit.
Queso fresco	This slightly salty Mexican cheese has a dry texture and mild flavor. Also called queso blanco, it is best crumbled over finished dishes.

Swiss

Feta

Roquefort

Cheddar

Stilton

Manchego

Havarti

Asiago

Chèvre

Provolone

Parmigiano-Reggiano

Muenster

Fresh Mozzarella

Gouda

Camembert

White Cheddar

Brie

Name	Description
Soft-Ripened Cheeses	
Soft-ripened cheeses become soft at room temperature and are prized for their unique flavors.	
Brie and Camembert	These rich, mild, and creamy French cow's milk cheeses are best eaten at room temperature. The interior should bulge when fully ripened. The bloomy white rind is edible. Brie and Camembert are popular warmed and/or in pastry crusts with crackers or bread and fresh fruit.
Semisoft Cheeses	
Semisoft cheeses have a smooth interior and a high moisture content.	
Gouda	Originally from Holland, this cow's milk cheese has a creamy texture and nutty, caramel-like flavor. The high fat content makes it a good melting cheese; it's great for fondue.
Havarti	This traditional Danish cheese has a buttery yet tangy flavor and melts nicely for sandwiches and sauces.
Muenster	American Muenster (not to be confused with French Muenster) is rich and mild. Try it in grilled cheese sandwiches or with sliced apples.
Port du Salut	This cow's milk cheese from France has a buttery, savory flavor. It's lovely on a platter with fresh fruit.
Semifirm Cheeses	
Semifirm cheeses have been pressed during cheesemaking to remove moisture. As they age they become even more firm and pungent.	
Cheddar/White Cheddar	Age determines whether this cow's milk cheese has a mild or sharp flavor. The color ranges from cream to pumpkin orange. It's the ultimate cheese for traditional macaroni and cheese.
Gouda (aged)	As Gouda ages, the mild, buttery flavor becomes more earthy and caramel-like. Aged Gouda is a good melting cheese for topping French onion soup.
Provolone	This cow's milk cheese originated in Italy. The flavor of a young provolone is mild—when aged it is somewhat sharp. Young provolone lends itself well to melting on a pizza.
Swiss	A mild, slightly nutty flavor and small holes characterize this American cow's milk cheese. It is a great choice for sandwiches or fondue.
Hard Cheeses	
In general, cheeses become firmer and more pungent as they age. The texture of hard cheeses is suitable for grating, and the taste is sharp.	
Asiago (aged)	This cow's milk cheese has a nutty, sharp, and pleasantly salty flavor. Grate this Italian cheese over pasta or serve with figs, grapes, pears, and apples.
Manchego (aged)	From Spain, this sheep's milk cheese has a mellow, nutty flavor. It's satisfying with a fruity wine or eaten on its own.
Parmigiano-Reggiano	A rich, sharp flavor distinguishes this Italian cow's milk cheese. It is the quintessential cheese in risotto and for grating as a finishing touch to pasta.
Blue	
Blue cheeses have distinctive blue veins created by the addition of mold during the cheesemaking process. The flavor is mild to assertive and quite pungent.	
Gorgonzola	This cow's milk cheese from Italy has a rich, slightly pungent flavor. The aroma and flavor of aged Gorgonzola is quite strong. Partner it with pears and apples or crumble over potatoes.
Maytag Blue	Soft and crumbly in texture, this blue cheese is made in Iowa and has a salty, slightly peppery flavor. It is lovely served crumbled over salads.
Roquefort	This pungent, slightly salty blue cheese is made from sheep's milk and has a creamy texture. It is the star of Roquefort salad dressing and is great with fruit for dessert.
Stilton	The creamy yet slightly crumbly texture of this English cheese makes it especially good alone or served with port or dry red wine.

Parmigiano-Reggiano

Chile Rellenos Casserole VEGETARIAN

Prep: 20 minutes **Bake:** 15 minutes **Oven:** 450°F
Stand: 5 minutes **Makes:** 4 servings

- 2 **large fresh poblano chile peppers, fresh Anaheim chile peppers, or green sweet peppers (8 ounces)**
- 1 **cup shredded Monterey Jack cheese with jalapeño peppers or Mexican-blend cheese (4 ounces)**
- 3 **eggs, beaten**
- ¼ **cup milk**
- ⅓ **cup all-purpose flour**
- ½ **teaspoon baking powder**
- ¼ **teaspoon cayenne pepper**
- ⅛ **teaspoon salt**
- ½ **cup shredded Monterey Jack cheese with jalapeño peppers or Mexican-blend cheese (2 ounces)**
  Picante sauce (optional)
  Dairy sour cream (optional)

1. Preheat oven to 450°F. Quarter the peppers and remove seeds, stems, and veins (see tip, page 74). Immerse peppers into boiling water for 3 minutes; drain. Invert peppers on paper towels to drain well. Place the peppers in a well-greased 2-quart square baking dish. Top with the 1 cup cheese.

2. In a medium bowl combine eggs and milk. Add flour, baking powder, cayenne pepper, and salt. Beat until smooth with a rotary beater. Pour egg mixture over peppers and cheese.

3. Bake, uncovered, for about 15 minutes or until a knife inserted into the egg mixture comes out clean. Sprinkle with ½ cup cheese. Let stand about 5 minutes or until cheese melts. If desired, serve with picante sauce and sour cream.

Per serving: 286 cal., 18 g total fat (10 g sat. fat), 206 mg chol.,
466 mg sodium, 14 g carbo., 0 g fiber, 18 g pro.
Daily Values: 26% vit. A, 207% vit. C, 38% calcium, 13% iron
Exchanges: 1 Vegetable, ½ Starch, 2 High-Fat Meat

Low-Fat Chile Rellenos Casserole: Prepare as above, except use reduced-fat Monterey Jack cheese with jalapeño peppers or reduced-fat Mexican-blend cheese. Substitute ¾ cup refrigerated or frozen egg product (thawed) for the eggs and fat-free milk for the milk.

Per serving: 207 calories, 9 g total fat (6 g sat. fat), 30 mg chol.,
569 mg sodium, 15 g carbo., 1 g fiber, 18 g pro.
Daily Values: 25% vit. A, 213% vit. C, 38% calcium, 15% iron
Exchanges: ½ Starch, 1 Vegetable, 2 Lean Meat

Grilled Cheese Sandwich

Pair this classic sandwich—or one of its delicious variations—with a steaming cup of soup for a warming lunch or light dinner.

Place one slice of white or whole wheat bread on work surface; top with 1 or 2 ounces of sliced American, cheddar, Monterey Jack, or Havarti cheese, cutting the cheese so it covers the bread. Top with another slice of bread; spread bread with butter. Place sandwich, buttered side down, in a skillet over medium heat. Carefully spread unbuttered bread with butter. Cook for 2 to 3 minutes per side or until cheese is melted.

Grilled Swiss and Corned Beef Sandwich: Prepare as above, except use process Swiss cheese and top cheese with 1 tablespoon bottled Thousand Island salad dressing, if desired, and 1 ounce thinly sliced corned beef.

Grilled Cheese and Caramelized Onion Sandwich: Slice half of a small onion. In a small skillet, cook onion in 2 teaspoons butter over medium heat about 10 minutes or until onion is soft and golden brown. Sprinkle lightly with salt. Prepare Grilled Cheese Sandwich as above, except top desired cheese with caramelized onions.

Grilled Provolone and Pepperoni Sandwich: Prepare Grilled Cheese Sandwich as above, except use provolone or mozzarella cheese and top cheese with 1 tablespoon pizza sauce and 5 to 6 slices (½ ounce) thinly sliced pepperoni.

Grilled Cheese and Fruit Sandwich: Prepare Grilled Cheese Sandwich as above, except top cheese with several thin slices of apple or pear.

Cheese Soufflé

This golden cheese soufflé is best when made with a variety of cheeses. See photo, page 221.

Prep: 50 minutes **Bake:** 40 minutes
Oven: 350°F **Makes:** 4 servings

>   4 egg yolks
>   4 egg whites
>   ¼ cup butter or margarine
>   ¼ cup all-purpose flour
>   ¼ teaspoon dry mustard
>   Dash cayenne pepper
>   1 cup milk
>   2 cups shredded cheddar, Colby, Havarti,
>   and/or process Swiss cheese (8 ounces)

1. Allow the egg yolks and egg whites to stand at room temperature for 30 minutes.

2. Preheat oven to 350°F. For cheese sauce, in a medium saucepan melt butter; stir in flour, dry mustard, and cayenne pepper. Add milk all at once. Cook and stir over medium heat until thickened and bubbly. Remove from heat. Add cheese, a little at a time, stirring until cheese melts. In a medium bowl beat egg yolks with a fork until combined. Slowly add cheese sauce to egg yolks, stirring constantly. Cool slightly. In a large mixing bowl beat whites with an electric mixer on medium to high speed until stiff peaks form (tips stand straight). Gently fold about 1 cup of the stiffly beaten egg whites into cheese sauce (see photo, below). Gradually pour cheese sauce over remaining stiffly beaten egg whites, folding to combine. Pour into an ungreased 2-quart soufflé dish.

3. Bake for about 40 minutes or until a knife inserted near center comes out clean. Serve immediately.

Per serving: 466 cal., 37 g total fat (20 g sat. fat), 301 mg chol., 530 mg sodium, 10 g carbo., 0 g fiber, 23 g pro.
Daily Values: 26% vit. A, 50% calcium, 7% iron
Exchanges: ½ Other Carbo., 1 Medium-Fat Meat, 2 High-Fat Meat, 3 Fat

To fold some of the egg whites into the cheese sauce, use a spatula to cut down through the mixture, scrape across the bottom of the bowl, and come up to the surface.

Serving a Soufflé

A soufflé begins with an egg yolk-based sauce that is lightened with stiffly beaten egg whites.

Light and airy, a soufflé demands to be served immediately after it comes out of the oven.

● To cut your soufflé into serving-size wedges, insert two forks back to back and gently pull the soufflé apart.

● Use a large serving spoon to transfer the soufflé wedges to individual plates.

Hard-Cooked Eggs

Minimize the chance of having a harmless but unattractive green ring form around the yolk by timing the cooking carefully. Cool hard-cooked eggs in ice water.

Start to Finish: 25 minutes **Makes:** 6 hard-cooked eggs

>   6 large eggs*
>   Cold water

1. Place eggs in a single layer in a large saucepan (do not stack eggs). Add enough cold water to cover the eggs by at least 1 inch. Bring to a rapid boil over high heat (water will have large, rapidly breaking bubbles). Remove from heat, cover, and let stand for 15 minutes; drain.

2. Run cold water over the eggs or place them in ice water until cool enough to handle; drain.

3. To peel a hard-cooked egg, gently tap it on the countertop, then roll it between the palms of your hands. Peel off the eggshell, starting at the large end.

*Note: If you have extra-large eggs, let them stand in the boiled water for 18 minutes.

Per egg: 78 cal., 5 g total fat (2 g sat. fat), 212 mg chol., 62 mg sodium, 1 g carbo., 0 g fiber, 6 g pro.
Daily Values: 6% vit. A, 3% calcium, 3% iron
Exchanges: 1 Medium-Fat Meat

Deviled Eggs FAST

Start to Finish: 25 minutes **Makes:** 12 servings

    6 Hard-Cooked Eggs (page 228)
    ¼ cup mayonnaise or salad dressing
    1 teaspoon yellow mustard
    1 teaspoon vinegar
       Paprika or parsley sprigs (optional)

1. Halve hard-cooked eggs lengthwise and remove yolks. Set whites aside. Place yolks in a small bowl; mash with a fork. Add mayonnaise, mustard, and vinegar; mix well. If desired, season with *salt* and *black pepper*. Stuff egg white halves with yolk mixture. Cover and chill until serving time (up to 24 hours). If desired, garnish with paprika and/or parsley.

Greek-Style Deviled Eggs: Prepare as above, except fold 2 tablespoons crumbled feta cheese, 1 tablespoon finely chopped pitted kalamata olives, and 2 teaspoons snipped fresh oregano into yolk mixture.

Curry-and-Crab Deviled Eggs: Prepare as above, except omit mustard and vinegar. Stir the mayonnaise, 2 teaspoons Dijon-style mustard, 1 teaspoon snipped fresh chives, and ½ teaspoon curry powder into mashed yolks; mix well. Fold in ¼ cup drained, flaked canned crabmeat.

Per plain, Greek-style, or curry-and-crab egg half: 72 cal., 6 g total fat (1 g sat. fat), 109 mg chol., 64 mg sodium, 0 g carbo., 0 g fiber, 3 g pro.
Daily Values: 3% vit. A, 1% calcium, 2% iron
Exchanges: ½ Medium-Fat Meat, 1 Fat

Chipotle Deviled Eggs: Prepare as above, except omit mayonnaise, mustard, and vinegar. Stir ¼ cup dairy sour cream, 1 tablespoon finely chopped green onion, and 1 teaspoon finely chopped canned chipotle peppers in adobo sauce into yolk mixture.

Per egg half: 48 cal., 3 g total fat (1 g sat. fat), 108 mg chol., 35 mg sodium, 1 g carbo., 0 g fiber, 3 g pro.
Daily Values: 4% vit. A, 2% calcium, 2% iron
Exchanges: ½ Medium-Fat Meat, ½ Fat

Egg Salad Sandwiches
FAST   VEGETARIAN

Egg salad tastes just as good today as it did 60 years ago. This recipe gives you the basic salad as well as Greek- and California-style options.

Start to Finish: 15 minutes **Makes:** 2 sandwiches

    4 hard-cooked eggs (page 228), chopped
    2 tablespoons finely chopped green onion

    1 tablespoon diced pimiento
    2 tablespoons mayonnaise or salad dressing
    2 teaspoons yellow mustard
       Salt
       Black pepper
    4 slices bread, 2 small pita bread rounds
       (halved crosswise), or 2 bagels (split)
       Lettuce leaves

1. In a medium bowl combine chopped egg, green onion, and pimiento. Stir in mayonnaise and mustard. Add salt and pepper to taste. Spread egg mixture on two slices of bread, in pita halves, or on bagel bottoms. Top with lettuce and, if not using pitas, remaining bread slices or bagel tops.

Greek-Style Egg Salad Sandwiches: Prepare as above, except omit the pimiento and mustard. Stir ½ cup crumbled feta cheese, ¼ cup finely chopped seeded tomato, and 2 tablespoons sliced, pitted ripe olives into egg mixture. Use 6 slices of bread, 3 pitas, or 3 bagels. Makes 3 sandwiches.

Per plain or Greek-style sandwich: 398 cal., 23 g total fat (5 g sat. fat), 434 mg chol., 679 mg sodium, 28 g carbo., 2 g fiber, 17 g pro.
Daily Values: 21% vit. A, 20% vit. C, 14% calcium, 20% iron
Exchanges: 2 Starch, 2 Medium-Fat Meat, 2 Fat

California-Style Egg Salad Sandwiches: Prepare as above, except omit pimiento and lettuce. Substitute avocado slices and thin slices of Monterey Jack cheese. Makes 2 sandwiches.

Per sandwich: 568 cal., 38 g total fat (12 g sat. fat), 454 mg chol., 899 mg sodium, 32 g carbo., 4 g fiber, 25 g pro.
Daily Values: 19% vit. A, 35% calcium, 21% iron
Exchanges: 2 Starch, 2 Medium-Fat Meat, 1 High-Fat Meat, 3½ Fat

Deviled Eggs

Poached Eggs

Start to Finish: 10 minutes **Makes:** 4 poached eggs

> **1 to 2 teaspoons instant chicken bouillon granules (optional)**
> **1 to 4 eggs**

1. If desired, lightly grease a medium skillet (for three or four eggs) or a 1-quart saucepan (for one or two eggs) with *cooking oil* or *shortening*. Half fill the skillet with *water*. If desired, stir in bouillon granules. Bring the water to boiling; reduce heat to simmering (bubbles should begin to break the surface of the water).

2. Break one of the eggs into a measuring cup. Holding the lip of the cup as close to the water as possible, carefully slide egg into simmering water (see photo 1, below). Repeat with remaining eggs, allowing each egg an equal amount of space.

3. Simmer eggs, uncovered, for 3 to 5 minutes or until the whites are completely set and yolks begin to thicken but are not hard. Remove eggs with a slotted spoon. Season to taste with *salt* and *black pepper*.

Poaching pan directions: Lightly grease each cup of an egg-poaching pan. Place poacher cups over the pan of boiling water (water should not touch bottoms of cups); reduce heat to simmering. Break an egg into a measuring cup. Carefully slide egg into a poacher cup. Repeat with remaining eggs (see photo 2, below). Cover and cook for 4 to 6 minutes or until the whites are completely set and yolks begin to thicken but are not hard. Run a knife around edges to loosen eggs. Invert poacher cups to remove eggs.

Per egg: 78 cal., 5 g total fat (2 g sat. fat), 212 mg chol., 62 mg sodium, 1 g carbo., 0 g fiber, 6 g pro.
Daily Values: 6% vit. A, 3% calcium, 3% iron
Exchanges: 1 Medium-Fat Meat

1. Using a measuring cup with a handle, gently slide each egg into the simmering water, taking care to not break the egg.

2. If using an egg-poaching pan, gently slide each egg from a measuring cup into a greased poacher cup.

Eggs Benedict

This classic breakfast or brunch specialty easily inspires delicious variations. See photo, page 221.

Start to Finish: 35 minutes **Makes:** 4 servings

> **4 eggs**
> **1 recipe Hollandaise Sauce (page 518)**
> **2 English muffins, split**
> **4 slices Canadian-style bacon**
> **Paprika (optional)**

1. Lightly grease a medium skillet. Half fill the skillet with *water.* Bring water to boiling; reduce heat to simmering (bubbles should begin to break the surface of the water). Break one of the eggs into a measuring cup. Holding the lip of the cup as close to the water as possible, carefully slide egg into simmering water (see photo 1, below left). Repeat with remaining eggs, allowing each egg an equal amount of space.

2. Simmer eggs, uncovered, for 3 to 5 minutes or until the whites are completely set and yolks begin to thicken but are not hard. Remove eggs with a slotted spoon and place them in a large pan of warm water to keep them warm. Prepare the Hollandaise Sauce.

3. Meanwhile, place muffin halves, cut sides up, on a baking sheet. Broil 3 to 4 inches from the heat 2 minutes or until toasted. Top each muffin half with a slice of Canadian-style bacon; broil 1 minute more or until meat is heated.

4. To serve, top each bacon-topped muffin half with an egg; spoon Hollandaise Sauce over eggs. If desired, sprinkle with paprika.

Crab Benedict: Prepare as above, except substitute one 6.5-ounce can crabmeat, drained, flaked, and cartilage removed, for the Canadian-style bacon.

Salmon Benedict: Prepare as above, except substitute 4 ounces thinly sliced lox-style smoked salmon for the Canadian-style bacon and stir 1 tablespoon drained capers into the Hollandaise Sauce. Do not use the paprika.

Mushrooms Benedict: Prepare as above, except in a large skillet cook 2 cups sliced fresh assorted mushrooms in 2 tablespoons hot butter until mushrooms are tender. Continue as directed, using the mushrooms instead of the Canadian-style bacon and sprinkling with 1 tablespoon snipped fresh basil instead of the paprika.

Make-ahead directions: Prepare the eggs and toast English muffins as on page 230. Place muffin halves in a greased 8×8×2-inch baking pan. Top each muffin half with a slice of Canadian-style bacon and one cooked egg. Cover and chill for up to 24 hours. To serve, prepare one recipe Mock Hollandaise Sauce (see page 519); spoon sauce over eggs. Bake, covered, in a 350°F oven about 25 minutes or until heated through.

Per serving plain, crab, salmon, or mushroom variations:
442 cal., 36 g total fat (19 g sat. fat), 451 mg chol., 836 mg sodium, 14 g carbo., 1 g fiber, 16 g pro.
Daily Values: 30% vit. A, 3% vit. C, 10% calcium, 12% iron
Exchanges: 1 Starch, 2 Medium-Fat Meat, 4½ Fat

Fried Eggs `FAST`

Eggs are rich in protein, low in sodium, and contain important vitamins and minerals for good health. They are also inexpensive and easy to prepare for any meal of the day.

Start to Finish: 10 minutes **Makes:** 4 fried eggs

> **2 teaspoons butter or margarine, or nonstick cooking spray**
> **4 eggs**
> **Salt (optional)**
> **Black pepper (optional)**

1. In a large skillet melt butter over medium heat. (Or coat an unheated skillet with nonstick cooking spray.) Break eggs into skillet. If desired, sprinkle with salt and pepper. Reduce heat to low; cook eggs for 3 to 4 minutes or until whites are completely set and yolks start to thicken.

2. For fried eggs over easy or over hard, turn the eggs and cook 30 seconds more (over easy) or 1 minute more (over hard).

Steam-Basted Fried Eggs: Prepare as above, except when egg edges turn white add 1 to 2 teaspoons water. Cover skillet and cook eggs for 3 to 4 minutes more or until yolks begin to thicken but are not hard.

Per egg: 91 cal., 7 g total fat (3 g sat. fat), 217 mg chol., 84 mg sodium, 0 g carbo., 0 g fiber, 6 g pro.
Daily Values: 6% vit. A, 3% calcium, 5% iron
Exchanges: 1 Medium-Fat Meat, ½ Fat

Baked Eggs

Serve these eggs with croissants or hearty bread and fresh fruit for an easy brunch.

Prep: 10 minutes **Bake:** 25 minutes
Oven: 325°F **Makes:** 3 servings

> **Butter or margarine**
> **6 eggs**
> **Snipped fresh chives or desired herb**
> **6 tablespoons shredded cheddar, Swiss, or Monterey Jack cheese (optional)**

1. Generously grease three 10-ounce casseroles with butter. Carefully break two of the eggs into each casserole; sprinkle with chives, *salt*, and *black pepper*. Set casseroles in a 13×9×2-inch baking pan; place on oven rack. Pour hot *water* around casseroles in pan to a depth of 1 inch.

2. Bake in a 325°F oven about 25 minutes or until the eggs are firm and the whites are opaque. If desired, after 20 minutes of baking, sprinkle shredded cheese on eggs. Bake for 5 to 10 minutes more or until eggs are cooked and cheese melts.

Per 2 eggs: 167 cal., 12 g total fat (4 g sat. fat), 430 mg chol., 147 mg sodium, 1 g carbo., 0 g fiber, 13 g pro.
Daily Values: 15% vit. A, 5% calcium, 8% iron
Exchanges: 2 Medium-Fat Meat, ½ Fat

Egg Sandwiches

Egg sandwiches are perfect for the time-pressured cook or a family on the go. They can be prepared in about 10 minutes and make a terrific option for breakfast, lunch, or a light dinner.

Classic Egg Sandwich: Prepare Fried Eggs (see recipe, left) or Scrambled Eggs (see recipe, page 234). For each open-face sandwich, spread one slice of bread, toasted, or English muffin, split and toasted, with butter or margarine. Top with cooked egg. If desired, add one of the following toppings:

● Cheese and crisp-cooked bacon or Canadian-style bacon
● Sliced fresh tomatoes and fresh basil leaves
● Fresh baby spinach and shaved ham
● Fresh arugula and finely shredded Parmesan cheese

Huevos Rancheros

Huevos Rancheros VEGETARIAN

Huevos rancheros is Spanish for "rancher's eggs." With eggs, vegetables, and corn tortillas, this dish is a meal in itself.

Start to Finish: 40 minutes
Oven: 300°F **Makes:** 4 servings

3 tablespoons olive oil or cooking oil
5 6-inch corn tortillas
½ cup chopped onion (1 medium)
2 cloves garlic, minced
1 14.5-ounce can diced tomatoes, drained
1 or 2 chipotle peppers in adobo sauce, chopped (see tip, page 74), or ½ of a 4-ounce can diced green chile peppers, drained
2 tablespoons snipped fresh cilantro
¼ teaspoon ground cumin
8 eggs
½ cup shredded Monterey Jack cheese or crumbled queso fresco (2 ounces)
Snipped fresh cilantro or parsley (optional)

1. In a 12-inch skillet heat 2 tablespoons of the oil. Dip tortillas, one at a time, into the oil just until hot. Drain on paper towels (do not stack), reserving oil in skillet. Keep four tortillas warm on a baking sheet in a 300°F oven. Reserve remaining tortilla.

2. For salsa, cook onion and garlic in the reserved oil for 2 to 3 minutes or until tender. Stir in drained tomatoes, chile peppers, cilantro, and cumin. Bring to boiling; reduce heat. Simmer, uncovered, for 5 minutes. Transfer mixture to a blender or food processor. Tear reserved tortilla into pieces; add to blender or

food processor. Cover and blend or process until a coarse puree results. Keep warm.

3. In the skillet heat the remaining 1 tablespoon oil over medium heat. Carefully break eggs into skillet. When whites are set and edges turn white, add 1 tablespoon *water.* Cover skillet and cook eggs to desired doneness (3 to 4 minutes for soft-set yolks or 4 to 5 minutes for firm-set yolks).

4. Place a warm tortilla on each of four dinner plates. Top each with two fried eggs. Spoon some of the warm salsa over the eggs. Sprinkle with cheese. If desired, garnish with cilantro.

Per serving: 413 cal., 26 g total fat (7 g sat. fat), 437 mg chol., 397 mg sodium, 27 g carbo., 3 g fiber, 20 g pro.
Daily Values: 31% vit. A, 29% vit. C, 23% calcium, 22% iron
Exchanges: ½ Vegetable, 1½ Starch, 2 Medium-Fat Meat, ½ High-Fat Meat, 2 Fat

Vegetable Frittata with Cheese FAST VEGETARIAN

Start to Finish: 25 minutes **Makes:** 4 servings

8 eggs, slightly beaten
1 tablespoon snipped fresh basil or 1 teaspoon dried basil, crushed
1 cup frozen whole kernel corn or cut fresh corn
½ cup chopped zucchini
⅓ cup thinly sliced green onion (3)
2 tablespoons olive oil
¾ cup chopped roma tomato (2)
½ cup shredded cheddar cheese (2 ounces)

1. In a bowl combine eggs and basil; set aside. In a large broilerproof skillet cook corn, zucchini, and green onion in hot oil. Cook and stir for 3 minutes; add tomato. Cook, uncovered, over medium heat about 5 minutes or until the vegetables are crisp-tender, stirring occasionally.

2. Pour the egg mixture over vegetables in the skillet. Cook over medium heat. As mixture sets, run a spatula around edge of skillet, lifting egg mixture so uncooked portion flows underneath (see photo 1, page 234). Continue cooking and lifting edges until egg mixture is almost set (surface will be moist). Sprinkle with cheese.

3. Broil 4 to 5 inches from heat about 1 minute or until cheese melts. Cut into quarters.

Per quarter: 313 cal., 22 g total fat (7 g sat. fat), 440 mg chol., 220 mg sodium, 13 g carbo., 2 g fiber, 18 g pro.
Daily Values: 22% vit. A, 19% vit. C, 16% calcium, 12% iron
Exchanges: 1 Vegetable, ½ Starch, 2 Medium-Fat Meat, 2 Fat

Mediterranean Frittata (FAST) (VEGETARIAN)

Start to Finish: 25 minutes **Makes:** 4 servings

- **1 cup chopped onion**
- **2 cloves garlic, minced**
- **3 tablespoons olive oil**
- **8 eggs, beaten**
- **¼ cup half-and-half, light cream, or milk**
- **½ cup crumbled feta cheese (2 ounces)**
- **½ cup chopped bottled roasted red sweet peppers**
- **½ cup sliced kalamata or pitted ripe olives (optional)**
- **¼ cup slivered fresh basil**
- **⅛ teaspoon black pepper**
- **½ cup onion-and-garlic croutons, coarsely crushed**
- **2 tablespoons finely shredded Parmesan cheese**
- **Fresh basil leaves (optional)**

1. Preheat broiler. In a large broilerproof skillet cook onion and garlic in 2 tablespoons of the hot oil until onion is just tender.

2. Meanwhile, in a bowl beat together eggs and half-and-half. Stir in feta cheese, roasted sweet pepper, olives (if desired), basil, and black pepper. Pour egg mixture over onion mixture in skillet. Cook over medium heat. As mixture sets, run a spatula around the skillet edge, lifting egg mixture so uncooked portion flows underneath (see photo 1, page 234). Continue cooking and lifting edges until egg mixture is almost set (surface will be moist). Reduce heat as necessary to prevent overcooking.

3. In a small bowl combine the remaining 1 tablespoon oil, the crushed croutons, and Parmesan cheese; sprinkle mixture over frittata.

4. Broil 4 to 5 inches from heat for 1 to 2 minutes or until top is set and crumbs are golden. Cut frittata in quarters to serve. If desired, garnish with fresh basil leaves.

Per quarter: 370 cal., 28 g total fat (8 g sat. fat), 443 mg chol., 577 mg sodium, 12 g carbo., 2 g fiber, 17 g pro.
Daily Values: 15% vit. A, 90% vit. C, 19% calcium, 14% iron
Exchanges: 1 Other Carbo., 3 Medium-Fat Meat, 2 Fat

Mediterranean Frittata

Brunch: Endless Possibilities

Brunch, a combination of breakfast and lunch, has become a popular time to gather with family and friends. It's also a good opportunity for new cooks to practice their skills.

Brunch generally is served late morning and the menu often is simple, though elaborate fare also works—the choice is yours. As you plan your menu, consider the season and how many guests you will have. If you are entertaining more than six to eight guests, table space may become limited and you probably will want to serve a casual brunch buffet.

To keep your day stress-free, make ahead any dishes that you can: Stratas, quiches, and egg casseroles are all good make-ahead possibilities. To save time, consider stopping by your favorite bakery for muffins, bagels, croissants, quick breads, or coffee cake.

The produce department of your grocery store can be of help too, with a healthy offering of cut-up fresh fruit that you can serve on a platter with a dip or in a decorative serving bowl. Make sure you have a colorful variety of foods and choose familiar dishes if you don't know the particular likes and dislikes of your guests. You should also label any dishes that aren't easy to identify.

Beverage offerings often include hot coffee and tea, fruit juice, and milk, but you also might want to consider hot chocolate, iced tea, or an alcoholic option such as white wine, Champagne, Bloody Marys, or mimosas.

Scrambled Eggs

Start to Finish: 10 minutes **Makes:** 3 servings

> **6 eggs**
> **⅓ cup milk, half-and-half, or light cream**
> **¼ teaspoon salt**
> **Dash black pepper**
> **1 tablespoon butter or margarine**

1. In a bowl beat together eggs, milk, salt, and pepper with a rotary beater. In a skillet melt butter over medium heat; pour in egg mixture. Cook over medium heat, without stirring, until mixture begins to set on the bottom and around edges.

2. With a spatula or a large spoon, lift and fold the partially cooked egg mixture so that the uncooked portion flows underneath (see photo 1, right). Continue cooking over medium heat for 2 to 3 minutes or until egg mixture is cooked through, but is still glossy and moist (see photo 2, right). Immediately remove from heat.

Per serving: 196 cal., 15 g total fat (5 g sat. fat), 436 mg chol., 375 mg sodium, 2 g carbo., 14 g pro.
Daily Values: 13% vit. A, 8% calcium, 10% iron
Exchanges: 2 Medium-Fat Meat, 1 Fat

Low-Fat Scrambled Eggs: Prepare as above, except substitute 3 whole eggs and 5 egg whites for the 6 whole eggs. Substitute fat-free milk for the milk. Omit the butter and coat an unheated nonstick skillet with nonstick cooking spray before cooking the egg mixture.

Per serving: 112 cal., 5 g total fat (2 g sat. fat), 212 mg chol., 368 mg sodium, 2 g carbo., 13 g pro.
Daily Values: 6% vit. A, 6% calcium, 6% iron
Exchanges: 1 Medium-Fat Meat, 1 Very Lean Meat

Spinach-Feta Scrambled Eggs: Prepare as above, except cook and stir 2 cups fresh baby spinach in the melted butter until limp. Add egg mixture and continue as directed. Fold in ½ cup crumbled feta cheese with garlic and herbs after the eggs begin to set.

Per serving: 250 cal., 19 g total fat (8 g sat. fat), 452 mg chol., 599 mg sodium, 4 g carbo., 17 g pro.
Daily Values: 52% vit. A, 9% vit. C, 20% calcium, 14% iron
Exchanges: ½ Vegetable, 2½ Medium-Fat Meat, 1 Fat

Cheese-and-Onion Scrambled Eggs: Prepare as above, except cook 1 sliced green onion in the melted butter for 30 seconds; add egg mixture and continue as directed. Fold in ½ cup shredded American cheese after eggs begin to set.

Per serving: 269 cal., 20 g total fat (9 g sat. fat), 454 mg chol., 657 mg sodium, 3 g carbo., 18 g pro.
Daily Values: 18% vit. A, 2% vit. C, 19% calcium, 11% iron
Exchanges: 2½ Medium-Fat Meat, 1½ Fat

Denver Scrambled Eggs: Prepare as at left, except omit salt and increase butter to 2 tablespoons. In the melted butter cook ⅓ cup diced cooked ham; ¼ cup chopped onion; one 2-ounce can mushroom stems and pieces, drained; and 2 tablespoons finely chopped green sweet pepper. Add egg mixture to skillet and continue as directed.

Per serving: 268 cal., 20 g total fat (8 g sat. fat), 455 mg chol., 485 mg sodium, 5 g carbo., 17 g pro.
Daily Values: 16% vit. A, 11 vit. C, 9% calcium, 12% iron
Exchanges: ½ Vegetable, 2½ Medium-Fat Meat, 1½ Fat

Breakfast Burritos: Prepare as at left, except omit the salt and butter. In the skillet cook 4 ounces bulk pork sausage, ¼ cup chopped onion, and 2 tablespoons finely chopped green sweet pepper over medium heat until meat is brown and vegetables are tender. Drain off fat. Add egg mixture to skillet with sausage mixture and continue as directed. To serve, warm four 10-inch flour tortillas. Place one-fourth of the egg mixture onto each tortilla just below the center. Divide ½ cup of shredded Monterey Jack cheese (2 ounces) and ¼ cup bottled salsa among the tortillas. Fold bottom edge of each tortilla up and over the filling. Fold opposite sides in. Roll up from bottom. Serve with additional salsa. Makes 4 burritos.

Per burrito: 399 cal., 23 g total fat (9 g sat. fat), 352 mg chol., 584 mg sodium, 25 g carbo., 1 g fiber, 21 g pro.
Daily Values: 12% vit. A, 10% vit. C, 22% calcium, 18% iron
Exchanges: 1½ Starch, 2½ Medium-Fat Meat, 2 Fat

1. As the egg mixture begins to set, lift and fold it, allowing the uncooked egg mixture to flow underneath the cooked mixture.

2. The egg mixture is done when it is set but still looks glossy and moist. Avoid overcooking eggs as it makes them dry and rubbery.

Scrambled Egg Pizza

3. In a medium bowl beat together eggs and milk. In the same skillet melt butter over medium heat; pour in egg mixture. Cook, without stirring, until mixture begins to set on the bottom and around edges. Using a large spatula, lift and fold partially cooked eggs so that the uncooked portion flows underneath (see photo 1, page 234). Continue cooking over medium heat for 2 to 3 minutes or until egg mixture is cooked through but is still glossy and moist (see photo 2, page 234). Remove from heat.

4. Sprinkle half of the shredded cheese over the hot crust. Top with scrambled eggs, zucchini mixture, bacon, and remaining cheese. Bake for 5 to 8 minutes more or until cheese melts.

Per slice: 287 cal., 15 g total fat (6 g sat. fat), 193 mg chol., 455 mg sodium, 23 g carbo., 2 g fiber, 16 g pro.
Daily Values: 9% vit. A, 2% vit. C, 16% calcium, 6% iron
Exchanges: 1½ Starch, 1½ Medium-Fat Meat, 1½ Fat

Easy Scrambled Egg Pizza: Prepare as at left, except omit the bread dough and Step 1. Substitute one 12-inch Italian bread shell (Boboli) and continue as directed, baking according to the bread shell package. Or substitute one 13.8-ounce package refrigerated pizza dough, baking as directed on the pizza dough package.

Per slice: 290 cal., 16 g total fat (6 g sat.), 195 mg chol., 451 mg sodium, 21 g carbo., 1 g fiber, 16 g pro.
Daily Values: 9% vit. A, 3% vit. C, 21% calcium, 10% iron
Exchanges: 1½ Starch, 1½ Medium-Fat Meat, 1½ Fat

Sausage-Mushroom Scrambled Egg Pizza: Prepare as at left, except omit the zucchini, crushed red pepper, oil, and bacon. After preparing crust, in a large skillet cook 8 ounces bulk pork sausage or Italian sausage and the sliced mushrooms until meat is brown; remove from skillet and drain. Continue as directed in Steps 3 and 4, substituting the sausage-mushroom mixture for the zucchini mixture and bacon.

Per slice: 333 cal., 19 g total fat (8 g sat.), 208 mg chol., 573 mg sodium, 23 g carbo., 2 g fiber, 19 g pro.
Daily Values: 9% vit. A, 16% calcium, 7% iron
Exchanges: 1½ Starch, 1 High-Fat Meat, 1 Medium-Fat Meat, 1 Fat

Scrambled Egg Pizza

For a rustic pizza crust, leave the dough edges free-form. For a decorative crust, snip the dough edges every inch.

Start to Finish: 45 minutes
Oven: 375°F **Makes:** 10 slices

- 1 16-ounce loaf frozen whole wheat bread dough, thawed
- 1 cup chopped zucchini or green sweet pepper
- 1 cup sliced fresh mushrooms
- ¼ teaspoon crushed red pepper (optional)
- 1 tablespoon cooking oil
- 8 eggs
- ½ cup milk
- 1 tablespoon butter or margarine
- 1½ cups shredded cheddar or mozzarella cheese (6 ounces)
- 2 strips bacon, crisp-cooked, drained, and crumbled

1. Grease a 13-inch pizza pan; set aside. On a lightly floured surface, roll bread dough into a 14-inch circle. If dough is difficult to roll out, stop and let it rest a few minutes. Transfer dough to prepared pan. Build up edges slightly. Prick dough generously with a fork. Bake in a 375°F oven for 15 to 20 minutes or until light brown.

2. Meanwhile, in a large skillet cook zucchini, mushrooms, and, if desired, crushed red pepper in hot oil 5 minutes or until vegetables are almost tender. Remove zucchini mixture and drain.

French Omelet

Cover each omelet with foil to keep it warm while preparing any additional omelets.

Start to Finish: 10 minutes **Makes:** 1 omelet

Filling (optional)
2 eggs
2 tablespoons water
⅛ teaspoon salt
Dash ground black pepper
1 tablespoon butter

1. If desired, prepare filling; keep warm.

2. In a small bowl combine eggs, water, salt, and pepper. Beat until combined, but not frothy, with a fork. Heat an 8-inch nonstick skillet with flared sides over medium-high heat until hot.

3. Melt butter in skillet. Add egg mixture to skillet; lower heat to medium. Immediately begin stirring the eggs gently but continuously with a wooden or plastic spatula until mixture resembles small pieces of cooked egg surrounded by liquid egg (see photo 1, right). Stop stirring. Cook for 30 to 60 seconds more or until egg mixture is set and shiny.

4. If desired, spoon filling across the center. With a spatula, lift and fold an omelet edge about a third of the way toward the center (see photo 2, right). Fold the opposite omelet edge toward the center and transfer to a warm plate.

Per omelet: 255 cal., 22 g total fat (9 g sat. fat), 455 mg chol., 518 mg sodium, 1 g carbo., 0 g fiber, 13 g pro.
Daily Values: 17% vit. A, 6% calcium, 10% iron
Exchanges: 2 Medium-Fat Meat, 2 Fat

Lower-Cholesterol Omelet: Prepare as above, except substitute 2 egg whites for one of the whole eggs.

Per omelet: 216 cal., 17 g total fat (8 g sat. fat), 244 mg chol., 559 mg sodium, 1 g carbo., 0 g fiber, 14 g pro.
Daily Values: 12% vit. A, 4% calcium, 6% iron
Exchanges: 1 Very Lean Meat, 1 Medium-Fat Meat, 2 Fat

Mushroom Omelet: Prepare as above, except for filling, in the 8-inch skillet cook ⅓ cup sliced fresh mushrooms in 1 teaspoon butter until tender. Remove from skillet; keep warm. Add filling in Step 4 as directed.

Per omelet: 300 cal., 27 g total fat (11 g sat. fat), 466 mg chol., 548 mg sodium, 2 g carbo., 0 g dietary fiber, 14 g pro.
Daily Values: 26% vit. A, 6% calcium, 11% iron
Exchanges: ½ Vegetable, 2 Medium-Fat Meat, 3 Fat

Cheese Omelet: Prepare as at left, except omit salt. In Step 4, sprinkle ¼ cup shredded cheddar, Swiss, or Monterey Jack cheese across center of omelet for filling.

Per omelet: 370 cal., 32 g total fat (15 g sat. fat), 485 mg chol., 403 mg sodium, 1 g carbo., 0 g fiber, 20 g pro.
Daily Values: 23% vit. A, 26% calcium, 11% iron
Exchanges: 1 High-Fat Meat, 2 Medium-Fat Meat, 2½ Fat

Denver Omelet: Prepare as at left, except for filling, in the 8-inch skillet cook 2 tablespoons chopped green sweet pepper, 2 tablespoons chopped onion, and ⅛ teaspoon dried basil, crushed, in 2 teaspoons butter until tender. Stir in ¼ cup finely chopped cooked ham. Remove from skillet; keep warm. Add filling in Step 4 as directed.

Per omelet: 394 cal., 33 g total fat (14 g sat. fat), 496 mg chol., 1,017 mg sodium, 5 g carbo., 1 g fiber, 19 g pro.
Daily Values: 23% vit. A, 29% vit. C, 8% calcium, 13% iron
Exchanges: ½ Vegetable, 2½ Medium-Fat Meat, 4 Fat

1. As the egg mixture cooks, use a wooden or plastic spatula to stir it gently but continuously until it resembles small pieces of cooked egg surrounded by liquid egg.

2. When the egg mixture is set and looks shiny, spoon desired filling across its center. Loosen omelet edges from skillet. Fold one edge, then the other, over filling, allowing edges to overlap in the center.

Egg Substitutes

Refrigerated or frozen egg products are easy to use, readily available, and enable anyone on a cholesterol-restricted diet to enjoy great-tasting egg dishes. These products are based mostly on egg whites and contain less fat than whole eggs and no cholesterol. Use ¼ cup of either refrigerated or frozen egg product for each whole egg in scrambled egg dishes, omelets, quiches, and stratas. To replace hard-cooked eggs in salads and other recipes, cook the egg product as you would cook an omelet and cut it up.

Orange Blintz Casserole

Orange Blintz Casserole

Prep: 25 minutes **Bake:** 45 minutes **Oven:** 350°F
Cool: 30 minutes **Makes:** 12 servings

- 6 eggs
- 2 egg whites
- 1½ cups dairy sour cream
- 2 teaspoons finely shredded orange peel
- ½ cup orange juice
- ¼ cup butter, softened
- 1 cup all-purpose flour
- ½ cup sugar
- 2 teaspoons baking powder
- 1 12-ounce carton cottage cheese (2 cups)
- 1 8-ounce package cream cheese, softened and cut up
- 2 egg yolks
- 2 tablespoons sugar
- 2 teaspoons vanilla
- ½ cup orange marmalade, melted
  Orange slices (optional)

1. Grease a 3-quart rectangular baking dish; set aside. For batter, in a blender or food processor combine eggs, egg whites, sour cream, orange peel, orange juice, and butter. Cover and blend or process until smooth. Add flour, ½ cup sugar, and baking powder. Cover; blend or process until smooth. Transfer to a bowl; set aside.

2. For filling, in blender or food processor combine cottage cheese, cream cheese, egg yolks, the 2 tablespoons sugar, and vanilla. Cover; blend or process until smooth. Pour 2 cups of the batter into prepared dish. Spoon filling over

batter in dish; swirl filling with a knife. Pour remaining batter evenly over filling mixture.

3. Bake in a 350°F oven for 45 minutes or until puffed and lightly golden. Cool 30 minutes on a wire rack (edges may fall). Drizzle with orange marmalade. If desired, garnish with orange slices.

Per serving: 346 cal., 20 g total fat (11 g sat. fat), 186 mg chol., 306 mg sodium, 30 g carbo., 0 g fiber, 11 g pro.
Daily Values: 16% vit. A, 14% vit. C, 10% calcium, 7% iron
Exchanges: 2 Other Carbo., 1 Lean Meat, ½ Medium-Fat Meat, 3 Fat

Farmer's Casserole LOW FAT

See photo, page 221.

Prep: 25 minutes **Bake:** 40 minutes **Oven:** 350°F
Stand: 5 minutes **Makes:** 6 servings

- Nonstick cooking spray
- 3 cups frozen shredded hash brown potatoes
- ¾ cup shredded Monterey Jack cheese with jalapeño peppers or shredded cheddar cheese (3 ounces)
- 1 cup diced cooked ham or Canadian-style bacon, or cooked breakfast sausage
- ¼ cup sliced green onion (2)
- 4 eggs, beaten, or 1 cup refrigerated or frozen egg product, thawed
- 1½ cups milk

1. Coat a 2-quart square baking dish with nonstick cooking spray. Arrange hash brown potatoes evenly in the dish. Sprinkle with cheese, ham, and green onion.

2. In a medium bowl combine eggs, milk, ⅛ teaspoon *salt*, and ⅛ teaspoon *black pepper*. Pour egg mixture over layers in dish.

3. Bake, uncovered, in a 350°F oven for 40 minutes or until a knife inserted near center comes out clean. Let stand 5 minutes before serving.

Farmer's Casserole for 12: Prepare as above, except double all ingredients and use a 3-quart rectangular baking dish. Bake, uncovered, in a 350°F oven for 45 to 55 minutes or until a knife inserted near the center comes out clean. Let stand 5 minutes before serving.

Make-ahead directions: Prepare as above through Step 2. Cover and chill for up to 24 hours. Bake, uncovered, in a 350°F oven for 50 to 55 minutes or until a knife inserted near the center comes out clean. Let stand 5 minutes before serving.

Per 4×2½-inch piece: 265 cal., 12 g total fat (6 g sat. fat), 175 mg chol., 590 mg sodium, 23 g carbo., 2 g fiber, 17 g pro.
Daily Values: 11% vit. A, 13% vit. C, 21% calcium, 11% iron
Exchanges: 1½ Starch, 2 Medium-Fat Meat

Quiche

Quiche

This versatile recipe can fit into any lifestyle—the classic version, lower-fat, or vegetarian. Serve for brunch or dinner with fresh fruit and brioche.

Prep: 25 minutes **Bake:** 52 minutes **Oven:** 450°F/325°F
Stand: 10 minutes **Makes:** 6 slices

- 1 **recipe Pastry for Single-Crust Pie (see page 453) or ½ of a 15-ounce package rolled refrigerated unbaked piecrust (1 piecrust)**
- 4 **eggs, beaten**
- 1½ **cups half-and-half, light cream, or milk**
- ¼ **cup sliced green onion (2)**
- ¼ **teaspoon salt**
- ⅛ **teaspoon black pepper**
  Dash ground nutmeg
- ¾ **cup chopped cooked ham, chicken, or crabmeat (about 3½ ounces)**
- 1½ **cups shredded Swiss, cheddar, Monterey Jack, and/or Havarti cheese (6 ounces)**
- 1 **tablespoon all-purpose flour**

1. Prepare and roll out Pastry for Single-Crust Pie. Line a 9-inch pie plate with pastry. Trim; crimp edge as desired. Line unpricked pastry with a double thickness of foil. Bake in a 450°F oven for 8 minutes. Remove foil. Bake for 4 to 5 minutes more or until pastry is set and dry. Remove from oven. Reduce oven temperature to 325°F.

2. Meanwhile, in a medium bowl stir together eggs, half-and-half, green onion, salt, pepper, and nutmeg. Stir in ham. In a small bowl toss together the cheese and flour. Add to egg mixture; mix well.

3. Pour egg mixture into hot, baked pastry shell. Bake in the 325°F oven for 40 to 45 minutes or until a knife inserted near center comes out clean. If necessary, cover edge of crust with foil to prevent overbrowning. Let stand 10 minutes before serving.

Per slice: 453 cal., 31 g total fat (14 g sat. fat), 199 g chol., 540 mg sodium, 25 g carbo., 1 g fiber, 19 g pro.
Daily Values: 13% vit. A, 3% vit. C, 31% calcium, 12% iron
Exchanges: 1½ Starch, 2 Medium-Fat Meat, 4 Fat

Lower-Fat Quiche: Prepare as at left, except substitute Oil Pastry (see page 453) for the Pastry for Single-Crust Pie; 1 cup refrigerated or frozen egg product, thawed, for the eggs; fat-free milk for the half-and-half; and reduced-fat cheddar, Swiss, or Monterey Jack cheese for the cheese.

Per slice: 341 cal., 17 g total fat (6 g sat. fat), 31 mg chol., 762 mg sodium, 26 g carbo., 1 g fiber, 19 g pro.
Daily Values: 20% vit. A, 2% vit. C, 29% calcium, 14% iron
Exchanges: 1½ Starch, 2 Very Lean Meat, 2½ Fat

Spinach and Bacon Quiche

No time to make your own pastry? Use a rolled, refrigerated, unbaked piecrust instead.

Prep: 25 minutes **Bake:** 57 minutes **Stand:** 10 minutes
Oven: 450°F/325°F **Makes:** 6 slices

- 1 **recipe Pastry for Single-Crust Pie (see page 453)**
- ½ **cup chopped onion (1 medium)**
- 6 **slices bacon, chopped**
- 8 **eggs, beaten**
- ½ **cup dairy sour cream**
- ½ **cup half-and-half, light cream, or milk**
- ¼ **teaspoon salt**
- ⅛ **teaspoon ground white pepper**
  Dash ground nutmeg (optional)
- 3 **cups lightly packed chopped fresh spinach**
- ⅔ **cup shredded mozzarella cheese (3 ounces)**
- ½ **cup shredded Swiss cheese (2 ounces)**
  Cherry tomatoes, cut up (optional)

1. Prepare and roll out Pastry for Single-Crust Pie. Line a 9-inch pie plate with the pastry. Trim; crimp edge as desired. Line the unpricked pastry shell with a double thickness of foil. Bake in a 450°F oven for 8 minutes. Remove foil. Bake for 4 to 5 minutes more or until pastry is set and dry. Remove from oven. Reduce oven temperature to 325°F.

2. Meanwhile, in a large skillet cook onion and bacon until onion is tender and bacon is crisp. Drain onion mixture on paper towels.

3. In a bowl stir together eggs, sour cream, half-and-half, salt, pepper, and, if desired, nutmeg. Stir in onion mixture, spinach, and cheeses.

4. Pour egg mixture into the hot baked pastry shell. Bake in the 325°F oven for 45 to 50 minutes or until a knife inserted near the center comes out clean. If necessary, cover edge of crust with foil to prevent overbrowning. Let stand for 10 minutes before serving. If desired, garnish with cherry tomatoes.

Per slice: 478 cal., 34 g total fat (13 g sat. fat), 323 mg chol., 550 mg sodium, 23 g carbo., 1 g fiber, 21 g pro.
Daily Values: 42% vit. A, 9% vit. C, 24% calcium, 17% iron
Exchanges: 1 Vegetable, 1 Starch, 1½ Medium-Fat Meat, ½ High-Fat Meat, 4½ Fat

Spinach Quiche: Prepare as on page 238, except omit the bacon. Cook the onion in 1 tablespoon butter or margarine. Stir into egg mixture with spinach and cheeses.

Per slice: 449 cal., 32 g total fat (13 g sat. fat), 321 mg chol., 437 mg sodium, 23 g carbo., 1 g fiber, 18 g pro.
Daily Values: 43% vit. A, 9% vit. C, 24% calcium, 16% iron
Exchanges: 1 Starch, 1 Vegetable, 1½ Medium-Fat Meat, 5 Fat

Cheese-and-Mushroom Brunch Eggs VEGETARIAN

Use fat-free milk and refrigerated or frozen egg product for a lower-fat version.

Prep: 30 minutes **Bake:** 15 minutes **Oven:** 350°F
Stand: 10 minutes **Makes:** 6 servings

- 2 tablespoons butter or margarine
- 2 tablespoons all-purpose flour
- 1⅓ cups milk or fat-free milk
- ½ cup shredded Swiss or Gruyère cheese (2 ounces)
- ¼ cup grated Parmesan cheese
- ⅛ teaspoon salt
- ⅛ teaspoon ground nutmeg
- 1½ cups sliced fresh mushrooms, such as button, shiitake, or cremini
- ¼ cup thinly sliced green onion (2)
- 1 tablespoon butter
- 12 eggs, beaten, or 3 cups refrigerated or frozen egg product, thawed
  Tomato slices, cut in half (optional)

1. For sauce, in a medium saucepan melt the 2 tablespoons butter. Stir in flour. Cook and stir for 1 minute. Add milk all at once. Cook and stir over medium heat until thickened and bubbly. Stir in Swiss cheese, Parmesan cheese, salt, and nutmeg. Cook and stir over medium heat until cheeses melt. Remove from heat; set aside.

2. In a large nonstick skillet cook mushrooms and green onion in the 1 tablespoon hot butter until tender. Add eggs. Cook over medium heat without stirring until eggs begin to set on the bottom and around the edges. Using a large spatula, lift and fold the partially cooked eggs so that the uncooked portion flows underneath (see photo 1, page 234). Continue cooking until eggs are cooked through, but still glossy and moist (see photo 2, page 234).

3. Transfer half of the scrambled egg mixture to a 2-quart square baking dish. Drizzle half of the sauce over egg mixture. Top with the remaining scrambled egg mixture and remaining sauce.

4. Bake, uncovered, in a 350°F oven for 15 to 20 minutes or until heated through. If desired, top with tomato slices. Let stand 10 minutes before serving.

Cheese-and-Mushroom Brunch Eggs for 12: Prepare as at left, except double all ingredients, use a 12-inch nonstick skillet, and work in batches. Cook half the mushrooms and green onions in 1 tablespoon hot butter until tender. Beat 12 eggs together and add them to mushroom mixture in skillet. Cook egg mixture as in Step 2. Transfer scrambled egg mixture to a 3-quart rectangular baking dish. Repeat with remaining mushrooms, green onions, butter, and eggs. Top egg mixture in dish with half of the sauce. Top with remaining scrambled egg mixture and remaining sauce. Bake, uncovered, in a 350°F oven about 25 minutes or until heated through. If desired, top with tomato slices. Let stand 10 minutes before serving. Makes 12 servings.

Per cup: 295 cal., 21 g total fat (9 g sat. fat), 455 mg chol., 328 mg sodium, 7 g carbo., 0 g fiber, 19 g pro.
Daily Values: 29% vit. A, 1% vit. C, 17% calcium, 11% iron.
Exchanges: 1 Other Carbo., 2½ Medium-Fat Meat, 1½ Fat

Easy Cheese-and-Mushroom Brunch Eggs: Prepare as at left, except omit the first seven ingredients and Step 1. Substitute one 16-ounce jar purchased light Alfredo sauce for the prepared sauce. Continue as directed.

Per cup: 331 cal., 23 g total fat (11 g sat. fat), 462 mg chol., 833 mg sodium, 12 g carbo., 0 g fiber, 19 g pro.
Daily Values: 29% vit. A, 1% vit. C, 17% calcium, 11% iron.
Exchanges: 1 Other Carbo., 2½ Medium-Fat, 1½ Fat

Ham-Asparagus Strata

Prep: 25 minutes **Chill:** 2 hours **Bake:** 1 hour
Oven: 325°F **Stand:** 10 minutes **Makes:** 6 servings

- 4 **English muffins, torn or cut into bite-size pieces (4 cups)**
- 2 **cups cubed cooked ham or chicken (10 ounces)**
- 1 **10-ounce package frozen cut asparagus or frozen cut broccoli, thawed and well drained, or 2 cups cut-up cooked fresh asparagus or broccoli**
- 4 **ounces process Swiss cheese, torn, or process Gruyère cheese, cut up**
- 4 **eggs, beaten**
- ¼ **cup dairy sour cream**
- 1¼ **cups milk**
- 2 **tablespoons finely chopped onion**
- 1 **tablespoon Dijon-style mustard**

1. Grease a 2-quart square baking dish. Spread half of the English muffin pieces in the dish. Add the ham, asparagus, and cheese. Top with the remaining English muffin pieces.

2. In a bowl whisk together the eggs and sour cream. Stir in milk, onion, mustard, and ⅛ teaspoon *black pepper*.* Pour evenly over the layers in dish. Cover and chill for 2 to 24 hours.

3. Bake, uncovered, in a 325°F oven for 60 to 65 minutes or until the internal temperature registers 170°F on an instant-read thermometer. Let stand for 10 minutes before serving.

*Note: If using chicken, add ¼ teaspoon *salt.*

Per 4×2½-inch piece: 349 cal., 16 g total fat (7 g sat. fat), 193 mg chol., 1,224 mg sodium, 25 g carbo., 2 g fiber, 26 g pro. **Daily Values:** 20% vit. A, 26% vit. C, 32% calcium, 15% iron **Exchanges:** ½ Vegetable, 1½ Starch, 3 Lean Meat, 2 Fat

Easy Brunch Menu

Keep your brunch stress-free by assembling the main dish, such as strata, the night before.

- *Sliced melon and berries*
- *Assorted muffins served with whipped butter and/or jams*
- *Cheesy Sausage Strata (right)*
- *Oven-roasted potatoes*
- *Fruit juice, milk, hot coffee, and/or hot tea*

Cheesy Sausage Strata

Use day-old French or Italian bread from the bakery for a strata because it readily soaks up the egg mixture. This flavorful dish is hearty enough to be served for dinner as well as brunch.

Prep: 30 minutes **Stand:** 15 minutes + 10 minutes
Bake: 45 minutes **Oven:** 325°F **Makes:** 6 servings

- 8 **ounces bulk Italian or pork sausage**
- ⅓ **cup chopped onion**
- ⅓ **cup chopped red sweet pepper**
- 1 **clove garlic, minced**
- 5 **cups French or Italian bread cubes (5 ounces)**
- 1½ **cups shredded Monterey Jack cheese (6 ounces)**
- 4 **eggs, beaten**
- 2 **cups milk**
- ¼ **teaspoon salt**
- 1 **tablespoon snipped fresh cilantro or parsley**

1. In a large skillet cook sausage, onion, sweet pepper, and garlic until sausage is cooked and vegetables are tender. Drain off fat. Set aside.

2. Place bread cubes in 2-quart square baking dish. Spoon sausage mixture over bread cubes. Sprinkle with 1 cup Monterey Jack cheese.

3. In a medium bowl combine eggs, milk, salt, and cilantro. Pour egg mixture evenly over layers in baking dish. Using the back of a spoon, gently press down on layers. Let stand for 15 minutes.

4. Bake, uncovered, in a 325°F oven about 45 minutes or until a knife inserted near center comes out clean. Sprinkle with remaining cheese. Let stand for 10 minutes before serving.

Overnight Strata: Prepare as above through Step 3. Cover and refrigerate overnight or up to 24 hours. Bake in a 325°F oven about 1 hour or until the internal temperature registers 170°F on an instant-read thermometer. Let stand for 10 minutes before serving.

Per 4×2½-inch piece: 375 cal., 23 g total fat (11 g sat. fat), 198 mg chol., 684 mg sodium, 18 g carbo., 1 g fiber, 21 g pro. **Daily Values:** 16% vit. A, 24% vit. C, 34% calcium, 10% iron **Exchanges:** 1 Starch, 2 High-Fat Meat, ½ Medium-Fat Meat, 1 Fat

Cookies & Bars

Coconut Macaroons, 247

Toffee Bars, 262

Jam Thumbprints, 251

Cookies & Bars Essentials

Looking for some useful tips on making and baking the best cookies your family has ever tasted? These baking basics will get you on the right path for cookie success.

Butter Is Better, But ...

It's true—nothing is better for the flavor, richness, texture, and color of cookies than real dairy butter, which is why all the recipes in this chapter call for it. However, margarine can be substituted for butter if it contains enough fat. For best results, choose a stick margarine with at least 80 percent vegetable oil or one that contains at least 100 calories per tablespoon. Substituting shortening for butter will give cookies a softer, more cakelike texture and a different flavor.

Sheet Success

If your cookie sheets are thin, warped, or dark from years of baked-on grease, it's time  to go shopping. Purchase shiny, heavy-gauge cookie sheets that have low or no sides. Use jelly-roll pans (15×10×1-inch baking pans) only for bar cookies since their 1-inch sides prevent other cookie types from browning properly. Let hot cookie sheets cool between batches.

To the Freezer

Are you concerned you'll have no time for last-minute holiday cookie baking? Get a head start by freezing baked and cooled cookies. Most cookies can be frozen for months, ready to be pulled out at a moment's notice.
- Use airtight plastic bags and containers specifically labeled for freezer storage. Separate layers of cookies with sheets of waxed paper.
- Tightly seal filled bags and containers and freeze for up to three months. For best results, don't frost or glaze cookies before freezing. Instead, freeze unfrosted cookies, thaw, then frost before serving.
- Most cookie dough—except bar batters and meringue or macaroon mixtures—can be frozen in an airtight freezer container for up to six months. Thaw dough in its container in the refrigerator. Shape and bake as directed.

Shipping Out

Sending cookies, not crumbs, to loved ones through the mail is possible—with a little care. For best results, send crisp or firm varieties—including most slice-and-bake, bar, and drop cookies—and avoid frosted, moist, thin, or filled types. Wrap baked and cooled cookies individually, in back-to-back pairs, or in stacks in plastic wrap. Line a sturdy box with bubble wrap and pack cookies in layers of packing peanuts or tissue paper so they won't have room to shift. Write "perishable" on the box and ship early in the week so your package won't be delayed over a weekend.

Tricks of the Trade

Microplane Grater: This supersharp device grates the peel off citrus fruit in seconds, leaving you with mounds of zest and time to spare. It's also great for ginger. Fine, medium, and coarse graters are available.

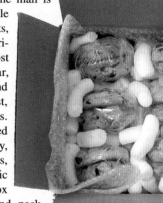

Nut Chopper: Tired of chopping nuts with a knife and watching them roll all over? With this device, nuts are contained and can be chopped in seconds. It also works for onions and garlic.

Nonstick Baking Mat: Prevent cookies from sticking to cookie sheets by lining the sheets with this reusable mat (see photo, above left). It's also perfect for kneading and rolling dough.

Chocolate Chip Cookies

Prep: 40 minutes **Bake:** 8 minutes per batch
Oven: 375°F **Makes:** about 60 cookies

- ¾ **cup butter, softened**
- ¼ **cup shortening**
- 1 **cup packed brown sugar**
- ½ **cup granulated sugar**
- ¾ **teaspoon baking soda**
- ½ **teaspoon salt**
- 2 **eggs**
- 1 **teaspoon vanilla**
- 2½ **cups all-purpose flour**
- 1 **12-ounce package (2 cups) semisweet chocolate pieces or miniature candy-coated semisweet chocolate pieces**
- 1½ **cups chopped walnuts or pecans (optional)**

1. Preheat oven to 375°F. In a large mixing bowl beat butter and shortening with an electric mixer on medium to high speed for 30 seconds. Add the brown sugar, granulated sugar, baking soda, and salt. Beat until mixture is combined, scraping sides of bowl. Beat in eggs and vanilla until combined. Beat in as much of the flour as you can with the mixer. Stir in remaining flour. Stir in chocolate pieces and, if desired, walnuts.

2. Drop dough by rounded teaspoons 2 inches apart onto an ungreased cookie sheet (see photo, below). Bake for 8 to 9 minutes or until edges are light brown. Transfer to a wire rack; cool.

Sizing Up

When making drop cookies, have you ever questioned what is meant by "a rounded teaspoon"? It's not what you might think. When a recipe advises dropping dough from teaspoons, it's referring to spoons from your flatware versus measuring spoons. Use a spatula or another spoon to push the dough from the first spoon and reshape the mound accordingly. For the most uniform sizes, purchase a small ice cream scoop at a kitchen shop. It will ensure that every mound of dough will be the same size for even baking and the cookies will have the same round shape.

Macadamia Nut and White Chocolate Chip Cookies: Prepare as at left, except substitute white baking pieces for the semisweet chocolate pieces. Stir in one 3½-ounce jar macadamia nuts, chopped, with the baking pieces.

Per cookie regular or macadamia nut variation: 92 cal., 5 g total fat (2 g sat. fat), 13 mg chol., 55 mg sodium, 13 g carbo., 1 g fiber, 1 g pro.
Daily Values: 2% vit. A, 1% calcium, 3% iron
Exchanges: 1 Other Carbo., 1 Fat

Big Chocolate Chip Cookies: Prepare as at left, except use a ¼-cup measure or scoop to drop mounds of dough about 4 inches apart onto an ungreased cookie sheet. If desired, flatten dough mounds to circles about ¾ inch thick. Bake in a 375°F oven for 10 to 12 minutes or until edges are light brown. Cool on cookie sheet 1 minute. Transfer to a wire rack and let cool. Makes about 20 cookies.

Per cookie: 307 cal., 16 g total fat (8 g sat. fat), 44 mg chol., 185 mg sodium, 42 g carbo., 2 g fiber, 4 g pro.
Daily Values: 5% vit. A, 2% calcium, 9% iron
Exchanges: 2 Other Carbo., ½ Starch, 3 Fat

Chocolate Chip Cookie Bars: Prepare as at left, except press dough into an ungreased 15×10×1-inch baking pan. Bake in a 375°F oven for 15 to 20 minutes or until golden. Cool on a wire rack. Cut into bars. Makes 48 bars.

Per bar: 115 cal., 6 g total fat (3 g sat. fat), 16 mg chol., 69 mg sodium, 16 g carbo., 1 g fiber, 1 g pro.
Daily Values: 2% vit. A, 1% calcium, 3% iron
Exchanges: 1 Other Carbo., 1 Fat

Oatmeal Cookies

Prep: 25 minutes **Bake:** 8 minutes per batch
Oven: 375°F **Makes:** about 48 cookies

- ¾ **cup butter, softened**
- 1 **cup packed brown sugar**
- ½ **cup granulated sugar**
- 1 **teaspoon baking powder**
- ¼ **teaspoon baking soda**
- ½ **teaspoon ground cinnamon (optional)**
- ¼ **teaspoon ground cloves (optional)**
- 2 **eggs**
- 1 **teaspoon vanilla**
- 1½ **cups all-purpose flour**
- 2 **cups rolled oats**

1. Preheat oven to 375°F. In a mixing bowl beat butter with an electric mixer on medium to high speed for 30 seconds. Add brown sugar, granulated sugar, baking powder, baking soda, ¼ teaspoon *salt,* and, if desired, cinnamon and cloves. Beat until combined, scraping sides of bowl. Beat in eggs and vanilla. Beat in as much of the flour as you can. Stir in remaining flour. Stir in rolled oats.

2. Drop dough by rounded teaspoons 2 inches apart onto an ungreased cookie sheet (see photo, page 244). Bake for 8 to 10 minutes or until edges are light brown. Cool on cookie sheet 1 minute. Transfer to a wire rack and let cool.

Oatmeal-Raisin Cookies: Prepare as on page 244, except after stirring in the oats, stir in 1 cup raisins or snipped dried tart cherries. Makes about 54 cookies.

Oatmeal-Chip Cookies: Prepare as on page 244, except after stirring in oats, stir in 1 cup semisweet chocolate, butterscotch-flavored, or peanut butter-flavored pieces and ½ cup chopped walnuts or pecans. Makes about 54 cookies.

Per cookie regular, oatmeal-raisin, or oatmeal-chip variations: 86 cal., 4 g total fat (2 g sat. fat), 17 mg chol., 51 mg sodium, 12 g carbo., 1 g fiber, 1 g pro.
Daily Values: 3% vit. A, 1% calcium, 2% iron
Exchanges: 1 Other Carbo., ½ Fat

Big Oatmeal Cookies: Prepare as on page 244, except use a ¼-cup measure or scoop to drop mounds of dough 4 inches apart onto an ungreased cookie sheet. Press into 3-inch circles. Bake in a 375°F oven for 10 to 12 minutes or until edges are light brown. Cool on cookie sheet 1 minute. Transfer to a wire rack and let cool. Makes about 10 cookies.

Per cookie: 415 cal., 17 g total fat (10 g sat. fat), 82 mg chol., 242 mg sodium, 60 g carbo., 3 g fiber, 6 g pro.
Daily Values: 12% vit. A, 7% calcium, 12% iron
Exchanges: 4 Other Carbo., 3 Fat

Ranger Cookies

Ranger Cookies

Filled with oats, coconut, and raisins, these energy-packed cookies are ideal for a late-afternoon snack. Take them on long hikes and car trips to keep the munchies at bay.

Prep: 25 minutes **Bake:** 8 minutes per batch
Oven: 375°F **Makes:** about 48 cookies

- ½ **cup butter, softened**
- ½ **cup granulated sugar**
- ½ **cup packed brown sugar**
- ½ **teaspoon baking powder**
- ¼ **teaspoon baking soda**
- 1 **egg**
- 1 **teaspoon vanilla**
- 1¼ **cups all-purpose flour**
- 1 **cup quick-cooking rolled oats**
- 1 **cup coconut**
- 1 **cup raisins, dried cherries, dried cranberries, or mixed dried fruit bits**

1. Preheat oven to 375°F. In a large mixing bowl beat butter with electric mixer on medium to high speed for 30 seconds. Add granulated sugar, brown sugar, baking powder, and baking soda. Beat until combined, scraping sides of bowl occasionally. Beat in egg and vanilla until combined. Beat in as much of the flour as you can with the mixer. Stir in any remaining flour. Stir in rolled oats, coconut, and raisins.

2. Drop dough by rounded teaspoons 2 inches apart onto an ungreased cookie sheet (see photo, page 244). Bake for 8 to 10 minutes or until edges are light brown and centers are set. Cool on cookie sheet 1 minute. Transfer to a wire rack and let cool.

Per cookie: 74 cal., 3 g total fat (2 g sat. fat), 10 mg chol., 34 mg sodium, 11 g carbo., 1 g fiber, 1 g pro.
Daily Values: 1% vit. A, 1% calcium, 2% iron
Exchanges: 1 Other Carbo., ½ Fat

Big Ranger Cookies: Prepare as above, except use a ⅓-cup measure or scoop to drop mounds of dough 2 inches apart on an ungreased cookie sheet. Press into 3-inch circles. Bake in a 375°F oven for 10 to 12 minutes or until edges are light brown and centers are set. Cool on cookie sheet 1 minute. Transfer to a wire rack and let cool. Makes about 10 cookies.

Per cookie: 355 cal., 15 g total fat (9 g sat. fat), 47 mg chol., 162 mg sodium, 53 g carbo., 3 g fiber, 5 g pro.
Daily Values: 6% vit. A, 1% vit. C, 3% calcium, 9% iron
Exchanges: 1 Starch, ½ Fruit, 2 Other Carbo., 3 Fat

Peanut Butter-Oatmeal Rounds

Prep: 30 minutes **Bake:** 10 minutes per batch
Oven: 375°F **Makes:** about 48 cookies

- ¾ **cup butter, softened**
- ½ **cup peanut butter**
- 1 **cup granulated sugar**
- ½ **cup packed brown sugar**
- 1 **teaspoon baking powder**
- ½ **teaspoon baking soda**
- 2 **eggs**
- 1 **teaspoon vanilla**
- 1¼ **cups all-purpose flour**
- 2 **cups rolled oats**
- 1 **cup chopped cocktail peanuts or semisweet chocolate pieces**

1. Preheat oven to 375°F. In a large mixing bowl beat butter and peanut butter with an electric mixer on medium to high speed about 30 seconds or until combined. Add granulated sugar, brown sugar, baking powder, and baking soda. Beat until combined, scraping sides of bowl occasionally. Beat in eggs and vanilla until combined. Beat in as much of the flour as you can with the mixer. Stir in any remaining flour. Stir in rolled oats and peanuts.

2. Drop dough by rounded teaspoons 2 inches apart onto an ungreased cookie sheet (see photo, page 244). Bake about 10 minutes or until edges are light brown. Transfer to a wire rack; cool.

Chocolate-Peanut Butter-Oatmeal Rounds: Prepare as above, except melt and cool 3 ounces unsweetened chocolate. After beating in the eggs and vanilla, stir in chocolate.

Per cookie regular or chocolate variation: 114 cal., 6 g total fat (2 g sat. fat), 17 mg chol., 82 mg sodium, 12 g carbo., 1 g fiber, 3 g pro.
Daily Values: 3% vit. A, 2% calcium, 3% iron
Exchanges: 1 Other Carbo., 1 Fat

 **Chocolate Fudgies**

Using only ¼ cup flour results in a thin dough.

Prep: 20 minutes **Bake:** 8 minutes per batch
Oven: 350°F **Makes:** about 36 cookies

- 1 **12-ounce package (2 cups) semisweet chocolate pieces**
- 2 **ounces unsweetened chocolate, chopped**
- 2 **tablespoons butter**
- 2 **eggs**
- ⅔ **cup sugar**

- ¼ **cup all-purpose flour**
- 1 **teaspoon vanilla**
- ¼ **teaspoon baking powder**
- 1 **cup chopped nuts**

1. Preheat oven to 350°F. Grease a cookie sheet; set aside. In a medium saucepan heat and stir 1 cup of the chocolate pieces, the unsweetened chocolate, and butter until melted. Remove from heat; add the eggs, sugar, flour, vanilla, and baking powder. Beat with a wooden spoon until combined, scraping sides of pan. Stir in remaining 1 cup chocolate pieces and nuts.

2. Drop dough by rounded teaspoons 2 inches apart onto the prepared cookie sheet (see photo, page 244). Bake for 8 to 10 minutes or until surfaces are dull and crackled. Cool on cookie sheet 2 minutes. Transfer to a wire rack; cool.

Per cookie: 102 cal., 7 g total fat (3 g sat. fat), 14 mg chol., 12 mg sodium, 11 g carbo., 1 g fiber, 1 g pro.
Daily Values: 1% vit. A, 1% calcium, 4% iron
Exchanges: 1 Other Carbo., 1 Fat

Sour Cream-Chocolate Drops

Prep: 25 minutes **Bake:** 8 minutes per batch
Oven: 350°F **Makes:** about 42 cookies

- ½ **cup butter, softened**
- 1 **cup packed brown sugar**
- ½ **teaspoon baking soda**
- ¼ **teaspoon salt**
- 1 **egg**
- 1 **teaspoon vanilla**
- 2 **ounces unsweetened chocolate, melted and cooled**
- 1 **8-ounce carton dairy sour cream**
- 2 **cups all-purpose flour**
- 1 **recipe Chocolate Buttercream Frosting (page 247)**

1. Preheat oven to 350°F. In a mixing bowl beat butter with an electric mixer on medium speed for 30 seconds. Add brown sugar, baking soda, and salt. Beat until combined, scraping sides of bowl occasionally. Beat in egg and vanilla. Add melted chocolate; beat until combined. Beat in sour cream. Beat in as much of the flour as you can with the mixer. Stir in any remaining flour.

2. Drop by slightly rounded teaspoons 2 inches apart onto an ungreased cookie sheet (see photo, page 244). Bake for 8 to 10 minutes or until edges are firm. Transfer to a wire rack; cool. Frost with Chocolate Buttercream Frosting.

Chocolate Buttercream Frosting: In a medium mixing bowl beat ¼ cup butter with an electric mixer on medium speed until fluffy. Gradually add 1 cup powdered sugar and ⅓ cup unsweetened cocoa powder, beating well. Slowly beat in 3 tablespoons half-and-half, light cream, or milk and 1 teaspoon vanilla. Gradually beat in 1½ cups powdered sugar. If necessary, beat in additional half-and-half to make spreadable.

Per cookie: 138 cal., 7 g total fat (4 g sat. fat), 20 mg chol., 71 mg sodium, 19 g carbo., 0 g fiber, 2 g pro.
Daily Values: 4% vit. A, 3% calcium, 5% iron
Exchanges: 1 Other Carbo., 1½ Fat

Coconut Macaroons EASY

All the rage in Paris 100 years ago, these chewy coconut bites are still a popular treat. For an extra-special snack, drizzle melted chocolate over the tops of the cookies. See photo, page 241.

Prep: 15 minutes **Bake:** 20 minutes per batch
Oven: 325°F **Makes:** about 30 cookies

   2⅔ **cups flaked coconut (7 ounces)**
    ⅔ **cup sugar**
    ⅓ **cup all-purpose flour**
    ¼ **teaspoon salt**
     3 **egg whites**
    ½ **teaspoon vanilla or ¼ teaspoon**
        almond extract
     4 **ounces semisweet chocolate (optional)**
     1 **teaspoon shortening (optional)**

1. Preheat oven to 325°F. Lightly grease and flour a large cookie sheet or line it with parchment paper; set aside. In a medium mixing bowl combine coconut, sugar, flour, and salt. Stir in egg whites and vanilla.

2. Drop mixture by rounded teaspoons 2 inches apart onto the prepared cookie sheet (see photo, page 244). Bake for 20 to 25 minutes or until edges are light brown. Transfer cookies to a wire rack and let cool.

3. If desired, in a small saucepan melt chocolate and shortening over low heat, stirring often. Dip bottoms of cookies in melted chocolate or drizzle melted chocolate over tops in a crisscross pattern (see tip, right).

Per cookie: 73 cal., 4 g total fat (4 g sat. fat), 0 mg chol., 57 mg sodium, 10 g carbo., 1 g fiber, 1 g pro.
Exchanges: ½ Other Carbo., 1 Fat

Almond Meringues

Prep: 15 minutes **Bake:** 20 minutes per batch
Oven: 325°F **Makes:** about 30 cookies

     2 **egg whites**
    ½ **teaspoon vanilla**
    ⅔ **cup sugar**
     1 **8-ounce can almond paste***

1. Preheat oven to 325°F. Lightly grease a cookie sheet; set aside. In a medium mixing bowl beat egg whites and vanilla with an electric mixer on high speed until soft peaks form (tips curl; see photo 1, page 182). Gradually add sugar, about 1 tablespoon at a time, beating until stiff peaks form (tips stand straight; see photo 2, page 182). Crumble almond paste; stir in ½ cup of the beaten egg white mixture. Fold this mixture into remaining egg white mixture.

2. Drop mixture by rounded teaspoons 2 inches apart onto the prepared cookie sheet (see photo, page 244). Bake for about 20 minutes or until edges are light brown. Transfer to a wire rack and let cool.

***Note:** Only use almond paste made without syrup or liquid glucose.

Per cookie: 52 cal., 2 g total fat (0 g sat. fat), 0 mg chol., 4 mg sodium, 8 g carbo., 0 g fiber, 1 g pro.
Daily Values: 1% calcium, 1% iron
Exchanges: ½ Other Carbo., ½ Fat

Coconut Meringues: Prepare as above, except omit almond paste and fold 1⅓ cups flaked coconut into the beaten egg white mixture.

Lemon-Coconut Meringues: Prepare as above, except omit almond paste and vanilla. Add 1 tablespoon lemon juice and 1 teaspoon finely shredded lemon peel. Fold 1⅓ cups flaked coconut into the beaten egg white mixture.

Per cookie coconut or lemon-coconut variations: 32 cal., 1 g total fat (1 g sat. fat), 0 mg chol., 4 mg sodium, 6 g carbo., 0 g fiber, 0 g pro.
Exchanges: ½ Other Carbo.

Drizzle and Pipe

To drizzle melted chocolate or pipe toppings and fillings over cookies and bars, use a pastry bag fitted with a small, plain tip. If you don't own a pastry bag, fill a heavy-duty resealable plastic bag with the mixture and snip a small hole in one corner of the bag. Pipe out the mixture as desired.

Old-Fashioned Sugar Cookies

Old-Fashioned Sugar Cookies

This is the simple version of sugar cookies. Instead of rolling out the dough and cutting it into shapes, just form the dough into balls, roll them in sugar, and pop them in the oven.

Prep: 30 minutes **Chill:** 2 hours **Bake:** 9 minutes per batch
Oven: 375°F **Makes:** about 48 cookies

  1 **cup butter, softened**
1½ **cups sugar**
  2 **eggs**
  1 **teaspoon cream of tartar**
  1 **teaspoon baking soda**
  1 **teaspoon vanilla**
  ¼ **teaspoon salt**
2¾ **cups all-purpose flour**
  ¼ **to ⅓ cup sugar**

1. In a large mixing bowl beat the butter with an electric mixer on medium to high speed for 30 seconds. Add the 1½ cups sugar; beat until combined. Beat in eggs, cream of tartar, baking soda, vanilla, and salt until combined. Beat in as much of the flour as you can with the mixer. Stir in remaining flour. Cover and chill for 2 to 3 hours.

2. Preheat oven to 375°F. Shape dough into 1-inch balls. Roll balls in the ¼ cup sugar to coat. Place balls 2 inches apart on an ungreased cookie sheet.

3. Bake for 9 to 12 minutes or until light brown. Transfer to a wire rack and let cool.

Per cookie: 90 cal., 4 g total fat (2 g sat. fat), 20 mg chol., 70 mg sodium, 12 g carbo., 0 g fiber, 1 g pro.
Daily Values: 3% vit. A, 2% iron
Exchanges: 1 Other Carbo., ½ Fat

Snickerdoodles

Prep: 25 minutes **Chill:** 1 hour
Bake: 10 minutes per batch **Oven:** 375°F
Makes: about 36 cookies

  ½ **cup butter, softened**
  1 **cup sugar**
  ¼ **teaspoon baking soda**
  ¼ **teaspoon cream of tartar**
  1 **egg**
  ½ **teaspoon vanilla**
1½ **cups all-purpose flour**
  2 **tablespoons sugar**
  1 **teaspoon ground cinnamon**

1. In a medium mixing bowl beat butter with an electric mixer for 30 seconds. Add the 1 cup sugar, baking soda, and cream of tartar. Beat until combined, scraping sides of bowl occasionally. Beat in egg and vanilla until combined. Beat in as much of the flour as you can with the mixer. Stir in any remaining flour. Cover and chill dough about 1 hour or until easy to handle.

2. Preheat oven to 375°F. Combine the 2 tablespoons sugar and the cinnamon. Shape dough into 1-inch balls. Roll balls in sugar mixture to coat. Place 2 inches apart on an ungreased cookie sheet. Bake 10 to 11 minutes or until edges are golden. Transfer to a wire rack; cool.

Per cookie: 69 cal., 3 g total fat (2 g sat. fat), 13 mg chol., 38 mg sodium, 10 g carbo., 0 g fiber, 1 g pro.
Daily Values: 2% vit. A, 2% iron
Exchanges: ½ Other Carbo., ½ Fat

Sandies

Prep: 25 minutes **Bake:** 15 minutes per batch
Oven: 325°F **Makes:** about 48 cookies

  1 **cup butter, softened**
  ½ **cup powdered sugar**
  1 **tablespoon water**
  1 **teaspoon vanilla**
  2 **cups all-purpose flour**
1½ **cups finely chopped pecans**
  1 **cup powdered sugar**

1. Preheat oven to 325°F. Beat butter with an electric mixer on medium to high speed for 30 seconds. Add the ½ cup powdered sugar. Beat until combined, scraping sides of bowl. Beat in water and vanilla until combined. Beat in as much of the flour as you can with the mixer. Stir in any remaining flour. Stir in pecans.

2. Shape dough into 1-inch balls or 2×½-inch logs. Place 1 inch apart on an ungreased cookie sheet. Bake about 15 minutes or until bottoms are light brown. Transfer to a wire rack and let cool. Place the 1 cup powdered sugar in a plastic bag; gently shake cooled cookies in bag to coat.

Per cookie: 91 cal., 7 g total fat (3 g sat. fat), 11 mg chol., 41 mg sodium, 8 g carbo., 0 g fiber, 1 g pro.
Daily Values: 3% vit. A, 2% iron
Exchanges: ½ Other Carbo., 1½ Fat

Macadamia Nut Cookies

FAVORITE Macadamia Nut Cookies

Surprised to see ½ cup cornstarch in these cookies? It's actually the cornstarch that gives the cookies their tender, melt-in-your-mouth texture.

Prep: 25 minutes **Bake:** 12 minutes per batch
Oven: 350°F **Makes:** about 36 cookies

>   2 **cups all-purpose flour**
>   1 **cup powdered sugar**
> ½ **cup cornstarch**
>   1 **cup butter**
> ½ **cup chopped macadamia nuts or toasted walnuts (see tip, page 265)**
>   1 **egg yolk**
> 1½ **teaspoons finely shredded orange peel**
>   2 **tablespoons orange juice**
>   1 **recipe Orange Frosting**

1. Preheat oven to 350°F. Combine flour, powdered sugar, and cornstarch. Using a pastry blender, cut in butter until mixture resembles coarse crumbs. Stir in macadamia nuts. In a bowl combine egg yolk, orange peel, and orange juice. Add egg yolk mixture to flour mixture, stirring until moistened. Knead dough in bowl until it forms a ball.

2. Shape dough into 1¼-inch balls. Place balls 2 inches apart on an ungreased cookie sheet. Dip the bottom of a glass in *granulated sugar* and flatten each ball to ¼-inch thickness.

3. Bake for 12 to 15 minutes or until edges are set and surfaces are dry. Transfer to a wire rack; cool. Frost with Orange Frosting. If desired, sprinkle with additional finely chopped *macadamia nuts*.

Orange Frosting: Combine 1 cup powdered sugar, 2 tablespoons softened butter, and ½ teaspoon finely shredded orange peel. Stir in 1 to 2 tablespoons orange juice to make spreadable.

Per cookie: 124 cal., 8 g total fat (3 g sat. fat), 22 mg chol., 2 mg sodium, 13 g carbo., 0 g fiber, 1 g pro.
Daily Values: 4% vit. A, 1% vit. C, 5% calcium, 2% iron
Exchanges: 1 Other Carbo., 1½ Fat

Peanut Butter Cookies

Drizzle cookies with melted chocolate for an unbeatable taste sensation.

Prep: 25 minutes **Bake:** 7 minutes per batch
Oven: 375°F **Makes:** about 36 cookies

> ½ **cup butter, softened**
> ½ **cup peanut butter**
> ½ **cup granulated sugar**
> ½ **cup packed brown sugar or ¼ cup honey**
> ½ **teaspoon baking soda**
> ½ **teaspoon baking powder**
>   1 **egg**
> ½ **teaspoon vanilla**
> 1¼ **cups all-purpose flour**

1. Beat butter and peanut butter with an electric mixer on medium to high speed for 30 seconds. Add the granulated sugar, brown sugar, baking soda, and baking powder. Beat until combined, scraping sides of bowl. Beat in the egg and vanilla until combined. Beat in as much of the flour as you can with the mixer. Stir in remaining flour. If necessary, cover and chill dough until easy to handle.

2. Preheat oven to 375°F. Shape dough into 1-inch balls. Roll balls in additional *granulated sugar* to coat. Place balls 2 inches apart on an ungreased cookie sheet. Flatten by making crisscross marks with the tines of a fork. Bake for 7 to 9 minutes or until bottoms are light brown. Transfer to a wire rack and let cool.

Per cookie: 87 cal., 5 g total fat (2 g sat. fat), 13 mg chol., 70 mg sodium, 10 g carbo., 0 g fiber, 2 g pro.
Daily Values: 2% vit. A, 1% calcium, 2% iron
Exchanges: ½ Other Carbo., 1 Fat

Peanut Butter Blossoms

If you want to go the healthful route with these cookies, use only 1 cup all-purpose flour and add ¾ cup whole wheat flour.

Prep: 25 minutes **Bake:** 10 minutes per batch
Oven: 350°F **Makes:** about 54 cookies

- ½ **cup shortening**
- ½ **cup peanut butter**
- ½ **cup granulated sugar**
- ½ **cup packed brown sugar**
- 1 **teaspoon baking powder**
- ⅛ **teaspoon baking soda**
- 1 **egg**
- 2 **tablespoons milk**
- 1 **teaspoon vanilla**
- 1¾ **cups all-purpose flour**
- ¼ **cup granulated sugar**
  Milk chocolate kisses or stars (about 54)

1. Preheat oven to 350°F. In a large mixing bowl beat shortening and peanut butter with an electric mixer on medium to high speed for 30 seconds. Add the ½ cup granulated sugar, brown sugar, baking powder, and baking soda. Beat until combined, scraping sides of bowl occasionally. Beat in egg, milk, and vanilla until combined. Beat in as much of the flour as you can with the mixer. Stir in any remaining flour.

2. Shape dough into 1-inch balls. Roll balls in the ¼ cup granulated sugar. Place 2 inches apart on an ungreased cookie sheet. Bake for 10 to 12 minutes or until edges are firm and bottoms are light brown. Immediately press a chocolate kiss into each cookie's center. Transfer to a wire rack and let cool.

Per cookie: 94 cal., 5 g total fat (2 g sat. fat), 5 mg chol., 28 mg sodium, 11 g carbo., 0 g fiber, 2 g pro.
Daily Values: 2% calcium, 2% iron
Exchanges: 1 Other Carbo., 1 Fat

Ginger Cookies

Sugar and spice and everything nice is exactly what makes up these chewy little snacks. For big after-school appetites, try the Big Ginger Cookies.

Prep: 20 minutes **Bake:** 8 minutes per batch
Oven: 350°F **Makes:** about 120 cookies

- 4½ **cups all-purpose flour**
- 4 **teaspoons ground ginger**
- 2 **teaspoons baking soda**
- 1½ **teaspoons ground cinnamon**
- 1 **teaspoon ground cloves**
- ¼ **teaspoon salt**
- 1½ **cups shortening**
- 2 **cups sugar**
- 2 **eggs**
- ½ **cup molasses**
- ¾ **cup sugar**

1. Preheat oven to 350°F. In a medium bowl stir together flour, ginger, baking soda, cinnamon, cloves, and salt; set aside. In a large mixing bowl beat shortening with an electric mixer on low speed for 30 seconds. Add the 2 cups sugar. Beat until combined, scraping sides of bowl occasionally. Beat in eggs and molasses until combined. Beat in as much of the flour mixture as you can with the mixer. Stir in any remaining flour mixture.

2. Shape dough into 1-inch balls. Roll balls in the ¾ cup sugar. Place 1½ inches apart on an ungreased cookie sheet. Bake for 8 to 9 minutes or until bottoms are light brown and tops are puffed (do not overbake). Cool on cookie sheet 1 minute. Transfer to a wire rack and let cool.

Per cookie: 61 cal., 3 g total fat (1 g sat. fat), 4 mg chol., 28 mg sodium, 9 g carbo., 0 g fiber, 1 g pro.
Daily Values: 1% calcium, 2% iron
Exchanges: ½ Other Carbo., ½ Fat

Big Ginger Cookies: Prepare as above, except use a ¼-cup measure or scoop to shape dough into 2-inch balls; roll in sugar. Place 2½ inches apart on an ungreased cookie sheet. Bake in a 350°F oven for 11 to 13 minutes or until

Peanut Butter Blossoms

bottoms are light brown and tops are puffed (do not overbake). Cool on cookie sheet 2 minutes. Transfer to a wire rack and let cool. Makes about 24 cookies.

Per cookie: 306 cal., 13 g total fat (3 g sat. fat), 18 mg chol., 138 mg sodium, 45 g carbo., 1 g fiber, 3 g pro.
Daily Values: 1% vit. A, 1% vit. C, 3% calcium, 10% iron
Exchanges: 3 Other Carbo., 2½ Fat

Jam Thumbprints

Use a variety of jam flavors, such as strawberry, cherry, or apricot, for these little thumbprints. For a completely different twist, spoon frosting or purchased citrus curd into the centers. See photo, page 241.

Prep: 25 minutes Chill: 1 hour Bake: 10 minutes per batch
Oven: 375°F Makes: about 42 cookies

  2 eggs
  ⅔ cup butter, softened
  ½ cup sugar
  1 teaspoon vanilla
  1½ cups all-purpose flour
  1 cup finely chopped walnuts
  ⅓ to ½ cup jam or preserves

1. Separate eggs; place yolks and whites in separate bowls. Cover and chill egg whites until needed. In a large mixing bowl beat butter with an electric mixer on medium to high speed for 30 seconds. Add sugar. Beat until combined, scraping sides of bowl occasionally. Beat in egg yolks and vanilla until combined. Beat in as much of the flour as you can with the mixer. Stir in any remaining flour. Cover and chill dough about 1 hour or until easy to handle.

2. Preheat oven to 375°F. Grease a cookie sheet; set aside. Shape dough into 1-inch balls. Slightly beat reserved egg whites. Roll balls in egg whites, then in walnuts to coat. Place balls 1 inch apart on the prepared cookie sheet. Using your thumb, make an indentation in the center of each ball of dough.

3. Bake for 10 to 12 minutes or until edges are light brown. (To re-press centers, see tip, right.) Transfer to a wire rack and let cool. Just before serving, fill cookie centers with jam.

Per cookie: 82 cal., 5 g total fat (2 g sat. fat), 18 mg chol., 35 mg sodium, 8 g carbo., 0 g fiber, 1 g pro.
Daily Values: 3% vit. A, 1% calcium, 2% iron
Exchanges: ½ Other Carbo., 1 Fat

Chocolate Crinkles

Prep: 25 minutes Chill: 2 hours Bake: 8 minutes per batch
Oven: 375°F Makes: about 60 cookies

  4 eggs
  1¾ cups granulated sugar
  4 ounces unsweetened chocolate, melted and cooled
  ½ cup cooking oil
  2 teaspoons baking powder
  2 teaspoons vanilla
  2 cups all-purpose flour
  Powdered sugar

1. In a large mixing bowl beat eggs, granulated sugar, chocolate, oil, baking powder, and vanilla with an electric mixer until combined. Gradually beat in as much of the flour as you can with the mixer. Stir in any remaining flour. Cover and chill dough 2 hours or overnight or until dough is easy to handle.

2. Preheat oven to 375°F. Lightly grease a cookie sheet. Shape dough into 1-inch balls. Roll balls in powdered sugar to coat generously. Place balls 1 inch apart on prepared cookie sheet. Bake for 8 to 10 minutes or until edges are set and tops are dry (do not overbake). Transfer to a wire rack and let cool. (Cookies will deflate slightly upon cooling.) If desired, sift additional *powdered sugar* over the tops of cookies.

Per cookie: 66 cal., 3 g total fat (1 g sat. fat), 14 mg chol., 13 mg sodium, 9 g carbo., 0 g fiber, 1 g pro.
Daily Values: 1% calcium, 3% iron
Exchanges: ½ Other Carbo., ½ Fat

Leaving Prints Behind

It may seem obvious, but if you've never made thumbprint cookies, you might not understand the name. Before each delicate nibble is placed in the oven, the baker must press a thumb into the center of each cookie. After the cookies are baked and cooled, the indentations are filled with spoonfuls of sweet filling.

Sometimes a cookie's indentation will puff up during baking. If this happens, upon removing a cookie sheet from the oven, simply re-press your thumb (or if cookies are too hot, use the bowl of a measuring teaspoon) into each puffed-up cookie. Cool completely before filling. Enjoy!

Chocolaty Caramel Thumbprints

Chocolaty Caramel Thumbprints

If you wish to indulge in a decadent pleasure, this is the cookie for you! These irresistible chocolate goodies are rolled in pecans, filled with a thick caramel topping, and finished with a fine drizzle of chocolate.

Prep: 30 minutes **Chill:** 2 hours **Bake:** 10 minutes per batch
Oven: 350°F **Makes:** about 36 cookies

 1 **egg**
 ½ **cup butter, softened**
 ⅔ **cup sugar**
 2 **tablespoons milk**
 1 **teaspoon vanilla**
 1 **cup all-purpose flour**
 ⅓ **cup unsweetened cocoa powder**
 ¼ **teaspoon salt**
 16 **vanilla caramels, unwrapped**
 3 **tablespoons whipping cream**
 1¼ **cups finely chopped pecans**
 ½ **cup (3 ounces) semisweet chocolate pieces**
 1 **teaspoon shortening**

1. Separate egg; place yolk and white in separate bowls. Cover and chill egg white until needed. In a large mixing bowl beat butter with an electric mixer for 30 seconds. Add sugar and beat well. Beat in egg yolk, milk, and vanilla.

2. In another bowl stir together the flour, cocoa powder, and salt. Add flour mixture to butter mixture and beat until well combined. Wrap the cookie dough in plastic wrap and chill about 2 hours or until easy to handle.

3. Preheat oven to 350°F. Lightly grease a cookie sheet. In a small saucepan heat and stir caramels and whipping cream over low heat until mixture is smooth. Set aside.

4. Slightly beat reserved egg white. Shape the dough into 1-inch balls. Roll the balls in egg white, then in pecans to coat. Place balls 1 inch apart on prepared cookie sheet. Using your thumb, make an indentation in the center of each cookie.

5. Bake about 10 minutes or until edges are firm. Remove from oven. (To re-press centers, see tip, page 251.) Spoon melted caramel mixture into cookie centers. (If necessary, reheat caramel mixture to keep it spoonable.) Transfer to a wire rack and let cool.

6. In another small saucepan heat and stir chocolate pieces and shortening over low heat until chocolate is melted and mixture is smooth. Let cool slightly. Drizzle chocolate mixture over tops of cookies (see tip, page 247). Let stand until chocolate is set.

Per cookie: 114 cal., 7 g total fat (3 g sat. fat), 15 mg chol., 49 mg sodium, 12 g carbo., 1 g fiber, 1 g pro.
Daily Values: 2% vit. A, 2% calcium, 3% iron
Exchanges: 1 Other Carbo., 1½ Fat

Buried Cherry Cookies

Each of these hidden-gem cookies is topped with a bit of luscious chocolate frosting before baking. The result is chocolate-cherry perfection.

Prep: 30 minutes **Bake:** 10 minutes per batch
Oven: 350°F **Makes:** about 42 cookies

 1 **10-ounce jar maraschino cherries (about 42)**
 ½ **cup butter, softened**
 1 **cup sugar**
 ¼ **teaspoon baking powder**
 ¼ **teaspoon baking soda**
 ¼ **teaspoon salt**
 1 **egg**
 1½ **teaspoons vanilla**
 ½ **cup unsweetened cocoa powder**
 1½ **cups all-purpose flour**
 1 **cup semisweet chocolate pieces***
 ½ **cup sweetened condensed milk or low-fat sweetened condensed milk**

1. Preheat oven to 350°F. Drain cherries, reserving juice. Halve any large cherries. In a medium mixing bowl beat butter with an electric mixer on medium to high speed for 30 seconds.

Add the sugar, baking powder, baking soda, and salt. Beat until combined, scraping sides of bowl occasionally. Beat in egg and vanilla until combined. Beat in cocoa powder and as much of the flour as you can with the mixer. Stir in any remaining flour.

2. Shape dough into 1-inch balls. Place balls about 2 inches apart on an ungreased cookie sheet. Press your thumb into the center of each ball. Place a cherry in each center.

3. For frosting, in a small saucepan combine chocolate pieces and sweetened condensed milk. Cook and stir over low heat until chocolate melts. Stir in 4 teaspoons reserved cherry juice. (If you prefer a thinner frosting, add additional cherry juice.) Spoon 1 teaspoon frosting over each cherry, spreading to cover (see photo, below).

4. Bake about 10 minutes or until edges are firm. Cool on cookie sheet 1 minute. Transfer to a wire rack and let cool.

*Note: Do not substitute imitation chocolate pieces for semisweet chocolate pieces.

Per cookie: 97 cal., 4 g total fat (2 g sat. fat), 13 mg chol., 56 mg sodium, 14 g carbo., 0 g fiber, 1 g pro.
Daily Values: 2% vit. A, 3% calcium, 3% iron
Exchanges: 1 Other Carbo., 1 Fat

Top each cherry-filled piece of dough with about 1 teaspoon of the chocolate frosting. Carefully smooth the frosting over the top of the cherry so it is completely covered.

Cookie Press

Spritz cookies just wouldn't be the same if they weren't pumped out of the traditional cookie press into their classic shapes. The cookie press, or cookie gun, is a hollow tube fitted with a nozzle (most come with a variety of design templates) on one end and a pump or squeeze handle on the other. The tube is filled with cookie dough, which then is squeezed out through the template or nozzle onto cookie sheets.

Spritz

Because this recipe yields so many cookies, it's the perfect choice for a holiday cookie exchange. To spice it up a little, try making some or all of the variations listed below.

Prep: 25 minutes **Bake:** 8 minutes per batch
Oven: 375°F **Makes:** about 84 cookies

- 1½ **cups butter, softened**
- 1 **cup granulated sugar**
- 1 **teaspoon baking powder**
- 1 **egg**
- 1 **teaspoon vanilla**
- ¼ **teaspoon almond extract (optional)**
- 3½ **cups all-purpose flour**
  Colored sugar (optional)
- 1 **recipe Powdered Sugar Icing (page 184) (optional)**

1. Preheat oven to 375°F. In a large mixing bowl beat butter with an electric mixer on medium to high speed for 30 seconds. Add granulated sugar and baking powder. Beat until combined, scraping sides of bowl occasionally. Beat in egg, vanilla, and, if desired, almond extract until combined. Beat in as much of the flour as you can with the mixer. Stir in any remaining flour.

2. Force unchilled dough through a cookie press onto an ungreased cookie sheet. If desired, sprinkle shaped dough with colored sugar. Bake for 8 to 10 minutes or until edges are firm but not brown. Transfer to a wire rack and let cool. If desired, drizzle with Powdered Sugar Icing.

Chocolate Spritz: Prepare as above, except reduce flour to 3¼ cups and add ¼ cup unsweetened cocoa powder with the sugar.

Nutty Spritz: Prepare as above, except reduce sugar to ⅔ cup and flour to 3¼ cups. After adding flour, stir in 1 cup finely ground almonds or hazelnuts (filberts), toasted (see tip, page 265).

Peppermint Spritz: Prepare as above, except substitute 1 teaspoon of peppermint extract or 14 drops of peppermint oil for the vanilla and almond extracts. If desired, drizzle cookies with Powdered Sugar Icing and immediately sprinkle with finely crushed striped peppermint candies.

Per cookie regular, chocolate, nutty, or peppermint variations: 58 cal., 4 g total fat (2 g sat. fat), 12 mg chol., 28 mg sodium, 6 g carbo., 0 g fiber, 1 g pro.
Daily Values: 2% vit. A, 1% iron
Exchanges: ½ Starch, ½ Fat

Pecan Tassies

These delectable one-bite delights look and taste like miniature pecan pies. During the holiday season, fill small baskets or boxes with both the Pecan and Fudgy Brownie Tassies and give them as gifts. Or serve them as the finishing touch at an early afternoon luncheon.

Prep: 30 minutes **Bake:** 25 minutes
Oven: 325°F **Makes:** 24 cookies

- ½ **cup butter, softened**
- 1 **3-ounce package cream cheese, softened**
- 1 **cup all-purpose flour**
- 1 **egg**
- ¾ **cup packed brown sugar**
- 1 **tablespoon butter, melted**
- ⅔ **cup coarsely chopped pecans**

1. Preheat oven to 325°F. For pastry, in a mixing bowl beat the ½ cup butter and cream cheese until combined. Stir in the flour. Press a rounded teaspoon of pastry evenly into the bottom and up the sides of 24 ungreased 1¾-inch muffin cups.

2. For pecan filling, in a mixing bowl beat egg, brown sugar, and the 1 tablespoon melted butter until combined. Stir in pecans. Spoon about 1 heaping teaspoon of filling into each pastry-lined muffin cup. Bake for 25 to 30 minutes or until pastry is golden and filling is puffed. Cool slightly in pan. Carefully transfer to a wire rack and let cool.

Fudgy Brownie Tassies: Prepare as above, except instead of pecan filling, in a small saucepan heat and stir ½ cup semisweet chocolate pieces and 2 tablespoons butter or margarine over low heat until melted; remove from heat. Stir in ⅓ cup granulated sugar, 1 beaten egg, and 1 teaspoon vanilla. If desired, place 1 hazelnut (filbert), almond, macadamia nut, or walnut piece in each pastry-lined muffin cup. Spoon about 1 teaspoon of the chocolate mixture into each pastry-lined muffin cup. Bake in a 325°F oven for 20 to 25 minutes or until pastry is golden and filling is puffed. Continue as directed above.

Per cookie pecan or fudgy variation: 120 cal., 8 g total fat (4 g sat. fat), 25 mg chol., 62 mg sodium, 11 g carbo., 0 g fiber, 1 g pro.
Daily Values: 5% vit. A, 1% calcium, 3% iron
Exchanges: ½ Other Carbo., 1½ Fat

Almond Biscotti

Almond Biscotti [LOW FAT]

Prep: 25 minutes **Bake:** 45 minutes **Oven:** 325°F
Cool: 15 minutes **Makes:** about 84 cookies

- 2¾ **cups all-purpose flour**
- 1½ **cups sugar**
- 1½ **teaspoons baking powder**
- 1 **teaspoon salt**
- 2 **eggs**
- 2 **egg yolks**
- 6 **tablespoons butter, melted**
- 1½ **teaspoons finely shredded orange or lemon peel (optional)**
- 1 **cup coarsely chopped almonds**

1. Preheat oven to 325°F. Lightly grease two cookie sheets; set aside. In a bowl combine flour, sugar, baking powder, and salt. Make a well in the center of the flour mixture. Place eggs and egg yolks in the well and stir into the flour mixture. Add butter and, if desired, orange peel; stir until dough starts to form a ball. Stir in almonds.

2. Turn dough out onto a lightly floured surface; divide into three equal portions. Shape each portion into a 14-inch-long loaf. Place loaves about 3 inches apart on prepared cookie sheets; flatten loaves slightly until about 1½ inches wide (see photo, below). Bake 25 to 30 minutes or until firm and light brown. Cool on cookie sheets for 15 minutes.

3. Transfer baked loaves to a cutting board. Use a serrated knife to cut each loaf diagonally into ½-inch slices. Place slices on cookie sheets. Bake for 10 minutes. Turn slices over; bake for 10 to 15 minutes more or until crisp and dry. Cool.

Hazelnut or Pistachio Biscotti: Prepare as on page 254, except substitute 1 cup chopped hazelnuts (filberts) or pistachios for the almonds. For hazelnuts, use the orange peel option; for pistachios, use the lemon peel option.

Cashew-Chocolate Biscotti: Prepare as on page 254, except omit the citrus peel and substitute ½ cup chopped cashews and ½ cup finely chopped bittersweet chocolate for the almonds.

Per cookie almond, hazelnut, pistachio, or cashew-chocolate variations: 47 cal., 2 g total fat (1 g sat. fat), 12 mg chol., 40 mg sodium, 7 g carbo., 0 g fiber, 1 g pro.
Daily Values: 1% vit. A, 1% calcium, 2% iron
Exchanges: ½ Other Carbo., ½ Fat

Place the dough loaves about 3 inches apart on cookie sheets. Gently pat them until each one is about 1½ inches wide.

Double Chocolate Biscotti

Prep: 30 minutes Bake: 35 minutes Oven: 375°F/325°F
Cool: 1 hour Makes: about 24 cookies

- ½ **cup butter, softened**
- ⅔ **cup sugar**
- ¼ **cup unsweetened cocoa powder**
- 2 **teaspoons baking powder**
- 2 **eggs**
- 1¾ **cups all-purpose flour**
- ¾ **cup white baking pieces**
- ½ **cup large semisweet chocolate pieces**

1. Preheat oven to 375°F. Lightly grease a cookie sheet. Beat butter with an electric mixer on medium to high speed for 30 seconds. Add sugar, cocoa powder, and baking powder. Beat until combined, scraping sides of bowl. Beat in eggs until combined. Beat in as much of the flour as you can with the mixer. Stir in remaining flour. Stir in white baking pieces and chocolate pieces.

2. Divide dough in half; shape into two 9-inch-long loaves. Place loaves on prepared cookie sheet; flatten slightly until about 2 inches wide (see photo, left).

3. Bake for 20 to 25 minutes or until a wooden toothpick inserted near centers comes out clean. Cool on cookie sheet for 1 hour. (For easier slicing, wrap cooled loaves in plastic wrap and let stand overnight at room temperature.)

4. Preheat oven to 325°F. Use a serrated knife to cut each loaf diagonally into ½-inch slices. Place slices on an ungreased cookie sheet. Bake for 8 minutes. Turn cookies over; bake for 7 to 9 minutes more or until crisp and dry. Cool.

Per cookie: 157 cal., 8 g total fat (5 g sat. fat), 29 mg chol., 91 mg sodium, 19 g carbo., 0 g fiber, 2 g pro.
Daily Values: 4% vit. A, 4% calcium, 4% iron
Exchanges: 1½ Other Carbo., 1½ Fat

Santa's Whiskers

Prep: 20 minutes Chill: 2 hours
Bake: 10 minutes per batch Oven: 375°F
Makes: about 60 cookies

- ¾ **cup butter, softened**
- ¾ **cup sugar**
- 1 **tablespoon milk**
- 1 **teaspoon vanilla**
- 2 **cups all-purpose flour**
- ¾ **cup finely chopped candied red or green cherries**
- ⅓ **cup finely chopped pecans**
- ¾ **cup shredded coconut**

1. Beat butter with an electric mixer on medium to high speed for 30 seconds. Add sugar. Beat until combined, scraping sides of bowl. Beat in milk and vanilla until combined. Beat in as much of the flour as you can with the mixer. Stir in remaining flour. Stir in cherries and pecans.

2. Divide dough in half; shape into two 8-inch-long rolls. Roll in coconut. Wrap in plastic wrap or waxed paper. Chill for 2 to 24 hours or until firm enough to slice (see tip, page 257).

3. Preheat oven to 375°F. Cut rolls into ¼-inch slices. Place slices 1 inch apart on an ungreased cookie sheet. Bake for 10 to 12 minutes or until edges are golden. Transfer to a rack; let cool.

Per cookie: 65 cal., 3 g total fat (2 g sat. fat), 7 mg chol., 30 mg sodium, 8 g carbo., 0 g fiber, 1 g pro.
Daily Values: 2% vit. A, 1% iron
Exchanges: ½ Other Carbo., ½ Fat

Brown Sugar-Hazelnut Rounds

Also known as filberts and cobnuts, grape-size hazelnuts have a sweet, rich flavor that is popular in savory and sweet dishes. This slice-and-bake cookie showcases the nut in its ground form.

Prep: 25 minutes **Chill:** 6 hours **Bake:** 7 minutes per batch
Oven: 375°F **Makes:** about 60 cookies

- ½ **cup shortening**
- ½ **cup butter, softened**
- 1¼ **cups packed brown sugar**
- ½ **teaspoon baking soda**
- ¼ **teaspoon salt**
- 1 **egg**
- 1 **teaspoon vanilla**
- 2½ **cups all-purpose flour**
- ¾ **cup ground hazelnuts (filberts) or pecans, toasted (see tip, page 265)**
- 1 **recipe Browned Butter Icing (optional)**

1. In a large mixing bowl beat shortening and butter with an electric mixer on medium to high speed for 30 seconds. Add brown sugar, baking soda, and salt. Beat until combined, scraping sides of bowl occasionally. Beat in egg and vanilla until combined. Beat in as much of the flour as you can with the mixer. Stir in any remaining flour. Stir in hazelnuts.

2. Divide dough in half. Shape each half into a 10-inch-long roll. Wrap in plastic wrap or waxed paper. Chill for 6 hours or overnight or until firm enough to slice (see tip, page 257).

3. Preheat oven to 375°F. Cut rolls into ¼-inch slices with a serrated knife (see photo 2, page 257). Place slices 1 inch apart on an ungreased cookie sheet. Bake for 7 to 8 minutes or until edges are firm and light brown. Transfer cookies to a wire rack and let cool. If desired, drizzle cookies with Browned Butter Icing.

Per cookie: 89 cal., 5 g total fat (2 g sat. fat), 9 mg chol., 38 mg sodium, 11 g carbo., 0 g fiber, 1 g pro.
Daily Values: 1% vit. A, 1% calcium, 2% iron
Exchanges: 1 Other Carbo., 1 Fat

Browned Butter Icing: In a small saucepan heat 2 tablespoons butter over medium heat until butter turns the color of light brown sugar, stirring frequently. Remove from heat. Slowly beat in 1½ cups powdered sugar, 1 teaspoon vanilla, and enough milk (1 to 2 tablespoons) to make of drizzling consistency.

Cranberry-Orange Pinwheels

Cranberry-Orange Pinwheels

Perfect for a tea, these soft cookies are a delightful sight with their pretty red swirl of cranberry filling.

Prep: 30 minutes **Chill:** 5 hours **Bake:** 10 minutes per batch
Oven: 375°F **Makes:** about 60 cookies

- 1 **cup cranberries**
- 1 **cup pecans**
- ¼ **cup packed brown sugar**
- 1 **cup butter, softened**
- 1½ **cups granulated sugar**
- ½ **teaspoon baking powder**
- ½ **teaspoon salt**
- 2 **eggs**
- 2 **teaspoons finely shredded orange peel**
- 3¼ **cups all-purpose flour**

1. For filling, in a food processor* combine cranberries, pecans, and brown sugar. Cover and process until cranberries and pecans are finely chopped. Set filling aside.

2. In a large mixing bowl beat butter with an electric mixer on medium to high speed for 30 seconds. Add granulated sugar, baking powder, and salt. Beat until combined, scraping sides of bowl occasionally. Add eggs and orange peel; beat until combined. Beat in as much of the flour as you can with the mixer. Stir in remaining flour. Divide dough in half; cover and chill about 1 hour or until easy to handle.

3. Between waxed paper, roll half of dough into a 10-inch square. Spread half of the filling over dough to within ½ inch of edges; roll up dough (see photo 1, below right). Moisten edges; pinch to seal. Wrap in plastic wrap. Repeat with remaining dough and filling. Chill for 4 to 24 hours (see tip, below right).

4. Preheat oven to 375°F. Cut rolls into ¼-inch slices (see photo 2, below right). Place slices 2 inches apart on an ungreased cookie sheet. Bake for 10 to 12 minutes or until edges are firm and bottoms are light brown. Cool on cookie sheet for 1 minute. Transfer to a wire rack and let cool.

*Note: If you don't have a food processor, finely chop the cranberries and pecans; stir in brown sugar. Continue as directed.

Per cookie: 89 cal., 5 g total fat (2 g sat. fat), 16 mg chol., 47 mg sodium, 11 g carbo., 0 g fiber, 1 g pro.
Daily Values: 2% vit. A, 1% vit. C, 1% calcium, 2% iron
Exchanges: ½ Other Carbo., 1 Fat

Date Pinwheels

Prep: 40 minutes **Chill:** 1 hour **Freeze:** 2 hours
Bake: 8 minutes per batch **Oven:** 375°F
Makes: about 64 cookies

1 8-ounce package (1⅓ cups) pitted whole dates, finely chopped
½ cup water
⅓ cup granulated sugar
2 tablespoons lemon juice
½ teaspoon vanilla
½ cup shortening
½ cup butter, softened
½ cup granulated sugar
½ cup packed brown sugar
½ teaspoon baking soda
¼ teaspoon salt
1 egg
2 tablespoons milk
1 teaspoon vanilla
3 cups all-purpose flour

1. For filling, in a medium saucepan combine dates, water, and the ⅓ cup granulated sugar. Bring to boiling; reduce heat. Cook and stir about 2 minutes or until thick. Stir in lemon juice and the ½ teaspoon vanilla; cool.

2. In a large mixing bowl beat shortening and butter with an electric mixer on medium to high speed for 30 seconds. Add the ½ cup granulated sugar, the brown sugar, baking soda, and salt.

Beat until combined, scraping sides of bowl occasionally. Beat in egg, milk, and the 1 teaspoon vanilla until combined. Beat in as much of the flour as you can with the mixer. Stir in any remaining flour. Divide dough in half. Cover and chill dough about 1 hour or until easy to handle.

3. Roll half of the dough between pieces of waxed paper into a 12×10-inch rectangle. Spread with half of the filling; roll up dough (see photo 1, below). Moisten edges; pinch to seal. Wrap in plastic wrap. Repeat with remaining dough and filling. Freeze 2 to 24 hours (see tip, below).

4. Preheat oven to 375°F. Grease a cookie sheet. Cut rolls into ¼-inch slices (see photo 2, below). Place slices 1 inch apart on prepared cookie sheet. Bake for 8 to 10 minutes or until edges are light brown. Cool on cookie sheet 1 minute. Transfer to a wire rack and let cool.

Per cookie: 75 cal., 3 g total fat (1 g sat. fat), 7 mg chol., 32 mg sodium, 11 g carbo., 0 g fiber, 1 g pro.
Daily Values: 1% vit. A, 1% calcium, 2% iron
Exchanges: 1 Other Carbo., ½ Fat

1. After spreading the dough rectangle with filling, roll the dough starting from one of the long sides. Use the waxed paper beneath it to lift and guide the roll.

2. Once the chilled roll is firm, use a sharp knife to cut it into ¼-inch slices. (See tip, below.)

Round 'em Up

Do your slice-and-bake rolls flatten while chilling, freezing, or slicing? Try this:

● Cut rolls of dough longer than 8 inches in half crosswise.
● Wrap rolls in plastic wrap; twist ends.
● Place wrapped rolls in tall glasses and lay the glasses on their sides in the refrigerator (or freezer for faster chilling).
● Slice rolls using a sharp serrated or thin-bladed knife. Rotate rolls while cutting them to prevent flattening one side.

Shortbread

Prep: 15 minutes **Bake:** 25 minutes
Oven: 325°F **Makes:** 16 wedges

> 1¼ cups all-purpose flour
> 3 tablespoons granulated sugar
> ½ cup butter

1. Preheat oven to 325°F. Combine flour and sugar. Using a pastry blender, cut in butter until mixture resembles fine crumbs and starts to cling. Knead until smooth and form into a ball.

2. To make wedges,* on an ungreased cookie sheet, pat dough into an 8-inch circle. Make a scalloped edge (see photo 1, right). Cut circle into 16 wedges (see photo 2, right). Leave wedges in circle. Bake for 25 to 30 minutes or until bottom starts to brown and center is set. Recut circle into wedges while warm. Cool on cookie sheet 5 minutes. Cool on a wire rack.

*Note: For rounds, on a lightly floured surface, roll dough until ½ inch thick. Using a 1½-inch cookie cutter, cut into 24 rounds. Place 1 inch apart on an ungreased cookie sheet. Bake for 20 to 25 minutes. For strips, on a lightly floured surface, roll dough into an 8×6-inch rectangle about ½ inch thick. Using a knife, cut into twenty-four 2×1-inch strips (see photo 3, right). Place 1 inch apart on an ungreased cookie sheet. Bake for 20 to 25 minutes.

Butter-Pecan Shortbread: Prepare as above, except substitute brown sugar for the granulated sugar. After cutting in butter, stir in 2 tablespoons finely chopped pecans. Drizzle with ½ teaspoon vanilla before kneading.

Lemon-Poppy Seed Shortbread: Prepare as above, except stir 1 tablespoon poppy seeds into flour mixture and add 1 teaspoon finely shredded lemon peel with the butter.

Oatmeal Shortbread: Prepare as above, except reduce flour to 1 cup. After cutting in butter, stir in ⅓ cup quick-cooking rolled oats.

Spiced Shortbread: Prepare as above, except substitute brown sugar for the granulated sugar and stir ½ teaspoon ground cinnamon, ¼ teaspoon ground ginger, and ⅛ teaspoon ground cloves into the flour mixture.

Per wedge regular, butter-pecan, lemon-poppy seed, oatmeal, or spiced variations: 98 cal., 6 g total fat (4 g sat. fat), 16 mg chol., 62 mg sodium, 10 g carbo., 0 g fiber, 1 g pro.
Daily Values: 5% vit. A, 3% iron
Exchanges: ½ Starch, 1 Fat

1. Crimp the edges of the shortbread circle using your thumbs and one forefinger.

2. Cut the circle into wedges before it's baked. If you cut it after it's baked, it is likely to break into pieces.

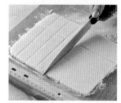

3. To make shortbread strips that are uniform in size, mark a long side of the rectangle at 1-inch intervals and a short side at 2-inch intervals. Cut across the rectangle using a sharp knife or pizza cutter.

Sugar Cookie Cutouts

Prep: 30 minutes **Chill:** 30 minutes
Bake: 7 minutes per batch **Oven:** 375°F
Makes: about 36 cookies

> ⅔ cup butter, softened
> ¾ cup granulated sugar
> 1 teaspoon baking powder
> 1 egg
> 1 tablespoon milk
> 1 teaspoon vanilla
> 2 cups all-purpose flour
> 1 recipe Powdered Sugar Icing (page 184) (optional)

Cookie Cutout Perfection

For pretty-as-a-picture cookie cutouts:

● Work with half of the dough at a time, keeping the other half in the refrigerator.
● Cover the rolling pin with a fabric stockinette. Excess flour toughens dough, so use only the minimum amount.
● Dip cookie cutter in flour each time you use it to prevent the dough from sticking.
● Transfer cookies to a cookie sheet using a wide metal spatula.
● Bake similar-size cookies together to prevent overbrowning of the smaller ones.

1. Preheat oven to 375°F. In a large mixing bowl beat butter on medium to high speed for 30 seconds. Add granulated sugar, baking powder, and ¼ teaspoon *salt*. Beat until combined, scraping sides of bowl occasionally. Beat in egg, milk, and vanilla. Beat in as much of the flour as you can with the mixer. Stir in any remaining flour. Divide dough in half. If necessary, cover and chill dough about 30 minutes or until easy to handle.

2. On a lightly floured surface, roll half the dough at a time until ⅛ inch thick. Using a 2½-inch cookie cutter, cut dough into desired shapes. Place 1 inch apart on an ungreased cookie sheet.

3. Bake for 7 to 8 minutes or until edges are firm and bottoms are barely light brown. Transfer to a wire rack and let cool. If desired, frost with Powdered Sugar Icing.

Candy Windowpane Cutouts: Prepare as on page 258, except place dough cutouts on a foil-lined cookie sheet. Cut small shapes out of the cutouts' centers. Finely crush 3 ounces hard candy (about ½ cup). Fill each center cutout with candy. Bake as directed; cool on foil. Store tightly covered.

Per cookie regular or candy windowpane variation: 73 cal.,
4 g total fat (2 g sat. fat), 16 mg chol., 66 mg sodium, 9 g carbo.,
0 g fiber, 1 g pro.
Daily Values: 3% vit. A, 1% calcium, 2% iron
Exchanges: ½ Other Carbo., 1 Fat

Gingerbread Cutouts

Prep: 35 minutes **Chill:** 3 hours **Bake:** 5 minutes per batch
Oven: 375°F **Makes:** about 36 cookies

- ½ **cup shortening**
- ½ **cup sugar**
- 1 **teaspoon baking powder**
- 1 **teaspoon ground ginger**
- ½ **teaspoon baking soda**
- ½ **teaspoon ground cinnamon**
- ½ **teaspoon ground cloves**
- ½ **cup molasses**
- 1 **egg**
- 1 **tablespoon vinegar**
- 2½ **cups all-purpose flour**
- 1 **recipe Powdered Sugar Icing (page 184) (optional)**

1. In a mixing bowl beat shortening with an electric mixer on medium to high speed for 30 seconds. Add sugar, baking powder, ginger, baking soda, cinnamon, and cloves. Beat until

combined, scraping sides of bowl occasionally. Beat in molasses, egg, and vinegar until combined. Beat in as much of the flour as you can with the mixer. Stir in remaining flour. Divide dough in half. Cover and chill dough about 3 hours or until easy to handle.

2. Preheat oven to 375°F. Grease a cookie sheet. On a lightly floured surface, roll half of the dough at a time until ⅛ inch thick. Using a 2½-inch cookie cutter, cut into desired shapes. Place 1 inch apart on prepared cookie sheet.

3. Bake for 5 to 6 minutes or until edges are light brown. Cool on cookie sheet 1 minute. Transfer to a wire rack and let cool. If desired, decorate cookies with Powdered Sugar Icing. If desired, before icing dries, sprinkle with *decorative candies* and *colored sugars*.

Per cookie: 81 cal., 3 g total fat (1 g sat. fat), 6 mg chol.,
32 mg sodium, 12 g carbo., 0 g fiber, 1 g pro.
Daily Values: 2% calcium, 4% iron
Exchanges: 1 Other Carbo., ½ Fat

Gingerbread People Cutouts: Prepare as at left, except roll dough until ¼ inch thick. Cut with 4½- to 6-inch people-shaped cookie cutters. Bake in a 375°F oven for 6 to 8 minutes or until edges are light brown. Makes about 18 cookies.

Per cookie: 161 cal., 6 g total fat (1 g sat. fat), 12 mg chol.,
65 mg sodium, 25 g carbo., 1 g fiber, 2 g pro.
Daily Values: 1% vit. C, 4% calcium, 8% iron
Exchanges: 1½ Other Carbo., 1 Fat

Gingerbread People Cutouts

Chocolate-Buttermilk Brownies

Chocolate-Buttermilk Brownies

This chocolaty dessert—known to some as Texas sheet cake and/or chocolate-buttermilk sheet cake—used to be found in the cake chapter. But because the texture is so rich and decadent, it fits much better under the definition of "brownie."

Prep: 30 minutes **Bake:** 25 minutes
Oven: 350°F **Cool:** 1 hour **Makes:** 24 brownies

- 2 **cups all-purpose flour**
- 2 **cups sugar**
- 1 **teaspoon baking soda**
- ¼ **teaspoon salt**
- 1 **cup butter**
- ⅓ **cup unsweetened cocoa powder**
- 2 **eggs**
- ½ **cup buttermilk or sour milk (see tip, page 169)**
- 1½ **teaspoons vanilla**
- 1 **recipe Chocolate-Buttermilk Frosting**

1. Preheat oven to 350°F. Grease a 15×10×1-inch or a 13×9×2-inch baking pan; set aside. In a medium bowl stir together flour, sugar, baking soda, and salt; set aside.

2. In a medium saucepan combine butter, cocoa powder, and 1 cup *water.* Bring mixture just to boiling, stirring constantly. Remove from heat. Add the cocoa mixture to flour mixture and beat with an electric mixer on medium to high speed until thoroughly combined. Add eggs, buttermilk, and vanilla. Beat for 1 minute (batter will be thin). Pour batter into the prepared pan.

3. Bake about 25 minutes for the 15×10×1-inch pan, 35 minutes for the 13×9×2-inch pan, or until a wooden toothpick inserted in the middle comes out clean.

4. Pour warm Chocolate-Buttermilk Frosting over brownies, spreading evenly. Cool in pan on wire rack for 1 hour. Cut into bars.

Chocolate-Buttermilk Frosting: In a saucepan combine ¼ cup butter, 3 tablespoons unsweetened cocoa powder, and 3 tablespoons buttermilk. Bring to boiling. Remove from heat. Add 2¼ cups powdered sugar and ½ teaspoon vanilla. Beat until smooth. If desired, stir in ¾ cup coarsely chopped pecans, toasted (see tip, page 265).

Chocolate-Cinnamon-Buttermilk Brownies: Prepare as at left, except add 1 teaspoon ground cinnamon to the flour mixture.

Per brownie regular or cinnamon variation: 244 cal., 11 g total fat (6 g sat. fat), 45 mg chol., 193 mg sodium, 35 g carbo., 0 g fiber, 2 g pro.
Daily Values: 8% vit. A, 4% calcium, 5% iron
Exchanges: 2 Other Carbo., 2 Fat

Fudgy Brownies

Prep: 20 minutes **Bake:** 30 minutes
Oven: 350°F **Makes:** 16 brownies

- ½ **cup butter**
- 3 **ounces unsweetened chocolate, coarsely chopped**
- 1 **cup sugar**
- 2 **eggs**
- 1 **teaspoon vanilla**
- ⅔ **cup all-purpose flour**
- ¼ **teaspoon baking soda**
- ½ **cup chopped almonds or pecans (optional)**
- 1 **recipe Chocolate-Cream Cheese Frosting (page 261) (optional)**

1. Preheat oven to 350°F. In a medium saucepan melt butter and unsweetened chocolate over low heat, stirring constantly. Remove from heat; cool.

2. Grease an 8×8×2-inch or 9×9×2-inch baking pan; set aside. Stir sugar into cooled chocolate mixture in saucepan. Add the eggs, one at a time, beating with a wooden spoon just until combined. Stir in the vanilla.

3. In a small mixing bowl stir together the flour and baking soda. Add flour mixture to chocolate mixture; stir just until combined. If desired, stir in nuts. Spread the batter into the prepared pan.

4. Bake for 30 minutes for 8-inch pan or 25 minutes for 9-inch pan. Cool in pan on a wire rack. If desired, frost with Chocolate-Cream Cheese Frosting. Cut into bars.

Per brownie: 157 cal., 10 g total fat (6 g sat. fat), 43 mg chol., 90 mg sodium, 18 g carbo., 1 g fiber, 2 g pro.
Daily Values: 5% vit. A, 1% calcium, 4% iron
Exchanges: 1 Other Carbo., 2 Fat

Chocolate-Cream Cheese Frosting: In a saucepan melt 1 cup semisweet chocolate pieces over low heat, stirring constantly. Remove from heat; cool slightly. In a small bowl stir together two 3-ounce packages softened cream cheese and ½ cup powdered sugar. Stir in melted chocolate until smooth.

Cake Brownies

The thick, fudgy frosting perfectly complements the mellow chocolate flavor of these soft brownies. Because the same bowl or saucepan is used for melting the butter and mixing the batter, this recipe is a snap to make and simple to clean up after.

Prep: 30 minutes **Bake:** 15 minutes **Oven:** 350°F
Cool: 2 hours **Makes:** 48 brownies

- ¾ cup butter
- 1¼ cups sugar
- ½ cup unsweetened cocoa powder
- 2 eggs
- 1 teaspoon vanilla
- 1½ cups all-purpose flour
- 1 teaspoon baking powder
- ¼ teaspoon baking soda
- 1 cup milk
- 1 cup chopped walnuts or pecans
- ½ recipe No-Cook Fudge Frosting (page 186)

1. Preheat oven to 350°F. Grease a 15×10×1-inch baking pan; set aside. In a large microwave-safe bowl microwave butter on 100 percent power (high) for 1½ to 2 minutes or until melted. (Or melt butter over medium heat in a medium saucepan; remove saucepan from heat before continuing.) Stir in sugar and cocoa powder until combined. Add eggs and vanilla. Using a wooden spoon, beat mixture lightly just until combined.

2. In a small bowl combine flour, baking powder, and baking soda. Alternately add flour mixture and milk to chocolate mixture, beating after each addition. Stir in walnuts.

3. Pour batter into prepared baking pan. Bake for 15 to 18 minutes or until a wooden toothpick inserted near the center comes out clean. Cool on a wire rack 2 hours. Frost with No-Cook Fudge Frosting. Cut into bars.

Per brownie: 146 cal., 7 g total fat (3 g sat. fat), 23 mg chol., 72 mg sodium, 19 g carbo., 0 g fiber, 2 g pro.
Daily Values: 4% vit. A, 4% calcium, 3% iron
Exchanges: 1 Other Carbo., 1½ Fat

Chocolate-Caramel Bars

With a thick, buttery crust heaped with pecans, coconut, caramel, and milk chocolate, these bars are an exercise in sinful delight.

Prep: 20 minutes **Bake:** 40 minutes **Oven:** 350°F
Cool: 10 minutes **Makes:** 48 bars

- 1 cup all-purpose flour
- ½ cup packed brown sugar
- ½ cup butter
- 2 cups coarsely chopped pecans
- 1 cup flaked coconut
- 1 14-ounce can (1¼ cups) sweetened condensed milk
- 2 teaspoons vanilla
- 20 vanilla caramels, unwrapped
- 2 tablespoons milk
- 1 cup milk chocolate pieces or semisweet chocolate pieces

1. Preheat oven to 350°F. For crust, in a medium bowl stir together the flour and brown sugar. Using a pastry blender, cut in the butter until the mixture resembles coarse crumbs. Press crumb mixture into the bottom of an ungreased 13×9×2-inch baking pan (see tip, page 263). Bake for 15 minutes. Sprinkle pecans and coconut over hot crust.

2. For filling, combine sweetened condensed milk and vanilla; pour over pecans and coconut. Bake for 25 to 30 minutes more or until the filling is set. Cool on a wire rack for 10 minutes.

3. Meanwhile, in a small saucepan combine caramels and milk. Cook and stir over medium low heat just until caramels melt. Drizzle caramel mixture over filling. Sprinkle with chocolate pieces. Cool completely. Cut into bars.

Per bar: 142 cal., 8 g total fat (3 g sat. fat), 10 mg chol., 46 mg sodium, 16 g carbo., 1 g fiber, 2 g pro.
Daily Values: 2% vit. A, 4% calcium, 2% iron
Exchanges: 1 Other Carbo., 1½ Fat

Chocolate Revel Bars

The thick oat mixture used for the crust of these snack bars is also used as a dappled topping on the chocolate filling.

Prep: 30 minutes **Bake:** 25 minutes
Oven: 350°F **Makes:** 60 bars

- 1 cup butter, softened
- 2 cups packed brown sugar
- 1 teaspoon baking soda
- 2 eggs
- 2 teaspoons vanilla
- 2½ cups all-purpose flour
- 3 cups quick-cooking rolled oats
- 1½ cups semisweet chocolate pieces
- 1 14-ounce can (1¼ cups) sweetened condensed milk or low-fat sweetened condensed milk
- ½ cup chopped walnuts or pecans
- 2 teaspoons vanilla

1. Preheat oven to 350°F. Set aside 2 tablespoons of the butter. In a large mixing bowl beat the remaining butter with an electric mixer on medium to high speed for 30 seconds. Add the brown sugar and baking soda. Beat until combined, scraping sides of bowl occasionally. Beat in eggs and 2 teaspoons vanilla until combined. Beat in as much of the flour as you can with the mixer. Stir in any remaining flour. Stir in the rolled oats.

2. For filling, in a medium saucepan combine the reserved 2 tablespoons butter, the chocolate pieces, and sweetened condensed milk. Cook over low heat until chocolate melts, stirring occasionally. Remove from heat. Stir in walnuts and 2 teaspoons vanilla.

3. Press two-thirds (about 3⅓ cups) of the rolled oats mixture into the bottom of an ungreased 15×10×1-inch baking pan (see tip, page 263). Spread filling evenly over the rolled oats mixture. Dot remaining oats mixture on filling (see photo, above right).

4. Bake about 25 minutes or until top is light brown (chocolate filling will still look moist). Cool in pan on a wire rack. Cut into bars.

Peanut Butter-Chocolate Revel Bars: Prepare as above, except substitute ½ cup peanut butter for the 2 tablespoons butter when making the chocolate filling and substitute peanuts for the walnuts or pecans.

Whole Wheat-Chocolate Revel Bars: Prepare as at left, except reduce the all-purpose flour to 1½ cups and add 1 cup whole wheat flour.

Per bar chocolate, peanut butter, or whole wheat variations: 146 cal., 6 g total fat (3 g sat. fat), 18 mg chol., 68 mg sodium, 21 g carbo., 1 g fiber, 2 g pro.
Daily Values: 3% vit. A, 3% calcium, 4% iron
Exchanges: 1½ Other Carbo., 1 Fat

Separate the remaining rolled oat mixture into pieces, flatten them with your fingers, and place them on top of the chocolate filling.

Toffee Bars `EASY`

The crust is the most time-consuming part of these super-simple bar cookies, and even that takes only a few minutes. See photo, page 241.

Prep: 15 minutes **Bake:** 15 minutes **Oven:** 350°F
Cool: 30 minutes **Makes:** 36 bars

- ½ cup butter, softened
- ¾ cup packed brown sugar
- 1 egg
- ½ teaspoon vanilla
- 1 cup all-purpose flour
- ⅛ teaspoon salt
- ¾ cup semisweet chocolate pieces
- ⅓ cup chopped walnuts or pecans
- ⅓ cup chocolate-covered toffee pieces

1. Preheat oven to 350°F. In a large mixing bowl beat butter with an electric mixer on medium to high speed for 30 seconds. Add the brown sugar, egg, and vanilla. Beat until combined, scraping sides of bowl occasionally. Beat in flour and salt until combined.

2. Spread dough evenly in an ungreased 13×9×2-inch baking pan (see tip, page 263). Bake for about 15 minutes or until edges begin to brown and surface is dry. Remove from oven and immediately sprinkle with chocolate pieces. Let stand about 2 minutes or until chocolate is softened; spread evenly. Sprinkle with walnuts and toffee pieces. Cool in pan on a wire rack 30 minutes. Cut into bars.

Per bar: 88 cal., 5 g total fat (2 g sat. fat), 14 mg chol., 46 mg sodium, 9 g carbo., 1 g fiber, 1 g pro.
Daily Values: 2% vit. A, 1% calcium, 2% iron
Exchanges: ½ Other Carbo., 1 Fat

Blondies

These moist bars essentially are light-colored brownies, hence the fun name. Here brown sugar replaces the chocolate used in brownies to give these treats a butterscotch flavor.

Prep: 20 minutes **Bake:** 25 minutes
Oven: 350°F **Makes:** 36 bars

> 2 cups packed brown sugar
> ⅔ cup butter
> 2 eggs
> 2 teaspoons vanilla
> 2 cups all-purpose flour
> 1 teaspoon baking powder
> ¼ teaspoon baking soda
> 1½ cups chopped almonds, pecans, or cashews

1. Preheat oven to 350°F. Grease a 13×9×2-inch baking pan (see tip, below right); set aside. In a medium saucepan heat and stir brown sugar and butter over medium heat until butter melts and mixture is smooth. Cool slightly. Stir in eggs, one at a time. Stir in vanilla. Stir in flour, baking powder, and baking soda.

2. Spread batter in prepared baking pan. Sprinkle with almonds. Bake for 25 to 30 minutes or until a wooden toothpick inserted near center comes out clean. Cool slightly in pan on a wire rack. Cut into bars while warm.

Chocolate-Chunk Blondies: Prepare as above, except reduce almonds to ¾ cup and add ¾ cup semisweet or white chocolate pieces with the almonds. When checking doneness, be careful not to insert toothpick into chocolate pieces.

Per bar plain or chocolate-chunk variation: 137 cal., 7 g total fat (2 g sat. fat), 21 mg chol., 50 mg sodium, 18 g carbo., 1 g fiber, 2 g pro.
Daily Values: 3% vit. A, 3% calcium, 5% iron
Exchanges: 1 Other Carbo., 1½ Fat

Pecan Pie Bars

This dessert has the irresistible flavor of pecan pie in the fun-to-eat shape of a bar.

Prep: 25 minutes **Bake:** 40 minutes
Oven: 350°F **Makes:** 24 bars

> 1¼ cups all-purpose flour
> ½ cup powdered sugar
> ¼ teaspoon salt
> ½ cup butter
> 2 eggs, slightly beaten
> 1 cup chopped pecans

> ½ cup packed brown sugar
> ½ cup light-colored corn syrup
> 2 tablespoons butter, melted
> 1 teaspoon vanilla

1. Preheat oven to 350°F. For crust, in a medium bowl combine flour, powdered sugar, and salt. Using a pastry blender, cut in the ½ cup butter until mixture resembles coarse crumbs. Pat crumb mixture into an ungreased 11×7×1½-inch baking pan (see tip, below). Bake about 20 minutes or until light brown.

2. Meanwhile, for filling, in a medium bowl stir together eggs, pecans, brown sugar, corn syrup, the 2 tablespoons melted butter, and the vanilla. Pour over the baked crust, spreading evenly.

3. Bake about 20 minutes more or until the filling is set. Cool in pan on a wire rack. Cut into bars. Cover and store in the refrigerator.

Per bar: 150 cal., 9 g total fat (3 g sat. fat), 31 mg chol., 76 mg sodium, 17 g carbo., 1 g fiber, 2 g pro.
Daily Values: 4% vit. A, 1% calcium, 3% iron
Exchanges: 1 Other Carbo., 1½ Fat

Foiled Again!

Lining a pan with foil is the miracle method for removing bars from pans.

Removing bar cookies from a pan can be difficult, even if you've greased the pan with shortening. How can you get around this? Try lining your pans with foil. It means the baked goody lifts out cleanly, your pan doesn't get scratched from cutting the bars, and cleanup is a breeze—just throw away the foil.

Here's how to do it:
- Flip your pan over and shape foil around the outside, extending it about 1 inch past the edges (for easy gripping and lifting).
- Place the foil lining in the pan; grease foil if the recipe specifies a greased pan.
- Spread batter or dough in lined pan. Then bake and cool as directed.
- To remove, grasp the foil overhang and lift out the baked treat in a block. Place on a cutting board and cut into bars.

Lemon Bars

Lemon Bars

The luscious lemon filling on these all-time favorite bars gets its citrusy nuance from plenty of lemon juice and a dab of shredded lemon peel. A light sprinkle of powdered sugar is all the garnish these bars need.

Prep: 25 minutes **Bake:** 33 minutes
Oven: 350°F **Makes:** 36 bars

  2 cups all-purpose flour
  ½ cup powdered sugar
  2 tablespoons cornstarch
  ¼ teaspoon salt
  ¾ cup butter
  4 eggs, lightly beaten
1½ cups granulated sugar
  3 tablespoons all-purpose flour
  1 teaspoon finely shredded lemon peel
  ¾ cup lemon juice
  ¼ cup half-and-half, light cream, or milk
    Powdered sugar

1. Preheat oven to 350°F. Grease a 13×9×2-inch baking pan (see tip, page 263). In a bowl combine the 2 cups flour, the ½ cup powdered sugar, the cornstarch, and salt. Using a pastry blender, cut in butter until mixture resembles coarse crumbs. Press mixture into the bottom of prepared pan. Bake 18 to 20 minutes or until edges are golden.

2. Meanwhile, for filling, in a medium bowl stir together eggs, the granulated sugar, the 3 tablespoons flour, the lemon peel, lemon juice, and half-and-half. Pour filling over hot crust. Bake for 15 to 20 minutes more or until center is set.

Cool completely in pan on a wire rack. Sift with powdered sugar. Cut into bars. Cover and store in the refrigerator.

Per bar: 114 cal., 5 g total fat (3 g sat. fat), 35 mg chol., 65 mg sodium, 16 g carbo., 0 g fiber, 2 g pro.
Daily Values: 4% vit. A, 4% vit. C, 1% calcium, 3% iron
Exchanges: 1 Other Carbo., 1 Fat

Fruit-Filled Oatmeal Bars

If using the canned pie filling, try flavors such as cherry, peach, apple, or blueberry. For the option of fruit preserves, strawberry, raspberry, and apricot are all divine choices.

Prep: 20 minutes **Bake:** 30 minutes
Oven: 350°F **Makes:** 25 bars

1 cup all-purpose flour
1 cup quick-cooking rolled oats
⅔ cup packed brown sugar
¼ teaspoon baking soda
½ cup butter
1 21-ounce can pie filling or 1½ cups fruit
  preserves

1. Preheat oven to 350°F. Grease a 9×9×2-inch or 11×7×1½-inch baking pan (see tip, page 263). In a medium bowl combine the flour, rolled oats, brown sugar, and baking soda. Using a pastry blender, cut in butter until the mixture resembles coarse crumbs. Measure ½ cup of the crumb mixture; set aside.

2. Press remaining crumb mixture into the bottom of prepared baking pan. If using pie filling, coarsely snip or chop any large pieces of fruit. Spread desired filling over crust. Sprinkle with reserved crumb mixture. Bake for 30 to 35 minutes or until the top is golden. Cool in pan on a wire rack. Cut into bars.

Raisin-Filled Oatmeal Bars: Prepare as above, except substitute raisin filling for canned pie filling. To prepare raisin filling, in a medium saucepan combine ¾ cup water, 2 tablespoons sugar, and 2 teaspoons cornstarch. Add 1¼ cups golden raisins. Cook and stir until thickened and bubbly.

Mincemeat-Filled Oatmeal Bars: Prepare as above, except use 1½ cups canned mincemeat instead of the canned pie filling.

Per bar fruit, raisin, or mincemeat variations: 113 cal., 4 g total fat (2 g sat. fat), 10 mg chol., 47 mg sodium, 18 g carbo., 1 g fiber, 1 g pro.
Daily Values: 3% vit. A, 1% vit. C, 1% calcium, 3% iron
Exchanges: 1 Other Carbo., 1 Fat

Apple Pastry Bars

This pastry treat may not look like apple pie, but it's composed of exactly the same flavors. For an extra-special snack, sprinkle with powdered sugar and top with spoonfuls of whipped cream.

Prep: 45 minutes **Chill:** 4 hours **Bake:** 40 minutes
Oven: 375°F **Makes:** 32 bars

- 2½ **cups all-purpose flour**
- 1 **teaspoon salt**
- 1 **cup shortening**
- 1 **egg yolk**
  Milk
- 1 **cup cornflakes**
- 8 **to 10 (about 2½ pounds total) tart baking apples, peeled and sliced ¼ inch thick (8 cups) (see tip, page 435)**
- ½ **cup granulated sugar**
- 1 **teaspoon ground cinnamon**
- 1 **egg white**
- 1 **tablespoon water**
  Powdered sugar (optional)
  Whipped cream (optional)

1. For pastry, in a large bowl stir together the flour and salt. Using a pastry blender, cut in shortening until mixture resembles coarse crumbs. Lightly beat egg yolk in a glass measuring cup. Add enough milk to egg yolk to make ⅔ cup; mix well. Stir egg yolk mixture into flour mixture; mix well. Divide dough in half. Cover and chill dough for 4 to 24 hours.

2. Preheat oven to 375°F. On a lightly floured surface, roll half of the dough into an 18×12-inch rectangle. Fit dough rectangle into and up the sides of an ungreased 15×10×1-inch baking pan. Sprinkle with cornflakes; top with apples. Combine granulated sugar and cinnamon; sprinkle over apples. Roll the remaining dough into a 16×12-inch rectangle; place over apples. Seal edges; cut slits in top for steam to escape. Beat egg white and water; brush over pastry.

3. Bake for 40 to 45 minutes or until golden. Cool in pan on a wire rack. Serve warm or cool. If desired, top with powdered sugar and/or whipped cream.

Per bar: 123 cal., 7 g total fat (2 g sat. fat), 7 mg chol., 84 mg sodium, 15 g carbo., 1 g fiber, 1 g pro.
Daily Values: 1% vit. A, 2% vit. C, 1% calcium, 4% iron
Exchanges: ½ Starch, ½ Other Carbo., 1 Fat

Banana Bars

Prep: 30 minutes **Bake:** 25 minutes
Oven: 350°F **Makes:** 36 bars

- ½ **cup butter, softened**
- 1⅓ **cups granulated sugar**
- 1½ **teaspoons baking powder**
- ½ **teaspoon baking soda**
- ¼ **teaspoon salt**
- 1 **egg**
- 1 **cup mashed bananas (2 to 3 medium)**
- ½ **cup dairy sour cream**
- 1 **teaspoon vanilla**
- 2 **cups all-purpose flour**
- 1 **cup chopped pecans or walnuts, toasted (see tip, below)**
- 1 **recipe Powdered Sugar Icing (page 184)**

1. Preheat oven to 350°F. Lightly grease a 15×10×1-inch baking pan (see tip, page 263); set aside. In a large mixing bowl beat butter with an electric mixer on medium to high speed for 30 seconds. Add granulated sugar, baking powder, baking soda, and salt; beat until combined, scraping sides of bowl occasionally. Beat in the egg, mashed bananas, sour cream, and vanilla until combined. Beat or stir in the flour. Stir in pecans. Pour the batter into the prepared baking pan, spreading evenly.

2. Bake about 25 minutes or until a wooden toothpick inserted near center comes out clean. Cool completely in pan on a wire rack. Drizzle with Powdered Sugar Icing. Cut into bars.

Per bar: 105 cal., 6 g total fat (2 g sat. fat), 14 mg chol., 67 mg sodium, 13 g carbo., 1 g fiber, 1 g pro.
Daily Values: 2% vit. A, 1% vit. C, 1% calcium, 2% iron
Exchanges: 1 Other Carbo., 1 Fat

Give a Toast

Nuts, seeds, and coconut get an outstanding flavor boost when toasted in the oven.

Toasting is a must when you're looking for taste. Follow these steps:
- Spread nuts, seeds, or shredded coconut in a single layer in a shallow baking pan.
- Bake in a 350°F oven for 5 to 10 minutes or until the pieces are golden brown.
- Check the pieces frequently to make sure they aren't getting too brown. If they start to burn, they go quickly and generally can't be salvaged. Stir once or twice.

Carrot and Zucchini Bars

Carrot and Zucchini Bars

What a delicious way to get your family to eat their veggies! No one will ever know the healthful ingredients these moist, heavenly bars contain.

Prep: 20 minutes **Bake:** 25 minutes
Oven: 350°F **Makes:** 36 bars

   1½ **cups all-purpose flour**
    1 **teaspoon baking powder**
    ½ **teaspoon ground ginger**
    ¼ **teaspoon baking soda**
    2 **eggs, slightly beaten**
   1½ **cups shredded carrot (about 3 medium)**
    1 **cup shredded zucchini (about 1 medium)**
    ¾ **cup packed brown sugar**
    ½ **cup raisins**
    ½ **cup chopped walnuts**
    ½ **cup cooking oil**
    ¼ **cup honey**
    1 **teaspoon vanilla**
    1 **recipe Citrus-Cream Cheese Frosting**

1. Preheat oven to 350°F. In a large bowl combine flour, baking powder, ginger, and baking soda. In another large bowl stir together eggs, carrot, zucchini, brown sugar, raisins, walnuts, oil, honey, and vanilla. Add carrot mixture to flour mixture, stirring just until combined. Spread batter in an ungreased 13×9×2-inch baking pan.

2. Bake about 25 minutes or until a wooden toothpick inserted near the center comes out clean. Cool in pan on a wire rack. Frost with Citrus-Cream Cheese Frosting. Cut into bars.

Citrus-Cream Cheese Frosting: In a bowl beat one 8-ounce package softened cream cheese and 1 cup powdered sugar with an electric mixer on medium speed until fluffy. Stir in 1 teaspoon finely shredded lemon peel.

Per bar: 125 cal., 7 g total fat (2 g sat. fat), 19 mg chol., 44 mg sodium, 16 g carbo., 1 g fiber, 2 g pro.
Daily Values: 13% vit. A, 1% vit. C, 18% calcium, 1% iron
Exchanges: 1 Other Carbo., 1 Fat

Pumpkin Bars

Prep: 35 minutes **Bake:** 25 minutes **Oven:** 350°F
Cool: 2 hours **Makes:** 48 bars

    2 **cups all-purpose flour**
   1½ **cups sugar**
    2 **teaspoons baking powder**
    2 **teaspoons ground cinnamon**
    1 **teaspoon baking soda**
    ¼ **teaspoon salt**
    ¼ **teaspoon ground cloves**
    4 **eggs, beaten**
    1 **15-ounce can pumpkin**
    1 **cup cooking oil**
    ½ **recipe Cream Cheese Frosting (page 185)**

1. Preheat oven to 350°F. In a bowl stir together the flour, sugar, baking powder, cinnamon, baking soda, salt, and cloves. Stir in the eggs, pumpkin, and oil until combined. Spread batter into an ungreased 15×10×1-inch baking pan.

2. Bake for 25 to 30 minutes or until a wooden toothpick inserted near the center comes out clean. Cool in pan on wire rack 2 hours. Spread with Cream Cheese Frosting. Cut into bars.

Applesauce Bars: Prepare as above, except omit pumpkin and use one 15-ounce jar applesauce.

Per bar pumpkin or applesauce variation: 133 cal., 7 g total fat (2 g sat. fat), 23 mg chol., 78 mg sodium, 17 g carbo., 1 g fiber, 1 g pro.
Daily Values: 44% vit. A, 1% vit. C, 2% calcium, 3% iron
Exchanges: 1 Other Carbo., 1½ Fat

Don't Be Square!
Think outside the box for fun-shaped bars.

● For triangles, cut the block into 2½-inch squares; cut the squares in half diagonally.
● For diamonds, cut lines 1½ inches apart down the length of the pan. Then cut straight lines 1½ inches apart diagonally across the pan.

Fast and Flavorful Fix-Ups

Packaged products and premade bakery foods can cut kitchen time in half. The recipes here and on page 268 use store-bought items that result in homemade flavor.

Lemon Cornmeal Cookies LOW FAT EASY

Prep: 15 minutes **Bake:** 7 minutes per batch
Oven: 375°F **Makes:** about 60 cookies

- 1 8½-ounce package corn muffin mix
- ½ cup quick-cooking rolled oats
- ¼ cup sugar
- 2 tablespoons butter, softened
- 2 teaspoons milk
- 1 egg, slightly beaten
- 1 teaspoon finely shredded lemon peel
- 1 teaspoon poppy seeds

1. Preheat oven to 375°F. Line a cookie sheet with parchment paper. In a bowl stir together corn muffin mix, oats, sugar, butter, milk, egg, lemon peel, and poppy seeds until combined.

2. Drop dough by teaspoons 2 inches apart onto prepared cookie sheet. Bake for 7 to 9 minutes or until light brown. Transfer to a wire rack and let cool.

Per cookie: 27 cal., 1 g total fat (0 g sat. fat), 5 mg chol., 32 mg sodium, 4 g carbo., 0 g fiber, 1 g pro.
Daily Values: 1% iron
Exchanges: ½ Other Carbo.

Shortcut Baklava

Prep: 15 minutes **Bake:** 25 minutes **Oven:** 375°F
Cool: 10 minutes **Makes:** 16 wedges

- 1 15-ounce package rolled refrigerated unbaked piecrust (2 crusts)
- 1 cup finely chopped walnuts
- ⅓ cup sugar
- 2 tablespoons honey
- 1 teaspoon ground cinnamon
- 1 teaspoon lemon juice
- 1 tablespoon honey
  Cinnamon-sugar

1. Preheat oven to 375°F. Let piecrusts stand according to package directions. Unroll; place a crust on an ungreased cookie sheet. For filling, in a small bowl stir together walnuts, sugar, the 2 tablespoons honey, the cinnamon, and lemon juice. Spread over piecrust on cookie sheet, leav-

ing about a ½-inch border. Top with remaining piecrust. Seal piecrust edges by pressing with the tines of a fork. Prick top piecrust with a fork. In a small bowl stir together the 1 tablespoon honey and 1 teaspoon *water*. Brush mixture over top. Sprinkle lightly with cinnamon-sugar.

2. Bake about 25 minutes or until golden. Cool on cookie sheet on a wire rack for 10 minutes. Cut into 16 wedges. Cool completely.

Per wedge: 197 cal., 12 g total fat (3 g sat. fat), 5 mg chol., 99 mg sodium, 22 g carbo., 1 g fiber, 2 g pro.
Daily Values: 1% vit. C, 1% calcium, 2% iron
Exchanges: 1½ Other Carbo., 2½ Fat

Peanut Butter Brownies

Prep: 15 minutes **Bake:** 30 minutes **Oven:** 350°F
Cool: 1 hour **Makes:** 64 brownies

- 1 18- to 21-ounce package fudge brownie mix
- ½ cup chopped peanuts (optional)
- 1 3-ounce package cream cheese, softened
- ½ cup creamy peanut butter
- 2 tablespoons milk
- 1 egg yolk
- 1 16-ounce can chocolate frosting
- ½ cup creamy peanut butter
  Chopped peanuts (optional)

1. Preheat oven to 350°F. Lightly grease a 13×9×2-inch baking pan; set aside. Prepare brownie batter according to package directions. If desired, stir in the ½ cup peanuts. Spread batter in prepared pan. In a medium mixing bowl beat together cream cheese, ½ cup peanut butter, milk, and egg yolk with an electric mixer until smooth. Pipe mixture over brownie batter in pan (see tip, page 247). Bake for 30 minutes. Cool in pan on a wire rack for 1 hour.

2. In a medium bowl stir together the frosting and the remaining ½ cup peanut butter. Spread over cooled brownies. If desired, sprinkle with peanuts. Cut into small brownies.

Per brownie: 101 cal., 6 g total fat (1 g sat. fat), 10 mg chol., 73 mg sodium, 11 g carbo., 0 g fiber, 2 g pro.
Daily Values: 1% calcium, 2% iron
Exchanges: 1 Other Carbo., 1 Fat

Five-Layer Bars `EASY`

Prep: 10 minutes **Bake:** 37 minutes
Oven: 350°F **Makes:** 30 bars

- **2 13-ounce packages soft coconut macaroon cookies (32 cookies)**
- **¾ cup sweetened condensed milk**
- **¾ cup semisweet chocolate pieces**
- **¾ cup raisins or dried cranberries**
- **1 cup coarsely chopped peanuts**

1. Preheat oven to 350°F. Grease a 13×9×2-inch baking pan. Arrange cookies in the bottom of prepared pan. Press cookies together to form a crust. Bake for 12 minutes. Drizzle crust evenly with condensed milk. Sprinkle with chocolate pieces, raisins, and peanuts. Bake about 25 minutes or until edges are light brown. Cool in pan on a wire rack. Cut into bars.

Per bar: 181 cal., 7 g total fat (4 g sat. fat), 3 mg chol., 86 mg sodium, 28 g carbo., 1 g fiber, 3 g pro.
Daily Values: 1% vit. C, 3% calcium, 2% iron
Exchanges: 2 Other Carbo., 1½ Fat

No-Bake Favorites

Interested in delicious cookies without using the oven? It can be done. These ideas will get you started. Try some of your own creations using supermarket products. Different spreads, frostings, jams, and decorations can turn plain purchased cookies into works of art—and taste!

Lemon Snaps: In a medium mixing bowl beat ¼ cup lemon or orange curd and 2 tablespoons softened butter with an electric mixer on medium to high speed for 30 seconds. Add ¾ cup powdered sugar. Beat until smooth. Spread frosting on about 30 purchased gingersnap cookies. Sprinkle with chopped nuts, toasted (see tip, page 265). For a variety of flavors, spread the frosting on an assortment of sugar cookies and shortbread cookies too.

Candy Bar Cookie Shells: Divide 1 cup chopped candy bars among 30 purchased baked miniature phyllo dough shells (two 2.1-ounce packages). In a saucepan combine ½ cup semisweet chocolate pieces and ½ cup sweetened condensed milk. Heat and stir over medium heat until melted and smooth. Spoon chocolate mixture over candy in shells. Sprinkle with chopped nuts, toasted (see tip, page 265). Let stand about 30 minutes or until chocolate is set. Cover and store in refrigerator.

Butterscotch Bars: Crush one 9-ounce package of chocolate wafers (for a total of 2 cups). In a large bowl stir together 6 tablespoons melted butter, 1 cup creamy peanut butter, and 1½ cups powdered sugar. Stir in chocolate wafer crumbs. Press mixture into the bottom of an ungreased 13×9×2-inch baking pan.

In a heavy medium saucepan combine one 11-ounce package butterscotch-flavored pieces (2 cups) and ¼ cup whipping cream. Stir over low heat until pieces are just melted.

Carefully spoon butterscotch mixture over crumb mixture, spreading evenly. Sprinkle ¾ cup chopped peanuts over butterscotch mixture. Cover and chill at least 2 hours. Cut into bars. Cover and store in refrigerator.

Chocolate-Mint Sandwich Cookies: In a small bowl stir together 1 cup canned whipped chocolate or vanilla frosting and 24 chopped chocolate-mint layered candies. Spread frosting mixture on the flat side of 12 purchased soft chocolate cookies. Top each frosted cookie with an another cookie, flat side down.

Chocolate-Peanut Butter Sandwich Cookies: Prepare Chocolate-Mint Sandwich Cookies as directed above, except omit chocolate-mint layered candies. Stir 2 tablespoons creamy peanut butter and ¼ cup chopped cocktail peanuts into the frosting. If desired, the frosting mixture also can be spread on vanilla wafers or peanut butter cookies.

ABC Sandwich Cookies: In a small bowl stir together 2 ounces cream cheese (tub-style) and 1 tablespoon strawberry preserves. If desired, stir in one drop of red food coloring. Spread cream cheese mixture on the flat sides of 16 plain and/or chocolate shortbread alphabet cookies. Top each cookie with another cookie, flat side down. Alternately, spread the cream cheese mixture on purchased regular shortbread cookies, vanilla wafers, or soft sugar cookies.

Desserts

Cherry Cobbler, 272

Almond Panna Cotta, 278

Blueberry-Sour Cream Dessert, 276

Desserts Essentials

For many, the best part of dinner comes at the end—dessert. Use these tips to add the perfect finishing touches to your meal's sweet conclusion.

Ripe Is Best

Fruit isn't the only food that tastes better when it's ripe. Ripening, or hardening, a frozen dessert improves the dessert's texture and keeps it from melting too quickly at room temperature.

● For a traditional-style ice cream freezer, after churning remove the lid and dasher and cover the top with waxed paper or foil. Plug the lid's hole with cloth, then replace the lid on the can. Fill the outer freezer bucket with ice and rock salt—enough to cover the top of the freezer can—in a ratio of 4 cups ice to 1 cup rock salt. Let stand at room temperature about 4 hours.

● For an ice cream freezer with an insulated freezer bowl, transfer the ice cream to a freezer-proof container, cover, and store in your freezer for 4 hours (or per manufacturer's directions).

| Grated | Shaved | Curls |

Chocolate Finishes

It's hard to outdo the seductive flavor and texture of chocolate, even as a garnish. For any dessert, these finishes are supreme.

Grated: Rub a solid piece of chocolate across either the fine or coarse grate of a handheld grater.

Shaved: Make short strokes with a vegetable peeler across a solid piece of chocolate.

Curls: Draw a vegetable peeler across the narrow side of a chocolate bar (milk chocolate is best).

Magic Whipper

Real whipped cream has never been so easy to make! Just pour your whipping cream into the whipped cream maker bottle, press the button, and, with the help of the attached gas canister, you'll have instant fresh whipped cream. Find this device at cooking shops.

Candied Nuts

Sprinkle these nuts on ice cream, desserts, and even salads for an unbeatable flavor boost.

Line a baking sheet with foil; butter the foil. Set aside. Spread 3 cups pecan halves or whole almonds in a shallow baking pan. Bake in a 325°F oven for 10 minutes, stirring once. Meanwhile, heat ½ cup sugar in a heavy 10-inch skillet over medium-high heat, shaking skillet occasionally to heat sugar evenly (see photo 1, page 290). Do not stir. Heat until some of the sugar is melted (it should look syrupy); begin to stir only the melted sugar to keep it from over-browning. Stir in remaining sugar as it melts. Reduce heat to medium-low; continue to cook until all the sugar is melted and golden, about 5 minutes. Add 2 tablespoons butter to melted sugar in skillet, stirring until butter melts and mixture is combined. Remove from heat. Stir in ½ teaspoon vanilla. Add warm nuts to skillet, stirring to coat. Pour nut mixture onto the prepared baking sheet. Cool completely. Break apart. Makes about 4⅓ cups.

Whipped Cream

Fresh whipped cream is divine on any dessert.

In a chilled mixing bowl add 1 cup whipping cream, 2 tablespoons sugar, and ½ teaspoon vanilla. Beat with an electric mixer on medium speed until soft peaks form.

If desired, add one of the following ingredients with the vanilla: 2 tablespoons unsweetened cocoa powder plus 1 tablespoon additional sugar; 2 tablespoons amaretto, coffee, hazelnut, orange, or praline liqueur; ½ teaspoon finely shredded citrus peel; or ¼ teaspoon ground cinnamon, nutmeg, or ginger.

Strawberry Shortcakes

Strawberry Shortcakes

Prep: 30 minutes **Bake:** 12 minutes
Oven: 400°F **Makes:** 8 shortcakes

    1½ cups all-purpose flour
    ¼ cup sugar
    1 teaspoon baking powder
    ¼ teaspoon baking soda
    ¼ teaspoon salt
    ⅓ cup cold butter
    1 egg, slightly beaten
    ½ cup dairy sour cream
    2 tablespoons milk
    5 cups sliced strawberries
    3 tablespoons sugar
    1 recipe Whipped Cream (page 271)

1. Preheat oven to 400°F. Lightly grease a baking sheet; set aside. In a medium bowl combine flour, the ¼ cup sugar, the baking powder, baking soda, and salt. Using a pastry blender, cut in butter until mixture resembles coarse crumbs. In a small bowl combine egg, sour cream, and milk. Add to flour mixture, stirring with a fork just until moistened.

2. Drop dough into eight mounds onto prepared baking sheet.* Bake for 12 to 15 minutes or until golden. Transfer to a wire rack; let cool.

3. Meanwhile, combine 4 cups of the strawberries and the 3 tablespoons sugar. Using a potato masher, mash berries slightly; set aside. To serve, split shortcakes in half; fill with strawberry mixture and Whipped Cream. Top with remaining sliced strawberries.

*Note: For a whole shortcake, spread all the dough into a greased 8×1½-inch round baking pan. Bake in a 400°F oven for 18 to 20 minutes or until a wooden toothpick comes out clean. Cool in pan for 10 minutes. Remove from pan; cool. Continue as directed in Step 3. Cut into wedges.

Mixed Berry or Mixed Fruit Shortcakes: Prepare as at left, except use 5 cups mixed fresh berries (such as raspberries, blueberries, or blackberries) or 5 cups mixed fresh fruit (such as sliced peaches, nectarines, bananas, and/or halved grapes) instead of sliced strawberries. Do not mash mixed fruit.

Strawberry-Lemon-Poppy Seed Shortcakes: Prepare as at left, except stir 1 tablespoon poppy seeds and 1 teaspoon finely shredded lemon peel into flour mixture after cutting in butter.

Per individual shortcake strawberry, mixed berry, mixed fruit, or lemon-poppy seed variations: 373 cal., 22 g total fat (14 g sat. fat), 93 mg chol., 225 mg sodium, 39 g carbo., 5 g fiber, 5 g pro. Daily Values: 16% vit. A, 89% vit. C, 7% calcium, 9% iron Exchanges: 1 Starch, ½ Fruit, 1 Other Carbo., 4½ Fat

Strawberry-Nut Shortcakes: Prepare as at left, except stir ½ cup chopped walnuts into flour mixture after cutting in butter.

Per individual shortcake: 416 cal., 27 g total fat (14 g sat. fat), 93 mg chol., 226 mg sodium, 40 g carbo., 3 g fiber, 6 g pro. Daily Values: 16% vit. A, 89% vit. C, 8% calcium, 10% iron Exchanges: 1 Starch, ½ Fruit, 1 Other Carbo., 5 Fat

Cherry Cobbler

This six-in-one recipe gives you plenty of fruit choices. You can try a different flavor almost every day of the week! See photo, page 269.

Prep: 40 minutes **Bake:** 20 minutes
Cool: 1 hour **Oven:** 400°F **Makes:** 6 servings

    1 cup all-purpose flour
    2 tablespoons sugar
    1½ teaspoons baking powder
    ¼ teaspoon salt
    ½ teaspoon ground cinnamon (optional)
    ¼ cup butter or margarine
    6 cups fresh or frozen unsweetened pitted tart
      red cherries
    1 cup sugar
    2 tablespoons cornstarch
    1 egg
    ¼ cup milk
      Vanilla ice cream (optional)

1. Preheat oven to 400°F. For topping, in a medium bowl stir together flour, the 2 tablespoons sugar, the baking powder, salt, and, if desired, cinnamon. Cut in butter until mixture resembles coarse crumbs; set aside.

2. For filling, in a large saucepan combine the cherries, the 1 cup sugar, and the cornstarch. Cook over medium heat until cherries release juices, stirring occasionally. Continue to cook, stirring constantly, over medium heat until thickened and bubbly. Keep filling hot.

3. In a small bowl stir together egg and milk. Add to flour mixture, stirring just until moistened. Transfer hot filling to a 2-quart square baking dish. Using a spoon, immediately drop topping into six mounds on top of filling.

4. Bake for 20 to 25 minutes or until topping is golden brown. Let cool in pan on a wire rack about 1 hour. If desired, serve with ice cream.

Per biscuit + ½ cup filling: 386 cal., 10 g total fat (5 g sat. fat), 58 mg chol., 236 mg sodium, 73 g carbo., 3 g fiber, 5 g pro. **Daily Values:** 40% vit. A, 21% vit. C, 7% calcium, 9% iron **Exchanges:** 1 Fruit, 1 Starch, 3 Other Carbo., 1½ Fat

Rhubarb Cobbler: Prepare as on page 272, except use 6 cups fresh or frozen unsweetened sliced rhubarb instead of cherries.

Per biscuit + ½ cup filling: 346 cal., 10 g total fat (5 g sat. fat), 93 mg chol., 248 mg sodium, 59 g carbo., 3 g fiber, 6 g pro. **Daily Values:** 9% vit. A, 16% vit. C, 15% calcium, 8% iron **Exchanges:** 1 Starch, ½ Fruit, 3 Other Carbo., 1½ Fat

Blueberry or Peach Cobbler: Prepare as on page 272, except, for filling, in a saucepan combine ⅓ to ⅔ cup sugar, ¼ cup water, and 1 tablespoon cornstarch. Stir in 5 cups fresh or frozen blueberries or unsweetened peach slices. Cook and stir until slightly thickened and bubbly.

Apple or Pear Cobbler: Prepare as on page 272, except, for filling, cook and stir 6 cups sliced, cored, and peeled cooking apples or pears; ⅓ to ½ cup sugar; and 1 tablespoon lemon juice until boiling, stirring occasionally once fruit begins to release juices; reduce heat. Simmer, covered, about 5 minutes or until fruit is almost tender, stirring occasionally. Combine 2 tablespoons water and 1 tablespoon cornstarch; add to filling. Cook and stir until thickened and bubbly.

Per biscuit + ½ cup blueberry, peach, apple, or pear filling variations: 278 cal., 10 g total fat (5 g sat. fat), 58 mg chol., 233 mg sodium, 44 g carbo., 6 g fiber, 4 g pro. **Daily Values:** 8% vit. A, 20% vit. C, 5% calcium, 8% iron **Exchanges:** 1 Starch, 1 Fruit, 1 Other Carbo., 1½ Fat

Fruit Crisp

Prep: 30 minutes **Bake:** 30 minutes
Oven: 375°F **Makes:** 6 servings

 - **5 cups sliced, peeled cooking apples, pears, peaches, or apricots or frozen unsweetened peach slices**
 - **2 to 4 tablespoons granulated sugar**
 - **½ cup regular rolled oats**
 - **½ cup packed brown sugar**
 - **¼ cup all-purpose flour**
 - **¼ teaspoon ground nutmeg or cinnamon**
 - **¼ cup butter or margarine**
 - **¼ cup chopped nuts or coconut**
 - **Vanilla ice cream (optional)**

1. Preheat oven to 375°F. If fruit is frozen, thaw but do not drain. Place fruit in a 2-quart square baking dish. Stir in the granulated sugar.

2. For topping, in a medium bowl combine the oats, brown sugar, flour, and nutmeg. Cut in butter until mixture resembles coarse crumbs. Stir in the nuts. Sprinkle topping over filling.

3. Bake for 30 to 35 minutes (40 minutes for thawed fruit) or until fruit is tender and topping is golden. Cool slightly. If desired, serve warm with ice cream.

Blueberry Crisp: Prepare filling as above, except use 5 cups fresh or frozen blueberries for the fruit. Use 4 tablespoons granulated sugar and add 3 tablespoons all-purpose flour to the blueberry mixture.

Per ½ cup fruit or blueberry variation: 319 cal., 13 g total fat (6 g sat. fat), 22 mg chol., 92 mg sodium, 53 g carbo., 5 g fiber, 3 g pro. **Daily Values:** 7% vit. A, 1% vit. C, 4% calcium, 7% iron **Exchanges:** 1 Fruit, 2½ Other Carbo., 1½ Fat

Cherry Crisp: Prepare filling as above, except use 5 cups fresh or frozen unsweetened pitted tart red cherries for the fruit, increase granulated sugar to ½ cup, and add 3 tablespoons all-purpose flour to the cherry mixture.

Rhubarb Crisp: Prepare filling as above, except use 5 cups fresh or frozen unsweetened sliced rhubarb for the fruit. If rhubarb is frozen, thaw but do not drain. Increase granulated sugar to ¾ cup and add 3 tablespoons all-purpose flour to the rhubarb mixture.

Per ½ cup cherry or rhubarb variations: 360 cal., 13 g total fat (6 g sat. fat), 22 mg chol., 92 mg sodium, 61 g carbo., 4 g fiber, 4 g pro. **Daily Values:** 8% vit. A, 12% vit. C, 12% calcium, 8% iron **Exchanges:** 1 Fruit, 3 Other Carbo., 1½ Fat

Apple Dumplings

Divine pastry-wrapped apples are worth the effort.

Prep: 45 minutes **Bake:** 1 hour
Oven: 350°F **Makes:** 6 dumplings

- 2 **cups water**
- 1¼ **cups sugar**
- ½ **teaspoon ground cinnamon**
- ¼ **cup butter or margarine**
- 2 **cups all-purpose flour**
- ½ **teaspoon salt**
- ⅔ **cup shortening**
- ⅓ to ½ **cup half-and-half, light cream, or whole milk**
- 2 **tablespoons chopped golden raisins or raisins**
- 2 **tablespoons chopped walnuts**
- 1 **tablespoon honey**
- 2 **tablespoons sugar**
- ½ **teaspoon ground cinnamon**
- 6 **small cooking apples (about 1½ pounds) (see tip, page 435)**
- 1 **tablespoon butter or margarine**

1. Preheat oven to 350°F. For sauce, in a medium saucepan combine water, the 1¼ cups sugar, and the ½ teaspoon cinnamon. Bring to boiling; reduce heat. Simmer, uncovered, for 5 minutes. Stir in the ¼ cup butter. Set aside.

2. Meanwhile, for pastry, in a medium bowl combine the flour and salt. Using a pastry blender, cut in shortening until pieces are pea size. Sprinkle 1 tablespoon of the half-and-half over part of the mixture; gently toss with a fork. Push moistened dough to the side of the bowl. Repeat moistening dough, using 1 tablespoon of the half-and-half at a time, until all of the dough is moistened. Form dough into a ball. On a lightly floured surface, roll dough to an 18×12-inch rectangle. Using a sharp knife, cut dough rectangle into six 6-inch squares.

3. In a small bowl combine the raisins, walnuts, and honey. In another small bowl stir together the 2 tablespoons sugar and the ½ teaspoon cinnamon. Set aside.

4. Peel and core the apples (see photo 1, above right). Place an apple on each pastry square. Fill apple centers with raisin mixture. Sprinkle with sugar-cinnamon mixture; dot with the 1 tablespoon butter. Moisten edges of each pastry square with water; gather corners over

apples (see photo 2, below). Pinch to seal. Place dumplings in a 13×9×2-inch baking pan. Reheat sauce to boiling and pour over dumplings. Bake, uncovered, about 1 hour or until apples are tender and pastry is golden. To serve, spoon sauce over dumplings.

Per dumpling: 586 cal., 36 g total fat (18 g sat. fat), 32 mg chol., 306 mg sodium, 68 g carbo., 4 g fiber, 1 g pro.
Daily Values: 10% vit. A, 9% vit. C, 4% calcium, 3% iron
Exchanges: 1 Fruit, 3½ Other Carbo., 5 Fat

1. Using an apple corer, twist and remove each apple's core.

2. Brush the edges of the pastry squares with water. Gather the four corners at the top of the apple and firmly pinch edges together to form a tight seal.

Caramel Apple Pudding Cake

Prep: 25 minutes **Bake:** 35 minutes
Oven: 350°F **Makes:** 12 servings

- 2 **cups thinly sliced, peeled tart cooking apples (see tip, page 435)**
- 3 **tablespoons lemon juice**
- ½ **teaspoon ground cinnamon**
- ⅛ **teaspoon ground nutmeg**
- ¼ **cup raisins or dried cherries**
- 1 **cup all-purpose flour**
- ¾ **cup packed brown sugar**
- 1 **teaspoon baking powder**
- ¼ **teaspoon baking soda**
- ½ **cup milk**
- 2 **tablespoons butter, melted**
- 1 **teaspoon vanilla**
- ½ **cup chopped pecans or walnuts**
- ¾ **cup caramel ice cream topping**
- ½ **cup water**
- 1 **tablespoon butter or margarine**
  Vanilla ice cream (optional)

1. Preheat oven to 350°F. Grease a 2-quart square baking dish. Arrange apple slices in bottom of dish; sprinkle with lemon juice, cinnamon, and nutmeg. Top evenly with raisins.

2. In a large bowl combine flour, brown sugar, baking powder, and baking soda. Add milk, the 2 tablespoons melted butter, and the vanilla; mix well. Stir in pecans. Spread batter evenly over apple mixture.

3. In a saucepan combine caramel topping, water, and the 1 tablespoon butter; bring to boiling. Pour mixture over batter in baking dish.

4. Bake about 35 minutes or until set in center. Serve warm. To serve, spoon cake, apples, and caramel mixture into dessert bowls. If desired, top with ice cream.

Per ½ cup: 316 cal., 9 g total fat (3 g sat. fat), 11 mg chol., 176 mg sodium, 58 g carbo., 3 g fiber, 3 g pro.
Daily Values: 3% vit. A, 7% vit. C, 7% calcium, 7% iron
Exchanges: ½ Fruit, ½ Starch, 3 Other Carbo., 1½ Fat

Caramel Apple Crepes

If you're pressed for time, substitute purchased crepes for the homemade recipe below. Warm crepes according to package, then follow Steps 3 and 4.

Start to Finish: 45 minutes **Makes:** 6 servings

- ¾ **cup all-purpose flour**
- ⅓ **cup water**
- ⅓ **cup milk**
- 2 **eggs**
- 2 **tablespoons sugar**
- 4 **teaspoons cooking oil**
- 1 **recipe Caramel Apple Sauce**
- 1 **recipe Candied Nuts (page 271) (optional)**
  Vanilla ice cream (optional)

1. For crepes, in a blender combine flour, water, milk, eggs, sugar, and oil. Cover and blend until smooth, stopping and scraping the sides of container as necessary.

2. Heat a lightly greased 6-inch skillet over medium heat; remove from heat. Spoon 2 tablespoons of batter into the skillet; lift and tilt skillet to spread batter evenly. Return skillet to heat; brown on one side only. Invert pan over paper towels; remove crepe from pan. Repeat with remaining batter, making 12 crepes total. (Adjust heat as necessary during cooking.)

3. Prepare Caramel Apple Sauce and, if desired, Candied Nuts.

4. To serve, fold the crepes in half, browned sides out. Fold in half again, forming a triangle. Place two crepes on each of six dessert plates.

Pour warm Caramel Apple Sauce over crepes. If desired, sprinkle with Candied Nuts and serve with ice cream.

Caramel Apple Sauce: In a medium saucepan cook 1½ cups peeled, thinly sliced apples in 1 tablespoon butter over medium heat about 5 minutes or until tender. Stir in ½ cup packed brown sugar and 2 teaspoons cornstarch. Stir in ½ cup whipping cream and 1 tablespoon apple brandy or apple juice. Cook and stir over medium heat until thickened and bubbly. Cook and stir for 2 minutes more. Makes about 1½ cups.

Per 2 crepes + ¼ cup sauce: 311 cal., 15 g total fat (7 g sat. fat), 104 mg chol., 60 mg sodium, 40 g carbo., 1 g fiber, 5 g pro.
Daily Values: 10% vit. A, 2% vit. C, 6% calcium, 8% iron
Exchanges: ½ Starch, 2 Other Carbo., 3 Fat

Bananas Foster

The rum in this dessert is lit on fire for an impressive presentation. Watch your fingers!

Start to Finish: 15 minutes **Makes:** 4 servings

- ⅓ **cup butter**
- ⅓ **cup packed brown sugar**
- 3 **ripe bananas, bias-sliced (2 cups)**
- ¼ **teaspoon ground cinnamon**
- 2 **tablespoons crème de cacao or banana liqueur**
- ¼ **cup rum**
- 2 **cups vanilla ice cream**

1. In a large skillet melt butter; stir in brown sugar until melted. Add bananas; cook and gently stir over medium heat about 2 minutes or until heated through. Sprinkle with cinnamon. Stir in crème de cacao.

2. In a small saucepan heat rum until it almost simmers. Ignite rum (see photo, below). Pour over bananas; stir gently to coat. Spoon sauce over ice cream and serve immediately.

Per ½ cup ice cream + about ⅓ cup banana sauce: 483 cal., 24 g total fat (15 g sat. fat), 72 mg chol., 225 mg sodium, 57 g carbo., 2 g fiber, 3 g pro.
Daily Values: 19% vit. A, 14% vit. C, 11% calcium, 4% iron
Exchanges: 1 Fruit, 2½ Other Carbo., 5 Fat

To ignite the rum in the saucepan, use a long fireplace match. Carefully pour the flaming rum over the bananas in the skillet. When the flame dies, serve the banana sauce over ice cream.

Cranberry Strudel Rolls

Cranberry Strudel Rolls

To keep phyllo from drying out while you work, cover the stack and remove sheets as needed.

Prep: 30 minutes **Bake:** 15 minutes
Oven: 375°F **Makes:** 12 rolls

  1 **cup cranberries**
  ⅔ **cup finely chopped, peeled apple (1 small)**
  ¼ **cup golden raisins**
  ¼ **cup finely chopped walnuts**
  ⅓ **cup sugar**
  ½ **teaspoon ground cinnamon**
  ½ **teaspoon finely shredded orange peel**
10 **sheets frozen phyllo dough (14×9-inch rectangles), thawed**
  ¼ **cup butter, melted**

1. Preheat oven to 375°F. Line a baking sheet with parchment paper or foil; set aside. In a saucepan combine cranberries and ⅓ cup *water.* Bring to boiling; reduce heat. Simmer, uncovered, about 3 minutes or until cranberries pop. Drain cranberries; discard liquid. Return cranberries to saucepan.

2. Add apple, raisins, and nuts to cranberries in saucepan. Add sugar, cinnamon, and orange peel; toss gently until mixed. Set aside.

3. Unroll phyllo dough. Layer five phyllo sheets on your work surface, brushing each sheet lightly with some of the melted butter. Repeat with remaining phyllo sheets and more of the melted butter to form a second stack. Cut each phyllo stack crosswise into thirds, then lengthwise in half to form 12 stacked squares total.

4. Spoon a rounded tablespoon of the fruit mixture near the bottom edge of a phyllo square. Fold bottom edge over fruit mixture, then fold in sides. Roll up around filling. Place on prepared baking sheet. Repeat with remaining phyllo squares and cranberry mixture. Brush tops with the remaining melted butter.

5. Bake for 15 to 18 minutes or until rolls are golden. (Rolls may leak slightly.) Transfer to a wire rack and cool. If desired, sift *powdered sugar* over tops and serve with *whipped cream.*

Per roll: 122 cal., 6 g total fat (2 g sat. fat), 11 mg chol., 74 mg sodium, 16 g carbo., 1 g fiber, 1 g pro.
Daily Values: 3% vit. A, 3% vit. C, 1% calcium, 3% iron
Exchanges: 1 Other Carbo., 1½ Fat

Blueberry-Sour Cream Dessert

See photo, page 269.

Prep: 40 minutes **Bake:** 50 minutes **Oven:** 400°F/350°F
Cool: 1 hour **Chill:** overnight **Makes:** 12 wedges

  1 **recipe Dessert Crust**
  3 **cups fresh or frozen blueberries**
  ⅓ **cup sugar**
  3 **tablespoons quick-cooking tapioca**
  ¼ **cup water**
  1 **teaspoon ground cinnamon**
  1 **teaspoon finely shredded lemon peel**
  ¼ **teaspoon ground nutmeg**
  3 **egg yolks, slightly beaten**
2½ **cups dairy sour cream**
  ½ **cup sugar**
  1 **teaspoon vanilla**

1. Prepare and bake Dessert Crust. Reduce oven temperature to 350°F. In a medium saucepan combine blueberries, the ⅓ cup sugar, the tapioca, water, cinnamon, lemon peel, and nutmeg. Let stand for 15 minutes. Cook and stir mixture over medium heat until blueberries release juices and mixture is bubbly. Turn into baked Dessert Crust.

2. In a medium mixing bowl combine egg yolks, sour cream, the ½ cup sugar, and the vanilla. Pour evenly over blueberry mixture.

3. Bake about 50 minutes or until sour cream layer is set when gently shaken. Cool in pan on a wire rack for 1 hour. With a sharp knife, loosen crust from side of pan; remove side. Cover and chill overnight before serving. To serve, if desired, garnish with additional blueberries.

Dessert Crust: Preheat oven to 400°F. Beat ½ cup butter, softened, with an electric mixer on medium to high speed for 30 seconds. Beat in ¼ cup sugar, ½ teaspoon baking powder, and ¼ teaspoon salt until combined. Beat in 1 egg yolk. Add 1½ cups all-purpose flour; beat until combined. (Mixture will be crumbly.) Work dough mixture with your hands just until mixture holds together. Press the mixture onto the bottom and 1½ inches up the sides of a 9-inch springform pan. Bake about 12 minutes or until edges are light brown. Cool on a wire rack.

Per wedge: 323 cal., 18 g total fat (10 g sat. fat), 107 mg chol., 141 mg sodium, 37 g carbo., 2 g fiber, 4 g pro.
Daily Values: 12% vit. A, 7% vit. C, 7% calcium, 6% iron
Exchanges: ½ Starch, 2 Other Carbo., 3½ Fat

Rhubarb Meringue Layers

Prep: 30 minutes **Bake:** 68 minutes
Oven: 350°F **Makes:** 16 squares

- 2 **cups all-purpose flour**
- 1 **tablespoon sugar**
- 1 **cup butter**
- 2 **cups sugar**
- ¼ **cup all-purpose flour**
- ⅛ **teaspoon salt**
- 1 **cup half-and-half or light cream**
- 6 **egg yolks, beaten**
- 5 **cups fresh or frozen (thawed, undrained) unsweetened sliced rhubarb**
- 6 **egg whites**
- ¾ **cup sugar**
- 2 **teaspoons vanilla**
- 1 **cup flaked coconut**

1. Preheat oven to 350°F. Lightly grease a 13×9×2-inch baking pan. For crust, in a large bowl combine the 2 cups flour and the 1 tablespoon sugar. Using a pastry blender, cut in butter until mixture resembles coarse crumbs. Press mixture into bottom of pan. Bake 10 minutes.

2. For custard, in a saucepan combine the 2 cups sugar, the ¼ cup flour, and the salt; add half-and-half and egg yolks. Cook and stir until thickened. Sprinkle rhubarb over crust and spoon custard over top. Bake for 40 minutes.

3. For meringue, in a bowl combine egg whites, the ¾ cup sugar, and the vanilla; beat on medium speed about 5 minutes or until soft peaks form (tips curl; see photo 1, page 182). Spoon on top of custard; carefully spread to edges. Sprinkle

with coconut. Bake 18 to 20 minutes more or until golden. Cool on a wire rack. Store, loosely covered, in refrigerator up to 24 hours.

Per square: 389 cal., 18 g total fat (10 g sat. fat), 115 mg chol., 158 mg sodium, 52 g carbo., 2 g fiber, 5 g pro.
Daily Values: 11% vit. A, 4% vit. C, 11% calcium, 6% iron
Exchanges: ½ Starch, 3 Other Carbo., 3½ Fat

Creamy Strawberry Squares

Love peaches? Next time, substitute fresh peach slices for the strawberries and peach-flavored gelatin for the strawberry gelatin.

Prep: 30 minutes **Bake:** 20 minutes **Oven:** 350°F
Chill: 4½ hours **Makes:** 15 squares

- 1½ **cups all-purpose flour**
- ¾ **cup butter, melted**
- ¾ **cup chopped pecans**
- 1 **cup granulated sugar**
- ¼ **cup all-purpose flour**
- 3 **tablespoons strawberry-flavored gelatin**
- 1 **cup water**
- 2 **cups powdered sugar**
- 1 **8-ounce package cream cheese, softened**
- 1 **8-ounce carton frozen whipped dessert topping, thawed**
- 3 **cups sliced strawberries**

1. Preheat oven to 350°F. For crust, combine the 1½ cups flour and the butter; stir in pecans. Pat pecan mixture evenly into the bottom of an ungreased 3-quart rectangular baking dish. Bake about 20 minutes or until golden brown around the edges. Cool in pan.

2. For strawberry topping, in a medium saucepan combine granulated sugar, the ¼ cup flour, and strawberry-flavored gelatin; stir in water. Cook and stir until thickened and bubbly. Cook and stir 1 minute more. Remove from heat. Cover surface and chill about 30 minutes or until partially set (consistency of unbeaten egg whites).

3. In a large mixing bowl gradually add powdered sugar to cream cheese, beating with an electric mixer on medium speed until combined. Add whipped topping by spoonfuls; beat until smooth. Spread cream cheese mixture over cooled crust. Arrange sliced strawberries on cream cheese layer. Spoon strawberry topping over strawberries. Cover; chill for 4 to 24 hours.

Per square: 389 cal., 22 g total fat (11 g sat. fat), 42 mg chol., 127 mg sodium, 46 g carbo., 2 g fiber, 4 g pro.
Daily Values: 10% vit. A, 28% vit. C, 3% calcium, 6% iron
Exchanges: ½ Starch, 2½ Other Carbo., 4½ Fat

Mixed Berry Clafouti

This dessert of French origin consists of a layer of fruit topped with a puddinglike batter.

Prep: 30 minutes **Bake:** 50 minutes
Oven: 375°F **Makes:** 8 servings

  1 teaspoon butter
⅔ cup whipping cream
⅓ cup milk
  3 eggs
⅓ cup all-purpose flour
¼ cup granulated sugar
  2 tablespoons butter, melted
  1 teaspoon vanilla
¼ teaspoon almond extract (optional)
  3 cups mixed berries, such as blueberries, raspberries, and/or sliced strawberries
  1 tablespoon powdered sugar

1. Preheat oven to 375°F. Grease the bottom and sides of a 9-inch pie plate or eight 6-ounce custard dishes with the 1 teaspoon butter.

2. In a medium mixing bowl combine whipping cream, milk, eggs, flour, granulated sugar, the 2 tablespoons melted butter, vanilla, almond extract (if desired), and ⅛ teaspoon *salt*. Beat with an electric mixer on low speed until smooth. Arrange mixed berries in prepared pie plate or dishes. Pour batter over fruit. If using custard dishes, place on a baking sheet.

3. Bake for 50 to 55 minutes for pie plate, 25 to 30 minutes for custard dishes, or until puffed and light brown. Cool slightly. Sift powdered sugar over top(s) and serve warm.

Per about ⅓ cup: 204 cal., 13 g total fat (8 g sat. fat), 117 mg chol., 99 mg sodium, 18 g carbo., 3 g fiber, 4 g pro.
Daily Values: 11% vit. A, 9% vit. C, 4% calcium, 4% iron
Exchanges: ½ Fruit, 1 Other Carbo., 2½ Fat

Almond Panna Cotta

In Italian, panna cotta means "cooked cream," which is a fairly accurate description of this custardlike dessert. Unlike traditional custard, however, this dish is thickened with gelatin instead of eggs. See photo, page 269.

Prep: 25 minutes **Chill:** 6 hours **Makes:** 6 desserts

  1 cup whole blanched almonds, toasted (see tip, page 265)
⅔ cup sugar
  1 envelope unflavored gelatin

  2 cups whipping cream
½ cup milk
⅛ teaspoon salt
  1 recipe Mocha Sauce
     Sliced almonds, toasted (optional)

1. Place almonds in a food processor and process until finely ground into a smooth butter.

2. In a medium saucepan stir together sugar and gelatin. Add whipping cream. Heat and stir until gelatin is dissolved. Remove from heat. Stir in the almond butter, the milk, and salt. Pour into six 6-ounce ramekins or custard dishes. Cover and chill for 6 to 24 hours or until set.

3. Prepare Mocha Sauce. To serve, loosen panna cotta from sides of dishes with a knife. Invert onto six dessert plates. Spoon or drizzle some Mocha Sauce around each panna cotta. Serve with additional Mocha Sauce and, if desired, garnish with sliced almonds.

Mocha Sauce: In a small heavy saucepan heat and stir 4 ounces chopped bittersweet or semisweet chocolate over low heat until melted. Stir in ⅔ cup whipping cream, ¼ cup sugar, and 1 teaspoon instant espresso coffee powder or regular instant coffee crystals. Cook and stir over medium-low heat about 3 minutes or until mixture just boils around edges. Remove from heat. Cool for 15 minutes before serving. Cover and store in the refrigerator for up to 3 days.

Per dessert + about 2½ tablespoons sauce: 730 cal., 59 g total fat (30 g sat. fat), 148 mg chol., 110 mg sodium, 49 g carbo., 4 g fiber, 10 g pro.
Daily Values: 32% vit. A, 1% vit. C, 15% calcium, 9% iron
Exchanges: 3 Other Carbo., 1 High-Fat Meat, 10 Fat

Chocolate Fondue

Fast, easy, and an absolute must for any party, Chocolate Fondue is a winner all around. Your hardest task may be getting the guests to sample the other foods.

Start to Finish: 15 minutes **Makes:** 8 servings

  8 ounces semisweet chocolate, coarsely chopped
  1 14-ounce can (1¼ cups) sweetened condensed milk
⅓ cup milk
     Assorted dippers, such as angel food or pound cake cubes, brownie squares, marshmallows, whole strawberries, banana slices, pineapple chunks, or dried apricots

1. In a medium heavy saucepan heat and stir chocolate over low heat until melted. Stir in sweetened condensed milk and milk; heat through. Transfer to a fondue pot; keep warm.

2. Serve fondue sauce immediately with assorted dippers. Swirl pieces as you dip. If the fondue mixture thickens, stir in additional milk.

Per ¼ cup fondue: 299 cal., 13 g total fat (8 g sat. fat), 18 mg chol., 68 mg sodium, 44 g carbo., 2 g fiber, 6 g pro. **Daily Values:** 4% vit. A, 2% vit. C, 15% calcium, 9% iron **Exchanges:** 3 Other Carbo., 2½ Fat

Chocolate-Peanut Fondue: Prepare as above, except stir ½ cup creamy peanut butter in with the milk.

Per ¼ cup fondue: 400 cal., 22 g total fat (18 g sat. fat), 18 mg chol., 140 mg sodium, 47 g carbo., 3 g fiber, 10 g pro. **Daily Values:** 3% vit. A, 2% vit. C, 16% calcium, 10% iron **Exchanges:** 3 Other Carbo., 1 High-Fat Meat, 2½ Fat

Candy Cane-Brownie Trifles

If you need a dessert that's dressed to impress, this is definitely it! Thick chunks of brownies are layered with a luscious chocolate sauce and ample spoonfuls of peppermint-flavored whipped cream.

Prep: 1 hour **Bake:** per package directions **Oven:** per package directions **Makes:** 16 servings

- 1 **19.5- to 20-ounce package brownie mix**
- 1 **recipe Chocolate-Peppermint Sauce**
- 2 **cups whipping cream**
- ¼ **cup powdered sugar**
- ½ **teaspoon peppermint extract or 2 tablespoons peppermint schnapps**
- 1 **to 2 drops red food coloring**
- 1 **cup crushed candy canes or peppermint sticks (about 6 ounces or twelve 5-inch candy canes)**

1. Prepare and bake brownies in a 13×9×2-inch baking pan according to package directions. Cool completely on a wire rack. Cut brownies into bite-size chunks; set aside. Meanwhile, prepare Chocolate-Peppermint Sauce.

2. For whipped cream, in a chilled extra-large mixing bowl combine whipping cream, powdered sugar, peppermint extract, and food coloring. Beat with the chilled beaters of an electric mixer on medium speed until soft peaks form (tips curl; see photo 1, page 182).

3. In 16 martini glasses or dessert cups alternately layer brownie chunks, Chocolate-Peppermint Sauce, peppermint-flavored whipped cream, and crushed candy canes, ending with peppermint-flavored whipped cream and crushed candy canes. Serve immediately.

Chocolate-Peppermint Sauce: In a medium heavy saucepan combine 6 ounces coarsely chopped semisweet chocolate and 3 tablespoons butter; cook and stir over low heat until melted. Stir in 1¼ cups half-and-half or light cream, ¾ cup granulated sugar, and 3 tablespoons light-colored corn syrup. Bring to a gentle boil over medium heat. Boil gently, stirring frequently, about 8 minutes or until sauce is reduced to about 2⅓ cups. Remove from heat. Stir in ¼ teaspoon peppermint extract or 1 tablespoon peppermint schnapps. Cool to room temperature (mixture thickens as it cools).

One-Bowl Candy Cane-Brownie Trifle: Place one-third of the brownie chunks in a 3-quart glass trifle bowl or serving bowl. Drizzle with one-fourth of the Chocolate-Peppermint Sauce. Sprinkle with one-fourth of the crushed candy canes. Top with one-third of the whipped cream mixture. Repeat layers twice more. Drizzle with remaining Chocolate-Peppermint sauce; sprinkle with remaining crushed candies. If desired, garnish with candy canes. Serve immediately.

Per about ⅔ cup: 508 cal., 28 g total fat (13 g sat. fat), 79 mg chol., 175 mg sodium, 62 g carbo., 1 g fiber, 5 g pro. **Daily Values:** 12% vit. A, 1% vit. C, 7% calcium, 11% iron **Exchanges:** 4 Other Carbo., 6 Fat

Candy Cane-Brownie Trifles

Chocolate Pot de Crème `EASY`

Prep: 10 minutes **Cook:** 10 minutes
Chill: 4 hours **Makes:** 8 desserts

> 2 **cups whipping cream**
> 6 **ounces semisweet chocolate, coarsely
>   chopped**
> ⅓ **cup sugar**
> 4 **egg yolks, beaten**
> 1 **teaspoon vanilla**
>   **White chocolate curls (see tip, page 271)
>   (optional)**

1. In a medium heavy saucepan combine the whipping cream, chocolate, and sugar. Cook and stir over medium heat about 10 minutes or until mixture comes to a full boil and thickens. (If chocolate flecks remain, use a wire whisk to beat mixture until blended.)

2. Gradually stir all of the hot mixture into the beaten egg yolks; stir in vanilla. Divide chocolate mixture evenly among eight small cups. Cover and chill for 4 to 24 hours before serving. If desired, garnish with white chocolate curls.

Mocha Pot de Crème: Prepare as above, except add 1 tablespoon instant espresso coffee powder or 2 tablespoons instant coffee crystals to whipping cream mixture before heating.

Per individual dessert chocolate or mocha variation: 375 cal., 32 g total fat (18 g sat. fat), 189 mg chol., 26 mg sodium, 22 g carbo., 4 g pro.
Daily Values: 21% vit. A, 1% vit. C, 5% calcium, 8% iron
Exchanges: 1½ Other Carbo., 6½ Fat

Springform Pans

What is this elusive pan used for so many dessert recipes? Here is the springform pan scoop:

A springform pan is round with a 2- to 3-inch-high side. What makes it special is that the side is not attached to the bottom. When the side spring, or clamp, is released, the side loosens and can be removed, leaving the dessert on the pan bottom, where it easily can be sliced and served.

Resist the temptation to use a regular cake pan for desserts that specifically call for a springform pan. They simply can't hold the same volume, and removal of the dessert (especially cheesecakes) will be close to impossible.

Chocolate Truffle Dessert Cake

If you love the luscious decadence of chocolate truffle candies, this dessert has your name written all over it.

Prep: 40 minutes **Bake:** 45 minutes **Oven:** 325°F
Cool: 4⅓ hours **Makes:** 16 slices

> 1 **cup pecans, toasted (see tip, page 265) and
>   coarsely ground**
> 1 **cup graham cracker crumbs**
> ¼ **cup butter or margarine, melted**
> 2 **tablespoons sugar**
> 2 **8-ounce packages semisweet chocolate,
>   cut up**
> 1 **cup whipping cream**
> 6 **eggs, beaten**
> ¾ **cup sugar**
> ⅓ **cup all-purpose flour**
>   **Whipped cream (optional)**

1. Preheat oven to 325°F. Grease sides and bottom of a 9-inch springform pan. For crust, in a medium bowl combine pecans, graham cracker crumbs, melted butter, and the 2 tablespoons sugar. Press mixture onto bottom and about 1½ inches up sides of prepared pan; set aside.

2. In a large saucepan cook and stir chocolate and whipping cream over low heat until the chocolate melts. Transfer the chocolate mixture to a medium bowl; set aside.

3. In a large mixing bowl combine eggs, the ¾ cup sugar, and the flour; beat about 10 minutes or until thick and lemon colored. Fold one-fourth of the egg mixture into chocolate mixture. Fold chocolate-egg mixture into remaining egg mixture. Pour batter into crust-lined pan.

4. Bake about 45 minutes or until puffed around edge and halfway to center (the center will be slightly soft). Cool in pan on a wire rack for 20 minutes. Remove sides of pan. Cool for 4 hours. If desired, serve with whipped cream. Cover and store in the refrigerator.

Orange-Chocolate Truffle Dessert Cake: Prepare as above, except stir 2 teaspoons finely shredded orange peel into the egg mixture after beating.

Per slice chocolate or orange-chocolate variation: 369 cal., 25 g total fat (12 g sat. fat), 109 mg chol., 89 mg sodium, 35 g carbo., 3 g fiber, 6 g pro.
Daily Values: 9% vit. A, 1% vit. C, 3% calcium, 13% iron
Exchanges: 2 Other Carbo., 4½ Fat

Chocolate Soufflé

Few desserts come close to the romance and wonderment of this inflated egg-based masterpiece. To prevent deflation, test for doneness while the soufflé is still in the oven.

Prep: 25 minutes **Bake:** 40 minutes
Oven: 350°F **Makes:** 6 wedges

    Butter
    Sugar
  2 tablespoons butter or margarine
  3 tablespoons all-purpose flour
  ¾ cup milk
  ½ cup semisweet chocolate pieces
  4 egg yolks, beaten
  4 egg whites
  ½ teaspoon vanilla
  ¼ cup sugar

1. Preheat oven to 350°F. Butter the sides of a 1½-quart soufflé dish. For a collar on the soufflé dish, measure enough foil to wrap around the top of the dish and add 3 inches. Fold the foil into thirds lengthwise. Lightly grease one side with butter; sprinkle with sugar. Place foil, sugar side in, around the outside of the dish so that the foil extends about 2 inches above the dish. Tape ends of foil together. Sprinkle inside of dish with sugar; set dish aside.

2. In a small saucepan melt the 2 tablespoons butter. Stir in flour; add milk all at once. Cook and stir until thickened and bubbly. Add chocolate; stir until melted. Remove from heat. Gradually stir chocolate mixture into beaten egg yolks. Set aside.

3. Beat egg whites and vanilla until soft peaks form (see photo 1, page 182). Gradually add the ¼ cup sugar, beating until stiff peaks form (see photo 2, page 182). Fold 1 cup of the beaten egg whites into chocolate mixture. Fold chocolate-egg whites mixture into remaining beaten egg whites. Transfer to the prepared dish.

4. Bake for 40 to 45 minutes or until a knife inserted near the center comes out clean. Serve soufflé immediately. To serve, insert two forks back to back; gently pull soufflé apart into six equal-size wedges. Use a spoon to transfer to plates. If desired, top with *whipped cream*.

Per wedge: 216 cal., 12 g total fat (7 g sat. fat), 155 mg chol., 100 mg sodium, 22 g carbo., 1 g fiber, 6 g pro.
Daily Values: 9% vit. A, 6% calcium, 6% iron
Exchanges: 1½ Other Carbo., 2 Fat

 # Brownie Pudding Cake EASY

First appearing on the pages of a 1944 issue of Better Homes and Gardens® *magazine, this recipe was a shining example of wartime restraint—it skimps on sugar and uses no butter or eggs. Nevertheless, it has been a favorite ever since.*

Prep: 15 minutes **Bake:** 40 minutes **Oven:** 350°F
Cool: 45 minutes **Makes:** 6 servings

  1 cup all-purpose flour
  ¾ cup granulated sugar
  2 tablespoons unsweetened cocoa powder
  2 teaspoons baking powder
  ¼ teaspoon salt
  ½ cup milk
  2 tablespoons cooking oil
  1 teaspoon vanilla
  ½ cup chopped walnuts
  ¾ cup packed brown sugar
  ¼ cup unsweetened cocoa powder
  1½ cups boiling water
    Vanilla ice cream (optional)

1. Preheat oven to 350°F. Grease an 8×8×2-inch baking pan; set aside. In a medium bowl stir together the flour, granulated sugar, the 2 tablespoons cocoa powder, the baking powder, and salt. Stir in the milk, oil, and vanilla. Stir in the walnuts.

2. Pour batter into prepared baking pan. In a small bowl stir together the brown sugar and the ¼ cup cocoa powder. Stir in the boiling water. Slowly pour brown sugar mixture over batter.

3. Bake for 40 minutes. Transfer to a wire rack and cool for 45 to 60 minutes. Serve warm. Spoon cake into dessert bowls; spoon pudding from the bottom of the pan over cake. If desired, serve with vanilla ice cream.

Per ½ cup: 412 cal., 13 g total fat (2 g sat. fat), 2 mg chol., 254 mg sodium, 72 g carbo., 1 g fiber, 6 g pro.
Daily Values: 1% vit. A, 1% vit. C, 21% calcium, 14% iron
Exchanges: 4 Other Carbo., 2 Fat

As if by Magic

Popular in the 1930s and 1940s, pudding cake continues to be a favorite today because of its almost magical results.

When the batter bakes, a rich cake layer rises to the top, leaving a creamy pudding layer on the bottom. It's easy to make and there's no need for frosting!

Baby Lava Cakes

The name for these cute little desserts comes from the "lava" center of rich, gooey chocolate nestled in each small cake. Sometimes they're called mini molten chocolate cakes for the same reason.

Prep: 15 minutes **Chill:** 45 minutes **Bake:** 13 minutes
Oven: 400°F **Cool:** 2 minutes **Makes:** 6 cakes

- ¾ **cup semisweet chocolate pieces**
- 2 **tablespoons whipping cream**
- 1 **cup semisweet chocolate pieces**
- ¾ **cup butter**
- 3 **eggs**
- 3 **egg yolks**
- ⅓ **cup granulated sugar**
- 1½ **teaspoons vanilla**
- ⅓ **cup all-purpose flour**
- 3 **tablespoons unsweetened cocoa powder**
  Powdered sugar (optional)

1. For filling, in a small heavy saucepan combine the ¾ cup chocolate pieces and whipping cream. Cook and stir over low heat until chocolate melts. Remove pan from heat. Cool, stirring occasionally. Cover and chill about 45 minutes or until firm.

2. Meanwhile, in a medium heavy saucepan cook and stir the 1 cup chocolate pieces and the butter over low heat until melted. Remove from heat; cool.

3. Preheat oven to 400°F. Form chilled chocolate filling into six balls of equal size; set aside. Lightly grease and flour six 6-ounce soufflé or custard dishes. Place dishes in a 15×10×1-inch baking pan; set aside.

4. In a mixing bowl beat eggs, egg yolks, granulated sugar, and vanilla with an electric mixer on high speed about 5 minutes or until lemon colored. Beat in cooled chocolate-butter mixture on medium speed. Sift flour and cocoa powder over mixture; beat on low speed just until combined. Spoon ⅓ cup batter into each dish; add one ball of filling to each dish. Spoon remaining batter into dishes.

5. Bake about 13 minutes or until cake edges feel firm. Cool in dishes 2 to 3 minutes. Using a knife, loosen cakes from sides of dishes. Invert onto dessert plates. If desired, sift with powdered sugar. Serve immediately.

Make-ahead directions: Prepare as at left through Step 4. Cover; chill until ready to bake or up to 4 hours. Let stand at room temperature for 30 minutes before baking as directed.

Per cake: 621 cal., 47 g total fat (27 g sat. fat), 285 mg chol.,
291 mg sodium, 50 g carbo., 3 g fiber, 8 g pro.
Daily Values: 26% vit. A, 8% calcium, 16% iron
Exchanges: 3 Other Carbo., 8 Fat

Triple Chocolate Tiramisu

FAVORITE Triple Chocolate Tiramisu

This classic Italian dessert is simplified by using purchased ladyfingers rather than homemade sponge cake.

Prep: 30 minutes **Chill:** 6 hours **Makes:** 12 squares

- 2 **3-ounce packages ladyfingers, split**
- ¼ **cup brewed espresso or strong coffee**
- 1 **8-ounce carton mascarpone cheese**
- 1 **cup whipping cream**
- ¼ **cup powdered sugar**
- 1 **teaspoon vanilla**
- ⅓ **cup chocolate liqueur**
- 1 **ounce white chocolate baking squares or white baking bars, grated (see tip, page 271)**
- 1 **ounce bittersweet chocolate, grated**
  Unsweetened cocoa powder
  Chopped chocolate-covered coffee beans (optional)

1. Line the bottom of an 8×8×2-inch baking pan with enough ladyfingers to cover; cut to fit. Drizzle half of the espresso over ladyfingers.

2. In a medium mixing bowl beat the mascarpone cheese, whipping cream, powdered sugar, and vanilla with an electric mixer just until stiff peaks form (tips stand straight; see photo 2, page 182), scraping sides of bowl occasionally. Beat in the chocolate liqueur just until combined.

3. Evenly spread half of the mascarpone mixture over ladyfingers. Sprinkle white chocolate and bittersweet chocolate over the mascarpone mixture. Top with another layer of ladyfingers (reserve any remaining ladyfingers for another use), remaining espresso, and remaining mascarpone mixture.

4. Cover and chill for 6 to 24 hours. Sift cocoa powder over top of dessert. If desired, garnish with chocolate-covered coffee beans.

Per square: 256 cal., 19 g total fat (11 g sat. fat), 104 mg chol., 42 mg sodium, 17 g carbo., 0 g fiber, 6 g pro.
Daily Values: 6% vit. A, 1% vit. C, 2% calcium, 3% iron
Exchanges: 1 Other Carbo., 4 Fat

Hazelnut Meringue Shells

Prep: 45 minutes **Bake:** 35 minutes **Oven:** 300°F
Stand: 1 hour **Chill:** 2 hours **Makes:** 8 meringue shells

- 4 **egg whites**
- 1 **teaspoon vanilla**
- ¼ **teaspoon cream of tartar**
- 1⅓ **cups sugar**
- 1 **cup ground hazelnuts (filberts)**
- 1 **3-ounce package cream cheese, softened**
- 2 **tablespoons butter or margarine, softened**
- ⅓ **cup sugar**
- 1 **cup whipping cream**
- 3 **tablespoons coffee liqueur or strong coffee**

1. Allow egg whites to stand at room temperature for 30 minutes. Line a large baking sheet with parchment paper or foil. Draw eight 3-inch circles 3 inches apart on the paper or foil.

2. Preheat oven to 300°F. For meringue, in a large mixing bowl combine egg whites, vanilla, and cream of tartar. Beat with an electric mixer on medium speed until soft peaks form (tips curl; see photo 1, page 182). Add the 1⅓ cups sugar, 1 tablespoon at a time, beating on high speed until stiff peaks form (tips stand straight; see photo 2, page 182) and sugar is almost dissolved (about 7 minutes). Gently fold ground hazelnuts into egg white mixture.

3. Spread meringue over circles on paper, building up sides to form shells. Bake for 35 minutes. Turn oven off. Let meringues dry in oven with door closed for 1 hour. Lift meringues off paper. Transfer to a wire rack; cool completely.

4. For filling, in a mixing bowl beat cream cheese and butter until smooth; beat in the ⅓ cup sugar. Add whipping cream and coffee liqueur. Beat on low speed until combined; beat on medium speed just until soft peaks form.

5. Transfer meringue shells to a platter. Fill shells with whipped cream mixture. Cover loosely and chill for 2 to 24 hours. If desired, before serving sprinkle with coarsely chopped *hazelnuts* (filberts) and garnish with *Chocolate Shapes* (see below).

Per meringue shell + ¼ cup filling: 504 cal., 32 g total fat (12 g sat. fat), 53 mg chol., 121 mg sodium, 50 g carbo., 2 g fiber, 6 g pro.
Daily Values: 16% vit. A, 2% vit. C, 50% calcium, 1% iron
Exchanges: 3 Other Carbo., 5½ Fat

Hooray for Chocolate!

For the chocoholics at your table, try these deliciously beautiful decorations:

Chocolate Shapes: Melt 1 ounce semisweet chocolate. Fill a heavy-duty resealable plastic bag with the melted chocolate (see tip, page 247) and pipe into eight desired shapes onto a sheet of waxed paper. Allow shapes to set at room temperature. (To set quickly, place shapes in the freezer for 1 to 2 minutes.) Carefully remove chocolate shapes from waxed paper. Arrange shapes on desserts.

Chocolate Plate Painting: In a small saucepan heat and stir 2 ounces semisweet chocolate and 1 tablespoon butter over low heat until melted. Cool slightly. Fill a squeeze bottle or heavy-duty resealable plastic bag (see tip, page 247)  with chocolate mixture. Drizzle over dessert plates in various designs, being as simple or as creative with your designs as you like. Consider squiggles, crisscross lines, elaborate filigrees, or words. Set desserts on top of chocolate on plates. For a different taste sensation, try drizzling Raspberry Sauce (page 524) on plates.

Meringue Shells with Fruit

For a beautiful dessert that's low in fat and calories, try filling these crunchy shells with low- or fat-free yogurt. Or skip the creamy filling altogether and serve with just the fresh fruit.

Prep: 45 minutes **Bake:** 35 minutes **Oven:** 300°F
Stand: 1 hour **Makes:** 6 meringue shells

  2 **egg whites**
  ½ **teaspoon vanilla**
  ⅛ **teaspoon cream of tartar**
  ½ **cup sugar**
  1 **recipe Fluffy Lemon Filling or 1½ cups
       Lemon Curd (page 292), purchased lemon
       curd, or vanilla or lemon yogurt or pudding**
  2 **cups sliced strawberries**
  1 **kiwifruit, peeled and sliced**

1. Allow egg whites to stand at room temperature for 30 minutes. Line a large baking sheet with parchment paper or foil. Draw six 3- to 4-inch circles 3 inches apart on the paper or foil; set aside.

2. Preheat oven to 300°F. For meringue, in a medium mixing bowl beat egg whites, vanilla, and cream of tartar with electric mixer on medium speed until soft peaks form (tips curl; see photo 1, page 182). Add sugar, 1 tablespoon at a time, beating on high speed until stiff peaks form (tips stand straight; see photo 2, page 182) and sugar is almost dissolved (about 7 minutes).

3. Spread meringue over circles on paper, building up sides to form shells. Bake for 35 minutes. Turn off oven; let meringues dry in oven with door closed for 1 hour. Lift meringues off paper. Transfer to a wire rack; cool completely.

4. Meanwhile, make Fluffy Lemon Filling. To serve, spoon lemon filling into shells. Arrange fruit on top of filling. Serve immediately.

Fluffy Lemon Filling: In a medium bowl stir together one 10-ounce jar purchased lemon curd and ½ of an 8-ounce carton frozen whipped topping, thawed. Makes 1½ cups.

Per meringue shell + ¼ cup Fluffy Lemon Filling + about ⅓ cup
fruit: 299 cal., 6 g total fat (4 g sat. fat), 35 mg chol., 55 mg sodium,
61 g carbo., 6 g fiber, 2 g pro.
Daily Values: 68% vit. C, 1% calcium, 2% iron
Exchanges: ½ Fruit, 3½ Other Carbo., ½ Very Lean Meat, 1 Fat

Cheesecake Supreme

Prep: 30 minutes **Bake:** 40 minutes **Oven:** 375°F
Cool: 2 hours **Chill:** 4 hours **Makes:** 12 slices

  1½ **cups finely crushed graham crackers**
  ¼ **cup finely chopped walnuts**
  1 **tablespoon sugar**
  ½ **teaspoon ground cinnamon (optional)**
  ½ **cup butter, melted**
  3 **8-ounce packages cream cheese, softened**
  1 **cup sugar**
  2 **tablespoons all-purpose flour**
  1 **teaspoon vanilla**
  ¼ **cup milk**
  3 **eggs, slightly beaten**
  ½ **teaspoon finely shredded lemon peel
       (optional)**
  1 **recipe Raspberry Sauce (page 524) (optional)**

1. Preheat oven to 375°F. For crust, in a bowl combine crushed graham crackers, walnuts, the 1 tablespoon sugar, and, if desired, the cinnamon. Stir in melted butter. Press the crumb mixture onto the bottom and about 2 inches up the sides of an 8- or 9-inch springform pan; set aside.

2. For filling, in a large mixing bowl beat cream cheese, the 1 cup sugar, the flour, and vanilla with an electric mixer until combined. Beat in milk until smooth. Stir in eggs and, if desired, lemon peel.

3. Pour filling into crust-lined pan. Place pan in a shallow baking pan (see optional water bath method, page 285). Bake for 40 to 45 minutes for the 8-inch pan, 35 to 40 minutes for the 9-inch pan, or until a 2½-inch area around the outside edge appears set when gently shaken.

4. Cool in pan on a wire rack for 15 minutes. Using a small sharp knife, loosen the crust from pan sides; cool for 30 minutes. Remove sides of pan; cool cheesecake completely on rack. Cover and chill at least 4 hours before serving. If desired, serve with Raspberry Sauce.

Sour Cream Cheesecake: Prepare as above, except reduce cream cheese to 2 packages. Omit the milk and add two 8-ounce cartons dairy sour cream. Bake 45 to 50 minutes for 8-inch pan or 40 to 45 minutes for 9-inch pan.

Per slice regular or sour cream variation: 426 cal.,
32 g total fat (17 g sat. fat), 138 mg chol., 303 mg sodium,
29 g carbo., 1 g fiber, 8 g pro.
Daily Values: 22% vit. A, 7% calcium, 8% iron
Exchanges: 2 Other Carbo., 6 Fat

Chocolate Marble Cheesecake: Prepare as on page 284, except omit lemon peel. Melt 4 ounces semisweet chocolate. Stir the melted chocolate into half of the filling. Pour plain filling into the crust; pour chocolate filling into the crust. Use a narrow metal spatula to gently swirl the fillings.

Per slice: 473 cal., 35 g total fat (19 g sat. fat), 137 mg chol., 34 carbo., 326 mg sodium, 1 g fiber, 8 g pro.
Daily Values: 22% vit. A, 7% calcium, 11% iron
Exchanges: 2 Other Carbo., 7 Fat

Fat-Free Cheesecake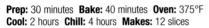

Prep: 30 minutes **Bake:** 40 minutes **Oven:** 375°F
Cool: 2 hours **Chill:** 4 hours **Makes:** 12 slices

> **Butter**
> ⅓ **cup finely crushed graham crackers**
> 3 **8-ounce packages fat-free cream cheese, softened**
> 1 **cup sugar**
> 2 **tablespoons all-purpose flour**
> 1 **teaspoon vanilla**
> ¼ **cup milk**
> ½ **cup refrigerated or frozen egg product (thawed)**
> ½ **teaspoon finely shredded lemon peel (optional)**
> **Strawberries, raspberries, and blueberries**

1. Preheat oven to 375°F. Generously butter the bottom and sides of an 8- or 9-inch springform pan. For crust, sprinkle crushed graham crackers on bottom and sides of prepared pan; set aside.

2. For filling, in a large mixing bowl beat cream cheese, sugar, flour, and vanilla with an electric mixer until combined. Beat in milk until smooth. Stir in egg product and, if desired, lemon peel.

3. Pour filling into crust-lined pan. Place pan in a shallow baking pan (see optional water bath method, right). Bake for 40 to 45 minutes for the 8-inch pan, 35 to 40 minutes for the 9-inch pan, or until a 2½-inch area around the outside edge appears set when gently shaken.

4. Cool in pan on a wire rack for 15 minutes. Using a small sharp knife, loosen the crust from sides of pan; cool for 30 minutes more. Remove the sides of the pan; cool cheesecake completely on rack. Cover and chill at least 4 hours before serving. Serve with berries.

Per slice: 135 cal., 0 g total fat (0 g sat. fat), 9 mg chol., 32 mg sodium, 23 g carbo., 0 g fiber, 10 g pro.
Daily Values: 3% vit. A, 20% calcium, 2% iron
Exchanges: 1½ Other Carbo.

Cheesecake Chat

Bathing Beauties

Long, hot baths aren't just for you anymore! As an alternate method, try baking your cheesecake in a water bath to keep it creamy and smooth.

Prepare crust as directed. Place the crust-lined springform pan on a double layer of 18×12-inch heavy-duty aluminum foil. Bring edges of foil up and mold around pan sides to form a watertight seal. Prepare filling and pour it into prepared pan. Place springform pan in a roasting pan. Pour enough hot water into roasting pan to reach halfway up the sides of the springform pan. Bake as directed. When done, cheesecake edges will be set, but center will jiggle slightly when pan is gently shaken. Turn oven off and allow cheesecake to sit in oven for 1 hour. Remove springform pan from water bath; cool and chill as directed.

Cut!

Slice cheesecake perfectly every time.

Start by choosing the right tool for the job—a long, thin-blade knife is ideal. Serrated knives can make your slices look chunky because clumps tend to form under the ridges of the blade as you cut. Before making each slice, dip the knife in hot water and wipe it dry with a towel. This helps make clean cuts and prevents the filling from dragging down with the knife.

Some for Later

No matter how great the cheesecake, there's bound to be some left. Save it and indulge another day.

For the fridge: Cover the cake with plastic wrap and chill for up to 3 days.
For the freezer: Place a whole or cut cheesecake in a freezer-safe bag or container or wrap in plastic wrap and foil. Freeze a whole cheesecake for up to a month and pieces for up to 2 weeks.
Thawing out: Loosen wrapping and thaw a whole cheesecake in the refrigerator for 24 hours or pieces at room temperature for 30 minutes.

Maple-Pumpkin Cheesecake

Maple-Pumpkin Cheesecake

Perfect for fall, winter, the holidays, or anytime really, this cheesecake is a surefire crowd-pleaser. To speed up the recipe, use the option of purchased caramel ice cream topping for the sauce.

Prep: 40 minutes **Bake:** 68 minutes **Oven:** 325°F
Cool: 1¾ hours **Chill:** 4 hours **Makes:** 12 slices

- 1½ cups finely crushed graham crackers
- ⅓ cup granulated sugar
- ⅓ cup butter, melted
- 3 8-ounce packages cream cheese, softened
- 1 cup canned pumpkin
- ⅔ cup packed brown sugar
- ¼ cup pure maple syrup or maple-flavored syrup
- 1½ teaspoons vanilla
- 3 eggs, slightly beaten
- ½ cup Caramel Sauce (page 526) or purchased caramel ice cream topping

1. Preheat oven to 325°F. In a medium bowl combine finely crushed graham crackers, granulated sugar, and melted butter. Press crumb mixture onto the bottom and 1½ inches up the sides of an ungreased 9-inch springform pan. Bake for 8 minutes. Remove from oven. Transfer to a wire rack; cool completely.

2. Meanwhile, for filling, in an extra-large mixing bowl beat cream cheese with an electric mixer on medium to high speed until smooth. Add pumpkin, brown sugar, maple syrup, and vanilla. Beat cream cheese mixture until well combined. Fold in eggs.

3. Pour filling into crust-lined pan. Place springform pan in a shallow baking pan (see optional water bath method, page 285). Bake for 60 to 70 minutes or until center appears nearly set when gently shaken.

4. Cool in springform pan on a wire rack for 15 minutes. Using a small thin knife, loosen crust from sides of springform pan. Cool for 30 minutes more. Remove sides of springform pan; cool for 1 hour. Cover and chill for at least 4 hours or up to 24 hours. To serve, spoon or drizzle Caramel Sauce over top of cheesecake.

Make-ahead directions: Prepare, bake, and cool as directed through Step 4. Cover with plastic wrap and refrigerate for up to 2 days. Or carefully transfer cheesecake to a plate and place in a freezer bag or airtight container. Freeze for up to 1 month. Thaw frozen cheesecake in the refrigerator for 24 hours. To serve, top with Caramel Sauce.

Per slice: 447 cal., 29 g total fat (17 g sat. fat), 133 mg chol., 302 mg sodium, 42 g carbo., 1 g fiber, 7 g pro.
Daily Values: 84% vit. A, 1% vit. C, 9% calcium, 12% iron
Exchanges: 2½ Other Carbo., 5½ Fat

 # Bread Pudding

This is comfort food for the soul. Settle in on a cold winter's night with a bowlful of this rich delight.

Prep: 30 minutes **Bake:** 50 minutes
Oven: 350°F **Makes:** 8 servings

- 4 cups dried white or cinnamon swirl bread cubes (6 to 7 slices)*
- ⅓ cup raisins, dried cranberries, or other snipped dried fruit
- 2 eggs, slightly beaten
- 2 cups milk
- ¼ cup butter, melted
- ½ cup sugar
- 1 teaspoon ground cinnamon
- ½ teaspoon ground nutmeg
- 1 teaspoon vanilla
  Butterscotch Sauce (page 526) or Bourbon Sauce (page 526) (optional)

1. Preheat oven to 350°F. Grease a 1½-quart casserole; set aside. In a large bowl combine bread cubes and raisins.

2. In a bowl combine eggs, milk, melted butter, sugar, cinnamon, nutmeg, and vanilla. Stir into bread mixture. Pour into the prepared casserole.

3. Bake, uncovered, for 50 to 55 minutes or until puffed and a knife inserted near the center comes out clean. Cool slightly. If desired, serve with warm Butterscotch Sauce.

*Note: For dry bread cubes, cut bread into ½-inch cubes. Spread cubes in a 15×10×1-inch baking pan. Bake in a 300°F oven for 10 to 15 minutes or until dry, stirring twice; cool.

Pear-Ginger Bread Pudding: Prepare as on page 286, except substitute snipped dried pears for the raisins, 1 tablespoon finely chopped crystallized ginger for the cinnamon, and 1 teaspoon finely shredded orange peel for nutmeg.

Per ¾ cup regular or pear-ginger variation: 220 cal., 9 g total fat (4 g sat. fat), 74 mg chol., 218 mg sodium, 30 g carbo., 1 g fiber, 5 g pro.
Daily Values: 7% vit. A, 1% vit. C, 11% calcium, 7% iron
Exchanges: 1 Starch, 1 Other Carbo., 2 Fat

Chocolate Chip Bread Pudding: Prepare as on page 286, except substitute chocolate milk for the milk and semisweet chocolate pieces for the raisins. Omit nutmeg and add ½ cup chopped pecans, toasted (see tip, page 265). Omit sauce.

Per ¾ cup: 287 cal., 15 g total fat (5 g sat. fat), 71 mg chol., 226 mg sodium, 34 g carbo., 2 g fiber, 6 g pro.
Daily Values: 8% vit. A, 1% vit. C, 12% calcium, 9% iron
Exchanges: 1 Starch, 1 Other Carbo., 3 Fat

Baked Rice Pudding LOW FAT

Baking this pudding in a water bath is worth the effort—the end result is deliciously creamy.

Prep: 25 minutes **Bake:** 50 minutes
Oven: 325°F **Makes:** 6 servings

  3 eggs, slightly beaten
1½ cups milk
  ⅓ cup sugar
  1 teaspoon vanilla
  ¼ teaspoon salt
  1 cup cooked rice (see tip, right)
  ½ cup raisins, dried cherries, dried cranberries, or mixed dried fruit bits (optional)
     Ground nutmeg or cinnamon (optional)
  1 recipe Raspberry Sauce (page 524) (optional)

1. Preheat oven to 325°F. In a medium bowl stir eggs, milk, sugar, vanilla, and salt with a wire whisk until combined but not foamy. Stir in cooked rice and, if desired, raisins. Pour rice mixture into a 1½-quart casserole. Place casserole in a 2-quart square baking dish on an oven rack. Pour boiling *water* into the baking dish until water comes halfway up the sides of the casserole.

2. Bake, uncovered, for 30 minutes; stir. If desired, sprinkle with nutmeg. Bake for 20 to 25 minutes more or until a knife inserted near the center comes out clean. Remove casserole from baking dish and let baked pudding cool slightly in casserole on a wire rack. Serve warm or cold. If desired, serve with Raspberry Sauce. To store, cover and chill up to 24 hours.

Per ½ cup: 144 cal., 4 g total fat (1 g sat. fat), 111 mg chol., 161 mg sodium, 21 g carbo., 0 g fiber, 6 g pro.
Daily Values: 5% vit. A, 8% calcium, 5% iron
Exchanges: ½ Starch, 1 Other Carbo., ½ Medium-Fat Meat, ½ Fat

Saucepan Rice Pudding LOW FAT EASY

Simple to make, low in fat, and only one saucepan to clean when you're finished: Who could ask for more in a dessert?

Start to Finish: 40 minutes **Makes:** 6 servings

  3 cups milk
  ⅓ cup uncooked long grain rice
  ⅓ cup raisins or mixed dried fruit bits
  ¼ cup sugar
  1 teaspoon vanilla
  ¼ teaspoon ground nutmeg

1. In a medium saucepan bring milk just to boiling. Stir in uncooked rice and raisins. Cook, covered, over low heat for 30 to 40 minutes or until most of the milk is absorbed, stirring occasionally. (Mixture may appear curdled.)

2. Remove saucepan from heat. Stir in sugar and vanilla. Spoon into dessert dishes. Sprinkle with nutmeg. Serve warm or chilled.

Per ½ cup: 155 cal., 3 g total fat (2 g sat. fat), 9 mg chol., 63 mg sodium, 28 g carbo., 1 g fiber, 5 g pro.
Daily Values: 5% vit. A, 2% vit. C, 16% calcium, 4% iron
Exchanges: ½ Milk, 1½ Other Carbo.

The "Rice" Stuff

If your package of rice doesn't tell you how to make the 1 cup of rice you need for rice pudding, try this:

For 1 cup cooked rice, combine ⅓ cup uncooked long grain rice and ⅔ cup water in a small saucepan. Bring to boiling; reduce heat. Cover and simmer for 15 minutes or until rice is tender and liquid is absorbed, stirring once. Leftover rice works well too!

Cream Puff Know-How

For crisp, tender, and puffed-to-perfection results, remember the following:

● Use large eggs.
● Measure water carefully.
● Add the flour promptly after the butter melts and the water boils. This prevents the water from boiling away in the saucepan.
● Cool the dough for precisely 10 minutes (set a timer) before beating in the first egg.
● Remove puffs from the oven only when they are golden brown, firm, and dry.
● Fill puffs just before serving.

Cream Puffs

Looking for finger foods to serve at potlucks? Try filling half the Mini Puffs, right, with Chicken Salad (page 494) for a starter and the rest with pudding for dessert.

Prep: 25 minutes **Cool:** 10 minutes **Bake:** 30 minutes
Oven: 400°F **Makes:** 12 cream puffs

   1 **cup water**
   ½ **cup butter**
   ⅛ **teaspoon salt**
   1 **cup all-purpose flour**
   4 **eggs**
   3 **cups whipped cream, pudding, or ice cream**
      Powdered sugar (optional)

1. Preheat oven to 400°F. Grease a baking sheet. In a medium saucepan combine the water, butter, and salt. Bring to boiling. Add flour all at once, stirring vigorously. Cook and stir until mixture forms a ball (see photo 1, right). Remove from heat. Cool for 10 minutes. Add eggs one at a time, beating well with a wooden spoon after each addition (see photo 2, right).

2. Drop 12 heaping tablespoons of dough onto prepared baking sheet. Bake for 30 to 35 minutes or until golden brown and firm; cool.

3. Cut tops from puffs; remove soft dough from inside. Fill with whipped cream. Replace tops. If desired, sift powdered sugar over tops.

Per cream puff: 238 cal., 21 g total fat (12 g sat. fat), 134 mg chol., 140 mg sodium, 9 g carbo., 0 g fiber, 4 g pro. **Daily Values:** 17% vit. A, 3% calcium, 4% iron **Exchanges:** ½ Other Carbo., 4 Fat

Éclairs: Prepare as at left, except spoon dough into a pastry bag fitted with a large plain round tip (about ½-inch opening). Pipe 12 strips of dough 3 inches apart onto a greased baking sheet, making each strip 4 inches long, 1 inch wide, and ¾ inch high. Bake, cool, and split as in Steps 2 and 3. Fill éclairs with whipped cream. Frost with Chocolate Glaze (page 168). Makes 12 éclairs.

Per éclair: 361 cal., 27 g total fat (16 g sat. fat), 142 mg chol., 27 g carbo., 171 mg sodium, 1 g fiber, 5 g pro. **Daily Values:** 19% vit. A, 3% calcium, 7% iron **Exchanges:** 1½ Other Carbo., 5 Fat

Mini Puffs: Prepare as at left, except drop dough by rounded teaspoons 2 inches apart onto greased baking sheets. Bake one sheet at a time in a 400°F oven for 25 minutes (keep remaining dough covered while first batch bakes). Cool, split, and fill as in Steps 2 and 3. Makes about 30 mini puffs.

Per mini puff: 94 cal., 8 g total fat (5 g sat. fat), 53 mg chol., 4 g carbo., 46 mg sodium, 0 g fiber, 2 g pro. **Daily Values:** 6% vit. A, 13% calcium, 2% iron **Exchanges:** 2 Fat

1. Add flour to the butter-water mixture; stir vigorously until the dough forms a ball that doesn't separate.

2. Cool the mixture for 10 minutes, then add the eggs one at a time. Beat the dough until smooth after each egg is added.

Vanilla Pudding EASY

On a diet? Try the Lower-Fat Pudding variation.

Prep: 10 minutes **Cook:** 20 minutes
Chill: 4 hours **Makes:** 4 servings

   ¾ **cup sugar**
   3 **tablespoons cornstarch**
   3 **cups whole milk or reduced-fat (2%) milk**
   4 **egg yolks, beaten**
   1 **tablespoon butter or margarine**
   1½ **teaspoons vanilla**

1. In a saucepan combine sugar and cornstarch. Stir in milk. Cook and stir over medium heat until thickened and bubbly. Cook and stir for

2 minutes more. Remove from heat. Gradually stir 1 cup of the milk mixture into egg yolks.

2. Add egg mixture to milk mixture in saucepan. Bring to a gentle boil; reduce heat. Cook and stir for 2 minutes. Remove from heat. Stir in butter and vanilla. Pour pudding into a bowl. Cover surface with plastic wrap. Serve warm or cold. (Do not stir during chilling.)

Chocolate Pudding: Prepare as on page 288, except add ⅓ cup unsweetened cocoa powder along with the sugar. Decrease cornstarch to 2 tablespoons and milk to 2⅔ cups.

Per about ¾ cup vanilla or chocolate variation: 357 cal., 13 g total fat (7 g sat. fat), 231 mg chol., 109 mg sodium, 51 g carbo., 0 g fiber, 9 g pro.
Daily Values: 10% vit. A, 21% calcium, 3% iron
Exchanges: 1 Milk, 2½ Other Carbo., 2½ Fat

Lower-Fat Vanilla or Chocolate Pudding: Prepare as on page 288 or above, except substitute fat-free milk for whole milk.

Per about ¾ cup lower-fat vanilla or chocolate variations: 309 cal., 8 g total fat (3 g sat. fat), 217 mg chol., 111 mg sodium, 51 g carbo., 0 g fiber, 9 g pro.
Daily Values: 14% vit. A, 19% calcium, 8% iron
Exchanges: 1 Fat-Free Milk, 2½ Other Carbo., 1½ Fat

Crème Brûlée

Caramelized sugar drizzled over a creamy custard led the French to call this dessert crème brûlée, which means "burnt cream."

Prep: 10 minutes **Bake:** 30 minutes **Oven:** 325°F
Chill: 1 hour **Stand:** 20 minutes **Makes:** 6 desserts

 1¾ **cups half-and-half or light cream**
 5 **egg yolks, slightly beaten**
 ⅓ **cup sugar**
 1 **teaspoon vanilla**
 ⅛ **teaspoon salt**
 ¼ **cup sugar**

1. Preheat oven to 325°F. In a small heavy saucepan heat half-and-half over medium-low heat just until bubbly. Remove from heat; set aside.

2. Meanwhile, in a medium bowl combine egg yolks, the ⅓ cup sugar, the vanilla, and salt. Beat with a wire whisk just until combined. Slowly whisk the hot half-and-half into the egg mixture.

3. Place six 6-ounce custard dishes in a 3-quart rectangular baking dish. Divide custard mixture evenly among the dishes. Place baking dish on oven rack. Pour boiling *water* into the baking dish to reach halfway up the custard dish sides.

4. Bake for 30 to 40 minutes or until a knife inserted near the center of each custard comes out clean. Remove dishes from the water; cool on a wire rack. Cover and chill for at least 1 hour and up to 8 hours.

5. Before serving, let custards stand at room temperature for 20 minutes. Meanwhile, in a heavy 8-inch skillet heat the ¼ cup sugar over medium-high heat until sugar begins to melt, shaking skillet occasionally to heat sugar evenly (see photo 1, page 290). Do not stir. Once the sugar starts to melt, reduce heat to low and cook about 5 minutes more or until all of the sugar is melted and golden, stirring as needed with a wooden spoon.

6. Quickly drizzle the caramelized sugar over custards. (If sugar hardens in the skillet, return to heat; stir until melted.) Serve immediately.

Amaretto Crème Brûlée: Prepare as at left, except stir 2 tablespoons amaretto or coffee liqueur into the custard mixture.

Maple Crème Brûlée: Prepare as at left, except reduce the ⅓ cup sugar to 3 tablespoons and stir 2 tablespoons of maple-flavored syrup and 1 teaspoon maple extract into custard mixture.

Per individual dessert regular, amaretto, or maple variations: 209 cal., 12 g total fat (6 g sat. fat), 197 mg chol., 84 mg sodium, 22 g carbo., 0 g fiber, 4 g pro.
Daily Values: 9% vit. A, 1% vit. C, 9% calcium, 2% iron
Exchanges: 1½ Other Carbo., ½ Medium-Fat Meat, 2 Fat

Crème Brûlée

Caramel Flans

Caramelized sugar is added to the dishes first to create the luscious rivers of caramel that spill out over these flans when they are unmolded.

Prep: 25 minutes **Bake:** 30 minutes **Oven:** 325°F
Stand: 10 minutes **Makes:** 4 flans

- ⅓ **cup sugar**
- 3 **eggs, beaten**
- 1½ **cups half-and-half**
- ⅓ **cup sugar**
- 1 **teaspoon vanilla**
  Ground nutmeg or cinnamon (optional)

1. To caramelize sugar, in an 8-inch heavy skillet cook ⅓ cup sugar over medium-high heat until sugar begins to melt, shaking the skillet occasionally (see photo 1, below). Do not stir. When sugar starts to melt, reduce heat to low and cook 5 minutes or until all of the sugar is melted, stirring as needed with a wooden spoon. Divide the caramelized sugar among four 6-ounce custard dishes; tilt dishes to coat bottoms. Let stand for 10 minutes.

2. Meanwhile, preheat oven to 325°F. Combine eggs, half-and-half, ⅓ cup sugar, and vanilla. Beat until well combined but not foamy. Place the custard dishes in a 2-quart square baking dish. Divide egg mixture among custard dishes. If desired, sprinkle with nutmeg. Place baking dish on an oven rack. Pour boiling *water* into the baking dish around custard dishes to a depth of 1 inch. Bake for 30 to 45 minutes or until a knife inserted near the centers comes out clean (see photo 2, above right).

3. Remove dishes from water. Cool slightly on a wire rack and unmold. (Or cool completely in custard dishes. Cover; chill until serving time.) To unmold, loosen flan edges with a knife. Invert a dessert plate over each dish; turn plate and dish over together. Remove custard dishes.

Per flan: 298 cal., 14 g total fat (8 g sat. fat), 192 mg chol., 90 mg sodium, 36 g carbo., 0 g fiber, 7 g pro.
Daily Values: 10% vit. A, 1% vit. C, 11% calcium, 4% iron
Exchanges: 2½ Other Carbo., 1 Medium-Fat Meat, 2 Fat

1. While the sugar is heating on the stove, shake the pan occasionally. Do not stir the sugar until it begins to melt. The sugar is done cooking when it is syrupy and golden.

2. Insert the tip of a knife in the middle of each custard. If the knife comes out clean, that custard is cooked.

Baked Custard: Prepare as at left, except omit the ⅓ cup sugar that is caramelized in Step 1. Divide egg mixture among custard cups or one 3½-cup soufflé dish. Bake individual custards as directed, or bake in soufflé dish for 50 to 60 minutes. Serve custard warm or chilled.

Per custard: 166 cal., 6 g total fat (2 g sat. fat), 166 mg chol., 93 mg sodium, 26 g carbo., 0 g fiber, 8 g pro.
Daily Values: 9% vit. A, 1% vit. C, 13% calcium, 3% iron
Exchanges: 1 Other Carbo., ½ Milk, 1 Fat

Orange Sherbet `NO FAT`

Prep: 20 minutes **Freeze:** per manufacturer's directions
Ripen: 4 hours (optional) **Makes:** 6 cups

- 1½ **cups sugar**
- 1 **envelope unflavored gelatin**
- 3¾ **cups orange juice**
- 1 **cup milk**
- 1 **teaspoon grated orange peel**

1. In a saucepan combine sugar and gelatin. Stir in 2 cups of the orange juice. Cook and stir until sugar and gelatin dissolve. Remove from heat. Stir in remaining orange juice, the milk, orange peel, and, if desired, a few drops of *orange food coloring*. (Mixture may appear curdled.)

2. Transfer mixture to a 4-quart ice cream freezer; freeze according to manufacturer's directions.* If desired, ripen 4 hours (see tip, page 271).

*Note: If you don't have access to an ice cream freezer, transfer mixture to a 13×9×2-inch baking pan. Cover; freeze several hours or until almost firm. Break mixture into small chunks; transfer to a large chilled mixing bowl. Beat with an electric mixer until smooth but not melted. Return to pan. Cover and freeze until firm.

Per ½ cup: 140 cal., 1 g total fat (0 g sat. fat), 2 mg chol., 12 mg sodium, 33 g carbo., 0 g fiber, 2 g pro.
Daily Values: 4% vit. A, 65% vit. C, 3% calcium, 1% iron
Exchanges: ½ Milk, 1½ Other Carbo.

 **Vanilla Ice Cream** `EASY`

Prep: 5 minutes **Freeze:** per manufacturer's directions
Ripen: 4 hours (optional) **Makes:** 8 cups

> 4 **cups half-and-half, light cream, or milk**
> 1½ **cups sugar**
> 1 **tablespoon vanilla**
> 2 **cups whipping cream**

1. In a large bowl combine half-and-half, sugar, and vanilla. Stir until sugar dissolves. Stir in whipping cream. Freeze cream mixture in a 4- or 5-quart ice cream freezer according to the manufacturer's directions. If desired, ripen 4 hours (see tip, page 271).

Mocha Ice Cream: Prepare as above, except dissolve 2 tablespoons instant coffee crystals in cream mixture and, if desired, stir ½ cup miniature semisweet chocolate pieces into cream mixture before freezing. Makes 8 cups.

Chocolate-Almond Ice Cream: Prepare as above, except reduce sugar to 1 cup. Before freezing, stir one 16-ounce can chocolate-flavored syrup and ½ cup chopped almonds, toasted (see tip, page 265), into cream mixture. Makes 10 cups.

Per ½ cup vanilla, mocha, or chocolate-almond variations:
253 cal., 18 g total fat (11 g sat. fat), 63 mg chol., 36 mg sodium, 22 g carbo., 0 g fiber, 2 g pro.
Daily Values: 14% vit. A, 1% vit. C, 8% calcium,
Exchanges: 1½ Other Carbo., 3 Fat

Strawberry or Peach Ice Cream: Prepare as above, except in a blender blend 4 cups fresh strawberries or cut-up, peeled peaches until nearly smooth. Stir blended fruit into cream mixture before freezing. Makes 10 cups.

Per ½ cup strawberry or peach variations: 212 cal., 15 g total fat (9 g sat. fat), 51 mg chol., 29 mg sodium, 19 g carbo., 1 g fiber, 2 g pro.
Daily Values: 11% vit. A, 29% vit. C, 71% calcium, 1% iron
Exchanges: ½ Fruit, 1 Other Carbo., 3 Fat

Pecan Praline Ice Cream: Prepare as above, except line a baking sheet with foil; grease foil. In a skillet cook ½ cup chopped pecans, ¼ cup sugar, and 1 tablespoon butter or margarine over medium-high heat until sugar begins to melt, shaking skillet occasionally. Do not stir. Reduce heat to low; cook until sugar turns golden, stirring frequently. Spread on prepared sheet. Cool; break into chunks. Stir nut mixture into cream mixture before freezing. Makes 8 cups.

Per ½ cup: 295 cal., 21 g total fat (12 g sat. fat), 65 mg chol., 44 mg sodium, 25 g carbo., 0 g fiber, 3 g pro.
Daily Values: 15% vit. A, 1% vit. C, 9% calcium, 1% iron
Exchanges: 1½ Other Carbo., 3 Fat

Butterscotch Crunch Squares

Prep: 40 minutes **Bake:** 10 minutes **Oven:** 400°F
Freeze: 6 hours **Stand:** 5 minutes **Makes:** 12 squares

> 1 **cup all-purpose flour**
> ¼ **cup quick-cooking rolled oats**
> ¼ **cup packed brown sugar**
> ½ **cup butter**
> ½ **cup chopped pecans or walnuts**
> ½ **cup butterscotch-flavored ice cream topping**
> ½ **gallon butter brickle or vanilla ice cream**

1. Preheat oven to 400°F. Combine the flour, oats, and brown sugar. Cut in butter until mixture resembles coarse crumbs. Stir in nuts. Pat nut mixture lightly into an ungreased 13×9×2-inch baking pan. Bake for 10 to 15 minutes. While warm, stir nut mixture to crumble; cool.

2. Spread half of the crumbs in a 9×9×2-inch pan; drizzle half of the ice cream topping over crumbs in pan. Place ice cream in a chilled bowl; stir to soften. Spread ice cream evenly over topping-drizzled crumbs. Drizzle with remaining topping; sprinkle with remaining crumbs. Cover and freeze at least 6 hours or until firm. Let stand at room temperature for 5 to 10 minutes before serving.

Per square: 450 cal., 28 g total fat (15 g sat. fat), 112 mg chol., 156 mg sodium, 46 g carbo., 1 g fiber, 5 g pro.
Daily Values: 18% vit. A, 13% calcium, 6% iron
Exchanges: ½ Starch, 2½ Other Carbo., 4½ Fat

Butterscotch Crunch Squares

Cinnamon Gelato

Prep: 20 minutes **Cool:** 30 minutes
Chill: 4 hours **Freeze:** per manufacturer's directions
Ripen: 4 hours (optional) **Makes:** 5 cups

  1 **cup sugar**
1½ **teaspoons ground cinnamon**
  3 **cups whole milk**
  1 **cup whipping cream**
  6 **egg yolks, slightly beaten**
  1 **teaspoon vanilla**

1. In a saucepan combine sugar and cinnamon. Stir in milk, cream, and egg yolks. Heat and stir over medium heat until mixture thickens slightly. Remove from heat. Stir in vanilla.

2. Place saucepan in ice water. Let stand about 30 minutes or until cool, stirring occasionally. Cover surface of custard with plastic wrap. Chill for 4 to 24 hours.

3. Freeze custard in a 4- to 5-quart ice cream freezer according to manufacturer's directions. If desired, ripen 4 hours (see tip, page 271).

Chocolate-Pistachio Gelato: Prepare as above, except omit cinnamon and add 6 ounces finely chopped bittersweet chocolate to milk mixture before heating. Stir ⅔ cup chopped pistachio nuts into chilled custard mixture just before freezing. Makes about 7 cups.

Coconut Gelato: Prepare as above, except omit cinnamon and substitute 1 cup unsweetened coconut milk for 1 cup of the whole milk. Stir

**Chocolate-Pistachio Gelato,
Coconut Gelato, and
Blackberry Gelato**

1 cup coconut, toasted (see tip, page 265), into chilled custard mixture before freezing. Makes about 5½ cups.

Per ½ cup cinnamon, chocolate-pistachio, or coconut variations: 235 cal., 14 g total fat (8 g sat. fat), 163 mg chol., 46 mg sodium, 24 g carbo., 0 g fiber, 4 g pro.
Daily Values: 11% vit. A, 11% calcium, 2% iron
Exchanges: 1½ Other Carbo., 3 Fat

Blackberry Gelato: Prepare as at left, except omit cinnamon. Place one 16-ounce package thawed frozen blackberries in a food processor; process until smooth. Pour puree through a fine-mesh sieve; discard seeds. Stir blackberry puree into chilled custard mixture just before freezing. Makes about 7 cups.

Per ½ cup: 165 cal., 9 g total fat (5 g sat. fat), 102 mg chol., 27 mg sodium, 19 g carbo., 1 g fiber, 3 g pro.
Daily Values: 8% vit. A, 2% vit. C, 8% calcium, 2% iron
Exchanges: 1 Other Carbo., 2 Fat

Lemon Curd `EASY`

Prep: 5 minutes **Cook:** 8 minutes
Chill: 1 hour **Makes:** 2 cups

  1 **cup sugar**
  2 **tablespoons cornstarch**
  3 **teaspoons finely shredded lemon peel**
  6 **tablespoons lemon juice**
  6 **tablespoons water**
  6 **egg yolks, beaten**
  ½ **cup butter or margarine, cut up**

1. In a saucepan stir together sugar and cornstarch. Stir in lemon peel, lemon juice, and water. Cook and stir over medium heat until thickened and bubbly.

2. Stir half of the lemon mixture into the egg yolks. Return egg mixture to the saucepan. Cook, stirring constantly, over medium heat until mixture comes to a gentle boil. Cook and stir for 2 minutes more. Remove from heat. Add butter; stir until melted. Remove from heat. Cover surface with plastic wrap. Chill 1 hour.

Per 2 tablespoons: 128 cal., 8 g total fat (4 g sat. fat), 96 mg chol., 65 mg sodium, 14 g carbo., 0 g fiber, 1 g pro.
Daily Values: 7% vit. A, 5% vit. C, 1% calcium, 1% iron
Exchanges: 1 Other Carbo., 1½ Fat

Orange Curd: Prepare as above, except decrease sugar to ¾ cup; substitute orange peel for the lemon peel and ¾ cup orange juice for the lemon juice and water. Makes about 1½ cups.

Per 2 tablespoons: 160 cal., 11 g total fat (6 g sat. fat), 128 mg chol., 87 mg sodium, 15 g carbo., 0 g fiber, 2 g pro.
Daily Values: 10% vit. A, 14% vit. C, 2% calcium, 2% iron
Exchanges: 1 Other Carbo., 2 Fat

Fish & Shellfish

Fish Tacos, 300

Stir-Fried Shrimp and Broccoli, 310

Salmon-Vegetable Bake, 300

Caesar Salmon Pizzas (FAST) 308

CANNED FISH

FISH FILLETS

FISH STEAKS

SAUCES & ACCOMPANIMENTS

SHELLFISH *See also Shrimp*

SHRIMP

TIPS

Fish & Shellfish Essentials

Every good fishmonger offers an enticing array of fish and shellfish. Get acquainted with the many types of seafood and try some flavorful new recipes in this chapter.

Market Forms:

Fish are available in several forms. Here's what the market terms mean:

Drawn: Whole fish with internal organs removed; may or may not be scaled.

Dressed: Ready to cook; organs, scales, gills, and fins have been removed. Pan-dressed fish have heads and tails removed.

Steak: Ready to cook; a crosscut slice ½ to 1 inch thick from a large, dressed fish.

Fillet: Ready to cook; a boneless piece cut from the side and away from the backbone; may or may not be skinned.

| Dressed | Steak | Fillet |

Storing Fresh Fish

Cook fish the same day you buy it. If that's not possible, wrap fresh fish loosely in plastic wrap, store in the coldest part of the refrigerator, and use it within two days. Cover and chill leftover cooked fish; use it within two days.

Shopping for Fish

Trust your eyes and nose when buying fish.
Look for fish with:
● Clear, bright, bulging eyes with black pupils
● Shiny, taut, bright skin
● Red gills that are not slippery
● Flesh that feels firm, elastic, and tight to bone
● Moist, cleanly cut fillets and steaks
Avoid fish with:
● Strong "fishy" odor
● Dull, bloody, or sunken eyes
● Fading skin with bruises, red spots, or browning or yellowing flesh edges
● Ragged-cut fillets and steaks

You can store frozen fish in a freezer (set at 0°F or lower) for up to three months. If you cut your own fillets or steaks, put them in resealable freezer bags or wrap in moisture- and vapor-proof wrap before freezing.

For safety and best quality, thaw fish or shellfish slowly in the refrigerator. Place the unopened package in a container in the refrigerator, allowing a 1-pound package to thaw overnight. If necessary, you can place the wrapped package under cold running water for 1 to 2 minutes to hasten thawing. Don't thaw fish or shellfish in warm water or at room temperature and do not refreeze fish; both are unsafe.

Selecting and Storing Shellfish

Shellfish quality can make or break a recipe.

When purchasing live crabs and lobsters, look for:
● Hard shells (except for soft-shell crabs).
● Vigorous activity; the lobster's or crab's legs should move when the body is touched.
● Lobster tail that curls under the body when it is lifted.

To store: Lobsters should be cooked live or killed immediately before cooking. Ideally, live lobsters and crabs should be cooked on the day they are purchased. Otherwise, place them on a tray and refrigerate them covered with a damp towel. Or place them on damp newspapers in an insulated cooler half-filled with ice. Cook within one day.

Lobster

How Much Fish to Buy

Use these guidelines to determine how much fish to buy for each serving:

- 12 ounces to 1 pound of whole fish
- 8 ounces of drawn or dressed fish
- 4 to 5 ounces of steaks or fillets
- 1 pound of live crabs
- 3 to 4 ounces of shelled shrimp
- One 1- to 1½-pound whole lobster, one 8-ounce lobster tail, or 4 to 5 ounces of cooked lobster meat

Clams   Mussels   Oysters

When purchasing live clams, mussels, and oysters, look for:

- Tightly closed shells. Mussels may gape slightly but should close when tapped; oysters should always be tightly closed.
- Clean, unbroken, moist shells; mussels should have beards.
- Fresh scent (not a strong fishy odor).

To store: Refrigerate live clams, mussels, and oysters covered with a moist cloth in an open container for up to one to two days.

When purchasing shucked clams, oysters, and scallops, look for:

- Plump meats in clear liquor (juices) without shell particles or grit; the liquor should not exceed 10 percent of total volume.
- Fresh oceanlike scent (not sour or sulfurlike).
- Scallops that are firm and moist, retaining their shape when touched.

To store: Refrigerate shucked clams, oysters, and scallops covered in the liquor for up to two days or freeze for up to three months.

When purchasing shrimp, look for:

- Firm meat.
- Translucent, moist shells without black spots.
- Fresh scent (not an ammonia odor, which indicates spoilage).
- Absence of vein, if peeled and deveined.

To store: Refrigerate fresh shrimp in a covered container for up to two days. Keep frozen shrimp in the freezer for up to six months.

Peeling and Deveining Shrimp

1. To peel a shrimp, open the shell lengthwise down the body. Starting at the head end, peel back the shell. Gently pull on the tail to remove it, or leave it intact, if you prefer.

2. To devein a shrimp, use a sharp knife to make a shallow slit along the back from the head to the tail end. Locate the black vein.

3. If the vein is visible, hold the shrimp under cold running water to rinse it away. Or use the tip of a knife to remove the vein, then rinse the shrimp.

Questions about Food Safety?

Call the U.S. Food and Drug Administration's Center for Food Safety and Applied Nutrition Outreach Center, 888/723-3366, weekdays from 10 a.m. to 4 p.m. (Eastern Standard Time).

Crab

Pan-Fried Fish `FAST`

An easy, family-pleasing way to cook fish, pan-frying produces a light, crisp coating. This recipe offers the options of a spicy coating and a crunchy potato chip coating.

Prep: 10 minutes **Cook:** 6 minutes per batch
Makes: 4 servings

- 1 **pound fresh or frozen fish fillets, ½ to ¾ inch thick**
- 1 **egg, beaten**
- 2 **tablespoons water**
- ⅔ **cup cornmeal or fine dry bread crumbs**
- ½ **teaspoon salt**
  Dash black pepper
  Shortening or cooking oil for frying

1. Thaw fish, if frozen. Rinse fish; pat dry with paper towels. Cut into four serving-size pieces, if necessary. In a shallow dish combine egg and water. In another shallow dish stir together cornmeal, salt, and pepper. Dip fish into egg mixture (see photo 1, above right); coat fish with cornmeal mixture.

2. In a large skillet heat ¼ inch of melted shortening or oil. Add half of the fish in a single layer, frying one side until golden. (If fillets have skin, fry skin side last.) Turn carefully (see photo 2, above right); fry until second side is golden and fish begins to flake when tested with a fork. Allow 3 to 4 minutes per side. Drain on paper towels. Keep warm in a 300°F oven while frying remaining fish.

Spicy Hot Pan-Fried Fish: Prepare as above, except omit black pepper. Reduce cornmeal to ¼ cup and combine with ¼ cup all-purpose flour, ¾ teaspoon cayenne pepper, ½ teaspoon chili powder, ½ teaspoon garlic powder, and ½ teaspoon paprika.

Per piece plain or spicy variation: 277 cal., 11 g total fat (3 g sat. fat), 102 mg chol., 369 mg sodium, 18 g carbo., 2 g fiber, 24 g pro.
Daily Values: 4% vit. A, 2% vit. C, 3% calcium, 9% iron
Exchanges: 1 Starch, 3 Very Lean Meat, 2 Fat

Potato Chip Pan-Fried Fish: Prepare as above, except substitute 1⅓ cups finely crushed potato chips (about 4 cups chips) or saltine crackers for the cornmeal and omit salt.

Per piece: 303 cal., 18 g total fat (4 g sat. fat), 102 mg chol., 185 mg sodium, 10 g carbo., 1 g fiber, 23 g pro.
Daily Values: 2% vit. A, 22% vit. C, 4% calcium, 6% iron
Exchanges: ½ Starch, 3 Very Lean Meat, 3½ Fat

1. First dip each fish piece in the egg mixture, turning the fish to coat both sides. This will ensure that the seasoned cornmeal mixture will cling to the fish.

2. When the fish is golden, carefully lift it with a wide metal spatula, steadying it with a narrow metal spatula. Turn the fish over and cook the second side.

Hush Puppies `FAST`

For best results, fry five or six at a time and let the oil temperature return to 375°F before frying more.

Prep: 10 minutes **Cook:** 3 minutes per batch
Makes: 14 to 18 hush puppies

- 1 **cup cornmeal**
- ¼ **cup all-purpose flour**
- 2 **teaspoons sugar**
- ¾ **teaspoon baking powder**
- ¼ **teaspoon baking soda**
- ¼ **teaspoon salt**
- 1 **egg, beaten**
- ½ **cup buttermilk or sour milk (see tip, page 169)**
- ¼ **cup sliced green onion (2)**
  Shortening or cooking oil for deep-fat frying

1. In a medium bowl stir together cornmeal, flour, sugar, baking powder, baking soda, and salt. Make a well in center of flour mixture; set aside.

2. In another bowl combine egg, buttermilk, and green onion. Add egg mixture all at once to flour mixture. Stir just until moistened (batter should be lumpy).

3. Drop batter by tablespoons into deep, hot fat (375°F). Fry about 3 minutes or until golden, turning once. Drain on paper towels. Serve warm.

Per hush puppy: 95 cal., 5 g total fat (1 g sat. fat), 15 mg chol., 100 mg sodium, 11 g carbo., 1 g fiber, 2 g pro.
Daily Values: 1% vit. A, 1% vit. C, 3% calcium, 4% iron
Exchanges: 1 Starch, ½ Fat

Crispy Oven-Fried Fish

 LOW FAT FAST

Prep: 20 minutes **Bake:** 4 to 6 minutes per ½-inch thickness **Oven:** 450°F **Makes:** 4 servings

> 1 **pound fresh or frozen skinless fish fillets, ½ to ¾ inch thick**
> ¼ **cup milk**
> ⅓ **cup all-purpose flour**
> ⅓ **cup fine dry bread crumbs**
> ¼ **cup grated Parmesan cheese**
> ½ **teaspoon dried dill**
> ⅛ **teaspoon black pepper**
> 2 **tablespoons butter, melted**

1. Thaw fish, if frozen. Rinse fish; pat dry with paper towels. Cut into four serving-size pieces, if necessary. Measure thickness of fish.

2. Place milk in a shallow dish. Place flour in a second shallow dish. In a third shallow dish combine bread crumbs, cheese, dill, and pepper. Add melted butter; stir until combined. Dip fish in milk; coat with flour. Dip again in milk, then in crumb mixture to coat all sides. Place fish on a greased baking sheet. Bake, uncovered, in a 450°F oven for 4 to 6 minutes per ½-inch thickness or until fish begins to flake when tested with a fork.

Per piece: 242 cal., 9 g total fat (5 g sat. fat), 71 mg chol., 423 mg sodium, 13 g carbo., 1 g fiber, 24 g pro.
Daily Values: 7% vit. A, 2% vit. C, 14% calcium, 8% iron
Exchanges: 1 Starch, 3 Very Lean Meat, 1 Fat

Fish and Chips

Start to Finish: 50 minutes **Makes:** 4 servings

> 1 **pound fresh or frozen skinless fish fillets, about ½ inch thick**
> 1¼ **pounds medium potatoes (about 4)**
> **Cooking oil for deep-fat frying**
> 1 **cup all-purpose flour**
> 1 **cup beer**
> 2 **eggs**
> ½ **teaspoon baking powder**
> ½ **teaspoon salt**
> ½ **teaspoon black pepper**
> **Coarse salt (optional)**
> 1 **recipe Tartar Sauce (page 522), malt vinegar, or cider vinegar (optional)**

1. Thaw fish, if frozen; cut into 3×2-inch pieces. Rinse fish; pat dry with paper towels. Cover and refrigerate until needed.

2. For chips, cut potatoes lengthwise into ⅜-inch-wide wedges. Pat dry with paper towels. In a 3-quart saucepan or deep-fat fryer heat 2 inches cooking oil to 375°F. Fry potatoes, one-fourth at a time, for 4 to 6 minutes or until light brown. Remove potatoes; drain on paper towels. Sprinkle lightly with *salt*. Transfer potatoes to a wire rack on a baking sheet, arranging them in a single layer. Keep warm in a 300°F oven.

3. Meanwhile, for batter, in a medium mixing bowl combine flour, beer, eggs, baking powder, the ½ teaspoon salt, and the pepper. Beat with a rotary beater or wire whisk until smooth. Dip fish into batter. Fry fish in the hot (375°F) oil, one or two pieces at a time, until coating is golden brown and fish begins to flake when tested with a fork (about 3 to 4 minutes), turning once. Remove fish and drain on paper towels. Transfer fish to a second baking sheet; keep warm in the 300°F oven while frying remaining fish. To serve, if desired, sprinkle fish and chips with coarse salt and pass Tartar Sauce.

Per 3 ounces fish + about 12 chips: 721 cal., 40 g total fat (10 g sat. fat), 208 mg chol., 454 mg sodium, 52 g carbo., 3 g fiber, 31 g pro.
Daily Values: 4% vit. A, 38% vit. C, 18% calcium, 25% iron
Exchanges: 3½ Starch, 3 Very Lean Meat, 7 Fat

Easy Fish Sandwiches FAST

Start to Finish: 25 minutes **Makes:** 4 sandwiches

> 4 **frozen battered or breaded fish fillets**
> 3 **tablespoons mayonnaise or salad dressing**
> 1 **teaspoon finely shredded lime peel**
> 2 **teaspoons lime juice**
> 1 **cup packaged shredded cabbage with carrot (coleslaw mix) or shredded cabbage**
> 4 **3½- to 4-inch French-style rolls, split**
> ½ **cup bottled salsa**
> ½ **cup sliced, pitted kalamata olives**
> 2 **tablespoons capers, drained**

1. Cook fish according to package directions. Meanwhile, in a medium bowl stir together mayonnaise, lime peel, and lime juice. Add cabbage; stir until combined. Set aside. Hollow out top half of each roll, leaving a ½-inch-thick shell. Place a fish fillet on the bottom half of each roll. Top with cabbage mixture and salsa. Sprinkle with olives and capers. Add roll tops.

Per sandwich: 383 cal., 22 g total fat (3 g sat. fat), 26 mg chol., 1,165 mg sodium, 37 g carbo., 3 g fiber, 12 g pro.
Daily Values: 43% vit. A, 16% vit. C, 7% calcium, 15% iron
Exchanges: 1 Vegetable, 2 Starch, 1 Very Lean Meat, 3½ Fat

Veracruz-Style Red Snapper `LOW FAT`

Start to Finish: 40 minutes **Makes:** 6 servings

1½ **pounds fresh or frozen skinless red snapper, mahi mahi, or other fish fillets**
⅓ **cup all-purpose flour**
½ **teaspoon salt**
⅛ **teaspoon black pepper**
2 **tablespoons olive oil**
1 **large onion, sliced and separated into rings**
2 **cloves garlic, minced**
2 **large tomatoes, chopped (2 cups)**
¼ **cup sliced pimiento-stuffed olives**
2 **tablespoons lime juice**
2 **tablespoons capers, drained**
1 **to 2 fresh jalapeño or serrano chile peppers, seeded and chopped (see tip, page 74)**
1 **tablespoon snipped fresh oregano**
   Salt and black pepper
3 **cups hot cooked rice**

1. Thaw fish, if frozen. Rinse fish; pat dry with paper towels. Cut fish into six serving-size pieces, if necessary. Measure thickness of fish. In a shallow dish combine flour, ¼ teaspoon of the salt, and the black pepper. Coat fish on both sides with flour mixture.

2. In a 12-inch skillet cook fish in 1 tablespoon hot oil over medium heat until golden, adding additional oil to skillet during cooking, if necessary. (Allow 5 to 6 minutes per ½-inch thickness.) Transfer to a serving platter; cover and keep warm.

3. Meanwhile, for sauce, in a medium saucepan cook onion and garlic in the remaining 1 tablespoon hot oil until onion is tender. Stir in the remaining ¼ teaspoon salt, the tomato, olives, lime juice, capers, and chile pepper. Bring to boiling; reduce heat. Simmer, uncovered, about 5 minutes or until desired consistency is reached. Stir in oregano. Season to taste with additional salt and black pepper.

4. To serve, spoon sauce over fish. Serve with hot cooked rice.

Per piece + ⅓ cup sauce + ½ cup rice: 317 cal., 8 g total fat (1 g sat. fat), 30 mg chol., 507 mg sodium, 34 g carbo., 2 g fiber, 27 g pro.
Daily Values: 14% vit. A, 22% vit. C, 5% calcium, 13% iron
Exchanges: ½ Vegetable, 2 Starch, 3 Very Lean Meat, 1 Fat

Crunchy Catfish `FAST`

Prep: 20 minutes **Cook:** 6 minutes **Makes:** 4 servings

1 **pound fresh or frozen catfish fillets, about ½ inch thick**
¼ **cup all-purpose flour**
1 **egg, beaten**
3 **tablespoons Dijon-style mustard**
1 **tablespoon milk**
¼ **teaspoon black pepper**
1 **cup coarsely crushed pretzels (about 2 cups whole pretzels)**
2 **tablespoons cooking oil**
   Thin lemon slices (optional)

1. Thaw fish, if frozen. Rinse fish; pat dry with paper towels. Cut into four serving-size pieces, if necessary. Place flour in a shallow dish. In a second shallow dish combine the egg, mustard, milk, and pepper, beating with a whisk or fork until smooth. In a third shallow dish place the coarsely crushed pretzels. Coat both sides of fillets with flour. Dip fillets in the mustard mixture; coat with crushed pretzels.

2. In a large skillet cook fish in hot oil over medium heat for 3 to 4 minutes per side or until golden and fish begins to flake when tested with a fork. (Reduce heat as necessary to prevent burning.) If desired, serve with lemon slices.

Per piece: 364 cal., 18 g total fat (4 g sat. fat), 106 mg chol., 504 mg sodium, 26 g carbo., 1 g fiber, 23 g pro.
Daily Values: 3% vit. A, 2% vit. C, 5% calcium, 11% iron
Exchanges: 1½ Starch, 3 Very Lean Meat, 3 Fat

Veracruz-Style Red Snapper

Fish Tacos FAST

See photo, page 293.

Start to Finish: 20 minutes **Oven:** 450°F
Makes: 4 servings

- 12 **ounces fresh or frozen skinless fish fillets**
- 1 **tablespoon olive oil**
- ¼ **teaspoon ground cumin**
- ⅛ **teaspoon garlic powder**
- 3 **tablespoons mayonnaise or salad dressing**
- 1 **teaspoon lime juice**
- 1½ **cups packaged shredded cabbage with carrot (coleslaw mix) or shredded cabbage**
- 8 **corn taco shells, warmed according to package directions**
- 1 **recipe Mango Salsa**

1. Thaw fish, if frozen. Rinse fish; pat dry with paper towels. Cut fish crosswise into ¾-inch slices. Place fish in a single layer in a greased shallow baking pan. Combine olive oil, cumin, and garlic powder. Brush over fish. Bake in a 450°F oven for 4 to 6 minutes or until fish begins to flake when tested with a fork.

2. Meanwhile, in a medium bowl stir together mayonnaise and lime juice. Add cabbage; toss to coat. To serve, spoon some of the coleslaw mixture into each taco shell; add fish slices and top with Mango Salsa.

Mango Salsa: In a medium bowl combine ¾ cup chopped, peeled mango or peach; half of a medium red sweet pepper, seeded and finely chopped; 2 tablespoons thinly sliced green onion; half of a jalapeño chile pepper, seeded and finely chopped (see tip, page 74); 1½ teaspoons olive oil; ¼ teaspoon finely shredded lime peel; 1½ teaspoons lime juice; 1½ teaspoons vinegar; ¼ teaspoon salt; and ⅛ teaspoon black pepper. Makes 1 cup.

Per 2 tacos: 322 cal., 19 g total fat (3 g sat. fat), 44 mg chol., 353 mg sodium, 21 g carbo., 3 g fiber, 17 g pro.
Daily Values: 21% vit. A, 73% vit. C, 5% calcium, 5% iron
Exchanges: ½ Vegetable, 1 Starch, 2 Very Lean Meat, 3½ Fat

Easy Weeknight Dinner

Base a satisfying menu on seafood tacos, a Baja California specialty.

- *Fish Tacos (above)*
- *Black beans and rice*
- *Caramel Flans (page 290)*

Salmon-Vegetable Bake LOW FAT

See photo, page 293.

Prep: 30 minutes **Bake:** 30 minutes
Oven: 350°F **Makes:** 4 packets

- 1 **pound fresh or frozen skinless salmon, cod, or flounder fillets, about ¾ inch thick**
- 2 **cups thinly sliced carrot (4)**
- 2 **cups sliced fresh mushrooms**
- ½ **cup sliced green onion (4)**
- 2 **teaspoons finely shredded orange peel**
- 2 **teaspoons snipped fresh oregano or ½ teaspoon dried oregano, crushed**
- ¼ **teaspoon salt**
- ¼ **teaspoon black pepper**
- 4 **cloves garlic, halved**
- 4 **teaspoons olive oil**
  Salt and black pepper
- 2 **medium oranges, thinly sliced**
- 4 **sprigs fresh oregano (optional)**

1. Thaw fish, if frozen. Rinse fish; pat dry with paper towels. Cut into four serving-size pieces, if necessary; set aside. In a small saucepan cook carrot, covered, in a small amount of boiling water for 2 minutes. Drain and set aside. Tear off four 24-inch pieces of 18-inch-wide heavy foil. Fold each in half to make four 18×12-inch pieces.

2. In a large bowl combine carrot, mushrooms, green onion, orange peel, oregano, the ¼ teaspoon salt, the ¼ teaspoon pepper, and garlic.

3. Divide vegetables among the four pieces of foil, placing vegetables in center of each piece. Place one salmon piece on top of each vegetable portion. Drizzle 1 teaspoon of the oil over each salmon piece. Sprinkle each lightly with additional salt and pepper; top with orange slices and, if desired, a sprig of oregano. Bring together two opposite foil edges and seal with a double fold. Fold remaining edges together to completely enclose the food, allowing space for steam to build. Place the foil packets in a single layer in a 15×10×1-inch baking pan.

4. Bake in a 350°F oven about 30 minutes or until carrot is tender and fish begins to flake when tested with a fork. Open packets carefully to allow steam to escape. To serve, transfer the packets to plates.

Per packet: 252 cal., 10 g total fat (1 g sat. fat), 59 mg chol., 393 mg sodium, 18 g carbo., 4 g fiber, 26 g pro.
Daily Values: 314% vit. A, 73% vit. C, 8% calcium, 10% iron
Exchanges: 2 Vegetable, ½ Fruit, 3 Lean Meat

Salmon with Pesto Mayo `EASY`

If you have purchased dried-tomato pesto on hand, you can substitute it for the basil pesto.

Start to Finish: 15 minutes   **Makes:** 4 servings

- **4 5- to 6-ounce fresh or frozen skinless salmon fillets**
- **¼ cup mayonnaise or salad dressing**
- **3 tablespoons purchased basil pesto**
  Shaved Parmesan cheese (optional)

1. Thaw fish, if frozen. Rinse fish; pat dry with paper towels. Measure thickness of fish.

2. Place fish fillets on the greased unheated rack of a broiler pan, tucking under thin edges. Broil 4 inches from the heat for 4 to 6 minutes per ½-inch thickness or until fish begins to flake when tested with a fork. (If fillets are 1 inch or more thick, carefully turn once halfway through broiling.)

3. Meanwhile, for topping, in a small bowl stir together mayonnaise and pesto. Spoon mayonnaise mixture over fillets. Broil about 1 minute more or until topping is bubbly. If desired, garnish with shaved Parmesan cheese.

Per fillet + 2 tablespoons topping: 440 cal., 34 g total fat (5 g sat. fat), 94 mg chol., 256 mg sodium, 2 g carbo., 0 g fiber, 30 g pro.
Daily Values: 1% vit. A, 8% vit. C, 2% calcium, 3% iron
Exchanges: 4 Lean Meat, 5 Fat

Salmon in Phyllo

Don't be afraid of phyllo dough. The trick is keeping it from drying out and becoming brittle. Let it thaw in the refrigerator and keep the unused sheets covered with plastic wrap as you work.

Prep: 30 minutes   **Bake:** 18 minutes
Oven: 375°F   **Makes:** 4 packets

- **1 1-pound fresh or frozen salmon fillet**
- **½ cup butter, melted**
- **2 tablespoons snipped fresh dill or 1 teaspoon dried dill**
  Dash salt
  Dash black pepper
- **16 sheets frozen phyllo dough (14×9-inch rectangles), thawed**
- **1 recipe Mustard Cream Sauce**

1. Thaw salmon, if frozen. Rinse salmon; pat dry with paper towels. Remove skin from salmon. Cut salmon into four serving-size pieces.

Tuck thin salmon edges under to make pieces of even thickness. Brush some of the melted butter over each salmon portion. Sprinkle with dill, salt, and pepper. Set aside.

2. Unfold the phyllo dough; cover with plastic wrap. Lay one sheet of phyllo dough on a work surface; brush with some of the melted butter. Top with another sheet of phyllo dough. Brush with more melted butter. Add six more sheets of dough (making a total of eight sheets), brushing each sheet with butter. Cut dough crosswise into two 9×7-inch rectangles. Place a salmon fillet, buttered side down, in the middle of a dough rectangle. Fold a long side of the dough over the salmon; repeat with the other long side, pressing lightly. Fold up ends (see photo, below). Brush with melted butter. Place the packet, seam side down, in a shallow baking pan. Brush top with butter. Repeat with remaining phyllo, butter, and salmon.

3. Bake in a 375°F oven for 18 to 20 minutes or until phyllo dough is golden and fish begins to flake when tested with a fork. Serve with Mustard Cream Sauce.

Mustard Cream Sauce: In a small bowl stir together ½ cup purchased crème fraîche or dairy sour cream, 1 tablespoon Dijon-style mustard, 1 teaspoon snipped fresh dill or ¼ teaspoon dried dill, and ⅛ teaspoon salt. If necessary, stir in enough milk to reach desired consistency. Makes about ½ cup.

Per packet + 2 tablespoons sauce: 645 cal., 48 g total fat (21 g sat. fat), 158 mg chol., 667 mg sodium, 25 g carbo., 1 g fiber, 27 g pro.
Daily Values: 16% vit. A, 7% vit. C, 5% calcium, 11% iron
Exchanges: 1½ Other Carbo., 3 Lean Meat, 8 Fat

Place a salmon fillet in the center of a phyllo rectangle. Fold the long phyllo edges over the fillet and lightly press the edges together to seal. Fold up the remaining edges to complete a packet. Brush with melted butter.

Red Snapper with Carrot and Fennel

Red Snapper with Carrot and Fennel **LOW FAT**

Prep: 25 minutes **Bake:** 12 minutes
Oven: 450°F **Makes:** 4 servings

  1 **pound fresh or frozen skinless red snapper, grouper, or ocean perch fillets, about ½ inch thick**
  2 **cups sliced fennel bulb (1 large)**
  1 **cup chopped onion (1 large)**
  1 **cup chopped carrot (2 medium)**
  2 **cloves garlic, minced**
  1 **tablespoon olive oil**
  ¼ **cup dry white wine or reduced-sodium chicken broth**
  2 **tablespoons snipped fresh dill or 1½ teaspoons dried dill**
  ¼ **teaspoon salt**
  ¼ **teaspoon black pepper**
     Fresh dill sprigs (optional)

1. Thaw fish, if frozen. Rinse fish; pat dry. Sprinkle lightly with *salt* and *black pepper;* set aside. In a large skillet cook fennel, onion, carrot, and garlic in hot oil over medium heat for 7 to 9 minutes or until vegetables are tender and light brown. Remove from heat. Stir in wine, dill, the ¼ teaspoon salt, and the ¼ teaspoon pepper.

2. Reserve ¼ cup of the vegetable mixture; spoon remaining vegetable mixture into a 2-quart baking dish. Place fish on top of vegetables, tucking under any thin edges. Spoon reserved vegetable mixture on top of fish.

3. Bake, uncovered, in a 450°F oven about 12 minutes or until fish begins to flake when tested with a fork. To serve, transfer fish and vegetables to dinner plates and, if desired, garnish with dill sprigs.

Per 3 ounces fish + 1 cup vegetables: 198 cal., 5 g total fat (1 g sat. fat), 42 mg chol., 299 mg sodium, 11 g carbo., 3 g fiber, 25 g pro.
Daily Values: 76% vit. A, 19% vit. C, 8% calcium, 5% iron
Exchanges: 1½ Vegetable, 3 Very Lean Meat, 1 Fat

Red Snapper with Orange-Ginger Sauce **LOW FAT** **FAST**

Prep: 20 minutes **Cook:** 4 to 6 minutes per ½-inch thickness **Makes:** 4 servings

  1 **pound fresh or frozen skinless red snapper, grouper, or ocean perch fillets, ½ to ¾ inch thick**
  ⅛ **teaspoon black pepper**
  1 **cup reduced-sodium chicken broth**
  ¼ **cup sliced green onion (2)**
  ⅓ **cup orange juice**
  2 **tablespoons reduced-sodium soy sauce**
  1 **tablespoon honey**
  1 **teaspoon toasted sesame oil**
  ½ **teaspoon grated fresh ginger or ¼ teaspoon ground ginger**
  6 **cups torn mixed greens, such as spinach, Swiss chard, and/or mustard, beet, or collard greens**

1. Thaw fish, if frozen. Rinse fish; pat dry with paper towels. Cut fish into four serving-size pieces, if necessary. Sprinkle with pepper. In a large skillet combine broth and green onion. Bring to boiling; add fish. Return to boiling; reduce heat. Simmer, covered, for 4 to 6 minutes per ½-inch thickness of fish or until fish begins to flake when tested with a fork. Remove fish, discarding cooking liquid; set fish aside and keep warm.

2. For sauce, in same skillet combine orange juice, soy sauce, honey, sesame oil, and ginger. Bring to boiling. Boil gently, uncovered, for 1 minute, stirring once. Remove from heat.

3. Place greens in a large bowl. Pour half of the sauce over greens, tossing to coat.

4. To serve, arrange greens on a platter. Place fish on top of greens and drizzle with remaining sauce.

Per piece + 1 cup greens: 177 cal., 4 g total fat (1 g sat. fat), 41 mg chol., 563 mg sodium, 9 g carbo., 1 g fiber, 26 g pro.
Daily Values: 89% vit. A, 41% vit. C, 8% calcium, 12% iron
Exchanges: 1½ Vegetable, 3½ Very Lean Meat, ½ Fat

Sesame-Teriyaki Sea Bass LOW FAT FAST

Regular sesame seeds are available in your supermarket. You can find black sesame seeds in the Asian foods section or at an Asian market.

Start to Finish: 25 minutes **Makes:** 4 servings

- **4 4-ounce fresh or frozen sea bass, rockfish, or other fish fillets, ½ to ¾ inch thick**
- **¼ teaspoon black pepper**
- **3 tablespoons soy sauce**
- **¼ cup sweet rice wine (mirin)**
- **2 teaspoons honey**
- **2 teaspoons cooking oil**
- **2 teaspoons sesame seeds and/or black sesame seeds, toasted (see tip, page 265)**

1. Thaw fish, if frozen. Rinse fish; pat dry with paper towels. Sprinkle fish with pepper; set aside.

2. For glaze, in a small saucepan combine soy sauce, rice wine, and honey. Bring to boiling; reduce heat. Simmer, uncovered, about 10 minutes or until glaze is slightly thickened and reduced to ⅓ cup; set aside.

3. Meanwhile, in a large nonstick skillet cook fish in hot oil over medium heat until fish is golden and begins to flake when tested with a fork, turning once. (Allow 4 to 6 minutes per ½-inch thickness.) Drain fish on paper towels.

4. To serve, transfer fish to a platter, drizzle with glaze, and sprinkle with sesame seeds.

Per fillet: 196 cal., 5 g total fat (1 g sat. fat), 46 mg chol., 783 mg sodium, 13 g carbo., 0 g fiber, 23 g pro.
Daily Values: 6% vit. A, 2% vit. C, 3% calcium, 4% iron
Exchanges: 1 Other Carbo., 3½ Very Lean Meat, ½ Fat

Cilantro-Lime Orange Roughy LOW FAT FAST

Start to Finish: 15 minutes **Makes:** 4 servings

- **1¼ pounds fresh or frozen orange roughy, ocean perch, cod, or haddock fillets, ¾ to 1 inch thick**
- **Salt and black pepper**
- **¼ cup snipped fresh cilantro**
- **1 tablespoon butter, melted**
- **1 teaspoon finely shredded lime peel**
- **1 tablespoon lime juice**

1. Thaw fish, if frozen. Rinse fish; pat dry with paper towels. Cut fish into four serving-size pieces, if necessary; sprinkle with salt and pepper.

2. Place fish on the greased unheated rack of a broiler pan, tucking under any thin edges to make pieces of uniform thickness. Broil 4 to 5 inches from heat until fish begins to flake when tested with a fork. (Allow 4 to 6 minutes per ½-inch thickness of fish.)

3. Meanwhile, in a small bowl stir together cilantro, melted butter, lime peel, and lime juice. To serve, spoon cilantro mixture over fish.

Per 4 ounces: 127 cal., 4 g total fat (2 g sat. fat), 36 mg chol., 259 mg sodium, 1 g carbo., 0 g fiber, 21 g pro.
Daily Values: 10% vit. A, 6% vit. C, 5% calcium, 2% iron
Exchanges: 3 Very Lean Meat, ½ Fat

Pesto-Topped Flounder Packets

Prep: 20 minutes **Bake:** 15 minutes
Oven: 400°F **Makes:** 4 packets

- **4 6-ounce fresh or frozen flounder, sole, or catfish fillets, about ½ inch thick**
- **2 tablespoons lemon juice**
- **2 tablespoons finely chopped shallots (1)**
- **⅛ teaspoon black pepper**
- **1 clove garlic, minced**
- **¼ cup purchased basil pesto or Classic Genovese Pesto (see page 427)**

1. Thaw fish, if frozen. Rinse fish; pat dry with paper towels. Tear off four 24-inch pieces of 12-inch-wide heavy foil. Fold each in half to make four 12-inch squares. Place each fillet on a square of heavy foil. Tuck under thin edges of fish to make pieces of uniform thickness.

2. In a small bowl stir together lemon juice, shallots, pepper, and garlic; spoon over fish. Top with pesto. Bring together two opposite foil edges and seal with a double fold. Fold remaining edges together to completely enclose food, allowing space for steam to build. Place foil packets in a single layer in a 15×10×1-inch baking pan.

3. Bake in a 400°F oven about 15 minutes or until fish begins to flake when tested with a fork. Open packets carefully to allow steam to escape. To serve, transfer packets to plates.

Per packet: 344 cal., 23 g total fat (3 g sat. fat), 81 mg chol., 207 mg sodium, 5 g carbo., 0 g fiber, 29 g pro.
Daily Values: 3% vit. A, 8% vit. C, 2% calcium, 5% iron
Exchanges: 4 Lean Meat, 2½ Fat

Shrimp-Topped Sole

Shrimp-Topped Sole LOW FAT

Prep: 20 minutes **Bake:** 15 minutes
Oven: 425°F **Makes:** 6 servings

- 6 4- to 5-ounce fresh or frozen sole fillets, ½ inch thick
- 8 ounces peeled, deveined, cooked medium shrimp, coarsely chopped, or 6 ounces cooked lump crabmeat (about 1½ cups)
- 1 6.5-ounce container semisoft cheese with dried tomato and basil*
- 6 tablespoons finely shredded Parmesan cheese
- ¼ cup thinly sliced fresh basil or snipped Italian parsley

1. Thaw fish, if frozen. Rinse fish; pat dry with paper towels. Arrange fish in a single layer in a greased 15×10×1-inch baking pan. Sprinkle with *salt* and freshly ground *black pepper.*

2. In a medium bowl combine shrimp and semisoft cheese. Spoon mixture on top of the fish, spreading with the back of a spoon to cover the fillets. Sprinkle with Parmesan cheese. Bake in a 425°F oven about 15 minutes or until fish begins to flake when tested with a fork. To serve, sprinkle with fresh basil.

*Note: If you can't find this product, combine 2 tablespoons snipped oil-packed dried tomatoes with half of an 8-ounce tub cream cheese spread with chive and onion or one 5.2-ounce container semisoft cheese with garlic and herb.

Per fillet: 258 cal., 12 g total fat (7 g sat. fat), 146 mg chol., 455 mg sodium, 2 g carbo., 0 g fiber, 31 g pro.
Daily Values: 13% vit. A, 4% vit. C, 13% calcium, 10% iron
Exchanges: 4½ Very Lean Meat, 2 Fat

Steamed Fish and Vegetables LOW FAT FAST

Start to Finish: 20 minutes **Makes:** 2 servings

- 2 6-ounce fresh or frozen fish fillets, ½ to ¾ inch thick
  Whole fresh basil leaves
- 2 teaspoons shredded fresh ginger
- 1 cup thinly sliced sweet pepper (1 large)
- 8 ounces fresh asparagus spears, trimmed

1. Thaw fish, if frozen. Rinse fish; pat dry with paper towels. Using a sharp knife, make bias cuts ¾ inch apart into the fish fillets. Tuck a basil leaf into each cut. Rub fillets with ginger.

2. Place sweet pepper and asparagus in a steamer basket. Place fish on top of vegetables. Place basket into a large, deep saucepan or wok over 1 inch of boiling water. Cover and steam for 6 to 8 minutes or until fish begins to flake when tested with a fork.

Per fillet + 1 cup vegetables: 143 cal., 1 g total fat (0 g sat. fat), 34 mg chol., 89 mg sodium, 6 g carbo., 2 g fiber, 27 g pro.
Daily Values: 18% vit. A, 73% vit. C, 8% calcium, 10% iron
Exchanges: 1 Vegetable, 3½ Very Lean Meat

Steamed Orange Roughy
LOW FAT FAST

Start to Finish: 20 minutes **Makes:** 4 servings

- 1 to 1¼ pounds fresh or frozen orange roughy, ocean perch, or cod fillets
- 1 medium onion, sliced
- ¼ teaspoon garlic salt
- 4 celery stalks, leafy ends only
- 1 recipe desired sauce (page 305)

1. Thaw fish, if frozen. Rinse fish; pat dry with paper towels. Cut fish into four serving-size pieces, if necessary. Measure thickness of fish; set aside. Fill a large skillet with water to a depth of 1 inch. Bring water to boiling; reduce heat.

2. Meanwhile, arrange onion slices in the bottom of a steamer basket. Place fish on top of onion. Sprinkle fish with garlic salt and a dash *black pepper.* Place steamer over simmering water. Place celery on fish. Cover and simmer gently until fish begins to flake when tested with a fork. Allow 4 to 6 minutes per ½-inch thickness of fish. Discard vegetables. Serve fish with sauce.

Per piece (without sauce): 92 cal., 1 g total fat (0 g sat. fat), 23 mg chol., 160 mg sodium, 3 g carbo., 1 g fiber, 17 g pro.
Daily Values: 2% vit. A, 6% vit. C, 5% calcium, 2% iron
Exchanges: 2½ Very Lean Meat

Fillets and Spinach with Balsamic Vinaigrette LOW FAT   FAST

This one-pan meal combines three powerhouse foods—fish, spinach, and sweet peppers. Healthful eating never looked more inviting or tasted better.

Start to Finish: 30 minutes **Makes:** 4 servings

> 1 **pound fresh or frozen skinless haddock, cod, or other fish fillets, ¾ to 1 inch thick**
> 4 **cups fresh baby spinach leaves, trimmed**
> 1 **medium onion, cut into thin wedges**
> 3 **tablespoons olive oil or cooking oil**
> 1 **medium red or yellow sweet pepper, cut into thin strips**
> ⅛ **teaspoon salt**
> ⅛ **teaspoon black pepper**
> 2 **tablespoons balsamic vinegar**
> 1 **tablespoon honey**

1. Thaw fish, if frozen. Rinse fish; pat dry with paper towels. Cut fish into four serving-size pieces, if necessary. Set aside. Place spinach in a large bowl; set aside.

2. In a large skillet cook onion in 1 tablespoon hot oil over medium heat for 5 to 6 minutes or until tender and slightly golden. Add sweet pepper; cook and stir for 1 minute more. Remove from heat. Stir onion mixture into spinach; transfer to a serving platter. Set aside.

3. Meanwhile, sprinkle fish with salt and black pepper. In same large skillet cook fish in the remaining 2 tablespoons hot oil over medium-high heat for 4 minutes. Carefully turn fish. Reduce heat to medium; cook about 3 minutes more or until fish begins to flake when tested with a fork. Place fish on top of wilted spinach mixture; cover to keep warm.

4. For vinaigrette, in a small bowl stir together the balsamic vinegar and honey. Add to skillet. Cook and stir until heated through, scraping up any browned bits. To serve, spoon vinaigrette over fish and spinach mixture.

Per piece + 1 cup vegetable mixture + 1 tablespoon dressing: 225 cal., 11 g total fat (2 g sat. fat), 49 mg chol., 159 mg sodium, 10 g carbo., 2 g fiber, 22 g pro.
Daily Values: 71% vit. A, 93% vit. C, 6% calcium, 8% iron
Exchanges: 2 Vegetable, 2½ Very Lean Meat, 2 Fat

Sassy Sauces
These sauces are tasty with any fish type.

Curry Mayonnaise: In a small bowl combine ¼ cup mayonnaise or salad dressing, ¼ cup dairy sour cream, 2 tablespoons frozen orange juice concentrate, and ¾ to 1 teaspoon curry powder. Stir in 4 to 5 tablespoons milk to reach drizzling consistency. Cover and chill for up to 24 hours. Makes ½ cup.

Greek Tomato Relish: In a small bowl combine 3 roma tomatoes, seeded and chopped; ½ cup chopped, pitted kalamata olives; ⅓ cup finely chopped red onion; 2 tablespoons olive oil; 1 tablespoon snipped fresh oregano; and 1 tablespoon red wine vinegar. Season to taste with black pepper. Cover and chill for 2 to 24 hours. Makes 1½ cups.

Savory Strawberry Salsa: In a medium bowl combine 2 cups strawberries, coarsely chopped; 1 cup coarsely chopped seeded, peeled avocado; ½ cup coarsely chopped seeded cucumber; 2 tablespoons honey; 1 teaspoon finely shredded lime peel; 2 tablespoons lime juice; 1 to 2 tablespoons seeded and finely chopped fresh jalapeño chile pepper (see tip, page 74); and ¼ teaspoon coarsely cracked black pepper. Cover and chill for 2 to 24 hours. Makes about 3 cups.

Tangy Coconut Sauce: In a small saucepan combine ⅓ cup coconut milk and 1 teaspoon cornstarch. Cook and stir over low heat for 3 to 5 minutes. Let cool. Meanwhile, in a small bowl combine 2 to 4 teaspoons wasabi paste, 2 teaspoons grated fresh ginger, and 1 teaspoon lime juice. Stir in cooled coconut milk mixture. Cover; chill for 2 to 24 hours. Makes about ½ cup.

Tuna with Mango-Mint Salsa

Tuna with Mango-Mint Salsa LOW FAT

Meaty and firm-textured, tuna can be slightly pink in the center when cooked.

Prep: 30 minutes **Chill:** 2 hours
Cook: 8 minutes **Makes:** 4 steaks

- 1 mango, seeded, peeled, and chopped
- ½ cup chopped peeled jicama
- ¼ cup finely chopped red onion
- ¼ cup snipped fresh mint
- ½ to 1 teaspoon finely chopped canned chipotle pepper in adobo sauce
- 1 tablespoon olive oil
- 1 tablespoon honey
- 4 6-ounce fresh or frozen tuna steaks, cut 1 inch thick
- 1 tablespoon olive oil

1. For salsa, in a medium bowl stir together mango, jicama, onion, mint, and chipotle pepper. Drizzle with 1 tablespoon oil and the honey; stir to combine. Cover and chill for 2 to 24 hours.

2. Thaw fish, if frozen. Rinse fish; pat dry with paper towels. In a large skillet cook fish in 1 tablespoon hot oil over medium-high heat for 4 to 6 minutes per side or until fish begins to flake when tested with a fork. Serve fish with salsa.

Per steak + ⅓ cup salsa: 306 cal., 8 g total fat (1 g sat. fat), 76 mg chol., 68 mg sodium, 16 g carbo., 1 g fiber, 40 g pro.
Daily Values: 10% vit. A, 40% vit. C, 4% calcium, 14% iron
Exchanges: 1 Other Carbo., 6 Very Lean Meat, 1 Fat

Marinated Fish Steaks LOW FAT EASY

Prep: 15 minutes **Marinate:** 30 minutes
Broil: 8 minutes **Makes:** 4 servings

- 1 pound fresh or frozen salmon, swordfish, or halibut steaks, cut 1 inch thick
- 2 tablespoons lime juice or lemon juice
- 1 tablespoon snipped fresh oregano or thyme, or ½ teaspoon dried oregano or thyme, crushed
- 2 teaspoons olive oil
- 1 teaspoon lemon-pepper seasoning
- 2 cloves garlic, minced
- 4 lime wedges

1. Thaw fish, if frozen. Rinse fish steaks; pat dry with paper towels. Cut into four serving-size pieces, if necessary. For marinade, in a shallow dish combine lime juice, oregano, oil, lemon-pepper seasoning, and garlic. Add fish; turn to coat. Cover and marinate in refrigerator for 30 minutes to 1½ hours, turning fish pieces occasionally. Drain fish, reserving marinade.

2. Place fish on the greased unheated rack of a broiler pan. Broil 4 inches from the heat for 8 to 12 minutes or until fish begins to flake when tested with a fork, turning once and brushing with reserved marinade halfway through cooking. Discard any remaining marinade. Before serving, squeeze the juice from one lime wedge over each piece.

Per piece: 158 cal., 6 g total fat (1 g sat. fat), 59 mg chol., 348 mg sodium, 2 g carbo., 0 g fiber, 23 g pro.
Daily Values: 3% vit. A, 7% vit. C, 2% calcium, 5% iron
Exchanges: 3 Lean Meat

 Basil Halibut Steaks

Prep: 25 minutes **Broil:** 8 minutes **Makes:** 4 steaks

- 4 5- to 6-ounce fresh or frozen halibut steaks, cut 1 inch thick
- ½ cup chopped onion (1 medium)
- 1 clove garlic, minced
- 1 tablespoon olive oil
- 2 cups chopped, peeled tomato (4 medium)
- 4 tablespoons snipped fresh basil
- 2 tablespoons butter, melted
  Nonstick cooking spray

1. Thaw fish, if frozen. Rinse fish steaks; pat dry with paper towels. Set aside. In a medium skillet cook onion and garlic in hot oil until tender. Stir in tomato, ¼ teaspoon *salt*, and

¼ teaspoon *black pepper.* Bring to boiling; reduce heat. Simmer, uncovered, for 15 minutes. Stir in 2 tablespoons of the basil.

2. Meanwhile, combine remaining basil and melted butter; brush over one side of steaks.

3. Lightly coat the unheated rack of a broiler pan with cooking spray. Place fish, brushed sides up, on broiler pan. Broil 4 inches from the heat for 8 to 12 minutes or until fish begins to flake when tested with a fork, turning once halfway through cooking.

4. Season fish to taste with additional salt and pepper. Serve with tomato mixture.

Per steak: 274 cal., 13 g total fat (4 g sat. fat), 61 mg chol., 273 mg sodium, 8 g carbo., 2 g fiber, 31 g pro.
Daily Values: 33% vit. A, 32% vit. C, 9% calcium, 10% iron
Exchanges: 1 Vegetable, 4 Very Lean Meat, 2½ Fat

Poached Fish Steaks with Peppers LOW FAT

Prep: 25 minutes **Cook:** 8 minutes **Makes:** 4 steaks

> 4   5- to 6-ounce fresh or frozen tuna, halibut, or salmon steaks, cut 1 inch thick
> 1½   cups dry white wine or chicken broth
> 1½   cups chopped yellow sweet pepper (2 medium)
> 3   tablespoons capers, drained
> ¼ to ½   teaspoon crushed red pepper
> 4   cloves garlic, minced
> 2   tablespoons basil-flavored oil or olive oil
> Coarsely chopped fresh parsley

1. Thaw fish, if frozen. Rinse fish steaks; pat dry with paper towels. In a large skillet combine wine, 1 cup *water*, sweet pepper, capers, crushed red pepper, and garlic. Bring to boiling; reduce heat. Simmer, uncovered, for 7 minutes, stirring occasionally.

2. Place fish in a single layer in the liquid in the skillet. Season fish with *salt* and *black pepper.* Spoon liquid over fish. Return to simmer. Cook, covered, for 8 to 12 minutes or until fish begins to flake when tested with a fork. Transfer fish to a serving platter. Drain peppers and capers from poaching liquid; discard liquid. Drizzle cooked fish with the oil and serve with pepper mixture. Sprinkle with parsley.

Per steak: 288 cal., 11 g total fat (2 g sat. fat), 54 mg chol., 433 mg sodium, 7 g carbo., 1 g fiber, 37 g pro.
Daily Values: 11% vit. A, 289% vit. C, 10% calcium, 12% iron
Exchanges: ½ Vegetable, 5 Very Lean Meat, 2 Fat

Herbed Trout with Lemon Butter

Prep: 20 minutes **Bake:** 15 minutes
Oven: 450°F **Makes:** 4 trout

> 4   8- to 10-ounce fresh or frozen dressed, boned rainbow trout or other dressed fish
> ¼   cup butter, melted
> 1   teaspoon finely shredded lemon peel (set aside)
> 3   tablespoons lemon juice
> ¼   cup finely chopped onion
> 1   tablespoon snipped fresh rosemary or tarragon
> ½   teaspoon salt
> ¼   teaspoon black pepper
> Snipped fresh parsley (optional)
> Lemon wedges

1. Thaw fish, if frozen. Rinse fish; pat dry with paper towels. On a cutting board, spread each fish open, skin side down. In a small bowl stir together melted butter and lemon juice. Set half of the butter mixture aside. Brush remaining half of the butter mixture over fish. In a small bowl stir together lemon peel, onion, rosemary, salt, and pepper. Sprinkle onion mixture over fish. Fold fish closed. Place fish on a greased 15×10×1-inch baking pan.

2. Bake in a 450°F oven about 15 minutes or until fish begins to flake when tested with a fork. If desired, sprinkle fish with parsley. Serve fish with reserved butter mixture and lemon wedges.

Per trout: 311 cal., 20 g total fat (8 g sat. fat), 116 mg chol., 427 mg sodium, 2 g carbo., 0 g fiber, 30 g pro.
Daily Values: 15% vit. A, 17% vit. C, 10% calcium, 3% iron
Exchanges: 4 Very Lean Meat, 4 Fat

Seafood Dinner

Lemon and butter accent the delicate flavor of baked trout. Try drizzling some of the lemon-butter mixture over the rice.

- *Herbed Trout with Lemon Butter (above)*
- *Hot cooked rice*
- *Steamed snow peas*
- *Apple salad*
- *Chocolate mousse*

Tuna-Noodle Casserole

We brought this classic casserole in sync with today's tastes by seasoning it with zippy dry mustard and stirring in cheddar cheese and roasted red sweet pepper.

Prep: 25 minutes **Bake:** 20 minutes
Oven: 375°F **Makes:** 4 servings

    3 cups medium noodles (4 ounces) or 1 cup
        elbow macaroni (3½ ounces)
    ½ cup soft bread crumbs
    1 tablespoon butter, melted
    1 cup chopped celery (2 stalks)
    ¼ cup chopped onion
    ¼ cup butter or margarine
    ¼ cup all-purpose flour
    ½ teaspoon salt
    ½ teaspoon dry mustard
    ¼ teaspoon black pepper
    2 cups milk
    1 9- or 9.25-ounce can tuna, drained and
        broken into chunks, or two 6-ounce cans
        skinless, boneless salmon, drained
    1 cup cheddar cheese cubes (4 ounces)
    ¼ cup chopped roasted red sweet pepper or
        pimiento

1. Cook noodles according to package directions. Drain and set aside. Meanwhile, combine bread crumbs and 1 tablespoon melted butter; set aside.

2. For sauce, in a medium saucepan cook celery and onion in ¼ cup hot butter until tender. Stir in flour, salt, dry mustard, and black pepper. Add milk all at once; cook and stir until slightly thickened and bubbly. Combine cooked noodles, sauce, tuna, cheese cubes, and roasted pepper. Transfer to a 1½-quart casserole. Sprinkle with crumb mixture. Bake, uncovered, in a 375°F oven for 20 to 25 minutes or until bubbly and top is golden.

Per 1⅓ cups: 588 cal., 34 g total fat (18 g sat. fat), 127 mg chol., 986 mg sodium, 37 g carbo., 2 g fiber, 34 g pro.
Daily Values: 24% vit. A, 47% vit. C, 39% calcium, 13% iron
Exchanges: 2½ Starch, 4 Very Lean Meat, 5 Fat

Vegetable Tuna-Noodle Casserole: Prepare as above, except add 1 cup frozen vegetables, thawed, with the tuna and use a 2-quart casserole. Makes 4 servings.

Per 1½ cups: 615 cal., 34 g total fat (18 g sat. fat), 127 mg chol., 1,002 mg sodium, 43 g carbo., 4 g fiber, 35 g pro.
Daily Values: 63% vit. A, 50% vit. C, 40% calcium, 16% iron
Exchanges: 3 Starch, 4 Very Lean Meat, 5 Fat

Caesar Salmon Pizzas

Caesar Salmon Pizzas FAST

Plan on one pizza per diner for a main dish. To serve as an appetizer, cut each pizza in quarters.

Prep: 15 minutes **Bake:** 8 minutes
Oven: 400°F **Makes:** 2 pizzas

    2 6-inch Italian bread shells (Boboli)
    ¼ cup bottled creamy Caesar salad dressing
    2 cups torn fresh spinach
    2 ounces smoked salmon, flaked, and skin
        and bones removed
    ¼ cup walnut pieces, toasted (see tip,
        page 265)
    ¼ cup finely shredded Parmesan cheese
        (1 ounce)
    2 tablespoons thinly sliced green onion (1)
    1 teaspoon capers, drained (optional)

1. Lightly spread bread shells with some of the Caesar salad dressing. Place the bread shells on a baking sheet.

2. Top bread shells with spinach, salmon, walnuts, half of the Parmesan cheese, the green onion, and, if desired, capers.

3. Bake in a 400°F oven for 8 to 10 minutes or just until heated through. Drizzle with remaining Caesar dressing; sprinkle with remaining Parmesan cheese.

Per pizza: 652 cal., 39 g total fat (6 g sat. fat), 19 mg chol., 1,480 mg sodium, 54 g carbo., 4 g fiber, 26 g pro.
Daily Values: 20% vit. A, 15% vit. C, 33% calcium, 32% iron
Exchanges: 1 Vegetable, 3 Starch, 3 Lean Meat, 6 Fat

Salmon Patties

Start to Finish: 30 minutes **Makes:** 4 servings

- 1 **egg, beaten**
- ¼ **cup milk**
- ¼ **cup chopped green onion (2)**
- 1 **tablespoon snipped fresh dill or 1 teaspoon dried dill**
- ¼ **teaspoon black pepper**
- 1 **14.75-ounce can salmon, drained, flaked, and skin and bones removed**
- ¼ **cup fine dry bread crumbs**
- 1 **tablespoon cooking oil**
- 1 **recipe Honey-Mustard Sauce or Tartar Sauce (page 522) (optional)**

1. In a medium bowl combine the egg, milk, green onion, dill, and pepper. Add salmon and bread crumbs; mix well. Form mixture into eight ½-inch-thick patties. In a large skillet cook patties in hot oil over medium-low heat about 6 minutes or until golden brown, turning once. If desired, serve with Honey-Mustard Sauce.

Per 2 patties: 231 cal., 12 g total fat (3 g sat. fat), 112 mg chol., 656 mg sodium, 6 g carbo., 0 g fiber, 24 g pro.
Daily Values: 4% vit. A, 2% vit. C, 26% calcium, 9% iron
Exchanges: ½ Starch, 3 Very Lean Meat, 1½ Fat

Honey-Mustard Sauce: In a small bowl stir together ¼ cup mayonnaise or salad dressing and 1 tablespoon honey mustard. Cover and chill until serving time.

Baked Coconut Shrimp with Curried Apricot Sauce

Prep: 30 minutes **Bake:** 10 minutes
Oven: 400°F **Makes:** 6 servings

- 24 **fresh or frozen jumbo shrimp in shells**
- 1 **cup mayonnaise or salad dressing**
- 3 **tablespoons apricot preserves**
- 1 **teaspoon curry powder**
- 2 **tablespoons cooking oil**
- 1½ **cups shredded unsweetened coconut, toasted (see tip, page 265)**
- ¼ **cup cornstarch**
- 1 **tablespoon sugar**
- ½ **teaspoon salt**
- 3 **egg whites, slightly beaten**

1. Thaw shrimp, if frozen. Peel and devein shrimp, leaving tails intact (see photos, page 296). Rinse shrimp; pat dry with paper towels. Set aside.

2. For sauce, in a small bowl stir together mayonnaise, apricot preserves, and curry powder. Cover and chill until ready to serve.

3. Spread the oil on bottom of a 15×10×1-inch baking pan; set pan aside. In a shallow dish combine coconut, cornstarch, sugar, and salt. Place the egg whites in a small shallow dish. Dip shrimp into the egg whites; coat shrimp with coconut mixture, pressing the mixture firmly onto the shrimp. Arrange shrimp in the prepared pan. Bake in a 400°F oven about 10 minutes or until shrimp are opaque and coconut is golden, turning once. Serve with sauce.

Per 4 shrimp + 3 tablespoons sauce: 545 cal., 42 g total fat (11 g sat. fat), 172 mg chol., 585 mg sodium, 19 g carbo., 2 g fiber, 23 g pro.
Daily Values: 5% vit. A, 6% vit. C, 7% calcium, 17% iron
Exchanges: 1 Other Carbo., 3 Very Lean Meat, 5 Fat

Garlic-and-Herb Shrimp Saute

Spur-of-the-moment hosting is no hassle with this simple but delightfully sumptuous entrée.

Start to Finish: 25 minutes **Makes:** 4 servings

- 1½ **pounds fresh or frozen large shrimp in shells**
- ⅓ **cup thinly sliced leek (1 medium) or thinly sliced green onion (3)**
- ½ **teaspoon dried basil, oregano, or tarragon, crushed**
- 4 **cloves garlic, minced**
- 2 **tablespoons olive oil**
- 2 **tablespoons dry white wine or dry sherry**
- 1 **tablespoon lemon juice**
- ¼ **teaspoon salt**
- ¼ **teaspoon black pepper**
- 1 **tablespoon snipped fresh parsley**

1. Thaw shrimp, if frozen. Peel and devein shrimp, leaving tails intact (see photos, page 296). Rinse shrimp; pat dry with paper towels. Set aside.

2. In a large skillet cook and stir shrimp, leek, basil, and garlic in hot oil over medium heat for 2 to 4 minutes or until shrimp are opaque. Carefully add wine, lemon juice, salt, and pepper to skillet. Cook and stir just until heated through. Stir in parsley.

Per 4 ounces: 211 cal., 9 g total fat (1 g sat. fat), 194 mg chol., 337 mg sodium, 4 g carbo., 0 g fiber, 26 g pro.
Daily Values: 8% vit. A, 11% vit. C, 8% calcium, 18% iron
Exchanges: 4 Very Lean Meat, 1½ Fat

Shrimp Scampi `FAST`

Prep: 15 minutes **Broil:** 5 minutes **Makes:** 4 servings

- 1½ **pounds fresh or frozen large shrimp in shells**
- ¼ **cup butter, melted**
- ¼ **cup olive oil**
- 6 **cloves garlic, minced**
- 2 **tablespoons snipped fresh parsley**
- 1 **teaspoon finely shredded lemon peel**
- ¼ **teaspoon salt**
- ¼ **teaspoon black pepper**

1. Thaw shrimp, if frozen. Peel and devein shrimp, leaving tails intact (see photos, page 296). Rinse shrimp; pat dry with paper towels. Set aside.

2. In a 13×9×2-inch baking pan combine butter, oil, and garlic. Broil 4 to 5 inches from the heat for 2 minutes. Add shrimp, parsley, lemon peel, salt, and pepper to baking pan. Toss ingredients to coat shrimp. Broil for 2 minutes. Turn shrimp over and broil about 1 minute more or until shrimp are opaque. If desired, serve with *lemon wedges.*

Per 4 ounces: 370 cal., 28 g total fat (8 g sat. fat), 226 mg chol., 423 mg sodium, 3 g carbo., 0 g fiber, 26 g pro.
Daily Values: 15% vit. A, 11% vit. C, 8% calcium, 17% iron
Exchanges: 4 Very Lean Meat, 5½ Fat

Shrimp Tips

Raw shrimp in the shell, available fresh or frozen, is sold by the pound. Use this list as a reference for market names and the number of shrimp per pound.

Market Name	Number per Pound
Colossal	Fewer than 15
Extra Jumbo	16 to 20
Jumbo	20 to 25
Extra large	26 to 30
Large	31 to 40
Medium large	36 to 40
Medium	41 to 50
Small	50 to 60
Extra Small	61 to 70

Equivalents: 12 ounces raw shrimp in the shell is equal to 8 ounces raw, shelled shrimp, one 4.5-ounce can shrimp, or 1 cup cooked, shelled shrimp.

Stir-Fried Shrimp and Broccoli `LOW FAT`

Wok or skillet—either pan works fine for stir-frying. Keep the food moving so it cooks quickly and evenly in the hot pan. See photo, page 293.

Start to Finish: 45 minutes **Makes:** 4 servings

- 1 **pound fresh or frozen medium shrimp in shells or 12 ounces fresh or frozen scallops**
- ⅓ **cup water**
- ¼ **cup soy sauce**
- 2 **tablespoons rice vinegar or 1 tablespoon cider vinegar**
- 1 **tablespoon cornstarch**
- 1½ **teaspoons sugar**
- 2 **cloves garlic, minced**
- 1 **tablespoon cooking oil**
- 2 **cups broccoli florets**
- 1 **cup thinly bias-sliced carrot (2)**
- 1 **small onion, halved lengthwise and sliced**
- 1 **cup sliced fresh mushrooms**
- 2 **cups hot cooked rice or 8 ounces packaged dried vermicelli or fusilli, cooked and drained**
- ¼ **cup cashews or sliced almonds, toasted (see tip, page 265)**

1. Thaw shrimp or scallops, if frozen. If using shrimp, peel and devein, leaving tails intact (see photos, page 296). If using scallops, cut any large scallops in half. Rinse shrimp or scallops; pat dry with paper towels. Set aside. In a small bowl combine water, soy sauce, vinegar, cornstarch, and sugar; set aside.

2. In a wok or a 12-inch skillet cook and stir garlic in hot oil over medium-high heat for 15 seconds. (Add more oil as necessary during cooking.) Add broccoli, carrot, and onion. Cook and stir for 3 minutes. Add mushrooms; cook and stir for 1 to 2 minutes more or until vegetables are crisp-tender. Remove vegetables from wok with slotted spoon. Stir soy sauce mixture. Add to wok; cook and stir until slightly thickened and bubbly. Add shrimp or scallops; cook about 3 minutes or until shrimp or scallops are opaque. Stir in vegetables; heat through. Serve with rice and sprinkle with cashews.

Per 1 cup shrimp and vegetable mixture + ½ cup rice: 446 cal., 10 g total fat (2 g sat. fat), 129 mg chol., 1,075 mg sodium, 57 g carbo., 4 g fiber, 31 g pro.
Daily Values: 186% vit. A, 67% vit. C, 9% calcium, 28% iron
Exchanges: 2 Vegetable, 3 Starch, 2½ Very Lean Meat, 1½ Fat

Shrimp Creole `LOW FAT`

Prep: 25 minutes **Cook:** 15 minutes **Makes:** 4 servings

- 1 **pound fresh or frozen medium shrimp in shells**
- ½ **cup chopped onion (1 medium)**
- ½ **cup chopped celery (1 stalk)**
- ½ **cup chopped green sweet pepper (1 small)**
- 2 **cloves garlic, minced**
- 2 **tablespoons butter or margarine**
- 1 **14.5-ounce can diced tomatoes, undrained**
- ½ **teaspoon paprika**
- ¼ **teaspoon salt**
- ⅛ **to ¼ teaspoon cayenne pepper**
- 2 **tablespoons snipped fresh parsley**
- 2 **cups hot cooked rice**

1. Thaw shrimp, if frozen. Peel and devein shrimp, removing tails (see photos, page 296). Rinse shrimp; pat dry. Set aside.

2. In a skillet cook onion, celery, sweet pepper, and garlic in hot butter over medium heat about 5 minutes or until tender. Stir in undrained tomatoes, paprika, salt, and cayenne pepper. Bring to boiling; reduce heat. Simmer, uncovered, for 5 to 8 minutes or until thickened.

3. Stir shrimp and parsley into tomato mixture. Cook, stirring frequently, for 2 to 4 minutes or until shrimp are opaque. Serve over rice.

Per 1 cup shrimp mixture + ½ cup rice: 290 cal., 8 g total fat (3 g sat. fat), 145 mg chol., 498 mg sodium, 32 g carbo., 2 g fiber, 21 g pro.
Daily Values: 16% vit. A, 57% vit. C, 11% calcium, 16% iron
Exchanges: 1 Vegetable, 1½ Starch, 2½ Very Lean Meat, 1 Fat

Fish Creole: Prepare as above, except substitute 12 ounces fresh or frozen skinless, firm-fleshed fish fillets (such as catfish, cod, or grouper) for the shrimp. Thaw fish, if frozen. Rinse fish and cut into 1-inch pieces. Add fish to tomato mixture with parsley. Cook, stirring frequently, about 3 minutes or until fish begins to flake when tested with a fork.

Per 1 cup fish mixture + ½ cup rice: 269 cal., 7 g total fat (3 g sat. fat), 52 mg chol., 418 mg sodium, 31 g carbo., 2 g fiber, 18 g pro.
Daily Values: 14% vit. A, 55% vit. C, 8% calcium, 7% iron.
Exchanges: 1 Vegetable, 1½ Starch, 2 Very Lean Meat, 1 Fat

Crawfish Étouffée

Prep: 25 minutes **Cook:** 50 minutes **Makes:** 6 servings

- ⅓ **cup cooking oil**
- ⅓ **cup all-purpose flour**
- 2 **cups chopped onion (2 large)**
- 1 **cup chopped celery (2 stalks)**
- ½ **cup chopped green sweet pepper (1 small)**
- 1 **14-ounce can chicken broth**
- ¼ **cup sliced green onion (2)**
- ¼ **cup snipped fresh parsley**
- 6 **cloves garlic, minced**
- 1 **teaspoon seasoned salt**
- 1 **bay leaf**
- 1 **pound fresh or frozen peeled, cooked crawfish, thawed, or 1½ pounds shrimp, peeled, deveined, and coarsely chopped**
- 3 **cups hot cooked rice**

1. For roux, in a large skillet heat the ⅓ cup oil over medium heat for 3 minutes. Gradually stir in the flour until smooth. Cook over medium-low heat about 20 minutes or until the mixture is dark reddish brown, stirring frequently.

2. Add onion, celery, and sweet pepper; cook over medium heat for 10 minutes, stirring occasionally. Stir in broth, green onion, parsley, garlic, seasoned salt, and bay leaf.

3. Bring to boiling; reduce heat. Simmer, covered, 10 minutes. Add crawfish; cook until warmed through (if using shrimp, cook until shrimp are opaque). Discard bay leaf. Serve over rice.

Per 1 cup crawfish mixture + ½ cup rice: 329 cal., 13 g total fat (2 g sat. fat), 40 mg chol., 648 mg sodium, 36 g carbo., 3 g fiber, 17 g pro.
Daily Values: 12% vit. A, 42% vit. C, 8% calcium, 13% iron
Exchanges: ½ Vegetable, 2 Starch, 2 Very Lean Meat, 2 Fat

Shrimp Creole

Scallops with Dill Sauce

Scallops with Dill Sauce `FAST`

Prep: 20 minutes **Broil:** 8 minutes **Makes:** 4 kabobs

- 1 **pound fresh or frozen sea scallops**
- 3 **tablespoons butter, melted**
- ¼ **teaspoon black pepper**
- ⅛ **teaspoon paprika**
- 1 **recipe Dill Sauce**

1. Thaw scallops, if frozen. Rinse scallops; pat dry with paper towels. Halve any large scallops. Thread scallops onto four 8- to 10-inch skewers, leaving a ¼-inch space between pieces. Preheat broiler. Place skewers on the greased unheated rack of a broiler pan.

2. In a small bowl stir together melted butter, pepper, and paprika. Brush half of the mixture over scallops. Broil about 4 inches from the heat for 8 to 10 minutes or until scallops are opaque, turning and brushing with the remaining melted butter mixture halfway through broiling. Serve scallops with Dill Sauce.

Dill Sauce: In a small bowl stir together ⅔ cup mayonnaise, 1 tablespoon finely chopped onion, 2 teaspoons lemon juice, and 1½ teaspoons snipped fresh dill or ½ teaspoon dried dill.

Per kabob + 3 tablespoons sauce: 451 cal., 39 g total fat (9 g sat. fat), 88 mg chol., 475 mg sodium, 3 g carbo., 0 g fiber, 19 g pro.
Daily Values: 7% vit. A, 7% vit. C, 3% calcium, 2% iron
Exchanges: 3 Very Lean Meat, 7½ Fat

Seared Scallops in Garlic Butter `LOW FAT` `FAST`

Start to Finish: 20 minutes **Makes:** 4 servings

- 1 **pound fresh or frozen sea scallops**
- 3 **cloves garlic, minced**
- 2 **tablespoons butter**
- 2 **tablespoons dry white wine**
- 1 **tablespoon snipped fresh chives or parsley**
- ⅛ **teaspoon salt**

1. Thaw scallops, if frozen. Rinse scallops; pat dry with paper towels.

2. In a 12-inch skillet cook garlic in 1 tablespoon hot butter over medium-high heat for 30 seconds. Add the scallops. Cook, stirring frequently, for 2 to 3 minutes or until scallops turn opaque. Remove from skillet and transfer to a serving platter. Add the remaining 1 tablespoon butter and the wine to the skillet. Cook and stir to loosen any browned bits. Pour over scallops; sprinkle with chives and salt.

Seared Shrimp in Garlic Butter: Prepare as above, except substitute 1½ pounds fresh or frozen medium shrimp in shells for the scallops. Thaw shrimp, if frozen. Peel and devein shrimp, leaving tails intact. Rinse shrimp; pat dry with paper towels. Cook shrimp in butter and garlic for 1 to 3 minutes or until shrimp turn opaque. Continue as above.

Per 3 ounces scallops or shrimp variation: 183 cal., 8 g total fat (4 g sat. fat), 189 mg chol., 303 mg sodium, 2 g carbo., 0 g fiber, 23 g pro.
Daily Values: 9% vit. A, 5% vit. C, 7% calcium, 14% iron
Exchanges: 3 Very Lean Meat, 1½ Fat

The Scoop on Scallops

You'll find two types of scallops at the market. They differ in size, so be sure to buy the type specified in your recipe.

Sea scallops are harvested off the New England coast. On average, there are 20 to 40 of them per pound.

Bay scallops are smaller than sea scallops, averaging from 70 to 100 per pound. Sweet and mild-tasting, they cook quickly.

Crab Cakes

Prep: 40 minutes **Chill:** 1 hour
Cook: 6 minutes per batch **Makes:** 4 servings

- 2 **tablespoons chopped green onion (1)**
- 1 **tablespoon butter**
- 1 **tablespoon all-purpose flour**
- ¼ **teaspoon seafood seasoning**
- ½ **cup milk**
- 1 **6- to 8-ounce package frozen lump crabmeat, thawed, or one 6-ounce can crabmeat, drained, flaked, and cartilage removed**
- 2 **tablespoons panko (Japanese-style bread crumbs) or fine dry bread crumbs**
- ¾ **cup panko (Japanese-style bread crumbs) or fine dry bread crumbs**
- 1 **egg**
- ¼ **cup all-purpose flour**
- 2 **tablespoons cooking oil**
- ¼ **cup Chutney Mustard**

1. In a small saucepan cook onion in hot butter until tender. Stir in the 1 tablespoon flour, seafood seasoning, and ⅛ teaspoon *black pepper.* Add milk all at once. Cook and stir until thickened and bubbly. Transfer to a medium bowl. Cover and chill about 1 hour or until cold.

2. Stir crabmeat and the 2 tablespoons panko into chilled sauce. Place the ¾ cup panko in a shallow dish. In a second shallow dish beat together egg and 1 teaspoon *water.* Place the ¼ cup flour in a third shallow dish.

3. Form about 2 tablespoons of the crab mixture into a small patty. Dip patty into flour. Carefully turn to coat. Dip in egg mixture, then in bread crumbs. Set on a sheet of waxed paper. Repeat with remaining crab mixture, flour, egg mixture, and crumbs.

4. In a large skillet heat oil over medium heat. Add crab cakes, half at a time. Cook about 3 minutes on each side or until golden and heated through. Serve with Chutney Mustard. (Chill leftover Chutney Mustard for another use.)

Chutney Mustard: In a small bowl combine ½ cup purchased chutney (snip any large pieces), 1½ teaspoons Dijon-style mustard, and 1 teaspoon lemon juice.

Per 2 crab cakes + 1 tablespoon mustard: 274 cal., 13 g total fat (3 g sat. fat), 106 mg chol., 274 mg sodium, 24 g carbo., 1 g fiber, 14 g pro.
Daily Values: 7% vit. A, 10% vit. C, 10% calcium, 8% iron
Exchanges: 1 Starch, ½ Other Carbo., 1½ Very Lean Meat, 2 Fat

Fried Soft-Shell Crabs `LOW FAT`

Live soft-shell crabs are available mid-May through September. Cleaned and frozen soft-shells can be purchased year-round. If using frozen crabs, begin preparation with Step 2.

Prep: 30 minutes **Cook:** 2½ minutes per batch
Makes: 4 servings

- 4 **large or 8 small live soft-shell blue crabs**
- 1 **egg, beaten**
- ¼ **cup milk**
- ½ **cup all-purpose flour**
- ¼ **teaspoon salt**
- ⅛ **teaspoon cayenne pepper**
  Shortening or cooking oil for frying

1. Immerse crabs in ice water. (This numbs them and makes them easier to handle.) To clean each crab, hold it between its back legs. Insert a knife into the brain at top of the skull to kill it. Using kitchen scissors, remove the head by cutting horizontally across the body ½ inch behind the eyes. Lift one pointed side of the soft top shell to expose the gills (the spongy projectiles). Using your fingers, push up on the gills and pull off. Replace the soft top shell over the body. Repeat on the other side. Turn crab over. Fold back the tail flap (apron); twist off and discard. Thoroughly rinse crabs under cold running water and pat dry with paper towels.

2. In a shallow dish combine egg and milk. In another shallow dish combine flour, salt, and cayenne pepper. Dip crabs in egg mixture; roll in flour mixture, coating evenly.

3. In a medium or large skillet heat ½ inch shortening over medium heat to 365°F. Carefully add two or three crabs, back sides down. Fry for 1½ to 2 minutes or until golden. Turn carefully. Fry for 1 to 2 minutes more or until crabs are crisp and golden. Drain on paper towels. Keep warm in a 300°F oven while frying the remaining crabs.

Per 1 large or 2 small crabs: 169 cal., 9 g total fat (2 g sat. fat), 104 mg chol., 375 mg sodium, 13 g carbo., 0 g fiber, 9 g pro.
Daily Values: 5% vit. A, 1% vit. C, 19% calcium, 9% iron
Exchanges: 1 Starch, 1 Very Lean Meat, 1½ Fat

Broiled Crab Legs

If split crab legs aren't available from your grocer, purchase whole legs. See the photo below for directions on splitting crab legs at home.

Start to Finish: 15 minutes **Makes:** 4 servings

- 1½ **pounds fresh or frozen crab legs, split (see photo, below)**
-   3 **tablespoons unsalted butter, melted**
-   1 **tablespoon snipped fresh basil or**
      1 **teaspoon dried basil, crushed**
-   ½ **teaspoon finely shredded lemon peel**
-   1 **tablespoon lemon juice**
-   1 **recipe Clarified Butter (optional) (right)**

1. Thaw crab legs, if frozen. Rinse and pat dry with paper towels. Place crab legs, cut sides up, on the greased unheated rack of a broiler pan. Stir together melted butter, basil, lemon peel, and lemon juice. Brush crab legs with butter mixture. Broil 4 to 6 inches from the heat for 3 to 4 minutes or until heated through. If desired, serve crab legs with Clarified Butter.

Per 4 ounces: 154 cal., 10 g total fat (6 g sat. fat), 64 mg chol., 799 mg sodium, 0 g carbo., 0 g fiber, 15 g pro.
Daily Values: 8% vit. A, 13% vit. C, 5% calcium, 3% iron
Exchanges: 2 Very Lean Meat, 2 Fat

Using kitchen shears, cut through the lighter-colored underside of each crab leg. Lay a partially split leg on a cutting board. Cut through the hard shell with a sharp knife, completely splitting the leg.

Boiled Lobster

Prep: 35 minutes **Cook:** 20 minutes **Makes:** 2 lobsters

-   8 **quarts water**
-   2 **teaspoons salt**
-   2 **1- to 1½-pound live lobsters**
-   1 **recipe Clarified Butter**

1. In a 12-quart kettle bring water and salt to boiling. Grasp lobsters just behind the eyes; rinse them under cold running water. Quickly plunge lobsters headfirst into the boiling water. Return to boiling; reduce heat. Simmer, covered, for 20 minutes. Drain lobsters, remove bands or pegs on large claws.

2. When cool enough to handle, place each lobster on its back. Separate the lobster tail from the body (see photo 1, above right). Cut away the tail membrane to expose the meat (see photo 2, below). Remove and discard the black vein running through the tail. Remove meat from tail. Twist the large claws away from the body (see photo 3, below). Using a nutcracker, break open the claws (see photo 4, below). Remove the meat from the claws. Crack the shell on remaining part of the body; remove meat with a small fork. Discard the green tomalley (liver) and the coral roe (found in female lobsters). Serve lobster meat with Clarified Butter.

Clarified Butter: Melt ¼ cup butter over very low heat without stirring; cool slightly. Pour off clear top layer; discard milky bottom layer.

Per lobster + 2 tablespoons butter: 340 cal., 25 g total fat (15 g sat. fat), 158 mg chol., 1,023 mg sodium, 2 g carbo., 0 g fiber, 26 g pro.
Daily Values: 21% vit. A, 9% calcium, 3% iron
Exchanges: 4 Very Lean Meat, 4½ Fat

1. To remove the tail from a lobster, twist the tail and body in opposite directions.

2. Using kitchen shears, cut away the membrane from the tail to expose the meat. Discard the intestinal vein that runs through the tail.

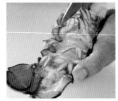

3. Twist off the large claws where they join the body.

4. Pull off and discard the small pincer from each claw. Using a nutcracker, break open the claws. Use a seafood fork to remove the meat.

Broiled Lobster Tails with Garlic-Chili Butter `FAST`

Prep: 15 minutes **Broil:** 12 minutes **Makes:** 4 servings

- **4 8-ounce fresh or frozen lobster tails**
- **1 clove garlic, minced**
- **1 teaspoon finely shredded orange peel**
- **½ teaspoon chili powder**
- **¼ cup butter**
- **1 recipe Clarified Butter (optional) (page 314)**

1. Thaw lobster tails, if frozen. Preheat broiler. Butterfly the lobster tails by cutting through the center of the hard top shells and meat. Spread the tail halves apart. Place lobster tails, meat sides up, on the unheated rack of a broiler pan.

2. In a small skillet cook garlic, orange peel, and chili powder in butter over medium heat about 30 seconds or until garlic is tender. Brush mixture over lobster meat.

3. Broil 4 inches from heat for 12 to 14 minutes or until lobster meat is opaque. If desired, serve with Clarified Butter.

Per lobster tail: 238 cal., 14 g total fat (6 g sat. fat), 167 mg chol., 509 mg sodium, 1 g carbo., 0 g fiber, 27 g pro.
Daily Values: 11% vit. A, 2% vit. C, 7% calcium, 2% iron
Exchanges: 3½ Very Lean Meat, 3 Fat

Oysters au Gratin

Prep: 30 minutes **Bake:** 10 minutes
Oven: 400°F **Makes:** 4 servings

- **2 pints shucked oysters (see photos 1 and 2, above right)**
- **3 tablespoons butter**
- **1 cup sliced fresh mushrooms**
- **1 clove garlic, minced**
- **2 tablespoons all-purpose flour**
- **¾ cup milk**
- **¼ cup dry white wine**
- **2 tablespoons snipped fresh parsley**
- **½ teaspoon Worcestershire sauce**
- **¾ cup soft bread crumbs**
- **¼ cup grated Parmesan cheese**
- **1 tablespoon butter, melted**

1. Rinse oysters; pat dry with paper towels. In a large skillet cook and stir oysters in 1 tablespoon hot butter over medium heat for 3 to 4 minutes or until oyster edges curl; drain. Divide oysters among four 8- to 10-ounce casseroles or four 10-ounce custard cups.

2. For sauce, in the same skillet cook mushrooms and garlic in the remaining 2 tablespoons hot butter until tender. Stir in flour. Add milk all at once. Cook and stir until thickened and bubbly. Stir in wine, parsley, and Worcestershire sauce. Spoon over oysters. In a small bowl toss together bread crumbs, Parmesan cheese, and the 1 tablespoon melted butter. Sprinkle over casseroles. Bake in a 400°F oven about 10 minutes or until crumbs are brown.

Per casserole: 345 cal., 19 g total fat (10 g sat. fat), 98 mg chol., 722 mg sodium, 23 g carbo., 1 g fiber, 18 g pro.
Daily Values: 15% vit. A, 24% vit. C, 26% calcium, 78% iron
Exchanges: 1½ Starch, 2 Very Lean Meat, 3½ Fat

1. To shuck an oyster, hold the oyster in a heavy towel or mitt. Insert an oyster knife tip into the hinge between the shells. Move blade along the inside of the upper shell to free muscle, twisting the knife to pry the shell open.

2. Slide the knife under the oyster to sever the muscle from the bottom shell.

Broiled Lobster Tails with Garlic-Chili Butter

Selecting and Cooking Shellfish

Refer to these directions for cooking fresh shellfish. Many types of shellfish are available partially prepared or even cooked. Ask at the fish and shellfish counter for additional information when making purchases.

Shellfish Type	Amount Per Serving	Preparing	Cooking
Clams	6 clams in the shell	Scrub live clams under cold running water. For 24 clams in shells, in an 8-quart Dutch oven combine 4 quarts of cold water and ⅓ cup salt. Add clams and soak for 15 minutes; drain and rinse. Discard water. Repeat.	For 24 clams in shells, add ½ inch water to an 8-quart kettle; bring to boiling. Place clams in a steamer basket. Steam, covered, for 5 to 7 minutes or until clams open. Discard any that do not open.
Crabs, hard-shell	1 pound live crabs	Grasp live crabs from behind, firmly holding the back two legs on each side. Rinse under cold running water.	To boil 3 pounds live hard-shell blue crabs, in a 12- to 16-quart kettle bring 8 quarts water and 2 teaspoons salt to boiling. Add crabs. Simmer, covered, for 10 minutes or until crabs turn pink; drain. (To crack and clean a crab, see page 317.)
Crawfish	1 pound live crawfish	Rinse live crawfish under cold running water. For 4 pounds crawfish, in a 12- to 16-quart kettle combine 8 quarts cold water and ⅓ cup salt. Add crawfish. Soak for 15 minutes; rinse and drain.	For 4 pounds live crawfish, in a 12- to 16-quart kettle bring 8 quarts water and 2 teaspoons salt to boiling. Add crawfish. Simmer, covered, 5 to 8 minutes or until shells turn red; drain.
Lobster tails	One 8-ounce frozen lobster tail	Thaw frozen lobster tails in the refrigerator.	For four 8-ounce lobster tails, in a 3-quart saucepan bring 6 cups water and 1½ teaspoons salt to boiling. Add tails; simmer, uncovered, for 8 to 12 minutes or until shells turn bright red and meat is tender. Drain. (To boil a live lobster, see page 314.)
Mussels	12 mussels in shells	Scrub live mussels under cold running water. Using your fingers, pull out the beards that are visible between the shells. Soak as for clams, above.	For 24 mussels, add ½ inch water to an 8-quart kettle; bring to boiling. Place mussels in a steamer basket. Steam, covered, for 5 to 7 minutes or until shells open. Discard any that do not open.
Oysters	6 oysters in shells	Scrub live oysters under cold running water. For easier shucking, chill first. Shuck, reserving bottom shells, if desired (see photos, page 315).	See Oysters au Gratin, page 315; Oyster Stuffing, page 480.
Shrimp	6 ounces shrimp in shells or 3 to 4 ounces peeled, deveined shrimp	To peel shrimp, open the shell down the underside. Starting at the head end, pull back the shell. Gently pull on the tail to remove. Use a sharp knife to remove the black vein that runs along the center of the back. Rinse under cold running water (see photos, page 296).	For 1 pound shrimp, in a 3-quart saucepan bring 4 cups water and 1 teaspoon salt to boiling. Add shrimp. Simmer, uncovered, for 1 to 3 minutes or until shrimp turn opaque, stirring occasionally. Rinse under cold running water; drain and chill, if desired.

Cracking and Cleaning Cooked Crab

Cracking and cleaning hard-shell crabs, such as the Atlantic blue crab or the Pacific Dungeness (shown below), may be intimidating at first, but the reward is well worth the effort. The rich, sweet-tasting meat is delicious simply dipped in buter, chilled and tossed in salads, or as an added surprise to soups or stews. Follow these steps to get every last bit of the flavorful meat.

1. Turn the crab on its back. Using your thumb, fold back the tail flap (apron), twist off, and discard.

2. Holding the crab with the top shell in one hand, grasp the bottom shell at the point where the apron was removed. Pull the top shell away from the body of the crab and discard.

3. Discard the crab's internal organs, mouth, and appendages at the front; rinse crab. Using a small knife, remove the spongy gills from each side of the top of the crab.

4. Twist off the claws and legs. Use a nutcracker to crack each joint; pick out the meat. Cut the crab body into quarters. Use a small fork to remove the meat.

Cooking Fish

Minutes count when cooking fish. Weigh dressed fish or use a ruler to measure the thickness of the fillets and steaks in order to better estimate when to check for doneness. Properly cooked fish is opaque, flakes when tested with a fork, and comes away from the bones readily; the juices should be a milky white.

Cooking Method	Preparation	Fresh or Thawed Fillets or Steaks	Dressed
Bake	Place in a single layer in a greased shallow baking pan. For fillets, tuck under any thin edges. Brush with melted butter or margarine.	Bake, uncovered, in a 450°F oven for 4 to 6 minutes per ½-inch thickness.	Bake, uncovered, in a 350°F oven for 6 to 9 minutes per 8 ounces.
Broil	Preheat broiler. Place fish on greased unheated rack of a broiler pan. For fillets, tuck under any thin edges. Brush with melted butter or margarine.	Broil 4 inches from the heat for 4 to 6 minutes per ½-inch thickness. If fish is 1 inch or more thick, turn once halfway through broiling.	Not recommended.
Microwave	Arrange fish in a single layer in a shallow baking dish. For fillets, tuck under any thin edges. Cover with vented plastic wrap.	Cook on 100% power (high). For ½ pound of ½-inch-thick fillets, allow 1½ to 2 minutes; for 1 pound of ½-inch-thick fillets, allow 2½ to 4 minutes. For 1 pound of ¾- to 1-inch-thick steaks, allow 3 to 5 minutes.	Not recommended.
Poach	Add 1½ cups water, broth, or wine to a large skillet. Bring to boiling. Add fish. Return to boiling; reduce heat.	Simmer, uncovered, for 4 to 6 minutes per ½-inch thickness.	Simmer, covered, for 6 to 9 minutes per 8 ounces.

Guide to Fish Types

Use this guide to become acquainted with various types of fish. Note that the flavors range from delicate to pronounced. This list makes it easy to substitute one type of fish for another.

Types	Market Forms	Texture	Flavor	Substitutions
Freshwater Fish				
Catfish	Whole, fillets, steaks	Firm	Mild	Grouper, rockfish, sea bass, tilapia
Lake trout (North American char)	Whole, fillets, steaks	Slightly firm	Moderate	Pike, sea trout, whitefish
Rainbow trout	Fillets	Slightly firm	Delicate	Salmon, sea trout
Tilapia	Whole, dressed, fillets	Slightly firm	Delicate	Catfish, flounder, orange roughy
Whitefish	Whole, fillets	Moderately firm	Delicate	Cod, lake trout, salmon, sea bass
Saltwater Fish				
Atlantic ocean perch (redfish)	Whole, fillets	Slightly firm	Mild	Orange roughy, rockfish, snapper
Cod	Fillets, steaks	Moderately firm	Delicate	Flounder, haddock, pollack
Flounder	Whole, fillets	Fine	Delicate to mild	Cod, orange roughy, sea trout, sole, whitefish, whiting
Grouper	Whole, dressed, fillets	Moderately firm	Mild	Mahi mahi, sea bass
Haddock	Fillets	Moderately firm	Delicate	Cod, grouper, halibut, lake trout, sole, whitefish, whiting
Halibut*	Fillets, steaks	Firm	Delicate	Cod, grouper, red snapper, sea bass
Mackerel*	Whole	Delicate	Pronounced	Mahi mahi, swordfish, tuna
Mahi mahi (dolphinfish)	Whole, fillets	Firm	Mild to moderate	Grouper, orange roughy, red snapper
Orange roughy	Fillets	Moderately firm	Delicate	Cod, flounder, haddock, ocean perch, sea bass, sole
Red snapper	Whole, fillets	Moderately firm	Mild to moderate	Grouper, lake trout, ocean perch, rockfish, whitefish
Rockfish	Whole, fillets	Slightly firm	Mild to moderate	Cod, grouper, ocean perch, red snapper
Salmon*	Whole, fillets, steaks	Moderately firm	Mild to moderate	Rainbow trout, swordfish, tuna
Shark (mako)	Fillets, steaks	Firm, dense	Moderate	Swordfish, tuna
Sole	Fillets	Fine	Delicate	Flounder, haddock, halibut, pollack
Swordfish*	Loins, steaks	Firm, dense	Mild to moderate	Halibut, shark, tuna
Tuna*	Loins, steaks	Firm	Mild to moderate	Mackerel, salmon, shark, swordfish

*Good source of Omega-3 fatty acids

Grilling

Mustard-Marinated Flank
Steak with Yam Fries, 324

Maple-Smoked Salmon Fillet, 346

Glazed Country Ribs, 328

Grilling Essentials

The recipes in this chapter are suitable for charcoal or gas grills and include directions for both. Recipes and tips for using an indoor grill, smoker, and turkey fryer also are included.

Direct vs. Indirect Grilling

Decide your grilling method depending on the food you plan to cook.

Direct grilling is best for tender, thin, or small foods that cook in 30 minutes or less, including burgers, steaks, chops, chicken pieces, brats or frankfurters, and vegetables. For this method, place the food on the grill rack directly over the heat source, either with or without the lid closed (check the grill manufacturer's directions). For even cooking, turn foods only once during the cooking time.

| Direct Grilling | Indirect Grilling |

Use **indirect grilling** for large roasts, ribs, whole birds, and whole fish. This method positions the food on the grill rack away from or to the side of the heat source and with the grill cover closed. Heat inside the grill reflects off the lid and other interior surfaces, cooking from all sides and eliminating the need to turn the food.

Get Fired Up!

Whether you're cooking with charcoal or gas, setting up your grill is easy.

For a charcoal grill: Prepare the fire. About 25 to 30 minutes prior to cooking, remove the grill cover and open all vents. Place briquettes on lower charcoal grate.

For **direct cooking**, use enough briquettes to cover the charcoal grate completely with one layer. Then pile these briquettes into a pyramid in the center of the grate.

For **indirect cooking,** the number of briquettes you need to use is based on your grill size.

Grill diameter in inches	Briquettes needed on each side to start	Briquettes to add per side for longer grilling
26¾	30	9
22½	25	8
18½	16	5

Apply fire starter, use an electric starter, or place briquettes in a chimney starter. If using a liquid starter, wait 1 minute before igniting the fire. Let the fire burn for 25 to 30 minutes or until the coals are covered with a light coating of gray ash.

Using long-handled tongs, arrange the coals according to the cooking method you are using:

For **direct cooking,** spread coals evenly across the bottom of the grill, covering an area 3 inches larger on all sides than the food you are cooking.

For **indirect cooking,** arrange coals to one side of the grill; place the drip pan on the other side. Or place the drip pan in the center; arrange the coals into two equal piles on each side of the pan.

Install the grill rack and check the cooking temperature.

For a gas grill: Open the lid. Turn the gas valve "on" and turn burners on high. Ignite as directed by the manufacturer. Close the lid and preheat the grill (usually with all burners on high for 10 to 15 minutes).

For **indirect cooking** method, turn off the burners directly below the food. Adjust the burner controls to the temperature needed for cooking.

Hand Check

To judge how hot your grill is, carefully place the palm of your hand just above the grill rack and count the number of seconds you can hold it in that position.

Time	Thermometer	Temperature	Visual
2 seconds	400°F to 450°F	Hot (high)	Coals glowing and lightly covered with gray ash
3 seconds	375°F to 400°F	Medium-high	
4 seconds	350°F to 375°F	Medium	Coals glowing through a layer of ash
5 seconds	325°F to 350°F	Medium-low	
6 seconds	300°F to 325°F	Low	Coals burning down and covered with a thick layer of ash

Hot or Not?

Coals are ready for grilling when they are covered with gray ash, typically after 25 to 30 minutes.

To check the temperature of the coals, use a built-in or separate flat grill thermometer. Or carefully place the palm of your hand above the grill rack at cooking level and count the number of seconds you can hold it there. For example, "One, I love grilling; two, I love grilling," and so on. When grilling indirectly, hot coals will provide medium-hot heat and medium-hot coals will provide medium heat.

Adjusting the Heat

● If the coals are too hot, raise the grill rack, spread the coals apart, close the air vents halfway, or remove some briquettes. For a gas or electric grill, adjust the burner to a lower setting.

● If the coals are too cool, use long-handled tongs to tap ashes off the burning coals, move the coals together, add briquettes, lower the rack, or open the vents. For a gas or electric grill, adjust the burner to a higher setting.

● Not everyone judges the temperature of coals alike. For perfectly done food, use the timings as a guide and watch all foods on the grill closely.

Safety First

● Allow coals to burn completely and let the ashes cool for 24 hours before disposing of them.

● Let your grill cool completely before covering or storing it.

● Use charcoal or gas grills outside only—never in a garage, porch, or enclosed area.

● Periodically test your gas grill for leaks and clean the venturi tubes regularly according to the manufacturer's directions.

● Don't use lighter fluid, an electric starter, or a chimney starter with instant-lighting briquettes.

● Never leave a grill unattended or try to move it while it's in use or hot.

Controlling Flare-Ups

Fat and meat juices dripping onto hot coals may cause small blazes, called flare-ups, which can make your meat taste charred. To control flare-ups, raise the grill rack, cover the grill, space the hot coals farther apart, or remove a few coals. As a last resort, remove the food from the grill and mist the fire with water from a spray bottle. When the flame subsides, return the food to the grill.

To prevent flare-ups on a gas grill, after each use burn off the residue by turning the grill setting to high for 10 to 15 minutes and closing the lid. Once the grill has cooled, use a brass-bristle brush to remove any baked-on food from the grill rack.

Grilling Fork   **Brass-Bristle Brush**   **Basting Brush**

Hamburgers `EASY`

Prep: 10 minutes **Grill:** 14 minutes **Makes:** 4 hamburgers

- 1½ pounds lean ground beef
- 4 hamburger buns, split
    Cheese slices, lettuce leaves, tomato slices, onion slices, and/or pickle slices (optional)

1. Lightly shape ground beef into four ¾-inch-thick patties.

2. For a charcoal grill, grill patties on the rack of an uncovered grill directly over medium coals for 14 to 18 minutes or until done (160°F), turning once halfway through grilling. (For a gas grill, preheat grill. Reduce heat to medium. Place patties on grill rack over heat. Cover; grill as above.)

3. Remove burgers from grill. Season with salt and black pepper. Serve burgers in buns. If desired, top burgers with cheese, lettuce, tomato, onion, and/or pickles.

Per hamburger: 395 cal., 18 g total fat (7 g sat. fat), 107 mg chol., 412 mg sodium, 21 g carbo., 1 g fiber, 35 g pro.
Daily Values: 7% calcium, 25% iron
Exchanges: 1½ Starch, 4½ Lean Meat, ½ Fat

Cheeseburgers

Serve these burgers open-face on slices of Texas toast for a knife-and-fork meal. Red sweet peppers make a good substitute for poblano chile peppers.

Prep: 30 minutes **Chill:** 1 hour
Grill: 14 minutes **Makes:** 4 cheeseburgers

- ¼ cup finely chopped onion
- 2 large poblano peppers, roasted, seeded, and chopped (see tip, page 74)
- 2 tablespoons chili powder
- 1½ pounds lean ground beef
- 3 ounces Monterey Jack cheese with jalapeño peppers or Monterey Jack cheese, shredded (¾ cup)
- 4 large hamburger buns, split and toasted
    Assorted condiments

1. In a bowl combine onion, poblano peppers, chili powder, 1 teaspoon *salt*, and ½ teaspoon *black pepper*. Add ground beef; mix well. Shape mixture into four ¾-inch-thick patties. Place on a tray; cover and chill for 1 to 2 hours.

2. For a charcoal grill, grill patties on the rack of an uncovered grill directly over medium coals for 14 to 18 minutes or until done (160°F), turning once halfway through grilling. Top burgers with cheese during the last 1 minute of grilling.

(For a gas grill, preheat grill. Reduce heat to medium. Place patties on grill rack over heat. Cover; grill as at left.) Serve burgers on buns with desired condiments.

Per cheeseburger: 552 cal., 30 g total fat (12 g sat. fat), 120 mg chol., 1,008 mg sodium, 30 g carbo., 3 g fiber, 39 g pro.
Daily Values: 37% vit. A, 212% vit. C, 15% calcium, 36% iron
Exchanges: 2 Starch, 4 Medium-Fat Meat, 1 High-Fat Meat

Spicy Grilled Brisket `LOW FAT`

Prep: 25 minutes **Soak:** 1 hour **Grill:** 3 hours
Stand: 10 minutes **Makes:** 15 servings

- 4 to 6 cups mesquite wood chips
- 1 4- to 5-pound fresh beef brisket
- 1 tablespoon cooking oil
- 2 tablespoons paprika
- 1 tablespoon coarse salt or coarse kosher salt
- 1 tablespoon black pepper
- 1 teaspoon cayenne pepper
- 1 teaspoon dried thyme, crushed
- 3 cups bottled barbecue sauce

1. At least 1 hour before grilling, soak wood chips in enough water to cover.

2. Trim fat from brisket. Brush brisket with oil. For rub, in a small bowl stir together paprika, salt, black pepper, cayenne pepper, and thyme. Sprinkle rub evenly over all sides of meat; rub in with your fingers.

3. Drain wood chips. For a charcoal grill, arrange medium-low coals around a drip pan. Test for low heat above pan. Sprinkle some of the drained chips over the coals. Place brisket on grill rack over drip pan. Cover and grill for 3 to 3¾ hours or until meat is tender. Add more wood chips every 30 minutes. (For a gas grill, preheat grill. Reduce heat to low. Adjust for indirect cooking. Add wood chips according to manufacturer's directions. Place meat on a rack in a roasting pan; place pan on grill rack over burner that is off. Grill as above.)

4. Meanwhile, warm bottled barbecue sauce in a saucepan over low heat. Let meat stand for 10 minutes. To serve, slice meat thinly across the grain. Serve with barbecue sauce.

Per 3 ounces: 253 cal., 9 g total fat (2 g sat. fat), 71 mg chol., 956 mg sodium, 15 g carbo., 1 g fiber, 27 g pro.
Daily Values: 19% vit. A, 19% vit. C, 3% calcium, 18% iron
Exchanges: 1 Other Carbo., 3½ Lean Meat

Mustard-Marinated Flank Steak with Yam Fries

This savory steak also makes fabulous sandwiches. Layer the sliced meat in kaiser rolls with your favorite fixings. See photo, page 319.

Prep: 20 minutes **Marinate:** 2 hours
Grill: 17 minutes **Makes:** 4 to 6 servings

- 1 1¼- to 1½-pound beef flank steak
- ½ teaspoon black pepper
- 1 cup bottled Italian salad dressing
- ½ cup yellow mustard
- 4 to 6 kaiser rolls (optional)
- 1 recipe Yam Fries

1. Trim fat from steak. Score both sides of steak in a diamond pattern, making shallow diagonal cuts at 1-inch intervals. Rub pepper into steak. Place steak in a resealable plastic bag set in a shallow dish.

2. For marinade, in a small bowl stir together Italian dressing and mustard. Pour marinade over steak; seal bag. Marinate in the refrigerator for 2 to 24 hours, turning bag occasionally. Drain steak, reserving marinade.

3. For a charcoal grill, grill steak on the rack of an uncovered grill directly over medium coals for 17 to 21 minutes for medium doneness (160°F), turning and brushing once with marinade halfway through grilling. (For a gas grill, preheat grill. Reduce heat to medium. Place steak on grill rack over heat. Cover and grill as above.)

4. To serve, thinly slice steak diagonally across the grain. If desired, layer steak slices on kaiser rolls. Serve with Yam Fries.

Yam Fries: Peel 1 pound yams and/or sweet potatoes; cut into ¼-inch diagonal slices. In a medium bowl stir together 2 tablespoons peanut oil or cooking oil, ½ teaspoon salt, and, if desired, ¼ teaspoon cayenne pepper. Gently toss yam slices in oil mixture. Arrange yam slices in a grill wok. For a charcoal grill, place wok on the rack of an uncovered grill directly over medium coals. Grill about 15 minutes or until yam slices are tender, turning occasionally. (For a gas grill, preheat grill. Reduce heat to medium. Place wok on grill rack over heat. Cover and grill as above.)

Per 4 ounces steak + ½ cup fries: 694 cal., 46 g total fat (10 g sat. fat), 57 mg chol., 1,179 mg sodium, 36 g carbo., 4 g fiber, 35 g pro.
Daily Values: 435% vit. A, 34% vit. C, 6% calcium, 21% iron
Exchanges: 1½ Starch, 1 Other Carbo., 4½ Lean Meat, 6 Fat

Roasted Garlic Steak LOW FAT

Don't be shy about the garlic. Roasting it on the grill tames the flavor, a great complement to beef.

Prep: 15 minutes **Grill:** 30 minutes **Makes:** 6 servings

- 1 or 2 whole garlic bulb(s)
- 3 to 4 teaspoons snipped fresh basil or 1 teaspoon dried basil, crushed
- 1 tablespoon snipped fresh rosemary or 1 teaspoon dried rosemary, crushed
- 2 tablespoons olive oil or cooking oil
- 1½ pounds boneless beef ribeye steaks or sirloin steak, cut 1 inch thick
- 1 to 2 teaspoons cracked black pepper

1. With a sharp knife, cut off the top ½ inch of the garlic bulb(s) to expose the ends of the individual cloves. Leaving garlic bulb(s) whole, remove any loose, papery outer layers.

2. Fold a 20×18-inch piece of heavy foil in half crosswise. Trim into a 10-inch square. Place garlic bulb(s), cut ends up, in center of foil square. Sprinkle garlic with basil and rosemary and drizzle with oil. Bring up opposite edges of foil and seal with a double fold. Fold remaining edges together to completely enclose garlic, leaving space for steam to build.

3. For a charcoal grill, grill garlic on the rack of an uncovered grill directly over medium coals about 30 minutes or until garlic feels soft when packet is squeezed, turning garlic occasionally.

4. Meanwhile, trim fat from steaks. Sprinkle pepper and ½ teaspoon *salt* over both sides of steaks; rub in with your fingers. While garlic is grilling, add steaks to grill. Grill to desired doneness, turning once halfway through grilling. For ribeye steaks, allow 11 to 15 minutes for medium rare (145°F) and 14 to 18 minutes for medium (160°F). For sirloin steak, allow 14 to 18 minutes for medium rare (145°F) and 18 to 22 minutes for medium (160°F.) (For a gas grill, preheat grill. Reduce heat to medium. Place garlic on grill over heat; while garlic is grilling, add steaks. Cover and grill as above.)

5. To serve, cut steaks into six pieces. Remove garlic from foil, reserving the oil mixture. Squeeze garlic pulp onto steaks. Mash pulp with a fork; spread over steaks. Drizzle with oil mixture.

Per 3 ounces: 189 cal., 9 g total fat (2 g sat. fat), 52 mg chol., 139 mg sodium, 4 g carbo., 0 g fiber, 22 g pro.
Daily Values: 1% vit. A, 6% vit. C, 3% calcium, 14% iron
Exchanges: 3 Lean Meat, ½ Fat

Steak and Potato Kabobs LOW FAT

Bottled salad dressing makes a quick marinade for this meat-and-potato meal on a stick.

Prep: 20 minutes **Marinate:** 4 hours
Grill: 12 minutes **Makes:** 4 servings

- 1 boneless beef sirloin steak, cut 1 inch thick
- ¼ cup bottled red wine vinegar and oil salad dressing
- 2 tablespoons snipped fresh thyme or 2 teaspoons dried thyme, crushed
- 2 tablespoons Worcestershire sauce
- ¼ teaspoon garlic powder
- 2 medium yellow and/or green sweet peppers, cut into 1-inch pieces
- 1 medium red onion, cut into wedges
- ½ of a 20-ounce package refrigerated potato wedges (about 32 wedges)

1. Trim fat from steak. Cut steak into 1-inch cubes. Place steak cubes in a resealable plastic bag set in a shallow dish. For marinade, in a bowl combine salad dressing, thyme, Worcestershire sauce, and garlic powder. Pour over steak; seal bag. Marinate in the refrigerator for 4 to 6 hours, turning bag occasionally.

2. Drain steak, reserving marinade. On eight 10-inch metal skewers, alternately thread steak, sweet pepper, red onion, and potato, leaving a ¼-inch space between pieces.

3. For a charcoal grill, grill kabobs on the rack of an uncovered grill directly over medium coals until meat reaches desired doneness, turning once and brushing occasionally with reserved marinade up to the last 5 minutes of grilling. Allow 12 to 14 minutes for medium doneness (160°F). (For a gas grill, preheat grill. Reduce heat to medium. Place kabobs on grill rack over heat. Cover and grill as above.) Discard any remaining marinade.

Per 2 kabobs: 230 cal., 5 g total fat (2 g sat. fat), 69 mg chol., 230 mg sodium, 17 g carbo., 4 g fiber, 27 g pro.
Daily Values: 8% vit. A, 85% vit. C, 2% calcium, 24% iron
Exchanges: ½ Vegetable, 1 Starch, 3½ Very Lean Meat, ½ Fat

Skewer Secrets

Skewers are perfect for cooking small pieces of meat and vegetables on the grill. Here are a few tips for success:

- Cut pieces of food into uniform sizes to ensure even cooking.
- Leave ¼-inch spaces between food pieces on skewers.
- Rub metal skewers with oil before threading with food to keep food from sticking; clean metal skewers well.
- Soak wooden skewers in water for 30 minutes before threading with food to prevent them from burning on the grill.
- Thread larger food pieces on two parallel skewers to stabilize the food and allow for easier turning.

Steak and Potato Kabobs

Chipotle Pork Wraps

Chipotle Pork Wraps

Prep: 40 minutes   **Grill:** 4 hours
Stand: 30 minutes   **Makes:** 8 to 10 wraps

- 1 4- to 5-pound boneless pork shoulder roast
- 2 teaspoons ground chipotle chile powder
- 1 teaspoon salt
- ½ teaspoon black pepper
- 2 medium red onions, cut into ½-inch-thick slices
- 1 tablespoon olive oil
- 1 recipe Chipotle Mayonnaise or 1 cup chipotle-flavored light mayonnaise dressing
- 8 to 10 8-inch flour tortillas
- 2 cups shredded Monterey Jack cheese (8 ounces)

1. Trim fat from meat. In a small bowl stir together chile powder, salt, and pepper. Sprinkle mixture evenly over all sides of meat; rub in with your fingers.

2. For a charcoal grill, arrange medium-hot coals around a drip pan. Test for medium heat above pan. Place meat on grill rack over drip pan. Cover; grill about 4 hours or until meat is very tender. Brush onion slices lightly with oil; place on grill rack directly over coals the last 20 minutes of grilling, turning once. (For a gas grill, preheat grill. Reduce heat to medium. Adjust for indirect cooking. Grill as above, except place meat on a rack in a roasting pan, place pan on grill rack over burner that is off.) Remove meat from grill. Cover with foil and let stand for 30 minutes.

3. Shred pork with two forks (see photo, page 327). Spread some of the Chipotle Mayonnaise on one side of each tortilla. Top each tortilla with meat, grilled onion slices, and Monterey Jack cheese. Tightly roll up each tortilla.

Chipotle Mayonnaise: In a small bowl stir together 1 cup mayonnaise or salad dressing and 2 to 3 canned chipotle peppers in adobo sauce, drained and finely chopped. Cover and chill until serving time or up to 1 week. Makes 1 cup.

Per wrap: 653 cal., 44 g total fat (12 g sat. fat), 133 mg chol., 1,159 mg sodium, 25 g carbo., 1 g fiber, 38 g pro.
Daily Values: 12% vit. A, 7% vit. C, 28% calcium, 20% iron
Exchanges: 1½ Starch, 5 Medium-Fat Meat, 3½ Fat

Barbecued Pork Sandwiches

The saucy, well-seasoned pork mixture makes a delicious filling for tacos and pita bread halves or a topping for baked potatoes.

Prep: 40 minutes   **Grill:** 4 hours
Stand: 30 minutes   **Makes:** 12 to 16 sandwiches

- 1 4½- to 5-pound boneless pork shoulder roast
- ½ teaspoon salt
- ½ teaspoon black pepper
- ¼ teaspoon celery seeds
- ⅛ teaspoon onion powder
- ⅛ teaspoon garlic powder
- ⅛ teaspoon ground cloves
- Dash cayenne pepper
- 1 8-ounce can tomato sauce
- 1 cup ketchup
- 1 cup chopped onion (1 large)
- ½ cup chopped green sweet pepper
- ¼ cup vinegar
- 2 tablespoons packed brown sugar
- 2 tablespoons Worcestershire sauce
- 1 tablespoon yellow mustard
- 2 teaspoons chili powder
- 2 cloves garlic, minced
- 12 to 16 French-style rolls, split and toasted

1. Trim fat from meat. In a small bowl combine salt, black pepper, celery seeds, onion powder, garlic powder, cloves, and cayenne pepper. Sprinkle mixture evenly over all sides of meat; rub in with your fingers.

2. For a charcoal grill, arrange medium-hot coals around a drip pan. Test for medium heat above pan. Place meat on grill rack over drip pan. Cover and grill about 4 hours or until meat is very tender. (For a gas grill, preheat grill. Reduce heat to medium. Adjust for indirect cooking. Grill as on page 326, except place meat on a rack in a roasting pan. Place pan on grill rack over burner that is off.) Remove meat from grill; cover with foil and let stand for 30 minutes.

3. Meanwhile, for sauce, in a large saucepan combine tomato sauce, ketchup, onion, sweet pepper, vinegar, brown sugar, Worcestershire sauce, mustard, chili powder, and garlic. Bring to boiling; reduce heat. Simmer, covered, for 15 minutes.

4. Shred pork with two forks (see photo, below). Stir shredded pork into sauce; heat through. Spoon pork onto toasted rolls.

Per sandwich: 405 cal., 14 g total fat (5 g sat. fat), 114 mg chol., 823 mg sodium, 30 g carbo., 2 g fiber, 37 g pro.
Daily Values: 12% vit. A, 22% vit. C, 9% calcium, 21% iron
Exchanges: 2 Starch, 4½ Lean Meat

After grilling the pork roast until it's extremely tender, use two forks to gently separate the meat into thin strands.

Pork with Melon-Tomato Relish

Prep: 20 minutes **Grill:** 30 minutes
Stand: 10 minutes **Makes:** 4 servings

  3 tablespoons olive oil
  3 tablespoons white wine vinegar
  ¼ teaspoon salt
  ⅛ teaspoon black pepper
  1 1-pound pork tenderloin
  ½ of a small cantaloupe
  ½ of a small honeydew melon
  1 cup yellow, red, and/or orange pear-shape tomatoes, halved or quartered
  1 small red onion, halved and thinly sliced
  ⅓ cup fresh mint leaves

1. In a small bowl whisk together oil, vinegar, salt, and pepper. Brush 1 tablespoon of the oil mixture over the tenderloin. Reserve remaining oil mixture to use in the relish.

2. For a charcoal grill, arrange hot coals around a drip pan. Test for medium-high heat above pan. Place meat on grill rack over pan. Cover; grill for 30 to 35 minutes or until a meat

thermometer registers 155°F. (For a gas grill, preheat grill. Reduce heat to medium. Adjust for indirect cooking. Grill as above.) Remove meat from grill. Cover with foil and let stand for 10 minutes. (The meat's temperature will rise 5°F during standing.)

3. Meanwhile, for relish, cut either the cantaloupe or honeydew melon half into bite-size pieces. Cut remaining melon half into four wedges. In a medium bowl combine melon pieces, tomato, onion, and mint. Add reserved oil mixture; toss to coat.

4. Slice pork diagonally. Serve with relish spooned over melon wedges.

Per 3 ounces pork + ½ cup salsa + ⅛ melon: 292 cal., 14 g total fat (3 g sat. fat), 73 mg chol., 211 mg sodium, 15 g carbo., 2 g fiber, 26 g pro.
Daily Values: 88% vit. A, 122% vit. C, 3% calcium, 19% iron
Exchanges: ½ Vegetable, 1 Fruit, 3½ Lean Meat, ½ Fat

Pork with Melon-Tomato Relish

Summer Porch Picnic

A simple pork tenderloin paired with refreshing melon makes an easy saladlike supper.

● *Pork with Melon-Tomato Relish (left)*
● *Multigrain rolls or ciabatta slices*
● *Brownies with ice cream*

Chuck Wagon Baby Back Ribs

To protect the roasting pan from blackening as the ribs cook, wrap the outside with heavy foil.

Prep: 20 minutes **Grill:** 1½ hours **Makes:** 4 servings

> 4 to 5 pounds pork loin back ribs or meaty pork spareribs
> 1 recipe Chuck Wagon Rub
> 1 cup dry red wine
> 1 cup pineapple juice
> ½ cup honey
> ½ cup cider vinegar
> ½ cup soy sauce
> ¼ cup yellow mustard
> 2 tablespoons bourbon
> 1 teaspoon bottled hot pepper sauce

1. Trim fat from ribs. Sprinkle Chuck Wagon Rub evenly over both sides of ribs; rub in with your fingers. Cut ribs into two- or three-rib portions.

2. For sauce, in a large bowl combine wine, pineapple juice, honey, vinegar, soy sauce, mustard, bourbon, and hot pepper sauce.

3. Place rib portions, bone sides down, in a large roasting pan. Pour sauce over ribs. For a charcoal grill, arrange medium-hot coals around the edge of grill. Test for medium heat above center of grill. Place uncovered roasting pan on center of grill rack. Cover; grill for 1½ to 1¾ hours or until ribs are tender, spooning sauce over ribs every 20 to 25 minutes. (For a gas grill, preheat grill. Reduce heat to medium. Adjust for indirect cooking. Grill as above, except place roasting pan on grill rack over burner that is off.)

Chuck Wagon Rub: Combine 1 tablespoon black pepper, 2 teaspoons kosher salt, 2 teaspoons chili powder, 1 teaspoon sugar, 1 teaspoon onion powder, 1 teaspoon garlic powder, 1 teaspoon dried parsley, and 1 teaspoon dried oregano, crushed.

Per ¼ ribs: 731 cal., 21 g total fat (7 g sat. fat), 135 mg chol., 3,106 mg sodium, 52 g carbo., 2 g fiber, 68 g pro.
Daily Values: 13% vit. A, 18% vit. C, 10% calcium, 27% iron
Exchanges: 3½ Other Carbo., 10 Very Lean Meat, 3½ Fat

With a sharp knife, cut between the bones to separate the ribs into serving-size portions of two or three ribs each.

 Glazed Country Ribs `EASY`

See photo, page 319.

Prep: 15 minutes **Grill:** 1½ hours **Makes:** 4 servings

> 1 cup ketchup
> ½ cup water
> ¼ cup finely chopped onion
> ¼ cup cider vinegar or wine vinegar
> ¼ cup mild-flavored molasses
> 2 tablespoons Worcestershire sauce
> 2 teaspoons chili powder
> 2 cloves garlic, minced
> 2½ to 3 pounds pork country-style ribs

1. For sauce, in a medium saucepan combine the ketchup, water, onion, vinegar, molasses, Worcestershire sauce, chili powder, and garlic. Bring to boiling; reduce heat. Simmer, uncovered, for 10 to 15 minutes or until desired consistency, stirring often.

2. Trim fat from ribs. For a charcoal grill, arrange medium-hot coals around a drip pan. Test for medium heat above pan. Place ribs, bone sides down, on grill rack over pan. (Or place ribs in a rib rack; place on grill rack.) Cover and grill for 1½ to 2 hours or until tender, brushing occasionally with sauce during the last 10 minutes of grilling. (For a gas grill, preheat grill. Reduce heat to medium. Adjust for indirect cooking. Grill as above, except place ribs in a roasting pan, place pan on grill rack over burner that is off.) Pass the remaining sauce with ribs.

Per ¼ ribs: 431 cal., 18 g total fat (6 g sat. fat), 112 mg chol., 852 mg sodium, 34 g carbo., 1 g fiber, 33 g pro.
Daily Values: 22% vit. A, 21% vit. C, 11% calcium, 20% iron
Exchanges: 2 Other Carbo., 4 Medium-Fat Meat

Tangy Peanut-Sauced Ribs

Peanut butter, ginger, and cayenne pepper combine to give these ribs an exotic Asian flavor.

Prep: 20 minutes **Grill:** 1½ hours **Makes:** 4 servings

> 4 pounds meaty pork spareribs or pork loin back ribs
> ¼ cup hot water
> ¼ cup peanut butter
> 2 tablespoons lime juice
> 2 tablespoons sliced green onion (1)
> ½ teaspoon grated fresh ginger or ¼ teaspoon ground ginger
> ¼ teaspoon cayenne pepper

1. Trim fat from ribs. Cut ribs into four serving-size pieces (see photo, page 328). For a charcoal grill, arrange medium-hot coals around a drip pan. Test for medium heat above pan. Place ribs, bone sides down, on grill rack over drip pan. (Or place ribs in a rib rack; place on grill rack.) Cover and grill for 1½ to 1¾ hours or until tender. (For a gas grill, preheat grill. Reduce heat to medium. Adjust for indirect cooking. Place ribs in a roasting pan, place pan on grill rack over burner that is off, and grill as above.)

2. Meanwhile, for sauce, in a small saucepan gradually stir hot water into peanut butter (mixture will stiffen at first). Stir in lime juice, green onion, ginger, and cayenne pepper. Cook and stir over low heat until heated through. Spoon sauce over ribs.

Per ¼ ribs: 802 cal., 62 g total fat (21 g sat. fat), 214 mg chol., 241 mg sodium, 4 g carbo., 1 g fiber, 56 g pro.
Daily Values: 2% vit. A, 6% vit. C, 10% calcium, 21% iron
Exchanges: 8 High-Fat Meat

Homemade Pork Sausage Links EASY

Slide these skewered and grilled pork links into buns for a meal you can wrap your hands around.

Prep: 15 minutes Chill: 8 hours
Grill: 14 minutes Makes: 4 sandwiches

    3 tablespoons finely snipped fresh basil
    1 teaspoon sugar
    1 teaspoon fennel seeds
    1 teaspoon crushed red pepper
    ¾ teaspoon salt
    ½ teaspoon black pepper
    1 clove garlic, minced
 1½ pounds ground pork
    4 frankfurter buns, split and toasted
    ¼ cup Bacon and Brown Sugar Mustard

1. In a bowl combine basil, sugar, fennel seeds, red pepper, salt, black pepper, and garlic. Add ground pork; mix well. Divide pork mixture into four equal portions. Shape each portion around a flat-sided metal skewer into a 6-inch-long link.

2. For a charcoal grill, grill links on the rack of an uncovered grill directly over medium coals for 14 to 18 minutes or until done (160°F), turning once halfway through grilling. (For a gas grill, preheat grill. Reduce heat to medium. Place links on grill rack over heat. Cover and grill as above.)

3. To serve, use the tines of a fork to slide the pork links from the skewers. Serve in toasted buns with Bacon and Brown Sugar Mustard.

Bacon and Brown Sugar Mustard: In a small bowl stir together ¾ cup yellow mustard; 3 slices bacon, crisp-cooked, drained, and finely crumbled; and 4 teaspoons packed brown sugar. Cover and chill for 8 hours to 2 days. Makes 1 cup.

Per sandwich: 349 cal., 15 g total fat (5 g sat. fat), 81 mg chol., 856 mg sodium, 25 g carbo., 2 g fiber, 26 g pro.
Daily Values: 3% vit. A, 4% vit. C, 9% calcium, 18% iron
Exchanges: 2 Starch, 3 Medium-Fat Meat

Lemon-and-Herb-Rubbed Chops LOW FAT EASY

Prep: 15 minutes Grill: 35 minutes Makes: 4 chops

    4 pork loin chops, cut 1¼ inches thick
 1½ teaspoons finely shredded lemon peel
    1 teaspoon dried rosemary, crushed
    ½ teaspoon salt
    ½ teaspoon dried sage, crushed
    ½ teaspoon black pepper
    8 cloves garlic, minced

1. Trim fat from chops. For rub, in a small bowl combine lemon peel, rosemary, salt, sage, pepper, and garlic. Sprinkle rub evenly over both sides of chops; rub in with your fingers.

2. For a charcoal grill, arrange medium-hot coals around a drip pan. Test for medium heat above pan. Place chops on grill rack over pan. Cover; grill for 35 to 40 minutes or until chops are slightly pink in center and juices run clear (160°F), turning once halfway through grilling. (For a gas grill, preheat grill. Reduce heat to medium. Adjust for indirect cooking. Place meat on grill rack. Grill as above.)

Per chop: 292 cal., 10 g total fat (4 g sat. fat), 105 mg chol., 371 mg sodium, 3 g carbo., 1 g fiber, 43 g pro.
Daily Values: 1% vit. A, 6% vit. C, 5% calcium, 8% iron
Exchanges: 6 Very Lean Meat, 1½ Fat

Friday Night Dinner
Start the weekend with delicious pork.
- Lemon-and-Herb-Rubbed Chops (above)
- Grilled potatoes and asparagus spears
- Tossed greens salad
- Apple Crumb Pie (page 436)

Lamb Chops and Beans with Chile Butter

Lamb chops slathered with a spicy butter are a great choice for a casual backyard meal. The butter enhances other meats and poultry too.

Prep: 25 minutes **Chill:** 1 hour
Grill: 12 minutes **Makes:** 4 servings

- **8 lamb loin chops, cut 1 inch thick**
  Salt and black pepper
- **1 15-ounce can cannellini or pinto beans, rinsed and drained**
- **½ cup chopped celery**
- **¼ cup chopped green onion (2)**
- **1 recipe Chile Butter**
- **1 tablespoon lime juice**
  Lime wedges (optional)

1. Trim fat from chops. Sprinkle chops lightly with salt and pepper. For a charcoal grill, grill chops on the rack of an uncovered grill directly over medium coals to desired doneness, turning once halfway through grilling. Allow 12 to 14 minutes for medium-rare (145°F) and 15 to 17 minutes for medium doneness (160°F). (For a gas grill, preheat grill. Reduce heat to medium. Place chops on grill rack over heat. Cover and grill as above.)

2. Meanwhile, in a medium saucepan combine beans, celery, green onion, and 2 tablespoons of the Chile Butter. Cook over medium heat until heated through, stirring occasionally. Stir in lime juice. Top each lamb chop with a slice of Chile Butter and serve with the bean mixture. If desired, garnish with lime wedges.

Chile Butter: In a small bowl stir together ½ cup softened butter; ¼ cup finely snipped fresh cilantro; 2 fresh jalapeño chile peppers, seeded and finely chopped (see tip, page 74); 1 clove garlic, minced; and 1 teaspoon chili powder. Place on waxed paper; form into a log. Wrap well; chill for 1 hour or overnight. Store in refrigerator for up to 2 weeks or freeze for up to 1 month.

Per 2 chops + ½ cup beans: 478 cal., 32 g total fat (18 g sat. fat), 156 mg chol., 661 mg sodium, 17 g carbo., 6 g fiber, 36 g pro.
Daily Values: 30% vit. A, 15% vit. C, 7% calcium, 23% iron
Exchanges: ½ Vegetable, 1 Starch, 4½ Lean Meat, 3 Fat

Greek Lamb Platter

Greek Lamb Platter

Prep: 20 minutes **Marinate:** 8 hours
Grill: 8 minutes **Makes:** 6 servings

- **1½ to 2 pounds boneless leg of lamb**
- **1 tablespoon finely shredded lemon peel**
- **⅔ cup lemon juice**
- **6 tablespoons olive oil**
- **⅓ cup snipped fresh oregano**
- **½ teaspoon salt**
- **⅛ teaspoon black pepper**
- **½ cup snipped fresh parsley**
- **2 ounces crumbled feta cheese (½ cup)**
- **¼ cup sliced, pitted kalamata olives or other ripe olives**
- **¼ teaspoon ground cinnamon**
- **¼ teaspoon black pepper**
- **2 pounds roma tomatoes, halved**

1. Trim fat from lamb. Cut lamb across the grain into ½- to ¾-inch slices. Place lamb in a large resealable plastic bag set in a shallow dish. For marinade, in a small bowl stir together lemon peel, ⅓ cup of the lemon juice, 4 tablespoons of the oil, the oregano, salt, and the ⅛ teaspoon pepper. Pour marinade over lamb; seal bag. Marinate in the refrigerator for 8 to 24 hours, turning bag occasionally.

2. In a large bowl combine remaining ⅓ cup lemon juice, 1 tablespoon of the remaining oil, the parsley, feta cheese, olives, cinnamon, and the ¼ teaspoon pepper; set aside. Drain lamb, discarding marinade. Brush tomatoes with remaining 1 tablespoon oil.

3. For a charcoal grill, grill lamb and tomatoes on the rack of an uncovered grill directly over medium coals until lamb reaches desired doneness and tomatoes are slightly charred, turning once halfway through grilling. Allow about 8 minutes for medium-rare (145°F) or about 10 minutes for medium doneness (160°F). (For a gas grill, preheat grill. Reduce heat to medium. Place meat and tomatoes on grill rack over heat. Cover and grill as above.)

4. Transfer tomatoes to a cutting board; cool slightly and coarsely chop. Toss tomatoes with feta cheese mixture. Serve with lamb.

Per 3 ounces lamb + ¾ cup tomato mixture: 256 cal., 14 g total fat (4 g sat. fat), 66 mg chol., 493 mg sodium, 11 g carbo., 0 g fiber, 22 g pro.
Daily Values: 15% vit. A, 80% vit. C, 6% calcium, 18% iron
Exchanges: 2 Vegetable, 2½ Lean Meat, 1½ Fat

Barbecue Chicken

Prep: 45 minutes **Marinate:** 2 hours
Grill: 50 minutes **Makes:** 6 servings

   3 to 4 pounds meaty chicken pieces (breast halves, thighs, and drumsticks)
1½ cups dry sherry
   1 cup finely chopped onion (1 large)
  ¼ cup lemon juice
   2 bay leaves
   6 cloves garlic, minced
   1 15-ounce can tomato puree
  ¼ cup honey
   3 tablespoons mild-flavored molasses
  ½ teaspoon dried thyme, crushed
¼ to ½ teaspoon cayenne pepper
   2 tablespoons white vinegar

1. Place chicken in a resealable plastic bag set in a shallow dish. For marinade, combine sherry, onion, lemon juice, bay leaves, and garlic. Pour over chicken; seal bag. Marinate in the refrigerator for 2 to 4 hours, turning bag occasionally. Drain chicken, reserving marinade. Cover and chill chicken until ready to grill.

2. For sauce, in a saucepan combine reserved marinade, tomato puree, honey, molasses, 1 teaspoon *salt,* thyme, cayenne pepper, and ¼ teaspoon *black pepper.* Bring to boiling; reduce heat. Simmer, uncovered, about 30 minutes or until reduced to 2 cups. Remove from heat; remove bay leaves. Stir in vinegar.

3. For a charcoal grill, arrange medium-hot coals around a drip pan. Test for medium heat above the pan. Place chicken pieces, bone sides down, on grill rack over drip pan. Cover and grill for 50 to 60 minutes or until chicken is no longer pink (170°F for breast halves, 180°F for thighs and drumsticks), brushing with some of the sauce during the last 15 minutes of grilling. (For a gas grill, preheat grill. Reduce heat to medium. Adjust for indirect cooking. Place chicken pieces on grill rack; grill as above.) Reheat and pass the remaining sauce with chicken.

Per 2 pieces: 503 cal., 18 g total fat (5 g sat. fat), 129 mg chol., 779 mg sodium, 35 g carbo., 2 g fiber, 35 g pro.
Daily Values: 22% vit. A, 29% vit. C, 7% calcium, 18% iron
Exchanges: 1 Vegetable, 2 Other Carbo., 5 Lean Meat, 2 Fat

Chicken with Firecracker Barbecue Sauce LOW FAT

Prep: 25 minutes **Grill:** 12 minutes **Makes:** 6 servings

  ¼ cup chipotle peppers in adobo sauce
  ⅓ cup finely chopped onion
   3 cloves garlic, minced
   1 cup ketchup
   3 tablespoons white wine vinegar
   3 tablespoons full-flavored molasses
   1 tablespoon Worcestershire sauce
   6 skinless, boneless chicken breast halves

1. For sauce, remove any stems from chipotle peppers. Place peppers and adobo sauce in a blender. Cover and blend until smooth. Set aside.

2. Lightly coat an unheated medium saucepan with *nonstick cooking spray.* Cook onion and garlic in saucepan until tender. Stir in chipotle pepper mixture, ketchup, vinegar, molasses, and Worcestershire sauce. Bring to boiling; reduce heat. Simmer, uncovered, about 10 minutes or until sauce is slightly thickened.

3. For a charcoal grill, grill chicken on the rack of an uncovered grill directly over medium coals for 12 to 15 minutes or until chicken is no longer pink (170°F), turning once halfway through grilling and brushing with sauce during the last 5 minutes of grilling. (For a gas grill, preheat grill. Reduce heat to medium. Place chicken on grill rack over heat. Cover and grill as above.) Bring remaining sauce to boiling; pass with chicken.

Per breast half: 207 cal., 2 g total fat (0 g sat. fat), 66 mg chol., 612 mg sodium, 20 g carbo., 1 g fiber, 27 g pro.
Daily Values: 11% vit. A, 14% vit. C, 5% calcium, 10% iron
Exchanges: 1½ Other Carbo., 3½ Very Lean Meat

Honey-Dijon Barbecued Chicken EASY

Prep: 15 minutes **Marinate:** 8 hours
Grill: 50 minutes **Makes:** 4 servings

- 1 2½- to 3-pound broiler-fryer chicken, quartered
- ½ cup white Zinfandel wine, apple juice, or apple cider
- ¼ cup olive oil or cooking oil
- ¼ cup honey
- ¼ cup Dijon-style mustard
- ½ teaspoon black pepper
- ¼ teaspoon salt
- 4 cloves garlic, minced
   Grilled vegetables (optional)

1. Place chicken in a resealable plastic bag set in a shallow dish. For marinade, in a bowl combine wine, oil, honey, mustard, pepper, salt, and garlic. Pour marinade over chicken; seal bag. Marinate in the refrigerator for 8 to 24 hours, turning bag occasionally. Drain chicken, reserving marinade.

2. For a charcoal grill, arrange medium-hot coals around a drip pan. Test for medium heat above pan. Place chicken pieces, bone sides up, on grill rack over drip pan. Cover and grill for 50 to 60 minutes or until chicken is no longer pink (170°F for breast portions, 180°F for thigh portions), brushing once with reserved marinade after 30 minutes of grilling. (For a gas grill,

preheat grill. Reduce heat to medium. Adjust for indirect cooking. Grill as at left.) Discard any remaining marinade. If desired, serve with grilled vegetables.

Per ¼ chicken: 597 cal., 40 g total fat (10 g sat. fat), 172 mg chol., 384 mg sodium, 11 g carbo., 0 g fiber, 45 g pro.
Daily Values: 5% vit. A, 6% vit. C, 4% calcium, 13% iron
Exchanges: ½ Other Carbo., 6½ Medium-Fat Meat, 1½ Fat

Beer Can Chicken

Prep: 30 minutes **Grill:** 1¼ hours
Stand: 10 minutes **Makes:** 4 to 6 servings

- 2 teaspoons salt
- 2 teaspoons packed brown sugar
- 2 teaspoons paprika
- 1 teaspoon dry mustard
- ½ teaspoon black pepper
- ½ teaspoon dried thyme, crushed
- ¼ teaspoon garlic powder
- 1 12-ounce can beer
- 1 3½- to 4-pound whole broiler-fryer chicken
- 2 tablespoons butter or margarine, softened
- 1 lemon quarter

1. For rub, in a small bowl combine salt, brown sugar, paprika, dry mustard, pepper, thyme, and garlic powder. Discard about half of the beer from the can. Add 1 teaspoon of the rub to the half-empty can (beer will foam up).

2. Remove neck and giblets from chicken. Sprinkle 1 teaspoon of the rub inside the body cavity. Rub the outside of the chicken with butter and sprinkle with the remaining rub.

3. Hold the chicken upright with the opening of the body cavity at the bottom and lower it onto the beer can so the can fits into the cavity. Pull the chicken legs forward so the bird rests on its legs and the can. Twist wing tips behind back. Stuff the lemon quarter in the neck cavity to seal in steam.

4. For a charcoal grill, arrange medium-hot coals around a drip pan. Test for medium heat above pan. Stand chicken upright on grill rack over drip pan. Cover and grill for 1¼ to 1¾ hours or until chicken is no longer pink (180°F in thigh muscle). If necessary, tent chicken with foil to prevent over-browning. (For a gas grill, preheat grill. Reduce heat to medium. Adjust

Honey-Dijon Barbecued Chicken

for indirect cooking. If necessary, remove upper grill racks so chicken will stand upright. Grill as on page 332.) Holding chicken by the can, carefully remove it from grill. Cover with foil; let stand for 10 minutes. To pull the can from the chicken, use a hot pad to grasp the can and heavy tongs to grasp the chicken.

Per ¼ chicken: 635 cal., 45 g total fat (15 g sat. fat), 217 mg chol., 1,180 mg sodium, 3 g carbo., 0 g fiber, 51 g pro.
Daily Values: 19% vit. A, 6% vit. C, 4% calcium, 14% iron
Exchanges: 7 Medium-Fat Meat, 2 Fat

Chicken Fajitas with Jicama Relish

Prep: 45 minutes **Marinate:** 1 hour
Grill: 12 minutes **Makes:** 8 fajitas

- 4 skinless, boneless chicken breast halves
- ½ cup bottled Italian salad dressing
- ½ teaspoon chili powder
- ½ teaspoon ground cumin
- 2 small sweet peppers, quartered lengthwise and seeded
- 1 small red onion, cut into ½-inch-thick slices
- 8 10-inch flour tortillas, warmed*
- 1 recipe Jicama Relish
- 1 16-ounce jar salsa

1. Place chicken in a resealable plastic bag set in a shallow dish. For marinade, combine Italian dressing, chili powder, and cumin. Pour over chicken; seal bag. Marinate in the refrigerator for 1 to 24 hours, turning bag occasionally. Drain chicken, reserving marinade. Brush marinade over sweet pepper and red onion.

2. For a charcoal grill, place chicken, pepper, and onion on the rack of an uncovered grill directly over medium coals. Grill until chicken is no longer pink (170°F) and vegetables are crisp-tender, turning once halfway through grilling. Allow 12 to 15 minutes for chicken, 8 to 10 minutes for vegetables. (For a gas grill, preheat grill. Reduce heat to medium. Place chicken and vegetables on grill rack over heat. Cover and grill as above.)

3. Remove chicken and vegetables from grill; carefully slice into thin bite-size strips. Spoon chicken and vegetable mixture onto warmed tortillas. Top with Jicama Relish and salsa; roll up.

*Note: Wrap tortillas tightly in foil. Place on edge of grill rack; heat for 10 minutes, turning once.

Jicama Relish: Combine one 15-ounce can black beans, rinsed and drained; 1 cup chopped, peeled jicama; 1 large tomato, chopped; 1 medium avocado, halved, seeded, peeled, and chopped; and ½ cup snipped fresh cilantro.

Per fajita + ½ cup jicama mixture: 396 cal., 16 g total fat (3 g sat. fat), 41 mg chol., 720 mg sodium, 42 g carbo., 6 g fiber, 25 g pro.
Daily Values: 38% vit. A, 91% vit. C, 11% calcium, 22% iron
Exchanges: ½ Vegetable, 2½ Starch, 2½ Very Lean Meat, 2½ Fat

Cacciatore-Style Chicken Kabobs with Linguine

Prep: 30 minutes **Marinate:** 2 hours
Grill: 12 minutes **Makes:** 4 servings

- 1 pound skinless, boneless chicken breast halves
- ½ cup bottled Italian salad dressing
- 1 medium red sweet pepper, cut into 1-inch pieces
- 1 10-ounce package frozen artichoke hearts, cooked according to package directions
- 8 medium fresh mushrooms
- 1 16-ounce jar pasta sauce
- 8 ounces dried linguine
  Shredded fresh Parmesan cheese (optional)

1. Cut chicken into 1-inch pieces. Place pieces in a resealable plastic bag set in a shallow dish. Pour Italian dressing over chicken; seal bag. Marinate in the refrigerator for 2 to 8 hours, turning bag occasionally. Drain chicken, reserving marinade.

2. On four medium skewers, alternately thread chicken, sweet pepper, and half of the artichoke hearts, leaving a ¼-inch space between pieces. Place two mushrooms on the end of each skewer. Brush kabobs with reserved marinade.

3. For a charcoal grill, grill kabobs on the rack of an uncovered grill directly over medium coals for 12 to 14 minutes or until chicken is no longer pink (170°F), turning once halfway through grilling. Brush with ¼ cup of the pasta sauce during the last 5 minutes of grilling. (For a gas grill, preheat grill. Reduce heat to medium. Place chicken on grill rack over heat. Cover and grill as above.)

4. Meanwhile, cook pasta according to package directions. Heat remaining artichoke hearts in remaining pasta sauce. Spoon over servings of linguine; top each with a kabob. If desired, sprinkle with Parmesan cheese.

Per kabob + 1 cup pasta: 720 cal., 28 g total fat (9 g sat. fat), 90 mg chol., 1,443 mg sodium, 69 g carbo., 9 g fiber, 51 g pro.
Daily Values: 41% vit. A, 118% vit. C, 51% calcium, 25% iron
Exchanges: 1 Vegetable, 3 Starch, 1½ Other Carbo., 5½ Very Lean Meat, 3½ Fat

New England Grilled Turkey

Because a turkey releases a lot of drippings as it grills, you may prefer to omit the drip pan and place the turkey on a rack in a roasting pan. Place the pan in the center of the grill, not directly over the heat source.

Prep: 40 minutes **Brine:** 12 hours **Grill:** 2½ hours
Stand: 15 minutes **Makes:** 8 to 12 servings + leftovers

- 1 8- to 10-pound whole turkey
- 4 cups hot water
- 1¼ cups kosher salt
- 1 cup pure maple syrup
- 1 6-ounce can apple juice concentrate, thawed
- 16 cups cold water
- ¼ teaspoon whole black peppercorns
- 4 whole cloves
- 3 cloves garlic, crushed
- ½ cup butter, softened
- 1 teaspoon ground sage
- 1 recipe Gingered Cranberry Sauce

1. Thaw turkey, if frozen. For brine, in a deep pot combine hot water, salt, maple syrup, and juice concentrate. Stir until salt dissolves. Add cold water, peppercorns, cloves, and garlic.

2. Remove neck and giblets from turkey. Add turkey to brine; weight it so it is covered by brine. Cover; place in the refrigerator overnight. Drain turkey and pat dry. Combine butter and sage; set aside. Starting at the neck on one side of the breast, slip your fingers between skin and meat, loosening skin as you work toward the tail end. Once your entire hand is under the skin, free the skin around thigh and leg area up to, but not around, the tip of the drumstick. Repeat on the other side of the breast. Rub sage butter under skin, directly on meat. Skewer neck skin to back. Twist wing tips behind back. Sprinkle surface and cavity of turkey with *salt* and *black pepper*. Tuck drumsticks under band of skin or tie to tail. If desired, insert a meat thermometer into the center of an inside thigh muscle.

3. For a charcoal grill, arrange medium-hot coals around a drip pan. Test for medium heat above the pan. Place turkey on grill rack over drip pan. Cover; grill for 2½ to 3 hours or until thermometer registers 180°F and turkey is no longer pink, adding fresh coals every 45 to 60 minutes and cutting band of skin or string the last hour of grilling. (For a gas grill, preheat

grill, reduce heat to medium. Adjust for indirect cooking. Grill as at left.)

4. Remove turkey from grill. Cover with foil; let stand for 15 minutes before carving. Serve with Gingered Cranberry Sauce.

Gingered Cranberry Sauce: In a medium saucepan combine 1 cup sugar and 1 cup water. Bring to boiling, stirring to dissolve sugar. Boil rapidly for 5 minutes. Add 2 cups fresh cranberries, ½ cup snipped dried apples, 1½ teaspoons grated fresh ginger, and 1 teaspoon finely shredded lemon peel. Return to boiling; reduce heat. Boil gently, uncovered, over medium heat for 3 to 4 minutes or until cranberry skins pop, stirring occasionally. Remove from heat. Serve warm or chilled. Makes 2½ cups.

Per 4 ounces turkey + ⅓ cup sauce: 430 cal., 18 g total fat (9 g sat. fat), 150 mg chol., 1,107 mg sodium, 34 g carbo., 2 g fiber, 32 g pro.
Daily Values: 8% vit. A, 7% vit. C, 4% calcium, 14% iron
Exchanges: ½ Fruit, 2 Other Carbo., 4½ Lean Meat, 1 Fat

Teriyaki Turkey Tenderloins LOW FAT

Prep: 25 minutes **Marinate:** 1 hour
Grill: 16 minutes **Makes:** 4 servings

- 2 8-ounce turkey breast tenderloins
- ¼ cup soy sauce
- 2 tablespoons packed brown sugar
- 2 tablespoons lemon juice
- 1 tablespoon cooking oil
- 1 teaspoon grated fresh ginger
- 1 clove garlic, minced
- 1 recipe Hot Pineapple Slaw (page 335)

1. Place turkey tenderloins in a resealable plastic bag set in a shallow dish. For marinade, in a small bowl combine soy sauce, brown sugar, lemon juice, oil, ginger, and garlic. Pour marinade over turkey; seal bag. Marinate in the refrigerator for 1 to 2 hours, turning once. Drain turkey, reserving marinade.

2. For a charcoal grill, grill turkey on the rack of an uncovered grill directly over medium coals for 16 to 20 minutes or until turkey is no longer pink (170°F), turning once and brushing with marinade halfway through cooking. (For a gas grill, preheat grill. Reduce heat to medium. Place turkey on grill rack over heat. Cover and grill as above.) Slice turkey and serve with Hot Pineapple Slaw.

Hot Pineapple Slaw: In a saucepan cook ¼ cup thinly sliced green onion and ⅛ teaspoon crushed red pepper in 1 tablespoon cooking oil for 2 minutes. Stir in 2 cups shredded napa cabbage, 1 cup bite-size fresh pineapple pieces, ¼ cup green sweet pepper cut into thin strips, 1 teaspoon toasted sesame oil, and dash salt. Heat and stir until cabbage just wilts. Makes about 3 cups.

Per 3 ounces + ¾ cup slaw: 239 cal., 8 g total fat (1 g sat. fat), 68 mg chol., 557 mg sodium, 12 g carbo., 2 g fiber, 29 g pro. **Daily Values:** 11% vit. A, 45% vit. C, 6% calcium, 9% iron **Exchanges:** ½ Vegetable, 4 Very Lean Meat, 1 Fat

Teriyaki Turkey Tenderloins

Keep It Clean

Clean your grill each time you use it.

For a charcoal grill, let the coals die down and the grill rack cool slightly. Brush off any debris using a brass-bristle grill brush or crumpled aluminum foil. For a more thorough cleaning, wash the grill rack using a mild soap and a fine steel wool pad.

For a gas grill, burn off any residue by covering the grill and turning the grill on high until the smoke subsides (about 10 to 15 minutes). Turn it off and allow it to cool slightly. Then brush the grill rack with a brass-bristle grill brush or crumpled aluminum foil.

Turkey Steaks with Sweet Pepper-Citrus Salsa

Precut turkey breast tenderloin steaks are available in most supermarkets. If you find only whole tenderloins, buy three 8-ounce tenderloins and halve them horizontally.

Prep: 15 minutes **Marinate:** 2 hours
Grill: 12 minutes **Makes:** 6 steaks

> 6 ½-inch-thick turkey breast tenderloin steaks (about 1½ pounds)
> ⅓ cup olive oil
> ¼ cup lemon juice
> 1 teaspoon finely shredded orange peel
> ¼ cup orange juice
> ¼ teaspoon salt
> ¼ teaspoon black pepper
> 4 cloves garlic, minced
> 1 recipe Sweet Pepper-Citrus Salsa

1. Place turkey in a resealable plastic bag set in a shallow bowl. For marinade, in a small bowl combine oil, lemon juice, orange peel, orange juice, salt, pepper, and garlic. Pour over turkey; seal bag. Marinate in the refrigerator for 2 to 4 hours, turning bag occasionally.

2. Drain turkey, reserving marinade. For a charcoal grill, grill turkey on the rack of an uncovered grill directly over medium coals for 12 to 15 minutes or until no longer pink (170°F), turning once halfway through grilling and brushing with marinade during the first 6 minutes of grilling. (For a gas grill, preheat grill. Reduce heat to medium. Place turkey on grill rack over heat. Cover and grill as above.) Serve with Sweet Pepper-Citrus Salsa.

Sweet Pepper-Citrus Salsa: In a small bowl combine one 7-ounce jar roasted red sweet peppers, drained and chopped; 1 orange, peeled, seeded, and cut up; 2 green onions, sliced; 2 tablespoons balsamic vinegar; and 1 tablespoon snipped fresh basil or 1 teaspoon dried basil, crushed. Cover and chill until serving time. Makes 1½ cups.

Per steak + ¼ cup salsa: 262 cal., 13 g total fat (2 g sat. fat), 70 mg chol., 141 mg sodium, 8 g carbo., 1 g fiber, 29 g pro. **Daily Values:** 2% vit. A, 138% vit. C, 3% calcium, 10% iron **Exchanges:** 1 Vegetable, 4 Very Lean Meat, 2 Fat

Glazed Turkey Burgers

For best results, treat the ground meat mixture gently when shaping and grilling it. Never press burgers with a spatula to hasten cooking. This forces out the juices that carry flavor and lend moistness.

Prep: 20 minutes **Grill:** 14 minutes **Makes:** 4 burgers

- 1 tablespoon yellow mustard
- 1 tablespoon cherry, apricot, peach, or pineapple preserves
- 1 egg, beaten
- ¼ cup quick-cooking rolled oats
- ¼ cup finely chopped celery
- 3 tablespoons snipped dried tart cherries or dried apricots (optional)
- ¼ teaspoon salt
- ⅛ teaspoon black pepper
- 1 pound uncooked ground turkey or chicken
- 4 kaiser rolls or hamburger buns, split and toasted
  Mayonnaise or salad dressing, lettuce leaves, and/or tomato slices (optional)

1. For glaze, in a small bowl stir together mustard and preserves; set aside. In a medium bowl combine egg, rolled oats, celery, dried cherries (if desired), salt, and pepper. Add ground turkey; mix well. Shape turkey mixture into four ¾-inch-thick patties.

2. For a charcoal grill, grill patties on the rack of an uncovered grill directly over medium coals for 14 to 18 minutes or until no longer pink (165°F), turning once halfway through grilling and brushing with glaze during the last minute of grilling. (For a gas grill, preheat grill. Reduce heat to medium. Place patties on grill rack over heat. Cover and grill as above.)

3. Serve burgers on buns. Brush any remaining glaze over burgers. If desired, serve burgers with mayonnaise, lettuce, and tomato.

Per burger: 397 cal., 14 g total fat (3 g sat. fat), 143 mg chol., 599 mg sodium, 38 g carbo., 2 g fiber, 28 g pro.
Daily Values: 2% vit. A, 2% vit. C, 9% calcium, 21% iron
Exchanges: 2½ Starch, 2½ Medium-Fat Meat

Salmon and Vegetable Packets

Served in its foil pouch, this fish and vegetable entrée makes a great-tasting meal with few dishes to wash.

Prep: 40 minutes **Grill:** 12 minutes per ½-inch thickness
Makes: 4 servings

- 1 pound fresh or frozen skinless salmon, cod, tilapia, or orange roughy fillets, ½ to ¾ inch thick
- 2 cups thin bite-size strips carrot
- 2 cups bite-size strips red sweet pepper
- 12 fresh asparagus spears (about 12 ounces), trimmed
- 4 small yellow summer squash (about 1 pound), cut into ¼-inch slices
- ½ cup dry white wine or chicken broth
- 2 teaspoons snipped fresh rosemary or ½ teaspoon dried rosemary, crushed
- 2 cloves garlic, minced
- 2 tablespoons butter or margarine, cut up
  Hot cooked white or brown rice (optional)

1. Thaw fish, if frozen. Rinse fish; pat dry with paper towels. Measure thickness of fish. Cut into four equal pieces. Set aside.

2. Tear off eight 18-inch squares of heavy-duty foil. Place two squares together to form four stacks. Coat one side of each stack with *nonstick cooking spray*. Divide carrot, sweet pepper, and asparagus among stacks. Top with fish and squash.

3. For seasoning, in a small bowl combine wine, rosemary, ¼ teaspoon *salt,* ¼ teaspoon *black pepper,* and garlic. Drizzle over fish and vegetables; top with butter. Bring up opposite edges of each foil stack; seal with a double fold. Fold remaining edges to completely enclose the fish and vegetables, leaving space for steam to build.

4. For a charcoal grill, grill foil packets on the rack of an uncovered grill directly over medium coals for 12 to 14 minutes per ½-inch thickness of fish or until fish begins to flake when tested with a fork and vegetables are tender, carefully opening packets to check doneness. (For a gas grill, preheat grill. Reduce heat to medium. Place foil packets on grill rack over heat. Cover and grill as above.) If desired, serve with hot cooked rice.

Per packet: 308 cal., 14 g total fat (5 g sat. fat), 76 mg chol., 320 mg sodium, 15 g carbo., 5 g fiber, 27 g pro.
Daily Values: 177% vit. A, 212% vit. C, 9% calcium, 12% iron
Exchanges: 2½ Vegetable, 3 Very Lean Meat, 3 Fat

Caramelized Salmon with Orange-Pineapple Salsa LOW FAT

The orange-scented sugar rub turns an inviting golden brown during grilling.

Prep: 20 minutes **Marinate:** 8 hours
Grill: 14 minutes **Makes:** 4 servings

- 1 1½-pound fresh or frozen salmon fillet (with skin), 1 inch thick
- 2 tablespoons sugar
- 2½ teaspoons finely shredded orange peel
- 1 teaspoon salt
- ¼ teaspoon freshly ground black pepper
- 2 oranges, peeled, sectioned, and coarsely chopped
- 1 cup chopped fresh pineapple or canned crushed pineapple, drained
- 2 tablespoons snipped fresh cilantro
- 1 tablespoon finely chopped shallot
- 1 fresh jalapeño chile pepper, seeded and finely chopped (see tip, page 74)

1. Thaw fish, if frozen. Rinse fish; pat dry with paper towels. Place fish, skin side down, in a shallow dish. In a small bowl stir together sugar, 1½ teaspoons of the orange peel, salt, and pepper. Sprinkle mixture evenly over fish (not on skin side); rub in with your fingers. Cover and marinate in the refrigerator for 8 to 24 hours.

2. Meanwhile, for salsa, in a small bowl stir together remaining 1 teaspoon orange peel, the orange, pineapple, cilantro, shallot, and jalapeño pepper. Cover and chill until ready to serve or up to 24 hours.

3. Drain fish, discarding any liquid. For a charcoal grill, arrange medium-hot coals around a drip pan. Test for medium heat above the pan. Place fish, skin side down, on greased grill rack over drip pan. Cover and grill for 14 to 18 minutes or until fish begins to flake when tested with a fork. (For a gas grill, preheat grill. Reduce heat to medium. Adjust for indirect cooking. Grill as above.)

4. To serve, cut the fish into four equal pieces, cutting to, but not through, the skin. Carefully slip a metal spatula between the fish and the skin, lifting the fish away from the skin. Serve fish with salsa.

Per piece + ½ cup salsa: 258 cal., 6 g total fat (1 g sat. fat), 81 mg chol., 688 mg sodium, 20 g carbo., 2 g fiber, 32 g pro.
Daily Values: 10% vit. A, 75% vit. C, 6% calcium, 9% iron
Exchanges: 1½ Fruit, 4½ Very Lean Meat

Orange and Dill Sea Bass LOW FAT FAST

For remarkable flavor, grill fish fillets on a bed of orange slices. It's even better than cooked fish drizzled with lemon juice.

Prep: 15 minutes **Grill:** 6 minutes **Makes:** 4 servings

- 4 5- to 6-ounce fresh or frozen sea bass or orange roughy fillets, cut ¾ inch thick
- 2 tablespoons snipped fresh dill
- 2 tablespoons olive oil
- ¼ teaspoon salt
- ¼ teaspoon white pepper
- 4 large oranges, cut into ¼-inch slices
- 1 orange, cut into wedges

1. Thaw fish, if frozen. Rinse fish; pat dry with paper towels. In a small bowl stir together dill, olive oil, salt, and white pepper. Brush both sides of fish fillets with dill mixture.

2. For a charcoal grill, arrange a layer of orange slices on greased grill rack directly over medium coals. Arrange fish on orange slices. Cover and grill for 6 to 9 minutes or until fish begins to flake when tested with a fork (do not turn fish). (For a gas grill, preheat grill. Reduce heat to medium. Arrange orange slices and fish on greased grill rack over heat. Cover and grill as above.)

3. To serve, use a spatula to transfer fish and grilled orange slices to a serving platter. Squeeze the juice from orange wedges over fish.

Per fillet: 268 cal., 10 g total fat (2 g sat. fat), 58 mg chol., 242 mg sodium, 18 g carbo., 3 g fiber, 28 g pro.
Daily Values: 11% vit. A, 133% vit. C, 7% calcium, 4% iron
Exchanges: 1 Fruit, 4 Very Lean Meat, 1½ Fat

Is It Done Yet?

Use these tips to determine fish doneness.

● If grilling fish with its skin on, let the skin become crisp and brown and allow it to pull away from the grill before turning.

● Check the flesh at the thickest part of a fillet, steak, or whole fish. When cooked, the flesh will be opaque and moist, and will begin to pull away from the bones. A fork can pull cooked fish apart into large flakes.

● To test thicker, denser fish steaks for doneness, insert an instant-read thermometer horizontally. When steaks are done, the internal temperature should read 140°F.

Tuna Steaks with Cumin Tartar Sauce

Tuna Steaks with Cumin Tartar Sauce

To toast cumin seeds for the tartar sauce, place them in a small nonstick skillet. Heat over medium heat for several minutes until the seeds are fragrant, stirring occasionally.

Prep: 25 minutes **Marinate:** 30 minutes
Grill: 8 minutes **Makes:** 4 steaks

    4 **6-ounce fresh or frozen tuna steaks, cut 1 inch thick**
   ¼ **cup cooking oil**
    3 **tablespoons lemon juice**
    1 **teaspoon cumin seeds, toasted**
   ¼ **teaspoon black pepper**
    2 **cloves garlic, minced**
    1 **recipe Cumin Tartar Sauce**

1. Thaw fish, if frozen. Rinse fish; pat dry with paper towels. Place fish in a resealable plastic bag set in a shallow dish. For marinade, in a small bowl stir together oil, lemon juice, cumin seeds, pepper, and garlic. Pour over fish; seal bag and turn to coat fish. Marinate in the refrigerator for 30 to 60 minutes, turning fish once. Drain fish, reserving marinade.

2. For a charcoal grill, grill fish on the greased rack of an uncovered grill directly over medium coals for 8 to 12 minutes or until fish begins to flake when tested with a fork and center of fish is still slightly pink; halfway through grilling

gently turn and brush with remaining marinade. Discard any remaining marinade. (For a gas grill, preheat grill. Reduce heat to medium. Place fish on greased grill rack over heat. Cover and grill as above.) Serve with Cumin Tartar Sauce.

Cumin Tartar Sauce: Finely chop any large fruit pieces in 2 tablespoons mango chutney. In a small bowl combine chutney, ⅓ cup mayonnaise or salad dressing, 1 teaspoon Dijon-style mustard, 1 teaspoon lemon juice, and 1 teaspoon cumin seeds, toasted. Cover and chill until serving time. Makes ½ cup.

Per steak + 2 tablespoons sauce: 520 cal., 37 g total fat (6 g sat. fat), 77 mg chol., 231 mg sodium, 6 g carbo., 0 g fiber, 40 g pro.
Daily Values: 68% vit. A, 14% vit. C, 3% calcium, 14% iron
Exchanges: ½ Other Carbo., 6 Very Lean Meat, 6 Fat

Blackened Swordfish with Hominy Dirty Rice

Like blackened fish, dirty rice is a Louisiana specialty, made by adding ground chicken livers to the rice. This less traditional version includes pork sausage and hominy.

Prep: 30 minutes **Cook:** 15 minutes
Grill: 8 minutes **Makes:** 4 servings

    4 **4- to 5-ounce fresh or frozen swordfish or tuna steaks, cut 1 inch thick**
    1 **teaspoon black pepper**
    1 **teaspoon paprika**
   ½ **teaspoon salt**
   ½ **teaspoon white pepper**
   ½ **teaspoon cayenne pepper**
   ½ **teaspoon dried thyme, crushed**
    4 **cloves garlic, minced**
    3 **tablespoons butter or margarine, melted**
    1 **recipe Hominy Dirty Rice (page 339)**

1. Thaw fish, if frozen. Rinse fish; pat dry with paper towels. In a small bowl combine black pepper, paprika, salt, white pepper, cayenne pepper, thyme, and garlic. Stir in melted butter. Brush both sides of fish with melted butter mixture.

2. For a charcoal grill, grill fish on the greased rack of an uncovered grill directly over medium coals for 8 to 12 minutes or until fish begins to flake when tested with a fork, turning once halfway through grilling. (For a gas grill, preheat grill. Reduce heat to medium. Place fish on greased grill rack over heat. Cover and grill as above.) Serve with Hominy Dirty Rice.

Hominy Dirty Rice: In a large skillet cook 8 ounces bulk pork sausage, ¼ cup finely chopped onion, 3 tablespoons finely chopped celery, 3 tablespoons finely chopped green sweet pepper, 3 tablespoons finely chopped red sweet pepper, and 2 tablespoons minced garlic over medium heat for 4 to 5 minutes or until sausage is no longer pink and vegetables are tender. Drain off fat, if necessary. Stir in 1½ cups chilled cooked white rice, ⅔ cup chicken broth, ⅓ cup hominy, ¼ teaspoon black pepper, and ⅛ to ¼ teaspoon cayenne pepper. Bring mixture to boiling; reduce heat. Simmer, uncovered, about 5 minutes or until mixture is heated through and most of the liquid has been absorbed, stirring occasionally.

Per steak + ½ cup rice: 504 cal., 27 g total fat (12 g sat. fat), 106 mg chol., 1,001 mg sodium, 26 g carbo., 2 g fiber, 34 g pro.
Daily Values: 26% vit. A, 44% vit. C, 6% calcium, 16% iron
Exchanges: 1½ Other Carbo., 2 Very Lean Meat, 2 High-Fat Meat, 2 Fat

Cilantro-Lime Trout `EASY`

Prep: 15 minutes **Grill:** 8 minutes **Makes:** 4 servings

- **4** 8- to 10-ounce fresh or frozen dressed trout, heads removed
- **3** tablespoons lime juice
- **2** tablespoons olive oil
- **2** tablespoons snipped fresh cilantro or parsley
- **½** teaspoon salt
- **¼** teaspoon cracked black pepper
  Lime wedges

1. Thaw trout, if frozen. Rinse trout; pat dry with paper towels. In a small bowl combine lime juice and oil. Brush the inside and outside of each trout with juice mixture. Sprinkle cilantro, salt, and pepper evenly inside the cavity of each trout.

2. For a charcoal grill, place trout in a well-greased grill basket. Place basket on the rack of an uncovered grill directly over medium coals. Grill for 8 to 12 minutes or until trout begins to flake when tested with a fork, turning basket once halfway through grilling. (For a gas grill, preheat grill. Reduce heat to medium. Place fish in well-greased grill basket. Place grill basket on grill rack over heat. Cover; grill as above.) Serve trout with lime wedges.

Per trout: 259 cal., 14 g total fat (3 g sat. fat), 83 mg chol., 342 mg sodium, 1 g carbo., 0 g fiber, 30 g pro.
Daily Values: 10% vit. A, 13% vit. C, 10% calcium, 3% iron
Exchanges: 4 Very Lean Meat, 2½ Fat

Marinate Safely

When used properly, marinades impart wonderful flavor to grilled foods. Follow these simple safety guidelines:

Always marinate food in the refrigerator. If the marinade is to be used later for basting, reserve some before it contacts any raw meat. If it is to be served as a sauce, boil it thoroughly to destroy harmful bacteria.

Shrimp Scampi Kabobs `LOW FAT`

Prep: 25 minutes **Grill:** 6 minutes **Makes:** 4 servings

- **1** pound fresh or frozen medium shrimp in shells (26 to 30)
- **2** tablespoons butter or margarine
- **1** tablespoon olive oil or cooking oil
- **3** cloves garlic, minced
- **¼** cup dry white wine
- **2** tablespoons snipped fresh parsley
- **1** teaspoon finely shredded lemon peel
- **¼** teaspooon black pepper
- **6** green onions, cut into 1-inch pieces
- **1** large red sweet pepper, cut into 1-inch pieces

1. Thaw shrimp, if frozen. Peel shrimp, leaving tails intact. Devein shrimp (see photos, page 296). In a small saucepan combine butter and oil. Add garlic and cook over medium-high heat for 2 minutes; remove from heat. Stir in wine, parsley, lemon peel, and black pepper; set aside.

2. Thread shrimp, green onion pieces, and sweet pepper pieces onto eight 8- to 10-inch skewers. (If using wooden skewers, soak them in water for at least 30 minutes before threading with food to prevent burning when grilling.) Brush with half of the garlic mixture.

3. Grill kabobs on a grill rack directly over medium heat for 6 to 8 minutes or until shrimp turn opaque, turning once and brushing with garlic mixture halfway through grilling. (For a gas grill, preheat grill. Reduce heat to medium. Place shrimp on grill rack over heat. Cover and grill as above.) Place on a platter. Drizzle with remaining garlic mixture.

Per 2 kabobs: 206 cal., 11 g total fat (4 g sat. fat), 145 mg chol., 157 mg sodium, 6 g carbo., 2 g fiber, 18 g pro.
Daily Values: 39% vit. A, 141% vit. C, 7% calcium, 15% iron
Exchanges: ½ Vegetable, 2½ Very Lean Meat, 2 Fat

Glazed Prosciutto-Wrapped Shrimp `LOW FAT`

Prep: 30 minutes **Grill:** 6 minutes **Makes:** 4 servings

- **24** fresh or frozen large shrimp in shells
- **½** cup bourbon grilling sauce
- **½** teaspoon chili powder
- **8** thin slices prosciutto
   Hot couscous (optional)
   Snipped fresh parsley (optional)

1. Thaw shrimp, if frozen. Peel and devein shrimp (see photos, page 296). Set aside. In a small bowl stir together grilling sauce and chili powder. Cut each prosciutto slice lengthwise into three strips. Wrap one prosciutto strip around each shrimp. Thread wrapped shrimp on four long metal skewers, leaving ¼-inch spaces between pieces. Brush shrimp with sauce.

2. For a charcoal grill, grill shrimp on the rack of an uncovered grill directly over medium coals for 6 to 9 minutes or until shrimp are opaque, turning once halfway through grilling and brushing occasionally with sauce. (For a gas grill, preheat grill. Reduce heat to medium. Place shrimp on grill rack over heat. Cover and grill as above.) If desired, serve with couscous and sprinkle with parsley.

Per 6 shrimp: 195 cal., 4 g total fat (1 g sat. fat), 207 mg chol., 932 mg sodium, 5 g carbo., 0 g fiber, 32 g pro.
Daily Values: 12% vit. A, 7% vit. C, 7% calcium, 18% iron
Exchanges: 4½ Very Lean Meat, ½ Fat

Glazed Prosciutto-Wrapped Shrimp

Vegetable Pizzas

For crispier crusts, grill untopped pita breads on the grill rack directly over medium coals for 1 to 2 minutes or until lightly toasted.

Prep: 25 minutes **Grill:** 10 minutes **Makes:** 4 servings

- **1** medium zucchini, quartered lengthwise
- **1** small yellow summer squash, quartered lengthwise
- **1** small red sweet pepper, quartered lengthwise
- **2** tablespoons olive oil
- **1** large ripe tomato, seeded and chopped
- **¼** cup mayonnaise or salad dressing
- **3** tablespoons purchased basil pesto
- **4** 6- to 7-inch pita breads or individual pizza crusts (such as Boboli)
- **1** cup shredded mozzarella or smoked provolone cheese

1. Brush zucchini, summer squash, and sweet pepper with olive oil; sprinkle with ¼ teaspoon *salt* and ⅛ teaspoon *black pepper*. For a charcoal grill, grill vegetables on the rack of an uncovered grill directly over medium coals until crisp-tender, turning once halfway through grilling. Allow 8 to 10 minutes for sweet pepper and 5 to 6 minutes for zucchini and summer squash. Remove vegetables from grill.

2. Chop grilled vegetables. In a medium bowl combine chopped vegetables, tomato, mayonnaise, and pesto. Spread vegetable mixture over one side of pitas. Sprinkle with shredded cheese. Place on grill rack. Cover and grill for 2 to 3 minutes or until pitas are lightly toasted, vegetables are heated, and cheese melts. Carefully remove from grill. (For a gas grill, preheat grill. Reduce heat to medium. Cover and grill vegetables and pitas as above.)

Per pizza: 513 cal., 33 g total fat (6 g sat. fat), 34 mg chol., 821 mg sodium, 41 g carbo., 3 g fiber, 14 g pro.
Daily Values: 24% vit. A, 74% vit. C, 21% calcium, 12% iron
Exchanges: 1½ Vegetable, 2 Starch, 1 Medium-Fat Meat, 5 Fat

Seafood Pizza: Prepare as above, except add 5 ounces smoked salmon; one 9½ ounce can tuna, well drained; or 5 ounces chopped cooked, peeled, deveined shrimp to vegetable mixture.

Per pizza: 555 cal., 34 g total fat (7 g sat. fat), 42 mg chol., 1,099 mg sodium, 41 g carbo., 3 g fiber, 21 g pro.
Daily Values: 25% vit. A, 74% vit. C, 21% calcium, 14% iron
Exchanges: 1½ Vegetable, 2 Starch, 1 Medium-Fat Meat, 1 Lean Meat, 5 Fat

Corn on the Cob with Herb Butter

Buy the freshest ears of sweet corn you can find. The quicker the corn gets from the field to your grill, the better.

Prep: 20 minutes **Grill:** 25 minutes **Makes:** 6 servings

> 6 **fresh ears corn (with husks)**
> 6 **tablespoons butter or margarine, softened**
> 36 **sprigs or leaves of cilantro or basil**
> **Lime or lemon wedges (optional)**

1. Carefully peel back corn husks but do not remove. Remove and discard the silks. Gently rinse corn; pat dry. Spread softened butter over ears of corn. Space six herb sprigs or leaves evenly around each ear, gently pressing them into butter. Carefully fold husks back around ears. Tie husks at the top with string.

2. For a charcoal grill, grill corn on the rack of an uncovered grill directly over medium coals for 25 to 30 minutes or until corn kernels are tender, turning and rearranging occasionally. (For a gas grill, preheat grill. Reduce heat to medium. Place corn on grill rack over heat. Cover and grill as above.)

3. To serve, remove string from corn; peel back husks. If desired, squeeze lime juice over corn.

Per ear: 185 cal., 13 g total fat (8 g sat. fat), 33 mg chol., 138 mg sodium, 17 g carbo., 2 g fiber, 3 g pro.
Daily Values: 15% vit. A, 9% vit. C, 1% calcium, 3% iron
Exchanges: 1 Starch, 2½ Fat

Grilling Indoors

Tabletop grills let you grill year-round.

● Most indoor grills have nonstick grill racks, so you only need to grease the rack if you're cooking poultry, fish, seafood, or vegetables. For those foods, before preheating lightly coat the rack with nonstick cooking spray or brush it with cooking oil. To protect a grill's nonstick surface, use only plastic or wooden utensils. When the food is cooked, transfer it to a cutting board before dividing into servings.

● When cooking with a covered grill, use meat of uniform thickness so the lid touches the entire surface of the meat and closes completely. Otherwise you'll have to turn the meat once halfway through grilling.

Chipotle Pork Soft Tacos

Strips of marinated pork, rather than ground beef, stuff these tacos. The marinade's chipotle peppers provide the heat.

Prep: 15 minutes **Marinate:** 2 hours
Grill: 6 minutes (covered) or 12 minutes (uncovered)
Makes: 4 servings

> 4 **boneless pork loin chops, cut ¾ inch thick**
> ¼ **cup sherry vinegar**
> 1 **tablespoon packed brown sugar**
> 1 **teaspoon dried thyme, crushed**
> ½ **teaspoon salt**
> ½ **teaspoon ground cumin**
> ¼ **teaspoon black pepper**
> **Dash ground cloves**
> 2 **chipotle chile peppers in adobo sauce, finely chopped (about 2 tablespoons)**
> 4 **cloves garlic, minced**
> 8 **6-inch flour tortillas**
> **Shredded lettuce**
> **Chopped tomato**
> **Shredded Monterey Jack cheese with jalapeño peppers**
> **Dairy sour cream**

1. Place chops in a resealable plastic bag set in a large bowl. For marinade, in a small bowl stir together vinegar, brown sugar, thyme, salt, cumin, black pepper, cloves, chipotle peppers, and garlic. Pour marinade over pork in bag; seal bag. Marinate in the refrigerator for 2 to 4 hours, turning bag occasionally. Drain, discarding marinade.

2. Preheat indoor electric grill. Place pork on the grill rack. If using a covered grill, close lid. Grill until an instant-read thermometer inserted into the sides of chops registers 160°F. For a covered grill, allow 6 to 8 minutes. For an uncovered grill, allow 12 to 15 minutes, turning once halfway through grilling. Slice pork across the grain into bite-size strips.

3. Place tortillas on grill rack. Grill for 20 to 30 seconds or until warm, turning once if using an uncovered grill. Serve pork on tortillas with lettuce, tomato, cheese, and sour cream.

Per 2 tacos: 534 cal., 24 g total fat (11 g sat. fat), 107 mg chol., 540 mg sodium, 34 g carbo., 2 g fiber, 43 g pro.
Daily Values: 15% vit. A, 12% vit. C, 30% calcium, 18% iron
Exchanges: 2 Starch, 5 Lean Meat, 2 Fat

Chicken and Roasted Pepper Sandwiches

Chicken and Roasted Pepper Sandwiches

Prep: 15 minutes **Marinate:** 15 minutes
Grill: 4 minutes (covered) or 10 minutes (uncovered)
Makes: 4 sandwiches

- ¼ **cup olive oil**
- 4 **teaspoons red wine vinegar**
- 1 **tablespoon snipped fresh thyme**
- ½ **teaspoon salt**
- ¼ **teaspoon crushed red pepper**
- 4 **skinless, boneless chicken breast halves**
- 8 **¾-inch bias-cut slices Italian bread**
- ¼ **cup semisoft cheese with herbs or semisoft goat cheese (chèvre)**
- 1 **cup roasted red sweet peppers (about one 7-ounce jar), cut into strips**
- ½ **cup fresh basil, watercress, or baby spinach leaves**

1. For marinade, in a small bowl whisk together oil, vinegar, thyme, salt, and crushed red pepper. Reserve 2 tablespoons of mixture; set aside.

2. Place chicken between two sheets of plastic wrap; pound lightly with the flat side of a meat mallet to about ½-inch thickness. Place in a resealable plastic bag set in a shallow dish. Add remaining marinade; seal bag. Marinate at room temperature about 15 minutes or in the refrigerator for up to 1 hour, turning bag once.

3. Lightly coat the rack of an indoor electric grill with *nonstick cooking spray*. Preheat grill. Drain chicken, discarding marinade. Place chicken on grill rack. If using a covered grill, close the

lid. Grill until chicken is no longer pink (170°F). For a covered grill, allow 3 to 4 minutes. For an uncovered grill, allow 8 to 10 minutes, turning once halfway through grilling.

4. Brush cut sides of bread with the reserved marinade. Place bread, cut sides down, on grill rack. If using a covered grill, close the lid. Grill until lightly toasted. For a covered grill, allow 1 to 2 minutes. For an uncovered grill, allow 2 to 4 minutes, turning once halfway through grilling. Remove bread from grill.

5. To serve, place each chicken breast on a grilled bread slice. Spread with cheese and top with sweet pepper and basil. Top with remaining grilled bread slices.

Per sandwich: 381 cal., 12 g total fat (3 g sat. fat), 69 mg chol., 585 mg sodium, 33 g carbo., 3 g fiber, 33 g pro.
Daily Values: 8% vit. A, 172% vit. C, 8% calcium, 19% iron
Exchanges: ½ Vegetable, 2 Starch, 4 Very Lean Meat, 1½ Fat

Herb-Pepper Sirloin Steak

Prep: 10 minutes **Grill:** 5 minutes (covered) or 12 minutes (uncovered) **Makes:** 4 servings

- 1 **tablespoon ketchup**
- 1 **teaspoon snipped fresh rosemary or ¼ teaspoon dried rosemary, crushed**
- 1 **teaspoon snipped fresh basil or ¼ teaspoon dried basil, crushed**
- ¼ **teaspoon coarsely ground black pepper**
  Dash garlic powder
  Dash ground cardamom (optional)
- 1 **1-pound boneless beef sirloin steak, cut 1 inch thick**

1. Preheat indoor electric grill. In a small bowl stir together ketchup, rosemary, basil, pepper, garlic powder, and, if desired, cardamom. Trim fat from steak. Coat both sides of steak with ketchup mixture.

2. Place steak on the grill rack. If using a covered grill, close lid. Grill until steak is desired doneness. For a covered grill, allow 5 to 7 minutes for medium rare or 7 to 9 minutes for medium. For an uncovered grill, allow 12 to 15 minutes for medium rare or 15 to 18 minutes for medium, turning once halfway through grilling. To serve, cut into four equal pieces.

Per 3 ounces: 144 cal., 4 g total fat (1 g sat. fat), 53 mg chol., 105 mg sodium, 1 g carbo., 0 g fiber, 24 g pro.
Daily Values: 1% vit. A, 1% vit. C, 2% calcium, 14% iron
Exchanges: 3½ Very Lean Meat, ½ Fat

Smoking Essentials

Now that you've mastered the grill, it's time to give something new a try. For unbeatable flavor, smoking is the answer. And it's so easy! Read on for hints, tips, and tricks.

What Is Smoking?

Smoking requires low temperatures (180°F to 220°F) and long cooking times—up to three times as long as grilling times. The low heat causes the wood chunks to smolder, rather than burn, generating smoke that infuses food with flavor. Smoking can be done in a smoker or a grill. Smoke only those foods that can handle the assertive smoke flavor, such as beef, lamb, pork, poultry, oily fish, and game.

Tips for Smoking Success

The most common type of smoker is a vertical water smoker. They're easy to use, compact, and affordably priced. Follow these simple steps for best results:

● Maintain temperature by adding 8 to 10 fresh briquettes every hour. Do not add instant-start charcoal briquettes during the cooking process.

● Keep the water pan full, replenishing it as needed with hot tap water. The water helps keep the temperature steady and adds moisture to keep meats tender.

● Resist the temptation to peek. Heat and smoke escape each time you open the lid, sacrificing aroma and flavor.

● Start with a small amount of wood to see how you like the flavor and add more for more intense smoky taste. Don't overdo it, though, and don't add wood after the first half of smoking. Adding wood too late in the process can impart a bitter flavor.

Don't Have a Traditional Smoker?

Here's how to turn your grill into a smoker.
For a charcoal grill:
1. Soak wood chips or chunks in water for at least 1 hour. Drain and shake off excess water before adding to the fire.
2. Using long-handled tongs, arrange hot ash-covered coals around a foil pan that's filled with 1 inch of hot water.

3. Add presoaked chunks or chips to coals.
4. Place food on grill rack and cover.
5. Check food, temperature, and water pan once every hour.
6. Do not add additional wood during the last half of smoking. Too much exposure to smoke imparts a bitter flavor to food.

For a gas grill:
1. Soak wood chips or chunks in water for at least 1 hour; soak aromatic twigs 30 minutes. Drain; shake off water before adding to the fire.
2. If your grill is equipped with a smoker box attachment, before firing up the grill, fill water pan on smoker attachment with hot tap water. Place presoaked chunks/chips in the compartment as directed by manufacturer's instructions. If you don't have an attachment, use a foil pan (separate from the water pan) or a foil packet with holes punched in the bottom. Place pan on rack directly over heat source.
3. Place food on center of grill rack and cover.
4. Check food, temperature, and water pan once every hour.

Food and Wood Pairings

Wood type	Characteristics	Pair with
Alder	Delicate	Fish, pork, and poultry
Apple or cherry	Delicate, slightly sweet and fruity	Veal, pork, and poultry
Hickory	Strong and hearty, smoky	Brisket, ribs, pork chops, and game
Mesquite	Light, sweet	Most meats and vegetables
Oak	Assertive but versatile	Beef, pork, and poultry
Pecan	Similar to hickory but more subtle	Pork, poultry, and fish
Seaweed	Tangy, smoky	Shellfish

Texas-Style Beef Ribs

Add additional coals and water as needed to maintain temperature and moisture. Pass any remaining sauce with ribs.

Per 2 ribs: 443 cal., 18 g total fat (7 g sat. fat), 88 mg chol., 992 mg sodium, 32 g carbo., 1 g fiber, 38 g pro.
Daily Values: 11% vit. A, 20% vit. C, 7% calcium, 22% iron
Exchanges: 2 Other Carbo., 5 Lean Meat, 1 Fat

Steak with Creamy Horseradish Sauce

Prep: 15 minutes **Chill:** 1 hour **Soak:** 1 hour
Smoke: 2 hours **Makes:** 6 servings

- 1 2- to 2½-pound beef sirloin steak, cut 1½ inches thick
- ¾ teaspoon ground cumin
- ½ teaspoon cracked black pepper
- 4 cloves garlic, minced
- 6 to 8 oak or hickory wood chunks
- 1 recipe Creamy Horseradish Sauce

1. Trim fat from steak. Place steak in a shallow dish. For rub, in a small bowl combine cumin, pepper, ½ teaspoon *salt,* and garlic. Sprinkle rub evenly over one side of steak; rub in with your fingers. Cover and chill for 1 to 4 hours.

2. At least 1 hour before smoke cooking, soak wood chunks in enough water to cover. Drain before using.

3. In a smoker arrange preheated coals, drained wood chunks, and water pan according to the manufacturer's directions. Pour water into pan. Place steak, seasoned side up, on the grill rack over water pan. Cover; smoke until steak reaches desired doneness. Allow about 2 hours for medium rare (145°F) or about 2½ hours for medium doneness (160°F). Add additional coals and water as needed.

4. To serve, thinly slice steak across the grain and serve with Creamy Horseradish Sauce.

Creamy Horseradish Sauce: In a small bowl stir together ⅓ cup dairy sour cream, 2 tablespoons Dijon-style mustard, 1 tablespoon snipped fresh chives, and 2 teaspoons prepared horseradish. In a chilled mixing bowl beat ¼ cup whipping cream with an electric mixer on medium speed until soft peaks form. Fold whipped cream into sour cream mixture. Makes ¾ cup.

Per 4 ounces + 2 tablespoons sauce: 261 cal., 13 g total fat (6 g sat. fat), 110 mg chol., 212 mg sodium, 2 g carbo., 0 g fiber, 33 g pro.
Daily Values: 5% vit. A, 2% vit. C, 4% calcium, 23% iron
Exchanges: 5 Lean Meat

Texas-Style Beef Ribs

Prep: 30 minutes **Soak:** 1 hour
Smoke: 2½ hours **Makes:** 6 servings

- 6 to 8 mesquite or hickory wood chunks
- 6 pounds beef back ribs (about 12 ribs)
- 1 cup finely chopped onion
- ½ cup honey
- ½ cup ketchup
- 1 4-ounce can diced green chile peppers
- 1 tablespoon chili powder
- ½ teaspoon dry mustard
- 2 cloves garlic, minced

1. At least 1 hour before smoke cooking, soak wood chunks in enough water to cover. Drain before using.

2. Trim fat from ribs. For rub, in a small bowl combine 1½ teaspoons *salt* and 1½ teaspoons *black pepper.* Sprinkle rub evenly over ribs; rub in with your fingers.

3. For sauce, in a small saucepan combine onion, honey, ketchup, undrained chile peppers, chili powder, mustard, and garlic. Cook and stir over low heat for 10 to 15 minutes or until desired consistency.

4. In a smoker arrange preheated coals, drained wood chunks, and water pan according to manufacturer's directions. Pour water into pan. Place ribs, bone sides down, on grill rack over water pan. (Or place ribs in a rib rack and place on grill rack.) Cover and smoke for 2½ to 3 hours or until ribs are tender, brushing once with the sauce during the last 15 minutes of smoking.

Mustard-Bourbon-Glazed Ribs

Country-style ribs are the meatiest type of pork ribs. They take on plenty of flavor from the rub, tangy-sweet sauce, and fragrant smoke.

Prep: 15 minutes **Chill:** 1 hour **Soak:** 1 hour
Smoke: 2 hours **Makes:** 4 servings

- 1½ teaspoons black pepper
- ¾ teaspoon paprika
- ½ teaspoon garlic salt or onion salt
- 3 to 3½ pounds pork country-style ribs
- 8 to 10 oak or hickory wood chunks
- ⅓ cup brown mustard
- ⅓ cup bourbon or orange juice
- 2 tablespoons mild-flavored molasses
- 2 tablespoons soy sauce
- 1 to 2 tablespoons packed brown sugar

1. For rub, in a small bowl combine pepper, paprika, and garlic salt. Trim fat from ribs. Place ribs in a shallow dish. Sprinkle rub evenly over ribs; rub in with your fingers. Cover and chill for 1 to 4 hours.

2. At least 1 hour before smoke cooking, soak wood chunks in enough water to cover. Drain before using.

3. In a smoker arrange preheated coals, drained wood chunks, and water pan according to manufacturer's directions. Pour water into pan. Place ribs, bone sides down, on grill rack over water pan. Cover and smoke for 2 to 2½ hours or until tender. Add additional coals and water as needed to maintain temperature and moisture.

4. Meanwhile, for sauce, in a small saucepan whisk together mustard, bourbon, molasses, soy sauce, and brown sugar. Cook and stir until mixture comes to boiling; reduce heat. Simmer, uncovered, about 10 minutes or until mixture is desired consistency.

5. Just before serving, brush ribs with some of the sauce. Pass remaining sauce with the ribs.

Per ¼ ribs: 410 cal., 16 g total fat (5 g sat. fat), 121 mg chol.,
958 mg sodium, 13 g carbo., 1 g fiber, 39 g pro.
Daily Values: 4% vit. A, 3% vit. C, 10% calcium, 18% iron
Exchanges: 1 Other Carbo., 5½ Lean Meat, ½ Fat

Jerk-Style Smoked Chicken

Authentic Jamaican jerk chicken is spiced with thyme, allspice, and Scotch bonnet peppers before it's slowly cooked over the wood of the allspice tree. In this recipe, fruit wood chunks provide a similar flavor.

Prep: 15 minutes **Marinate:** 1 hour **Soak:** 1 hour
Smoke: 1½ hours **Makes:** 6 servings

- 3 pounds meaty chicken pieces (breasts, thighs, and drumsticks)
- ½ cup tomato juice
- ⅓ cup finely chopped onion (1 small)
- 2 tablespoons water
- 2 tablespoons lime juice
- 1 tablespoon cooking oil
- 1 tablespoon Pickapeppa sauce (optional)
- ½ teaspoon salt
- 4 cloves garlic, minced
- 6 to 8 fruit wood chunks
- 1 to 2 tablespoons Jamaican jerk seasoning
  Lime wedges

1. If desired, remove skin from chicken. Place chicken in a resealable plastic bag set in a deep dish. For marinade, in a bowl combine tomato juice, onion, water, lime juice, oil, Pickapeppa sauce (if desired), salt, and garlic. Pour over chicken; seal bag. Marinate in the refrigerator for 1 to 4 hours, turning bag occasionally.

2. At least 1 hour before smoke cooking, soak wood chunks in enough water to cover. Drain before using. Drain chicken, discarding marinade. Sprinkle jerk seasoning evenly over chicken; rub in with your fingers.

3. In a smoker arrange preheated coals, drained wood chunks, and water pan according to the manufacturer's directions. Pour water into pan. Place chicken, bone sides down, on the grill rack over water pan. Cover; smoke for 1½ to 2 hours or until chicken is tender and juices run clear (170°F for breasts, 180°F for thighs and drumsticks). Add additional coals and water as needed to maintain temperature and moisture. Serve chicken with lime wedges.

Per 2 pieces: 283 cal., 14 g total fat (4 g sat. fat), 104 mg chol.,
331 mg sodium, 3 g carbo., 0 g fiber, 34 g pro.
Daily Values: 2% vit. A, 8% vit. C, 3% calcium, 10% iron
Exchanges: 5 Very Lean Meat

Smoked Garlic Chicken

Fruit woods are good choices for smoking chicken or turkey because their mild-flavored smoke doesn't overpower the poultry.

Prep: 20 minutes **Soak:** 1 hour **Smoke:** 3¼ hours
Stand: 15 minutes **Makes:** 6 to 8 servings

    10 to 12 apple or cherry wood chunks
     1 6- to 7-pound whole roasting chicken
     1 lemon
     2 teaspoons dried parsley
    ½ teaspoon salt
    ¼ teaspoon black pepper
     2 cloves garlic, minced

1. At least 1 hour before smoke cooking, soak wood chunks in enough water to cover. Drain before using.

2. Rinse the inside of the chicken; pat dry with paper towels. Finely shred enough peel from the lemon to equal 2 teaspoons. For rub, in a small bowl combine lemon peel, parsley, salt, pepper, and garlic. Halve the lemon. Squeeze the juice from one half over the entire surface of the chicken. Sprinkle rub evenly over chicken; rub in with your fingers. Place both lemon halves in the chicken cavity. Skewer the neck skin to the back. Tie legs to tail. Twist wing tips under back.

3. Insert a meat thermometer into the center of an inside thigh muscle, making sure the tip does not touch bone.

4. In a smoker arrange preheated coals, drained wood chunks, and water pan according to the manufacturer's directions. Pour water into pan. Place chicken, breast side up, on grill rack over water pan. Cover and smoke for 3¼ to 4 hours or until thermometer registers 180°F. Add additional coals and water as needed to maintain temperature and moisture.

5. Remove chicken from smoker. Cover with foil and let stand for 15 minutes before carving. Remove and discard lemon halves from chicken cavity before serving.

Per ⅙ chicken: 690 cal., 50 g total fat (14 g sat. fat), 237 mg chol., 372 mg sodium, 1 g carbo., 0 g fiber, 56 g pro.
Daily Values: 7% vit. A, 5% vit. C, 4% calcium, 18% iron
Exchanges: 8 Lean Meat, 5½ Fat

Maple-Smoked Salmon Fillet

If you can find fresh Alaskan king salmon, buy it. Wild kings are available only for part of the year, but fortunately, it's during prime smoking time. See photo, page 319.

Prep: 30 minutes **Marinate:** 1 hour **Soak:** 1 hour
Smoke: 50 minutes **Makes:** 4 servings

     1 2-pound fresh or frozen salmon fillet
        (with skin), about 1 inch thick
     6 to 8 alder or apple wood chunks
    ½ cup pure maple syrup
     2 tablespoons water
     1 tablespoon coarsely cracked mixed
        peppercorns
    ¼ teaspoon salt
     2 tablespoons pure maple syrup

1. Thaw salmon, if frozen. Rinse salmon and pat dry with paper towels. At least 1 hour before smoke cooking, soak wood chunks in enough water to cover. Drain before using.

2. Place salmon in a large resealable plastic bag set in a baking dish. For marinade, in a small bowl combine the ½ cup maple syrup, the water, peppercorns, and salt. Pour marinade over salmon; seal bag. Marinate in refrigerator for 1 hour, turning bag occasionally. Drain salmon, discarding marinade.

3. In a smoker arrange preheated coals, drained wood chunks, and water pan according to the manufacturer's directions. Pour water into pan. Place salmon, skin side down, on grill rack over water pan. Cover and smoke for 45 to 60 minutes or until fish begins to flake when tested with a fork. Brush salmon with the 2 tablespoons maple syrup. Cover and smoke for 5 minutes more.

4. To serve, cut fish into four equal pieces, cutting to, but not through, the skin. Carefully slip a metal spatula between fish and skin, lifting fish away from skin.

Per piece: 516 cal., 25 g total fat (5 g sat. fat), 133 mg chol., 251 mg sodium, 26 g carbo., 1 g fiber, 45 g pro.
Daily Values: 2% vit. A, 13% vit. C, 7% calcium, 12% iron
Exchanges: 1½ Other Carbo., 6 Lean Meat, 2 Fat

Turkey Fryer Essentials

No matter what you're cooking in your turkey fryer, there are no shortcuts when it comes to safety in setting up and using the fryer.

Set Up and Take Down

● Read and follow manufacturer's instructions.
● Never operate a turkey fryer indoors or in a garage or other attached structure. Avoid cooking on a wooden deck, which can catch fire.
● Position the fryer on a level dirt or grassy area. You also can place the fryer on a concrete surface. To avoid grease stains, put a layer of sand under and around the fryer. The sand absorbs any oil that spills and easily cleans up when finished.
● Check the level of fuel in your propane tank. You will need about 1½ hours of fuel for deep-frying a turkey—half for bringing the oil up to temperature and half for the actual cooking.
● Never leave hot oil unattended. The oil stays hot for hours after you turn off the burner, so allow it to cool in a safe place.
● Keep kids and pets away from cooking area.

Equipment

● Wear heat-resistant gloves, long sleeves, and an apron to protect yourself from splattering oil.
● Use long-handled tongs, meat forks, slotted fry spoons, and/or a fry basket.
● Have plates, platters, and paper towels handy.
● Keep a fire extinguisher close at hand.

Cooking Oil Smoking Points

Oil	Oil Temperature
Safflower oil	450°F
Cottonseed oil	450°F
Canola oil	437°F
Soybean oil	410°F
Peanut oil	410°F
Corn oil	410°F

Working with Oil

● The oils listed in the chart above are best for deep-frying.
● Do not cover the pot when deep-frying.
● Do not overfill the fryer with oil.
● Make sure there is 5 to 6 inches from the top of the oil to the top of the pot for the oil to bubble up when cooking.

● Once the oil reaches the appropriate temperature, turn off the burner before slowly lowering the food into the hot oil. Relight the burner after the food is in the pot and turn it off again when you're ready to remove the food.
● Monitor the oil temperature by using a deep-fry thermometer.
● Allow oil to completely cool after use. To discard, ladle the oil back into original container.
● If you plan to reuse the oil, strain it through 100-percent-cotton cheesecloth and store in a covered container in the refrigerator. You can reuse the oil once or twice within one month only if the food cooked in the oil didn't burn.

Calculating Fry Time

Food	Minutes/ Pound	Oil Temperature*
Turkey, whole	3	350°F
Turkey breast with bone	8	350°F
Turkey legs	8	350°F
Chicken, whole	7	350°F
Cornish hens	8	350°F
Duck, whole	10	350°F

*To maintain recommended temperatures, oil must be 10°F hotter before food is added.

Cajun Deep-Fried Turkey

If the turkey has not reached 180°F when you check for doneness, remove the thermometer and slowly lower the turkey back into the oil. Fry 3 to 5 minutes more and check temperature again.

Prep: 30 minutes **Fry:** 24 minutes
Stand: 15 minutes **Makes:** 10 to 12 servings + leftovers

- 1 8- to 10-pound turkey
  Peanut oil
- 1½ teaspoons salt
- 1½ teaspoons sweet paprika
- ¾ teaspoon dried thyme, crushed
- ¾ teaspoon black pepper
- ½ teaspoon garlic powder
- ½ teaspoon onion powder
- ¼ teaspoon cayenne pepper

1. Remove neck, giblets, and tail from turkey. Rinse inside of turkey; pat dry with paper towels. If present, remove and discard the plastic leg holder and pop-up timer. Preheat oil to 350°F.

2. For rub, in a small bowl combine salt, paprika, thyme, black pepper, garlic powder, onion powder, and cayenne pepper. Slip your fingers between turkey skin and meat to loosen the skin over the breast and leg areas. Lift skin and spread some of the rub directly over breast, thigh, and drumstick meat. Season body cavity with any remaining rub. Tuck the ends of the drumsticks under the band of skin across the tail

Cajun Deep-Fried Turkey

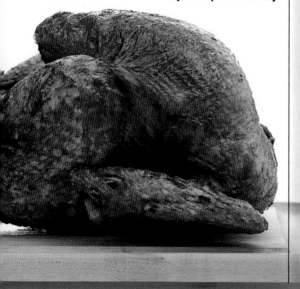

or tie legs with 100-percent-cotton string. Twist wing tips under back.

3. Place turkey, breast side down, in turkey rack. Use grab hook to slowly lower turkey into hot oil. Be cautious of splattering oil. Maintain oil temperature around 350°F. Fry turkey for 24 to 30 minutes (3 minutes per pound). Remove turkey from hot oil to check doneness by inserting an instant-read meat thermometer into the meaty part of the thigh. Turkey is done when thermometer registers 180°F.

4. Remove turkey from hot oil; drain on a wire rack. Let stand 15 minutes before carving.

Per 4 ounces: 390 cal., 28 g total fat (6 g sat. fat), 119 mg chol., 424 mg sodium, 1 g carbo., 0 g fiber, 32 g pro.
Daily Values: 4% vit. A, 3% calcium, 13% iron
Exchanges: 4½ Lean Meat, 3 Fat

Turkey-Frying Tips

For a tender, tasty bird, follow these tips:

- Select turkeys that weigh 12 pounds or less. If you need to serve more people, consider frying two smaller turkeys.
- Never fry a turkey that's too big for the fryer pot. The pot must be big enough to hold the turkey and enough oil to completely cover the turkey (up to 5 gallons).
- To determine the amount of oil needed, place the unwrapped, frozen turkey in the empty fryer pot; fill the pot with enough water to cover the bird by 1 to 2 inches. Remove the bird and mark the waterline. This is the level of oil you'll need. Dry the pot thoroughly before adding oil.
- Rinse inside of thawed turkey; thoroughly pat dry inside and out with paper towels.
- Make sure the equipment is dry before frying. All food that goes into the fryer must be blotted dry.
- Do not stuff the bird.
- Remove all plastic parts, including the tie that holds the turkey legs together and the pop-up timer.
- Check the internal temperature of turkey for doneness by inserting an instant-read thermometer into the meaty part of the thigh. When the turkey is done, thermometer should register 180°F.
- Let the turkey stand for 15 minutes before carving to serve.

Thanksgiving-Style Turkey Sandwiches

Thanksgiving-Style Turkey Sandwiches

Prep: 45 minutes **Fry:** 48 minutes **Stand:** 15 minutes
Makes: 24 sandwiches

  1 **6- to 8-pound turkey breast with bone**
     Peanut oil
     Salt
     Black pepper
  1 **recipe Orange-Walnut Cream Cheese Spread**
 24 **sweet Hawaiian or egg bread rolls, split**
 24 **lettuce leaves**
  1 **16-ounce can whole cranberry sauce,**
     drained

1. Rinse inside of turkey breast; pat dry with paper towels. If present, remove and discard pop-up timer. Preheat oil to 350°F.

2. Place turkey breast, breast side up, in a basket. Slowly lower basket into hot oil. Be cautious of splattering oil. Maintain oil temperature around 350°F. Fry turkey breast for 48 to 64 minutes (8 minutes per pound). Remove turkey from hot oil to check doneness. Insert a meat thermometer into the thickest part of the breast without touching bone. Turkey is done when thermometer reads 170°F. Remove turkey breast from hot oil; drain on a wire rack. Let stand for 15 minutes before carving.

3. To serve, thinly slice turkey breast. Season to taste with salt and pepper. Spread Orange-Walnut Cream Cheese Spread on bottoms of rolls. Top each with lettuce, turkey, and a spoonful of cranberry sauce. Top with roll tops.

Orange-Walnut Cream Cheese Spread: In a small bowl combine one 8-ounce package cream cheese, softened; 2 tablespoons chopped walnuts; 1 tablespoon honey; and ½ teaspoon finely shredded orange peel.

Per 2 sandwiches: 962 cal., 49 g total fat (14 g sat. fat), 186 mg chol., 450 mg sodium, 75 g carbo., 5 g fiber, 54 g pro.
Daily Values: 15% vit. A, 2% vit. C, 9% calcium, 34% iron
Exchanges: 3 Starch, 2 Other Carbo., 6½ Lean Meat, 5½ Fat

Maple-Mustard Glazed Chicken

Prep: 30 minutes **Fry:** 35 minutes **Stand:** 15 minutes
Makes: 6 to 8 servings

     Peanut oil
  1 **5- to 6-pound whole roasting chicken**
  1 **recipe Maple-Mustard Glaze**

1. Preheat oil to 350°F. Remove neck and giblets from chicken. Rinse inside of chicken; pat dry with paper towels. Skewer neck skin to back. Tie legs to tail with 100-percent-cotton string. Twist wing tips under back.

2. Place chicken, breast side up, in basket. Slowly lower basket into hot oil. Be cautious of splattering oil. Maintain oil temperature around 350°F. Fry chicken for 35 to 42 minutes (7 minutes per pound).

3. Remove chicken from hot oil to check doneness. Insert a meat thermometer into the meaty part of the thigh. Chicken is done when thermometer reads 180°F. Remove chicken from hot oil; drain on wire rack. Spoon Maple-Mustard Glaze over hot chicken. Let stand 15 minutes before carving.

Maple-Mustard Glaze: In a small saucepan combine ¼ cup pure maple syrup, 3 tablespoons butter or margarine, 2 tablespoons frozen orange juice concentrate, 2 tablespoons coarse-grain brown mustard, and ¼ to ½ teaspoon cayenne pepper. Bring to boiling; reduce heat. Simmer, uncovered, for 2 to 3 minutes. Remove saucepan from heat; stir in ¼ cup finely chopped pecans, toasted, and 1 to 1½ teaspoons finely shredded orange peel.

Per ⅙ chicken: 719 cal., 55 g total fat (15 g sat. fat), 205 mg chol., 230 mg sodium, 6 g carbo., 0 g fiber, 47 g pro.
Daily Values: 8% vit. A, 8% vit. C, 3% calcium, 15% iron
Exchanges: ½ Other Carbo., 6½ Medium-Fat Meat, 4½ Fat

Chicken Fried Steak For-a-Crowd

Chicken Fried Steak For-a-Crowd

If you prefer a more traditional take on this hearty favorite, serve with a purchased homestyle gravy mix that's prepared according to package directions.

Prep: 20 minutes **Fry:** 4 minutes per batch
Oven: 300°F **Makes:** 12 servings

  2 **cups all-purpose flour**
  2 **teaspoons black pepper**
1½ **teaspoons salt**
  1 **teaspoon dried thyme, crushed**
 ½ **teaspoon cayenne pepper (optional)**
  2 **eggs, beaten**
  1 **egg white**
  1 **cup milk**
  2 **cups cracker meal**
 12 **4- to 6-ounce beef cubed steaks**
    Peanut oil
    Bottled salsa (optional)

1. In a large shallow dish combine flour, black pepper, salt, thyme, and, if desired, cayenne pepper. In another shallow dish combine eggs, egg white, and milk. Place cracker meal in another shallow dish.

2. Dip each steak in flour mixture. Dip each steak in egg mixture, then coat with the cracker meal. Place coated steaks on wire racks; let stand for 10 minutes.

3. Meanwhile, preheat oil to 360°F. Fry steaks, three or four at a time, about 4 minutes or until golden. Do not crowd. Be cautious of splattering oil. Maintain oil temperature around 360°F. Remove steaks from hot oil; drain on wire racks. Keep warm in a 300°F oven while frying remaining steaks. If desired, serve with salsa.

Per steak: 360 cal., 11 g total fat (2 g sat. fat), 86 mg chol., 376 mg sodium, 31 g carbo., 1 g fiber, 32 g pro.
Daily Values: 2% vit. A, 4% calcium, 24% iron
Exchanges: 2 Starch, 3½ Very Lean Meat, 1½ Fat

Steaks and Fries

To prevent oil from splattering bare arms, long oven mitts are a necessity.

Prep: 25 minutes **Fry:** 5 minutes per batch (potatoes); 4 minutes per batch (steak) **Oven:** 300°F
Makes: 6 servings

    Peanut oil
  6 **medium baking potatoes (2 pounds)**
  6 **beef ribeye or top loin steaks, cut 1 inch thick (about 4 pounds)**
1½ **to 2 teaspoons Key West seasoning, Cajun seasoning, or lemon-pepper seasoning**
    Bottled barbecue sauce (optional)

1. Preheat oil to 350°F. Peel potatoes. Cut potatoes lengthwise into ¼-inch-wide sticks. Place potato sticks in a large bowl of ice water; soak for 10 minutes. Drain potatoes; pat dry with paper towels. Fry potatoes, one-third at a time, in a basket for 5 to 6 minutes or until crisp and golden. Be cautious of splattering oil. Maintain oil temperature around 350°F. Remove potatoes from hot oil; drain on wire racks. Keep warm in a 300°F oven while frying remaining potatoes and steaks.

2. Place each steak on a clean, heavy-duty, long-handled barbecue fork. Fry steaks, two or three at a time, for 4 to 6 minutes or to desired doneness. Remove steaks from hot oil; drain on wire racks.

3. Sprinkle fries with seasoning blend. If desired, serve steaks with barbecue sauce.

Per steak + 1 cup fries: 705 cal., 31 g total fat (9 g sat. fat), 144 mg chol., 291 mg sodium, 33 g carbo., 3 g fiber, 70 g pro.
Daily Values: 6% vit. A, 53% vit. C, 4% calcium, 37% iron
Exchanges: 1 Starch, 1 Other Carbo., 9 Very Lean Meat, 1 Fat

Pork Chops on a Stick

Pork Chops on a Stick

Kids of any age find food cooked on a stick irresistible, and these pork chops are no exception. They cook in a jiffy too.

Prep: 15 minutes **Marinate:** 1 hour
Fry: 5 minutes per batch **Makes:** 8 servings

  8 6-ounce boneless pork loin chops,
     about 1 inch thick
  ½ cup bottled Italian salad dressing
    Peanut oil
  8 8×¼-inch-thick wooden skewers or dowels
    Honey mustard or bottled barbecue sauce

1. Place chops in a resealable plastic bag set in a shallow dish. Pour salad dressing over chops; seal bag. Marinate in the refrigerator for 1 hour, turning bag occasionally.

2. Meanwhile, preheat oil to 350°F. Drain chops, discarding marinade. Insert a wooden skewer into a short side of each chop. Fry the chops, half at a time, for 5 to 8 minutes or until 160°F. (To test for doneness, carefully remove one chop from the hot oil. Insert an instant-read thermometer horizontally into chop.) Be cautious of splattering oil. Maintain oil temperature around 350°F. Remove chops from hot oil and drain on wire racks. Serve chops with honey mustard.

Per chop: 344 cal., 19 g total fat (5 g sat. fat), 93 mg chol., 243 mg sodium, 3 g carbo., 0 g fiber, 37 g pro.
Daily Values: 1% vit. C, 1% calcium, 8% iron
Exchanges: 5 Very Lean Meat, 3½ Fat

Italian-Style Corn Dogs

Make cornmeal fritters by spooning rounded tablespoons of the remaining batter into the hot oil. Fry 2 to 3 minutes or until golden, turning once.

Prep: 30 minutes **Fry:** 3 minutes per batch
Makes: 12 servings

  12 uncooked Italian sausage links
  ½ cup water
    Peanut oil
  1½ cups yellow cornmeal
  1 cup all-purpose flour
  ½ cup grated Romano or Parmesan cheese
  2 teaspoons baking powder
  1 teaspoon salt
  2 eggs, beaten
  1¼ cups half-and-half or light cream
  12 10×¼-inch wooden skewers or dowels
    Warm marinara sauce (optional)

1. Use the tines of a fork to prick several holes in each sausage link. In a large skillet cook sausage links over medium heat about 5 minutes or until brown, turning frequently. Carefully add the water. Bring to boiling; reduce heat. Simmer, covered, for 5 minutes. Uncover and cook, turning frequently, until liquid evaporates and sausages are done (160°F). Drain on paper towels.

2. Preheat oil to 375°F. For batter, in a large bowl combine cornmeal, flour, Romano cheese, baking powder, and salt. Make a well in center of cornmeal mixture. In a medium bowl combine eggs and half-and-half. Add egg mixture to cornmeal mixture. Stir just until moistened.

3. Insert a wooden skewer into one end of each sausage link. Dip sausage links into batter, using a spoon to coat all sides evenly.

4. Fry corn dogs, three at a time, about 3 minutes or until golden. Do not crowd. Be cautious of splattering oil. Maintain oil temperature around 375°F. Remove corn dogs from hot oil; drain on wire racks. If desired, serve with warm marinara sauce.

Per corn dog: 539 cal., 36 g total fat (14 g sat. fat), 125 mg chol., 928 mg sodium, 23 g carbo., 2 g fiber, 22 g pro.
Daily Values: 4% vit. A, 2% vit. C, 11% calcium, 9% iron
Exchanges: 1½ Starch, 2½ High-Fat Meat, 3½ Fat

Shrimp and Vegetable Tempura

Prep: 25 minutes **Fry:** 3 minutes per batch
Makes: 4 servings

        Peanut oil
 12 large fresh or frozen shrimp in shells
        (about 6 ounces)
 1½ cups all-purpose flour
  ½ teaspoon cayenne pepper
  1 12-ounce can light-color beer
  3 medium red, yellow, and/or orange sweet
        peppers, cut into ½-inch rings
  3 cups broccoli florets
  1 recipe Soy Dipping Sauce

1. Preheat oil to 350°F. Thaw shrimp, if frozen. Peel and devein shrimp; if desired, remove tails (see photos, page 296). Rinse shrimp and pat dry. For batter, in a large bowl combine flour, 1½ teaspoons *salt*, 1 teaspoon *black pepper*, and cayenne pepper. Slowly whisk in beer until batter is smooth. Dip shrimp, sweet peppers, and broccoli into batter; let excess drip off.

2. Fry shrimp and vegetables, five or six pieces at a time, for 3 to 4 minutes or until crisp and golden. Do not crowd. Be cautious of splattering oil. Maintain oil temperature at 350°F. Remove shrimp and vegetables from hot oil; drain on wire racks. Serve with Soy Dipping Sauce.

Soy Dipping Sauce: In a bowl combine ¼ cup reduced-sodium soy sauce, 3 tablespoons rice vinegar, 2 tablespoons honey, 1 tablespoon thinly sliced green onion, and 2 teaspoons lime juice. Stir until honey dissolves. Makes ⅔ cup.

Per 3 shrimp + ½ cup vegetables + 3 tablespoons sauce: 448 cal., 15 g total fat (3 g sat. fat), 65 mg chol., 55 g carbo., 5 g fiber, 17 g pro.
Daily Values: 70% vit. A, 386% vit. C
Exchanges: 1½ Vegetable, 1½ Starch, 1½ Other Carbo., 3 Fat

Sweet-and-Savory Potato Chips

Prep: 25 minutes **Fry:** 3 minutes per batch
Makes: 12 to 16 servings

        Peanut oil
  3 medium sweet potatoes (1 pound)
  3 medium baking potatoes (1 pound)
        Coarse salt

1. Preheat oil to 350°F. Peel potatoes; cut into very thin slices (about ¹⁄₁₆ inch thick). Place potato slices in a bowl of ice water; soak for 10 minutes. Drain potato slices; pat dry with paper towels.

2. Fry potato slices, half at a time, in a basket for 3 to 5 minutes or until crisp and golden. Do not crowd. Be cautious of splattering oil. Maintain oil temperature at 350°F. Remove potatoes from the hot oil; drain on wire racks. Sprinkle with coarse salt. If desired, fry chips up to 2 days ahead; store in an airtight container.

Per ¾ cup: 96 cal., 5 g total fat (1 g sat. fat), 0 mg chol., 48 mg sodium, 13 g carbo., 2 g fiber, 1 g pro.
Daily Values: 99% vit. A, 21% vit. C, 2% calcium, 4% iron
Exchanges: 1 Starch, 1 Fat

Mozzarella Cheese Sticks

Freeze the sticks at least 1 hour so cheese doesn't ooze out before the hot oil browns the coating.

Prep: 20 minutes **Freeze:** 1 hour
Fry: 2 minutes per batch **Makes:** 12 sticks

  ¾ cup all-purpose flour
  2 eggs, slightly beaten
  2 tablespoons water
 12 mozzarella cheese sticks or one 16-ounce
        block mozzarella cheese, cut into twelve
        4×½-inch sticks
  1 cup fine dry Italian bread crumbs
        Peanut oil
  ¾ cup marinara sauce

1. In a shallow dish combine flour, ½ teaspoon *salt*, and ½ teaspoon *black pepper*. In another shallow dish combine eggs and water. Dip cheese sticks in egg mixture, then coat with flour mixture. Dip cheese sticks again in egg mixture, then coat with bread crumbs. Place cheese sticks on a baking sheet. Cover and freeze for 1 hour or up to 2 days.*

2. Preheat oil to 350°F. Preheat basket in hot oil. Fry cheese sticks, half at a time, in the basket for 2 to 2½ minutes or until crisp and golden. Do not crowd. Be cautious of splattering oil. Maintain oil temperature at around 350°F. Remove sticks from hot oil; drain on wire racks. Warm marinara sauce in a small saucepan. Serve with cheese sticks.

***Note:** If sticks have been frozen longer than 1 hour, let stand at room temperature for 15 minutes before frying.

Per 1 stick + 1 tablespoon sauce: 250 cal., 16 g total fat (6 g sat. fat), 65 mg chol., 569 mg sodium, 15 g carbo.,1 g fiber, 12 g pro.
Daily Values: 7% vit. A, 21% calcium, 4% iron
Exchanges: ½ Starch, ½ Other Carbo., 1½ Medium-Fat Meat, 1½ Fat

Wisconsin Fish Boil

The Wisconsin fish boil is a very popular activity for tourists who visit Door County, Wisconsin. The custom, more than 100 years old, started when Scandinavian lumberjacks shared the cooking technique with residents of the area.

Prep: 20 minutes **Cook:** 26 minutes **Makes:** 16 servings

> 6 **pounds fresh or frozen whitefish or halibut steaks, 1 inch thick**
> 4 **gallons water**
> 1 **cup salt**
> 4 **pounds small red potatoes**
> 2 **1-pound packages peeled baby carrots**
> 2 **pounds boiling onions (about 32)**
> 1 **recipe Butter Sauce**
>   **Freshly ground black pepper (optional)**

1. Thaw fish, if frozen. Rinse fish; pat dry with paper towels. Place water and salt in boiling pot of a 30- to 34-quart turkey fryer. Bring to boiling. Meanwhile, place potatoes, carrots, and onions in basket. Carefully lower basket into boiling water. Cover and boil vegetables for 18 minutes.

2. Carefully add fish steaks to basket. Cover and boil for 8 to 11 minutes more or until fish flakes easily when tested with a fork and vegetables are tender.

3. Carefully lift basket from turkey fryer; remove fish and vegetables. Serve with Butter Sauce. If desired, season to taste with pepper.

Butter Sauce: In a small saucepan whisk together ¾ cup butter, ⅓ cup Dijon-style mustard, and ¼ cup snipped fresh dill or flat-leaf parsley until butter is melted and sauce is combined.

Per 4 ounces + 1 tablespoon sauce: 445 cal., 20 g total fat (7 g sat. fat), 117 mg chol., 464 mg sodium, 30 g carbo., 4 g fiber, 37 g pro.
Daily Values: 145% vit. A, 36% vit. C, 10% calcium, 13% iron
Exchanges: 1½ Vegetable, 1½ Starch, 4 Very Lean Meat, 3 Fat

Direct-Grilling Poultry

If desired, remove skin from poultry. For a charcoal grill, place poultry on grill rack, bone side up, directly over medium coals (see page 322). Grill, uncovered, for the time given below or until the proper temperature is reached and meat is no longer pink, turning once halfway through grilling. For a gas grill, preheat grill. Reduce heat to medium. Place poultry on grill rack, bone side down, over heat. Cover and grill.

Test for doneness using a meat thermometer (use an instant-read thermometer to test small portions). Thermometer should register 180°F, except in breast meat when thermometer should register 170°F. If desired, during last 5 to 10 minutes of grilling, brush often with a sauce.

Type of Bird	Weight	Grilling Temperature	Approximate Direct-Grilling Time	Doneness
Chicken				
Chicken breast half, skinned and boned	4 to 5 ounces	Medium	12 to 15 minutes	170°F
Chicken, broiler-fryer, half or quarters	1½- to 1¾-pound half or 12- to 14-ounce quarters	Medium	40 to 50 minutes	180°F
Chicken thigh, skinned and boned	4 to 5 ounces	Medium	12 to 15 minutes	180°F
Meaty chicken pieces (breast halves, thighs, and drumsticks)	2½ to 3 pounds total	Medium	35 to 45 minutes	180°F
Turkey				
Turkey breast tenderloin	8 to 10 ounces (¾ to 1 inch thick)	Medium	16 to 20 minutes	170°F

All cooking times are based on poultry removed directly from refrigerator.

Indirect-Grilling Poultry

For a charcoal grill, arrange medium-hot coals around a drip pan. Test for medium heat (see page 322). Place unstuffed poultry, breast side up, on grill rack over drip pan. Cover; grill for the time given below or until poultry is no longer pink (180°F for most cuts, 170°F for breast meat), adding more charcoal as necessary. Or if desired, place whole birds on a rack in a roasting pan and omit the drip pan. For a gas grill, preheat grill. Reduce heat to medium. Adjust heat for indirect cooking (see page 321). Test for doneness using a meat or instant-read thermometer. For whole birds, insert meat thermometer into center of the inside thigh muscle, away from bone (see photo 5, page 478). (Poultry sizes vary; use times as a general guide.)

Type of Bird	Weight	Grilling Temperature	Approximate Indirect-Grilling Time	Doneness
Chicken				
Chicken breast half, skinned and boned	4 to 5 ounces	Medium	15 to 18 minutes	170°F
Chicken, broiler-fryer, half	1½ to 1¾ pounds	Medium	1 to 1¼ hours	180°F
Chicken, broiler-fryer, quarters	12 to 14 ounces each	Medium	50 to 60 minutes	180°F
Chicken thigh, skinned and boned	4 to 5 ounces	Medium	15 to 18 minutes	180°F
Chicken, whole	2½ to 3 pounds 3½ to 4 pounds 4½ to 5 pounds	Medium Medium Medium	1 to 1¼ hours 1¼ to 1¾ hours 1¾ to 2 hours	180°F 180°F 180°F
Meaty chicken pieces (breast halves, thighs, and drumsticks)	2½ to 3 pounds total	Medium	50 to 60 minutes	180°F
Game				
Cornish game hen, halved lengthwise	10 to 12 ounces each	Medium	40 to 50 minutes	180°F
Cornish game hen, whole	1¼ to 1½ pounds	Medium	50 to 60 minutes	180°F
Pheasant, quartered	½ to ¾ pound each	Medium	50 to 60 minutes	180°F
Pheasant, whole	2 to 3 pounds	Medium	1 to 1½ hours	180°F
Quail, semiboneless	3 to 4 ounces	Medium	15 to 20 minutes	180°F
Squab	12 to 16 ounces	Medium	¾ to 1 hour	180°F
Turkey				
Turkey breast, half	2 to 2½ pounds	Medium	1¼ to 2 hours	170°F
Turkey breast tenderloin	8 to 10 ounces (¾ to 1 inch thick)	Medium	25 to 30 minutes	170°F
Turkey breast tenderloin steak	4 to 6 ounces	Medium	15 to 18 minutes	170°F
Turkey breast, whole	4 to 6 pounds 6 to 8 pounds	Medium Medium	1¾ to 2¼ hours 2½ to 3½ hours	170°F 170°F
Turkey drumstick	½ to 1 pound	Medium	¾ to 1¼ hours	180°F
Turkey thigh	1 to 1½ pounds	Medium	50 to 60 minutes	180°F
Turkey, whole	6 to 8 pounds 8 to 12 pounds 12 to 16 pounds	Medium Medium Medium	1¾ to 2¼ hours 2½ to 3½ hours 3 to 4 hours	180°F 180°F 180°F

All cooking times are based on poultry removed directly from refrigerator.

Direct-Grilling Meat

For a charcoal grill, place meat on grill rack directly over medium coals (see page 322). Grill, uncovered, for the time given below or to desired doneness, turning once halfway through grilling. For a gas grill, preheat grill. Reduce heat to medium. Place meat on grill rack over heat. Cover the grill. Test for doneness using a meat thermometer.

Cut	Thickness/Weight	Grilling Temperature	Approximate Direct-Grilling Time	Doneness
Beef				
Boneless steak (beef top loin [strip], ribeye, shoulder top blade [flat-iron], tenderloin)	1 inch 1 inch 1½ inches 1½ inches	Medium Medium Medium Medium	10 to 12 minutes 12 to 15 minutes 15 to 19 minutes 18 to 23 minutes	145°F medium rare 160°F medium 145°F medium rare 160°F medium
Boneless top sirloin steak	1 inch 1 inch 1½ inches 1½ inches	Medium Medium Medium Medium	14 to 18 minutes 18 to 22 minutes 20 to 24 minutes 24 to 28 minutes	145°F medium rare 160°F medium 145°F medium rare 160°F medium
Boneless tri-tip steak (bottom sirloin)	¾ inch ¾ inch 1 inch 1 inch	Medium Medium Medium Medium	9 to 11 minutes 11 to 13 minutes 13 to 15 minutes 15 to 17 minutes	145°F medium rare 160°F medium 145°F medium rare 160°F medium
Flank steak	1¼ to 1¾ pounds	Medium	17 to 21 minutes	160°F medium
Steak with bone (porterhouse, T-bone, rib)	1 inch 1 inch 1½ inches 1½ inches	Medium Medium Medium Medium	10 to 13 minutes 12 to 15 minutes 18 to 21 minutes 22 to 25 minutes	145°F medium rare 160°F medium 145°F medium rare 160°F medium
Ground Meat Patties				
Patties (beef, lamb, pork, or veal)	½ inch ¾ inch	Medium Medium	10 to 13 minutes 14 to 18 minutes	160°F medium 160°F medium
Lamb				
Chop (loin or rib)	1 inch 1 inch	Medium Medium	12 to 14 minutes 15 to 17 minutes	145°F medium rare 160°F medium
Chop (sirloin)	¾ to 1 inch	Medium	14 to 17 minutes	160°F medium
Miscellaneous				
Kabobs (beef or lamb)	1-inch cubes	Medium	8 to 12 minutes	160°F medium
Kabobs (pork or veal)	1-inch cubes	Medium	10 to 14 minutes)	160°F medium
Sausages, cooked (frankfurters, smoked bratwurst, etc.)		Medium	3 to 7 minutes	Heated through
Pork				
Chop (boneless top loin)	¾ to 1 inch 1¼ to 1½ inches	Medium Medium	7 to 9 minutes 14 to 18 minutes	160°F medium 160°F medium
Chop with bone (loin or rib)	¾ to 1 inch 1¼ to 1½ inches	Medium Medium	11 to 13 minutes 16 to 20 minutes	160°F medium 160°F medium
Veal				
Chop (loin or rib)	1 inch	Medium	12 to 15 minutes	160°F medium

All cooking times are based on meat removed directly from refrigerator.

Indirect-Grilling Meat

For a charcoal grill, arrange medium-hot coals around a drip pan. Test for medium heat above pan, unless chart says otherwise. Place meat, fat side up, on grill rack over drip pan. Cover and grill for the time given below or to desired temperature, adding more charcoal to maintain heat as necessary. For a gas grill, preheat grill. Reduce heat to medium. Adjust heat for indirect cooking (see page 321). To test for doneness, insert a meat thermometer (see tip, page 367), using an instant-read thermometer to test small portions. Temperature should register the "final grilling temperature." Remove meat from grill. For larger cuts, such as roasts, cover with foil and let stand 15 minutes before slicing. The meat's temperature will rise 10°F during the time it stands. Thinner cuts, such as steaks, do not have to stand.

Cut	Thickness/ Weight	Approximate Indirect-Grilling Time	Final Grilling Temperature (when to remove from grill)	Final Doneness Temperature (after 15 minutes of standing)
Beef				
Boneless top sirloin steak	1 inch	22 to 26 minutes	145°F medium rare	No standing time
	1 inch	26 to 30 minutes	160°F medium	No standing time
	1½ inches	32 to 36 minutes	145°F medium rare	No standing time
	1½ inches	36 to 40 minutes	160°F medium	No standing time
Boneless tri-tip roast (bottom sirloin)	1½ to 2 pounds	35 to 40 minutes	135°F	145°F medium rare
	1½ to 2 pounds	40 to 45 minutes	150°F	160°F medium
Flank steak	1¼ to 1¾ pounds	23 to 28 minutes	160°F medium	No standing time
Rib roast (chine bone removed) (medium-low heat)	4 to 6 pounds	2 to 2¾ hours	135°F	145°F medium rare
	4 to 6 pounds	2½ to 3¼ hours	150°F	160°F medium
Ribeye roast (medium-low heat)	4 to 6 pounds	1¼ to 1¾ hours	135°F	145°F medium rare
	4 to 6 pounds	1½ to 2¼ hours	150°F	160°F medium
Steak (porterhouse, rib, ribeye, shoulder blade [flat-iron], T-bone, tenderloin, top loin [strip])	1 inch	16 to 20 minutes	145°F medium rare	No standing time
	1 inch	20 to 24 minutes	160°F rmedium	No standing time
	1½ inches	22 to 25 minutes	145°F medium rare	No standing time
	1½ inches	25 to 28 minutes	160°F medium	No standing time
Tenderloin roast (medium-high heat)	2 to 3 pounds	¾ to 1 hour	135°F	145°F medium rare
	4 to 5 pounds	1 to 1¼ hours	135°F	145°F medium rare
Ground Meat				
Patties (beef, lamb, pork, or veal)	½ inch	15 to 18 minutes	160°F medium	No standing time
	¾ inch	20 to 24 minutes	160°F medium	No standing time
Lamb				
Boneless leg roast (medium-low heat)	3 to 4 pounds	1½ to 2¼ hours	135°F	145°F medium rare
	3 to 4 pounds	1¾ to 2½ hours	150°F	160°F medium
	4 to 6 pounds	1¾ to 2½ hours	135°F	145°F medium rare
	4 to 6 pounds	2 to 2¾ hours	150°F	160°F medium
Boneless sirloin roast (medium-low heat)	1½ to 2 pounds	1 to 1¼ hours	135°F	145°F medium rare
	1½ to 2 pounds	1¼ to 1½ hours	150°F	160°F medium
Chop (loin or rib)	1 inch	16 to 18 minutes	145°F medium rare	No standing time
	1 inch	18 to 20 minutes	160°F medium	No standing time
Leg of lamb (with bone) (medium-low heat)	5 to 7 pounds	1¾ to 2¼ hours	135°F	145°F medium rare
	5 to 7 pounds	2¼ to 2¾ hours	150°F	160°F medium

All cooking times are based on meat removed directly from refrigerator.

Cut	Thickness/ Weight	Approximate Indirect-Grilling Time	Final Grilling Temperature (when to remove from grill)	Final Doneness Temperature (after 15 minutes of standing)
Pork				
Boneless top loin roast (medium-low heat)	2 to 3 pounds (single loin) 3 to 5 pounds (double loin, tied)	1 to 1½ hours 1½ to 2¼ hours	150°F 150°F	160°F medium 160°F medium
Chop (boneless top loin)	¾ to 1 inch 1¼ to 1½ inch	20 to 24 minutes 30 to 35 minutes	160°F medium 160°F medium	No standing time No standing time
Chop (loin or rib)	¾ to 1 inch 1¼ to 1½ inch	22 to 25 minutes 35 to 40 minutes	160°F medium 160°F medium	No standing time No standing time
Country-style ribs		1½ to 2 hours	Tender	No standing time
Ham, cooked (boneless) (medium-low heat)	3 to 5 pounds 6 to 8 pounds	1¼ to 2 hours 2 to 2¾ hours	140°F 140°F	No standing time No standing time
Ham, cooked (slice) (medium-high heat)	1 inch	20 to 24 minutes	140°F	No standing time
Loin back ribs or spareribs		1½ to 1¾ hours	Tender	No standing time
Loin center rib roast (backbone loosened) (medium-low heat)	3 to 4 pounds 4 to 6 pounds	1¼ to 2 hours 2 to 2¾ hours	150°F 150°F	160°F medium 160°F medium
Sausages, uncooked (bratwurst, Polish, or Italian sausage links)	about 4 per pound	20 to 30 minutes	160°F medium	No standing time
Smoked shoulder picnic (with bone), cooked (medium-low heat)	4 to 6 pounds	1½ to 2¼ hours	140°F heated through	No standing time
Tenderloin (medium-high heat)	¾ to 1 pound	30 to 35 minutes	155°F	160°F medium
Veal				
Chop (loin or rib)	1 inch	19 to 23 minutes	160°F medium	No standing time

All cooking times are based on meat removed directly from refrigerator.

Direct-Grilling Fish

Thaw fish or seafood, if frozen. Rinse fish or seafood; pat dry. Place fish fillets in a well-greased grill basket. For fish steaks and whole fish, grease the grill rack. Thread scallops or shrimp on skewers, leaving a ¼-inch space between pieces. For a charcoal grill, place fish on the grill rack directly over medium coals. Grill, uncovered, for the time given below or until fish begins to flake when tested with a fork (seafood should look opaque), turning once halfway through grilling. For a gas grill, preheat grill. Reduce heat to medium. Place fish on grill rack over heat. Cover the grill. If desired, brush fish with melted butter or margarine after turning.

Form of Fish	Thickness, Weight, or Size	Grilling Temperature	Approximate Direct-Grilling Time	Doneness
Dressed whole fish	½ to 1½ pounds	Medium	6 to 9 minutes per 8 ounces	Flakes
Fillets, steaks, cubes (for kabobs)	½ to 1 inch thick	Medium	4 to 6 minutes per ½-inch thickness	Flakes
Lobster tails	6 ounces 8 ounces	Medium Medium	10 to 12 minutes 12 to 15 minutes	Opaque Opaque
Sea Scallops (for kabobs)	12 to 15 per pound	Medium	5 to 8 minutes	Opaque
Shrimp (for kabobs)	20 per pound 12 to 15 per pound	Medium Medium	5 to 8 minutes 7 to 9 minutes	Opaque Opaque

All cooking times are based on fish or seafood removed directly from refrigerator.

Indirect-Grilling Fish

Thaw fish or seafood, if frozen. Rinse fish or seafood; pat dry. Place fish fillets in a well-greased grill basket. For fish steaks and whole fish, grease grill rack. Thread scallops or shrimp on skewers, leaving a ¼-inch space between pieces. For a charcoal grill, arrange medium-hot coals around drip pan. Test for medium heat above the pan. Place fish on grill rack over drip pan. Cover and grill for the time given below or until fish begins to flake when tested with a fork (seafood should look opaque), turning once halfway through grilling, if desired. For a gas grill, preheat grill. Reduce heat to medium. Adjust heat for indirect cooking (see page 321). If desired, brush with melted butter or margarine halfway through grilling.

Form of Fish	Thickness, Weight, or Size	Grilling Temperature	Approximate Indirect-Grilling Time	Doneness
Dressed fish	½ to 1½ pounds	Medium	15 to 20 minutes per 8 ounces	Flakes
Fillets, steaks, cubes (for kabobs)	½ to 1 inch thick	Medium	7 to 9 minutes per ½-inch thickness	Flakes
Sea scallops (for kabobs)	12 to 15 per pound	Medium	11 to 14 minutes	Opaque
Shrimp (for kabobs)	20 per pound 12 to 15 per pound	Medium Medium	8 to 10 minutes 9 to 11 minutes	Opaque Opaque

All cooking times are based on fish or seafood removed directly from refrigerator.

Direct-Grilling Vegetables

Before grilling, rinse, trim, cut up, and precook vegetables as directed below. To precook vegetables, bring a small amount of water to boiling in a saucepan; add desired vegetable and simmer, covered, for the time specified in the chart. Drain well. Generously brush vegetables with olive oil, butter, or margarine before grilling to prevent vegetables from sticking to the grill rack. Place vegetables on a piece of heavy foil or directly on the grill rack. (If putting vegetables directly on grill rack, lay them perpendicular to wires of the rack so they won't fall into the coals.)

For a charcoal grill, place vegetables on rack directly over medium coals. Grill, uncovered, for the time given below or until crisp-tender, turning occasionally. For a gas grill, preheat grill. Reduce heat to medium. Place vegetables on grill rack directly over heat. Cover the grill. Monitor the grilling closely so vegetables don't char.

Vegetable	Preparation	Precooking Time	Approximate Direct-Grilling Time
Asparagus	Snap off and discard tough bases of stems. Precook, then tie asparagus in bundles with strips of cooked green onion tops.	3 minutes	3 to 5 minutes
Baby carrots, fresh	Cut off carrot tops. Wash and peel carrots.	3 to 5 minutes	3 to 5 minutes
Corn on the cob	Peel back the corn husks but do not remove. Remove corn silks. Rinse corn; pat dry. Fold husks back around cobs. Tie husk tops with 100-percent-cotton kitchen string.	Do not precook.	25 to 30 minutes
Eggplant	Cut off top and blossom ends. Cut eggplant crosswise into 1-inch slices.	Do not precook.	8 minutes
Fennel	Snip off feathery leaves. Cut off stems.	10 minutes; then cut into 6 to 8 wedges	8 minutes
Leeks	Cut off green tops; trim bulb roots and remove 1 or 2 layers of white skin.	10 minutes or until almost tender; halve lengthwise	5 minutes
New potatoes	Halve potatoes.	10 minutes or until almost tender	10 to 12 minutes
Potatoes	Scrub potatoes; prick with a fork. Wrap individually in a double thickness of foil.	Do not precook.	1 to 2 hours
Sweet peppers	Remove stems. Halve peppers lengthwise. Remove seeds and membranes. Cut into 1-inch-wide strips.	Do not precook.	8 to 10 minutes
Tomatoes	Remove cores; cut in half crosswise.	Do not precook.	5 minutes
Zucchini or yellow summer squash	Wash; cut off ends. Quarter lengthwise.	Do not precook.	5 to 6 minutes

Indoor Electric Grills

If grilling poultry, fish, or seafood, lightly grease the rack of an indoor electric grill or lightly coat with cooking spray. Preheat grill. Place meat, poultry, fish, or seafood on grill rack. (For fish fillets, tuck under any thin edges.) If using a grill with a cover, close the lid. Grill for the time given below or until done. If using a grill without a cover, turn food once halfway through grilling. The following times should be used as general guidelines. Test for doneness using a meat thermometer. Refer to your owner's manual for preheating directions, suggested cuts for grilling, and recommended grilling times.

Cut or Type	Thickness, Weight, or Size	Covered Grilling Time	Uncovered Grilling Time	Doneness
Beef				
Boneless steak (ribeye, tenderloin, top loin)	1 inch	4 to 6 minutes 6 to 8 minutes	8 to 12 minutes 12 to 15 minutes	145°F medium rare 160°F medium
Boneless top sirloin steak	1 inch	5 to 7 minutes 7 to 9 minutes	12 to 15 minutes 15 to 18 minutes	145°F medium rare 160°F medium
Flank steak		7 to 9 minutes	12 to 14 minutes	160°F medium
Ground meat patties	½ to ¾ inch	5 to 7 minutes	14 to 18 minutes	160°F medium
Steak with bone (porterhouse, rib, T-bone)	1 inch	Not recommended Not recommended	8 to 12 minutes 12 to 15 minutes	145°F medium rare 160°F medium
Lamb				
Chop (loin or rib)	1 inch	6 to 8 minutes	12 to 15 minutes	160°F medium
Veal				
Chop (boneless loin)	¾ inch	4 to 5 minutes	7 to 9 minutes	160°F medium
Pork				
Chop (boneless top loin)	¾ inch	6 to 8 minutes	12 to 15 minutes	160°F medium
Sausages, cooked (frankfurters, smoked bratwurst, etc.)	6 per pound	2½ to 3 minutes	5 to 6 minutes	140°F heated through
Poultry				
Chicken breast half, skinned and boned	4 to 5 ounces	4 to 6 minutes	12 to 15 minutes	170°F
Fish and Seafood				
Fillets or steaks	½ to 1 inch	2 to 3 minutes per ½-inch thickness	4 to 6 minutes per ½-inch thickness	Flakes
Sea scallops	15 to 20 per pound	2½ to 4 minutes	6 to 8 minutes	Opaque
Shrimp	41 to 50 per pound	2½ to 4 minutes	6 to 8 minutes	Opaque

All cooking times are based on food removed directly from refrigerator.

Meat

Fajitas, 374   Tuscan Lamb Chop Skillet, 402   New Orleans-Style Muffuletta, 398

Meat Essentials

Meat serves as the mainstay of many meals. The following information will help you determine how much to buy and how to handle it safely.

Buying Meat

For boneless roasts and steaks, plan on three to four servings per pound. For bone-in roasts and steaks, allow two to three servings per pound. And for bony cuts, plan on one or two servings per pound.

Storing Meat

Refrigerate meat in the coldest part of the refrigerator as soon as possible after purchase. If you don't plan to use fresh ground and cubed meat within two days and steaks, chops, and roasts within three days, store the meat in the freezer. For meat that's to be used within a week after buying, you can freeze it in the transparent, film-wrapped supermarket packaging. For longer storage, however, overwrap the meat with moisture- and vaporproof wrap, such as freezer paper, heavy foil, or food-safe freezer bags. Label and date the package; freeze meat quickly and maintain the freezer temperature at 0°F or below.

For best quality, freeze uncooked roasts, chops, and steaks up to 12 months, uncooked ground meats up to four months, and cooked meat up to three months. Thaw meat in the refrigerator on a plate or in a pan to catch any juices. Do not thaw on the counter at room temperature.

Handling Meat Safely

Wash your hands with hot, soapy water before and after touching raw meat. Clean everything that the raw meat touches, including utensils, countertops, cutting boards, and dishes. If you use any utensils or plates for raw meat, don't use them for other food preparation or for cooked meat without first washing and sanitizing them. To avoid confusion, reserve one cutting board just for raw meats and designate another board for cooked meat and other foods.

Cook ground meat to an internal temperature of 160°F. When cooking ground meat patties, their internal color is not a reliable doneness indicator; use an instant-read thermometer to check for doneness (see tip, page 367). Cook other beef and lamb cuts to at least 145°F

Browning Meat

When cooking ground meat for mixtures, break up meat in a skillet with a spoon until meat is crumbly, brown, and no longer pink (see photo).

To brown larger pieces of meat for pot roasting, use a heavy pan and cook over medium heat in a small amount of hot oil until meat develops a rich color (see photo).

(medium rare) and all pork to at least 160°F (medium), including the standing time, using a meat thermometer to determine doneness.

For make-ahead cooking, do not partially cook meat, poultry, or fish, then finish cooking it later because safe temperatures may not be maintained between cooking periods, even if you store the food in the refrigerator.

If a recipe specifies marinating the meat, keep meat in the refrigerator. Discard any leftover marinade or bring it to a full, rolling boil to destroy any bacteria that may be present.

**Standing Rib
Roast, page 367**

Beef Cuts

These two pages contain a drawing and labeled photos to help you identify the cuts of beef and suggested cooking methods. The drawing illustrates wholesale cuts, showing in general where those cuts are located on the animal. The photos of the retail cuts are divided into the same categories as those on the drawing, which should make it easier to determine where the cuts originate.

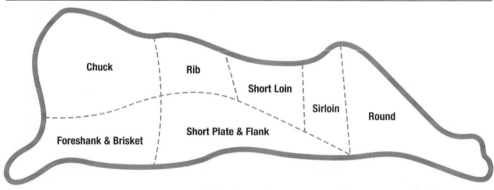

Chuck

Rib

Short Loin

Sirloin

Round

Foreshank & Brisket

Short Plate & Flank

Chuck

Chuck arm pot roast (boneless)
Braise, cook in liquid

Chuck top blade steak (boneless)
Braise, broil, cook in liquid, grill, skillet-cook

Chuck shoulder steak (boneless)
Braise, cook in liquid, tenderize before broiling or grilling, skillet-cook

Shoulder center steak (Ranch steak)
Broil, grill, skillet-cook

Chuck shoulder pot roast (boneless)
Braise, cook in liquid

Shoulder top blade steak (Flat-iron)
Broil, grill, skillet-cook

Shoulder petite tender
Broil, grill, roast, skillet-cook

Chuck 7-bone pot roast
Braise, cook in liquid

Chuck short ribs
Braise, cook in liquid

Sirloin

Tri-tip steak
Broil, grill, skillet-cook, stir-fry

Top sirloin steak (boneless)
Broil, grill, skillet-cook, stir-fry

Tri-tip roast
Grill, roast

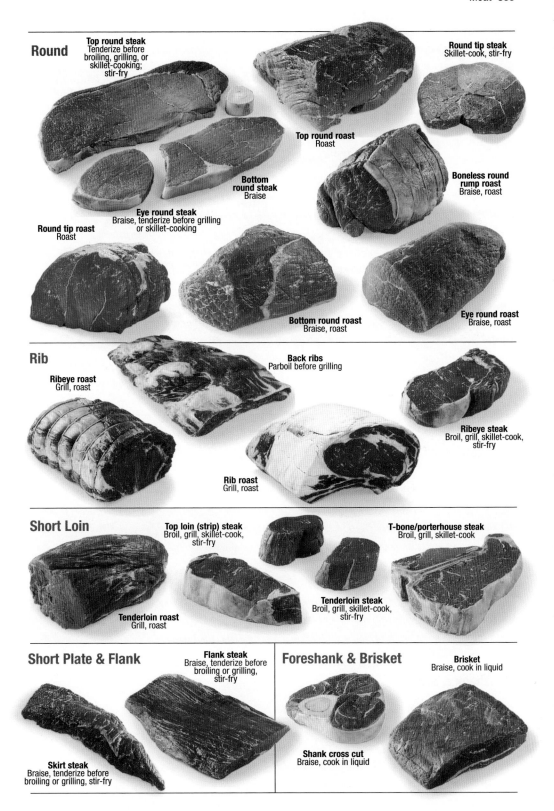

Round

Top round steak
Tenderize before broiling, grilling, or skillet-cooking; stir-fry

Round tip steak
Skillet-cook, stir-fry

Top round roast
Roast

Boneless round rump roast
Braise, roast

Bottom round steak
Braise

Eye round steak
Braise, tenderize before grilling or skillet-cooking

Round tip roast
Roast

Bottom round roast
Braise, roast

Eye round roast
Braise, roast

Rib

Ribeye roast
Grill, roast

Back ribs
Parboil before grilling

Ribeye steak
Broil, grill, skillet-cook, stir-fry

Rib roast
Grill, roast

Short Loin

Top loin (strip) steak
Broil, grill, skillet-cook, stir-fry

T-bone/porterhouse steak
Broil, grill, skillet-cook

Tenderloin steak
Broil, grill, skillet-cook, stir-fry

Tenderloin roast
Grill, roast

Short Plate & Flank

Flank steak
Braise, tenderize before broiling or grilling, stir-fry

Skirt steak
Braise, tenderize before broiling or grilling, stir-fry

Foreshank & Brisket

Brisket
Braise, cook in liquid

Shank cross cut
Braise, cook in liquid

Veal Cuts

This page contains a drawing and labeled photos to help you identify cuts of veal and suggested cooking methods. The drawing illustrates wholesale cuts; the photos are of retail cuts.

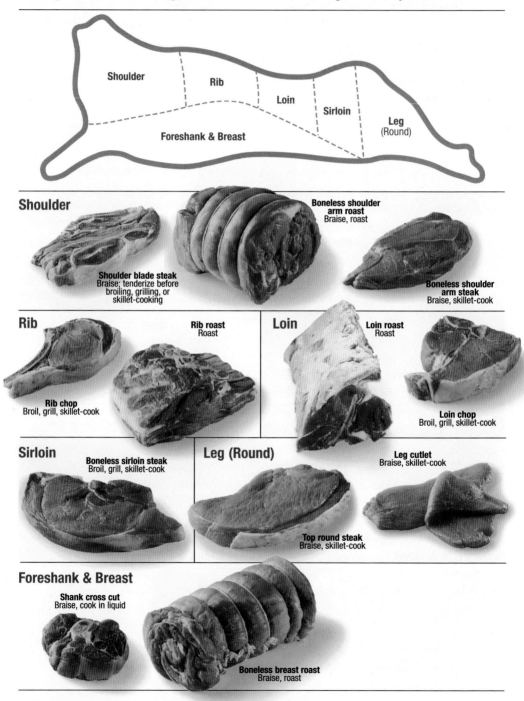

Shoulder

Rib

Loin

Sirloin

Leg
(Round)

Foreshank & Breast

Shoulder

Boneless shoulder arm roast
Braise, roast

Shoulder blade steak
Braise; tenderize before broiling, grilling, or skillet-cooking

Boneless shoulder arm steak
Braise, skillet-cook

Rib

Rib roast
Roast

Rib chop
Broil, grill, skillet-cook

Loin

Loin roast
Roast

Loin chop
Broil, grill, skillet-cook

Sirloin

Boneless sirloin steak
Broil, grill, skillet-cook

Leg (Round)

Leg cutlet
Braise, skillet-cook

Top round steak
Braise, skillet-cook

Foreshank & Breast

Shank cross cut
Braise, cook in liquid

Boneless breast roast
Braise, roast

Standing Rib Roast

See photo, page 363.

Prep: 10 minutes **Roast:** 1¾ hours **Oven:** 350°F
Stand: 15 minutes **Makes:** 12 to 16 servings

- **1 4- to 6-pound beef rib roast**
- **1 recipe Oven-Browned Potatoes or Yorkshire Pudding**
- **1 recipe Horseradish Sauce (page 520) (optional)**

1. Season meat with *salt* and *black pepper*. Place meat, fat side up, in a 15½×10½×2-inch roasting pan. Insert an oven-going meat thermometer into center (see tip, right), making sure it doesn't touch bone. Roast, uncovered, in a 350°F oven. For medium rare, roast 1¾ to 2¼ hours or until meat thermometer registers 135°F. Cover with foil; let stand 15 minutes. Temperature of meat after standing should be 145°F. (For medium, roast 2¼ to 2¾ hours or until thermometer registers 150°F. Cover; let stand 15 minutes. Temperature of meat after standing should be 160°F.)

2. Meanwhile, prepare Oven-Browned Potatoes or Yorkshire Pudding.

Per 4 ounces: 354 cal., 29 g total fat (12 g sat. fat), 88 mg chol.,
83 mg sodium, 0 g carbo., 0 g fiber, 22 g pro.
Daily Values: 1% calcium, 13% iron
Exchanges: 3½ High-Fat Meat

Oven-Browned Potatoes: Peel 4 pounds medium potatoes; cut into quarters. Cook in boiling salted water for 10 minutes; drain. About 30 to 40 minutes before roast is done (the roast temperature should be about 100°F), arrange potatoes around roast, turning to coat in drippings. Continue roasting. Serve with the roast.

Per cup: 110 cal., 0 g total fat (0 g sat. fat), 0 mg chol.,
4 mg sodium, 23 g carbo., 3 g fiber, 4 g pro.
Daily Values: 34% vit. C, 1% calcium, 7% iron
Exchanges: 1½ Starch

Yorkshire Pudding: After removing meat from oven, increase oven temperature to 450°F. Measure pan drippings. If necessary, add enough cooking oil to drippings to equal ¼ cup; return to pan. In a mixing bowl combine 4 eggs and 2 cups milk. Add 2 cups all-purpose flour and ¼ teaspoon salt. Beat with an electric mixer until smooth. Stir into drippings in roasting pan. Bake 20 to 25 minutes or until puffy and golden. Cut into 12 squares. Serve at once with roast.

Per square: 154 cal., 7 g total fat (3 g sat. fat), 79 mg chol.,
90 mg sodium, 17 g carbo., 1 g fiber, 5 g pro.
Daily Values: 4% vit. A, 1% vit. C, 6% calcium, 6% iron
Exchanges: 1 Starch, 1½ Fat

Meat Thermometer Usage

Check the meat's doneness with a meat thermometer. Use the doneness test and temperature given in each recipe and in the cooking charts on pages 405–408.

Dial oven-going meat thermometer: Use this thermometer type for roasts and larger cuts of meat. Before starting to roast or grill, insert the thermometer stem at least 2 inches into the center of the largest muscle or thickest portion of the uncooked meat (see photo, below). The thermometer should not touch fat, bone, or pan. It can remain in the meat while it is roasting or grilling. When the meat reaches the desired final temperature, push the stem in a little farther. If the temperature drops, continue cooking the meat; if it stays the same, remove the meat from the oven or grill. Cover the meat with foil and let it stand about 15 minutes before carving; during this time the meat's temperature will rise 5°F to 10°F.

Dial instant-read thermometer: Use this thermometer type to check a food's doneness; do not leave it in food during cooking. Insert the thermometer stem at least 2 inches into the food. It will register the temperature in 15 to 20 seconds. To get an accurate reading of thinner foods, such as burgers and chops, insert the stem into the side (see photo, above).

Digital instant-read thermometer: Use this thermometer type to check the doneness of larger cuts as well as thinner foods, such as burgers, steaks, and chops; do not leave it in food while food is cooking. Insert the thermometer stem at least ½ inch into the food (see photo, above). It will register the temperature in about 10 seconds.

Steak au Poivre (FAST)

Start to Finish: 30 minutes **Makes:** 4 servings

- 1 tablespoon cracked black pepper
- 4 beef tenderloin steaks or 2 beef top loin steaks, cut 1 inch thick (1 pound)
- 2 tablespoons butter or margarine
- ¼ cup brandy or beef broth
- ¼ cup beef broth
- ½ cup whipping cream (no substitutes)
- 2 teaspoons Dijon-style mustard

1. Use your fingers to press the pepper onto both sides of the steaks. If using top loin steaks, cut each steak in half crosswise. In a large skillet cook steaks in hot butter over medium heat to desired doneness, turning once. For tenderloin steaks, allow 10 to 13 minutes for medium rare (145°F) to medium (160°F). For top loin steaks, allow 12 to 15 minutes for medium rare to medium. Transfer steaks to a serving platter, reserving drippings in skillet; keep warm.

2. Remove skillet from burner and allow to stand for 1 minute. For sauce, combine brandy and beef broth (or all beef broth); carefully stir into drippings in skillet, scraping up crusty browned bits. Stir in whipping cream and mustard. Bring to boiling. Boil gently, uncovered, over medium heat for 5 to 6 minutes or until mixture is reduced to ½ cup, stirring occasionally. Spoon sauce over steaks to serve.

Per steak + 2 tablespoons sauce: 370 cal., 25 g total fat (13 g sat. fat), 114 mg chol., 192 mg sodium, 2 g carbo., 0 g fiber, 25 g pro.
Daily Values: 13% vit. A, 1% vit. C, 4% calcium, 20% iron
Exchanges: 3½ Lean Meat, 4 Fat

Steak with Pan Sauce (FAST)

Start to Finish: 20 minutes **Makes:** 2 servings

- 5 tablespoons cold unsalted butter
- 2 beef steaks, such as top loin, ribeye, or tenderloin, cut about ¾ inch thick
- ⅓ cup dry red wine or apple juice
- ¼ cup reduced-sodium beef broth
- 2 tablespoons finely chopped shallot or 1 clove garlic, minced
- 1 tablespoon whipping cream (no substitutes)
  Salt and black pepper

1. Heat a large skillet over medium-high heat (if possible, do not use a nonstick skillet). Add 1 tablespoon of the butter; reduce heat to medium. Add steaks; cook about 3 minutes per side

or until medium rare (145°F). Transfer steaks to a platter; cover with foil to keep warm (steaks will continue to cook as they stand). Drain fat from skillet.

2. Add wine, broth, and shallot to hot skillet. Using a wire whisk, stir and scrape up any browned bits. Continue to cook over medium heat 3 to 4 minutes or until liquid is reduced to about 2 tablespoons. Reduce heat to medium low.

3. Stir in cream; stir in remaining butter, 1 tablespoon at a time (see photo 1, below), whisking until butter is melted and sauce has thickened slightly (see photo 2, below). Season to taste with salt and pepper. Spoon sauce over steaks.

Per steak + 2 tablespoons sauce: 654 cal., 45 g total fat (25 g sat. fat), 199 mg chol., 325 mg sodium, 3 g carbo., 0 g fiber, 53 g pro.
Daily Values: 28% vit. A, 1% vit. C, 4% calcium, 25% iron
Exchanges: 7 Lean Meat, 6 Fat

Pan Sauce Flavor Variations:
- Stir 1 teaspoon snipped fresh thyme, tarragon, or oregano in with the shallot.
- Stir ½ teaspoon Dijon-style mustard in with the shallot.
- Stir ½ teaspoon balsamic vinegar into the finished sauce.
- Stir ½ teaspoon capers into the finished sauce.

1. After stirring cream into the reduced sauce, add butter, 1 tablespoon at a time, incorporating it with a wire whisk.

2. When the pan sauce has been properly cooked, it should be slightly thickened and have a sheen.

Beef Tenderloin with Mushrooms (FAST)

Start to Finish: 20 minutes **Makes:** 4 servings

- 4 beef tenderloin steaks, cut ¾ inch thick (1 pound)
- 1 tablespoon Dijon-style mustard or coarse-grain brown mustard
- 2 tablespoons olive oil

2 **4-ounce packages sliced cremini, shiitake, or portobello mushrooms or one 8-ounce package sliced button mushrooms (about 3 cups)**
⅓ **cup dry red wine or sherry**
1 **tablespoon Worcestershire sauce for chicken**
2 **teaspoons snipped fresh thyme**

1. Trim fat from steaks. Spread mustard evenly over both sides of steaks. In a large skillet heat 1 tablespoon of the oil over medium-high heat. Add steaks; reduce heat to medium. Cook to desired doneness; turn once. Allow 7 to 9 minutes for medium rare (145°F) to medium (160°F). Transfer steaks to serving platter; keep warm.

2. Add remaining 1 tablespoon oil to drippings in skillet. Add mushrooms; cook and stir for 4 minutes. Stir in wine, Worcestershire sauce, and thyme. Simmer, uncovered, for 3 minutes. Spoon sauce over steaks to serve.

Per steak + ⅓ cup sauce: 231 cal., 13 g total fat (3 g sat. fat), 52 mg chol., 115 mg sodium, 3 g carbo., 1 g fiber, 21 g pro.
Daily Values: 2% vit. C, 2% calcium, 17% iron
Exchanges: ½ Vegetable, 3 Lean Meat, 1 Fat

Beef Stroganoff [FAST]

Start to Finish: 30 minutes **Makes:** 4 servings

12 **ounces boneless beef sirloin steak**
1 **8-ounce carton dairy sour cream**
2 **tablespoons all-purpose flour**
½ **cup water**
2 **teaspoons instant beef bouillon granules**
¼ **teaspoon black pepper**
2 **cups sliced fresh mushrooms**
½ **cup chopped onion (1 medium)**
1 **clove garlic, minced**
2 **tablespoons butter or margarine**
2 **cups hot cooked noodles**

1. If desired, partially freeze beef for easier slicing. Trim fat from meat. Thinly slice meat across the grain into bite-size strips (see photo, page 371). In a small bowl stir together sour cream and flour. Stir in water, bouillon granules, and pepper; set aside.

2. In a large skillet cook and stir the meat, mushrooms, onion, and garlic in hot butter over medium-high heat about 5 minutes or until desired doneness. Drain off fat.

3. Stir sour cream mixture into meat mixture in skillet. Cook and stir until thickened and bubbly. Cook and stir for 1 minute more. Serve mixture over noodles.

Per about 1 cup mixture + ½ cup noodles: 427 cal., 23 g total fat (13 g sat. fat), 119 mg chol., 575 mg sodium, 29 g carbo., 2 g fiber, 26 g pro.
Daily Values: 14% vit. A, 3% vit. C, 9% calcium, 23% iron
Exchanges: 2 Starch, 3 Lean Meat, 2 Fat

Blackened Beef Stir-Fry [LOW FAT] [FAST]

Start to Finish: 25 minutes **Makes:** 4 servings

12 **ounces boneless beef top sirloin steak or top round steak**
2¼ **teaspoons blackened seasoning for beef**
⅔ **cup water**
2 **tablespoons tomato paste**
2 **teaspoons cornstarch**
½ **teaspoon instant beef bouillon granules**
1 **tablespoon cooking oil**
1 **16-ounce package frozen stir-fry vegetables (any combination)**
3 **cups hot cooked rice**

1. If desired, partially freeze beef for easier slicing. Trim fat from beef. Thinly slice meat across grain into thin bite-size strips (see photo, page 371). Sprinkle steak strips with 2 teaspoons of the blackened seasoning; toss to coat.

2. For sauce, in a small bowl stir together the remaining ¼ teaspoon blackened seasoning, water, tomato paste, cornstarch, and bouillon granules; set aside.

3. In a wok or large skillet heat oil over medium-high heat. Add stir-fry vegetables; cook and stir for 2 to 3 minutes or until crisp-tender. Remove vegetables from wok. Add beef strips to hot wok. (Add more oil as necessary during cooking.) Cook and stir for 2 to 3 minutes or until meat is slightly pink in center.

4. Push meat from center of wok. Stir sauce. Add sauce to center of wok. Cook and stir until thickened and bubbly. Return vegetables to wok. Stir to coat all ingredients with sauce. Heat through. Serve over rice.

Per 1 cup stir-fry + ¾ cup rice: 342 cal., 7 g total fat (2 g sat. fat), 40 mg chol., 367 mg sodium, 43 g carbo., 3 g fiber, 25 g pro.
Daily Values: 20% vit. A, 29% vit. C, 5% calcium, 21% iron
Exchanges: 1½ Vegetable, 2 Starch, 2½ Very Lean Meat, 1 Fat

Beef and Sweet Onion Sandwiches `LOW FAT` `FAST`

Start to Finish: 30 minutes **Makes:** 6 sandwiches

- 1 to 1½ pounds boneless beef sirloin steak or top round steak, cut 1 inch thick
- ½ teaspoon coarsely ground black pepper
- 1 tablespoon cooking oil
- ½ of a large sweet onion, such as Vidalia or Walla Walla, sliced (about 1½ cups)
- 3 tablespoons Dijon-style mustard
- 1 16-ounce loaf Italian flatbread (focaccia) or twelve 1-inch slices sourdough or marbled rye bread
- 2 cups fresh spinach leaves or fresh basil leaves
- 1 cup roasted red sweet peppers, drained and cut into ½-inch strips (about ½ of a 12-ounce jar)

1. Trim fat from steak. Use your fingers to press black pepper onto both sides of steak. In a large skillet cook steak in hot oil over medium heat for 15 to 20 minutes or until desired doneness (145°F for medium rare to 160°F for medium), turning once. Remove from skillet; keep warm.

2. Add onion to drippings in skillet. (Add more oil, if necessary.) Cook for 5 to 10 minutes or until onion is nearly tender, stirring occasionally. Stir in mustard; remove from heat.

3. Meanwhile, if using Italian flatbread, cut it into six wedges; split each wedge in half horizontally. If using sourdough slices, toast them, if desired. To serve, cut steak into bite-size strips. Top bottom halves of Italian flatbread wedges or six bread slices with spinach, steak strips, roasted pepper strips, onion mixture, and remaining bread wedges or slices.

Per sandwich: 335 cal., 8 g total fat (3 g sat. fat), 46 mg chol., 227 mg sodium, 41 g carbo., 4 g fiber, 26 g pro.
Daily Values: 19% vit. A, 121% vit. C, 10% calcium, 18% iron
Exchanges: 1 Vegetable, 2½ Starch, 2 Lean Meat

Broiled Sirloin with Simmered Vegetables `LOW FAT`

Start to Finish: 1 hour **Makes:** 4 servings

- 4 slices bacon
- 4 small onions, peeled and cut into 1-inch slices
- 8 small carrots, halved lengthwise
- 4 small red potatoes, cut up (1 pound)
- ½ cup beef broth
- ¼ cup beer or beef broth
- 1 tablespoon packed brown sugar
- 1 teaspoon dried thyme, crushed
- 1¼ pounds boneless beef top sirloin steak, cut 1½ to 2 inches thick
- ¼ teaspoon salt
- ¼ teaspoon black pepper
  Snipped fresh thyme (optional)

1. In a 12-inch skillet cook bacon over medium heat until crisp. Remove from skillet; drain bacon on paper towels. Drain all but about 1 tablespoon of the drippings from the skillet.

2. In the skillet brown onions on both sides, about 3 minutes per side. Remove onions; set aside. Add carrot to skillet; cook about 5 minutes or until light brown, turning occasionally. Remove skillet from heat. Carefully add potato, broth, beer, brown sugar, and ½ teaspoon of the dried thyme. Return onions to skillet. Return skillet to range top. Bring to boiling; reduce heat. Simmer, covered, for 30 to 35 minutes or until vegetables are tender.

3. Meanwhile, preheat broiler. Season beef with the remaining dried thyme, salt, and pepper. Place meat on the unheated rack of broiler pan. Broil 4 to 5 inches from heat for 25 to 27 minutes for medium rare (145°F) or 30 to 32 minutes for medium (160°F), turning once halfway through broiling. Cut into four pieces.

4. Remove vegetables from skillet with a slotted spoon. Gently boil juices, uncovered, for 1 to 2 minutes or until slightly thickened. Divide steak, vegetables, and bacon among four dinner plates; spoon juices over the top. If desired, sprinkle with fresh thyme.

Per 4 ounces beef + 1⅓ cups vegetables: 396 cal., 12 g total fat (4 g sat. fat), 94 mg chol., 451 mg sodium, 33 g carbo., 5 g fiber, 36 g pro.
Daily Values: 309% vit. A, 38% vit. C, 6% calcium, 34% iron
Exchanges: 1 Vegetable, 2 Starch, 4 Lean Meat

 Southwestern Tri-Tip Roast `LOW FAT` `EASY`

Prep: 15 minutes **Chill:** 6 hours **Roast:** 30 minutes
Oven: 425°F **Stand:** 15 minutes **Makes:** 6 to 8 servings

- 1 dried chipotle chile pepper, broke open, seeded, and crushed (about 2 teaspoons) (see tip, page 74)
- 1 tablespoon snipped fresh oregano or 1 teaspoon dried oregano, crushed
- 1 tablespoon olive oil

1 **teaspoon ground cumin**
½ **teaspoon salt**
2 **cloves garlic, minced**
1 **1½- to 2-pound boneless beef tri-tip roast (bottom sirloin)**

1. For rub, combine chipotle peppers, oregano, oil, cumin, salt, and garlic. Spread rub over meat's surface using your glove-covered hands; rub it in. Cover and chill for 6 to 24 hours.

2. Place meat on a rack in a shallow roasting pan. Insert an oven-going meat thermometer into center of roast (see tip, page 367). Roast in a 425°F oven. For medium rare, roast for 30 to 35 minutes or until meat thermometer registers 135°F. Cover with foil and let stand 15 minutes. The temperature of meat after standing should be 145°F. (For medium, roast for 40 to 45 minutes or until meat thermometer registers 150°F. Cover and let stand 15 minutes. The temperature of the meat after standing should be 160°F.)

Per 4 ounces: 156 cal., 7 g total fat (2 g sat. fat), 45 mg chol., 248 mg sodium, 1 g carbo., 0 g fiber, 21 g pro.
Daily Values: 2% vit. A, 1% vit. C, 1% calcium, 11% iron
Exchanges: 3 Lean Meat

Szechwan Beef Stir-Fry

Szechwan Beef Stir-Fry LOW FAT

Start to Finish: 40 minutes **Makes:** 4 servings

12 **ounces boneless beef top round steak or sirloin steak**
3 **tablespoons dry sherry or orange juice**
3 **tablespoons soy sauce**
2 **tablespoons water**
2 **tablespoons bottled hoisin sauce**

1 **tablespoon grated fresh ginger or ½ teaspoon ground ginger**
2 **teaspoons cornstarch**
1 **teaspoon sugar**
2 **cloves garlic, minced**
¼ **to ½ teaspoon crushed red pepper (optional)**
1 **tablespoon cooking oil**
1 **cup thinly bias-sliced carrot**
1 **14-ounce can whole baby corn, drained**
1 **red sweet pepper, cut into 1-inch pieces**
2 **cups hot cooked rice**
Thinly sliced green onion (optional)

1. If desired, partially freeze beef for easier slicing. Trim fat from meat. Thinly slice meat across the grain into bite-size strips (see photo, below). Set aside.

2. For sauce, in a small bowl stir together sherry, soy sauce, water, hoisin sauce, ginger, cornstarch, sugar, garlic, and, if desired, crushed red pepper; set aside.

3. In a wok or large skillet heat oil over medium-high heat. (Add more oil, if necessary, during cooking.) Add carrot; cook and stir in hot oil for 2 minutes. Add corn and sweet pepper. Cook and stir for 1 to 2 minutes more or until vegetables are crisp-tender. Remove from wok.

4. Add beef strips to hot wok. Cook and stir for 2 to 3 minutes or until meat is slightly pink in center. Push meat from center of wok.

5. Stir sauce. Add sauce to center of wok. Cook and stir until thickened and bubbly. Return cooked vegetables to wok; stir to coat all ingredients with sauce. Cook and stir for 1 to 2 minutes more or until heated through. Serve immediately with rice. If desired, sprinkle with green onion.

Per 1¼ cups stir-fry + ½ cup rice: 317 cal., 7 g total fat (1 g sat. fat), 48 mg chol., 859 mg sodium, 35 g carbo., 3 g fiber, 24 g pro.
Daily Values: 85% vit. A, 84% vit. C, 4% calcium, 17% iron
Exchanges: ½ Vegetable, 2 Starch, 2½ Very Lean Meat, 1½ Fat

To make it easier to slice meat or poultry for stir-frying, partially freeze it. For a more tender final product, thinly slice the meat or poultry across the grain into bite-size pieces.

Swiss Steak

Swiss Steak LOW FAT

Prep: 25 minutes **Cook:** 1¼ hours **Makes:** 4 servings

- 1 **pound boneless beef round steak,
  cut ¾ inch thick**
- 2 **tablespoons all-purpose flour**
- ¼ **teaspoon salt**
- ¼ **teaspoon black pepper**
- 1 **tablespoon cooking oil**
- 1 **14.5-ounce can diced tomatoes with basil,
  garlic, and oregano, undrained**
- 1 **small onion, sliced and separated into rings**
- ½ **cup sliced celery (1 stalk)**
- ½ **cup sliced carrot (1 medium)**
- 1 **recipe Mashed Potatoes (page 587) or
  one 24-ounce package refrigerated
  mashed potatoes heated according to
  package directions**

1. Trim fat from meat. Cut meat into four serving-size pieces. Combine flour, salt, and pepper. With the notched side of a meat mallet, pound flour mixture into meat.

2. In a large skillet brown meat on both sides in hot oil. Drain off fat. Add undrained tomatoes, onion, celery, and carrot. Bring to boiling; reduce heat. Simmer, covered, about 1¼ hours or until meat is tender. Skim off fat. Serve with Mashed Potatoes.

Oven directions: Prepare meat in skillet as above. Transfer meat to a 2-quart square baking dish. In the same skillet combine undrained tomatoes, onion, celery, and carrot. Bring to boiling, scraping up any browned bits. Pour over meat. Cover and bake in a 350°F oven about 1 hour or until tender. Serve as at left.

Per 3 ounces beef + ⅔ cup vegetables and sauce + ¾ cup potatoes: 386 cal., 12 g total fat (5 g sat. fat), 80 mg chol., 1,101 mg sodium, 39 g carbo., 3 g fiber, 31 g pro.
Daily Values: 50% vit. A, 45% vit. C, 11% calcium, 28% iron
Exchanges: 1 Vegetable, 2 Starch, 3½ Very Lean Meat, 2 Fat

Chicken Fried Steak

Prep: 20 minutes **Cook:** 1 hour **Makes:** 4 servings

- 1 **pound boneless beef top round steak,
  cut ½ inch thick**
- ¾ **cup fine dry bread crumbs**
- 1½ **teaspoons snipped fresh basil or oregano or
  ½ teaspoon dried basil or oregano, crushed**
- ½ **teaspoon salt**
- ¼ **teaspoon black pepper**
- 1 **egg, beaten**
- 1 **tablespoon milk**
- 2 **tablespoons cooking oil**
- 1 **small onion, sliced and separated into rings**
- 2 **tablespoons all-purpose flour**
- 1⅓ **cups milk**
  Salt and black pepper (optional)

1. Trim fat from meat. Cut meat into four serving-size pieces. Place each piece of meat between two pieces of plastic wrap. Working from center to edges, pound meat lightly with the flat side of a meat mallet to ¼-inch thickness. Remove plastic wrap.

2. In a shallow dish or on waxed paper combine bread crumbs, basil, the ½ teaspoon salt, and the ¼ teaspoon pepper. In a second shallow dish combine egg and the 1 tablespoon milk. Dip meat pieces into egg mixture; coat with bread crumb mixture.

3. In a 12-inch skillet cook meat, half at a time, in hot oil over medium heat about 6 minutes or until brown, turning once. (Add more oil, if necessary.) Return all meat to skillet. Reduce heat to medium low. Cook, covered, for 45 to 60 minutes more or until meat is tender. Transfer meat to a serving platter, reserving drippings in skillet. Cover and keep warm.

4. For gravy, cook onion in reserved drippings until tender but not brown. (Add more oil, if necessary.) Stir in flour. Gradually stir in the 1⅓ cups milk. Cook and stir over medium heat until thickened and bubbly. Cook and stir for

1 minute more. If desired, season to taste with salt and pepper. Serve gravy with meat.

Per 3½ ounces beef + ¼ cup gravy: 351 cal., 13 g total fat (3 g sat. fat), 108 mg chol., 578 mg sodium, 23 g carbo., 1 g fiber, 34 g pro.
Daily Values: 5% vit. A, 3% vit. C, 17% calcium, 21% iron
Exchanges: 1½ Starch, 4 Lean Meat

Beef and Noodles   `LOW FAT`

In some parts of the country, this meat-and-pasta combo is served over mashed potatoes.

Prep: 30 minutes   Cook: 1¾ hours   Makes: 4 servings

    1 pound boneless beef round steak or
       chuck roast
    ¼ cup all-purpose flour
    1 tablespoon cooking oil
    ½ cup chopped onion (1 medium)
    2 cloves garlic, minced
    3 cups beef broth
    1 teaspoon dried marjoram or basil, crushed
    ¼ teaspoon black pepper
    8 ounces frozen noodles
    2 tablespoons snipped fresh parsley

1. Trim fat from meat. Cut meat into ¾-inch cubes. Coat meat with the flour. In a large saucepan brown half of the coated meat in hot oil. Remove from saucepan. Brown the remaining coated meat with the onion and garlic, adding more oil, if necessary. Drain off fat. Return all meat to the saucepan.

2. Stir in the broth, marjoram, and pepper. Bring to boiling; reduce heat. Simmer, covered, for 1¼ to 1½ hours or until meat is tender.

3. Stir noodles into broth mixture. Bring to boiling; reduce heat. Cook, uncovered, for 25 to 30 minutes or until noodles are tender. To serve, sprinkle with parsley.

Per 1⅛ cups: 351 cal., 12 g total fat (3 g sat. fat), 94 mg chol., 677 mg sodium, 29 g carbo., 1 g fiber, 31 g pro.
Daily Values: 3% vit. A, 7% vit. C, 3% calcium, 25% iron
Exchanges: 2 Starch, 3½ Lean Meat

Cubed Steaks with Tomato-Mushroom Sauce   `EASY`

Prep: 15 minutes   Cook: 30 minutes   Makes: 4 servings

    4 4-ounce beef cubed steaks
    2 tablespoons cooking oil
    1 cup sliced fresh mushrooms
    ½ cup chopped onion (1 medium)

    1 clove garlic, minced
    1 14.5-ounce can diced tomatoes with basil,
       garlic, and oregano, undrained
    1 10.75-ounce can reduced-fat and
       reduced-sodium condensed cream of
       mushroom soup
    3 cups hot cooked noodles

1. In a 12-inch skillet brown steaks on both sides in hot oil over medium-high heat. Remove steaks from skillet. Add mushrooms, onion, and garlic to skillet; cook until onion is tender.

2. Stir in the undrained tomatoes and soup. Return steaks to skillet, turning to coat with sauce. Bring to boiling; reduce heat. Simmer, covered, about 30 minutes or until steaks are tender. Serve with noodles.

Per steak + ¾ cup sauce + ¾ cup noodles: 468 cal., 15 g total fat (3 g sat. fat), 108 mg chol., 916 mg sodium, 48 g carbo., 2 g fiber, 34 g pro.
Daily Values: 13% vit. A, 14% vit. C, 9% calcium, 36% iron
Exchanges: 1½ Vegetable, 2½ Starch, 3½ Lean Meat, 1 Fat

Oven-Barbecued Beef Brisket   `LOW FAT`   `EASY`

Prep: 15 minutes   Bake: 3 hours
Oven: 325°F   Makes: 10 to 12 servings

    1 3- to 3½-pound fresh beef brisket
    ¾ cup water
    ½ cup chopped onion (1 medium)
    3 tablespoons Worcestershire sauce
    2 tablespoons cider vinegar or white wine
       vinegar
    1 tablespoon chili powder
    1 teaspoon instant beef bouillon granules
    ⅛ teaspoon cayenne pepper
    2 cloves garlic, minced
    1½ cups bottled barbecue sauce

1. Trim fat from meat. Place meat in a 13×9×2-inch baking pan. In a small bowl stir together water, onion, Worcestershire sauce, vinegar, chili powder, bouillon granules, cayenne pepper, and garlic. Pour over meat. Cover with foil.

2. Bake in a 325°F oven about 3 hours or until tender, turning once. Remove meat; discard juices. Thinly slice meat across the grain. Serve with barbecue sauce.

Per 2½ ounces beef + 2 tablespoons sauce: 244 cal., 7 g total fat (2 g sat. fat), 78 mg chol., 735 mg sodium, 0 g fiber, 29 g pro.
Daily Values: 8% vit. A, 3% vit. C, 2% calcium, 17% iron
Exchanges: 1 Other Carbo., 3½ Lean Meat

Fajitas

See photo, page 361.

Prep: 30 minutes **Chill:** 30 minutes
Oven: 350°F **Makes:** 4 to 6 servings

- **12** ounces beef flank steak or bite-size strips of chicken or turkey
- **1** tablespoon purchased fajita seasoning
- **4 to 6** flour tortillas (8 inch)
- **2** tablespoons cooking oil
- **1** cup thin strips of red or green sweet pepper
- **½** cup thinly sliced onion, separated into rings
- **¾** cup chopped tomato (1 medium)
- **1** tablespoon lime juice
- **1** recipe Chunky Guacamole (page 66) (optional)
   Bottled salsa (optional)
   Dairy sour cream (optional)
   Lime wedges

1. If desired, partially freeze beef for easier slicing. If using beef, thinly slice beef across the grain into bite-size strips (see photo, page 371). Place meat strips in a deep bowl. Sprinkle with 2 teaspoons of the fajita seasoning. Stir to coat. Cover and chill 30 minutes.

2. Wrap tortillas tightly in foil. Heat in a 350°F oven about 10 minutes or until heated through. In a 12-inch skillet heat 1 tablespoon of the oil over medium-high heat. Add the remaining 1 teaspoon seasoning, sweet pepper, and onion. Cook and stir about 3 minutes or until crisp-tender. Remove onion mixture from skillet.

3. Add the remaining 1 tablespoon oil and the meat to the skillet. Cook and stir for 2 to 3 minutes until desired doneness for beef or until poultry strips are no longer pink. Drain well. Return onion mixture to skillet. Stir in tomato. Cook and stir for 1 minute or until heated through. Remove skillet from heat; stir in lime juice.

4. To serve, fill warm tortillas with meat mixture. If desired, top meat mixture with Chunky Guacamole, salsa, and sour cream. Roll up tortillas. Serve with lime wedges.

Per 1 tortilla + ¾ cup meat mixture: 312 cal., 15 g total fat (4 g sat. fat), 34 mg chol., 319 mg sodium, 21 g carbo., 2 g fiber, 21 g pro.
Daily Values: 34% vit. A, 90% vit. C, 4% calcium, 15% iron
Exchanges: 1 Vegetable, 1 Starch, 2½ Lean Meat, 1½ Fat

Flank Steak Bordelaise

Flank Steak Bordelaise

Because flank steak is often in demand, you may have to place an order with your butcher to get one.

Prep: 30 minutes **Marinate:** 6 hours
Broil: 15 minutes **Makes:** 4 servings

- **1** pound beef flank steak
- **⅓** cup red wine vinegar
- **¼** cup chopped onion
- **2** tablespoons cooking oil
- **1** tablespoon Worcestershire sauce
- **¼** teaspoon dry mustard
- **2** cloves garlic, minced
- **¼** cup chopped green onion (2)
- **2** tablespoons butter or margarine
- **1** tablespoon all-purpose flour
- **½** teaspoon dried thyme, crushed
- **1** 14-ounce can beef broth
- **¼** cup dry red wine or 1 tablespoon red wine vinegar
- **2½** cups thin zucchini strips
- **1** cup thin carrot strips
- **1** clove garlic, minced
- **1** tablespoon butter or margarine
- **⅓** cup walnuts, toasted (see tip, page 265) and coarsely chopped
   Salt and black pepper

1. Score both sides of steak in a diamond pattern by making shallow diagonal cuts at 1-inch intervals. Place meat in a large resealable plastic bag set in a shallow dish. For marinade, in a small bowl combine the ⅓ cup wine vinegar, onion, oil, Worcestershire sauce, dry mustard, and the

2 cloves garlic. Pour marinade over meat; seal bag. Turn to coat meat. Marinate in the refrigerator for at least 6 hours or up to 24 hours, turning bag several times.

2. For sauce, in a medium saucepan cook green onion in the 2 tablespoons hot butter over medium heat until tender. Stir in the flour and thyme. Stir in broth and wine. Bring to boiling, stirring occasionally; reduce heat. Boil gently, uncovered, for 15 to 20 minutes or until reduced to about 1 cup; keep warm.

3. Drain steak, discarding marinade. Pat steak dry with paper towels. Preheat broiler. Place steak on the unheated rack of a broiler pan. Broil 3 to 4 inches from the heat for 15 to 18 minutes or until medium doneness (160°F), turning once. Slice steak thinly across the grain.

4. Meanwhile, combine zucchini, carrot, and the 1 clove garlic; place in a steamer basket over boiling water. Steam about 4 minutes or just until tender. Transfer to a bowl. Stir in the 1 tablespoon butter and walnuts. Season to taste with salt and pepper.

5. To serve, spoon some of the sauce over steak; pass the remaining sauce. Serve the vegetable mixture with the steak. If desired, garnish with fresh *herb sprigs.*

Per 3 ounces beef + ½ cup vegetables + ¼ cup sauce: 400 cal., 26 g total fat (9 g sat. fat), 70 mg chol., 575 mg sodium, 11 g carbo., 3 g fiber, 29 g pro.
Daily Values: 76% vit. A, 26% vit. C, 8% calcium, 17% iron
Exchanges: 1 Vegetable, 4 Lean Meat, 3 Fat

Beef Pot Roast LOW FAT

Prep: 20 minutes **Cook:** 1¾ hours
Makes: 8 to 10 servings

- 1 2½- to 3-pound boneless beef chuck pot roast
- 2 tablespoons cooking oil
- 1 tablespoon Worcestershire sauce
- 1 teaspoon instant beef bouillon granules
- 1 teaspoon dried basil, crushed
- ½ teaspoon salt
- 1 pound tiny new potatoes or 4 medium potatoes or sweet potatoes
- 1 pound carrots or 6 medium parsnips, peeled and cut into 2-inch pieces
- 2 small onions, cut into wedges
- 2 stalks celery, bias-sliced into 1-inch pieces

- ½ cup cold water
- ¼ cup all-purpose flour
     Black pepper (optional)

1. Trim fat from meat. In a 4- to 6-quart Dutch oven brown meat in hot oil. Drain off fat. Combine ¾ cup *water,* Worcestershire sauce, bouillon granules, basil, and salt. Pour over meat. Bring to boiling; reduce heat. Simmer, covered, for 1 hour.

2. If using new potatoes, peel a strip of skin from the center of each. If using medium potatoes or sweet potatoes, peel and quarter. Add potato, carrot, onion, and celery to meat. Return to boiling; reduce heat. Simmer, covered, for 45 to 60 minutes more or until meat and vegetables are tender, adding *water* if necessary. Transfer meat and vegetables to a platter, reserving juices in Dutch oven. Keep warm.

3. For gravy, measure juices; skim fat. If necessary, add enough *water* to juices to equal 1½ cups. Return to Dutch oven. In a small bowl stir the ½ cup cold water into flour until smooth. Stir into juices in pan. Cook and stir over medium heat until thickened and bubbly. Cook and stir for 1 minute more. If desired, season with pepper. Serve gravy with meat and vegetables.

Oven directions: Prepare meat as above in an oven-going Dutch oven. Combine the ¾ cup *water,* Worcestershire sauce, bouillon granules, basil, and salt. Pour over meat. Bake, covered, in a 325°F oven for 1 hour. Prepare potatoes as directed. Add vegetables to meat in Dutch oven. Cover and bake for 45 to 60 minutes more or until tender. Prepare gravy in a saucepan and serve as above.

Slow cooker directions: Trim fat from meat. Place vegetables in a 4½- or 5-quart slow cooker. Cut meat to fit, if necessary; place on top of vegetables. Combine the ¾ cup *water,* Worcestershire sauce, bouillon granules, basil, and salt. Add to cooker. Cover and cook on low-heat setting for 9 to 11 hours or on high-heat setting for 4½ to 5½ hours. Prepare gravy in a medium saucepan on the range top and serve as above.

Per 3 ounces beef + ¾ cup vegetables + ¼ cup gravy: 294 cal., 9 g total fat (2 g sat. fat), 84 mg chol., 433 mg sodium, 20 g carbo., 3 g fiber, 33 g pro.
Daily Values: 124% vit. A, 20% vit. C, 5% calcium, 27% iron
Exchanges: 1 Vegetable, 1 Starch, 4 Very Lean Meat, 1 Fat

Winter Pot Roast

Winter Pot Roast

Prep: 30 minutes **Cook:** 2 hours **Makes:** 6 to 8 servings

- 1 2½- to 3-pound boneless beef chuck arm or shoulder pot roast
- 1 tablespoon cooking oil
- 1 14-ounce can beef broth
- 1 tablespoon finely shredded lemon peel
- 2 teaspoons dried oregano, crushed
- ½ teaspoon salt
- ¼ teaspoon black pepper
- 2 cloves garlic, minced
- 6 to 8 medium carrots and/or parsnips, peeled and cut into 1½-inch pieces
- 1 large onion, cut into wedges
- 1 cup pitted dried plums (prunes), halved
- ½ cup dried apricots, halved
- ⅓ cup cold water
- ¼ cup all-purpose flour
- 3 to 4 cups hot cooked noodles

1. Trim fat from meat. In a 4- to 6-quart Dutch oven brown meat in hot oil. Combine broth, lemon peel, oregano, salt, pepper, and garlic. Pour over meat. Bring to boiling; reduce heat. Simmer, covered, for 1½ hours.

2. Add carrot, onion, plums, and apricots. Return to boiling; reduce heat. Simmer, covered, for 30 to 40 minutes more or until meat and vegetables are tender. Transfer meat, vegetables, and fruit to a platter, reserving juices in Dutch oven; keep warm.

3. For gravy, measure juices; skim fat. If necessary, add enough *water* to juices to equal

2½ cups. Return to Dutch oven. In a small bowl stir ⅓ cup cold water into flour until smooth. Stir into juices. Cook and stir over medium heat until thickened and bubbly. Cook and stir for 1 minute more. Season to taste. Serve with meat, vegetables, fruit, and noodles.

Oven directions: Prepare meat as at left in an oven-going Dutch oven. Combine broth, lemon peel, oregano, salt, pepper, and garlic. Pour over meat. Bake, covered, in a 325°F oven for 1½ hours. Add carrot, onion, plums, and apricots. Cover and bake for 30 to 40 minutes more or until meat and vegetables are tender. Transfer meat, vegetables, and fruit to a platter, reserving juices. Keep warm. Prepare gravy in a saucepan and serve as above.

Per 4 ounces beef + 1 cup vegetables + ½ cup noodles: 604 cal., 23 g total fat (8 g sat. fat), 140 mg chol., 476 mg sodium, 58 g carbo., 7 g fiber, 42 g pro.
Daily Values: 335% vit. A, 15% vit. C, 8% calcium, 41% iron
Exchanges: 1 Vegetable, 1½ Fruit, 2 Starch, 5 Lean Meat, 1 Fat

Beef and Broccoli Noodle Bowl

Start to Finish: 30 minutes **Makes:** 4 servings

- 8 ounces dried wide noodles (3 cups)
- 3 cups broccoli florets
- 12 ounces boneless beef chuck eye steak or beef shoulder top blade steak (flat iron)
- 1 medium onion, cut into ½-inch slices
- 2 cloves garlic, minced
- 1 tablespoon cooking oil
- 1 tablespoon all-purpose flour
- ¼ teaspoon salt
- ¼ teaspoon black pepper
- 1 14-ounce can beef broth
- ¼ cup tomato paste
- 1 teaspoon prepared horseradish

1. Cook noodles according to package directions, adding broccoli the last 3 minutes of cooking; drain and keep warm.

2. If desired, partially freeze beef for easier slicing. Trim fat from meat. Cut into thin bite-size strips (see photo, page 371). In a large skillet cook meat, onion, and garlic in hot oil until onion is tender and meat reaches desired doneness; remove skillet from heat. Sprinkle flour, salt, and pepper over meat. Stir to coat.

3. Add beef broth, tomato paste, and horseradish to skillet with beef. Cook and stir until thickened and bubbly. Cook and stir for 1 minute more. Remove from heat. To serve, divide noodle mixture among four bowls. Spoon beef mixture on top of noodle mixture.

Per ¾ cup beef mixture + 2 cups noodle mixture: 413 cal., 10 g total fat (2 g sat. fat), 106 mg chol., 604 mg sodium, 52 g carbo., 4 g fiber, 30 g pro.
Daily Values: 9% vit. A, 106% vit. C, 6% calcium, 29% iron
Exchanges: 1½ Vegetable, 3 Starch, 2½ Lean Meat, ½ Fat

Zesty Short Ribs

These ribs are made in two steps—first they're simmered until tender, then broiled with sauce.

Prep: 20 minutes **Cook:** 1½ hours
Broil: 10 minutes **Makes:** 4 servings

  3 **to 4 pounds beef short ribs, cut into serving-size pieces**
⅓ **cup ketchup**
⅓ **cup bottled chili sauce**
¼ **cup molasses**
  3 **tablespoons lemon juice**
  2 **tablespoons yellow mustard**
¼ **teaspoon cayenne pepper**

1. Trim fat from ribs. Place ribs in a 4- to 6-quart Dutch oven. Add *water* to cover ribs. Bring to boiling; reduce heat. Simmer, covered, for 1½ to 2 hours or until ribs are tender; drain.

2. Preheat broiler. For sauce, combine ketchup, chili sauce, molasses, lemon juice, mustard, and cayenne pepper. Place ribs on the unheated rack of a broiler pan. Brush with some of the sauce. Broil 4 to 5 inches from the heat for 10 to 15 minutes or until heated through, turning often and brushing with sauce. Heat any remaining sauce and pass with ribs.

Per 5 ounces ribs + 3 tablespoons sauce: 489 cal., 23 g total fat (9 g sat. fat), 106 mg chol., 1,048 mg sodium, 27 g carbo., 1 g fiber, 43 g pro.
Daily Values: 19% vit. A, 17% vit. C, 9% calcium, 28% iron
Exchanges: 2 Other Carbo., 5 Medium-Fat Meat

Meat Loaf LOW FAT

Serve a slice of this meat for pure comfort, especially when accompanied with mashed potatoes.

Prep: 20 minutes **Bake:** 70 minutes **Oven:** 350°F
Stand: 10 minutes **Makes:** 8 servings

  2 **eggs, beaten**
¾ **cup milk**
⅔ **cup fine dry bread crumbs or**
     2 cups soft bread crumbs (2½ slices)
¼ **cup finely chopped onion**
  2 **tablespoons snipped fresh parsley**
  1 **teaspoon salt**
½ **teaspoon dried leaf sage, basil, or oregano, crushed**
⅛ **teaspoon black pepper**
1½ **pounds lean ground beef, ground lamb, or ground pork**
¼ **cup ketchup**
  2 **tablespoons packed brown sugar**
  1 **teaspoon dry mustard**

1. In a medium bowl combine eggs and milk; stir in bread crumbs, onion, parsley, salt, sage, and pepper. Add ground meat; mix well. Lightly pat mixture into an 8×4×2-inch loaf pan.

2. Bake in a 350°F oven for 1 to 1¼ hours or until internal temperature registers 160°F on an instant-read thermometer. Spoon off fat. In a small bowl combine ketchup, brown sugar, and mustard; spread over meat. Bake for 10 minutes more. Let stand for 10 minutes before cutting into eight slices.

Ham Loaf: Prepare as above, except use soft bread crumbs. Substitute ½ teaspoon dry mustard for dried herb and omit the salt. For the ground meat, use 12 ounces lean ground beef or pork and 12 ounces ground cooked ham. Bake and let stand as above.

Per slice plain or ham variation: 225 cal., 10 g total fat (4 g sat. fat), 108 mg chol., 676 mg sodium, 13 g carbo., 1 g fiber, 19 g pro.
Daily Values: 5% vit. A, 5% vit. C, 6% calcium, 13% iron
Exchanges: 1 Other Carbo., 2½ Lean Meat, ½ Fat

Meat Loaf

Basil Pan Burgers `FAST`

The color of cooked meat is not a good indication of doneness. To be certain your burgers are cooked, insert a meat thermometer into a burger's side.

Prep: 15 minutes **Cook:** 12 minutes
Makes: 4 sandwiches

- 1 egg, slightly beaten
- ¼ cup chopped onion
- ¼ cup grated Parmesan cheese
- 2 tablespoons fine dry bread crumbs
- 2 tablespoons snipped fresh basil or 1 teaspoon dried basil, crushed
- 2 tablespoons ketchup
- ¼ teaspoon salt
- ¼ teaspoon black pepper
- 1 clove garlic, minced
- 1 pound lean ground beef
  Nonstick cooking spray
- 4 whole wheat hamburger buns, split and toasted
  Fresh basil leaves (optional)
- 4 tomato slices

1. In a medium bowl combine egg, onion, Parmesan cheese, bread crumbs, 2 tablespoons fresh basil, ketchup, salt, pepper, and garlic. Add beef; mix well. Shape beef mixture into four ¾-inch-thick patties.

2. Lightly coat a heavy skillet with cooking spray (or use a heavy nonstick skillet).* Preheat skillet over medium-high heat until hot. Add patties. Reduce heat to medium and cook, uncovered, for 12 to 15 minutes or until temperature registers 160°F on an instant-read thermometer, turning patties once halfway through cooking. If patties brown too quickly, reduce heat to medium low. Serve patties on buns with basil leaves (if desired) and tomato slices.

*Note: To prepare on an indoor grill, preheat grill according to manufacturer's directions. Place patties on grill rack. If using a covered grill, close lid. Grill until internal temperature reaches 160°F. For a covered grill, allow 5 to 7 minutes. For an uncovered grill, allow 14 to 18 minutes, turning once halfway through grilling. Serve as above.

Per sandwich: 365 cal., 16 g total fat (6 g sat. fat), 129 mg chol., 651 mg sodium, 26 g carbo., 2 g fiber, 29 g pro.
Daily Values: 7% vit. A, 7% vit. C, 13% calcium, 24% iron
Exchanges: 2 Starch, 3½ Lean Meat

Hamburger Pie

Hamburger Pie

Prep: 30 minutes **Bake:** 30 minutes
Oven: 350°F **Makes:** 6 servings

- 1 recipe Mashed Potatoes (page 587) or one 24-ounce package refrigerated mashed potatoes
- 1¼ pounds lean ground beef
- ½ cup chopped onion (1 medium)
- ¼ teaspoon salt
  Dash black pepper
- 2½ cups frozen cut green beans, thawed
- 1 10.75-ounce can condensed tomato soup
- ½ cup shredded process American cheese (2 ounces)

1. Prepare Mashed Potatoes (if using); set aside. In a large skillet cook meat and onion until meat is brown and onion is tender. Drain off fat. Add salt and pepper. Stir in thawed beans and soup. Pour into a greased 2-quart rectangular baking dish or casserole.

2. Spoon Mashed Potatoes in mounds on beef mixture. (If desired, use a pastry bag and a large star tip to pipe potatoes onto mixture.) Sprinkle cheese over potatoes. Bake, uncovered, in a 350°F oven for 30 to 35 minutes or until mixture is bubbly and cheese begins to brown.

Per 1 cup beef mixture + ½ cup potatoes: 376 cal., 16 g total fat (8 g sat. fat), 80 mg chol., 796 mg sodium, 34 g carbo., 4 g fiber, 23 g pro.
Daily Values: 14% vit. A, 43% vit. C, 10% calcium, 18% iron
Exchanges: ½ Vegetable, 1½ Starch, ½ Other Carbo., 2½ Lean Meat, 1½ Fat

Swedish Meatballs

These meatballs feature a blend of ground meats. A touch of spice gives them an extra flavor boost.

Start to Finish: 50 minutes **Makes:** 5 or 6 servings

- 1 egg, beaten
- ¼ cup milk
- ¾ cup soft bread crumbs (1 slice)
- ½ cup finely chopped onion (1 medium)
- ¼ cup snipped fresh parsley
- ¼ teaspoon black pepper
- ⅛ teaspoon ground allspice or nutmeg
- 8 ounces ground beef or ground veal
- 8 ounces ground pork or ground lamb
- 1 tablespoon butter or margarine
- 2 tablespoons all-purpose flour
- 2 teaspoons instant beef bouillon granules
- ⅛ teaspoon black pepper
- 2 cups milk
- 3 cups hot cooked noodles
  Snipped fresh parsley (optional)

1. In a large bowl combine egg and the ¼ cup milk. Stir in bread crumbs, onion, the ¼ cup parsley, the ¼ teaspoon pepper, and allspice. Add meats. Mix well. Shape into 30 meatballs.*

2. In a large skillet cook half the meatballs at a time in hot butter over medium heat about 10 minutes or until done (an instant-read thermometer inserted into meatballs should register 160°F), turning to brown evenly. Remove meatballs from skillet, reserving drippings; drain meatballs on paper towels. Measure 2 tablespoons drippings; if necessary, add *cooking oil* to make 2 tablespoons.

3. Stir flour, bouillon granules, and the ⅛ teaspoon pepper into drippings. Stir in the 2 cups milk. Cook and stir over medium heat until thickened and bubbly. Cook and stir for 1 minute more. Return meatballs to skillet. Heat through. Serve over noodles. If desired, sprinkle with additional snipped parsley.

*Note: If desired, use a melon baller or small cookie scoop to shape the meatballs.

Per about ¾ cup meatballs and sauce + ½ cup noodles:
518 cal., 29 g total fat (12 g sat. fat), 160 mg chol., 602 mg sodium, 37 g carbo., 2 g fiber, 26 g pro.
Daily Values: 11% vit. A, 11% vit. C, 18% calcium, 20% iron
Exchanges: 2½ Starch, 2½ High-Fat Meat, 1½ Fat

Upside-Down Pizza Casserole

Prep: 20 minutes **Bake:** 15 minutes
Oven: 400°F **Makes:** 5 servings

- 1½ pounds lean ground beef
- 1 15-ounce can Italian-style tomato sauce
- 1 4-ounce can sliced mushrooms, drained
- ¼ cup sliced, pitted ripe olives (optional)
- 1 to 1½ cups shredded mozzarella cheese
- 1 10-ounce package (10) refrigerated biscuits

1. Preheat oven to 400°F. In a large skillet cook beef until brown. Drain off fat. Stir in tomato sauce, mushrooms, and, if desired, olives. Heat through. Transfer mixture to a 2-quart rectangular baking dish. Sprinkle with cheese. Flatten each biscuit with your hands. Arrange the biscuits on top of cheese. Bake for 15 to 17 minutes or until biscuits are golden.

Per about 1 cup mixture + 2 biscuits: 507 cal., 26 g total fat (10 g sat. fat), 103 mg chol., 1,251 mg sodium, 33 g carbo., 3 g fiber, 35 g pro.
Daily Values: 3% vit. A, 10% vit. C, 16% calcium, 26% iron
Exchanges: ½ Vegetable, 2 Starch, 4 Medium-Fat Meat, 1 Fat

Chili-Pasta Skillet [LOW FAT]

Prep: 10 minutes **Cook:** 25 minutes **Makes:** 6 servings

- 1 pound lean ground beef
- ¾ cup chopped onion
- 1 15- or 15.5-ounce can red kidney beans, black beans, or red beans, rinsed and drained
- 1 14.5-ounce can diced tomatoes, undrained
- 1 8-ounce can tomato sauce
- 1 4-ounce can diced green chile peppers, drained
- ½ cup dried elbow macaroni (2 ounces)
- 2 to 3 teaspoons chili powder
- ½ teaspoon garlic salt
- ½ cup shredded Monterey Jack or cheddar cheese (2 ounces)

1. In a large skillet cook meat and onion until meat is brown and onion is tender. Drain off fat. Stir in beans, undrained tomatoes, tomato sauce, chile peppers, macaroni, chili powder, and garlic salt. Bring to boiling; reduce heat. Simmer, covered, about 20 minutes or until macaroni is tender, stirring often. Remove from heat; sprinkle with cheese. Cover and let stand about 2 minutes or until cheese melts.

Per cup: 289 cal., 11 g total fat (5 g sat. fat), 56 mg chol., 622 mg sodium, 27 g carbo., 5 g fiber, 23 g pro.
Daily Values: 7% vit. A, 27% vit. C, 15% calcium, 18% iron
Exchanges: 1 Vegetable, 1½ Starch, 2 Medium-Fat Meat

Stuffed Cabbage Rolls

Prep: 30 minutes **Bake:** 35 minutes
Oven: 350°F **Stand:** 2 minutes **Makes:** 4 servings

> 12 ounces ground beef, ground pork, ground lamb, or bulk pork sausage
> ⅓ cup chopped onion (1 small)
> 1 cup canned diced tomatoes, undrained
> ⅓ cup uncooked long grain rice
> 1 teaspoon dried oregano or thyme, crushed
> ¼ teaspoon black pepper
> 8 medium to large cabbage leaves
> ½ cup shredded Swiss cheese (2 ounces)
> 1 15-ounce can tomato sauce
> 1 teaspoon sugar

1. In a large skillet cook meat and onion until meat is brown and onion is tender. Drain off fat. Stir in undrained tomatoes, ½ cup *water*, rice, ½ teaspoon of the oregano, and the pepper. Bring to boiling; reduce heat. Simmer, covered, about 20 minutes or until the rice is tender.

2. Meanwhile, trim the heavy vein from each cabbage leaf (see photo, below). Immerse leaves, four at a time, into boiling water for 2 to 3 minutes or just until limp.

3. Stir ¼ cup of the cheese into the meat mixture. Place about ⅓ cup of the meat mixture on each cabbage leaf. Fold in sides. Starting at an unfolded edge, carefully roll up each leaf, making sure folded sides are included in the roll.

4. For sauce, in a small bowl stir together tomato sauce, sugar, and remaining ½ teaspoon oregano. Pour half the sauce into a 2-quart square baking dish. Arrange cabbage rolls on the sauce in the dish. Spoon remaining sauce over cabbage rolls. Bake, covered, in a 350°F oven for 35 to 40 minutes or until heated through. Sprinkle with the remaining ¼ cup cheese. Let stand about 2 minutes or until cheese melts.

Per 2 rolls + about ⅓ cup sauce: 353 cal., 16 g total fat (7 g sat. fat), 63 mg chol., 827 mg sodium, 28 g carbo., 4 g fiber, 25 g pro.
Daily Values: 31% vit. A, 57% vit. C, 21% calcium, 22% iron
Exchanges: 2½ Vegetable, 1 Starch, 2½ Medium-Fat Meat, ½ Fat

Trim away the heavy vein off the back of each cabbage leaf so that it's even with the rest of the leaf. Rolling the leaves around the stuffing will be easier.

Super Burritos

Prep: 40 minutes **Bake:** 20 minutes
Oven: 350°F **Makes:** 8 burritos

> 1 pound lean ground beef
> 1 cup chopped onion (1 large)
> ½ cup chopped green sweet pepper (1 small)
> 1 clove garlic, minced
> ¼ cup water
> 1 tablespoon medium or hot chili powder
> ¼ teaspoon ground cumin
> ¼ teaspoon salt
> 1 cup cooked rice
> 1 4-ounce can diced green chile peppers, drained
> 8 10-inch flour tortillas
> 1½ cups shredded Monterey Jack or cheddar cheese (6 ounces)
> 1 cup chopped tomato (1 large)
> 2 cups shredded lettuce
> 1 recipe Chunky Guacamole (page 66) or frozen avocado dip (guacamole), thawed
> Bottled salsa (optional)

1. For filling, in a large skillet cook ground beef, onion, sweet pepper, and garlic until meat is brown and onion is tender. Drain off fat. Stir in water, chili powder, cumin, and salt. Cook about 5 minutes or until most of the water has evaporated. Remove from heat. Stir in cooked rice and chile peppers.

2. Meanwhile, wrap tortillas tightly in foil. Heat in a 350°F oven for 10 minutes to soften. (When ready to fill tortillas, remove only half of them at a time, keeping remaining tortillas warm in the oven.)

3. Spoon about ½ cup filling onto each tortilla just below the center. Top filling with cheese and tomato. Fold bottom edge of each tortilla up and over filling (see photo 1, page 381). Fold opposite sides in and over filling (see photo 2, page 381). Roll up from the bottom. Secure with wooden toothpicks.

4. Arrange burritos, seam sides down, on a baking sheet. Bake in a 350°F oven for 10 to 12 minutes or until heated through. Remove and discard toothpicks. Serve warm burritos on lettuce with Chunky Guacamole and, if desired, salsa.

Per burrito: 429 cal., 23 g total fat (8 g sat. fat), 55 mg chol., 462 mg sodium, 37 g carbo., 5 g fiber, 21 g pro.
Daily Values: 32% vit. A, 44% vit. C, 26% calcium, 20% iron
Exchanges: ½ Vegetable, 2½ Starch, 2 Medium-Fat Meat, 1½ Fat

Chicken or Steak Burritos: Prepare as on page 380, except omit the ground beef. Partially freeze 1 pound skinless, boneless chicken breast halves or 1 pound beef flank steak for easier slicing. Cut chicken into thin bite-size strips and cut beef across the grain into thin bite-size strips (see photo, page 371). Heat 1 tablespoon cooking oil in skillet. Cook chicken or beef, onion, sweet pepper, and garlic in hot oil until chicken is no longer pink or steak reaches desired doneness and onion is tender. Stir in water, chili powder, cumin, and salt. Cook about 5 minutes or until most of the water has evaporated. Remove from heat. Stir in cooked rice and chile peppers. Continue with Step 2 on page 380.

Per burrito: 415 cal., 20 g total fat (6 g sat. fat), 52 mg chol., 472 mg sodium, 37 g carbo., 5 g fiber, 24 g pro.
Daily Values: 32% vit. A, 44% vit. C, 26% calcium, 17% iron
Exchanges: ½ Vegetable, 2 Starch, 1 Very Lean Meat, 1 High-Fat Meat, 2 Fat

1. To make a burrito, first fold the bottom edge of a softened tortilla up and over the filling.

2. Hold the bottom of the tortilla over the filling while folding in the sides. Starting from the folded bottom edge, roll up the tortilla to enclose the filling.

Fiesta Supper

For a family-style Mexican fiesta, let diners top their burritos with desired accompaniments.

- *Super Burritos (page 380)*
- *Buttered corn*
- *Salad greens with mandarin oranges and citrus vinaigrette dressing*
- *Baked Custard (page 290)*

Tostada Pizza

Start to Finish: 40 minutes **Oven:** 400°F
Makes: 6 servings

- **1 pound lean ground beef**
- **¾ cup water**
- **1 4-ounce can diced green chile peppers, drained**
- **2 tablespoons taco seasoning mix**
- **1 teaspoon chili powder**
- **1 tablespoon cornmeal**
- **1 13.8-ounce package refrigerated pizza dough**
- **1 15-ounce can pinto beans, rinsed and drained**
- **1 cup shredded cheddar or Monterey Jack cheese (4 ounces)**
- **1 cup shredded lettuce**
- **1 medium tomato, chopped**
- **½ cup thinly sliced green onion (4)**
- **Bottled taco sauce (optional)**

1. In a large skillet cook ground beef until brown. Drain off fat. Stir in the water, chile peppers, taco seasoning mix, and chili powder. Bring to boiling; reduce heat. Simmer, uncovered, for 15 to 20 minutes or until most of the liquid has evaporated.

2. Meanwhile, preheat oven to 400°F. Grease a baking sheet and sprinkle with the cornmeal. Unroll pizza dough onto the baking sheet. Bake for 5 minutes.

3. In a small bowl mash pinto beans with a fork. Spread beans over partially baked dough to within ½ inch of edges. Spoon meat mixture over beans. Bake, uncovered, about 10 minutes more or until crust is just golden. Sprinkle with the cheese. Bake for 1 to 2 minutes more or until cheese melts. Top with lettuce, tomato, and green onion. Cut into 12 pieces. If desired, serve with taco sauce.

Per 2 pieces: 423 cal., 17 g total fat (7 g sat. fat), 67 mg chol., 939 mg sodium, 41 g carbo., 6 g fiber, 28 g pro.
Daily Values: 24% vit. A, 23% vit. C, 20% calcium, 23% iron
Exchanges: ½ Vegetable, 2½ Starch, 3 Medium-Fat Meat

Taco Pizza: Prepare as above, except top with crushed tortilla chips or corn chips after green onion. If desired, serve with dairy sour cream.

Per 2 pieces: 470 cal., 20 g total fat (8 g sat. fat), 67 mg chol., 989 mg sodium, 47 g carbo., 6 g fiber, 29 g pro.
Daily Values: 24% vit. A, 23% vit. C, 22% calcium, 24% iron
Exchanges: ½ Vegetable, 3 Starch, 3 Medium-Fat Meat

Sloppy Joes [FAST]

Start to Finish: 25 minutes **Makes:** 6 sandwiches

- 1 **pound lean ground beef or ground pork**
- ½ **cup chopped onion (1 medium)**
- ½ **cup chopped green sweet pepper (1 small)**
- 1 **8-ounce can tomato sauce**
- 2 **tablespoons water**
- 1 to 1½ **teaspoons chili powder**
- 1 **teaspoon Worcestershire sauce**
- ½ **teaspoon garlic salt**
  Dash bottled hot pepper sauce
- 6 **kaiser rolls or hamburger buns, split and toasted**

1. In a large skillet cook meat, onion, and sweet pepper until meat is brown and vegetables are tender. Drain off fat. Stir in tomato sauce, water, chili powder, Worcestershire sauce, garlic salt, and hot pepper sauce. Bring to boiling; reduce heat. Simmer, uncovered, for 5 minutes. Serve on toasted rolls.

Sloppy Joes For-a-Crowd: In a 4- to 6-quart Dutch oven cook 3 pounds lean ground beef or ground pork, 1½ cups chopped onion, and 1½ cups chopped green sweet pepper until meat is brown and vegetables are tender. Drain off fat. Stir in one 15-ounce can tomato sauce, one 8-ounce can tomato sauce, ¼ cup water, 3 to 4 teaspoons chili powder, 1 tablespoon Worcestershire sauce, 1½ teaspoons garlic salt, and ¼ teaspoon bottled hot pepper sauce. Bring to boiling; reduce heat. Simmer, uncovered, for 10 minutes. Split and toast 18 kaiser rolls or hamburger buns. Serve mixture on toasted rolls. Makes 18 sandwiches.

Per sandwich: 369 cal., 16 g total fat (6 g sat. fat), 54 mg chol., 678 mg sodium, 35 g carbo., 2 g fiber, 20 g pro.
Daily Values: 12% vit. A, 26% vit. C, 7% calcium, 20% iron
Exchanges: 2½ Starch, 2 Medium-Fat Meat, ½ Fat

Ground Meat Know-How

Check out these buying and storing tips.

When purchasing ground meat, check the label for a "sell by" date. The package should be tightly wrapped and without holes. Store it in your refrigerator's coldest section up to two days. Freeze for longer storage; use within four months. Thaw in the refrigerator; cook as soon as possible.

French Dip Sandwiches

French Dip Sandwiches [FAST]

This sandwich makes great use of leftover or deli roast beef.

Start to Finish: 30 minutes **Makes:** 4 sandwiches

- 1 **large onion, sliced and separated into rings**
- 1 **clove garlic, minced**
- 1 **tablespoon butter or margarine**
- 1 **14-ounce can beef broth**
- ½ **teaspoon dried thyme, marjoram, or oregano, crushed**
- ¼ **teaspoon black pepper**
- 12 **ounces thinly sliced cooked beef**
- 4 **French-style rolls, split**

1. In a saucepan cook onion and garlic in hot butter until tender. Stir in broth, thyme, and pepper. Bring to boiling; reduce heat. Simmer, uncovered, for 10 minutes. Add beef. Return to boiling; reduce heat. Simmer, uncovered, about 5 minutes more or until beef is heated through.

2. If desired, toast rolls. Remove beef and onion from liquid. Arrange on rolls. Serve with dishes of broth mixture for dipping.

Per sandwich + about ⅓ cup broth: 472 cal., 17 g total fat (6 g sat. fat), 76 mg chol., 969 mg sodium, 47 g carbo., 3 g fiber, 31 g pro.
Daily Values: 3% vit. A, 4% vit. C, 10% calcium, 29% iron
Exchanges: 3 Starch, 3 Lean Meat, 1½ Fat

French Dip Sandwiches with Cheese and Veggies: Prepare as above, except use a large skillet. Add 1 cup sliced fresh mushrooms and 1 cup green sweet pepper strips with broth and seasonings. Continue cooking as above. Preheat broiler. Place vegetables and beef on bottom halves of rolls. Place a slice of provolone cheese on each sandwich. Place on broiler pan; broil about 4 inches from heat about 1 minute or until cheese melts. Add tops of rolls and serve as on page 382.

Per sandwich + about ⅓ cup broth: 560 cal., 23 g total fat (10 g sat. fat), 91 mg chol., 1,155 mg sodium, 50 g carbo., 4 g fiber, 38 g pro.
Daily Values: 9% vit. A, 46% vit. C, 26% calcium, 31% iron
Exchanges: ½ Vegetable, 3 Starch, 3 Lean Meat, 1 High-Fat Meat, 1 Fat

New England Boiled Dinner

Prep: 20 minutes **Cook:** 2½ hours **Makes:** 6 servings

- 1 2- to 2½-pound corned beef brisket
- 1 teaspoon whole black peppercorns*
- 2 bay leaves*
- 2 medium potatoes, peeled and quartered
- 3 medium carrots, quartered
- 2 medium parsnips or 1 medium rutabaga, peeled and cut into chunks
- 1 medium onion, cut into 6 wedges
- 1 small cabbage, cut into 6 wedges
  Salt and black pepper (optional)
- 1 recipe Horseradish Sauce (page 520), prepared horseradish, or mustard (optional)

1. Trim fat from meat. Place in a 4- to 6-quart Dutch oven; add juices and spices from package of corned beef. (*Add peppercorns and bay leaves if your brisket doesn't come with a packet of spices.) Add enough *water* to cover meat. Bring to boiling; reduce heat. Simmer, covered, about 2 hours or until almost tender.

2. Add potato, carrot, parsnip, and onion to meat. Return to boiling; reduce heat. Simmer, covered, for 10 minutes. Add cabbage. Cover and cook for 15 to 20 minutes more or until tender. Discard bay leaves. Thinly slice meat across the grain. Transfer meat and vegetables to a serving platter. If desired, season to taste with salt and pepper and serve with Horseradish Sauce.

Per about 3½ ounces beef + 1 cup vegetables: 357 cal., 18 g total fat (5 g sat. fat), 77 mg chol., 131 mg sodium, 23 g carbo., 5 g fiber, 25 g pro.
Daily Values: 193% vit. A, 104% vit. C, 6% calcium, 21% iron
Exchanges: 1½ Vegetable, 1 Starch, 2½ Medium-Fat Meat, 1 Fat

Corned Beef and Cabbage: Prepare as above, except omit the potato, carrot, and parsnip.

Per about 3½ ounces beef + ½ cup vegetables: 279 cal., 18 g total fat (5 g sat. fat), 77 mg chol., 112 mg sodium, 5 g carbo., 2 g fiber, 23 g pro.
Daily Values: 2% vit. A, 82% vit. C, 4% calcium, 17% iron
Exchanges: 1 Vegetable, 3 Medium-Fat Meat, ½ Fat

Corned Beef Hash

Turn extra potatoes and corned beef into a dinnertime favorite.

Prep: 20 minutes **Cook:** 10 minutes **Makes:** 4 servings

- 2 tablespoons butter or margarine
- 2 cups finely chopped cooked potatoes or frozen diced hash brown potatoes, thawed
- 1½ cups finely chopped cooked corned beef
- ½ cup chopped onion (1 medium)
- 2 tablespoons snipped fresh parsley
- 1 to 2 teaspoons Worcestershire sauce
- ⅛ teaspoon black pepper
- 2 tablespoons milk

1. In a large skillet melt butter over medium heat. Stir in potato, beef, onion, parsley, Worcestershire sauce, and pepper. Spread in an even layer in skillet. Cook over medium heat about 10 minutes or until potato is browned, turning occasionally. Stir in milk; heat through.

Per ¾ cup: 277 cal., 17 g total fat (7 g sat. fat), 73 mg chol., 727 mg sodium, 18 g carbo., 2 g fiber, 12 g pro.
Daily Values: 7% vit. A, 23% vit. C, 3% calcium, 9% iron
Exchanges: 1 Starch, 1½ Medium-Fat Meat, 1½ Fat

Reuben Sandwiches

Prep: 10 minutes **Cook:** 8 minutes **Makes:** 4 sandwiches

- 3 tablespoons butter or margarine, softened
- 8 slices dark rye or pumpernickel bread
- 3 tablespoons bottled Thousand Island or Russian salad dressing
- 6 ounces thinly sliced cooked corned beef, beef, pork, or ham
- 4 slices Swiss cheese (3 ounces)
- 1 cup sauerkraut, well drained

1. Spread butter on one side of each bread slice and salad dressing on the other. With the buttered sides down, top four slices with meat, cheese, and sauerkraut. Top with remaining bread slices, dressing sides down.

2. Preheat a large skillet over medium heat. Reduce heat to medium low. Cook two of the sandwiches at a time over medium-low heat for 4 to 6 minutes or until the bread is toasted and the cheese melts, turning once. Repeat with remaining sandwiches.

Per sandwich: 487 cal., 29 g total fat (13 g sat. fat), 89 mg chol., 1,509 mg sodium, 36 g carbo., 5 g fiber, 20 g pro.
Daily Values: 11% vit. A, 14% vit. C, 27% calcium, 20% iron
Exchanges: 2½ Starch, 1½ Medium-Fat Meat, 3½ Fat

Liver and Onions

Prep: 10 minutes **Cook:** 10 minutes **Makes:** 4 servings

- 1 **pound sliced beef liver**
- 2 **medium onions, sliced and separated into rings**
- 2 **tablespoons butter or margarine**
  Dash salt
  Dash black pepper
- 2 **teaspoons water**
- 2 **teaspoons lemon juice**
- 1 **teaspoon Worcestershire sauce**

1. Pat liver dry with paper towels; set aside. In a large skillet cook onion in hot butter over medium heat until tender. Remove onion from the skillet.

2. Add liver to skillet. Sprinkle with salt and pepper. Cook over medium heat for 3 minutes; turn. Return onion to skillet. Cook for 2 to 3 minutes more or until liver is slightly pink in center. Remove liver and onion from skillet. Stir in water, lemon juice, and Worcestershire sauce. Heat through. Pour over liver and onion.

Per 3 ounces liver + about ½ cup onions: 233 cal., 11 g total fat (5 g sat. fat), 418 mg chol., 197 mg sodium, 11 g carbo., 1 g fiber, 23 g pro.
Daily Values: 646% vit. A, 39% vit. C, 2% calcium, 44% iron
Exchanges: ½ Vegetable, ½ Starch, 3 Lean Meat, ½ Fat

Veal Marsala LOW FAT

Start to Finish: 35 minutes **Makes:** 4 servings

- 1 **pound veal leg round steak or veal sirloin steak (about 1 pound)**
- 3 **cups fresh mushrooms (such as cremini, porcini, baby portobello, or button), quartered, halved, or sliced**
- 4 **teaspoons olive oil or cooking oil**
- ¼ **teaspoon salt**
- ¼ **teaspoon black pepper**
- ¾ **cup dry Marsala**
- ½ **cup sliced green onion (4)**
- 1 **tablespoon snipped fresh sage or ½ teaspoon dried sage, crushed**
- 1 **tablespoon cold water**
- 1 **teaspoon cornstarch**
- ⅛ **teaspoon salt**
  Hot cooked noodles (optional)
  Fresh herb sprigs (optional)

Veal Marsala

1. Cut veal into four serving-size pieces. Place each veal piece between two pieces of plastic wrap. Use the flat side of a meat mallet to lightly pound each slice to about ⅛-inch thickness, working from center to edges. Remove plastic wrap. Set meat aside.

2. In a 12-inch skillet cook the mushrooms in 2 teaspoons of the hot oil for 4 to 5 minutes or until tender. Remove from skillet; set aside.

3. Sprinkle veal with the ¼ teaspoon salt and pepper. In the same skillet cook veal, half at a time, in the remaining 2 teaspoons hot oil over medium-high heat for 2 to 3 minutes or until no longer pink, turning once. Transfer to dinner plates; keep warm.

4. Add Marsala to drippings in skillet. Bring to boiling. Boil mixture gently, uncovered, for 1 minute, scraping up any browned bits. Return mushrooms to skillet; add green onion and sage. In a small bowl stir together cold water, cornstarch, and the ⅛ teaspoon salt; add to skillet. Cook and stir until slightly thickened and bubbly; cook and stir for 2 minutes more. To serve, spoon the mushroom mixture over meat. Serve immediately. If desired, serve with noodles and garnish with herb sprigs.

Per 2½ ounces veal + about ⅓ cup sauce: 251 cal., 8 g total fat (1 g sat. fat), 88 mg chol., 283 mg sodium, 7 g carbo., 1 g fiber, 27 g pro.
Daily Values: 1% vit. A, 4% vit. C, 2% calcium, 9% iron
Exchanges: 1 Vegetable, 3 Medium-Fat Meat, 1 Fat

Veal Chops with Mushroom Sauce

Start to Finish: 25 minutes **Makes:** 4 servings

> 4 veal loin chops or pork loin chops, cut ¾ inch thick (about 1¾ pounds)
> Salt and black pepper
> ¾ cup sliced fresh mushrooms
> 2 tablespoons sliced green onion (1)
> 1 tablespoon butter or margarine
> 1 tablespoon all-purpose flour
> 2 teaspoons snipped fresh thyme or ¼ teaspoon dried thyme, crushed
> 1 cup half-and-half, light cream, or milk
> 2 tablespoons dry white wine or 1 tablespoon water plus 2 teaspoons Worcestershire sauce for chicken
> Salt and black pepper (optional)

1. Preheat broiler. Place chops on the unheated rack of a broiler pan. Sprinkle lightly with salt and pepper. Broil 3 to 4 inches from the heat until meat is 160°F, turning once halfway through broiling. For veal, allow 14 to 16 minutes for medium; for pork, allow 9 to 12 minutes.

2. Meanwhile, for sauce, in a medium saucepan cook mushrooms and green onion in hot butter until tender. Stir in flour and dried thyme (if using). Add half-and-half all at once. Cook and stir until thickened and bubbly. Cook and stir for 1 minute more. Stir in wine and fresh thyme (if using). If desired, season sauce with salt and pepper. To serve, spoon some of the sauce over the chops. Pass any remaining sauce.

Per chop + ¼ cup sauce: 219 cal., 13 g total fat (7 g sat. fat), 97 mg chol., 267 mg sodium, 5 g carbo., 0 g fiber, 19 g pro.
Daily Values: 8% vit. A, 3% vit. C, 8% calcium, 5% iron
Exchanges: 1 Vegetable, 2½ Very Lean Meat, 2½ Fat

Osso Buco LOW FAT

Prep: 25 minutes **Cook:** 1¾ hours **Makes:** 6 servings

> 2 to 2½ pounds veal shanks or meaty lamb shanks, cut crosswise into 2- to 2½-inch slices
> 2 tablespoons all-purpose flour
> ¼ teaspoon lemon-pepper seasoning
> 2 tablespoons olive oil or cooking oil
> 1 14.5-ounce can diced tomatoes with basil, garlic, and oregano, undrained
> 1 cup chopped onion (1 large)
> ½ cup chopped celery (1 stalk)
> ½ cup chopped carrot (1 medium)
> ½ cup water
> ¼ cup dry white wine or water
> 1 teaspoon anchovy paste (optional)
> ½ teaspoon instant beef bouillon granules
> ½ teaspoon dried Italian seasoning, crushed
> ½ teaspoon finely shredded orange peel
> 1 clove garlic, minced
> 3 cups hot cooked rice or couscous
> 1 tablespoon snipped fresh parsley

1. Trim fat from meat. In a large resealable plastic bag combine the flour and lemon-pepper seasoning. Add veal slices to bag, seal, and shake to coat well. In a 4-quart Dutch oven brown veal in hot oil over medium-high heat. Drain off fat.

2. Add undrained tomatoes, onion, celery, carrot, water, wine, anchovy paste (if desired), bouillon granules, Italian seasoning, orange peel, and garlic to Dutch oven; stir to combine. Bring to boiling; reduce heat. Simmer, covered, for 1½ to 2 hours or until veal is tender. Remove veal, reserving vegetable mixture; keep warm.

3. Boil vegetable mixture gently, uncovered, about 15 minutes or until slightly thickened. Toss rice with parsley; place in a serving dish. Arrange meat on top of rice. Spoon the vegetable mixture over meat and rice.

Per ½ shank + about ½ cup vegetables + ½ cup rice: 316 cal., 8 g total fat (1 g sat. fat), 79 mg chol., 570 mg sodium, 34 g carbo., 2 g fiber, 24 g pro.
Daily Values: 32% vit. A, 14% vit. C, 9% calcium, 17% iron
Exchanges: 1 Vegetable, 1½ Starch, 2½ Lean Meat, ½ Fat

Company's Coming

This supper is special enough to serve guests.

- French Onion Soup (page 566)
- Veal Chops with Mushroom Sauce (left)
- Steamed rice
- Broccoli spears
- Tossed salad greens with Blue Cheese Dressing (page 509)
- Dinner Rolls (page 152) and butter
- Coffee ice cream with fudge sauce

Pork Cuts

These two pages contain a drawing and labeled photos to help you identify cuts of pork and suggested cooking methods. The drawing illustrates wholesale cuts, showing in general where cuts are located on the animal. Photos of retail cuts are divided into the same categories as those on the drawing, which should make it easier to determine where cuts originate.

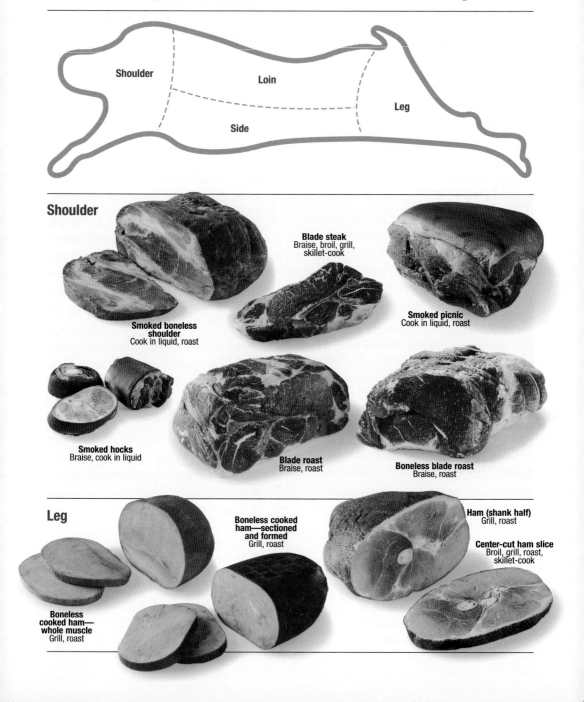

Shoulder

Loin

Leg

Side

Shoulder

Blade steak
Braise, broil, grill, skillet-cook

Smoked boneless shoulder
Cook in liquid, roast

Smoked picnic
Cook in liquid, roast

Smoked hocks
Braise, cook in liquid

Blade roast
Braise, roast

Boneless blade roast
Braise, roast

Leg

Boneless cooked ham—sectioned and formed
Grill, roast

Ham (shank half)
Grill, roast

Center-cut ham slice
Broil, grill, roast, skillet-cook

Boneless cooked ham— whole muscle
Grill, roast

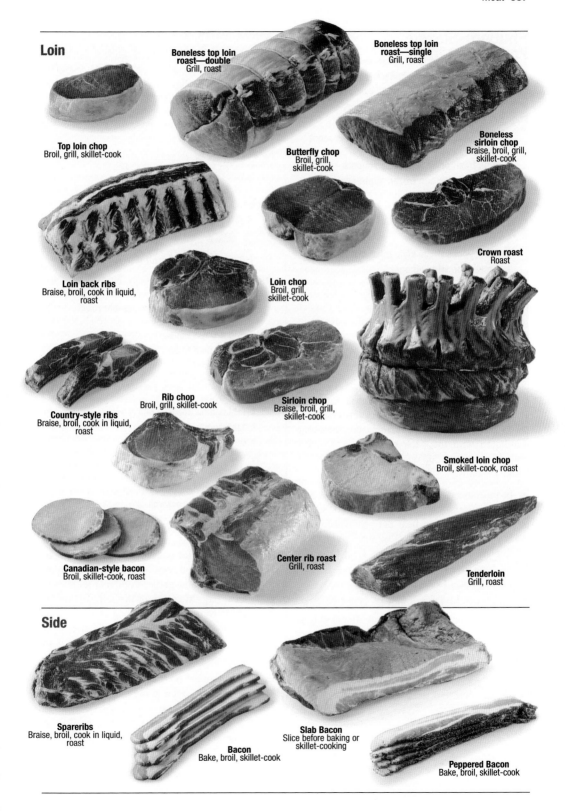

Loin

Boneless top loin roast—double
Grill, roast

Boneless top loin roast—single
Grill, roast

Top loin chop
Broil, grill, skillet-cook

Butterfly chop
Broil, grill, skillet-cook

Boneless sirloin chop
Braise, broil, grill, skillet-cook

Crown roast
Roast

Loin back ribs
Braise, broil, cook in liquid, roast

Loin chop
Broil, grill, skillet-cook

Country-style ribs
Braise, broil, cook in liquid, roast

Rib chop
Broil, grill, skillet-cook

Sirloin chop
Braise, broil, grill, skillet-cook

Smoked loin chop
Broil, skillet-cook, roast

Canadian-style bacon
Broil, skillet-cook, roast

Center rib roast
Grill, roast

Tenderloin
Grill, roast

Side

Spareribs
Braise, broil, cook in liquid, roast

Bacon
Bake, broil, skillet-cook

Slab Bacon
Slice before baking or skillet-cooking

Peppered Bacon
Bake, broil, skillet-cook

Rhubarb-Glazed Pork Roast `LOW FAT`

Make this in spring when rhubarb is in season or buy frozen rhubarb for year-round convenience.

Prep: 25 minutes **Roast:** 1¼ hours **Oven:** 325°F
Stand: 15 minutes **Makes:** 6 to 8 servings

- 1 2- to 3-pound boneless pork top loin roast (single loin)
- 4 cups fresh or frozen sliced rhubarb
- ½ of a 12-ounce can frozen apple-cranberry juice concentrate
- 2 tablespoons cornstarch
- 2 tablespoons cold water
- ⅓ cup honey
- 2 tablespoons Dijon-style mustard
- 1 tablespoon wine vinegar

1. Place roast on a rack in a shallow roasting pan. Insert an oven-going meat thermometer into center of roast (see tip, page 367). Roast in a 325°F oven for 1¼ hours to 1¾ hours or until the thermometer registers 150°F.

2. Meanwhile, for glaze, in a 2-quart saucepan combine rhubarb and juice concentrate. Bring to boiling; reduce heat. Simmer, covered, for 10 to 15 minutes or until rhubarb is very tender. Strain mixture into a 2-cup liquid measure, pressing out liquid with the back of a spoon; discard pulp. If necessary, add enough *water* to liquid to equal 1¼ cups.

3. In the saucepan stir together cornstarch and the cold water. Stir in rhubarb liquid. Cook and stir over medium heat until thickened and bubbly. Cook and stir for 2 minutes more. Stir in honey, mustard, and vinegar. Heat through. Brush some of the glaze onto the meat for the last 30 minutes of roasting.

4. Cover meat with foil and let stand 15 minutes. The temperature of the meat after standing should be 160°F. Reheat remaining glaze and pass with meat.

Per 4 ounces pork + 2 to 3 tablespoons glaze: 336 cal., 8 g total fat (3 g sat. fat), 83 mg chol., 85 mg sodium, 32 g carbo., 0 g fiber, 33 g pro.
Daily Values: 38% vit. C, 4% calcium, 8% iron
Exchanges: 2 Other Carbo., 4 Lean Meat

Apricot-Glazed Pork Roast: Prepare roast as at left, except substitute apricot glaze for rhubarb glaze. For apricot glaze, in a small saucepan combine ⅔ cup apricot preserves, 4 teaspoons lime juice, 2 teaspoons soy sauce, ¼ teaspoon grated fresh ginger or ⅛ teaspoon ground ginger, and dash cayenne pepper. Cook and stir until bubbly.

Per 4 ounces: 309 cal., 7 g total fat (3 g sat. fat), 83 mg chol., 168 mg sodium, 25 g carbo., 0 g fiber, 33 g pro.
Daily Values: 7% vit. C, 4% calcium, 7% iron
Exchanges: 1½ Other Carbo., 4 Lean Meat

Festive Pork Roast
`LOW FAT` `EASY`

Use leftovers the next day for a terrific sandwich.

Prep: 15 minutes **Marinate:** 6 hours **Roast:** 1¼ hours
Oven: 325°F **Stand:** 15 minutes **Makes:** 8 to 10 servings

- 1 3-pound boneless pork top loin roast (single loin)
- ¾ cup dry red wine
- ⅓ cup packed brown sugar
- ¼ cup vinegar
- ¼ cup ketchup
- ¼ cup water
- 1 tablespoon cooking oil
- 1 tablespoon soy sauce
- 1 teaspoon curry powder
- ½ teaspoon ground ginger
- ¼ teaspoon black pepper
- 1 clove garlic, minced
- 2 teaspoons cornstarch

1. Place roast in a large resealable plastic bag set in a large, deep bowl. For marinade, in a small bowl combine wine, brown sugar, vinegar, ketchup, water, oil, soy sauce, curry powder, ginger, pepper, and garlic. Pour marinade over meat; seal bag. Marinate in the refrigerator for 6 hours or overnight, turning bag several times. Drain meat, reserving 1¼ cups marinade; cover reserved marinade and chill. Pat meat dry with paper towels.

2. Place the meat on a rack in a shallow roasting pan. Insert an oven-going meat thermometer into center of roast (see tip, page 367). Roast in a 325°F oven for 1¼ to 1½ hours or until meat thermometer registers 150°F.

3. Meanwhile, for the sauce, in a small saucepan stir reserved marinade into the cornstarch.

Cook and stir until thickened and bubbly. Cook and stir 2 minutes more. Brush roast frequently with sauce after 1 hour of roasting.

4. Cover meat with foil and let stand 15 minutes. The temperature of the meat after standing should be 160°F. Bring remaining sauce to boiling and pass with meat.

Per 4¾ ounces pork + about 2 tablespoons sauce: 327 cal.,
11 g total fat (4 g sat. fat), 93 mg chol., 265 mg sodium,
12 g carbo., 0 g fiber, 38 g pro.
Daily Values: 2% vit. A, 3% vit. C, 5% calcium, 10% iron
Exchanges: 1 Other Carbo., 5 Very Lean Meat, 2 Fat

Festive Double-Loin Pork Roast: Prepare as on page 388, except use a 5-pound boneless pork top loin roast (double loin, tied) and double the marinade mixture. Reserve 2½ cups marinade for sauce and increase cornstarch to 4 teaspoons. Roast pork in a 325°F oven for 2 to 2½ hours or until thermometer registers 150°F. Let stand and serve as above. Makes 15 servings.

Per 4 ounces pork + about 2 tablespoons sauce: 306 cal.,
10 g total fat (3 g sat. fat), 82 mg chol., 272 mg sodium,
13 g carbo., 0 g fiber, 34 g pro.
Daily Values: 2% vit. A, 3% vit. C, 5% calcium, 9% iron
Exchanges: 1 Other Carbo., 5 Very Lean Meat, 2 Fat

Pork Medallions with Cranberry and Fig Chutney

Pork Medallions with Cranberry and Fig Chutney

LOW FAT   FAST

Start to Finish: 20 minutes **Makes:** 2 servings

  ½ cup fresh cranberries or ¼ cup canned
      whole cranberry sauce
  ¼ cup apple juice or apple cider
  2 tablespoons snipped dried figs

  1 tablespoon packed brown sugar or
      granulated sugar
  ½ teaspoon snipped fresh rosemary or
      ¼ teaspoon dried rosemary, crushed
    Salt
    Black pepper
  6 ounces pork tenderloin
  2 teaspoons cooking oil
    Hot cooked rice (optional)
    Fresh rosemary sprigs (optional)

1. For chutney, in a small heavy saucepan stir together the cranberries, apple juice, dried figs, brown sugar, and rosemary. Bring to boiling; reduce heat. Simmer, uncovered, for 5 to 8 minutes or until chutney reaches desired consistency, stirring occasionally. Season to taste with salt and pepper; set aside.

2. Meanwhile, trim fat from meat. Cut meat crosswise into six pieces. Press each piece with palm of your hand to make an even thickness. In a large nonstick skillet cook the pork in hot oil over medium-high heat for 2 to 3 minutes or until juices run clear, turning once.

3. To serve, spoon some of the warm chutney over pork and pass remaining chutney. If desired, serve with rice and garnish with rosemary sprigs.

Per 2½ ounces pork + ¼ cup chutney: 227 cal., 7 g total fat
(1 g sat. fat), 55 mg chol., 185 mg sodium, 23 g carbo., 3 g fiber,
18 g pro.
Daily Values: 1% vit. A, 8% vit. C, 3% calcium, 9% iron
Exchanges: 1½ Fruit, 2½ Very Lean Meat, 1 Fat

Cooking Bacon

Follow package directions for stove-top cooking or choose one of these methods.

To cook bacon in 400°F preheated oven, place slices side by side on a rack in a shallow baking pan with sides. Bake for 15 to 18 minutes or until crisp-cooked. Drain.

  To microwave bacon, place slices on a microwave-safe rack or a plate lined with microwave-safe paper towels. Cover bacon with a paper towel. Microwave bacon on 100 percent power (high) to desired doneness, rearranging bacon once. Allow 2 to 3 minutes for two slices, 3 to 4½ minutes for four slices, and 4 to 5 minutes for six slices.

Pork with Fennel and Pancetta `FAST`

Start to Finish: 30 minutes **Makes:** 4 servings

- 12 **ounces pork tenderloin**
- ¼ **cup all-purpose flour**
  Dash salt
  Dash black pepper
- 2 **tablespoons olive oil**
- 2 **ounces pancetta (Italian bacon) or bacon, finely chopped**
- 2 **fennel bulbs, trimmed and cut crosswise into ¼-inch slices**
- 1 **small onion, thinly sliced**
- 2 **cloves garlic, minced**
- 2 **tablespoons lemon juice**
- ½ **cup whipping cream**

1. Trim fat from meat. Cut meat crosswise into 1-inch slices. Place each slice between two pieces of plastic wrap. Use the flat side of a meat mallet to lightly pound each slice into a ¼-inch medallion. Remove plastic wrap.

2. In a shallow bowl combine flour, salt, and pepper; coat meat with flour mixture. In a large heavy skillet cook pork, half at a time, in hot oil over medium-high heat for 2 to 3 minutes or until meat is slightly pink in center, turning once. (Add more oil, if necessary.) Remove from skillet.

3. In the same skillet cook pancetta over medium-high heat until crisp. Add fennel, onion, and garlic. Cook for 3 to 5 minutes or until crisp-tender. Add lemon juice; stir in whipping cream. Bring to boiling; return meat to pan. Cook until meat is heated through and sauce is slightly thickened. To serve, spoon the sauce over the meat.

Per 2½ ounces pork + ½ cup vegetables: 417 cal., 29 g total fat (12 g sat. fat), 106 mg chol., 256 mg sodium, 18 g carbo., 4 g fiber, 22 g pro.
Daily Values: 12% vit. A, 33% vit. C, 9% calcium, 14% iron
Exchanges: 2 Vegetable, ½ Starch, 2½ Lean Meat, 4 Fat

Thai Pork and Vegetable Curry `FAST`

Canned coconut milk is a mixture of coconut meat and water that has been simmered and strained. Don't confuse it with cream of coconut, a sweetened product.

Start to Finish: 30 minutes **Makes:** 4 servings

- 1⅓ **cups dried orzo (about 8 ounces)**
- 12 **ounces pork tenderloin or lean boneless pork**
- 2 **tablespoons cooking oil**
- 8 **ounces green beans, bias-sliced into 1½-inch pieces (2 cups)***
- 1 **red sweet pepper, cut into thin bite-size strips**
- 2 **green onions, bias-sliced into ¼-inch pieces**
- 1 **14-ounce can reduced-fat unsweetened coconut milk**
- 4 **teaspoons bottled curry paste**
- 2 **teaspoons sugar**
- 2 **tablespoons lime juice**

1. Cook orzo according to package directions. Drain and keep warm. Thinly slice pork into bite-size strips (see photo, page 371).

2. Pour 1 tablespoon of the oil into a large non-stick skillet. Heat over medium-high heat. Add pork; cook and stir for 2 to 3 minutes or until no pink remains. Remove from skillet.

3. Add the remaining 1 tablespoon oil to skillet. Add green beans; cook and stir for 3 minutes. Add sweet pepper and green onion; cook and stir about 2 minutes more or until vegetables are crisp-tender. Add coconut milk, curry paste, and sugar. Reduce heat to low, stirring until combined. Stir in cooked pork and lime juice; heat through. Serve over hot orzo.

*Note: A 9-ounce package of frozen cut green beans, thawed, can be substituted for the fresh

Thai Pork and Vegetable Curry

beans. Add them to the skillet along with the sweet pepper and onion; cook as directed.

Per 1¼ cups mixture + ¾ cup orzo: 502 cal., 17 g total fat (5 g sat. fat), 50 mg chol., 447 mg sodium, 57 g carbo., 4 g fiber, 29 g pro.
Daily Values: 50% vit. A, 153% vit. C, 4% calcium, 26% iron
Exchanges: 2 Vegetable, 3 Starch, 2 Lean Meat, 2 Fat

Pork Chow Mein

Prep: 30 minutes **Cook:** 15 minutes
Makes: 4 to 6 servings

    1 pound lean boneless pork
    ¾ cup water
    3 tablespoons reduced-sodium soy sauce
    2 tablespoons cornstarch
    2 tablespoons dry sherry or water
    1 teaspoon instant chicken bouillon granules
    ¼ teaspoon black pepper
    1 tablespoon cooking oil
    2 teaspoons grated fresh ginger
    1 cup thinly bias-sliced celery (2 stalks)
    2 cups sliced fresh mushrooms
    2 cups fresh bean sprouts or one 16-ounce can bean sprouts, rinsed and drained
   10 green onions, bias-sliced into 1-inch pieces (1 cup)
    1 8-ounce can sliced water chestnuts or bamboo shoots, drained
    1 5-ounce can chow mein noodles

1. If desired, partially freeze meat for easier slicing. Thinly slice pork across the grain into bite-size strips (see photo, page 371). For sauce, in a bowl stir together water, soy sauce, cornstarch, sherry, bouillon granules, and pepper. Set mixture aside.

2. Pour oil into a wok or 12-inch skillet. (Add more oil as necessary during cooking.) Preheat over medium-high heat. Cook and stir ginger in hot oil for 15 seconds. Add celery; cook and stir for 2 minutes. Add mushrooms, fresh bean sprouts (if using), and green onion. Cook and stir for 1 to 2 minutes or until celery is crisp-tender. Remove vegetables from wok.

3. Add half of the pork to hot wok. Cook and stir for 2 to 3 minutes or until no pink remains. Remove from wok. Repeat with remaining pork. Return all meat to wok; push from center of wok.

4. Stir sauce; add to center of wok. Cook and stir until thickened and bubbly. Push meat into center; add cooked vegetables, water chestnuts,

and, if using, canned bean sprouts. Cook and stir until hot. Serve with chow mein noodles.

Per 1⅓ cups mixture + about ⅔ cup noodles: 475 cal., 21 g total fat (5 g sat. fat), 62 mg chol., 1,019 mg sodium, 39 g carbo., 4 g fiber, 34 g pro.
Daily Values: 11% vit. A, 26% vit. C, 9% calcium, 24% iron
Exchanges: 2 Vegetable, 1½ Starch, 3½ Very Lean Meat, 4 Fat

FAVORITE Cashew Pork and Vegetables

When stir-frying, test the oil's hotness by adding a vegetable piece. If the veggie sizzles, start frying.

Start to Finish: 45 minutes **Makes:** 4 servings

    1 pound lean boneless pork
    ¼ cup orange juice
    2 tablespoons bottled hoisin sauce
    ½ teaspoon ground ginger
    ⅛ teaspoon crushed red pepper (optional)
    2 cups fresh pea pods or one 6-ounce package frozen pea pods, thawed
    1 tablespoon cooking oil
    3 medium carrots, bias-sliced, or 1½ cups packaged fresh julienned carrots
    ¼ cup sliced green onion (2)
    2 cups hot cooked rice
    ½ cup cashews or peanuts

1. If desired, partially freeze meat for easier slicing. Thinly slice pork across the grain into bite-size strips (see photo, page 371). For sauce, stir together orange juice, hoisin sauce, ginger, and, if desired, crushed red pepper. Set aside.

2. If using fresh pea pods, remove strings and tips; set pea pods aside. Pour oil into a wok or large skillet. (Add more oil as necessary during cooking.) Preheat over medium-high heat. Stir in carrot. Cook and stir for 2 minutes. Add pea pods and green onion. Cook and stir for 2 to 3 minutes or until vegetables are crisp-tender. Remove vegetables from wok.

3. Add half of the pork to hot wok. Cook and stir for 2 to 3 minutes or until no pink remains; remove from wok. Repeat with remaining pork. Return all meat and vegetables to wok. Stir sauce; add to wok. Cook and stir until heated through. Stir in rice until coated. Top with nuts.

Per 2 cups: 453 cal., 18 g total fat (4 g sat. fat), 62 mg chol., 189 mg sodium, 41 g carbo., 4 g fiber, 32 g pro.
Daily Values: 104% vit. A, 62% vit. C, 8% calcium, 18% iron
Exchanges: 1 Vegetable, 1½ Starch, 1 Other Carbo., 4 Lean Meat, 1 Fat

Pork Pot Roast in Cider EASY

Prep: 15 minutes **Cook:** 1½ hours **Makes:** 4 servings

- 1 1½- to 2-pound boneless pork blade roast or sirloin roast
- 2 tablespoons cooking oil
- 1¼ cups apple cider or apple juice
- 2 teaspoons instant beef bouillon granules
- ½ teaspoon dry mustard
- ¼ teaspoon black pepper
- 3 medium red potatoes or round white potatoes, peeled (if desired) and quartered
- 3 medium carrots, cut into 2-inch pieces
- 3 medium parsnips, peeled and cut into 2-inch pieces
- 1 large onion, cut into wedges
- ¼ cup all-purpose flour

1. Trim fat from meat. In a 4- to 6-quart Dutch oven brown meat on all sides in hot oil. Drain off fat. Stir together cider, bouillon granules, mustard, and pepper. Pour over meat. Bring to boiling; reduce heat. Simmer, covered, 1 hour.

2. Add potato, carrot, parsnip, and onion. Simmer, covered, for 30 to 40 minutes more or until meat and vegetables are tender. Transfer meat and vegetables to a serving platter, reserving juices. Keep warm.

3. For gravy, measure juices; skim fat. If necessary, add enough *water* to juices to equal 1½ cups. Return to Dutch oven. Stir ⅓ cup *cold water* into flour. Stir into juices in pan. Cook and stir over medium heat until thickened and bubbly. Cook and stir for 1 minute more. To serve, remove string from meat, if present. Slice meat and serve with vegetables and gravy.

Slow cooker directions: Prepare meat as above. Place potato, carrot, parsnip, and onion in a 3½- or 4-quart slow cooker. Cut meat to fit, if necessary; place on top of vegetables. Stir together apple cider, bouillon granules, mustard, and pepper. Add to cooker. Cover and cook on low-heat setting for 8 to 10 hours or on high-heat setting for 4 to 5 hours or until tender. Transfer meat and vegetables to a serving platter; keep warm. Prepare gravy in a medium saucepan on the range top and serve as above.

Per 5 ounces pork + about ½ cup gravy: 538 cal., 17 g total fat (5 g sat. fat), 110 mg chol., 608 mg sodium, 56 g carbo., 7 g fiber, 39 g pro.
Daily Values: 287% vit. A, 53% vit. C, 7% calcium, 24% iron
Exchanges: 2 Vegetable, 3 Starch, 3½ Lean Meat, 1 Fat

Shredded Pork Sandwiches LOW FAT EASY

Prep: 15 minutes **Roast:** 2½ hours
Oven: 325°F **Makes:** 12 sandwiches

- 1 3-pound boneless pork shoulder blade roast
- 8 cloves garlic, minced
- 2 teaspoons ground coriander
- 2 teaspoons ground cumin
- 2 teaspoons dried oregano, crushed
- 1 teaspoon onion powder
- ½ teaspoon black pepper
- ½ teaspoon cayenne pepper
- 1 cup beef broth
- 12 hamburger buns or kaiser rolls, split and toasted

1. Trim fat from meat. In a small bowl combine garlic, coriander, cumin, oregano, onion powder, black and cayenne peppers, and ½ teaspoon *salt*; rub into meat. Place meat in a roasting pan that has a cover; add broth. Cover; roast in a 325°F oven for 2½ to 3 hours or until very tender.

2. Remove meat from cooking liquid with a slotted spoon. Remove and discard excess fat from cooking liquid. Reserve cooking liquid. When meat is cool enough to handle, shred it by pulling two forks through it in opposite directions. Stir in enough cooking liquid to moisten; reheat in a saucepan over medium heat, stirring frequently. Serve on toasted buns.

Slow cooker directions: Prepare meat as above. Place meat in a 3½- to 5-quart slow cooker; add beef broth. Cover and cook on low-heat setting for 8 to 10 hours or on high-heat setting for 4 to 5 hours. Continue as above.

Per sandwich: 302 cal., 11 g total fat (3 g sat. fat), 77 mg chol., 458 mg sodium, 23 g carbo., 1 g fiber, 27 g pro.
Daily Values: 1% vit. A, 2% vit. C, 10% calcium, 18% iron
Exchanges: 1½ Starch, 3 Lean Meat, ½ Fat

USDA Hotline

For more information on meat or poultry food safety, the United States Department of Agriculture Meat and Poultry Hotline is ready to help. Call weekdays from 10 a.m. to 4 p.m. (Eastern Standard Time). The toll-free number is 888/674-6854. For the hearing impaired (TTY), call 800/256-7072. Or send an e-mail to mphotline. fsis@usda.gov.

Shredded Pork Tacos `LOW FAT` `FAST`

Prep: 15 minutes **Cook:** 4 minutes **Makes:** 12 tacos

- 1 **17-ounce package refrigerated cooked pork roast**
- ¾ **cup bottled salsa**
- 12 **taco shells or six 6- to 8-inch flour tortillas**
- 2 **cups shredded lettuce**
- ½ **cup finely shredded Monterey Jack or anejo enchilada cheese (2 ounces)**
- ¼ **cup sliced, pitted ripe olives**
   Dairy sour cream (optional)
- 1 **medium avocado, halved, seeded, peeled, and chopped (optional)**

1. Place pork and juices in a 2-quart square microwave-safe baking dish. Cover loosely and microwave on 100 percent power (high) for 2 minutes. Shred pork by pulling two forks through it in opposite directions. Drain pork and return to baking dish. Stir in salsa. Cover loosely and microwave on high 2 minutes more or until hot. Keep warm.

2. Place taco shells on a baking sheet and heat according to package directions. (Or wrap flour tortillas tightly in foil. Heat in a 350°F oven about 10 minutes or until heated through.)

3. To assemble tacos, place pork mixture in warm taco shells. Top with lettuce, cheese, and olives. (If using flour tortillas, place pork mixture in center of warm tortillas and add remaining ingredients; fold tortillas in half.) If desired, serve with sour cream and avocado.

Per taco: 137 cal., 7 g total fat (2 g sat. fat), 28 mg chol., 295 mg sodium, 9 g carbo., 1 g fiber, 11 g pro.
Daily Values: 3% vit. A, 2% vit. C, 6% calcium, 5% iron
Exchanges: ½ Starch, 1½ Medium-Fat Meat

FAVORITE Honey-and-Apple Ribs

Prep: 40 minutes **Bake:** 1¾ hours
Oven: 350°F **Makes:** 4 servings

- 3 **pounds pork country-style ribs**
- ½ **cup chopped onion (1 medium)**
- 2 **cloves garlic, minced**
- 1 **tablespoon cooking oil**
- ¾ **cup bottled chili sauce**
- ½ **cup apple juice, apple cider, or light beer**
- ¼ **cup honey**
- 2 **tablespoons Worcestershire sauce**
- ½ **teaspoon dry mustard**

1. Place the ribs in a shallow roasting pan. Bake, uncovered, in a 350°F oven for 1 hour. Drain off fat.

2. Meanwhile, for sauce, in a medium saucepan cook onion and garlic in hot oil until tender. Stir in chili sauce, apple juice, honey, Worcestershire sauce, and dry mustard. Bring to boiling; reduce heat. Simmer, uncovered, for 20 minutes. (You should have about 1½ cups sauce.)

3. Spoon ⅓ cup of the sauce over ribs. Bake, covered, for 45 to 60 minutes more or until tender, turning ribs and spooning ⅓ cup more of the sauce over ribs after 25 minutes. Heat remaining sauce until warm; pass with ribs.

Per ¼ recipe: 529 cal., 25 g total fat (8 g sat. fat), 135 mg chol., 730 mg sodium, 36 g carbo., 3 g fiber, 40 g pro.
Daily Values: 7% vit. A, 18% vit. C, 7% calcium, 16% iron
Exchanges: 2½ Other Carbo., 5 Medium-Fat Meat

Oven-Roasted Asian-Style Pork Ribs

Prep: 40 minutes **Bake:** 15 minutes
Oven: 350°F **Makes:** 4 servings

- 3 **pounds pork loin back ribs or pork spareribs**
- 3 **tablespoons pineapple, peach, or apricot preserves**
- ⅓ **cup ketchup**
- 2 **tablespoons soy sauce**
- 1 **teaspoon grated fresh ginger or ¼ teaspoon ground ginger**
- 1 **clove garlic, minced**

1. Cut ribs into serving-size pieces. Place ribs in a 4- to 6-quart Dutch oven. Add enough *water* to cover. Bring to boiling; reduce heat. Simmer, covered, for 20 to 30 minutes or until ribs are tender; drain.

2. Meanwhile, for sauce, cut up any large pieces of fruit in the preserves. In a bowl stir together preserves, ketchup, soy sauce, ginger, and garlic.

3. Brush some of the sauce over both sides of the ribs. Place ribs, bone sides down, in a shallow roasting pan. Bake, uncovered, in a 350°F oven for 15 to 20 minutes or until ribs are glazed and heated through. Brush with remaining sauce before serving.

Per ¼ recipe: 442 cal., 22 g total fat (7 g sat. fat), 101 mg chol., 797 mg sodium, 16 g carbo., 1 g fiber, 43 g pro.
Daily Values: 4% vit. A, 8% vit. C, 3% calcium, 8% iron
Exchanges: 1 Other Carbo., 5½ Medium-Fat Meat

Oven-Barbecued Ribs

Prep: 25 minutes **Bake:** 1½ hours
Oven: 350°F **Makes:** 4 servings

- **3 to 4 pounds pork loin back ribs**
- **¾ cup ketchup**
- **¾ cup water**
- **2 tablespoons vinegar**
- **2 tablespoons Worcestershire sauce**
- **1 teaspoon paprika**
- **1 teaspoon chili powder**
- **½ teaspoon black pepper**
- **¼ teaspoon salt**
- **¼ to ½ teaspoon cayenne pepper**
- **1 cup finely chopped onion (1 large)**

1. If desired, cut ribs into serving-size pieces. Place the ribs, bone sides down, in a large, shallow roasting pan. Bake, covered, in a 350°F oven for 1 hour. Carefully drain off fat.

2. Meanwhile, in a medium bowl combine the ketchup, water, vinegar, Worcestershire sauce, paprika, chili powder, black pepper, salt, and cayenne pepper. Stir in onion. Pour mixture over ribs. Bake, uncovered, for 30 minutes more or until ribs are tender, basting once with sauce. Pass sauce with ribs.

Per ¼ recipe: 408 cal., 15 g total fat (5 g sat. fat), 100 mg chol., 839 mg sodium, 18 g carbo., 1 g fiber, 48 g pro.
Daily Values: 18% vit. A, 17% vit. C, 4% calcium, 14% iron
Exchanges: 1 Other Carbo., 6½ Lean Meat

Spicy Pecan Pork Sandwiches FAST

Start to Finish: 30 minutes **Makes:** 4 sandwiches

- **4 boneless pork loin chops, cut ½ inch thick (about 1 pound)**
- **1 egg**
- **2 tablespoons Dijon-style mustard**
- **¼ to ½ teaspoon cayenne pepper**
- **½ cup fine dry bread crumbs**
- **½ cup ground toasted pecans**
- **¼ cup all-purpose flour**
- **2 tablespoons cooking oil**
- **Chipotle chile or sun-dried tomato-flavored light mayonnaise**
- **4 hoagie buns, kaiser rolls, or hamburger buns, split and toasted, or 8 slices whole wheat bread, toasted**
- **Lettuce leaves**
- **Tomato slices**

Spicy Pecan Pork Sandwiches

1. Place each pork chop between two pieces of plastic wrap. Use the flat side of a meat mallet to pound each chop to about ¼ inch thick. In a shallow dish beat together egg, mustard, and cayenne pepper just until combined. In a second dish stir together crumbs and pecans; place flour in a third dish. Coat each pork piece with flour, dip in egg mixture, then coat with crumbs.

2. In a 12-inch skillet cook pork slices in hot oil over medium-high heat for 6 to 8 minutes or until slightly pink in the center, turning once. (If necessary, reduce heat to medium to avoid burning.) Spread mayonnaise on buns. Serve pork in buns with lettuce and tomato slices.

Per sandwich: 634 cal., 31 g total fat (6 g sat. fat), 122 mg chol., 987 mg sodium, 51 g carbo., 4 g fiber, 38 g pro.
Daily Values: 9% vit. A, 9% vit. C, 14% calcium, 25% iron
Exchanges: ½ Vegetable, 3 Starch, 4 Very Lean Meat, 5½ Fat

Pesto-Stuffed Pork Chops

Prep: 20 minutes **Bake:** 35 minutes
Oven: 375°F **Makes:** 4 servings

- **3 tablespoons crumbled feta cheese**
- **2 tablespoons refrigerated basil pesto**
- **1 tablespoon pine nuts, toasted (see tip, page 265)**
- **4 pork loin chops or boneless pork loin chops, cut 1¼ inches thick**
- **1 teaspoon freshly ground black pepper**
- **1 teaspoon dried oregano, crushed**
- **2 cloves garlic, minced**
- **¼ teaspoon crushed red pepper**
- **¼ teaspoon dried thyme, crushed**
- **1 tablespoon balsamic vinegar**

1. For filling, in a small bowl stir together feta cheese, pesto, and pine nuts. Set aside.

2. Trim fat from chops. Make a pocket in each chop by cutting horizontally from the fat side almost to the bone or the opposite side (see photo, below). Divide filling among pockets in chops. If necessary, secure the openings with wooden toothpicks.

3. For rub, in a small bowl combine black pepper, oregano, garlic, crushed red pepper, and thyme. Rub evenly onto all sides of meat. Place chops on a rack in a shallow roasting pan. Bake in a 375°F oven for 35 to 45 minutes or until chops are 160°F and juices run clear. Brush vinegar onto chops the last 5 minutes of baking. Before serving, discard toothpicks.

Per chop: 358 cal., 18 g total fat (5 g sat. fat), 104 mg chol., 201 mg sodium, 4 g carbo., 0 g fiber, 41 g pro.
Daily Values: 2% vit. A, 2% vit. C, 6% calcium, 11% iron
Exchanges: 6 Lean Meat, ½ Fat

To make a pocket in a chop, use a sharp knife to cut a 2-inch-wide slit in its fatty side. Work the knife through the chop and almost to the other side, keeping the original slit as narrow as possible.

Rosemary Pork Chop Skillet

Start to Finish: 35 minutes **Makes:** 4 servings

- 1 **pound boneless pork sirloin chops, cut ½ inch thick**
- ½ **teaspoon salt**
- ½ **teaspoon black pepper**
- 1 **tablespoon olive oil**
- 2 **cups peeled and cubed (1 inch) winter squash, such as butternut, banana, and/or acorn**
- 1 **medium onion, cut into thin wedges**
- 2 **teaspoons snipped fresh rosemary**
- ¼ **cup chicken broth**
- ¼ **cup orange juice**
- 2 **medium zucchini, quartered lengthwise and cut into 1-inch pieces**
- 1 **teaspoon snipped fresh sage**

1. Trim fat from chops. Sprinkle chops with salt and pepper. In a 12-inch skillet brown chops in hot oil over medium-high heat about 4 minutes,

turning once. Combine squash, onion, and rosemary; spoon squash mixture over chops. Pour broth and orange juice over squash mixture and chops. Bring to boiling; reduce heat. Simmer, covered, for 10 minutes.

2. Add zucchini and sage. Cook, covered, about 5 minutes more or until chops are 160°F. Using a slotted spoon, transfer chops and vegetables to a serving platter, reserving juices. Cover chops and vegetables; keep warm.

3. Bring reserved juices in skillet to boiling; reduce heat. Simmer, uncovered, about 5 minutes or until liquid is reduced to about ¼ cup. Spoon over chops and vegetables to serve.

Per chop + about 1 cup vegetables: 220 cal., 8 g total fat (2 g sat. fat), 63 mg chol., 411 mg sodium, 15 g carbo., 2 g fiber, 24 g pro.
Daily Values: 111% vit. A, 49% vit. C, 7% calcium, 11% iron
Exchanges: 1 Starch, 3 Very Lean Meat, 1 Fat

Pork Chops with Black Bean Salsa FAST

For a speedy after-work supper for the family, serve these chops with hot cooked rice, glazed carrots, a tossed salad, and pears with cookies for dessert.

Start to Finish: 25 minutes **Makes:** 4 servings

- 4 **pork loin chops, cut 1¼ inches thick**
- 1 **teaspoon Jamaican jerk or Cajun seasoning**
- ⅛ **teaspoon black pepper**
- ⅔ **cup corn relish**
- ½ **of a 15-ounce can black beans, rinsed and drained**
- 1½ **teaspoons lime juice**
- ¼ **teaspoon ground cumin**
  Dairy sour cream (optional)

1. Preheat broiler. Trim fat from chops. Rub seasoning and pepper onto both sides of chops. Place pork chops on the unheated rack of a broiler pan. Broil 3 to 4 inches from the heat for 16 to 20 minutes or until 160°F, turning once halfway through broiling.

2. Meanwhile, for salsa, in a small bowl combine corn relish, black beans, lime juice, and cumin. Serve chops with salsa and, if desired, sour cream.

Per chop + ⅓ cup salsa: 470 cal., 13 g total fat (5 g sat. fat), 152 mg chol., 425 mg sodium, 21 g carbo., 3 g fiber, 64 g pro.
Daily Values: 2% vit. C, 6% calcium, 13% iron
Exchanges: 1½ Starch, 8½ Very Lean Meat, 1 Fat

Oven-Fried Pork Chops `FAST`

Prep: 10 minutes **Bake:** 20 minutes
Oven: 425°F **Makes:** 4 servings

- 4 pork loin chops, cut ¾ inch thick
- 2 tablespoons butter, melted
- 1 egg, beaten
- 2 tablespoons milk
- ¼ teaspoon black pepper
- 1 cup herb-seasoned stuffing mix, finely crushed

1. Trim fat from pork. Pour butter into a 13×9×2-inch baking pan, tilting pan to coat the bottom. In a shallow dish combine egg, milk, and pepper. Place stuffing mix in a second shallow dish. Dip chops into egg mixture. Coat both sides with stuffing mix. Place in prepared pan.

2. Bake, uncovered, in a 425°F oven for 10 minutes. Turn chops. Bake 10 to 15 minutes more or until 160°F and juices run clear.

Per chop: 289 cal., 13 g total fat (6 g sat. fat), 141 mg chol., 342 mg sodium, 12 g carbo., 1 g fiber, 29 g pro.
Daily Values: 7% vit. A, 2% vit. C, 5% calcium, 10% iron
Exchanges: 1 Starch, 3½ Lean Meat

Smoked Pork Chops with Curried Fruit `FAST`

Because the smoked chops are already cooked, all they need is a quick heating in a skillet.

Start to Finish: 20 minutes **Makes:** 4 servings

- 4 cooked smoked pork chops, cut ¾ inch thick
- 1 tablespoon cooking oil
- 1 8-ounce can pineapple chunks (juice pack)
- ⅓ cup chopped onion (1 small)
- 1 tablespoon butter or margarine
- 1½ teaspoons curry powder
- ¾ cup orange juice
- 1 tablespoon cornstarch
- 1 cup cranberries
- 1 11-ounce can mandarin orange sections, drained
- 2 cups hot cooked couscous or basmati rice (optional)

1. Trim fat from meat. In a 12-inch skillet cook chops in hot oil for 8 to 10 minutes or until hot, turning once.

2. Meanwhile, for sauce, drain pineapple, reserving juice. In a medium saucepan cook onion in hot butter until tender. Stir in curry powder. Cook and stir for 1 minute.

3. In a bowl stir together the reserved pineapple juice, orange juice, and cornstarch. Stir into saucepan. Add cranberries. Cook and stir over medium heat until thickened and bubbly. Cook and stir for 2 minutes more. Gently stir in pineapple and drained mandarin oranges; heat through. Serve sauce over pork chops. If desired, serve with couscous.

Per chop + about ⅔ cup sauce: 422 cal., 20 g total fat (7 g sat. fat), 92 mg chol., 2,162 mg sodium, 28 g carbo., 3 g fiber, 33 g pro.
Daily Values: 18% vit. A, 100% vit. C, 4% calcium, 15% iron
Exchanges: 2 Fruit, 4½ Lean Meat, 1 Fat

Pork and Green Chiles Casserole `EASY`

Diced green chile peppers and a little salsa add spunk to this hearty rice, bean, and pork dish.

Prep: 15 minutes **Bake:** 30 minutes **Oven:** 375°F
Stand: 5 minutes **Makes:** 6 servings

- 1 pound ground pork
- 1 15-ounce can pinto beans or black beans, rinsed and drained
- 1 10.75-ounce can condensed cream of chicken soup
- 1½ cups bottled salsa
- 1 4-ounce can diced green chile peppers, drained
- 1 cup quick-cooking brown rice
- ¼ cup water
- 1 teaspoon ground cumin
- ½ cup shredded cheddar cheese or Monterey Jack cheese with jalapeño peppers (2 ounces)

1. In a large skillet cook pork until no pink remains; drain. Stir in beans, soup, salsa, chile peppers, rice, water, and cumin. Heat and stir just until bubbly. Pour into a 2-quart casserole.

2. Bake, uncovered, in a 375°F oven for 30 to 35 minutes or until edges are bubbly. Remove from oven. Sprinkle with cheese; let stand for 5 minutes until cheese melts.

Per cup: 314 cal., 13 g total fat (6 g sat. fat), 49 mg chol., 820 mg sodium, 31 g carbo., 5 g fiber, 19 g pro.
Daily Values: 10% vit. A, 18% vit. C, 16% calcium, 13% iron
Exchanges: 2 Starch, 2 Medium-Fat Meat, ½ Fat

Glazed Ham `LOW FAT` `EASY`

Prep: 15 minutes **Bake:** 1½ hours
Oven: 325°F **Makes:** 16 to 20 servings

> 1 **5- to 6-pound cooked ham (rump half or shank portion)**
> 24 **whole cloves (optional)**
> 1 **recipe Orange Glaze, Chutney Glaze, or Raspberry-Chipotle Glaze**

1. Score ham by making diagonal cuts in a diamond pattern. If desired, stud ham with cloves. Place ham on a rack in a shallow roasting pan. Insert an oven-going meat thermometer into center of ham (see tip, page 367). The thermometer should not touch the bone. Bake in a 325°F oven for 1½ to 2¼ hours or until thermometer registers 140°F. Brush ham with some of the desired glaze during the last 20 minutes of baking. Serve with remaining glaze.

Orange Glaze: In a medium saucepan combine 2 teaspoons finely shredded orange peel, 1 cup orange juice, ½ cup packed brown sugar, 4 teaspoons cornstarch, and 1½ teaspoons dry mustard. Cook and stir over medium heat until thickened and bubbly. Cook and stir for 2 minutes more. Makes 1¼ cups glaze.

Chutney Glaze: In a food processor or blender combine one 9-ounce jar mango chutney, ¼ cup maple syrup, and 2 teaspoons stone-ground mustard. Cover and process or blend until smooth. Makes about 1¼ cups glaze.

Per 3 ounces ham + about 1 tablespoon orange or chutney glaze: 166 cal., 5 g total fat (2 g sat. fat), 47 mg chol., 1,078 mg sodium, 10 g carbo., 0 g fiber, 19 g pro.
Daily Values: 1% vit. A, 14% vit. C, 2% calcium, 8% iron
Exchanges: ½ Other Carbo., 3 Very Lean Meat, ½ Fat

Raspberry-Chipotle Glaze: In a medium saucepan combine 1½ cups seedless raspberry preserves; 2 tablespoons vinegar; 2 or 3 canned chipotle peppers in adobo sauce, drained and chopped (see tip, page 74); and 3 cloves garlic, minced. Cook and stir just until boiling; reduce heat. Cook, uncovered, 10 minutes more. Makes 1½ cups glaze.

Per 3 ounces ham + 1½ tablespoons glaze: 216 cal., 5 g total fat (2 g sat. fat), 47 mg chol., 1,104 mg sodium, 23 g carbo., 0 g fiber, 19 g pro.
Daily Values: 5% vit. C, 2% calcium, 8% iron
Exchanges: 1½ Other Carbo., 3 Very Lean Meat, ½ Fat

Ham with Five-Spice Vegetables `LOW FAT` `FAST`

Start to Finish: 20 minutes **Makes:** 4 servings

> 2 **cups sliced carrot (4 medium)**
> 1 **cup fresh or frozen sugar snap peas**
> 1 **cup packaged shredded broccoli**
> 1 **to 1½ pound cooked center-cut ham slice**
> 1 **teaspoon cooking oil**
> ½ **teaspoon five-spice powder**
> 1 **tablespoon honey**
> 1 **tablespoon reduced-sodium soy sauce**

1. In a medium covered saucepan cook carrot in a small amount of boiling water for 5 minutes. Add snap peas and broccoli; return to boiling. Cook, covered, 2 minutes or until crisp-tender; drain.

2. Meanwhile, trim fat from ham. Cut ham into four serving-size pieces. In a large skillet cook ham in hot oil over medium heat until heated through, turning once. Transfer ham to platter; keep warm. Stir five-spice powder into drippings in skillet. Stir in honey and soy sauce. Gently stir in cooked vegetables; heat through. Spoon vegetable mixture over ham.

Per 4 ounces ham + 1 cup vegetables: 222 cal., 7 g total fat (2 g sat. fat), 53 mg chol., 1,465 mg sodium, 16 g carbo., 4 g fiber, 24 g pro.
Daily Values: 328% vit. A, 39% vit. C, 6% calcium, 10% iron
Exchanges: 3 Vegetable, 3 Lean Meat

Ham Terms

Fully cooked: This is the most popular kind. It's ready to eat when you buy it. Heat it to an internal temperature of 140°F.

"Cook before eating" ham: This kind is not completely cooked during processing, so cook it to an internal temperature of 160°F (with standing time). If you're not sure whether a ham is fully cooked, heat it to 160°F.

Country or country-style ham: Distinctively flavored and specially processed, these hams are cured, may or may not be smoked, and usually are aged. They're often named for the city where they are processed. Follow package directions for cooking.

Rump and shank: The rump is the upper, meatier part of the leg; it contains the pelvic bone and some round leg bone. The lower, slightly pointed shank portion contains the shank bone and some leg bone.

Ham Balls in Barbecue Sauce

Prep: 20 minutes **Bake:** 45 minutes
Oven: 350°F **Makes:** 6 servings

  2 eggs, beaten
1½ cups soft bread crumbs (2 slices)
  ½ cup finely chopped onion (1 medium)
  2 tablespoons milk
  1 teaspoon dry mustard
  ¼ teaspoon black pepper
 12 ounces ground cooked ham
 12 ounces ground pork or ground beef
  ¾ cup packed brown sugar
  ½ cup ketchup
  2 tablespoons vinegar
  1 teaspoon dry mustard

1. In a large bowl combine eggs, bread crumbs, onion, milk, 1 teaspoon mustard, and pepper. Add ground ham and ground pork; mix well. Shape into 12 balls, using about ⅓ cup mixture for each. Place ham balls in a lightly greased 2-quart rectangular baking dish.

2. In a bowl combine brown sugar, ketchup, vinegar, and remaining 1 teaspoon mustard. Stir until sugar is dissolved. Pour over meatballs.

3. Bake, uncovered, in a 350°F oven about 45 minutes or until done (an instant-read thermometer inserted into the meatballs should register 160°F).

Per 2 ham balls: 427 cal., 19 g total fat (7 g sat. fat), 143 mg chol., 1,107 mg sodium, 42 g carbo., 1 g fiber, 23 g pro.
Daily Values: 6% vit. A, 11% vit. C, 9% calcium, 14% iron
Exchanges: 3 Other Carbo., 3 Medium-Fat Meat, ½ Fat

Ham Balls in Barbecue Sauce

New Orleans-Style Muffuletta `EASY`

See photo, page 361.

Prep: 10 minutes **Chill:** 4 hours **Makes:** 6 sandwiches

  ½ cup coarsely chopped, pitted ripe olives
  ½ cup chopped pimiento-stuffed green olives
  1 tablespoon snipped fresh parsley
  2 teaspoons lemon juice
  ½ teaspoon dried oregano, crushed
  1 tablespoon olive oil
  1 clove garlic, minced
  1 16-ounce loaf ciabatta or unsliced French bread
  6 lettuce leaves
  3 ounces thinly sliced salami, pepperoni, or summer sausage
  3 ounces thinly sliced cooked ham or turkey
  6 ounces thinly sliced provolone, Swiss, or mozzarella cheese
  1 or 2 medium tomatoes, thinly sliced
  ⅛ teaspoon coarsely ground black pepper

1. For olive relish, in a small bowl combine the ripe olives, green olives, parsley, lemon juice, and oregano. Cover and chill for 4 to 24 hours.

2. Stir together olive oil and garlic. Horizontally split the bread loaf and hollow out the inside of the top half, leaving a ¾-inch-thick shell.

3. Brush the bottom bread half with olive oil mixture. Top with lettuce, meats, cheese, and tomato; sprinkle with pepper. Stir olive relish. Mound on top of tomato. Add top of bread. To serve, cut into six portions.

Italian-Style Muffuletta: Prepare as above, except omit ripe and green olives, parsley, lemon juice, and oregano. Drain a 16-ounce jar of pickled mixed vegetables, reserving the liquid. Chop the vegetables, removing any pepperoncini stems present. In a medium bowl combine chopped vegetables; 2 tablespoons of the reserved liquid; ¼ cup chopped pimiento-stuffed green olives and/or pitted ripe olives; 1 clove garlic, minced; and 1 tablespoon olive oil. Assemble sandwich as above, spooning the pickled vegetable mixture on top of the tomato.

Per sandwich plain or Italian-style variation: 435 cal., 21 g total fat (8 g sat. fat), 41 mg chol., 1,512 mg sodium, 43 g carbo., 3 g fiber, 20 g pro.
Daily Values: 13% vit. A, 12% vit. C, 30% calcium, 18% iron
Exchanges: 1 Vegetable, 2½ Starch, 2 Medium-Fat Meat, 1½ Fat

FAVORITE Sausage and Pepper Sandwiches FAST

Top the veggies with a slice of mozzarella cheese, if you like; broil for a minute or two to melt it.

Prep: 5 minutes **Cook:** 25 minutes **Makes:** 4 sandwiches

- **4 uncooked sweet (mild) Italian sausage links (about 1 pound)**
- **½ cup water**
- **1 tablespoon cooking oil**
- **1 cup green sweet pepper strips (1 medium)**
- **1 cup red sweet pepper strips (1 medium)**
- **1 large onion, sliced and separated into rings**
- **¼ cup bottled Italian salad dressing**
- **1 tablespoon Dijon-style mustard**
- **4 French-style rolls or hoagie buns, split***

1. In a large skillet cook sausage links over medium heat about 5 minutes or until brown, turning frequently. Carefully add water. Bring to boiling; reduce heat. Simmer, covered, for 5 minutes. Uncover and cook sausages, turning frequently, until liquid evaporates and sausages are cooked through (160°F). Watch carefully so that sausages do not burn. Drain sausages on paper towels. Wipe out skillet, if necessary.

2. In the same skillet add the oil, sweet pepper, and onion. Cook and stir about 5 minutes or until vegetables are crisp-tender. Return sausage links to skillet. Combine the salad dressing and mustard. Stir into sausage mixture in skillet. Heat through.

3. To serve, hollow out bottoms of rolls. If desired, preheat broiler and toast roll halves 4 inches from the heat of the broiler for 2 to 3 minutes. Place sausages on roll bottoms. Top with sweet pepper mixture and roll tops.

*Note: If desired, do not split rolls horizontally. Instead, split them lengthwise, starting at the top and cutting almost to the bottom. Add cooked sausages and vegetable mixture.

Per sandwich: 567 cal., 38 g total fat (12 g sat. fat), 77 mg chol., 993 mg sodium, 29 g carbo., 3 g fiber, 21 g pro.
Daily Values: 34% vit. A, 116% vit. C, 7% calcium, 13% iron
Exchanges: 1 Vegetable, 1½ Starch, 2½ High-Fat Meat, 4 Fat

Sausage Information

Sausage Glossary

Fresh (Uncooked): Sausages made from fresh meat that was neither cooked nor cured during processing. Cook these sausages well before eating.

Uncooked and Smoked: Sausages made with fresh or cured meat that was smoked but not cooked during processing. Cook these sausages well before eating.

Cooked: Cured and fully cooked sausages. You can heat them before serving.

Cooked and Smoked: Ready-to-eat sausages made from fresh meat that was cured, smoked, and fully cooked during processing. Serve them cold or hot.

Dry and Semidry: Sausages made from fresh meat that was cured, dried, and possibly smoked during processing. Most dry sausages are salamis (highly seasoned with a characteristic fermented flavor). Most semidry sausages are a type of summer sausage (mildly seasoned and easy to store). Dry and semidry sausages need no cooking.

Cooking Sausages

Uncooked Patties: Place ½-inch-thick sausage patties in an unheated skillet and cook over medium-low heat for 10 to 12 minutes or until juices run clear, turning once (an instant-read thermometer inserted into a patty should register 160°F). Drain well. Or arrange patties on a rack in a shallow baking pan. Bake in a 400°F oven about 15 minutes or until juices run clear and the internal temperature reaches 160°F.

Uncooked Links: Place 1- to 1½-inch-diameter sausage links in an unheated skillet; add ½ inch water. Bring to boiling; reduce heat. Simmer, covered, about 15 minutes or until juices run clear; drain. Cook 1 to 2 minutes more or until browned, turning often.

Fully Cooked Links: Place sausage links in a saucepan. Cover with cold water. Bring to boiling; reduce heat. Simmer for 5 to 10 minutes or until heated through.

Lamb Cuts

This page contains a drawing and labeled photos to help you identify cuts of lamb and suggested cooking methods. The drawing illustrates wholesale cuts; photos are of retail cuts.

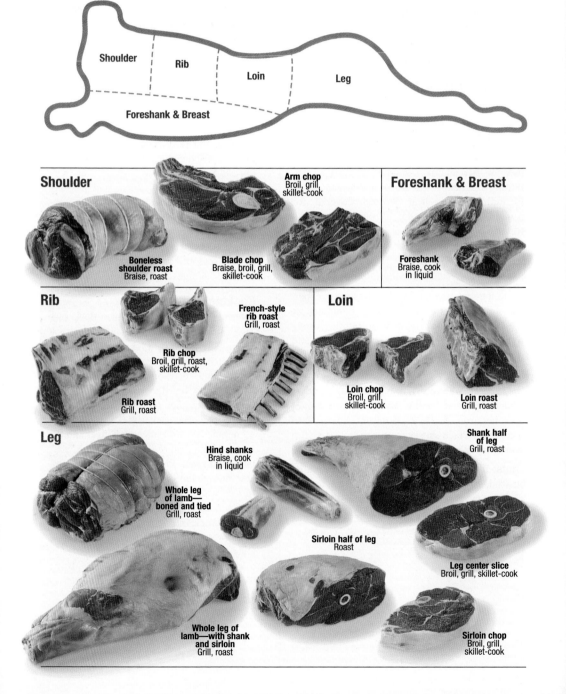

Shoulder

Rib

Loin

Leg

Foreshank & Breast

Shoulder

Arm chop
Broil, grill,
skillet-cook

Foreshank & Breast

**Boneless
shoulder roast**
Braise, roast

Blade chop
Braise, broil, grill,
skillet-cook

Foreshank
Braise, cook
in liquid

Rib

**French-style
rib roast**
Grill, roast

Loin

Rib chop
Broil, grill, roast,
skillet-cook

Rib roast
Grill, roast

Loin chop
Broil, grill,
skillet-cook

Loin roast
Grill, roast

Leg

Hind shanks
Braise, cook
in liquid

**Shank half
of leg**
Grill, roast

**Whole leg
of lamb—
boned and tied**
Grill, roast

Sirloin half of leg
Roast

Leg center slice
Broil, grill, skillet-cook

**Whole leg of
lamb—with shank
and sirloin**
Grill, roast

Sirloin chop
Broil, grill,
skillet-cook

Herb-Rubbed Leg of Lamb LOW FAT

You may need to special order this meat cut a few days ahead of when you plan to serve it.

Prep: 30 minutes **Roast:** 1¾ hours **Oven:** 325°F
Stand: 15 minutes **Makes:** 12 to 16 servings

- 1 **5- to 7-pound whole leg of lamb (with bone)**
  Lemon juice
- 2 **tablespoons snipped fresh parsley**
- 1 **tablespoon snipped fresh mint or basil or**
  1 teaspoon dried mint or basil, crushed
- 1 **tablespoon snipped fresh rosemary or**
  ½ teaspoon dried rosemary, crushed
- ½ **teaspoon onion salt**
- ¼ **teaspoon black pepper**
- 1 **or 2 cloves garlic, slivered**
  Mint jelly (optional)
- 1 **recipe Creamy Mustard Sauce (page 519) (optional)**

1. Trim fat from meat. Cut ½-inch-wide slits about 1 inch deep into roast. Drizzle lemon juice over meat's surface and into slits. In a bowl stir together parsley, mint, rosemary, onion salt, and pepper. Rub parsley mixture onto meat and into slits. Insert garlic into slits (see photo, below).

2. Place meat, fat side up, on a rack in a shallow roasting pan. Insert an oven-going meat thermometer into center of roast (see tip, page 367). The thermometer should not touch the bone. Roast, uncovered, in a 325°F oven. For medium rare, roast for 1¾ to 2¼ hours until meat thermometer registers 140°F. Cover with foil and let stand 15 minutes. The temperature of the meat after standing should be 145°F. (For medium, roast for 2¼ to 2¾ hours or until meat thermometer registers 155°F. Remove from oven. Cover and let stand 15 minutes. The temperature of the meat after standing should be 160°F.) If desired, serve with mint jelly and/or Creamy Mustard Sauce.

Per 4½ ounces: 150 cal., 5 g total fat (2 g sat. fat), 77 mg chol., 123 mg sodium, 0 g carbo., 0 g fiber, 25 g pro.
Daily Values: 1% vit. A, 3% vit. C, 1% calcium, 13% iron
Exchanges: 3½ Very Lean Meat, ½ Fat

Use a paring knife to cut ½-inch-wide slits about 1 inch deep into the lamb. Push the garlic slivers into the slits.

Lamb with Olive Tapenade

Prep: 30 minutes **Roast:** 1¾ hours **Oven:** 325°F
Stand: 15 minutes **Makes:** 8 servings

- 1 **cup pitted kalamata olives**
- 1 **tablespoon snipped fresh Italian parsley**
- 1 **tablespoon olive oil**
- 1 **teaspoon finely shredded lemon peel**
- 2 **teaspoons lemon juice**
- 1 **teaspoon snipped fresh rosemary**
- 1 **teaspoon snipped fresh thyme**
- ¼ **teaspoon freshly ground black pepper**
- 2 **cloves garlic, minced**
- 1 **3½- to 4-pound boneless leg of lamb, rolled and tied**
- ⅓ **cup dry red wine**
- 1 **teaspoon kosher salt**
- 1 **teaspoon freshly ground black pepper**

1. For olive tapenade, in a food processor combine olives, parsley, oil, lemon peel, lemon juice, rosemary, thyme, ¼ teaspoon pepper, and garlic. Cover and process until finely chopped, stopping to scrape down the sides of the food processor as necessary. Set aside.

2. Untie and unroll roast; trim fat. If necessary, place meat, boned side up, between two pieces of plastic wrap; pound meat with meat mallet to an even thickness. Spread tapenade over cut surface of meat. Roll up; tie securely with 100-percent-cotton kitchen string.

3. Place meat, seam side down, on a rack in a shallow roasting pan. In a small bowl combine red wine, salt, and the 1 teaspoon pepper. Roast meat in a 325°F oven for 1¾ to 2¼ hours or until an instant-read thermometer inserted into the center of the roast (see tip, page 367) registers 140°F (medium rare), basting with red wine mixture several times during roasting up until the last 10 minutes of roasting. Discard any remaining wine mixture. Remove roast from oven. Cover with foil and let stand 15 minutes. The temperature of the meat after standing should be 150°F. Remove string and slice the meat.

Per 5 ounces + 1½ tablespoons tapenade: 320 cal., 14 g total fat (4 g sat. fat), 127 mg chol., 591 mg sodium, 2 g carbo., 1 g fiber, 41 g pro.
Daily Values: 1% vit. A, 3% vit. C, 2% calcium, 20% iron
Exchanges: 5½ Lean Meat

Roast Rack of Lamb with Peach-Ginger Chutney LOW FAT

Prep: 20 minutes **Roast:** 45 minutes **Oven:** 325°F
Stand: 15 minutes **Makes:** 6 servings

- 2 1- to 1½-pound lamb rib roasts (6 to 8 ribs each), with or without backbone
- 3 tablespoons Dijon-style mustard
- 3 tablespoons lemon juice
- 1 tablespoon snipped fresh rosemary or thyme
- ½ teaspoon salt
- ¾ cup soft bread crumbs (1 slice)
- 1 tablespoon butter or margarine, melted
- 1 recipe Peach-Ginger Chutney (page 523)

1. Trim fat from meat. Stir together mustard, lemon juice, rosemary, and salt. Rub onto meat. In a bowl toss together bread crumbs and melted butter. Sprinkle onto meat.

2. Place meat on a rack in a shallow roasting pan. Insert an oven-going meat thermometer (see tip, page 367). The thermometer should not touch the bone. Roast, uncovered, in a 325°F oven. For medium rare, roast for 45 minutes to 1 hour or until meat thermometer registers 135°F. Cover with foil and let stand 15 minutes. The temperature of the meat after standing should be 145°F. (For medium, roast for 1 to 1½ hours or until meat thermometer registers 150°F. Cover and let stand 15 minutes. The temperature of the meat after standing should be 160°F.) Serve with warm Peach-Ginger Chutney.

Per 2 ribs + about ⅓ cup chutney: 299 cal., 9 g total fat (3 g sat. fat), 50 mg chol., 332 mg sodium, 41 g carbo., 3 g fiber, 16 g pro.
Daily Values: 11% vit. A, 16% vit. C, 5% calcium, 12% iron
Exchanges: 1 Fruit, 1½ Other Carbo., 2 Lean Meat, ½ Fat

Tuscan Lamb Chop Skillet LOW FAT FAST

See photo, page 361.

Start to Finish: 20 minutes **Makes:** 4 servings

- 8 lamb rib chops, cut 1 inch thick
- 2 teaspoons olive oil
- 3 cloves garlic, minced
- 1 19-ounce can cannellini beans (white kidney beans), rinsed and drained
- 1 cup canned Italian-style stewed tomatoes, undrained
- 1 tablespoon balsamic vinegar
- 2 teaspoons snipped fresh rosemary

1. Trim fat from chops. In a large skillet cook chops in hot oil over medium heat for 9 to 11 minutes for medium (160°F), turning once. Transfer chops to a plate; keep warm.

2. Stir garlic into drippings in skillet. Cook and stir for 1 minute. Stir in beans, undrained tomatoes, vinegar, and snipped rosemary. Bring to boiling; reduce heat. Simmer, uncovered, for 3 minutes. Top bean mixture in skillet with chops or spoon bean mixture onto four dinner plates and arrange two chops on each plate.

Per 2 chops + ½ cup vegetables: 245 cal., 9 g total fat (3 g sat. fat), 48 mg chol., 374 mg sodium, 23 g carbo., 7 g fiber, 23 g pro.
Daily Values: 2% vit. C, 6% calcium, 16% iron
Exchanges: 1½ Starch, 2½ Lean Meat

Lamb and Sweet Peppers

Lamb and Sweet Peppers FAST

Start to Finish: 25 minutes **Makes:** 4 servings

- 8 lamb rib or loin chops, cut 1 inch thick
   Salt and black pepper
- 3 small green, red, and/or yellow sweet peppers, cut into 1-inch pieces
- 2 cloves garlic, minced
- 1 tablespoon olive oil or cooking oil
- ¼ cup sliced, pitted green or ripe olives
- 1 tablespoon snipped fresh oregano
   Hot cooked rice (optional)

1. Preheat broiler. Trim fat from chops. Place chops on unheated rack of broiler pan. Broil chops 3 to 4 inches from heat for 10 to 15 minutes for medium (160°F), turning chops once halfway through broiling. Season with salt and black pepper. Transfer to a serving platter.

2. Meanwhile, in a large skillet cook sweet pepper and garlic in hot oil for 8 to 10 minutes or until crisp-tender. Add olives and oregano. Cook and stir until heated through. Spoon over chops. If desired, serve with rice.

Per 2 chops + ⅓ cup vegetables: 267 cal., 13 g total fat (4 g sat. fat), 100 mg chol., 454 mg sodium, 3 g carbo., 1 g fiber, 33 g pro.
Daily Values: 5% vit. A, 70% vit. C, 4% calcium, 19% iron
Exchanges: 1 Vegetable, 4½ Lean Meat

Lamb Chops with Sweet Potato Chutney LOW FAT

Start to Finish: 40 minutes Makes: 4 servings

 8 lamb rib or loin chops, cut 1 inch thick
 1 medium sweet potato, peeled and coarsely chopped (about 1½ cups)
 2 tablespoons finely chopped shallots
 ⅛ teaspoon crushed red pepper
 ¼ cup packed brown sugar
 ¼ cup vinegar
 2 tablespoons dried cranberries or currants
 ½ teaspoon grated fresh ginger

1. Preheat broiler. Trim fat from chops. Place chops on unheated rack of broiler pan; set aside.

2. For chutney, in a medium saucepan bring 1 cup of *lightly salted water* to boiling. Add the chopped sweet potato, cook for 5 minutes, and drain. Place shallot, crushed red pepper, brown sugar, vinegar, dried cranberries, and ginger in saucepan. Stir in sweet potato. Heat until vinegar bubbles; reduce heat. Simmer, covered, for 10 minutes, stirring occasionally. Remove cover and simmer 2 more minutes or until liquid is slightly thickened and sweet potato is tender.

3. Broil chops 3 to 4 inches from heat for 10 to 15 minutes for medium (160°F), turning chops once halfway through broiling. Serve chops with the chutney.

Per 2 chops + ⅓ cup chutney: 314 cal., 10 g total fat
(4 g sat. fat), 80 mg chol., 109 mg sodium, 29 g carbo., 2 g fiber,
25 g pro.
Daily Values: 129% vit. A, 2% vit. C, 5% calcium, 15% iron
Exchanges: ½ Starch, 1½ Other Carbo., 3 Lean Meat

Smoked Pork Chops with Sweet Potato Chutney:
Prepare as above, except substitute 4 cooked smoked pork chops, cut ¾ to 1 inch thick, for lamb. Broil chops until heated through (140°F), turning chops once halfway through broiling.

Per chop + ⅓ cup chutney: 299 cal., 7 g total fat (3 g sat. fat),
83 mg chol, 1,811 mg sodium, 29 g carbo., 2 g fiber, 28 g pro.
Daily Values: 122% vit. A, 2% vit. C, 3% calcium, 8% iron
Exchanges: ½ Starch, 1½ Other Carbo., 3½ Very Lean Meat, 1 Fat

Lamb Shanks with Beans LOW FAT

Prep: 30 minutes Stand: 1 hour
Cook: 2¼ hours Makes: 6 servings

 1¼ cups dry navy beans
 4 cups water
 4 meaty lamb shanks (about 4 pounds), cut into 3- to 4-inch pieces, or meaty veal shank cross cuts (about 3 pounds)
 1 tablespoon cooking oil
 1 medium onion, sliced and separated into rings
 2 cloves garlic, minced
 2 cups chicken broth
 1 teaspoon dried thyme, crushed
 ½ teaspoon salt
 ¼ teaspoon black pepper
 1 14.5-ounce can diced tomatoes, undrained

1. Rinse beans. In a 4- to 6-quart Dutch oven combine the beans and the water. Bring to boiling; reduce heat. Simmer, uncovered, for 2 minutes. Remove from heat. Do not drain. Cover and let stand for 1 hour. (Or add water to cover beans. Cover and let stand overnight.)

2. Drain and rinse beans. In the same pan brown lamb shanks on all sides in hot oil; remove from pan. Add onion and garlic to the same pan and cook until tender. Carefully stir in beans, shanks, chicken broth, thyme, salt, and pepper. Bring to boiling; reduce heat. Simmer, covered, for 2 to 2½ hours or until meat and beans are tender. (If necessary, add more chicken broth to keep mixture moist.)

3. Remove meat from pan. Let it cool slightly. When cool enough to handle, cut meat off bones and coarsely chop. Discard fat and bones. Skim fat from the top of the bean mixture. Stir in the meat and undrained tomatoes. Bring to boiling; reduce heat. Simmer, covered, for 10 to 15 minutes until flavors are blended.

Per 1½ cups: 434 cal., 10 g total fat (3 g sat. fat), 132 mg chol.,
766 mg sodium, 31 g carbo., 11 g fiber, 53 g pro.
Daily Values: 1% vit. A, 17% vit. C, 10% calcium, 36% iron
Exchanges: ½ Vegetable, 2 Starch, 6 Very Lean Meat, 1½ Fat

Dinner with Italian Flair

Serve this quick meal after a busy day.

● *Tuscan Lamb Chop Skillet (page 402)*
● *Tossed salad greens with vinaigrette*
● *Spumoni ice cream*

Braised Venison with Sour Cream Gravy LOW FAT

Braising is an excellent method for cooking less tender cuts of meat, such as a shoulder or rump.

Prep: 25 minutes **Cook:** 1½ hours
Makes: 6 to 8 servings

- 1 2- to 3-pound boneless venison shoulder or rump roast
- 1 tablespoon cooking oil
- 1 6-ounce can (⅔ cup) tomato juice
- ½ cup finely chopped onion (1 medium)
- ½ cup finely chopped carrot (1 medium)
- 1 teaspoon instant beef bouillon granules
- 3 tablespoons all-purpose flour
- ½ cup dairy sour cream
  Salt (optional)
  Black pepper (optional)
  Hot cooked noodles or mashed potatoes (optional)

1. Trim fat from meat. In a 4- to 6-quart Dutch oven brown meat on all sides in hot oil. Drain off fat. Add tomato juice, onion, carrot, and bouillon granules. Bring to boiling; reduce heat. Simmer, covered, for 1½ to 2 hours or until meat is tender. Transfer meat to a platter. Keep warm while preparing gravy.

2. For gravy, skim fat from vegetable mixture. Measure vegetable mixture. If necessary, add enough *water* to vegetable mixture to equal 2 cups. Return to Dutch oven. In a small bowl stir flour into sour cream. Stir into vegetable mixture in pan. Cook and stir over medium heat until thickened and bubbly. Cook and stir for 1 minute more. If desired, season to taste with salt and pepper. Serve gravy with meat and, if desired, noodles.

Slow cooker directions: Prepare meat as above. Place onion and carrot in a 3½- or 4-quart slow cooker. Cut meat to fit in cooker; place on top of vegetables. Combine tomato juice and bouillon granules. Add to cooker. Cover and cook on low-heat setting for 10 to 12 hours or on high-heat setting for 5 to 6 hours. Transfer meat to a serving platter; keep warm. Prepare gravy in a saucepan on the range top and serve as above.

Per 2 ounces venison + about ½ cup gravy: 211 cal., 8 g total fat (3 g sat. fat), 98 mg chol., 463 mg sodium, 7 g carbo., 1 g fiber, 26 g pro.
Daily Values: 57% vit. A, 11% vit. C, 3% calcium, 23% iron
Exchanges: 1 Vegetable, 3½ Very Lean Meat, 1½ Fat

Marinated Venison Chops LOW FAT

Prep: 12 minutes **Marinate:** 2 hours
Broil: 10 minutes **Makes:** 4 servings

- 4 8-ounce venison rib chops, cut 1 inch thick
- ¼ cup finely chopped green onion (2)
- 2 tablespoons lime juice
- 2 tablespoons soy sauce
- 2 tablespoons grated fresh ginger
- 1 tablespoon packed brown sugar
- 1 fresh jalapeño chile pepper, seeded and finely chopped (see tip, page 74)
- 2 cloves garlic, minced

1. Place chops in a resealable plastic bag set in a shallow dish. For marinade, in a small bowl combine green onion, lime juice, soy sauce, ginger, brown sugar, jalapeño pepper, and garlic. Pour marinade over chops; seal bag. Marinate in the refrigerator for 2 to 4 hours, turning bag occasionally. Drain chops, discarding marinade.

2. Preheat broiler. Place chops on the unheated rack of a broiler pan. Broil 3 to 4 inches from the heat for 10 to 12 minutes for medium (160°F), turning chops once halfway through broiling.

Per chop: 214 cal., 4 g total fat (1 g sat. fat), 144 mg chol., 306 mg sodium, 2 g carbo., 0 g fiber, 40 g pro.
Daily Values: 1% vit. A, 9% vit. C, 2% calcium, 33% iron
Exchanges: 6 Very Lean Meat

Pan Gravy for Roasted Meat

Make this basic gravy recipe to accompany a roast. If you don't get ¼ cup fat from the roast, add cooking oil to equal that amount. (A ¼-cup serving of gravy adds 71 calories and 6 grams fat to the meal.)

Remove roasted meat from pan and pour drippings into a large measuring cup, scraping out the crusty browned bits. Skim fat from drippings (see photo, page 483); reserve ¼ cup of the fat. Measure remaining drippings; for 2 cups of gravy add enough beef broth or water to equal 2 cups.

In a medium saucepan combine reserved fat and ¼ cup all-purpose flour. Gradually stir the 2 cups drippings into the flour mixture. Cook and stir over medium heat until thickened and bubbly. Cook and stir for 1 minute more. If desired, season to taste with salt and black pepper.

Broiling Meat

Preheat broiler. Place meat on the unheated rack of a broiler pan. For cuts less than 1½ inches thick, broil 3 to 4 inches from the heat. For 1½-inch-thick cuts, broil 4 to 5 inches from the heat. Broil for the time given or until done, turning meat over after half of the broiling time.

Cut	Thickness/Weight	Approximate Time	Doneness
Beef			
Boneless steak (ribeye, tenderloin, top loin)	1 inch	12 to 14 minutes	145°F medium rare
	1 inch	15 to 18 minutes	160°F medium
	1½ inches	18 to 21 minutes	145°F medium rare
	1½ inches	22 to 27 minutes	160°F medium
Boneless top sirloin steak	1 inch	15 to 17 minutes	145°F medium rare
	1 inch	20 to 22 minutes	160°F medium
	1½ inches	25 to 27 minutes	145°F medium rare
	1½ inches	30 to 32 minutes	160°F medium
Boneless tri-tip steak (bottom sirloin)	¾ inch	6 to 7 minutes	145°F medium rare
	¾ inch	8 to 9 minutes	160°F medium
	1 inch	9 to 10 minutes	145°F medium rare
	1 inch	11 to 12 minutes	160°F medium
Flank steak	1¼ to 1¾ pounds	15 to 18 minutes	160°F medium
Steak with bone (porterhouse, rib, T-bone)	1 inch	12 to 15 minutes	145°F medium rare
	1 inch	15 to 20 minutes	160°F medium
	1½ inches	20 to 25 minutes	145°F medium rare
	1½ inches	25 to 30 minutes	160°F medium
Ground Meat			
Patties (beef, lamb, pork, or veal)	½ inch	10 to 12 minutes	160°F medium
	¾ inch	12 to 14 minutes	160°F medium
Lamb			
Chop (loin or rib)	1 inch	10 to 15 minutes	160°F medium
Chop (sirloin)	1 inch	12 to 15 minutes	160°F medium
Pork			
Chop (boneless top loin)	¾ to 1 inch	9 to 11 minutes	160°F medium
	1¼ to 1½ inches	15 to 18 minutes	160°F medium
Chop with bone (loin or rib)	¾ to 1 inch	9 to 12 minutes	160°F medium
	1¼ to 1½ inches	16 to 20 minutes	160°F medium
Chop with bone (sirloin)	¾ to 1 inch	10 to 13 minutes	160°F medium
Ham slice, cooked	1 inch	12 to 15 minutes	140°F heated through
Sausages			
Frankfurters and sausage links, cooked		3 to 7 minutes	140°F heated through
Veal			
Chop (loin or rib)	¾ to 1 inch	14 to 16 minutes	160°F medium
	1½ inches	21 to 25 minutes	160°F medium

All cooking times are based on meat removed directly from refrigerator.

Roasting Meat

Place meat, fat side up, on a rack in a shallow roasting pan. (Roasts with a bone do not need a rack.) Insert a meat thermometer (see tip, page 367). Do not add water or liquid and do not cover. Roast in a 325°F oven (unless chart says otherwise) for the time given and until the thermometer registers the "final roasting temperature." (This will be 5°F to 10°F below the "final doneness temperature.") Remove the roast from the oven; cover with foil and let it stand 15 minutes before carving. The meat's temperature will rise 5°F to 10°F during the time it stands.

Cut	Weight	Approximate Roasting Time	Final Roasting Temperature (when to remove from oven)	Final Doneness Temperature (after standing 15 minutes)
Beef				
Boneless tri-tip roast (bottom sirloin) Roast at 425°F	1½ to 2 pounds	30 to 35 minutes 40 to 45 minutes	135°F 150°F	145°F medium rare 160°F medium
Eye round roast Roasting past medium rare is not recommended.	2 to 3 pounds	1½ to 1¾ hours	135°F	145°F medium rare
Ribeye roast Roast at 350°F	3 to 4 pounds 4 to 6 pounds 6 to 8 pounds	1½ to 1¾ hours 1¾ hours to 2 hours 1¾ hours to 2 hours 2 to 2½ hours 2 to 2¼ hours 2½ to 2¾ hours	135°F 150°F 135°F 150°F 135°F 150°F	145°F medium rare 160°F medium 145°F medium rare 160°F medium 145°F medium rare 160°F medium
Rib roast (chine bone removed) Roast at 350°F	4 to 6 pounds 6 to 8 pounds 8 to 10 pounds*	1¾ to 2¼ hours 2¼ to 2¾ hours 2¼ to 2½ hours 2¾ to 3 hours 2½ to 3 hours 3 to 3½ hours	135°F 150°F 135°F 150°F 135°F 150°F	145°F medium rare 160°F medium 145°F medium rare 160°F medium 145°F medium rare 160°F medium
Round tip roast	3 to 4 pounds 4 to 6 pounds 6 to 8 pounds	1¾ to 2 hours 2¼ to 2½ hours 2 to 2½ hours 2½ to 3 hours 2½ to 3 hours 3 to 3½ hours	135°F 150°F 135°F 150°F 135°F 150°F	145°F medium rare 160°F medium 145°F medium rare 160°F medium 145°F medium rare 160°F medium
Tenderloin roast Roast at 425°F	2 to 3 pounds 4 to 5 pounds	35 to 40 minutes 45 to 50 minutes 50 to 60 minutes 60 to 70 minutes	135°F 150°F 135°F 150°F	145°F medium rare 160°F medium 145°F medium rare 160°F medium
Top round roast Roasting past medium rare is not recommended.	4 to 6 pounds 6 to 8 pounds	1¾ to 2½ hours 2½ to 3 hours	135°F 135°F	145°F medium rare 145°F medium rare
Lamb				
Boneless leg roast	4 to 5 pounds 5 to 6 pounds	1¾ to 2¼ hours 2 to 2½ hours 2 to 2½ hours 2½ to 3 hours	135°F 150°F 135°F 150°F	145°F medium rare 160°F medium 145°F medium rare 160°F medium
Boneless shoulder roast	3 to 4 pounds 4 to 5 pounds	1½ to 2 hours 1¾ to 2¼ hours 2 to 2½ hours 2¼ to 3 hours	135°F 150°F 135°F 150°F	145°F medium rare 160°F medium 145°F medium rare 160°F medium

All cooking times are based on meat removed directly from refrigerator.
*Roasts weighing more than 8 pounds should be loosely covered with foil halfway through roasting.

Cut	Weight	Approximate Roasting Time	Final Roasting Temperature (when to remove from oven)	Final Doneness Temperature (after standing 15 minutes)
Lamb *(continued)*				
Boneless sirloin roast	1½ to 2 pounds	1 to 1¼ hours 1¼ to 1½ hours	135°F 150°F	145°F medium rare 160°F medium
Leg of lamb (with bone)	5 to 7 pounds 7 to 8 pounds	1¾ to 2¼ hours 2¼ to 2¾ hours 2¼ to 2¾ hours 2½ to 3 hours	135°F 150°F 135°F 150°F	145°F medium rare 160°F medium 145°F medium rare 160°F medium
Leg of lamb, shank half (with bone)	3 to 4 pounds	1¾ to 2¼ hours 2 to 2½ hours	135°F 150°F	145°F medium rare 160°F medium
Leg of lamb, sirloin half (with bone)	3 to 4 pounds	1½ to 2 hours 1¾ to 2¼ hours	135°F 150°F	145°F medium rare 160°F medium
Pork				
Boneless sirloin roast	1½ to 2 pounds	¾ to 1¼ hours	150°F	160°F medium
Boneless top loin roast (double loin)	3 to 4 pounds 4 to 5 pounds	1½ to 2¼ hours 2 to 2½ hours	150°F 150°F	160°F medium 160°F medium
Boneless top loin roast (single loin)	2 to 3 pounds	1¼ to 1¾ hours	150°F	160°F medium
Loin center rib roast (backbone loosened)	3 to 4 pounds 4 to 6 pounds	1¼ to 1¾ hours 1¾ to 2½ hours	150°F 150°F	160°F medium 160°F medium
Loin back ribs or spareribs		1½ to 1¾ hours	Tender	No standing time
Country-style ribs Roast at 350°F		1½ to 2 hours	Tender	No standing time
Crown roast	6 to 8 pounds	2½ to 3¼ hours	150°F	160°F medium
Tenderloin Roast at 425°F	¾ to 1 pound	25 to 35 minutes	155°F	160°F medium
Ham, cooked (boneless)	1½ to 3 pounds 3 to 5 pounds 6 to 8 pounds 8 to 10 pounds*	¾ to 1¼ hours 1 to 1¾ hours 1¾ to 2½ hours 2¼ to 2¾ hours	140°F 140°F 140°F 140°F	No standing time No standing time No standing time No standing time
Ham, cooked (with bone) (half or whole)	6 to 8 pounds 14 to 16 pounds*	1½ to 2¼ hours 2¾ to 3¾ hours	140°F 140°F	No standing time No standing time
Ham, cook before eating (with bone)	3 to 5 pounds 7 to 8 pounds 14 to 16 pounds*	1¾ to 3 hours 2½ to 3¼ hours 4 to 5¼ hours	150°F 150°F 150°F	160°F medium 160°F medium 160°F medium
Smoked shoulder picnic, cooked (with bone)	4 to 6 pounds	1¼ to 2 hours	140°F	No standing time
Veal				
Loin roast (with bone)	3 to 4 pounds	1¾ to 2¼ hours	150°F	160°F medium
Rib roast (chine bone removed)	4 to 5 pounds	1½ to 2¼ hours	150°F	160°F medium

All cooking times are based on meat removed directly from refrigerator.
*Roasts weighing more than 8 pounds should be loosely covered with foil halfway through roasting.

Skillet-Cooking Meat

Select a heavy skillet that is the correct size for the amount of meat you are cooking. (If the skillet is too large, the pan juices can burn.) Lightly coat the skillet with nonstick cooking spray. (Or use a heavy nonstick skillet.) Preheat skillet over medium-high heat until very hot. Add meat. Do not add any liquid and do not cover the skillet. Reduce heat to medium and cook for the time given or until done, turning meat occasionally. If meat browns too quickly, reduce heat to medium low.

Cut	Thickness	Approximate Cooking Time	Doneness
Beef			
Boneless chuck eye steak	¾ inch 1 inch	9 to 11 minutes 12 to 15 minutes	145°F med. rare to 160°F medium 145°F med. rare to 160°F medium
Boneless top sirloin steak	¾ inch 1 inch	10 to 13 minutes 15 to 20 minutes	145°F med. rare to 160°F medium 145°F med. rare to 160°F medium
Boneless tri-tip steak (bottom sirloin)	¾ inch 1 inch	6 to 9 minutes 9 to 12 minutes	145°F med. rare to 160°F medium 145°F med. rare to 160°F medium
Cubed steak	½ inch	5 to 8 minutes	160°F medium
Porterhouse or T-bone steak	¾ inch 1 inch	11 to 13 minutes 14 to 17 minutes	145°F med. rare to 160°F medium 145°F med. rare to 160°F medium
Ribeye steak	¾ inch 1 inch	8 to 10 minutes 12 to 15 minutes	145°F med. rare to 160°F medium 145°F med. rare to 160°F medium
Shoulder center steak (Ranch steak)	¾ inch 1 inch	9 to 12 minutes (turn twice) 13 to 16 minutes (turn twice)	145°F med. rare to 160°F medium 145°F med. rare to 160°F medium
Shoulder top blade steak (Flat-iron)	6 to 8 ounces	13 to 15 minutes (turn twice)	145°F med. rare to 160°F medium
Tenderloin steak	¾ inch 1 inch	7 to 9 minutes 10 to 13 minutes	145°F med. rare to 160°F medium 145°F med. rare to 160°F medium
Top loin steak	¾ inch 1 inch	10 to 12 minutes 12 to 15 minutes	145°F med. rare to 160°F medium 145°F med. rare to 160°F medium
Ground Meat			
Patties (beef, lamb, pork, or veal)	½ inch ¾ inch	9 to 12 minutes 12 to 15 minutes	160°F medium 160°F medium
Lamb			
Chop (loin or rib)	1 inch	9 to 11 minutes	160°F medium
Pork			
Canadian-style bacon	¼ inch	3 to 4 minutes	heated through
Chop (loin or rib) (with bone or boneless)	¾ to 1 inch	8 to 12 minutes	160°F medium
Cutlet	¼ inch	3 to 4 minutes	no longer pink
Ham slice, cooked	1 inch	14 to 16 minutes	140°F heated through
Tenderloin medallions	¼ to ½ inch	4 to 8 minutes	160°F medium
Veal			
Chop (loin or rib)	¾ to 1 inch	10 to 14 minutes	160°F medium
Cutlet	⅛ inch ¼ inch	2 to 4 minutes 4 to 6 minutes	no longer pink no longer pink

All cooking times are based on meat removed directly from refrigerator.

Pasta

Eight-Layer Casserole, 428

Fresh Tomato and Arugula Pasta with Chicken, 425

Cream-Sauced Pasta with Vegetables, 424

Pasta Essentials

In Italian, the word "pasta" means "paste"—a mixture of flour and water that can be cut or shaped and cooked in countless ways. Try something new from the recipes in this chapter.

Matching Sauces and Pasta

Choose the pasta that best complements your sauce.

● **Light, thin sauces** are best paired with thin, delicate pastas, such as angel hair (capellini) or thin spaghetti (vermicelli).

● **Chunky sauces** are best partnered with pastas with holes or ridges, such as mostaccioli, ziti, rotini, or radiatore.

● **Heavy sauces** complement sturdier pasta shapes, such as fettuccine, linguine, bucatini, or lasagna noodles.

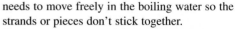

How Much to Cook

Figure the average diner will eat about 1 cup of cooked pasta. Here are guidelines for cooking the right amount of dried pasta for a specific number of people:

● 8 ounces uncooked small to medium pasta (rotini, wagon wheels, bow ties, penne, ziti, elbow macaroni) = 4 cups cooked

● 8 ounces uncooked long pasta (spaghetti, angel hair, linguine, fettuccine) = 1½-inch diameter bunch = 4 cups cooked

● 8 ounces uncooked egg noodles = 2½ cups cooked

Refrigerated Pasta: When buying refrigerated fresh pasta, plan on 3 ounces for each main-dish serving and 1½ to 2 ounces for each side-dish serving. To use fresh pasta instead of dried pasta in a recipe, substitute 6 to 8 ounces of refrigerated fresh pasta for 4 ounces of dried pasta.

Cooking Perfect Pasta

When cooking purchased dried pasta, check the package directions because cooking times for brands vary. Whichever brand you buy, follow these tips:

● Don't skimp on the cooking water. For 16 ounces of pasta, use 4 to 6 quarts of water in a large pot. This may look like a lot, but pasta needs to move freely in the boiling water so the strands or pieces don't stick together.

● Cover the pot to bring the water quickly to boiling. Keep the water boiling by adding the pasta slowly. Cook the pasta uncovered while maintaining a rolling boil.

● Drain cooked pasta in a colander and shake it well to get rid of excess water. Skip the rinse; rinsing removes the light coating of starch that covers the surface of each piece of pasta. That coating helps the sauce and seasonings cling. Rinse, using cool water, only if you plan to fill or layer the pasta or use the pasta in a salad.

Hot Pasta

Pasta continues to cook even after draining. Serve pasta immediately or it will become too soft. To keep pasta warm for a few minutes before serving, use one of the following suggestions:

● Return the drained, cooked pasta to the warm cooking pan. Stir in any additional ingredients or toss pasta with a little butter to help prevent it from sticking together. (If you add oil to the cooking water, it is not necessary to add more oil.) Cover and let the pasta stand for no more than 15 minutes.

● Fill a serving bowl with hot water and let it stand for a few minutes. Empty and dry the bowl; add the hot pasta and cover. Serve the pasta within 5 minutes.

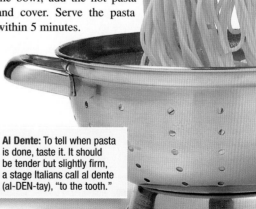

Al Dente: To tell when pasta is done, taste it. It should be tender but slightly firm, a stage Italians call al dente (al-DEN-tay), "to the tooth."

Pasta

Bow ties
(farfalle)

Spaghetti

Gnocchi

Campanelle

Penne

Ravioli

Manicotti

Mafalda

Orzo
(rosamarina)

Linguine

Fine egg
noodles

Couscous

Small shell
macaroni

Capellini

Rotini

Fusilli

Wide egg
noodles

Jumbo shell
macaroni

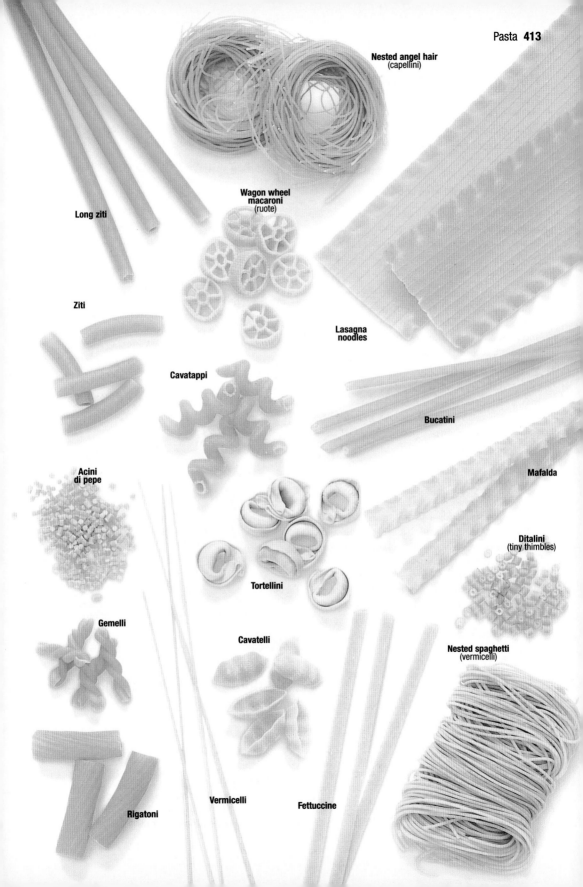

Nested angel hair
(capellini)

Long ziti

**Wagon wheel
macaroni**
(ruote)

Ziti

**Lasagna
noodles**

Cavatappi

Bucatini

**Acini
di pepe**

Mafalda

Tortellini

Ditalini
(tiny thimbles)

Gemelli

Cavatelli

Nested spaghetti
(vermicelli)

Rigatoni

Vermicelli

Fettuccine

Homemade Pasta LOW FAT

Prep: 1 hour **Cook:** see chart, below
Makes: 5 servings

   2⅓ cups all-purpose flour
     1 teaspoon dried basil or sage, crushed
     2 eggs
    ⅓ cup water
     1 teaspoon cooking oil or olive oil

1. In a large bowl stir together 2 cups of the flour, the basil, and ½ teaspoon *salt*. Make a well in the center of the flour mixture. In a small bowl beat eggs; add water and oil. Add egg mixture to flour mixture; stir to combine.

2. Sprinkle a clean kneading surface with the remaining ⅓ cup flour. Turn dough out onto floured surface. Knead until dough is smooth and elastic (8 to 10 minutes total). Cover and let the dough rest for 10 minutes.

3. Divide the dough into four equal portions. On a lightly floured surface, roll each portion into a 12-inch square (about ¹⁄₁₆ inch thick). Let stand, uncovered, about 20 minutes. Cut as desired (see photos 1 and 2, right). If using a pasta machine, pass each portion through machine according to manufacturer's directions until dough is ¹⁄₁₆ inch thick. Let stand, uncovered, about 20 minutes; cut as desired.

4. To serve pasta immediately, cook according to the chart, below left; drain.

5. To store cut pasta, hang it from a pasta-drying rack or spread it on a wire cooling rack. Let pasta dry about 1 hour or until completely dry. Place it in an airtight container and chill for up to 3 days. Or dry the pasta for at least 1 hour; place it in a freezer bag and freeze for up to 8 months.

Food processor directions: Place steel blade in food processor bowl. Add flour, basil, ½ teaspoon salt, and eggs to bowl. Cover and process until mixture forms fine crumbs, about the consistency of cornmeal. With the processor running, slowly pour the water and oil through the feed tube. Continue processing just until the dough forms a ball. Transfer dough to a lightly floured surface. Cover; let dough rest for 10 minutes. Continue as in Step 3.

Per cup cooked pasta: 250 cal., 4 g total fat (1 g sat. fat), 85 mg chol., 259 mg sodium, 45 g carbo., 2 g fiber, 9 g pro.
Daily Values: 2% calcium, 17% iron
Exchanges: 3 Starch

Cooking Homemade Pasta

In a large saucepan or kettle bring water (3 quarts water for 4 to 8 ounces pasta) to boiling. If desired, add 1 teaspoon salt and 1 tablespoon olive oil or cooking oil to the water to prevent pasta from sticking together. Add pasta a little at a time so the water does not stop boiling. Reduce heat slightly and boil, uncovered, stirring occasionally, for the time specified below or until the pasta is al dente. Test often for doneness near the end of the cooking time. Drain in a colander.

Homemade Pasta	Cooking Time
Bow ties	2 to 3 minutes
Fettuccine	1½ to 2 minutes
Lasagna	2 to 3 minutes
Linguine	1½ to 2 minutes
Noodles	1½ to 2 minutes
Ravioli	7 to 9 minutes
Tortellini	7 to 9 minutes

Allow 1 to 2 minutes more for dried or frozen pasta.

1. For linguine, fettuccine, or noodles, loosely roll up dough. Cut into ⅛-inch-wide strips for linguine or ¼-inch-wide strips for fettuccine or noodles. Separate the strips and cut into 12-inch lengths.

2. For lasagna noodles, use a fluted pastry wheel or a sharp knife to cut dough into 2½-inch-wide strips. Cut strips into desired lengths.

Homemade Spinach Pasta LOW FAT

Prep: 1 hour **Cook:** see chart, left
Makes: 6 servings

   2¾ cups all-purpose flour
    ½ teaspoon salt
     2 eggs
    ¼ cup water
    ¼ cup cooked spinach, well drained and finely chopped
     1 teaspoon cooking oil or olive oil

1. In a large bowl stir together 2 cups of the flour and the salt. Make a well in the center of the flour mixture. In a small bowl beat eggs. Add water, spinach, and oil. Add egg mixture to flour mixture; mix well.

2. Sprinkle a clean kneading surface with the remaining ¾ cup flour. Turn dough out onto floured surface. Knead dough until smooth and elastic (8 to 10 minutes total). Cover and let the dough rest for 10 minutes.

3. Divide dough into four equal portions. On a lightly floured surface, roll each portion into a 12-inch square (about ¹⁄₁₆ inch thick). If using a pasta machine, pass each portion through the machine according to the manufacturer's directions until dough is ¹⁄₁₆ inch thick. Let stand, uncovered, about 20 minutes. Cut as desired (see photos 1 and 2, page 414).

4. To serve pasta immediately, cook according to the chart on page 414; drain.

5. To store cut pasta, hang it from a pasta-drying rack or spread it on a wire cooling rack. Let pasta dry about 1 hour or until completely dry. Place it in an airtight container and chill for up to 3 days. Or dry the pasta for at least 1 hour and place it in a freezer bag or freezer container; freeze for up to 8 months.

Per cup cooked pasta: 242 cal., 3 g total fat (1 g sat. fat), 71 mg chol., 221 mg sodium, 44 g carbo., 2 g fiber, 8 g pro.
Daily Values: 14% vit. A, 1% vit. C, 3% calcium, 18% iron
Exchanges: 3 Starch

Homemade Noodles `LOW FAT`

Noodles are easier to make than you might expect and give old-fashioned flavor and texture.

Prep: 1 hour **Cook:** see chart, page 414 **Makes:** 5 servings

  2 cups all-purpose flour
  2 egg yolks, beaten
  1 egg, beaten
  ⅓ cup water
  1 teaspoon cooking oil or olive oil

1. In a large bowl stir together 1¾ cups of the flour and ½ teaspoon *salt*. Make a well in the center of the flour mixture. In a small bowl beat egg yolks and whole egg. Add water and oil. Add egg mixture to flour mixture; mix well.

2. Sprinkle a clean kneading surface with the remaining ¼ cup flour. Turn dough out onto floured surface. Knead until dough is smooth and elastic (8 to 10 minutes total). Cover and let the dough rest for 10 minutes.

3. Divide dough into four equal portions. On a lightly floured surface, roll each portion into a 12×9-inch rectangle (about ¹⁄₁₆ inch thick). If using a pasta machine, pass each portion through machine according to manufacturer's directions until dough is ¹⁄₁₆ inch thick. Let stand, uncovered, for 20 minutes. Lightly dust dough with flour. Loosely roll dough into a spiral; cut into ¼-inch-wide strips (see photo 1, page 414). Shake strips to separate; cut strips into 2- to 3-inch lengths.

4. To serve noodles immediately, cook according to the chart, page 414; drain.

5. To store cut noodles, hang them from a pasta-drying rack or spread them on a wire cooling rack. Let noodles dry about 1 hour or until completely dry. Place them in an airtight container and refrigerate for up to 3 days. Or dry the noodles for at least 1 hour and place them in a freezer bag or freezer container; freeze for up to 8 months.

Per ½ cup cooked noodles: 229 cal., 4 g total fat (1 g sat. fat), 128 mg chol., 249 mg sodium, 38 g carbo., 1 g fiber, 8 g pro.
Daily Values: 4% vit. A, 2% calcium, 15% iron
Exchanges: 2½ Starch, ½ Fat

Yolkless Noodles: Prepare as at left, except substitute 2 beaten egg whites for the 2 beaten egg yolks and 1 beaten egg. Increase the oil to 2 teaspoons.

Per cup cooked noodles: 204 cal., 2 g total fat (0 g sat. fat), 0 mg chol., 256 mg sodium, 38 g carbo., 1 g fiber, 7 g pro.
Daily Values: 1% calcium, 13% iron
Exchanges: 2½ Starch

Storing Pasta

● Uncooked purchased dried pasta keeps indefinitely in an airtight container in a cool, dry place.

● Refrigerated fresh pasta keeps for up to 5 days in its original packaging. If frozen, it will keep for up to 8 months.

● Cooked pasta can be refrigerated for 1 to 2 days sealed in an airtight container. Reheat the pasta in a sauce or clear broth.

● Freeze prepared pasta dishes, such as lasagna and baked cavatelli up to 2 months.

Spaghetti with Sauce and Meatballs

Spaghetti with Sauce `LOW FAT` `VEGETARIAN`

Prep: 20 minutes **Cook:** 40 minutes
Makes: 4 to 6 servings

- 1 **cup chopped onion (1 large)**
- ½ **cup chopped green sweet pepper**
- ¼ **cup chopped celery**
- 2 **cloves garlic, minced**
- 1 **tablespoon cooking oil**
- 6 **large tomatoes, peeled and chopped (4 cups), or two 14.5-ounce cans diced tomatoes, undrained**
- 1 **6-ounce can tomato paste**
- 2 **tablespoons snipped fresh parsley**
- 1 **tablespoon snipped fresh basil or 1 teaspoon dried basil, crushed**
- 1 **tablespoon snipped fresh oregano or 1 teaspoon dried oregano, crushed**
- 2 **teaspoons snipped fresh marjoram or ½ teaspoon dried marjoram, crushed**
- 1 **teaspoon sugar**
- 8 **ounces dried spaghetti or linguine**
   Finely shredded Parmesan cheese (optional)

1. In a Dutch oven cook onion, sweet pepper, celery, and garlic in hot oil over medium heat until vegetables are tender.

2. Stir in tomato, tomato paste, ⅓ cup *water,* parsley, dried herbs (if using), sugar, ½ teaspoon *salt,* and ¼ teaspoon *black pepper.* Bring to boiling; reduce heat. Simmer, covered, for 30 minutes. Uncover and simmer for 10 to 15 minutes more or to desired consistency, stirring occasionally. Stir in fresh herbs, if using.

3. Meanwhile, cook pasta according to package directions. Serve sauce over hot cooked pasta. If desired, sprinkle with Parmesan cheese.

Big-Batch Spaghetti Sauce: Prepare as at left, except use a large Dutch oven and 2 cups chopped onion, 1 cup chopped sweet pepper, ½ cup chopped celery, 4 cloves garlic, 2 tablespoons cooking oil, two 28-ounce cans diced tomatoes, one 6-ounce can tomato paste, ⅔ cup water, ¼ cup fresh parsley, 2 tablespoons fresh basil or 2 teaspoons dried basil, 2 tablespoons fresh oregano or 2 teaspoons dried oregano, 1 tablespoon fresh marjoram or 1 teaspoon dried marjoram, 1 teaspoon sugar, 1 teaspoon salt, and ½ teaspoon black pepper. Simmer, uncovered, for 30 minutes or to desired consistency. Serve as above.

Make-ahead directions: Place sauce in freezer containers. Seal and freeze up to 3 months. To use, thaw overnight in the refrigerator. Transfer to saucepan and heat through.

Per 1 cup pasta + ⅔ cup sauce: 325 cal., 5 g total fat (1 g sat. fat), 0 mg chol., 342 mg sodium, 62 g carbo., 7 g fiber, 12 g pro.
Daily Values: 28% vit. A, 104% vit. C, 5% calcium, 22% iron
Exchanges: 2 Vegetable, 3 Starch, 1 Fat

Spaghetti with Meat Sauce: Prepare as at left, except omit the oil. In a large saucepan cook 12 ounces ground beef or bulk pork sausage with the onion, sweet pepper, celery, and garlic until meat is brown; drain. Continue as in Step 2.

Per 1 cup pasta + ¾ cup sauce: 459 cal., 12 g total fat (4 g sat. fat), 53 mg chol., 386 mg sodium, 62 g carbo., 7 g fiber, 28 g pro.
Daily Values: 28% vit. A, 104% vit. C, 5% calcium, 31% iron
Exchanges: 3½ Starch, 2 Vegetable, 2 Medium-Fat Meat, 1 Fat

Spaghetti with Sauce and Meatballs: Prepare sauce as at left. Meanwhile, in a large bowl combine 1 egg; ¾ cup soft bread crumbs (1 slice); ¼ cup finely chopped onion; 2 tablespoons finely chopped green sweet pepper; ¼ teaspoon dried oregano, crushed; and ¼ teaspoon salt. Add 12 ounces ground beef or bulk pork sausage; mix well. Shape into 24 meatballs. Arrange meatballs in a 15×10×1-inch baking pan. Bake in a 350°F oven for 15 to 20 minutes or until done (160°F); drain. Stir meatballs into sauce. Serve as above.

Per 1 cup pasta + 6 meatballs + ⅔ cup sauce: 535 cal., 17 g total fat (5 g sat. fat), 107 chol., 593 mg sodium, 67 g carbo., 7 g fiber, 31 g pro.
Daily Values: 30% vit. A, 112% vit. C, 7% calcium, 34% iron
Exchanges: 3½ Starch, 2 Vegetable, 2 Medium-Fat Meat, 1 Fat

One-Pot Spaghetti

Start to Finish: 40 minutes **Makes:** 4 servings

- 8 ounces ground beef or bulk pork sausage
- 1 cup sliced fresh mushrooms or one 6-ounce jar sliced mushrooms, drained
- ½ cup chopped onion (1 medium)
- 1 clove garlic, minced
- 1 14-ounce can chicken broth or beef broth
- 1 6-ounce can tomato paste
- 1 teaspoon dried Italian seasoning
- 6 ounces dried spaghetti, broken
- ¼ cup grated Parmesan cheese

1. In a large saucepan cook the ground beef, fresh mushrooms (if using), onion, and garlic until meat is brown and onion is tender; drain.

2. Stir in canned mushrooms (if using), broth, 1¾ cups *water,* tomato paste, Italian seasoning, and ¼ teaspoon *black pepper.* Bring mixture to boiling. Add broken spaghetti, a little at a time, stirring constantly. Return to boiling; reduce heat. Boil gently, uncovered, for 17 to 20 minutes or until spaghetti is tender and sauce is desired consistency, stirring frequently. Serve with Parmesan cheese.

Per 1½ cups: 394 cal., 15 g total fat (6 g sat. fat), 39 mg chol., 926 mg sodium, 44 g carbo., 4 g fiber, 22 g pro.
Daily Values: 23% vit. A, 33% vit. C, 13% calcium, 20% iron
Exchanges: 1 Vegetable, 2½ Starch, 2 Medium-Fat Meat, ½ Fat

Spaghetti with Beef and Mushroom Sauce (LOW FAT) (EASY)

Prep: 15 minutes **Cook:** 20 minutes **Makes:** 6 servings

- 1 pound lean ground beef
- ½ cup chopped onion (1 medium)
- 1 10.75-ounce can condensed cream of mushroom soup
- 1 15-ounce can tomato sauce
- 1 4-ounce can sliced mushrooms, drained (optional)
- 1 teaspoon dried Italian seasoning, crushed
- ¼ teaspoon black pepper
- 12 ounces dried spaghetti
  Grated Parmesan cheese (optional)

1. In a large saucepan cook the ground beef and onion until meat is brown and onion is tender; drain. Stir in mushroom soup, tomato sauce, mushrooms (if desired), Italian seasoning, and pepper. Bring to boiling; reduce heat. Simmer, covered, for 20 minutes, stirring occasionally.

2. Meanwhile, cook spaghetti according to package directions; drain. Serve sauce over hot spaghetti. If desired, sprinkle with Parmesan cheese.

Per 1 cup pasta + ⅔ cup sauce: 398 cal., 11 g total fat (4 g sat. fat), 49 mg chol., 711 mg sodium, 51 g carbo., 3 g fiber, 22 g pro.
Daily Values: 2% vit. C, 3% calcium, 20% iron
Exchanges: ½ Vegetable, 3 Starch, 2 Lean Meat, 1 Fat

Pasta with Bolognese Sauce

Prep: 40 minutes **Cook:** 45 minutes
Makes: 5 to 6 servings

- 12 ounces bulk sweet Italian sausage or ground beef
- 1 cup chopped onion (1 large)
- ½ cup chopped green sweet pepper
- ½ cup chopped carrot (1)
- ¼ cup chopped celery
- 4 cloves garlic, minced
- 3 pounds roma tomatoes, peeled, seeded, and chopped (about 4 cups), or two 14.5-ounce cans tomatoes, undrained and cut up
- 1 6-ounce can tomato paste
- ½ cup dry red wine or beef broth
- 2 tablespoons snipped fresh basil or 1½ teaspoons dried basil, crushed
- 1 tablespoon snipped fresh oregano or 1 teaspoon dried oregano, crushed
- 2 teaspoons snipped fresh marjoram or ½ teaspoon dried marjoram, crushed
- ¼ cup whipping cream
- 2 tablespoons snipped fresh parsley
- 10 ounces dried pasta, such as spaghetti, linguine, or penne

1. In a large saucepan cook the sausage, onion, sweet pepper, carrot, celery, and garlic until meat is brown and onion is tender; drain.

2. Stir in tomato, tomato paste, wine, dried herbs (if using), ½ teaspoon *salt,* and ¼ teaspoon *black pepper.* Bring to boiling; reduce heat. Simmer, covered, for 30 minutes. Uncover; simmer about 10 minutes more or to desired consistency, stirring occasionally. Stir in whipping cream, parsley, and fresh herbs (if using); heat through.

3. Meanwhile, cook pasta according to package directions; drain. Serve sauce over hot pasta.

Per 1½ cups pasta + ½ cup sauce: 549 cal., 21 g total fat (9 g sat. fat), 62 mg chol., 656 mg sodium, 62 g carbo., 5 g fiber, 21 g pro.
Daily Values: 59% vit. A, 68% vit. C, 7% calcium, 20% iron
Exchanges: 2 Vegetable, 3½ Starch, 1 High-Fat Meat, 2 Fat

Fettuccine Alfredo

The butter-and-cream sauce is satiny smooth and divinely rich. Even a small portion satisfies.

Start to Finish: 35 minutes **Makes:** 4 servings

- 8 **ounces dried fettuccine**
- 2 **tablespoons butter**
- 1 **cup whipping cream**
- ½ **teaspoon salt**
- ⅛ **teaspoon freshly ground black pepper**
- ½ **cup freshly grated Parmesan cheese**
   Grated or finely shredded Parmesan cheese (optional)

1. Cook pasta according to package directions.

2. Meanwhile, in a large saucepan melt butter. Add cream, salt, and pepper. Bring to boiling; reduce heat. Boil gently, uncovered, for 3 to 5 minutes or until mixture begins to thicken. Remove from heat and stir in the ½ cup grated Parmesan cheese. Drain pasta. Add pasta to hot sauce. Toss to combine. Transfer to warm serving dish. Serve immediately. If desired, sprinkle with additional Parmesan cheese.

Per 1¼ cups: 515 cal., 32 g total fat (19 g sat. fat), 107 mg chol., 512 mg sodium, 45 g carbo., 1 g fiber, 12 g pro.
Daily Values: 22% vit. A, 1% vit. C, 16% calcium, 10% iron
Exchanges: 3 Starch, 1 Lean Meat, 5 Fat

Chicken and Tomato Fettuccine Alfredo: Prepare as above, except stir 1½ cups chopped cooked chicken and ¼ cup drained oil-packed snipped dried tomatoes into the thickened cream mixture and heat through before adding the ½ cup Parmesan cheese.

Per 1¼ cups: 629 cal., 37 total fat (20 g sat. fat), 154 mg chol., 575 mg sodium, 46 g carbo., 2 g fiber, 28 g pro.
Daily values: 25% vit. A, 12% vit. C, 17% calcium, 14% iron
Exchanges: 3 Starch, 2 Lean Meat, 6 Fat

Shrimp Fettuccine Alfredo: Prepare as above, except stir 12 ounces cooked medium shrimp and 1 tablespoon snipped fresh basil or 1 teaspoon dried basil into the thickened cream mixture and heat through before adding the ½ cup Parmesan cheese.

Per 1¼ cups: 599 cal., 33 total fat (19 g sat. fat), 273 mg chol., 703 mg sodium, 45 g carbo., 21 g fiber, 30 g pro.
Daily values: 27% vit. A, 4% vit. C, 20% calcium, 25% iron
Exchanges: 3 Starch, 1 Lean Meat, 1½ Very Lean Meat, 5½ Fat

Fettuccine alla Carbonara FAST

Start to Finish: 25 minutes **Makes:** 4 servings

- 6 **slices bacon, cut into 1-inch pieces**
- 6 **ounces dried fettuccine or linguine**
- 1 **egg, beaten**
- 1 **cup half-and-half, light cream, or milk**
- 2 **tablespoons butter or margarine**
- ½ **cup grated Parmesan or Romano cheese**
- ¼ **cup snipped fresh parsley**
   Coarsely ground black pepper

1. Cook bacon until crisp; drain.

2. Cook pasta according to package directions; drain and keep warm.

3. Meanwhile, for sauce, in a saucepan combine egg, half-and-half, and butter. Cook and stir over medium heat until egg mixture just coats a metal spoon (about 6 minutes); do not boil. Immediately pour sauce over pasta; stir gently to coat.

4. Add cooked bacon, Parmesan cheese, and parsley; stir gently to combine. Season with pepper. Serve immediately.

Per 1¼ cups: 422 cal., 23 g total fat (13 g sat. fat), 110 mg chol., 489 mg sodium, 35 g carbo., 1 g fiber, 17 g pro.
Daily Values: 17% vit. A, 9% vit. C, 26% calcium, 11% iron
Exchanges: 2½ Starch, 1½ Medium-Fat Meat, 2½ Fat

Chicken Pad Thai

The noodles will seem too firm after soaking but will be perfect after stir-frying.

Prep: 25 minutes **Cook:** 12 minutes **Makes:** 4 servings

- 8 **ounces rice noodles (Vietnamese bahn pho or Thai sen-mee)**
- ¼ **cup salted peanuts, finely chopped**
- ½ **teaspoon grated lime peel**
- 3 **tablespoons fish sauce**
- 2 **tablespoons fresh lime juice**
- 2 **tablespoons packed brown sugar**
- 4½ **teaspoons rice vinegar**
- 1 **tablespoon Asian chile sauce with garlic**
- 3 **tablespoons cooking oil**
- 1 **pound skinless, boneless chicken breast, cut into bite-size strips**
- 1 **tablespoon finely chopped garlic**
- 1 **egg, lightly beaten**
- 1 **cup fresh bean sprouts**
- ⅓ **cup sliced green onion (3)**
- 2 **tablespoons snipped fresh cilantro**

1. Place noodles in a large bowl. Add enough *hot water* to cover them; let stand for 10 to 15 minutes or until the noodles are pliable but not soft. Drain well in a colander.

2. Meanwhile, for peanut topping, combine peanuts and lime peel; set aside.

3. In a small bowl combine fish sauce, lime juice, brown sugar, rice vinegar, and chile sauce; stir until smooth. Set aside.

4. In a 12-inch nonstick skillet heat 1 tablespoon of the oil over medium-high heat. Add chicken and garlic; cook and stir about 6 minutes or until chicken is no longer pink. Transfer to a bowl.

5. Add egg to the hot skillet and cook for 30 seconds. Turn egg with spatula and cook for 30 to 60 seconds more, just until set. Remove egg from skillet; chop egg and set aside.

6. In same skillet heat remaining 2 tablespoons oil over high heat for 30 seconds. Add drained noodles and the sprouts; stir-fry for 2 minutes. Add fish sauce mixture and chicken; cook for 1 to 2 minutes more or until heated through. Divide noodle mixture among four plates. Sprinkle each serving with egg, peanut topping, green onion, and cilantro.

Per 1¼ cups: 565 cal., 19 g total fat (3 g sat. fat), 119 mg chol., 945 mg sodium, 63 g carbo., 3 g fiber, 34 g pro.
Daily Values: 7% vit. A, 17% vit. C, 10% calcium, 14% iron
Exchanges: 3 Starch, 1 Other Carbo., 3½ Very Lean Meat, 3 Fat

Chicken Pad Thai

Lemon Chicken Pasta Toss `LOW FAT`

Multigrain pasta has the nutritional advantages of a whole grain product plus a pleasantly chewy texture. In addition to penne, you may find it in the form of rotini and spaghetti.

Prep: 20 minutes **Cook:** 20 minutes **Makes:** 4 servings

- 2 **cups dried multigrain penne (6 ounces)**
- 12 **ounces skinless, boneless chicken breast halves, cut into 1-inch pieces**
- 2 **tablespoons all-purpose flour**
- 2 **tablespoons olive oil**
- ⅓ **cup finely chopped shallot (3)**
- 2 **cloves garlic, minced**
- ¾ **cup chicken broth**
- 3 **tablespoons lemon juice**
- ¼ **teaspoon salt**
- ¼ **teaspoon black pepper**
- 3 **tablespoons capers, drained**
- 3 **tablespoons snipped fresh Italian parsley**
  Freshly grated Parmesan cheese (optional)

1. Cook pasta according to package directions; drain. Return pasta to hot saucepan; cover and keep warm.

2. Meanwhile, in a bowl toss together chicken and flour until chicken is lightly coated. In a large skillet cook and stir chicken in 1 tablespoon of the oil over medium-high heat for 6 to 8 minutes or until chicken is no longer pink. Remove chicken from pan; set aside.

3. Reduce heat to medium. Add remaining oil to skillet. Add shallot and garlic; cook and stir about 1 minute or until tender. Carefully stir in broth, lemon juice, salt, and pepper. Cook, uncovered, for 2 to 3 minutes or until reduced to about ⅔ cup. Stir in chicken, capers, and parsley; heat through.

4. Toss pasta with chicken mixture. If desired, serve with Parmesan cheese.

Lemon Shrimp Pasta Toss: Prepare as above, except substitute 12 ounces peeled, deveined shrimp for the chicken. Cook and stir in skillet for 2 to 3 minutes or until shrimp are opaque.

Per 1½ cups chicken or shrimp variation: 339 cal., 9 g total fat (1 g sat. fat), 50 mg chol., 589 mg sodium, 36 g carbo., 4 g fiber, 29 g pro.
Daily Values: 9% vit. A, 18% vit. C, 4% calcium, 15% iron
Exchanges: 2½ Starch, 3 Very Lean Meat, 1 Fat

White Bean and Sausage Rigatoni

Like many northern Italian specialties, this one-dish meal stretches flavorful sausage with white beans. Cannellini are traditional, but any white bean will work.

Start to Finish: 20 minutes **Makes:** 4 servings

- 2 cups dried rigatoni (8 ounces)
- 1 15-ounce can white kidney beans (cannellini), Great Northern beans, or navy beans, rinsed and drained
- 1 14.5-ounce can Italian-style stewed tomatoes, undrained
- 8 ounces cooked smoked turkey sausage, halved lengthwise and cut into ½-inch slices
- ⅓ cup thinly sliced fresh basil or 1 tablespoon dried basil, crushed
- ¼ cup shredded Asiago or Parmesan cheese (1 ounce)

1. Cook pasta according to package directions. Drain; return pasta to saucepan.

2. Meanwhile, in a large saucepan combine beans, undrained tomatoes, sausage, and dried basil (if using). Cook and stir until heated through. Add bean mixture and fresh basil (if using) to pasta; stir gently to combine. To serve, sprinkle each serving with cheese.

Per 2 cups: 432 cal., 10 g total fat (3 g sat. fat), 46 mg chol., 961 mg sodium, 65 g carbo., 7 g fiber, 25 g pro.
Daily Values: 4% vit. A, 3% vit. C, 11% calcium, 23% iron
Exchanges: ½ Vegetable, 4 Starch, 2 Lean Meat

White Bean and Sausage Rigatoni

Bow Ties with Sausage and Sweet Peppers

Start to Finish: 25 minutes **Makes:** 4 servings

- 4 cups dried large bow ties (8 ounces)
- 12 ounces spicy Italian sausage links
- 2 medium red sweet peppers, cut into ¾-inch pieces (1½ cups)
- ½ cup vegetable broth or beef broth
- ¼ teaspoon coarsely ground black pepper
- ¼ cup snipped fresh Italian parsley

1. Cook pasta according to package directions. Drain; keep warm.

2. Meanwhile, cut the sausage into 1-inch pieces. In a large skillet cook sausage and sweet pepper over medium-high heat until sausage is brown; drain.

3. Add the broth and black pepper to skillet. Bring to boiling; reduce heat. Simmer, uncovered, for 5 minutes. Remove from heat. Pour over pasta; add parsley. Stir gently to coat.

Per 2 cups: 476 cal., 20 g total fat (8 g sat. fat), 57 mg chol., 597 mg sodium, 47 g carbo., 3 g fiber, 20 g pro.
Daily Values: 62% vit. A, 151% vit. C, 3% calcium, 16% iron
Exchanges: 1 Vegetable, 3 Starch, 2 High-Fat Meat

Fettuccine with Asparagus and Ham

Start to Finish: 25 minutes **Makes:** 4 servings

- 8 ounces dried fettuccine, broken
- 1 pound fresh asparagus, bias-sliced into 1½-inch pieces
- 1 tablespoon olive oil or cooking oil
- 4 roma tomatoes, chopped (2 cups)
- 3 ounces cooked ham, cut into thin strips (½ cup)
- ⅓ cup grated Parmesan cheese

1. Cook fettuccine according to package directions. Drain; keep warm.

2. Meanwhile, in a large skillet cook and stir asparagus in hot oil about 4 minutes or until nearly tender. Add tomato and ham; cook about 2 minutes more or until heated through. Add asparagus mixture to fettuccine; stir gently to combine. Sprinkle with Parmesan cheese. Season to taste with *salt* and *black pepper*.

Per 1½ cups: 350 cal., 9 g total fat (3 g sat. fat), 21 mg chol., 744 mg sodium, 47 g carbo., 3 g fiber, 19 g pro.
Daily Values: 11% vit. A, 46% vit. C, 14% calcium, 15% iron
Exchanges: 1 Vegetable, 2½ Starch, 1½ Medium-Fat Meat

Pasta with White Clam Sauce FAST

Start to Finish: 30 minutes **Makes:** 4 servings

- **10 ounces dried linguine or fettuccine**
- **2 6.5-ounce cans chopped or minced clams**
  Half-and-half, light cream, or whole milk (about 2 cups)
- **½ cup chopped onion (1 medium)**
- **2 cloves garlic, minced**
- **2 tablespoons butter or margarine**
- **¼ cup all-purpose flour**
- **2 teaspoons snipped fresh oregano or ½ teaspoon dried oregano, crushed**
- **¼ teaspoon salt**
- **¼ cup snipped fresh parsley**
- **¼ cup dry white wine, nonalcoholic dry white wine, or chicken broth**
- **¼ cup finely shredded Parmesan cheese**

1. Cook pasta according to package directions. Drain; keep warm. Meanwhile, drain canned clams, reserving the juice from one of the cans (you should have about ½ cup). Add enough of the half-and-half to the reserved clam juice to equal 2½ cups liquid. Set clams and clam juice mixture aside.

2. In a medium saucepan cook onion and garlic in hot butter until tender but not brown. Stir in flour, dried oregano (if using), salt, and ⅛ teaspoon *black pepper*. Add clam juice mixture all at once. Cook and stir until thickened and bubbly. Cook and stir for 1 minute more. Stir in drained clams, fresh oregano (if using), parsley, and wine; heat through. Serve over warm pasta. Sprinkle with Parmesan cheese.

Per 1¼ cups pasta + ¾ cup sauce: 595 cal., 23 g total fat (13 g sat. fat), 88 mg chol., 369 mg sodium, 69 g carbo., 2 g fiber, 25 g pro.
Daily Values: 24% vit. A, 26% vit. C, 25% calcium, 71% iron
Exchanges: 4½ Starch, 2 Very Lean Meat, 4 Fat

Salmon-Sauced Pasta FAST

Start to Finish: 20 minutes **Makes:** 4 servings

- **2⅔ cups dried cavatappi or penne (8 ounces)**
- **3 cups broccoli florets**
- **1 small green or red sweet pepper, cut into bite-size strips**
- **½ cup chopped onion (1 medium)**
- **1 tablespoon butter or margarine**
- **1 10-ounce container refrigerated Alfredo sauce**
- **¼ cup milk**
- **⅛ teaspoon black pepper**
- **3 ounces lox-style smoked salmon, coarsely chopped**
- **2 teaspoons snipped fresh dill or ½ teaspoon dried dill**

1. Cook pasta according to package directions, except add broccoli the last 3 minutes of cooking. Drain; keep warm.

2. Meanwhile, for sauce, in a medium saucepan cook and stir sweet pepper and onion in hot butter until tender. Stir in Alfredo sauce, milk, and black pepper; heat through. Gently stir in salmon and dill; heat through. Serve sauce over hot pasta mixture.

Per 1½ cups pasta + ⅔ cup sauce: 530 cal., 28 g total fat (2 g sat. fat), 50 mg chol., 737 mg sodium, 55 g carbo., 4 g fiber, 18 g pro.
Daily Values: 13% vit. A, 121% vit. C, 7% calcium, 14% iron
Exchanges: 1 Vegetable, 3 Starch, 1 Very Lean Meat, 5 Fat

Crab and Spinach Pasta with Fontina

Keep these five ingredients on hand, and you can make this tasty recipe at your convenience.

Prep: 30 minutes **Bake:** 30 minutes **Oven:** 375°F
Stand: 10 minutes **Makes:** 6 servings

- **3½ cups dried bow ties (8 ounces)**
- **1 10-ounce package frozen chopped spinach, thawed and well drained**
- **2 6- to 6.5-ounce cans crabmeat, drained, flaked, and cartilage removed**
- **1 26-ounce jar tomato-based pasta sauce**
- **1½ cups shredded fontina cheese (6 ounces)**

1. Cook pasta according to package directions; drain. Meanwhile, in a medium bowl combine spinach and crabmeat.

2. Cover bottom of a 2-quart square baking dish with 1 cup of the pasta sauce. Top with pasta. Top pasta evenly with crab mixture. Sprinkle with half of the cheese. Top with remaining sauce. Sprinkle with remaining cheese.

3. Bake, uncovered, in a 375°F oven for 30 to 35 minutes or until sauce is bubbly around edges and cheese is slightly golden brown. Let stand for 10 minutes before serving.

Per 1½ cups: 377 cal., 11 g total fat (6 g sat. fat), 83 mg chol., 1,064 mg sodium, 45 g carbo., 5 g fiber, 29 g pro.
Daily Values: 74% vit. A, 23% vit. C, 29% calcium, 19% iron
Exchanges: 1½ Vegetable, 2 Starch, ½ Other Carbo., 1 High-Fat Meat, 1½ Very Lean Meat

Pasta with Shrimp and Asparagus

Pasta with Shrimp and Asparagus

Start to Finish: 40 minutes **Makes:** 4 servings

- 1 pound fresh or frozen shrimp in shells or 8 ounces chilled cooked shrimp
- 1 pound thin fresh asparagus spears
- 8 ounces dried linguine
- 3 cloves garlic, minced
- 1 tablespoon olive oil
- 8 medium roma tomatoes, seeded and coarsely chopped (4 cups)
- 2 tablespoons tomato paste
- ⅓ cup dry white wine
- ½ teaspoon salt
- ¼ teaspoon freshly ground black pepper
- 1 tablespoon butter or margarine
- 2 tablespoons finely shredded fresh basil
  Salt and freshly ground balck pepper

1. Thaw shrimp, if frozen. Peel and devein shrimp, leaving tails intact, if desired (see page 296). Rinse shrimp; pat dry with paper towels. Set aside.

2. Snap off and discard woody bases from asparagus spears. Bias-slice the asparagus into 1- to 1½-inch pieces. Cook pasta according to package directions; drain. Return pasta to pan; cover and keep warm.

3. Meanwhile, in a large skillet cook and stir garlic in hot oil over medium heat for 15 seconds. Add tomato and tomato paste; cook and stir for 3 minutes.

4. Add asparagus, wine, the ½ teaspoon salt, and the ¼ teaspoon pepper. Bring to boiling; reduce heat. Cook, uncovered, for 3 minutes. Stir in shrimp. Cook, uncovered, for 2 to 3 minutes more or until shrimp are opaque. Stir in butter until melted.

5. To serve, add the shrimp mixture and basil to pasta; toss gently to coat. Season to taste with additional salt and black pepper.

Per 1¾ cups: 425 cal., 9 g total fat (3 g sat. fat), 137 mg chol., 529 mg sodium, 55 g carbo., 5 g fiber, 28 g pro.
Daily Values: 43% vit. A, 47% vit. C, 9% calcium, 32% iron
Exchanges: 1½ Vegetable, 3 Starch, 2½ Very Lean Meat, ½ Fat

Shanghai Pasta

Start to Finish: 30 minutes **Makes:** 4 servings

- 8 ounces dried fusilli, linguine, or spaghetti
- 3 tablespoons soy sauce
- 1 tablespoon bottled plum sauce
- 1 teaspoon toasted sesame oil
- ½ teaspoon red chile paste (optional)
- 1 medium red and/or green sweet pepper, cut into bite-size pieces
- 1 cup fresh green beans, cut into 1-inch pieces, or 1 cup pea pods, trimmed
- 1 tablespoon cooking oil
- 12 ounces frozen peeled and deveined large shrimp without tails, thawed (26 to 30 shrimp per pound count)
- 1 teaspoon grated fresh ginger
- ¼ teaspoon black pepper
- 2 cloves garlic, minced
- 2 green onions, bias-sliced into 1-inch pieces
- 2 teaspoons sesame seeds, toasted (see tip, page 265)

1. Cook pasta according to package directions; drain. Set aside; keep warm. For sauce, stir together soy sauce, plum sauce, sesame oil, and, if desired, chile paste; set aside.

2. In a wok or large skillet stir-fry sweet pepper and beans in hot oil for 5 minutes. Push from center of wok. Add shrimp, ginger, black pepper, and garlic to center of wok. Cook and stir for 2 to 3 minutes or until shrimp are opaque. Stir in sauce. Stir in pasta; heat through. To serve, top with green onion and sesame seeds.

Per 1¼ cups: 387 cal., 8 g total fat (1 g sat. fat), 129 mg chol., 850 mg sodium, 51 g carbo., 3 g fiber, 27 g pro.
Daily Values: 39% vit. A, 92% vit. C, 8% calcium, 27% iron
Exchanges: ½ Vegetable, 2½ Starch, ½ Other Carbo., 3 Very Lean Meat, 1 Fat

Linguine with Scallops and Capers LOW FAT FAST

Prep: 15 minutes **Cook:** 15 minutes **Makes:** 6 servings

- 1 pound fresh or frozen scallops
- 12 ounces dried linguine
- 2 tablespoons butter
- 2 tablespoons olive oil
- 1 14-ounce can chicken broth
- ¾ cup dry vermouth or dry white wine
- 3 tablespoons lemon juice
- ¾ cup sliced green onion (6)
- ¾ cup snipped fresh parsley
- 2 tablespoons capers, drained
- 1 teaspoon dried dill
- ¼ teaspoon black pepper

1. Thaw scallops, if frozen. Cut any large scallops in half; set aside. Cook linguine according to package directions; drain and keep warm.

2. Meanwhile, in a 12-inch skillet cook and stir scallops in hot butter and oil over medium-high heat about 2 minutes or until scallops are opaque. Remove scallops with slotted spoon; reserve juices in skillet.

3. Stir broth, vermouth, and lemon juice into juices in skillet. Bring to boiling; reduce heat. Simmer, uncovered, for 8 to 10 minutes or until liquid is reduced to about 1¼ cups. Stir in green onion, parsley, capers, dill, and pepper. Simmer, uncovered, for 1 minute more. Add scallops. Cook and stir just until heated through. Pour over linguine; toss gently to combine.

Per 1 cup pasta + ¾ cup sauce: 398 cal., 10 g total fat (3 g sat. fat), 36 mg chol., 516 mg sodium, 47 g carbo., 2 g fiber, 21 g pro.
Daily Values: 19% vit. A, 30% vit. C, 6% calcium, 16% iron
Exchanges: 2½ Starch, ½ Other Carbo., 2 Very Lean Meat, 2 Fat

Creamy Herbed Pasta
FAST VEGETARIAN

Reduced-fat cream cheese is the base for the quick sauce. It nicely coats any shape of pasta.

Start to Finish: 30 minutes **Makes:** 4 servings

- 4 cups dried rigatoni or other dried pasta (10 ounces)
- ¼ cup snipped fresh basil or 1 tablespoon dried basil, crushed
- 4 cloves garlic, minced
- 1 tablespoon olive oil or cooking oil

- ½ of an 8-ounce package reduced-fat cream cheese (Neufchâtel)
- ½ cup low-fat cottage cheese
- ⅓ cup finely shredded Parmesan cheese
- ¾ cup milk
- ¼ cup snipped fresh parsley
- ¼ teaspoon salt
- 2 tablespoons dry white wine or milk

1. Cook pasta according to package directions; drain and keep warm.

2. Meanwhile, for sauce, in a heavy medium saucepan cook basil and garlic in hot oil about 30 seconds. Reduce heat. Add cream cheese, cottage cheese, and Parmesan cheese. Cook and stir until nearly smooth. Stir in milk, parsley, and salt until combined; add wine. Bring to a gentle boil; reduce heat. Cook and stir for 2 to 3 minutes or until slightly thickened. Serve sauce over hot pasta.

Per 1½ cups pasta + ½ cup sauce: 448 cal., 14 g total fat (7 g sat. fat), 31 mg chol., 511 mg sodium, 58 g carbo., 2 g fiber, 20 g pro.
Daily Values: 18% vit. A, 11% vit. C, 20% calcium, 15% iron
Exchanges: 4 Starch, 1 Lean Meat, 1½ Fat

Creamy Ham and Broccoli Pasta: Prepare as above, except omit parsley and wine. Stir ¾ cup chopped cooked broccoli and ¾ cup chopped cooked ham into thickened sauce; heat through.

Per 1½ cups pasta + ⅔ cup sauce: 493 cal., 16 g fat (7 g sat. fat), 45 mg chol., 850 mg sodium, 61 g carbo., 3 g fiber, 25 g pro.
Daily Values: 23% vit. A, 36% vit. C, 21% calcium, 16% iron
Exchanges: 4 Starch, 2 Lean Meat, 1½ Fat

Creamy Smoked Chicken Pasta: Prepare as above, except stir 1 cup chopped smoked chicken or turkey into thickened sauce; heat through.

Per 1½ cups pasta + ⅔ cup sauce: 486 cal., 15 g fat (7 g sat. fat), 46 mg chol., 884 mg sodium, 60 g carbo., 2 g fiber, 27 g pro.
Daily Values: 18% vit. A, 11% vit. C, 20% calcium, 15% iron
Exchanges: 4 Starch, 2 Lean Meat, 1½ Fat

Creamy Pasta with Scallops: Halve 12 ounces sea scallops. In a large saucepan cook and stir scallops in 1 tablespoon hot oil for 1 to 2 minutes or until scallops are opaque. Remove from pan; set aside. In same saucepan prepare sauce as above, except stir scallops into thickened sauce; heat through.

Per 1½ cups pasta + ⅔ cup sauce: 553 cal., 18 g fat (7 g sat. fat), 59 mg chol., 627 mg sodium, 60 g carbo., 2 g fiber, 34 g pro.
Daily Values: 19% vit. A, 14% vit. C, 22% calcium, 16% iron
Exchanges: 4 Starch, 1 Lean Meat, 2 Very Lean Meat, 2 Fat

Rotini and Sweet Pepper Primavera `LOW FAT` `FAST` `VEGETARIAN`

Start to Finish: 20 minutes **Makes:** 4 servings

- 1 **pound fresh asparagus spears**
- 3 **cups dried rotini or gemelli (8 ounces)**
- 1 **large red or yellow sweet pepper, cut into 1-inch pieces**
- 1 **cup sliced zucchini or yellow summer squash**
- 1 **10-ounce container refrigerated light Alfredo sauce**
- 2 **tablespoons snipped fresh tarragon or thyme**
- ¼ **teaspoon crushed red pepper**

1. Snap off and discard woody bases from asparagus spears. Bias-slice the asparagus into 1-inch pieces.

2. Cook pasta according to package directions, adding asparagus, sweet pepper, and squash the last 3 minutes of cooking; drain. Return pasta mixture to hot saucepan to keep warm.

3. Meanwhile, for sauce, in a small saucepan combine Alfredo sauce, the 2 tablespoons tarragon, and crushed red pepper. Cook and stir over medium heat about 5 minutes or until sauce is heated through. Pour sauce over pasta mixture; stir gently to coat.

Per 1½ cups: 353 cal., 9 g total fat (4 g sat. fat), 23 mg chol., 326 mg sodium, 55 g carbo., 4 g fiber, 11 g pro.
Daily Values: 47% vit. A, 107% vit. C, 18% calcium, 13% iron
Exchanges: 2 Vegetable, 3 Starch, 1½ Fat

Cream-Sauced Pasta with Vegetables `FAST` `VEGETARIAN`

See photo, page 409.

Start to Finish: 30 minutes **Makes:** 4 servings

- 8 **ounces dried mafalda or 3 cups dried rotini**
- 1 **medium onion, halved lengthwise and thinly sliced**
- 2 **cloves garlic, minced**
- 1 **tablespoon olive oil or butter**
- 1¼ **pounds fresh asparagus, trimmed and cut into 2-inch pieces (2 cups)**
- 1 **medium yellow summer squash or zucchini, halved lengthwise and sliced (2 cups)**
- ½ **teaspoon salt**
- ¼ **teaspoon black pepper**
- 1 **cup whipping cream**
- 4 **roma tomatoes, seeded and chopped (2 cups)**

1. Cook pasta according to package directions; drain. Return pasta to hot pan and keep warm.

2. Meanwhile, in a large skillet cook onion and garlic in hot oil over medium heat about 3 minutes or until nearly tender, stirring occasionally. Add asparagus, squash, salt, and pepper to skillet. Cook for 3 to 5 minutes more or until vegetables are crisp-tender, stirring occasionally. Add vegetables to pasta in pan.

3. Add whipping cream to skillet; bring to boiling. Boil gently for 5 minutes or until reduced to ¾ cup. To serve, pour reduced cream over pasta mixture; stir gently to coat. Stir in tomato.

Per 2 cups: 494 cal., 27 g total fat (14 g sat. fat), 82 mg chol., 323 mg sodium, 54 g carbo., 5 g fiber, 12 g pro.
Daily Values: 44% vit. A, 34% vit. C, 9% calcium, 21% iron
Exchanges: 1½ Vegetable, 3 Starch, 5 Fat

Cream-Sauced Pasta with Sausage: Prepare as above, except stir 9 ounces fully cooked Italian sausage links, cut into bite-size pieces, into reduced cream; heat through. Makes 5 servings.

Per 2 cups: 559 cal., 35 g total fat (16 g sat. fat), 106 mg chol., 4 mg sodium, 44 g carbo., 4 g fiber, 19 g pro.
Daily Values: 35% vit. A, 29% vit. C, 8% calcium, 21% iron
Exchanges: 1½ Vegetable, 2½ Starch, 1½ High-Fat Meat, 4 Fat

Tortellini with Roasted Red Pepper Sauce `LOW FAT` `FAST`

Start to Finish: 20 minutes **Makes:** 6 servings

- 2 **9-ounce packages refrigerated meat- or cheese-filled tortellini or one 7- to 8-ounce package dried cheese-filled tortellini**
- 2 **12-ounce jars roasted red sweet peppers, drained**
- 1 **cup chopped onion (1 large)**
- 4 **cloves garlic, minced**
- 1 **tablespoon olive oil**
- 2 **tablespoons snipped fresh basil or 1 teaspoon dried basil, crushed**
- 1 **teaspoon sugar**
- ½ **teaspoon salt**
- ¼ **cup finely shredded Asiago or Parmesan cheese**

1. Cook the tortellini according to package directions; drain. Return pasta to hot pan and keep warm.

2. Meanwhile, place roasted sweet peppers in a food processor. Cover and process until almost smooth; set aside.

3. For sauce, in a medium saucepan cook the onion and garlic in hot oil over medium heat until tender. Add pureed peppers, basil, sugar, and salt. Cook and stir until heated through. Pour sauce over tortellini; toss to coat. Sprinkle with Asiago cheese.

Per cup: 324 cal., 8 g total fat (1 g sat. fat), 55 mg chol., 633 mg sodium, 47 g carbo., 2 g fiber, 16 g pro.
Daily Values: 1% vit. A, 230% vit. C, 5% calcium, 4% iron
Exchanges: 1 Vegetable, 2½ Starch, 1 Lean Meat, 1 Fat

Mushroom Stroganoff
LOW FAT VEGETARIAN

The meaty texture of mushrooms makes this meatless pasta entrée especially satisfying.

Start to Finish: 35 minutes **Makes:** 4 servings

- 8 ounces dried fettuccine
- 1 8-ounce carton light dairy sour cream
- 2 tablespoons all-purpose flour
- ¾ cup water
- 1 vegetable bouillon cube, crumbled
- ¼ teaspoon black pepper
- 2 medium onions, cut into thin wedges
- 2 tablespoons butter or margarine
- 4½ cups (about 12 ounces) sliced mushrooms (such as shiitake [stems removed], button, and/or cremini)
- 1 clove garlic, minced
- Snipped fresh chives

1. Cook fettuccine according to package directions; drain and keep warm. In a small bowl stir together the sour cream and flour. Stir in the water, bouillon, and pepper; set aside.

2. In a large skillet cook onion in hot butter over medium heat about 5 minutes or until onion is tender, stirring frequently. Stir in mushrooms and garlic. Cook and stir about 5 minutes more or until vegetables are tender. Remove mushroom mixture from skillet and add to drained pasta; keep warm.

3. Wipe out skillet. Stir the sour cream mixture into the skillet. Cook and stir until thickened and bubbly. Cook and stir for 1 minute more. Pour the sour cream mixture over the pasta and mushroom mixture, stirring gently to coat. To serve, sprinkle with chives.

Per 2 cups: 459 cal., 12 g total fat (7 g sat. fat), 35 mg chol., 355 mg sodium, 76 g carbo., 6 g fiber, 14 g pro.
Daily Values: 13% vit. A, 5% vit. C, 14% calcium, 15% iron
Exchanges: 2 Vegetable, 4 Starch, 1½ Fat

Fresh Tomato and Arugula Pasta
LOW FAT FAST VEGETARIAN

See photo of Fresh Tomato and Arugula Pasta with Chicken, page 409.

Start to Finish: 30 minutes **Makes:** 4 servings

- 2⅔ cups dried ziti or mostaccioli (8 ounces)
- 1 medium onion, thinly sliced
- 2 cloves garlic, minced
- 1 tablespoon olive oil
- 3 cups coarsely chopped, seeded tomato (6 medium)
- ⅛ to ¼ teaspoon crushed red pepper (optional)
- 4 cups arugula and/or spinach, coarsely chopped
- ¼ cup pine nuts or slivered almonds, toasted (see tip, page 265)
- ¼ cup crumbled Gorgonzola cheese or Parmesan cheese (1 ounce)

1. Cook pasta according to package directions; drain and keep warm.

2. Meanwhile, in a large skillet cook onion and garlic in hot olive oil over medium heat until onion is tender. Add tomato, ½ teaspoon *salt*, ¼ teaspoon *black pepper,* and, if desired, crushed red pepper. Cook and stir over medium-high heat about 2 minutes or until tomato is warm and releases some of its juices. Stir in arugula; heat just until greens wilt.

3. To serve, top pasta with tomato mixture; sprinkle with toasted pine nuts and cheese.

Per 1 cup pasta + ¾ cup sauce: 362 cal., 12 g total fat (3 g sat. fat), 6 mg chol., 424 mg sodium, 53 g carbo., 4 g fiber, 13 g pro.
Daily Values: 33% vit. A, 36% vit. C, 11% calcium, 19% iron
Exchanges: 2 Vegetable, 3 Starch, ½ High-Fat Meat, 1 Fat

Fresh Tomato and Arugula Pasta with Chicken: Prepare as above, except stir 2 cups chopped deli-roasted chicken into tomato mixture along with arugula.

Per 1 cup pasta + ½ cup sauce: 495 cal., 17 g total fat (4 g sat. fat), 69 mg chol., 53 g carbo., 4 g fiber, 34 g pro.
Daily Values: 34% vit. A, 36% vit. C, 12% calcium, 23% iron
Exchanges: 2 Vegetable, 3 Starch, ½ High-Fat Meat, 2½ Lean Meat, ½ Fat

Farmer's Market Supper

Enjoy fresh flavor any time of year.

- *Fresh Tomato and Arugula Pasta (above)*
- *Olive focaccia wedges*
- *Blackberry Gelato (page 292)*

Herbed Pasta Primavera

Herbed Pasta Primavera

LOW FAT · VEGETARIAN · WHOLE GRAIN

Start to Finish: 40 minutes **Makes:** 4 servings

1¾ cups dried multigrain or whole wheat penne pasta (8 ounces)

8 ounces packaged peeled baby carrots, halved lengthwise (1¾ cups)

1 tablespoon olive oil

8 ounces fresh green beans, trimmed and cut into 2-inch pieces (1½ cups)

½ cup sliced green onion or chopped onion

¾ cup chicken broth

2 cloves garlic, minced

1 medium zucchini and/or yellow summer squash, halved lengthwise and sliced ¼ inch thick (2 cups)

2 tablespoons snipped fresh basil or 1 teaspoon dried basil, crushed

¼ teaspoon salt

¼ cup sliced almonds, toasted (see tip, page 265)

Grated or finely shredded Parmesan cheese (optional)

Cracked black pepper

1. Cook pasta according to package directions; drain. Return penne to hot saucepan; cover and keep warm.

2. Meanwhile, in a large skillet cook and stir carrots in hot olive oil for 5 minutes. Add green beans, green onion, broth, and garlic. Reduce heat and simmer, uncovered, for 3 minutes, stirring occasionally. Stir in squash. Simmer, uncovered, for 4 to 5 minutes or until vegetables are crisp-tender, stirring occasionally.

3. Toss vegetable mixture, basil, and salt with pasta. Sprinkle with almonds, cheese (if desired), and pepper.

Per 1¾ cups: 284 cal., 9 g total fat (1 g sat. fat), 0 mg chol., 375 mg sodium, 42 g carbo., 7 g fiber, 12 g pro.
Daily Values: 12% vit. A, 35% vit. C, 9% calcium, 15% iron
Exchanges: 2 Vegetable, 2 Starch, 1½ Fat

Rigatoni and Eggplant with Dried Tomato Pesto VEGETARIAN

Start to Finish: 35 minutes
Oven: 425°F **Makes:** 4 servings

1 medium onion, cut into 8 wedges

2 tablespoons olive oil

1 medium eggplant (about 1 pound), halved lengthwise

2 cups dried rigatoni or penne (6 ounces)

⅓ recipe Dried Tomato Pesto or ⅓ cup purchased dried tomato pesto

¼ teaspoon coarsely ground black pepper

2 tablespoons crumbled goat cheese or feta cheese (optional)

1. Place onion wedges in a large shallow baking pan; brush with 1 tablespoon of the olive oil. Roast onion in a 425°F oven for 10 minutes; stir. Brush eggplant halves with remaining 1 tablespoon olive oil. Place eggplant in pan, cut sides down. Roast 15 minutes more or until onion is golden brown and eggplant is tender.

2. Meanwhile, cook pasta according to package directions; drain. Add pesto and pepper to pasta; stir gently to coat. Transfer pasta to a warm serving dish; keep warm.

3. Cut eggplant into ½-inch-thick slices. Gently stir eggplant and onion into pasta; season to taste with *salt*. If desired, top with cheese.

Dried Tomato Pesto: Drain ¾ cup oil-packed dried tomatoes, reserving oil. Add enough olive oil to reserved oil to make ½ cup; set aside. Place tomatoes, ¼ cup pine nuts or slivered almonds, ¼ cup snipped fresh basil, ½ teaspoon salt, and 8 cloves garlic, chopped, in a food processor. Cover; process until finely chopped. With machine running, slowly add the ½ cup oil, processing until almost smooth. Divide pesto into three portions. Chill extra portions for up to 2 days or freeze for up to 3 months.

Per 2 cups: 370 cal., 19 g total fat (3 g sat. fat), 0 mg chol., 121 mg sodium, 43 g carbo., 5 g fiber, 8 g pro.
Daily Values: 4% vit. A, 18% vit. C, 3% calcium, 12% iron
Exchanges: 2½ Vegetable, 2 Starch, 3½ Fat

Pleasures of Pesto

For six side-dish servings, cook 6 ounces dried pasta according to package directions, drain, and toss with ¼ cup pesto.

Classic Genovese Pesto: In a food processor or blender combine ⅓ cup olive oil; 2 cups firmly packed fresh basil leaves; ½ cup pine nuts; ½ cup grated Parmesan cheese; 3 to 4 cloves garlic, peeled and quartered; and ¼ teaspoon salt. Cover and process or blend until nearly smooth, stopping and scraping sides as necessary and adding enough of 2 tablespoons additional olive oil to reach desired consistency. Add black pepper to taste. Makes ¾ cup.

Per tablespoon: 92 cal., 9 g total fat (2 g sat. fat), 3 mg chol., 111 mg sodium, 2 g carbo., 0 g fiber, 3 g pro.
Daily Values: 6% vit. A, 3% vit. C, 6% calcium, 5% iron
Exchanges: 2 Fat

Greek Pesto: In a food processor or blender combine ⅓ cup olive oil; 2 cups firmly packed fresh lemon basil leaves or basil leaves; one 2.25-ounce can sliced, pitted ripe olives; ½ cup crumbled feta cheese; 4 cloves garlic, peeled and quartered; and ¼ teaspoon salt. Cover and process or blend as above, adding enough of 2 tablespoons additional olive oil to reach desired consistency. Add black pepper to taste. Makes 1⅓ cups.

Per tablespoon: 45 cal., 4 g total fat (1 g sat. fat), 3 mg chol., 94 mg sodium, 1 g carbo., 0 g fiber, 1 g pro.
Daily Values: 4% vit. A, 2% vit. C, 3% calcium, 2% iron
Exchanges: 1 Fat

Thai Pesto: In a food processor or blender combine ⅓ cup olive oil, 2 cups firmly packed fresh basil leaves, ½ cup peanuts, ½ cup crumbled goat cheese, 1 teaspoon finely shredded lime peel, ½ teaspoon crushed red pepper, and ¼ teaspoon salt. Cover and process or blend as above, adding enough of 2 tablespoons additional olive oil to reach desired consistency. Add black pepper to taste. Makes 1 cup.

Per tablespoon: 81 cal., 8 g total fat (2 g sat. fat), 3 mg chol., 74 mg sodium, 1 g carbo., 1 g fiber, 2 g pro.
Daily Values: 5% vit. A, 2% vit. C, 2% calcium, 2% iron
Exchanges: 2 Fat

To store: Divide pesto into ¼-cup portions. Place portions in airtight containers; chill for 2 days or freeze for 3 months.

FAVORITE ▼ Spaghetti Pie LOW FAT

To form the crust, use a large wooden spoon or a rubber spatula to press the spaghetti onto the bottom and up the sides of the pie plate.

Prep: 30 minutes **Bake:** 20 minutes
Oven: 350°F **Makes:** 6 servings

- 4 ounces dried spaghetti
- 1 tablespoon butter or margarine
- 1 egg, beaten
- ¼ cup grated Parmesan cheese
- 8 ounces ground beef or bulk Italian sausage
- ½ cup chopped onion (1 medium)
- ½ cup chopped green sweet pepper
- 1 clove garlic, minced
- 1 8-ounce can tomato sauce
- 1 teaspoon dried oregano, crushed
  Nonstick cooking spray
- 1 cup low-fat cottage cheese, drained
- ½ cup shredded part-skim mozzarella cheese (2 ounces)

1. Cook spaghetti according to package directions; drain. Return spaghetti to hot saucepan and keep warm.

2. Stir butter into hot pasta until melted. Stir in egg and Parmesan cheese; set aside.

3. Meanwhile, in a medium skillet cook ground beef, onion, sweet pepper, and garlic over medium heat until meat is brown and onion is tender. Drain off fat. Stir in tomato sauce and oregano; heat through.

4. Coat a 9-inch pie plate with nonstick cooking spray. Press spaghetti mixture onto bottom and up sides of pie plate, forming a crust. Spread cottage cheese on the bottom and up the sides of pasta crust. Spread meat mixture over cottage cheese. Sprinkle with mozzarella cheese.

5. Bake in a 350°F oven for 20 to 25 minutes or until bubbly and heated through. To serve, cut into wedges.

Per wedge: 270 cal., 11 g total fat (6 g sat. fat), 76 mg chol., 500 mg sodium, 20 g carbo., 1 g fiber, 21 g pro.
Daily Values: 7% vit. A, 17% vit. C, 16% calcium, 11% iron
Exchanges: ½ Vegetable, 1 Starch, 2½ Medium-Fat Meat

Eight-Layer Casserole

See photo, page 409.

Prep: 30 minutes **Bake:** 55 minutes **Oven:** 350°F
Stand: 10 minutes **Makes:** 8 servings

- **3 cups dried medium noodles (6 ounces)**
- **1 pound ground beef**
- **2 8-ounce cans tomato sauce**
- **1 teaspoon dried basil, crushed**
- **½ teaspoon sugar**
- **½ teaspoon garlic powder**
- **¼ teaspoon salt**
- **¼ teaspoon black pepper**
- **1 8-ounce carton dairy sour cream**
- **1 8-ounce package cream cheese, softened**
- **½ cup milk**
- **⅓ cup chopped onion (1 small)**
- **1 10-ounce package frozen chopped spinach, thawed and well drained**
- **1 cup shredded cheddar cheese (4 ounces)**

1. Grease a 2-quart casserole or a 2-quart square baking dish; set aside. Cook noodles according to package directions; drain and set aside.

2. Meanwhile, in a large skillet cook beef over medium heat until brown. Drain off fat. Stir tomato sauce, basil, sugar, garlic powder, salt, and pepper into skillet. Bring to boiling; reduce heat. Simmer, uncovered, for 5 minutes.

3. In a medium mixing bowl beat together the sour cream and cream cheese with an electric mixer on medium speed until smooth. Stir in milk and onion. In prepared casserole or baking dish layer half of the noodles (about 2 cups), half of the meat mixture (about 1½ cups), half of the cream cheese mixture (about 1 cup), and all of the spinach. Top with the remaining meat mixture and noodles. Cover and chill remaining cream cheese mixture.

4. Cover casserole or baking dish with lightly greased foil. Bake in a 350°F oven about 45 minutes or until heated through. Uncover; spread with remaining cream cheese mixture. Sprinkle with the cheddar cheese. Bake, uncovered, about 10 minutes more or until cheese melts. Let stand for 10 minutes before serving.

Make-ahead directions: Prepare as above through Step 3. Cover with lightly greased foil and chill for up to 24 hours. Bake in a 350°F oven about 1 hour or until heated through.

Uncover; spread with remaining cream cheese mixture. Sprinkle with the cheddar cheese. Bake, uncovered, about 10 minutes more or until cheese melts. Let stand for 10 minutes before serving.

Per 1½ cups: 472 cal., 30 g total fat (17 g sat. fat), 127 mg chol., 683 mg sodium, 25 g carbo., 3 g fiber, 27 g pro.
Daily Values: 9% vit. A, 14% vit. C, 34% calcium, 13% iron
Exchanges: 1 Vegetable, 1 Starch, 3 Medium-Fat Meat, 3 Fat

Lasagna

Prep: 45 minutes **Bake:** 30 minutes **Oven:** 375°F
Stand: 10 minutes **Makes:** 8 servings

- **12 ounces bulk Italian or pork sausage or ground beef**
- **1 cup chopped onion (1 large)**
- **2 cloves garlic, minced**
- **1 14.5-ounce can diced tomatoes, undrained**
- **1 8-ounce can tomato sauce**
- **1 tablespoon dried Italian seasoning, crushed**
- **1 teaspoon fennel seeds, crushed (optional)**
- **6 dried lasagna noodles**
- **1 egg, beaten**
- **1 15-ounce container ricotta cheese or 2 cups cream-style cottage cheese, drained**
- **¼ cup grated Parmesan cheese**
- **1½ cups shredded mozzarella cheese (6 ounces)**
- **Grated Parmesan cheese (optional)**

1. For sauce, in a large saucepan cook sausage, onion, and garlic over medium heat until meat is brown; drain off fat. Stir undrained tomatoes, tomato sauce, Italian seasoning, fennel seeds (if desired), and ¼ teaspoon *black pepper* into meat mixture. Bring to boiling; reduce heat. Simmer, covered, for 15 minutes, stirring occasionally.

2. Meanwhile, cook lasagna noodles according to package directions. Drain noodles; rinse with cold water. Drain well; set aside.

3. For filling, combine egg, ricotta, and the ¼ cup Parmesan cheese; set aside.

4. Spread about ½ cup of the sauce over the bottom of a 2-quart rectangular baking dish. Layer half of the cooked noodles in the dish, trimming or overlapping as necessary to fit. Spread with half of the filling. Top with half of the remaining sauce and half of the mozzarella cheese. Repeat layers. If desired, sprinkle additional Parmesan cheese over top.

5. Place baking dish on a baking sheet. Bake in a 375°F oven for 30 to 35 minutes or until heated through. Let stand for 10 minutes before serving.

Make-ahead directions: Prepare as on page 428 through Step 4. Cover unbaked lasagna; chill for up to 24 hours. To serve, bake, covered, in a 375°F oven for 40 minutes. Uncover; bake about 20 minutes more or until heated through. Let stand for 10 minutes before serving.

Per 3½×2¾-inch piece: 441 cal., 22 g total fat (11 g sat. fat), 97 mg chol., 658 mg sodium, 33 g carbo., 2 g fiber, 24 g pro.
Daily Values: 9% vit. A, 14% vit. C, 34% calcium, 13% iron
Exchanges: 1 Vegetable, 2 Starch, 2 High-Fat Meat, 1 Fat

Quick Lasagna: Prepare as on page 428, except omit tomatoes, tomato sauce, Italian seasoning, fennel seeds, and black pepper. Instead, stir a 26-ounce jar tomato pasta sauce into the meat mixture; do not simmer. Skip Step 2 and substitute 6 no-boil lasagna noodles (one-third of a 9-ounce package) for the cooked noodles in Step 4.

Per 3½×2¾-inch piece: 391 cal., 24 g total fat (11 g sat. fat), 97 mg chol., 1,047 mg sodium, 18 g carbo., 2 g fiber, 22 g pro.
Daily Values: 15% vit. A, 9% vit. C, 33% calcium, 8% iron
Exchanges: 1 Starch, 1 Vegetable, 2½ High-Fat Meat, 1 Fat

Vegetable Lasagna

Prep: 40 minutes **Bake:** 35 minutes **Oven:** 350°F
Stand: 10 minutes **Makes:** 12 servings

   9 or 10 dried lasagna noodles
   2 eggs, beaten
   2 cups cream-style cottage cheese, drained
   1 15-ounce carton ricotta cheese
   2 teaspoons dried Italian seasoning, crushed
   2 cups sliced fresh mushrooms
   1 cup chopped onion (1 large)
   4 cloves garlic, minced
   2 tablespoons olive oil or cooking oil
   2 tablespoons all-purpose flour
 1¼ cups milk
   1 10-ounce package frozen chopped spinach, thawed and well drained
   1 10-ounce package frozen chopped broccoli, thawed and well drained
   1 cup shredded carrot
   ¾ cup shredded Parmesan cheese (3 ounces)
   1 8-ounce package shredded mozzarella cheese (2 cups)

1. Cook noodles according to package directions. Drain; set aside.

2. In a bowl combine eggs, cottage cheese, ricotta cheese, and Italian seasoning; set aside.

3. In a large skillet cook mushrooms, onion, and garlic in hot oil until tender. Stir in the flour and ½ to 1 teaspoon *black pepper*; add milk all at once. Cook and stir until slightly thickened and bubbly. Remove from heat. Stir in the spinach, broccoli, carrot, and ½ cup of the Parmesan cheese.

4. In a greased 3-quart rectangular baking dish layer one-third of the noodles, trimming or overlapping as necessary to fit. Spread with one-third of the cottage cheese mixture, then one-third of the vegetable mixture. Sprinkle with one-third of the mozzarella. Repeat layers twice. Sprinkle with remaining ¼ cup Parmesan.

5. Bake, uncovered, in a 350°F oven about 35 minutes or until heated through. Let stand for 10 minutes before serving.

Quick Vegetable Lasagna: Prepare as above, except substitute 12 no-boil lasagna noodles for the dried lasagna noodles and skip Step 1, increase milk to 2 cups, and spread ½ cup of the vegetable mixture in bottom of the dish before adding the first layer of noodles.

Make-ahead directions: Prepare as above through Step 4. Cover unbaked lasagna; chill for up to 24 hours. To serve, bake, covered, in a 375°F oven for 40 minutes. Uncover; bake about 20 minutes more or until heated through. Let stand for 10 minutes before serving.

Per 3¼×3-inch piece: 322 cal., 15 g total fat (8 g sat. fat), 78 mg chol., 388 mg sodium, 25 g carbo., 3 g fiber, 22 g pro.
Daily Values: 107% vit. A, 24% vit. C, 37% calcium, 10% iron
Exchanges: 2 Vegetable, 1 Starch, 2 Medium-Fat Meat, 1 Fat

Vegetable Lasagna

Baked Cavatelli

Italian sausage links are available either mild (sometimes labeled "sweet") or hot—use whichever you prefer.

Prep: 25 minutes **Bake:** 30 minutes **Oven:** 375°F
Makes: 5 or 6 servings

- 2⅓ cups dried cavatelli or wagon wheel macaroni (7 ounces)
- 12 ounces uncooked Italian sausage links, sliced ½ inch thick, or ground beef
- ¾ cup chopped onion
- 2 cloves garlic, minced
- 1 26-ounce jar pasta sauce
- 1 cup shredded mozzarella cheese (4 ounces)
- ¼ teaspoon black pepper

1. Cook pasta according to package directions; drain and set aside.

2. In a large skillet cook the sausage, onion, and garlic over medium heat until sausage is brown; remove from skillet; drain off fat.

3. In a large bowl stir together pasta sauce, ¾ cup of the mozzarella cheese, and the pepper. Add the cooked pasta and the drained sausage mixture. Stir gently to combine. Spoon the mixture into a 2-quart casserole.*

4. Bake, covered, in a 375°F oven for 25 to 30 minutes or until nearly heated through. Uncover; sprinkle with the remaining ¼ cup mozzarella cheese. Bake about 5 minutes more or until cheese melts.

*Note: For individual portions, spoon the mixture into five or six individual (8- to 10-ounce) casseroles. Place the casseroles on a large baking sheet. Cover casseroles with foil and bake in a 375°F oven for 15 to 20 minutes or until nearly heated through. Uncover, sprinkle with remaining ¼ cup cheese, and bake about 5 minutes more or until cheese melts.

Per 2 cups: 503 cal., 24 g total fat (9 g sat. fat), 58 mg chol., 1,464 mg sodium, 43 g carbo., 4 g fiber, 23 g pro.
Daily Values: 14% vit. A, 13% vit. C, 23% calcium, 15% iron
Exchanges: 1 Vegetable, 2½ Starch, 1 Fat

Prosciutto, Spinach, and Pasta Casserole LOW FAT

Prosciutto (proh-SHOO-toh) is a spicy cured ham. Substitute cooked lean ham, if you like.

Prep: 25 minutes **Cook:** 25 minutes **Oven:** 350°F
Stand: 5 minutes **Makes:** 6 servings

- 2⅔ cups dried bow ties, penne, or ziti (8 ounces)
- 2 medium onions, cut into thin wedges, or 5 medium leeks, sliced
- 2 cloves garlic, minced
- 1 tablespoon butter or margarine
- ¼ cup all-purpose flour
- ½ teaspoon anise seeds, crushed
- 1¾ cups milk
- 1½ cups chicken broth
- ¼ cup grated Parmesan cheese
- 1 10-ounce package frozen chopped spinach, thawed and well drained
- 2 ounces prosciutto, cut into thin bite-size strips
- 1 medium tomato, seeded and chopped

1. Cook the pasta according to the package directions; drain. Rinse pasta with cold water; drain again. Set aside.

2. In a large saucepan cook onion and garlic, covered, in hot butter about 5 minutes or until onion is tender, stirring occasionally. Stir in flour and anise seeds. Add the milk and chicken broth all at once. Cook and stir until slightly thickened and bubbly. Stir in Parmesan cheese. Stir in the cooked pasta, spinach, and prosciutto. Spoon the mixture into a 2-quart casserole.

3. Bake, covered, in a 350°F oven for 25 to 30 minutes or until heated through. Let stand about 5 minutes. To serve, stir gently and top with chopped tomato.

Per 1½ cups: 288 cal., 7 g total fat (3 g sat. fat), 21 mg chol., 627 mg sodium, 42 g carbo., 3 g fiber, 15 g pro.
Daily Values: 81% vit. A, 20% vit. C, 23% calcium, 14% iron
Exchanges: 1 Vegetable, 2½ Starch, ½ Medium-Fat Meat

Italian Family Dinner

Bring a taste of Tuscany to your table.

- Prosciutto, Spinach, and Pasta Casserole (above)
- Steamed zucchini with pine nuts
- Basil garlic bread
- Apple and pear wedges with biscotti

Spinach-Stuffed Pasta Shells

Spinach-Stuffed Pasta Shells `VEGETARIAN`

A shredded cheese blend plus a jar of your favorite pasta sauce deliver an easy weeknight dinner with old-fashioned flavor.

Prep: 25 minutes **Bake:** 40 minutes
Oven: 350°F **Makes:** 4 servings

- **12 dried jumbo shell macaroni**
- **1 10-ounce package frozen chopped spinach, thawed**
- **2 eggs**
- **1 8-ounce package shredded Italian cheese blend (2 cups)**
- **1 cup ricotta cheese**
- **1 26- to 32-ounce jar pasta sauce**

1. Cook pasta according to package directions; drain. Rinse pasta with cold water; drain again. Set aside. Meanwhile, drain thawed spinach well, pressing out excess liquid.

2. For filling, in a medium bowl beat eggs. Stir in spinach, 1½ cups of the Italian cheese blend, and the ricotta cheese. Spoon a rounded 2 tablespoons of the filling into each jumbo shell. Place shells in 2-quart square baking dish. Pour pasta sauce over shells.

3. Bake, covered, in a 350°F oven about 40 minutes or until heated through. Sprinkle with remaining ½ cup Italian cheese blend before serving.

Make-ahead directions: Prepare as above through Step 2. Cover unbaked casserole with plastic wrap, then foil. Chill for up to 24 hours.

To bake, remove plastic wrap and cover with foil. Bake in a 375°F oven for 50 to 55 minutes or until heated through.

Per 3 shells: 592 cal., 31 g total fat (14 g sat. fat), 117 mg chol., 2,049 mg sodium, 52 g carbo., 12 g fiber, 34 g pro.
Daily Values: 213% vit. A, 57% vit. C, 57% calcium, 26% iron
Exchanges: 1½ Vegetable, 1½ Starch, 1½ Other Carbo., 3½ Medium-Fat Meat, 2 Fat

FAVORITE Spinach Manicotti

Three different cheeses—Swiss, ricotta, and Parmesan—plus spinach are the major ingredients in this tasty main dish.

Prep: 40 minutes **Bake:** 30 minutes **Oven:** 350°F
Stand: 10 minutes **Makes:** 4 servings

- **8 dried manicotti shells**
- **¼ cup sliced green onion (2)**
- **1 clove garlic, minced**
- **2 tablespoons butter or margarine**
- **2 tablespoons all-purpose flour**
- **1⅓ cups milk**
- **3 ounces process Swiss cheese slices, torn**
- **⅓ cup chicken broth**
- **1 egg, beaten**
- **1 10-ounce package frozen chopped spinach, thawed and well drained**
- **¾ cup ricotta cheese**
- **½ cup grated Parmesan cheese**
- **¼ teaspoon finely shredded lemon peel**

1. Cook manicotti according to package directions; drain. Rinse pasta with cold water; drain. Cool pasta in a single layer on greased foil.

2. Meanwhile, for sauce, in a medium saucepan cook green onion and garlic in hot butter over medium heat until tender. Stir in flour. Add milk all at once. Cook and stir until thickened and bubbly. Add Swiss cheese and broth, stirring until cheese melts.

3. For filling, in a medium bowl stir together egg, spinach, ricotta cheese, Parmesan cheese, and lemon peel. Use a small spoon to fill manicotti shells with spinach mixture. Arrange filled shells in a 2-quart rectangular baking dish. Pour sauce over filled shells.

4. Bake, covered, in a 350°F oven for 30 to 35 minutes or until heated through. Let stand for 10 minutes before serving.

Per 2 shells: 487 cal., 25 g total fat (15 g sat. fat), 128 mg chol., 572 mg sodium, 38 g carbo., 3 g fiber, 28 g pro.
Daily Values: 130% vit. A, 18% vit. C, 69% calcium, 16% iron
Exchanges: 1 Vegetable, 2 Starch, 3 Medium-Fat Meat, 1½ Fat

Macaroni and Cheese (VEGETARIAN)

Prep: 25 minutes **Bake:** 25 minutes **Oven:** 350°F
Stand: 10 minutes **Makes:** 4 servings

  2 cups dried elbow macaroni (8 ounces)
  ½ cup chopped onion (1 medium)
  2 tablespoons butter or margarine
  2 tablespoons all-purpose flour
  ⅛ teaspoon black pepper
  2½ cups milk
  1½ cups shredded cheddar cheese (6 ounces)
  1½ cups shredded American cheese (6 ounces)

1. Cook macaroni according to package directions; drain and set aside.

2. Meanwhile, for cheese sauce, in a medium saucepan cook onion in hot butter until tender. Stir in flour and pepper. Add milk all at once. Cook and stir over medium heat until slightly thickened and bubbly. Add cheeses, stirring until melted. Stir in cooked macaroni. Transfer mixture to a 2-quart casserole.

3. Bake, uncovered, in a 350°F oven for 25 to 30 minutes or until bubbly and heated through. Let stand for 10 minutes before serving.

Per 1½ cups: 692 cal., 37 g total fat (23 g sat. fat), 112 mg chol., 1,012 mg sodium, 56 g carbo., 2 g fiber, 33 g pro.
Daily Values: 30% vit. A, 4% vit. C, 77% calcium, 14% iron
Exchanges: 3½ Starch, 3 High-Fat Meat, 2 Fat

Saucepan Macaroni and Cheese: Prepare as above, except reduce milk to 2 cups. After draining macaroni, immediately return macaroni to the saucepan. Pour cheese sauce over macaroni; stir to coat macaroni with sauce. Cook over low heat for 2 to 3 minutes or until heated through, stirring frequently. Let stand for 10 minutes before serving.

Per 1½ cups: 677 cal., 37 g total fat (23 g sat. fat), 110 chol., 997 mg sodium, 54 g carbo., 2 g fiber, 32 g pro.
Daily Values: 29% vit. A, 4% vit. C, 73% calcium, 13% iron
Exchanges: 3½ Starch, 3 High-Fat Meat, 2½ Fat

Macaroni and Cheese with Caramelized Onions

Prep: 25 minutes **Bake:** 30 minutes **Oven:** 350°F
Stand: 10 minutes **Makes:** 4 servings

  4 strips bacon
  1 large sweet onion, halved and thinly sliced
  1½ cups regular or multigrain dried elbow macaroni (6 ounces)
  2 cups shredded mozzarella cheese (8 ounces)
  4 ounces processed Gruyère cheese, shredded, or blue cheese, crumbled
  1 cup half-and-half or light cream
  ⅛ teaspoon black pepper

1. In a large skillet cook bacon over medium heat until crisp, turning once. Drain bacon on paper towels; crumble. Reserve bacon drippings in skillet.

2. Cook onion in reserved bacon drippings over medium heat for 5 to 8 minutes or until onion is tender and golden brown. Set aside.

3. In a large saucepan cook macaroni according to package directions. Drain and return to saucepan. Stir in the crumbled bacon, onion, 1½ cups of the mozzarella cheese, the Gruyère cheese, half-and-half, and pepper. Toss gently to combine. Spoon into a 1½-quart casserole.

4. Bake, uncovered, in a 350°F oven for 20 minutes. Stir gently. Top with the remaining mozzarella cheese. Bake about 10 minutes more or until top of casserole is brown and bubbly. Let stand 10 minutes.

Per 1½ cups: 632 cal., 39 g total fat (21 g sat. fat), 110 mg chol., 617 mg sodium, 37 g carbo., 4 g fiber, 33 g pro.
Daily Values: 17% vit. A, 5% vit. C, 65% calcium, 11% iron
Exchanges: ½ Vegetable, 2 Starch, 2 Medium-Fat Meat, 1½ High-Fat Meat, 3½ Fat

Macaroni and Cheese with Caramelized Onions

Pies & Tarts

Country Peach Tart, 450

Butterscotch-Pecan Tart, 448

Apple Pie, 436

Pies & Tarts Essentials

Once you try your hand at baking these crust-encased desserts, you'll understand where the phrase "easy as pie" comes from. Before you start, check out the tips below.

On the Edge

A pie is just a pie ... or is it? Make your crusted dessert stand out with a special edge.

1. Favorite Flute: Fold under pastry edge as directed. Place one of your thumbs against the inside edge of the pastry. Using the thumb and index finger of your other hand, press the pastry from the outside into your first thumb to form a crimp. Continue around the edge.

2. Circle Around: Trim the pastry even with the pie plate edge. With a cookie cutter, cut small circles from an additional pastry. Brush pastry edge with water. Place the circles around the pastry edge, overlapping them slightly.

3. Easy Finish: Fold under pastry edge as directed. Use a spoon to press a design into edge.

4. The Weave: Trim the pastry even with the pie plate edge. Cut pastry at ½- to 1-inch intervals. Fold every other section in toward the center.

The Craft of Crust

Measure accurately: Too much flour or water will make a crust tough, while too much shortening will make it crumbly.

Less is more: To roll out pastry, cover your rolling pin with a stockinette and use a pastry cloth. Lightly flour both, but avoid using excess flour.

Cover up: To protect the edge from over-browning, fold a 12-inch square of foil into quarters. Cut a 7-inch circle out of the center. Unfold the foil square and loosely mold it over the edge of the pie.

Buy it: For a speedy alternative, try purchased rolled refrigerated unbaked piecrusts. Your pie will still come from the heart, even if part of it came from the supermarket.

Apple of My Eye

So many apples—so little time! But which are good for baking? For best results, try combining some of the sweet and tart varieties below.

Sweet

Braeburn: This red- and gold-speckled apple is juicy sweet with spicy, pearlike undertones.

Golden Delicious: This apple has crisp yellow to yellow-green skin and a deliciously sweet, mellow flavor. The flesh is soft, rich, and creamy.

Jonagold: A sweet-tart favorite, this juicy red-blushed apple is a cross between Golden Delicious and Jonathan. The flavors are more distinct than Golden Delicious but retain the same rich buttery undertones.

Tart

Cortland: With a firm, dense flesh, this red-hued apple has a crisp, snappy flavor.

Granny Smith: Puckery, sharp, and zingy— Granny Smith's flavor is slightly reminiscent of sour apple-flavor candy. This firm apple holds its shape well when cooked.

Jonathan: Pleasantly sweet and tart, this red apple is a juicy favorite. Keep in mind, however, it does not perform well when baked whole.

Granny Smith · Jonagold · Braeburn · Cortland · Jonathan · Golden Delicious

Apple Pie

See photo, page 433.

Prep: 30 minutes **Bake:** 1 hour
Oven: 375°F **Makes:** 8 slices

- 1 **recipe Pastry for Double-Crust Pie (page 454)**
- 6 **cups thinly sliced, peeled cooking apples (about 2¼ pounds) (see page 435)**
- 1 **tablespoon lemon juice (optional)**
- ¾ **cup sugar**
- 2 **tablespoons all-purpose flour**
- ½ **teaspoon ground cinnamon**
- ⅛ **teaspoon ground nutmeg**
- ⅓ **cup dried cranberries (optional)**

1. Preheat oven to 375°F. Prepare and roll out Pastry for Double-Crust Pie. Line a 9-inch pie plate with a pastry circle (see photo 2, page 454).

2. If desired, sprinkle apples with lemon juice. In a large bowl stir together sugar, flour, cinnamon, and nutmeg. Add apple slices and, if desired, cranberries. Gently toss until coated.

3. Transfer apple mixture to the pastry-lined pie plate. Trim bottom pastry to edge of pie plate. Cut slits in remaining pastry circle; place on filling and seal (see photo 4, page 454). Crimp edge as desired (see page 435).

4. If desired, brush top pastry with *milk* and sprinkle with additional sugar. To prevent over-browning, cover edge of pie with foil (see page 435). Bake for 40 minutes. Remove foil. Bake 20 minutes more or until fruit is tender and filling is bubbly. Cool on a wire rack. To serve warm, let pie cool at least 2 hours.

Apple Crumb Pie: Prepare as at left, except substitute 1 recipe Pastry for Single-Crust Pie (page 453) for Pastry for Double-Crust Pie. Fill pastry-lined pie plate as at left. Prepare 1 recipe Crumb Topping (page 439). Sprinkle over apple mixture. Do not brush top with milk or sprinkle with sugar. Bake as directed above.

Per slice regular or crumb variation: 395 cal., 18 g total fat (4 g sat. fat), 0 mg chol., 219 mg sodium, 57 g carbo., 3 g fiber, 4 g pro. Daily Values: 1% vit. A, 6% vit. C, 1% calcium, 10% iron Exchanges: 1 Fruit, 3 Other Carbo., 3½ Fat

Cherry Pie

When they're in season in early summer, try using fresh cherries. Three good pie varieties are Early Richmond, English Morello, and Montmorency.

Prep: 30 minutes **Stand:** 15 minutes **Bake:** 55 minutes
Oven: 375°F **Makes:** 8 slices

- 1¼ **cups sugar**
- 3 **tablespoons cornstarch or quick-cooking tapioca**
- 5½ **cups fresh or frozen unsweetened pitted tart red cherries**
- 1 **recipe Pastry for Double-Crust Pie (page 454)**

1. In a large bowl stir together sugar and cornstarch. Add cherries; gently toss until coated. Let mixture stand about 15 minutes or until a syrup forms, stirring occasionally. (If using frozen cherries, let cherry mixture stand 45 minutes or until fruit is partially thawed but still icy.)

2. Preheat oven to 375°F. Prepare and roll out Pastry for Double-Crust Pie. Line a 9-inch pie plate with a pastry circle (see photo 2, page 454).

3. Stir cherry mixture; transfer to pastry-lined pie plate. Trim bottom pastry to edge of pie plate. Cut slits in remaining pastry; place on filling and seal (see photo 4, page 454). Crimp edge as desired (see page 435).

4. If desired, brush top pastry with *milk* and sprinkle with additional sugar. Place pie on a baking sheet. To prevent overbrowning, cover edge of pie with foil (see page 435). Bake for 30 minutes (or 50 minutes for partially thawed frozen fruit). Remove foil. Bake for 25 to 30 minutes or until filling is bubbly and pastry is golden. Cool on a wire rack.

Freeze for Later

Special occasions are hectic enough without last-minute baking. Instead, prepare your fruit pies now and freeze them.

To freeze a baked fruit pie: Let it cool completely. Place it in a freezer bag; seal, label, and freeze for up to 4 months. To serve, thaw the pie at room temperature.

To freeze an unbaked fruit pie: Before assembling, treat light-color fruit with ascorbic-acid color-keeper. Assemble pie in a metal pie pan. Place in a freezer bag; seal, label, and freeze for up to 4 months. To bake, unwrap frozen pie; cover with foil. Bake in a 450°F oven for 15 minutes. Reduce temperature to 375°F; bake 15 minutes. Uncover; bake for 55 to 60 minutes or until filling is bubbly and crust is golden.

Lattice Cherry Pie: Prepare as on page 436, except follow directions for Pastry for Lattice-Top Pie (page 454).

Per slice regular or lattice variation: 446 cal., 18 g total fat (4 g sat. fat), 0 mg chol., 221 mg sodium, 69 g carbo., 3 g fiber, 4 g pro.
Daily Values: 19% vit. A, 3% vit. C, 2% calcium, 11% iron
Exchanges: ½ Fruit, 4 Other Carbo., 3½ Fat

Raspberry-Cherry Pie: Prepare as on page 436, except use 3 cups fresh or frozen unsweetened pitted tart cherries and 2 cups fresh or frozen lightly sweetened raspberries.

Per slice: 488 cal., 18 g total fat (4 g sat. fat), 0 mg chol., 221 mg sodium, 80 g carbo., 5 g fiber, 4 g pro.
Daily Values: 11% vit. A, 19% vit. C, 2% calcium, 12% iron
Exchanges: ½ Fruit, 5 Other Carbo., 3½ Fat

 Berry Pie

Raspberries, blueberries, and blackberries—oh my!

Prep: 30 minutes **Bake:** 50 minutes
Oven: 375°F **Makes:** 8 slices

- 1 recipe Pastry for Double-Crust Pie (page 454)
- 1 recipe desired Berry Pie Filling (see chart, below)
- 2 teaspoons finely shredded lemon peel or ½ teaspoon ground cinnamon

1. Preheat oven to 375°F. Prepare and roll out Pastry for Double-Crust Pie. Line a 9-inch pie plate with a pastry circle (see photo 2, page 454).

2. In a large bowl prepare the desired Berry Pie Filling, first combining sugar and flour in the amounts specified for desired berries. Stir in desired berries and lemon peel. Gently toss berries until coated. (If using frozen fruit, let mixture stand for 45 minutes or until fruit is partially thawed but still icy.)

3. Transfer berry mixture to the pastry-lined pie plate. Trim bottom pastry to edge of pie plate.

Cut slits in remaining pastry circle; place on filling and seal (see photo 4, page 454). Crimp edge as desired (see page 435).

4. If desired, brush top pastry with *milk* and sprinkle with additional sugar. To prevent over-browning, cover edge of pie with foil (see page 435). Bake for 25 minutes (or 50 minutes for frozen fruit). Remove foil. Bake pie for 25 to 30 minutes more or until filling is bubbly and pastry is golden. Cool on a wire rack.

Lattice Berry Fruit Pie: Prepare as at left, except follow directions for Pastry for Lattice-Top Pie (page 454).

Per slice regular or lattice variation: 373 cal., 18 g total fat (4 g sat. fat), 0 mg chol., 222 mg sodium, 50 g carbo., 4 g fiber, 5 g pro.
Daily Values: 2% vit. A, 49% vit. C, 2% calcium, 11% iron
Exchanges: 1 Fruit, 2½ Other Carbo., 3½ Fat

Berry Pie

Berry Pie Filling

Berry pickers, take notice! No matter what berries are in season or grown locally, you'll find a pie filling, below, that includes them. For a quick substitute, frozen berries work just as well.

Berries	Amount	Sugar	All-Purpose Flour
Blackberries, fresh or frozen	5 cups	¾ to 1 cup	⅓ cup
Blueberries, fresh or frozen	5 cups	⅔ to ¾ cup	3 tablespoons
Raspberries, fresh or frozen	5 cups	¾ to 1 cup	⅓ cup
Mixed berries (2 cups halved strawberries, 2 cups blueberries, and 1 cup blackberries or raspberries)	5 cups	½ to ⅔ cup	⅓ cup

Cranberry-Apricot Pie

This pie also looks divine with a lattice-top crust, so if you prefer, follow the directions for Pastry for Lattice-Top Pie (page 454). Brush all the pastry strips with the egg white mixture, then sprinkle half the strips with the sugar mixture.

Prep: 30 minutes **Bake:** 50 minutes
Oven: 375°F **Makes:** 8 slices

- 1 recipe Pastry for Double-Crust Pie (page 454)
- ½ cup sugar
- 3 tablespoons cornstarch
- 1½ teaspoons pumpkin pie spice
- ¼ teaspoon salt
- 3 15.25-ounce cans apricot halves, drained and cut into quarters
- ½ cup dried cranberries, snipped
- 1 egg white
- 1 tablespoon milk
- 1 tablespoon sugar
- ¼ teaspoon pumpkin pie spice

1. Preheat oven to 375°F. Prepare and roll out Pastry for Double-Crust Pie. Line a 9-inch pie plate with a pastry circle (see photo 2, page 454). Trim pastry edge (see photo 3, page 454).

2. In a large bowl combine the ½ cup sugar, the cornstarch, the 1½ teaspoons pumpkin pie spice, and the salt. Stir in apricots and cranberries. Spoon fruit mixture into pastry-lined pie plate.

3. Roll out remaining pastry into a circle about 12 inches in diameter. Using a 1- to 1½-inch cookie cutter, cut 36 to 40 shapes from the remaining pastry circle. In a small bowl stir together egg white and milk. Brush egg white mixture over pastry shapes; reserve remaining egg white mixture. Stir together the 1 tablespoon sugar and the ¼ teaspoon pumpkin pie spice. Sprinkle half of the pastry shapes with the sugar mixture. Arrange about 10 of the shapes, alternating brushed and sprinkled, in a circle on the fruit mixture. Brush pie edge with remaining egg white mixture. Place the remaining pastry shapes around the pie edge.

4. To prevent overbrowning, cover edge of pie with foil (see page 435). Bake for 35 minutes. Remove foil; bake for 15 minutes more. Cool on a wire rack.

Per slice: 437 cal., 18 g total fat (4 g sat. fat), 0 mg chol., 308 mg sodium, 67 g carbo., 4 g fiber, 5 g pro.
Daily Values: 55% vit. A, 13% vit. C, 3% calcium, 12% iron
Exchanges: 2 Fruit, 2½ Other Carbo., 2½ Fat

Peach Pie

For a real flavor sensation, try topping the pie with candied pecans (see variation, below).

Prep: 30 minutes **Stand:** 20 minutes **Bake:** 50 minutes
Oven: 375°F **Makes:** 8 slices

- ½ to ⅔ cup sugar
- 2 tablespoons quick-cooking tapioca
- ¼ teaspoon ground cinnamon
- ¼ teaspoon ground nutmeg
- 6 cups thinly sliced, peeled peaches or frozen unsweetened peach slices
- 1 recipe Pastry for Double-Crust Pie (page 454)

1. For filling, in a large bowl stir together sugar, tapioca, cinnamon, and nutmeg. Add peaches. Gently toss peaches until coated. Let peach mixture stand 20 minutes, stirring occasionally. (If using frozen peaches, let mixture stand 45 minutes.)

2. Preheat oven to 375°F. Prepare and roll out Pastry for Double-Crust Pie. Line a 9-inch pie plate with a pastry circle (see photo 2, page 454).

3. Stir peach mixture. Transfer peach mixture to the pastry-lined pie plate. Trim bottom pastry to edge of pie plate (see photo 3, page 454). Cut slits in the remaining pastry circle. Place pastry circle on filling and seal (see photo 4, page 454). Crimp edge as desired (see page 435).

4. Place pie plate on a baking sheet. To prevent overbrowning, cover edge of pie with foil (see page 435). Bake for 25 minutes (or 50 minutes for frozen fruit). Remove foil. Bake 25 to 30 minutes more or until filling is bubbly and pastry is golden. Cool on a wire rack.

Per slice: 380 cal., 17 g total fat (4 g sat. fat), 0 mg chol., 219 mg sodium, 53 g carbo., 4 g fiber, 4 g pro.
Daily Values: 14% vit. A, 14% vit. C, 1% calcium, 9% iron
Exchanges: 1 Fruit, 2½ Other Carbo., 3 Fat

Peach Pie with Candied Pecan Topping: Prepare as above, except while pie is baking, prepare the pecan topping. In a small saucepan combine ⅓ cup packed brown sugar, 2 tablespoons butter, 1 tablespoon water, and 1 teaspoon cornstarch. Cook and stir over medium heat until bubbly. Stir in ¾ cup chopped pecans. When pie is done baking, spread warm pecan mixture over hot crust. Bake 5 minutes. Cool on a wire rack.

Per slice: 500 cal., 28 g total fat (7 g sat. fat), 8 mg chol., 169 mg sodium; 61 g carbo., 4 g fiber, 5 g pro.
Daily Values: 16% vit. A, 14% vit. C, 3% calcium, 11% iron
Exchanges: 1 Fruit, 3 Other Carbo., 5 Fat

Rhubarb Pie

Although it is most often used as a fruit, in the botanical world rhubarb is considered a vegetable. Perfect for jams and sauces, its tart flavor also is delicious with this pie's sweet crumb topping.

Prep: 30 minutes **Bake:** 45 minutes
Oven: 375°F **Makes:** 8 slices

> 1 **recipe Pastry for Single-Crust Pie (page 453)**
> 1 **recipe Crumb Topping**
> ¾ **cup sugar**
> ⅓ **cup all-purpose flour**
> ½ **teaspoon ground cinnamon (optional)**
> 6 **cups fresh or frozen unsweetened, sliced rhubarb**

1. Preheat oven to 375°F. Prepare and roll out Pastry for Single-Crust Pie. Line a 9-inch pie plate with the pastry circle and trim (see photos 2 and 3, page 454). Crimp edge as desired (see page 435). Prepare Crumb Topping; set aside.

2. In a large bowl stir together sugar, flour, and, if desired, cinnamon. Add rhubarb. Gently toss rhubarb until coated. (If using frozen fruit, let mixture stand for 45 minutes or until fruit is partially thawed but still icy.)

3. Transfer rhubarb mixture to the pastry-lined pie plate. Sprinkle Crumb Topping evenly over rhubarb mixture.

4. To prevent overbrowning, cover edge of pie with foil (see page 435). Bake for 25 minutes (or 60 minutes for frozen fruit). Remove foil. Bake for 20 to 30 minutes more or until filling in center is bubbly and topping is golden. Cool on a wire rack.

Crumb Topping: Stir together ½ cup all-purpose flour and ½ cup packed brown sugar. Using a pastry blender, cut in 3 tablespoons butter until mixture resembles coarse crumbs.

Double-Crust Rhubarb Pie: Prepare as above, except substitute 1 recipe Pastry for Double-Crust Pie (page 454) for Pastry for Single-Crust Pie and omit Crumb Topping. Follow directions for Pastry for Double-Crust Pie. If desired, brush top pastry with milk and sprinkle with additional sugar before baking.

Per slice regular or double-crust variation: 365 cal., 13 g total fat (5 g sat. fat), 12 mg chol., 129 mg sodium, 58 g carbo., 2 g fiber, 4 g pro.
Daily Values: 5% vit. A, 10% vit. C, 10% calcium, 10% iron
Exchanges: 1 Fruit, 3 Other Carbo., 2½ Fat

FAVORITE Fresh Strawberry Pie

During the hot days of summer, cool off with a glass of lemonade and a slice of this fresh-from-the-berry-patch pie. When peaches are in season, switch it up by trying the variation, below.

Prep: 1 hour **Chill:** 1 hour **Makes:** 8 slices

> 1 **recipe Baked Pastry Shell (page 453)**
> 8 **cups medium fresh strawberries**
> ⅔ **cup water**
> ⅔ **cup sugar**
> 2 **tablespoons cornstarch**
>   **Several drops red food coloring (optional)**
>   **Whipped cream (optional)**

1. Prepare Baked Pastry Shell and set aside. Meanwhile, remove stems from strawberries. Cut any large strawberries in half lengthwise.

2. For glaze, in a blender or food processor combine 1 cup of the strawberries and the water. Cover and blend or process until smooth. Add enough additional water to the mixture to equal 1½ cups. In a medium saucepan combine sugar and cornstarch; stir in blended strawberry mixture. Cook and stir over medium heat until mixture is thickened and bubbly. Cook and stir 2 minutes more. If desired, stir in red food coloring. Remove from heat; cool for 10 minutes without stirring.

3. Spread about ¼ cup of the glaze over bottom and sides of Baked Pastry Shell. Arrange half of the remaining strawberries with stem ends down in the pastry shell.

4. Carefully spoon half of the remaining glaze over strawberries, making sure all berries are covered. Arrange remaining berries over first layer. Spoon remaining glaze over berries, covering them. Chill for 1 to 2 hours. (After 2 hours, filling may begin to water out.) If desired, top with whipped cream.

Fresh Peach Pie: Prepare as above, except substitute 6 cups sliced, peeled peaches for the strawberries and omit the food coloring.

Per slice strawberry or peach variation: 253 cal., 9 g total fat (2 g sat. fat), 0 mg chol., 75 mg sodium, 42 g carbo., 4 g fiber, 3 g pro.
Daily Values: 1% vit. A, 136% vit. C, 2% calcium, 8% iron
Exchanges: 1 Fruit, 2 Other Carbo., 1½ Fat

Pecan-Topped Pumpkin Pie

Pecan-Topped Pumpkin Pie

Prep: 30 minutes **Bake:** 1 hour
Oven: 375°F **Makes:** 8 slices

- 1 recipe Deep-Dish Pie Pastry
- 1¼ cups coarsely chopped pecans or walnuts
- ¾ cup packed brown sugar
- 1 15-ounce can pumpkin (about 1¾ cups)
- 1½ cups half-and-half or light cream
- ¾ cup granulated sugar
- 3 eggs, slightly beaten
- 1½ teaspoons pumpkin pie spice
- 3 tablespoons butter, melted

1. Preheat oven to 375°F. Prepare the Deep-Dish Pie Pastry. Line a 9-inch deep-dish pie plate with pastry circle; trim (see photos 2 and 3, page 454). Crimp as desired (see page 435).

2. In a small bowl combine pecans and brown sugar. Spread ¾ cup pecan mixture in the bottom of the pastry-lined pie plate; reserve remaining pecan mixture. For filling, combine pumpkin, half-and-half, granulated sugar, eggs, pumpkin pie spice, and ¼ teaspoon *salt*; mix well.

3. Place the pastry-lined pie plate on the oven rack. Carefully pour filling over the pecan mixture in pastry shell. Bake about 50 minutes or just until set in center. Stir melted butter into remaining pecan mixture. Sprinkle pecan mixture over pie filling; bake for 10 minutes more or until topping is bubbly around edges. Cool on a wire rack. Cover and chill within 2 hours.

Deep-Dish Pie Pastry: In a medium bowl stir together 1½ cups flour and ¼ teaspoon salt. Using a pastry blender, cut in 6 tablespoons shortening until pieces are pea size (see photo 1, page 454). Sprinkle 1 tablespoon cold water over part of the flour mixture; gently toss with fork. Push moistened pastry to the side of bowl. Repeat, using 1 tablespoon water at a time, until all the flour mixture is moistened and forms a ball (about 5 to 6 tablespoons cold water). On a lightly floured surface, slightly flatten pastry. Roll pastry from center to edges into a 12-inch circle.

Per slice: 579 cal., 34 g total fat (10 g sat. fat), 108 mg chol., 235 mg sodium, 65 g carbo., 4 g fiber, 8 g pro.
Daily Values: 173% vit. A, 5% vit. C, 11% calcium, 17% iron
Exchanges: 1 Starch, 3 Other Carbo., ½ Medium-Fat Meat, 6 Fat

Pumpkin Pie

Prep: 30 minutes **Bake:** 50 minutes
Oven: 375°F **Makes:** 8 slices

- 1 recipe Pastry for Single-Crust Pie (page 453)
- 1 15-ounce can pumpkin (about 1¾ cups)
- ½ cup sugar
- 1 teaspoon ground cinnamon
- ½ teaspoon ground ginger
- ¼ teaspoon ground nutmeg
- 2 eggs, slightly beaten
- ¾ cup half-and-half, light cream, or milk

1. Preheat oven to 375°F. Prepare and roll out Pastry for Single-Crust Pie. Line a 9-inch pie plate with the pastry circle and trim (see photos 2 and 3, page 454). Crimp edge as desired (see page 435).

Fresh from the Patch

For fresh pumpkin pie filling, choose a medium-size pie pumpkin (pie varieties are labeled "sugar" or "sweet" pumpkins and are higher in natural sugar than decorating types). To pick the right size, remember, a 6-pound pumpkin makes about 2 cups pulp; a 15-ounce can of pumpkin equals about 1¾ cups pulp. To bake, cut pumpkin into 5-inch pieces. Scrape away strings; arrange in a single layer, rind sides up, in a baking pan. Cover pan with foil; bake in a 375°F oven for 1 hour or until tender. Scoop pulp from the rind. Blend pulp in a blender until smooth. Strain liquid from the pulp.

2. For filling, in a bowl combine pumpkin, sugar, cinnamon, ginger, and nutmeg. Add eggs; beat lightly with a fork until combined. Gradually add half-and-half; stir just until combined.

3. Place the pastry-lined pie plate on the oven rack. Carefully pour filling into pastry shell. To prevent overbrowning, cover edge of the pie with foil (see page 435). Bake for 25 minutes. Remove foil. Bake about 25 minutes more or until a knife inserted near the center comes out clean. Cool on a wire rack. Cover and chill within 2 hours.

Per slice: 255 cal., 13 g total fat (4 g sat. fat), 61 mg chol., 94 mg sodium, 31 g carbo., 2 g fiber, 5 g pro.
Daily Values: 238% vit. A, 4% vit. C, 5% calcium, 11% iron
Exchanges: 2 Other Carbo., 2½ Fat

Sweet Potato Pie

Be sure to use dark-skinned sweet potatoes with orange flesh. Pale sweet potatoes won't do for this!

Prep: 30 minutes **Bake:** 35 minutes **Oven:** 375°F
Cool: 30 minutes **Makes:** 8 slices

   1 **recipe Baked Pastry Shell (page 453)**
   2 **cups cooked, mashed orange sweet potatoes* or one 17.2-ounce can sweet potatoes, drained and mashed**
   ½ **cup sugar**
   ½ **teaspoon ground cinnamon**
   ¼ **teaspoon ground allspice**
   ¼ **teaspoon ground nutmeg**
   3 **eggs, slightly beaten**
   1 **cup buttermilk or dairy sour cream**

1. Prepare Baked Pastry Shell; set aside. Preheat oven to 375°F. For filling, stir together sweet potatoes, sugar, cinnamon, allspice, nutmeg, and ⅛ teaspoon *salt*. Add eggs; beat lightly with a fork just until combined. Gradually stir in buttermilk until thoroughly combined.

2. Place the Baked Pastry Shell on the oven rack. Pour filling into pastry shell. Bake 35 to 40 minutes or until a knife inserted near the center comes out clean and edges are puffed. To serve warm, cool on a wire rack for at least 30 minutes. If desired, serve with *whipped cream*. Cover and chill within 2 hours.

***Note:** To cook sweet potatoes, see page 610.

Per slice: 290 cal., 11 g total fat (3 g sat. fat), 81 mg chol., 190 mg sodium, 42 g carbo., 3 g fiber, 6 g pro.
Daily Values: 263% vit. A, 18% vit. C, 7% calcium, 10% iron
Exchanges: 1 Starch, 2 Other Carbo., 1½ Fat

Streusel-Topped Sweet Potato Pie: Prepare as at left, except bake for 15 minutes and prepare streusel topping. Combine ¼ cup all-purpose flour, ¼ cup packed brown sugar, ⅛ teaspoon ground cinnamon, and ⅛ teaspoon ground nutmeg. Cut in 2 tablespoons butter until mixture resembles coarse crumbs. Stir in ¼ cup chopped hazelnuts (filberts) or toasted almonds (see tip, page 265). Sprinkle partially baked pie with streusel topping. Bake for 20 to 25 minutes more or until a knife inserted near center comes out clean. Cool on a wire rack for 30 minutes.

Per slice: 383 cal., 17 g total fat (5 g sat. fat), 89 mg chol., 215 mg sodium; 52 g carbo., 3 g fiber, 7 g pro.
Daily Values: 265% vit. A, 19% vit. C, 9% calcium, 13% iron
Exchanges: 1 Starch, 2½ Other Carbo., 3 Fat

Custard Pie

Prep: 25 minutes **Bake:** 52 minutes **Oven:** 450°F/350°F
Cool: 1 hour **Makes:** 8 slices

   1 **recipe Pastry for Single-Crust Pie (page 453)**
   4 **eggs**
   ½ **cup sugar**
   2 **teaspoons vanilla**
   ⅛ **teaspoon ground nutmeg**
   2 **cups half-and-half, light cream, or whole milk**

1. Preheat oven to 450°F. Prepare and roll out Pastry for Single-Crust Pie. Line a 9-inch pie plate with the pastry circle and trim (see photos 2 and 3, page 454). Crimp edge as desired (see page 435). Line pastry with a double thickness of foil. Bake for 8 minutes. Remove foil. Bake for 4 to 5 minutes or until set and dry. Remove from oven; reduce oven temperature to 350°F.

2. Meanwhile, for filling, in a bowl slightly beat eggs with a fork. Stir in sugar, vanilla, ⅛ teaspoon *salt*, and nutmeg. Gradually stir in half-and-half until mixture is thoroughly combined.

3. Place the partially baked pastry shell on the oven rack. Pour filling into shell. To prevent overbrowning, cover edge of pie with foil (see page 435). Bake in the 350°F oven for 25 minutes. Remove foil. Bake for 15 to 20 minutes or until a knife inserted near the center comes out clean. To serve warm, cool on a wire rack for at least 1 hour. Cover and chill within 2 hours. For longer storage cover and refrigerate for 2 days.

Per slice: 305 cal., 18 g total fat (7 g sat. fat), 128 mg chol., 166 mg sodium, 29 g carbo., 0 g fiber, 7 g pro.
Daily Values: 8% vit. A, 1% vit. C, 8% calcium, 7% iron
Exchanges: 2 Other Carbo., 3½ Fat

Vanilla Cream Pie

Prep: 45 minutes **Bake:** 30 minutes **Oven:** 325°F
Cool: 1 hour **Chill:** 3 hours **Makes:** 8 slices

    1 recipe Baked Pastry Shell (page 453)
    4 eggs
    ¾ cup sugar
    ¼ cup cornstarch
   2½ cups half-and-half, light cream, or milk
    1 tablespoon butter or margarine
   1½ teaspoons vanilla
    1 recipe Four Egg White Meringue (page 443)

1. Prepare Baked Pastry Shell. Separate egg yolks from whites. Set aside yolks for filling and whites for Four Egg White Meringue.

2. Preheat oven to 325°F. For filling, in a medium saucepan combine sugar and cornstarch. Gradually stir in half-and-half. Cook and stir over medium-high heat until thickened and bubbly; reduce heat. Cook and stir for 2 minutes more. Remove from heat. Slightly beat egg yolks with a fork. Gradually stir about 1 cup of the hot filling into yolks. Add egg yolk mixture to saucepan. Bring to a gentle boil; reduce heat. Cook and stir for 2 minutes. Remove from heat. Stir in butter and vanilla. Keep filling warm. Prepare Four Egg White Meringue.

3. Pour warm filling into Baked Pastry Shell. Spread meringue over warm filling; seal to edge (see photo, page 443). Bake for 30 minutes. Cool on a wire rack 1 hour. Chill for 3 to 6 hours before serving; cover for longer storage.

Per slice: 425 cal., 21 g total fat (9 g sat. fat), 138 mg chol., 151 mg sodium, 51 g carbo., 1 g fiber, 7 g pro.
Daily Values: 11% vit. A, 1% vit. C, 10% calcium, 7% iron
Exchanges: 3½ Other Carbo., 4 Fat

Coconut Cream Pie: Prepare as above, except stir in 1 cup flaked coconut with butter and vanilla. Sprinkle another ⅓ cup flaked coconut over meringue before baking.

Banana Cream Pie: Prepare as above, except before adding filling, arrange 3 medium bananas, sliced (about 2¼ cups), over bottom of shell.

Per slice coconut or banana variations: 482 cal., 25 g total fat (13 g sat. fat), 138 mg chol., 154 mg sodium, 56 g carbo., 1 g fiber, 8 g pro.
Daily Values: 11% vit. A, 1% vit. C, 10% calcium, 8% iron
Exchanges: 4 Other Carbo., 5 Fat

Dark Chocolate Cream Pie: Prepare as above, except increase the sugar to 1 cup. Stir in 3 ounces chopped unsweetened chocolate with the half-and-half.

Sour Cream-Raisin Pie: Prepare as at left, except decrease sugar to ⅔ cup and increase the cornstarch to ⅓ cup. Fold in 1 cup raisins and ½ cup dairy sour cream with the butter. Heat filling mixture through but do not boil.

Per slice chocolate or raisin variations: 504 cal., 27 g total fat (13 g sat. fat), 138 mg chol., 153 mg sodium, 60 g carbo., 2 g fiber, 8 g pro.
Daily Values: 11% vit. A, 1% vit. C, 10% calcium, 10% iron
Exchanges: 4 Other Carbo., 5½ Fat

🏅 Lemon Meringue Pie

For best flavor, use freshly squeezed lemon juice.

Prep: 40 minutes **Bake:** 15 minutes **Oven:** 350°F
Cool: 1 hour **Chill:** 3 hours **Makes:** 8 slices

    1 recipe Baked Pastry Shell (page 453)
    3 eggs
   1½ cups sugar
    3 tablespoons all-purpose flour
    3 tablespoons cornstarch
    2 tablespoons butter or margarine
    1 to 2 teaspoons finely shredded lemon peel
    ⅓ cup lemon juice
    1 recipe Meringue for Pie (page 443)

1. Prepare Baked Pastry Shell; set aside. Separate egg yolks from whites. Set aside yolks for filling and whites for Meringue for Pie.

2. Preheat oven to 350°F. For filling, in a medium saucepan combine sugar, flour, cornstarch, and a dash of *salt*. Gradually stir in 1½ cups *water*. Cook and stir over medium-high heat until mixture is thickened and bubbly; reduce heat. Cook and stir for 2 minutes more. Remove from heat. Slightly beat egg yolks with a fork. Gradually stir about 1 cup of the hot filling into yolks. Return egg yolk mixture to saucepan. Bring to a gentle boil; reduce heat. Cook and stir 2 minutes more. Remove from heat. Stir in butter and lemon peel. Gently stir in lemon juice. Keep filling warm. Prepare Meringue for Pie.

3. Pour warm filling into Baked Pastry Shell. Spread meringue over warm filling; seal to edge (see photo, page 443). Bake for 15 minutes. Cool on a wire rack 1 hour. Chill 3 to 6 hours before serving; cover for longer storage.

Per slice: 395 cal., 14 g total fat (5 g sat. fat), 88 mg chol., 182 mg sodium, 65 g carbo., 1 g fiber, 5 g pro.
Daily Values: 5% vit. A, 8% vit. C, 2% calcium, 7% iron
Exchanges: 4½ Other Carbo., 2½ Fat

Meringue for Pie

Pie meringue is thick and fluffy, a perfect melt-in-the-mouth topping. Composed primarily of whipped egg whites and sugar and baked only until the top is golden brown, it remains soft and airy. Hard meringue (see page 284) is formed into shells and baked at a low temperature until crisp and dry. Filled with yogurt or ice cream, hard meringues make a sumptuous dessert too.

Prep: 10 minutes **Stand:** 30 minutes
Makes: 8 servings (tops one 9-inch pie)

- **3 egg whites**
- **½ teaspoon vanilla**
- **¼ teaspoon cream of tartar**
- **6 tablespoons sugar**

1. Allow egg whites to stand at room temperature for 30 minutes. In a large mixing bowl combine egg whites, vanilla, and cream of tartar. Beat with an electric mixer on medium speed about 1 minute or until soft peaks form (tips curl; see photo 1, page 182).

2. Gradually add sugar, 1 tablespoon at a time, beating on high speed about 4 minutes more or until mixture forms stiff, glossy peaks (tips stand straight; see photo 2, page 182) and sugar dissolves (rub a small amount between two fingers; it should feel completely smooth).

3. Immediately spread meringue over hot pie filling, carefully sealing to edge of pastry to prevent shrinkage (see photo, below). Bake as directed in recipes.

Per serving: 42 cal., 0 g total fat (0 g sat. fat), 0 mg chol., 21 mg sodium, 9 g carbo., 0 g fiber, 1 g pro.
Exchanges: ½ Other Carbo.

Four Egg White Meringue: Prepare as above, except use 4 egg whites, 1 teaspoon vanilla, ½ teaspoon cream of tartar, and ½ cup sugar. Beat about 5 minutes or until stiff peaks form.

Per serving: 57 cal., 0 g total fat (0 g sat. fat), 0 mg chol., 28 mg sodium, 12 g carbo., 0 g fiber, 2 g pro.
Exchanges: 1 Other Carbo.

After pouring hot pie filling into the baked shell, spoon meringue over it. Gently spread meringue to the edges of the crust to seal and prevent the meringue from shrinking.

The Facts on Fluff

Making Meringue

Fluffy meringue turns regular pies into mouthwatering masterpieces. For perfect results, follow these need-to-know tips:

Volume control: Allow egg whites to stand at room temperature for 30 minutes to produce a meringue with volume.

Bowl basics: Use the size bowl called for in the recipe because meringue inflates considerably during beating. Copper, stainless-steel, and glass bowls work best.

Lather up: Clean all your bowls and utensils with hot soapy water and carefully dry them before you begin. Even a little oil or grease residue will make a meringue flat and unusable.

Perfect peaks: Once all the sugar has been added to the meringue, continue beating until stiff peaks form and the sugar is completely dissolved. Underbeating may cause shrinkage during baking.

Moisture maintenance: Prevent beading—the small beads of moisture that seep from the surface of the meringue—by not overbaking the meringue.

No tears: Prevent weeping—the watery layer that forms between the meringue and filling layers—by spooning the meringue onto the filling when the filling is still hot. This helps the bottom of the meringue cook at the same rate as the top.

Tidbits on Meringue-Topped Pies

● After removing a meringue-topped pie from the oven, let it cool at room temperature for 1 hour. After cooling, chill the pie, uncovered, for 3 to 6 hours before serving.
● For longer storage, insert several toothpicks into the meringue halfway between the center and edge of the pie. Drape plastic wrap over the toothpicks and chill for up to 2 days. Whipped cream-topped pies can be stored for up to 4 hours.
● Before cutting each slice from a meringue-topped pie, dip the knife in water and do not dry it off. This will prevent meringue from sticking to the knife.

Strawberry Chiffon Pie

Strawberry Chiffon Pie

Prep: 40 minutes **Chill:** 5 hours **Makes:** 8 slices

    1 recipe Baked Pastry Shell (page 453)
    1 envelope unflavored gelatin
    ¾ cup sugar
    ⅓ cup water
    3 egg yolks, beaten
    3 tablespoons lemon juice
      Dash salt
  2½ cups fresh strawberries, crushed (about
      1½ cups after crushing)
    ¾ cup whipping cream

1. Prepare Baked Pastry Shell; set aside. In a saucepan combine gelatin and sugar. Stir in water, egg yolks, lemon juice, and salt. Cook and stir over medium heat until boiling; remove from heat. Transfer gelatin mixture to a bowl; stir in crushed strawberries. Cover; chill for 1 to 1¼ hours or until partially set (consistency of unbeaten egg whites), stirring occasionally.

2. In a chilled mixing bowl beat the whipping cream with an electric mixer until stiff peaks form (see photo 2, page 182). Fold whipped cream into strawberry mixture. Cover and chill about 20 minutes or until mixture mounds when spooned. Spoon filling into cooled pastry shell. Cover; chill at least 4 hours or until firm. If desired, garnish with halved *strawberries*.

Per slice: 326 cal., 19 g total fat (8 g sat. fat), 108 mg chol., 105 mg sodium, 37 g carbo., 1 g fiber, 4 g pro.
Daily Values: 9% vit. A, 49% vit. C, 3% calcium, 7% iron
Exchanges: 1 Starch, 1½ Other Carbo., 3½ Fat

Reduced-Fat Strawberry Chiffon Pie: Prepare as at left, except omit the whipping cream. Combine 2 tablespoons dried egg whites* and 6 tablespoons lukewarm water. Stir 2 minutes or until completely dissolved. Beat with an electric mixer on medium speed until stiff peaks form. Fold into chilled strawberry mixture.

***Note:** Check the baking supply section of your local supermarket for dried egg whites.

Per slice: 254 cal., 10 g total fat (3 g sat. fat), 77 mg chol., 115 mg sodium; 36 g carbo., 1 g fiber, 5 g pro.
Daily Values: 2% vit. A, 48% vit. C, 2% calcium, 7% iron
Exchanges: 1 Starch, 1½ Other Carbo., 2 Fat

French Silk Pie

Prep: 40 minutes **Chill:** 5 hours **Makes:** 8 slices

    1 recipe Baked Pastry Shell (page 453)
    1 cup whipping cream
    1 cup semisweet chocolate pieces (6 ounces)
    ⅓ cup butter
    ⅓ cup sugar
    2 egg yolks, beaten
    3 tablespoons crème de cacao or whipping
      cream
    1 cup whipped cream

1. Prepare Baked Pastry Shell; set aside. In a medium heavy saucepan combine 1 cup whipping cream, the chocolate pieces, butter, and sugar. Cook over low heat, stirring constantly, until chocolate is melted (about 10 minutes). Remove from heat. Gradually stir half of the hot mixture into egg yolks. Return egg mixture to chocolate mixture in saucepan. Cook over medium-low heat, stirring constantly, until mixture is slightly thickened and begins to bubble (about 5 minutes). Remove from heat. (Mixture may appear slightly curdled.) Stir in the 3 tablespoons crème de cacao. Place the saucepan in a bowl of ice water, stirring occasionally, until the mixture stiffens and becomes hard to stir (about 20 minutes).

2. Transfer the chocolate mixture to a medium mixing bowl. Beat chocolate mixture with an electric mixer on medium to high speed for 2 to 3 minutes or until light and fluffy. Spread filling in the Baked Pastry Shell. Cover and chill for 5 to 24 hours. To serve, top with whipped cream.

Per slice: 533 cal., 41 g total fat (21 g sat. fat), 137 mg chol., 168 mg sodium, 31 g carbo., 3 g fiber, 4 g pro.
Daily Values: 21% vit. A, 4% calcium, 6% iron
Exchanges: 2 Other Carbo., 8 Fat

Chocolate-Peanut Butter Pie

Prep: 25 minutes **Chill:** 2 hours **Makes:** 10 slices

- 1 recipe Chocolate Wafer Crust (page 454)
- 1 8-ounce package cream cheese, softened
- ¾ cup peanut butter
- 1 cup powdered sugar
- 2 tablespoons milk
- 1 teaspoon vanilla
- 1 cup whipping cream
- 2 tablespoons powdered sugar
- ¾ cup miniature semisweet chocolate pieces

1. Prepare Chocolate Wafer Crust; set aside. Chill a medium mixing bowl and beaters.

2. For filling, in a large mixing bowl beat cream cheese and peanut butter until smooth. Add the 1 cup powdered sugar, milk, and vanilla; beat until combined.

3. In the chilled mixing bowl beat whipping cream and the 2 tablespoons powdered sugar with the chilled beaters of an electric mixer until soft peaks form (tips curl; see photo 1, page 182). Gently fold about one-third of the whipped cream into the peanut butter mixture. Fold remaining whipped cream and miniature chocolate pieces into peanut butter mixture. Spoon into Chocolate Wafer Crust. If desired, sprinkle with coarsely chopped *peanuts*. Cover and chill about 2 hours or until set.

Per slice: 512 cal., 39 g total fat (18 g sat. fat), 77 mg chol., 343 mg sodium, 32 g carbo., 3 g fiber, 8 g pro.
Daily Values: 18% vit. A, 5% calcium, 5% iron
Exchanges: 2 Other Carbo., 8 Fat

Chocolate Bar Pie

This pie has kid appeal written all over it!

Prep: 40 minutes **Bake:** 12 minutes **Oven:** 325°F
Freeze: 8 hours **Stand:** 10 minutes **Makes:** 8 slices

- 1 recipe Walnut Crust
- 6 1- to 1.5-ounce bars milk chocolate with almonds, chopped
- 15 large marshmallows or 1½ cups tiny marshmallows
- ½ cup milk
- 1 cup whipping cream
- ½ teaspoon vanilla
   Whipped cream (optional)
   Coarsely chopped chocolate-covered English toffee or milk chocolate bars with almonds (optional)

1. Chill a medium mixing bowl and beaters. Prepare and bake Walnut Crust; set aside. Meanwhile, for filling, in a medium saucepan combine the six chopped chocolate bars, the marshmallows, and milk. Cook and stir over medium-low heat until chocolate and marshmallows are melted. Remove from heat. Let the chocolate mixture stand until cooled to room temperature (about 30 minutes).

2. In the chilled mixing bowl beat the 1 cup whipping cream and the vanilla with an electric mixer on medium speed until soft peaks form (tips curl; see photo 1, page 182).

3. Fold whipped cream mixture into cooled chocolate mixture. Spoon chocolate mixture into crust. Freeze about 8 hours or until firm.

4. To serve, remove the pie from the freezer and let stand about 10 minutes before cutting. If desired, garnish with additional whipped cream and chopped chocolate-covered English toffee.

Walnut Crust: Preheat oven to 325°F. In a medium bowl combine 1½ cups (6 ounces) walnuts, coarsely ground; 3 tablespoons butter, melted; and 2 tablespoons sugar. Press onto the bottom and sides of a 9-inch pie plate to form a firm, even crust. Bake for 12 to 14 minutes or until edges are golden. Cool on a wire rack.

Per slice: 464 cal., 38 g total fat (14 g sat. fat), 57 mg chol., 78 mg sodium, 27 g carbo., 2 g fiber, 7 g pro.
Daily Values: 13% vit. A, 1% vit. C, 10% calcium, 6% iron
Exchanges: 2 Other Carbo., ½ High-Fat Meat, 6½ Fat

Chocolate Bar Pie

Pecan Pie

Prep: 25 minutes **Bake:** 45 minutes
Oven: 350°F **Makes:** 8 slices

    1 recipe Pastry for Single-Crust Pie (page 453)
    3 eggs, slightly beaten
    1 cup light-colored corn syrup
    ⅔ cup sugar
    ⅓ cup butter or margarine, melted
    1 teaspoon vanilla
    1¼ cups pecan halves or chopped macadamia
       nuts

1. Preheat oven to 350°F. Prepare and roll out Pastry for Single-Crust Pie. Line a 9-inch pie plate with the pastry circle and trim (see photos 2 and 3, page 454). Crimp edge as desired (see page 435).

2. For filling, in a medium bowl combine eggs, corn syrup, sugar, butter, and vanilla; mix well. Stir in pecan halves.

3. Place the pastry-lined pie plate on the oven rack. Carefully pour the filling into the pastry shell. To prevent overbrowning, cover edge of pie with foil (see page 435). Bake about 25 minutes. Remove foil. Bake for 20 to 25 minutes more or until a knife inserted near the center comes out clean. Cool on a wire rack. Cover and chill within 2 hours.

Per slice: 536 cal., 31 g total fat (8 g sat. fat), 101 mg chol., 205 mg sodium, 64 g carbo., 2 g fiber, 6 g pro.
Daily Values: 7% vit. A, 3% calcium, 9% iron
Exchanges: 1 Starch, 3 Other Carbo., ½ Medium-Fat Meat, 5 Fat

Chocolate Pecan Pie: Prepare as above, except before adding the filling to the pastry-lined pie plate, pat ½ cup semisweet chocolate pieces onto the bottom of pastry.

Per slice: 581 cal., 33 g total fat (9 g sat. fat), 101 mg chol., 205 mg sodium, 71 g carbo., 3 g fiber, 7 g pro.
Daily Values: 7% vit. A, 3% calcium, 11% iron
Exchanges: 1 Starch, 3½ Other Carbo., ½ Medium-Fat Meat, 5½ Fat

Brownie-Walnut Pie

See photo, page 515.

Prep: 40 minutes **Bake:** 50 minutes
Oven: 350°F **Makes:** 8 slices

    ½ cup butter or margarine
    3 ounces unsweetened chocolate, cut up
    1 recipe Pastry for Single-Crust Pie (page 453)
    3 eggs, beaten
    1½ cups sugar
    ½ cup all-purpose flour
    1 teaspoon vanilla
    1 cup chopped walnuts
    1 recipe Hot Fudge Sauce (page 525) or
       fresh fruit, such as raspberries, sliced
       strawberries, or sliced peaches (optional)

1. For filling, in a small heavy saucepan melt butter and chocolate over low heat, stirring frequently. Cool 20 minutes.

2. Preheat oven to 350°F. Prepare and roll out Pastry for Single-Crust Pie. Line a 9-inch pie plate with the pastry circle and trim (see photos 2 and 3, page 454). Crimp edge as desired (see page 435).

3. For filling, combine eggs, sugar, flour, and vanilla; stir in the chocolate mixture and nuts.

4. Pour filling into pastry-lined pie plate. Bake for 50 to 55 minutes or until a knife inserted near the center comes out clean. Cool on a wire rack. If desired, serve with Hot Fudge Sauce or fresh fruit.

Per slice: 597 cal., 38 g total fat (15 g sat. fat), 113 mg chol., 223 mg sodium, 61 g carbo., 3 g fiber, 9 g pro.
Daily Values: 12% vit. A, 4% calcium, 14% iron
Exchanges: 4 Other Carbo., 7½ Fat

Chocolate Macaroon Pie

Prep: 30 minutes **Bake:** 40 minutes **Oven:** 350°F
Chill: 3 hours **Stand:** 30 minutes **Makes:** 10 slices

    1 recipe Butter Pastry
    ½ cup sugar
    ½ cup light-colored corn syrup
    4 ounces semisweet chocolate, chopped
    ¾ cup shredded coconut
    3 eggs, slightly beaten
    ¼ cup butter, melted
    1 tablespoon maraschino cherry juice
    ¼ teaspoon almond extract

1. Prepare Butter Pastry. Preheat oven to 350°F. In a saucepan combine the sugar and corn syrup. Cook and stir until mixture begins to boil. Remove from heat. Stir in chocolate, coconut, eggs, butter, cherry juice, and almond extract. Pour mixture into pastry shell. To prevent overbrowning, cover edge with foil (see page 435).

2. Bake for 40 to 50 minutes or until a knife inserted near the center comes out clean. Cool on a wire rack. Cover and chill for 3 to 24 hours. Let stand at room temperature about 30 minutes before serving.

3. If desired, garnish with *whipped cream* and whole *maraschino cherries*.

Butter Pastry: In a large bowl stir together 1¼ cups flour, 1 tablespoon sugar, and ⅛ teaspoon salt. Using a pastry blender, cut in 6 tablespoons butter until pieces are pea size. Gently stir in one slightly beaten egg. Using your fingers, gently knead dough just until a ball forms. Cover dough with plastic wrap and chill for 30 to 60 minutes or until dough is easy to handle. On a lightly floured surface, use your hands to slightly flatten the dough. Roll dough from center to edges into a circle 12 inches in diameter. Wrap pastry around the rolling pin. Unroll pastry into a 9-inch pie plate without stretching it (see photo 2, page 454). Trim pastry to ½ inch beyond the edge of the pie plate; fold under extra pastry (see photo 3, page 454). Crimp as desired (see page 435). Do not prick pastry.

Per slice: 357 cal., 19 g total fat (12 g sat. fat), 115 mg chol., 162 mg sodium, 44 g carbo., 2 g fiber, 5 g pro.
Daily Values: 9% vit. A, 2% calcium, 10% iron
Exchanges: ½ Starch, 2½ Other Carbo., 4 Fat

Warm Up with Frozen Pies

It doesn't get easier (or more delicious) than an ice cream pie. Take your pick from among these choices for your favorite flavor combinations, toppings, and add-ins.

Strawberry Ice Cream Pie: In a large chilled bowl stir 2 pints (4 cups) strawberry ice cream until softened but not melted. If desired, stir in ½ cup sliced almonds, toasted (see tip, page 265). Spoon ice cream mixture into a purchased graham cracker crumb pie shell,* spreading evenly. Cover; freeze 4 hours or until firm. To serve, let pie stand at room temperature 10 to 15 minutes before slicing. Top slices with warmed hot fudge ice cream topping and, if desired, whole strawberries, whipped cream, and additional toasted almonds.

Mint Ice Cream Pie: In a large chilled bowl stir 2 pints (4 cups) mint-chocolate chip or peppermint ice cream until softened but not melted. Spoon ice cream into a purchased chocolate-flavored crumb pie shell,* spreading evenly. Cover; freeze for 4 hours or until firm. To serve, let pie stand at room temperature for 10 to 15 minutes before slicing. Top slices with warmed hot fudge ice cream topping and, if desired, coarsely chopped chocolate-mint layered candies or crushed peppermint candies.

S'mores Ice Cream Pie: In a large chilled bowl stir 2 pints (4 cups) chocolate ice cream until softened but not melted. Stir in 1 cup miniature marshmallows. Spoon ice cream mixture into a purchased graham cracker crumb or chocolate-flavored crumb pie shell,* spreading evenly. Cover; freeze for at least 4 hours or until firm. To serve, let pie stand at room temperature for 10 to 15 minutes before slicing. Top slices with warmed hot fudge ice cream topping and marshmallows. If desired, top with whipped cream.

Caramel-Butter Pecan Ice Cream Pie: In a large chilled bowl stir 2 pints (4 cups) butter pecan ice cream until softened but not melted. Spoon ice cream into a purchased graham cracker crumb pie shell,* spreading evenly. Cover; freeze at least 4 hours or until firm. To serve, let pie stand at room temperature for 10 to 15 minutes before slicing. Top slices with caramel ice cream topping and, if desired, whipped cream and chopped, toasted pecans.

***Note:** For a better-tasting, easier-to-cut crust, brush purchased crumb pie shell with slightly beaten egg white, bake for 5 minutes in a 375°F oven, and cool completely before filling.

Mint Ice Cream Pie

Butterscotch-Pecan Tart

This decadent pie will have you dancing at the dinner table. If your taste buds can handle the delight, top each slice with whipped cream and chocolate curls. See photo, page 433.

Prep: 30 minutes **Bake:** 15 minutes
Oven: 400°F/350°F **Makes:** 10 slices

  - 1 recipe Rich Tart Pastry (page 452)
  - 3 cups pecan halves
  - 1 recipe Creamy Butterscotch Sauce
  - ⅔ cup semisweet chocolate pieces (4 ounces)
  - ⅓ cup butterscotch-flavored pieces (2 ounces)
    Whipped cream (optional)
    Chocolate curls (see tip, page 271) (optional)

1. Preheat oven to 400°F. Prepare Rich Tart Pastry, rolling it into an 11-inch circle. Transfer pastry circle to a 9-inch tart pan that has a removable bottom. Press pastry into fluted sides of tart pan; trim edges. Line the pastry shell with a double thickness of foil. Bake for 10 minutes. Remove foil. Bake for 5 to 6 minutes or until light brown. Cool slightly on a wire rack. Reduce oven temperature to 350°F.

2. For filling, toast pecans in the oven (see tip, page 265). Meanwhile, prepare Creamy Butterscotch Sauce. Transfer 1¼ cups of the butterscotch sauce to a medium heatproof bowl. Stir in warm pecans, chocolate pieces, and butterscotch-flavored pieces, stirring until the pieces are melted. Pour filling into pastry shell.

3. Bake about 15 minutes or until filling edges are bubbly; cool on rack. Remove pan sides. Serve with remaining butterscotch sauce and, if desired, whipped cream and chocolate curls.

Creamy Butterscotch Sauce: In a medium heavy saucepan melt ½ cup butter over low heat, stirring often. Increase heat to medium. Stir in ⅔ cup granulated sugar, ⅔ cup packed dark brown sugar, ¾ cup light-colored corn syrup, 2 tablespoons water, and ¼ teaspoon salt. Bring to boiling, stirring constantly; reduce heat. Simmer, uncovered, for 5 minutes, stirring often. Remove from heat. Carefully stir in ¾ cup whipping cream and 2 teaspoons vanilla. Cover and chill remaining sauce for up to 2 weeks. Makes about 2⅔ cups.

Per slice: 536 cal., 39 g total fat (14 g sat. fat), 75 mg chol., 126 mg sodium, 47 g carbo., 4 g fiber, 5 g pro.
Daily Values: 10% vit. A, 1% vit. C, 5% calcium, 10% iron
Exchanges: ½ Starch, 3 Other Carbo., 5 Fat

☙FAVORITE Browned Butter Tart

Vanilla beans often can be found in the spice aisles of large supermarkets and natural foods stores. They're somewhat expensive but are considered well worth the price because they impart such an outstanding vanilla flavor.

Prep: 40 minutes **Bake:** 35 minutes **Oven:** 350°F
Cool: 1 hour **Makes:** 12 slices

  - 1 recipe Rich Tart Pastry (page 452)
  - 3 eggs
  - 1¼ cups sugar
  - ½ cup all-purpose flour
  - 1 vanilla bean, split lengthwise, or 1 teaspoon vanilla
  - ¾ cup butter
  - 3 cups assorted mixed berries or assorted cut-up fresh fruit
    Whipped cream (optional)

1. Preheat oven to 350°F. Prepare and roll out Rich Tart Pastry. Transfer pastry circle to a 10-inch tart pan that has a removable bottom. Press pastry into fluted sides of tart pan; trim edges. Set aside.

2. For filling, in a large bowl slightly beat eggs with a fork. Stir in sugar, flour, and, if using, liquid vanilla; set aside. In a medium heavy saucepan combine the vanilla bean (if using) and butter. Cook over medium-high heat until the butter turns the color of light brown sugar. Remove from heat. Remove and discard vanilla bean. Slowly add the browned butter to the egg mixture, stirring until combined. Pour filling into the pastry-lined tart pan.

3. Bake about 35 minutes or until the top is crisp and golden. To serve warm, cool in pan on a wire rack for 1 hour.

4. To serve, remove sides of the tart pan. Serve with assorted mixed berries and, if desired, whipped cream. Cover and chill within 2 hours.

Per slice: 365 cal., 21 g total fat (13 g sat. fat), 138 mg chol., 156 mg sodium, 40 g carbo., 3 g fiber, 4 g pro.
Daily Values: 15% vit. A, 11% vit. C, 3% calcium, 8% iron
Exchanges: ½ Starch, 4 Other Carbo., 4½ Fat

Fresh Fruit and Cream Tarts

Fresh Fruit and Cream Tarts

Berries, papaya, and kiwifruits work exceptionally well with the rich Pastry Cream in these tarts, but they're not the only options. Try other fruits—such as seasonal favorites—for different flavors, textures, and shapes. Turn each tart into art!

Prep: 40 minutes **Bake:** 13 minutes **Oven:** 450°F
Chill: 4 hours **Makes:** 8 tarts

- 1 **recipe Rich Tart Pastry (page 452)**
- 1 **recipe Pastry Cream**
- 2 **cups fresh fruit such as sliced strawberries; raspberries; blackberries; peeled, sliced papaya; and/or peeled, sliced kiwifruits**

1. Preheat oven to 450°F. Prepare Rich Tart Pastry through Step 1; divide pastry into eight portions. On a floured surface, use your hands to slightly flatten each portion. Roll pastry from center to edges into circles about 5 inches in diameter. Transfer each pastry circle to a 4-inch tart pan that has a removable bottom. Press pastry into fluted sides of tart pans; trim edges. Prick bottoms and sides of pastry shells. Line pastry shells with a double thickness of foil. Place on a baking sheet. Bake for 8 minutes. Remove foil. Bake for 5 to 6 minutes more or until shells are golden. Cool on a wire rack.

2. Meanwhile, prepare and chill Pastry Cream. To serve, divide the chilled Pastry Cream among the baked pastry shells. Arrange fresh fruit on top of each tart. Remove sides of tart pans.

Pastry Cream: In a medium heavy saucepan stir together ½ cup sugar, 4 teaspoons cornstarch, and ¼ teaspoon salt. Gradually stir in 2 cups half-and-half or light cream. If desired, add 1 vanilla bean, split lengthwise. Cook and stir over medium heat until thickened and bubbly. Cook and stir for 1 minute more. Gradually stir half of the hot mixture into 4 beaten egg yolks. Return all of the egg yolk mixture to the saucepan. Bring to a gentle boil; reduce heat. Cook and stir for 2 minutes. Remove from heat. Remove vanilla bean. Strain into a bowl. If not using vanilla bean, stir in 1 teaspoon vanilla. Place bowl of Pastry Cream in a bowl of ice water; chill for 5 minutes, stirring occasionally. Cover surface with plastic wrap. Chill about 4 hours or until cold; do not stir. Makes 2 cups.

Whole Fresh Fruit and Cream Tart: Prepare as at left, except roll out Rich Tart Pastry as directed on page 452 and transfer pastry circle to a 10-inch tart pan that has a removable bottom. Press pastry into fluted sides of tart pan and trim edges. Do not prick pastry. Bake and cool as at left. To serve, fill cooled pastry shell with Pastry Cream and top with fruit. Makes 8 slices.

Per individual tart or slice whole tart variation: 386 cal., 23 g total fat (13 g sat. fat), 211 mg chol., 228 mg sodium, 40 g carbo., 1 g fiber, 6 g pro.
Daily Values: 18% vit. A, 36% vit. C, 9% calcium, 8% iron
Exchanges: 1 Starch, 1½ Other Carbo., 4½ Fat

Praising Pastry Cream

Pastry Cream is tops when it comes to luscious fillings. This egg-based puddinglike dessert cream blends wonderfully with fresh fruit, either alone or in a variety of desserts. It also can be spooned into Cream Puffs and Éclairs (recipes, page 288) or Meringue Shells (page 284). Use a pastry bag to pipe it into doughnuts, Danish pastries, and cupcakes, or spread it between cake layers before frosting the cake. When alternately layered with cubes of purchased pound cake and cut-up fruit, Pastry Cream helps make a delicious trifle.

Key Lime Tart

FAVORITE
Key Lime Tart

The filling's smooth green color comes from the optional food coloring. Without it, the filling's color is pale and creamy, with an almost buttery appearance. Either way, it looks and tastes superb.

Prep: 20 minutes **Bake:** 15 minutes **Oven:** 350°F
Cool: 1 hour **Chill:** 2 hours **Makes:** 8 slices

   1 **recipe Baked Pastry Tart Shell (page 453)**
   4 **egg yolks**
   1 **14-ounce can sweetened condensed milk (1¼ cups)**
   1 **teaspoon finely shredded lime peel**
   ½ **cup lime juice (10 to 12 Key limes or 4 to 6 Persian limes) or bottled Key lime juice**
      Few drops green food coloring (optional)
      Whipped cream

1. Prepare Baked Pastry Tart Shell; set aside. Preheat oven to 350°F. For filling, in a medium bowl beat egg yolks with a wire whisk or fork. Gradually stir in sweetened condensed milk; add lime peel, lime juice, and, if desired, food coloring. Mix well (mixture will thicken slightly).

2. Spoon filling into Baked Pastry Tart Shell. Bake for 15 to 20 minutes or until set. Cool on a wire rack for 1 hour. Chill for 2 to 3 hours before serving; cover for longer storage.

3. To serve, remove sides of tart pan. Pipe whipped cream (see tip, page 247) onto slices.

Per slice: 330 cal., 15 g total fat (6 g sat. fat), 119 mg chol., 141 mg sodium, 42 g carbo., 1 g fiber, 7 g pro.
Daily Values: 6% vit. A, 10% vit. C, 16% calcium, 7% iron
Exchanges: 1 Starch, 2 Other Carbo., 2½ Fat

Country Peach Tart

See photo, page 433.

Prep: 30 minutes **Bake:** 35 minutes **Oven:** 375°F
Cool: 30 minutes **Makes:** 8 slices

   1 **recipe Pastry for Single-Crust Pie (page 453)**
   ¼ **cup sugar**
   4 **teaspoons all-purpose flour**
   ¼ **teaspoon ground nutmeg**
   3 **cups sliced, peeled peaches or nectarines (1 pound)**
   1 **tablespoon lemon juice**
   1 **tablespoon sliced almonds**

1. Preheat oven to 375°F. Line a baking sheet with foil; sprinkle with flour. Prepare Pastry for Single-Crust Pie through Step 2. Roll pastry into a 13-inch circle on prepared baking sheet.

2. For filling, in a large bowl stir together sugar, flour, and nutmeg. Add peaches and lemon juice; toss until coated. Mound filling in center of pastry, leaving the outer 2 inches uncovered. Fold uncovered pastry up over filling (see photo, below). Sprinkle filling with sliced almonds. Lightly brush pastry top and sides with *milk*.

3. Bake for 35 to 40 minutes or until filling is bubbly and crust is golden. If necessary, cover edge of tart with foil to prevent overbrowning (see page 435). Cool 30 minutes on the baking sheet. If desired, dust edges with *powdered sugar* and serve with *whipped cream.*

Country Pear Tart: Prepare 1 recipe Browned Butter Pastry (page 453) through Step 2 of pastry recipe. Prepare filling as above, except substitute 4 cups sliced, peeled pears (1⅓ pounds) for the peaches and 1 tablespoon finely chopped crystallized ginger or ¼ teaspoon ground ginger for the nutmeg. Assemble tart as above, except after brushing pastry edges with milk, sprinkle with additional granulated sugar. Bake as above. Do not dust with powdered sugar.

Per slice peach or pear variation: 233 cal., 9 g total fat (2 g sat. fat), 0 mg chol., 74 mg sodium, 36 g carbo., 3 g fiber, 3 g pro.
Daily Values: 14% vit. A, 16% vit. C, 1% calcium, 6% iron
Exchanges: 1 Fruit, 1½ Other Carbo., 1½ Fat

With your hands, gently fold the pastry edges over the filling. Pleat the pastry as necessary to keep it flat against the fruit.

Dried Fruit Tart

For an easy lattice topping, instead of interweaving the pastry strips, simply lay half of the strips on the filling at 1-inch intervals and arrange the remaining strips perpendicular to and on top of the first strips.

Prep: 35 minutes **Bake:** 45 minutes
Oven: 375°F **Makes:** 12 slices

  1 recipe Pastry for Lattice-Top Pie (page 454)
1²⁄₃ cups apple juice or apple cider
  ¾ cup snipped dried apricots or peaches
  ¾ cup snipped dried pitted plums (prunes)
  ½ cup dried tart cherries or raisins
  ⅓ cup packed brown sugar
  ¼ cup all-purpose flour
  ¼ teaspoon ground nutmeg
  1 cup chopped, peeled cooking apple or pear
  ½ cup broken walnuts

1. Preheat oven to 375°F. Prepare and roll out Pastry for Lattice-Top Pie. Transfer a pastry circle to a 10- or 11-inch tart pan that has a removable bottom. Press pastry into fluted sides of tart pan and trim edges. Cut remaining pastry circle into ½-inch-wide strips for lattice top.

2. For filling, in a medium saucepan combine apple juice, apricots, plums, and cherries. Bring to boiling; reduce heat. Simmer, covered, for 10 minutes. Remove from heat. Meanwhile, in a bowl stir together brown sugar, flour, and nutmeg; add chopped apple and walnuts. Gradually stir dried fruit mixture into apple mixture.

3. Transfer filling to pastry-lined tart pan. Top with pastry strips in lattice pattern (see photos 1 through 3, below and right). If desired, brush pastry strips with *milk* and sprinkle with *granulated sugar*. Bake about 45 minutes or until filling is bubbly and pastry is golden. Cool on a wire rack. To serve, remove sides of tart pan.

Per slice: 333 cal., 15 g total fat (3 g sat. fat), 0 mg chol., 152 mg sodium, 47 g carbo., 3 g fiber, 4 g pro.
Daily Values: 16% vit. A, 2% vit. C, 3% calcium, 12% iron
Exchanges: 1½ Fruit, 1½ Other Carbo., 3 Fat

1. To create a lattice top, lay half of the pastry strips over filling at 1-inch intervals.

2. Fold every other pastry strip in half. Place a pastry strip across the middle of the tart, perpendicular to the first strips. Unfold the folded strips; fold the unfolded strips in half and add another strip.

3. Continue in this manner until the pie is covered with a lattice top. Use your fingers to trim all the strips even with the edge of the pan. Press the strips against the edge to seal.

Nut and Chocolate Chip Tart

This luscious pie filling is just like that used for pecan pie, only with chocolate pieces and a variety of rich, salty nuts instead of just pecans.

Prep: 30 minutes **Bake:** 40 minutes
Oven: 350°F **Makes:** 8 slices

  1 recipe Pastry for Single-Crust Pie (page 453)
  3 eggs
  1 cup light-colored corn syrup
  ½ cup packed brown sugar
  ⅓ cup butter, melted and cooled
  1 teaspoon vanilla
  1 cup coarsely chopped salted mixed nuts
  ½ cup miniature semisweet chocolate pieces

1. Preheat oven to 350°F. Prepare and roll out Pastry for Single-Crust Pie. Transfer the pastry circle to an 11-inch tart pan that has a removable bottom. Press pastry into fluted sides of tart pan and trim edges. Do not prick pastry.

2. For filling, in a large bowl beat eggs slightly with a fork. Stir in corn syrup. Add brown sugar, melted butter, and vanilla, stirring until sugar is dissolved. Stir in nuts and chocolate pieces. Place pastry-lined tart pan on a baking sheet; place baking sheet on the oven rack. Carefully pour filling into tart pan. Bake about 40 minutes or until a knife inserted near the center comes out clean. Cool on a wire rack.

3. To serve, remove sides from tart pan. Cover and chill within 2 hours.

Per slice: 439 cal., 23 g total fat (8 g sat. fat), 80 mg chol., 210 mg sodium, 52 g carbo., 2 g fiber, 6 g pro.
Daily Values: 6% vit. A, 3% calcium, 8% iron
Exchanges: ½ Starch, 3 Other Carbo., 5 Fat

Teeny-Tiny Tartlets

Paper-thin and irresistibly flaky phyllo dough now comes conveniently packaged as miniature prebaked shells, which serve as the perfect vessels for sweet or savory fillings. If you like, experiment with a variety of other fillings and toppers.

Chocolate and Fruit Tartlets: Combine 2 tablespoons each of snipped dried apricots and snipped dried cherries. Spoon fruit mixture evenly into 15 baked miniature phyllo dough shells (one 2.1-ounce package). In a small bowl combine ⅓ cup chocolate-hazelnut spread, 1 tablespoon orange juice, and 1 teaspoon brandy or orange juice. Spoon into shells on top of fruit. Sprinkle with 2 tablespoons finely chopped almonds, toasted (see tip, page 265). Hold at room temperature for up to 8 hours.

Fruit-Topped Phyllo Tartlets: In a small bowl stir 2 tablespoons powdered sugar into 4 ounces (half of an 8-ounce package) cream cheese until smooth. Spoon cream cheese mixture into 15 baked miniature phyllo dough shells (one 2.1-ounce package). Using a knife, chop about 15 fresh strawberries or seedless grapes. Toss with about 2 tablespoons pourable strawberry all-fruit topping. Divide fruit evenly among tartlets. Serve immediately or cover and chill up to 4 hours before serving. Top with whipped cream before serving.

Mini Apple-Pecan Tartlets: Using a knife, chop the apples in 1 cup canned apple pie filling. Spoon about 1 tablespoon filling into each of 15 baked miniature phyllo dough shells (one 2.1-ounce package). Sprinkle filling with 2 tablespoons finely chopped pecans, toasted (see tip, page 265). If desired, pipe whipped cream (see tip, page 247) on top of each mini tartlet and sprinkle with cinnamon-sugar. Serve within 30 minutes.

Little Lemon Tartlets: Stir ⅓ cup purchased lemon curd to loosen it. Spoon 2 teaspoons curd into each of 15 baked miniature phyllo dough shells (one 2.1-ounce package). Top lemon curd in each tartlet with a fresh raspberry. If desired, sift with powdered sugar before serving. Serve within 1 hour.

Rich Tart Pastry

Sugar, butter, and egg yolks are the "rich" additions.

Prep: 15 minutes **Chill:** 30 minutes
Makes: 1 tart crust (8 servings)

- 1¼ **cups all-purpose flour**
- ¼ **cup sugar**
- ½ **cup cold butter**
- 2 **egg yolks, beaten**
- 1 **tablespoon ice water**

1. In a medium bowl stir together flour and sugar. Using a pastry blender, cut in butter until pieces are pea size (see photo 1, page 454). In a small bowl stir together egg yolks and ice water. Gradually stir egg yolk mixture into flour mixture. Using your fingers, gently knead the pastry just until a ball forms. Cover pastry with plastic wrap and chill for 30 to 60 minutes or until pastry is easy to handle.

2. On a floured surface, use your hands to slightly flatten the pastry. Roll pastry from center to edges into a circle 12 inches in diameter.

3. Wrap pastry circle around the rolling pin. Unroll it into a 10-inch tart pan that has a removable bottom. Ease pastry into pan without stretching it (see photo 2, page 454). Press pastry into fluted sides of tart pan; trim edges. Do not prick pastry. Fill and bake pastry as directed in recipes.

Per serving: 217 cal., 14 g total fat (8 g sat. fat), 86 mg chol., 126 mg sodium, 21 g carbo., 1 g fiber, 3 g pro.
Daily Values: 11% vit. A, 1% calcium, 6% iron
Exchanges: 1 Starch, 1½ Other Carbo., 2½ Fat

Oil Pastry for Single-Crust Pie `EASY`

Prep: 10 minutes **Makes:** 1 piecrust (8 servings)

- 1⅓ cups all-purpose flour
- ¼ teaspoon salt
- ¼ cup cooking oil
- 3 to 4 tablespoons milk

1. In a medium bowl stir together flour and salt. Add oil and 3 tablespoons milk all at once to flour mixture. Stir lightly with a fork until combined. If necessary, stir in 1 tablespoon additional milk to moisten (pastry will appear crumbly). Form pastry into a ball.

2. On a lightly floured surface, use your hands to slightly flatten pastry ball. Roll pastry from center to edges into a circle 12 inches in diameter (press any cracks back together). Ease pastry into pie plate without stretching it (see photo 2, page 454). Trim pastry to ½ inch beyond edge of pie plate. Fold under extra pastry (see photo 3, page 454). Crimp edge as desired (see page 435). Do not prick pastry. Fill and bake pastry as directed in recipes.

Per serving: 133 cal., 7 g total fat (1 g sat. fat), 1 mg chol., 76 mg sodium, 15 g carbo., 1 g fiber, 2 g pro.
Daily Values: 1% calcium, 5% iron
Exchanges: 1 Starch, 1½ Fat

Pastry for Single-Crust Pie

For a flavor boost, use butter-flavored shortening.

Prep: 10 minutes **Makes:** 1 piecrust (8 servings)

- 1¼ cups all-purpose flour
- ¼ teaspoon salt
- ⅓ cup shortening
- 4 to 5 tablespoons cold water

1. In a medium bowl stir together flour and salt. Using a pastry blender, cut in shortening until pieces are pea size (see photo 1, page 454).

2. Sprinkle 1 tablespoon of the water over part of the flour mixture; gently toss with a fork. Push moistened pastry to the side of the bowl. Repeat moistening flour mixture, using 1 tablespoon of the water at a time, until all the flour mixture is moistened. Form pastry into a ball.

3. On a lightly floured surface, use your hands to slightly flatten pastry. Roll pastry from center to edges into a circle about 12 inches in diameter.

4. Wrap pastry circle around the rolling pin. Unroll into a 9-inch pie plate. Ease into pie plate without stretching it (see photo 2, page 454).

5. Trim pastry to ½ inch beyond edge of pie plate. Fold under extra pastry (see photo 3, page 454). Crimp edge as desired (see page 435). Do not prick pastry. Fill and bake pastry as directed in recipes.

Browned Butter Pastry: Prepare as at left, except reduce shortening to 2 tablespoons and melt ¼ cup butter over medium heat until butter turns the color of light brown sugar. Cover; chill browned butter until solid, about 45 minutes. Add 1 tablespoon sugar to the flour mixture. Using a pastry blender, cut in browned butter and shortening. Continue with Step 2.

Food processor directions: Place steel blade in food processor bowl. Add flour, salt, and shortening. Cover and process with on/off turns until most of mixture resembles cornmeal but a few larger pieces remain. With food processor running, quickly add 3 tablespoons water through feed tube. Stop processor as soon as all water is added; scrape down sides. Process with two on/off turns (mixture may not all be moistened). Remove pastry from bowl; shape into a ball. Continue with Step 3 at left.

Baked Pastry Shell: Prepare as at left, except prick bottom and sides of pastry with a fork. Line pastry with a double thickness of foil. Bake in a 450°F oven for 8 minutes. Remove foil. Bake 5 to 6 minutes more or until crust is golden. Cool on a wire rack.

Baked Pastry Tart Shell: Prepare as at left through Step 3. Wrap pastry circle around the rolling pin. Unroll it into a 10-inch tart pan with a removable bottom. Ease pastry into pan without stretching it (see photo 1, page 454). Press pastry into fluted sides of tart pan and trim edges. Prick pastry with a fork. Line pastry with a double thickness of foil. Bake in a 450°F oven for 8 minutes. Remove foil. Bake 6 to 8 minutes more or until golden. Cool on a wire rack.

Per serving regular, browned butter, food processor, pastry shell, or pastry tart shell variations: 140 cal., 9 g total fat (2 g sat. fat), 0 mg chol., 73 mg sodium, 14 g carbo., 0 g fiber, 2 g pro.
Daily Values: 4% iron
Exchanges: 1 Starch, 1½ Fat

Graham Cracker Crust ⬤EASY

Prep: 10 minutes **Chill:** 1 hour
Makes: 1 piecrust (8 servings)

⅓ **cup butter**
¼ **cup sugar**
1¼ **cups finely crushed graham crackers (about 18)**

1. Melt butter; stir in sugar. Add crushed crackers; toss to mix well. Spread in a 9-inch pie plate; press evenly onto bottom and sides. Chill about 1 hour. (Or bake in a 375°F oven for 4 to 5 minutes or until edges are light brown. Cool completely on a wire rack before filling.) Fill as directed in recipes.

Chocolate Wafer, Gingersnap, or Vanilla Wafer Crust: Prepare as above, except omit sugar and substitute 1½ cups finely crushed chocolate wafers (about 25), 1¼ cups finely crushed gingersnaps (20 to 22), or 1½ cups finely crushed vanilla wafers (about 44) for the graham crackers. Do not bake the chocolate wafer variation.

Per serving graham cracker, chocolate wafer, gingersnap, or vanilla wafer variations: 154 cal., 9 g total fat (5 g sat. fat), 22 mg chol., 154 mg sodium, 17 g carbo., 0 g fiber, 1 g pro.
Daily Values: 6% vit. A, 1% calcium, 3% iron
Exchanges: 2 Other Carbo., 2 Fat

Pastry for Double-Crust Pie

To make perfect pastry, follow the tips on page 435.

Prep: 15 minutes **Makes:** 2 piecrusts (8 servings)

2¼ **cups all-purpose flour**
¾ **teaspoon salt**
⅔ **cup shortening**
8 **to 10 tablespoons cold water**

1. In a medium bowl stir together flour and salt. Using a pastry blender, cut in shortening until pieces are pea size (see photo 1, right).

2. Sprinkle 1 tablespoon of the water over part of the flour mixture; toss with a fork. Push moistened pastry to side of bowl. Repeat moistening flour mixture, using 1 tablespoon of the water at a time, until flour mixture is moistened. Divide pastry in half; form halves into balls.

3. On lightly floured surface, use your hands to slightly flatten one pastry ball. Roll it from center to edges into a circle 12 inches in diameter.

4. Wrap pastry circle around the rolling pin. Unroll pastry into a 9-inch pie plate. Ease pastry into pie plate without stretching it (see photo 2, below). Trim pastry even with rim of pie plate. Transfer desired filling to pastry-lined pie plate.

5. Roll remaining ball into a circle 12 inches in diameter. Cut slits in pastry. Place pastry circle on filling; trim to ½ inch beyond edge of plate. Fold top pastry under bottom pastry (see photo 4, below). Crimp edge as desired (see page 435). Bake as directed in recipes.

Pastry for Lattice-Top Pie: Prepare as at left, except trim bottom pastry to ½ inch beyond edge of pie plate. Roll out remaining pastry and cut into ½-inch-wide strips. Transfer desired filling to pastry-lined pie plate. Weave strips over filling in a lattice pattern (see photos 1, 2, and 3, page 451). Press strip ends into bottom pastry rim. Fold bottom pastry over strip ends; seal and crimp edge. Bake as directed in recipes.

Per serving regular or lattice variation: 269 cal., 17 g total fat (4 g sat. fat), 0 mg chol., 219 mg sodium, 25 g carbo., 1 g fiber, 3 g pro.
Daily Values: 1% calcium, 8% iron
Exchanges: 1½ Starch, 3½ Fat

1. Use a pastry blender to combine the flour mixture and the shortening. For best results, the pieces should be pea size before adding water.

2. To transfer a pastry circle to a pie plate, wrap it around a rolling pin. Unroll the pastry over the plate, being careful not to stretch it. Stretching the pastry will cause it to shrink during baking.

3. For a single-crust pie, trim the pastry to ½ inch beyond the edge of the plate. Fold the pastry under, even with the pie plate's edge, and crimp as desired (see page 435).

4. For a double-crust pie, trim the bottom pastry even with the plate's edge; fill. Top with second pastry circle. Lift the bottom pastry slightly; fold the top pastry under. Crimp as desired (see page 435).

Poultry

Poultry Essentials

Poultry is inexpensive, versatile, and easy to prepare. In fact, chicken tops beef and pork as one of America's most popular foods.

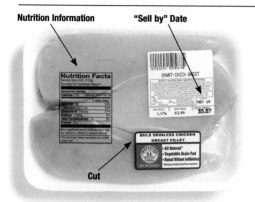

Nutrition Information   "Sell by" Date

Cut

Look at the Label

The labels on poultry are loaded with valuable information:

Type of cut: whole, cut-up, or parts.

"Sell by" date: This tells you not to buy the package after that date. Cook poultry within 3 days of that date too.

"Use by" date: If there is no "sell by" date, then a "use by" date indicates when raw poultry should be cooked or frozen. Precooked chicken should be eaten or frozen by the "use by" date.

Other info: Handling and cooking tips and a nutrition facts panel are also on the label.

Safety First

Storage: Store raw poultry in original package in the coldest part of the refrigerator up to 2 days.

Freeze poultry in its original package up to 2 months at 0°F. To freeze it longer, wrap the package with foil. Whole poultry will keep up to 1 year; cut-up pieces up to 9 months. (Never freeze stuffed poultry.)

Careful thawing: Never thaw poultry on the countertop. Thaw it in a dish in the refrigerator, allowing 9 hours for parts and 24 hours for every 5 pounds of whole birds.

For quick thawing, place poultry in an airtight bag in a sink of cold water. Allow 30 minutes per pound, changing the water every 30 minutes. Cook water-thawed poultry soon after thawing.

Keep it clean: Wash work surfaces and utensils in hot soapy water before and right after handling raw poultry to prevent spread of bacteria.

Use separate cutting boards for raw poultry and other foods, such as vegetables.

Never use the same plate for uncooked and cooked poultry.

Is It Done?

● A thermometer is the most accurate way to check doneness. Dark meat is done at 180°F, white meat at 170°F, and ground poultry at 165°F. See page 478 for tips on using a thermometer.

● No thermometer? Pierce thickest part with a fork. The meat should be tender and no longer pink in the center; juices should run clear.

Good to Know

● Rinsing raw poultry isn't necessary. The less you handle it, the better. You may rinse cavities of whole birds that will be stuffed, however. Drain well and pat dry with paper towels.

● Discard used marinades. Instead, reserve some unused marinade to serve with the dish.

● Do not partially cook poultry, refrigerate it, then finish it later. Bacteria can grow.

● Serve cooked poultry immediately; refrigerate leftovers within 2 hours.

Rotisserie Versatility

Use the flavorful meat from deli rotisserie chicken in one of the following ways:

● Layer shredded chicken on buns and top with barbecue sauce.

● Simmer chicken chunks with enchilada sauce to use in tacos or in pasta sauce to spoon over hot cooked pasta.

● Toss chicken shreds in a favorite salad.

● Top a pizza crust with pesto, chicken, and smoked mozzarella.

Buttermilk-Brined Fried Chicken

While the brine contains a significant amount of salt, it is the salt that brings out amazing flavors.

Prep: 30 minutes **Chill:** 2 hours
Cook: 12 minutes per batch **Makes:** 6 servings

- 3 cups buttermilk
- ⅓ cup coarse salt
- 2 tablespoons sugar
- 2½ to 3 pounds meaty chicken pieces (breast halves, thighs, and drumsticks)
- 2 cups all-purpose flour
- ¼ teaspoon salt
- ¼ teaspoon black pepper
- ¾ cup buttermilk
  Cooking oil

1. For brine, in a resealable plastic bag set in a bowl combine the 3 cups buttermilk, the coarse salt, and sugar. Cut chicken breasts in half crosswise. Add all chicken pieces to the brine; seal bag. Chill for 2 to 4 hours; remove chicken from brine. Drain chicken; pat dry with paper towels. Discard brine.

2. In a large bowl stir together flour, the ¼ teaspoon salt, and pepper. Place the ¾ cup buttermilk in a shallow dish. Coat chicken with flour mixture, dip in the buttermilk, and coat again with flour mixture.

3. Meanwhile, in a deep, heavy Dutch oven or kettle or a deep-fat fryer heat 1½ inches oil to 350°F. Using tongs, carefully add a few pieces of chicken to hot oil. (Oil temperature will drop; maintain temperature at 325°F.) Fry chicken for 12 to 15 minutes or until chicken is no longer pink (170°F for breasts; 180°F for thighs

and drumsticks) and coating is golden, turning once. Drain on a wire rack or on paper towels. If desired, keep fried chicken warm in a 300°F oven while frying remaining chicken pieces.

Spicy Buttermilk-Brined Fried Chicken: Prepare as at left, except add 1½ teaspoons cayenne pepper to the flour mixture.

Per 3 ounces plain or spicy variation: 549 cal., 30 g total fat (6 g sat. fat), 88 mg chol., 1,191 mg sodium, 35 g carbo., 1 g fiber, 34 g pro.
Daily Values: 2% vit. C, 9% calcium, 19% iron
Exchanges: 2½ Starch, 3½ Medium-Fat Meat, 2 Fat

Pecan Buttermilk-Brined Fried Chicken: Prepare as at left, except reduce the flour to 1¼ cups and add ¾ cup ground pecans to the flour mixture.

Per 3 ounces: 585 cal., 40 g total fat (7 g sat. fat), 88 mg chol., 1,191 mg sodium, 25 g carbo., 2 g fiber, 33 g pro.
Daily Values: 1% vit. A, 2% vit. C, 10% calcium, 17% iron
Exchanges: 1½ Starch, 3½ Medium-Fat Meat, 4 Fat

★FAVORITE Maryland Fried Chicken with Creamy Gravy

What sets this fried chicken apart is that the pieces simmer in milk. Serve it with Mashed Potatoes (page 587).

Prep: 20 minutes **Cook:** 55 minutes **Makes:** 6 servings

- 1 egg, beaten
- 3 tablespoons milk
- 1 cup finely crushed saltine crackers (28 crackers)
- 1 teaspoon dried thyme, crushed
- ½ teaspoon paprika
- ⅛ teaspoon black pepper
- 2½ to 3 pounds meaty chicken pieces (breast halves, thighs, and drumsticks)
- 2 to 3 tablespoons cooking oil
- 1 cup milk
- 1 recipe Creamy Gravy (page 459)

1. In a small bowl combine the egg and the 3 tablespoons milk. In a shallow bowl combine crushed crackers, thyme, paprika, and pepper. Dip chicken pieces, one at a time, in egg mixture; roll in cracker mixture.

2. In a large skillet brown chicken in hot oil over medium heat for 10 to 15 minutes, turning occasionally. Drain well.

3. Add the 1 cup milk to skillet. Heat just to boiling. Reduce heat to medium low; partially cover skillet. Cook for 35 minutes. Uncover;

Buttermilk-Brined Fried Chicken

cook about 10 minutes more or until chicken is no longer pink (170°F for breasts; 180°F for thighs and drumsticks). Transfer chicken to a serving platter, reserving drippings for gravy. Cover chicken; keep warm. Prepare Creamy Gravy.

Creamy Gravy: Skim fat from drippings. Reserve 3 tablespoons of the drippings in skillet. In a screw-top jar combine ¾ cup milk, 3 tablespoons all-purpose flour, ¼ teaspoon salt, and ⅛ teaspoon black pepper; cover and shake until well combined. Add to skillet. Stir in an additional 1 cup milk. Cook over medium heat, stirring constantly, until thickened and bubbly. Cook and stir for 1 minute more. (If desired, thin with additional milk.) Makes about 1¾ cups.

Per 3 ounces chicken + ¼ cup gravy: 404 cal., 20 g total fat (5 g sat. fat), 131 mg chol., 423 mg sodium, 19 g carbo., 1 g fiber, 35 g pro.
Daily Values: 8% vit. A, 17% calcium, 14% iron
Exchanges: ½ Milk, 1 Starch, 4 Lean Meat, 1½ Fat

Pan-Fried Chicken with Gravy

Hold the chicken in a 300°F oven to keep it warm while you make the gravy.

Prep: 25 minutes **Cook:** 35 minutes **Makes:** 6 servings

- ⅓ cup all-purpose flour
- 1½ teaspoons poultry seasoning or paprika; dried basil or marjoram, crushed; or ½ teaspoon garlic powder or onion powder
- ½ teaspoon salt
- ¼ teaspoon black pepper
- 2½ to 3 pounds meaty chicken pieces (breast halves, thighs, and drumsticks)
  Cooking oil
- 1 recipe Gravy

1. In a plastic bag combine flour, poultry seasoning, salt, and pepper. Add chicken pieces, a few at a time, shaking to coat.

2. In a large heavy skillet heat ¼ to ½ inch oil over medium-high heat until hot enough to sizzle a drop of water. Reduce heat.

3. Add chicken to the skillet. (Do not crowd skillet. If necessary, use two skillets.) Cook, uncovered, over medium heat for 15 minutes, turning to brown evenly. Reduce heat; cover tightly. Cook for 15 minutes. Uncover and cook for 5 to 10 minutes more or until chicken is no longer pink (170°F for breasts; 180°F for thighs and drumsticks). Drain on paper towels, reserv-

ing drippings for gravy. Transfer chicken to a serving platter; keep warm. Prepare Gravy.

Oven directions: Prepare as at left, except brown chicken in a large ovenproof skillet. (Or brown chicken in a regular skillet; transfer to a 15×10×1-inch baking pan, arranging bone sides down.) Bake, uncovered, in a 375°F oven for 35 to 40 minutes or until chicken is no longer pink. Do not turn.

Gravy: Reserve 2 tablespoons of the drippings in skillet. Add 2 tablespoons all-purpose flour, ⅛ teaspoon black pepper, and, if desired, 1 teaspoon instant chicken bouillon granules, stirring until smooth. Add 1⅔ cups whole milk all at once. Cook and stir over medium heat until thickened and bubbly. Cook and stir for 1 minute more. (If desired, thin with additional milk.) Season to taste with salt. Makes 1⅔ cups.

Per 3 ounces chicken + ¼ cup gravy: 409 cal., 27 g total fat (6 g sat. fat), 93 mg chol., 444 mg sodium, 10 g carbo., 0 g fiber, 31 g pro.
Daily Values: 3% vit. A, 1% vit. C, 11% calcium, 11% iron
Exchanges: ½ Starch, 4 Lean Meat, 3 Fat

Lemon-Mustard Chicken LOW FAT FAST

Prep: 10 minutes **Broil:** 20 minutes **Makes:** 6 servings

- 2½ to 3 pounds meaty chicken pieces (breast halves, thighs, and drumsticks)
- 2 tablespoons cooking oil
- 1 tablespoon Dijon-style mustard
- 1 tablespoon lemon juice
- 1½ teaspoons lemon-pepper seasoning
- 1 teaspoon dried oregano or basil, crushed
- ⅛ teaspoon cayenne pepper

1. Preheat broiler. Skin chicken. Place chicken, bone sides up, on the unheated rack of a broiler pan. Broil 4 to 5 inches from the heat for 15 to 20 minutes or until light brown.

2. Meanwhile, in a bowl stir together oil, mustard, lemon juice, lemon-pepper seasoning, oregano, and cayenne pepper. Brush mustard mixture on chicken. Turn chicken; brush with remaining mixture. Broil for 5 to 10 minutes more or until chicken is no longer pink (170°F for breasts; 180°F for thighs and drumsticks).

Per 3 ounces: 207 cal., 11 g total fat (2 g sat. fat), 77 mg chol., 355 mg sodium, 1 g carbo., 0 g fiber, 25 g pro.
Daily Values: 1% vit. A, 2% vit. C, 2% calcium, 7% iron
Exchanges: 3½ Medium-Fat Meat, ½ Fat

Oven-Fried Chicken

Oven-frying chicken cuts back on the fat and effort. Fried tenders are a kid-friendly favorite.

Prep: 20 minutes **Bake:** 45 minutes
Oven: 375°F **Makes:** 6 servings

> 1 **egg, beaten**
> 3 **tablespoons milk**
> 1¼ **cups crushed cornflakes or finely crushed rich round crackers (about 35 crackers)**
> 1 **teaspoon dried thyme, crushed**
> ½ **teaspoon paprika**
> ¼ **teaspoon salt**
> ⅛ **teaspoon black pepper**
> 2 **tablespoons butter or margarine, melted**
> 2½ **to 3 pounds meaty chicken pieces (breast halves, thighs, and drumsticks)**

1. In a small bowl combine egg and milk. For coating, in a shallow dish combine crushed cornflakes, thyme, paprika, salt, and pepper; stir in melted butter. Skin chicken. Dip chicken pieces, one at a time, into egg mixture; coat with crumb mixture.

2. In a greased 15×10×1-inch baking pan, arrange chicken, bone sides down, so the pieces aren't touching. Sprinkle chicken pieces with any remaining crumb mixture so they are generously coated.

3. Bake, uncovered, in a 375°F oven for 45 to 55 minutes or until chicken is no longer pink (170°F for breasts; 180°F for thighs and drumsticks). Do not turn pieces while baking.

Oven-Fried Parmesan Chicken: Prepare as above, except omit thyme and salt and reduce crushed cornflakes to ½ cup. For coating, combine cornflakes; ½ cup grated Parmesan cheese; 1 teaspoon dried oregano, crushed; the paprika; and pepper. Stir in melted butter.

Per 3 ounces regular or Parmesan variation: 336 cal., 16 g total fat (5 g sat. fat), 133 mg chol., 351 mg sodium, 16 g carbo., 0 g fiber, 31 g pro.
Daily Values: 6% vit. A, 3% calcium, 25% iron
Exchanges: 1 Starch, 4 Lean Meat, 1 Fat

Oven-Fried Chicken Breast Tenders: Prepare as above, except substitute 1½ pounds chicken tenders* for the meaty chicken pieces, increase crushed cornflakes to 1¾ cups, and place tenders in a single layer on a 15×10×1-inch baking pan. Bake, uncovered, in a 400°F oven for 10 to 12 minutes or until chicken is no longer pink. Do not turn tenders while baking.

***Note:** To make chicken tenders, cut 1½ pounds of boneless, skinless chicken breast halves lengthwise into 1-inch strips.

Per 4 tenders: 250 cal., 7 g total fat (3 g sat. fat), 112 mg chol., 336 mg sodium, 16 g carbo., 0 g fiber, 29 g pro.
Daily Values: 7% vit. A, 3% calcium, 23% iron
Exchanges: 1 Starch, 3½ Very Lean Meat, 1 Fat

Chicken and Dumplings

⟨FAVORITE⟩ Chicken and Dumplings LOW FAT

Prep: 30 minutes **Cook:** 47 minutes **Makes:** 6 servings

> 2½ **to 3 pounds meaty chicken pieces (breast halves, thighs, and drumsticks)**
> 3 **cups water**
> 1 **medium onion, cut into wedges**
> ¾ **teaspoon salt**
> ½ **teaspoon dried sage or marjoram, crushed**
> ¼ **teaspoon black pepper**
> 1 **bay leaf**
> 1 **cup sliced celery (2 stalks)**
> 1 **cup thinly sliced carrot (2 medium)**
> 1 **cup sliced fresh mushrooms**
> 1 **recipe Dumplings (page 461)**
> ½ **cup cold water**
> ¼ **cup all-purpose flour**

1. Skin chicken. In a 4-quart Dutch oven combine chicken, the 3 cups water, onion, salt, sage, pepper, and bay leaf. Bring to boiling; reduce heat. Simmer, covered, for 25 minutes. Add celery, carrot, and mushrooms. Return to boiling; reduce heat. Simmer, covered, about 10 minutes more or until vegetables are tender and chicken is no longer pink (170°F for breasts; 180°F for thighs and drumsticks). Discard bay leaf. Arrange chicken pieces on top of vegetables.

2. Meanwhile, prepare Dumplings. Spoon batter into six mounds on top of chicken. (Do not spoon batter into liquid.) Return to boiling; reduce heat. Simmer, covered, for 12 to 15 minutes or until a wooden toothpick inserted into dumplings comes out clean. With a slotted spoon, transfer chicken, dumplings, and vegetables to a serving platter; keep warm.

3. For gravy, pour 2 cups cooking liquid into a large measuring cup. Skim fat from liquid (see photo, page 483); discard fat. Pour liquid into Dutch oven. Stir the ½ cup cold water into flour; stir into the liquid in Dutch oven. Cook and stir over medium heat until mixture is thickened and bubbly. Cook and stir for 1 minute more. Serve gravy over chicken, vegetables, and dumplings.

Dumplings: In a medium bowl combine 1 cup all-purpose flour, 1 teaspoon baking powder, and ½ teaspoon salt. Cut in 2 tablespoons shortening until mixture resembles coarse crumbs. Add ½ cup buttermilk, stirring just until moistened.

Per 3 ounces chicken + ½ cup vegetable mixture + 1 dumpling: 322 cal., 11 g total fat (3 g sat. fat), 77 mg chol., 672 mg sodium, 25 g carbo., 2 g fiber, 29 g pro.
Daily Values: 103% vit. A, 6% vit. C, 10% calcium, 15% iron
Exchanges: 1 Vegetable, 1½ Starch, 3 Medium-Fat Meat

Oven-Barbecued Chicken LOW FAT EASY

See photo, page 455.

Prep: 10 minutes **Bake:** 45 minutes
Oven: 375°F **Makes:** 6 servings

  2½ **to 3 pounds meaty chicken pieces**
      (breast halves, thighs, and drumsticks)
   ½ **cup chopped onion (1 medium)**
   1 **clove garlic, minced**
   1 **tablespoon cooking oil**
   ¾ **cup bottled chili sauce**
   2 **tablespoons honey**
   2 **tablespoons soy sauce**
   1 **tablespoon yellow mustard**
   ½ **teaspoon prepared horseradish**
   ¼ **teaspoon crushed red pepper**

1. Skin chicken. Arrange chicken, bone sides up, in a 15×10×1-inch baking pan. Bake in a 375°F oven for 25 minutes.

2. For sauce, in a saucepan cook onion and garlic in hot oil until tender but not brown. Stir in chili sauce, honey, soy sauce, mustard, horseradish, and crushed red pepper; heat through.

3. Turn chicken bone sides down. Brush half of the sauce over the chicken. Bake for 20 to 30 minutes more or until chicken is no longer pink (170°F for breasts; 180°F for thighs and drumsticks). Reheat remaining sauce; pass with the chicken.

Per 3 ounces chicken + 2 tablespoons sauce: 244 cal., 9 g total fat (2 g sat. fat), 77 mg chol., 807 mg sodium, 15 g carbo., 2 g fiber, 26 g pro.
Daily Values: 4% vit. A, 10% vit. C, 2% calcium, 8% iron
Exchanges: 1 Other Carbo., 3½ Medium-Fat Meat

Chicken Cacciatore LOW FAT

Start to Finish: 1 hour **Makes:** 6 servings

  2½ **to 3 pounds meaty chicken pieces**
      (breast halves, thighs, and drumsticks)
   2 **tablespoons olive oil**
  1½ **cups sliced fresh mushrooms**
   1 **medium onion, sliced**
   1 **clove garlic, minced**
   1 **14.5-ounce can diced tomatoes, undrained**
   1 **6-ounce can tomato paste**
   ¾ **cup dry white wine**
   1 **teaspoon sugar**
   1 **teaspoon dried Italian seasoning, crushed**
   ½ **teaspoon salt**
   ⅛ **teaspoon black pepper**
   1 **tablespoon snipped fresh parsley**
     Hot cooked fettuccine or linguine (optional)

1. Skin chicken. In a large skillet brown chicken on all sides in hot oil over medium heat about 15 minutes, turning occasionally. Remove chicken from skillet, reserving drippings in skillet; set chicken aside.

2. Add mushrooms, onion, and garlic to skillet. Cook and stir about 5 minutes or until vegetables are just tender. Return chicken to skillet.

3. Meanwhile, in a medium bowl combine undrained tomatoes, tomato paste, wine, sugar, Italian seasoning, salt, and pepper. Pour over chicken in skillet. Bring to boiling; reduce heat. Simmer, covered, for 30 to 35 minutes or until chicken is no longer pink (170°F for breasts; 180°F for thighs and drumsticks), turning once during cooking. Sprinkle with parsley. If desired, serve over hot cooked pasta.

Per 3 ounces chicken + ½ cup vegetable mixture: 280 cal., 11 g total fat (2 g sat. fat), 77 mg chol., 396 mg sodium, 12 g carbo., 2 g fiber, 28 g pro.
Daily Values: 1% vit. A, 26% vit. C, 5% calcium, 13% iron
Exchanges: 2 Vegetable, 3½ Medium-Fat Meat, 2½ Fat

Coq au Vin

Prep: 35 minutes **Cook:** 35 minutes **Makes:** 6 servings

- 2½ to 3 pounds meaty chicken pieces (breast halves, thighs, and drumsticks)
- 2 tablespoons cooking oil
  Salt and black pepper
- 12 to 18 pearl onions or shallots, peeled
- 1¼ cups Pinot Noir or Burgundy
- 1 cup whole fresh mushrooms
- 1 cup thinly sliced carrot (2 medium)
- ¼ cup chicken broth or water
- 1 tablespoon snipped fresh parsley
- 1½ teaspoons snipped fresh marjoram or ½ teaspoon dried marjoram, crushed
- 1½ teaspoons snipped fresh thyme or ½ teaspoon dried thyme, crushed
- 1 bay leaf
- 2 cloves garlic, minced
- 2 tablespoons all-purpose flour
- 2 tablespoons butter or margarine, softened
- 2 slices bacon, crisp-cooked, drained, and crumbled
  Snipped fresh parsley (optional)
  Hot cooked noodles (optional)

1. Skin chicken. In a large skillet brown chicken on all sides in hot oil over medium heat about 15 minutes, turning occasionally. Drain fat. Season chicken with salt and pepper. Add onions, Pinot Noir, mushrooms, carrot, broth, the 1 tablespoon parsley, dried marjoram (if using), dried thyme (if using), bay leaf, and garlic. Bring to boiling; reduce heat. Simmer, covered, for 35 to 40 minutes or until chicken is no longer pink (170°F for breasts; 180°F for thighs and drumsticks). If using, add fresh marjoram and thyme. Discard bay leaf. Transfer chicken and vegetables to a serving platter.

2. In a bowl stir together flour and softened butter to make a smooth paste. Stir into wine mixture in skillet. Cook and stir until thickened and bubbly. Cook and stir for 1 minute more. Season to taste with additional salt and pepper.

3. Pour sauce over chicken and vegetables. Sprinkle with bacon. If desired, top with additional parsley and serve with hot cooked noodles.

Per 3 ounces chicken + ½ cup vegetable mixture: 318 cal., 16 g total fat (5 g sat. fat), 89 mg chol., 211 mg sodium, 7 g carbo., 1 g fiber, 27 g pro.
Daily Values: 107% vit. A, 6% vit. C, 3% calcium, 10% iron
Exchanges: 1 Vegetable, 3½ Medium-Fat Meat

Chicken and Noodles LOW FAT

Homemade noodles make this the perfect main dish for a family meal; a small salad and dinner rolls would complete it.

Prep: 30 minutes **Cook:** 30 minutes **Makes:** 6 servings

- 3 chicken legs (thigh-drumstick piece)
- 3 cups water
- 2 bay leaves
- 1 teaspoon dried thyme, crushed
- ¾ teaspoon salt
- ¼ teaspoon black pepper
- 1½ cups chopped onion (3 medium)
- 2 cups sliced carrot (4 medium)
- 1 cup sliced celery (2 stalks)
- 1 recipe Homemade Noodles (page 415) or one 12-ounce package frozen noodles
- 1 cup frozen peas (optional)
- 1 cup milk
- 2 tablespoons all-purpose flour

1. Skin chicken. If necessary, cut up chicken to fit pan. In a 4-quart Dutch oven combine chicken, water, bay leaves, thyme, salt, and pepper. Add onion, carrot, and celery. Bring to boiling; reduce heat. Simmer, covered, for 20 to 30 minutes or until chicken is tender and no longer pink. Discard bay leaves. Remove chicken from Dutch oven; cool slightly. Remove meat from bones; discard bones. Chop chicken; set aside.

2. Bring broth mixture to boiling. Add noodles; cook for 5 minutes (15 minutes if using frozen noodles). If desired, stir in frozen peas. In a screw-top jar combine milk and flour; cover and shake until smooth. Stir into noodle mixture. Cook and stir until thickened and bubbly. Stir in chopped chicken. Cook and stir for 1 to 2 minutes more or until mixture is heated through.

Per 1⅓ cups: 359 cal., 8 g total fat (2 g sat. fat), 176 mg chol., 641 mg sodium, 44 g carbo., 3 g fiber, 26 g pro.
Daily Values: 95% vit. A, 8% vit. C, 11% calcium, 20% iron
Exchanges: 1 Vegetable, 2½ Starch, 2½ Lean Meat

Greek Dinner

Remember this easy meal for a hectic day.

- *Kalamata Lemon Chicken (page 463)*
- *Fresh spinach salad*
- *Warm pita bread wedges*
- *Ice cream with fresh berries*

Chicken with Black Beans and Rice

This colorful one-dish meal goes together quickly and is sure to please the whole family.

Prep: 20 minutes **Bake:** 45 minutes
Oven: 375°F **Makes:** 6 servings

- ¼ cup all-purpose flour
- 1½ teaspoons chili powder
- ¼ teaspoon salt
- ¼ teaspoon black pepper
- 2½ to 3 pounds meaty chicken pieces (breast halves, thighs, and drumsticks)
- 2 tablespoons cooking oil
- 1 15-ounce can black beans, rinsed and drained
- 1 14.5-ounce can diced tomatoes with onion and green pepper, undrained
- 1 cup tomato juice
- 1 cup frozen whole kernel corn
- ⅔ cup uncooked long grain rice
- ⅛ to ¼ teaspoon cayenne pepper
- 2 cloves garlic, minced

1. In a large resealable plastic bag combine flour, 1 teaspoon of the chili powder, the salt, and black pepper. Add chicken pieces, half at a time. Seal bag; shake to coat.

2. In a large skillet brown chicken on all sides in hot oil over medium heat about 10 minutes, turning occasionally. Remove chicken from skillet and set aside; discard drippings. Add the remaining ½ teaspoon chili powder, the beans, undrained tomatoes, tomato juice, corn, rice, cayenne pepper, and garlic to the skillet. Bring to boiling. Transfer rice mixture to a 3-quart rectangular baking dish. Arrange chicken pieces on top of rice mixture.

3. Bake, covered, in a 375°F oven for 45 to 50 minutes or until chicken is no longer pink (170°F for breasts; 180°F for thighs and drumsticks) and rice is tender.

Per 3 ounces chicken + ⅔ cup rice mixture: 437 cal., 16 g total fat (4 g sat. fat), 86 mg chol., 634 mg sodium, 40 g carbo., 5 g fiber, 35 g pro.
Daily Values: 8% vit. A, 29% vit. C, 8% calcium, 21% iron
Exchanges: 1 Vegetable, 2 Starch, 4 Lean Meat, ½ Fat

Kalamata Lemon Chicken

Kalamata Lemon Chicken LOW FAT EASY

To save time, skip the browning step.

Prep: 10 minutes **Bake:** 35 minutes
Oven: 400°F **Makes:** 4 servings

- 1 to 1¼ pounds skinless, boneless chicken thighs
- 1 tablespoon olive oil
- ⅔ cup dried orzo
- ½ cup drained, pitted kalamata olives
- 1 14-ounce can chicken broth
- ½ of a lemon, cut into wedges or chunks
- 1 tablespoon lemon juice
- 1 teaspoon dried Greek seasoning
- ¼ teaspoon salt
- ¼ teaspoon freshly ground black pepper
  Hot chicken broth (optional)
  Fresh oregano leaves (optional)

1. In a 4-quart Dutch oven brown chicken in hot oil about 5 minutes, turning once. Stir in orzo, olives, broth, lemon wedges, lemon juice, Greek seasoning, salt, and pepper. Transfer mixture to a 2-quart rectangular baking dish.

2. Bake, covered, in a 400°F oven about 35 minutes or until chicken is tender and no longer pink (180°F). If desired, serve in shallow bowls with additional hot broth and topped with fresh oregano.

Per 3 ounces chicken + ½ cup orzo: 309 cal., 11 g total fat (2 g sat. fat), 91 mg chol., 837 mg sodium, 24 g carbo., 2 g fiber, 27 g pro.
Daily Values: 1% vit. A, 14% vit. C, 2% calcium, 12% iron
Exchanges: 1½ Starch, 3 Lean Meat, ½ Fat

Cheese-Stuffed Chicken Breasts

For added flavor, spoon warmed pasta sauce over these filled chicken breasts.

Prep: 20 minutes **Bake:** 45 minutes
Oven: 375°F **Makes:** 6 servings

> 6 chicken breast halves
> ½ cup ricotta cheese
> ½ cup shredded fontina or mozzarella cheese (2 ounces)
> ⅓ cup grated Parmesan or Romano cheese
> 2 teaspoons snipped fresh basil or ½ teaspoon dried basil, crushed
> 1 teaspoon snipped fresh oregano or ¼ teaspoon dried oregano, crushed
> ¼ teaspoon lemon-pepper seasoning
> 2 tablespoons butter or margarine, melted

1. Using your fingers, gently separate the chicken skin from the meat of the breast halves along rib edges (see photo, below).

2. For stuffing, in a small bowl combine the cheeses, basil, oregano, and lemon-pepper seasoning. Spoon a rounded tablespoon of cheese mixture under the skin of each breast half. Place chicken, bone sides down, in a 3-quart rectangular baking dish. Brush chicken with melted butter. Bake in a 375°F oven for 45 to 55 minutes or until no longer pink (170°F).

Per breast half: 346 cal., 22 g total fat (10 g sat. fat), 116 mg chol., 356 mg sodium, 1 g carbo., 0 g fiber, 35 g pro.
Daily Values: 10% vit. A, 2% vit. C, 20% calcium, 6% iron
Exchanges: 5 Lean Meat, 1½ Fat

To make a pocket for stuffing, start along the rib edge of a bone-in, skin-on chicken breast. Use your fingers to gently separate the skin from the meat, leaving the skin attached along the breast bone.

Chicken Cordon Bleu

"Cordon bleu" [kor-dohn-BLUH] is a French term describing a dish of chicken or veal that has been pounded thin, layered with Swiss cheese and ham, rolled, and cooked until golden brown.

Prep: 20 minutes **Cook:** 20 minutes **Makes:** 4 servings

> 4 skinless, boneless chicken breast halves
> 4 slices prosciutto or cooked ham
> 4 slices Swiss cheese (3 ounces)
> 1 tablespoon butter or margarine

1. Place each chicken breast half between two pieces of plastic wrap. Using the flat side of a meat mallet, pound chicken lightly into rectangles about ⅛ inch thick (see photo 2, page 465). Remove plastic wrap.

2. Place a slice of prosciutto and a slice of cheese on each chicken piece. Fold in side edges; roll up from bottom edge (see photo 3, page 465). Secure with wooden toothpicks.

3. In a medium skillet cook rolls in hot butter over medium-low heat for 20 to 25 minutes or until no longer pink (170°F), turning to brown evenly. Remove toothpicks before serving.

Per roll: 290 cal., 13 g total fat (7 g sat. fat), 113 mg chol., 911 mg sodium, 1 g carbo., 40 g pro.
Daily Values: 6% vit. A, 2% vit. C, 22% calcium, 6% iron
Exchanges: 5½ Lean Meat

Chicken Kiev

Prep: 20 minutes **Chill:** 1 hour **Cook:** 5 minutes
Bake: 15 minutes **Oven:** 400°F **Makes:** 4 servings

> 1 tablespoon chopped green onion
> 1 tablespoon snipped fresh parsley
> 1 clove garlic, minced
> ½ of a ¼-pound stick of butter, chilled
> 1 egg, beaten
> 1 tablespoon water
> ¼ cup all-purpose flour
> ½ cup fine dry bread crumbs
> 4 skinless, boneless chicken breast halves
> Salt and black pepper
> 1 tablespoon butter
> 1 tablespoon cooking oil

1. In a small bowl combine green onion, parsley, and garlic; set aside. Cut chilled butter into four 2½×½-inch sticks (see photo 1, page 465). In a shallow bowl stir together egg and water. Place flour in a second shallow bowl. Place bread crumbs in a third shallow bowl. Set all three bowls aside.

2. Place each chicken breast half between two pieces of plastic wrap. Using the flat side of a meat mallet, pound chicken lightly into rectangles about ⅛ inch thick (see photo 2, page 465). Remove plastic wrap. Sprinkle with salt and pepper. Divide green onion mixture among chicken pieces. Place a butter stick in center of each chicken piece. Fold in side edges; roll up from bottom edge (see photo 3, page 465).

3. Coat chicken rolls with flour. Dip in egg mixture; coat with bread crumbs. Dip in egg mixture again; coat with additional bread crumbs. (Coat ends well to seal in the butter.) Place coated chicken rolls in a 2-quart rectangular baking dish. Cover and chill for 1 to 24 hours.

4. In a large skillet melt the 1 tablespoon butter over medium-high heat; add oil. Add chilled chicken rolls. Cook about 5 minutes or until golden brown, turning to brown all sides. Return rolls to baking dish. Bake, uncovered, in a 400°F oven for 15 to 18 minutes or until chicken is no longer pink (170°F). To serve, spoon any drippings over rolls.

Per roll: 377 cal., 22 g total fat (11 g sat. fat), 160 mg chol., 499 mg sodium, 13 g carbo., 1 g fiber, 30 g pro.
Daily Values: 15% vit. A, 5% vit. C, 5% calcium, 11% iron
Exchanges: 1 Starch, 4 Lean Meat, 2 Fat

Cheesy Chicken Rolls: Prepare as on page 464, except substitute 2½×½-inch sticks of caraway, blue, Gruyère, or cheddar cheese for the butter. If using caraway or blue cheese, omit parsley. If using Gruyère cheese, substitute 2 teaspoons snipped fresh tarragon for the parsley. If using cheddar cheese, substitute 2 teaspoons snipped fresh thyme for parsley.

Per roll: 328 cal., 15 g total fat (6 g sat. fat), 142 mg chol., 479 mg sodium, 13 g carbo., 1 g fiber, 33 g pro.
Daily Values: 9% vit. A, 5% vit. C, 15% calcium, 12% iron
Exchanges: 1 Starch, 4 Lean Meat, ½ Fat

1. For the Chicken Kiev filling, cut the half stick of butter in half lengthwise, then cut each portion in half lengthwise again to get four 2½×½-inch sticks.

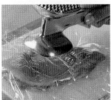

2. Lightly pound skinless, boneless chicken breast halves using the flat side of a meat mallet. Work from the center to the edges until the thickness is even and the breast halves are rectangular.

3. Place filling on pounded breast halves. Fold in side edges and roll up from the bottom edge, pressing firmly to seal in the filling.

Chicken Marsala `LOW FAT`

Marsala is a fortified Italian wine that ranges from extremely sweet (a dessert wine) to dry (an apéritif). Choose a dry type for this dish.

Start to Finish: 35 minutes **Makes:** 4 servings

- ¼ cup all-purpose flour
- ½ teaspoon dried marjoram, crushed
- ⅛ teaspoon salt
- ⅛ teaspoon black pepper
- 4 skinless, boneless chicken breast halves
- 2 cups sliced fresh mushrooms
- ¼ cup sliced green onion (2)
- 3 tablespoons butter or margarine
- ½ cup chicken broth
- ½ cup dry Marsala or dry sherry
  Hot cooked pasta, such as angel hair or linguine (optional)

1. In a shallow bowl stir together flour, marjoram, salt, and pepper. Place each chicken breast half between two pieces of plastic wrap. Using the flat side of a meat mallet, pound chicken lightly to about ¼ inch thick (see photo 2, left). Remove plastic wrap. Lightly coat chicken pieces on both sides with flour mixture; shake off excess.

2. In a large skillet cook mushrooms and green onion in 1 tablespoon hot butter over medium-high heat until tender; remove from skillet. In the same skillet cook chicken in the remaining 2 tablespoons hot butter for 5 to 6 minutes, turning to brown evenly.

3. Remove skillet from heat. Return mushrooms and green onion to skillet. Carefully add broth and Marsala to skillet. Bring mixture to boiling; reduce heat. Simmer, uncovered, for 2 minutes more, stirring occasionally. Season sauce to taste with additional salt and pepper. To serve, spoon mushroom mixture over chicken. If desired, serve over pasta.

Per breast half: 298 cal., 12 g total fat (6 g sat. fat), 90 mg chol., 329 mg sodium, 10 g carbo., 1 g fiber, 30 g pro.
Daily Values: 8% vit. A, 4% vit. C, 3% calcium, 10% iron
Exchanges: 1½ Vegetable, 3½ Very Lean Meat, 3 Fat

Sauteed Chicken with Five Easy Sauces

Pounding chicken breasts to a thin, even thickness really speeds up cooking time. Follow these classic techniques to make one of five different sauces perfect for accompanying chicken breasts. What's your mood tonight?

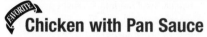
Chicken with Pan Sauce

Start to Finish: 35 minutes **Makes:** 4 servings

- **4 skinless, boneless chicken breast halves**
- **¼ teaspoon salt**
- **¼ teaspoon freshly ground black pepper**
- **5 tablespoons cold butter**
- **⅔ cup dry white wine**
- **½ cup chicken broth**
- **¼ cup finely chopped shallot (2) or onion**
- **2 tablespoons whipping cream**

1. Place each chicken breast half between two pieces of plastic wrap. Using the flat side of a meat mallet, pound the chicken lightly to about ¼ inch thick (see photo 2, page 465). Remove plastic wrap. Sprinkle with salt and pepper.

2. In a large skillet melt 1 tablespoon of the butter over medium-high heat. Reduce heat to medium. Cook chicken for 6 to 8 minutes or until no longer pink, turning once. Transfer chicken to a platter; keep warm.

3. Add wine, broth, and shallot to hot skillet. Cook and stir, scraping up browned bits from the bottom of the pan. Bring to boiling. Boil gently for 10 to 15 minutes or until liquid is reduced to ¼ cup.* Reduce heat to medium low.

4. Stir in cream. Add the remaining 4 tablespoons butter, 1 tablespoon at a time, stirring after each addition until butter is melted. Sauce should be slightly thickened. Season with additional salt and pepper. To serve, spoon sauce over chicken.

*Note: It is important to reduce the liquid to ¼ cup or the sauce will be too thin.

Balsamic-Caper Sauce: Prepare as above, except stir 2 teaspoons balsamic vinegar and 2 teaspoons drained capers into finished sauce.

Lemon-Herb Sauce: Prepare as above, except stir 2 teaspoons fresh lemon juice and 2 teaspoons snipped fresh thyme, chervil, or parsley into the finished sauce.

Mushroom-Tomato Sauce: Prepare as at left through Step 1. In a large skillet cook 1 cup sliced fresh shiitake, porcini, or button mushrooms in 1 tablespoon of the butter over medium heat until tender. Remove mushrooms from skillet. Continue as directed in Step 2, using the same skillet. Along with the cream, add cooked mushrooms and 2 tablespoons snipped, drained, oil-packed dried tomatoes. There will be only 3 tablespoons of butter to add in Step 4. Stir 2 teaspoons snipped fresh basil or parsley into the finished sauce.

Mustard Sauce: Prepare as at left, except stir 1 tablespoon snipped Italian parsley and 2 teaspoons Dijon-style mustard into the finished sauce.

Per breast half + 2 tablespoons sauce all variations: 325 cal., 20 g total fat (10 g sat. fat), 117 mg chol., 444 mg sodium, 2 g carbo., 0 g fiber, 27 g pro.
Daily Values: 14% vit. A, 1% vit. C, 3% calcium, 6% iron
Exchanges: 4 Very Lean Meat, 4 Fat

1. Brown pounded breast halves quickly in butter until golden and no longer pink inside. Place on a warm platter and cover with foil to keep warm; set aside.

2. After adding the wine, broth, and shallot, scrape the flavorful browned bits from the bottom of the pan. Boil the liquid to reduce it and concentrate the flavors.

3. Stir in cream, then butter, 1 tablespoon at a time, to thicken the sauce.

Baked Chicken Chiles Rellenos (LOW FAT)

Normally, it's the chiles that are stuffed for chiles rellenos, but this dish puts them on the inside.

Prep: 35 minutes **Bake:** 25 minutes
Oven: 375°F **Makes:** 6 servings

- 6 **skinless, boneless chicken breast halves**
- ⅓ **cup all-purpose flour**
- 3 **tablespoons cornmeal**
- ¼ **teaspoon cayenne pepper**
- 1 **egg**
- 1 **tablespoon water**
- 1 **4-ounce can whole green chile peppers, rinsed, seeded, and cut in half lengthwise (6 pieces total) (see tip, page 74)**
- 2 **ounces Monterey Jack cheese, cut into six 2×½-inch sticks**
- 2 **tablespoons snipped fresh cilantro or fresh parsley**
- ¼ **teaspoon black pepper**
- 2 **tablespoons butter or margarine, melted**
- 1 **8-ounce jar green or red salsa**

1. Place each chicken breast half between two pieces of plastic wrap. Using the flat side of a meat mallet, pound chicken lightly into rectangles about ⅛ inch thick (see photo 2, page 465). Remove plastic wrap.

2. In a shallow dish combine the flour, cornmeal, and cayenne pepper. Place egg in a second shallow dish; add water and beat lightly to combine.

3. Place a chile pepper half on each chicken piece near an edge. Place a stick of cheese on each chile pepper half. Sprinkle with snipped cilantro and the black pepper. Fold in side edges; roll up from the edge with cheese and chile pepper (see photo 3, page 465). Secure with wooden toothpicks.

4. Dip chicken rolls in egg mixture; coat with cornmeal mixture. Place rolls, seam sides down, in a shallow baking pan. Drizzle with butter.

5. Bake, uncovered, in a 375°F oven for 25 to 30 minutes or until chicken is no longer pink (170°F). Remove toothpicks. Meanwhile, heat salsa; serve over chicken.

Per roll: 260 cal., 10 g total fat (5 g sat. fat), 120 mg chol., 381 mg sodium, 10 g carbo., 1 g fiber, 31 g pro.
Daily Values: 14% vit. A, 22% vit. C, 13% calcium, 10% iron
Exchanges: ½ Vegetable, ½ Starch, 4 Lean Meat

Pepper-Lime Chicken (LOW FAT) (EASY)

Use any leftover Pepper-Lime Chicken in Chicken Burritos (page 474) or Tex-Mex Chicken and Rice Casserole (page 473). Served cold, this chicken would be great in a salad too.

Prep: 10 minutes **Marinate:** 30 minutes
Broil: 12 minutes **Makes:** 6 servings

- 6 **skinless, boneless chicken breast halves**
- 1 **teaspoon finely shredded lime peel**
- ⅓ **cup lime juice**
- 3 **tablespoons cooking oil**
- 1 **teaspoon dried thyme or basil, crushed**
- ½ **teaspoon coarsely ground black pepper**
- ¼ **teaspoon salt**
- 2 **cloves garlic, minced**
  Bottled salsa (optional)
  Lime wedges (optional)

1. Place chicken breast halves in a resealable plastic bag set in a shallow dish. For marinade, stir together lime peel, lime juice, oil, thyme, pepper, salt, and garlic. Pour over chicken; seal bag. Marinate in refrigerator for 30 minutes.

2. Preheat broiler. Drain chicken, reserving marinade. Place chicken on the unheated rack of a broiler pan. Broil 4 to 5 inches from the heat about 6 minutes or until light brown.

3. Turn chicken and brush lightly with reserved marinade. Discard any remaining marinade. Broil for 6 to 8 minutes more or until chicken is no longer pink (170°F). If desired, serve with salsa and lime wedges.

Per breast half: 240 cal., 9 g total fat (2 g sat. fat), 88 mg chol., 180 mg sodium, 2 g carbo., 0 g fiber, 35 g pro.
Daily Values: 2% vit. A, 8% vit. C, 8% calcium, 7% iron
Exchanges: 5 Very Lean Meat, 1½ Fat

Pepper-Lime Chicken

Chicken Parmigiana

Chicken Parmigiana

Prep: 30 minutes **Cook:** 25 minutes **Makes:** 4 servings

- 1 **small onion, chopped (⅓ cup)**
- 1 **clove garlic, minced**
- 1 **tablespoon butter or margarine**
- 1 **14.5-ounce can diced tomatoes, undrained**
- ½ **teaspoon sugar**
- ⅛ **teaspoon salt**
  Dash black pepper
- ¼ **cup snipped fresh basil**
- 4 **skinless, boneless chicken breast halves**
- ⅓ **cup seasoned fine dry bread crumbs**
- 4 **tablespoons grated Parmesan cheese**
- ½ **teaspoon dried oregano, crushed**
- 1 **egg, beaten**
- 2 **tablespoons milk**
- 3 **tablespoons olive oil or cooking oil**
- ¼ **cup shredded mozzarella cheese (1 ounce)**

1. For sauce, in a medium saucepan cook onion and garlic in hot butter over medium heat until tender. Carefully stir in the undrained tomatoes, sugar, salt, and pepper. Bring to boiling; reduce heat. Simmer, uncovered, about 10 minutes or to desired consistency, stirring occasionally. Stir in basil. Set aside; keep warm.

2. Meanwhile, place each chicken breast half between two pieces of plastic wrap. Using flat side of a meat mallet, pound chicken lightly to about ¼ inch thick (see photo 2, page 465). Remove plastic wrap.

3. In a shallow dish stir together bread crumbs, 3 tablespoons of the Parmesan cheese, and the

oregano. In a second dish stir together the egg and milk. Dip chicken in egg mixture, then in crumb mixture to coat.

4. In a large skillet cook chicken in hot oil over medium heat for 2 to 3 minutes per side or until golden. Transfer chicken to a serving platter.

5. Spoon sauce over chicken. Top with mozzarella and remaining 1 tablespoon Parmesan. Let stand about 2 minutes or until cheese melts.

Veal Parmigiana: Prepare as at left, except substitute 1 pound boneless veal sirloin or round steak for chicken. Cut meat into four pieces and pound to ¼ inch thick as at left.

Per 3 ounces chicken or veal + ⅓ cup sauce: 379 cal., 20 g total fat (6 g sat. fat), 137 mg chol., 711 mg sodium, 15 g carbo., 1 g fiber, 34 g pro.
Daily Values: 8% vit. A, 24% vit. C, 18% calcium, 11% iron
Exchanges: 1 Vegetable, ½ Other Carbo., 4½ Very Lean Meat, 3½ Fat

Creamy Tomato Chicken Parmigiana: Prepare as at left, except after simmering the sauce to desired consistency, slowly add 3 tablespoons whipping cream, half-and-half, or light cream, stirring constantly. Cook and stir for 3 minutes more, then stir in basil.

Per 3 ounces chicken + ⅓ cup sauce: 418 cal., 24 g total fat (9 g sat. fat), 152 mg chol., 715 mg sodium, 15 g carbo., 1 g fiber, 34 g pro.
Daily Values: 11% vit. A, 24% vit. C, 19% calcium, 11% iron
Exchanges: 1 Vegetable, ½ Other Carbo., 4½ Very Lean Meat, 4 Fat

Chicken with Creamy Mushrooms **FAST**

If you can't find premarinated chicken breasts, you can substitute unmarinated breasts.

Start to Finish: 30 minutes **Makes:** 6 servings

- 1 **pound sliced fresh mushrooms, such as button or shiitake (6 cups)**
- 3 **tablespoons butter**
- 6 **Italian-marinated skinless, boneless chicken breast halves**
- 3 **tablespoons rice vinegar or white wine vinegar**
- 1½ **cups whipping cream**
- 3 **tablespoons capers, drained**
- ¼ **teaspoon freshly ground black pepper**

1. In a large skillet cook mushrooms in 1 tablespoon hot butter over medium-high heat about 5 minutes or until tender. Remove mushrooms from skillet.

2. Reduce heat to medium. Add the remaining 2 tablespoons butter and the chicken breast halves to skillet. Cook for 8 to 10 minutes or until no longer pink (170°F), turning once. Remove chicken from skillet and keep warm.

3. Add vinegar to skillet, stirring to loosen browned bits in bottom of skillet. Return skillet to heat. Stir in cream, capers, and pepper. Bring to boiling. Boil gently, uncovered, for 2 to 3 minutes or until sauce is slightly thickened. Return mushrooms to skillet; heat through. Top chicken with mushroom sauce.

Per breast half + ¼ cup sauce: 456 cal., 34 g total fat (19 g sat. fat), 183 mg chol., 967 mg sodium, 7 g carbo., 1 g fiber, 33 g pro.
Daily Values: 22% vit. A, 1% vit. C, 5% calcium, 5% iron
Exchanges: 1 Vegetable, 4½ Very Lean Meat, 6 Fat

Chicken Breasts with Tomatillo Salsa LOW FAT FAST

Start to Finish: 25 minutes **Makes:** 4 servings

> 2 **tablespoons yellow cornmeal**
> 2 **tablespoons all-purpose flour**
> 1 **tablespoon chili powder**
> ½ **teaspoon salt**
> ¼ **teaspoon black pepper**
> 4 **skinless, boneless chicken breast halves**
> 2 **tablespoons cooking oil**
> 1 **13-ounce can tomatillos, rinsed and drained**
> 3 **tablespoons snipped fresh cilantro**
> 3 **tablespoons finely chopped onion**
> 2 **tablespoons lime juice**
> 1 **fresh jalapeño chile pepper, seeded and finely chopped (see tip, page 74)**

1. In a resealable plastic bag combine cornmeal, flour, chili powder, salt, and pepper. Add a few chicken pieces. Seal bag; shake to coat. Remove coated chicken pieces. Repeat with remaining chicken.

2. In a large skillet cook chicken in hot oil over medium heat for 8 to 10 minutes or until chicken is no longer pink (170°F), turning once.

3. Meanwhile, for salsa, coarsely chop tomatillos (you should have about 1 cup). In a small bowl stir together chopped tomatillos, the cilantro, onion, lime juice, and jalapeño pepper. Serve salsa over chicken.

Per breast half + ¼ cup salsa: 258 cal., 9 g total fat (1 g sat. fat), 66 mg chol., 1,065 mg sodium, 16 g carbo., 3 g fiber, 27 g pro.
Daily Values: 22% vit. A, 15% vit. C, 4% calcium, 20% iron
Exchanges: 1½ Vegetable, ½ Starch, 3 Very Lean Meat, 1½ Fat

Chicken Lo Mein LOW FAT

Keep tossing the cooked noodles when combining them with the rest of the ingredients so they get coated by the oyster sauce mixture and heated without becoming crunchy or tough.

Prep: 35 minutes **Cook:** 16 minutes **Makes:** 6 servings

> 1¼ **to 1½ pounds skinless, boneless chicken breast halves**
> 10 **ounces dried Chinese egg noodles, spaghetti, or angel hair pasta**
> ¼ **cup oyster sauce**
> ¼ **cup reduced-sodium soy sauce**
> 2 **tablespoons rice wine or dry sherry**
> 1 **tablespoon cooking oil**
> 1 **tablespoon toasted sesame oil**
> 2 **teaspoons finely chopped fresh ginger**
> 1 **medium red onion, halved lengthwise and thinly sliced (1 cup)**
> 8 **ounces fresh mushrooms, sliced (3 cups)**
> 2 **cups sugar snap pea pods, halved**

1. Cut chicken into bite-size strips; set aside. Cook noodles according to package directions until tender; drain. Rinse with cold water; drain well. Set noodles aside.

2. For sauce, in a small bowl stir together oyster sauce, soy sauce, and rice wine. Set aside.

3. Pour cooking oil and sesame oil into a wok or large nonstick skillet. (If necessary, add more oil during cooking.) Heat over medium-high heat. Add ginger; cook and stir for 30 seconds. Add onion; cook and stir for 2 minutes. Add mushrooms; cook and stir for 2 minutes. Add pea pods; cook and stir for 1 minute. Remove vegetables from wok.

4. Add half the chicken to wok; cook and stir for 3 to 4 minutes or until no longer pink. Remove from wok. Repeat with remaining chicken. Return all chicken to wok. Add the cooked noodles, vegetables, and sauce. Using two spatulas or wooden spoons, lightly toss the mixture about 3 minutes or until heated through.

Per 1⅓ cups: 409 cal., 9 g total fat (2 g sat. fat), 100 mg chol., 747 mg sodium, 48 g carbo., 4 g fiber, 33 g pro.
Daily Values: 2% vit. A, 24% vit. C, 7% calcium, 19% iron
Exchanges: 1 Vegetable, 2½ Starch, 3 Very Lean Meat, 1½ Fat

Garlic Chicken Stir-Fry `LOW FAT`

Prep: 25 minutes **Marinate:** 30 minutes
Cook: 6 minutes **Makes:** 4 servings

- 12 **ounces skinless, boneless chicken breast halves**
- 1 **cup water**
- 3 **tablespoons reduced-sodium soy sauce**
- 1 **tablespoon rice vinegar or white wine vinegar**
- 1 **tablespoon cornstarch**
- 2 **tablespoons cooking oil**
- 10 **green onions, bias-sliced into 1-inch pieces**
- 1 **cup thinly sliced fresh mushrooms**
- 12 **cloves garlic, peeled and finely chopped**
- ½ **cup sliced water chestnuts**
- 2 **cups hot cooked white, jasmine, or basmati rice**

1. Cut chicken into ½-inch pieces. Place chicken in a resealable plastic bag set in a shallow dish. For marinade, stir together water, soy sauce, and vinegar. Pour over chicken; seal bag. Marinate in the refrigerator for 30 minutes. Drain chicken, reserving the marinade. Stir cornstarch into reserved marinade; set aside.

2. Pour oil into a wok or large skillet. (If necessary, add more oil during cooking.) Heat over medium-high heat. Add green onion, mushrooms, and garlic to wok; cook and stir for 1 to 2 minutes or until tender. Remove vegetables from wok.

3. Add chicken to wok; cook and stir for 2 to 3 minutes or until no longer pink. Push chicken from center of wok. Stir marinade mixture; add to center of wok. Cook and stir until thickened and bubbly. Push chicken into center of wok. Return cooked vegetables to wok. Add water chestnuts. Cook and stir about 1 minute more or until heated through. Serve with rice.

Per 1 cup + ½ cup rice: 313 cal., 9 g total fat (2 g sat. fat), 49 mg chol., 490 mg sodium, 33 g carbo., 2 g fiber, 25 g pro.
Daily Values: 9% vit. A, 18% vit. C, 7% calcium, 14% iron
Exchanges: ½ Vegetable, 2 Starch, 2½ Very Lean Meat, 1½ Fat

Garlic Chicken Stir-Fry with Cashews: Prepare as above, except stir ½ teaspoon crushed red pepper into marinade. Stir in 1 cup cashews with water chestnuts.

Per 1 cup + ½ cup rice: 511 cal., 25 g total fat (5 g sat. fat), 49 mg chol., 495 mg sodium, 44 g carbo., 3 g fiber, 30 g pro.
Daily Values: 10% vit. A, 18% vit. C, 9% calcium, 25% iron
Exchanges: ½ Vegetable, 2½ Starch, 3 Very Lean Meat, 4 Fat

Thai Chicken Stir-Fry

Thai Chicken Stir-Fry `LOW FAT`

Start to Finish: 35 minutes **Makes:** 4 servings

- 1 **pound skinless, boneless chicken breast halves**
- ¼ **cup rice wine**
- 3 **tablespoons reduced-sodium soy sauce**
- 2 **tablespoons water**
- 1 **tablespoon fish sauce (optional)**
- 1½ **teaspoons cornstarch**
- ½ **teaspoon crushed red pepper**
- 1 **tablespoon cooking oil**
- 1 **teaspoon grated fresh ginger**
- 2 **cloves garlic, minced**
- 1½ **cups bias-sliced carrot (3 medium)**
- 2 **cups fresh pea pods, tips and strings removed, or one 6-ounce package frozen pea pods, thawed**
- 4 **green onions, bias-sliced into 1-inch pieces**
- ⅓ **cup dry-roasted peanuts**
- 2 **cups hot cooked rice**
  Chopped peanuts (optional)

1. Cut chicken into 1-inch pieces; set aside. For sauce, stir together rice wine, soy sauce, water, fish sauce (if desired), cornstarch, and crushed red pepper. Set aside.

2. Pour oil into a wok or large skillet. (If necessary, add more oil during cooking.) Heat over medium-high heat. Add ginger and garlic; cook and stir for 15 seconds. Add carrot; cook and stir for 2 minutes. Add pea pods and green onion; cook and stir about 2 minutes more or until vegetables are crisp-tender. Remove vegetables from wok.

3. Add half the chicken to hot wok. Cook and stir for 3 to 4 minutes or until chicken is no longer pink. Remove from wok. Repeat with remaining chicken. Return all chicken to wok. Push chicken from center of wok. Stir sauce; add to center of wok. Cook and stir until thickened and bubbly. Push chicken into center of wok. Return vegetables to wok. Stir in the ⅓ cup peanuts. Cook and stir for 1 to 2 minutes more or until heated through. Serve with rice. If desired, sprinkle with additional chopped peanuts.

Per 1 cup + ½ cup rice: 435 cal., 12 g total fat (2 g sat. fat), 66 mg chol., 646 mg sodium, 46 g carbo., 3 g fiber, 34 g pro.
Daily Values: 106% vit. A, 15% vit. C, 9% calcium, 17% iron
Exchanges: 1 Vegetable, 2 Starch, ½ Other Carbo., 3½ Very Lean Meat, 2 Fat

Basil Chicken in Coconut-Curry Sauce

This is a mildly spicy dish. For more kick, add another jalapeño chile pepper or two.

Prep: 25 minutes **Chill:** 1 hour
Cook: 20 minutes **Makes:** 4 servings

   2 teaspoons curry powder
   ½ teaspoon cracked black pepper
   ¼ teaspoon chili powder
   4 skinless, boneless chicken breast halves
   1 tablespoon olive oil
   ½ of a large red onion, cut into thin wedges
   2 fresh jalapeño chile peppers, seeded and finely chopped (see tip, page 74)
   5 cloves garlic, minced
   1 13.5- or 14-ounce can unsweetened coconut milk
   1 tablespoon cornstarch
   3 tablespoons snipped fresh basil
   1 teaspoon grated fresh ginger
   3 cups hot cooked rice

1. In a medium bowl combine curry powder, black pepper, ¼ teaspoon *salt*, and chili powder. Cut chicken into 1-inch pieces. Add to spice mixture; toss to coat. Cover and chill for 1 to 2 hours to allow spices to penetrate meat.

2. Pour oil into a wok or large skillet; heat over medium-high heat. Add onion, jalapeño pepper, and garlic; cook and stir about 8 minutes or until crisp-tender. Remove from wok. Add half the chicken to wok. Cook and stir for 4 to 6 minutes or until chicken is no longer pink. Remove from wok. Repeat with remaining chicken.

3. Stir together coconut milk, cornstarch, and ¼ teaspoon *salt* until smooth. Carefully add to wok. Cook and stir until slightly thickened and bubbly. Return chicken and the onion mixture to wok. Stir in basil and ginger. Cook and stir about 2 minutes or until heated through. Serve over hot rice.

Per 1 cup + ¾ cup rice: 520 cal., 23 g total fat (17 g sat. fat), 66 mg chol., 382 mg sodium, 44 g carbo., 2 g fiber, 32 g pro.
Daily Values: 5% vit. A, 11% vit. C, 5% calcium, 21% iron
Exchanges: 2½ Starch, ½ Other Carbo., 3½ Very Lean Meat, 4 Fat

FAVORITE Southwest-Style Chicken Burgers

See photo, page 455.

Prep: 20 minutes **Broil:** 15 minutes **Makes:** 4 sandwiches

   1 egg, slightly beaten
   ¼ cup finely crushed nacho-flavor or plain tortilla chips
   3 tablespoons finely chopped green sweet pepper
   ¾ teaspoon chili powder
   ¼ teaspoon salt
   ¼ teaspoon black pepper
   1 pound ground uncooked chicken or turkey
   2 ounces Monterey Jack cheese with jalapeño peppers, sliced
   4 kaiser rolls or hamburger buns, split and toasted
   1 avocado, halved, seeded, peeled, and sliced
   4 lettuce leaves
   ¼ cup bottled salsa

1. Preheat broiler. In a medium bowl stir together egg, tortilla chips, sweet pepper, chili powder, salt, and black pepper. Add chicken; mix well. (Mixture will be wet.) Shape chicken mixture into four ¾-inch-thick patties.

2. Place patties on the unheated rack of a broiler pan. Broil 4 to 5 inches from heat for 14 to 18 minutes or until no longer pink (165°F), turning once halfway through broiling time. Top burgers with cheese. Broil about 1 minute more or until cheese melts.

3. Serve burgers on toasted rolls; top with avocado, lettuce, and salsa.

Per sandwich: 522 cal., 26 g total fat (5 g sat. fat), 66 mg chol., 698 mg sodium, 39 g carbo., 4 g fiber, 32 g pro.
Daily Values: 16% vit. A, 19% vit. C, 21% calcium, 23% iron
Exchanges: 2½ Starch, 3½ Medium-Fat Meat, 1½ Fat

Greek-Style Turkey Burgers

A tomato, cucumber, and olive salsa tops these flavorful ground poultry burgers. Feta cheese completes the Greek experience.

Prep: 25 minutes **Broil:** 11 minutes **Makes:** 4 sandwiches

- 1 egg, slightly beaten
- ¼ cup fine dry bread crumbs or ¾ cup soft whole wheat bread crumbs
- 1 tablespoon milk
- 2 teaspoons dried Greek seasoning
- ¼ teaspoon salt
- 1 pound ground uncooked turkey or chicken
- 4 soft pita bread rounds, or 4 whole wheat hamburger buns, split and toasted
- 1 recipe Greek Salsa
- ¼ cup crumbled feta cheese

1. Preheat broiler. In a medium bowl stir together egg, bread crumbs, milk, Greek seasoning, and salt. Add ground turkey; mix well. Shape turkey mixture into four ½-inch-thick oval or round patties.

2. Place patties on the unheated rack of a broiler pan. Broil 4 to 5 inches from heat for 11 to 13 minutes or until no longer pink (165°F), turning once halfway through broiling time.

3. Serve the burgers in pita bread rounds. Top with Greek Salsa and sprinkle with feta cheese.

Greek Salsa: In a bowl stir together 2 tablespoons white wine vinegar, 2 teaspoons olive oil, and 1 teaspoon dried Greek seasoning. Stir in 1 cup finely chopped tomato, ¼ cup finely chopped cucumber, and ¼ cup finely chopped, pitted kalamata or ripe olives. Makes 1⅓ cups.

Per sandwich + ⅓ cup salsa: 448 cal., 17 g total fat (5 g sat. fat), 151 mg chol., 1,033 mg sodium, 42 g carbo., 3 g fiber, 29 g pro. **Daily Values:** 10% vit. A, 10% vit. C, 14% calcium, 21% iron **Exchanges:** 2 Starch, ½ Other Carbo., 3 Medium-Fat Meat, ½ Fat

Deep-Dish Chicken Pot Pie

Use the flavorful meat from a supermarket deli rotisserie chicken in this classic comfort food. See photo, page 455.

Prep: 50 minutes **Bake:** 30 minutes **Oven:** 400°F **Stand:** 20 minutes **Makes:** 6 servings

- 1 recipe Pastry Topper
- 1 cup chopped leek (3 medium) or onion (1 large)
- 1 cup sliced fresh mushrooms
- ¾ cup sliced celery (1½ stalks)
- ½ cup chopped red sweet pepper (1 small)
- 2 tablespoons butter or margarine
- ⅓ cup all-purpose flour
- 1 teaspoon poultry seasoning
- ¼ teaspoon salt
- ¼ teaspoon black pepper
- 1½ cups chicken broth
- 1 cup half-and-half, light cream, or milk
- 2½ cups chopped cooked chicken
- 1 cup frozen peas and carrots
- 1 egg, beaten

1. Prepare Pastry Topper; set aside.

2. In a large saucepan cook leek, mushrooms, celery, and sweet pepper in hot butter over medium heat for 4 to 5 minutes or until vegetables are tender. Stir in the flour, poultry seasoning, salt, and black pepper. Add broth and half-and-half all at once. Cook and stir until thickened and bubbly. Stir in chicken and peas and carrots. Pour into a 2-quart rectangular baking dish.

3. Place pastry over chicken mixture in dish. Turn edges of pastry under; flute to edges of dish. Brush pastry with some of the egg. If desired, place cutout pastry shapes on top of pastry. Brush again with egg.

4. Bake, uncovered, in a 400°F oven for 30 to 35 minutes or until crust is golden brown. Let stand for 20 minutes before serving.

Pastry Topper: In a medium bowl stir together 1¼ cups all-purpose flour and ¼ teaspoon salt. Using a pastry blender, cut in ⅓ cup shortening until dough pieces are pea size. Sprinkle 1 tablespoon cold water over part of the mixture; gently toss with a fork. Push moistened dough to side of bowl. Sprinkle an additional 3 to 4 tablespoons cold water over remaining flour mixture, 1 tablespoon at a time, tossing with a fork until all dough is moistened. Form into a ball. On a lightly floured surface, roll dough into a 13×9-inch rectangle. Using a sharp knife, cut slits in pastry to allow steam to escape. Or if desired, use a small cookie cutter to cut shapes from pastry.

Per cup: 471 cal., 26 g total fat (10 g sat. fat), 113 mg chol., 543 mg sodium, 33 g carbo., 3 g fiber, 26 g pro. **Daily Values:** 26% vit. A, 42% vit. C, 9% calcium, 19% iron **Exchanges:** 2 Vegetable, 1½ Starch, 2½ Lean Meat, 3½ Fat

Pulled Chicken Sandwiches FAST

Pick up a rotisserie chicken from your supermarket's deli on the way home, and your dinner is halfway finished.

Prep: 25 minutes **Cook:** 7 minutes **Makes:** 6 sandwiches

- 1 1¾- to 2-pound purchased rotisserie chicken
- 1 medium onion, cut into ¼-inch slices
- 1 tablespoon olive oil
- ⅓ cup cider vinegar or white wine vinegar
- ½ cup tomato sauce
- 3 to 4 tablespoons seeded and finely chopped fresh red and/or green serrano chile peppers (see tip, page 74)
- 2 tablespoons snipped fresh thyme
- 2 tablespoons molasses
- 2 tablespoons water
- ½ teaspoon salt
- 6 kaiser rolls or hamburger buns, split
  Bread-and-butter pickle slices or sweet pickle slices

1. Cut the meat from the chicken, discarding skin and bones. Using two forks or your fingers, pull meat into shreds.

2. In a large skillet cook onion in hot oil over medium heat about 5 minutes or until tender, stirring occasionally to separate slices into rings. Add vinegar. Cook and stir for 1 minute more.

3. Stir in tomato sauce, serrano pepper, thyme, molasses, water, and salt. Bring to boiling. Add the chicken, stirring gently to coat. Heat through. Serve on split rolls with pickle slices.

Per sandwich: 668 cal., 18 g total fat (4 g sat. fat), 126 mg chol., 1,485 mg sodium, 76 g carbo., 3 g fiber, 50 g pro.
Daily Values: 9% vit. A, 19% vit. C, 14% calcium, 26% iron
Exchanges: 5 Starch, 5 Lean Meat

Tex-Mex Chicken and Rice Casserole LOW FAT

If you wish, use leftover Pepper-Lime Chicken (page 467) for the cooked chicken in this crowd-pleasing casserole.

Prep: 20 minutes **Bake:** 25 minutes **Oven:** 425°F
Stand: 5 minutes **Makes:** 6 servings

- ½ cup chopped onion (1 medium)
- 1 tablespoon olive oil
- 1 6.9-ounce package chicken-flavored rice and vermicelli mix
- 1 14-ounce can chicken broth
- 2 cups water
- 2 cups chopped cooked chicken
- 1 cup chopped, seeded tomato (2 medium)
- 3 tablespoons canned diced green chile peppers, drained
- 1½ teaspoons chili powder
- 1 teaspoon dried basil, crushed
- ⅛ teaspoon ground cumin
- ½ cup shredded cheddar cheese (2 ounces)

1. In a saucepan cook onion in hot oil over medium heat until tender. Stir in rice and vermicelli mix (including seasoning package); cook and stir for 2 minutes. Stir in broth and water. Bring to boiling; reduce heat. Simmer, covered, for 20 minutes (liquid will not be fully absorbed).

2. Transfer the rice mixture to a large bowl. Stir in chicken, tomato, chile peppers, chili powder, basil, cumin, and ⅛ teaspoon *black pepper*. Transfer to a 2-quart casserole.

3. Bake, covered, in a 425°F oven for 25 minutes. Uncover and sprinkle with cheese. Let stand about 5 minutes or until cheese melts.

Make-ahead directions: Prepare as above through Step 2. Cover and chill for up to 24 hours. Bake, covered, in a 425°F oven about 40 minutes or until heated through. Uncover and sprinkle with cheese. Let stand for 5 minutes.

Per cup: 280 cal., 10 g total fat (4 g sat. fat), 52 mg chol., 931 mg sodium, 28 g carbo., 2 g fiber, 20 g pro.
Daily Values: 13% vit. A, 11% vit. C, 10% calcium, 11% iron
Exchanges: 2 Starch, 2 Lean Meat, ½ Fat

Tex-Mex Chicken and Rice Casserole

Chicken Burritos

For an extra flavor kick, shred leftover Pepper-Lime Chicken (page 467) for this recipe.

Prep: 20 minutes **Bake:** 30 minutes
Oven: 350°F **Makes:** 8 servings

- 8 8- to 10-inch flour tortillas
- 1½ cups shredded cooked chicken, beef, or pork
- 1 cup bottled salsa
- 1 3.125-ounce can jalapeño-flavored bean dip
- 1 teaspoon fajita seasoning
- 8 ounces Monterey Jack cheese or cheddar cheese, cut into eight 5×½-inch sticks
  Shredded lettuce (optional)
  Dairy sour cream (optional)
  Bottled salsa (optional)

1. Wrap tortillas in foil; heat in a 350°F oven about 10 minutes or until heated through.

2. Meanwhile, in a large bowl stir together shredded chicken, the 1 cup salsa, the bean dip, and fajita seasoning.

3. To assemble, place ⅓ cup chicken mixture onto each tortilla near the edge. Top chicken mixture with a stick of cheese. Fold in tortilla sides and roll up, starting from the edge with the filling. Place filled tortillas, seam sides down, in a greased 3-quart rectangular baking dish.

4. Bake, uncovered, in a 350°F oven about 30 minutes or until heated through. If desired, serve with shredded lettuce, sour cream, and additional salsa.

Per burrito: 261 cal., 13 g total fat (6 g sat. fat), 48 mg chol., 441 mg sodium, 18 g carbo., 1 g fiber, 17 g pro.
Daily Values: 8% vit. A, 4% vit. C, 25% calcium, 9% iron
Exchanges: 1 Starch, 2 Lean Meat, 1½ Fat

Chicken Enchiladas

If you prefer a red sauce on your enchiladas, omit the soup, sour cream, and 1 cup milk. Stir the reserved chile peppers into 2½ cups of purchased enchilada sauce. Bake as directed.

Prep: 30 minutes **Bake:** 40 minutes
Oven: 350°F **Makes:** 6 servings

- ¼ cup slivered almonds
- ¼ cup chopped onion
- 2 tablespoons butter or margarine
- 1 4-ounce can diced green chile peppers, drained
- 1 3-ounce package cream cheese, softened
- 1 tablespoon milk
- ¼ teaspoon ground cumin
- 2 cups chopped cooked chicken or turkey
- 12 7-inch flour tortillas or 6-inch corn tortillas
- 1 10.75-ounce can reduced-fat condensed cream of chicken or cream of mushroom soup
- 1 8-ounce carton light dairy sour cream
- 1 cup milk
- ¾ cup shredded Monterey Jack or cheddar cheese (3 ounces)
- 2 tablespoons slivered almonds

1. In a medium skillet cook the ¼ cup almonds and the onion in hot butter over medium heat until onion is tender and nuts are lightly toasted. Remove from heat. Stir in 1 tablespoon of the canned green chile peppers; reserve remaining peppers for sauce.

2. In a medium bowl stir together cream cheese, the 1 tablespoon milk, and the cumin; add nut mixture and chicken. Stir until combined. Spoon about 3 tablespoons of the chicken mixture onto each tortilla near the edge; roll up. Place filled tortillas, seam sides down, in a greased 3-quart rectangular baking dish. Set aside.

3. For sauce, in a medium bowl combine the reserved chile peppers, the soup, sour cream, and the 1 cup milk. Pour evenly over the tortillas in the baking dish. Cover with foil. Bake in a 350°F oven about 35 minutes or until heated through. Remove foil. Sprinkle enchiladas with Monterey Jack cheese and the 2 tablespoons almonds. Return to oven; bake about 5 minutes more or until cheese melts.

Per 2 enchiladas: 538 cal., 30 g total fat (13 g sat. fat), 100 mg chol., 635 mg sodium, 38 g carbo., 3 g fiber, 29 g pro.
Daily Values: 20% vit. A, 12% vit. C, 34% calcium, 17% iron
Exchanges: 2½ Starch, 3 Lean Meat, 4 Fat

Mexican Dinner

Here's a family-pleasing menu perfect for a weeknight sit-down dinner.

- *Chicken Burritos (left) or Chicken Enchiladas (left)*
- *Spanish Rice (page 88)*
- *Refried black beans*
- *Tortilla chips*
- *Sliced fresh fruit*

Chicken Tetrazzini

Half-and-half makes this dish very creamy. For more or less richness, substitute cream or milk.

Prep: 30 minutes **Bake:** 15 minutes
Oven: 350°F **Makes:** 6 servings

- 8 ounces dried spaghetti or linguine
- 2 cups sliced fresh mushrooms
- ½ cup sliced green onion (4)
- 2 tablespoons butter or margarine
- ¼ cup all-purpose flour
- ⅛ teaspoon black pepper
- ⅛ teaspoon ground nutmeg
- 1¼ cups chicken broth
- 1¼ cups half-and-half, light cream, or milk
- 2 cups chopped cooked chicken or turkey
- 2 tablespoons dry sherry (optional)
- ¼ cup grated Parmesan cheese
- ¼ cup sliced almonds, toasted (see tip, page 265)
- 2 tablespoons snipped fresh parsley (optional)

1. Cook spaghetti according to package directions; drain.

2. Meanwhile, in a large saucepan cook mushrooms and green onion in hot butter over medium heat until tender. Stir in flour, pepper, and nutmeg. Add broth and half-and-half all at once. Cook and stir until thickened and bubbly. Stir in chicken, sherry (if desired), and half of the Parmesan cheese. Gently stir in spaghetti.

3. Transfer pasta mixture to a 2-quart rectangular baking dish. Sprinkle with the remaining Parmesan cheese and the almonds. Bake, uncovered, in a 350°F oven for 15 minutes. If desired, sprinkle with parsley before serving.

Per cup: 404 cal., 18 g total fat (8 g sat. fat), 74 mg chol., 342 mg sodium, 37 g carbo., 2 g fiber, 24 g pro.
Daily Values: 8% vit. A, 4% vit. C, 13% calcium, 14% iron
Exchanges: ½ Vegetable, 2 Starch, 2½ Lean Meat, 2 Fat

Herb-Roasted Chicken

Only a little prep is needed for this simple recipe. To make it more of a meal, try the variation with roasted vegetables.

Prep: 20 minutes **Roast:** 1¼ hours **Oven:** 375°F
Stand: 10 minutes **Makes:** 4 servings

- 1 3½- to 4-pound whole broiler chicken
- 2 tablespoons butter or margarine, melted
- 2 cloves garlic, minced
- 1 teaspoon dried basil, crushed
- ½ teaspoon ground sage
- ½ teaspoon dried thyme, crushed
- ¼ teaspoon salt
- ¼ teaspoon lemon-pepper seasoning or ground black pepper

1. Rinse the chicken body cavity; pat dry with paper towels. Skewer neck skin of chicken to back (see photo 2, page 478); tie legs to tail. Twist wing tips under back (see photo 4, page 478). Place chicken, breast side up, on a rack in a shallow roasting pan. Brush chicken with melted butter and rub with minced garlic.

2. In a small bowl stir together basil, sage, thyme, salt, and lemon-pepper seasoning; rub onto chicken. If desired, insert a meat thermometer into center of an inside thigh muscle (see photo 5, page 478). (The thermometer should not touch bone.)

3. Roast, uncovered, in a 375°F oven for 1¼ to 1½ hours or until drumsticks move easily in their sockets and chicken is no longer pink (180°F). Remove chicken from oven. Cover; let stand for 10 minutes before carving.

Per 4 ounces: 625 cal., 45 g total fat (14 g sat. fat), 217 mg chol., 408 mg sodium, 1 g carbo., 0 g fiber, 50 g pro.
Daily Values: 11% vit. A, 7% vit. C, 4% calcium, 14% iron
Exchanges: 7 Medium-Fat Meat, 2 Fat

Herb-Roasted Chicken and Vegetables: Prepare as above, except before roasting chicken, in a large saucepan bring lightly salted water to boiling. Add 1 pound red potatoes, quartered (or halved, if small); 3 carrots, halved lengthwise and cut into 1-inch pieces; and 1 medium turnip, peeled and cut into 1½-inch pieces. Return to boiling; reduce heat. Simmer, covered, for 5 minutes; drain. Add drained vegetables and 1 medium onion, cut into 1-inch chunks, to the bottom of the roasting pan around chicken. Drizzle vegetables with 2 tablespoons melted butter or margarine and sprinkle with ¼ teaspoon salt and ¼ teaspoon black pepper. Roast as directed above, stirring vegetables once or twice during roasting.

Per 4 ounces chicken + ⅔ cup vegetables: 799 cal., 51 g total fat (17 g sat. fat), 233 mg chol., 657 mg sodium, 28 g carbo., 4 g fiber, 54 g pro.
Daily Values: 119% vit. A, 50% vit. C, 9% calcium, 24% iron
Exchanges: 1 Vegetable, 1½ Starch, 7 Medium-Fat Meat, 2½ Fat

One-Dish Turkey and Biscuits LOW FAT

Serve this creamy comfort food on a chilly day.

Prep: 30 minutes **Bake:** 20 minutes
Oven: 425°F **Makes:** 4 servings

      1 cup chicken broth
    ½ cup finely chopped onion (1 medium)
    ½ cup finely chopped celery (1 stalk)
  1½ cups frozen peas and carrots
  1½ cups milk
      3 tablespoons all-purpose flour
      2 cups cubed cooked turkey breast
    ½ teaspoon dried sage, crushed
    ⅛ teaspoon black pepper
  1¼ cups packaged biscuit mix
      2 teaspoons dried parsley flakes, crushed

1. In a medium saucepan stir together broth, onion, and celery. Bring to boiling; reduce heat. Simmer, covered, for 5 minutes. Add peas and carrots; return to boiling.

2. In a small bowl stir together 1 cup of the milk and the flour until smooth; stir into vegetable mixture in saucepan. Cook and stir until thickened and bubbly. Stir in turkey, sage, and pepper. Transfer to a 2-quart casserole.

3. In a small bowl combine biscuit mix, the remaining ½ cup milk, and the parsley. Stir with a fork just until moistened. Spoon biscuit mixture into eight mounds on top of the hot turkey mixture in casserole. Bake, uncovered, in a 425°F oven for 20 to 25 minutes or until biscuits are golden brown.

Per 1 cup + 2 biscuits: 368 cal., 9 g total fat (3 g sat. fat), 68 mg chol., 853 mg sodium, 41 g carbo., 3 g fiber, 30 g pro. **Daily Values:** 105% vit. A, 14% vit. C, 21% calcium, 18% iron **Exchanges:** ½ Milk, ½ Vegetable, 2 Starch, 2½ Very Lean Meat, 1½ Fat

Artichoke-Turkey Casserole

Prep: 20 minutes **Bake:** 40 minutes **Oven:** 350°F
Stand: 10 minutes **Makes:** 4 servings

    ½ cup chopped carrot (1 medium)
    ½ cup chopped red sweet pepper (1 small)
    ¼ cup sliced green onion (2)
      1 tablespoon butter or margarine
      1 10.75-ounce can condensed cream of chicken soup
      1 8- to 9-ounce package frozen artichoke hearts, thawed and cut up

  1½ cups chopped cooked turkey or chicken
      1 cup cooked long grain rice or wild rice
    ⅔ cup milk
    ½ cup shredded mozzarella cheese (2 ounces)
    ½ teaspoon dried thyme, crushed
      2 slices bacon, crisp-cooked, drained, and crumbled
      3 tablespoons grated Parmesan cheese

1. In a large skillet cook carrot, sweet pepper, and green onion in hot butter over medium heat until carrot is crisp-tender. Remove from heat. Stir in soup, artichoke hearts, turkey, rice, milk, mozzarella cheese, thyme, and bacon. Transfer turkey mixture to a 2-quart rectangular baking dish. Sprinkle with Parmesan cheese.

2. Bake, covered, in a 350°F oven for 20 minutes. Uncover and bake for 20 to 25 minutes more or until bubbly. Let stand for 10 minutes before serving.

Make-ahead directions: Prepare as above through Step 1. Cover and chill for up to 24 hours. Bake, covered, in a 350°F oven for 30 minutes. Uncover and bake about 20 minutes more or until bubbly.

Per 1¼ cups: 372 cal., 16 g total fat (7 g sat. fat), 71 mg chol., 916 mg sodium, 27 g carbo., 5 g fiber, 28 g pro. **Daily Values:** 113% vit. A, 62% vit. C, 27% calcium, 14% iron **Exchanges:** 1 Vegetable, 1½ Starch, 3 Lean Meat, 1½ Fat

Honey-Mustard-Glazed Turkey Breast

Prep: 20 minutes **Roast:** 1¼ hours **Oven:** 325°F
Stand: 10 minutes **Makes:** 6 servings

      1 2- to 2½-pound turkey breast portion with bone
      1 tablespoon cooking oil
    ¼ teaspoon salt
    ⅛ teaspoon black pepper
      1 recipe Honey-Mustard Glaze (page 477)

1. Place turkey breast, bone side down, on a rack in a shallow roasting pan. Brush with oil; sprinkle with salt and pepper. Insert a meat thermometer into thickest part of the breast. (The thermometer should not touch bone.)

2. Roast turkey, uncovered, in a 325°F oven for 1¼ to 1½ hours or until juices run clear and turkey is no longer pink (170°F), brushing with Honey-Mustard Glaze several times during the last 15 minutes of roasting. Transfer turkey to a cutting board; let stand for 10 to 15 minutes before carving. Heat any remaining glaze; serve with turkey.

Honey-Mustard Glaze: In a small bowl stir together ¼ cup honey, 1 tablespoon Dijon-style mustard, 1 tablespoon Worcestershire sauce for chicken, and 1 tablespoon butter, melted.

Maple-Barbecue-Glazed Turkey Breast: Prepare as on page 476, except omit Honey-Mustard Glaze. In a small saucepan stir together ¼ cup pure maple syrup, 1 tablespoon bottled chili sauce, 1 tablespoon cider vinegar, 2 teaspoons Worcestershire sauce, ¼ teaspoon dry mustard, and ¼ teaspoon black pepper. Heat and stir over medium heat until slightly thickened. Substitute for Honey-Mustard Glaze.

Per 3 ounces honey-mustard or maple-barbecue variation: 282 cal., 13 g total fat (4 g sat. fat), 88 mg chol., 268 mg sodium, 13 g carbo., 0 g fiber, 28 g pro.
Daily Values: 1% vit. A, 3% calcium, 9% iron
Exchanges: 1 Other Carbo., 4 Lean Meat

Spice-Rubbed Turkey with
Cranberry Barbecue Sauce

Spice-Rubbed Turkey with Cranberry Barbecue Sauce LOW FAT

For a more crusty, blackened-spice look, rub the spice mixture on the outside of the turkey breast. Be sure to cover with foil during the last 30 minutes to prevent burning.

Prep: 25 minutes **Roast:** 20 minutes + 1 hour
Oven: 400°F/350°F **Stand:** 10 minutes
Makes: 10 servings

    Nonstick cooking spray
2 tablespoons packed dark brown sugar
2 teaspoons paprika
2 teaspoons garlic powder

1½ teaspoons salt
1 teaspoon ground cumin
1 teaspoon chili powder
¾ teaspoon freshly ground black pepper
2 3- to 3½-pound turkey breast portions with bone
1 cup chopped onion (1 large)
1 tablespoon cooking oil
1 16-ounce can whole cranberry sauce
⅓ cup bottled chili sauce
1 tablespoon cider vinegar
1 teaspoon Worcestershire sauce
¼ teaspoon freshly ground black pepper

1. Coat a large shallow roasting pan and roasting rack with cooking spray. In a small bowl combine brown sugar, paprika, garlic powder, salt, cumin, chili powder, and the ¾ teaspoon pepper; set aside.

2. Place turkey breasts, bone sides down, on the rack in prepared pan. Starting at the breast bones, use your fingers to loosen the skin from the meat, leaving skin attached at the top. Spread spice mixture evenly under skin over the breast meat. Insert a meat thermometer into thickest part of the breast. (The thermometer should not touch bone.)

3. Roast turkey, uncovered, on the lower rack of a 400°F oven for 20 minutes. Reduce the oven temperature to 350°F; roast for 1 to 1½ hours longer or until juices run clear and turkey is no longer pink (170°F), occasionally spooning pan juices over turkey. Transfer turkey to a cutting board. Let stand, covered with foil, for 10 to 15 minutes before slicing.

4. Meanwhile, for barbecue sauce, in a medium saucepan cook onion in hot oil over medium heat about 5 minutes or until tender. Add cranberry sauce, chili sauce, vinegar, Worcestershire sauce, and the ¼ teaspoon pepper. Bring to boiling; reduce heat. Simmer, uncovered, about 5 minutes or until thickened, stirring occasionally. Serve with the turkey.

Per 4 ounces turkey + ¼ cup sauce: 413 cal., 7 g total fat (2 g sat. fat), 167 mg chol., 707 mg sodium, 26 g carbo., 1 g fiber, 57 g pro.
Daily Values: 6% vit. A, 3% vit. C, 5% calcium, 17% iron
Exchanges: 1½ Other Carbo., 8 Very Lean Meat, 1 Fat

Roast Turkey

Roast Turkey `LOW FAT` `EASY`

If you wish, fill a turkey with any of the stuffings listed on pages 480 to 482. Because stuffed turkeys take longer to roast, be sure to check the roasting times for various-size turkeys on page 488.

Prep: 15 minutes **Roast:** 2¾ hours **Oven:** 325°F
Stand: 15 minutes **Makes:** 12 servings

　1　8- to 10-pound turkey
　　Salt (optional)
　　Stuffing (optional)
　　Cooking oil

1. Rinse the turkey body cavity; pat dry with paper towels. If desired, season body cavity with salt. If desired, spoon stuffing loosely into neck and body cavities (see photo 1, right). Skewer turkey neck skin to back (see photo 2, right).

2. Tuck drumstick ends under the band of skin across the tail, if available. If there is no band of skin, tie the drumsticks securely to the tail (see photo 3, right). Twist wing tips under the back (see photo 4, right).

3. Place turkey, breast side up, on a rack in a shallow roasting pan. Brush with oil. If desired, insert a meat thermometer into the center of an inside thigh muscle (see photo 5, right). The thermometer should not touch bone. Cover turkey loosely with foil.

4. Roast in a 325°F oven for 2¼ hours. Remove foil; cut band of skin or string between drumsticks so thighs will cook evenly. Continue roasting for 30 to 45 minutes more (1 to 1¼ hours if stuffed) or until the thermometer

registers 180°F; if stuffed, the center of the stuffing should register 165°F. (The juices should run clear and drumsticks should move easily in their sockets.)

5. Remove turkey from oven. Cover with foil; let stand for 15 to 20 minutes before carving. Transfer turkey to a cutting board. Carve turkey (see carving tips, page 479).

Per 4 ounces: 255 cal., 12 g total fat (3 g sat. fat), 101 mg chol., 83 mg sodium, 0 g carbo., 0 g fiber, 35 g pro. **Daily Values:** 3% calcium, 12% iron
Exchanges: 5 Lean Meat

1. Lightly spoon some stuffing into the neck cavity. Don't pack it in tightly; it won't cook through.

2. After adding stuffing to the neck cavity, pull the neck skin over the stuffing and onto the back of the turkey; secure neck skin with a small skewer.

3. Loosely fill the body cavity with stuffing. (Use no more than ¾ cup stuffing per pound of turkey.) If there is a band of skin at the tail, tuck the legs under it; if there is not a band, tie legs to tail with kitchen string.

4. To prevent the wing tips from overbrowning and for a neater appearance, twist the wing tips under the back of the turkey.

5. Insert a thermometer into the center of an inside thigh muscle. The tip should not touch bone. After roasting, use an instant-read thermometer to check the stuffing (165°F) and thigh (180°F) in several places.

Carving a Roasted Turkey

For carving, use a long, sharp knife and a cutting board with grooves for catching juices.

1. With the turkey on a large cutting board, remove the drumstick/ thigh portions by pulling the legs away from the body of the turkey and cutting the joints that attach the thighs to the body.

2. With the drumstick/thigh portions on the cutting board, cut through their joints to separate them. Place drumsticks on a serving platter. Holding each thigh firmly on the cutting board with a meat fork, cut slices of meat away from the bone. Arrange slices on platter with drumsticks.

3. Holding the turkey firmly with a meat fork, carve each entire breast half away from the breast bone and rib cage. Place whole breast halves on the cutting board.

4. Slice breast halves crosswise (across the grain). Arrange slices on platter. If desired, cut wings* off turkey frame, cutting at the joints, and arrange them on the platter. (For a serving presentation, see photo, page 478, top left.)

*Note: Or leave wings attached to the turkey frame and use the frame to make Turkey Frame Soup (page 555).

Maple-Brined Turkey `LOW FAT`

Prep: 20 minutes **Marinate:** 12 hours **Roast:** 2¾ hours
Oven: 325°F **Stand:** 15 minutes **Makes:** 12 servings

- 1½ **gallons water**
- 1½ **cups pure maple syrup or maple-flavored syrup**
- 1 **cup coarse salt**
- ¾ **cup packed brown sugar**
- 1 **8- to 10-pound turkey (not self-basting type)**
  Cooking oil

1. For brine, in a 10-quart pot combine water, syrup, salt, and brown sugar; stir to dissolve sugar and salt. Set aside.

2. Rinse the turkey body cavity; remove any excess fat from cavity. Add turkey to brine in pot. Cover and marinate in the refrigerator for 12 to 24 hours.

3. Remove turkey from brine; discard brine. Drain turkey; pat dry with paper towels. Place turkey, breast side up, on a rack in a shallow roasting pan. Tuck drumstick ends under the band of skin across the tail, if available. If there is no band of skin, tie drumsticks securely to the tail (see photo 3, page 478). Twist wing tips under the back (see photo 4, page 478). Brush with oil. If desired, insert a meat thermometer into center of an inside thigh muscle (see photo 5, page 478). The thermometer should not touch bone. Cover turkey loosely with foil.

4. Roast turkey in a 325°F oven for 2¼ hours. Remove foil; cut band of skin or string between drumsticks so thighs will cook evenly. Continue roasting, uncovered, for 30 to 45 minutes more or until the thermometer registers 180°F. (The juices should run clear and drumsticks should move easily in sockets.)

5. Remove turkey from oven. Cover with foil; let stand for 15 to 20 minutes before carving. Transfer turkey to a cutting board. Carve turkey (see carving tips, above).

Per 4 ounces: 280 cal., 11 g total fat (3 g sat. fat), 101 mg chol., 1,250 mg sodium, 7 g carbo., 0 g fiber, 36 g pro.
Daily Values: 4% calcium, 13% iron
Exchanges: ½ Other Carbo., 4½ Lean Meat

Classic Giblet Stuffing

Giblets refer to the heart, liver, gizzard and, sometimes, the neck of poultry.

Prep: 35 minutes **Bake:** 35 minutes
Oven: 325°F **Makes:** 10 to 12 servings

- Turkey giblets
- 1 cup finely chopped celery (2 stalks)
- ½ cup chopped onion (1 medium)
- ½ cup butter or margarine
- 1 tablespoon snipped fresh sage or
  1 teaspoon poultry seasoning or ground sage
- ¼ teaspoon black pepper
- ⅛ teaspoon salt
- 8 cups dry bread cubes (see tip, page 481)
- 1 to 1¼ cups chicken broth or water

1. Rinse giblets; refrigerate liver. In a small saucepan cook the remaining giblets, covered, in enough boiling water to cover for 1 hour. Add liver. Simmer, covered, for 20 to 30 minutes more or until tender. Drain* and chop giblets; set aside.

2. In the same saucepan cook celery and onion in hot butter over medium heat until tender but not brown; remove from heat. Stir in giblets, sage, pepper, and salt. Place the bread cubes in an extra-large bowl; add onion mixture. Drizzle with enough broth to moisten, tossing lightly to combine. Transfer bread mixture to a 2-quart casserole.** Bake, covered, in a 325°F oven for 35 to 40 minutes or until heated through.

*Note: If desired, reserve 1 to 1¼ cups of the giblet cooking broth and substitute for the chicken broth.

**Note: Or use bread mixture to stuff an 8- to 10-pound turkey. (See stuffing tips, page 481, and see roasting chart, page 488, for doneness temperatures and roasting times.) Reduce broth to ¾ to 1 cup.

Oyster Stuffing: Prepare as above, except omit the giblets and use a medium saucepan. Add 1 pint shucked oysters, drained and chopped, to the cooked vegetables. Cook and stir for 2 minutes more. Stir in seasonings. Continue as above, except reduce broth to ¼ cup.

Per ¾ cup plain or oyster variation: 189 cal., 11 g total fat (6 g sat. fat), 62 mg chol., 379 mg sodium, 16 g carbo., 1 g fiber, 5 g pro.
Daily Values: 18% vit. A, 2% vit. C, 4% calcium, 9% iron
Exchanges: 1 Starch, 2½ Fat

Chestnut Stuffing: Prepare as at left, except omit the giblets. With a knife, cut an X in the shells of 1 pound fresh chestnuts (3 cups). Spread chestnuts on a large baking sheet. Roast chestnuts in a 400°F oven for 15 minutes; cool. Peel and coarsely chop chestnuts. (Or use one 8-ounce jar or one 10-ounce can whole, peeled chestnuts, drained and chopped.) Add chestnuts with seasonings. Use ¾ cup to 1 cup broth.

Per ¾ cup: 271 cal., 12 g total fat (6 g sat. fat), 27 mg chol., 376 mg sodium, 37 g carbo., 5 g fiber, 4 g pro.
Daily Values: 8% vit. A, 34% vit. C, 6% calcium, 8% iron
Exchanges: 2½ Starch, 2 Fat

Old-Fashioned Bread Stuffing EASY

Prep: 15 minutes **Bake:** 30 minutes
Oven: 325°F **Makes:** 12 to 14 servings

- 1½ cups chopped celery (3 stalks)
- 1 cup chopped onion (1 large)
- ½ cup butter or margarine
- 1 tablespoon snipped fresh sage or
  1 teaspoon poultry seasoning or ground sage
- ¼ teaspoon black pepper
- 12 cups dry bread cubes (see tip, page 481)
- 1 to 1¼ cups chicken broth

1. In a large skillet cook celery and onion in hot butter until tender but not brown. Remove from heat. Stir in sage and pepper. Place the bread cubes in a large bowl; add onion mixture. Drizzle with enough chicken broth to moisten, tossing lightly to combine. Transfer bread mixture to a 2-quart casserole.* Bake, covered, in a 325°F oven for 30 to 45 minutes or until heated through.

*Note: Or use bread mixture to stuff a 10- to 12-pound turkey. (See stuffing tips, page 481, and see roasting chart, page 488, for doneness temperatures and roasting times.) Reduce broth to ¾ to 1 cup.

Per ⅔ cup: 181 cal., 10 g total fat (5 g sat. fat), 22 mg chol., 342 mg sodium, 20 g carbo., 1 g fiber, 4 g pro.
Daily Values: 6% vit. A, 2% vit. C, 5% calcium, 7% iron
Exchanges: 1½ Starch, 1½ Fat

Mediterranean-Style Stuffing

Prep: 30 minutes **Bake:** 40 minutes
Oven: 375°F/325°F **Makes:** 6 to 8 servings

> 8 cups Italian bread cubes (about 8 ounces)
> ¾ cup chopped red or yellow sweet pepper (1 medium)
> ½ cup chopped onion (1 medium)
> 3 cloves garlic, minced
> ¼ cup olive oil
> 1 tablespoon lemon juice
> 1 teaspoon dried rosemary, crushed
> ⅛ teaspoon cayenne pepper
> ¼ cup snipped fresh parsley
> 1 to 1¼ cups chicken broth

1. Place bread cubes in a single layer in a 15×10×1-inch baking pan. Bake in a 375°F oven about 10 minutes or until golden, stirring once; set aside. Reduce oven temperature to 325°F.

2. In a skillet cook sweet pepper, onion, and garlic in hot oil about 4 minutes or until tender; remove from heat. Stir in lemon juice, rosemary, and cayenne pepper. In a large bowl toss bread cubes, onion mixture, and parsley. Drizzle with enough broth to moisten; toss lightly to combine. Transfer mixture to a 1½-quart casserole.* Bake, covered, for 20 minutes. Uncover; bake about 20 minutes more or until heated through.

*Note: Or use bread mixture to stuff an 8-pound turkey. (See stuffing tips, right, and see roasting chart, page 488, for doneness temperatures and roasting times.) Reduce broth to ¾ to 1 cup.

Per ¾ cup: 202 cal., 11 g total fat (2 g sat. fat), 0 mg chol., 390 mg sodium, 22 g carbo., 2 g fiber, 4 g pro.
Daily Values: 23% vit. A, 60% vit. C, 4% calcium, 8% iron
Exchanges: 1½ Starch, 2 Fat

Wild Rice Stuffing

Prep: 15 minutes **Cook:** 45 minutes **Makes:** 6 servings

> ¼ cup uncooked wild rice
> ¼ cup uncooked brown rice
> 1 teaspoon instant chicken bouillon granules
> ⅛ to ¼ teaspoon ground sage or nutmeg
> 2 cups sliced fresh mushrooms
> ½ cup chopped celery (1 stalk)
> ⅓ cup sliced green onion (3)
> ½ cup sliced almonds or pine nuts, toasted (see tip, page 265) (optional)

1. Rinse uncooked wild rice in a strainer under cold water about 1 minute; drain. In a medium saucepan combine wild rice, 1¾ cups *water,* uncooked brown rice, bouillon granules, and sage. Bring to boiling; reduce heat. Simmer, covered, for 20 minutes.

2. Add mushrooms, celery, and green onion. Cook, covered, over medium-low heat about 25 minutes more or just until vegetables are tender, stirring frequently. If desired, stir in almonds. Serve immediately, or cool and use to stuff a 3½- to 4-pound broiler-fryer chicken (see stuffing tips, below).

Make-ahead directions: Prepare as above, except transfer stuffing to a 1-quart casserole. Cover and chill for up to 24 hours. Stir in ¼ cup water. Bake, covered, in a 375°F oven about 30 minutes or until heated through.

Per ½ cup: 66 cal., 1 g total fat (0 g sat. fat), 0 mg chol., 155 mg sodium, 13 g carbo., 1 g fiber, 3 g pro.
Daily Values: 1% vit. A, 3% vit. C, 1% calcium, 3% iron
Exchanges: 1 Vegetable, ½ Starch

Stuffing Tips

● To make dry bread cubes, cut fresh bread into ½-inch cubes. (Twelve to 14 bread slices will yield 8 cups bread cubes.) Spread cubes in a 15½×10½×2-inch baking pan. Bake in a 300°F oven for 10 to 15 minutes or until cubes are dry, stirring twice; cool. (Cubes will continue to dry and crisp as they cool.) Or let bread cubes stand loosely covered at room temperature for 8 to 12 hours.

● Estimate ¾ cup stuffing for each pound of turkey or other poultry.

● Do not stuff poultry until just before roasting it.

● Spoon stuffing loosely into bird to give stuffing room to expand. Also, if stuffing is too tightly packed, it will not reach a safe temperature by the time the bird is done.

● Stuffing temperature should reach at least 165°F. Insert a thermometer into the center of stuffing to check it.

● Stuffing doesn't have to be baked in a bird. Bake all of it or any that wouldn't fit in the bird in a covered casserole in a 325°F oven for 30 to 45 minutes or until heated through.

Sausage Stuffing

Sausage Stuffing

Make Corn Bread (page 134) for this recipe or prepare one 8-ounce package corn muffin mix.

Prep: 30 minutes **Bake:** 30 minutes
Oven: 325°F **Makes:** 10 to 12 servings

   12 ounces bulk pork sausage
   ¾ cup finely chopped onion (1 large)
   ½ cup chopped green sweet pepper (1 small)
   ½ cup chopped celery (2 stalks)
   ½ cup butter or margarine
    5 cups dry white bread cubes
       (see tip, page 481)
 4½ cups crumbled corn bread
    1 teaspoon poultry seasoning
   ⅛ teaspoon black pepper
   ¾ cup chopped pecans, toasted (see tip,
       page 265) (optional)
 1¼ to 1½ cups chicken broth

1. In a large skillet brown sausage over medium heat; drain well. Remove sausage from skillet; set aside.

2. In the same skillet cook onion, sweet pepper, and celery in hot butter over medium heat until tender; set aside.

3. In a large bowl combine bread cubes and corn bread. Add cooked sausage, onion mixture, poultry seasoning, black pepper, and, if desired, pecans. Drizzle with enough broth to moisten (about 1¼ cups), tossing lightly to combine. Transfer bread mixture to a 2-quart casserole.* Bake, covered, in a 325°F oven for 30 to 45 minutes or until heated through.

*Note: Or use bread mixture to stuff an 8- to 10-pound turkey. (See stuffing tips, page 481, and see roasting chart, page 488, for doneness temperatures and roasting times.) Reduce broth to ¾ to 1 cup.

Quick Sausage Stuffing: Prepare as at left, except substitute 3 cups corn bread stuffing mix (one 8-ounce package) for the crumbled corn bread. Reduce poultry seasoning to ½ teaspoon; omit black pepper. Substitute water for broth.

Per ¾ cup regular or quick variation: 373 cal., 24 g total fat (10 g sat. fat), 62 mg chol., 686 mg sodium, 29 g carbo., 1 g fiber, 8 g pro.
Daily Values: 8% vit. A, 12% vit. C, 7% calcium, 8% iron
Exchanges: 2 Starch, ½ High-Fat Meat, 3½ Fat

Giblet Gravy

Prep: 15 minutes **Cook:** 1½ hours **Makes:** 2½ cups

       Whole turkey or chicken
    4 ounces turkey or chicken giblets,
       including the neck
    1 stalk celery with leaves, cut up
   ½ small onion, cut up
       Pan drippings from roasted turkey or
       chicken
   ¼ cup all-purpose flour
   ¼ teaspoon salt
   ¼ teaspoon black pepper

1. Roast turkey or chicken according to roasting chart on page 488. Rinse giblets; refrigerate liver. In a medium saucepan combine remaining giblets, the celery, onion, and enough lightly salted *water* to cover. Bring to boiling; reduce heat. Simmer, covered, for 1 hour. Add liver. Simmer, covered, about 30 minutes more for turkey (10 minutes more for chicken) or until tender. Remove giblets; finely chop. Discard neck. Strain broth (see photo, page 548). Discard vegetables. Chill giblets and broth while turkey or chicken roasts.

2. Transfer roasted turkey or chicken to a serving platter; pour pan drippings into a large measuring cup. Skim and reserve fat from drippings (see photo, page 483). Pour ¼ cup of the fat into a medium saucepan (discard remaining fat). Stir in flour, salt, and pepper.

3. Add enough reserved broth to drippings in measuring cup to equal 2 cups. Add broth mixture all at once to flour mixture in the saucepan. Cook and stir over medium heat until thickened and bubbly. Cook and stir for 1 minute more. Stir in chopped giblets. Heat through.

Per ⅓ cup: 85 cal., 7 g total fat (4 g sat. fat), 56 mg chol., 150 mg sodium, 3 g carbo., 0 g fiber, 3 g pro.
Daily Values: 22% vit. A, 1% vit. C, 1% calcium, 6% iron
Exchanges: ½ Very Lean Meat, 1½ Fat

Pan Gravy ⟮FAST⟯

Start to Finish: 15 minutes Makes: 2 cups

> **Pan drippings from roasted poultry**
> ¼ **cup all-purpose flour**
> **Chicken broth**
> **Salt and black pepper**

1. Pour pan drippings into a large measuring cup. Scrape the browned bits from the pan into the cup. Skim and reserve fat from the drippings (see photo, below).

2. Pour ¼ cup of the fat into a medium sauce-pan (discard remaining fat). Stir in flour. Add enough broth to drippings in the measuring cup to equal 2 cups. Add broth mixture all at once to flour mixture in saucepan. Cook and stir over medium heat until thickened and bubbly. Cook and stir for 1 minute more. Season to taste with salt and pepper.

Per ¼ cup: 77 cal., 6 g total fat (4 g sat. fat), 16 mg chol., 256 mg sodium, 3 g carbo., 0 g fiber, 2 g pro.
Daily Values: 5% vit. A, 2% iron
Exchanges: 1½ Fat

Making Gravy

● For the best flavor, skim and reserve fat from pan drippings to make gravy.
● Combine the fat with flour to make a roux, a smooth mixture that thickens broth and pan drippings without creating lumps.
● If you don't skim enough fat from the pan drippings to make gravy, use an equal measure of melted butter.
● To skim the fat off roast poultry or meat drippings, pour the drippings into a glass measure. Tip the mea-sure and use a metal spoon to carefully remove the clear fat that rises to the top.

Crimson Cherry-Glazed Holiday Hens

A whole game hen makes a spectacular entrée for a special occasion. If it's too much food, cut each roasted hen in half for smaller servings.

Prep: 20 minutes Roast: 1 hour Oven: 375°F
Cook: 20 minutes Makes: 4 servings

> 2 **cloves garlic**
> 4 **24-ounce Cornish game hens**
> 1 **tablespoon olive oil**
> ½ **teaspoon salt**
> ¼ **teaspoon black pepper**
> ⅓ **cup sliced or chopped shallot**
> 2 **tablespoons butter**
> 1 **12-ounce jar red cherry preserves (with whole cherries)**
> ¼ **cup red wine vinegar**
> ½ **teaspoon ground allspice**
> ¼ **teaspoon ground cloves**

1. Cut one of the cloves of garlic in half and rub the skin of each hen with cut side of garlic clove. Mince remaining garlic clove and set aside. Tie drumsticks to tail. Brush hens with olive oil and sprinkle with the salt and pepper. Place hens, breast sides up, on a rack in a shallow roast-ing pan; twist wing tips under back (see photo 4, page 478).

2. Roast, uncovered, in a 375°F oven for 1 to 1¼ hours or until an instant-read thermometer inserted into the thigh of each hen registers 180°F and juices run clear. (The thermometer should not touch bone.)

3. Meanwhile, in a small saucepan cook minced garlic and shallot in hot butter over medium heat about 3 minutes or until tender, stirring often. Stir in preserves, vinegar, allspice, and cloves. Bring to boiling; reduce heat. Boil gently, uncovered, about 20 minutes or until it reaches desired glazing consistency. To serve, spoon glaze over hens.

Per hen + ¼ cup glaze: 1,124 cal., 63 g total fat (19 g sat. fat), 431 mg chol., 564 mg sodium, 62 g carbo., 1 g fiber, 72 g pro.
Daily Values: 13% vit. A, 18% vit. C, 7% calcium, 20% iron
Exchanges: 4 Other Carbo., 10 Medium-Fat Meat, 3 Fat

Spiced Game Hens

If you can find it, use hot paprika rather than sweet in this recipe.

Prep: 25 minutes **Marinate:** 2 hours
Roast: 1 hour **Oven:** 375°F **Makes:** 4 servings

- ¼ cup lemon juice
- 2 tablespoons olive oil
- 1 tablespoon paprika
- 1 teaspoon salt
- 1 teaspoon ground coriander
- ½ teaspoon ground turmeric
- ¼ teaspoon black pepper
- 4 cloves garlic, minced
- 2 24-ounce Cornish game hens
- ½ cup reduced-sodium chicken broth

1. For marinade, in a small bowl combine lemon juice, olive oil, paprika, salt, coriander, turmeric, pepper, and garlic. Set mixture aside.

2. Using a long, heavy knife or kitchen shears, halve each Cornish hen lengthwise, cutting through the breast bone just off-center and through the center of the backbone. If desired, remove each backbone.

3. Place hen halves in a large resealable plastic bag. Pour marinade over hens. Seal bag; chill for 2 hours, turning bag once.

4. Remove hens from bag and place them, cut sides down, in a 3-quart rectangular baking dish. Pour lemon mixture from bag over hens. Pour broth around hens in dish. Season hens with additional salt and pepper.

5. Roast hens, covered, in a 375°F oven for 40 minutes. Uncover and continue roasting for 20 to 35 minutes more or until an instant-read thermometer inserted into the thigh of each hen registers 180°F and juices run clear. (The thermometer should not touch bone.)

Per half hen: 410 cal., 30 g total fat (7 g sat. fat), 173 mg chol., 813 mg sodium, 4 g carbo., 1 g fiber, 31 g pro.
Daily Values: 17% vit. A, 15% vit. C, 3% calcium, 10% iron
Exchanges: 4½ Medium-Fat Meat, 1½ Fat

Duckling Information

For more information on duckling and links to related sites, visit The Duckling Council's website at www.duckling.org.

Roast Duckling with Raspberry Sauce EASY

Prep: 15 minutes **Roast:** 1½ hours **Oven:** 350°F
Stand: 15 minutes **Cook:** 13 minutes **Makes:** 4 servings

- 1 4- to 6-pound domestic duckling
  Salt and black pepper
- ⅓ cup orange juice
- ¼ cup chicken broth
- 2 tablespoons blackberry brandy or orange juice
- 1 cup fresh or frozen lightly sweetened raspberries
- ⅓ cup seedless raspberry preserves
- ¼ teaspoon ground ginger
- ⅛ teaspoon ground allspice
- 1 tablespoon butter or margarine
- ¼ cup coarsely chopped walnuts, toasted
- 1 teaspoon snipped fresh sage

1. Rinse the duckling body cavity; pat dry with paper towels. Skewer neck skin to back (see photo 2, page 478); tie legs to tail. Twist wing tips under back (see photo 4, page 478). Place duck, breast side up, on a rack in a shallow roasting pan. Using a fork, prick skin generously. Sprinkle with salt and pepper.

2. Roast duckling, uncovered, in a 350°F oven for 1½ to 2 hours or until the drumsticks move easily in their sockets (180°F). Cover and let stand for 15 minutes before carving.

3. Meanwhile, for sauce, in a small saucepan combine orange juice, broth, and brandy. Bring to boiling. Cook, uncovered, over medium-high heat about 8 minutes or until sauce is reduced to ¼ cup. Stir in ¼ cup of the raspberries, raspberry preserves, ginger, allspice, and dash *salt*. Simmer, uncovered, for 5 minutes, stirring occasionally. Remove saucepan from heat; stir in butter. Stir in remaining raspberries, the walnuts, and sage. (If using frozen raspberries, heat until thawed and the sauce is heated through.)

4. To carve duckling, if desired, remove the skin. Using a sharp knife, cut duckling along the backbone. Cut downward, removing meat from ribs. Cut the wings and legs from the duckling. Slice breast meat. Serve with raspberry sauce.

Per 4 ounces duck + ¼ cup sauce: 537 cal., 27 g total fat (7 g sat. fat), 224 mg chol., 275 mg sodium, 25 g carbo., 3 g fiber, 44 g pro.
Daily Values: 6% vit. A, 41% vit. C, 4% calcium, 30% iron
Exchanges: 1½ Other Carbo., 6 Lean Meat, 2 Fat

Roast Duckling with Wild Mushroom Sauce

Prep: 25 minutes **Roast:** 1½ hours **Oven:** 350°F
Stand: 15 minutes **Cook:** 35 minutes **Makes:** 4 servings

- 1 4- to 6-pound domestic duckling
- ¼ cup broken dried mushrooms
- 1 cup frozen small whole onions, thawed
- 2 tablespoons butter or margarine
- 2 teaspoons sugar
- 4 teaspoons all-purpose flour
- 1½ cups beef broth
- 1 tablespoon tomato paste
- ½ teaspoon dried savory, sage, or thyme, crushed
- ½ teaspoon Worcestershire sauce

1. Rinse the duckling body cavity; pat dry with paper towels. Skewer neck skin to back (see photo 2, page 478); tie legs to tail. Twist wing tips under back (see photo 4, page 478). Place duck, breast side up, on a rack in a shallow roasting pan. Using a fork, prick the skin generously.

2. Roast duckling, uncovered, in a 350°F oven for 1½ to 2 hours or until the drumsticks move easily in their sockets (180°F). Cover and let stand for 15 minutes before carving.

3. Meanwhile, for sauce, pour enough *boiling water* over dried mushrooms to cover. Let stand for 30 minutes; drain. In a saucepan, cook mushrooms and onions in hot butter over medium heat about 15 minutes or until tender. Stir in sugar; cook and stir for 5 to 7 minutes or until vegetables are glazed. Stir in flour; cook and stir for 3 to 5 minutes more or until flour is brown. Add broth, tomato paste, savory, and Worcestershire sauce. Bring to boiling; reduce heat. Simmer, uncovered, for 10 to 15 minutes or until sauce is reduced to about 1⅔ cups.

4. To carve duckling, if desired, remove the skin. Using a sharp knife, cut duckling along the backbone. Cut downward, removing the meat from the ribs. Cut the wings and legs from the duckling. Slice breast meat. Serve with mushroom sauce.

Per 4 ounces duck + ⅓ cup sauce: 452 cal., 24 g total fat
(9 g sat. fat), 232 mg chol., 473 mg sodium, 11 g carbo., 1 g fiber,
45 g pro.
Daily Values: 7% vit. A, 12% vit. C, 3% calcium, 31% iron
Exchanges: 1 Vegetable, ½ Starch, 6 Lean Meat, 1 High-Fat Meat,
1 Fat

Orange-Ginger Duck

Prep: 25 minutes **Marinate:** 4 hours **Cook:** 35 minutes
Roast: 15 minutes **Oven:** 425°F **Makes:** 6 servings

- 6 boneless duck breast halves (with skin)
- 1 tablespoon finely shredded orange peel
- 1 cup orange juice
- 1 cup dry white wine
- 6 tablespoons honey
- 4 tablespoons grated fresh ginger
- 1 tablespoon olive oil
- ¼ cup chicken broth
- 1 tablespoon soy sauce
  - Salt and black pepper
- 3 cups hot cooked rice

1. Trim excess fat from duck (do not remove the skin). Score the skin in a diamond pattern. Place duck in a resealable plastic bag set in a bowl. For marinade, combine orange peel, orange juice, ½ cup of the wine, 4 tablespoons of the honey, and 3 tablespoons of the ginger. Pour over duck in bag; seal. Refrigerate for 4 to 24 hours, turning bag occasionally.

2. Remove duck from marinade; set aside. Transfer marinade (about 1¾ cups) to a large saucepan. Add remaining ½ cup wine. Bring to boiling; reduce heat. Boil gently, uncovered, for 20 to 25 minutes or until reduced to 1¼ cups (watch carefully as mixture may foam over).

3. In a large skillet cook duck in hot oil over medium-high heat about 10 minutes or until browned, turning once (watch for spattering). Transfer duck, skin side up, to a 3-quart rectangular baking dish. Roast in a 425°F oven about 15 minutes or until an instant-read thermometer registers 160°F; cover loosely with foil if duck begins to spatter.

4. Meanwhile, for glaze, add remaining 2 tablespoons honey, remaining 1 tablespoon ginger, the broth, and soy sauce to reduced marinade. Bring to boiling. Boil gently, uncovered, about 15 minutes or until reduced to about ⅔ cup, stirring frequently. Season to taste with salt and pepper. To serve, slice duck breasts and arrange on rice; spoon glaze over duck.

Per breast half + ½ cup rice + 2 tablespoons glaze: 469 cal.,
15 g total fat (4 g sat. fat), 154 mg chol., 402 mg sodium,
46 g carbo., 1 g fiber, 31 g pro.
Daily Values: 3% vit. A, 45% vit. C, 3% calcium, 28% iron
Exchanges: 1½ Starch, 1½ Other Carbo., 4 Lean Meat, 1 Fat

Duck Breast with Pears and Balsamic Vinaigrette

Duck breast is a red meat, so it is OK to leave it a little pink in the middle. Cook it to 165°F if you prefer it more well done.

Prep: 20 minutes **Cook:** 20 minutes **Roast:** 25 minutes
Oven: 350°F **Stand:** 10 minutes **Makes:** 4 servings

- 2 pears, cored and sliced
- 2 tablespoons butter
- ⅛ teaspoon coarsely ground black pepper
- 4 boneless duck breast halves (with skin)
- ¼ teaspoon salt
- ¼ teaspoon freshly ground black pepper
- 2 tablespoons balsamic vinegar
- 1 teaspoon Dijon-style mustard
- ½ teaspoon dried thyme, crushed
- 4 cups fresh baby spinach
- ¼ cup chopped walnuts, toasted
  (see tip, page 265)

1. In a large ovenproof skillet cook pears in hot butter over medium heat for 8 to 10 minutes or until golden brown and tender, stirring frequently. Sprinkle with coarsely ground pepper; remove from skillet and set aside.

2. Trim excess fat from duck (do not remove skin). Score the skin in a diamond pattern. Season duck breasts with salt and the freshly ground pepper.

3. In the same skillet cook duck breasts, skin sides down, over medium heat for 5 minutes. Turn and cook about 5 minutes more or until browned. Drain, reserving 2 tablespoons fat. Roast duck breasts in a 350°F oven in the

uncovered skillet for 25 to 30 minutes or until an instant-read thermometer inserted into the breast registers 155°F. Remove duck from pan; cover and let stand for 10 minutes.

4. For vinaigrette, in a screw-top jar combine reserved duck fat, the vinegar, mustard, and thyme. Cover and shake well to combine.

5. Slice duck breasts. To serve, arrange spinach on serving plates. Top with pears, duck breast slices, and toasted walnuts. Drizzle vinaigrette over top.

Per breast half + ¾ cup pears + 1 cup spinach: 573 cal.,
33 g total fat (9 g sat. fat), 286 mg chol., 411 mg sodium,
18 g carbo., 4 g fiber, 51 g pro.
Daily Values: 63% vit. A, 29% vit. C, 7% calcium, 44% iron
Exchanges: 1 Vegetable, 1 Fruit, 7 Lean Meat, 2 Fat

Pheasant Marsala

Substitute a cut-up broiler-fryer chicken or bone-in chicken thighs for pheasant, if desired.

Prep: 45 minutes **Bake:** 40 minutes
Oven: 325°F **Makes:** 4 servings

- 1 2- to 2½-pound pheasant, cut up
- 2 tablespoons cooking oil
- 2 tablespoons butter or margarine
  Salt
  Black pepper
- 3 cups sliced fresh mushrooms
- 1 medium onion, cut into wedges
- 2 cloves garlic, minced
- ½ cup chicken broth
- ¼ cup dry Marsala
- 1 teaspoon finely shredded orange peel
- 1 8-ounce carton dairy sour cream
- 2 tablespoons all-purpose flour
- ¼ teaspoon salt

1. Remove skin from pheasant. In a large skillet cook pheasant in hot oil and butter over medium heat until brown, turning once. Place in a 2-quart rectangular baking dish. Sprinkle with salt and pepper. Add mushrooms, onion, and garlic to skillet. Cook and stir over medium heat for 2 to 3 minutes or until onion is tender. Stir in broth, Marsala, and orange peel. Pour broth mixture over pheasant in baking dish.

2. Bake pheasant, covered, in a 325°F oven about 40 minutes or until an instant-read thermometer inserted into the breast registers 170°F. (Thermometer should not touch bone.)

Duck Breast with Pears and Balsamic Vinaigrette

3. Using a slotted spoon, transfer the pheasant and vegetables to a serving platter. Cover and keep warm.

4. For sauce, pour cooking juices into a medium saucepan. In a small bowl stir together sour cream, flour, and the ¼ teaspoon salt. Whisk sour cream mixture into the pan juices until smooth. Cook and stir until thickened and bubbly. Cook and stir for 1 minute more. Spoon some of the sauce over pheasant and vegetables; pass remaining sauce.

Per 3 ounces pheasant + ½ cup sauce: 534 cal., 33 g total fat (15 g sat. fat), 155 mg chol., 577 mg sodium, 12 g carbo., 1 g fiber, 46 g pro.
Daily Values: 18% vit. A, 20% vit. C, 11% calcium, 16% iron
Exchanges: 1 Vegetable, ½ Starch, 6 Very Lean Meat, 6 Fat

Wine-Marinated Pheasant

Look for domestic pheasant near the frozen turkeys or Cornish game hens in large supermarkets or specialty stores.

Prep: 35 minutes **Marinate:** 6 hours **Roast:** 1¼ hours
Oven: 350°F **Makes:** 4 servings

  1 **small onion, thinly sliced**
  ¾ **cup dry white wine**
  ¼ **cup lime juice or lemon juice**
  2 **tablespoons cooking oil**
  ½ **teaspoon dried savory, crushed**
  ¼ **teaspoon salt**
  ¼ **teaspoon bottled hot pepper sauce**
  1 **2- to 2½-pound pheasant**
  1 **tablespoon butter or margarine**
  4 **teaspoons all-purpose flour**
  ½ **cup chicken broth**
  2 **tablespoons snipped fresh Italian parsley**
     Black pepper

1. For marinade, in a small bowl combine onion, wine, lime juice, oil, savory, salt, and hot pepper sauce.

2. Place pheasant in a large resealable plastic bag set in a bowl. Pour marinade over pheasant. Seal bag; turn pheasant to coat well. Marinate in the refrigerator for 6 to 24 hours, turning bag occasionally. Remove pheasant from bag, reserving marinade.

3. Tie legs of pheasant to the tail (see photo 3, page 478). Twist wing tips under back (see photo 4, page 478). Place pheasant, breast side up, on a rack in a shallow roasting pan. Cover pheasant with foil, leaving air space between bird and foil. Lightly press the foil to the ends of drumsticks and neck to enclose bird.

4. Roast in a 350°F oven for 1¼ to 1½ hours. After about 1 hour of roasting, remove foil and cut string between drumsticks. Continue roasting until drumsticks move easily in their sockets and juices run clear (180°F). (Check the thigh temperature in several places with an instant-read thermometer. The thermometer should not touch bone.)

5. Meanwhile, strain marinade, reserving ½ cup. In a medium saucepan melt butter over medium heat; stir in flour. Add the reserved ½ cup marinade and the chicken broth. Cook and stir until thickened and bubbly; cook and stir for 1 minute more. Stir in parsley. Season to taste with black pepper.

Per 3 ounces pheasant + ¼ cup sauce: 480 cal., 27 g total fat (8 g sat. fat), 146 mg chol., 341 mg sodium, 3 g carbo., 0 g fiber, 45 g pro.
Daily Values: 10% vit. A, 22% vit. C, 3% calcium, 14% iron
Exchanges: 6½ Lean Meat, 2½ Fat

Hunter's Dinner

Showcase a favorite game bird with this menu.

- *Wine-Marinated Pheasant (left)*
- *Wild rice pilaf*
- *Tossed mixed greens salad*
- *Roasted acorn squash wedges*
- *Dinner Rolls (page 152)*
- *Pecan pie*

Roasting Poultry

To prepare a bird for roasting, follow the steps below (see photos, page 478). Because birds vary in size and shape, use the times as general guides. To stuff a bird, see the photos on page 478 and tips on page 481.

1. If desired, thoroughly rinse a whole bird's body and neck cavities. Pat dry with paper towels. If desired, sprinkle the body cavity with salt.

2. For an unstuffed bird, if desired, place quartered onions and celery in body cavity. To stuff a bird (do not stuff a duckling or goose), just before roasting loosely spoon some stuffing into the neck and body cavities. For both a stuffed and unstuffed bird, pull neck skin to the back and fasten with a short skewer. If a band of skin crosses tail, tuck drumsticks under band. If there is no band, tie drumsticks to tail with kitchen string. Twist the wing tips under the back.

3. Place bird, breast side up, on a rack in a shallow roasting pan; brush with cooking oil or melted butter and, if desired, sprinkle with a crushed dried herb, such as thyme or oregano. (When cooking a domestic duckling or goose, use a fork to prick skin generously all over and omit cooking oil or butter.) For large birds, insert a meat thermometer into center of one of the inside thigh muscles. The thermometer should not touch the bone.

4. Cover Cornish game hen, pheasant, squab, and whole turkey with foil, leaving air space between bird and foil. Lightly press the foil to the ends of drumsticks and neck to enclose bird. Leave all other types of poultry uncovered.

5. Roast in an uncovered pan. Two-thirds through roasting time, cut the band of skin or string between drumsticks. Uncover large birds the last 45 minutes of roasting; uncover small birds the last 30 minutes of roasting. Continue roasting until the meat thermometer registers 180°F in thigh muscle (check temperature of thigh in several places) or until drumsticks move easily in their sockets and juices run clear. (For a whole or half turkey breast, the thermometer should register 170°F.) Center of stuffing should register 165°F. Remove bird from oven; cover. Allow whole birds and turkey portions to stand for 15 minutes before carving.

Type of Bird	Weight	Oven Temperature	Roasting Time
Chicken			
Capon	5 to 7 pounds	325°F	1¾ to 2½ hours
Meaty pieces (breast halves, drumsticks, and thighs with bone)	2½ to 3 pounds	375°F	45 to 55 minutes
Whole	2½ to 3 pounds 3½ to 4 pounds 4½ to 5 pounds	375°F 375°F 375°F	1 to 1¼ hours 1¼ to 1¾ hours 1½ to 2 hours
Game			
Cornish game hen	1¼ to 1½ pounds	375°F	1 to 1¼ hours
Duckling, domestic	4 to 6 pounds	350°F	1½ to 2 hours
Goose, domestic	7 to 8 pounds 8 to 10 pounds	350°F 350°F	2 to 2½ hours 2½ to 3 hours
Pheasant	2 to 3 pounds	350°F	1¼ to 1½ hours
Squab, domestic	12 to 16 ounces	375°F	45 to 60 minutes
Turkey			
Boneless whole	2½ to 3½ pounds 4 to 6 pounds	325°F 325°F	2 to 2½ hours 2½ to 3½ hours
Breast, whole	4 to 6 pounds 6 to 8 pounds	325°F 325°F	1½ to 2¼ hours 2¼ to 3¼ hours
Drumstick	1 to 1½ pounds	325°F	1¼ to 1¾ hours
Thigh	1½ to 1¾ pounds	325°F	1½ to 1¾ hours
Whole (unstuffed)*	8 to 12 pounds 12 to 14 pounds 14 to 18 pounds 18 to 20 pounds 20 to 24 pounds	325°F 325°F 325°F 325°F 325°F	2¾ to 3 hours 3 to 3¾ hours 3¾ to 4¼ hours 4¼ to 4½ hours 4½ to 5 hours

*Stuffed birds generally require 15 to 45 minutes more roasting time than unstuffed birds. Always verify doneness temperatures of poultry and stuffing with a meat thermometer.

Broiling Poultry

If desired, remove the skin from the poultry; sprinkle with salt and black pepper. Preheat broiler for 5 to 10 minutes. Arrange the poultry on the unheated rack of the broiler pan with the bone side up. If desired, brush poultry with cooking oil. Place the pan under the broiler so the surface of the poultry is 4 to 5 inches from the heat; chicken and Cornish game hen halves should be 5 to 6 inches from the heat. Turn the pieces over when brown on one side, usually after half of the broiling time. Chicken halves and quarters and meaty pieces should be turned after 20 minutes. Brush again with oil. The poultry is done when the meat is no longer pink and the juices run clear (180°F for thighs and drumsticks; 170°F for breast meat; 165°F for patties; 160°F for duck breast). If desired, brush with a sauce the last 5 minutes of cooking.

Type of Bird	Thickness/Weight	Broiling Time
Chicken		
Broiler-fryer, half	1¼ to 1½ pounds	28 to 32 minutes
Broiler-fryer, quarter	10 to 12 ounces	28 to 32 minutes
Kabobs (boneless breast, cut into 2½-inch strips and threaded loosely onto skewers)		8 to 10 minutes
Meaty pieces (breast halves, drumsticks, and thighs with bone)	2½ to 3 pounds	25 to 35 minutes
Skinless, boneless breast halves	4 to 5 ounces	12 to 15 minutes
Game		
Cornish game hen, half	10 to 12 ounces	25 to 35 minutes
Boneless duck breast, skin removed	6 to 8 ounces	14 to 16 minutes
Turkey		
Breast cutlet	2 ounces	6 to 8 minutes
Breast tenderloin steak (to make ½-inch-thick steaks, cut turkey tenderloin in half horizontally)	4 to 6 ounces	8 to 10 minutes
Patties (ground uncooked turkey or chicken)	¾ inch thick ½ inch thick	14 to 18 minutes 11 to 13 minutes

Want More Info?

For answers to all your poultry questions, call the United States Department of Agriculture's Meat and Poultry Hotline, 888-674-6854 (888-MPHotline) from 10 a.m. to 4 p.m. weekdays (Eastern Standard Time). For the hearing impaired (TTY), call 800-256-7072. Send e-mail inquiries to mphotline.fsis@usda.gov. Or visit the National Chicken Council's website at www.eatchicken.com.

Skillet-Cooking Poultry

Select a heavy skillet that is the right size for the amount of poultry being cooked. (If the skillet is too large, pan juices can burn. If it's too small, poultry will steam instead of brown.) If the skillet is not nonstick, lightly coat it with nonstick cooking spray or 2 to 3 teaspoons of oil. Preheat skillet over medium-high heat until hot. Add poultry. Do not add any liquid and do not cover the skillet. Reduce heat to medium; cook for the time given or until done, turning poultry occasionally. (If poultry browns too quickly, reduce heat to medium low.) Poultry is done when the meat is no longer pink and the juices run clear (180°F for thighs; 170°F for breast meat; 165°F for patties).

Type of Bird	Thickness/Weight	Approximate Cooking Time
Chicken		
Breast tenders	1 to 2 ounces	6 to 8 minutes
Skinless, boneless breast halves	3 to 5 ounces	8 to 12 minutes
Skinless, boneless thighs	3 to 4 ounces	14 to 18 minutes
Turkey		
Breast tenderloin steaks (to make ½-inch-thick steaks, cut turkey tenderloin in half horizontally)	4 to 6 ounces	15 to 18 minutes
Patties (ground uncooked turkey or chicken)	¾ inch thick	12 to 14 minutes

Microwaving Poultry

Arrange bone-in pieces in a microwave-safe baking dish with meaty portions toward edges of dish and thin boneless portions tucked under. Do not crowd the pieces in the dish. Cover with waxed paper. (Or for skinless poultry, cover with a lid or vented plastic wrap.) Microwave on 100 percent power (high) for the time given or until no longer pink, rearranging and turning pieces over after half of the cooking time.

Type of Bird	Amount	Power Level	Cooking Time
Chicken			
Breast halves (with bone)	Two 6-ounce Two 8-ounce	100% (high) 100% (high)	6 to 9 minutes 8 to 11 minutes
Drumsticks	2 drumsticks 6 drumsticks	100% (high) 100% (high)	3½ to 5 minutes 6 to 10 minutes
Meaty pieces (breast halves, drumsticks, and thighs with bone)	2½ to 3 pounds	100% (high)	9 to 17 minutes
Skinless, boneless breast halves	Two 4- to 5-ounce Four 4- to 5-ounce	100% (high) 100% (high)	4 to 7 minutes 5 to 8 minutes
Game			
Cornish game hen, halved	1¼ to 1½ pounds	100% (high)	7 to 10 minutes
Turkey			
Breast tenderloins	Two 8- to 10-ounce	100% (high)	8 to 12 minutes
Breast tenderloin steaks (to make ½-inch-thick steaks, cut turkey tenderloin in half horizontally)	Four 4-ounce	100% (high)	5 to 8 minutes

Salads & Dressings

Waldorf Salad, 508

White Corn and Baby Pea Salad, 499

Italian Basil, Tomato, and Pasta Salad, 506

Salads & Dressings Essentials

Today's salads are more than simple greens topped with a bland bottled dressing. They run the gamut from a meal starter to a side dish to a complete dinner on one plate.

Using Salad Greens

When cutting or tearing greens for a salad, be sure the resulting pieces are uniformly bite size. If they are too large it makes for messy and difficult eating. If tossing greens with vinaigrette or other dressing, do so just before serving so your greens don't wilt. Some salads that have mayonnaise-based dressings actually benefit from standing overnight to let the flavors blend.

Homemade Salad Dressings

You'll be amazed at how refreshing and wonderful homemade dressings can be and how easily they come together. The most important tool for making homemade dressings is a screw-top jar.

For many recipes you simply combine ingredients in the screw-top jar, shake, and serve. If you do store the dressing, it can remain in this container for up to two weeks, depending on the recipe. (See individual recipes for storage information.) Just be sure to shake it well to combine ingredients each time you serve it. If the dressing is oil-based, let it come to room temperature before shaking and serving.

Mayonnaise serves as the base for many salad dressings. You can use store-bought or homemade Mayonnaise (page 509) for any of the recipes in this cookbook. In fact, mayo from scratch is another simple and quick process—it takes about 15 minutes from start to finish—and you'll be amazed at how great it can make your salads.

Croutons

Homemade croutons (such as Parmesan Croutons, page 496) are simple to prepare. Store cubed bread heels and/or bread that has expired in the freezer so you have it on hand when you are ready to make croutons. Store cubes for no more than six months.

Preparing Salad Greens

When you purchase greens, choose those that look the freshest and have no brown spots. Use greens as soon as you can after purchase.

To wash your greens, first remove and discard the roots, then separate the leaves. Swirl leaves around in a bowl or clean sink filled with cold water for about 30 seconds. Remove leaves and shake them gently to let dirt and other debris fall into the water. Repeat this process, using fresh water each time, until the water remains clear.

Dry lettuce is important; the drier it is the better dressings cling to it. A salad spinner works wonders for drying greens. Many spinners start with the touch of a button and stop on their own when the greens are dry. If you don't have access to one, pat each leaf dry with a clean paper towel. Once the greens are dry, do not cut or tear them until you use them. Washed greens can be stored in the refrigerator in a resealable bag lined with paper towels. See page 514 for storage times for specific greens.

Chef's Salad `FAST`

Give this classic a new look every time by choosing different greens, meats, cheeses, and dressings.

Start to Finish: 30 minutes **Makes:** 4 main-dish servings

- 4 **cups torn iceberg or leaf lettuce**
- 4 **cups torn romaine or fresh spinach**
- 4 **ounces cooked ham, chicken, turkey, beef, pork, or lamb, cut into bite-size strips (1 cup)**
- 4 **ounces thinly sliced Swiss, cheddar, American, or provolone cheese, cut into thin strips (1 cup)**
- 2 **Hard-Cooked Eggs (page 228), sliced**
- 2 **medium tomatoes, cut into wedges, or 8 cherry tomatoes, halved**
- 1 **small green or red sweet pepper, cut into bite-size strips (⅓ cup)**
- 1 **cup Parmesan Croutons (page 496) or purchased croutons (optional)**
- ½ **cup Creamy French Dressing (page 509), Buttermilk Dressing (page 510), Creamy Italian Dressing (page 511), or other salad dressing**

1. In a large salad bowl toss together greens. Divide greens among four large salad plates. Arrange meat, cheese, egg, tomato, and sweet pepper on top of the greens. If desired, sprinkle with Parmesan Croutons. Drizzle desired salad dressing over all, passing any of the remaining dressing.

Per 2 cups: 472 cal., 40 g total fat (10 g sat. fat), 145 mg chol., 621 mg sodium, 13 g carbo., 3 g fiber, 19 g pro.
Daily Values: 59% vit. A, 74% vit. C, 32% calcium, 11% iron
Exchanges: 2½ Vegetable, 2 Medium-Fat Meat, 6 Fat

Chicken Salad

Serve this versatile salad over mixed salad greens or on your favorite bread. If serving as a sandwich, be sure to finely chop the chicken.

Prep: 20 minutes **Chill:** 1 hour
Makes: 4 main-dish servings

- 2 **cups chopped cooked chicken or turkey (8 ounces)**
- ½ **cup chopped celery (1 stalk)**
- ¼ **cup thinly sliced green onion (2)**
- ⅓ **to ½ cup mayonnaise or salad dressing**
- 1 **teaspoon snipped fresh basil or ¼ teaspoon dried basil, crushed**
- ¼ **teaspoon salt**
- ½ **teaspoon finely shredded lemon peel (optional)**
- **Bread or mixed salad greens (optional)**

1. In a medium bowl combine chicken, celery, and green onion. For dressing, in a small bowl stir together mayonnaise, basil, salt, and, if desired, lemon peel. Pour dressing over chicken mixture; toss to coat. Cover and chill for 1 to 4 hours. Serve as a sandwich filling on bread slices or over salad greens.

Curried Chicken Salad: Prepare as above, except reduce mayonnaise to ¼ cup, omit the basil, and add 2 tablespoons chutney and 1 teaspoon curry powder. Before serving, stir in 2 tablespoons coarsely chopped, toasted cashews or almonds (see tip, page 265).

Per 1⅛ cups plain or curried variation: 269 cal., 20 g total fat (3 g sat. fat), 75 mg chol., 331 mg sodium, 1 g carbo., 0 g fiber, 20 g pro.
Daily Values: 4% vit. A, 3% vit. C, 2% calcium, 5% iron
Exchanges: 3 Very Lean Meat, 2½ Fat

Grape and Nut Chicken Salad: Prepare as above, except stir ¾ cup red and/or green seedless grapes, halved, into the chicken mixture before chilling. Before serving, stir in ⅓ cup coarsely chopped toasted walnuts or pecans (see tip, page 265).

Per 1⅛ cups: 355 cal., 26 g total fat (4 g sat. fat), 75 mg chol., 332 mg sodium, 8 g carbo., 1 g fiber, 22 g pro.
Daily Values: 4% vit. A, 8% vit. C, 3% calcium, 8% iron
Exchanges: 3 Very Lean Meat, 2½ Fat, ½ Other Carbo.

Ham Salad `EASY`

Prep: 15 minutes **Chill:** 1 hour
Makes: 4 to 6 main-dish servings

- 2½ **cups cubed cooked ham (10 ounces)**
- ½ **cup finely chopped celery (1 stalk)**
- ¼ **cup thinly sliced green onion (2)**
- ⅓ **cup mayonnaise**
- 2 **teaspoons sweet pickle relish**
- 1 **teaspoon snipped fresh basil or sage or ¼ teaspoon dried basil or sage, crushed**
- 4 **croissants or cantaloupe wedges**

1. Place ham cubes in a food processor. Cover and process until finely chopped. In a medium bowl combine chopped ham, celery, and green onion. For dressing, in a small bowl combine mayonnaise, pickle relish, and basil. Pour over ham mixture; stir gently to coat. Cover and chill for 1 to 4 hours. Serve ham salad on croissants or over wedges of cantaloupe.

Per ½ cup: 486 cal., 33 g total fat (11 g sat. fat), 92 mg chol., 1,494 mg sodium, 31 g carbo., 3 g fiber, 17 g pro.
Daily Values: 11% vit. A, 8% vit. C, 5% calcium, 11% iron
Exchanges: 2 Starch, 2 Lean Meat, 5 Fat

Tuna Salad

Tuna or Salmon Salad

Prep: 20 minutes **Chill:** 1 hour
Makes: 4 main-dish servings

> 1 **12-ounce can solid white tuna or one
>   14.75-ounce can salmon, drained, flaked,
>   and skin and bones removed**
> ½ **cup chopped celery (1 stalk)**
> ¼ **cup thinly sliced green onion (2)**
> 3 **tablespoons chopped sweet pickle**
> ⅓ **cup mayonnaise or salad dressing**
> 1 **tablespoon lemon juice**
> 2 **teaspoons snipped fresh dill or ½ teaspoon
>   dried dill**
>   **Bread or mixed salad greens (optional)**

1. In a medium bowl combine tuna, celery, green onion, and pickle. For dressing, in a small bowl stir together mayonnaise, lemon juice, and dill. Add to tuna mixture; toss to coat. Cover and chill for 1 to 24 hours before serving. Serve as a sandwich filling on bread slices or over salad greens.

Per ½ cup: 255 cal., 17 g total fat (3 g sat. fat), 49 mg chol., 521 mg sodium, 4 g carbo., 1 g fiber, 20 g pro.
Daily Values: 3% vit. A, 6% vit. C, 2% calcium, 6% iron
Exchanges: 3 Very Lean Meat, 3 Fat

Salad Niçoise

You can cook and chill the beans and potatoes for this French-inspired salad a day before serving.

Prep: 35 minutes **Chill:** 2 hours
Makes: 4 main-dish servings

> 8 **ounces fresh green beans (2 cups)**
> 12 **ounces tiny new potatoes, scrubbed and
>   sliced (2 medium)**

> 1 **recipe Niçoise Dressing or ½ cup bottled
>   balsamic vinaigrette salad dressing**
>   **Boston or Bibb lettuce leaves**
> 1½ **cups flaked cooked tuna or salmon
>   (8 ounces) or one 9.25-ounce can chunk
>   white tuna (water pack), drained and
>   broken into chunks**
> 2 **medium tomatoes, cut into wedges**
> 2 **Hard-Cooked Eggs (page 228), sliced**
> ½ **cup pitted ripe olives (optional)**
> ¼ **cup thinly sliced green onion (2)**
> 4 **anchovy fillets, drained, rinsed, and patted
>   dry (optional)**
>   **Fresh tarragon (optional)**

1. Wash green beans; remove ends and strings. In a large saucepan cook green beans and potato, covered, in a small amount of boiling lightly salted water for 10 to 15 minutes or just until tender. Drain; place vegetables in a medium bowl. Cover and chill for 2 to 24 hours.

2. Prepare Niçoise Dressing. To serve, line four salad plates with lettuce leaves. Arrange chilled vegetables, tuna, tomato, egg, and, if desired, olives on the lettuce-lined plates. Sprinkle each serving with green onion. If desired, top each salad with an anchovy fillet and garnish with tarragon. Shake dressing; drizzle dressing over each salad.

Niçoise Dressing: In a screw-top jar combine ¼ cup olive oil or salad oil; ¼ cup white wine vinegar or white vinegar; 1 teaspoon honey; 1 teaspoon snipped fresh tarragon or ¼ teaspoon dried tarragon, crushed; 1 teaspoon Dijon-style mustard; ¼ teaspoon salt; and dash black pepper. Cover and shake well. Makes about ½ cup.

Per 2 cups: 348 cal., 17 g total fat (3 g sat. fat), 139 mg chol., 228 mg sodium, 24 g carbo., 4 g fiber, 24 g pro.
Daily Values: 26% vit. A, 56% vit. C, 8% calcium, 17% iron
Exchanges: 2 Vegetable, 1 Starch, 2½ Lean Meat, 2 Fat

For the Bride or Baby

This light and delicious menu is perfect for a bridal or baby shower.

- *Tuna or Salmon Salad (left)*
- *Chicken Salad (page 494)*
- *Melon and Berries Salad (page 506)*
- *Purchased cheesecake with strawberries*

Couscous Chicken Salad `LOW FAT` `EASY`

Quick-cooking couscous is a tiny, grain-shape pasta made from semolina flour, a product of durum wheat. Once cooked and fluffed, couscous is a good substitute for rice or polenta.

Start to Finish: 15 minutes **Makes:** 4 main-dish servings

- 1 **14-ounce can chicken broth**
- 1¼ **cups quick-cooking couscous**
- ½ **cup mango chutney, large pieces cut up**
- ¼ **cup bottled olive oil and vinegar salad dressing, white wine vinaigrette, or roasted garlic vinaigrette salad dressing**
- 1 **6-ounce package cooked, refrigerated lemon-pepper or Italian-style chicken breast strips, cut into bite-size pieces (about 1½ cups)**
- ½ **cup golden raisins (optional)**
- 1 **cup coarsely chopped, seeded cucumber or radishes**
- **Salt**
- **Black pepper**
- 1 **small cucumber, cut into spears**

1. In a medium saucepan bring chicken broth to boiling. Stir in couscous. Cover and remove from heat. Let stand for 5 minutes. Fluff couscous lightly with a fork.

2. In a medium bowl combine mango chutney and salad dressing. Add chicken, raisins (if desired), chopped cucumber, and couscous. Toss to coat. Season to taste with salt and pepper. Serve with cucumber spears.

Per 1⅓ cups: 418 cal., 10 g total fat (1 g sat. fat), 28 mg chol., 873 mg sodium, 62 g carbo., 4 g fiber, 19 g pro.
Daily Values: 6% vit. A, 17% vit. C, 4% calcium, 9% iron
Exchanges: ½ Vegetable, 2 Starch, 2 Carbo., 2½ Very Lean Meat, 1½ Fat

Caesar Salad `FAVORITE`

Using cooked egg yolk as opposed to the traditional raw egg makes this classic salad safer to eat.

Prep: 30 minutes **Chill:** 2 hours **Bake:** 20 minutes
Oven: 300°F **Makes:** 6 side-dish servings

- 3 **cloves garlic**
- 3 **anchovy fillets**
- 3 **tablespoons lemon juice**
- 3 **tablespoons olive oil**
- 1 **tablespoon Dijon-style mustard**
- ½ **teaspoon Worcestershire sauce**
- 1 **Hard-Cooked Egg yolk (page 228)**
- 1 **clove garlic, halved**
- 10 **cups torn romaine**
- 1 **recipe Parmesan Croutons or 2 cups purchased garlic-Parmesan croutons**
- ¼ **cup grated Parmesan cheese or ½ cup Parmesan curls (4 ounces)**
- **Freshly ground black pepper**

1. For dressing, in a blender or food processor combine the three garlic cloves, the anchovy fillets, and lemon juice. Cover and blend or process until mixture is nearly smooth, stopping to scrape down sides as needed. Add oil, mustard, Worcestershire sauce, and cooked egg yolk. Cover and blend or process until smooth. Cover surface with plastic wrap; chill for 2 to 24 hours.

2. To serve, rub inside of a wooden salad bowl with cut edges of the halved garlic clove; discard garlic clove. Add romaine and croutons to bowl. Pour dressing over salad; toss lightly to coat. Sprinkle Parmesan cheese over top; toss gently. To serve, divide salad among salad plates; sprinkle pepper over each salad.

Parmesan Croutons: Cut four ½-inch-thick slices French bread into ¾-inch cubes; set aside. In a large skillet melt ¼ cup butter or margarine. Remove from heat. Stir in 3 tablespoons grated Parmesan cheese and ⅛ teaspoon garlic powder. Add bread cubes, stirring until cubes are coated with butter mixture. Spread bread cubes in a single layer in a shallow baking pan. Bake in a 300°F oven for 10 minutes; stir. Bake about 10 minutes more or until bread cubes are crisp and golden. Cool completely; store in an airtight container for up to 1 week. Makes about 2 cups (sixteen 2-tablespoon servings).

Per ½ cup: 243 cal., 19 g total fat (8 g sat. fat), 64 mg chol., 409 mg sodium, 13 g carbo., 2 g fiber, 7 g pro.
Daily Values: 57% vit. A, 44% vit. C, 16% calcium, 10% iron
Exchanges: 1 Vegetable, ½ Starch, 4 Fat

Chicken Caesar Salad: Prepare as above, except add 2 cups chopped cooked chicken with the romaine. Makes 6 main-dish servings.

Per cup: 331 cal., 22 g total fat (9 g sat. fat), 106 mg chol., 450 mg sodium, 13 g carbo., 2 g fiber, 21 g pro.
Daily Values: 57% vit. A, 44% vit. C, 16% calcium, 14% iron
Exchanges: 1 Vegetable, ½ Starch, 2½ Very Lean Meat, 4 Fat

Packaged Greens

If you're running short on time, choose a salad mix from the produce section of your supermarket. Not only do these handy mixes shave minutes from your prep time, they allow you to add variety to any salad. Because they are packaged in a specially designed wrapper that allows the greens to "breathe," store any leftovers in the original bag. If refrigerated immediately, unopened packages will keep for up to 14 days. Even if the package label says the greens have been prewashed, be sure to wash them again to remove all grit and dirt.

Layered Vegetable Salad

Prep: 35 minutes **Chill:** 4 hours
Makes: 8 to 10 side-dish servings

- **6 cups torn mixed salad greens**
- **1 15-ounce can garbanzo beans (chickpeas), rinsed and drained, or one 10-ounce package frozen peas, thawed**
- **1 cup cherry tomatoes, quartered or halved**
- **1 cup thinly sliced fennel bulb or broccoli florets**
- **1 cup chopped red sweet pepper (1 large)**
- **1 cup diced cooked ham (6 ounces)**
- **¼ cup thinly sliced green onion (2)**
- **1 cup mayonnaise, light mayonnaise dressing, or salad dressing**
- **2 tablespoons milk**
- **1 tablespoon snipped fennel tops (optional)**
- **⅛ teaspoon ground white pepper or black pepper**
- **¾ cup shredded smoked cheddar cheese or cheddar cheese (3 ounces)**

1. Place greens in the bottom of a 3-quart clear salad bowl. Layer in the following order: beans, tomato, fennel, sweet pepper, ham, and onion.

2. For dressing, stir together mayonnaise, milk, snipped fennel tops (if desired), and ground pepper. Spoon dressing over salad. Cover tightly with plastic wrap. Chill for 4 to 24 hours.

3. Before serving, top salad with shredded cheese; toss lightly to coat evenly.

Per 1¾ cups: 352 cal., 29 g total fat (6 g sat. fat), 34 mg chol., 676 mg sodium, 13 g carbo., 6 g fiber, 10 g pro.
Daily Values: 9% vit. A, 84% vit. C, 12% calcium, 7% iron
Exchanges: 1 Vegetable, ½ Starch, 1 Lean Meat, 5 Fat

Chicken Fiesta Salad

Prep: 30 minutes **Chill:** 4 hours
Makes: 4 main-dish servings

- **4 cups torn iceberg, Boston, or Bibb lettuce**
- **½ cup shredded Monterey Jack cheese with jalapeño peppers (2 ounces)**
- **½ of a 15-ounce can black beans, pinto beans, or garbanzo beans (chickpeas), rinsed and drained (1 cup)**
- **8 ounces chopped cooked chicken or turkey (about 1½ cups)**
- **2 small tomatoes, cut into thin wedges**
- **1 cup jicama (about 4 ounces), cut into bite-size strips, or 1 cup shredded carrot**
- **½ cup sliced, pitted ripe olives (optional)**
- **1 recipe Chile Dressing**
- **¾ cup tortilla chips (optional)**

1. Place the lettuce in the bottom of a 2-quart clear salad bowl. Layer ingredients in the following order: cheese, beans, chicken, tomato, jicama, and, if desired, olives. Spread Chile Dressing evenly over salad, sealing to edge of bowl. Cover salad tightly with plastic wrap. Chill for 4 to 24 hours. To serve, toss lightly to coat evenly. If desired, sprinkle with tortilla chips.

Chile Dressing: In a small bowl stir together ½ cup mayonnaise or salad dressing, one 4-ounce can chopped undrained green chile peppers, 1½ teaspoons chili powder, and 1 clove garlic, minced. Makes about ¾ cup.

Per 2⅓ cups: 444 cal., 32 g total fat (7 g sat. fat), 73 mg chol., 460 mg sodium, 17 g carbo., 5 g fiber, 26 g pro.
Daily Values: 21% vit. A, 50% vit. C, 18% calcium, 14% iron
Exchanges: 2 Vegetable, ½ Starch, 2½ Lean Meat, 4½ Fat

Chicken Fiesta Salad

Avocados and Discoloration

Ripe avocados—which are a fruit, not a vegetable—can be stored in the refrigerator up to 4 days. Because they discolor rapidly once cut, add them to dishes at the last minute. To diminish discoloration, brush cut sides of an avocado with lemon juice.

Taco Salad

You generally can find premade tortilla cups in a supermarket deli. Or, if you prefer, serve this salad on crushed tortilla chips.

Prep: 30 minutes **Bake:** 15 minutes **Oven:** 350°F
Makes: 6 main-dish servings

    8 ounces lean ground beef or uncooked
       ground turkey
    3 cloves garlic, minced
    1 15-ounce can dark red kidney beans, rinsed
       and drained
    1 8-ounce bottle taco sauce
    ¾ cup frozen whole kernel corn, thawed
       (optional)
    6 cups shredded leaf or iceberg lettuce
    2 medium tomatoes, chopped
    1 large green sweet pepper, chopped (1 cup)
    ½ cup thinly sliced green onion (4)
    6 purchased tortilla cups*
    1 medium avocado, halved, pitted, peeled, and
       chopped (½ cup)
    ¾ cup shredded sharp cheddar cheese
       (3 ounces)
       Dairy sour cream (optional)

1. In a medium saucepan cook ground beef and garlic until beef is brown. Drain off fat. Stir in kidney beans, taco sauce, and, if desired, corn. Bring to boiling; reduce heat. Simmer, covered, for 10 minutes.

2. Meanwhile, in an extra-large bowl combine lettuce, tomatoes, sweet pepper, and green onion. To serve, divide lettuce mixture among the tortilla cups. Top each serving with some of the meat mixture and avocado. Sprinkle with cheese. If desired, serve with sour cream.

***Note:** If tortilla cups are not available for purchase, lightly brush one side of six 9- or 10-inch flour tortillas with a small amount of water or lightly coat with nonstick cooking spray. Coat six small oven-safe bowls or six 16-ounce casseroles with nonstick cooking spray. Press tortillas, coated sides up, into prepared bowls or casseroles (see photo, below), pleating as necessary. Place a ball of foil in each tortilla. Bake in a 350°F oven for 15 to 20 minutes or until light brown. Remove the foil; let tortilla cups cool. Remove cups from the bowls. Serve immediately or store in an airtight container for up to 5 days. Makes 6 tortilla cups.

Per 2 cups: 412 cal., 18 g total fat (6 g sat. fat), 35 mg chol., 632 mg sodium, 45 g carbo., 8 g fiber, 21 g pro.
Daily Values: 37% vit. A, 74% vit. C, 22% calcium, 26% iron
Exchanges: 3 Starch, 2 Medium-Fat Meat, ½ Fat

With the coated side up, fit each coated tortilla into bowl or casserole, creating loose pleats. Place a ball of foil in each cupped tortilla so the tortilla holds its shape while it bakes.

Spinach, Avocado, and Orange Salad `FAST`

Serve this immediately so the avocados don't brown.

Start to Finish: 20 minutes **Makes:** 6 side-dish servings

    1 6-ounce package fresh baby spinach or
       8 cups fresh baby spinach and/or assorted
       torn greens
    2 oranges or 3 tangerines, peeled and
       sectioned
    1 cup fresh raspberries or quartered
       strawberries
    2 avocados, halved, seeded, peeled, and sliced
    ¼ cup raspberry vinegar
    ¼ cup olive oil
    1 teaspoon Dijon-style mustard
    2 teaspoons granulated sugar or honey

1. Place spinach on a large serving platter or divide among individual salad plates. Cut orange sections into bite-size pieces. Arrange raspberries, orange, and avocado on spinach.

2. For dressing, in a screw-top jar combine vinegar, oil, Dijon-style mustard, and sugar. Cover and shake well. Pour over the spinach mixture. If desired, sprinkle with *ground black pepper*.

Per 1⅔ cups: 202 cal., 18 g total fat (2 g sat. fat), 47 mg sodium, 11 g carbo., 6 g fiber, 2 g pro.
Daily Values: 56% vit. A, 47% vit. C, 5% calcium, 8% iron
Exchanges: 1 Vegetable, ½ Fruit, 3½ Fat

White Corn and Baby Pea Salad `LOW FAT` `EASY`

For the most punch, be sure to use fresh mint on this super-easy, colorful salad. See photo, page 491.

Prep: 15 minutes **Chill:** 1 hour
Makes: 10 to 12 side-dish servings

- 1 **16-ounce package frozen white whole kernel corn (shoe peg), thawed**
- 1 **16-ounce package frozen baby peas, thawed**
- 1 **cup chopped, peeled jicama (4 ounces)**
- ⅔ **cup sliced celery (about 1½ stalks)**
- ½ **cup thinly sliced green onion (4)**
- ¼ **cup chopped red and/or orange sweet pepper (½ small)**
- ½ **cup seasoned rice vinegar**
- 2 **tablespoons packed brown sugar**
- 2 **tablespoons snipped fresh mint**
- 2 **tablespoons salad oil**
- ½ **teaspoon salt**
- ¼ **teaspoon ground white pepper or black pepper**

1. In a large bowl combine corn, peas, jicama, celery, green onion, and sweet pepper.

2. For dressing, in a screw-top jar combine vinegar, brown sugar, mint, oil, salt, and white pepper. Cover and shake well. Pour the dressing over vegetable mixture; toss to coat. Cover and chill for 1 to 4 hours.

Per ⅔ cup: 112 cal., 2 g total fat (0 g sat. fat), 297 mg sodium, 22 g carbo., 3 g fiber, 3 g pro.
Daily Values: 23% vit. A, 39% vit. C, 2% calcium, 8% iron
Exchanges: ½ Vegetable, 1 Starch, ½ Fat

 **Wilted Spinach Salad** `FAST`

As a timesaver use presliced mushrooms from your supermarket's produce section. If you want to add an extra kick, use peppered bacon.

Start to Finish: 25 minutes **Makes:** 4 side-dish servings

- 8 **cups fresh baby spinach or torn spinach (5 ounces)**
- 1 **cup sliced fresh mushrooms**
- ¼ **cup thinly sliced green onion (2)**
   Dash black pepper (optional)
- 3 **slices bacon**
- ¼ **cup vinegar**
- 2 **teaspoons sugar**
- ½ **teaspoon dry mustard**
- 1 **Hard-Cooked Egg (page 228), chopped**

1. In a large bowl combine spinach, mushrooms, and green onion. If desired, sprinkle with pepper; set aside.

2. For dressing, in a 12-inch skillet cook bacon until crisp. Remove bacon, reserving 2 tablespoons drippings in skillet (add *salad oil*, if necessary to make 2 tablespoons). Or, if desired, substitute 2 tablespoons *salad oil* for bacon drippings. Crumble bacon; set aside. Stir vinegar, sugar, and dry mustard into drippings. Bring to boiling; remove from heat. Add the spinach mixture. Toss mixture in skillet for 30 to 60 seconds or until spinach is just wilted.

3. Transfer spinach mixture to a serving dish. Add crumbled bacon and chopped egg; toss to combine. Serve salad immediately.

Wilted Garden Greens Salad: Prepare as above, except omit the spinach and egg; substitute 8 cups (5 ounces) arugula or torn leaf lettuce.

Per cup spinach or garden greens variation: 145 cal., 11 g total fat (4 g sat. fat), 64 mg chol., 161 mg sodium, 6 g carbo., 2 g fiber, 6 g pro.
Daily Values: 115% vit. A, 18% vit. C, 7% calcium, 12% iron
Exchanges: 2 Vegetable, ½ Lean Meat, 1½ Medium-Fat Meat

Sunny Broccoli Salad

Make this flavor-packed salad a day ahead and refrigerate. For convenience use precooked bacon and cut-up broccoli from your supermarket's produce section.

Prep: 20 minutes **Chill:** 2 hours
Makes: 12 to 16 side-dish servings

- 1 **cup mayonnaise or reduced-fat mayonnaise**
- ½ **cup raisins**
- ¼ **cup finely chopped red onion (about half of 1 small)**
- 3 **tablespoons sugar**
- 2 **tablespoons vinegar**
- 7 **cups chopped fresh broccoli florets**
- ½ **cup shelled sunflower seeds**
- 8 **slices bacon, crisp-cooked, drained, and crumbled**

1. In a large bowl combine mayonnaise, raisins, onion, sugar, and vinegar. Add broccoli and stir to coat. Cover and chill in the refrigerator for at least 2 hours or up to 24 hours. Before serving, stir in sunflower seeds and bacon.

Per ½ cup: 247 cal., 20 g total fat (3 g sat. fat), 18 mg chol., 216 mg sodium, 13 g carbo., 2 g fiber, 5 g pro.
Daily Values: 7% vit. A, 77% vit. C, 4% calcium, 6% iron
Exchanges: ½ Vegetable, ½ Other Carbo., 4½ Fat

Greek Salad

Greek Salad ⬭FAST⬭

*Most supermarkets carry pitted kalamata olives—
a huge timesaver for a busy cook.*

Start to Finish: 15 minutes **Makes:** 6 side-dish servings

- 6 **cups torn mixed salad greens or romaine**
- 2 **medium tomatoes, cut into wedges, or
8 cherry tomatoes, halved**
- 1 **small cucumber, halved lengthwise and
thinly sliced**
- 1 **small red onion, cut into thin wedges**
- ½ **cup pitted kalamata olives**
- ½ **cup crumbled feta cheese (2 ounces)**
- 1 **recipe Greek Vinaigrette**
- 2 **small pita bread rounds, cut into wedges
(optional)**

1. In a salad bowl combine salad greens, tomato, cucumber, onion, olives, and feta cheese.
Add Greek Vinaigrette; toss to coat. If desired,
serve with pita bread wedges.

Greek Vinaigrette: In a screw-top jar combine
2 tablespoons olive oil or salad oil; 2 tablespoons lemon juice; 2 teaspoons snipped fresh
oregano or ½ teaspoon dried oregano, crushed;
⅛ teaspoon salt; and ⅛ teaspoon black pepper.
Cover and shake well. Makes about ¼ cup.

Per ¾ cup: 105 cal., 8 g total fat (2 g sat. fat), 8 mg chol.,
286 mg sodium, 7 g carbo., 2 g fiber, 2 g pro.
Daily Values: 12% vit. A, 19% vit. C, 7% calcium, 3% iron
Exchanges: 1½ Vegetable, 1½ Fat

Marinated Cucumbers
⬭LOW FAT⬭ ⬭EASY⬭

*For added color and flavor, stir in 1 cup halved
cherry tomatoes and 1 medium green, red, or yellow
sweet pepper, cut into strips.*

Prep: 15 minutes **Chill:** 4 hours
Makes: 6 side-dish servings

- 2 **tablespoons vinegar**
- 2 **tablespoons salad oil**
- ½ **teaspoon sugar**
- ½ **teaspoon salt**
- ¼ **teaspoon celery seeds**
- 1 **large cucumber, peeled (if desired), halved
lengthwise, and thinly sliced (3 cups)**
- 1 **small onion, thinly sliced (about ⅔ cup)**

1. For marinade, in a covered nonreactive container combine vinegar, oil, sugar, salt, and
celery seeds. Add cucumber and onion; toss to
coat. Cover and chill for at least 4 hours or up to
3 days, stirring occasionally.

Per ⅔ cup: 54 cal., 5 g total fat (1 g sat. fat), 0 mg chol.,
195 mg sodium, 3 g carbo., 1 g fiber, 0 g pro.
Daily Values: 1% vit. A, 3% vit. C, 12% calcium, 1% iron
Exchanges: ½ Vegetable, 1 Fat

Creamy Cucumbers ⬭LOW FAT⬭ ⬭EASY⬭

*Sour cream makes these cucumbers rich in flavor.
Dill adds extra freshness.*

Prep: 15 minutes **Chill:** 4 hours
Makes: 6 side-dish servings

- ½ **cup dairy sour cream or plain yogurt**
- 1 **tablespoon vinegar**
- ½ **teaspoon salt**
- ¼ **teaspoon dried dill**
  Dash black pepper
- 1 **large cucumber, peeled (if desired), halved
lengthwise, and thinly sliced (3 cups)**
- ⅓ **cup thinly sliced onion (about half of
1 small)**

1. In a medium nonreactive bowl combine
sour cream, vinegar, salt, dill, and pepper. Add
cucumber and onion; toss to coat. Cover and
chill for 4 hours or up to 3 days, stirring occasionally. Stir before serving.

Per ½ cup: 45 cal., 3 g total fat (2 g sat. fat), 7 mg chol.,
204 mg sodium, 3 g carbo., 1 g pro.
Daily Values: 3% vit. A, 3% vit. C, 3% calcium, 1% iron
Exchanges: ½ Vegetable, ½ Fat

Broccoli-Cauliflower Salad

Tote this salad to a potluck and watch it disappear. Be sure it doesn't sit out for more than 2 hours.

Prep: 20 minutes **Chill:** 4 hours
Makes: 8 to 10 side-dish servings

    4 cups small cauliflower florets
    3 cups small broccoli florets
    ½ cup thinly sliced green onion (4)
    ¾ cup sliced radishes
    ½ cup shredded carrot
    1 cup mayonnaise or salad dressing
    2 tablespoons sugar
    1 tablespoon lemon juice
    2 teaspoons prepared horseradish
    ½ teaspoon salt
    ½ teaspoon black pepper
    6 slices bacon, crisp-cooked, drained, and
       crumbled

1. In a large bowl layer cauliflower, broccoli, green onion, radishes, and carrot; set aside.

2. For dressing, in a medium bowl combine mayonnaise, sugar, lemon juice, horseradish, salt, and pepper; spread over vegetables. Sprinkle with bacon. Cover and chill in the refrigerator for at least 4 hours or up to 24 hours. Stir to coat before serving.

Per ¾ cup: 267 cal., 24 g total fat (4 g sat. fat), 16 mg chol., 451 mg sodium, 11 g carbo., 2 g fiber, 4 g pro.
Daily Values: 24% vit. A, 96% vit. C, 4% calcium, 5% iron
Exchanges: 2 Vegetable, 5 Fat

Sesame Noodle Slaw

The Oriental noodles are crunchy when you first make this cabbage salad. If you prefer softer noodles, chill the salad to give them time to absorb some of the soy-vinegar dressing.

Prep: 20 minutes **Bake:** 10 minutes **Oven:** 300°F
Chill: 30 minutes **Makes:** 8 side-dish servings

    ½ cup slivered almonds
    2 tablespoons sesame seeds
    ⅓ cup salad oil
    3 tablespoons vinegar
    2 tablespoons reduced-sodium soy sauce
    1 3-ounce package chicken-flavor ramen
       noodles
    1 tablespoon sugar
    ¼ teaspoon black pepper
    ½ of a medium head cabbage, cored and
       shredded (about 6 cups)
    ⅓ to ½ cup thinly sliced green onion (3 or 4)

1. Spread almonds and sesame seeds in a shallow baking pan. Bake in a 300°F oven about 10 minutes or until toasted, stirring once; cool.

2. Meanwhile, for dressing, in a screw-top jar combine oil, vinegar, soy sauce, seasoning packet from ramen noodles, sugar, and pepper. Cover and shake well.

3. In a large bowl layer cabbage, green onion, and toasted nuts. Break noodles into small pieces. Sprinkle onto salad.

4. Add dressing; toss gently to coat. Cover and chill at least 30 minutes or up to 4 hours.

Per cup: 211 cal., 16 g total fat (3 g sat. fat), 0 mg chol., 360 mg sodium, 14 g carbo., 3 g fiber, 4 g pro.
Daily Values: 3% vit. A, 30% vit. C, 6% calcium, 6% iron
Exchanges: 1 Vegetable, ½ Starch, 3 Fat

Sesame Chicken and Noodle Slaw: Prepare as above, except layer 1½ cups chopped cooked chicken or pork with the cabbage and onion. Makes 4 main-dish servings.

Per 2¼ cups: 523 cal., 37 g total fat (7 g sat. fat), 47 mg chol., 450 mg sodium, 28 g carbo., 6 g fiber, 24 g pro.
Daily Values: 6% vit. A, 37% vit. C, 16% calcium, 16% iron
Exchanges: ½ Vegetable, 1 Starch, 2½ Lean Meat, 7 Fat

Salad Oils

Nut oils: Almond oil is pale in color with a delicate, sweet flavor. Other nut oils, such as hazelnut and walnut, are golden with rich aromas and the pronounced flavor of the derivative nut. Refrigerate to store.

Olive oils: This versatile oil is made from pressed olives. Extra virgin olive oil, made from the first pressing of olives, is considered the finest type. With the most robust olive flavor and aroma, it has a rich golden-to-green hue. It's also the most expensive. Products labeled "olive oil" are usually lighter in color and have a more delicate taste. Store olive oils in a cool, dark place for up to 6 months or refrigerate them up to 1 year. Chilled olive oil becomes thick and cloudy; let it stand at room temperature until it becomes liquid and clear.

Salad or vegetable oils: The most common varieties are made from soybeans, sunflowers, corn, peanuts, canola, and safflower. All are light yellow and have a neutral flavor. Store at room temperature and use within 6 months.

Vinaigrette Coleslaw LOW FAT

Prep: 20 minutes **Chill:** 2 hours
Makes: 6 side-dish servings

> 3 tablespoons cider vinegar
> 2 tablespoons sugar
> 2 tablespoons salad oil
> ½ teaspoon celery or caraway seeds (optional)
> ¼ teaspoon dry mustard
> ¼ teaspoon salt
> ⅛ to ¼ teaspoon black pepper
> 4 cups shredded green and/or red cabbage
> 1 cup shredded carrot (2 medium)
> ¼ cup thinly sliced green onion (2)

1. For vinaigrette, in a screw-top jar combine vinegar, sugar, oil, celery seeds (if desired), mustard, salt, and pepper. Cover and shake well. In a large bowl combine cabbage, carrot, and green onion. Pour vinaigrette over cabbage mixture. Toss to coat. Cover and chill 2 to 24 hours.

Easy Vinaigrette Coleslaw: Prepare as above, except substitute 5 cups packaged coleslaw mix for the cabbage and carrot.

Per ¾ cup regular or easy variation: 78 cal., 5 g total fat (1 g sat. fat), 120 mg sodium, 9 g carbo., 2 g fiber, 1 g pro. **Daily Values:** 51% vit. A, 28% vit. C, 3% calcium, 3% iron **Exchanges:** 1 Vegetable, 1 Fat

Creamy Coleslaw

Prep: 20 minutes **Chill:** 2 hours
Makes: 6 side-dish servings

> ½ cup mayonnaise or salad dressing
> 1 tablespoon vinegar
> 1 to 2 teaspoons sugar
> ½ teaspoon celery seeds
> ¼ teaspoon salt
> 4 cups shredded green and/or red cabbage
> 1 cup shredded carrot (2 medium)
> ¼ cup thinly sliced green onion (2)

1. For dressing, in a large bowl stir together mayonnaise, vinegar, sugar, celery seeds, and salt.

2. Add cabbage, carrot, and onion. Toss lightly to coat. Cover and chill 2 to 24 hours.

Easy Creamy Coleslaw: Prepare as above, except substitute 5 cups packaged coleslaw mix for cabbage and carrot.

Per ¾ cup regular or easy variation: 158 cal., 15 g total fat (3 g sat. fat), 7 mg chol., 220 mg sodium, 6 g carbo., 2 g fiber, 1 g pro. **Daily Values:** 51% vit. A, 28% vit. C, 35% calcium, 3% iron **Exchanges:** 1 Vegetable, 3 Fat

Mesclun with Pears and Blue Cheese

Mesclun with Pears and Blue Cheese FAST

Mesclun is a mix of young salad greens. Most supermarkets sell bagged varieties.

Start to Finish: 25 minutes **Makes:** 8 side-dish servings

> 10 cups mesclun or torn romaine
> 3 medium red and/or green pears, cored and thinly sliced
> ¼ cup pear nectar
> 2 tablespoons walnut oil or salad oil
> 2 tablespoons white wine vinegar
> 1 teaspoon Dijon-style mustard
> ⅛ teaspoon ground ginger
> ⅛ teaspoon black pepper
> ½ cup broken walnuts, toasted (see tip, page 265) or 1 recipe Candied Nuts (page 271)
> ½ cup crumbled blue cheese (2 ounces)

1. In a large salad bowl lightly toss mesclun and pear.

2. For dressing, in a screw-top jar combine pear nectar, oil, vinegar, mustard, ginger, and pepper. Cover and shake well. Pour dressing over salad; toss lightly to coat.

3. Divide evenly among salad plates. Sprinkle each serving with nuts and cheese.

Per 1⅓ cups: 152 cal., 11 g total fat (2 g sat. fat), 5 mg chol., 110 mg sodium, 13 g carbo., 3 g fiber, 4 g pro. **Daily Values:** 6% vit. A, 10% vit. C, 7% calcium, 4% iron **Exchanges:** 1 Vegetable, ½ Fruit, 2 Fat

Balsamic-Dressed Mesclun with Pears: Prepare as on page 502, except omit dressing. Toss salad with ½ cup Balsamic Vinaigrette (page 511) or bottled balsamic vinaigrette.

Per 1⅓ cups: 183 cal., 13 g total fat (3 g sat. fat), 5 mg chol., 107 mg sodium, 15 g carbo., 3 g fiber, 4 g pro.
Daily Values: 6% vit. A, 10% vit. C, 7% calcium, 5% iron
Exchanges: 1 Vegetable, ½ Fruit, 2½ Fat

German-Style Potato Salad

Traditionally this hearty salad is served warm, but it also tastes great cold the next day.

Start to Finish: 45 minutes
Makes: 4 to 6 side-dish servings

- 1¼ **pounds red or white potatoes (about 4 medium)**
- ¼ **teaspoon salt**
- 4 **slices bacon**
- ½ **cup chopped onion (1 medium)**
- 1 **tablespoon all-purpose flour**
- 1 **tablespoon sugar**
- ½ **teaspoon salt**
- ½ **teaspoon celery seeds**
- ½ **teaspoon dry mustard**
- ⅛ **to ¼ teaspoon black pepper**
- ⅔ **cup water**
- ¼ **cup vinegar**

1. In a medium saucepan place potatoes, the ¼ teaspoon salt, and enough water to cover. Bring to boiling; reduce heat. Simmer, covered, 20 to 25 minutes or until just tender. Drain well; cool slightly. Halve, peel, and cut potatoes into ¼-inch slices. Set aside.

2. For dressing, in a large skillet cook bacon over medium heat until crisp. Remove bacon, reserving 2 tablespoons drippings in skillet. Drain bacon on paper towels. Crumble the bacon and set aside.

3. Add onion to the reserved drippings. Cook over medium heat until tender. Stir in flour, sugar, the ½ teaspoon salt, the celery seeds, dry mustard, and pepper. Stir in the ⅔ cup water and the vinegar. Cook and stir until thickened and bubbly. Gently stir in the potato and bacon. Cook, stirring gently, for 1 to 2 minutes more or until heated through. Transfer to a serving bowl. If desired, sprinkle with *parsley*.

Per cup: 235 cal., 10 g total fat (4 g sat. fat), 11 mg chol., 402 mg sodium, 33 g carbo., 3 g fiber, 5 g pro.
Daily Values: 35% vit. C, 2% calcium, 8% iron
Exchanges: 2 Starch, 1½ Fat

Marinated Potato Salad

For the most nutritious version, leave the skin on the potatoes because that's where most of their nutrients and vitamins are found.

Cook: 25 minutes **Prep:** 20 minutes **Chill:** 4 hours
Stand: 30 minutes **Makes:** 10 side-dish servings

- 2 **pounds red potatoes (6 medium)**
- ⅓ **cup olive oil**
- ⅓ **cup white wine vinegar**
- 2 **teaspoons Dijon-style mustard**
- 1½ **teaspoons Italian seasoning, crushed**
- ½ **teaspoon salt**
- ¼ **teaspoon black pepper**
- ¾ **cup chopped red sweet pepper (1 medium)**
- 1 **cup cherry tomatoes, halved**
- 1 **9-ounce package frozen artichoke hearts, thawed (optional)**
- ½ **cup sliced green onion (4)**

1. In a large saucepan cook potatoes, covered, in a large amount of boiling salted water for 25 to 30 minutes or just until tender. Drain well; cool slightly. If desired, peel potatoes. Cut into ½-inch cubes. Transfer to a large bowl.

2. For dressing, in a screw-top jar combine oil, vinegar, mustard, Italian seasoning, salt, and black pepper. Cover; shake well. Pour over potato. Add sweet pepper, tomato, artichoke hearts (if desired), and green onion. Toss gently to mix. Cover and chill for 4 to 24 hours, stirring once or twice. Let stand at room temperature 30 minutes before serving.

Per ¾ cup: 126 cal., 7 g total fat (1 g sat. fat), 148 mg sodium, 13 g carbo., 2 g fiber, 2 g pro.
Daily Values: 11% vit. A, 60% vit. C, 2% calcium, 7% iron
Exchanges: 1 Starch, 1½ Fat

Greek Potato Salad: Prepare as above, except omit mustard, tomato, and artichoke hearts. Substitute Greek seasoning for Italian seasoning and stir in 4 ounces feta cheese, crumbled; ½ cup oil-packed dried tomatoes, drained and snipped; and ½ cup pitted kalamata olives, chopped, with the green onion.

Per ¾ cup: 191 cal., 11 g total fat (3 g sat. fat), 10 mg chol., 375 mg sodium, 19 g carbo., 2 g fiber, 4 g pro.
Daily Values: 11% vit. A, 47% vit. C, 8% calcium, 10% iron
Exchanges: 1 Starch, 2½ Fat

Classic Potato Salad

Boiling the potatoes in their skins prevents them from absorbing too much water during cooking, ensuring firm potatoes for salads.

Cook: 20 minutes **Prep:** 20 minutes **Chill:** 6 hours
Makes: 12 side-dish servings

- 2 **pounds potatoes (6 medium)**
- ¼ **teaspoon salt**
- 1¼ **cups mayonnaise or salad dressing**
- 1 **tablespoon yellow mustard**
- ½ **teaspoon salt**
- ¼ **teaspoon black pepper**
- 1 **cup thinly sliced celery (2 stalks)**
- ⅓ **cup chopped onion (1 small)**
- ½ **cup chopped sweet or dill pickle or sweet or dill pickle relish**
- 6 **Hard-Cooked Eggs (page 228), coarsely chopped**
  Lettuce leaves (optional)
  Paprika (optional)

1. In a medium saucepan place potatoes, the ¼ teaspoon salt, and enough water to cover. Bring to boiling; reduce heat. Simmer, covered, for 20 to 25 minutes or just until tender. Drain well; cool slightly. Peel and cube the potatoes.

2. Meanwhile, for dressing, in a large bowl combine mayonnaise, mustard, the ½ teaspoon salt, and the pepper.

3. Stir in the celery, onion, and pickle. Add the potato and egg. Toss lightly to coat. Cover and chill for 6 to 24 hours.

4. To serve, if desired, line a salad bowl with lettuce leaves. Transfer the potato salad to the bowl. If desired, sprinkle with paprika.

Per ½ cup: 277 cal., 21 g total fat (4 g sat. fat), 120 mg chol., 337 mg sodium, 18 g carbo., 2 g fiber, 5 g pro.
Daily Values: 5% vit. A, 17% vit. C, 3% calcium, 4% iron
Exchanges: 1 Starch, 4 Fat

Perfect Potluck Party

Don't stress out the next time you host an open house. Try this easy, party-perfect menu.

- *Asiago Cheese Dip (page 531)*
- *Purchased barbecue pork sandwiches*
- *Potluck Pasta Salad (right)*
- *Three-Bean Salad (page 505)*
- *Ice cream sundaes*

Potluck Pasta Salad

Potluck Pasta Salad

This crowd-pleasing salad offers versatility: You can use any type of pasta, whatever vegetables are in season, and your favorite cheese.

Prep: 30 minutes **Chill:** 2 hours
Makes: 16 side-dish servings

- 3 **cups dried wagon wheel macaroni, rotini, or other desired pasta (8 ounces)**
- 1 **medium yellow summer squash or zucchini, halved lengthwise and sliced (2 cups)**
- 1 **cup frozen peas, thawed; shelled fresh peas, cooked and cooled (page 609); or frozen whole kernel corn, thawed**
- 1 **medium red sweet pepper, cut into strips (about ½ cup)**
- 8 **ounces smoked cheddar cheese or cheddar cheese, cubed (2 cups)**
- 1 **6-ounce can pitted ripe olives, drained and coarsely chopped**
- 1 **cup cherry tomatoes, halved**
- ½ **cup chopped red onion (1 medium)**
- 2 **tablespoons snipped fresh oregano or basil or 2 teaspoons dried oregano or basil, crushed**
- 1 **cup bottled balsamic vinaigrette or red wine vinaigrette salad dressing**

1. Cook pasta according to package directions; drain. Rinse with cold water; drain again.

2. In a large bowl combine pasta, squash, peas, sweet pepper, cheese, olives, tomato, onion, and oregano. Add dressing to pasta mixture; toss gently to coat. Cover and chill for 2 to 24 hours.

Per cup: 182 cal., 11 g total fat (4 g sat. fat), 15 mg chol., 368 mg sodium, 16 g carbo., 2 g fiber, 6 g pro.
Daily Values: 15% vit. A, 31% vit. C, 12% calcium, 6% iron
Exchanges: ½ Vegetable, 1 Starch, ½ High-Fat Meat, 1 Fat

Macaroni Salad

You can choose this creamy pasta salad's flavor— sweet or savory—depending on your choice of pickle relish (or pickles)—sweet or dill.

Prep: 30 minutes **Chill:** 4 to 24 hours
Makes: 6 side-dish servings

 1 **cup elbow macaroni or wagon wheel macaroni (3 ounces)**
 ¾ **cup cubed cheddar or American cheese (3 ounces)**
 ½ **cup thinly sliced celery (1 stalk)**
 ½ **cup frozen peas**
 ½ **cup thinly sliced radishes**
 2 **tablespoons thinly sliced green onion (1) or chopped onion**
 ½ **cup mayonnaise or salad dressing**
 ¼ **cup sweet or dill pickle relish or chopped sweet or dill pickle**
 2 **tablespoons milk**
 2 **tablespoons horseradish mustard (optional)**
 ¼ **teaspoon salt**
   Dash black pepper
 2 **Hard-Cooked Eggs (page 228), coarsely chopped**
   Milk (optional)

1. Cook pasta according to package directions. Drain pasta. Rinse with cold water; drain again. In a large bowl combine cooked pasta, cheese, celery, peas, radishes, and green onion.

2. For dressing, in a small bowl stir together the mayonnaise, pickle relish, the 2 tablespoons milk, the horseradish mustard (if desired), salt, and pepper.

3. Pour dressing over pasta mixture. Add chopped egg. Toss lightly to coat. Cover and chill for 4 to 24 hours. Before serving, if necessary, stir in additional milk to moisten.

Per ⅔ cup: 311 cal., 22 g total fat (6 g sat. fat), 97 mg chol., 411 mg sodium, 20 g carbo., 1 g fiber, 9 g pro.
Daily Values: 8% vit. A, 9% vit. C, 13% calcium, 7% iron
Exchanges: 1½ Starch, 1 High-Fat Meat, 2 Fat

Three-Bean Salad

Prep: 15 minutes **Chill:** 4 hours
Makes: 6 side-dish servings

 1 **16-ounce can cut wax beans, black beans, or garbanzo beans (chickpeas), rinsed and drained**
 1 **8-ounce can cut green beans or lima beans, rinsed and drained**
 1 **8-ounce can red kidney beans, rinsed and drained**
 ½ **cup chopped green sweet pepper (1 medium)**
 ⅓ **cup chopped red onion (about half of 1 small)**
 ¼ **cup vinegar**
 2 **tablespoons sugar**
 2 **tablespoons salad oil**
 ½ **teaspoon celery seeds**
 ½ **teaspoon dry mustard**
 1 **clove garlic, minced**

1. In a bowl combine wax beans, green beans, red kidney beans, sweet pepper, and onion.

2. For dressing, in a screw-top jar combine vinegar, sugar, oil, celery seeds, dry mustard, and garlic. Cover and shake well. Pour over vegetables; stir lightly. Cover and chill for 4 to 24 hours, stirring often.

Per ¾ cup: 120 cal., 5 g total fat (1 g sat. fat), 0 mg chol., 419 mg sodium, 17 g carbo., 5 g fiber, 4 g pro.
Daily Values: 6% vit. A, 30% vit. C, 5% calcium, 10% iron
Exchanges: 2 Vegetable, ½ Starch, 1 Fat

Types of Vinegar

Balsamic vinegar: Gets its sweetness and dark color from aging in barrels.

Cider vinegar: Made from fermented cider; has a bite and a subtle apple flavor.

Fruit vinegar: Made by steeping fruits in cider or white wine vinegar.

Herb vinegar: Made by infusing fresh herbs in white wine or cider vinegar.

Rice vinegar: Made from rice wine or sake; clear to pale gold in color with a tang and sweet flavor; available plain or seasoned.

White or distilled vinegar: Made from grain alcohol; colorless; has the strongest and sharpest flavor of all vinegars.

Wine vinegar: Reflects the color and flavor of the source: red, white, or rosé wine; Champagne; or sherry.

Italian Basil, Tomato, and Pasta Salad

Just about any tubular-type pasta would work for this recipe. See photo, page 491.

Prep: 45 minutes **Chill:** 4 hours
Makes: 8 side-dish servings

¼ cup red wine vinegar
¼ cup olive oil
2 teaspoons Dijon-style mustard
¼ teaspoon salt
⅛ teaspoon black pepper
1 clove garlic, minced
¼ cup slivered fresh basil
8 ounces fresh green beans, trimmed and cut up, or one 9-ounce package frozen cut green beans (about 2 cups)
4 ounces dried gnocchi, rotini, bow ties, or penne pasta (about 1¼ cups)
2 cups cherry tomatoes, halved
½ cup salami, cubed (optional)
½ cup finely shredded Parmesan cheese (2 ounces)
1 cup loosely packed fresh baby spinach leaves or arugula
Freshly ground black pepper

1. For dressing, in a screw-top jar combine vinegar, oil, mustard, salt, the ⅛ teaspoon pepper, and the garlic. Cover and shake well. Add basil. Cover and shake gently to combine.

2. Meanwhile, cook fresh green beans, covered, in a small amount of boiling water for 12 to 15 minutes or until crisp-tender. (Or cook frozen beans according to package directions until crisp-tender.) Drain; rinse with cold water. Drain well.

3. Cook pasta according to package directions; drain. Rinse with cold water; drain well.

4. In an extra-large bowl combine cooked green beans, pasta, tomato, salami (if desired), and Parmesan cheese. Pour dressing over pasta mixture. Toss lightly to coat. Cover and chill at least 4 hours or up to 24 hours. Add spinach leaves just before serving, tossing gently to combine. Sprinkle with the freshly ground black pepper.

Per cup: 161 cal., 9 g total fat (2 g sat. fat), 5 mg chol., 230 mg sodium, 15 g carbo., 2 g fiber, 6 g pro.
Daily Values: 20% vit. A, 17% vit. C, 11% calcium, 6% iron
Exchanges: ½ Vegetable, 1 Starch, ½ Lean Meat, 1 Fat

Melon and Berries Salad NO FAT EASY

Prep: 20 minutes **Chill:** up to 24 hours
Makes: 4 to 6 side-dish servings

2 cups chilled cantaloupe cubes or balls
2 cups chilled honeydew melon cubes or balls
1 tablespoon honey
1 teaspoon fresh lime juice
1 tablespoon snipped fresh mint
1 cup fresh blueberries and/or red raspberries

1. In a medium bowl combine cantaloupe and honeydew melon. Drizzle honey and lime juice over melon; gently toss to mix. Cover and chill for up to 24 hours.

2. Just before serving, add mint and toss gently to mix. Sprinkle with fresh berries.

Per 1¼ cups: 96 cal., 0 g total fat (0 g sat. fat), 0 mg chol., 29 mg sodium, 24 g carbo., 2 g fiber, 1 g pro.
Daily Values: 55% vit. A, 83% vit. C, 2% calcium, 4% iron
Exchanges: 1½ Fruit

Melon and Berries Salad

Berry Salad NO FAT EASY

Prep: 10 minutes **Chill:** 4¾ hours
Makes: 8 side-dish servings

1 10-ounce package frozen sliced strawberries in syrup, thawed
1 10-ounce package frozen red raspberries in syrup, thawed
1 6-ounce package strawberry- or raspberry-flavored gelatin
1¼ cups boiling water
½ cup apple juice or cranberry juice
1 tablespoon lemon juice

1. Drain strawberries and raspberries, reserving syrup. In a medium bowl combine gelatin and boiling water, stirring until gelatin dissolves. Stir in reserved syrup, apple juice, and lemon juice. Chill about 45 minutes or until partially set (the consistency of unbeaten egg whites).

2. Fold in berries. Pour into a 5- or 5½-cup mold. Cover and chill for 4 hours or until firm. Unmold salad (see photo, below) onto a serving plate.

Per ½ cup: 144 cal., 0 g total fat (0 g sat. fat), 0 mg chol.,
55 mg sodium, 33 g carbo., 1 g fiber, 2 g pro.
Daily Values: 1% vit. A, 16% vit. C, 2% iron
Exchanges: 1 Fruit, 1 Other Carbo.

To unmold a gelatin salad, set the mold in a bowl or sink filled with warm water for several seconds or until the salad edges appear to pull away from the mold.

Layered Cranberry-Apple Mold LOW FAT

Prep: 1½ hours **Chill:** 6 hours
Makes: 12 side-dish servings

  1 6-ounce package lemon-flavored gelatin
 ½ cup sugar
  1 cup boiling water
1½ cups cranberry-apple drink
  1 16-ounce can whole cranberry sauce
  1 1.3-ounce envelope dessert topping mix
  1 large apple, cored and finely chopped
    (1¼ cups)
 ¼ cup mayonnaise or salad dressing
    Sugared cranberries* (optional)
    Fresh mint (optional)

1. In a medium bowl dissolve gelatin and sugar in the boiling water. Stir in cranberry-apple drink. Transfer 1¾ cups of the mixture to a second bowl; cover and chill second bowl about 30 minutes or until mixture is partially set (the consistency of unbeaten egg whites). Set remaining gelatin mixture aside.

2. Fold cranberry sauce into partially set gelatin mixture; pour into an 8-cup ring mold or 2-quart square dish. Cover and chill about 30 minutes or until almost firm. Chill remaining gelatin mixture about 30 minutes or until partially set (the consistency of unbeaten egg whites).

3. Meanwhile, prepare topping mix according to package directions. Fold topping, apple, and mayonnaise into partially set gelatin mixture. Spoon over chilled layer in mold or dish.

4. Cover and chill about 6 hours or until firm. Unmold gelatin (see photo, left) onto platter. If desired, garnish with sugared cranberries and fresh mint.

*Note: For sugared cranberries, freeze cranberries; roll in sugar to coat.

Per ½ cup: 228 cal., 5 g total fat (2 g sat. fat), 3 mg chol.,
91 mg sodium, 45 g carbo., 1 g fiber, 2 g pro.
Daily Values: 1% vit. A, 18% vit. C, 2% calcium, 1% iron
Exchanges: 3 Other Carbo., 1 Fat

Apple-Rice Salad WHOLE GRAIN

Use Granny Smith apples in this crunchy salad.

Prep: 50 minutes **Chill:** 2 hours
Makes: 6 side-dish servings

 ⅓ cup uncooked brown rice
 ⅓ cup uncooked wild rice, rinsed and drained
1¾ cups water
  2 cups chopped apple (about 2 medium)
  1 cup thinly sliced celery (2 stalks)
 ¼ cup shelled sunflower seeds
 ¼ cup dried currants or dried cranberries
  2 tablespoons balsamic vinegar
  1 tablespoon olive oil
  2 teaspoons honey
  2 teaspoons brown or Dijon-style mustard
  2 teaspoons finely shredded orange peel
 ¼ teaspoon salt
  1 clove garlic, minced
    Lettuce leaves

1. In a medium saucepan combine the brown rice, wild rice, and water. Bring to boiling; reduce heat. Simmer, covered, for 40 to 45 minutes or until rice is tender; drain. Transfer to a large bowl; cover and chill for 2 hours.

2. Add apple, celery, sunflower seeds, and currants to the chilled rice mixture; stir to combine. For dressing, in a screw-top jar combine vinegar, oil, honey, mustard, orange peel, salt, and garlic. Cover and shake well. Pour over rice mixture; toss gently to coat. Serve immediately on lettuce leaves or cover and chill up to 4 hours.

Per ¾ cup: 191 cal., 6 g total fat (1 g sat. fat), 0 mg chol.,
143 mg sodium, 32 g carbo., 4 g fiber, 4 g pro.
Daily Values: 5% vit. A, 12% vit. C, 3% calcium, 7% iron
Exchanges: 1 Fruit, 1 Starch, 1 Fat

Five-Cup Fruit Salad `EASY`

For a richer flavor, toast the pecans (see tip, page 265). Walnuts or slivered almonds would make a fine substitute for the pecans.

Prep: 10 minutes **Chill:** 2 hours
Makes: 6 side-dish servings

   1 **8-ounce can pineapple chunks**
   1 **11-ounce can mandarin orange sections, drained**
   1 **cup coconut**
   1 **cup tiny marshmallows**
   1 **8-ounce carton dairy sour cream**
   2 **tablespoons chopped pecans**

1. Drain pineapple chunks, reserving 1 tablespoon juice. In a medium bowl combine reserved juice, pineapple chunks, mandarin orange sections, coconut, marshmallows, and sour cream. Cover and chill for 2 to 24 hours. Before serving, sprinkle with pecans.

Per ¾ cup: 279 cal., 16 g total fat (12 g sat. fat), 17 mg chol., 94 mg sodium, 33 g carbo., 2 g fiber, 3 g pro.
Daily Values: 15% vit. A, 24% vit. C, 5% calcium, 2% iron
Exchanges: 1 Fruit, 1 Other Carbo., 3½ Fat

Waldorf Salad

If desired, increase seedless green grapes to ½ cup and omit the dried fruit. You also can substitute ¼ cup mixed dried fruit for the raisins. Low-fat mayonnaise works as well as regular mayonnaise. See photo, page 491.

Prep: 20 minutes **Chill:** up to 8 hours
Makes: 6 side-dish servings

   2 **cups chopped apple and/or pear**
   2 **teaspoons lemon juice**
   ¼ **cup chopped celery (½ stalk)**
   ¼ **cup chopped walnuts or pecans, toasted (see tip, page 265)**
   ¼ **cup raisins, snipped pitted whole dates, or dried tart cherries**
   ¼ **cup seedless green grapes, halved**
   ⅓ **cup mayonnaise or salad dressing**

1. In a medium bowl toss apple with lemon juice. Stir in celery, nuts, raisins, and grapes. Stir in mayonnaise until combined. Serve immediately or cover and chill for up to 8 hours.

Per ½ cup: 164 cal., 13 g total fat (2 g sat. fat), 9 mg chol., 80 mg sodium, 12 g carbo., 2 g fiber, 1 g pro.
Daily Values: 48% vit. A, 4% vit. C, 1% calcium, 2% iron
Exchanges: 1 Fruit, 2½ Fat

Fruit Salad with Cranberry Dressing `LOW FAT`

The brilliant ruby red color of cranberries brightens this refreshing winter fruit salad.

Prep: 25 minutes **Chill:** 2 hours
Makes: 6 side-dish servings

   2 **cups cranberries**
   ⅓ **cup water**
   1 **cup sugar**
   ¼ **cup orange juice**
      Bibb lettuce leaves
   2 **large oranges, peeled and sectioned (2 cups)**
   ½ **large pineapple, peeled, cored, sliced, and cut into wedges**
   2 **large ripe pears, cored and sliced into wedges* (2 cups)**
   2 **kiwifruits and/or golden kiwifruits, peeled and sliced lengthwise into wedges (1 cup)**

1. For dressing, in a medium saucepan combine cranberries and water. Bring to boiling; reduce heat. Simmer, covered, for 4 to 5 minutes or until berries just begin to pop. Remove saucepan from heat; stir in sugar and orange juice. When cool, press mixture through a sieve. Discard cranberry skins. Cover and chill the dressing about 2 hours or until thoroughly chilled. (The dressing will thicken slightly as it chills.)

2. To serve, line six small bowls or plates with lettuce leaves. Arrange fruit on lettuce leaves. Drizzle with dressing.

***Note:** To prevent pears from darkening, brush cut edges with lemon juice.

Per ¾ cup: 231 cal., 1 g total fat (0 g sat. fat), 0 mg chol., 4 mg sodium, 58 g carbo., 5 g fiber, 2 g pro.
Daily Values: 11% vit. A, 113% vit. C, 5% calcium, 5% iron
Exchanges: 2 Fruit, 2 Other Carbo.

Using Olive Oil in Dressings

Because olive oil thickens and becomes cloudy when chilled, a salad dressing made with olive oil may do the same. If you've chilled an olive-oil-based salad dressing, before serving let it stand at room temperature for about 30 minutes or until it becomes easy to pour or drizzle.

Mayonnaise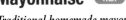

Traditional homemade mayonnaise contains raw eggs, which can be unsafe to eat. This recipe uses egg product, so you can serve it without worry.

Start to Finish: 15 minutes **Makes:** about 2 cups

- ½ teaspoon dry mustard
- ¼ teaspoon salt
- ¼ teaspoon paprika (optional)
- ⅛ teaspoon cayenne pepper
- ¼ cup refrigerated or frozen egg product, thawed
- 2 tablespoons vinegar or lemon juice
- 2 cups salad oil or 1½ cups salad oil and ½ cup olive oil

1. In a medium mixing bowl combine mustard, salt, paprika (if desired), and cayenne pepper. Add egg product and vinegar. Beat mixture with an electric mixer on medium speed until combined.

2. With mixer running, add 2 tablespoons of the salad oil, 1 teaspoon at a time. Slowly add the remaining oil in a thin, steady stream. (This should take about 5 minutes.) Cover and store in the refrigerator for up to 2 weeks. Stir well before using.

Food processor directions: Use only half the amount of each ingredient, except use the ¼ cup egg product. In a food processor combine all ingredients except salad oil; process until combined. With the processor running, add 1 cup oil in a thin, steady stream. (When necessary, stop processor and scrape down sides of bowl.) Makes about 1 cup.

Blender directions: Use only half of each ingredient, except use the ¼ cup egg product. In a blender combine all ingredients except salad oil. Cover and blend for 5 seconds. With blender running slowly, add 1 cup oil in a thin, steady stream. (When necessary, stop blender and use a rubber scraper to scrape the sides of the blender.) Makes about 1 cup.

Per tablespoon: 122 cal., 14 g total fat (2 g sat. fat), 0 mg chol., 22 mg sodium, 0 g carbo., 0 g fiber, 0 g pro.
Exchanges: 2½ Fat

Creamy French Dressing

Start to Finish: 15 minutes **Makes:** about 1⅓ cups

- 3 tablespoons vinegar
- 2 tablespoons sugar
- 2 teaspoons paprika
- 1 teaspoon Worcestershire sauce (optional)
- ¼ teaspoon salt
- ¼ teaspoon dry mustard
  Dash cayenne pepper
- 1 clove garlic, minced
- ¾ cup salad oil or olive oil

1. In a small mixing bowl, blender, or food processor combine vinegar, sugar, paprika, Worcestershire sauce (if desired), salt, mustard, cayenne pepper, and garlic. With mixer, blender, or food processor running, slowly add oil in a thin, steady stream. (This should take 2 to 3 minutes.) Continue mixing, blending, or processing until mixture reaches desired consistency.

2. Serve immediately or cover and store in the refrigerator for up to 2 weeks. Stir or shake well before using.

Per tablespoon: 74 cal., 8 g total fat (1 g sat. fat), 0 mg chol., 28 mg sodium, 1 g carbo., 0 g fiber, 0 g pro.
Daily Values: 2% vit. A, 1% vit. C, 1% calcium, 1% iron
Exchanges: 1½ Fat

Blue Cheese Dressing

There are many varieties of blue cheese from which to choose. See page 226 for descriptions to help you match one to your taste.

Start to Finish: 10 minutes **Makes:** about 1¼ cups

- ½ cup plain yogurt or dairy sour cream
- ¼ cup cream-style cottage cheese
- ¼ cup mayonnaise or salad dressing
- ¾ cup crumbled blue cheese (3 ounces)
- 1 to 2 tablespoons milk (optional)

1. In a blender or food processor combine yogurt, cottage cheese, mayonnaise, and ¼ cup of the blue cheese. Cover and blend or process until smooth. Stir in remaining blue cheese. If necessary, stir in milk to make a dressing with the desired consistency. Serve immediately or cover and store in the refrigerator for up to 2 weeks. Stir well before using.

Per tablespoon: 44 cal., 4 g total fat (1 g sat. fat), 7 mg chol., 100 mg sodium, 1 g carbo., 0 g fiber, 2 g pro.
Daily Values: 1% vit. A, 4% calcium
Exchanges: 1 Fat

Left to right: Honey-Mustard Dressing,
Thousand Island Dressing,
Russian Dressing

Honey-Mustard Dressing

This kid-favorite dressing makes a great dip for fried or baked chicken nuggets or strips.

Start to Finish: 10 minutes   **Makes:** about 1 cup

- ¼ to ⅓ cup coarse-grain mustard
- ¼ cup olive oil or salad oil
- ¼ cup lemon juice
- ¼ cup honey
- 2 cloves garlic, minced

1. In a screw-top jar combine mustard, oil, lemon juice, honey, and garlic. Cover and shake well. Serve immediately or cover and store in refrigerator for up to 2 weeks. Stir or shake well before using.

Per tablespoon: 51 cal., 4 g total fat (0 g sat. fat), 0 mg chol., 52 mg sodium, 5 g carbo., 0 g fiber, 0 g pro.
Daily Values: 3% vit. C
Exchanges: 1 Fat

Russian Dressing

For added kick, use hot-style Hungarian paprika.

Start to Finish: 10 minutes   **Makes:** ⅔ cup

- ¼ cup salad oil
- ¼ cup ketchup
- 1 tablespoon sugar
- 1 tablespoon white wine vinegar or vinegar
- 1 tablespoon lemon juice
- 1 teaspoon Worcestershire sauce
- ½ teaspoon paprika
- ¼ teaspoon salt
- ⅛ teaspoon black pepper

1. In a screw-top jar combine the oil, ketchup, sugar, vinegar, lemon juice, Worcestershire sauce, paprika, salt, and pepper. Cover and shake well.

2. Serve immediately or cover and store in the refrigerator for up to 2 weeks. Stir or shake well before using.

Per tablespoon: 61 cal., 6 g total fat (1 g sat. fat), 0 mg chol., 135 mg sodium, 3 g carbo., 0 g fiber, 0 g pro.
Daily Values: 3% vit. A, 3% vit. C, 1% calcium, 1% iron
Exchanges: 1 Fat

Thousand Island Dressing

Worcestershire sauce gives this classic dressing a tangy flavor, while horseradish gives it a punch. Use it to dress salads or Reuben Sandwiches (page 383).

Start to Finish: 15 minutes   **Makes:** 1½ cups

- 1 cup mayonnaise or salad dressing
- ¼ cup bottled chili sauce
- 2 tablespoons sweet pickle relish
- 2 tablespoons finely chopped green or red sweet pepper
- 2 tablespoons finely chopped onion
- 1 teaspoon Worcestershire sauce or prepared horseradish
  Milk (optional)

1. In a small bowl combine mayonnaise and chili sauce. Stir in relish, sweet pepper, onion, and Worcestershire sauce.

2. Serve immediately or cover and store in refrigerator for up to 1 week. Before serving, if necessary, stir in 1 to 2 tablespoons milk until dressing reaches desired consistency.

Per tablespoon: 70 cal., 7 g total fat (1 g sat. fat), 5 mg chol., 97 mg sodium, 1 g carbo., 0 g fiber, 0 g pro.
Daily Values: 1% vit. A, 2% vit. C
Exchanges: 1½ Fat

Buttermilk Dressing   EASY

Prep: 10 minutes   **Chill:** 30 minutes   **Makes:** 1¼ cups

- ¾ cup buttermilk
- ½ cup mayonnaise or salad dressing
- 1 tablespoon snipped fresh Italian parsley or 1 teaspoon dried parsley, crushed
- ¼ teaspoon onion powder
- ¼ teaspoon dry mustard
- ¼ teaspoon black pepper
- 1 clove garlic, minced
  Buttermilk (optional)

1. In a small bowl stir together the ¾ cup buttermilk, the mayonnaise, parsley, onion powder, mustard, pepper, and garlic. If necessary, stir in additional buttermilk until dressing reaches desired consistency.

2. Cover and chill dressing for 30 minutes before serving or cover and store in the refrigerator for up to 1 week. Stir or shake well before using.

Peppercorn-Buttermilk Dressing: Prepare as above, except substitute ½ teaspoon cracked black pepper for the ¼ teaspoon black pepper.

Bacon-Buttermilk Dressing: Prepare as above, except cook 4 slices bacon until crisp; drain and crumble, reserving 1 tablespoon bacon drippings. Stir crumbled bacon and bacon drippings into dressing just before serving. Store in refrigerator for up to 3 days. Makes about 1⅓ cups.

Per tablespoon all variations: 44 cal., 4 g total fat (1 g sat. fat), 4 mg chol., 44 mg sodium, 1 g carbo., 0 g pro.
Daily Values: 1% vit. C, 1% calcium
Exchanges: 1 Fat

Creamy Italian Dressing

Start to Finish: 15 minutes **Makes:** about 1 cup

- ¾ **cup mayonnaise or salad dressing**
- ¼ **cup dairy sour cream**
- 2 **teaspoons white wine vinegar or white vinegar**
- 1 **clove garlic, minced**
- ½ **teaspoon dried Italian seasoning, crushed**
- ¼ **teaspoon dry mustard**
- ⅛ **teaspoon salt**

1. In a small bowl stir together mayonnaise, sour cream, vinegar, garlic, Italian seasoning, mustard, and salt.

2. Serve immediately or cover and store in the refrigerator for up to 1 week. Before serving, if necessary, stir in *milk* until dressing reaches desired consistency.

Creamy Garlic Dressing: Prepare as above, except add 2 additional cloves garlic, minced.

Creamy Parmesan Dressing: Prepare as above, except omit dry mustard and salt. Stir in 3 tablespoons grated Parmesan cheese and, if desired, ¼ teaspoon coarsely ground black pepper.

Per tablespoon all variations: 82 cal., 9 g total fat (2 g sat. fat), 9 mg chol., 3 mg sodium, 0 g carbo., 0 g fiber, 0 g pro.
Daily Values: 1% calcium
Exchanges: 2 Fat

Fresh Herb Vinaigrette FAST

When your summer garden is bursting with fresh herbs, use a combination of all three called for here to pack even more flavor into this versatile vinaigrette. Drizzle it over your favorite mixed greens and top with some freshly grated Parmesan or Asiago cheese for a fabulous meal starter.

Start to Finish: 10 minutes **Makes:** about ¾ cup

- ⅓ **cup olive oil or salad oil**
- ⅓ **cup white or red wine vinegar, rice vinegar, or white vinegar**
- 1 **to 2 teaspoons sugar**
- 1 **tablespoon snipped fresh thyme, oregano, or basil, or ½ teaspoon dried thyme, oregano, or basil, crushed**
- ¼ **teaspoon dry mustard or 1 teaspoon Dijon-style mustard**
- ⅛ **teaspoon black pepper**
- 1 **clove garlic, minced**

1. In a screw-top jar combine oil, vinegar, sugar, herb, mustard, pepper, and garlic. Cover and shake well. Serve immediately or cover and store in refrigerator for up to 3 days if using fresh herb. If using dried herb, store covered in refrigerator up to 1 week. Stir or shake well before using.

Ginger Vinaigrette: Prepare as above, except substitute rice vinegar instead of the listed vinegar options, substitute 2 teaspoons honey for the sugar, substitute 1 teaspoon grated fresh ginger for the herb, and add 2 teaspoons soy sauce.

Raspberry Vinaigrette: Prepare as above, except substitute raspberry or red wine vinegar instead of the listed vinegar options, omit the sugar, and add 3 tablespoons seedless raspberry preserves.

Balsamic Vinaigrette: Prepare as above, except use balsamic or white balsamic vinegar instead of the listed vinegar options.

Orange Balsamic Vinaigrette: Prepare Balsamic Vinaigrette as above, except reduce the balsamic vinegar to 3 tablespoons and add ½ teaspoon finely shredded orange peel and ¼ cup orange juice.

Per tablespoon all variations: 57 cal., 6 g total fat (1 g sat. fat), 0 mg chol., 0 mg sodium, 1 g carbo., 0 g fiber, 0 g pro.
Daily Values: 1% vit. C, 1% iron
Exchanges: 1½ Fat

Orange-Poppy Seed Dressing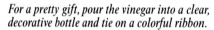

Drizzle this sweet dressing over greens or your favorite fruit salad.

Start to Finish: 15 minutes **Makes:** ⅔ cup

> 2 **tablespoons honey**
> 1½ **teaspoons finely shredded orange peel**
> 2 **tablespoons orange juice**
> 2 **tablespoons vinegar**
> 1 **tablespoon finely chopped onion**
> ⅛ **teaspoon salt**
>   **Dash black pepper**
> ⅓ **cup salad oil**
> 1 **teaspoon poppy seeds**

1. In a small food processor or a blender combine honey, orange peel, orange juice, vinegar, onion, salt, and pepper. Cover and process or blend until combined. With processor or blender running, slowly add oil in a steady stream until mixture is thickened. Stir in poppy seeds.

2. Serve immediately or cover and store in refrigerator for up to 1 week. Stir or shake well before using.

Per tablespoon: 80 cal., 7 g total fat (1 g sat. fat), 0 mg chol.,
29 mg sodium, 4 g carbo., 0 g carbo., 0 g fiber, 0 g pro.
Daily Values: 3% vit. C, 1% calcium
Exchanges: 1½ Fat

Fruit Vinegar

For a pretty gift, pour the vinegar into a clear, decorative bottle and tie on a colorful ribbon.

Prep: 15 minutes **Stand:** 2 weeks
Makes: about 1½ cups

> 1 **cup fresh or frozen unsweetened tart red cherries, blueberries, or raspberries**
> 2 **cups white wine vinegar**

1. Thaw fruit, if frozen. In a small stainless-steel or enamel saucepan combine fruit and vinegar. Bring to boiling; reduce heat. Boil gently, uncovered, for 3 minutes. Remove from heat and cover loosely with 100-percent-cotton cheesecloth; cool.

2. Pour mixture into a clean 1-quart jar. Cover jar tightly with a nonmetallic lid (or cover with plastic wrap and tightly seal with a metal lid). Let stand in a cool, dark place for 2 weeks.

3. Line a colander with several layers of 100-percent-cotton cheesecloth. Pour vinegar mixture through the colander and let it drain into a bowl. Discard the fruit.

4. Transfer strained vinegar to a clean 1-pint jar or bottle. If desired, add a few pieces of fresh fruit to the jar or bottle (the fruit must be completely submerged in the vinegar). Cover the jar or bottle tightly with a nonmetallic lid (or cover with plastic wrap and tightly seal with a metal lid). Store vinegar in a cool, dark place for up to 6 months.

Per tablespoon: 7 cal., 0 g total fat (0 g sat. fat), 0 mg chol.,
1 mg sodium, 0 g carbo., 0 g fiber, 0 g pro.
Daily Values: 1% iron
Exchanges: Free

Herb Vinegar NO FAT

Prep: 15 minutes **Stand:** 2 weeks **Makes:** about 2 cups

> ½ **cup tightly packed fresh tarragon, thyme, mint, rosemary, or basil leaves**
> 2 **cups white wine vinegar or cider vinegar**

1. Wash desired herbs; pat dry with paper towels. In a small stainless-steel or enamel saucepan combine the herbs and vinegar. Bring almost to boiling. Remove from heat and cover loosely with 100-percent-cotton cheesecloth; cool. Pour mixture into a clean 1-quart jar, making sure herbs are completely submerged in the vinegar. Cover jar tightly with a nonmetallic lid (or cover the jar with plastic wrap and tightly seal with a metal lid). Let stand in a cool, dark place for 2 weeks.

2. Line a colander with several layers of 100-percent-cotton cheesecloth. Pour vinegar mixture through the colander and let it drain into a bowl. Discard herbs.

3. Transfer strained vinegar to a clean 1½-pint jar or bottle. If desired, add a small sprig (2 to 3 inches long) of fresh herb to the jar (the sprig must be completely submerged in the vinegar). Cover jar with a nonmetallic lid (or cover with plastic wrap and tightly seal with a metal lid). Store vinegar in a cool, dark place for up to 6 months.

Per tablespoon: 5 cal., 0 g total fat (0 g sat. fat), 0 mg chol.,
1 mg sodium, 0 g carbo., 0 g fiber, 0 g pro.
Exchanges: Free

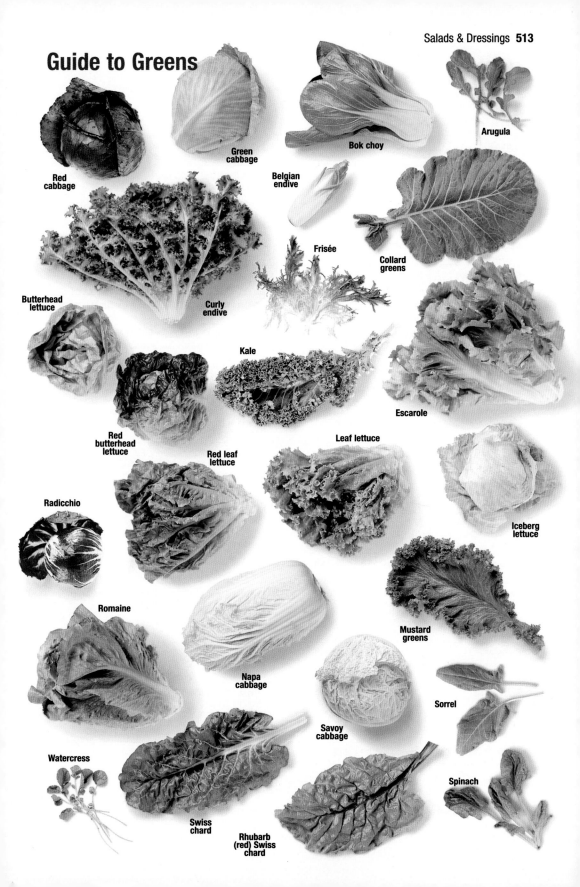

Guide to Greens

Red
cabbage

Green
cabbage

Bok choy

Arugula

Belgian
endive

Collard
greens

Frisée

Butterhead
lettuce

Curly
endive

Kale

Escarole

Red
butterhead
lettuce

Red leaf
lettuce

Leaf lettuce

Iceberg
lettuce

Radicchio

Romaine

Mustard
greens

Napa
cabbage

Sorrel

Savoy
cabbage

Watercress

Spinach

Swiss
chard

Rhubarb
(red) Swiss
chard

Guide to Greens

Type	Weight at Purchase	Amount After Preparation	Preparation and Storage*
Arugula	1 ounce	1 cup torn	Rinse thoroughly in cold water to remove all sand; pat dry. Refrigerate in plastic bag for up to 2 days.
Bok choy	1¼ pounds (1 head)	7 cups sliced stems and shredded leaves	Trim base; pull stalks apart. Rinse in cold water; pat dry. Refrigerate in plastic bag for up to 3 days.
Cabbage	2 pounds (1 head)	12 cups shredded or 10 cups coarsely chopped	Refrigerate in plastic bag for up to 5 days. Rinse in cold water just before using; pat dry.
Cabbage, napa	2 pounds (1 head)	12 cups sliced stems and shredded leaves	Cut off bottom core. Rinse in cold water; pat dry. Refrigerate in plastic bag for up to 3 days.
Cabbage, savoy	1¾ pounds (1 head)	12 cups coarsely shredded	Refrigerate in plastic bag for up to 5 days. Wash in cold water just before using; pat dry.
Collard greens	8 ounces	6 cups torn, stems removed	Wash in cold water; pat dry. Refrigerate in plastic bag for up to 5 days.
Endive, Belgian	4 ounces (1 head)	20 leaves	Cut off bottom core. Rinse in cold water; pat dry. Refrigerate in plastic bag and use within 1 day.
Endive, curly	12 ounces (1 head)	14 cups torn	Rinse in cold water; pat dry. Refrigerate, tightly wrapped, for up to 3 days.
Escarole	8 ounces (1 head)	7 cups torn	Rinse in cold water; pat dry. Refrigerate, tightly wrapped, for up to 3 days.
Frisée	8 ounces	7 cups torn	Rinse in cold water; pat dry. Refrigerate in plastic bag for up to 3 days.
Kale	8 ounces	7 cups torn, heavy vein removed	Wash in cold water; pat dry. Refrigerate in plastic bag for up to 3 days (longer storage increases its bitterness).
Lettuce, butterhead (Bibb or Boston)	8 ounces (1 head)	6 cups torn	Cut off bottom core. Rinse in cold water; pat dry. Refrigerate in plastic bag for up to 5 days.
Lettuce, iceberg	1¼ pounds (1 head)	10 cups torn or 12 cups shredded	Remove core. Rinse (core side up) under cold running water; invert to drain. Refrigerate in plastic bag for up to 5 days.
Lettuce, leaf	12 ounces (1 head)	10 cups torn	Cut off bottom core. Rinse in cold water; pat dry. Refrigerate in plastic bag for up to 5 days.
Mustard greens	8 ounces	8 cups torn	Refrigerate in plastic bag for up to 3 days. Wash in cold water just before using; pat dry.
Radicchio	8 ounces (1 head)	5½ cups torn	Rinse in cold water; pat dry. Refrigerate in plastic bag for up to 1 week.
Romaine	1 pound (1 head)	10 cups torn	Cut off bottom core. Rinse leaves in cold water; pat dry. Refrigerate in plastic bag for up to 5 days. Before using, remove fibrous rib from each leaf.
Sorrel	1 ounce	1 cup torn	Rinse in cold water; pat dry. Refrigerate in plastic bag for up to 3 days.
Spinach	1 pound	12 cups torn, stems removed	Rinse thoroughly in cold water to remove all sand; pat dry. Refrigerate in plastic bag for up to 3 days.
Swiss chard	1 pound	12 cups	Rinse in cold water; pat dry. Refrigerate in plastic bag for up to 3 days.
Watercress	4 ounces	2⅓ cups, stems removed	Rinse in cold water. Wrap in damp paper towels; refrigerate in plastic bag for up to 2 days.

*Line a plastic storage bag with paper towels. For more information, see "Preparing Salad Greens," page 493.

Sauces & Relishes

Hot Fudge Sauce, 525

Zesty Fruit Relish, 523

Béarnaise Sauce, 519

Sauces & Relishes Essentials

Sauces add flavor, texture, and color to sweet and savory dishes. Some, such as relishes, offer contrasting flavors, while others, such as pan sauces, extend the flavors of foods.

Types of Sauces

Sauces generally are defined by how they are thickened. Most sauces in this book are thickened in one of four ways:

Cornstarch-thickened: Cornstarch is commonly used to thicken fruit or dessert sauces to achieve a glossy, translucent appearance. To prevent lumps, cornstarch first is combined with a cold liquid. That mixture is added to a hot base, which is cooked until the sauce is thick and bubbly.

Egg-thickened: The proteins in egg yolks provide thickening power in a variety of sauces. But yolks are delicate and need to be heated gently and finished over low heat to avoid lumps. Some egg-thickened sauces are made in a double boiler. For others, the eggs are tempered before being added to a hot base. (Tempering involves whisking a little hot base into the eggs, then adding the egg mixture back into the base.)

Reduction: A reduction is a sauce thickened by simply boiling away (evaporating) its liquid. As the liquid evaporates, the sauce thickens and flavors intensify. Make a quick sauce for meats and roasted vegetables by reducing broth, wine, vinegar, or another liquid with seasonings. (See pan sauces for chicken on page 466 and for steak on page 368.)

Roux-thickened: A roux is a mixture of equal parts fat and flour that is cooked to remove the raw flour flavor and to prevent lumps. A white sauce is the classic roux-thickened sauce and is the base for many other sauces.

Medium white sauces (see recipe, page 518) are used for scalloped and creamed dishes; thin white sauces are used for creamed soups or creamed vegetables. To make a thin white

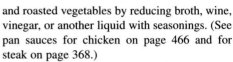
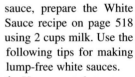

1

sauce, prepare the White Sauce recipe on page 518 using 2 cups milk. Use the following tips for making lump-free white sauces.

1. Use a wooden spoon to cook and stir flour, fat, and seasonings in a small heavy saucepan over low heat until evenly combined and lump-free. This makes the roux.

2. Slowly add all the milk to the roux. Stir constantly with a whisk to evenly blend the roux and milk.

3. Stir the sauce over medium heat until the mixture bubbles across the entire surface. Cook and stir 1 minute more to completely cook the flour in the sauce.

3

Successful Sauces

● Prevent lumps in sauces thickened with flour or cornstarch by stirring them constantly while they are cooking. If lumps do form, use a whisk to beat them out. If all else fails, strain the sauce through a fine-mesh sieve before serving.

● Cook sauces over low to medium heat unless directed otherwise. Do not cook sauces longer than the specified time. High heat and long cooking can cause sauces to curdle or break down.

● Prevent a "skin" from forming on a sauce (especially a milk-based sauce, such as a custard) by placing plastic wrap directly on its surface before chilling or while holding a warm sauce before serving.

White Sauce [FAST]

This basic sauce, also known as béchamel sauce, is the base for many other sauces, some of which are included as variations below.

Start to Finish: 15 minutes **Makes:** 1½ cups

    2 tablespoons butter or margarine
    2 tablespoons all-purpose flour
    ¼ teaspoon salt
      Dash black pepper
 1½ cups milk

1. In a small saucepan melt butter over medium heat. Stir in flour, salt, and pepper (see photo 1, page 517). Stir in milk (see photo 2, page 517). Cook and stir over medium heat until thickened and bubbly (see photo 3, page 517). Cook and stir for 1 minute more.

Curry Sauce: Prepare as above, except cook 1 teaspoon curry powder in the melted butter for 1 minute before adding the flour. Stir 2 tablespoons snipped chutney into the cooked sauce. Serve with fish or poultry.

Herb-Garlic Sauce: Prepare as above, except cook 2 cloves garlic, minced, in the melted butter for 30 seconds. Stir in ½ teaspoon caraway seeds; celery seeds; or dried basil, oregano, or sage, crushed, with the flour. Serve with vegetables or poultry.

Lemon-Chive Sauce: Prepare as above, except stir in 2 tablespoons snipped fresh chives and 1 teaspoon finely shredded lemon peel with the flour. Serve with vegetables, poultry, or fish.

Per 2 tablespoons plain, curry, herb-garlic, or lemon-chive variations: 38 cal., 3 g total fat (2 g sat. fat), 8 mg chol., 84 mg sodium, 2 g carbo., 0 g fiber, 1 g pro.
Daily Values: 3% vit. A, 4% calcium
Exchanges: ½ Fat

Cheese Sauce: Prepare as above, except omit salt. Over low heat, stir 1½ cups shredded American, process Swiss, or Gruyère cheese; ½ cup crumbled blue cheese; or ¾ cup grated Parmesan cheese into the cooked sauce until cheese melts. Serve with vegetables. Makes about 2 cups.

Per 2 tablespoons: 85 cal., 6 g total fat (4 g sat. fat), 20 mg chol., 230 mg sodium, 3 g carbo., 0 g fiber, 5 g pro.
Daily Values: 5% vit. A, 15% calcium, 1% iron
Exchanges: ½ High-Fat Meat, ½ Fat

Hollandaise Sauce

Well-known for its use in classic Eggs Benedict (page 230), this sauce is best made in a double boiler to prevent it from curdling.

Prep: 50 minutes **Cook:** 10 minutes **Makes:** ¾ cup

    ½ cup unsalted butter (1 stick)
    3 egg yolks, beaten
    1 tablespoon lemon juice
    1 tablespoon water
      Salt
      White pepper

1. Cut the butter into thirds and bring it to room temperature; allow about 45 minutes.

2. In the top of a double boiler combine egg yolks, lemon juice, and water. Add a piece of the butter. Place over gently boiling water (upper pan should not touch water). Cook, stirring rapidly with a whisk, until butter melts and sauce begins to thicken (see photo 1, below). (Sauce may appear to curdle at this point but will smooth out when remaining butter is added.) Add the remaining butter, a piece at a time, stirring constantly until melted. Continue to cook and stir for 2 to 2½ minutes more or until sauce thickens (see photo 2, below). Immediately remove from heat. If sauce is too thick or curdles, immediately whisk in 1 to 2 tablespoons *hot water*. Season to taste with salt and white pepper. Serve with cooked vegetables, poultry, fish, or eggs.

Per 2 tablespoons: 174 cal., 19 g total fat (11 g sat. fat), 150 mg chol., 54 mg sodium, 0 g carbo., 0 g fiber, 2 g pro.
Daily Values: 15% vit. A, 2% vit. C, 2% calcium, 2% iron
Exchanges: 4 Fat

1. After adding one piece of butter, cook and stir the sauce until it starts to thinly coat a spoon.

2. Continue cooking over boiling water, adding remaining butter pieces and stirring with a whisk until the butter melts and sauce becomes thicker.

Mock Hollandaise Sauce `EASY`

Start to Finish: 10 minutes **Makes:** ½ cup

 ¼ cup dairy sour cream
 ¼ cup mayonnaise or salad dressing
 1 teaspoon lemon juice
 ½ teaspoon yellow mustard

1. In a small saucepan stir together sour cream, mayonnaise, lemon juice, and mustard. Cook and stir over medium-low heat until hot. If desired, thin with a little *milk*. Serve with vegetables, poultry, fish, or eggs.

Per 2 tablespoons: 125 cal., 13 g total fat (3 g sat. fat), 13 mg chol., 92 mg sodium, 1 g carbo., 0 g fiber, 1 g pro.
Daily Values: 3% vit. A, 1% vit. C, 2% calcium
Exchanges: 2½ Fat

Béarnaise Sauce `FAST`

See photo, page 515.

Start to Finish: 15 minutes **Makes:** about 1 cup

 3 tablespoons white wine vinegar
 1 teaspoon finely chopped green onion
 1 teaspoon snipped fresh tarragon or
 ¼ teaspoon dried tarragon, crushed
 ¼ teaspoon snipped fresh chervil or
 dash dried chervil, crushed
 ⅛ teaspoon white pepper
 4 egg yolks, beaten
 1 tablespoon water
 ½ cup butter, cut into thirds, softened (1 stick)

1. In a small saucepan stir together vinegar, green onion, tarragon, chervil, and white pepper. Bring to boiling. Boil, uncovered, about 2 minutes or until reduced by about half.

2. In the top of a double boiler combine vinegar mixture, egg yolks, and water. Add a piece of the butter. Place over gently boiling water (upper pan should not touch water). Cook, stirring rapidly with a whisk, until butter melts and sauce begins to thicken (see photo 1, page 518). Add the remaining butter, a piece at a time, stirring constantly until melted. Continue to cook and stir for 1 to 2 minutes more or until sauce is thickened (see photo 2, page 518). Immediately remove from heat. If sauce is too thick or curdles, immediately whisk in 1 to 2 tablespoons *hot water*. Serve with beef, pork, or poultry.

Per 2 tablespoons: 139 cal., 15 g total fat (8 g sat. fat), 139 mg chol., 128 mg sodium, 0 g carbo., 0 g fiber, 2 g pro.
Daily Values: 12% vit. A, 2% calcium, 2% iron
Exchanges: 3 Fat

Beurre Blanc `FAST`

Start to Finish: 20 minutes **Makes:** 1 cup (unstrained)

 ¼ cup dry white wine
 2 tablespoons finely chopped shallot
 1 tablespoon white wine vinegar
 2 tablespoons whipping cream
 (no substitutes)
 ¾ cup cold unsalted butter, cut into
 2-tablespoon pieces (1½ sticks)
 Salt and ground white pepper

1. In a small saucepan* stir together the wine, shallot, and vinegar. Bring to boiling; reduce heat to medium. Boil gently, uncovered, for 7 to 9 minutes or until almost all of the liquid has evaporated. Stir in the cream. Bring to boiling and cook about 1 minute to reduce the cream slightly. Reduce heat to medium low.

2. Using a wire whisk, stir in the butter, a piece at a time, allowing each piece to melt before adding the next. Allow about 8 minutes (see photos 1 and 2, below). Strain sauce, if desired. Season to taste with salt and white pepper. Serve immediately over fish or vegetables.

*Note: Use a stainless-steel saucepan as vinegar may react with aluminum and cause curdling.

Lemony Beurre Blanc: Prepare as above, except substitute lemon juice for the vinegar. If desired, garnish with finely shredded lemon peel.

Creamy Mustard Sauce: Prepare as above, except whisk in 2 teaspoons Dijon-style mustard before serving.

Per 2 tablespoons plain, lemony, or mustard variations: 182 cal., 20 g total fat (12 g sat. fat), 54 mg chol., 41 mg sodium, 1 g carbo., 0 g fiber, 0 g pro.
Daily Values: 13% vit. A, 1% calcium
Exchanges: 4 Fat

1. Using a stainless-steel wire whisk, stir in the butter, a piece at a time, allowing each piece to melt before adding the next.

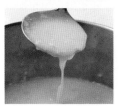

2. The cooked sauce should have a satiny finish. For a completely smooth sauce, use a fine-mesh sieve to strain out the shallot pieces.

Sauce Provençal

Start to Finish: 25 minutes **Makes:** 1¾ cups

- ¼ cup finely chopped onion
- 1 clove garlic, minced
- 2 tablespoons olive oil
- ¼ cup dry white wine
- ¼ cup chicken broth
- 1½ cups chopped, peeled, seeded tomato
- 1 tablespoon snipped fresh parsley
- 2 teaspoons snipped fresh thyme
- ¼ teaspoon salt

1. In a medium saucepan cook onion and garlic in hot oil over medium-high heat until tender but not brown. Stir in wine and broth. Bring to boiling; reduce heat. Boil gently, uncovered, about 8 minutes or until reduced to ¼ cup. Stir in tomato, parsley, thyme, and salt; heat through. Serve with fish, chicken, couscous, or pasta.

Per 2 tablespoons: 29 cal., 2 g total fat (0 g sat. fat), 0 mg chol., 59 mg sodium, 2 g carbo., 0 g fiber, 0 g pro.
Daily Values: 4% vit. A, 12% vit. C, 1% iron
Exchanges: ½ Fat

Bordelaise Sauce

Beurre manié, a butter-flour paste, thickens bordelaise sauce.

Start to Finish: 40 minutes **Makes:** about 1 cup

- 1¼ cups reduced-sodium beef broth
- ¾ cup dry red wine
- 2 tablespoons finely chopped shallot or onion
- 3 tablespoons butter or margarine, softened
- 1 tablespoon all-purpose flour
- ¼ teaspoon salt
- 1 tablespoon snipped fresh parsley (optional)

1. In a medium saucepan stir together broth, wine, and shallot. Bring just to boiling; reduce heat. Simmer, uncovered, skimming the surface often with a spoon, for 25 to 30 minutes or until reduced to 1 cup.

2. With a fork, in a small bowl stir together butter and flour. Whisk butter mixture into wine mixture, 1 teaspoon at a time, whisking constantly (mixture will thicken). Cook and stir for 1 minute more. Stir in salt and, if desired, parsley. Serve with beef or lamb.

Per 2 tablespoons: 64 cal., 4 g total fat (3 g sat. fat), 11 mg chol., 175 mg sodium, 2 g carbo., 0 g fiber, 1 g pro.
Daily Values: 3% vit. A, 2% iron
Exchanges: 1½ Fat

Barbecue Sauce LOW FAT

Slather this traditional sauce over grilled meats or use in any recipe calling for barbecue sauce.

Start to Finish: 40 minutes **Makes:** about 1⅓ cups

- ½ cup finely chopped onion (1 medium)
- 2 cloves garlic, minced
- 1 tablespoon olive oil or cooking oil
- ¾ cup apple juice
- ½ of a 6-ounce can tomato paste (⅓ cup)
- ¼ cup vinegar
- 2 tablespoons packed brown sugar
- 2 tablespoons molasses
- 1 tablespoon paprika
- 1 tablespoon prepared horseradish
- 1 tablespoon Worcestershire sauce
- 1 teaspoon salt
- ½ teaspoon black pepper

1. In a medium saucepan cook onion and garlic in hot oil over medium heat until onion is tender. Stir in apple juice, tomato paste, vinegar, brown sugar, molasses, paprika, horseradish, Worcestershire sauce, salt, and pepper. Bring to boiling; reduce heat. Simmer, uncovered, about 30 minutes or until desired consistency is reached, stirring occasionally. Serve with chicken, pork, or beef. (Cover and chill any leftovers for up to 3 days.)

Per 2 tablespoons: 52 cal., 2 g total fat (0 g sat. fat), 1 mg chol., 238 mg sodium, 9 g carbo., 1 g fiber, 1 g pro.
Daily Values: 7% vit. A, 5% vit. C, 2% calcium, 4% iron
Exchanges: ½ Other Carbo., ½ Fat

Horseradish Sauce EASY

Serve with Standing Rib Roast (page 367) or New England Boiled Dinner (page 383).

Start to Finish: 10 minutes **Makes:** 1 cup

- 1 cup whipping cream
- 4 to 5 tablespoons prepared horseradish

1. In a mixing bowl beat whipping cream until soft peaks form. Fold in horseradish. Cover and chill for up to 24 hours. Serve with beef or pork.

Per tablespoon: 27 cal., 3 g total fat (2 g sat. fat), 10 mg chol., 5 mg sodium, 0 g carbo., 0 g fiber, 0 g pro.
Daily Values: 2% vit. A, 1% calcium
Exchanges: ½ Fat

Chimichurri Sauce

Chimichurri Sauce

In Argentina this robust sauce is commonly found on every table. Serve it with meat, poultry, or fish.

Prep: 15 minutes **Chill:** 2 hours **Makes:** ⅔ cup

 1¼ cups packed fresh Italian parsley
 ¼ cup olive oil
 2 tablespoons fresh oregano or basil
 1 shallot, peeled
 3 to 4 cloves garlic, peeled
 2 tablespoons cider vinegar or red wine vinegar
 1 tablespoon lemon juice
 ¼ to ½ teaspoon crushed red pepper

1. In a food processor or blender combine parsley, oil, oregano, shallot, garlic, vinegar, lemon juice, ½ teaspoon *salt,* and crushed red pepper. Cover and process or blend just until chopped and a few herb leaves are still visible. Cover and chill for 2 hours before serving. (Cover and chill any leftovers for up to 1 week.)

Per tablespoon: 55 cal., 5 g total fat (1 g sat. fat), 0 mg chol., 121 mg sodium, 2 g carbo., 0 g fiber, 0 g pro.
Daily Values: 14% vit. A, 19% vit. C, 2% calcium, 3% iron
Exchanges: 1 Fat

Cocktail Sauce

Start to Finish: 10 minutes **Makes:** about 1 cup

 ¾ cup bottled chili sauce
 2 tablespoons lemon juice
 2 tablespoons thinly sliced green onion (1)
 1 tablespoon prepared horseradish
 2 teaspoons Worcestershire sauce
  Several dashes bottled hot pepper sauce

1. In a small bowl stir together chili sauce, lemon juice, green onion, horseradish, Worcestershire sauce, and hot pepper sauce. Transfer to a storage container. Cover and chill for up to 2 weeks. Serve with fish or seafood.

Per 2 tablespoons: 30 cal., 0 g total fat (0 g sat. fat), 1 mg chol., 321 mg sodium, 6 g carbo., 1 g fiber, 1 g pro.
Daily Values: 4% vit. A, 10% vit. C, 1% calcium, 2% iron
Exchanges: ½ Other Carbo.

Yogurt-Dill Sauce

Start to Finish: 5 minutes **Makes:** 1 cup

 1 8-ounce carton plain yogurt
 1 tablespoon snipped fresh dill or
  1 teaspoon dried dill
 ¼ teaspoon finely shredded lemon peel
 ¼ teaspoon black pepper
 1 small clove garlic, minced

1. In a small bowl stir together yogurt, dill, lemon peel, pepper, and garlic. Cover and chill until serving time. Serve with fish or seafood.

Yogurt-Cucumber-Mint Sauce: Prepare as above, except omit dill and lemon peel. Stir in ⅓ cup finely chopped cucumber and 1 teaspoon snipped fresh mint. Serve with fish or lamb.

Per 2 tablespoons dill or cucumber-mint variation: 18 cal., 1 g total fat (1 g sat. fat), 4 mg chol., 13 mg sodium, 1 g carbo., 0 g fiber, 1 g pro.
Daily Values: 1% vit. A, 1% vit. C, 4% calcium
Exchanges: Free

Honey-Mustard Sauce
NO FAT EASY

Prep: 10 minutes **Cook:** 5 minutes **Makes:** ½ cup

 ⅓ cup honey
 2 tablespoons packed brown sugar
 2 tablespoons Dijon-style mustard
 2 tablespoons apple juice or cider
 1 tablespoon finely chopped onion or
  1 teaspoon dried minced onion
 ⅛ teaspoon cayenne pepper

1. In a small saucepan stir together honey, sugar, mustard, apple juice, onion, and cayenne pepper. Bring just to boiling; reduce heat. Simmer, uncovered, for 5 to 7 minutes or until sugar dissolves and sauce is slightly thickened.

Per tablespoon: 61 cal., 0 g total fat (0 g sat. fat), 0 mg chol., 92 mg sodium, 16 g carbo., 0 g fiber, 1 g pro.
Daily Values: 1% calcium, 1% iron
Exchanges: 1 Other Carbo.

Tartar Sauce

Prep: 10 minutes **Chill:** 2 hours **Makes:** 1 cup

- ¾ **cup mayonnaise or salad dressing**
- ¼ **cup drained dill or sweet pickle relish**
- 2 **tablespoons finely chopped onion**
- 1 **tablespoon snipped fresh parsley**
- 2 **teaspoons capers, drained (optional)**

1. In a small bowl stir together the mayonnaise, pickle relish, onion, parsley, and, if desired, capers. Cover and chill for at least 2 hours before serving. Serve with fish or seafood. (Cover and chill any leftovers for up to 1 week.)

Per 2 tablespoons: 159 cal., 17 g total fat (2 g sat. fat), 8 mg chol., 168 mg sodium, 2 g carbo., 0 g fiber, 0 g pro.
Daily Values: 1% vit. C
Exchanges: 3½ Fat

Lower-Fat Tartar Sauce: Prepare as above, except substitute ½ cup light mayonnaise dressing or salad dressing and ¼ cup plain low-fat yogurt for the ¾ cup mayonnaise.

Per 2 tablespoons: 63 cal., 5 g total fat (1 g sat. fat), 5 mg chol., 151 mg sodium, 5 g carbo., 0 g fiber, 0 g pro.
Daily Values: 1% vit. A, 1% vit. C, 2% calcium
Exchanges: 1 Fat

Sweet-and-Sour Sauce

Start to Finish: 20 minutes **Makes:** 1½ cups

- ½ **cup packed brown sugar**
- 4 **teaspoons cornstarch**
- ½ **cup chicken broth**
- ⅓ **cup red wine vinegar**
- ¼ **cup finely chopped green sweet pepper**
- 2 **tablespoons chopped pimiento**
- 2 **tablespoons corn syrup**
- 2 **tablespoons soy sauce**
- 1½ **teaspoons grated fresh ginger**
- 1 **clove garlic, minced**

1. In a small saucepan stir together brown sugar and cornstarch. Stir in broth, vinegar, sweet pepper, pimiento, corn syrup, soy sauce, ginger, and garlic. Cook and stir until thickened and bubbly. Cook and stir for 2 minutes more. Serve warm with egg rolls and wontons or use in recipes calling for sweet-and-sour sauce. (Cover and chill any leftovers for up to 3 days.)

Per 2 tablespoons: 52 cal., 0 g total fat (0 g sat. fat), 0 mg chol., 213 mg sodium, 13 g carbo., 0 g fiber, 0 g pro.
Daily Values: 1% vit. A, 8% vit. C, 1% calcium, 2% iron
Exchanges: 1 Other Carbo.

Cranberry Relish

Prep: 15 minutes **Chill:** 2 hours **Makes:** about 2½ cups

- ¾ **cup apple juice or orange juice**
- ½ **to ⅔ cup sugar**
- ¼ **teaspoon ground cinnamon**
- ¼ **teaspoon ground nutmeg**
- **Dash ground cloves**
- 1 **12-ounce package cranberries (3 cups)**
- ½ **cup golden raisins**
- ½ **cup chopped pecans**

1. In a medium saucepan stir together apple juice, sugar, cinnamon, nutmeg, and cloves. Cook and stir over medium heat until sugar is dissolved. Add the cranberries and raisins. Bring to boiling; reduce heat. Cook and stir for 3 to 4 minutes or until cranberries pop. Remove from heat. Stir in pecans. Transfer to a bowl. Cover and chill for at least 2 hours. Serve with poultry, pork, or ham. (Cover and chill any leftovers for up to 2 days.)

Per 2 tablespoons: 63 cal., 2 g total fat (0 g sat. fat), 0 mg chol., 2 mg sodium, 12 g carbo., 1 g fiber, 0 g pro.
Daily Values: 4% vit. C, 1% calcium, 1% iron
Exchanges: 1 Other Carbo.

Cranberry Sauce

Start to Finish: 20 minutes **Makes:** about 2 cups

- 1 **cup sugar**
- 1 **cup water**
- 2 **cups cranberries (8 ounces)**

1. In a medium saucepan stir together sugar and water. Bring to boiling, stirring to dissolve sugar. Boil rapidly for 5 minutes. Add cranberries. Return to boiling; reduce heat. Boil gently, uncovered, over medium-high heat for 3 to 4 minutes or until cranberries pop, stirring occasionally. Remove from heat. Serve warm or chilled with poultry or pork.

Molded Cranberry Sauce: Prepare as above, except gently boil cranberry mixture for 13 to 16 minutes or until a drop of it gels on a cold plate. Pour into a 1½-cup mold and chill until firm. To unmold, see tip, page 507.

Per 2 tablespoons: 53 cal., 0 g total fat (0 g sat. fat), 0 mg chol., 1 mg sodium, 14 g carbo., 1 g fiber, 0 g pro.
Daily Values: 3% vit. C
Exchanges: 1 Other Carbo.

Mango-Ginger Chutney

Mango-Ginger Chutney

This sweet and tangy chutney is delicious served as a condiment with roasted or grilled meat. It freezes well, so make a double batch.

Prep: 20 minutes **Cook:** 15 minutes
Makes: about 2½ cups

½ cup packed brown sugar
½ cup dried tart red cherries or raisins
⅓ cup vinegar
¼ cup chopped onion
1 teaspoon grated fresh ginger
¼ teaspoon crushed red pepper
3 cups chopped, peeled mangoes
(about 3 mangoes)

1. In a medium saucepan stir together brown sugar, dried cherries, vinegar, onion, ginger, and crushed red pepper. Bring to boiling; reduce heat. Simmer, uncovered, for 15 minutes, stirring occasionally. Stir in mangoes; heat through. Let cool. Cover and chill up to 4 weeks. (Or freeze in an airtight container for up to 12 months.) Serve with beef, lamb, pork, or poultry.

Peach-Ginger Chutney: Prepare as above, except substitute 3 cups chopped, peeled fresh peaches or frozen peach slices, thawed, for the mangoes.

Per ¼ cup mango or peach variation: 104 cal., 0 g total fat (0 g sat. fat), 0 mg chol., 6 mg sodium, 27 g carbo., 1 g fiber, 1 g pro.
Daily Values: 48% vit. A, 29% vit. C, 2% calcium, 2% iron
Exchanges: 1 Fruit, 1 Other Carbo.

Cranberry-Cherry Chutney NO FAT EASY

Prep: 15 minutes **Cook:** 10 minutes **Chill:** 4 hours
Makes: 1½ cups

⅔ cup cranberry juice
½ cup sugar
1½ cups cranberries (6 ounces)
½ cup dried tart or sweet cherries
½ teaspoon finely shredded orange peel
⅛ teaspoon ground allspice

1. In a medium saucepan stir together cranberry juice and sugar; heat over medium heat, stirring until sugar is dissolved. Add cranberries, dried cherries, orange peel, allspice, and dash *salt.* Bring to boiling; reduce heat. Simmer, uncovered, for 10 to 12 minutes or until mixture thickens (the mixture will thicken further upon chilling). Transfer to a bowl. Cover and chill at least 4 hours. Serve with poultry, pork, or ham.

Per 2 tablespoons: 63 cal., 0 g total fat (0 g sat. fat), 0 mg chol., 13 mg sodium, 16 g carbo., 1 g fiber, 0 g pro.
Daily Values: 3% vit. A, 12% vit. C, 1% iron
Exchanges: 1 Other Carbo.

Zesty Fruit Relish

See photo, page 515.

Prep: 25 minutes **Chill:** 4 hours **Makes:** about 3 cups

2 cups chopped fresh cranberries (8 ounces)
¾ cup finely chopped, peeled pear (1 small)
½ cup finely chopped, peeled apple (1 small)
½ cup finely chopped, peeled, seeded orange
2 tablespoons finely chopped shallot
(1 medium)
2 tablespoons thinly sliced green onion (1)
1 to 2 fresh jalapeño chile peppers, seeded and finely chopped (see tip, page 74)
⅓ cup sugar
1 tablespoon lime juice
1 tablespoon white wine vinegar
½ teaspoon salt

1. In a medium nonmetal bowl stir together cranberries, pear, apple, orange, shallot, green onion, and jalapeño pepper. Stir in the sugar, lime juice, vinegar, and salt. Cover and chill for at least 4 hours or up to 24 hours. Stir before serving. Serve with ham, poultry, or pork.

Per ¼ cup: 50 cal., 0 g total fat (0 g sat. fat), 0 mg chol., 98 mg sodium, 13 g carbo., 2 g fiber, 0 g pro.
Daily Values: 2% vit. A, 18% vit. C, 1% calcium, 1% iron
Exchanges: ½ Fruit, ½ Other Carbo.

Raspberry Sauce NO FAT

Prep: 20 minutes **Chill:** 1 hour **Makes:** about 1 cup

- **3 cups fresh or frozen slightly sweetened raspberries**
- **⅓ cup sugar**
- **1 teaspoon cornstarch**

1. Thaw berries, if frozen. Do not drain. Place half of the berries in a food processor or blender. Cover and process or blend until berries are smooth. Press berries through a fine-mesh sieve; discard seeds. Repeat with remaining berries. (You should have about 1¼ cups sieved puree.)

2. In a small saucepan stir together sugar and cornstarch. Add raspberry puree. Cook and stir over medium heat until thickened and bubbly. Cook and stir for 2 minutes more. Transfer to a bowl. Cover and chill for at least 1 hour. Serve over angel food cake, cheesecake, or ice cream. (Cover and chill leftovers for up to 1 week.)

Per 2 tablespoons: 55 cal., 0 g total fat (0 g sat. fat), 0 mg chol., 0 mg sodium, 14 g carbo., 3 g fiber, 0 g pro.
Daily Values: 1% vit. A, 19% vit. C, 1% calcium, 1% iron
Exchanges: 1 Other Carbo.

Strawberry Sauce: Prepare as above, except substitute 3 cups fresh strawberries or one 16-ounce package frozen unsweetened whole strawberries, thawed, for the raspberries and do not sieve; use a medium saucepan and reduce sugar to ¼ cup. Makes about 2 cups.

Per 2 tablespoons: 20 cal, 0 g total fat (0 g sat. fat), 0 mg chol., 0 mg sodium, 5 g carbo., 1 g fiber, 0 g pro.
Daily Values: 26% vit. C, 1% iron
Exchanges: ½ Other Carbo.

Lemon Sauce FAST

Start to Finish: 20 minutes **Makes:** 1⅓ cups

- **⅔ cup sugar**
- **4 teaspoons cornstarch**
- **¼ cup water**
- **2 teaspoons finely shredded lemon peel**
- **¼ cup lemon juice**
- **2 egg yolks, beaten**
- **6 tablespoons butter, cut up**
- **¼ cup half-and-half, light cream, or milk**

1. In a small saucepan stir together sugar and cornstarch. Stir in water, lemon peel, and juice. Cook and stir over medium heat until thickened and bubbly. Cook and stir 1 minute more.

2. Place egg yolks in a medium bowl. Gradually stir hot mixture into egg yolks. Return egg mixture to saucepan. Cook and stir for 2 minutes more. Gradually stir in butter until melted. Stir in half-and-half. Serve warm. (Cover and chill any leftovers for up to 3 days.)

Orange Sauce: Prepare as above, except substitute orange peel for lemon peel and ½ cup orange juice for the water and lemon juice.

Per 2 tablespoons lemon or orange variation: 126 cal., 8 g total fat (5 g sat. fat), 59 mg chol., 72 mg sodium, 13 g carbo., 0 g fiber, 1 g pro.
Daily Values: 7% vit. A, 5% vit. C, 1% calcium, 1% iron
Exchanges: 1 Other Carbo., 1½ Fat

Cherry Sauce NO FAT EASY

Start to Finish: 15 minutes **Makes:** 2 cups

- **½ cup sugar**
- **2 tablespoons cornstarch**
- **½ cup water**
- **2 cups fresh or frozen pitted tart cherries**
- **1 tablespoon orange or cherry liqueur, cherry brandy, or orange juice**
- **Few drops red food coloring (optional)**

1. In a saucepan combine sugar and cornstarch; stir in water. Add cherries. Cook and stir over medium heat until thickened and bubbly. Cook and stir 2 minutes more. Remove from heat.

2. Stir in liqueur and, if desired, food coloring. Serve warm or cooled to room temperature. (Cover and chill any leftovers for up to 3 days.)

Per 2 tablespoons: 39 cal., 0 g total fat (0 g sat. fat), 0 mg chol., 1 mg sodium, 10 g carbo., 0 g fiber, 0 g pro.
Daily Values: 5% vit. A, 3% vit. C
Exchanges: ½ Other Carbo.

Cherry Sauce

Rhubarb Sauce

For 3 cups sliced rhubarb you need about 1 pound whole rhubarb.

Start to Finish: 20 minutes **Makes:** 2 cups

>   3 cups sliced fresh or frozen rhubarb
>   ½ to ⅔ cup sugar
>   1 strip orange peel (optional)

1. Thaw rhubarb, if frozen; set aside. In a medium saucepan stir together sugar, ¼ cup *water,* and, if desired, orange peel. Bring to boiling; stir in rhubarb. Return to boiling; reduce heat. Simmer, covered, about 5 minutes or until rhubarb is tender. Remove the orange peel, if using. Serve warm over cake or ice cream. (Cover and chill any leftovers for up to 3 days.)

Per 2 tablespoons: 28 cal., 0 g total fat (0 g sat. fat), 0 mg chol.,
1 mg sodium, 7 g carbo., 0 g fiber, 0 g pro.
Daily Values: 3% vit. C, 2% calcium
Exchanges: ½ Other Carbo.

Custard Sauce

For a brandied version of this classic sauce, also called crème anglaise, stir in 1 to 2 tablespoons brandy after removing sauce from heat.

Prep: 15 minutes **Chill:** 2 hours
Makes: about 2 cups

>   5 egg yolks, beaten
>   1½ cups whole milk
>   ¼ cup sugar
>   1½ teaspoons vanilla

1. In a heavy saucepan stir together egg yolks, milk, and sugar. Cook and stir continuously with a wooden spoon or heatproof rubber spatula over medium heat until mixture thickens and just coats the back of a clean metal spoon. Remove pan from heat. Stir in vanilla. Quickly cool the custard sauce by placing the saucepan in a large bowl of ice water for 1 to 2 minutes, stirring constantly.

2. Pour custard sauce into a bowl. Cover the surface with plastic wrap to prevent a skin from forming. Chill for at least 2 hours, without stirring, before serving. Serve over fresh fruit, baked fruit tarts, or dessert soufflés. (Cover and chill any leftovers for up to 3 days.)

Chocolate Custard Sauce: Prepare as above, except add ¼ cup unsweetened Dutch-process cocoa powder or unsweetened cocoa powder and, if desired, a dash ground cinnamon with the sugar. (If necessary, use a whisk to combine the ingredients.)

Per 2 tablespoons plain or chocolate variation: 43 cal.,
2 g total fat (1 g sat. fat), 66 mg chol., 12 mg sodium, 4 g carbo.,
0 g fiber, 2 g pro.
Daily Values: 2% vit. A, 3% calcium, 1% iron
Exchanges: ½ Other Carbo., ½ Fat

Hot Fudge Sauce

See photo, page 515.

Start to Finish: 15 minutes **Makes:** 1½ cups

>   ¾ cup semisweet chocolate pieces
>   ¼ cup butter
>   ⅔ cup sugar
>   1 5-ounce can evaporated milk (⅔ cup)

1. In a small heavy saucepan melt the chocolate and butter over medium heat. Add the sugar; gradually stir in the evaporated milk. Bring mixture to boiling; reduce heat. Boil gently over low heat for 8 minutes, stirring frequently. Remove from heat. Cool slightly. Serve warm over ice cream. (Cover and chill any leftovers for up to 3 days.)

Peanut Butter-Fudge Sauce: Prepare as above, except after boiling for 8 minutes, stir in ¼ cup peanut butter. Makes 1¾ cups sauce.

Per 2 tablespoons plain or peanut butter variation: 146 cal.,
8 g total fat (5 g sat. fat), 14 mg chol., 54 mg sodium, 15 g carbo.,
2 g fiber, 1 g pro.
Daily Values: 4% vit. A, 3% calcium
Exchanges: 1 Other Carbo., 1½ Fat

Vanilla Sauce

Start to Finish: 10 minutes **Makes:** 1¼ cups

>   ½ cup sugar
>   1 tablespoon cornstarch
>   1 cup boiling water
>   2 tablespoons butter
>   1 teaspoon vanilla paste or vanilla
>   Dash salt

1. In a medium saucepan stir together sugar and cornstarch. Slowly stir in water. Bring to boiling over medium heat; reduce heat. Boil gently for 5 minutes; remove from heat. Stir in butter, vanilla paste, and salt. Serve over gingerbread, apple dumplings, or your favorite berry pie. (Cover and chill any leftovers for up to 3 days.)

Per 2 tablespoons: 63 cal., 2 g total fat (2 g sat. fat), 7 mg chol.,
40 mg sodium, 10 g carbo., 0 g fiber, 0 g pro.
Daily Values: 2% vit. A
Exchanges: ½ Other Carbo., ½ Fat

Caramel Sauce

Prep: 20 minutes **Cool:** 15 minutes
Chill: up to 2 weeks **Stand:** 1 hour **Makes:** 1½ cups

- ½ **cup whipping cream**
- ½ **cup butter (1 stick)**
- ¾ **cup packed dark brown sugar**
- 2 **tablespoons light-colored corn syrup**
- 1 **teaspoon vanilla**

1. In a medium heavy saucepan stir together whipping cream, butter, brown sugar, and corn syrup. Bring to boiling over medium-high heat, whisking occasionally; reduce heat to medium. Boil gently for 3 minutes more. Remove from heat; stir in vanilla. Transfer sauce to a storage jar with a lid. Let cool for 15 minutes. Cover and chill for up to 2 weeks. Let stand at room temperature for 1 hour before serving.

Per 2 tablespoons: 339 cal., 19 g total fat (10 g sat. fat), 56 mg chol., 139 mg sodium, 42 g carbo., 2 g fiber, 2 g pro.
Daily Values: 13% vit. A, 5% vit. C, 4% calcium, 4% iron
Exchanges: 3 Other Carbo., 4 Fat

Butterscotch Sauce

Butterscotch Sauce `FAST`

Prep: 10 minutes **Cook:** 5 minutes **Makes:** 1½ cups

- ½ **cup butter or unsalted butter (1 stick)**
- ½ **cup half-and-half or light cream**
- ½ **cup granulated sugar**
- ½ **cup packed brown sugar**
- 1 **teaspoon vanilla**

1. In a medium saucepan combine butter, half-and-half, granulated sugar, and brown sugar. Cook and stir over medium heat for 5 to 8 minutes or until mixture is slightly thickened

and just comes to a full boil. Remove from heat; stir in vanilla. Serve warm. (Cover and chill any leftovers for up to 3 days. Reheat before serving.)

Per 2 tablespoons: 154 cal., 9 g total fat (5 g sat. fat), 25 mg chol., 66 mg sodium, 18 g carbo., 0 g fiber, 0 g pro.
Daily Values: 6% vit. A, 2% calcium, 1% iron
Exchanges: 1 Other Carbo., 2 Fat

Hard Sauce `EASY`

"Hard" simply means that the sauce has the consistency of butter.

Prep: 10 minutes **Chill:** 30 minutes **Makes:** ⅔ cup

- 1 **cup powdered sugar**
- ¼ **cup butter, softened**
- ½ **teaspoon vanilla or 1 tablespoon brandy or rum**

1. In a small mixing bowl beat together powdered sugar and butter with an electric mixer on medium speed for 3 to 5 minutes or until mixture is well combined. Beat in vanilla. Spoon into a serving bowl. Cover and chill for 30 minutes before serving. Serve as a topping for warm spice cake or bread pudding.

Orange Hard Sauce: Prepare as above, except substitute ¼ teaspoon finely shredded orange peel and 1 tablespoon orange juice or orange liqueur for the vanilla.

Per tablespoon plain or orange variation: 83 cal., 5 g total fat (3 g sat. fat), 13 mg chol., 50 mg sodium, 10 g carbo., 0 g fiber, 0 g pro.
Daily Values: 4% vit. A
Exchanges: ½ Other Carbo., 1 Fat

Bourbon Sauce `EASY`

Start to Finish: 10 minutes **Makes:** ⅔ cup

- ¼ **cup butter**
- ½ **cup sugar**
- 1 **egg yolk, beaten**
- 2 **tablespoons water**
- 1 **to 2 tablespoons bourbon**

1. In a small saucepan melt the butter. Stir in the sugar, egg yolk, and water. Cook and stir over medium-low heat for 5 to 6 minutes or until sugar dissolves and mixture boils. Remove from heat; stir in bourbon. Serve warm over bread pudding or ice cream.

Per 2 tablespoons: 180 cal., 11 g total fat (6 g sat. fat), 69 mg chol., 101 mg sodium, 119 g carbo., 0 g fiber, 1 g pro.
Daily Values: 9% vit. A, 1% calcium, 1% iron
Exchanges: 1½ Other Carbo., 2 Fat

Slow Cooker Recipes

Five-Spice Chicken Wings, 531   Meatball and Vegetable Stew, 536   Ranch Pork Roast, 538

Slow Cooker Recipes Essentials

Using a slow cooker is an enormous timesaver when it comes to preparing meals for busy families. Spend a little time in the morning and come home to a delicious hot dinner.

Slow Cooker Styles

Continuous slow cooker: This electric appliance cooks foods at a low wattage. The heating elements wrap around the sides of the ceramic liner and remain on continuously. There are two heat settings—low (about 200°F) and high (about 300°F)—and, in some models, automatic (cooker shifts from high to low or to warm automatically). The ceramic liner may or may not be removable. All of the slow cooker recipes in this book were tested in this style cooker.

Continuous Slow Cooker   **Multipurpose Slow Cooker**

Multipurpose slow cooker: In this type of cooker, the heating element is located below the food container. It cycles on and off during operation, and a dial indicates cooking temperatures in degrees. Because the recipes in this book need continuous slow cooking, they will not cook properly in this type of cooker.

Play It Safe

Safety first: A safe slow cooker cooks food slowly enough for all-day cooking but hot enough to keep food out of the bacterial "danger zone" (between 40°F and 140°F). To find out if your cooker is safe to use, fill the cooker one-half to two-thirds full of water. Heat it on low for 8 hours with the lid on. Check the water temperature with an accurate food thermometer. (Do this quickly since the temperature drops fast when the lid is removed.) The water temperature should be about 185°F. If it's not, replace your slow cooker.

Thaw it out: Thaw raw meat and poultry completely in the refrigerator before adding it to the cooker. If it thaws as it cooks, it will stay in that bacterial danger zone too long.

Leftovers: Do not leave leftovers to cool down in the slow cooker. Transfer warm leftovers quickly to storage containers, cover, and refrigerate or freeze them. Never reheat leftovers in the slow cooker.

Slow Cooker Basics

The one-half to two-thirds rule: For best results, a slow cooker must be at least half full and no more than two-thirds full. Many of our recipes give a range of cooker sizes (from 3½ to 6 quarts). Be sure to use a cooker that's within the specified range so the food cooks properly.

Keep a lid on it: Most slow cooker recipes do not require stirring, so no peeking! The domed lid allows condensation to run down inside, forming a water seal that keeps in heat. Lifting the lid drops the temperature in the cooker by 10°F to 15°F, and the heat doesn't recover quickly on the low-heat setting. If you really must lift the lid to stir a high-heat recipe, do so quickly, then add 15 to 20 minutes per hour of cooking time.

Automatic Timers

Automatic timers can help ensure dinner is ready at just the right time.

For recipes that may be ready before you are, start the slow cooker with an automatic timer (like those used for lamps). Make sure the timer is set to start within 2 hours of adding ingredients to the cooker and that the food is well chilled when it goes in.

Meet the Meats

Less tender (and less expensive) cuts of meat are perfect for long, slow, moist cooking.

Beef: Arm pot roast, blade steak, brisket, chuck pot roast, chuck short ribs, flank steak, round steak, rump roast, shank cross cuts, shoulder steak, stew meat

Pork: Blade roast, boneless pork shoulder roast (butt roast), country-style ribs, sirloin chops, sirloin roast, smoked pork hocks

Chicken and turkey: Breast halves (bone-in), drumsticks, thighs (bone-in or boneless)

Cut the fat: Because it provides low, moist heat, slow cooking requires little fat. Choose lean cuts of meat and trim away as much fat as possible. Remove the skin from poultry. Use a slotted spoon to transfer cooked meat and vegetables to a serving platter. Skim off any visible fat from cooking liquid if using the liquid as a sauce.

Not too big: Do not cook large pieces of meat or a whole chicken in the slow cooker because it will be in the bacterial "danger zone" too long. Halve any roasts that are larger than 2½ pounds.

Brown for flavor: Browning meat and poultry before placing them in the slow cooker adds a lot of flavor to recipes. Dredging them in flour before browning helps thicken the cooking liquid too. After browning, drain any fat from the skillet before adding meat to the cooker, or use a slotted spoon to transfer meat.

Ahead of the game: If your morning schedule doesn't allow time to prep ingredients for long-cooking recipes, do most of the work the night before. Chop vegetables, brown ground meats completely, place the items in separate containers, and refrigerate overnight. (Meat cubes and poultry should be browned right before adding them to the slow cooker rather than browning and chilling them since browning doesn't cook them through.) Place everything in the slow cooker in the morning, and away you go.

Ingredient Ideas

Using your beans: Dried beans take longer to cook in a slow cooker than on the stove top, so they usually will not be tender at the end of cooking if added directly to a recipe. If a recipe has sugar or acidic ingredients, the beans must be cooked completely before adding (follow package directions to cook beans). For all other recipes, precook beans for about 10 minutes, then drain and add to the cooker. Soaking dried beans overnight isn't enough to ensure they'll be tender.

Getting the veggies done: Meat cooks faster than vegetables, so cut the vegetables into small, uniform pieces and place them close to the heat, either around the sides of the slow cooker or at the bottom under the meat and liquid.

Avoid curdling: Dairy ingredients break down during long cooking. Add milk, cream, sour cream, and cream cheese during the last 15 to 30 minutes of cooking. Evaporated milk does not curdle and can often be used as a substitute.

High-Altitude Slow Cooking

High altitudes require you add about 30 minutes for each hour of cooking time called for in a slow-cooking recipe.

Adapting Favorite Recipes

Use the following tips to make many of your favorite recipes in the slow cooker:

● Start with a recipe that has a less tender cut of meat.

● Find a recipe in this chapter that is similar to yours and use it as a guide for quantities, piece sizes, liquid levels, and cooking times.

● Cut vegetables into bite-size pieces; place them at the bottom of the slow cooker so they'll cook evenly and completely.

● Trim the meat, cut it to the right size for the slow cooker, and brown it, if desired.

● Unless your dish contains long grain rice, reduce the liquids in the recipe you are adapting by about half.

Five-Spice Chicken Wings

See photo, page 527.

Prep: 20 minutes **Bake:** 20 minutes **Oven:** 375°F
Cook: 4 to 5 hours (low) or 2 to 2½ hours (high)
Makes: about 16 appetizers

> 3 **pounds chicken wings (about 16)**
> 1 **cup bottled plum sauce**
> 2 **tablespoons butter, melted**
> 1 **teaspoon five-spice powder**
> **Thin orange wedges and pineapple slices (optional)**

1. If desired, use a knife to cut off tips of the wings; discard tips. In a foil-lined 15×10×1-inch baking pan arrange wings in a single layer. Bake in a 375°F oven for 20 minutes. Drain well.

2. For sauce, in a 3½- or 4-quart slow cooker stir together plum sauce, melted butter, and five-spice powder. Add wings, stirring to coat.

3. Cover and cook on low-heat setting for 4 to 5 hours or on high-heat setting for 2 to 2½ hours. Serve immediately or keep warm on low-heat setting up to 2 hours. If desired, garnish with orange wedges and pineapple slices.

Kentucky Chicken Wings: Prepare as above, except omit the plum sauce and five-spice powder; substitute ½ cup pure maple syrup and ½ cup whiskey.

Per wing five-spice or Kentucky variation: 176 cal.,
13 g total fat (3 g sat. fat), 70 mg chol., 82 mg sodium,
6 g carbo., 0 g fiber, 12 g pro.
Daily Values: 1% vit. A, 2% calcium
Exchanges: ½ Other Carbo., 2 Lean Meat, 1 Fat

Asiago Cheese Dip `EASY`

Keep this party-perfect dip warm on low-heat setting for up to 2 hours. Stir just before serving.

Prep: 15 minutes **Cook:** 3 to 4 hours (low) or
1½ to 2 hours (high) **Makes:** 6½ cups

> 1 **cup water or chicken broth**
> 4 **ounces dried tomatoes (not oil packed)**
> 4 **8-ounce cartons dairy sour cream**
> 1¼ **cups mayonnaise**
> ½ **of an 8-ounce package cream cheese, cut up**
> 1 **cup sliced fresh mushrooms**
> 1 **cup thinly sliced green onion (8)**
> 1½ **cups shredded Asiago cheese (6 ounces)**
> **Thinly sliced green onion**
> **Toasted baguette slices (optional)**

1. In a medium saucepan bring the water to boiling. Remove from heat and add the dried tomatoes. Cover and let stand for 5 minutes. Drain and discard the liquid; chop the tomatoes (you should have about 1¼ cups).

2. Meanwhile, in a 3½- or 4-quart slow cooker combine sour cream, mayonnaise, cream cheese, mushrooms, the 1 cup green onion, and the Asiago cheese. Stir in the chopped tomatoes. Cover and cook on low-heat setting for 3 to 4 hours or on high-heat setting for 1½ to 2 hours. Stir before serving and sprinkle with additional sliced green onion. Keep warm on low-heat setting for 1 to 2 hours. If desired, serve with toasted baguette slices.

Per ¼ cup: 194 cal., 18 g total fat (8 g sat. fat), 29 mg chol.,
237 mg sodium, 5 g carbo., 1 g fiber, 4 g pro.
Daily Values: 7% vit. A, 4% vit. C, 10% calcium, 3% iron
Exchanges: 4 Fat

Bacon-Horseradish Dip

Prep: 25 minutes **Cook:** 4 to 5 hours (low) or
2 to 2½ hours (high) **Makes:** 5 cups

> 3 **8-ounce packages cream cheese, softened and cut up**
> 3 **cups shredded cheddar cheese (12 ounces)**
> 1 **cup half-and-half or light cream**
> ⅓ **cup chopped green onion (3)**
> 3 **tablespoons prepared horseradish**
> 1 **tablespoon Worcestershire sauce**
> 3 **cloves garlic, minced**
> ½ **teaspoon coarsely ground black pepper**
> 12 **slices bacon, crisp-cooked, cooled, and finely crumbled (1 cup)**
> **Corn chips, toasted baguette slices or pita wedges, or assorted crackers (optional)**

1. In a 3½- or 4-quart slow cooker stir together cream cheese, cheddar cheese, half-and-half, green onion, horseradish, Worcestershire sauce, garlic, and pepper.

2. Cover and cook on low-heat setting for 4 to 5 hours or on high-heat setting for 2 to 2½ hours, stirring once halfway through cooking. Stir in the crumbled bacon. Keep warm on low-heat setting for 1 to 2 hours. If desired, serve with your choice of dippers.

Per ¼ cup: 227 cal., 21 g total fat (13 g sat. fat), 63 mg chol.,
282 mg sodium, 2 g carbo., 0 g fiber, 8 g pro.
Daily Values: 15% vit. A, 1% vit. C, 17% calcium, 4% iron
Exchanges: 1 High-Fat Meat, 3 Fat

Wild Rice with Pecans and Cherries LOW FAT

This out-of-the-ordinary dish is a great addition to your big holiday dinner. It's an easy make-ahead and is sure to be ready when the turkey is.

Prep: 20 minutes **Cook:** 5 to 6 hours (low)
Stand: 10 minutes **Makes:** 15 side-dish servings

- 3 14-ounce cans chicken broth
- 2½ cups uncooked wild rice, rinsed and drained
- 1 cup coarsely shredded carrot (2 medium)
- 1 4.5-ounce jar sliced mushrooms, drained
- 2 tablespoons butter or margarine, melted
- 2 teaspoons dried marjoram, crushed
- ¼ teaspoon salt
- ¼ teaspoon black pepper
- ⅔ cup dried tart cherries
- ⅔ cup sliced green onion (5)
- ½ cup coarsely chopped pecans, toasted

1. In a 3½- or 4-quart slow cooker stir together chicken broth, wild rice, carrot, mushrooms, melted butter, marjoram, salt, and pepper.

2. Cover and cook on low-heat setting for 5 to 6 hours. Turn off cooker. Stir in cherries and green onion. Cover; let stand for 10 minutes.

3. Just before serving, sprinkle with pecans. Serve with a slotted spoon.

Per ⅔ cup: 169 cal., 5 g total fat (1 g sat. fat), 4 mg chol., 423 mg sodium, 27 g carbo., 3 g fiber, 5 g pro.
Daily Values: 43% vit. A, 3% vit. C, 2% calcium, 5% iron
Exchanges: 1½ Starch, ½ Other Carbo., ½ Fat

Maple-Orange Sweet Potatoes and Carrots LOW FAT

Orange juice and apricots bring extra dimensions of sweetness and tang to this colorful side dish.

Prep: 20 minutes **Cook:** 8 to 9 hours (low) or 4 to 4½ hours (high) **Makes:** 10 side-dish servings

- Nonstick cooking spray
- 16 ounces small carrots with tops, trimmed, or one 16-ounce package peeled fresh baby carrots
- 2 pounds sweet potatoes, peeled and cut into 1½-inch pieces
- 1 cup snipped dried apricots
- ½ cup pure maple syrup
- ¼ cup frozen orange juice concentrate, thawed
- ¼ cup water
- 2 tablespoons butter or margarine, melted
- ½ teaspoon salt
- ¼ teaspoon white pepper
- ¼ teaspoon ground cinnamon

1. Lightly coat the inside of a 3½- or 4-quart slow cooker with cooking spray. Add carrots. Top with sweet potatoes and dried apricots.

2. In a small bowl stir together maple syrup, orange juice concentrate, water, melted butter, salt, white pepper, and cinnamon. Pour over potato mixture in cooker.

3. Cover and cook on low-heat setting for 8 to 9 hours or on high-heat setting for 4 to 4½ hours. Serve with a slotted spoon.

Per ⅔ cup: 194 cal., 3 g total fat (2 g sat. fat), 7 mg chol., 168 mg sodium, 42 g carbo., 5 g fiber, 2 g pro.
Daily Values: 487% vit. A, 41% vit. C, 5% calcium, 8% iron
Exchanges: ½ Vegetable, ½ Fruit, 1 Starch, 1 Other Carbo., ½ Fat

Maple-Orange Sweet Potatoes and Carrots

Savory Stuffing with Fruit and Pecans

Cooking the stuffing in a slow cooker gives you room in the oven for other dishes.

Prep: 25 minutes **Cook:** 4½ to 5 hours (low) or 2¼ to 2½ hours (high) **Makes:** 10 to 12 side-dish servings

- ½ **cup apple juice**
- 1 **6-ounce package mixed dried fruit bits (1½ cups)**
- 1 **cup finely chopped celery (2 stalks)**
- ½ **cup sliced green onion (4)**
- ½ **cup butter or margarine**
- 2 **tablespoons snipped fresh parsley**
- 1 **teaspoon dried sage, crushed**
- ½ **teaspoon dried thyme, crushed**
- ½ **teaspoon dried marjoram, crushed**
- ½ **teaspoon salt**
- ¼ **teaspoon black pepper**
- 10 **cups dry bread cubes***
- ½ **cup broken pecans, toasted (see tip, page 265)**
- 1 **to 1½ cups chicken broth**

1. In a small saucepan heat apple juice until boiling. Stir in dried fruit bits. Remove from heat; cover and let stand until needed.

2. In a medium saucepan cook celery and green onion in hot butter over medium heat until tender but not brown; remove from heat. Stir in parsley, sage, thyme, marjoram, salt, and pepper.

3. Place dry bread cubes in a large bowl. Add undrained fruit, the vegetable mixture, and pecans. Drizzle with enough of the broth to moisten, tossing lightly. Transfer stuffing mixture to a 3½- or 4-quart slow cooker.

4. Cover and cook on low-heat setting for 4½ to 5 hours or on high-heat setting for 2¼ to 2½ hours.

***Note:** To prepare the 10 cups dry bread cubes, cut 14 to 16 slices of bread into ½-inch cubes and spread in a large roasting pan. Bake, uncovered, in a 300°F oven for 10 to 15 minutes or until dry, stirring twice. Or let bread stand, loosely covered, at room temperature for 8 to 12 hours.

Per ⅔ cup: 279 cal., 15 g total fat (7 g sat. fat), 27 mg chol., 528 mg sodium, 33 g carbo., 2 g fiber, 4 g pro.
Daily Values: 9% vit. A, 5% vit. C, 6% calcium, 10% iron
Exchanges: ½ Fruit, 1½ Starch, 3 Fat

Mediterranean-Style Pot Roast LOW FAT

Prep: 20 minutes **Cook:** 8 to 10 hours (low) or 4 to 5 hours (high) **Makes:** 6 main-dish servings

- 1 **2- to 3-pound boneless beef chuck pot roast**
- 1 **tablespoon cooking oil**
- 1 **medium onion, sliced**
- 1 **14.5-ounce can diced tomatoes with basil, oregano, and garlic, undrained**
- ¼ **cup sliced, pitted ripe olives**
- 1 **tablespoon Worcestershire sauce**
- 2 **teaspoons dried herbes de Provence, crushed**
- 1 **teaspoon coarsely ground black pepper**
- ½ **cup crumbled feta cheese (2 ounces)**

1. Trim fat from meat. If necessary, cut meat to fit into a 3½- or 4-quart slow cooker. In a large skillet brown meat on all sides in hot oil. Drain off fat. Set aside.

2. Place onion in cooker; top with meat. In a medium bowl combine undrained tomatoes, olives, Worcestershire sauce, herbes de Provence, and pepper; pour over meat in cooker.

3. Cover and cook on low-heat setting for 8 to 10 hours or on high-heat setting for 4 to 5 hours.

4. Remove meat from cooker. Cut meat into six serving-size pieces. Arrange meat on a serving platter. Using a slotted spoon, transfer vegetables to serving platter, reserving juices. Spoon enough of the juices over meat and vegetables to moisten. Sprinkle with feta cheese.

Per 4 ounces beef + ½ cup vegetables: 274 cal., 10 g total fat (4 g sat. fat), 98 mg chol., 641 mg sodium, 9 g carbo., 1 g fiber, 35 g pro.
Daily Values: 10% vit. A, 10% vit. C, 11% calcium, 30% iron
Exchanges: 1 Vegetable, 4½ Lean Meat

Thanksgiving Feast

Borrow a friend's slow cooker so you can make these two side dishes.

- *Roast Turkey (page 478)*
- *Savory Stuffing with Fruit and Pecans (left)*
- *Maple-Orange Sweet Potatoes and Carrots (page 532)*
- *Steamed peas with red sweet pepper*
- *Mashed potatoes and gravy*
- *Favorite pie*

Shredded-Beef Sandwiches EASY

After slow cooking, a tough cut like pot roast just falls apart—perfect for sandwiches.

Prep: 15 minutes **Cook:** 11 to 12 hours (low) or 5½ to 6 hours (high) **Makes:** 8 sandwiches

- 1 3-pound beef chuck pot roast
- 1 large onion, cut up
- 3 bay leaves
- ½ teaspoon salt
- ¼ teaspoon garlic powder
- ⅛ teaspoon ground cloves
- ⅓ cup cider vinegar
- 8 French rolls, split and toasted, if desired
  Spinach or lettuce leaves (optional)

1. Trim fat from meat. If necessary, cut meat to fit into a 3½- or 4-quart slow cooker. Place meat and onion in cooker. Add bay leaves, salt, garlic powder, and cloves; pour vinegar over meat in cooker.

2. Cover and cook on low-heat setting for 11 to 12 hours or on high-heat setting for 5½ to 6 hours. Remove meat from cooker. Discard bay leaves. Using two forks, pull meat apart into shreds, discarding any bones and fat. Strain juices and reserve; skim off fat.

3. If desired, line rolls with spinach leaves. Place shredded meat on rolls. Drizzle meat with some of the strained juices. Serve remaining juices with sandwiches for dipping.

Per sandwich: 449 cal., 23 g total fat (9 g sat. fat), 109 mg chol., 480 mg sodium, 22 g carbo., 2 g fiber, 36 g pro.
Daily Values: 2% vit. C, 5% calcium, 27% iron
Exchanges: 1½ Starch, 4½ Medium-Fat Meat

Vegetable-Beef Soup LOW FAT

Prep: 25 minutes **Cook:** 8 to 10 hours (low) or 4 to 5 hours (high) **Makes:** 6 main-dish servings

- 1 pound boneless beef chuck pot roast, cut into ¾-inch pieces
- 1 tablespoon cooking oil
- 4 cups water
- 1 14.5-ounce can diced tomatoes, undrained
- 2 cups frozen mixed vegetables
- 2 cups frozen diced hash brown potatoes or 2 medium potatoes, peeled and chopped
- 1 1-ounce envelope onion soup mix (½ of a 2-ounce package)
- 1 teaspoon instant beef bouillon granules

- ⅛ teaspoon black pepper
- 1 clove garlic, minced, or ⅛ teaspoon garlic powder

1. In a large skillet brown meat pieces, half at a time, in hot oil. Drain fat. In a 3½- or 4-quart slow cooker place meat and remaining ingredients.

2. Cover and cook on low-heat setting for 8 to 10 hours or on high-heat setting for 4 to 5 hours.

Per 1½ cups: 289 cal., 12 g total fat (4 g sat. fat), 48 mg chol., 519 mg sodium, 26 g carbo., 3 g fiber, 19 g pro.
Daily Values: 49% vit. A, 28% vit. C, 6% calcium, 19% iron
Exchanges: 2 Vegetable, 1 Starch, 1½ Very Lean Meat, 1 Fat

Beef Brisket with Barbecue Sauce

Prep: 25 minutes **Cook:** 10 to 12 hours (low) or 5 to 6 hours (high) **Makes:** 6 to 8 main-dish servings

- ¾ cup water
- ¼ cup Worcestershire sauce
- 1 tablespoon cider vinegar
- 1 teaspoon instant beef bouillon granules
- ½ teaspoon dry mustard
- ½ teaspoon chili powder
- ¼ teaspoon cayenne pepper
- 2 cloves garlic, minced
- 1 2½-pound fresh beef brisket
- ½ cup ketchup
- 2 tablespoons packed brown sugar
- 2 tablespoons butter or margarine

1. For cooking liquid, in a bowl combine water, Worcestershire sauce, vinegar, bouillon, mustard, chili powder, cayenne pepper, and garlic. Reserve ½ cup; cover and chill. Trim fat from meat. If necessary, cut meat to fit into a 3½- or 4-quart slow cooker.* Place meat in cooker. Pour remaining liquid over meat.

2. Cover and cook on low-heat setting for 10 to 12 hours or on high-heat setting for 5 to 6 hours. For sauce, in a small saucepan combine the ½ cup reserved cooking liquid, ketchup, brown sugar, and butter. Heat through; pass sauce with meat.

*Note: If you only have a 5- or 6-quart slow cooker, double the cooking liquid ingredients; reserve ½ cup. Leave all other ingredients the same. Prepare as above. Makes 6 to 8 servings.

Per 3 ounces beef + ¼ cup sauce: 488 cal., 33 g total fat (13 g sat. fat), 131 mg chol., 672 mg sodium, 11 g carbo., 0 g fiber, 35 g pro.
Daily Values: 10% vit. A, 8% vit. C, 4% calcium, 23% iron
Exchanges: ½ Other Carbo., 5 Medium-Fat Meat, 2 Fat

Pepper Steak

Pepper Steak EASY

If you can't find Italian-style stewed tomatoes and tomato paste, use the plain varieties and add 1 teaspoon dried Italian seasoning, crushed.

Prep: 15 minutes **Cook:** 10 to 12 hours (low) or 5 to 6 hours (high) **Makes:** 4 main-dish servings

- **1 pound boneless beef round steak, cut ¾ to 1 inch thick**
- **Salt**
- **Black pepper**
- **1 tablespoon cooking oil**
- **1 14.5-ounce can Italian-style stewed tomatoes, undrained**
- **3 tablespoons Italian-style tomato paste**
- **1 teaspoon Worcestershire sauce**
- **1 16-ounce package frozen pepper stir-fry vegetables (yellow, green, and red sweet peppers and onion)**

1. Trim fat from meat. Cut meat into four pieces; sprinkle lightly with salt and black pepper. In a large skillet brown meat on both sides in hot oil. Transfer to a 3½- or 4-quart slow cooker. In a bowl stir together undrained tomatoes, tomato paste, and Worcestershire sauce; pour over meat in cooker. Top with frozen stir-fry vegetables.

2. Cover and cook on low-heat setting for 10 to 12 hours or on high-heat setting for 5 to 6 hours or until meat and vegetables are tender.

Per 3 ounces beef + ½ cup vegetables: 344 cal., 18 g total fat (6 g sat. fat), 71 mg chol., 496 mg sodium, 17 g carbo., 4 g fiber, 25 g pro.
Daily Values: 42% vit. A, 34% vit. C, 6% calcium, 20% iron
Exchanges: 3 Vegetable, 2½ Medium-Fat Meat, 1 Fat

Beef and Chipotle Burritos

Chipotle peppers are smoked jalapeños that are usually canned in a rich adobo sauce. Look for them with other canned chile peppers in the Mexican foods section of your supermarket.

Prep: 20 minutes **Cook:** 8 to 10 hours (low) or 4 to 5 hours (high) **Makes:** 6 burritos

- **1½ pounds boneless beef round steak, cut ¾ inch thick**
- **1 14.5-ounce can diced tomatoes, undrained**
- **⅓ cup chopped onion (1 small)**
- **1 to 2 canned chipotle peppers in adobo sauce, chopped (see tip, page 74)**
- **1 teaspoon dried oregano, crushed**
- **¼ teaspoon ground cumin**
- **1 clove garlic, minced**
- **6 9- to 10-inch tomato-flavored or plain flour tortillas, warmed**
- **¾ cup shredded sharp cheddar cheese (3 ounces)**
- **1 recipe Pico de Gallo Salsa**
- **Shredded jicama or radishes (optional)**
- **Dairy sour cream (optional)**

1. Trim fat from meat. Cut meat into six pieces. In a 3½- or 4-quart slow cooker place meat, undrained tomatoes, onion, chipotle pepper, oregano, cumin, and garlic.

2. Cover and cook on low-heat setting for 8 to 10 hours or on high-heat setting for 4 to 5 hours. Remove meat from cooker. Using two forks, pull meat apart into shreds. Place shredded meat in a large bowl. Stir in enough cooking liquid to reach desired consistency. Divide meat among warm tortillas, spooning it just below the centers. Top with cheese, Pico de Gallo Salsa, and, if desired, jicama and sour cream. Roll up tortillas.

Pico de Gallo Salsa: In a small bowl combine 1 cup finely chopped tomatoes; 2 tablespoons finely chopped onion; 2 tablespoons snipped fresh cilantro; 1 fresh serrano chile pepper, seeded and finely chopped (see tip, page 74); and dash sugar. Cover; chill several hours.

Per burrito: 361 cal., 13 g total fat (5 g sat. fat), 71 mg chol., 433 mg sodium, 29 g carbo., 2 g fiber, 30 g pro.
Daily Values: 11% vit. A, 30% vit. C, 19% calcium, 26% iron
Exchanges: 1 Vegetable, 1½ Starch, ½ Medium-Fat Meat

Deviled Steak Strips LOW FAT EASY

For a smooth sauce, grind the tapioca in a clean coffee grinder or blender before adding it to the slow cooker.

Prep: 15 minutes **Cook:** 7 to 9 hours (low) or 3½ to 4½ hours (high) **Makes:** 6 to 8 main-dish servings

- 2 pounds boneless beef round steak
- 1 15-ounce can tomato sauce
- 1 cup chopped onion (1 large)
- 1 cup water
- 3 tablespoons quick-cooking tapioca
- 3 tablespoons horseradish mustard
- 3 cloves garlic, minced
- 2 teaspoons instant beef bouillon granules
- ¼ teaspoon black pepper
- 3 cups hot cooked noodles or mashed potatoes

1. Trim fat from meat. Thinly slice meat across the grain into bite-size strips. In a 3½- or 4-quart slow cooker stir together tomato sauce, onion, water, tapioca, mustard, garlic, bouillon, and pepper. Stir meat strips into onion mixture.

2. Cover and cook on low-heat setting for 7 to 9 hours or on high-heat setting for 3½ to 4½ hours. Serve over hot cooked noodles.

For a 1½-quart slow cooker: Prepare as above, except use 12 ounces round steak, one 8-ounce can tomato sauce, ½ cup chopped onion, ¼ cup water, 1 tablespoon tapioca, 1 tablespoon mustard, 2 cloves garlic, 1 teaspoon bouillon granules, and ⅛ teaspoon pepper. Cover and cook on low-heat setting for 6 to 8 hours or on high-heat setting for 3 to 4 hours. If the cooker does not have heat settings, cook for 5 to 6 hours. Makes 2 to 3 servings.

Per 1 cup + ½ cup noodles: 325 cal., 4 g total fat (1 g sat. fat), 86 mg chol., 754 mg sodium, 32 g carbo., 2 g fiber, 37 g pro. Daily Values: 3% vit. C, 3% calcium, 25% iron Exchanges: ½ Vegetable, 1½ Starch, 4½ Very Lean Meat, 1 Fat

Meatball and Vegetable Stew EASY

Frozen meatballs added straight from the bag make this recipe extra easy. See photo, page 527.

Prep: 10 minutes **Cook:** 6 to 8 hours (low) or 3 to 4 hours (high) **Makes:** 4 main-dish servings

- 1 16- to 18-ounce package frozen cooked meatballs
- ½ of a 16-ounce package (about 2 cups) frozen broccoli, corn, and red sweet peppers, or other mixed vegetables
- 1 14.5-ounce can diced tomatoes with onion and garlic or stewed tomatoes, undrained
- 1 12-ounce jar mushroom gravy
- ⅓ cup water
- 1½ teaspoons dried basil, crushed

1. In a 3½- or 4-quart slow cooker place meatballs and mixed vegetables. In a bowl stir together undrained tomatoes, gravy, water, and basil; pour over meatballs and vegetables in cooker.

2. Cover and cook on low-heat setting for 6 to 8 hours or on high-heat setting for 3 to 4 hours.

For a 5- or 6-quart slow cooker: Prepare as above, except double all ingredients. Makes 8 servings.

Per 1½ cups: 458 cal., 32 g total fat (14 g sat. fat), 87 mg chol., 2,003 mg sodium, 23 g carbo., 5 g fiber, 21 g pro. Daily Values: 69% vit. A, 31% vit. C, 9% calcium, 20% iron Exchanges: 1½ Vegetable, 1 Starch, 2 Medium-Fat Meat, 4 Fat

FAVORITE Spaghetti Sauce Italiano

Prep: 25 minutes **Cook:** 8 to 10 hours (low) or 4 to 5 hours (high) **Makes:** 6 to 8 main-dish servings

- 1 pound bulk Italian sausage or ground beef
- 1 cup chopped onion (1 large)
- 2 cloves garlic, minced
- 2 14.5-ounce cans diced tomatoes, undrained
- 1 6-ounce can tomato paste
- 2 4-ounce cans mushroom stems and pieces, drained
- 1 bay leaf
- 2 teaspoons dried Italian seasoning, crushed
- 1 cup chopped green sweet pepper (1 large)
- 12 to 16 ounces dried spaghetti, cooked and drained

  Finely shredded or grated Parmesan cheese (optional)

1. In a large skillet cook the sausage, onion, and garlic over medium heat until meat is brown and onion is tender. Drain off fat.

2. Meanwhile, in a 3½- or 4-quart slow cooker stir together undrained tomatoes, tomato paste, mushrooms, bay leaf, Italian seasoning, ½ teaspoon *salt*, and ¼ teaspoon *black pepper*. Stir in meat mixture.

3. Cover and cook on low-heat setting for 8 to 10 hours or on high-heat setting for 4 to 5 hours. Stir in sweet pepper. Discard bay leaf. Serve sauce over hot cooked spaghetti. If desired, sprinkle with Parmesan cheese.

Spicy Tomato-Cream Sauce: Prepare as above, except use hot Italian sausage and stir ½ cup whipping cream into sauce just before serving.

Per 1 cup sauce + 1 cup spaghetti regular or spicy variation: 517 cal., 18 g total fat (7 g sat. fat), 51 mg chol., 1,015 mg sodium, 61 g carbo., 5 g fiber, 22 g pro.
Daily Values: 2% vit. A, 69% vit. C, 10% calcium, 23% iron
Exchanges: 2 Vegetable, 3 Starch, 2 High-Fat Meat, ½ Fat

Pulled Pork with Root Beer Sauce `LOW FAT`   `EASY`

Look for root beer concentrate with the extracts in the spice section of your supermarket.

Prep: 15 minutes **Cook:** 8 to 10 hours (low) or 4 to 5 hours (high) **Makes:** 8 to 10 sandwiches

- 1 2½- to 3-pound pork sirloin roast
- ½ teaspoon salt
- ½ teaspoon black pepper
- 1 tablespoon cooking oil
- 2 medium onions, cut into thin wedges
- 1 cup root beer*
- 6 cloves garlic, minced
- 3 cups root beer* (two 12-ounce cans or bottles)
- 1 cup bottled chili sauce
- ¼ teaspoon root beer concentrate (optional)
   Several dashes bottled hot pepper sauce (optional)
- 8 to 10 hamburger buns, split (toasted, if desired)
   Lettuce leaves (optional)
   Tomato slices (optional)

1. Trim fat from meat. If necessary, cut meat to fit into a 3½- to 5-quart slow cooker. Sprinkle meat with the salt and pepper. In a large skillet brown meat on all sides in hot oil. Drain off fat. Transfer meat to cooker. Add onion, the 1 cup root beer, and the garlic.

Pulled Pork with Root Beer Sauce

2. Cover and cook on low-heat setting for 8 to 10 hours or on high-heat setting for 4 to 5 hours.

3. Meanwhile, for sauce, in a saucepan stir together the 3 cups root beer and the chili sauce. Bring to boiling; reduce heat. Simmer, uncovered, stirring occasionally, about 30 minutes or until mixture is reduced to 2 cups. If desired, add root beer concentrate and hot pepper sauce.

4. Transfer meat to a cutting board or serving platter. Using two forks, pull meat apart into shreds. Using a slotted spoon, transfer onion to serving platter; discard cooking juices. If desired, line buns with lettuce leaves and tomato slices. Place shredded meat and onion on rolls. Drizzle meat with some of the root beer sauce.

*Note: Do not use diet root beer.

Per sandwich: 433 cal., 12 g total fat (3 g sat. fat), 89 mg chol., 877 mg sodium, 45 g carbo., 3 g fiber, 35 g pro.
Daily Values: 4% vit. A, 14% vit. C, 10% calcium, 17% iron
Exchanges: 2 Starch, 1 Other Carbo., 4 Lean Meat

Potluck or Picnic Fare

Take your slow cooker along for a crowd-pleasing meal of pork sandwiches.

- *Pulled Pork with Root Beer Sauce (left)*
- *Creamy deli coleslaw*
- *Dill pickle spears*
- *Potato chips or corn chips*
- *Root beer*
- *Brownies or chocolate chip cookies*

 **Ranch Pork Roast** EASY

See photo, page 527.

Prep: 15 minutes **Cook:** 9 to 10 hours (low) or
4½ to 5 hours (high) **Makes:** 6 main-dish servings

- 1 2½-pound boneless pork shoulder roast
  Nonstick cooking spray
- 1 pound new red-skinned potatoes, halved
- 1 10.75-ounce can condensed cream of chicken soup
- 1 8-ounce package cream cheese, softened and cut up
- 1 0.4-ounce envelope ranch dry salad dressing mix

1. Trim fat from meat. Lightly coat a large skillet with cooking spray; heat skillet over medium heat. In hot skillet brown meat on all sides. Remove from heat.

2. Place potatoes in a 3½- or 4-quart slow cooker. Place meat on potatoes. In a bowl whisk together soup, cream cheese, and dressing mix. Spoon over meat and potatoes in cooker.

3. Cover and cook on low-heat setting for 9 to 10 hours or on high-heat setting for 4½ to 5 hours.

Per 5 ounces pork + ⅔ cup sauce: 521 cal., 31 g total fat
(15 g sat. fat), 173 mg chol., 757 mg sodium, 16 g carbo., 1 g fiber,
42 g pro.
Daily Values: 15% vit. A, 17% vit. C, 9% calcium, 21% iron
Exchanges: 1 Starch, 5½ Lean Meat, 3 Fat

Creamy Ranch Potatoes: Prepare as above, except omit pork roast, use 2½ pounds potatoes, and substitute one 8-ounce carton dairy sour cream for cream cheese. Cover and cook on low-heat setting for 7 to 8 hours or on high-heat setting for 3½ to 4 hours. Stir before serving. Makes 6 side-dish servings.

Per cup: 245 cal., 12 g total fat (6 g sat. fat), 17 mg chol.,
517 mg sodium, 30 g carbo., 2 g fiber, 5 g pro.
Daily Values: 6% vit. A, 31% vit. C, 7% calcium, 12% iron
Exchanges: 2 Starch, 2 Fat

Sauerkraut and Pork Shoulder Roast LOW FAT EASY

Serve this German-style pork with spaetzle, mashed potatoes, noodles, or boiled new potatoes.

Prep: 15 minutes **Cook:** 8 to 10 hours (low) or
4 to 5 hours (high) **Makes:** 8 main-dish servings

- 1 14.5-ounce can sauerkraut with caraway seeds, rinsed and drained
- 1 2½-pound boneless pork shoulder roast
  Salt and black pepper

- 2 tablespoons Dijon-style mustard
- 1 cup beer or nonalcoholic beer

1. Place sauerkraut in a 3½- or 4-quart slow cooker. Trim fat from meat. If necessary, cut meat to fit into the slow cooker. Lightly sprinkle meat with salt and pepper. Spread mustard over meat. Place meat on top of sauerkraut in cooker. Pour beer over the meat.

2. Cover and cook on low-heat setting for 8 to 10 hours or on high-heat setting for 4 to 5 hours. Transfer meat to a cutting board; cool slightly. Slice meat, discarding any fat. Serve meat with sauerkraut.

Per 4 ounces pork + ¼ cup sauerkraut: 230 cal., 10 g total fat
(3 g sat. fat), 92 mg chol., 546 mg sodium, 4 g carbo., 1 g fiber,
29 g pro.
Daily Values: 15% vit. A, 83% vit. C, 3% calcium, 14% iron
Exchanges: 4 Lean Meat

Open-Face Pork Sandwiches: Prepare as above, except toast 8 rye bread slices; spread one side of each slice with 2 teaspoons Dijon-style mustard. Arrange slices on baking sheet. Using two forks, pull meat apart into shreds. Top each bread slice with drained sauerkraut, shredded meat, and 2 tablespoons shredded Swiss cheese. Place under broiler 3 to 4 inches from the heat. Broil for 2 to 3 minutes or until cheese melts. Makes 8 sandwiches.

Per sandwich: 372 cal., 15 g total fat (6 g sat. fat), 105 mg chol.,
1,024 mg sodium, 22 g carbo., 3 g fiber, 37 g pro.
Daily Values: 3% vit. A, 15% vit. C, 17% calcium, 21% iron
Exchanges: 1 Starch, ½ Other Carbo., 4½ Lean Meat

Country-Style Pork Ribs

Prep: 15 minutes **Cook:** 10 to 12 hours (low) or
5 to 6 hours (high) + 10 minutes
Makes: 4 to 6 main-dish servings

- 1 large onion, sliced and separated into rings
- 2½ to 3 pounds country-style pork ribs
- 1½ cups vegetable juice cocktail
- ½ of a 6-ounce can (⅓ cup) tomato paste
- ¼ cup molasses
- 3 tablespoons cider vinegar
- 1 teaspoon dry mustard
- ¼ teaspoon salt
- ¼ teaspoon black pepper
- ⅛ teaspoon dried thyme, crushed
- ⅛ teaspoon dried rosemary, crushed

1. Place onion in a 3½- to 6-quart slow cooker. Place ribs on top of onion in cooker. In a medium bowl stir together remaining ingredients.

Reserve 1 cup juice mixture for sauce; cover and chill. Pour remaining juice mixture over ribs in the cooker.

2. Cover and cook on low-heat setting for 10 to 12 hours or on high-heat setting for 5 to 6 hours.

3. For sauce, heat reserved juice mixture to boiling; reduce heat. Simmer, uncovered, for 10 minutes. Transfer ribs to serving platter; discard cooking liquid. Serve sauce with ribs.

Per 6 ounces pork + ¼ cup sauce: 354 cal., 13 g total fat (4 g sat. fat), 101 mg chol., 518 mg sodium, 26 g carbo., 2 g fiber, 33 g pro.
Daily Values: 22% vit. A, 54% vit. C, 10% calcium, 20% iron
Exchanges: 1 Vegetable, 1½ Other Carbo., 4 Lean Meat, ½ Fat

Pork and Edamame Soup

Edamame (green soybeans) add color and nutrition to this soup.

Prep: 25 minutes **Cook:** 7 to 8 hours (low) or 3½ to 4 hours (high), + 5 minutes **Makes:** 6 main-dish servings

- **2 pounds boneless pork shoulder roast**
- **1 tablespoon cooking oil**
- **2 14-ounce cans chicken broth**
- **1 12-ounce package frozen edamame**
- **1 8-ounce can sliced water chestnuts, drained**
- **1 cup chopped red sweet pepper (1 large)**
- **2 tablespoons light soy sauce**
- **1 tablespoon bottled hoisin sauce**
- **2 teaspoons grated fresh ginger**
- **¼ to ½ teaspoon crushed red pepper**
- **6 cloves garlic, minced**
- **1 3-ounce package ramen noodles, broken**

1. Trim fat from meat. Cut meat into 1-inch pieces. In a large skillet brown meat, half at a time, in hot oil. Drain off fat.

2. Transfer meat to a 3½- or 4-quart slow cooker. Stir in broth, edamame, water chestnuts, sweet pepper, soy sauce, hoisin sauce, ginger, crushed red pepper, and garlic.

3. Cover and cook on low-heat setting for 7 to 8 hours or on high-heat setting for 3½ to 4 hours. Skim off fat. Stir in ramen noodles (reserve seasoning packet for another use). Cover and cook for 5 minutes more.

Per 1½ cups: 400 cal., 15 g total fat (4 g sat. fat), 111 mg chol., 906 mg sodium, 22 g carbo., 7 g fiber, 41 g pro.
Daily Values: 29% vit. A, 85% vit. C, 8% calcium, 23% iron
Exchanges: 1½ Starch, 2 Very Lean Meat, 3½ Lean Meat, ½ Fat

Irish Stew

Prep: 30 minutes **Cook:** 10 to 12 hours (low) or 5 to 6 hours (high) **Makes:** 4 or 5 main-dish servings

- **1 pound lean boneless lamb**
- **1 tablespoon cooking oil**
- **2½ cups peeled turnip cut into ½-inch pieces (2 medium)**
- **1½ cups carrot cut into ½-inch pieces (3 medium)**
- **1½ cups peeled potato cut into ½-inch pieces (2 medium)**
- **2 medium onions, cut into wedges**
- **¼ cup quick-cooking tapioca**
- **½ teaspoon salt**
- **¼ teaspoon black pepper**
- **¼ teaspoon dried thyme, crushed**
- **3 cups beef broth**

1. Cut meat into 1-inch pieces. In a large skillet brown meat, half at a time, in hot oil. Drain off fat. In a 3½- or 4-quart slow cooker stir together turnip, carrot, potato, onion, tapioca, salt, pepper, and thyme. Stir in meat and the beef broth.

2. Cover and cook on low-heat setting for 10 to 12 hours or on high-heat setting for 5 to 6 hours.

Per 1½ cups: 442 cal., 22 g total fat (9 g sat. fat), 75 mg chol., 1,037 mg sodium, 35 g carbo., 5 g fiber, 25 g pro.
Daily Values: 231% vit. A, 45% vit. C, 6% calcium, 19% iron
Exchanges: 1 Vegetable, 2 Starch, 2½ Lean Meat, 2 Fat

Pork and Edamame Soup

Moroccan Lamb Shanks

Moroccan Lamb Shanks

If you can't find lamb shanks halved crosswise, ask the butcher to cut them for you.

Prep: 25 minutes **Cook:** 9 to 10 hours (low) or 4½ to 5 hours (high) **Makes:** 6 main-dish servings

    3½ pounds lamb shanks, halved crosswise
        (3 to 4 shanks)
      Salt
      Black pepper
    ¼ cup all-purpose flour
    2 tablespoons cooking oil
    ½ cup dried apricots
    ½ cup pitted dried plums (prunes), halved
    ½ cup raisins
    ¾ cup beef broth
    2 tablespoons sugar
    2 tablespoons cider vinegar
    2 tablespoons lemon juice
    ½ teaspoon ground allspice
    ½ teaspoon ground cinnamon
    1 tablespoon cornstarch
    1 tablespoon cold water
    4 cups hot cooked rice

1. Sprinkle lamb shanks with salt and pepper. Coat with flour. In a large skillet brown meat on all sides in hot oil. Drain off fat. In a 3½- or 4-quart slow cooker stir together apricots, plums, raisins, broth, sugar, vinegar, lemon juice, allspice, and cinnamon. Add meat to cooker.

2. Cover and cook on low-heat setting for 9 to 10 hours or on high-heat setting for 4½ to 5 hours or until lamb is tender. Transfer shanks to a serving platter; keep warm.

3. For gravy, strain cooking juices into a glass measuring cup, reserving the fruit. Skim fat from juices. Measure juices, adding water, if necessary, to equal 1½ cups. Pour into a medium saucepan. Combine cornstarch and the cold water; stir into juices in saucepan. Cook and stir over medium heat until thickened and bubbly; cook and stir for 2 minutes more. Stir in reserved fruit. Heat through. To serve, place lamb shanks on hot cooked rice and spoon gravy over top.

Per ½ shank + ¾ cup rice + ⅓ cup sauce: 543 cal., 13 g total fat (4 g sat. fat), 116 mg chol., 241 mg sodium, 65 g carbo., 3 g fiber, 42 g pro.
Daily Values: 22% vit. A, 6% vit. C, 4% calcium, 34% iron
Exchanges: 1 Fruit, 3 Starch, 4½ Lean Meat

Tuscan Lamb Shanks

Pesto sauce is a simple way to infuse a dish with a great deal of flavor. For even more flavor, sprinkle a pesto-seasoned dish such as this one with shredded lemon peel and snipped fresh parsley.

Prep: 20 minutes **Cook:** 10 to 12 hours (low) or 5 to 6 hours (high) **Makes:** 6 to 8 main-dish servings

    1 16-ounce package frozen Italian vegetables
        (zucchini, carrots, cauliflower, lima beans,
        Italian beans)
    1 14.5-ounce can diced tomatoes with basil,
        garlic, and oregano, undrained
    1 15- or 19-ounce can cannellini (white
        kidney) beans, rinsed and drained
    1 14-ounce can chicken broth
    ½ cup refrigerated basil pesto
    3 to 3½ pounds lamb shanks, halved
        crosswise (3 to 4 shanks)

1. In a large bowl stir together the frozen vegetables, undrained tomatoes, beans, broth, and pesto. Place lamb shanks in a 5- or 6-quart slow cooker. Pour vegetable mixture over the meat.

2. Cover and cook on low-heat setting for 10 to 12 hours or on high-heat setting for 5 to 6 hours. Using a slotted spoon, transfer meat and vegetables to a serving platter.

Per ½ shank + ¾ cup vegetables: 350 cal., 16 g total fat (1 g sat. fat), 67 mg chol., 989 mg sodium, 24 g carbo., 5 g fiber, 29 g pro.
Daily Values: 53% vit. A, 17% vit. C, 9% calcium, 19% iron
Exchanges: 1½ Vegetable, 1 Starch, 3 Lean Meat, 1½ Fat

Spicy Chicken with Peppers and Olives LOW FAT

Purchased pasta sauce makes the difference in this recipe. If spicy red pepper sauce is not available, substitute your favorite variety.

Prep: 20 minutes **Cook:** 6 to 7 hours (low) or 3 to 3½ hours (high) **Makes:** 6 main-dish servings

- 2½ to 3 pounds meaty chicken pieces (breasts, thighs, and drumsticks), skinned
  Salt
  Black pepper
- ½ cup coarsely chopped yellow sweet pepper (1 small)
- ½ cup sliced, pitted ripe olives and/or pimiento-stuffed green olives
- 1 26-ounce jar spicy red pepper pasta sauce
  Hot cooked pasta (optional)

1. Place the chicken pieces in a 3½- or 4-quart slow cooker. Sprinkle lightly with salt and black pepper. Add sweet pepper and olives to cooker. Pour pasta sauce over chicken mixture in cooker.

2. Cover and cook on low-heat setting for 6 to 7 hours or on high-heat setting for 3 to 3½ hours. If desired, serve chicken and sauce over hot cooked pasta.

Per 6 ounces chicken + ⅔ cup sauce: 239 cal., 10 g total fat (2 g sat. fat), 77 mg chol., 592 mg sodium, 10 g carbo., 3 g fiber, 27 g pro.
Daily Values: 10% vit. A, 79% vit. C, 8% calcium, 12% iron
Exchanges: 1 Vegetable, ½ Other Carbo., 3½ Lean Meat

Hearty Tuscan Dinner

A few simple additions complete this rich, warming meal.

- *Tuscan Lamb Shanks (page 540)*
- *Hot cooked fettuccine or penne pasta*
- *Fresh spinach salad with bottled balsamic vinaigrette*
- *Crusty country Italian bread*
- *Purchased gelato*

Italian Chicken and Pasta LOW FAT EASY

You can vary this recipe every time you make it. For the pasta, prepare spinach or red pepper fettuccine. Use regular frozen green beans instead of Italian-style or try a different kind of mushroom.

Prep: 15 minutes **Cook:** 5 to 6 hours (low) or 2½ to 3 hours (high) **Makes:** 4 main-dish servings

- 1 9-ounce package frozen Italian-style green beans
- 1 cup fresh mushrooms, quartered
- 1 small onion, cut into ¼-inch-thick slices
- 12 ounces skinless, boneless chicken thighs, cut into 1-inch pieces
- 1 14.5-ounce can Italian-style stewed tomatoes, undrained
- 1 6-ounce can Italian-style tomato paste
- 1 teaspoon dried Italian seasoning, crushed
- 2 cloves garlic, minced
- 6 ounces dried fettuccine, cooked and drained
  Finely shredded or grated Parmesan cheese (optional)

1. In a 3½- or 4-quart slow cooker stir together green beans, mushrooms, and onion. Place chicken on vegetables in cooker.

2. In a small bowl stir together undrained tomatoes, tomato paste, Italian seasoning, and garlic. Pour over chicken in cooker.

3. Cover and cook on low-heat setting for 5 to 6 hours or on high-heat setting for 2½ to 3 hours. Serve chicken mixture over hot fettuccine. If desired, sprinkle with Parmesan cheese.

For a 1½-quart slow cooker: Prepare as above, except use 1 cup green beans, ½ cup mushrooms, 1 small onion, 8 ounces chicken thighs, one 8-ounce can tomato sauce, ½ teaspoon Italian seasoning, 1 clove garlic, and 3 ounces dried fettuccine. Omit stewed tomatoes. Cover and cook as above. If the cooker does not have heat settings, cook for 4 to 5 hours. Stir 1 chopped roma tomato into cooker just before serving. Makes 2 servings.

Per 1½ cups chicken mixture + ¾ cup fettuccine: 405 cal., 7 g total fat (2 g sat. fat), 75 mg chol., 728 mg sodium, 55 g carbo., 4 g fiber, 28 g pro.
Daily Values: 7% vit. A, 46% vit. C, 15% calcium, 26% iron
Exchanges: 3½ Vegetable, 2½ Starch, 2 Lean Meat

Chicken with Mushroom Stuffing

Chicken with Mushroom Stuffing

Putting the stuffing on top of the chicken in the cooker keeps both of them moist and flavorful.

Prep: 40 minutes **Cook:** 4 to 5 hours (high)
Makes: 8 main-dish servings

    Nonstick cooking spray
  2 tablespoons finely shredded lemon peel
  1 tablespoon ground sage
  1 tablespoon seasoned salt
1½ teaspoons black pepper
  8 small chicken legs (drumstick-thigh portion) (about 5 pounds), skinned
  4 cups quartered or sliced fresh mushrooms, such as cremini, baby portobellos, shiitakes, and/or buttons
  2 cloves garlic, thinly sliced
¼ cup butter
  8 cups sourdough baguette cut into 1-inch pieces (about 10 ounces)
  1 cup coarsely shredded carrot (2 medium)
  1 cup chicken broth
¼ cup chopped walnuts, toasted (see tip, page 265)
  3 tablespoons snipped fresh Italian parsley

1. Lightly coat inside of a 6-quart slow cooker with cooking spray. Reserve 1 teaspoon lemon peel. Combine remaining lemon peel, sage, seasoned salt, and pepper. Rub 3 tablespoons sage mixture onto chicken legs. Place legs in cooker.

2. In a large skillet cook mushrooms and garlic in hot butter over medium heat for 3 to 5 minutes or just until tender. Stir in the remaining tablespoon sage mixture. Transfer mushroom mixture to a large bowl. Add baguette pieces and carrot. Drizzle with broth, tossing gently to combine. Lightly pack stuffing on top of chicken in cooker.

3. Cover and cook on high-heat setting for 4 to 5 hours. Using a slotted spoon, transfer stuffing and chicken to a serving platter; discard juices in cooker. In a small bowl combine the reserved 1 teaspoon lemon peel, the walnuts, and parsley. Before serving, sprinkle nut mixture over chicken and stuffing.

Per 1 leg + ¾ cup stuffing: 412 cal., 17 g total fat (5 g sat. fat), 146 mg chol., 1,450 mg sodium, 27 g carbo., 3 g fiber, 39 g pro. **Daily Values:** 45% vit. A, 17% vit. C, 7% calcium, 19% iron **Exchanges:** ½ Vegetable, 1½ Starch, 5 Lean Meat

FAVORITE Creamy Chicken and Noodles LOW FAT

Prep: 25 minutes **Cook:** 8 to 9 hours (low) or 4 to 4½ hours (high) **Makes:** 6 main-dish servings

  2 cups sliced carrot (4 medium)
1½ cups chopped onion (3 medium)
  1 cup sliced celery (2 stalks)
  2 tablespoons snipped fresh parsley
  1 bay leaf
  3 medium chicken legs (drumstick-thigh portion) (about 2 pounds), skinned
  2 10.75-ounce cans reduced-fat and reduced-sodium condensed cream of chicken soup
½ cup water
  1 teaspoon dried thyme, crushed
¼ teaspoon black pepper
 10 ounces dried wide noodles (about 5 cups)
  1 cup frozen peas
    Salt (optional)
    Black pepper (optional)

1. In a 3½- or 4-quart slow cooker place carrot, onion, celery, parsley, and bay leaf. Place chicken on top of vegetables. In a medium bowl stir together soup, water, thyme, and the ¼ teaspoon pepper. Pour over chicken and vegetables in cooker.

2. Cover and cook on low-heat setting for 8 to 9 hours or on high-heat setting for 4 to 4½ hours. Remove chicken from cooker; cool slightly. Discard bay leaf.

3. Cook noodles according to package directions; drain. Stir peas into soup mixture in cooker. Remove chicken meat from bones; discard bones. Cut meat into bite-size pieces; stir into soup mixture in cooker. To serve, spoon chicken mixture over noodles; toss gently to combine. If desired, season to taste with salt and pepper.

Per 1½ cups chicken mixture + ¾ cup noodles: 396 cal., 7 g total fat (1 g sat. fat), 114 mg chol., 554 mg sodium, 56 g carbo., 5 g fiber, 26 g pro.
Daily Values: 213% vit. A, 21% vit. C, 6% calcium, 20% iron
Exchanges: 1 Vegetable, 3½ Starch, 2 Very Lean Meat

Chicken with Creamy Chive Sauce EASY

Prep: 15 minutes **Cook:** 4 to 5 hours (low)
Makes: 6 main-dish servings

  6 skinless, boneless chicken breast halves (about 1¾ pounds)
  ¼ cup butter or margarine
  1 0.7-ounce package Italian salad dressing mix
  1 10.75-ounce can condensed golden mushroom soup
  ½ cup dry white wine
  ½ of an 8-ounce tub cream cheese with chives and onion
    Hot cooked pasta (optional)

1. Place chicken in a 3½- or 4-quart slow cooker. In a medium saucepan melt the butter over medium heat. Stir in dressing mix. Stir in mushroom soup, wine, and cream cheese until combined. Pour over the chicken in cooker.

2. Cover and cook on low-heat setting for 4 to 5 hours. Serve chicken with sauce. If desired, serve with hot cooked pasta and sprinkle with snipped *fresh chives.*

Per chicken breast half + ½ cup sauce: 342 cal., 17 g total fat (9 g sat. fat), 117 mg chol., 1,119 mg sodium, 7 g carbo., 0 g fiber, 32 g pro.
Daily Values: 17% vit. A, 4% calcium, 6% iron
Exchanges: ½ Other Carbo., 4½ Very Lean Meat, 3½ Fat

White Chicken Chili LOW FAT

Prep: 25 minutes **Cook:** 8 to 10 hours (low) or 4 to 5 hours (high) **Makes:** 6 main-dish servings

  3 15- to 15.5-ounce cans Great Northern, pinto, or cannellini (white kidney) beans, rinsed and drained
2½ cups chopped cooked chicken
  1 cup chopped onion (1 large)
1½ cups chopped red, green, and/or yellow sweet pepper (2 medium)

  2 fresh jalapeño chile peppers, seeded and chopped (see tip, page 74)
  2 cloves garlic, minced
  2 teaspoons ground cumin
  ½ teaspoon salt
  ½ teaspoon dried oregano, crushed
3½ cups chicken broth
    Shredded Monterey Jack cheese (optional)
    Broken tortilla chips (optional)

1. In a 3½- or 4-quart slow cooker stir together the drained beans, chicken, onion, sweet pepper, jalapeño pepper, garlic, cumin, salt, and oregano. Stir in chicken broth.

2. Cover and cook on low-heat setting for 8 to 10 hours or on high-heat setting for 4 to 5 hours. If desired, top each serving with shredded cheese and broken tortilla chips.

Per 1½ cups: 422 cal., 6 g total fat (2 g sat. fat), 52 mg chol., 709 mg sodium, 54 g carbo., 13 g fiber, 38 g pro.
Daily Values: 42% vit. A, 112% vit. C, 16% calcium, 28% iron
Exchanges: ½ Vegetable, 3½ Starch, 4 Very Lean Meat

Smoky Chicken and Cheesy Potato Casserole

Smoked chicken and cheese add their distinctive flavors to this creamy comfort-food casserole.

Prep: 20 minutes **Cook:** 5 to 6 hours (low)
Makes: 6 main-dish servings

    Nonstick cooking spray
  1 10.75-ounce can condensed cream of chicken with herbs soup
  1 8-ounce carton dairy sour cream
  6 ounces smoked cheddar cheese, shredded (1½ cups)
  1 28-ounce package frozen diced hash brown potatoes with onion and peppers, thawed
  3 cups chopped smoked or roasted chicken or turkey
    Crushed croutons (optional)

1. Lightly coat the inside of a 3½- or 4-quart slow cooker with cooking spray. In the cooker stir together the soup, sour cream, cheese, potatoes, and chicken.

2. Cover and cook on low-heat setting for 5 to 6 hours. If desired, top each serving with crushed croutons.

Per 1¼ cups: 399 cal., 20 g total fat (12 g sat. fat), 80 mg chol., 1,313 mg sodium, 31 g carbo., 3 g fiber, 25 g pro.
Daily Values: 20% vit. A, 25% vit. C, 27% calcium, 10% iron
Exchanges: 2 Starch, 2 Very Lean Meat, 1 High-Fat Meat, 1½ Fat

Hot Kielbasa and Potato Salad

juices over the spinach on each plate. Using a slotted spoon, remove potatoes and sausage from cooker; arrange on top of spinach.

Per 1½ cups: 339 cal., 10 g total fat (3 g sat. fat), 70 mg chol., 1,227 mg sodium, 43 g carbo., 7 g fiber, 23 g pro.
Daily Values: 86% vit. A, 41% vit. C, 8% calcium, 15% iron
Exchanges: 2 Vegetable, 1 Starch, 1 Other Carbo., 2½ Lean Meat

Chicken and Sausage Gumbo

Save time by making the roux (thickener) ahead and refrigerating it.

Prep: 40 minutes **Cook:** 6 to 7 hours (low) or 3 to 3½ hours (high) **Makes:** 6 main-dish servings

- ⅓ cup all-purpose flour
- ⅓ cup cooking oil
- 3 cups water
- 12 ounces cooked smoked turkey sausage links, quartered lengthwise and sliced
- 1½ cups chopped cooked chicken or 12 ounces skinless, boneless chicken breasts or thighs, cut into ¾-inch pieces
- 2 cups sliced okra or one 10-ounce package frozen whole okra, partially thawed and cut into ½-inch slices
- 1 cup chopped onion (1 large)
- ½ cup chopped green sweet pepper (1 small)
- ½ cup chopped celery (1 stalk)
- 4 cloves garlic, minced
- ½ teaspoon salt
- ½ teaspoon black pepper
- ¼ teaspoon cayenne pepper
- 3 cups hot cooked rice

1. For roux, in a medium heavy saucepan stir together flour and oil until smooth. Cook and stir constantly over medium-high heat for 5 minutes. Reduce heat to medium. Cook and stir constantly about 15 minutes more or until a dark reddish brown color is reached; cool.

2. Place water in a 3½- or 4-quart slow cooker. Stir in the roux. Add sausage, chicken, okra, onion, sweet pepper, celery, garlic, salt, black pepper, and cayenne pepper.

3. Cover and cook on low-heat setting for 6 to 7 hours or on high-heat setting for 3 to 3½ hours. Skim off fat. Serve gumbo over hot cooked rice.

Per 1½ cups gumbo + ⅔ cup rice: 419 cal., 20 g total fat (4 g sat. fat), 66 mg chol., 759 mg sodium, 36 g carbo., 2 g fiber, 22 g pro.
Daily Values: 5% vit. A, 33% vit. C, 6% calcium, 12% iron
Exchanges: 1 Vegetable, 2 Starch, 2½ Lean Meat, 2 Fat

Hot Kielbasa and Potato Salad LOW FAT

Kielbasa, another name for Polish sausage, makes this German-style potato salad hearty enough to be a main dish. Fresh spinach makes it a meal.

Prep: 25 minutes **Cook:** 6 to 8 hours (low) or 4 to 4½ hours (high) **Makes:** 4 main-dish servings

- 10 to 12 whole tiny new potatoes (about 12 ounces)
- 1 pound cooked turkey kielbasa or smoked sausage, cut into 1-inch pieces
- 1 cup chopped onion (1 large)
- 1 cup chopped celery (2 stalks)
- 1 cup water
- ⅔ cup cider vinegar
- ¼ cup sugar
- 2 tablespoons quick-cooking tapioca
- ¾ teaspoon celery seeds
- ¼ teaspoon black pepper
- 6 cups fresh baby spinach leaves

1. Cut potatoes into halves or quarters. Place potatoes in a 3½- or 4-quart slow cooker. Add sausage, onion, and celery. In a medium bowl stir together the water, vinegar, sugar, tapioca, celery seeds, and pepper. Pour over vegetables and sausage in cooker.

2. Cover and cook on low-heat setting for 6 to 8 hours or on high-heat setting for 4 to 4½ hours.

3. To serve, divide spinach among four salad dishes. Drizzle 2 tablespoons of the cooking

Soups & Stews

Red and Green Gazpacho, 569

Polenta Beef Stew, 550

Cheesy Vegetable and
Ham Chowder, 558

Soups & Stews Essentials

Making soup can take hours or minutes. Whatever amount of time you invest, your soup will soothe as well as nourish.

Soup Basics

One of the many great things about making soup is that it doesn't require a lot of fancy equipment or advanced cooking techniques. A Dutch oven or a slow cooker, a good knife, a cutting board, measuring cups and spoons, stirring spoons, and ladles are all you need.

All soups are cooked in a liquid, usually a stock or broth. There are four types of stocks or broths: poultry, meat, vegetable, or seafood. Stocks and broths generally are interchangeable. Broths tend to be lighter tasting than stocks, which often have a more intense flavor. Although homemade broths are ideal (see recipes on pages 548 and 549), many of the stocks and broths available for purchase taste great and, most important, are convenient. For the most natural flavor, use reduced-sodium broths and adjust the seasoning according to your taste.

Serving Soup

Enjoy soup at the correct temperature—hot or cold—with these easy tips. To warm bowls, preheat your oven to its lowest temperature, then turn it off. Place the bowls in the oven for 5 to 10 minutes before serving. To chill your bowls, place them in the refrigerator for 10 to 15 minutes before serving.

Top It Off

Toppings really add to the flavor of a soup. Try one of these:

- Bacon, crisp-cooked and crumbled
- Cheeses, shredded
- Croutons (purchased or homemade)
- Green onion, thinly sliced
- Olive oil
- Pesto
- Phyllo dough, cut into strips and baked
- Pine nuts, toasted
- Popped popcorn
- Puff pastry, cut into triangles or squares and baked
- Salsa
- Sliced almonds, toasted
- Sour cream, crème fraîche, or yogurt
- Tapenade
- Tortilla chips, crumbled
- Wonton strips, crispy fried

Storing Leftovers

Many soup recipes make large quantities, providing welcome leftovers. A lot of soups taste even better a day after making them because flavors have a chance to meld.

For short-term storage, ladle the cooled soup into a container that has a cover and store it in the refrigerator for up to 3 days. For longer storage, ladle cooled soup into an airtight container, cover, and freeze for up to 6 months. For food safety reasons always defrost soups in the refrigerator, not at room temperature.

Perfectly Pureed

Creamy soups generally are pureed. Many vegetable or bean soups are partially pureed. You can use an immersion blender, blender, or food processor to blend soups. An immersion blender allows you to leave the soup in the Dutch oven, making it easier, safer, and less messy to use than a blender or food processor. If using a blender, make sure the lid is secure. Remove the round plastic piece in the center of the lid and hold a kitchen towel over the opening; this will allow the steam to escape as you blend. Always blend on low speed to avoid a dangerous expulsion.

Beef Broth `LOW FAT`

If the soup bones you use to make this broth are meaty, they will yield 3 to 4 cups of meat that you can save to add to soups, stews, or casserole dishes.

Prep: 30 minutes **Bake:** 30 minutes **Oven:** 450°F
Cook: 3½ hours **Makes:** 8 to 9 cups

  4 **pounds meaty beef soup bones (beef shank cross cuts or short ribs)**
  ½ **cup water**
  3 **carrots, cut up**
  2 **medium onions, unpeeled and cut up**
  2 **stalks celery with leaves, cut up**
  1 **tablespoon dried basil or thyme, crushed**
1½ **teaspoons salt**
10 **whole black peppercorns**
  8 **sprigs fresh parsley**
  4 **bay leaves**
  2 **cloves garlic, unpeeled and halved**
10 **cups water**

1. Place soup bones in a large shallow roasting pan. Bake in a 450°F oven about 30 minutes or until well browned, turning once. Place soup bones in a large kettle. Pour the ½ cup water into the roasting pan and scrape up browned bits; add water mixture to kettle. Stir in carrot, onion, celery, basil, salt, peppercorns, parsley, bay leaves, and garlic. Add the 10 cups water. Bring to boiling; reduce heat. Simmer, covered, for 3½ hours. Remove soup bones from broth.

2. Strain broth (see photo, below right). Discard vegetables and seasonings. If desired, clarify broth* (see note, right). If using the broth while hot, skim fat (see tip, page 552). Or chill broth; lift off fat. If desired, when bones are cool enough to handle, remove meat; reserve meat for another use. Discard bones. Place broth and reserved meat in separate containers. Cover and chill for up to 3 days or freeze for up to 6 months.

Per cup: 20 cal., 1 g total fat (1 g sat. fat), 5 mg chol., 409 mg sodium, 1 g carbo., 0 g fiber, 2 g pro.
Daily Values: 1% calcium, 1% iron
Exchanges: Free

Chicken Broth `LOW FAT`

Prep: 25 minutes **Cook:** 2½ hours
Makes: about 6 cups

  3 **pounds bony chicken pieces (wings, backs, and/or necks)**
  3 **stalks celery with leaves, cut up**
  2 **carrots, cut up**
  1 **large onion, unpeeled and cut up**
  1 **teaspoon salt**
  1 **teaspoon dried thyme, sage, or basil, crushed**
  ½ **teaspoon whole black peppercorns or ¼ teaspoon black pepper**
  4 **sprigs fresh parsley**
  2 **bay leaves**
  2 **garlic cloves, unpeeled and halved**
  6 **cups cold water**

1. If using wings, cut each wing at joints into three pieces. Place chicken pieces in a 6-quart kettle. Add celery, carrot, onion, salt, thyme, peppercorns, parsley, bay leaves, and garlic. Add the 6 cups water. Bring to boiling; reduce heat. Simmer, covered, for 2½ hours. Remove chicken pieces from broth.

2. Strain broth (see photo, below). Discard vegetables and seasonings. If desired, clarify broth.* If using the broth while hot, skim fat (see tip, page 552). Or chill broth; lift off fat. If desired, when bones are cool enough to handle, remove meat and reserve it for another use; discard bones. Place broth and reserved meat in separate containers. Cover and chill for up to 3 days or freeze for up to 6 months.

***Note:** To clarify hot, strained broth, return the broth to the kettle. Combine ¼ cup cold water and 1 beaten egg white. Stir water mixture into broth. Bring to boiling. Remove from heat. Let stand for 5 minutes; strain again (see photo, below).

Per cup: 30 cal., 2 g total fat (1 g sat. fat), 5 mg chol., 435 mg sodium, 1 g carbo., 0 g fiber, 2 g pro.
Daily Values: 1% calcium, 1% iron
Exchanges: ½ Fat

Line a large colander or sieve with two layers of 100-percent-cotton cheesecloth. Set the colander in a large heatproof bowl; carefully pour broth mixture into the lined colander.

Vegetable Stock `LOW FAT`

The herb you choose will depend on the type of soup in which you plan to use the stock. For example, for a fish or seafood soup, use dill. For an Italian-style soup, use basil. Or for chicken soup, use rosemary or marjoram.

Prep: 30 minutes **Cook:** 2 hours
Makes: about 8 cups

- 4 **medium carrots**
- 3 **medium potatoes**
- 2 **medium parsnips, turnips, or rutabagas**
- 1 **small head cabbage**
- 4 **medium yellow onions, unpeeled**
- 1 **tablespoon olive oil**
- 8 **cups water**
- 1 **teaspoon salt**
- ½ **teaspoon dried dill, basil, rosemary, or marjoram, crushed**

1. Scrub carrots, potatoes, and parsnips. Cut off root and stem ends of all vegetables. Do not peel vegetables, unless coated with wax. Cut carrots, potatoes, parsnips, and cabbage into 2-inch pieces. Cut onions into wedges.

2. In a 7- to 8-quart Dutch oven cook and stir vegetables in hot oil over medium-high heat about 15 minutes or until vegetables start to brown. Stir in water, salt, dill, and ½ teaspoon *black pepper.* Bring to boiling; reduce heat. Simmer, covered, for 2 hours.

3. Strain stock (see photo, page 548). Discard vegetable mixture. Place stock in storage containers. Cover and chill for up to 3 days or freeze up to 6 months.

Per cup: 15 cal., 2 g total fat (0 g sat. fat), 0 mg chol., 295 mg sodium, 0 g carbo., 0 g fiber, 0 g pro.
Exchanges: Free

Adding Herbs

Herbs are a flavorful addition to soups.

You can use fresh or dried herbs. They differ only in when they should be added to the soup kettle. Dried herbs usually are added at the beginning of cooking so they have time to rehydrate and release their flavors. Fresh herbs usually are added just before serving so they retain their flavors and color. Fresh herbs in soups should appear bright and green—not wilted and dark.

Barley-Beef Soup

Barley-Beef Soup `LOW FAT`

Prep: 25 minutes **Cook:** 1¾ hours
Makes: 8 main-dish servings

- 12 **ounces beef stew meat, cut into 1-inch cubes**
- 1 **tablespoon cooking oil**
- 4 **14-ounce cans beef broth**
- 1 **cup chopped onion (1 large)**
- ½ **cup chopped celery (1 stalk)**
- 1 **teaspoon dried oregano or basil, crushed**
- 2 **cloves garlic, minced**
- 1 **bay leaf**
- 1 **cup frozen mixed vegetables**
- 1 **14.5-ounce can diced tomatoes, undrained**
- 1 **cup ½-inch slices peeled parsnip or ½-inch cubes peeled potato**
- ⅔ **cup quick-cooking barley**

1. In a Dutch oven brown meat in hot oil. Stir in broth, onion, celery, oregano, ½ teaspoon *black pepper,* garlic, and bay leaf. Bring to boiling; reduce heat. Simmer, covered, for 1½ hours.

2. Stir in frozen vegetables, undrained tomatoes, parsnip, and barley. Return to boiling; reduce heat. Simmer, covered, about 15 minutes more or until meat and vegetables are tender. Discard bay leaf.

Slow cooker directions: Brown meat as above; drain off fat. In a 6-quart slow cooker combine meat and remaining ingredients, substituting regular barley for quick-cooking barley. Cover; cook on low-heat setting for 8 to 10 hours or on high-heat setting for 4 to 5 hours.

Per 1⅓ cups: 171 cal., 4 g total fat (1 g sat. fat), 25 mg chol., 865 mg sodium, 20 g carbo., 4 g fiber, 13 g pro.
Daily Values: 10% vit. A, 20% vit. C, 5% calcium, 11% iron
Exchanges: 1 Vegetable, 1 Starch, 1½ Very Lean Meat

Old-Fashioned Beef Stew

Pork stew meat and boneless lamb are tasty alternatives for this stew. For pork, only simmer about 30 minutes in Step 1. If using slow cooker directions, prepare as directed for any type of meat.

Prep: 20 minutes **Cook:** 1½ hours
Makes: 5 main-dish servings

    2 tablespoons all-purpose flour
   12 ounces beef stew meat, cut into ¾-inch cubes
    2 tablespoons cooking oil
    3 cups vegetable juice
    1 cup water
    1 medium onion, cut into thin wedges
    1 tablespoon Worcestershire sauce
  1½ teaspoons instant beef bouillon granules
    1 teaspoon dried oregano, crushed
    ½ teaspoon dried marjoram, crushed
    ¼ teaspoon black pepper
    1 bay leaf
    3 cups cubed potato (about 3 medium)
  1½ cups frozen cut green beans
    1 cup frozen whole kernel corn
    1 cup sliced carrot (2 medium)

1. Place flour in a plastic bag. Add meat cubes, a few at a time, shaking to coat. In a Dutch oven or large saucepan brown meat in hot oil; drain fat. Stir in vegetable juice, water, onion, Worcestershire sauce, bouillon granules, oregano, marjoram, pepper, and bay leaf. Bring to boiling; reduce heat. Simmer, covered, for 1 to 1¼ hours or until meat is nearly tender.

2. Stir in potato, green beans, corn, and carrot. Return to boiling; reduce heat. Simmer, covered, about 30 minutes more or until meat and vegetables are tender. Discard bay leaf.

Slow cooker directions: Prepare and brown meat as above. In a 3½- or 4-quart slow cooker layer meat, onion, potato, green beans, corn, and carrot. Decrease vegetable juice to 2 cups. Combine vegetable juice, water, Worcestershire sauce, bouillon granules, oregano, marjoram, pepper, and bay leaf. Pour over meat and vegetables in slow cooker. Cover and cook on low-heat setting for 10 to 12 hours or on high-heat setting for 5 to 6 hours or until meat and vegetables are tender. Discard bay leaf.

Per 1⅓ cups: 331 cal., 13 g total fat (4 g sat. fat), 43 mg chol., 744 mg sodium, 36 g carbo., 6 g fiber, 18 g pro.
Daily Values: 162% vit. A, 97% vit. C, 6% calcium, 21% iron
Exchanges: 1 Vegetable, 2 Starch, 1½ Medium-Fat Meat, ½ Fat

 Polenta Beef Stew

See photo, page 545.

Prep: 25 minutes **Cook:** 2 hours
Makes: 8 main-dish servings

    ¼ cup all-purpose flour
    2 teaspoons Italian seasoning
    1 teaspoon garlic powder
    2 pounds boneless beef chuck steak, cut into 1-inch pieces
    ½ cup chopped onion (1 medium)
    1 teaspoon snipped fresh rosemary or ¼ teaspoon dried rosemary, crushed
    6 cloves garlic, minced
    1 14-ounce can beef broth
  1½ cups dry red wine
    8 ounces boiling onions
    5 medium carrots, cut into 1-inch chunks
    1 recipe Polenta
    ½ cup snipped fresh Italian parsley
    ¼ cup tomato paste

1. Place flour, Italian seasoning, garlic powder, ½ teaspoon *salt,* and ½ teaspoon *black pepper* in a plastic bag. Add meat pieces, a few at a time, shaking to coat. In a Dutch oven brown meat, one-third at a time, in 2 tablespoons hot *olive oil;* drain fat. Return all meat to Dutch oven; add chopped onion, dried rosemary (if using), and garlic. Cook and stir until onion is tender. Stir in broth and wine. Bring to boiling; reduce heat. Simmer, covered, for 1½ hours.

2. Stir in boiling onions and carrot. Bring to boiling; reduce heat. Simmer, covered, about 30 minutes more or until meat and vegetables are tender. Meanwhile, prepare Polenta. Just before serving, stir fresh rosemary (if using), parsley, and tomato paste into stew. Serve with Polenta.

Polenta: In a saucepan bring 3 cups milk just to a simmer over medium heat. In a bowl combine 1 cup cornmeal, 1 cup water, and 1 teaspoon salt. Stir cornmeal mixture slowly into hot milk. Bring mixture to boiling, stirring frequently. Reduce heat to low. Cook for 10 to 15 minutes or until mixture is thick, stirring occasionally. (If mixture is too thick, stir in additional milk.) Stir in 2 tablespoons butter or margarine until melted.

Per cup + about ½ cup polenta: 508 cal., 26 g total fat (10 g sat. fat), 88 mg chol., 736 mg sodium, 32 g carbo., 4 g fiber, 29 g pro.
Daily Values: 205% vit. A, 22% vit. C, 16% calcium, 25% iron
Exchanges: 1 Vegetable, 2 Starch, 3 Lean Meat, 3 Fat

Beef Bourguignon

Prep: 30 minutes **Cook:** 1¼ hours
Makes: 6 main-dish servings

- 1 **pound boneless beef chuck roast, cut into ¾-inch cubes**
- 1 **tablespoon cooking oil**
- 1½ **cups chopped onion (3 medium)**
- 2 **cloves garlic, minced**
- 1½ **cups Pinot Noir or Burgundy wine**
- ¾ **cup beef broth**
- 1 **teaspoon dried thyme, crushed**
- ¾ **teaspoon dried marjoram, crushed**
- ½ **teaspoon salt**
- 2 **bay leaves**
- 3 **cups whole fresh mushrooms**
- 2 **cups ¾-inch pieces carrot (4 medium)**
- 1 **cup pearl onions, peeled, or frozen small whole onions**
- 2 **tablespoons all-purpose flour**
- 2 **tablespoons butter or margarine, softened**
- 2 **slices bacon, crisp-cooked, drained, and crumbled**
- 3 **cups hot cooked noodles or 1 recipe Mashed Potatoes (page 587)**

1. In a 4-quart Dutch oven brown half of the meat in hot oil; remove meat from Dutch oven. Add remaining meat, chopped onion, and garlic. Cook and stir until meat is brown and onion is tender. Return all meat to Dutch oven.

2. Stir in wine, broth, thyme, marjoram, salt, ¼ teaspoon *black pepper*, and bay leaves. Bring to boiling; reduce heat. Simmer, covered, for

45 minutes. Add mushrooms, carrot, and pearl onions. Return to boiling; reduce heat. Simmer, covered, for 25 to 30 minutes more or until meat and vegetables are tender. Discard bay leaves.

3. In a small bowl stir together flour and butter to make a smooth paste; stir into meat mixture. Cook and stir until thickened and bubbly. Cook and stir for 1 minute more. Stir in crumbled bacon. Serve with hot noodles.

Slow cooker directions: Brown meat, chopped onion, and garlic in hot oil as above. In a 3½- or 4-quart slow cooker layer mushrooms, carrot, and pearl onions. Omit flour and butter or margarine. Sprinkle with 3 tablespoons quick-cooking tapioca. Place meat mixture on top of vegetables. Add thyme, marjoram, salt, pepper, and bay leaves. Decrease wine to 1¼ cups and beef broth to ½ cup; pour over meat. Cover and cook on low-heat setting for 10 to 12 hours or on high-heat setting for 5 to 6 hours or until meat and vegetables are tender. Discard bay leaves. Stir in bacon.

Per cup + ½ cup noodles: 395 cal., 14 g total fat (5 g sat. fat), 87 mg chol., 436 mg sodium, 35 g carbo., 4 g fiber, 23 g pro. **Daily Values:** 210% vit. A, 12% vit. C, 6% calcium, 25% iron **Exchanges:** 2 Vegetable, 1½ Starch, 2 Lean Meat, 2½ Fat

Broth Substitutions

When a recipe calls for chicken or beef broth or vegetable stock, you can make your own using one of the recipes on pages 548 and 549. Or choose a store-bought variety, below.

Canned Broths: Canned chicken and beef broth are ready to use straight from the can (low-sodium versions are available too).

Bouillon: Instant bouillon granules or cubes can be purchased in beef, chicken, or vegetable variety. Mix 1 teaspoon of granules, or 1 small cube, with 1 cup water.

Condensed Broths: Cans of condensed chicken or beef broth also are available. Dilute them for use according to the label directions on the can.

Teriyaki Beef Soup LOW FAT

Sesame oil and crushed red pepper give this soup a well-rounded flavor.

Start to Finish: 40 minutes **Makes:** 4 main-dish servings

    8 ounces boneless beef sirloin steak
    1 tablespoon cooking oil
    2 14-ounce cans lower-sodium beef broth
    1 cup water
    1 cup bite-size strips carrot (2 medium)
   ⅓ cup uncooked long grain rice
    1 tablespoon grated fresh ginger
    3 cloves garlic, minced
    2 cups coarsely chopped broccoli
   ¼ cup sliced green onion (2)
    3 tablespoons teriyaki sauce
    1 teaspoon toasted sesame oil
   ¼ teaspoon crushed red pepper

1. Trim fat from beef. Cut beef into bite-size strips. In a large skillet cook and stir beef in hot oil over medium-high heat for 2 to 3 minutes or until beef is brown. Remove beef with a slotted spoon; set aside.

2. In the same skillet combine broth, water, carrot, uncooked rice, ginger, and garlic. Bring to boiling; reduce heat. Simmer, covered, about 15 minutes or until carrot and rice are tender.

3. Stir in beef, broccoli, green onion, teriyaki sauce, sesame oil, and crushed red pepper. Simmer, covered, for 3 minutes more.

Per 1½ cups: 223 cal., 7 g total fat (2 g sat. fat), 34 mg chol., 889 mg sodium, 21 g carbo., 2 g fiber, 17 g pro.
Daily Values: 74% vit. A, 62% vit. C, 6% calcium, 16% iron
Exchanges: 1 Vegetable, 1 Starch, 2 Very Lean Meat, 1 Fat

Vegetable-Beef Soup LOW FAT

Prep: 25 minutes **Cook:** 1 hour 25 minutes
Makes: 8 main-dish servings

  1½ pounds boneless beef chuck roast, cut into
       1-inch cubes, or beef stew meat
    1 tablespoon cooking oil
    4 14-ounce cans beef broth
    1 teaspoon dried oregano, crushed
   ½ teaspoon dried marjoram, crushed
    2 bay leaves
    2 cups chopped, peeled tomato (2 large) or
       one 14.5-ounce can diced tomatoes,
       undrained
    1 10-ounce package frozen whole kernel corn
  1½ cups cubed, peeled potato (2 medium)

    1 cup frozen cut green beans
    1 cup sliced carrot (2 medium)
    1 cup sliced celery (2 stalks)
   ½ cup chopped onion (1 medium)

1. In a 6- to 8-quart Dutch oven brown meat, half at a time, in hot oil; drain fat. Return all meat to Dutch oven. Stir in beef broth, oregano, marjoram, ¼ teaspoon *black pepper,* and bay leaves. Bring to boiling; reduce heat. Simmer, covered, for 1 hour. Discard bay leaves. If necessary, skim fat (see tip, below).

2. Stir in tomato, corn, potato, green beans, carrot, celery, and onion. Return to boiling; reduce heat. Simmer, covered, about 25 minutes more or until vegetables are tender.

Per 1⅔ cups: 208 cal., 6 g total fat (1 g sat. fat), 52 mg chol., 821 mg sodium, 19 g carbo., 3 g fiber, 22 g pro.
Daily Values: 45% vit. A, 25% vit. C, 4% calcium, 19% iron
Exchanges: 1 Vegetable, 1 Starch, 2½ Very Lean Meat, ½ Fat

Skimming Fat from Broth

Make your homemade soups as low-fat and low-calorie as possible by skimming off extra fat with these techniques.

To remove fat from hot soup or broth, use a large metal spoon and skim off the fat that rises to the top (see photo, top).

You also can cover and refrigerate the soup or broth for 6 to 8 hours or until the fat solidifies on the surface. Then use a spoon to lift off the hardened fat (see photo, middle).

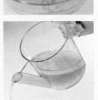

A useful skimming tool is a fat-separating pitcher (see photo, bottom), which has a spout connected near the bottom. To use it, pour hot broth into the pitcher, allow it to stand for a few minutes, then pour the broth out. Because fat rises, it gets left behind.

Another tool is a fat-skimming ladle. Slots near the upper edge catch the fat, which stays in the ladle.

Chipotle Steak Chili

Chili [LOW FAT]

This recipe can be made with ground beef or steak.

Prep: 25 minutes **Cook:** 20 minutes
Makes: 8 main-dish servings

- 1½ **pounds lean ground beef**
- 2 **cups chopped onion (2 large)**
- 1 **cup chopped green sweet pepper (1 large)**
- 4 **cloves garlic, minced**
- 2 **15- to 16-ounce cans kidney beans, pinto beans, and/or black beans, rinsed and drained**
- 2 **14.5-ounce cans diced tomatoes, undrained**
- 1 **15-ounce can tomato sauce**
- 1 **cup water**
- 2 **tablespoons chili powder**
- 1 **teaspoon dried basil, crushed**
- ½ **teaspoon black pepper**
  Shredded cheddar cheese (optional)
  Dairy sour cream (optional)

1. In a 4-quart Dutch oven cook ground beef, onion, sweet pepper, and garlic until meat is brown and onion is tender; drain fat. Stir in kidney beans, undrained tomatoes, tomato sauce, water, chili powder, basil, and black pepper. Bring to boiling; reduce heat. Simmer, covered, for 20 minutes, stirring occasionally. If desired, top each serving with cheese and/or sour cream.

Chipotle Steak Chili: Prepare as above, except substitute 1½ pounds boneless beef shoulder top blade steak (flat-iron), cut into ¾-inch cubes, for the ground beef. In a Dutch oven brown meat, half at a time, in 1 tablespoon hot cooking oil. Remove meat, reserving drippings in pan. Cook onion, sweet pepper, and garlic in drippings until tender; drain fat. Return meat to Dutch oven. Stir in 1 to 2 teaspoons chopped chipotle chile peppers in adobo sauce. Continue as directed, except reduce the water to ½ cup and simmer, covered, about 1 hour or until the meat is tender.

Per 1½ cups chili or 1¼ cups steak chili variation: 288 cal., 8 g total fat (3 g sat. fat), 54 mg chol., 639 mg sodium, 32 g carbo., 8 g fiber, 24 g pro.
Daily Values: 13% vit. A, 49% vit. C, 9% calcium, 22% iron
Exchanges: 1½ Vegetable, 1½ Starch, 2½ Lean Meat

Hamburger-Barley Soup [LOW FAT]

If you're strapped for time, substitute 4½ cups fresh stir-fry veggies from the produce section of the supermarket for the vegetables.

Prep: 30 minutes **Cook:** 20 minutes
Makes: 8 main-dish servings

- 1½ **pounds lean ground beef**
- 2 **cups thinly sliced carrot (4 medium)**
- 1 **cup chopped onion (1 large)**
- 1 **cup sliced celery (2 stalks)**
- ½ **cup chopped green sweet pepper (1 medium)**
- 1 **clove garlic, minced**
- 3 **14-ounce cans beef broth**
- 1 **28-ounce can diced tomatoes, undrained**
- 1 **8-ounce can tomato sauce**
- ½ **cup quick-cooking barley**
- 2 **bay leaves**
- 1 **teaspoon Worcestershire sauce**
- 1 **teaspoon dried oregano, crushed, or 1 tablespoon snipped fresh oregano**
- ¼ **teaspoon black pepper**
- ¼ **teaspoon salt**

1. In a 5- to 6-quart Dutch oven cook beef, carrot, onion, celery, sweet pepper, and garlic over medium heat until meat is brown and vegetables are tender. Drain well; return to Dutch oven.

2. Stir in broth. Add undrained tomatoes, tomato sauce, barley, bay leaves, Worcestershire sauce, dried oregano (if using), black pepper, and salt. Bring to boiling; reduce heat. Simmer, covered, about 20 minutes or until barley is tender. Stir in fresh oregano, if using. Discard bay leaves.

Per 1⅔ cups: 237 cal., 8 g total fat (3 g sat. fat), 54 mg chol., 990 mg sodium, 20 g carbo., 3 g fiber, 19 g pro.
Daily Values: 68% vit. A, 36% vit. C, 7% calcium, 15% iron
Exchanges: 2 Vegetable, ½ Fruit, 2 Lean Meat, ½ Fat

Old-Fashioned Chicken Noodle Soup <small>LOW FAT</small>

Prep: 20 minutes **Cook:** 1 hour 40 minutes
Makes: 8 main-dish servings

- 1 3½- to 4-pound chicken, cut up, or 2½ pounds meaty chicken pieces
- 8 cups water
- ½ cup chopped onion (1 medium)
- 2 teaspoons salt
- ¼ teaspoon black pepper
- 1 bay leaf
- 1 cup chopped carrot (2 medium)
- 1 cup chopped celery (2 stalks)
- 1½ cups dried egg noodles
- 2 tablespoons snipped fresh parsley

1. In a 6- to 8-quart Dutch oven combine chicken, water, onion, salt, pepper, and bay leaf. Bring to boiling; reduce heat. Simmer, covered, about 1½ hours or until chicken is tender.

2. Remove chicken from broth. When cool enough to handle, remove meat from bones. Discard bones and skin. Cut meat into bite-size pieces; set aside. Discard bay leaf. Skim fat from broth (see tip, page 552).

3. Bring broth to boiling. Stir in carrot and celery. Simmer, covered, about 5 minutes. Stir in noodles. Simmer, covered, about 5 minutes more or until noodles are tender but still firm. Stir in chicken and parsley; heat through.

Per 1⅓ cups: 152 cal., 3 g total fat (1 g sat. fat), 73 mg chol., 684 mg sodium, 8 g carbo., 1 g fiber, 22 g pro.
Daily Values: 37% vit. A, 8% vit. C, 3% calcium, 7% iron
Exchanges: ½ Starch, 3 Very Lean Meat

Chicken Stew with Cornmeal Dumplings

Serve the quintessential chicken soup in just 40 minutes using leftover chicken.

Start to Finish: 40 minutes **Makes:** 4 main-dish servings

- 1 14-ounce can chicken broth
- 1 10-ounce package frozen mixed vegetables
- 1 cup frozen small whole onions
- ½ cup water
- 2 teaspoons snipped fresh basil, oregano, or dill; or ½ teaspoon dried basil, oregano, or dill, crushed
- ½ teaspoon salt
- ⅛ teaspoon garlic powder
- ⅛ teaspoon black pepper
- 1 cup milk
- ⅓ cup all-purpose flour
- 2 cups cubed cooked chicken or turkey or two 5-ounce cans chunk-style chicken or turkey
- 1 recipe Cornmeal Dumplings

1. In a large saucepan combine broth, frozen vegetables, onions, water, dried herb (if using), salt, garlic powder, and pepper. Bring to boiling.

2. Meanwhile, in a small bowl combine milk and flour; stir into vegetable mixture. Stir in chicken. Cook and stir until thickened and bubbly. Stir in fresh herb, if using.

3. Drop dumpling mixture from a tablespoon to make four to eight mounds on top of stew. Simmer, covered (do not lift cover), over low heat for 10 to 12 minutes or until a wooden toothpick inserted into a dumpling comes out clean.

Cornmeal Dumplings: In a medium bowl stir together ½ cup all-purpose flour, ½ cup shredded cheddar cheese, ⅓ cup yellow cornmeal, 1 teaspoon baking powder, and dash black pepper. In a small bowl combine 1 egg, beaten; 2 tablespoons milk; and 2 tablespoons cooking oil. Add egg mixture to flour mixture, stirring with a fork just until combined.

Per 1½ cups stew + 1 dumpling: 510 cal., 21 g total fat (7 g sat. fat), 135 mg chol., 1,045 mg sodium, 46 g carbo., 5 g fiber, 35 g pro.
Daily Values: 81% vit. A, 17% vit. C, 33% calcium, 20% iron
Exchanges: 1½ Vegetable, 2½ Starch, 3½ Lean Meat, 1½ Fat

Tex-Mex Tortilla Soup

Although this delicious soup tastes like it simmered all day, it only takes 30 minutes to make.

Start to Finish: 30 minutes **Makes:** 6 main-dish servings

- 1 to 1¼ pounds skinless, boneless chicken thighs or breast halves
- 3 14-ounce cans reduced-sodium chicken broth
- 1 14.5-ounce can diced tomatoes, undrained
- ½ cup chopped onion (1 medium)
- ¼ cup chopped green sweet pepper
- 1 to 2 teaspoons chili powder
- ½ teaspoon ground cumin
- ⅛ teaspoon black pepper
- 1 cup frozen whole kernel corn
- 3 cups tortilla chips, coarsely crushed
- 1 cup shredded Monterey Jack cheese (4 ounces)

1 avocado, seeded, peeled, and cut into
   chunks (optional)
   Snipped fresh cilantro and/or sliced fresh
   jalapeño chile pepper (see tip, page 74)
   (optional)
   Lime wedges (optional)

1. Cut chicken into bite-size pieces; set aside. In
a 4-quart Dutch oven combine broth, undrained
tomatoes, onion, sweet pepper, chili powder,
cumin, and black pepper. Bring to boiling; add
chicken. Return to boiling; reduce heat. Simmer,
covered, for 10 minutes. Add corn. Return
to boiling; reduce heat. Simmer, covered, for
10 minutes more.

2. Sprinkle each serving with tortilla chips and
cheese. If desired, serve with avocado chunks,
snipped cilantro, sliced jalapeño chile pepper,
and lime wedges.

Per 1½ cups: 298 cal., 13 g total fat (5 g sat. fat), 77 mg chol.,
817 mg sodium, 21 g carbo., 2 g fiber, 25 g pro.
Daily Values: 8% vit. A, 29% vit. C, 21% calcium, 9% iron
Exchanges: ½ Vegetable, 1 Starch, 3 Lean Meat, 1 Fat

Chicken and Wild Rice Soup

*A Minnesota staple—nutty and chewy wild rice—
stars in this creamy soup. Wild rice isn't really rice
at all. It is a long-grain marsh grass.*

Prep: 30 minutes **Cook:** 55 minutes
Makes: 4 main-dish servings

   ½ cup finely chopped carrot (1 medium)
   ½ cup finely chopped onion (1 medium)
   ½ cup finely chopped celery (1 stalk)
   1 tablespoon butter or margarine
   4 cups chicken broth
   ¾ cup wild rice, rinsed and drained
   12 ounces skinless, boneless chicken breast
      halves, cut into ¾-inch pieces
   2 tablespoons all-purpose flour
   2 tablespoons butter or margarine, softened
   2 cups half-and-half or light cream

1. In a Dutch oven cook and stir carrot, onion,
and celery in hot butter about 5 minutes or
until tender. Add broth and wild rice. Bring
to boiling; reduce heat. Simmer, covered, for
30 minutes. Add chicken. Simmer, covered, for
20 to 25 minutes more or until rice is tender.

2. In a small bowl combine flour and softened
butter to make a smooth paste. Stir flour mixture
into the rice mixture. Cook and stir until thickened and bubbly. Cook and stir for 1 minute

more. Add half-and-half. Cook and stir over
medium heat until heated through. Season to
taste with *salt* and *black pepper.*

Per 1½ cups: 480 cal., 25 g total fat (14 g sat. fat), 119 mg chol.,
1,142 mg sodium, 35 g carbo., 3 g fiber, 30 g pro.
Daily Values: 48% vit. A, 5% vit. C, 16% calcium, 8% iron
Exchanges: ½ Vegetable, 2 Starch, 3½ Very Lean Meat, 4 Fat

Turkey Frame Soup LOW FAT

*This flavorful noodle soup is a great way to use
every morsel of your holiday bird.*

Prep: 30 minutes **Cook:** 1¾ hours
Makes: 4 main-dish servings

   1 meaty turkey frame
   8 cups water
   2 large onions, quartered
   1 cup sliced celery (2 stalks)
   1 tablespoon instant chicken bouillon
      granules
   3 cloves garlic, minced
      Chopped cooked turkey
   1 14.5-ounce can diced tomatoes, undrained
   1½ teaspoons dried oregano, basil, marjoram, or
      thyme, crushed
   ¼ teaspoon black pepper
   3 cups (any combination) sliced celery, carrot,
      parsnip, or mushrooms; chopped onion or
      rutabaga; or broccoli or cauliflower florets
   1½ cups dried medium noodles

1. Break turkey frame or cut in half with
kitchen shears. Place in an 8- to 10-quart kettle
or Dutch oven. Add water, onions, celery, bouillon granules, and garlic. Bring to boiling; reduce
heat. Simmer, covered, for 1½ hours.

2. Remove turkey frame. When cool enough to
handle, remove meat from bones; discard bones.
Coarsely chop meat. If necessary, add enough
chopped cooked turkey to equal 2 cups; set turkey aside.

3. Strain broth, discarding solids (see photo,
page 548). Skim fat from broth (see tip, page
552). Return broth to kettle. Stir in undrained
tomatoes, oregano, and pepper. Stir in vegetables. Return to boiling; reduce heat. Simmer,
covered, for 10 minutes. Stir in noodles. Simmer,
uncovered, for 8 to 10 minutes more or until
noodles are tender but still firm and vegetables
are tender. Stir in turkey; heat through.

Per 1¾ cups: 182 cal., 4 g total fat (1 g sat. fat), 52 mg chol.,
608 mg sodium, 17 g carbo., 2 g fiber, 20 g pro.
Daily Values: 54% vit. A, 30% vit. C, 8% calcium, 13% iron
Exchanges: 1 Vegetable, 1 Starch, 2 Very Lean Meat

Lentil and Sausage Soup

Lentil and Sausage Soup LOW FAT

For those who love beans but never have the time to allow them to soak and cook, here is a great alternative. Lentils require no soaking and much less cooking time than other legumes. They also are high in fiber.

Prep: 20 minutes **Cook:** 20 minutes
Makes: 5 main-dish servings

> 2 **14-ounce cans reduced-sodium chicken broth**
> 1½ **cups water**
> 1 **cup brown lentils, rinsed and drained**
> 1 **cup sliced celery (2 stalks)**
> 1 **cup sliced carrot (2 medium)**
> ½ **cup chopped onion (1 medium)**
> 1 **teaspoon snipped fresh thyme or
>   ½ teaspoon dried thyme, crushed**
> ⅛ **teaspoon cayenne pepper**
> 2 **cloves garlic, minced**
> 6 **ounces cooked smoked sausage links, quartered lengthwise and sliced**

1. In a large saucepan combine broth, water, lentils, celery, carrot, onion, dried thyme (if using), cayenne pepper, and garlic. Bring to boiling; reduce heat. Simmer, covered, for 20 to 25 minutes or until vegetables and lentils are tender. Stir in sausage and, if using, fresh thyme. Heat through.

Per 1⅓ cups: 294 cal., 11 g total fat (4 g sat. fat), 23 mg chol., 962 mg sodium, 28 g carbo., 13 g fiber, 21 g pro.
Daily Values: 124% vit. A, 11% vit. C, 5% calcium, 20% iron
Exchanges: 1 Vegetable, 1½ Starch, 2 Medium-Fat Meat

Black Bean Soup with Sausage LOW FAT

Prep: 1½ hours **Stand:** 1 hour **Cook:** 1 hour
Makes: 6 main-dish servings

> 1 **cup dry black beans**
> 2 **cups chicken broth**
> 2 **cups water**
> 1 **cup chopped onion (1 large)**
> 1 **cup chopped celery (2 stalks)**
> 1 **teaspoon ground coriander**
> ¼ **teaspoon salt**
> ⅛ **to ¼ teaspoon cayenne pepper**
> 4 **cloves garlic, minced**
> 8 **ounces cooked smoked turkey sausage or Polish sausage, chopped**
> **Dairy sour cream or shredded Monterey Jack cheese (optional)**
> **Snipped fresh cilantro (optional)**

1. Rinse beans. In a large saucepan or Dutch oven combine beans and 6 cups *water.* Bring to boiling; reduce heat. Simmer for 2 minutes. Remove from heat. Cover and let stand for 1 hour. (Or place beans in water in pan. Cover and let soak in a cool place for 6 to 8 hours or overnight.) Drain and rinse beans.

2. Return beans to saucepan. Stir in broth, the 2 cups water, onion, celery, coriander, salt, cayenne pepper, and garlic. Bring to boiling; reduce heat. Simmer, covered, for 1 to 1½ hours or until beans are tender.

3. If desired, mash beans slightly. Stir in sausage; heat through. If desired, serve topped with sour cream and cilantro.

Per 1¼ cups: 198 cal., 6 g total fat (2 g sat. fat), 29 mg chol., 682 mg sodium, 24 g carbo., 6 g fiber, 14 g pro.
Daily Values: 1% vit. A, 5% vit. C, 8% calcium, 13% iron
Exchanges: ½ Vegetable, 1½ Starch, 1 Lean Meat

Shortcut Black Bean Soup with Sausage: Prepare as above, except omit dry black beans and the 6 cups soaking water. Decrease chicken broth to 1½ cups. Rinse and drain two 15-ounce cans black beans. In a large saucepan combine beans, broth, water, onion, celery, coriander, salt, cayenne pepper, and garlic. Bring to boiling; reduce heat. Simmer, covered, about 15 minutes or until vegetables are tender. Stir in sausage; heat through. Makes 4 servings.

Per 1½ cups: 268 cal., 8 g total fat (2 g sat. fat), 1,421 mg sodium, 35 g carbo., 11 g fiber, 25 g pro.
Daily Values: 1% vit. A, 8% vit. C, 13% calcium, 19% iron
Exchanges: 1 Vegetable, 2 Starch, 2 Lean Meat

Italian Sausage-Bean Stew

Prep: 1½ hours **Stand:** 1 hour **Cook:** 1¼ hours
Makes: 8 main-dish servings

  2⅓ cups dry navy beans
    6 cups water
    1 pound uncooked Italian sausage links, cut
       into ½-inch slices
    1 cup chopped onion (1 large)
    1 clove garlic, minced
  3½ cups beef broth
   ¾ cup water
    1 teaspoon dried oregano, crushed
    2 bay leaves
    3 cups chopped cabbage
    1 14.5-ounce can diced tomatoes, undrained

1. Rinse beans. In a 4-quart Dutch oven combine beans and 6 cups water. Bring to boiling; reduce heat. Simmer, uncovered, for 2 minutes. Remove from heat. Cover and let stand for 1 hour. (Or place beans in water in Dutch oven. Cover and let soak in a cool place for 6 to 8 hours or overnight.) Drain and rinse beans; set aside.

2. In the same Dutch oven cook sausage, onion, and garlic over medium-high heat until meat is brown and onion is tender; drain off fat. Stir in beans, broth, the ¾ cup water, oregano, and bay leaves. Bring to boiling; reduce heat. Simmer, covered, for 1 to 1½ hours or until beans are tender, stirring occasionally. Stir in cabbage and undrained tomatoes. Return to boiling; reduce heat. Simmer, covered, 15 minutes more or until cabbage is tender. Discard bay leaves. Skim off fat. Season to taste with *salt* and *black pepper*.

Per 1⅓ cups: 391 cal., 14 g total fat (6 g sat. fat), 38 mg chol., 840 mg sodium, 41 g carbo., 15 g fiber, 22 g pro.
Daily Values: 1% vit. A, 27% vit. C, 12% calcium, 22% iron
Exchanges: 1 Vegetable, 2½ Starch, 2 Medium-Fat Meat, ½ Fat

White Chili with Sausage

Prep: 15 minutes **Cook:** 20 minutes
Makes: 6 to 8 main-dish servings

  1½ pounds bulk pork sausage
    1 cup chopped onion (1 large)
    4 cloves garlic, minced
    2 19-ounce cans cannellini beans, rinsed and
       drained
    2 14-ounce cans reduced-sodium chicken
       broth
    1 14.5-ounce can white or yellow whole
       kernel corn, drained

    1 fresh poblano chile pepper, seeded and
       finely chopped (see tip, page 74)
   ⅓ cup lime juice
   ¼ teaspoon ground white pepper
       Crushed white corn tortilla chips

1. In a 4-quart Dutch oven cook and stir sausage, onion, and garlic over medium heat until sausage is no longer pink. Stir in beans, broth, corn, chile pepper, lime juice, and white pepper. Bring to boiling; reduce heat. Simmer, covered, for 20 minutes. Serve with crushed chips.

Per 1⅔ cups: 660 cal., 37 g total fat (14 g sat. fat), 65 mg chol., 1,464 mg sodium, 54 g carbo., 10 g fiber, 28 g pro.
Daily Values: 1% vit. A, 49% vit. C, 7% calcium, 17% iron
Exchanges: 3½ Starch, 3 High-Fat Meat, 2 Fat

Pork and Orzo Soup with Spinach LOW FAT

Start to Finish: 50 minutes **Makes:** 6 main-dish servings

  1½ pounds boneless pork loin chops, cut into
       1-inch cubes
    2 tablespoons cooking oil
    4 cups water
    2 14-ounce cans chicken broth
    2 bay leaves
    1 teaspoon dried oregano, crushed, or
       1 tablespoon snipped fresh oregano
   ½ teaspoon dried marjoram, crushed, or
       1½ teaspoons snipped fresh marjoram
    1 cup bite-size strips carrot (2 medium)
    1 cup sliced celery (2 stalks)
   ¾ cup dried orzo (rosamarina)
    3 cups torn spinach or ½ of a 10-ounce
       package frozen chopped spinach, thawed
       and well drained

1. In a 4-quart Dutch oven cook the meat, half at a time, in hot oil over medium-high heat until brown. Drain fat.

2. Stir in water, broth, bay leaves, dried oregano (if using), dried marjoram (if using), ½ teaspoon *salt*, and ¼ teaspoon *black pepper*. Bring to boiling. Stir in carrot, celery, and orzo. Return to boiling; reduce heat. Simmer, covered, 15 minutes or until vegetables and pasta are tender.

3. Discard bay leaves. Stir in fresh herbs (if using) and spinach. Cook for 1 to 2 minutes more or just until spinach wilts.

Per 1¾ cups: 261 cal., 9 g total fat (3 g sat. fat), 62 mg chol., 709 mg sodium, 13 g carbo., 3 g fiber, 30 g pro.
Daily Values: 121% vit. A, 11% vit. C, 6% calcium, 17% iron
Exchanges: 1 Vegetable, ½ Starch, 3½ Very Lean Meat, 1½ Fat

Cheesy Vegetable and Ham Chowder

See photo, page 545.

Prep: 25 minutes **Cook:** 25 minutes
Makes: 6 main-dish servings

  2 **cups water**
  2 **cups chopped potato (2 medium)**
  ½ **cup chopped carrot (1 medium)**
  ½ **cup chopped celery (1 stalk)**
  ¼ **cup chopped onion (1 small)**
  ¼ **cup butter or margarine**
  ¼ **cup all-purpose flour**
  2 **cups milk**
2½ **cups shredded cheddar cheese or 10 ounces American cheese, torn**
  1 **15-ounce can cream-style corn**
  2 **cups cubed cooked ham**

1. In a large saucepan combine water, potato, carrot, celery, and onion. Bring to boiling; reduce heat. Simmer, covered, for 10 minutes. Do not drain.

2. Meanwhile, in a medium saucepan melt butter. Stir in flour and ¼ teaspoon *black pepper;* add milk all at once. Cook and stir over medium heat until thickened and bubbly.

3. Add cheese to milk mixture. Cook and stir until cheese melts. Add cheese mixture to potato mixture. Stir in corn and ham. Heat through but do not boil. If desired, season with additional pepper.

Per 1½ cups: 490 cal., 30 g total fat (16 g sat. fat), 103 mg chol., 1,198 mg sodium, 33 g carbo., 3 g fiber, 25 g pro.
Daily Values: 41% vit. A, 23% vit. C, 46% calcium, 12% iron
Exchanges: ½ Milk, 1½ Starch, 2½ High-Fat Meat, 1½ Fat

Ham and Bean Soup   LOW FAT

Prep: 1¾ hours **Stand:** 1 hour **Cook:** 1¼ hours
Makes: 5 main-dish servings

  1 **cup dry navy beans**
  4 **cups water**
  1 **to 1½ pounds meaty smoked pork hocks or one 1- to 1½-pound meaty ham bone**
  1 **tablespoon butter or margarine**
1½ **cups sliced celery (3 stalks)**
1½ **cups chopped onion (3 medium)**
  ¾ **teaspoon dried thyme, crushed**
  ¼ **to ½ teaspoon salt**
  ¼ **teaspoon black pepper**
  1 **bay leaf**
  4 **cups water**

1. Rinse beans. In a 4-quart Dutch oven combine the beans and 4 cups water. Bring to boiling; reduce heat. Simmer, uncovered, for 2 minutes. Remove from heat. Cover and let stand for 1 hour. (Or place beans in water in Dutch oven. Cover and let soak in a cool place for 6 to 8 hours or overnight.) Drain and rinse beans; set aside.

2. In the same Dutch oven brown pork hocks on all sides in hot butter over medium heat. Add celery and onion to Dutch oven. Cook and stir until vegetables are tender. Stir in beans, thyme, salt, pepper, bay leaf, and 4 cups water. Bring to boiling; reduce heat. Simmer, covered, for 1 to 1½ hours or until beans are tender. Remove pork hocks. When cool enough to handle, cut meat off bones; coarsely chop meat. Discard bones and bay leaf. Slightly mash beans in saucepan.

3. Stir in chopped meat; heat through. Season to taste with additional salt and pepper.

Per 1½ cups: 217 cal., 4 g total fat (2 g sat. fat), 21 mg chol., 492 mg sodium, 30 g carbo., 11 g fiber, 15 g pro.
Daily Values: 6% vit. A, 7% vit. C, 8% calcium, 14% iron
Exchanges: ½ Vegetable, 2 Starch, 1 Lean Meat

Vegetable, Ham, and Bean Soup: Prepare as above, except after slightly mashing beans, stir in 2 cups sliced carrot and 2 cups sliced parsnip or chopped, peeled rutabaga. Return to boiling; reduce heat. Simmer, covered, about 15 minutes more or until vegetables are tender. Stir in chopped meat; heat through.

Per 1½ cups: 277 cal., 5 g total fat (2 g sat. fat), 21 mg chol., 531 mg sodium, 45 g carbo., 15 g fiber, 16 g pro.
Daily Values: 111% vit. A, 17% vit. C, 12% calcium, 16% iron
Exchanges: 1½ Vegetable, 2 Starch, 1 Lean Meat

Easy Ham and Bean Soup: Prepare as above, except omit dry navy beans, pork hocks, and 8 cups water. Cook celery and onion in hot butter as directed in Step 2. Add 4 cups chicken broth; 1 cup cubed cooked ham (5 ounces); and two 15-ounce cans navy beans, rinsed and drained, along with thyme, black pepper, and bay leaf. Omit the salt. Bring to boiling; reduce heat. Simmer, uncovered, for 10 to 15 minutes or until heated through.

Per 1⅓ cups: 315 cal., 6 g total fat (2 g sat. fat), 25 mg chol., 2,023 mg sodium, 46 g carbo., 11 g fiber, 21 g pro.
Daily Values: 6% vit. A, 10% vit. C, 12% calcium, 22% iron
Exchanges: ½ Vegetable, 3 Starch, 1½ Lean Meat

Split Pea Soup LOW FAT

Prep: 20 minutes **Cook:** 1⅓ hours
Makes: 4 main-dish servings

2¾ cups water
1½ cups dry split peas, rinsed and drained
1 14-ounce can reduced-sodium chicken broth
1 to 1½ pounds meaty smoked pork hocks or one 1- to 1½-pound meaty ham bone
¼ teaspoon dried marjoram, crushed
Dash black pepper
1 bay leaf
½ cup chopped carrot (1 medium)
½ cup chopped celery (1 stalk)
½ cup chopped onion (1 medium)

1. In a large saucepan combine water, split peas, broth, pork hocks, marjoram, pepper, and bay leaf. Bring to boiling; reduce heat. Simmer, covered, for 1 hour, stirring occasionally. Remove pork hocks.

2. When cool enough to handle, cut meat off bones; coarsely chop meat. Discard bones. Return meat to saucepan. Stir in carrot, celery, and onion. Return to boiling; reduce heat. Simmer, covered, for 20 to 30 minutes more or until vegetables are tender. Discard bay leaf.

Slow cooker directions: In a 3½- or 4-quart slow cooker combine split peas, pork hocks, marjoram, pepper, bay leaf, carrot, celery, and onion. Pour water and chicken broth over all. Cover and cook on low-heat setting for 8 to 10 hours or on high-heat setting for 4 to 5 hours. Discard bay leaf. Remove pork hocks. Cut meat off bones; coarsely chop. Stir meat into soup.

Per 1½ cups: 320 cal., 4 g total fat (1 g sat. fat), 19 mg chol., 713 mg sodium, 49 g carbo., 20 g fiber, 25 g pro.
Daily Values: 36% vit. A, 8% vit. C, 7% calcium, 21% iron
Exchanges: ½ Vegetable, 3 Starch, 2 Very Lean Meat

Lamb Stew with Pasta

Lamb Stew with Pasta LOW FAT

Prep: 25 minutes **Cook:** 1 hour
Makes: 4 main-dish servings

1 pound lamb or beef stew meat
1 medium onion, sliced and separated into rings
2 tablespoons cooking oil
3½ cups water
¼ cup snipped dried tomatoes (not oil-packed)
1 teaspoon dried Italian seasoning, crushed
¼ teaspoon salt
¼ teaspoon black pepper
2 cups sliced fresh mushrooms
1 9-ounce package frozen cut green beans
1 cup thinly sliced carrot (2 medium)
¾ cup dried bow tie pasta
1 15-ounce can tomato sauce

1. In a large saucepan cook the lamb and onion in hot oil until the meat is brown.

2. Stir water, dried tomatoes, Italian seasoning, salt, and pepper into the lamb and onion mixture. Bring to boiling; reduce heat. Simmer, covered, about 45 minutes (or about 1¼ hours for beef) or until the meat is nearly tender.

3. Stir mushrooms, green beans, carrot, and pasta into meat mixture. Return to boiling; reduce heat. Simmer, covered, about 15 minutes more or until meat, vegetables, and pasta are tender. Stir in tomato sauce; heat through.

Per 1¾ cups: 309 cal., 12 g total fat (2 g sat. fat), 71 mg chol., 803 mg sodium, 24 g carbo., 5 g fiber, 29 g pro.
Daily Values: 73% vit. A, 20% vit. C, 6% calcium, 24% iron
Exchanges: 2½ Vegetable, 1 Starch, 3 Very Lean Meat, 1½ Fat

Soup Supper

Soups and stews make easy meals and need only a few sides.

- *Cheesy Vegetable and Ham Chowder (page 558)*
- *Buttermilk Biscuits (page 129)*
- *Mixed greens salad with herb vinaigrette*
- *Blueberry Crisp (page 273)*
- *Iced tea with lemon*

Lamb Cassoulet LOW FAT

This French stew contains lamb, beans, chicken, and vegetables. It is comfort food at its finest.

Prep: 30 minutes **Stand:** 1 hour **Cook:** 1½ hours
Makes: 6 main-dish servings

- 2 cups dry navy beans
- 8 cups water
- 1 pound lean boneless lamb, cut into 1-inch cubes
- 1 tablespoon cooking oil
- 1 cup chopped carrot (2 medium)
- ½ cup chopped green sweet pepper (1 medium)
- ½ cup chopped onion (1 medium)
- 1 tablespoon instant beef bouillon granules
- 1 tablespoon Worcestershire sauce
- 2 teaspoons snipped fresh thyme or 1 teaspoon dried thyme, crushed
- 3 cloves garlic, minced
- 2 bay leaves
- 4 cups water
- 8 ounces skinless, boneless chicken thighs, cut into 1-inch pieces
- 1 14.5-ounce can diced tomatoes, undrained
- ½ teaspoon salt
- Salt and black pepper

1. Rinse beans. In a 5- to 6-quart Dutch oven combine beans and the 8 cups water. Bring to boiling; reduce heat. Simmer, uncovered, for 2 minutes. Remove from heat. Cover and let stand for 1 hour. (Or place the beans in water in the Dutch oven. Cover and let soak in a cool place for 6 to 8 hours or overnight.) Drain and rinse beans.

2. In the same Dutch oven brown lamb, half at a time, in hot oil; drain fat. Return all lamb to Dutch oven. Add beans, carrot, sweet pepper, onion, bouillon granules, Worcestershire sauce, dried thyme (if using), garlic, and bay leaves to Dutch oven. Add 4 cups water. Bring to boiling; reduce heat. Simmer, covered, for 1 to 1½ hours or until beans are tender.

3. Stir in chicken, undrained tomatoes, salt, and, if using, fresh thyme. Return to boiling; reduce heat. Simmer, uncovered, for 30 minutes more. Discard bay leaves. Skim fat, if necessary. Season to taste with additional salt and pepper.

Per 1⅔ cups: 420 cal., 7 g total fat (2 g sat. fat), 78 mg chol., 857 mg sodium, 49 g carbo., 18 g fiber, 39 g pro.
Daily Values: 45% vit. A, 36% vit. C, 13% calcium, 30% iron
Exchanges: 1 Vegetable, 2½ Starch, 4 Very Lean Meat, 1½ Fat

Lamb and Vegetable Stew LOW FAT

Prep: 30 minutes **Cook:** 51 minutes
Makes: 5 main-dish servings

- 1 pound lean boneless lamb, cut into ¾-inch cubes
- 1 tablespoon cooking oil
- 1 14-ounce can beef broth
- 1 cup dry red wine or beef broth
- 1 tablespoon snipped fresh thyme or 1 teaspoon dried thyme, crushed
- 2 cloves garlic, minced
- 1 bay leaf
- 2 cups cubed, peeled butternut squash
- 1 cup ½-inch slices peeled parsnip
- 1 cup chopped, peeled sweet potato
- 1 cup sliced celery (2 stalks)
- 1 medium onion, cut into thin wedges
- ½ cup plain low-fat yogurt or dairy sour cream
- 3 tablespoons all-purpose flour

1. In a large saucepan brown meat, half at a time, in hot oil; drain fat. Return all meat to pan. Stir in broth, wine, dried thyme (if using), garlic, and bay leaf. Bring to boiling; reduce heat. Simmer, covered, for 20 minutes.

2. Stir in squash, parsnip, sweet potato, celery, and onion. Return to boiling; reduce heat. Simmer, covered, about 30 minutes more or until meat and vegetables are tender. Discard bay leaf.

3. In a small bowl combine yogurt, flour, and, if using, fresh thyme. Stir ½ cup of the hot liquid into the yogurt mixture. Add yogurt mixture to saucepan. Cook and stir until thickened and bubbly. Cook and stir for 1 minute more. Season to taste with *salt* and *black pepper.*

Per 1½ cups: 365 cal., 9 g total fat (2 g sat. fat), 75 mg chol., 397 mg sodium, 32 g carbo., 4 g fiber, 30 g pro.
Daily Values: 166% vit. A, 35% vit. C, 13% calcium, 22% iron
Exchanges: ½ Vegetable, 2 Starch, 3½ Lean Meat

Browning Meat

Recipes for stews often call for browning cubes of meat in oil.

Browning meat—sometimes coating the cubes with flour first—accomplishes a couple of things. It gives the meat a wonderful mahogany color and toothsome crust that cooking in liquid doesn't give, and it creates drippings that contribute flavor. The flour, if used, also helps thicken the stew.

Jambalaya

Jambalaya

Prep: 25 minutes **Cook:** 20 minutes
Makes: 6 main-dish servings

- 1 **pound fresh or frozen peeled and deveined shrimp**
- ½ **cup chopped onion (1 medium)**
- ½ **cup chopped celery (1 stalk)**
- ¼ **cup chopped green sweet pepper (1 small)**
- 2 **cloves garlic, minced**
- 2 **tablespoons cooking oil**
- 2 **cups chicken broth**
- 1 **14.5-ounce can diced tomatoes, undrained**
- 8 **ounces andouille or kielbasa sausage, halved lengthwise and cut into ½-inch slices**
- ¾ **cup uncooked long grain rice**
- 1 **teaspoon dried thyme, crushed**
- ½ **teaspoon dried basil, crushed**
- ¼ **teaspoon cayenne pepper**
- 1 **bay leaf**
- 1 **cup cubed cooked ham**

1. Thaw shrimp, if frozen. Rinse shrimp; set aside. In a 12-inch skillet cook onion, celery, sweet pepper, and garlic in hot oil over medium-high heat until tender. Stir in broth, undrained tomatoes, sausage, rice, thyme, basil, cayenne pepper, ¼ teaspoon *black pepper,* and bay leaf. Bring to boiling; reduce heat. Simmer, covered, for 15 minutes. Stir in shrimp. Return to boiling. Simmer, covered, about 5 minutes more or until shrimp turn opaque and rice is tender. Stir in ham; heat through. Discard bay leaf.

Per cup: 416 cal., 20 g total fat (6 g sat. fat), 154 mg chol., 1,199 mg sodium, 27 g carbo., 1 g fiber, 30 g pro.
Daily Values: 5% vit. A, 29% vit. C, 9% calcium, 22% iron
Exchanges: 1 Vegetable, 1½ Starch, 3½ Medium-Fat Meat

Hot-and-Sour Soup with Shrimp LOW FAT

Now you won't have to dine out to enjoy this classic Asian-style soup. The best part is that it only takes 35 minutes to make. (And it tastes great too!)

Start to Finish: 35 minutes
Makes: 4 main-dish servings

- 8 **ounces fresh or frozen peeled and deveined shrimp**
- 3½ **cups chicken broth**
- ½ **of a 15-ounce jar whole straw mushrooms, drained, or one 6-ounce jar sliced mushrooms, drained**
- ¼ **cup rice vinegar or white vinegar**
- 2 **tablespoons soy sauce**
- 1 **teaspoon sugar**
- 1 **teaspoon grated fresh ginger**
- ½ **teaspoon black pepper**
- 4 **ounces firm, silken-style tofu (fresh bean curd), cut into bite-size pieces**
- 1 **tablespoon cornstarch**
- 1 **tablespoon cold water**
- ½ **cup frozen peas**
- ½ **cup shredded carrot (1 medium)**
- 2 **tablespoons thinly sliced green onion (1)**
- 1 **egg, beaten**

1. Thaw shrimp, if frozen. Rinse shrimp; set aside. In a large saucepan combine broth, mushrooms, vinegar, soy sauce, sugar, ginger, and pepper. Bring to boiling; reduce heat. Simmer, covered, for 2 minutes. Stir in shrimp and tofu. Return to boiling; reduce heat. Simmer, covered, for 1 minute more.

2. Stir together cornstarch and cold water; stir into broth mixture. Cook and stir until slightly thickened and bubbly. Cook and stir for 2 minutes more. Stir in peas, carrot, and green onion. Pour egg into the soup in a steady stream, stirring a few times to create shreds.

Per 1½ cups: 195 cal., 6 g total fat (1 g sat. fat), 139 mg chol., 1,703 mg sodium, 11 g carbo., 3 g fiber, 22 g pro.
Daily Values: 76% vit. A, 10% vit. C, 9% calcium, 17% iron
Exchanges: ½ Vegetable, ½ Starch, 3 Very Lean Meat, 1 Fat

Easy Salmon Chowder

Easy Salmon Chowder   EASY

Open up a can of salmon, pull out some frozen vegetables and hash brown potatoes, add a few on-hand ingredients, and you have a quick supper.

Prep: 15 minutes **Cook:** 10 minutes
Makes: 4 main-dish servings

  2 cups frozen vegetables (such as broccoli, sweet pepper, and/or corn)
  2 tablespoons finely chopped, seeded fresh jalapeño chile pepper (see tip, page 74) (optional)
  1 tablespoon butter or margarine
  2 tablespoons all-purpose flour
  2 cups milk
  1 cup half-and-half or light cream
  2 cups frozen loose-pack hash brown potatoes with onions and peppers, thawed
  1 15-ounce can salmon, drained and flaked
  ¼ cup snipped fresh Italian parsley
  2 tablespoons lemon juice
  ½ teaspoon salt

1. In a large saucepan cook frozen vegetables and, if desired, jalapeño pepper in hot butter over medium heat for 3 to 5 minutes or until tender. Stir in flour. Stir in milk and half-and-half. Cook and stir until slightly thickened and bubbly. Cook and stir for 2 minutes more.

2. Stir in thawed hash brown potatoes, salmon, parsley, lemon juice, salt, and ½ teaspoon *black pepper.* Cook and stir until heated through.

Per 1½ cups: 383 cal., 19 g total fat (9 g sat. fat), 98 mg chol., 1,009 mg sodium, 23 g carbo., 4 g fiber, 30 g pro.
Daily Values: 34% vit. A, 94% vit. C, 48% calcium, 13% iron
Exchanges: ½ Milk, 1 Vegetable, 1 Starch, 3 Lean Meat, 2 Fat

Oyster Stew   FAST

Start to Finish: 20 minutes **Makes:** 4 main-dish servings

  ¼ cup finely chopped shallot or onion
  1 tablespoon butter or margarine
  1 pint shucked oysters, undrained
  ½ teaspoon salt
  2 cups half-and-half or light cream
  1 cup milk
  1 tablespoon snipped fresh parsley
  ¼ teaspoon white pepper
     Butter or margarine (optional)

1. In a large saucepan cook shallot in hot butter over medium heat until tender. Stir in undrained oysters and salt. Bring to boiling; reduce heat to medium. Cook for 3 to 5 minutes or until oysters curl around the edges, stirring occasionally.

2. Stir in half-and-half, milk, parsley, and pepper; heat through. If desired, top each serving with additional butter.

Per cup: 273 cal., 20 g total fat (12 g sat. fat), 100 mg chol., 573 mg sodium, 12 g carbo., 0 g fiber, 11 g pro.
Daily Values: 18% vit. A, 10% vit. C, 24% calcium, 28% iron
Exchanges: 1 Lean Meat, 3 Fat

New England Clam Chowder

Start to Finish: 45 minutes **Makes:** 4 main-dish servings

  1 pint shucked clams or two 6.5-ounce cans minced clams
  2 slices bacon, halved
  2½ cups chopped, peeled potato (3 medium)
  1 cup chopped onion (1 large)
  1 teaspoon instant chicken bouillon granules
  1 teaspoon Worcestershire sauce
  ¼ teaspoon dried thyme, crushed
  ⅛ teaspoon black pepper
  2 cups milk
  1 cup half-and-half or light cream
  2 tablespoons all-purpose flour

1. Chop fresh clams (if using), reserving juice; set clams aside. Strain clam juice to remove bits of shell. (Or drain canned clams, reserving the juice.) If necessary, add enough water to the reserved clam juice to equal 1 cup. Set clam juice aside.

2. In a large saucepan cook bacon until crisp. Remove bacon, reserving 1 tablespoon drippings in pan. Drain bacon on paper towels; crumble bacon and set aside.

3. Stir the reserved clam juice, potato, onion, bouillon granules, Worcestershire sauce, thyme, and pepper into saucepan. Bring to boiling; reduce heat. Simmer, covered, about 15 minutes or until potatoes are tender. With the back of a fork, mash potatoes slightly against the side of the pan.

4. Stir together milk, half-and-half, and flour; add to potato mixture. Cook and stir until slightly thickened and bubbly. Stir in clams. Return to boiling; reduce heat. Cook for 1 to 2 minutes more or until heated through. Sprinkle each serving with crumbled bacon.

Per 1½ cups: 376 cal., 15 g total fat (8 g sat. fat), 76 mg chol., 495 mg sodium, 35 g carbo., 2 g fiber, 24 g pro.
Daily Values: 17% vit. A, 49% vit. C, 28% calcium, 86% iron
Exchanges: 2½ Starch, 2½ Very Lean Meat, 2 Fat

Manhattan Clam Chowder LOW FAT

Start to Finish: 40 minutes **Makes:** 4 main-dish servings

- 1 **pint shucked clams or two 6.5-ounce cans minced clams**
- 1 **cup chopped celery (2 stalks)**
- ⅓ **cup chopped onion (1 small)**
- ¼ **cup chopped carrot (1 small)**
- 2 **tablespoons olive oil or cooking oil**
- 1 **8-ounce bottle clam juice or 1 cup chicken broth**
- 2 **cups cubed, unpeeled red potato (2 medium)**
- 1 **teaspoon dried thyme, crushed**
- ⅛ **teaspoon cayenne pepper**
- ⅛ **teaspoon black pepper**
- 1 **14.5-ounce can diced tomatoes, undrained**
- 2 **tablespoons purchased cooked bacon pieces or cooked crumbled bacon***

1. Chop fresh clams (if using), reserving juice; set clams aside. Strain clam juice to remove bits of shell. (Or drain canned clams, reserving juice.) If necessary, add enough water to reserved clam juice to equal 1½ cups. Set clam juice aside.

2. In a large saucepan cook celery, onion, and carrot in hot oil over medium heat until tender. Stir in the reserved 1½ cups clam juice and the 8 ounces clam juice. Stir in potato, thyme, cayenne pepper, and black pepper. Bring to boiling; reduce heat. Simmer, covered, for 10 minutes. Stir in clams, undrained tomatoes, and bacon. Return to boiling; reduce heat. Cook for 1 to 2 minutes more or until heated through.

*Note: If cooking your own bacon, cook 2 slices, reserving 2 tablespoons drippings. Omit oil. Cook celery, onion, and carrot in the reserved drippings.

Per 1½ cups: 254 cal., 9 g total fat (1 g sat. fat), 41 mg chol., 507 mg sodium, 24 g carbo., 3 g fiber, 19 g pro.
Daily Values: 47% vit. A, 61% vit. C, 12% calcium, 90% iron
Exchanges: 2 Vegetable, 1 Starch, 2 Very Lean Meat, 1½ Fat

Roasted Corn and Crab Soup LOW FAT

Start to Finish: 1 hour **Oven:** 450°F
Makes: 6 main-dish servings

- 1 **16-ounce package frozen whole kernel corn**
- 2 **cups chopped onion (2 large)**
- 1½ **cups coarsely chopped red sweet pepper (3 medium)**
- 1 **tablespoon cooking oil or butter**
- 4 **14-ounce cans chicken broth**
- ½ **teaspoon dried thyme, crushed**
- ⅛ **to ¼ teaspoon cayenne pepper**
- ⅓ **cup all-purpose flour**
- ½ **cup half-and-half or light cream**
- 4 **ounces cooked crabmeat, cut into bite-size pieces (⅔ cup)**

1. Thaw frozen corn; pat dry with paper towels. Line a 15×10×1-inch baking pan with foil; lightly grease foil. Spread corn in prepared pan. Bake in a 450°F oven for 10 minutes; stir. Bake about 10 minutes more until golden brown, stirring once or twice. Remove from oven; set aside.

2. In a 4-quart Dutch oven cook onion and sweet pepper in hot oil over medium heat for 3 to 4 minutes or until nearly tender. Add roasted corn, three cans of the broth, thyme, and cayenne pepper. Bring to boiling; reduce heat. Simmer, uncovered, for 15 minutes.

3. In a large screw-top jar combine remaining can of broth and the flour. Cover and shake well; stir into soup. Cook and stir until slightly thickened and bubbly. Cook and stir for 1 minute more. Stir in half-and-half; heat through. To serve, ladle soup into bowls; divide crabmeat among bowls.

Make-ahead directions: Prepare as above, except do not add crabmeat. Cool soup; cover and chill for up to 2 days. To serve, reheat soup. Ladle into bowls and divide crabmeat among the servings.

Per 1⅓ cups: 229 cal., 7 g total fat (2 g sat. fat), 26 mg chol., 907 mg sodium, 30 g carbo., 4 g fiber, 14 g pro.
Daily Values: 43% vit. A, 113% vit. C, 7% calcium, 9% iron
Exchanges: 1 Vegetable, 1½ Starch, 1 Very Lean Meat, 1 Fat

Corn Chowder

Prep: 30 minutes **Cook:** 15 minutes
Makes: 6 side-dish servings

- 6 **ears of fresh corn or 3 cups frozen whole kernel corn**
- ½ **cup chopped onion (1 medium)**
- ½ **cup chopped green sweet pepper (1 medium)**
- 1 **tablespoon cooking oil**
- 1 **14-ounce can chicken broth**
- 1 **cup cubed, peeled potato (1 medium)**
- 2 **tablespoons all-purpose flour**
- ½ **teaspoon salt**
- ¼ **teaspoon black pepper**
- 1½ **cups milk**
- 3 **slices bacon, crisp-cooked, drained, and crumbled, or 2 tablespoons purchased cooked bacon pieces**
- 2 **tablespoons snipped fresh parsley (optional)**

1. If using fresh corn, use a sharp knife to cut the kernels off the cobs (see photo, below); you should have about 3 cups corn kernels. Set corn kernels aside.

2. In a large saucepan cook onion and sweet pepper in hot oil until onion is tender but not brown. Stir in corn, broth, and potato. Bring to boiling; reduce heat. Simmer, covered, for 10 to 15 minutes or until vegetables are tender, stirring occasionally.

3. In a small bowl combine flour, salt, and black pepper. Stir milk into flour mixture; add to corn mixture in saucepan. Cook and stir until slightly thickened and bubbly. Cook and stir for 1 minute more. Add bacon; heat through. If desired, garnish each serving with parsley.

Corn and Crab Chowder: Prepare as above, except omit bacon. In Step 3, after cooking for 1 minute, stir in one 6- or 6.5-ounce can crabmeat, drained, flaked, and cartilage removed. Heat through.

Per cup corn or crab variation: 192 cal., 7 g total fat (2 g sat. fat), 9 mg chol., 572 mg sodium, 29 g carbo., 3 g fiber, 8 g pro.
Daily Values: 7% vit. A, 32% vit. C, 8% calcium, 5% iron
Exchanges: 2 Starch, 1 Fat

Hold the ear of corn so an end rests on a cutting board. Using a sharp knife, cut along the cob across the base of the kernels from the top end to the bottom end.

Butternut Squash and Carrot Soup

Butternut Squash and Carrot Soup LOW FAT

Prep: 30 minutes **Cook:** 25 minutes
Makes: 6 side-dish servings

- 3 **cups peeled, diced butternut squash (about 1 small)**
- 2 **cups thinly sliced carrot (4 medium)**
- ¾ **cup thinly sliced leek or chopped onion**
- 1 **tablespoon butter or margarine**
- 2 **14-ounce cans reduced-sodium chicken broth**
- ¼ **teaspoon ground white pepper**
- ¼ **teaspoon ground nutmeg**
- ¼ **cup half-and-half or light cream**
  Pumpkin seeds, toasted (optional) (see tip, page 265)

1. In a large covered saucepan cook squash, carrot, and leek in hot butter over medium heat about 8 minutes, stirring occasionally. Add broth. Bring to boiling; reduce heat. Simmer, covered, for 25 to 35 minutes or until vegetables are tender. Cool slightly.

2. Place one-third of the squash mixture in a food processor or blender. Cover and process or blend until almost smooth. Repeat with remaining squash mixture. Return all of mixture to the saucepan. Add white pepper and nutmeg; bring just to boiling. Add half-and-half; heat through. If desired, garnish each serving with pumpkin seeds.

Per cup: 82 cal., 3 g total fat (2 g sat. fat), 9 mg chol., 364 mg sodium, 12 g carbo., 2 g fiber, 3 g pro.
Daily Values: 107% vit. A, 14% vit. C, 5% calcium, 4% iron
Exchanges: ½ Vegetable, ½ Starch, ½ Fat

Cream of Vegetable Soup

Start to Finish: 25 minutes **Makes:** 4 side-dish servings

Desired vegetable (see variations, below)
1½ cups chicken broth or vegetable stock
1 tablespoon butter or margarine
1 tablespoon all-purpose flour
Seasoning (see variations, below)
¼ teaspoon salt
1 cup milk, half-and-half, or light cream

1. In a large saucepan cook desired vegetable, covered, in a large amount of boiling water according to directions in each variation. Drain well. Set aside 1 cup cooked vegetables.

2. In a food processor combine the remaining cooked vegetables and ¾ cup of the broth. Cover and process about 1 minute or until smooth. Set aside.

3. In same saucepan melt butter. Stir in flour, seasoning, salt, and dash *black pepper.* Add milk all at once. Cook and stir until slightly thickened and bubbly. Cook and stir 1 minute more.

4. Stir in the reserved cooked vegetable, blended vegetable mixture, and remaining ¾ cup broth. Cook and stir until heated through. If necessary, stir in additional milk to reach desired consistency. If desired, season to taste with additional salt and *black pepper.*

Cream of Potato Soup: Cook 5 medium potatoes, peeled and cubed, and ½ cup chopped onion as directed in Step 1 about 15 minutes or until tender; drain. Reserve 1 cup of potato-onion mixture. Process remaining mixture as directed in Step 2, except use all of the broth. Use ¼ teaspoon dried dill or basil, crushed, in Step 3.

Per cup potato variation: 236 cal., 5 g total fat (3 g sat. fat), 13 mg chol., 509 mg sodium, 40 g carbo., 3 g fiber, 8 g pro.
Daily Values: 5% vit. A, 47% vit. C, 10% calcium, 10% iron
Exchanges: 2½ Starch, ½ Fat

Cream of Cauliflower-Cheese Soup: Cook 4 cups fresh or frozen cauliflower florets as directed in Step 1 for 8 to 10 minutes or until tender; drain. Reserve 1 cup cauliflower florets. Process remaining cauliflower florets as directed in Step 2. Use ½ teaspoon celery seeds in Step 3. Stir in ½ cup shredded American cheese along with the blended vegetable mixture in Step 4. If desired, top each serving with additional shredded American cheese.

Cream of Broccoli-Cheese Soup: Cook 4 cups fresh or frozen chopped broccoli as directed in Step 1, at left, for 8 to 10 minutes or until tender; drain. Reserve 1 cup of broccoli. Process remaining broccoli as directed in Step 2. Use ¼ teaspoon lemon-pepper seasoning in Step 3. Stir in ½ cup shredded American cheese with the blended vegetable mixture in Step 4. If desired, top each serving with additional shredded cheese.

Per cup cauliflower-cheese or broccoli-cheese variation: 158 cal., 9 g total fat (6 g sat. fat), 26 mg chol., 729 mg sodium, 10 g carbo., 3 g fiber, 9 g pro.
Daily Values: 9% vit. A, 63% vit. C, 19% calcium, 5% iron
Exchanges: 2 Vegetable, ½ High-Fat Meat, 1½ Fat

Curried Sweet Potato Chowder

Start to Finish: 30 minutes **Makes:** 4 side-dish servings

1⅓ cups ½-inch peeled sweet potato cubes (3 medium)
⅓ cup finely chopped shallot (1 large)
1 tablespoon butter
½ teaspoon curry powder
1 tablespoon all-purpose flour
1½ cups milk
½ cup half-and-half or light cream
¾ cup frozen baby peas
¼ teaspoon salt
4 teaspoons pumpkin seeds, toasted (see tip, page 265)

1. In a medium saucepan cook and stir sweet potato and shallot in hot butter over medium heat for 2 minutes. Add curry powder and stir for 30 seconds. Stir in flour. Gradually stir in milk until smooth. Add half-and-half, peas, salt, and ⅛ teaspoon *black pepper.* Bring to boiling; reduce heat. Simmer, covered, 10 to 15 minutes or until potatoes are tender, stirring occasionally. Sprinkle each serving with pumpkin seeds.

Per ¾ cup: 208 cal., 10 g total fat (5 g sat. fat), 26 mg chol., 261 mg sodium, 21 g carbo., 3 g fiber, 8 g pro.
Daily Values: 151% vit. A, 28% vit. C, 16% calcium, 10% iron
Exchanges: ½ Milk, 1 Starch, 2 Fat

Lower-Fat Curried Sweet Potato Chowder: Prepare as above, except reduce butter to 2 teaspoons and substitute 1½ cups fat-free milk for the milk and ½ cup fat-free half-and-half for the half-and-half.

Per ¾ cup: 165 cal., 4 g total fat (2 g sat. fat), 7 mg chol., 269 mg sodium, 23 g carbo., 3 g fiber, 8 g pro.
Daily Values: 149% vit. A, 27% vit. C, 13% calcium, 12% iron
Exchanges: 1 Starch, ½ Milk, 1 Fat

New Potato Simmer

New Potato Simmer LOW FAT

Besides bright yellow-green napa cabbage, shredded spinach leaves are an option for a fresh and colorful garnish.

Prep: 15 minutes **Cook:** 20 minutes
Makes: 6 main-dish servings

- 1½ **pounds tiny new potatoes**
- 1 **pound smoked turkey breast or smoked chicken breast, shredded**
- 2 **14-ounce cans reduced-sodium chicken broth**
- ⅓ **cup sliced leek (1)**
- ⅓ **cup whipping cream**
- 3 **tablespoons Dijon-style mustard**
- 1 **tablespoon snipped fresh lemon thyme or regular fresh thyme**
- 1½ **cups shredded napa cabbage**

1. Cut any large potatoes in half. In a 4-quart Dutch oven combine potatoes, turkey, broth, and leek. Bring to boiling; reduce heat. Simmer, covered, for 15 minutes.

2. In a small bowl stir together cream and mustard; add to Dutch oven along with lemon thyme. Simmer, uncovered, about 5 minutes more or until potatoes are tender, stirring occasionally. Top each serving with ¼ cup cabbage.

Per 1⅓ cups: 243 cal., 8 g total fat (4 g sat. fat), 57 mg chol., 1,297 mg sodium, 23 g carbo., 3 g fiber, 19 g pro.
Daily Values: 9% vit. A, 41% vit. C, 5% calcium, 13% iron
Exchanges: 1½ Starch, 2 Very Lean Meat, 1½ Fat

Baked Potato Soup

Prep: 20 minutes **Bake:** 40 minutes **Oven:** 425°F
Cook: 20 minutes **Makes:** 5 to 6 main-dish servings

- 2 **large baking potatoes (about 8 ounces each)**
- 6 **tablespoons thinly sliced green onion (3)**
- 3 **tablespoons butter**
- 3 **tablespoons all-purpose flour**
- 2 **teaspoons snipped fresh dill or chives or ¼ teaspoon dried dill**
- ¼ **teaspoon salt**
- ¼ **teaspoon black pepper**
- 4 **cups milk**
- 1¼ **cups shredded American cheese (5 ounces)**
- 4 **slices bacon, crisp-cooked, drained, and crumbled**

1. Scrub potatoes with a vegetable brush; pat dry. Prick potatoes with a fork. Bake in a 425°F oven for 40 to 60 minutes or until tender; cool. Cut each potato lengthwise. Scoop out white portion of each potato. Break up any large pieces of potato; set aside. Discard potato skins.

2. In a large saucepan cook 3 tablespoons of the green onion in hot butter over medium heat until tender. Stir in flour, dill, salt, and pepper. Add milk all at once. Cook and stir for 12 to 15 minutes or until thickened and bubbly. Add the potato and 1 cup of the cheese; stir until cheese melts.

3. Top each serving with the remaining ¼ cup cheese, remaining 3 tablespoons green onion, and the bacon.

Per cup: 377 cal., 23 g total fat (14 g sat. fat), 67 mg chol., 801 mg sodium, 26 g carbo., 1 g fiber, 17 g pro.
Daily Values: 21% vit. A, 23% vit. C, 43% calcium, 7% iron
Exchanges: 1 Starch, 1 Milk, 1 High-Fat Meat, 2½ Fat

French Onion Soup FAST

Start to Finish: 30 minutes **Makes:** 6 side-dish servings

- 2 **cups thinly sliced yellow onion (2 large)**
- 2 **tablespoons butter or margarine**
- 4 **cups beef broth**
- 2 **tablespoons dry sherry or dry white wine (optional)**
- 1 **teaspoon Worcestershire sauce**
  Dash black pepper
- 6 **slices French bread, toasted**
- 1 **cup shredded Swiss, Gruyère, or Jarlsberg cheese (4 ounces)**

1. In a large saucepan cook onion, covered, in hot butter over medium-low heat for 8 to 10 minutes or until tender and golden, stirring occasionally. Stir in broth, dry sherry (if desired), Worcestershire sauce, and pepper. Bring to boiling; reduce heat. Simmer, covered, for 10 minutes.

2. Meanwhile, arrange toasted bread slices on a baking sheet. Evenly divide cheese among slices. Broil 3 to 4 inches from heat for 3 to 4 minutes or until cheese is light brown and bubbly. Top each serving with a bread slice.

Per ¾ cup + 1 slice cheese toast: 212 cal., 11 g total fat (6 g sat. fat), 31 mg chol., 778 mg sodium, 18 g carbo., 2 g fiber, 10 g pro.
Daily Values: 7% vit. A, 5% vit. C, 20% calcium, 6% iron
Exchanges: ½ Vegetable, 1 Starch, 1 High-Fat Meat, ½ Fat

Fresh Tomato Soup

See variation to serve this soup chilled.

Prep: 20 minutes **Cook:** 20 minutes **Cool:** 10 minutes
Makes: 4 side-dish servings

> 3 **medium tomatoes, peeled and quartered**
> 1½ **cups water**
> ½ **cup chopped onion (1 medium)**
> ½ **cup chopped celery (1 stalk)**
> ½ **of a 6-ounce can (⅓ cup) tomato paste**
> 2 **tablespoons snipped fresh cilantro or basil**
> 2 **teaspoons instant chicken bouillon granules**
> 1 **teaspoon sugar**
>   **Few dashes bottled hot pepper sauce**
>   **Snipped fresh cilantro or basil (optional)**

1. If desired, seed the tomatoes. In a large saucepan combine tomato, water, onion, celery, tomato paste, the 2 tablespoons cilantro, bouillon granules, sugar, and hot pepper sauce. Bring to boiling; reduce heat. Simmer, covered, about 20 minutes or until celery and onion are tender. Remove from heat; cool for 10 minutes.

2. Place half of the tomato mixture in a blender or food processor. Cover and blend or process until smooth. Repeat with the remaining mixture. Return all to the saucepan; heat through. If desired, garnish with additional cilantro.

Chilled Fresh Tomato Soup: Prepare as above, except after blending, cover and chill soup for up to 24 hours. If desired, top with sour cream.

Per cup: 54 cal., 0 g total fat (0 g sat. fat), 0 mg chol., 744 mg sodium, 12 g carbo., 3 g fiber, 2 g pro.
Daily Values: 25% vit. A, 45% vit. C, 3% calcium, 5% iron
Exchanges: 2 Vegetable

Spring Pea Soup LOW FAT

Prep: 25 minutes **Cook:** 10 minutes
Makes: 6 main-dish servings

> 5 **cups shelled peas**
> 2 **14-ounce cans chicken broth**
> 2 **small heads Boston or Bibb lettuce, torn into small pieces**
> 1½ **cups sliced green onion (12)**
> 3 **tablespoons snipped fresh tarragon**
> 1½ **to 2 cups half-and-half, light cream, or milk**
> 6 **slices French bread, toasted**
> 2 **ounces prosciutto, cut into thin strips**
> ⅓ **cup crumbled feta cheese**
>   **Fresh tarragon sprigs (optional)**

1. In a 4-quart Dutch oven combine peas and chicken broth. Bring to boiling; reduce heat. Simmer, covered, for 6 minutes. Add lettuce and green onion. Return to boiling; reduce heat. Simmer, covered, for 4 to 6 minutes more or until peas are tender. If desired, use a slotted spoon to remove ⅓ cup peas; reserve for garnish. Stir in tarragon. Cool slightly.

2. Transfer one-fourth of the soup to a blender or food processor. Cover and blend or process until nearly smooth. Repeat with remaining soup, blending or processing one-fourth at a time. Return all of the soup to Dutch oven. Stir in enough half-and-half to reach desired consistency; heat through. Do not boil. Add *salt* and *black pepper* to taste.

3. Top each serving with a slice of French bread, some prosciutto strips, and some feta cheese. Garnish each serving with reserved peas, and, if desired, a tarragon sprig.

Per 1⅓ cups + 1 slice bread and toppings: 304 cal., 11 g total fat (6 g sat. fat), 38 mg chol., 1,218 mg sodium, 36 g carbo., 7 g fiber, 16 g pro.
Daily Values: 96% vit. A, 50% vit. C, 19% calcium, 21% iron
Exchanges: 2 Starch, 1½ Vegetable, 1 Lean Meat, 1½ Fat

Summer Supper

A chilled soup for supper during the warm summer months is refreshing and light.

- *Chilled Fresh Tomato Soup (left)*
- *Nut Bread (page 131)*
- *Mixed baby greens salad with vinaigrette*
- *Cinnamon Gelato (page 292)*
- *Iced tea with orange slices*

Pumpkin Soup `LOW FAT` `FAST`

Coconut milk lends a wonderful flavor to this soup.

Prep: 15 minutes **Cook:** 10 minutes
Makes: 8 side-dish servings

- 1 cup sliced carrot (2 medium)
- ¾ cup coarsely chopped green sweet pepper (1 large)
- ½ cup chopped onion (1 medium)
- 1 tablespoon cooking oil
- 1 15-ounce can pumpkin
- 1 14-ounce can unsweetened light coconut milk
- 1 14-ounce can reduced-sodium chicken broth
- 2 tablespoons packed brown sugar
- 1 medium fresh jalapeño chile pepper, seeded and finely chopped (see tip, page 74)
- ¾ teaspoon salt
- ½ teaspoon ground ginger
- 2 tablespoons snipped fresh cilantro or parsley

1. In a large saucepan cook carrot, sweet pepper, and onion in hot oil over medium heat about 5 minutes or until vegetables are almost tender. Remove from heat. In a bowl combine pumpkin, coconut milk, and broth. Stir in brown sugar, jalapeño pepper, salt, and ginger. Stir pumpkin mixture into cooked vegetable mixture.

2. Bring to boiling; reduce heat. Simmer, uncovered, about 10 minutes or until heated through, stirring frequently. Stir in cilantro before serving.

Per ¾ cup: 94 cal., 5 g total fat (2 g sat. fat), 0 mg chol., 365 mg sodium, 13 g carbo., 2 g fiber, 2 g pro.
Daily Values: 201% vit. A, 25% vit. C, 3% calcium, 8% iron
Exchanges: ½ Vegetable, ½ Other Carbo., 1 Fat

Black Bean and Chipotle Pepper Soup `LOW FAT`

This soup is easy to put together after work, thanks to the convenience of canned beans. Just heat some corn tortillas and serve with Mexican beer or soda.

Prep: 15 minutes **Cook:** 30 minutes
Makes: 4 main-dish servings

- 1 cup chopped green sweet pepper (1 large)
- 1 cup chopped onion (1 large)
- 2 cloves garlic, minced
- 1 tablespoon olive oil or cooking oil
- 2 15-ounce cans black beans, rinsed and drained
- 1 14-ounce can beef broth
- 1 cup chopped tomato (2 medium)
- 2 tablespoons snipped fresh cilantro or parsley
- 1 tablespoon snipped fresh thyme or 1 teaspoon dried thyme, crushed
- 2 teaspoons snipped fresh oregano or ½ teaspoon dried oregano, crushed
- 2 teaspoons chopped canned chipotle pepper in adobo sauce (see tip, page 74)
- Dairy sour cream (optional)
- Fresh cilantro sprigs (optional)

1. In a large saucepan cook sweet pepper, onion, and garlic in hot oil over medium heat for 3 minutes. Stir in black beans, broth, tomato, snipped cilantro, thyme, oregano, and chipotle pepper. Bring to boiling; reduce heat. Simmer, covered, for 30 minutes.

2. If desired, mash beans slightly.* If desired, garnish with sour cream and cilantro sprigs.

***Note:** For a pureed bean soup, cool soup slightly. Place half of the soup in a food processor or blender. Cover and process or blend until smooth. Repeat with remaining soup.

Per 1⅓ cups: 207 cal., 4 g total fat (1 g sat. fat), 1 mg chol., 911 mg sodium, 37 g carbo., 12 g fiber, 16 g pro.
Daily Values: 14% vit. A, 60% vit. C, 10% calcium, 16% iron
Exchanges: 1 Vegetable, 2 Starch, ½ Very Lean Meat, ½ Fat

Vegetarian Chili `LOW FAT` `VEGETARIAN`

Start to Finish: 40 minutes **Makes:** 8 main-dish servings

- 1 cup chopped green sweet pepper (1 large)
- ½ cup chopped onion (1 medium)
- 3 cloves garlic, minced
- 1 tablespoon cooking oil
- 2 14.5-ounce cans diced tomatoes with chili spices or diced tomatoes, undrained
- 1 12-ounce can beer or one 14-ounce can vegetable broth
- 1 cup water
- 1 8-ounce can tomato sauce
- 3 to 4 teaspoons chili powder
- 1 tablespoon snipped fresh oregano or 1 teaspoon dried oregano, crushed
- 1 teaspoon ground cumin
- ½ teaspoon black pepper
- Several dashes bottled hot pepper sauce (optional)
- 3 15-ounce cans pinto beans, black beans, white kidney beans, and/or red kidney beans, rinsed and drained

2 **cups fresh or frozen whole kernel corn**

1 **cup chopped zucchini (1 medium)**

1 **cup shredded cheddar or Monterey Jack cheese (4 ounces) (optional)**

1. In a 5- or 6-quart Dutch oven cook sweet pepper, onion, and garlic in hot oil over medium heat until tender, stirring occasionally. Stir in undrained tomatoes, beer, water, tomato sauce, chili powder, dried oregano (if using), cumin, black pepper, and, if desired, hot pepper sauce. Bring to boiling; reduce heat. Simmer, covered, for 10 minutes.

2. Stir in beans, corn, and zucchini. Return to boiling; reduce heat. Simmer, uncovered, for 10 minutes more. Stir in fresh oregano, if using. If desired, top each serving with cheese.

Per 1½ cups: 256 cal., 3 g total fat (0 g sat. fat), 0 mg chol., 879 mg sodium, 46 g carbo., 11 g fiber, 13 g pro.
Daily Values: 30% vit. A, 55% vit. C, 9% calcium, 18% iron
Exchanges: 1½ Vegetable, 2 Starch, 1 Very Lean Meat, ½ Fat

Minestrone

This hearty vegetable soup tastes even better the day after you make it.

Prep: 15 minutes **Cook:** 10 minutes
Makes: 8 main-dish servings

3 **14-ounce cans beef broth**

1 **15-ounce can kidney beans, rinsed and drained**

1 **15-ounce can garbanzo beans (chickpeas), rinsed and drained**

1 **14.5-ounce can stewed tomatoes, undrained**

1 **11.5-ounce can vegetable juice**

1 **6-ounce can tomato paste**

2 **teaspoons sugar**

1 **teaspoon dried Italian seasoning, crushed**

1½ **cups frozen mixed vegetables (such as Italian blend)**

2 **cups fresh spinach leaves, cut into strips**

2 **cups cooked pasta, such as medium shell macaroni or mostaccioli**

Finely shredded Parmesan cheese (optional)

1. In a 4-quart Dutch oven combine broth, kidney beans, garbanzo beans, undrained tomatoes, vegetable juice, tomato paste, sugar, and Italian seasoning. Bring to boiling; add mixed vegetables. Reduce heat. Simmer, covered, about 10 minutes or until vegetables are tender.

2. Stir in spinach and cooked pasta; heat through. If desired, sprinkle with Parmesan cheese.

Make-ahead directions: Prepare as at left through Step 1, except cover and chill overnight. To serve, reheat soup over medium heat. Stir in spinach and cooked pasta; heat through.

Per 1½ cups: 223 cal., 2 g total fat (0 g sat. fat), 0 mg chol., 1,152 mg sodium, 43 g carbo., 8 g fiber, 11 g pro.
Daily Values: 48% vit. A, 48% vit. C, 8% calcium, 18% iron
Exchanges: 2 Vegetable, 2 Starch

Red and Green Gazpacho

Colorful tomatoes, tomatillos, cucumber, and cilantro combine in this make-ahead chilled soup. See photo, page 545.

Prep: 30 minutes **Chill:** 1 hour
Makes: 6 side-dish servings

3 **cups chopped red and/or partially green tomato (3 large)**

2 **11.5-ounce cans tomato juice (about 3 cups)**

½ **cup chopped tomatillo (2 medium) (optional)**

½ **cup chopped cucumber**

1 **large fresh jalapeño chile pepper, seeded and finely chopped (see tip, page 74)**

¼ **cup finely chopped green onion (2)**

1 **clove garlic, minced**

¼ **cup finely snipped fresh cilantro**

1 **tablespoon olive oil**

1 **tablespoon lime juice**

¼ **teaspoon salt**

¼ **teaspoon bottled hot pepper sauce**

1 **avocado, halved, seeded, peeled, and chopped (optional)**

Lime wedges

1. In a large bowl combine tomato, tomato juice, tomatillo (if using), cucumber, jalapeño pepper, green onion, garlic, cilantro, oil, lime juice, salt, and hot pepper sauce. Cover and chill at least 1 hour.

2. If desired, top each serving with avocado. Serve with lime wedges.

Per cup: 60 cal., 3 g total fat (0 g sat. fat), 0 mg chol., 398 mg sodium, 9 g carbo., 2 g fiber, 2 g pro.
Daily Values: 30% vit. A, 59% vit. C, 3% calcium, 5% iron
Exchanges: 1½ Vegetable, ½ Fat

Shrimp Gazpacho: Prepare as above, except before serving stir 8 ounces cooked, peeled, deveined, and chopped shrimp or 8 ounces lump crabmeat into soup.

Per cup: 98 cal., 3 g total fat (0 g sat. fat), 74 mg chol., 483 mg sodium, 9 g carbo., 2 g fiber, 10 g pro.
Daily Values: 32% vit. A, 60% vit. C, 4% calcium, 11% iron
Exchanges: 1½ Vegetable, 1 Very Lean Meat, ½ Fat

Strawberry-Melon Soup with Ginger Melon Balls

This flavorful soup is the perfect way to start a spring or summer brunch. Garnish with edible pesticide-free flowers, if you like.

Prep: 40 minutes **Cook:** 5 minutes **Chill:** overnight
Makes: 8 side-dish servings

- 1 **small cantaloupe**
- ½ **of a small honeydew melon**
- ½ **cup unsweetened pineapple juice**
- ⅓ **cup sugar**
- 1 **tablespoon grated fresh ginger**
- 1 **8-ounce carton dairy sour cream**
- 1 **6-ounce carton vanilla yogurt**
- 4 **cups fresh or frozen unsweetened strawberries**
- 2 **cups milk**

1. Using a small melon baller, scoop the cantaloupe and the honeydew into balls or use a knife to cut melons into cubes. You should have about 4 cups cantaloupe and 2 cups honeydew pieces. Set melon pieces aside.

2. In a small saucepan combine pineapple juice, sugar, and ginger. Bring to boiling, stirring until sugar dissolves; reduce heat. Simmer, uncovered, over medium heat for 5 to 7 minutes or until the mixture is the consistency of a thin syrup. Remove from heat; cool. Transfer syrup to a storage container. Add 2 cups of the cantaloupe pieces and all of the honeydew pieces. Cover and chill overnight.

3. Meanwhile, in a large bowl stir together sour cream and yogurt; set aside. In a blender or food processor cover and blend or process strawberries until smooth; add to sour cream mixture. Cover and blend or process remaining 2 cups cantaloupe pieces until smooth. Add pureed melon and milk to strawberry mixture; stir to combine. Cover and chill overnight.

4. To serve, drain melon balls, reserving syrup. Stir reserved syrup into the chilled soup. Ladle soup into chilled bowls; top with melon balls.

Per cup: 215 cal., 8 g total fat (5 g sat. fat), 18 mg chol., 76 mg sodium, 33 g carbo., 3 g fiber, 5 g pro.
Daily Values: 61% vit. A, 137% vit. C, 16% calcium, 4% iron
Exchanges: 1 Fruit, 1 Other Carbo., 1½ Fat

Fall Fruit Soup

Fall Fruit Soup

Prep: 10 minutes **Cook:** 5 minutes
Makes: 6 side-dish servings

- 1 **cup cranberries (4 ounces)**
- 1 **medium pear, cored and cut into bite-size pieces**
- 1 **medium cooking apple (such as Rome, Jonathan, or Fuji), cored and cut into bite-size pieces**
- 3 **plums, halved, pitted, and cut into thin slices**
- 3 **cups cranberry-apple juice**
- ¼ **cup packed brown sugar**
- 1 **tablespoon lemon juice**
- 2 **3-inch pieces stick cinnamon**

1. In a large saucepan combine cranberries, pear, apple, and plum. Stir in cranberry-apple juice, brown sugar, lemon juice, and cinnamon stick. Bring to boiling; reduce heat. Simmer, covered, for 5 to 6 minutes or until fruit is tender and skins on cranberries pop. Remove and discard cinnamon sticks.

Per cup: 174 cal., 0 g total fat (0 g sat. fat), 0 mg chol., 13 mg sodium, 45 g carbo., 3 g fiber, 1 g pro.
Daily Values: 3% vit. A, 80% vit. C, 2% calcium, 3% iron
Exchanges: 2½ Fruit, ½ Other Carbo.

Fall Brunch Menu

Serve this menu for a special gathering.

- *Fall Fruit Soup (above)*
- *Scones with butter*
- *Quiche (page 238)*
- *Hot tea with honey*

Vegetables & Fruits

Sour Cream and Chive
Mashed Potatoes, 587

Warm Citrus Fruit
with Brown Sugar, 596

Farm-Style Green Beans, 575

Vegetables & Fruits Essentials

Vegetables and fruits bring color, flavor, crunch, and a host of vitamins and minerals to meals and snacks. Here are some suggestions for maximizing their goodness.

Fresh from the Garden

Whether purchased from your supermarket, roadside stand, or farmer's market or picked from your garden, fresh vegetables and fruits are hard to top in flavor and texture. Choose those that are crisp, bright in color, and heavy for their size. Avoid any that are bruised, shriveled, moldy, or blemished. For information on selecting and storing specific vegetables and fruits, refer to the chart on pages 601–605.

Ripening Fruit

Some fruits are picked and shipped while still firm, so they may need additional ripening. To ripen fruit, place it in a small, clean paper bag. (A plastic bag is not suitable for ripening because it doesn't allow fruit to breathe and the trapped moisture can produce mold on the fruit.) Loosely close the bag and store it at room temperature. To speed up the ripening, place an apple or ripe banana in the bag with the underripe fruit. Check fruit daily and remove any that yields to gentle pressure. Enjoy the ripe fruit immediately or transfer it to the refrigerator for a couple of days. Refrigeration will slow down any further ripening.

Cooking Fresh Vegetables

Fresh vegetables can be cooked in many ways—simmered, steamed, stir-fried, roasted, or microwaved. For directions on simmering, steaming, and microwaving vegetables, refer to the charts on pages 606–610.

Stir-frying is a great way to maximize the flavor and texture of vegetables. It's best to cut the vegetable into bite-size pieces and, if you're cooking more than one type of vegetable, into pieces that will cook in about the same length of time. Heat oil in the wok or skillet before adding the vegetables. Once the oil is hot, add the vegetables in small batches and cook

Off-the-Shelf Veggies

When pressed for time, you can use frozen and canned vegetables.

Frozen vegetables are flash-frozen soon after picking. This helps to retain their vitamins and minerals at levels equal to or greater than fresh. Other advantages include year-round availability and ease of storage. If you're short on freezer space, canned vegetables may be even more convenient than frozen. If you are concerned about the sodium that traditionally is added during the canning process, look for products labeled low sodium or no salt added.

and stir just until crisp-tender. Stir-frying too many vegetables at once makes them steam and become mushy. You can add all the vegetables to the wok or skillet at the end and cook them just long enough to reheat.

Roasting is another easy cooking technique. It is well suited for root vegetables (beets, carrots, parsnips, potatoes, rutabagas, and sweet potatoes) because it brings out their subtle sweetness. It also gives the vegetables a great texture—a crisp crust with a tender interior. Other vegetables can be tossed with oil and roasted in the oven. Cooking times vary, so it's best to follow a recipe. Check the chapter divider (page 572) for roasted vegetable recipes.

Artichokes with Herb-Butter Sauce

Start to Finish: 35 minutes **Makes:** 2 servings

- 2 **artichokes (about 10 ounces each)**
  Lemon juice
- ¼ **cup butter**
- 1 **tablespoon lemon juice**
- 1 **teaspoon snipped fresh dill, tarragon, or oregano, or ¼ teaspoon dried dill, tarragon, or oregano, crushed**

1. Wash artichokes; trim stems and remove loose outer leaves. Cut 1 inch off the top of each artichoke; snip off the sharp leaf tips (see photo, right). Brush the cut edges with a little lemon juice. In a large saucepan or Dutch oven bring a large amount of lightly salted water to boiling; add artichokes. Return to boiling; reduce heat. Simmer, covered, for 20 to 30 minutes or until a leaf pulls out easily. Drain artichokes upside down on paper towels.

2. Meanwhile, for herb-butter sauce, melt butter. Stir in the 1 tablespoon lemon juice and the desired herb. Turn artichokes right side up; serve with the butter sauce.*

*Note: To eat an artichoke, pull off one leaf and dip the leaf base into sauce or dip. Draw the base of the leaf through your teeth, scraping off only tender flesh. Discard remainder of leaf. Continue removing leaves until the fuzzy choke appears. Scoop out the choke with a spoon; discard choke. If you have trouble getting the choke out, try loosening it with a grapefruit knife, then scooping with a spoon. Eat the remaining heart with a fork, dipping pieces into sauce or dip.

Per artichoke with 2 tablespoons sauce: 268 cal., 23 g total fat (15 g sat. fat), 61 mg chol., 278 mg sodium, 15 g carbo., 7 g fiber, 4 g pro.
Daily Values: 14% vit. A, 30% vit. C, 6% calcium, 9% iron
Exchanges: 2 Vegetable, 2 Fat

Artichokes with Honey-Mustard Dip: Prepare as above, except thoroughly chill artichokes after Step 1 and omit herb-butter sauce. For Honey-Mustard Dip, combine ½ cup mayonnaise or salad dressing, 1 tablespoon Dijon-style mustard, and 1 tablespoon honey. Cover; chill until serving time. Makes 4 appetizer servings.

Per ½ artichoke with 2 tablespoons dip: 251 cal., 22 g total fat (4 g sat. fat), 10 mg chol., 297 mg sodium, 12 g carbo., 3 g fiber, 3 g pro.
Daily Values: 12% vit. C, 3% calcium, 5% iron
Exchanges: 1 Vegetable, ½ Other Carbo., 4½ Fat

Artichokes with Curry Dip: Prepare as at left, except chill artichokes after Step 1 and omit herb-butter sauce. For Curry Dip, combine ½ cup mayonnaise or salad dressing, 1 teaspoon lemon juice, 1 teaspoon prepared horseradish, 1 teaspoon finely chopped onion, 1 teaspoon curry powder, and ⅛ teaspoon salt. Cover; chill for 2 to 24 hours. Makes 4 appetizer servings.

Per ½ artichoke with 2 tablespoons dip: 234 cal., 22 g total fat (4 g sat. fat), 10 mg chol., 338 mg sodium, 8 g carbo., 4 g fiber, 2 g pro.
Daily Values: 14% vit. C, 3% calcium, 5% iron
Exchanges: 1 Vegetable, 4½ Fat

Use kitchen scissors to cut 1 inch off the top of each artichoke and carefully snip off the leaves' sharp tips.

Roasted Asparagus with Gruyère `EASY`

Prep: 15 minutes **Roast:** 20 minutes
Oven: 400°F **Makes:** 6 servings

- 2 **pounds asparagus spears**
- 1 **small onion, cut into thin wedges**
- 1 **small red or yellow sweet pepper, cut into thin strips**
- 1 **tablespoon olive oil**
- ¼ **cup shredded Gruyère or Swiss cheese**

1. Snap off and discard woody bases from asparagus (see photo, below). Scrape off scales. Place asparagus, onion, and sweet pepper in a 15×10×1-inch baking pan. Drizzle vegetables with oil; toss to coat. Spread vegetables in a single layer. Sprinkle with ¼ teaspoon *salt* and ¼ teaspoon *black pepper.* Roast, uncovered, in a 400°F oven about 20 minutes or until asparagus is crisp-tender. Transfer to a serving platter; sprinkle with cheese.

Per ⅙ recipe: 73 cal., 4 g total fat (1 g sat. fat), 5 mg chol., 127 mg sodium, 4 g carbo., 2 g fiber, 4 g pro.
Daily Values: 5% vit. A, 94% vit. C, 6% calcium, 4% iron
Exchanges: 1 Vegetable, 1 Fat

Starting at the base of each asparagus spear and working toward the tip, bend the spear several times until you find a place where it breaks easily. Snap off the woody base at that point.

Asparagus-Snow Pea Stir-Fry

Asparagus-Snow Pea Stir-Fry

Start to Finish: 30 minutes **Makes:** 6 servings

- **1 pound asparagus spears**
- **1 tablespoon cooking oil**
- **2 teaspoons grated fresh ginger**
- **2 cloves garlic, minced**
- **1 medium red onion, cut into thin wedges**
- **1 medium red sweet pepper, cut into 1-inch pieces**
- **2 cups fresh sugar snap peas or frozen sugar snap peas**
- **1 tablespoon sesame seeds**
- **2 tablespoons soy sauce**
- **2 tablespoons rice vinegar**
- **1 tablespoon packed brown sugar**
- **1 teaspoon toasted sesame oil**

1. Snap off and discard woody bases from asparagus (see photo, page 574). If desired, scrape off scales. Bias-slice asparagus into 2-inch pieces (you should have about 3 cups).

2. In a wok or large skillet heat oil over medium-high heat. Add ginger and garlic; cook and stir for 15 seconds. Add asparagus, onion, and sweet pepper; cook and stir for 3 minutes. Add sugar snap peas and sesame seeds; cook and stir for 3 to 4 minutes or until vegetables are crisp-tender.

3. Add soy sauce, rice vinegar, brown sugar, and sesame oil to vegetable mixture; toss to coat. If desired, serve with a slotted spoon.

Per ⅔ cup: 106 cal., 4 g total fat (1 g sat. fat), 0 mg chol., 319 mg sodium, 14 g carbo., 3 g fiber, 4 g pro.
Daily Values: 18% vit. A, 80% vit. C, 5% calcium, 11% iron
Exchanges: 2 Vegetable, 1 Fat

Farm-Style Green Beans

See photo, page 571.

Prep: 20 minutes **Cook:** 10 minutes **Makes:** 8 servings

- **1 pound green beans**
- **4 slices bacon, cut up**
- **1 cup sliced onion (2 medium)**
- **2 cups chopped, seeded, peeled tomato**
- **½ teaspoon salt**

1. Remove ends and strings from beans. Leave whole or cut into 1-inch pieces. Set aside.

2. In a large skillet cook bacon until crisp. Remove bacon, reserving 3 tablespoons drippings. Drain bacon on paper towels; set aside. Cook the onion in the reserved drippings over medium heat until tender. Add tomato and salt. Cook, uncovered, about 5 minutes more or until most of the liquid is absorbed.

3. Meanwhile, in a medium saucepan cook the beans, covered, in a small amount of boiling salted water for 10 to 15 minutes or until crisp-tender; drain. Transfer beans to a serving bowl. Top beans with tomato mixture and bacon.

Per ⅔ cup: 99 cal., 7 g total fat (2 g sat. fat), 9 mg chol., 244 mg sodium, 8 g carbo., 3 g fiber, 3 g pro.
Daily Values: 14% vit. A, 24% vit. C, 3% calcium, 4% iron
Exchanges: 1½ Vegetable, 1½ Fat

Green Beans Amandine

Start to Finish: 30 minutes **Makes:** 3 servings

- **8 ounces fresh green beans or one 9-ounce package frozen cut or French-cut green beans**
- **2 tablespoons slivered almonds**
- **1 tablespoon butter or margarine**
- **1 teaspoon lemon juice**

1. Cut fresh beans into 1-inch pieces. (Slice French-cut beans lengthwise.) Cook fresh green beans, covered, in a small amount of boiling salted water for 10 to 15 minutes (5 to 10 minutes for French-cut beans) or until crisp-tender. (Cook frozen beans according to package directions.) Drain; keep warm.

2. Meanwhile, in saucepan cook and stir almonds in melted butter until golden. Remove from heat; stir in lemon juice. Stir into beans.

Per ½ cup: 89 cal., 7 g total fat (3 g sat. fat), 11 mg chol., 45 mg sodium, 6 g carbo., 3 g fiber, 2 g pro.
Daily Values: 11% vit. A, 15% vit. C, 4% calcium, 5% iron
Exchanges: 1 Vegetable, 1½ Fat

Home-Style Green Bean Bake `EASY`

Prep: 15 minutes **Bake:** 45 minutes
Oven: 350°F **Makes:** 6 servings

- 1 **10.75-ounce can condensed cream of mushroom soup or cream of celery soup**
- ½ **cup shredded cheddar cheese or American cheese (2 ounces)**
- 1 **2-ounce jar sliced pimiento, drained (optional)**
- 3 **14.5-ounce cans French-cut green beans or cut green beans, drained, or 6 cups frozen French-cut green beans or cut green beans, thawed and drained**
- 1 **2.8-ounce can french-fried onions**

1. In a large bowl combine soup, cheese, and, if desired, pimiento. Stir in green beans. Transfer mixture to a 1½-quart casserole.

2. Bake, covered, in a 350°F oven for 40 minutes. Remove from oven and stir; sprinkle with french-fried onions. Bake about 5 minutes more or until heated through.

Calico Bean Bake: Prepare as above, except substitute one 14.5-ounce can cut wax beans for 1 can of green beans.

Per cup home-style or calico variation: 194 cal., 12 g total fat (3 g sat. fat), 11 mg chol., 1,200 mg sodium, 16 g carbo., 2 g fiber, 5 g pro.
Daily Values: 12% vit. A, 7% vit. C, 11% calcium, 8% iron
Exchanges: 2 Vegetable, ½ Other Carbo., 2½ Fat

Roasted Beets

Prep: 20 minutes **Roast:** 50 minutes
Oven: 375°F **Makes:** 6 servings

- 1½ **pounds baby beets or 6 medium beets**
- 8 **ounces pearl onions**
- 2 **tablespoons olive oil**
- 6 **cloves garlic, minced**
- 1 **tablespoon snipped fresh thyme or basil**
- ½ **teaspoon salt**
- ¼ **teaspoon black pepper**
- 1 **tablespoon snipped fresh chives (optional)**

1. Scrub beets; trim off stem and root ends. If desired, peel the baby beets. (If using medium beets, peel them and cut into 1-inch pieces.) Set beets aside.

2. In a medium saucepan cook unpeeled onions in boiling water for 3 minutes; drain. Rinse onions with cold water. Carefully remove skins.

3. Place beets and onions in a 13×9×2-inch baking pan. In a small bowl combine olive oil, garlic, thyme, salt, and pepper. Drizzle over vegetables in pan. Toss lightly to coat.

4. Cover pan with foil and roast in a 375°F oven for 30 minutes; uncover and continue roasting for 20 to 30 minutes more or until vegetables are tender. If desired, sprinkle with chives.

Per ⅔ cup: 92 cal., 5 g total fat (1 g sat. fat), 0 mg chol., 252 mg sodium, 12 g carbo., 3 g fiber, 2 g pro.
Daily Values: 1% vit. A, 10% vit. C, 3% calcium, 5% iron
Exchanges: 2 Vegetable, 1 Fat

Broccoli and Peppers with Walnuts

Walnuts impart a rich, nutty flavor and a delightful crunch to this colorful stir-fry.

Start to Finish: 25 minutes **Makes:** 6 servings

- ¼ **cup chicken broth**
- 2 **tablespoons bottled oyster sauce**
- 1 **teaspoon finely shredded lemon peel**
- ⅛ **teaspoon cayenne pepper**
- 4 **teaspoons cooking oil**
- ½ **cup coarsely chopped walnuts**
- 1 **clove garlic, minced**
- 1 **pound broccoli, cut into 1-inch florets**
- 1 **medium red sweet pepper, cut into bite-size strips**

1. For sauce, in a small bowl combine chicken broth, oyster sauce, lemon peel, and cayenne pepper; set aside.

2. In a large nonstick skillet heat 2 teaspoons of the oil over medium heat. Add walnuts and garlic; cook and stir for 2 to 3 minutes or until nuts are lightly toasted. Remove the walnut mixture from the skillet; set aside.

3. In the same skillet heat the remaining oil over medium-high heat. Add broccoli and sweet pepper; cook and stir for 2 to 3 minutes or until vegetables are crisp-tender.

4. Stir sauce; add to skillet. Cook and stir for 1 minute. Transfer broccoli mixture to serving bowl. Sprinkle with walnut mixture.

Per ⅔ cup: 133 cal., 10 g total fat (1 g sat. fat), 0 mg chol., 299 mg sodium, 10 g carbo., 3 g fiber, 4 g pro.
Daily Values: 21% vit. A, 150% vit. C, 5% calcium, 7% iron
Exchanges: 2 Vegetable, 2 Fat

Broccoli-Cauliflower Bake

Broccoli-Cauliflower Bake

Prep: 20 minutes **Bake:** 20 minutes
Oven: 375°F **Makes:** 8 servings

- **4 cups broccoli florets***
- **3 cups cauliflower florets***
- **½ cup chopped onion (1 medium)**
- **1 tablespoon butter or margarine**
- **1 10.75-ounce can condensed cream of mushroom soup or cream of chicken soup**
- **3 ounces American cheese or process Swiss cheese, torn**
- **¼ cup milk**
- **½ teaspoon dried basil, thyme, or marjoram, crushed**
- **¾ cup soft bread crumbs (1 slice bread)**
- **1 tablespoon butter, melted**

1. In a large saucepan cook broccoli and cauliflower, covered, in a small amount of boiling lightly salted water for 6 to 8 minutes or until vegetables are almost crisp-tender. Drain well. Remove broccoli and cauliflower from saucepan; set aside.

2. In the same saucepan cook onion in 1 tablespoon hot butter over medium heat until tender, stirring occasionally. Stir in soup, cheese, milk, and basil. Cook and stir over medium-low heat until bubbly and cheese melts. Stir in cooked broccoli and cauliflower. Transfer vegetable mixture to a 1½-quart casserole. Toss together bread crumbs and the 1 tablespoon melted butter; sprinkle over vegetable mixture.

3. Bake, uncovered, in a 375°F oven about 20 minutes or until heated through.

*Note: If you like, substitute 8 cups frozen broccoli and cauliflower, thawed, for the fresh broccoli and cauliflower florets. Prepare as at left, except omit Step 1 and bake about 35 minutes or until heated through.

Per ⅔ cup: 141 cal., 9 g total fat (4 g sat. fat), 19 mg chol., 506 mg sodium, 11 g carbo., 3 g fiber, 5 g pro.
Daily Values: 10% vit. A, 81% vit. C, 11% calcium, 5% iron
Exchanges: 1 Vegetable, ½ High-Fat Meat, 1½ Fat

FAVORITE Broccoli and Rice Bake `EASY`

Rice, broccoli, and a savory soup-based sauce bake together for a true fix-and-forget favorite.

Prep: 15 minutes **Bake:** 65 minutes **Oven:** 350°F
Stand: 5 minutes **Makes:** 6 servings

- **1 10.75-ounce can condensed cream of broccoli or cream of chicken soup**
- **1¼ cups milk**
- **1 8-ounce carton dairy sour cream**
- **1 teaspoon dried basil, crushed**
- **¼ teaspoon salt**
- **⅛ teaspoon black pepper**
- **1 16-ounce package frozen cut broccoli**
- **1½ cups uncooked instant white rice**
- **½ cup shredded Swiss cheese (2 ounces)**

1. In a large bowl whisk together soup, milk, sour cream, basil, salt, and pepper. Stir in broccoli and uncooked rice. Spoon mixture into an ungreased 2-quart rectangular baking dish.

2. Bake, covered, in a 350°F oven about 65 minutes or until heated through. Uncover and sprinkle with Swiss cheese. Cover and let stand for 5 minutes before serving.

Per cup: 295 cal., 13 g total fat (8 g sat. fat), 31 mg chol., 511 mg sodium, 33 g carbo., 2 g fiber, 10 g pro.
Daily Values: 26% vit. A, 55% vit. C, 22% calcium, 8% iron
Exchanges: ½ Vegetable, 2 Starch, ½ Medium-Fat Meat, 2 Fat

Southern Sunday Dinner

Stir up a pitcher of lemonade and enjoy this fried chicken dinner on the back porch.

- *Buttermilk-Brined Fried Chicken (page 458)*
- *Broccoli and Rice Bake (above)*
- *Leaf lettuce with cherry tomatoes and vinaigrette dressing*
- *Dinner Rolls (page 152)*

Sauteed Broccoli Rabe

Leafy green broccoli rabe is a popular vegetable in Italy. In the United States, look for it with specialty produce in the fall, winter, and spring months.

Start to Finish: 20 minutes **Makes:** 6 servings

- 2 pounds broccoli rabe
- 1 large red sweet pepper, cut into bite-size strips
- 1 teaspoon dried basil, crushed
- ¼ teaspoon salt
- 3 cloves garlic, minced
- 2 tablespoons olive oil
  Crushed red pepper
  Lemon wedges

1. Wash broccoli rabe; remove and discard woody stems. Coarsely chop the leafy greens; set aside.

2. In a 12-inch skillet cook and stir sweet pepper, basil, salt, and garlic in hot oil over medium-high heat for 2 minutes. Add broccoli rabe. Using tongs, toss and cook vegetables for 4 to 6 minutes or until broccoli rabe is crisp-tender. Transfer to serving dish. Sprinkle with crushed red pepper. Serve with lemon wedges.

Per ½ cup: 103 cal., 5 g total fat (1 g sat. fat), 0 mg chol., 178 mg sodium, 7 g carbo., 4 g fiber, 6 g pro.
Daily Values: 52% vit. A, 161% vit. C, 28% calcium, 12% iron
Exchanges: 1½ Vegetable, 1 Fat

Caramelized Brussels Sprouts LOW FAT

Prep: 25 minutes **Cook:** 21 minutes **Makes:** 4 servings

- 1 pound small Brussels sprouts
- 2 tablespoons sugar
- 1 tablespoon butter
- 2 tablespoons red wine vinegar
- ¼ cup water
- ¼ teaspoon salt

1. Trim stems and remove any wilted outer leaves from Brussels sprouts; wash. Set aside.

2. In a large skillet heat the sugar over medium-high heat until it begins to melt, shaking pan occasionally to heat sugar evenly. Once sugar starts to melt, reduce heat and cook until sugar begins to turn brown. Add butter; stir until melted. Add the vinegar. Cook and stir for 1 minute.

3. Carefully add the water and salt. Bring to boiling; add the Brussels sprouts. Return to boiling; reduce heat. Simmer, covered, for 6 minutes.

Uncover and cook about 15 minutes more or until most of the liquid has been absorbed and the sprouts are glazed, occasionally stirring gently.

Per ½ cup: 94 cal., 3 g total fat (2 g sat. fat), 8 mg chol., 191 mg sodium, 15 g carbo., 4 g fiber, 3 g pro.
Daily Values: 16% vit. A, 108% vit. C, 4% calcium, 8% iron
Exchanges: 1 Vegetable, ½ Other Carbo., ½ Fat

Brined Skillet-Roasted Brussels Sprouts

Soaking Brussels sprouts in a brine solution makes this side dish extra flavorful.

Prep: 20 minutes **Stand:** 1 hour **Roast:** 25 minutes
Oven: 350°F **Makes:** 6 servings

- 1½ pounds Brussels sprouts
- 8 cups cold water
- ½ cup kosher salt
- ¼ cup olive oil
- 1 teaspoon mustard seeds
- ¼ teaspoon cracked black pepper
- ¼ teaspoon kosher salt (optional)

1. Trim stems and remove any wilted outer leaves from Brussels sprouts; wash. Halve any large Brussels sprouts; set aside.

2. For brine, in an extra-large bowl or deep container stir together the cold water and the ½ cup kosher salt until salt is completely dissolved. Add Brussels sprouts to brine mixture, making sure the sprouts are completely submerged (weigh down with a plate if necessary to keep sprouts submerged). Let stand at room temperature for 1 hour.

3. Drain Brussels sprouts; do not rinse. In a 12-inch cast-iron skillet or shallow roasting pan toss Brussels sprouts with olive oil to coat. Roast Brussels sprouts, uncovered, in a 350°F oven for 25 to 30 minutes or until tender, stirring once halfway through roasting.

4. Meanwhile, in a small skillet heat mustard seeds over medium-low heat about 5 minutes or until seeds are lightly toasted, shaking skillet occasionally. Remove seeds from skillet and crush them slightly. Add crushed seeds, cracked black pepper, and, if desired, the ¼ teaspoon kosher salt to cooked Brussels sprouts, tossing well. Serve immediately.

Per ½ cup: 126 cal., 9 g total fat (1 g sat. fat), 0 mg chol., 346 mg sodium, 9 g carbo., 4 g fiber, 4 g pro.
Daily Values: 14% vit. A, 108% vit. C, 4% calcium, 8% iron
Exchanges: 1½ Vegetable, 2 Fat

Sweet-and-Sour Cabbage `FAST`

Start to Finish: 15 minutes **Makes:** 3 or 4 servings

- **2 tablespoons packed brown sugar**
- **2 tablespoons vinegar**
- **2 tablespoons water**
- **1 tablespoon cooking oil**
- **¼ teaspoon caraway seeds**
- **¼ teaspoon salt**
  Dash black pepper
- **2 cups shredded red or green cabbage**
- **¾ cup chopped apple**

1. In a large skillet mix brown sugar, vinegar, water, oil, caraway seeds, salt, and pepper. Cook for 2 to 3 minutes or until hot and brown sugar is dissolved, stirring occasionally.

2. Stir in cabbage and apple. Cook, covered, over medium-low heat about 5 minutes or until cabbage is crisp-tender, stirring occasionally. Serve with a slotted spoon.

Per ⅔ cup: 94 cal., 5 g total fat (1 g sat. fat), 0 mg chol., 202 mg sodium, 14 g carbo., 2 g fiber, 1 g pro.
Daily Values: 1% vit. A, 47% vit. C, 3% calcium, 3% iron
Exchanges: 1 Vegetable, ½ Other Carbo., 1 Fat

Mustard-Glazed Cabbage `EASY`

Serve this peppy concoction as a flavorful side with roast beef or pork. If you have any leftovers, heat and serve as a condiment for deli sandwiches, burgers, or bratwurst.

Start to Finish: 20 minutes **Makes:** 6 servings

- **¼ cup water**
- **1 teaspoon instant beef bouillon granules**
- **6 cups packaged shredded cabbage with carrot (coleslaw mix)**
- **½ cup sliced green onion (4)**
- **¼ teaspoon salt**
- **⅛ teaspoon black pepper**
- **2 tablespoons butter or margarine, melted**
- **1 teaspoon Dijon-style mustard**
- **⅓ cup chopped pecans (optional)**

1. In a large saucepan combine the water and beef bouillon granules; heat over medium heat just until mixture begins to simmer. Stir in coleslaw mix, green onion, salt, and pepper. Cook, covered, over medium-low heat for 5 to 7 minutes or until crisp-tender, stirring once or twice. Drain, if necessary.

2. In a small bowl combine butter and mustard. If desired, add pecans; toss to coat. Pour butter mixture over cabbage mixture; toss to combine.

Per ½ cup: 55 cal., 4 g total fat (2 g sat. fat), 10 mg chol., 289 mg sodium, 4 g carbo., 2 g fiber, 1 g pro.
Daily Values: 24% vit. A, 43% vit. C, 4% calcium, 1% iron
Exchanges: 1 Vegetable, 1 Fat

Brown Sugar-Glazed Carrots

`LOW FAT`

Start to Finish: 25 minutes **Makes:** 4 servings

- **1 pound peeled baby carrots or medium carrots, halved lengthwise and cut into 2-inch pieces**
- **1 tablespoon butter or margarine**
- **1 tablespoon packed brown sugar**
  Dash salt
  Black pepper

1. In a medium saucepan cook carrots, covered, in a small amount of boiling salted water for 8 to 10 minutes or until crisp-tender. Drain; remove carrots from pan.

2. In the same saucepan combine butter, brown sugar, and salt. Cook and stir over medium heat until combined. Add carrots. Cook and stir about 2 minutes or until glazed. Season to taste with pepper.

Herbed-Glazed Carrots: Prepare as above, except substitute 1 tablespoon honey for the brown sugar and add 1 tablespoon snipped fresh thyme or ½ teaspoon dried thyme, crushed, to the butter mixture.

Per ¾ cup brown sugar or herb variation: 83 cal., 3 g total fat (2 g sat. fat), 8 mg chol., 111 mg sodium, 14 g carbo., 2 g fiber, 1 g pro.
Daily Values: 286% vit. A, 16% vit. C, 4% calcium, 7% iron
Exchanges: 1½ Vegetable, ½ Other Carbo., ½ Fat

Baby Vegetables

Diminutive baby vegetables are immature versions of regular varieties.

Artichokes, beets, carrots (not "baby-cut carrots"), corn, green beans, potatoes, yellow squash, and zucchini are commonly available. They are at their best when simply steamed and served with butter, salt, freshly ground pepper, and, if you wish, a snipped fresh herb.

Creamed Corn Casserole

Creamed Corn Casserole EASY

Prep: 15 minutes **Bake:** 50 minutes
Oven: 375°F **Makes:** 12 servings

   Nonstick cooking spray
2 **16-ounce packages frozen whole kernel corn**
2 **cups chopped red and/or green sweet pepper (2 large)**
1 **cup chopped onion (1 large)**
1 **tablespoon butter or margarine**
¼ **teaspoon black pepper**
1 **10.75-ounce can condensed cream of celery soup**
1 **8-ounce tub cream cheese spread with chive and onion or cream cheese spread with garden vegetables**
¼ **cup milk**

1. Coat a 2-quart casserole with cooking spray; set aside. Place corn in a colander. Run it under cool water to thaw; drain. Set aside.

2. In a large saucepan cook sweet pepper and onion in hot butter until tender. Stir in corn and black pepper. In a medium bowl whisk together soup, cream cheese spread, and milk. Stir soup mixture into corn mixture. Transfer to the prepared casserole.

3. Bake, covered, in a 375°F oven for 50 to 55 minutes or until casserole is heated through, stirring once.

Slow cooker directions: Prepare as above, except do not thaw the corn and omit the butter. In a 3½- or 4-quart slow cooker combine frozen corn, sweet pepper, onion, and black pepper.

In a medium bowl whisk together soup, cream cheese spread, and milk. Pour over the corn mixture in cooker. Cover and cook on low-heat setting for 8 to 10 hours or on high-heat setting for 4 to 5 hours. Stir before serving.

Per ½ cup: 176 cal., 9 g total fat (5 g sat. fat), 22 mg chol., 280 mg sodium, 22 g carbo., 3 g fiber, 4 g pro.
Daily Values: 12% vit. A, 38% vit. C, 4% calcium, 3% iron
Exchanges: 1½ Starch, 1½ Fat

Corn on the Cob EASY

What's a summer cookout without corn on the cob? For variety, serve a choice of plain butter plus one or more of the flavored variations.

Prep: 15 minutes **Cook:** 5 minutes **Makes:** 8 servings

8 **ears of corn**
   Butter, margarine, or 1 recipe Herb Butter, Cajun Butter, or Chipotle-Lime Butter
   Salt
   Black pepper

1. Remove husks from the ears of corn. Scrub with a stiff brush to remove silks; rinse. Cook, covered, in enough boiling lightly salted water to cover for 5 to 7 minutes or until tender. Serve with butter, salt, and black pepper.

Herb Butter: In a small mixing bowl beat ½ cup softened butter, 2 teaspoons snipped fresh thyme, and 2 teaspoons snipped fresh marjoram or oregano with an electric mixer on low speed until combined. Cover and chill for 1 to 24 hours.

Cajun Butter: In a small mixing bowl beat ½ cup softened butter, 1 teaspoon garlic salt, ¼ teaspoon black pepper, ¼ teaspoon cayenne pepper, ⅛ teaspoon ground ginger, and ⅛ teaspoon ground cloves with an electric mixer on low speed until combined. Cover and chill for 1 to 24 hours.

Chipotle-Lime Butter: In a small mixing bowl beat ½ cup softened butter, 1 teaspoon finely shredded lime peel, ½ teaspoon salt, ⅛ to ¼ teaspoon ground chipotle chile pepper, and dash cayenne pepper with electric mixer on low speed until combined. Cover and chill for 1 to 24 hours.

Per ear + 1 tablespoon plain or flavored butter: 179 cal., 13 g total fat (7 g sat. fat), 31 mg chol., 168 mg sodium, 17 g carbo., 2 g fiber, 3 g pro.
Daily Values: 11% vit. A, 10% vit. C, 1% calcium, 3% iron
Exchanges: 1 Starch, 2½ Fat

Scalloped Corn

Prep: 20 minutes **Bake:** 35 minutes **Oven:** 325°F
Stand: 15 minutes **Makes:** 8 servings

- ½ **cup chopped onion (1 medium)**
- ½ **cup chopped green or red sweet pepper (optional)**
- 2 **tablespoons butter or margarine**
- 1 **9- or 10-ounce package frozen whole kernel corn, thawed**
- ¼ **teaspoon salt**
- 2 **eggs, slightly beaten**
- 1 **14.75- or 16-ounce can cream-style corn**
- 1 **cup milk**
- ¾ **cup coarsely crushed rich round crackers (about 20 crackers)**
- ½ **cup shredded cheddar cheese (2 ounces)**

1. In a medium saucepan cook the onion and sweet pepper in hot butter about 5 minutes or until tender. Stir in thawed corn and salt. Remove from heat.

2. Meanwhile, in a large bowl stir together the eggs, cream-style corn, milk, and crushed crackers. Stir in the thawed corn mixture. Transfer to an ungreased 2-quart square or rectangular baking dish.

3. Bake, uncovered, in a 325°F oven for 35 to 40 minutes or until the center appears set. Sprinkle with the cheddar cheese. Let stand for 15 minutes before serving.

Per ⅔ cup: 199 cal., 10 g total fat (4 g sat. fat), 71 mg chol., 388 mg sodium, 24 g carbo., 2 g fiber, 7 g pro.
Daily Values: 8% vit. A, 8% vit. C, 11% calcium, 6% iron
Exchanges: 1½ Starch, ½ Medium-Fat Meat, 1 Fat

Eggplant Parmigiana

Eggplant looks sturdier than it really is; refrigerate for no more than 2 days.

Start to Finish: 30 minutes **Makes:** 4 servings

- 1 **small eggplant (12 ounces)**
- 1 **egg, slightly beaten**
- 1 **tablespoon water**
- ¼ **cup all-purpose flour**
- 2 **tablespoons cooking oil**
- ⅓ **cup grated Parmesan cheese**
- 1 **cup meatless spaghetti sauce**
- ¾ **cup shredded mozzarella cheese (3 ounces)**

1. Wash and peel eggplant; cut crosswise into ½-inch slices. Combine egg and water; dip eggplant slices into egg mixture, then into flour,
turning to coat both sides. In a large skillet cook eggplant, half at a time, in hot oil for 4 to 6 minutes or until golden, turning once. (If necessary, add additional oil.) Drain on paper towels.

2. Wipe skillet. Arrange the cooked eggplant slices in the skillet; sprinkle with Parmesan cheese. Top with spaghetti sauce and mozzarella cheese. Cook, covered, over medium-low heat for 5 to 7 minutes or until heated through.

Baked Eggplant Parmigiana: Prepare as above, except in Step 2, place the eggplant slices in a single layer in an ungreased 2-quart rectangular baking dish. (If necessary, cut slices to fit.) Sprinkle with Parmesan cheese. Top with spaghetti sauce and mozzarella cheese. Bake, uncovered, in a 400°F oven for 10 to 12 minutes or until heated through.

Per ¼ recipe regular or baked variation: 269 cal., 18 g total fat (6 g sat. fat), 76 mg chol., 660 mg sodium, 17 g carbo., 3 g fiber, 12 g pro.
Daily Values: 11% vit. A, 6% vit. C, 26% calcium, 7% iron
Exchanges: 2 Vegetable, ½ Starch, 1 High-Fat Meat, 2 Fat

Roasted Fennel and Onions `EASY`

Prep: 15 minutes **Roast:** 35 minutes
Oven: 400°F **Makes:** 6 servings

- 2 **medium fennel bulbs**
- 1 **large onion, cut into 1-inch wedges**
- 2 **tablespoons olive oil**
- ½ **teaspoon fennel seeds or dried Italian seasoning, crushed**
- ½ **teaspoon salt**
- ¼ **teaspoon black pepper**

1. Cut off and discard fennel stalks (see photo, page 582). Remove any wilted outer layers and cut a thin slice from the base of each fennel bulb. Wash bulbs and cut each one in half lengthwise. Cut halves lengthwise into 1-inch wedges. Place fennel and onion in a shallow roasting pan. Drizzle with olive oil; sprinkle with fennel seeds, salt, and pepper. Stir to coat.

2. Roast, uncovered, in a 400°F oven for 35 to 40 minutes or until vegetables are light brown and tender, stirring twice.

Per ½ cup: 75 cal., 5 g total fat (1 g sat. fat), 0 mg chol., 235 mg sodium, 8 g carbo., 3 g fiber, 1 g pro.
Daily Values: 2% vit. A, 19% vit. C, 5% calcium, 4% iron
Exchanges: 1½ Vegetable, 1 Fat

Baked Fennel with Parmesan

Prep: 25 minutes **Cook:** 5 minutes **Bake:** 55 minutes
Oven: 350°F/450°F **Makes:** 12 servings

- 6 **medium fennel bulbs**
- 2 **tablespoons butter, melted**
- 2 **tablespoons snipped fresh Italian parsley**
- 2 **tablespoons snipped fresh sage**
- ⅛ **teaspoon salt**
- ⅛ **teaspoon black pepper**
- ¼ **cup chicken broth**
- ¼ **cup dry white wine**
- ¾ **cup shredded Parmesan cheese (3 ounces)**
- 6 **slices bacon, crisp-cooked, drained, and crumbled**

1. Cut off and discard fennel stalks (see photo, below). Remove any wilted outer layers and cut a thin slice from the base of each bulb. Wash bulbs and cut each one into quarters. In a large saucepan cook fennel in a small amount of boiling salted water for 5 minutes. Drain; pat dry.

2. Lightly grease a 2-quart shallow baking dish. Arrange half of the fennel quarters in the baking dish. Drizzle half of the melted butter over the fennel. Sprinkle with half each of the parsley, sage, salt, and pepper. Add the remaining fennel. Drizzle with remaining butter; sprinkle with remaining parsley, sage, salt, and pepper. Pour chicken broth and wine along the sides of the baking dish, being careful not to wash off any of the butter or seasonings. Sprinkle with half of the Parmesan cheese.

3. Bake, covered, in a 350°F oven for 45 minutes. Increase the oven temperature to 450°F. Remove cover; sprinkle with the remaining cheese and the crumbled bacon. Bake, uncovered, for 10 to 15 minutes more or until fennel is tender and top is golden.

Per ¾ cup: 102 cal., 6 g total fat (3 g sat. fat), 12 mg chol., 269 mg sodium, 9 g carbo., 4 g fiber, 5 g pro.
Daily Values: 6% vit. A, 25% vit. C, 12% calcium, 6% iron
Exchanges: 1 Vegetable, ½ Medium-Fat Meat, 1 Fat

Using a sharp knife, carefully cut about 1 inch above the fennel bulb to remove the stalks. Discard the stalks, saving some wispy leaves for a garnish, if desired.

Collard Greens with Bacon

Prep: 30 minutes **Cook:** 1¼ hours **Makes:** 6 servings

- 1½ **pounds collard greens**
- 3 **slices bacon, chopped**
- 2 **cups water**
- 1 **7- to 8-ounce smoked pork hock**
- ½ **cup chopped onion (1 medium)**
- ½ **cup chopped green sweet pepper**
- 1 **teaspoon sugar**
- ¼ **teaspoon salt**
- ⅛ **teaspoon cayenne pepper**
- 4 **cloves garlic, minced**
  Red wine vinegar (optional)

1. Wash collard greens thoroughly in cold water; drain well. Remove and discard stems; trim bruised leaves. Coarsely chop leaves to measure 6 cups; set aside.

2. In a large saucepan cook bacon until crisp. Remove bacon, reserving drippings in saucepan. Drain bacon on paper towels and set aside. Add water, pork hock, onion, sweet pepper, sugar, salt, cayenne pepper, and garlic to saucepan. Bring to boiling; add chopped collard greens. Reduce heat. Simmer, covered, about 1¼ hours or until greens are tender. Remove from heat. Remove pork hock. Cover greens; keep warm.

3. When cool enough to handle, cut meat off pork hock. Chop or shred meat; discard bone. Return meat to greens mixture along with cooked bacon; heat through. Serve with a slotted spoon. If desired, sprinkle each serving with a little vinegar.

Per ½ cup: 158 cal., 13 g total fat (5 g sat. fat), 22 mg chol., 267 mg sodium, 5 g carbo., 2 g fiber, 5 g pro.
Daily Values: 28% vit. A, 31% vit. C, 6% calcium, 2% iron
Exchanges: 1 Vegetable, ½ Medium-Fat Meat, 2 Fat

Gingered Jerusalem Artichokes LOW FAT FAST

Wait until your dinner is ready to go on the table before you cook these slightly crunchy veggies. Once cooked, they soften if not eaten right away.

Start to Finish: 15 minutes **Makes:** 4 servings

- 1 **pound Jerusalem artichokes, peeled, if desired, and cut up**
- 1 **tablespoon butter or margarine**
- 2 **teaspoons grated fresh ginger**
- ¼ **cup Marsala, sherry, or apple juice**

1. In a large skillet cook and stir Jerusalem artichokes in hot butter over medium-high heat for 5 to 6 minutes or until crisp-tender. Add ginger; cook for 30 seconds. Remove from heat; stir in Marsala. Season to taste with *salt.*

Per ¾ cup: 110 cal., 3 g total fat (2 g sat. fat), 8 mg chol., 36 mg sodium, 16 g carbo., 1 g fiber, 2 g pro.
Daily Values: 3% vit. A, 5% vit. C, 1% calcium, 15% iron
Exchanges: 1 Starch, ½ Fat

Leeks au Gratin

Prep: 35 minutes **Cook:** 15 minutes **Bake:** 10 minutes
Oven: 450°F **Makes:** 8 to 10 servings

　8　**Hard-Cooked Eggs (page 228), peeled**
　10　**medium leeks**
　6　**tablespoons butter or margarine**
　2　**tablespoons all-purpose flour**
　1½　**cups milk**
　½　**cup white cheddar cheese, shredded (2 ounces)**
　¼　**cup grated Parmesan cheese**
　¼　**teaspoon cayenne pepper**
　　Salt
　　Black pepper

1. Quarter eggs lengthwise. Arrange in a single layer in a 1½- to 2-quart round or oval au gratin dish or 10-inch round quiche dish; set aside.

2. Remove green portions from leeks. Halve leeks lengthwise. Wash thoroughly; pat dry. Remove roots from leeks; cut leeks lengthwise into thin strips (you should have about 5 cups.) In a large skillet cook leek in 4 tablespoons hot butter over medium heat until tender, stirring occasionally. Spoon leek over egg in dish.

3. For sauce, melt the remaining 2 tablespoons butter in skillet; whisk in flour. Add milk; cook and stir until thickened and bubbly. Whisk in ¼ cup of the cheddar cheese, the Parmesan cheese, and cayenne pepper. Season to taste with salt and black pepper. Pour sauce over the leek and egg in dish. Sprinkle with remaining ¼ cup cheddar cheese.

4. Bake, uncovered, in a 450°F oven about 10 minutes or until edges are bubbly and top begins to brown.

Per ½ cup: 245 cal., 18 g total fat (10 g sat. fat), 248 mg chol., 268 mg sodium, 10 g carbo., 1 g fiber, 11 g pro.
Daily Values: 27% vit. A, 8% vit. C, 18% calcium, 9% iron
Exchanges: ½ Vegetable, ½ Other Carbo., 1½ Medium-Fat Meat, 1½ Fat

Mushroom Medley au Gratin

This creamy gratin showcases three types of mushrooms—shiitake, oyster, and button. It pairs deliciously with roast beef.

Prep: 35 minutes **Bake:** 15 minutes
Oven: 350°F **Makes:** 6 servings

　2　**tablespoons grated Parmesan cheese**
　2　**tablespoons fine dry bread crumbs**
　2　**teaspoons butter or margarine, melted**
　8　**ounces fresh shiitake mushrooms**
　4　**ounces fresh oyster mushrooms**
　1　**pound fresh button mushrooms, sliced**
　1　**clove garlic, minced**
　2　**tablespoons butter or margarine**
　2　**tablespoons all-purpose flour**
　2　**teaspoons Dijon-style mustard**
　1½　**teaspoons snipped fresh thyme or ½ teaspoon dried thyme, crushed**
　¼　**teaspoon salt**
　⅔　**cup milk**

1. In a small bowl stir together Parmesan cheese, bread crumbs, and the 2 teaspoons melted butter; set aside.

2. Separate caps and stems from shiitake and oyster mushrooms. (Reserve stems to use in stocks or discard.) Slice mushroom caps.

3. In a large skillet cook button mushrooms and garlic in the 2 tablespoons butter over medium-high heat about 5 minutes or until tender and most of the liquid has evaporated, stirring occasionally. Remove button mushroom mixture and set aside, reserving drippings in skillet.

4. Add shiitake and oyster mushrooms to the skillet. Cook for 7 to 8 minutes or until tender and most of the liquid has evaporated, stirring occasionally. Stir in flour, mustard, thyme, and salt. Add milk all at once. Cook and stir until thickened and bubbly. Cook and stir for 1 minute more. Stir in button mushroom mixture.

5. Transfer to a 1-quart au gratin dish or 1-quart casserole. Sprinkle with the bread crumb mixture. Bake, uncovered, in a 350°F oven for 15 minutes or until heated through.

Per ½ cup: 124 cal., 9 g total fat (4 g sat. fat), 18 mg chol., 256 mg sodium, 8 g carbo., 1 g fiber, 7 g pro.
Daily Values: 6% vit. A, 1% vit. C, 7% calcium, 6% iron
Exchanges: 1½ Vegetable, 2 Fat

Broiled Portobello Mushrooms (LOW FAT) (EASY)

Prep: 10 minutes **Broil:** 8 minutes **Makes:** 4 servings

- **2 extra-large portobello mushrooms**
- **¼ to ½ teaspoon crushed red pepper (optional)**
- **¼ teaspoon seasoned salt**
- **2 cloves garlic, minced**
- **2 teaspoons olive oil**
- **1 tablespoon snipped fresh basil**

1. Preheat broiler. Cut off mushroom stems even with caps; discard stems. Brush or lightly rinse mushrooms. Gently pat dry with paper towels. Place mushrooms, stem sides up, in a small shallow baking pan. Set aside.

2. In a small bowl combine the crushed red pepper (if desired), seasoned salt, and garlic. Sprinkle evenly over mushrooms. Drizzle olive oil evenly over mushrooms.

3. Transfer mushrooms to the unheated rack of a broiler pan. Broil 3 to 4 inches from the heat for 8 to 10 minutes or until mushrooms are tender. Sprinkle with snipped basil. Cut mushrooms in half; serve immediately.

Per ½ mushroom: 39 cal., 3 g total fat (0 g sat. fat), 0 mg chol., 78 mg sodium, 4 g carbo., 1 g fiber, 1 g pro.
Daily Values: 5% vit. C, 1% calcium, 8% iron
Exchanges: 1 Vegetable, ½ Fat

Bistro Mushrooms

Start to Finish: 20 minutes **Makes:** 4 servings

- **3 cups sliced cremini, shiitake, and/or button mushrooms (8 ounces)**
- **2 tablespoons olive oil, roasted garlic olive oil, or butter**
- **⅓ cup dry red wine, dry sherry, or beef broth**
- **1 tablespoon Worcestershire sauce for chicken**
- **2 teaspoons snipped fresh thyme**
- **Salt**
- **Black pepper**

1. In a large skillet cook and stir mushrooms in hot oil for 4 minutes. Stir in wine, Worcestershire sauce, and thyme. Simmer, uncovered, for 3 minutes. Season to taste with salt and pepper. Serve with beef, fish, pork, or poultry.

Per ⅓ cup: 92 cal., 8 g total fat (1 g sat. fat), 0 mg chol., 137 mg sodium, 3 g carbo., 0 g fiber, 2 g pro.
Daily Values: 1% vit. C, 1% calcium, 4% iron
Exchanges: ½ Vegetable, 1½ Fat

Glazed Parsnips and Carrots

Glazed Parsnips and Carrots

Fresh pears, dried cranberries, and orange juice add a pleasant fruity flavor to this winning vegetable combination.

Start to Finish: 20 minutes **Makes:** 6 servings

- **8 ounces parsnips, cut into thin strips (2¼ cups)**
- **8 ounces carrots, cut into thin strips (2¼ cups)**
- **¾ cup orange juice**
- **⅓ cup dried cranberries**
- **½ teaspoon ground ginger**
- **2 firm ripe pears, peeled, if desired, and sliced**
- **⅓ cup pecan halves**
- **3 tablespoons packed brown sugar**
- **2 tablespoons butter or margarine**

1. In a large nonstick skillet combine parsnip, carrot, orange juice, cranberries, and ginger. Bring to boiling; reduce heat to medium. Cook, uncovered, for 7 to 8 minutes or until vegetables are crisp-tender and most of the liquid has evaporated, stirring occasionally.

2. Stir pear, pecans, brown sugar, and butter into mixture in skillet. Cook, uncovered, for 2 to 3 minutes more or until vegetables are glazed.

Per ⅔ cup: 200 cal., 9 g total fat (3 g sat. fat), 11 mg chol., 59 mg sodium, 31 g carbo., 5 g fiber, 2 g pro.
Daily Values: 175% vit. A, 41% vit. C, 4% calcium, 5% iron
Exchanges: 1½ Vegetable, 1 Fruit, ½ Starch, 1½ Fat

Smothered Okra

Prep: 20 minutes **Cook:** 20 minutes **Makes:** 4 servings

- ½ cup chopped onion (1 medium)
- ½ cup chopped green sweet pepper
- 2 cloves garlic, minced
- 2 tablespoons butter or margarine
- 8 ounces whole okra, cut into ½-inch pieces (2 cups), or 2 cups frozen cut okra, thawed
- 2 cups chopped, peeled tomato (2 large)
- ½ teaspoon salt
- ⅛ teaspoon black pepper
- ⅛ teaspoon cayenne pepper (optional)
- 2 slices bacon, crisp-cooked, drained, and crumbled (optional)

1. In a large skillet cook and stir onion, sweet pepper, and garlic in hot butter over medium heat about 5 minutes or until tender. Stir in okra, tomato, salt, black pepper, and, if desired, cayenne pepper. Bring to boiling; reduce heat. Simmer, covered, about 20 minutes for fresh okra (10 minutes for frozen okra) or until okra is tender. If desired, sprinkle with bacon.

Per ⅔ cup: 106 cal., 7 g total fat (4 g sat. fat), 16 mg chol., 367 mg sodium, 12 g carbo., 4 g fiber, 2 g pro.
Daily Values: 25% vit. A, 72% vit. C, 6% calcium, 6% iron
Exchanges: 2½ Vegetable, 1 Fat

Sugar Snap Peas with Orange-Ginger Butter LOW FAT

Start to Finish: 25 minutes **Makes:** 4 servings

- 3 cups fresh sugar snap peas or frozen sugar snap peas
- 1 teaspoon grated fresh ginger
- 1 tablespoon butter or margarine
- 1 tablespoon orange marmalade
- 1 teaspoon cider vinegar
- ⅛ teaspoon black pepper

1. Remove strings and tips from peas. Cook fresh peas, covered, in small amount of boiling salted water 2 to 4 minutes or until crisp-tender. (Cook frozen peas according to the package directions.) Drain well.

2. Meanwhile, in a small pan cook ginger in hot butter for 1 minute. Stir in marmalade, vinegar, and pepper; cook and stir until marmalade melts. Pour over hot cooked peas; toss to coat.

Per ⅔ cup: 115 cal., 3 g total fat (2 g sat. fat), 8 mg chol., 53 mg sodium, 17 g carbo., 4 g fiber, 4 g pro.
Daily Values: 2% vit. A, 47% vit. C, 6% calcium, 10% iron
Exchanges: 3 Vegetable, 1 Fat

Peas, Carrots, and Mushrooms LOW FAT

Start to Finish: 25 minutes **Makes:** 6 servings

- ½ cup sliced carrot (1 medium)
- 1 10-ounce package frozen peas
- 2 cups sliced fresh mushrooms
- 2 green onions, cut into ½-inch pieces
- 1 tablespoon butter or margarine
- 1 tablespoon snipped fresh basil or ½ teaspoon dried basil, crushed
- ¼ teaspoon salt
   Dash black pepper

1. In a medium saucepan cook carrot, covered, in a small amount of boiling salted water for 3 minutes. Add the frozen peas. Return to boiling; reduce heat. Cook about 5 minutes more or until carrot and peas are crisp-tender. Drain well. Remove carrot and peas from saucepan; set aside.

2. In the same saucepan cook mushrooms and green onion in hot butter until tender. Stir in basil, salt, and pepper. Return carrot and peas to saucepan; heat through, stirring occasionally.

Per ⅔ cup: 69 cal., 3 g total fat (1 g sat. fat), 5 mg chol., 171 mg sodium, 9 g carbo., 3 g fiber, 4 g pro.
Daily Values: 42% vit. A, 13% vit. C, 2% calcium, 6% iron
Exchanges: ½ Vegetable, ½ Starch, ½ Fat

Peas in a Pod

You'll find two varieties of pea pods in your supermarket—snow peas and sugar snap peas. What's the difference between the two? Here's what you need to know about both varieties.

- Both snow pea pods and sugar snap peas are picked before the seed develops and, unlike regular green peas, are meant to be eaten pods and all.
- Snow peas, also called Chinese pea pods, have pale green, flat pods with small, immature-looking peas.
- Sugar snap peas are a cross between snow peas and green peas. They have plump pods with small, tender peas.
- Snow pea pods and sugar snap peas may be used interchangeably in recipes.

Baked Potatoes

Prep: 5 minutes **Bake:** 40 minutes
Oven: 425°F **Makes:** 4 servings

> **4** medium baking potatoes (6 to
> 8 ounces each)
> Shortening, butter, or margarine (optional)

1. Scrub potatoes thoroughly with a brush; pat dry. Prick potatoes with a fork. (If desired, for soft skins, rub potatoes with shortening or wrap each potato in foil.)

2. Bake potatoes in a 425°F oven for 40 to 60 minutes (or in a 350°F oven for 70 to 80 minutes) or until tender. To serve, roll each potato gently under your hand. Using a knife, cut an X in top of each potato. Press in and up on the ends of each potato.

Per potato: 125 cal., 0 g total fat (0 g sat. fat), 0 mg chol., 12 mg sodium, 28 g carbo., 3 g fiber, 4 g pro.
Daily Values: 38% vit. C, 2% calcium, 13% iron
Exchanges: 2 Starch

Baked Sweet Potatoes: Prepare as above, except substitute sweet potatoes or yams for the baking potatoes. If desired, serve sweet potatoes with butter and cinnamon-sugar.

Per sweet potato: 136 cal., 0 g total fat (0 g sat. fat), 0 mg chol., 17 mg sodium, 32 g carbo., 4 g fiber, 2 g pro.
Daily Values: 496% vit. A, 37% vit. C, 3% calcium, 4% iron
Exchanges: 2 Starch

Twice-Baked Potatoes

If you like, stir a little crumbled cooked bacon or finely chopped cooked ham into the mashed potato mixture.

Prep: 20 minutes **Bake:** 62 minutes **Oven:** 425°F
Stand: 10 minutes **Makes:** 4 servings

> **1** recipe Baked Potatoes (above)
> ½ cup dairy sour cream or plain yogurt
> ¼ teaspoon garlic salt
> ⅛ teaspoon black pepper
> Milk (optional)
> ¾ cup finely shredded cheddar cheese
> (3 ounces)
> **1** tablespoon snipped fresh chives (optional)

1. Bake potatoes as directed; let stand about 10 minutes. Cut a lengthwise slice off the top of each baked potato; discard skin from slices and place pulp in a bowl. Scoop pulp out of potatoes (see photo, above right); add pulp to the bowl.

2. Mash the potato pulp with a potato masher or an electric mixer on low speed. Add sour cream, garlic salt, and pepper; beat until smooth. (If necessary, stir in 1 to 2 tablespoons milk to reach desired consistency.) Season to taste with *salt* and additional pepper. Stir in ½ cup of the cheddar cheese and, if desired, chives. Divide the mashed potato mixture evenly among the potato shells. Place in a 2-quart baking dish.

3. Bake, uncovered, in a 425°F oven for 20 to 25 minutes or until light brown. Sprinkle with remaining cheese. Bake for 2 to 3 minutes more or until cheese melts.

Per potato: 277 cal., 13 g total fat (8 g sat. fat), 37 mg chol., 238 mg sodium, 30 g carbo., 3 g fiber, 11 g pro.
Daily Values: 8% vit. A, 39% vit. C, 23% calcium, 14% iron
Exchanges: 2 Starch, 1 High-Fat Meat, ½ Fat

Using a spoon, gently scoop out the cooked potato pulp, leaving ¼-inch shells.

Creamed Peas and New Potatoes

To ensure a velvety-smooth, rich-tasting sauce, be sure to use whole milk.

Start to Finish: 30 minutes **Makes:** 4 servings

> **10** to 12 tiny new potatoes (1 pound)
> 1½ cups shelled fresh peas or frozen
> peas
> ¼ cup chopped onion
> **1** tablespoon butter or margarine
> **1** tablespoon all-purpose flour
> ½ teaspoon salt
> Dash black pepper
> **1** cup whole milk
> Snipped fresh chives or dill (optional)

1. Scrub potatoes; cut any large potatoes in half. Peel a narrow strip from around the center of each whole potato. In a medium saucepan cook potatoes, covered, in a small amount of boiling salted water for 8 minutes. Add fresh peas and cook for 10 to 12 minutes more or until tender. (If using frozen peas, cook potatoes 14 minutes; add peas and cook 4 to 5 minutes more.) Drain; return vegetables to saucepan.

2. Meanwhile, in a small saucepan cook onion in hot butter until tender. Stir in flour, salt, and pepper. Add milk all at once. Cook and stir until thickened and bubbly. Cook and stir 1 minute more. Stir into potatoes and peas; heat through. Season to taste. If desired, sprinkle with chives.

Per ¾ cup: 180 cal., 5 g total fat (3 g sat. fat), 14 mg chol., 344 mg sodium, 27 g carbo., 4 g fiber, 7 g pro.
Daily Values: 11% vit. A, 49% vit. C, 10% calcium, 11% iron
Exchanges: 1½ Starch, 1 Fat

Mashed Potatoes EASY

Choose either the classic plain mashed potatoes or one of the flavorful variations. See photo of Sour Cream and Chive Mashed Potatoes, page 571.

Prep: 15 minutes **Cook:** 20 minutes **Makes:** 4 servings

- 1½ **pounds baking potatoes (such as russet or Yukon gold), peeled and quartered**
- ½ **teaspoon salt**
- 2 **tablespoons butter or margarine**
- 3 **to 5 tablespoons milk**
  Butter or margarine (optional)

1. In a medium saucepan cook potatoes and the ½ teaspoon salt, covered, in enough boiling water to cover for 20 to 25 minutes or until tender; drain. Mash with a potato masher or beat with an electric mixer on low speed. Add the 2 tablespoons butter. Season to taste with additional salt and *black pepper.* Gradually beat in enough milk to make potato mixture light and fluffy. If desired, serve with additional butter.

Per ¾ cup: 157 cal., 6 g total fat (4 g sat. fat), 16 mg chol., 344 mg sodium, 23 g carbo., 2 g fiber, 3 g pro.
Daily Values: 4% vit. A, 30% vit. C, 2% calcium, 5% iron
Exchanges: 1½ Starch, 1 Fat

Garlic Mashed Potatoes: Prepare as above, except add 4 peeled garlic cloves to water while cooking potatoes and substitute 2 tablespoons olive oil for the 2 tablespoons butter.

Per ¾ cup: 171 cal., 7 g total fat (1 g sat. fat), 1 mg chol., 303 mg sodium, 24 g carbo., 2 g fiber, 3 g pro.
Daily Values: 32% vit. C, 3% calcium, 6% iron
Exchanges: 1½ Starch, 1 Fat

Sour Cream and Chive Mashed Potatoes: Prepare as above, except add ½ cup dairy sour cream with the 2 tablespoons butter. Stir 2 tablespoons snipped fresh chives into the potatoes just before serving. If desired, sprinkle with additional snipped fresh chives.

Pesto Mashed Potatoes: Prepare as above, except add 2 tablespoons purchased pesto along with the 2 tablespoons butter.

Cheesy Chipotle Mashed Potatoes: Prepare as above, except stir ¼ cup shredded smoked cheddar or Monterey Jack cheese (2 ounces) and 1 teaspoon finely chopped chipotle pepper in adobo sauce into potatoes before serving.

Per ¾ cup sour cream and chive, pesto, or cheesy chipotle variations: 215 cal., 11 g total fat (7 g sat. fat), 31 mg chol., 437 mg sodium, 24 g carbo., 2 g fiber, 7 g pro.
Daily Values: 7% vit. A, 30% vit. C, 13% calcium, 6% iron
Exchanges: 1½ Starch, ½ High-Fat Meat, 2 Fat

FAVORITE Scalloped Potatoes

Prep: 30 minutes **Bake:** 85 minutes **Oven:** 350°F
Stand: 10 minutes **Makes:** 10 servings

- 1 **cup chopped onion (1 large)**
- 2 **cloves garlic, minced**
- ¼ **cup butter or margarine**
- ¼ **cup all-purpose flour**
- ½ **teaspoon salt**
- ¼ **teaspoon black pepper**
- 2½ **cups milk**
- 8 **cups thinly sliced red, white, long white, or yellow potatoes (about 2½ pounds)**

1. For sauce, in a medium saucepan cook onion and garlic in hot butter until tender. Stir in flour, salt, and pepper. Add milk all at once. Cook and stir over medium heat until thickened and bubbly. Remove from heat; set aside. Place half the sliced potatoes in a greased 3-quart rectangular dish. Top with half the sauce. Repeat layers.

2. Bake, covered, in a 350°F oven for 45 minutes. Uncover and bake for 40 to 50 minutes more or until potato is tender. Let stand, uncovered, for 10 minutes before serving.

Per ¾ cup: 178 cal., 6 g total fat (4 g sat. fat), 17 mg chol., 183 mg sodium, 27 g carbo., 2 g fiber, 5 g pro.
Daily Values: 5% vit. A, 34% vit. C, 9% calcium, 10% iron
Exchanges: 1½ Starch, 1 Fat

Cheesy Scalloped Potatoes: Prepare as above, except gradually add 1½ cups (6 ounces) shredded cheddar, Gruyère, or Swiss cheese to the thickened sauce, stirring until cheese melts.

Per ¾ cup: 247 cal., 12 g total fat (7 g sat. fat), 35 mg chol., 289 mg sodium, 27 g carbo., 2 g fiber, 9 g pro.
Daily Values: 9% vit. A, 34% vit. C, 22% calcium, 11% iron
Exchanges: 1½ Starch, ½ High-Fat Meat, 1½ Fat

Parmesan Potato Wedges

Parmesan Potato Wedges

Prep: 25 minutes **Bake:** 30 minutes
Oven: 425°F **Makes:** 6 servings

- 6 **medium baking potatoes (about 2 pounds)**
- ⅓ **cup butter, melted**
- 1 **clove garlic, minced**
- ¼ **cup grated Parmesan cheese**
- ½ **teaspoon Italian seasoning, crushed**

1. Line a 15×10×1-inch baking pan with parchment paper or foil; set aside. Cut each potato lengthwise into eight wedges. In a large bowl stir together butter, garlic, Parmesan cheese, Italian seasoning, ¼ teaspoon *salt*, and ⅛ teaspoon *black pepper.* Add potato wedges and stir to thoroughly coat. Place the wedges on the prepared baking pan.

2. Bake, uncovered, in a 425°F oven about 30 minutes or until tender.

Per 8 wedges: 194 cal., 12 g total fat (6 g sat. fat), 31 mg chol., 232 mg sodium, 19 g carbo., 2 g fiber, 4 g pro.
Daily Values: 7% vit. A, 30% vit. C, 6% calcium, 9% iron
Exchanges: 1½ Starch, 2 Fat

Creamy Potluck Potatoes `EASY`

Prep: 10 minutes **Bake:** 1¼ hours **Oven:** 350°F
Stand: 5 minutes **Makes:** 12 servings

- 1 **32-ounce package frozen loose-pack diced hash brown potatoes, thawed (7½ cups)**
- 1 **10.75-ounce can reduced-fat and reduced-sodium condensed cream of chicken soup**
- 1 **8-ounce carton dairy sour cream**
- 2 **tablespoons butter or margarine, melted**

- 1 **cup shredded cheddar cheese (4 ounces)**
- ¼ **cup sliced green onion (2)**
- ¼ **cup milk**
- ½ **teaspoon garlic salt**
- ¼ **teaspoon black pepper**

1. In a large bowl stir together the potatoes, soup, sour cream, and butter. Stir in ½ cup of the shredded cheese, 3 tablespoons of the green onion, the milk, garlic salt, and pepper. Transfer mixture to a 2-quart rectangular baking dish.

2. Bake, covered, in a 350°F oven about 1¼ hours or until potatoes are tender. Sprinkle with the remaining ½ cup cheddar cheese. Let stand for 5 minutes. Sprinkle with the remaining 1 tablespoon green onion.

Per ¾ cup: 176 cal., 10 g total fat (6 g sat. fat), 26 mg chol., 251 mg sodium, 17 g carbo., 1 g fiber, 5 g pro.
Daily Values: 6% vit. A, 11% vit. C, 11% calcium, 5% iron
Exchanges: 1 Starch, 2 Fat

French Fries

For zesty fries like those served at your favorite fast-food restaurant, combine ½ teaspoon seasoned salt and ½ teaspoon seasoned pepper; sprinkle lightly over the cooked fries.

Prep: 15 minutes **Cook:** 5 minutes per batch
Oven: 300°F **Makes:** 4 to 6 servings

- 4 **medium baking potatoes (6 to 8 ounces each)**
  Cooking oil or shortening for deep-fat frying
  Salt or seasoned salt (optional)

1. If desired, peel potatoes. To prevent darkening, immerse peeled potatoes in a bowl of ice water until ready to cut. Cut potatoes lengthwise into ⅜-inch-wide strips. Return potato strips to the ice water.

2. In a heavy, deep 3-quart saucepan or deep-fat fryer, heat oil to 365°F. To prevent splattering, pat potato strips dry. Using a spoon, carefully add potato strips, a few at a time, to hot oil. Fry for 5 to 6 minutes or until crisp and golden brown, turning once.

3. Using a slotted spoon, carefully remove french fries from hot oil; drain on paper towels. If desired, sprinkle with salt. Keep french fries warm in a 300°F oven while frying remaining potatoes.

Per ¼ recipe: 224 cal., 19 g total fat (3 g sat. fat), 0 mg chol., 5 mg sodium, 15 g carbo., 1 g fiber, 2 g pro.
Daily Values: 20% vit. C, 2% calcium, 5% iron
Exchanges: 1 Starch, 3 Fat

Cottage-Fried Potatoes EASY

Prep: 15 minutes **Cook:** 20 minutes **Makes:** 4 servings

> 2 **cloves garlic, minced**
> 3 **tablespoons butter or margarine**
> 3 **medium potatoes, peeled, if desired, and thinly sliced (1 pound)**
> 1 **small onion, thinly sliced**

1. In a large skillet cook and stir garlic in hot butter over medium heat for 15 seconds. (If necessary, add additional butter during cooking.) Layer potato and onion in skillet. Sprinkle with ¼ teaspoon *salt* and ⅛ teaspoon *black pepper.* Cook, covered, for 8 minutes, turning occasionally. Uncover; cook for 12 to 15 minutes more or until potatoes are tender and light brown, turning occasionally.

Per ⅔ cup: 152 cal., 9 g total fat (5 g sat. fat), 24 mg chol., 216 mg sodium, 16 g carbo., 2 g fiber, 2 g pro.
Daily Values: 6% vit. A, 23% vit. C, 2% calcium, 7% iron
Exchanges: 1 Starch, 2 Fat

Hash Brown Potatoes EASY

Prep: 10 minutes **Cook:** 18 minutes **Makes:** 4 servings

> 4 **medium potatoes (1½ pounds)**
> ¼ **cup finely chopped onion**
> ¼ **teaspoon salt**
> ⅛ **teaspoon black pepper**
> 3 **tablespoons butter or margarine**

1. Peel potatoes; coarsely shred to make 4½ cups. Rinse shredded potato and pat dry. Combine potato, onion, salt, and pepper.

2. In a 12-inch skillet melt butter. Using a pancake turner, pat potato mixture into skillet. Cook over medium-low heat about 10 minutes or until bottom of mixture is crisp. With the pancake turner, turn potato mixture in large sections. Cook for 8 to 10 minutes more or until golden.

Per ¾ cup: 186 cal., 9 g total fat (5 g sat. fat), 24 mg chol., 218 mg sodium, 24 g carbo., 2 g fiber, 3 g pro.
Daily Values: 6% vit. A, 31% vit. C, 1% calcium, 5% iron
Exchanges: 1½ Starch, 1½ Fat

Cheese-Topped Hash Browns: Prepare as above, except before serving sprinkle with ½ cup (2 ounces) finely shredded cheddar cheese. Cover and cook for 1 to 2 minutes more or until cheese melts.

Per ¾ cup: 243 cal., 14 g total fat (8 g sat. fat), 39 mg chol., 306 mg sodium, 24 g carbo., 2 g fiber, 6 g pro.
Daily Values: 8% vit. A, 31% vit. C, 12% calcium, 6% iron
Exchanges: ½ High-Fat Meat, 1½ Starch, 1½ Fat

Easy Roasted Potatoes EASY

To get these potatoes on the table faster, increase the oven temp to 425°F and roast, uncovered, for 25 to 30 minutes, stirring occasionally.

Prep: 10 minutes **Roast:** 55 minutes
Oven: 325°F **Makes:** 4 servings

> 3 **medium round red or white potatoes (1 pound), cut into eighths, or 10 to 12 tiny new potatoes (1 pound), halved**
> 2 **tablespoons olive oil**
> ½ **teaspoon onion powder**
> ⅛ **teaspoon paprika**
> 1 **clove garlic, minced**

1. Place potatoes in a greased 9×9×2-inch baking pan. In a small bowl combine oil, onion powder, ¼ teaspoon *salt*, ¼ teaspoon *black pepper*, paprika, and garlic. Drizzle oil mixture over potatoes, tossing to coat. Roast, uncovered, in a 325°F oven for 45 minutes. Stir potatoes; bake for 10 to 20 minutes more or until potatoes are tender and brown on the edges.

Per ¾ cup: 146 cal., 7 g total fat (1 g sat. fat), 0 mg chol., 154 mg sodium, 19 g carbo., 2 g fiber, 3 g pro.
Daily Values: 1% vit. A, 28% vit. C, 2% calcium, 9% iron
Exchanges: 1 Starch, 1½ Fat

Picking Potatoes

Which potato represents the best choice? The answer depends on the recipe.

Different potato types have different textures, depending on the starch content.

● High-starch potatoes, such as russets, have a light, mealy texture. They are best for baked potatoes, potato pancakes, french fries, and mashed potatoes.

● Medium-starch potatoes, such as Finnish yellow and Yukon gold, are all-purpose. They contain more moisture than high-starch potatoes, so they don't fall apart as easily. They're a good choice for roasting and scalloped potatoes.

● Low-starch potatoes, often called waxy potatoes, are dense and hold their shapes better than other potatoes, making them an ideal choice for salads and roasting. Most round red and round white varieties are low-starch potatoes. New potatoes also belong to this category.

Sweet Potato and Cranberry Saute `LOW FAT`

Dried cranberries add a burst of tang to these maple-glazed sweet potatoes.

Start to Finish: 30 minutes **Makes:** 4 servings

- ¾ cup apple juice or apple cider
- 1 pound sweet potatoes, peeled and cut into ¼-inch slices (about 3 cups)
- 1 cup coarsely chopped cooking apple
- 2 tablespoons dried cranberries
- 2 tablespoons pure maple syrup or maple-flavored syrup
- 2 tablespoons rum (optional)
- ¼ teaspoon salt
- 2 tablespoons chopped hazelnuts (filberts) or walnuts, toasted (see tip, page 265)

1. In a large skillet heat apple juice. Add sweet potato slices, spreading evenly. Cook, covered, over low heat about 12 minutes or until potato is nearly tender. Stir in apple, cranberries, maple syrup, rum (if desired), and salt. Cook, covered, over low heat for 3 to 4 minutes more or just until apple is tender.

2. Uncover; boil gently for 3 to 4 minutes more or until liquid is syrupy. Spoon into a serving bowl. Sprinkle with nuts.

Per cup: 197 cal., 3 g total fat (0 g sat. fat), 0 mg chol., 208 mg sodium, 42 g carbo., 5 g fiber, 3 g pro.
Daily Values: 274% vit. A, 7% vit. C, 5% calcium, 7% iron
Exchanges: 1 Fruit, 1 Starch, ½ Other Carbo., ½ Fat

Candied Sweet Potatoes

Family tradition prevails when it comes to topping this Thanksgiving classic. It's your choice—nuts or marshmallows.

Prep: 30 minutes **Bake:** 30 minutes **Oven:** 375°F
Stand: 5 minutes **Makes:** 6 servings

- 4 medium sweet potatoes or yams (about 2 pounds) or two 18-ounce cans sweet potatoes, drained
- ¼ cup pure maple syrup
- ¼ cup butter, melted
- ½ cup chopped pecans or walnuts, toasted if desired (see tip, page 265), or ¾ cup tiny marshmallows

1. Peel the fresh sweet potatoes; cut into 1½-inch chunks. Cook fresh sweet potato, covered, in enough boiling water to cover, for 10 to 12 minutes or just until tender; drain. (Cut up canned sweet potatoes.)

2. Transfer potato to a 2-quart rectangular baking dish. Add maple syrup and melted butter; stir gently to combine.

3. Bake, uncovered, in a 375°F oven for 30 to 35 minutes or until sweet potato is glazed, stirring gently twice. Sprinkle with nuts; let stand for 5 minutes before serving.

Candied Sweet Potatoes with Apples: Prepare as above, except reduce sweet potatoes to 1½ pounds (3 medium). In Step 2, combine prepared sweet potato and 1½ cups sliced apple in a 2-quart rectangular baking dish. Add the maple syrup, the melted butter, and ½ teaspoon ground cinnamon; stir gently to combine. Bake, uncovered, in a 375°F oven for 30 to 35 minutes or until potato and apple are glazed, stirring gently twice. Sprinkle with nuts; let stand for 5 minutes before serving.

Per ¾ cup regular or apple variation: 258 cal., 14 g total fat (5 g sat. fat), 20 mg chol., 113 mg sodium, 32 g carbo., 4 g fiber, 3 g pro.
Daily Values: 267% vit. A, 3% vit. C, 5% calcium, 6% iron
Exchanges: 1½ Starch, ½ Other Carbo., 2½ Fat

Caramelized Onions `EASY`

Prep: 5 minutes **Cook:** 16 minutes
Makes: 4 to 6 servings

- 2 tablespoons butter or margarine
- 2 large sweet onions (such as Vidalia or Walla Walla), halved lengthwise and thinly sliced or cut into ¾-inch chunks

1. In a large skillet melt the butter over medium-low heat. Add onion. Cook, covered, for 13 to 15 minutes or until onion is tender, stirring occasionally. Uncover; cook and stir over medium-high heat for 3 to 5 minutes more or until onion is golden.

Per ⅓ cup: 84 cal., 6 g total fat (4 g sat. fat), 16 mg chol., 64 mg sodium, 7 g carbo., 1 g fiber, 1 g pro.
Daily Values: 5% vit. A, 7% vit. C, 2% calcium, 1% iron
Exchanges: 1½ Vegetable, 1 Fat

Father's Day Cookout

Treat Dad to a special steak dinner.

- *Grilled beef ribeye steaks topped with Caramelized Onions (above)*
- *Corn on the Cob (page 580)*
- *Caesar Salad (page 496)*
- *Ice cream sundaes*

Sauteed Spinach with Bacon and Mustard `FAST`

When cooking spinach, use metal tongs to add it in small batches; lift and stir while it cooks. As the spinach in the skillet cooks down, add a little more.

Start to Finish: 15 minutes **Makes:** 4 to 6 servings

- **4 slices bacon, cut into 1-inch pieces**
- **3 6-ounce packages prewashed fresh baby spinach or two 10-ounce packages prewashed spinach**
- **1 tablespoon butter or margarine**
- **1 tablespoon Dijon-style mustard**
- **¼ teaspoon crushed red pepper**

1. In a 12-inch skillet cook bacon over medium heat until crisp. Remove bacon, reserving 1 tablespoon drippings in skillet. Drain bacon on paper towels.

2. Gradually add spinach to skillet, stirring frequently with metal tongs. Cook just until spinach is wilted (should take 2 to 3 minutes total). Transfer spinach from skillet to a colander; hold colander over sink and press lightly to drain. (If using larger spinach leaves, use kitchen scissors to snip them into smaller pieces.)

3. Melt butter in the same skillet over medium heat; stir in mustard and crushed red pepper. Add drained spinach; toss to coat. Top with cooked bacon and serve immediately.

Per ½ cup: 135 cal., 11 g total fat (4 g sat. fat), 18 mg chol., 340 mg sodium, 5 g carbo., 3 g fiber, 7 g pro.
Daily Values: 241% vit. A, 60% vit. C, 13% calcium, 20% iron
Exchanges: 1½ Vegetable, 2 Fat

Creamed Spinach

Baby spinach has smaller leaves and a milder flavor than regular spinach.

Start to Finish: 30 minutes **Makes:** 4 servings

- **4 6-ounce packages prewashed fresh baby spinach; two 10-ounce packages prewashed fresh spinach (large stems removed); or two 10-ounce packages frozen chopped spinach, thawed**
- **½ cup chopped onion (1 medium)**
- **2 to 3 cloves garlic, minced**
- **2 tablespoons butter**
- **1 cup whipping cream**
- **½ teaspoon black pepper**
- **¼ teaspoon salt**
- **¼ teaspoon ground nutmeg**

1. In a Dutch oven cook fresh spinach (if using) in rapidly boiling salted water for 1 minute. Drain well, squeezing out excess liquid. Pat spinach dry with paper towels. Snip spinach with kitchen shears to coarsely chop; set aside. (If using frozen spinach, drain well, squeezing out the excess liquid.)

2. In a large skillet cook onion and garlic in hot butter about 5 minutes or until onion is tender. Stir in whipping cream, pepper, salt, and nutmeg. Bring mixture to boiling; cook, uncovered, until cream begins to thicken. Add spinach. Simmer, uncovered, until desired consistency, stirring occasionally. Season to taste with additional salt and pepper. Serve immediately.

Per ½ cup: 312 cal., 29 g total fat (17 g sat. fat), 98 mg chol., 347 mg sodium, 11 g carbo., 4 g fiber, 6 g pro.
Daily Values: 340% vit. A, 83% vit. C, 22% calcium, 27% iron
Exchanges: 2 Vegetable, 6 Fat

Zucchini and Sweet Peppers with Feta `LOW FAT`

Bottled roasted sweet peppers, cumin, and feta cheese transform your garden zucchini into a Mediterranean treat.

Start to Finish: 25 minutes **Makes:** 6 servings

- **1 cup chopped onion (1 large)**
- **1 tablespoon olive oil or cooking oil**
- **3 medium zucchini, cut into ¼-inch slices (about 4 cups)**
- **2 tablespoons water**
- **½ teaspoon ground cumin**
- **½ cup bottled roasted red sweet peppers, drained and cut into strips**
  - **Salt**
  - **Black pepper**
- **2 tablespoons crumbled feta cheese**

1. In a large skillet cook and stir onion in hot oil over medium heat about 5 minutes or until tender. Add zucchini, water, and cumin to skillet; reduce heat. Simmer, covered, for 3 to 5 minutes or until zucchini is crisp-tender.

2. Stir roasted sweet pepper strips into zucchini mixture; heat through. Season to taste with salt and pepper. Sprinkle with feta cheese.

Per ⅔ cup: 56 cal., 3 g total fat (1 g sat. fat), 2 mg chol., 108 mg sodium, 6 g carbo., 2 g fiber, 2 g pro.
Daily Values: 7% vit. A, 72% vit. C, 4% calcium, 4% iron
Exchanges: 1 Vegetable, ½ Fat

Maple Acorn Squash `EASY`

Prep: 10 minutes **Bake:** 65 minutes
Oven: 350°F **Makes:** 2 servings

- 1 **medium acorn squash (about 1¼ pounds)**
- ¼ **cup maple syrup or 3 tablespoons packed brown sugar**
- 2 **tablespoons butter or margarine, melted**
- ½ **teaspoon finely shredded orange peel (optional)**
- ⅛ **teaspoon ground cinnamon or ground nutmeg**

1. Cut squash in half lengthwise; remove and discard seeds. Arrange the squash halves, cut sides down, in a 2-quart baking dish. Bake in a 350°F oven for 45 minutes. Turn squash halves cut sides up.

2. Meanwhile, in a small bowl stir together maple syrup, butter, orange peel (if desired), and cinnamon. Spoon maple syrup mixture into centers of squash halves. Bake for 20 to 25 minutes more or until squash is tender.

Per ½ squash: 299 cal., 12 g total fat (8 g sat. fat), 33 mg chol.,
134 mg sodium, 49 g carbo., 3 g fiber, 2 g pro.
Daily Values: 23% vit. A, 34% vit. C, 10% calcium, 11% iron
Exchanges: 1½ Starch, 2 Other Carbo., 1½ Fat

Squash, Pear, and Onion au Gratin

Prep: 25 minutes **Bake:** 1 hour
Oven: 350°F **Makes:** 6 servings

- 1½ **pounds butternut, buttercup, or banana squash**
- 1 **large onion, sliced and separated into rings (1 cup)**
- 1 **tablespoon butter or margarine**
- 1 **cup thinly sliced, peeled pear (1 medium)**
- 3 **tablespoons fine dry bread crumbs**
- 3 **slices bacon, crisp-cooked, drained, and crumbled**
- 2 **tablespoons chopped walnuts**
- 1 **tablespoon grated Romano cheese**
- 1 **tablespoon butter or margarine, melted**
- 2 **tablespoons snipped fresh parsley (optional)**

1. If using butternut squash, cut the squash in half lengthwise. Peel butternut, buttercup, or banana squash; slice crosswise into ½-inch slices. Remove and discard seeds; set squash slices aside.

2. Cook onion rings in 1 tablespoon hot butter for 5 to 10 minutes or until tender.

3. Arrange half of the squash slices in the bottom of a 2-quart square baking dish. Top with half of the pear slices. Repeat layers. Sprinkle lightly with *salt.* Cover with the cooked onion.

4. Bake, covered, in a 350°F oven about 45 minutes or until nearly tender.

5. Meanwhile, in a small bowl combine bread crumbs, bacon, walnuts, Romano cheese, and the 1 tablespoon melted butter; sprinkle over vegetables. Bake, uncovered, about 15 minutes more or until squash is tender. If desired, sprinkle with parsley.

Per cup: 153 cal., 8 g total fat (3 g sat. fat), 14 mg chol.,
270 mg sodium, 20 g carbo., 1 g fiber, 3 g pro.
Daily Values: 146% vit. A, 35% vit. C, 7% calcium, 6% iron
Exchanges: 1½ Starch, 1 Fat

Buttered Spaghetti Squash

Spaghetti squash is a tasty, low-calorie substitute for spaghetti.

Prep: 20 minutes **Bake:** 30 minutes
Oven: 350°F **Makes:** 6 servings

- 1 **medium spaghetti squash (2½ to 3 pounds)**
- ½ **cup finely shredded Parmesan cheese**
- 3 **tablespoons butter or margarine, cut up**
- 1 **tablespoon snipped fresh basil, oregano, or parsley**
- ¼ **teaspoon salt**

1. Halve squash lengthwise; remove and discard seeds. Place squash halves, cut sides down, in a large baking dish. Using a fork, prick the skin all over. Bake, uncovered, in a 350°F oven for 30 to 40 minutes or until tender.

2. Remove squash pulp from shell (see photo, page 593). Toss squash with ¼ cup of the Parmesan cheese, the butter, basil, and salt. Sprinkle with the remaining Parmesan cheese.

Per ¾ cup: 123 cal., 9 g total fat (4 g sat. fat), 21 mg chol.,
276 mg sodium, 10 g carbo., 0 g fiber, 3 g pro.
Daily Values: 6% vit. A, 4% vit. C, 12% calcium, 3% iron
Exchanges: ½ Starch, ½ Lean Meat, 1½ Fat

Spaghetti Squash with Marinara Sauce: Bake spaghetti squash as in Step 1. Omit Parmesan cheese, butter, basil, and salt. For marinara sauce, in a medium saucepan cook ¼ cup chopped onion and 2 cloves minced garlic in 1 tablespoon olive oil or cooking oil. Stir in one 14.5-ounce can diced tomatoes, undrained; 1 teaspoon dried Italian seasoning, crushed; ⅛ teaspoon fennel seeds, crushed; ¼ teaspoon salt; and ¼ teaspoon black pepper. Bring to boiling; reduce heat. Simmer, uncovered, for 10 to 15 minutes or until desired consistency is reached, stirring often. Remove the squash pulp from shell (see photo, below). Spoon sauce over squash. If desired, sprinkle with grated Parmesan cheese.

Per ¾ cup squash + ¼ cup sauce: 84 cal., 3 g total fat (0 g sat. fat), 0 mg chol., 233 mg sodium, 14 g carbo., 0 g fiber, 1 g pro.
Daily Values: 1% vit. A, 19% vit. C, 7% calcium, 5% iron
Exchanges: ½ Vegetable, ½ Starch, ½ Fat

With a fork, carefully rake the stringy pulp from the squash shell, separating the pulp into strands that look like spaghetti.

Fried Green Tomatoes EASY

This summertime classic is a great way to fix the surplus tomatoes from your garden.

Prep: 10 minutes **Cook:** 8 minutes per batch
Stand: 15 minutes **Makes:** 6 servings

    3 medium firm green tomatoes
    ½ teaspoon salt
    ¼ teaspoon black pepper
    ½ cup all-purpose flour
    ¼ cup milk
    2 eggs, slightly beaten
    ⅔ cup fine dry bread crumbs or cornmeal
    ¼ cup cooking oil

1. Cut unpeeled tomatoes into ½-inch slices; sprinkle slices with the salt and pepper. Let tomato slices stand for 15 minutes. Meanwhile, place flour, milk, eggs, and bread crumbs in separate shallow dishes.

2. Dip tomato slices in milk, then flour, then eggs, then bread crumbs, coating both sides. In a skillet fry the coated tomato slices, half at a time, in hot oil over medium heat for 4 to 6 minutes on each side or until brown. (If tomatoes begin to brown too quickly, reduce heat to medium low. If necessary, add additional oil.) If desired, season to taste with additional salt and pepper.

Per ⅙ recipe: 194 cal., 12 g total fat (2 g sat. fat), 72 mg chol., 465 mg sodium, 18 g carbo., 1 g fiber, 5 g pro.
Daily Values: 10% vit. A, 24% vit. C, 5% calcium, 8% iron
Exchanges: 1 Vegetable, 1 Starch, 2 Fat

Tomato Saute

Tomato Saute FAST

For a more substantial dish, spoon this quick-to-fix medley of warm grape tomatoes, shallot, thyme, and mozzarella cheese over pasta. It's also terrific over wilted greens.

Start to Finish: 15 minutes **Makes:** 4 servings

    2½ cups whole red grape or yellow teardrop
         tomatoes and/or cherry tomatoes
         Nonstick olive oil cooking spray
    ¼ cup sliced shallot
    1 teaspoon snipped fresh thyme
    1 clove garlic, minced
    ¼ teaspoon salt
    ¼ teaspoon black pepper
    4 ounces mozzarella cheese, cut into ½-inch
         cubes

1. Halve about 1½ cups of the tomatoes; set aside. Lightly coat a 10-inch nonstick skillet with cooking spray. Add shallot, thyme, and garlic. Cook and stir over medium heat for 2 to 3 minutes or until shallot is tender.

2. Add all of the tomatoes, the salt, and pepper. Cook and stir for 1 to 2 minutes or just until tomatoes are warmed. Remove from heat. Stir in mozzarella cheese.

Per ⅔ cup: 109 cal., 6 g total fat (4 g sat. fat), 20 mg chol., 237 mg sodium, 6 g carbo., 1 g fiber, 6 g pro.
Daily Values: 25% vit. A, 26% vit. C, 21% calcium, 3% iron
Exchanges: 1½ Vegetable, 1 Medium-Fat Meat

Ratatouille

This Mediterranean dish features eggplant and tomatoes. It is equally delicious served cold.

Start to Finish: 40 minutes **Makes:** 4 servings

- ½ cup chopped onion (1 medium)
- 1 clove garlic, minced
- 1 tablespoon olive oil or cooking oil
- 3 cups cubed, peeled eggplant
- 1 medium zucchini or yellow summer squash, halved lengthwise and cut into ¼-inch slices (1½ cups)
- 1 cup chopped, peeled tomato (2 medium) or one 14.5-ounce can diced tomatoes, drained
- ¾ cup chopped green sweet pepper (1 medium)
- 3 tablespoons dry white wine, chicken broth, or vegetable broth
- ¼ teaspoon salt
- ⅛ teaspoon black pepper
- 1 tablespoon snipped fresh basil or oregano

1. In a large skillet cook onion and garlic in hot oil over medium heat until onion is tender. Stir in eggplant, zucchini, tomato, sweet pepper, wine, salt, and pepper. Bring to boiling; reduce heat. Simmer, covered, about 10 minutes or until vegetables are tender. Uncover and cook about 5 minutes more or until most of the liquid has evaporated, stirring occasionally. Season to taste with additional salt and black pepper. Stir in basil just before serving.

Per ¾ cup: 82 cal., 4 g total fat (1 g sat. fat), 0 mg chol., 155 mg sodium, 10 g carbo., 4 g fiber, 2 g pro.
Daily Values: 12% vit. A, 58% vit. C, 3% calcium, 4% iron
Exchanges: 2 Vegetable, ½ Fat

Roasting Sweet Peppers

Bright and colorful, roasted sweet peppers are delicious in soups, stews, vegetable medleys, and salads. Follow these easy roasting directions.

Halve sweet peppers lengthwise; remove stems, seeds, and membranes. Place pepper halves, cut sides down, on a foil-lined baking sheet. Bake in a preheated 425°F oven for 20 to 25 minutes. Bring foil up around peppers to enclose. Let stand about 15 minutes or until cool. Use a sharp knife to loosen edges of the skins; gently pull off the skin in strips and discard.

Herbed Vegetable Medley

LOW FAT   EASY

Prep: 15 minutes **Cook:** 8 minutes **Makes:** 12 servings

- 1 pound packaged peeled baby carrots
- ¼ cup water
- 2 yellow or red sweet peppers, cut into 1-inch pieces
- 1 pound fresh sugar snap peas or snow peas, trimmed
- 1 tablespoon butter or margarine
- 2 tablespoons snipped fresh basil or dill
- ½ teaspoon salt
- ⅛ teaspoon black pepper

1. Cut any large baby carrots in half lengthwise. In a 12-inch skillet bring water to boiling. Add carrots and sweet pepper. Reduce heat to medium and cook, covered, about 5 minutes or until nearly tender, stirring once. Add sugar snap peas. Cook and stir, uncovered, 3 minutes more or until crisp-tender. Drain, if necessary. Stir in butter, basil, salt, and black pepper.

Per ⅔ cup: 54 cal., 1 g total fat (1 g sat. fat), 3 mg chol., 136 mg sodium, 9 g carbo., 2 g fiber, 2 g pro.
Daily Values: 84% vit. A, 97% vit. C, 3% calcium, 4% iron
Exchanges: 2 Vegetable

Veggie Mash

Adding cauliflower and carrot to classic mashed potatoes fortifies them with extra vitamins.

Start to Finish: 30 minutes **Makes:** 6 servings

- 3 medium baking potatoes (1 pound), peeled and cubed
- 1 cup coarsely chopped cauliflower
- ½ cup sliced carrot or coarsely chopped cauliflower
- ¼ cup light dairy sour cream
- ¼ teaspoon salt
- 2 tablespoons finely shredded Parmesan cheese

1. In a medium saucepan cook potato, cauliflower, and carrot, covered, in enough boiling salted water to cover for 15 to 20 minutes or until tender; drain. Mash with a potato masher or beat with an electric mixer on low speed. Add sour cream and salt. Mash or beat until combined. Season with additional salt and *black pepper*. Top servings with Parmesan cheese.

Per ½ cup: 113 cal., 4 g total fat (2 g sat. fat), 11 mg chol., 303 mg sodium, 13 g carbo., 2 g fiber, 6 g pro.
Daily Values: 54% vit. A, 25% vit. C, 17% calcium, 3% iron
Exchanges: 1 Vegetable, ½ Starch, 1 Fat

Rosemary Roasted Vegetables

Prep: 30 minutes **Roast:** 20 minutes
Oven: 425°F **Makes:** 12 servings

> 1 **pound Brussels sprouts**
> 12 **ounces green beans**
> 6 **green onions, trimmed and cut up**
> 12 **fresh rosemary sprigs**
> 8 **slices pancetta or bacon, partially cooked, drained, and cut up**
> 2 **tablespoons olive oil**
>   **Salt**
>   **Black pepper**
> 1 **lemon, halved**

1. Trim stems and remove any wilted outer leaves from Brussels sprouts; halve large Brussels sprouts. Wash Brussels sprouts and green beans; drain. In a large saucepan cook Brussels sprouts in a small amount of boiling lightly salted water for 3 minutes. Add green beans. Cook for 5 minutes more; drain.

2. Place Brussels sprouts and beans in a shallow roasting pan. Add green onion and rosemary sprigs; toss to combine. Top with partially cooked pancetta. Drizzle vegetable mixture with olive oil. Sprinkle with salt and pepper.

3. Roast, uncovered, in a 425°F oven about 20 minutes or until vegetables are crisp-tender and pancetta is crisp. Transfer vegetable mixture to a serving platter. Squeeze juice from the lemon over the vegetable mixture.

Per ½ cup: 143 cal., 10 g total fat (4 g sat. fat), 10 mg chol., 275 mg sodium, 6 g carbo., 3 g fiber, 4 g pro.
Daily Values: 10% vit. A, 51% vit. C, 3% calcium, 6% iron
Exchanges: 1½ Vegetable, 2 Fat

Breaded Veggies

For an appetizer, serve these oven-fried vegetables with ranch salad dressing for dipping.

Prep: 25 minutes **Bake:** 20 minutes
Oven: 400°F **Makes:** 6 servings

> ½ **cup seasoned fine dry bread crumbs**
> 2 **tablespoons grated Parmesan cheese**
> ¼ **teaspoon black pepper**
> 1 **egg, slightly beaten**
> 1 **tablespoon milk**
> 4 **cups cauliflower florets, broccoli florets, whole fresh button mushrooms, and/or packaged peeled baby carrots**
> 1 **tablespoon butter or margarine, melted**

1. Preheat oven to 400°F. Lightly grease a 15×10×1-inch baking pan; set the pan aside.

2. In a plastic bag combine bread crumbs, Parmesan cheese, and pepper. In a small bowl combine egg and milk.

3. Toss 1 cup of the vegetables in the egg mixture, letting excess drip off. Add vegetables to crumbs in plastic bag. Close bag and shake to coat well. Place coated vegetables on the prepared baking pan. Repeat with remaining vegetables. Drizzle melted butter over vegetables.

4. Bake about 20 minutes or until vegetables are golden brown, stirring twice during baking.

Per ⅔ cup: 93 cal., 4 g total fat (2 g sat. fat), 42 mg chol., 348 mg sodium, 11 g carbo., 2 g fiber, 5 g pro.
Daily Values: 3% vit. A, 52% vit. C, 6% calcium, 4% iron
Exchanges: 1 Vegetable, ½ Starch, ½ Fat

Baked Apples LOW FAT EASY

These fruit-stuffed apples make a tasty side dish for a roast pork dinner. Add the ice cream and they become a scrumptious dessert.

Prep: 15 minutes **Bake:** 40 minutes
Oven: 350°F **Makes:** 4 servings

> 4 **medium cooking apples, such as Rome Beauty, Granny Smith, or Jonathan**
> ½ **cup raisins, snipped pitted whole dates, or mixed dried fruit bits**
> 2 **tablespoons packed brown sugar**
> ½ **teaspoon ground cinnamon**
> ¼ **teaspoon ground nutmeg**
> ⅓ **cup apple juice or water**
>   **Ice cream or half-and-half (optional)**

1. Using an apple corer or a sharp knife, remove the cores from the apples. Peel a strip from the top of each apple. Place the apples in a 2-quart baking dish or casserole. Set aside.

2. In a small bowl stir together raisins, brown sugar, cinnamon, and nutmeg; spoon raisin mixture into centers of apples. Pour apple juice into casserole around the apples.

3. Bake, uncovered, in a 350°F oven for 40 to 45 minutes or until the apples are tender, basting occasionally with the apple juice in the casserole. Serve warm and, if desired, with ice cream.

Per apple: 164 cal., 1 g total fat (0 g sat. fat), 0 mg chol., 5 mg sodium, 42 g carbo., 5 g fiber, 1 g pro.
Daily Values: 1% vit. A, 12% vit. C, 3% calcium, 5% iron
Exchanges: 1½ Fruit, 1 Other Carbo.

Sauteed Apples and Mushrooms

Sauteed Apples and Mushrooms

Granny Smith apples give mushrooms a delightfully tart, fresh taste.

Start to Finish: 20 minutes **Makes:** 4 or 5 servings

- 2 **medium Granny Smith and/or Rome Beauty apples, cored and cut into ½-inch wedges (about 2½ cups)**
- ⅓ **cup sliced shallot (3)**
- 1 **tablespoon snipped fresh thyme or 1 teaspoon dried thyme, crushed**
- 2 **tablespoons butter**
- 8 **ounces small fresh mushrooms**
- 1 **tablespoon lemon juice**
- ¼ **teaspoon salt**
- ⅛ **teaspoon black pepper**

1. In a large skillet cook apple, shallot, and thyme in 1 tablespoon hot butter over medium heat about 5 minutes or just until apple is tender, stirring occasionally. Transfer apple mixture to a large bowl; set aside.

2. In the same skillet cook and stir mushrooms in the remaining 1 tablespoon hot butter about 5 minutes or until mushrooms are tender. If necessary, simmer, uncovered, until the liquid has evaporated. Stir in the apple mixture, the lemon juice, salt, and pepper. Cook and stir until heated through.

Per ¾ cup: 113 cal., 7 g total fat (4 g sat. fat), 15 mg chol., 191 mg sodium, 14 g carbo., 2 g fiber, 2 g pro.
Daily Values: 8% vit. A, 12% vit. C, 2% calcium, 4% iron
Exchanges: ½ Vegetable, ½ Fruit, 1½ Fat

Honey-Berry Compote NO FAT EASY

Add the raspberries or blackberries just before serving. These berries are more delicate than the blueberries and strawberries and will lose their texture if chilled too long in the dressing.

Prep: 15 minutes **Chill:** 2 hours **Makes:** 8 servings

- 2 **teaspoons finely shredded orange peel**
- ½ **cup orange juice**
- ¼ **cup honey**
- 1 **tablespoon snipped fresh mint (optional)**
- 2 **cups halved green or red seedless grapes**
- 2 **cups fresh blueberries**
- 2 **cups halved fresh strawberries**
- 2 **cups fresh raspberries and/or blackberries**
  Small fresh mint leaves (optional)

1. For dressing, in a small bowl whisk together orange peel, orange juice, honey, and, if desired, the 1 tablespoon snipped mint.

2. In a large serving bowl combine grapes, blueberries, and strawberries. Gently stir in dressing. Cover and chill for 2 to 24 hours.

3. Just before serving, stir in raspberries. If desired, garnish with fresh mint leaves.

Per cup: 105 cal., 0 g total fat (0 g sat. fat), 0 mg chol., 2 mg sodium, 26 g carbo., 5 g fiber, 1 g pro.
Daily Values: 2% vit. A, 73% vit. C, 2% calcium, 4% iron
Exchanges: 1 Fruit, ½ Other Carbo.

Warm Citrus Fruit with Brown Sugar EASY

Serve this warm medley of oranges, grapefruit, and pineapple for brunch. See photo, page 571.

Prep: 15 minutes **Broil:** 5 minutes **Makes:** 4 servings

- 2 **medium red grapefruit, peeled and sectioned, or 1½ cups drained refrigerated grapefruit sections**
- 2 **medium oranges, peeled and sectioned**
- 1 **cup fresh pineapple chunks or one 8-ounce can pineapple chunks, drained**
- 2 **tablespoons rum (optional)**
- ¼ **cup packed brown sugar**
- 2 **tablespoons butter or margarine, softened**

1. In a medium bowl combine grapefruit, orange, and pineapple. Transfer to a 1-quart broiler-safe au gratin dish or casserole.*

2. If desired, in a small saucepan heat rum until it almost simmers. Carefully pour over fruit. Stir gently to coat.

3. In a small bowl stir together brown sugar and butter until well mixed; sprinkle over fruit. Broil about 4 inches from the heat for 5 to 6 minutes until sugar is bubbly and fruit is warmed.

*Note: For individual servings, use four individual au gratin dishes and do not use the rum.

Per ¾ cup: 192 cal., 6 g total fat (4 g sat. fat), 16 mg chol., 68 mg sodium, 35 g carbo., 4 g fiber, 2 g pro.
Daily Values: 14% vit. A, 146% vit. C, 6% calcium, 4% iron
Exchanges: 1½ Fruit, 1 Other Carbo., 1 Fat

Warm Spiced Peaches

When fresh peach season rolls around, remember this sweet and spicy dish. Pluck a little basil from the garden to add a fresh finish.

Prep: 15 minutes **Bake:** 5 minutes
Oven: 350°F **Makes:** 4 servings

- 3 ripe medium peaches, peeled and sliced
- 2 teaspoons sugar
- ½ teaspoon ground cinnamon
- ½ teaspoon finely shredded orange peel
- ½ teaspoon vanilla
- ¼ teaspoon ground nutmeg
- 2 teaspoons snipped fresh basil or 1 teaspoon snipped fresh mint

1. In a medium bowl combine sliced peaches, sugar, cinnamon, orange peel, vanilla, and nutmeg; toss gently to combine. Divide peach mixture among four 5-inch individual quiche dishes or 10-ounce custard cups.

2. Bake, covered, in a 350°F oven for 5 to 10 minutes or until warm. Sprinkle with basil.

Per ½ cup: 66 cal., 0 g total fat (0 g sat. fat), 0 mg chol., 0 mg sodium, 17 g carbo., 3 g fiber, 1 g pro.
Daily Values: 14% vit. A, 15% vit. C, 1% iron
Exchanges: 1 Fruit

Sectioning Citrus

The trick to sectioning oranges and grapefruit is to remove the bitter white membrane while keeping the sweet sections intact.

Using a serrated knife, remove the peel. Holding the fruit over a bowl to catch the juice, cut between one section and the membrane, slicing to the fruit's center. Turn the knife and slide it up the other side of the section alongside the membrane. Place the section in a second bowl. Repeat with remaining sections.

Spiced Cantaloupe

Lime juice gives this dish some tang, while nutmeg gives it a hint of celebration.

Start to Finish: 10 minutes **Makes:** 4 servings

- 2 cups cubed cantaloupe
- 2 tablespoons lime juice
- 1 tablespoon sugar
- ¼ teaspoon ground nutmeg

1. In a medium bowl combine cantaloupe, lime juice, sugar, and nutmeg; toss gently to combine. Spoon into serving dishes.

Per ½ cup: 41 cal., 0 g total fat, 0 mg chol., 13 mg sodium, 10 g carbo., 1 g fiber, 1 g pro.
Daily Values: 54% vit. A, 53% vit. C, 1% calcium, 1% iron
Exchanges: ½ Fruit

Cinnamon Poached Pears

Savor the aromas of fresh ginger and stick cinnamon as the pears cook in the sweet syrup.

Prep: 20 minutes **Cook:** 15 minutes
Chill: 2 hours **Makes:** 8 servings

- 8 small to medium pears (about 3 pounds)
- 1 750-milliliter bottle dry white wine or 3 cups apple juice
- 2 cups water
- 1 cup sugar
- 1 2-inch piece peeled fresh ginger, cut into strips
- 3 inches stick cinnamon, broken

1. Peel pears, leaving stems intact. Cut a thin slice from the bottom of each pear so the pears stand up. Working through the bottom of each pear, use a melon baller to remove the core.

2. Meanwhile, in a 4-quart Dutch oven combine wine, water, sugar, ginger, and cinnamon. Cook, uncovered, over medium heat until gently boiling, stirring occasionally to dissolve sugar. Add the pears. Return liquid just to boiling. Reduce heat. Simmer, covered, about 15 minutes or just until pears are tender. Remove from heat; cool pears slightly in syrup. Transfer pears and syrup to an extra-large bowl. Cover and chill for 2 to 24 hours. Drain pears to serve.

Per pear: 110 cal., 0 g total fat (0 g sat. fat), 0 mg chol., 2 mg sodium, 27 g carbo., 5 g fiber, 1 g pro.
Daily Values: 1% vit. A, 8% vit. C, 1% calcium, 2% iron
Exchanges: 2 Fruit

Squash

Always bright and colorful, squash varies in size, shape, color, texture, and flavor. Most types of squash fall into two categories—summer and winter. Those considered summer squash are most readily available from early to late summer. These squash have thin, edible skins and soft seeds. Summer squashes cook quickly and have high water content and mild flavor. They are delicious when sauteed, steamed, or simmered. Winter squash are known for their thick skins and hard seeds. For most varieties, the flesh is deep yellow or orange. They can be baked, steamed, or simmered. Although some types are available year-round, the peak season is fall and winter.

Summer Squash

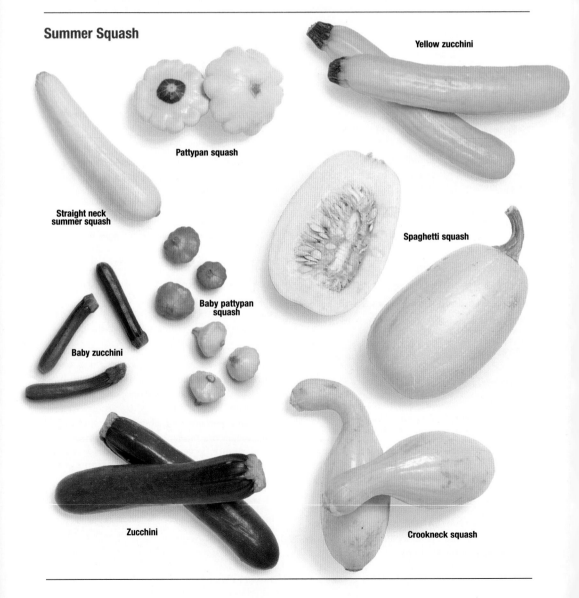

Yellow zucchini

Pattypan squash

Straight neck summer squash

Spaghetti squash

Baby pattypan squash

Baby zucchini

Zucchini

Crookneck squash

Winter Squash

Delicata
squash

Butternut squash

Carnival squash

Kabocha
squash

Buttercup squash

Golden nugget
squash

Pie pumpkin

Turban squash

Sweet dumpling
squash

Hubbard squash

Acorn squash

Potatoes

Potatoes vary in texture, shape, and color. Look for these varieties at your grocery store or farmer's market. Refer to page 589 for suggestions on how to use each type.

New potatoes

Sweet potatoes and yams

Long white potato

Yukon gold potatoes

Purple potatoes

Russet potatoes

Namé
(Cuban yam)

Fingerling potatoes

Round red potatoes

Onions

Vegetables of the onion family are valued for the pungent flavors they impart to a multitude of dishes. Try some of these in your favorite recipes.

Shallots

Green onions

Cipollini

Pearl onions

Yellow, white, and red onions

Boiling onions

Leek

Selecting Fresh Vegetables

When buying fresh vegetables, look for ones that are plump, crisp, brightly colored, and heavy for their size. Avoid any that are bruised, shriveled, moldy, or blemished. For specific vegetables, follow these guidelines for selecting and storing. For cooking information, see the charts on pages 606–610.

Vegetable	Peak Season	How to Choose	How to Store
Asparagus	Available March through June with peak season in April and May; available year-round in some areas.	Choose firm, straight stalks with compact, closed tips. Avoid stalks that are very thin (less than ⅛ inch) or very thick (more than ½ inch).	Wrap the bases of fresh asparagus spears in wet paper towels and keep tightly sealed in a storage container in the refrigerator for up to 4 days.
Beans, green: snap or string	Available April through September; available year-round in some areas.	Select fresh beans that are brightly colored and crisp. Avoid those that are bruised, scarred, or rusty with brown spots or streaks. Bulging, leathery beans are old.	Refrigerate in a covered container up to 5 days.
Beets	Available year-round with peak season from June through October.	Select small or medium beets; large beets tend to be pithy, tough, and less sweet.	Trim beet greens, leaving 1 to 2 inches of stem. Do not cut the long root. Store unwashed beets in an open container in the refrigerator for up to 1 week.
Bok choy	Available year-round.	Look for firm, white, bulblike bases with deep green leaves. Avoid soft spots on base or wilted, shriveled leaves.	Refrigerate in a plastic bag and use within 3 days.
Broccoli	Available year-round.	Look for firm stalks with tightly packed, deep green or purplish green heads. Avoid heads that are light green or yellowing.	Keep unwashed broccoli in a covered container in the refrigerator for up to 4 days.
Brussels sprouts	Available year-round with peak season from August through April.	Pick out the smaller sprouts that are vivid green; they will taste the sweetest. Large ones may be bitter.	Refrigerate in a covered container for up to 2 days.
Cabbage: green, napa, red, or savoy	Available year-round.	The head should feel heavy for its size, and its leaves should be unwithered, brightly colored, and free of brown spots.	Refrigerate in a covered container for up to 5 days.
Carrots	Available year-round.	Select straight, rigid, bright orange carrots.	Refrigerate in a plastic bag for up to 2 weeks.
Cauliflower	Available year-round.	Look for solid, heavy heads with bright green leaves. Avoid those with brown bruises or yellowed leaves.	Refrigerate in a covered container for up to 4 days.
Celery	Available year-round.	Look for crisp ribs that are firm, unwilted, and unblemished.	Refrigerate, tightly wrapped, for up to 2 weeks.
Cucumbers	Available year-round with peak season from late May through early September.	Select firm cucumbers without shriveled or soft spots. Edible wax sometimes is added to prevent moisture loss.	Keep salad cucumbers in refrigerator for up to 10 days. Pickling cucumbers should be picked and used the same day.

Selecting Fresh Vegetables (*continued*)

Vegetable	Peak Season	How to Choose	How to Store
Eggplant	Available year-round with peak season from July through September.	Look for plump, glossy eggplants that have fresh-looking, mold-free caps. Skip any that are scarred or bruised.	Refrigerate whole eggplants for up to 2 days.
Fennel	Available October through April; available year-round in some areas.	Look for crisp, clean bulbs without brown spots or blemishes. Tops should be bright green and fresh looking.	Refrigerate, tightly wrapped, for up to 5 days.
Leeks	Available year-round.	Look for leeks that have clean white ends and fresh green tops.	Refrigerate, tightly wrapped, for up to 5 days.
Mushrooms (all varieties)	Available year-round; morel mushrooms available April through June.	Mushrooms should be firm, fresh, plump, and bruise-free. Size is a matter of preference. Avoid spotted or slimy mushrooms.	Store unwashed mushrooms in the refrigerator for up to 2 days. A paper bag or damp cloth bag lets them breathe so they stay firm longer.
Okra	Available year-round with peak season from June through September.	Look for small, crisp, bright-color pods without brown spots or blemishes. Avoid shriveled pods.	Refrigerate, tightly wrapped, for up to 3 days.
Onions (all varieties)	Variety determines availability. Some varieties, such as white, red, pearl, and boiling onions, are available year-round. Various sweet onion varieties, such as Vidalia and Walla Walla, are available on and off throughout the year.	Select dry bulb onions that are firm, free from blemishes, and not sprouting.	Keep in a cool, dry, well-ventilated place for several weeks.
Peas, Pea pods	Peas: Available January through June with peak season from March through May. Pea pods: Available February through August.	Select fresh, crisp, bright-colored peas, snow peas, or sugar snap peas. Avoid shriveled pods or those with brown spots.	Store, tightly wrapped, in the refrigerator for up to 3 days.
Peppers: hot or sweet	Available year-round.	Fresh peppers, whether sweet or hot, should be brightly colored and have a good shape for the variety. Avoid shriveled, bruised, or broken peppers.	Refrigerate in a covered container for up to 5 days.
Potatoes	Available year-round.	Look for clean potatoes that have smooth, unblemished skins. They should be firm and have a shape that is typical for their variety. Avoid those that have green spots or are soft, moldy, or shriveled.	Store for several weeks in a dark, well-ventilated, cool place that is slightly humid but not wet. Bright lights cause potatoes to develop green patches that have a bitter flavor. Do not refrigerate; cold temperatures cause potatoes to turn overly sweet and to darken when cooked.
Root vegetables: parsnips, rutabagas, or turnips	Available year-round. Parsnips: Peak season from November through March. Rutabagas: Peak season from September through March. Turnips: Peak season from October through March.	Choose vegetables that are smooth-skinned and heavy for their size. Sometimes parsnips, rutabagas, and turnips are covered with a wax coating to extend storage; cut off this coating before cooking.	Refrigerate for up to 2 weeks.

Selecting Fresh Vegetables (*continued*)

Vegetable	Peak Season	How to Choose	How to Store
Spinach	Available year-round.	Leaves should be crisp and free of moisture. Avoid spinach with broken or bruised leaves.	Rinse leaves in cold water and thoroughly dry. Place the leaves in a storage container with a paper towel and refrigerate for up to 3 days.
Squash, winter	Some varieties available year-round with peak season from September through March.	Avoid cracked or bruised squash.	Store whole squash in a cool, dry place for up to 2 months. Refrigerate cut squash, wrapped in plastic, for up to 4 days.
Sweet potatoes, Yams	Available year-round with peak season from October through January.	Choose small to medium smooth-skinned potatoes that are firm and free of soft spots.	Store in a cool, dry, dark place for up to 1 week.
Tomatoes	Available year-round with peak season from June through early September.	Pick well-shaped, plump, fairly firm tomatoes.	Store at room temperature for up to 3 days. Do not store tomatoes in the refrigerator because they lose their flavor.
Zucchini, Summer squash	Some varieties available year-round with peak season from June through September.	It is almost impossible for tender-skinned zucchini to be blemish-free, but look for small ones that are firm and free of cuts and soft spots.	Refrigerate squash, tightly wrapped, for up to 5 days; fresh-from-the-garden squash may be stored for up to 2 weeks.

Selecting Fresh Fruit

When picking fruit, look for plumpness, tenderness, and bright color. Fruits should be heavy for their size and free from mold, mildew, bruises, cuts, or other blemishes. Tips for selecting and storing specific types of fruits are listed below and on the following pages. Some fruits are picked and shipped while still firm, so they may need additional ripening (see tip, page, 573).

Fruit	Peak Season	How To Choose	How to Store
Apples	Available year-round with peak season September through November.	Select firm apples, free from bruises or soft spots. Fruit is sold ready for eating. Select variety according to intended use.	Refrigerate for up to 6 weeks; store bulk apples in a cool, moist place.
Apricots	Available May through July.	Look for plump, fairly firm fruit with deep yellow or yellowish orange skin.	Ripen firm fruit as directed on page 573 until it yields to gentle pressure and is golden in color. Refrigerate ripe fruit for up to 2 days.
Avocados	Available year-round.	Avoid bruised fruit with gouges or broken skin. Soft avocados can be used immediately (and are especially good for guacamole).	Ripen firm fruit as directed on page 573 until it yields to gentle pressure. Store ripened fruit in the refrigerator for up to 4 days.
Bananas	Available year-round.	Choose bananas at any stage of ripeness, from green to yellow.	Ripen at room temperature until they have a bright yellow color. Overripe bananas are brown.

Selecting Fresh Fruit (continued)

Fruit	Peak Season	How to Choose	How to Store
Berries	Blackberries: Available June through August. Blueberries: Available late May through October. Boysenberries: Available late June through early August. Raspberries: Available year-round with peak season from May through September. Strawberries: Available year-round with peak season from June through September.	If picking your own, select berries that separate easily from their stems.	Refrigerate berries in a single layer, loosely covered, for up to 2 days. Rinse just before using.
Cantaloupe	Available year-round with peak season from June through September.	Select cantaloupe that has a sweet, aromatic scent; a strong smell could indicate overripeness. It should feel heavy for its size. Avoid wet, bruised, or cracked fruit.	Ripen as directed on page 573. Refrigerate whole melon up to 4 days. Refrigerate cut fruit in a covered container or tightly wrapped for up to 2 days.
Carambolas (Star fruit)	Available late August through February.	Look for firm, shiny-skinned golden fruit. Some browning on the edge of the fins is natural and does not affect the taste.	Ripen as directed on page 573. Refrigerate ripened fruit in a covered container or tightly wrapped for up to 1 week.
Cherries	Sweet: Available May through August with peak season in June and July. Tart: Available June through August with peak season in June and July.	Select firm, brightly colored fruit.	Refrigerate in a covered container for 2 to 3 days.
Cranberries	Available October through December with peak season in November.	Fruit is ripe when sold. Avoid soft, shriveled, or bruised cranberries.	Refrigerate for up to 4 weeks or freeze for up to 1 year.
Grapefruit	Available year-round.	Choose fully colored grapefruit with a nicely rounded shape. Juicy grapefruit will be heavy for its size.	Refrigerate for up to 2 weeks.
Grapes	Available year-round.	Look for plump grapes without bruises, soft spots, or mold. Bloom (a frosty white cast) is typical and doesn't affect quality.	Refrigerate in a covered container for up to 1 week.
Honeydew melon	Available year-round with peak season from June through September.	Choose one that is smooth-skinned and heavy for its size and that has a sweet, aromatic scent. Avoid wet, dented, bruised, or cracked fruit.	Ripen as directed on page 573. Refrigerate whole melon up to 4 days. Refrigerate cut fruit in a covered container or tightly wrapped for up to 3 days.
Kiwifruits	Available year-round.	Choose fruit that is free of wrinkles, bruises, and soft spots.	Ripen firm fruit as directed on page 573 until skin yields to gentle pressure; refrigerate up to 1 week.
Lemons, Limes	Available year-round.	Look for firm, well-shaped fruit with smooth, evenly yellow skin. Avoid bruised or wrinkled lemons.	Refrigerate for up to 2 weeks.
Mangoes	Available April through September with peak season from June through July.	Look for fully colored fruit that smells fruity and feels fairly firm when pressed.	Ripen firm fruit as directed on page 573 and refrigerate for up to 5 days.

Selecting Fresh Fruit (continued)

Fruit	Peak Season	How to Choose	How to Store
Oranges	Available year-round.	Choose oranges that are firm and heavy for their size. Brown specks or a slight greenish tinge on the surface of an orange will not affect the eating quality.	Refrigerate for up to 2 weeks.
Papayas	Available year-round.	Choose fruit that is at least half yellow and feels somewhat soft when pressed. The skin should be smooth.	Ripen as directed on page 573 until yellow. Refrigerate in a covered container for 1 to 2 days.
Peaches, Nectarines	Peaches: Available May through September. Nectarines: Available May through September with peak season in July and August.	Look for fruit with a golden yellow skin and no tinges of green. Ripe fruit should yield slightly to gentle pressure.	Ripen as directed on page 573. Refrigerate for up to 5 days.
Pears	Available year-round.	Skin color is not always an indicator of ripeness because skin color of some varieties does not change much as the pears ripen. Look for pears without bruises or cuts. Choose a variety according to intended use.	Ripen as directed on page 573 until skin yields to gentle pressure at the stem end. Refrigerate ripened fruit for several days.
Pineapple	Available year-round with peak season from March through July.	Look for a plump pineapple with a sweet, aromatic smell at the stem end. It should be slightly soft to the touch, heavy for its size, and have deep green leaves.	Refrigerate for up to 2 days. Cut pineapple lasts a few more days if placed in a tightly covered container and refrigerated.
Plantains	Available year-round.	Choose undamaged plantains. Slight bruises are acceptable because the skin is tough enough to protect the fruit. Choose plantains at any stage of ripeness, from green to dark brown or black, depending on intended use.	Ripen as directed on page 573. Color will change from green to yellow-brown to black. Black plantains are fully ripe. The starchy fruit must be cooked before eating.
Plums	Available May through October with peak season in June and July.	Find firm, plump, well-shaped fresh plums. Each should give slightly when gently pressed. Bloom (light gray cast) on the skin is natural and doesn't affect quality.	Ripen as directed on page 573. Refrigerate for up to 3 days.
Rhubarb	Available February through June with peak season from April through June.	Look for crisp stalks that are firm and tender. Avoid rhubarb that looks wilted or has very thick stalks.	Wrap stalks tightly in plastic wrap and refrigerate for up to 5 days.
Watermelon	Available May through September with peak season from mid-June through late August.	Choose watermelon that has a hard, smooth rind and is heavy for its size. Avoid wet, dented, bruised, or cracked fruit.	Watermelon does not ripen after it is picked. Refrigerate whole melon up to 4 days. Refrigerate cut fruit in a covered container or tightly wrapped for up to 3 days.

Cooking Fresh Vegetables

There are a several basic ways to cook fresh vegetables—on the range top (boiling or steaming), in the oven, and in the microwave oven. Keep in mind that cooking and steaming times may vary according the particular vegetable. The amounts given in this chart yield enough cooked vegetables for 4 servings, except where noted. Wash fresh vegetables with cool, clear tap water; scrub firm vegetables with a clean produce brush.

To steam vegetables, place a steamer basket in a saucepan. Add water to just below the bottom of the basket. Bring water to boiling. Add vegetables to steamer basket. Cover and reduce heat. Steam for the time specified in the chart or until vegetables reach desired doneness.

To microwave vegetables, use a microwave-safe baking dish or casserole and follow the directions in the chart, keeping in mind that times may vary depending on the microwave oven.

Vegetable and Amount	Preparation (Yield)	Conventional Cooking Directions	Microwave Cooking Directions
Artichokes 2 (10 ounces each) (2 servings)	Wash; trim stems. Cut off 1 inch from tops; snip off sharp leaf tips. Brush cut edges with lemon juice.	Cook, covered, in a large amount of boiling salted water for 20 to 30 minutes or until a leaf pulls out easily. (Or steam for 20 to 25 minutes.) Invert artichokes to drain.	Place in a casserole with 2 tablespoons water. Microwave, covered, on 100% power (high) for 7 to 9 minutes or until a leaf pulls out easily, rearranging artichokes once. Invert artichokes to drain.
Artichokes, baby 1 pound (6 to 8 whole)	Wash; trim stems. Cut off one-fourth from tops. Remove outer leaves until pale green petals are reached. Cut into halves or quarters. Cut out fuzzy centers, if necessary.	Cook, covered, in a large amount of boiling salted water for 15 minutes or until tender. (Or steam for 15 to 20 minutes.)	Place in a casserole with 2 tablespoons water. Microwave, covered, on 100% power (high) for 6 to 9 minutes or until tender.
Asparagus 1 pound (18 to 24 spears)	Wash; break off woody bases where spears snap easily. If desired, scrape off scales. Leave spears whole or cut into 1-inch pieces (2 cups pieces).	Cook, covered, in a small amount of boiling salted water for 3 to 5 minutes or until crisp-tender. (Or steam for 3 to 5 minutes.)	Place in a baking dish or casserole with 2 tablespoons water. Microwave, covered, on 100% power (high) for 3 to 6 minutes or until crisp-tender, rearranging or stirring once.
Beans: green, Italian green, purple, or yellow wax 12 ounces	Wash; remove ends and strings. Leave whole or cut into 1-inch pieces (2½ cups pieces). For French-cut beans, slice lengthwise.	Cook, covered, in a small amount of boiling salted water for 10 to 15 minutes for whole or cut beans (5 to 10 minutes for French-cut beans) or until crisp-tender. (Or steam whole, cut, or French-cut beans for 18 to 22 minutes.)	Place in a casserole with 2 tablespoons water. Microwave, covered, on 100% power (high) for 8 to 12 minutes for whole or cut beans (7 to 10 minutes for French-cut beans) or until crisp-tender, stirring once.
Beets 4 medium (1 pound)	For whole beets, cut off all but 1 inch of stems and roots; wash. Do not peel. (For microwaving, prick the skins of whole beets.) Or peel beets; cube or slice (2¾ cups cubes).	Cook, covered, in enough boiling salted water to cover for 35 to 45 minutes for whole beets (about 20 minutes for cubed or sliced beets) or until tender. Slip skins off whole beets.	Place in a casserole with 2 tablespoons water. Microwave whole, cubed, or sliced beets, covered, on 100% power (high) for 9 to 12 minutes or until tender, rearranging or stirring once. Slip skins off whole beets.

Cooking Fresh Vegetables (continued)

Vegetable and Amount	Preparation (Yield)	Conventional Cooking Directions	Microwave Cooking Directions
Broccoli 12 ounces	Wash; remove outer leaves and tough parts of stalks. Cut lengthwise into spears or cut into 1-inch florets (3 cups florets).	Cook, covered, in a small amount of boiling salted water for 8 to 10 minutes or until crisp-tender. (Or steam for 8 to 10 minutes.)	Place in a baking dish with 2 tablespoons water. Microwave, covered, on 100% power (high) for 5 to 8 minutes or until crisp-tender, rearranging or stirring once.
Brussels sprouts 12 ounces	Trim stems and remove any wilted outer leaves; wash. Cut large sprouts in half lengthwise (3 cups).	Cook, covered, in enough boiling salted water to cover for 10 to 12 minutes or until crisp-tender. (Or steam for 10 to 15 minutes.)	Place in a casserole with ¼ cup water. Microwave, covered, on 100% power (high) for 5 to 7 minutes or until crisp-tender, stirring once.
Cabbage Half of a 1½-pound head	Remove wilted outer leaves; wash. Cut into 4 wedges or coarsely chop (3 cups coarsely chopped).	Cook, uncovered, in a small amount of boiling water for 2 minutes. Cover; cook for 6 to 8 minutes more for wedges (3 to 5 minutes for pieces) or until crisp-tender. (Or steam wedges for 10 to 12 minutes.)	Place in a baking dish or casserole with 2 tablespoons water. Microwave, covered, on 100% power (high) for 9 to 11 minutes for wedges (4 to 6 minutes for pieces) or until crisp-tender, rearranging or stirring once.
Carrots 1 pound	Wash, trim, and peel or scrub. Cut into ¼-inch slices or into strips (2½ cups slices).	Cook, covered, in a small amount of boiling salted water for 7 to 9 minutes for slices (4 to 6 minutes for strips) or until crisp-tender. (Or steam slices for 8 to 10 minutes or strips for 5 to 7 minutes.)	Place in a casserole with 2 tablespoons water. Microwave, covered, on 100% power (high) for 6 to 9 minutes for slices (5 to 7 minutes for strips) or until crisp-tender, stirring once.
Carrots (packaged peeled baby carrots or small carrots with tops) 1 pound	Wash; trim and scrub, if necessary (3½ cups).	Cook, covered, in a small amount of boiling salted water for 8 to 10 minutes for baby carrots or 6 to 8 minutes for small carrots or until crisp-tender. (Or steam for 8 to 10 minutes.)	Place in a casserole with 2 tablespoons water. Microwave, covered, on 100% power (high) for 7 to 9 minutes or until crisp-tender, stirring once.
Cauliflower 12 ounces florets or 1½- to 2-pound head	Wash; remove leaves and woody stem. Leave whole or break into florets (3 cups florets).	Cook, covered, in a small amount of boiling salted water for 10 to 15 minutes for head (8 to 10 minutes for florets) or until crisp-tender. (Or steam head or florets for 8 to 12 minutes.)	Place in a casserole with 2 tablespoons water. Microwave, covered, on 100% power (high) for 9 to 11 minutes for head (7 to 10 minutes for florets) or until crisp-tender, turning or stirring once.
Celeriac 1 pound	Wash; trim off the leaves and ends. Peel off hairy brown skin. Cut into strips (3½ cups strips).	Cook, covered, in a small amount of boiling salted water for 5 to 6 minutes or until crisp-tender. (Or steam for 5 minutes.)	Place in a casserole with 2 tablespoons water. Microwave, covered, on 100% power (high) for 4 to 5 minutes or until crisp-tender, stirring once.
Celery 5 stalks	Remove leaves; wash stalks. Cut into ½-inch slices (2½ cups slices).	Cook, covered, in a small amount of boiling salted water for 6 to 9 minutes or until crisp-tender. (Or steam for 7 to 10 minutes.)	Place in a casserole with 2 tablespoons water. Microwave, covered, on 100% power (high) for 6 to 10 minutes or until crisp-tender, stirring once.

Cooking Fresh Vegetables (continued)

Vegetable and Amount	Preparation (Yield)	Conventional Cooking Directions	Microwave Cooking Directions
Chayote 1 pound	Wash, peel, halve lengthwise, and remove seed; cube (2 cups cubes).	Cook, covered, in a small amount of boiling salted water about 5 minutes or until crisp-tender. (Or steam about 8 minutes.)	Place in a casserole with 2 tablespoons water. Microwave, covered, on 100% power (high) for 5 to 6 minutes or until crisp-tender, stirring once.
Corn 4 ears	Remove husks. Scrub with a stiff brush to remove silks; rinse. Cut kernels from cob (2 cups kernels).	Cook, covered, in a small amount of boiling salted water for 4 minutes. (Or steam for 4 to 5 minutes.)	Place in a casserole with 2 tablespoons water. Microwave, covered, on 100% power (high) for 5 to 6 minutes, stirring once.
Corn on the cob (1 ear equals 1 serving)	Remove husks from fresh ears of corn. Scrub with a stiff brush to remove silks; rinse.	Cook, covered, in enough boiling lightly salted water to cover for 5 to 7 minutes or until kernels are tender.	Wrap each ear in waxed paper; place on microwave-safe paper towels in the microwave. Microwave on 100% power (high) for 3 to 5 minutes for 1 ear, 5 to 7 minutes for 2 ears, or 9 to 12 minutes for 4 ears, rearranging once.
Eggplant 1 pound	Wash and, if desired, peel. Cut into ¾-inch cubes (5 cups cubes).	Cook, covered, in a small amount of boiling water for 4 to 5 minutes or until tender. (Or steam for 4 to 5 minutes.)	Place in a casserole with 2 tablespoons water. Microwave, covered, on 100% power (high) for 6 to 8 minutes or until tender, stirring once.
Fennel 2 bulbs	Cut off and discard stalks, including feathery leaves. Remove wilted outer layer; cut off a thin slice from base. Wash; cut fennel lengthwise into quarters (2½ cups quarters).	Cook, covered, in a small amount of boiling water for 6 to 10 minutes or until tender. (Or steam for 6 to 8 minutes.)	Place in a casserole with ¼ cup water. Microwave, covered, on 100% power (high) for 6 to 8 minutes or until tender, rearranging once.
Greens: beet or chard 12 ounces	Wash thoroughly in cold water; drain well. Remove stems; trim bruised leaves. Tear into pieces (12 cups torn).	Cook, covered, in a small amount of boiling salted water for 8 to 10 minutes or until tender.	Not recommended.
Greens: kale, mustard, or turnip 12 ounces	Wash thoroughly in cold water; drain well. Remove stems; trim bruised leaves. Tear into pieces (12 cups torn).	Cook, covered, in a small amount of boiling salted water for 20 to 25 minutes or until tender.	Not recommended.
Jerusalem artichokes (Sunchokes) 1 pound	Wash, trim, and peel or scrub. Cut into ¼-inch slices (2 cups slices).	Cook, covered, in a small amount of boiling salted water for 7 to 9 minutes or until tender. (Or steam for 10 to 12 minutes.)	Place in a casserole with 2 tablespoons water. Microwave, covered, on 100% power (high) for 5 to 7 minutes or until tender, stirring once.
Jicama 10 ounces	Wash, trim, and peel. Cut into ½-inch cubes (2 cups cubes).	Cook, covered, in a small amount of boiling salted water about 5 minutes or until crisp-tender. (Or steam about 5 minutes.)	Place in a casserole with 2 tablespoons water. Microwave, covered, on 100% power (high) for 5 minutes or until crisp-tender, stirring once.

Cooking Fresh Vegetables (continued)

Vegetable and Amount	Preparation (Yield)	Conventional Cooking Directions	Microwave Cooking Directions
Kohlrabi 1 pound	Cut off leaves; wash. Peel; chop or cut into strips (3 cups strips).	Cook, covered, in a small amount of boiling salted water for 4 to 6 minutes or until crisp-tender. (Or steam about 6 minutes.)	Place in a casserole with 2 tablespoons water. Microwave, covered, on 100% power (high) for 5 to 7 minutes or until crisp-tender, stirring once.
Leeks 1½ pounds	Wash well; remove any tough outer leaves. Trim roots from base. Slit lengthwise and wash well. Cut into ½-inch slices (3 cups slices).	Cook, covered, in a small amount of boiling salted water for 4 to 5 minutes or until tender. (Or steam slices for 4 to 5 minutes.)	Place in a casserole with 2 tablespoons water. Microwave, covered, on 100% power (high) for 4 to 6 minutes or until tender, stirring once.
Mushrooms 1 pound	Wipe mushrooms with a damp towel or paper towel. Leave whole or slice (6 cups slices).	Cook sliced mushrooms in 2 tablespoons butter or margarine about 5 minutes. (Or steam whole mushrooms for 10 to 12 minutes.)	Place in a casserole with 2 tablespoons butter or margarine. Microwave, covered, on 100% power (high) for 4 to 6 minutes, stirring twice.
Okra 8 ounces	Wash; cut off stems. Cut into ½-inch slices (2 cups slices).	Cook, covered, in a small amount of boiling salted water for 8 to 10 minutes or until tender.	Place in a casserole with 2 tablespoons water. Microwave, covered, on 100% power (high) for 4 to 6 minutes or until tender, stirring once.
Onions: boiling or pearl 8 ounces boiling onions (10 to 12) 8 ounces pearl onions (24 to 30)	Peel boiling onions before cooking; peel pearl onions after cooking (2 cups).	Cook, covered, in a small amount of boiling salted water for 10 to 12 minutes (boiling onions) or 8 to 10 minutes (pearl onions). (Or steam boiling onions 12 to 15 minutes or pearl onions 10 to 12 minutes.)	Place in a casserole with 2 tablespoons water. Microwave, covered, on 100% power (high) for 3 to 5 minutes.
Parsnips 12 ounces	Wash, trim, and peel or scrub. Cut into ¼-inch slices (2 cups slices).	Cook, covered, in a small amount of boiling salted water for 7 to 9 minutes or until tender. (Or steam for 8 to 10 minutes.)	Place in a casserole with 2 tablespoons water. Microwave, covered, on 100% power (high) for 4 to 6 minutes or until tender, stirring once.
Peas, edible pod: snow peas or sugar snap peas 8 ounces	Remove strings and tips; wash (2 cups).	Cook, covered, in a small amount of boiling salted water for 2 to 4 minutes or until crisp-tender. (Or steam for 2 to 4 minutes.)	Place in a casserole with 2 tablespoons water. Microwave, covered, on 100% power (high) for 3 to 5 minutes or until crisp-tender, stirring once.
Peas, green 2 pounds	Shell and wash (3 cups shelled).	Cook, covered, in a small amount of boiling salted water for 10 to 12 minutes or until crisp-tender. (Or steam for 12 to 15 minutes.)	Place in a casserole with 2 tablespoons water. Microwave, covered, on 100% power (high) for 6 to 8 minutes or until crisp-tender, stirring once.
Peppers, sweet 2 large	Wash; remove stems, seeds, and membranes. Cut into rings or strips (2½ cups rings or strips).	Cook, covered, in a small amount of boiling salted water for 6 to 7 minutes or until crisp-tender. (Or steam for 6 to 7 minutes.)	Place in a casserole with 2 tablespoons water. Microwave, covered, on 100% power (high) for 4 to 6 minutes or until crisp-tender, stirring once.

Cooking Fresh Vegetables *(continued)*

Vegetable and Amount	Preparation (Yield)	Conventional Cooking Directions	Microwave Cooking Directions
Potatoes 1 pound	Wash, peel, and remove eyes, sprouts, or green areas. Cut into quarters or cubes (2¾ cups cubes).	Cook, covered, in enough boiling salted water to cover for 20 to 25 minutes for quarters (15 minutes for cubes) or until tender. (Or steam about 20 minutes.)	Place in a casserole with 2 tablespoons water. Microwave, covered, on 100% power (high) for 8 to 10 minutes or until tender, stirring once.
Rutabagas 1 pound	Wash and peel. Cut into ½-inch cubes (3 cups cubes).	Cook, covered, in a small amount of boiling salted water for 18 to 20 minutes or until tender. (Or steam for 18 to 20 minutes.)	Place in a casserole with 2 tablespoons water. Microwave, covered, on 100% power (high) for 11 to 13 minutes or until tender, stirring 3 times.
Spinach 1 pound	Wash and drain; remove stems and tear into pieces (12 cups torn).	Cook, covered, in a small amount of boiling salted water for 3 to 5 minutes or until tender; begin timing when steam forms. (Or steam for 3 to 5 minutes.)	Not recommended.
Squash: acorn, delicata, golden nugget, or sweet dumpling One 1¼-pound (2 servings)	Wash, halve, and remove seeds.	Place squash halves, cut sides down, in a baking dish. Bake in a 350°F oven for 45 to 55 minutes or until tender.	Place, cut sides down, in a baking dish with 2 tablespoons water. Microwave, covered, on 100% power (high) 7 to 10 minutes, rearranging once. Let stand, covered, 5 minutes.
Squash: banana, buttercup, butternut, hubbard, or turban One 1½-pound or a 1½-pound piece	Wash, halve lengthwise, and remove seeds.	Place squash halves, cut sides down, in a baking dish. Bake in a 350°F oven for 50 to 55 minutes or until tender.	Place, cut sides down, in a baking dish with 2 tablespoons water. Microwave, covered, on 100% power (high) for 9 to 12 minutes or until tender, rearranging once.
Squash: pattypan, sunburst, yellow, or zucchini 12 ounces	Wash; do not peel. Cut off ends. Cut into ¼-inch slices (3 cups slices).	Cook, covered, in a small amount of boiling salted water for 3 to 5 minutes or until crisp-tender. (Or steam for 4 to 6 minutes.)	Place in a casserole with 2 tablespoons water. Microwave, covered, on 100% power (high) for 4 to 5 minutes or until crisp-tender, stirring twice.
Squash, spaghetti One 2½- to 3-pound	Wash, halve lengthwise, and remove seeds.	Place squash halves, cut sides down, in a baking dish. Bake in a 350°F oven for 30 to 40 minutes or until tender.	Place, cut sides down, in a baking dish with ¼ cup water. Microwave, covered, on 100% power (high) for 17 to 20 minutes or until tender, rearranging once.
Sweet potatoes 1 pound	Wash, peel, and cut off woody portions and ends. Cut into quarters (for microwave) or cubes (2¾ cups cubes).	Cook, covered, in enough boiling salted water to cover for 25 to 30 minutes or until tender. (Or steam for 20 to 25 minutes.)	Place in a casserole with ½ cup water. Microwave, covered, on 100% power (high) for 10 to 13 minutes or until tender, stirring once.
Turnips 1 pound	Wash and peel. Cut into ½-inch cubes or strips (2¾ cups cubes).	Cook, covered, in a small amount of boiling salted water for 10 to 12 minutes or until tender. (Or steam for 10 to 15 minutes.)	Place in a casserole with 2 tablespoons water. Microwave, covered, on 100% power (high) for 10 to 12 minutes or until tender, stirring once.

20-Minute Meals

Hurry-Up Beef and Vegetable Stew, 614

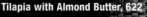

Tilapia with Almond Butter, 622

Ravioli Skillet, 624

20-Minute Meals Essentials

There's no need to spend hours in the kitchen to make mealtimes nourishing and pleasant for your family. The timesaving tips below and the recipes that follow prove it.

Make Extras

Get the most out of every minute you spend in the kitchen by following these tips.

● Cook extra batches of the foods you serve on the weekends and store them to serve during the week.

● Freeze homemade spaghetti sauces in meal-size portions. Reheat the frozen block of sauce in a saucepan on the range top.

● Whenever you grill out, cook up a bonus batch of meat—such as extra steaks, pork chops, or chicken breasts—that can be tossed into a satisfying main-dish salad the next day. Or transform them into quesadillas: Pile tortillas with shredded leftover meat, cheese, chopped tomato, and chopped onion. Cook them on a hot grill or in a skillet and serve with sour cream and salsa.

● If you have some extra chicken, place it in a freezer container and freeze for up to 3 months. A little bit of chicken left over from here and there can add up to the right amount for stirring into a salad, casserole, or omelet.

Swift Sides

It's easy to put a meal on the table fast if you start with ready-made entrées from the deli and heat-and-serve dishes from the meat department. Call on these strategies, and you're ready to round out the meal.

● Cook more rice than needed for one meal and divide it into meal-size portions. Store cooked rice in an airtight container in the refrigerator up to 1 week or in the freezer up to 6 months. To serve, place chilled or frozen rice in a saucepan, adding 2 tablespoons water or broth for each cup of rice. Cover and cook over low heat about 5 minutes or until heated through.

● Remember that couscous and orzo are two of the quickest-cooking sides. Look for preseasoned mixes for extra flavor fast.

● Stock up on frozen vegetables. They cook up bright and quickly at mealtimes.

● Stock up on heat-and-serve meats, such as kielbasa and other smoked sausages, that have a long shelf life when refrigerated. Keep these on hand and serve with refrigerated mashed potatoes and a frozen vegetable.

Depend on the Deli

Deli foods can be the starting point for terrific dinners, especially if you add a few fresh embellishments.

Satisfying Sandwiches: Stock high-quality breads (ciabatta, French loaves, country loaves) in the freezer and have an interesting assortment of deli meats and cheeses on hand to make grilled panini, Italian-sauced sandwiches, or subs.

Italian-Style Three-Bean Salad: Add ½ cup sliced hearts of palm; 1 medium tomato, chopped; and ½ teaspoon dried Italian seasoning, crushed, to 1 pint three-bean salad.

Main-Dish Three-Bean Salad: Add 1 cup cooked and drained shell macaroni, ½ cup cubed cheddar cheese, and 6 ounces cooked ham strips to 1 pint three-bean salad.

Veggie Macaroni Salad: Add ½ cup thawed frozen peas and 2 tablespoons sliced radishes to 1 pint macaroni salad.

Quick Onion-and-Herb Pot Roast LOW FAT

Sauteed onion and garlic lend their home-cooked flavor to a premade, store-bought pot roast.

Start to Finish: 20 minutes **Makes:** 4 servings

- 1 **large onion, thinly sliced**
- 1 **clove garlic, minced**
- 1 **tablespoon butter**
- 1 **16- or 17-ounce package refrigerated cooked beef pot roast with juices**
- 2 **teaspoons snipped fresh basil, oregano, and/or thyme**
  Salt and black pepper

1. In a large skillet cook onion and garlic in hot butter over medium heat about 5 minutes until nearly tender. Add pot roast with juices. Bring to boiling; reduce heat. Simmer, covered, about 10 minutes or until pot roast is heated through.

2. Transfer pot roast to a serving platter, reserving juices in skillet. Stir basil into skillet; season to taste with salt and pepper. To serve, pour juices over pot roast.

Per 3 ounces meat + ¼ cup onion mixture: 213 cal., 11 g total fat (5 g sat. fat), 72 mg chol., 488 mg sodium, 6 g carbo., 1 g fiber, 24 g pro.
Daily Values: 3% vit. A, 5% vit. C, 1% calcium, 9% iron
Exchanges: 1 Medium-Fat Meat, 1 Fat

Picante Pot Roast LOW FAT

Start to Finish: 20 minutes **Makes:** 4 servings

- 1 **16- or 17-ounce package refrigerated cooked beef pot roast with juices**
- 1½ **cups sliced fresh mushrooms**
- 1 **cup bottled picante sauce**
- 1 **14-ounce can chicken broth**
- 1 **cup quick-cooking couscous**
- 2 **tablespoons snipped fresh cilantro**
  Dairy sour cream (optional)
  Chopped fresh tomato (optional)
  Sliced avocado (optional)

1. Transfer liquid from pot roast package to a large skillet; add mushrooms and picante sauce. Cut pot roast into 1- to 1½-inch pieces; add to skillet. Bring to boiling; reduce heat. Simmer, covered, for 10 minutes.

2. Meanwhile, in a medium saucepan bring broth to boiling. Stir in couscous; cover and remove from heat. Let stand about 5 minutes or until liquid is absorbed. Fluff couscous with a fork. Stir in cilantro.

3. Spoon pot roast mixture over couscous. If desired, serve with sour cream, chopped tomato, and/or sliced avocado.

Per ¾ cup pot roast mixture + ¾ cup couscous: 370 cal., 9 g total fat (3 g sat. fat), 61 mg chol., 1,268 mg sodium, 44 g carbo., 3 g fiber, 31 g pro.
Daily Values: 6% vit. A, 3% vit. C, 4% calcium, 14% iron
Exchanges: 3 Starch, 3 Lean Meat

Hurry-Up Beef and Vegetable Stew LOW FAT

Forget hash and sandwiches—here's a tasty way to use leftover roast beef. See photo, page 611.

Start to Finish: 20 minutes **Makes:** 5 servings

- 2 **cups water**
- 1 **10.75-ounce can condensed golden mushroom soup**
- 1 **10.75-ounce can condensed tomato soup**
- ½ **cup dry red wine or beef broth**
- 2 **cups chopped cooked roast beef**
- 1 **16-ounce package frozen sugar snap pea stir-fry vegetables or one 16-ounce package frozen cut broccoli**
- ½ **teaspoon dried thyme, crushed**

1. In a 4-quart Dutch oven combine water, mushroom soup, tomato soup, and wine. Stir in beef, frozen vegetables, and thyme.

2. Cook over medium heat until bubbly, stirring frequently. Continue cooking, uncovered, for 4 to 5 minutes or until vegetables are crisp-tender, stirring occasionally.

Per 1½ cups: 304 cal., 10 g total fat (4 g sat. fat), 56 mg chol., 852 mg sodium, 24 g carbo., 4 g fiber, 23 g pro.
Daily Values: 13% vit. A, 36% vit. C, 5% calcium, 21% iron
Exchanges: 1 Vegetable, 2 Other Carbo., 3 Lean Meat

Picante Pot Roast

Steak and Mushrooms

Start to Finish: 20 minutes **Makes:** 4 servings

- **4 beef tenderloin steaks, cut ¾ inch thick (about 1 pound total)**
- **1 tablespoon olive oil**
- **3 cups sliced fresh mushrooms**
- **¼ cup seasoned beef broth**
- **¼ cup whipping cream**

1. Sprinkle steaks lightly with *salt* and *black pepper.* In a large skillet cook steaks in hot oil over medium-high heat for 7 to 9 minutes or to desired doneness (145°F for medium rare or 160°F for medium), turning once. Transfer steaks to a platter; keep warm.

2. In the same skillet cook and stir mushrooms over medium-high heat for 4 to 5 minutes or until tender. Stir in broth and cream. Cook and stir over medium-high heat for 2 minutes. Season sauce to taste with additional *salt* and *pepper.* Spoon mushroom mixture over steaks to serve.

Per steak + about ¼ cup mushroom mixture: 279 cal., 19 g total fat (7 g sat. fat), 90 mg chol., 189 mg sodium, 3 g carbo., 1 g fiber, 26 g pro.
Daily Values: 5% vit. A, 2% calcium, 19% iron
Exchanges: 1 Vegetable, 3 Lean Meat, 2 Fat

Fast Fajita Roll-Ups

Start to Finish: 20 minutes **Oven:** 350°F
Makes: 4 servings

- **12 ounces beef flank steak or sirloin steak or skinless, boneless chicken breast halves**
- **4 8-inch flour tortillas**
- **1 tablespoon cooking oil**
- **⅓ cup finely chopped onion (1 small)**
- **⅓ cup finely chopped green sweet pepper**
- **½ cup chopped tomato (1 medium)**
- **2 tablespoons bottled Italian salad dressing**
- **½ cup shredded cheddar cheese (2 ounces)**
- **¼ cup bottled salsa or taco sauce**
- **½ cup dairy sour cream (optional)**

1. If desired, partially freeze beef for easier slicing. If using beef, trim fat. Thinly slice meat into bite-size strips (see photo, page 371). Wrap tortillas in foil. Heat in a 350°F oven for 10 minutes. Meanwhile, heat oil in a 12-inch skillet over medium-high heat. Add meat, onion, and sweet pepper; cook and stir for 2 to 3 minutes or until beef reaches desired doneness or until chicken is no longer pink. Remove from heat. Drain well. Stir in tomato and salad dressing.

2. To serve, fill warm tortillas with meat mixture. Roll up tortillas. Serve with cheese, salsa, and, if desired, sour cream.

Per filled tortilla + 2 tablespoons cheese + 1 tablespoon salsa: 344 cal., 18 g total fat (7 g sat. fat), 49 mg chol., 424 mg sodium, 19 g carbo., 1 g fiber, 25 g pro.
Daily Values: 8% vit. A, 20% vit. C, 15% calcium, 15% iron
Exchanges: 1 Starch, ½ Other Carbo., 2½ Lean Meat, 2 Fat

Thai Beef Stir-Fry EASY

Start to Finish: 15 minutes **Makes:** 4 servings

- **4 ounces rice noodles**
- **1 16-ounce package frozen sweet pepper and onion stir-fry vegetables**
- **2 tablespoons cooking oil**
- **12 ounces beef stir-fry strips**
- **½ cup bottled Thai peanut stir-fry sauce**

1. Cook noodles according to package directions. Drain and set aside.

2. In a large skillet cook the vegetables in 1 tablespoon of the hot oil over medium-high heat for 2 to 3 minutes or just until tender. Drain; transfer vegetables to a bowl. In the skillet cook and stir beef strips in remaining 1 tablespoon hot oil for 2 to 3 minutes or until desired doneness. Return vegetables to skillet; add sauce. Stir to combine; heat through. Serve over noodles.

Per about ¾ cup stir-fry + ½ cup noodles: 404 cal., 16 g total fat (4 g sat. fat), 50 mg chol., 597 mg sodium, 39 g carbo., 3 g fiber, 23 g pro.
Daily Values: 42% vit. A, 28% vit. C, 3% calcium, 15% iron
Exchanges: 2 Vegetable, 2 Starch, 2 Lean Meat, 1½ Fat

Wrap It Up

Wrap a selection of ready-made ingredients in a flour tortilla or other wrap for a meal in minutes. Here are a few ideas.

- Horseradish sauce, thinly sliced roast beef, fresh arugula, thinly sliced red onion.
- Honey mustard, thinly sliced smoked turkey, fresh spinach, sweet pepper strips, thinly sliced onion.
- Chipotle chile-flavored light mayonnaise, deli-roasted chicken, baby lettuce, sliced avocado, crisp-cooked bacon.
- Sliced ham, fresh spinach, artichoke hearts, sliced cucumber, sliced tomato, feta cheese.

Beef and Cabbage Wraps

Start to Finish: 20 minutes **Oven:** 350°F
Makes: 4 servings

- 8 8-inch flour tortillas
- 12 ounces lean ground beef
- ½ cup chopped onion (1 medium)
- 2 cups packaged shredded cabbage with carrot (coleslaw mix)
- 1 cup frozen whole kernel corn
- ¼ cup bottled barbecue sauce
  Bottled barbecue sauce (optional)

1. Wrap tortillas tightly in foil. Heat in a 350°F oven about 10 minutes or until heated through.

2. Meanwhile, for filling, in a large skillet cook meat and onion until meat is brown and onion is tender. Drain off fat. Stir cabbage mix and corn into meat mixture in skillet. Cover and cook about 4 minutes or until vegetables are tender, stirring once. Stir in the barbecue sauce. Cook and stir until heated through.

3. To serve, spoon about ⅓ cup of the filling below center of each tortilla. Roll up from bottom. If desired, serve with additional barbecue sauce.

Per 2 wraps: 380 cal., 13 g total fat (4 g sat. fat), 54 mg chol., 408 mg sodium, 44 g carbo., 3 g fiber, 21 g pro.
Daily Values: 12% vit. A, 28% vit. C, 9% calcium, 21% iron
Exchanges: 1 Vegetable, 2 Starch, ½ Other Carbo., 3 Lean Meat

Skillet Tostadas

Nacho cheese soup and salsa add zesty flavor.

Start to Finish: 20 minutes **Makes:** 4 servings

- 8 ounces lean ground beef
- ½ cup chopped onion (1 medium)
- 1 15-ounce can light red kidney beans, rinsed and drained
- 1 11-ounce can condensed nacho cheese soup
- ⅓ cup bottled salsa
- 8 tostada shells
- 1 cup shredded taco cheese (4 ounces)
- 1⅓ cups shredded lettuce
- 1 cup chopped tomato
  Dairy sour cream or guacamole (optional)

1. In a large skillet cook meat and onion until meat is brown and onion is tender. Drain off fat. Stir kidney beans, soup, and salsa into meat mixture in skillet. Heat through.

2. Divide mixture among tostada shells. Top with cheese, lettuce, and tomato. If desired, serve with sour cream.

Per 2 tostadas: 482 cal., 15 g total fat (12 g sat. fat), 69 mg chol., 1,075 mg sodium, 42 g carbo., 8 g fiber, 22 g pro.
Daily Values: 43% vit. A, 19% vit. C, 29% calcium, 15% iron
Exchanges: ½ Vegetable, 2½ Starch, 3 Lean Meat, 1 Fat

Easy Meatball Panini

Start to Finish: 20 minutes **Makes:** 4 sandwiches

- 1 1-pound package frozen Italian-style cooked meatballs (16 to 32 meatballs)
- 1 8-ounce can pizza sauce or 1 cup bottled pasta sauce
- ½ cup water
- 4 ciabatta rolls or hoagie buns
- 4 slices provolone cheese or mozzarella cheese (4 ounces)
- 8 large fresh basil or spinach leaves (optional)

1. Preheat the broiler. In a large saucepan combine meatballs, pizza sauce, and water. Heat until sauce bubbles. Cook, covered, over medium-low heat for 10 minutes or until heated through, stirring occasionally.

2. Meanwhile, cut a thin slice from the tops of rolls; hollow out rolls, leaving ¼- to ½-inch-thick shells. (Discard or save bread from rolls for another use.) Place hollowed-out rolls and roll tops, cut sides up, on a baking sheet. Broil 3 to 4 inches from the heat for 1 to 2 minutes or until lightly toasted. Remove roll tops from baking sheet.

3. Spoon meatballs and sauce into toasted rolls. Top with cheese. Broil about 1 minute more or until cheese melts. To serve, top with basil leaves and replace roll tops.

Per sandwich: 864 cal., 42 g total fat (19 g sat. fat), 93 mg chol., 1,997 mg sodium, 83 g carbo., 8 g fiber, 38 g pro.
Daily Values: 5% vit. A, 5% vit. C, 37% calcium, 37% iron
Exchanges: 4 Starch, 1½ Other Carbo., 3½ High-Fat Meat, 2½ Fat

Greek-Style Sloppy Joes

Start to Finish: 20 minutes **Makes:** 6 sandwiches

- 1 pound lean ground lamb or ground beef
- ½ cup chopped onion (1 medium)
- 1 15-ounce can tomato sauce
- ⅓ cup bulgur
- 1 teaspoon dried oregano, crushed
- ½ teaspoon salt
- ¼ teaspoon black pepper

2 **cups shredded romaine lettuce**

6 **kaiser rolls, split and toasted**

4 **ounces crumbled feta cheese with tomato and basil or plain feta cheese**

1. In a large skillet cook ground meat and onion until meat is brown and onion is tender. Drain off fat. Stir tomato sauce, bulgur, oregano, salt, and pepper into meat mixture in skillet. Bring to boiling; reduce heat. Simmer, uncovered, about 5 minutes or until desired consistency is reached, stirring occasionally.

2. To assemble sandwiches, arrange romaine on bottom halves of toasted rolls. Spoon meat mixture onto romaine. Sprinkle with cheese; replace top halves of rolls.

Per sandwich: 418 cal., 17 g total fat (7 g sat. fat), 67 mg chol., 1,086 mg sodium, 42 g carbo., 4 g fiber, 23 g pro.
Daily Values: 24% vit. A, 9% vit. C, 18% calcium, 24% iron
Exchanges: 2½ Starch, ½ Other Carbo., 3 Medium-Fat Meat

Honey-Mustard Lamb Chops LOW FAT

Broil meat and vegetable at the same time.

Start to Finish: 20 minutes **Makes:** 4 servings

8 **small lamb loin chops, cut 1 inch thick (about 1½ pounds total)**

2 **medium zucchini and/or yellow summer squash, quartered lengthwise (2½ cups)**

Salt

Black pepper

2 **tablespoons Dijon-style mustard**

2 **tablespoons honey**

1 **tablespoon snipped fresh rosemary or 1 teaspoon dried rosemary, crushed**

1. Preheat broiler. Trim fat from chops. Season chops and zucchini with salt and pepper. Arrange chops and zucchini, cut sides down, on the unheated rack of a broiler pan. In a small bowl stir together mustard, honey, and rosemary. Brush some of the mustard mixture on the chops.

2. Broil chops and zucchini 3 to 4 inches from the heat for 5 minutes. Turn chops and zucchini; brush remaining mustard mixture on the chops and zucchini. Broil for 5 to 10 minutes more or until lamb reaches medium doneness (160°F) and zucchini is tender.

Per 2 chops + ½ cup zucchini: 183 cal., 5 g total fat (2 g sat. fat), 60 mg chol., 326 mg sodium, 14 g carbo., 1 g fiber, 22 g pro.
Daily Values: 4% vit. A, 28% vit. C, 4% calcium, 13% iron
Exchanges: 1 Vegetable, ½ Other Carbo., 3 Lean Meat

Medallions of Pork with Apples LOW FAT EASY

Start to Finish: 15 minutes **Makes:** 4 servings

1 **1-pound pork tenderloin**

2 **cloves garlic, minced**

2 **tablespoons olive oil or butter**

1 **20-ounce can sliced apples, drained**

2 **teaspoons snipped fresh thyme or ½ teaspoon dried thyme, crushed**

1. Cut pork crosswise into ½-inch slices. In a 12-inch skillet cook garlic in hot oil over medium-high heat for 15 seconds. Carefully place pork in the hot oil. Cook for 2 minutes on each side or until browned and no longer pink in center. Add apples and thyme to skillet. Cook, covered, for 1 minute or until apples are heated through.

Per 3 ounces pork + about ¾ cup apple mixture: 292 cal., 11 g total fat (2 g sat. fat), 73 mg chol., 61 mg sodium, 24 g carbo., 2 g fiber, 24 g pro.
Daily Values: 2% vit. A, 4% vit. C, 2% calcium, 10% iron
Exchanges: 1 Fruit, ½ Other Carbo., 3 Lean Meat, 1½ Fat

Easy Homemade Pizza

Fresh, home-baked pizza can be ready in minutes if Italian bread shells (Boboli) and a few other ingredients are on hand.

Place a bread shell on an ungreased baking sheet. If desired, top it with sauce; add your favorite toppings. Bake in a preheated 425°F oven about 10 minutes or until toppings are hot and cheese melts and is bubbly.

For sauce, try pizza, barbecue, or prepared Alfredo sauce—or use no sauce. Traditional melting cheeses for pizza include mozzarella, fontina, provolone, and Scamorza. Or experiment with cheddar, Gruyère, Gouda, Emmentaler, Jarlsberg, or kasseri. Even though feta and chèvre don't melt as smoothly as others, they add lots of flavor.

Here are a few tasty topping ideas:

● Barbecue sauce, shredded cooked chicken, sliced apples, smoked cheddar cheese.

● Cooked steak strips, roasted sweet pepper strips, sliced banana peppers, provolone cheese.

● Sliced pepperoni, sliced fresh mushrooms, sliced ripe olives, fontina cheese.

● Sliced prosciutto, fresh basil strips, mozzarella and Asiago cheeses.

Jamaican Pork Stir-Fry

Jamaican Pork Stir-Fry

Use instant rice to keep the prep time in check.

Start to Finish: 20 minutes **Makes:** 4 servings

- 1 16-ounce package frozen stir-fry vegetables (carrots, snap peas, mushrooms, and onions)
- 2 tablespoons cooking oil
- 12 ounces pork stir-fry strips
- 2 to 3 teaspoons Jamaican jerk seasoning
- ¾ cup bottled plum sauce
- 2 cups hot cooked rice or pasta
  Chopped peanuts

1. In a wok or large skillet cook and stir vegetables in hot oil over medium-high heat for 5 to 7 minutes or until vegetables are crisp-tender. Remove vegetables from wok.

2. Toss pork strips with Jamaican jerk seasoning until coated; add pork strips to the wok. (Add more oil, if necessary.) Cook and stir for 2 to 5 minutes or until no pink remains.

3. Add plum sauce to wok. Return vegetables to the wok. Gently toss all ingredients together to coat. Heat through. Serve over rice. Sprinkle with peanuts.

Per 1¼ cups stir-fry + ½ cup rice: 445 cal., 14 g total fat (3 g sat. fat), 46 mg chol., 804 mg sodium, 54 g carbo., 3 g fiber, 24 g pro.
Daily Values: 39% vit. A, 12% vit. C, 6% calcium, 11% iron
Exchanges: 1½ Vegetable, 1½ Starch, 1½ Other Carbo., 2½ Lean Meat, 1½ Fat

Tex-Mex Skillet

Start to Finish: 20 minutes **Makes:** 4 servings

- 8 ounces ground pork
- 4 ounces bulk chorizo sausage
- 1 10-ounce can diced tomatoes and green chiles, undrained
- 1 cup frozen whole kernel corn
- ¾ cup water
- ½ cup chopped red sweet pepper
- 1 cup uncooked instant rice
- ½ cup shredded cheddar cheese or Monterey Jack cheese (2 ounces)
  Flour tortillas, warmed (optional)
  Dairy sour cream (optional)

1. In a large skillet cook pork and sausage until meat is brown. Drain off fat. Stir in undrained tomatoes and green chiles, corn, water, and sweet pepper. Bring to boiling.

2. Stir uncooked rice into mixture in skillet. Remove skillet from heat. Top with cheese. Cover and let stand about 5 minutes or until rice is tender. If desired, serve in flour tortillas and top with sour cream.

Per cup: 401 cal., 20 g total fat (9 g sat. fat), 66 mg chol., 671 mg sodium, 34 g carbo., 3 g fiber, 22 g pro.
Daily Values: 21% vit. A, 72% vit. C, 14% calcium, 13% iron
Exchanges: 1 Vegetable, 2 Starch, 3 Medium-Fat Meat

Corn and Sausage Chowder

Start to Finish: 20 minutes **Makes:** 5 servings

- 1 20-ounce package refrigerated shredded hash brown potatoes
- 1 14-ounce can reduced-sodium chicken broth
- 1 10-ounce package frozen whole kernel corn
- 2 cups milk
- 12 ounces cooked link sausage, halved lengthwise and sliced
- ⅓ cup sliced green onion
- ¼ teaspoon black pepper
  Salt
  Bottled green or red hot pepper sauce (optional)
- 2 tablespoons snipped fresh cilantro

1. In a 4-quart Dutch oven combine potatoes, broth, and corn. Bring just to boiling; reduce heat. Simmer, covered, about 10 minutes or just until potatoes are tender, stirring occasionally.

2. Using a potato masher, slightly mash potatoes. Stir in milk, sausage, green onion, and pepper. Heat through. Season to taste with salt and, if desired, hot pepper sauce. Sprinkle with cilantro.

Per 1⅔ cups: 439 cal., 22 g total fat (8 g sat. fat), 65 mg chol., 873 mg sodium, 41 g carbo., 3 g fiber, 22 g pro.
Daily Values: 11% vit. A, 22% vit. C, 13% calcium, 8% iron
Exchanges: 1 Vegetable, ½ Milk, 2 Starch, 2 Medium-Fat Meat, 1 Fat

Crunchy Chicken Strips

Start to Finish: 20 minutes **Oven:** 425°F
Makes: 4 servings

    Nonstick cooking spray
2½ **cups crushed bite-size cheddar fish-shape crackers or pretzels**
⅔ **cup bottled buttermilk ranch salad dressing**
1 **pound chicken breast tenderloins**
    Bottled buttermilk ranch salad dressing (optional)

1. Preheat oven to 425°F. Line a 15×10×1-inch baking pan with foil; lightly coat foil with cooking spray. Set aside.

2. Place the crushed crackers in a shallow dish. Place the ranch dressing in a second dish. Dip chicken tenderloins into the dressing, allowing excess to drip off; dip into the crushed crackers to coat. Arrange chicken in prepared pan.

3. Bake for 10 to 15 minutes or until chicken is no longer pink (170°F). If desired, serve with additional ranch dressing.

Quicker Crunchy Chicken Strips: Prepare as above, except use one 10-ounce package of cooked refrigerated chicken breast strips instead of the chicken breast tenderloins and bake only 5 to 8 minutes or until heated through.

Per 3 ounces: 517 cal., 21 g total fat (2 g sat. fat), 66 mg chol., 1,060 mg sodium, 51 g carbo., 2 g fiber, 33 g pro.
Daily Values: 3% calcium, 10% iron
Exchanges: 3 Starch, 3 Very Lean Meat, 3 Fat

Chicken and Cheese Panini

Start to Finish: 20 minutes **Makes:** 4 sandwiches

4 **soft French or sourdough rolls (about 7×3 inches)**
¼ **cup mayonnaise or salad dressing**
8 **ounces sliced cooked chicken or smoked cooked chicken**
2 **ounces thinly sliced Canadian-style bacon or cooked ham**
8 **ounces sliced smoked cheddar cheese or provolone cheese**
    Fresh spinach leaves, mesclun, or baby lettuce
¼ **to ½ cup bottled fruit chutney**

1. Preheat a covered indoor grill. Meanwhile, split each roll in half horizontally. To assemble sandwiches, spread cut sides of roll halves with mayonnaise. Layer chicken, Canadian-style bacon, cheese, and spinach on bottom halves of rolls. Spread 1 to 2 tablespoons chutney on cut side of each roll top. Replace top halves of rolls.

2. Place sandwiches (two at a time, if necessary) in preheated grill, cover, and cook about 6 minutes or until cheese melts and rolls are crisp.

Per sandwich: 718 cal., 38 g total fat (16 g sat. fat), 122 mg chol., 1,240 mg sodium, 52 g carbo., 3 g fiber, 41 g pro.
Daily Values: 28% vit. A, 8% vit. C, 50% calcium, 20% iron
Exchanges: 3½ Starch, 4 Lean Meat, ½ High-Fat Meat, 4 Fat

Tortellini and Cheese

Keep the ingredients for this easy main dish on hand in the refrigerator and freezer.

Start to Finish: 20 minutes **Makes:** 4 servings

1 **9-ounce package refrigerated cheese-filled tortellini**
1 **cup frozen peas, corn, or pea pods**
1 **8-ounce tub cream cheese spread with garden vegetables or chive and onion**
½ **cup milk**
1 **9-ounce package frozen chopped cooked chicken breast**

1. In a large saucepan cook tortellini according to package directions. Place frozen vegetables in colander. Drain hot pasta over vegetables to thaw; return pasta-vegetable mixture to saucepan.

2. Meanwhile, in a small saucepan combine cream cheese and milk; heat and stir the mixture until cheese melts. Heat the chicken according to package directions.

3. Stir the cheese sauce into the cooked pasta-vegetable mixture. Cook and gently stir until heated through. Spoon into serving bowls. Top with chicken.

Per about 1⅓ cups: 505 cal., 26 g total fat (15 g sat. fat), 130 mg chol., 525 mg sodium, 32 g carbo., 2 g fiber, 32 g pro.
Daily Values: 33% vit. A, 11% vit. C, 24% calcium, 12% iron
Exchanges: 2 Starch, 2 Very Lean Meat, 2 High-Fat Meat, 1 Fat

Chicken and Biscuit Kabobs

Chicken and Biscuit Kabobs

You can substitute thick slices of fully cooked smoked sausage for the chicken. Thread it onto the skewers with the biscuit dough and bake the kabobs as directed.

Start to Finish: 20 minutes **Oven:** 400°F
Makes: 4 kabobs

- ½ of a 13.5-ounce package (12) frozen cooked breaded chicken breast chunks
- 1 4.5-ounce package (6) refrigerated buttermilk or country biscuits
- 1 medium zucchini and/or yellow summer squash, cut into 3×¾-inch strips
- ⅓ cup butter, melted*
- 3 tablespoons honey*

1. Preheat oven to 400°F. Arrange chicken chunks in a single layer on a microwave-safe plate. Microwave, uncovered, on 100 percent power (high) for 1 minute; the chicken will not be heated through but will be softened enough to allow skewers to be inserted easily.

2. Cut each biscuit in half with a kitchen scissors or knife. On four skewers, alternately thread chicken pieces, biscuit halves, and zucchini, leaving about ¼ inch of space between pieces. Place skewers on an ungreased baking sheet. Bake about 10 minutes or until biscuits are golden brown and chicken is heated through.

3. Meanwhile, whisk together melted butter and honey. Drizzle some of the mixture over kabobs. Pass remainder for dipping.

*Note: If desired, substitute ½ cup honey-butter for the melted butter and honey. Place in a microwave-safe bowl and microwave, uncovered, on 100 percent power (high) for 35 to 45 seconds or until melted.

Per kabob: 376 cal., 22 g total fat (9 g sat. fat), 57 mg chol., 649 mg sodium, 37 g carbo., 1 g fiber, 10 g pro.
Daily Values: 11% vit. A, 10% vit. C, 1% calcium, 6% iron
Exchanges: ½ Vegetable, 1 Starch, 1 Other Carbo., 1 Lean Meat, 4 Fat

FAVORITE Fettuccine with Chicken

To round out this meal, add a tossed salad made with packaged greens and bottled dressing and serve fresh fruit for dessert.

Start to Finish: 20 minutes **Makes:** 4 servings

- 1 9-ounce package refrigerated red sweet pepper fettuccine
- ¼ of a 7-ounce jar oil-packed dried tomato strips or pieces (¼ cup)
- 1 large zucchini or yellow summer squash, halved lengthwise and sliced (about 2 cups)
- 8 ounces packaged skinless, boneless chicken breast strips (stir-fry strips)
- 2 tablespoons olive oil
- ½ cup finely shredded Parmesan, Romano, or Asiago cheese (2 ounces)
  Freshly ground black pepper

1. Using kitchen scissors, cut fettuccine strands in half. Cook fettuccine in lightly salted boiling water according to package directions; drain. Return fettuccine to hot pan.

2. Meanwhile, drain tomatoes, reserving 2 tablespoons of the oil from the jar. Set drained tomatoes aside. In a large skillet heat 1 tablespoon of the reserved oil over medium-high heat. Add zucchini; cook and stir for 2 to 3 minutes or until crisp-tender. Remove from skillet. Add remaining 1 tablespoon reserved oil to skillet. Add chicken; cook and stir for 2 to 3 minutes or until no longer pink.

3. Add chicken, zucchini, drained tomatoes, and olive oil to cooked fettuccine; toss gently to combine. Sprinkle servings with cheese and season to taste with pepper.

Per 1½ cups pasta mixture + 2 tablespoons cheese: 389 cal., 14 g total fat (4 g sat. fat), 43 mg chol., 431 mg sodium, 40 g carbo., 3 g fiber, 27 g pro.
Daily Values: 6% vit. A, 24% vit. C, 23% calcium, 13% iron
Exchanges: ½ Vegetable, 2½ Starch, 2 Very Lean Meat, 2 Fat

Spring Greens and Roasted Chicken

Serve this salad for a light summer supper along with some rolls from the bakery.

Start to Finish: 20 minutes **Makes:** 6 servings

- 1 2.25-pound purchased roasted chicken, chilled
- 1 5-ounce package mixed salad greens (about 8 cups)
- 2 cups sliced fresh strawberries or blueberries
- 4 ounces Gorgonzola or blue cheese, crumbled (1 cup)
- ½ cup honey-roasted cashews or peanuts
- 1 lemon, halved
- 3 tablespoons olive oil
- ¼ teaspoon salt
- ¼ teaspoon black pepper

1. Remove and discard skin from chicken. Pull meat from bones, discarding bones. Shred meat (you should have about 3½ cups).

2. Place greens on a platter. Top with chicken, berries, cheese, and nuts. Drizzle with juice from the lemon and the oil; sprinkle with the salt and pepper.

Per 1⅓ cups: 377 cal., 27 g total fat (8 g sat. fat), 81 mg chol., 454 mg sodium, 9 g carbo., 2 g fiber, 27 g pro.
Daily Values: 8% vit. A, 52% vit. C, 12% calcium, 10% iron
Exchanges: 1 Vegetable, ½ Fruit, 3½ Lean Meat, 3 Fat

Southwestern Chicken Wraps EASY

Wraps make an easy lunch. Pick up some guacamole from the grocery store's refrigerated case and some precooked chicken from the meat case. Tomatoes and lettuce add freshness.

Start to Finish: 15 minutes **Makes:** 4 wraps

- ½ cup dairy sour cream
- 2 tablespoons purchased guacamole
- 4 10-inch dried tomato, spinach, and/or plain flour tortillas
- 2 5.5-ounce packages Southwestern-flavored refrigerated cooked chicken breast strips
- 2 roma tomatoes, sliced
- 2 cups shredded lettuce

1. In a small bowl stir together the sour cream and guacamole. Divide sour cream mixture among the tortillas, spreading it over one side of each tortilla.

2. Divide cooked chicken, tomato, and lettuce among tortillas. Roll up.

Per wrap: 397 cal., 13 g total fat (4 g sat. fat), 63 mg chol., 1,352 mg sodium, 44 g carbo., 2 g fiber, 26 g pro.
Daily Values: 44% vit. A, 22% vit. C, 9% calcium, 19% iron
Exchanges: 1 Vegetable, 2½ Starch, 3 Lean Meat

Smoked Turkey and Tortellini Salad LOW FAT

Turn this into a vegetarian salad by replacing the turkey with 1 cup chopped raw broccoli.

Start to Finish: 20 minutes **Makes:** 4 servings

- 1 9-ounce package refrigerated or one 7- to 8-ounce package dried cheese-filled tortellini
- 1 cup chopped cooked smoked turkey, ham, or chicken
- 8 cherry tomatoes, quartered
- ½ cup coarsely chopped green sweet pepper
- ¼ cup sliced, pitted ripe olives (optional)
- ¼ cup bottled Italian vinaigrette or balsamic vinaigrette salad dressing
  Black pepper

1. Cook tortellini according to package directions; drain. Rinse with cold water; drain again.

2. In a large bowl combine tortellini, turkey, tomato, sweet pepper, and, if desired, olives. Drizzle salad dressing over mixture; toss to coat. Season with black pepper. Serve immediately.

Per 1¼ cups: 290 cal., 10 g total fat (3 g sat. fat), 50 mg chol., 858 mg sodium, 34 g carbo., 1 g fiber, 18 g pro.
Daily Values: 6% vit. A, 32% vit. C, 12% calcium, 10% iron
Exchanges: ½ Vegetable, ½ Other Carbo., 2 Starch, 1 Lean Meat, 1 Fat

Smoked Turkey and Tortellini Salad

Chicken and Veggie Tacos (LOW FAT) (EASY)

Here's a chance to slide in some extra veggies where your kids might not notice. If you like, heat the taco shells according to package directions.

Start to Finish: 15 minutes **Makes:** 8 tacos

- 1 18-ounce tub refrigerated taco sauce with shredded chicken
- 8 taco shells
- 1 cup shredded, peeled jicama; shredded carrot; packaged shredded broccoli (broccoli slaw mix); or canned black beans, rinsed and drained
- ⅔ cup shredded Colby and Monterey Jack cheese (about 2 ounces)
  Light dairy sour cream (optional)

1. In a medium saucepan cook taco sauce with chicken over medium heat for 6 to 8 minutes or until heated through. Spoon chicken mixture into taco shells. Top with vegetables and cheese. If desired, serve with sour cream.

Per taco: 176 cal., 8 g total fat (3 g sat. fat), 37 mg chol., 602 mg sodium, 15 g carbo., 2 g fiber, 9 g pro.
Daily Values: 7% vit. A, 7% vit. C, 11% calcium, 5% iron
Exchanges: 1 Starch, 1 Lean Meat, 1 Fat

Tilapia with Almond Butter

Perch, sole, or other white-flesh fish fillets also work well in this recipe. See photo, page 611.

Start to Finish: 20 minutes **Makes:** 4 servings

- 3 cups snow pea pods, trimmed
- 4 4- to 5-ounce fresh skinless tilapia fillets
  Sea salt
  Freshly ground black pepper
- 1 teaspoon all-purpose flour
- 1 tablespoon olive oil
- 2 tablespoons butter
- ¼ cup sliced almonds

1. In a large saucepan bring lightly salted water to boiling. Add pea pods. Cook for 2 minutes. Drain and set aside.

2. Meanwhile, season fish with salt and pepper; sprinkle with flour. In a large skillet cook fish in hot oil over medium-high heat for 4 to 5 minutes or until fish is easy to remove with a spatula. (If necessary, cook half the fish at a time.) Gently turn fish and cook for 2 to 3 minutes more or until fish flakes easily when tested with a fork.

Place peas on serving plates; arrange fish on top of peas. Keep warm.

3. Reduce heat to medium. Add butter to skillet. When butter begins to melt, stir in almonds. Cook and stir for 30 to 60 seconds or until almonds are lightly toasted (do not let butter burn). Spoon butter mixture over fish fillets.

Per fillet + ¾ cup peas: 266 cal., 15 g total fat (5 g sat. fat), 71 mg chol., 210 mg sodium, 7 g carbo., 3 g fiber, 24 g pro.
Daily Values: 9% vit. A, 8% vit. C, 5% calcium, 6% iron
Exchanges: 1 Vegetable, 3 Very Lean Meat, 2½ Fat

Simple Salsa Fish (LOW FAT) (EASY)

Start to Finish: 15 minutes **Makes:** 4 servings

- 1 pound fresh or frozen skinless orange roughy or red snapper fillets, ½ to 1 inch thick
- ⅓ cup bottled salsa
- 1 clove garlic, minced
- 1 14-ounce can vegetable broth
- 1 cup quick-cooking couscous
- ¼ cup thinly sliced green onion (2) or coarsely chopped fresh cilantro
  Salt and black pepper
  Lime or lemon wedges

1. Thaw fish, if frozen. Preheat broiler. Rinse fish; pat dry with paper towels. Set aside. In a small bowl combine salsa and garlic; set aside.

2. In a medium saucepan bring broth to boiling. Stir in couscous; cover and remove from heat. Let stand about 5 minutes or until liquid is absorbed. Fluff couscous with a fork. Stir in green onion.

3. Meanwhile, measure thickness of fish. Place fish on the greased unheated rack of a broiler pan. Sprinkle fish lightly with salt and pepper.

4. Broil about 4 inches from the heat just until fish flakes easily when tested with a fork. Allow 4 to 6 minutes per ½-inch thickness of fish. (If fillets are 1 inch thick or more, turn once halfway through broiling.) Spoon salsa mixture over fish; broil about 1 minute more or until salsa is heated through. Arrange fish on couscous. Serve with lime wedges.

Per 3 ounces fish + ¾ cup couscous: 265 cal., 1 g total fat (0 g sat. fat), 22 mg chol., 529 mg sodium, 39 g carbo., 3 g fiber, 23 g pro.
Daily Values: 8% vit. A, 7% vit. C, 5% calcium, 6% iron
Exchanges: 2 Starch, 3 Very Lean Meat

No-Bake Tuna-Noodle Casserole LOW FAT

Start to Finish: 20 minutes **Makes:** 4 servings

- **8 ounces dried wagon wheel macaroni or medium shell macaroni**
- **¼ to ½ cup milk**
- **1 6.5-ounce container light semisoft cheese with cucumber and dill or garlic and herb**
- **1 12.25-ounce can solid white tuna (water pack), drained and broken into chunks**

1. Cook pasta in lightly salted water according to package directions; drain. Return pasta to pan.

2. Add ¼ cup of the milk and the cheese to the pasta. Cook and stir over medium heat until cheese is melted and pasta is coated, adding additional milk as needed to get a creamy consistency. Gently fold in tuna; heat through.

Per about 1½ cups: 417 cal., 10 g total fat (7 g sat. fat), 66 mg chol., 552 mg sodium, 45 g carbo., 2 g fiber, 33 g pro.
Daily Values: 2% vit. A, 7% calcium, 20% iron
Exchanges: 2 Starch, 1 Other Carbo., 4 Lean Meat

Italian-Style Fish

Italian-Style Fish LOW FAT

Purchase the mushrooms already sliced and the cheese already shredded for an easy main dish.

Start to Finish: 20 minutes **Makes:** 6 servings

- **1½ pounds fresh or frozen white-flesh fish fillets, ½ to 1 inch thick**
- **¼ teaspoon salt**
- **⅛ teaspoon black pepper**
- **2 cups sliced fresh mushrooms**
- **1 tablespoon cooking oil**
- **1 14.5-ounce can Italian-style stewed tomatoes, undrained**
- **1 10.75-ounce can condensed tomato bisque soup**
- **⅛ teaspoon black pepper**
- **4½ cups hot cooked linguine or other pasta**
- **⅓ cup finely shredded Parmesan cheese**

1. Thaw fish, if frozen. Preheat broiler. Rinse fish; pat dry with paper towels. If necessary, cut fish into six serving-size pieces. Measure thickness of fish. Place fish on the greased unheated rack of a broiler pan. Turn any thin portions under to make uniform thickness. Sprinkle with salt and ⅛ teaspoon pepper.

2. Broil about 4 inches from the heat just until fish flakes easily when tested with a fork. Allow 4 to 6 minutes per ½-inch thickness of fish. (If fillets are 1 inch thick or more, turn once halfway through broiling.)

3. Meanwhile, for sauce, in a medium saucepan cook mushrooms in hot oil until tender. Stir in undrained tomatoes, tomato bisque soup, and ⅛ teaspoon pepper. Cook and stir over medium heat until mixture is heated through. Spoon pasta onto plates; top with some of the sauce, fish fillets, and remaining sauce. Sprinkle with Parmesan cheese.

Per 3 ounces fish + ¾ cup pasta + ½ cup sauce: 369 cal., 7 g total fat (2 g sat. fat), 54 mg chol., 724 mg sodium, 45 g carbo., 3 g fiber, 29 g pro.
Daily Values: 4% vit. A, 7% vit. C, 11% calcium, 14% iron
Exchanges: 1 Vegetable, 2½ Starch, 3 Very Lean Meat, ½ Fat

Thawing Frozen Fish

For quality and food safety, the best place to thaw fish is in the refrigerator.

If you didn't get the fish out of the freezer in time, you can speed the thawing process by putting the package in a watertight plastic bag and submerging it in cold water. Change the water every 30 minutes to ensure that the food is kept cold—this is important to slow bacterial growth that can occur on the outer edges of the fish while the inner areas are still thawing. Never thaw fish on the counter or in the sink without cold water because harmful bacteria can multiply rapidly at room temperature.

Spinach-Pasta Salad with Shrimp

Start to Finish: 20 minutes **Makes:** 6 servings

- 1 **pound fresh or frozen cooked shrimp**
- 1 **cup dried shell pasta or elbow macaroni**
- 1 **cup chopped red sweet pepper**
- ⅓ **cup bottled creamy onion or Caesar salad dressing**
- 2 **tablespoons snipped fresh dill (optional)**
- 1 **6-ounce package baby spinach**
- 4 **ounces goat cheese, sliced, or feta cheese, crumbled**

1. Thaw shrimp, if frozen; rinse. Cook pasta following package directions; drain. Rinse with cold water; drain. In extra-large bowl combine shrimp, pasta, and sweet pepper. Drizzle with salad dressing. If desired, sprinkle with dill. Toss to coat. Season to taste with *salt* and freshly ground *black pepper*. Divide spinach among plates. Top with shrimp mixture and cheese.

Per 1¾ cups: 247 cal., 10 g total fat (4 g sat. fat), 156 mg chol., 435 mg sodium, 17 g carbo., 2 g fiber, 23 g pro.
Daily Values: 72% vit. A, 95% vit. C, 9% calcium, 23% iron
Exchanges: ½ Vegetable, 1 Starch, 2½ Very Lean Meat, ½ Medium-Fat Meat, 1 Fat

Ravioli Skillet

See photo, page 611.

Start to Finish: 15 minutes **Makes:** 4 servings

- 1 **14.5-ounce can Italian-style stewed tomatoes, undrained**
- 1 **14-ounce can vegetable broth**
- 2 **medium zucchini, halved lengthwise and sliced ½ inch thick (about 2½ cups)**
- 1 **9-ounce package refrigerated cheese ravioli**
- 1 **15-ounce can white kidney beans (cannellini), rinsed and drained**
- 2 **tablespoons grated Parmesan cheese**
- 2 **tablespoons snipped fresh basil or parsley**

1. In a large saucepan combine undrained tomatoes and broth; bring to boiling. Stir in zucchini and ravioli. Return to boiling; reduce heat. Boil gently, uncovered, for 6 to 7 minutes or until ravioli is tender and broth mixture is slightly thickened, stirring gently once or twice. Stir in beans; heat through. Sprinkle each serving with cheese and snipped basil.

Per 1½ cups: 335 cal., 11 g total fat (5 g sat. fat), 58 mg chol., 1,131 mg sodium, 47 g carbo., 7 g fiber, 19 g pro.
Daily Values: 6% vit. A, 11% vit. C, 25% calcium, 17% iron
Exchanges: 1½ Vegetable, 3 Starch, 1 Very Lean Meat, 1 Fat

Polenta and Beans

Start to Finish: 20 minutes **Makes:** 4 servings

- 1 **cup yellow cornmeal**
- 1 **15-ounce can black beans, rinsed and drained**
- 1 **14.5-ounce can diced tomatoes, undrained**
- 1 **cup bottled salsa with cilantro or other salsa**
- ¾ **cup shredded Mexican cheese blend**

1. For polenta, in a large saucepan bring 3 cups *water* to boiling. In a bowl combine cornmeal, 1 cup *cold water*, and ½ teaspoon *salt*. Stir cornmeal mixture slowly into boiling water. Cook and stir until mixture returns to boiling. Reduce heat to low. Cook 5 to 10 minutes or until mixture is thick, stirring occasionally. (If mixture gets too thick, stir in additional water.) Meanwhile, in a large skillet combine beans, undrained tomatoes, and salsa. Bring to boiling; reduce heat. Simmer, uncovered, 10 minutes, stirring frequently. Stir ½ cup of the cheese into polenta. Divide polenta among four shallow bowls. Top with bean mixture and remaining cheese.

Per ¾ cup bean mixture + about 1 cup polenta: 311 cal., 8 g total fat (4 g sat. fat), 19 mg chol., 751 mg sodium, 49 g carbo., 8 g fiber, 15 g pro.
Daily Values: 6% vit. A, 28% vit. C, 21% calcium, 13% iron
Exchanges: 2 Starch, 1 Other Carbo., 1 Very Lean Meat, 1 Medium-Fat Meat

Cashews and Vegetables

Start to Finish: 20 minutes **Makes:** 4 servings

- 1 **16-ounce package frozen broccoli stir-fry vegetables (broccoli, carrots, onions, red peppers, celery, water chestnuts, mushrooms)**
- 2 **tablespoons cooking oil**
- ¾ **cup whole raw cashews**
- ¾ **cup bottled stir-fry sauce with garlic**
- 3 **cups hot cooked linguine or Chinese noodles**

1. In a large skillet cook and stir vegetables in hot oil over medium-high heat for 5 to 7 minutes or until crisp-tender. Remove vegetables. Add cashews and, if necessary, more oil. Cook and stir for 2 to 5 minutes or until nuts are browned. Add sauce. Return vegetables to skillet; toss ingredients to coat. Heat through. Serve over pasta. If desired, sprinkle with sliced *green onion*.

Per about ¾ cup stir-fry + ¾ cup pasta: 452 cal., 23 g total fat (3 g sat. fat), 0 mg chol., 791 mg sodium, 49 g carbo., 5 g fiber, 13 g pro.
Daily Values: 30% vit. A, 42% vit. C, 12% calcium, 17% iron
Exchanges: 1 Vegetable, 2½ Starch, ½ Other Carbo., 4 Fat

Index

Note: Numbers in italics indicate photo pages for finished dishes.

Note: Numbers in italics indicate photo pages for finished dishes.

Note: Numbers in italics indicate photo pages for finished dishes.

Note: Numbers in italics indicate photo pages for finished dishes.

Note: Numbers in italics indicate photo pages for finished dishes.

Note: Numbers in italics indicate photo pages for finished dishes.

Note: Numbers in italics indicate photo pages for finished dishes.

Note: Numbers in italics indicate photo pages for finished dishes.

Note: Numbers in italics indicate photo pages for finished dishes.

Note: Numbers in italics indicate photo pages for finished dishes.

Note: Numbers in italics indicate photo pages for finished dishes.

Note: Numbers in italics indicate photo pages for finished dishes.

Note: Numbers in italics indicate photo pages for finished dishes.

Note: Numbers in italics indicate photo pages for finished dishes.

Note: Numbers in italics indicate photo pages for finished dishes.

Note: Numbers in italics indicate photo pages for finished dishes.

Note: Numbers in italics indicate photo pages for finished dishes.

Note: Numbers in italics indicate photo pages for finished dishes.

Note: Numbers in italics indicate photo pages for finished dishes.

Note: Numbers in italics indicate photo pages for finished dishes.

Note: Numbers in italics indicate photo pages for finished dishes.

Note: Numbers in italics indicate photo pages for finished dishes.

Note: Numbers in italics indicate photo pages for finished dishes.

Note: Numbers in italics indicate photo pages for finished dishes.

Note: Numbers in italics indicate photo pages for finished dishes.

Note: Numbers in italics indicate photo pages for finished dishes.

Note: Numbers in italics indicate photo pages for finished dishes.

Cooking at High Altitudes

When you cook at high altitudes, recipe adjustments need to be made to ensure the best results possible. Unfortunately, no simple formula exists for converting all recipes to high altitude recipes. If you live more than 1,000 feet above sea level, it will help you to understand ways in which altitude affects cooking and to become familiar with common cooking adjustments.

General High-Altitude Issues

Higher than 3,000 feet above sea level:
● Water boils at lower temperatures, causing moisture to evaporate more quickly. This can cause food to dry out during cooking and baking.
● Because of a lower boiling point, foods cooked in steam or boiling liquids take longer to cook.
● Lower air pressure may cause baked goods that use yeast, baking powder, baking soda, egg whites, or steam to rise excessively, then fall.

Suggestions for Baking

● For cakes leavened by air, such as angel food, beat the egg whites only to soft peaks; otherwise, the batter may expand too much.
● For cakes made with shortening, you may want to decrease the baking powder (start by decreasing it by ⅛ teaspoon per teaspoon called for); decrease the sugar (start by decreasing by about 1 tablespoon for each cup called for); and increase the liquid (start by increasing it 1 to 2 tablespoons for each cup called for). These estimates are based on an altitude of 3,000 feet above sea level—at higher altitudes, you may need to alter these measures proportionately. You can also try increasing the baking temperature by 15°F to 25°F to help set the batter.
● When making a rich cake, reduce the shortening by 1 to 2 tablespoons per cup and add one egg (for a 2-layer cake) to prevent cake from falling.
● Cookies generally yield acceptable results, but if you're not satisfied, try slightly increasing baking temperature; slightly decreasing the baking powder or soda, fat, and/or sugar; and/or slightly increasing the liquid ingredients and flour.
● Muffinlike quick breads and biscuits generally need little adjustment, but if you find that these goods develop a bitter or alkaline flavor, decrease the baking soda or powder slightly. Because cakelike quick breads are more delicate, you may need to follow adjustment guidelines for cakes.
● Yeast breads will rise more quickly at high altitudes. Allow unshaped dough to rise only until double in size, then punch the dough down. Repeat this rising step once more before shaping dough. Flour tends to be drier at high altitudes and sometimes absorbs more liquid. If your yeast dough seems dry, add more liquid and reduce the amount of flour the next time you make the recipe.
● Large cuts of meat may take longer to cook. Be sure to use a meat thermometer to determine proper doneness.

Suggestions for Range-Top Cooking

Candy-making: Rapid evaporation caused by cooking at high altitudes can cause candies to cook down more quickly. Therefore, decrease the final cooking temperature by the difference in boiling water temperature at your altitude and that of sea level (212°F). This is an approximate decrease of 2 degrees for every increase of 1,000 feet in elevation above sea level.
Canning and freezing foods: When canning at high altitudes, adjustments in processing time or pressure are needed to guard against contamination; when freezing, an adjustment in the blanching time is needed. See the Canning and Freezing chapter, especially the tip on page 214.
Deep-fat frying: At high altitudes, deep-fried foods can overbrown on the outside but remain underdone inside. While foods vary, a rough guideline is to lower the temperature of the fat about 3°F for every 1,000 feet in elevation above sea level.

Cooking Above 6,000 Feet

Cooking at altitudes higher than 6,000 feet above sea level poses further challenges because the dry air found at such elevations influences cooking. Call your local United States Department of Agriculture Extension Service Office for advice.

Further Information

For more information on cooking at high altitudes, contact your county extension office or write to Colorado State University, Department of Food Science and Human Nutrition Cooperative Extension, Fort Collins, CO 80523-1571. Please use this contact only for queries regarding high-altitude cooking.

Metric Information

The charts on this page provide a guide for converting measurements from the U.S. customary system, which is used throughout this book, to the metric system.

Product Differences

Most of the ingredients called for in the recipes in this book are available in most countries. However, some are known by different names. Here are some common American ingredients and their possible counterparts:
• Sugar (white) is granulated, fine granulated, or castor sugar.
• Powdered sugar is icing sugar.
• All-purpose flour is enriched, bleached or unbleached white household flour. When self-rising flour is used in place of all-purpose flour in a recipe that calls for leavening, omit the leavening agent (baking soda or baking powder) and salt.
• Light-colored corn syrup is golden syrup.
• Cornstarch is cornflour.
• Baking soda is bicarbonate of soda.
• Vanilla or vanilla extract is vanilla essence.
• Green, red, or yellow sweet peppers are capsicums or bell peppers.
• Golden raisins are sultanas.

Volume and Weight

The United States traditionally uses cup measures for liquid and solid ingredients. The chart below shows the approximate imperial and metric equivalents. If you are accustomed to weighing solid ingredients, the following approximate equivalents will be helpful.
• 1 cup butter, castor sugar, or rice = 8 ounces = ½ pound = 250 grams
• 1 cup flour = 4 ounces = ¼ pound = 125 grams
• 1 cup icing sugar = 5 ounces = 150 grams
• Canadian and U.S. volume for a cup measure is 8 fluid ounces (237 ml), but the standard metric equivalent is 250 ml.
• 1 British imperial cup is 10 fluid ounces.
• In Australia, 1 tablespoon equals 20 ml, and there are 4 teaspoons in the Australian tablespoon.
• Spoon measures are used for smaller amounts of ingredients. Although the size of the tablespoon varies slightly in different countries, for practical purposes and for recipes in this book, a straight substitution is all that's necessary. Measurements made using cups or spoons always should be level unless stated otherwise.

Common Weight Range Replacements

Imperial / U.S.	Metric
½ ounce	15 g
1 ounce	25 g or 30 g
4 ounces (¼ pound)	115 g or 125 g
8 ounces (½ pound)	225 g or 250 g
16 ounces (1 pound)	450 g or 500 g
1¼ pounds	625 g
1½ pounds	750 g
2 pounds or 2¼ pounds	1,000 g or 1 Kg

Oven Temperature Equivalents

Fahrenheit Setting	Celsius Setting	Gas Setting
300°F	150°C	Gas Mark 2 (very low)
325°F	160°C	Gas Mark 3 (low)
350°F	180°C	Gas Mark 4 (moderate)
375°F	190°C	Gas Mark 5 (moderate)
400°F	200°C	Gas Mark 6 (hot)
425°F	220°C	Gas Mark 7 (hot)
450°F	230°C	Gas Mark 8 (very hot)
475°F	240°C	Gas Mark 9 (very hot)
500°F	260°C	Gas Mark 10 (extremely hot)
Broil	Broil	Grill

*Electric and gas ovens may be calibrated using celsius. However, for an electric oven, increase celsius setting 10 to 20 degrees when cooking above 160°C. For convection or forced air ovens (gas or electric), lower the temperature setting 25°F/10°C when cooking at all heat levels.

Baking Pan Sizes

Imperial / U.S.	Metric
9×1½-inch round cake pan	22- or 23×4-cm (1.5 L)
9×1½-inch pie plate	22- or 23×4-cm (1 L)
8×8×2-inch square cake pan	20×5-cm (2 L)
9×9×2-inch square cake pan	22- or 23×4.5-cm (2.5 L)
11×7×1½-inch baking pan	28×17×4-cm (2 L)
2-quart rectangular baking pan	30×19×4.5-cm (3 L)
13×9×2-inch baking pan	34×22×4.5-cm (3.5 L)
15×10×1-inch jelly roll pan	40×25×2-cm
9×5×3-inch loaf pan	23×13×8-cm (2 L)
2-quart casserole	2 L

U.S. / Standard Metric Equivalents

⅛ teaspoon = 0.5 ml	
¼ teaspoon = 1 ml	
½ teaspoon = 2 ml	
1 teaspoon = 5 ml	
1 tablespoon = 15 ml	
2 tablespoons = 25 ml	
¼ cup = 2 fluid ounces = 50 ml	
⅓ cup = 3 fluid ounces = 75 ml	
½ cup = 4 fluid ounces = 125 ml	
⅔ cup = 5 fluid ounces = 150 ml	
¾ cup = 6 fluid ounces = 175 ml	
1 cup = 8 fluid ounces = 250 ml	
2 cups = 1 pint = 500 ml	
1 quart = 1 litre	